Claude Elwood Shannon

Claude Elwood Shannon

Collected Papers

Edited by

N.J.A. Sloane

Aaron D. Wyner

Mathematical Sciences Research Dept.
AT & T Bell Laboratories
Murray Hill, NJ 07974
USA

IEEE Information Theory Society, *Sponsor*

The Institute of Electrical and Electronics Engineers, Inc., New York

A JOHN WILEY & SONS, INC., PUBLICATION

IEEE PRESS
445 Hoes Lane, PO Box 1331
Piscataway, NJ 08855-1331

1992 Editorial Board
William Perkins, *Editor in Chief*

K. K. Agarwal	G. F. Hoffnagle	A. C. Schell
R. S. Blicq	J. D. Irwin	L. Shaw
R. C. Dorf	A. Michel	M. Simaan
D. M. Etter	E. K. Miller	Y. Sunahara
J. J. Farrell III	J. M. F. Moura	D. J. Wells
K. Hess	J. G. Nagle	

Dudley R. Kay, *Executive Editor*
Carrie Briggs, *Administrative Assistant*
Karen G. Miller, *Production Editor*

IEEE Information Theory Society, *Sponsor*
G. David Forney, Jr.
President

Library of Congress Cataloging-in-Publication Data

Shannon, Claude Elwood,
  [Works]
  Claude Elwood Shannon : collected papers / edited by N.J.A.
  Sloane, A.D. Wyner.
    p.   cm.
  Includes bibliographical references.
  ISBN 0-7803-0434-9
  1. Telecommunication.   2. Information theory.   3. Computers.
I. Sloane, N. J. A. (Neil James Alexander).   II. Wyner, A.
D. (Aaron D.)   III. Title.
TK5101.S448   1993
  621.382—dc20
                                            92-26762
                                              CIP

Contents

Part A: Communication Theory, Information Theory, Cryptography
[Bracketed numbers refer to the Bibliography]

ABSTRACTS, ETC.

Part B: Computers, Circuits, Games

PAPERS

Contents

Part C: Genetics

Introduction

The publication of Claude Shannon's collected papers is long overdue. A substantial collection of his papers was published in Russian in 1963 (see item [121] of his Bibliography), but no English edition has ever appeared. The editors were therefore commissioned by the Information Theory Society of the Institute of Electrical and Electronics Engineers to collect and publish his papers.

Since much of Shannon's work was never published, our first task was to assemble a complete bibliography. We did this by consulting Claude and Betty Shannon, who have been extremely helpful throughout this project and supplied us with copies of a number of unpublished items; many of Claude's friends and colleagues; the Bell Laboratories Archives; the National Archives in Washington; the National Security Agency; the patent records; Mathematical Reviews; and other sources. We believe the resulting bibliography of 127 items is reasonably complete.

The second step was to decide what to include. Our policy has been to include everything of importance. We have included all the published papers, and all the unpublished material that seemed of lasting value. Some war-time reports of very limited interest have been excluded, as well as the M.I.T. seminar notes. If an excluded paper has an abstract, we have printed it. We have made several sets of copies of the excluded material, and plan to deposit copies in the AT&T Bell Laboratories library at Murray Hill, New Jersey, the M.I.T. library, and the Library of Congress and the British Library.

The papers fall naturally into three groups: (A) communication theory, information theory and cryptography; (B) computers, circuits and games; (C) the hitherto unpublished doctoral dissertation on population genetics. Inside each group the papers are, with some exceptions, arranged in chronological order. Minor items (abstracts, book reviews, and so on) have been placed at the end of each section.

Most of the published works have been photographically reproduced from the originals, while the others have been typeset by computer at AT&T Bell Labs.

The "Notes" following each section give references to more recent work.

We should like to thank R. B. Blackman, P. Elias, E. N. Gilbert, R. Gnanadesikan, R. L. Graham, D. W. Hagelbarger, T. T. Kadota, H. O. Pollak, D. Slepian, E. Wolman and R. Wright for supplying us with copies of Shannon's papers. R. A. Matula, of the AT&T Bell Laboratories library staff, has been extremely helpful to us throughout this project. J. P. Buhler, J. H. Conway, J. F. Crow, R. L. Graham, D. S. Johnson, T. Nagylaki and K. Thompson kindly provided comments on some of the papers. We are very grateful to Susan Marko (sometimes assisted by Sue Pope), who expertly retyped many of Shannon's papers for us.

Biography of Claude Elwood Shannon

Claude Elwood Shannon was born in Petoskey, Michigan, on Sunday, April 30, 1916. His father, Claude Sr. (1862-1934), a descendant of early New Jersey settlers, was a businessman and, for a period, Judge of Probate. His mother, Mabel Wolf Shannon (1880-1945), daughter of German immigrants, was a language teacher and for a number of years Principal of Gaylord High School, in Gaylord, Michigan.

The first sixteen years of Shannon's life were spent in Gaylord, where he attended the Public School, graduating from Gaylord High School in 1932. As a boy, Shannon showed an inclination toward things mechanical. His best subjects in school were science and mathematics, and at home he constructed such devices as model planes, a radio-controlled model boat and a telegraph system to a friend's house half a mile away. The telegraph made opportunistic use of two barbed wires around a nearby pasture. He earned spending money from a paper route and delivering telegrams, as well as repairing radios for a local department store. His childhood hero was Edison, who he later learned was a distant cousin. Both were descendants of John Ogden, an important colonial leader and the ancestor of many distinguished people. Shannon's recent hero list, without deleting Edison, includes more academic types such as Newton, Darwin, Einstein and Von Neumann.

In 1932 he entered the University of Michigan, following his sister Catherine, who had just received a master's degree in mathematics there. While a senior, he was elected a member of Phi Kappa Phi and an associate member of Sigma Xi. In 1936 he obtained the degrees of Bachelor of Science in Electrical Engineering and Bachelor of Science in Mathematics. This dual interest in mathematics and engineering continued throughout his career.

In 1936 he accepted the position of research assistant in the Department of Electrical Engineering at the Massachusetts Institute of Technology. The position allowed him to continue studying toward advanced degrees while working part-time for the department. The work in question was ideally suited to his interests and talents. It involved the operation of the Bush differential analyzer, the most advanced calculating machine of that era, which solved by analog means differential equations of up to the sixth degree. The work required translating differential equations into mechanical terms, setting up the machine and running through the needed solutions for various initial values. In some cases as many as four assistants would be needed to crank in functions by following curves during the process of solution.

Also of interest was a complex relay circuit associated with the differential analyzer that controlled its operation and involved over one hundred relays. In studying and servicing this circuit, Shannon became interested in the theory and design of relay and switching circuits. He had studied symbolic logic and Boolean algebra at Michigan in mathematics courses, and realized that this was the appropriate mathematics for studying such two-valued systems. He developed these ideas during the summer of 1937, which he spent at Bell Telephone Laboratories in New York City, and, back at M.I.T., in his master's thesis, where he showed how Boolean algebra could be used in the analysis and synthesis of switching and computer circuits. The thesis, his first published paper, aroused considerable interest when it appeared in 1938 in the A.I.E.E. Transactions [1].[*] In 1940 it was awarded the Alfred Noble Prize of the

---

The numbers in square brackets refer to items in Shannon's bibliography.

combined engineering societies of the United States, an award given each year to a person not over thirty for a paper published in one of the journals of the participating societies. A quarter of a century later H. H. Goldstine, in his book *The Computer from Pascal to Von Neumann*, called this work "one of the most important master's theses ever written...a landmark in that it helped to change digital circuit design from an art to a science."

During the summer of 1938 he did research work at M.I.T. on the design of the Bush Rapid Selector, and was mainly involved with the vacuum tube circuits employed in this device. In September of 1938, at the suggestion of Vannevar Bush, Shannon changed from the Electrical Engineering Department to the Mathematics Department. He was awarded the Bolles Fellowship and was also a teaching assistant while working toward a doctorate in mathematics. Bush had just been made President of the Carnegie Institution in Washington, one of whose branches, in Cold Spring Harbor, N.Y., dealt with the science of genetics. He suggested to Shannon that algebra might be as useful in organizing genetic knowledge as it was in switching, and Shannon decided to look into this matter with a view toward using it for a doctoral thesis in mathematics. He spent the summer of 1939 at Cold Spring Harbor working under geneticist Dr. Barbara Burks exploring the possibility, and found it a suitable subject for a dissertation under the title "An Algebra for Theoretical Genetics" [3]. His Ph.D. supervisor at M.I.T. was Professor Frank L. Hitchcock, an algebraist. In the Spring of 1939 he was elected to full membership in Sigma Xi.

At about this time Shannon was also developing ideas both in computers and communications systems. In a letter of February 16, 1939 now in the Library of Congress archives ([2], included in Part A), he writes to Bush about trading relations between time, bandwidth, noise and distortion in communication systems, and also about a computer design for symbolic mathematical operations.

As the Spring of 1940 approached, Shannon had passed all requirements for both a master's in electrical engineering and a doctorate in mathematics – except for satisfying the language requirements, always his weakest subjects. Facing reality, he buckled down in the last few months, hired a French and German tutor and repeatedly worked his way through stacks of flash cards. He finally passed the language exams (it took two tries with German) and in the Spring of 1940 received the S.M. degree in Electrical Engineering and the degree of Doctor of Philosophy in Mathematics at the same commencement. His Ph.D. dissertation, [3], is published here for the first time (in Part D).

The Summer of 1940 was spent at Bell Telephone Laboratories doing further research on switching circuits. A new method of design was developed which greatly reduced the number of contacts needed to synthesize complex switching functions from earlier realizations. This was later published in a paper, "The Synthesis of Two-Terminal Switching Circuits" [50].

The academic year 1940-1941 was spent on a National Research Fellowship at the Institute for Advanced Study in Princeton working under Hermann Weyl. It was during this period that Shannon began to work seriously on his ideas relating to information theory and efficient communication systems.

Thornton C. Fry, head of the mathematics department at Bell Labs, was in charge of a committee on fire control systems for anti-aircraft use – the country was arming up at the time because of the spreading European war threats – and asked Shannon to join in this effort. Returning to Bell Labs, Shannon joined a team working on anti-aircraft directors – devices to observe enemy planes or missiles and calculate the aiming of counter missiles. This problem became crucial with the development of the German V1 and V2 rockets. Without the American anti-aircraft directors, the ravaging of England, bad as it was, would have been vastly worse.

Shannon spent fifteen years at Bell Laboratories in a very fruitful association. Many first-rate mathematicians and scientists were at the Labs – men such as John Pierce, known for satellite communication; Harry Nyquist, with numerous contributions to signal theory; Hendrik Bode of feedback fame; transistor inventors Brattain, Bardeen and Shockley; George Stibitz, who built an early (1938) relay computer; Barney Oliver, engineer extraordinaire; and many others.

During this period Shannon worked in many areas, most notably in information theory, a development which was published in 1948 as "A Mathematical Theory of Communication" [37]. In this paper it was shown that all information sources – telegraph keys, people speaking, television cameras and so on – have a "source rate" associated with them which can be measured in bits per second. Communication channels have a "capacity" measured in the same units. The information can be transmitted over the channel if and only if the source rate does not exceed the channel capacity (see the Preface to Part A).

This work on communication is generally considered to be Shannon's most important scientific contribution. In 1981 Professor Irving Reed, speaking at the International Symposium on Information Theory in Brighton, England, said, "It was thirty-four years ago, in 1948, that Professor Claude E. Shannon first published his uniquely original paper, 'A Mathematical Theory of Communication,' in the *Bell System Technical Journal*. Few other works of this century have had greater impact on science and engineering. By this landmark paper and his several subsequent papers on information theory he has altered most profoundly all aspects of communication theory and practice."

Shannon has rung many changes on the problems of information and noise. In a paper "Communication Theory of Secrecy Systems" [25] cryptography is related to communication in a noisy channel, the "noise" being in this case the scrambling by the key of the cryptographic system. This work later led to his appointment as a consultant on cryptographic matters to the United States Government.

Another problem, which he investigated jointly with E. F. Moore [88]–[90], was that of increasing the reliability of relay circuits by redundant use of contacts, each of which may be unreliable. Again this is a problem related to transmission in noisy channels.

Shannon has also applied these concepts to the problem of optimal investment strategies. The "noisy signal" is the stock market and related time series, and the problem is to maximize a utility function by proper choice and adjustment of a portfolio.

In a lighter vein and in the computer and artificial intelligence area, Shannon wrote a paper "Programming a Computer for Playing Chess" in 1950 [54]. At that time computers were slow, inept and very difficult to program. Since then, many chess-playing programs have been written, most of them following quite closely the system described in that early paper.

In 1965 he was invited to Russia to give lectures at an engineering conference. While there, he took the opportunity to meet Mikhail Botvinnik, for many years the World Chess Champion. Botvinnik, also an electrical engineer, had become interested in the chess programming problem. Shannon remembers the discussion as interesting but carried on through a somewhat noisy channel since the interpreters knew little of either chess or computers.

After the discussion, he asked Botvinnik for the pleasure of a chess game. Translators, guides and members of the American party watched with rapt attention as the epic battle unfolded. At one point Shannon had a slight edge (a rook for a knight and pawn), but alas the result was foregone – after forty-two moves Shannon tipped over his king – a message that needed no translation.

Further advances in chess programming continued through the next decades and in 1980 Shannon was invited, as an honored guest, to an International Computer Chess Championship held in Linz, Austria. Eighteen computers from Sweden, Germany, Russia, France, England, Canada and several from the United States were entered. Most of the computers remained at home but were linked electronically to the tournament hall in Linz. The winner, "Belle," developed by Ken Thompson and Joe Condon of Bell Laboratories, was not far from master playing strength.

Dr. Shannon enjoys constructing amusing if not utilitarian devices, and his house is filled with such brainchildren. Among these might be mentioned THROBAC (Thrifty ROman numerical BAckward looking Computer) [76], a calculator which performs all the arithmetic operations in the Roman numerical system; "turtles" which wander around the floor, backing up and turning from obstacles; game-playing machines of various types and sizes; and a three-ball juggling machine with two hands that bounce-juggles three balls on a drumhead.

The "Ultimate Machine," based on an idea of Marvin Minsky, was built in the early fifties. The operation and spirit were well described by Arthur C. Clarke in *Voice Across the Sea:* "Nothing could be simpler. It is merely a small wooden casket, the size and shape of a cigar box, with a single switch on one face. When you throw the switch, there is an angry, purposeful buzzing. The lid slowly rises, and from beneath it emerges a hand. The hand reaches down, turns the switch off and retreats into the box. With the finality of a closing coffin, the lid snaps shut, the buzzing ceases and peace reigns once more. The psychological effect, if you do not know what to expect, is devastating. There is something unspeakably sinister about a machine that does nothing – absolutely nothing – except switch itself off."

The maze-solving mouse Theseus, built in 1950, took a more positive approach to its universe. Controlled by a relay circuit, a lifesize magnetic mouse moved around a maze of twenty-five squares. The maze could be altered at will and the mouse would then search through the passageways until it found the arbitrarily placed goal. Having been through the maze, the mouse could be placed anywhere it had been and would go directly to the goal – placed in unfamiliar ground, it would search until it reached a known position and then proceed to the goal, adding the new knowledge to its memory. It appears to have been the first learning device of this level.

In the case of Theseus, both the "brain" and the "muscles" were separate from the mouse itself and were in fact under the maze. The brain was a circuit of about 100 relays, and the muscles a pair of motors driving an electromagnet which by magnetic action moved the mouse through the maze. With the development of solid state circuitry, self-contained mice became feasible. Compared to Theseus, the brains were smaller but the mice were bigger. By 1978 enough engineers had built maze-solving mice for the *IEEE Spectrum* to hold an "Amazing Micro Mouse Maze Contest," at which Theseus made a guest appearance.

A happy consequence of Shannon's sojourn at Bell Labs was his marriage to Mary Elizabeth (Betty) Moore. Betty, a graduate in mathematics of Douglass College, Rutgers University, worked as a numerical analyst (what was then called a "computer") in John Pierce's group. Her interests in handweaving and computing are currently combined in work with a computer-controlled loom, an area in which she pioneered in the sixties. Claude and Betty were married in 1949 and have three children, Robert, Andrew and Margarita. They live on Mystic Lake, in Winchester, Massachusetts.

In 1956 Dr. Shannon was invited to be a visiting professor at M.I.T. and, in 1957-58, a fellow at the Center for the Study of the Behavioral Sciences in Palo Alto, California. The following year he became a permanent member of the M.I.T. faculty as Donner Professor of

Science, where he continued research in various areas of communication theory. Among these were communications systems with feedback and a study of the rate at which it is possible to approach ideal coding as a function of delay. He continued his affiliation with Bell Telephone Laboratories until July 1, 1972.

Many of Shannon's papers have been translated into various foreign languages. Perhaps the most thorough job was that of Russian scientists, who have long been interested in information theory and computers and have contributed greatly to these fields. In 1963 he received three copies of an 830-page collection, in Russian, of his scientific papers [121]. Years later, on a visit to Russia, he was informed that his book had been collecting royalties to the amount of several thousand rubles, which translated roughly into the same number of dollars. Unfortunately, there was a catch – this could not be taken out of the country as money, but could only be spent in Russia. Curiously, nothing they might buy seemed suitable. The books were in Russian, Betty already had a fur coat, furniture was difficult to transport. They finally ended up with an array of eight musical instruments ranging from a bassoon to a balalaika. On the trip home the party was often taken for a traveling orchestra.

In his leisure time Shannon, in addition to the gadgeteering mentioned above, has a number of recreations. He tries to jog a mile or two each day, and enjoys sports like juggling which require good coordination. One Christmas, Betty, knowing his proclivities, gave him a unicycle. Within a few days he was riding around the block; in a few weeks he could juggle three balls while riding. In a few months he was building unusual cycles such as one with an eccentric wheel (the rider moved up and down as he pedalled forward). He is an easy mark for any new intellectual challenge – he designed a machine to solve the Rubik cube, and was observed trying to equal his son's record at Pac-Man.

Shannon plays the clarinet and enjoys music, especially the Dixieland popular in his youth. He likes poetry with a nod to T. S. Eliot, the Rubaiyat and Ogden Nash, and has been known to dash off a bit of light verse from time to time [127].

He holds honorary degrees from Yale (Master of Science, 1954), Michigan (1961), Princeton (1962), Edinburgh (1964), Pittsburgh (1964), Northwestern (1970), Oxford (1978), East Anglia (1982), Carnegie-Mellon (1984), Tufts (1987) and the University of Pennsylvania (1991).

His awards include the Alfred Noble Prize (1940), Morris Liebmann Memorial Award of the Institute of Radio Engineers (1949), Stuart Ballantine Medal of the Franklin Institute (1955), Research Corporation Award (1956), Rice University Medal of Honor (1962), Marvin J. Kelly Award (1962), I.E.E.E. Medal of Honor (1966), National Medal of Science (1966) presented by President Johnson, Golden Plate Award (1967), Harvey Prize, Technion, Haifa (1972) presented by the President of Israel, Jacquard Award (1978), Harold Pender Award (1978), Audio Engineering Society Gold Medal (1985), the Kyoto Prize (1985) and the Eduard Rhein Prize (1991).

He delivered the Vanuxem Lectures, Princeton (1958); the Steinmetz Lecture, Schenectady (1962); the Gibbs Lecture, American Mathematical Society (1965); the first Shannon Lecture, I.E.E.E. (1973); and the Chichele Lecture, Oxford (1978).

He has been Bolles Fellow at M.I.T. (1938-40); National Research Fellow at the Institute for Advanced Study in Princeton (1940-41); Fellow of the Center for Advanced Study in the Behavioral Sciences, Stanford (1957-58), Visiting Fellow at All Souls College, Oxford (1978); and is a Fellow of Muir College of the University of California, the I.E.E.E., and the Royal Society. He is (or has been) a member of the National Academy of Sciences, the National Academy of Engineering, the American Mathematical Society, the American Philosophical

Society, the Royal Irish Academy, the American Academy of Arts and Sciences, the Royal Netherlands Academy, the Leopoldina Academy of Leipzig, and Tau Beta Pi, Sigma Xi, Phi Kappa Phi and Eta Kappa Nu. For many years he was a member of the board of directors of Teledyne, Inc.

In 1983, Dr. Shannon wrote concerning information technologies: "The growth of both communication and computing devices has been explosive in the last century. It was about a hundred years ago that the telephone and phonograph were invented, and these were followed by radio, motion pictures and television. We now have vacuum tubes, transistors, integrated circuits, satellite communication and microwave cable. We have even talked to astronauts on the moon. Our life style has been totally changed by advances in communication.

"On the computing side we started the twentieth century with slide rules and adding machines. These were followed in quantum jumps by the Bush analog computers, Stibitz and Aiken relay computers, Eckert and Mauchly vacuum tube machines (ENIAC), transistor computers and, finally, the incredibly compact integrated circuit and chip computers. At each step the computers became faster, cheaper and more powerful. These hardware revolutions were matched by equally impressive developments in programming.

"What can we expect in the future? Three advances in the artificial intelligence area would be most welcome. (1) An optical sensor-computer combination capable of learning to recognize objects, people, etc., as our eyes and occipital cortex do. (2) A manipulator-computer combination capable of the purposeful operations of the human hand. (3) A computer program capable of at least some of the concept formation and generalizing abilities of the human brain.

"In the communication area our government might consider diverting a small fraction of its 'defense' budget to the construction of giant radio telescopes as proposed by the SETI (Search for Extraterrestrial Intelligence) program, to listen for evidence of intelligent life on other star systems – possibly as a joint venture with the Soviets. Who knows, perhaps E.T. would have words of wisdom for all of us!"

Shannon was recently interviewed by the *Scientific American* and the interviewer, John Horgan, reports that: "Claude E. Shannon can't sit still. We're at his home, a stuccoed Victorian edifice overlooking a lake north of Boston, and I'm trying to get him to recall how he came up with the theory of information. But Shannon, who is a boyish 73, with an elfish grin and a shock of snowy hair, is tired of expounding on his past. Wouldn't I rather see his toys?

"Without waiting for an answer, and over the mild protests of his wife, Betty, he leaps from his chair and disappears into the other room. When I catch up with him, he proudly shows me his seven chess-playing machines, gasoline-powered pogostick, hundred-bladed jackknife, two-seated unicycle and countless other marvels. Some of his personal creations – such as a juggling W. C. Fields mannequin and a computer called THROBAC that calculates in Roman numerals – are a bit dusty and in disrepair, but Shannon seems as delighted with everything as a 10-year-old on Christmas morning.

"Is this the man who, as a young engineer at Bell Laboratories in 1948, wrote the Magna Carta of the information age: *The Mathematical Theory of Communication?* Whose work Robert W. Lucky, executive director of research at AT&T Bell Laboratories, calls the greatest 'in the annals of technological thought?' Whose 'pioneering insight' IBM Fellow Rolf W. Landauer equates with Einstein's? Yes. This is also the man who invented a rocket-powered Frisbee and who juggled while riding a unicycle through the halls of Bell Labs. 'I've always pursued my interests without much regard to financial value or value to the world,' Shannon says. 'I've spent lots of time on totally useless things.'

···   ···   ···

''Shannon's ideas were almost too prescient to have an immediate practical impact. Vacuum-tube circuits simply could not calculate the complex codes needed to approach the Shannon limit. In fact, not until the early 1970's – with the advent of high-speed integrated circuits – did engineers begin fully to exploit information theory. Today Shannon's insights help shape virtually all systems that store, process or transmit information in digital form, from compact disks to computers, from facsimile machines to deep-space probes such as *Voyager*.

''Information theory has also infiltrated fields outside of communications, including linguistics, psychology, economics, biology, even the arts. In the early 1970's the *IEEE Transactions on Information Theory* published an editorial, titled ''Information Theory, Photosynthesis and Religion,'' decrying this trend. Yet Shannon himself suggests that applying information theory to biological systems may not be so farfetched, because in his view common principles underlie mechanical and living things. 'You bet,' he replies, when asked whether he thinks machines can think. 'I'm a machine and you're a machine, and we both think, don't we?'

''He built a 'mind-reading' machine [73] that played the game of penny-matching, in which one person tries to guess whether the other has chosen heads or tails. A colleague at Bell Labs, David W. Hagelbarger, built the prototype; the machine recorded and analyzed its opponent's past choices, looking for patterns that would foretell the next choice. Because it is almost impossible for a human to avoid falling into such patterns, the machine won more than 50 percent of the time. Shannon then built his own version and challenged Hagelbarger to a legendary dual. Shannon's machine won.''

This biographical sketch was based on the booklet *Claude E. Shannon, Medalist for 1983* that was issued when he was awarded the John Fritz medal. It has been supplemented by material from other sources, including a profile by John Horgan that appeared in the *Scientific American* of January 1990.

Another interview follows.

Profile of Claude Shannon*

Anthony Liversidge

Much to his discomfort, Claude Elwood Shannon, at seventy, is a living legend. What Louis Armstrong was to jazz, Shannon is to the electronic, digital information age, a founding father who laid down its most important principles. His contribution is saluted by the world. Diplomas and prizes stretch along a wall and up a spiral staircase in his home. There would surely be a Nobel too, if one existed in mathematics or information science.

But Shannon doesn't seek prominence. He is as content as an English country gentleman in his privacy. His face is so unfamiliar that when he arrived at a conference last year in Brighton, England, devoted to the field he founded, he was hardly recognized. In the dining hall, a man cried excitedly "Do you know who's coming? Claude Shannon!", when Shannon was sitting at the next table.

Not that he is unsociable. Out of the line of fire of the media, he laughs often, and is variously playful as a gadgeteer and a prankster. He is vividly remembered at Bell Labs for riding a unicycle down its long corridor and back again, juggling all the while. One of the plaques on his wall is from the Wham-O Company for his rocket powered Frisbee. At the end of the Brighton conference, he gave an amusing after dinner speech and pulling three tennis balls from his pockets, demonstrated a juggling "cascade."

Shannon's mathematical genius, on the other hand, is well recognized. He won fame first at 22 as a student at M.I.T., when he wrote an M.Sc. thesis which Howard Gardner, the Harvard mind theorist, in *The Mind's New Science*, judges "possibly the most important, and also the most famous, master's thesis of the century."

This prize winning paper, *A Symbolic Analysis of Relay and Switching Circuits*, put forward a very bright idea. Shannon saw that the branching network of strict logic, Boolean algebra, could be expressed by the relay switching circuits used in telephone exchanges. Essentially, "If the alarm clock rings and it is Monday, then you have to go to work" was equivalent to "If Switch A is closed, and Switch B is closed, then current flows through to the motor."

The insight was "monumental," says Marvin Minsky, M.I.T.'s Artificial Intelligence guru, because it helped to lay the groundwork for constructing computers. "You could use mathematics to calculate if a design was correct instead of using trial and error."

Ten years later, working at Bell Labs, Shannon came out with his masterwork, *The Mathematical Theory of Communication* (University of Illinois Press). At a stroke he transformed the understanding of the process of electronic communication, by providing it with a mathematics, a general set of theorems called 'information theory'. With lucid brilliance, Shannon wrote out the basic principles of the signaling of information. It was like Newton writing out the laws of motion for mechanics.

The slim paper exploded on the scene 'like a bomb', wrote John Pierce, a prominent colleague, and author of *Symbols, Signals and Noise* (Dover). Suddenly, engineers had a language to deal with the major puzzles of telephone and radio communications: how to

---

* This article appeared (in a slightly different form) in *Omni* magazine, August 1987.

measure information, and how to exploit fully the capacity of a telephone wire, microwaves, a fiber optic cable or any other channel of communication. So wide were the repercussions that Fortune magazine was soon calling the theory one of man's "proudest and rarest creations, a great scientific theory which could profoundly and rapidly alter man's view of his world."

What astonished engineers was Shannon's proof that however "noisy" a communications channel, it was always possible to send a signal without distortion. To do so, you have to encode the message in such a way that it is self checking. With the right code, signals could be received with as high accuracy as if there were no interference on the line.

A simple code might involve adding a symbol, a binary digit or "bit," every few bits of message to describe whether a previous group of bits add up to an odd or even number. English is another error correcting code. Noisy party conversation is intelligible partly because half the language is redundant. The extra symbols allow you to fill in what you miss.

Shannon had lit a beacon, showing such codes were possible. Over the next twenty-five years engineers steered into the dark by his light. Powerful codes were worked out, yielding super accurate communications hardware, from space probes and computers to disk drives and compact disc players. Drag a knife point across the surface of a compact disc, and error correcting codes will mask the flaw, thanks to Shannon.

Voyager II sending detailed pictures of Uranus and its ten newly discovered moons to Earth 1.8 million miles away is a tribute to Shannon's inspiration. So are the picture perfect digital TV's and VCR's now joining CD's on the home market. Information theory spurred the digital revolution, where information is sent in discrete bits rather than in the wave form of 'analog' signals, because Shannon's error correcting codes work naturally in digital.

A problem is that the name "information theory" is misleading. As opposed to everyday use, in Shannon's theory "information," like "force" or "energy" in mechanics, is defined very precisely as a commodity, measured in bits per second, unrelated to the meaning of the message. Like the driver of a truckload of sealed packing cases, a communications engineer is concerned only how to deliver the bits most efficiently.

Prompted by this misunderstanding, the short treatise, now in its eleventh printing, has inspired great claims that information theory has a significance far beyond communications engineering. Professors of the social sciences and other fields short of mathematical models rushed to adapt the ideas to their own ends. The formulation has been applied to everything from molecular biology and the brain to psychology, art, music, sociology, semantics and linguistics, economics and even landscape gardening.

A wave of enthusiasm for such work came in the fifties, then receded. Now there is renewed interest among some researchers. In one recent book, *Grammatical Man*, science author Jeremy Campbell found enough progress to argue that Shannon's theories are fundamental to understanding the universe, and that "to the powerful theories of chemistry and physics must be added a later arrival: a theory of information. Nature must be interpreted as matter, energy and information."

Shannon was in his mid-twenties when he worked out information theory. Born on the prairie in Gaylord, Michigan, he had gone to the University of Michigan, and then M.I.T., where he wrote his Ph.D. thesis on the mathematics of genes and heredity. He joined Bell Laboratories in 1941 and worked on cryptography. A theorem of Shannon's was behind the SIGSALY telephone, the huge speech scrambling apparatus which allowed Churchill to speak to Roosevelt from a special, toilet-sized booth through a coding system that even today is unbreakable.

Shannon left for M.I.T. in 1956, much to the regret of colleagues at Bell. "It was a big loss," says Edgar Gilbert, a colleague. "He was always generating interesting ideas. He would grasp the essence of a problem immediately, and come up with a totally different idea that shed a great deal of light on it."

At M.I.T. Shannon, made Donner Professor in 1958, gave "beautiful" lectures, says a colleague, took a few select graduate students in hand, and refined information theory. By the mid sixties, his preference for working at home became the rule (a friend borrowing his deserted office found a sizable uncashed check more than a year old). He retired in 1978, becoming Professor Emeritus, wealthy from investments in technological companies, some of them founded by his friends. One is Teledyne, where until recently Shannon served on the board of directors.

Not just a theorist, Shannon has always been fond of inventing and building gadgets and machines. A famous one was a mechanical white mouse which could learn its way through a maze, decades before the microchip. Another was Throbac, a calculator which operated in Roman numerals, and a 'mind reading' machine which anticipated whether a challenger would choose heads or tails. (Colleague David Hagelbarger invented this but Shannon's stripped down version outsmarted his "more conservative and pompous design," he says.)

Then there was Hex, a machine which played a board game. Shannon's prankish side came out in the design, which cunningly concealed the fact that the machine had an unfair advantage. A Harvard mathematician got very upset when he lost to Hex, which actually followed a childishly simple strategy, but took an impressively long time to "think." He was all set to try again, when Shannon took pity on him and confessed the truth.

None of these devices made his fortune, though there was one near miss. Shannon and Edward Thorp, author of *Beat The Dealer*, once took a trip to Las Vegas with their wives and a computer, intent on outsmarting the roulette wheels. Unfortunately, the analog computer and the ratio apparatus were primitive by modern standards and so the enterprise failed for technical reasons. This was a pity: a night of testing in Shannon's basement had turned a few hundred imaginary dollars into $24,000.

A visit to his large house, down a shady lane a few miles from M.I.T., suggests that home life for Shannon has not been dull. There is a pile of penciled manuscripts of his mathematical work. Around the house there are five pianos and thirty other musical instruments ranging from piccolos to trumpets. Among a sizeable collection of chess playing machines is one which moves the pieces with a three fingered arm, beeps and makes wry comments. (In 1950 Shannon wrote the pioneering treatise on how a computer could be programmed to play chess.) In the garage, there is a dusty pile of unicycles and penny farthings. The chair lift he built to take his three children 450 feet down to the lakeside has been taken down, however, now that they are grown.

For some time his current interest has been juggling, continuing a life long fascination with balance and controlled instability. His machines include a motorized, gasoline powered pogo stick, a unicycle with an off center wheel (it keeps a rider steady while juggling), and a tandem unicycle that no couple has yet been able to ride. He goes to juggling conventions, and is polishing a paper for *Scientific American*. In the toy room there is a machine with soft bean bags for hands which "juggles" steel balls. His model masterpiece is a tiny stage on which three clowns juggle eleven rings, seven balls and five clubs, all driven by a diabolical mechanism of clockwork and rods, invisible to the viewer in black light illumination.

When I visited him, Shannon was just back from Japan, where he had given a speech and collected a Kyoto award in company with Messaien the composer. He was entertainingly hospitable, ready to show off photos of his family, a computer printout of his stock selections, and all his toys. His gruff laugh made it clear that fun is still his life's motif. Betty Shannon, a math graduate who met Shannon at Bell Labs, was his partner in the constant merriment. Occasionally the overlay of disarming geniality was penetrated, as a question gave him pause. Under the beetle brows his eyes would show the canny depths of genius.

OMNI: How many balls can you juggle?

Shannon: I can do four. With five I don't last very long! I can get them up there, but catching them is a different matter!

OMNI: Did your genius come unannounced, or was there science and invention in your background?

Shannon: My grandfather was an inventor who had some patents, a washing machine, stuff like that. He was also very interested in determining the exact turn of the century, how it should be fixed – 1900 or 1901. He owned a farm, and was always inventing farm machinery.

My father Claude was judge of probate in Gaylord, a little town of about 3000 people in Michigan. Small enough that if you walked a couple of blocks, you'd be in the countryside. Here is a picture of me playing the E Flat alto horn in the town band. Here's my mother, who was principal of the high school in Gaylord. Very intelligent person, as was my father. My father was clever mathematically and knew what he was talking about, but he didn't work in mathematics. My mother got glowing recommendations from her University of Michigan professors in languages.

I don't think there was much scientific influence between my father and myself. He was a little distant, and by the time I got to be ten or fifteen he was practically seventy. Although he certainly helped me when he could. I used to work with erector sets, and a friend of mine and I had a telegraph system between our houses, half a mile away, and we built the parts for this line for Morse Code signalling. Later we scrounged telephone equipment from the local exchange and connected up a telephone. I was always interested in building things that had funny motions, but my interest gradually shifted into electronics.

OMNI: Funny motions?

Shannon: Yes, especially like those dancers I used to see as a young man on the stage burlesque theatre! They had an interesting motion. Cheap joke!

OMNI: When was the erector set?

Shannon: In the seventh grade or so. As a matter of fact when Betty and I got married I said I'd always wished I'd got a number ten erector set, as I had only got up to eight and a half, and she gave me one for Christmas!

Betty Shannon: I went out and gave him the biggest erector set you could buy in this country – it was fifty bucks and everyone thought I was insane!

Shannon: Giving it to a grown man! But the fact of the matter is that it was extremely useful and I used it to try out different things. Now I have a number ten Meccano set and two others as well.

OMNI: Ashley Montagu in *Growing Young* says that it's important to remain playful in spirit through life. You seem to agree with that?

Shannon: Yes, I certainly do. I am always building totally useless gadgets, some of which you can see around here, just because I think they're fun to make. They have no commercial value, but I think they may be amusing.

OMNI: Don't you ever worry about the fact that they are not useful?

Shannon: No. That would be the last thing! Here's a picture of me riding a unicycle and juggling at the same time. That was more than thirty years ago. As a matter of fact you wouldn't believe the number of unicycles we have in our garage outside, and similar wheeled vehicles of very odd types. I have a certain fascination for them.

OMNI: You once made an enormous impression riding a unicycle and juggling at the same time in the corridors of Bell Labs!

Shannon: Yes I did! That created quite a stir.

OMNI: Was it such a staid place, Bell Labs, that this could create such a sensation?

Shannon: Oh no. Those people are very far out. But this was something that had never happened in the hall before. Bell Labs was and is the freest research group in the country associated with a commercial firm.

I worked at Bell Labs for fifteen years, and after that I was a consultant there. They gave you great freedom. To begin with you could work on what you wanted, your own ideas; they didn't come and say, "work on this!" At least, not to me. Not only that, but the people in my department in the mathematics research group were all very bright and capable and I had a lot of interaction with them. Yes, it is a great place.

OMNI: Can Bell Labs take credit to some extent for your achievement?

Shannon: I think so. If I had been in another company, more aimed at a particular goal I wouldn't have had the freedom to work that way. I think I could have done it if I had been at a university. Most universities are totally free in which kind of research their professors do, M.I.T. for instance. Bell Labs was very open-minded.

OMNI: Shockley, the inventor of the transistor, was there at Bell Labs when you were there – did you know him well?

Shannon: I remember going into his office, where he had a little object on his desk and I said "What's that?," and he said "It's a solid state amplifier," and explained that it amplified like a vacuum tube. In other words this was the transistor in its first version. Right there I got a little grasp of its importance because of its small size. I consider Shockley and his team there and Bardeen as the inventors of the most important thing discovered this century.

OMNI: Was the university environment less conducive to you?

Shannon: I believe that scientists get their best work done before they are fifty, or even earlier than that. I did most of my best work while I was young.

OMNI: Is there some magical quality which disappears with age?

Shannon: It may be that our brains are not as sharp as when we are young. If you look at the history of great scientists, and read about Newton or Einstein or people in that class, you find that their greatest work was done at a fairly young age, usually between twenty and fifty.

OMNI: Some recent research suggests that the brain physically responds to stimulating interests even in old age, and with growth in dendrites, and so there doesn't seem to be an obvious physical reason why the brain should not operate as well later. The experiments have been on rats, rather than people, of course!

Shannon: What did they do, ask them a hard mathematical question?

OMNI: Did your ambition wane at all?

Shannon: I don't think I was ever motivated by the notion of winning prizes, although I have a couple of dozen of them in the other room. I was more motivated by curiosity. Never by the desire for financial gain. I just wondered how things were put together. Or what laws or rules govern a situation, or if there are theorems about what one can't or can do. Mainly because I wanted to know myself. After I had found the answers it was always painful to write them up or to publish them (which is how you get the acclaim). There are many things I have done and never written up at all. Too lazy, I guess. I have a file upstairs of unfinished papers.

OMNI: You weren't affected by your success in the stock market, were you? Did it take away the necessity to work so hard?

Shannon: Certainly not. It's true we have been very successful in stocks, not just Teledyne, but Hewlett Packard, Motorola and many other companies. Indeed I even did some work on the theory of stocks and the stock market, which is among other papers that I have not published. Everybody wants to know what's in them! (Laughs.) It's funny. I gave a talk at M.I.T. on this subject some twenty years ago and outlined the mathematics, but never published it, and to this day people ask about it. Just last year when we were over in Brighton more than one person came up to me and said "I heard you talked at M.I.T. about the stock market!" I was amazed that anybody would even have remembered it!

OMNI: So your stock market success was based on mathematics?

Shannon: Oh yes. Mathematics and some good friends! More important, that! One of my good friends since college days was Henry Singleton, who is head of Teledyne. He started his company and asked me if I would like to invest in him. I had a good opinion of him and we put as much as we could into Teledyne, and that's gone off like crazy. That was in 1961.

Betty Shannon: We had already had one good experience with Bill Harrison, that taught us what can happen if you're lucky in the market.

Shannon: He started Harrison Laboratories, which merged with Hewlett Packard. That was in 1953. We've had quite a few things like that. But in addition, we do study the graphs and charts. The bottom line is that the mathematics is not as important in my opinion as the people and the product.

OMNI: What was the lecture at M.I.T. about?

Shannon: The best way to balance a portfolio – the optimal amount you should have in different stocks, to maximize the logarithm of the current value of the portfolio, if that is the thing you are trying to maximize. But let me say that a lot of this is negated by the tax laws. If you make money it becomes very painful to sell that stock, because you have to pay a capital gains tax. This tends to negate all the theoretical thinking.

OMNI: It is not about when to buy or sell an individual stock?

Shannon: A lot of people look at the stock price, when they should be looking at the basic company and its earnings. There are many problems concerned with the prediction of stochastic processes, for example the earnings of companies. When we consider a new investment, we look carefully at the earnings of the company, and think a lot about the future prospects of the product. We're fundamentalists, not technicians.

OMNI: Are you lucky too?

Shannon: Far beyond any reasonable expectations.

You know economists talk about the efficient market, and say everything is equalized out and nobody can really make any money, it's all luck and so on. I don't believe that's true at all. These are our current stocks, some of which we have only held a short time. The annual growth rates are punched out by our machine there every night, a prehistoric Apple II which Steve Jobs wired together himself.

The annual compounded growth rates of these stocks since we bought them, most of them quite a few years ago, are 31% a year, 11%, 185% (that one we haven't had too long), 30%, 31%, 181%, 10%, 18%, 114%, 21%, 2% and 27%. (Laughs.) That's the full list of our holdings.

OMNI: Which companies are the big gainers?

Shannon: Teledyne for example, we have held for 25 years, and it's compounded 27 per cent a year. The difference between going up 27 per cent and 10 per cent, such as you might get in a bank, is incredible, especially when that happens for 25 years.

OMNI: Is there a future to using mathematics to predict fluctuations in stock prices?

Shannon: My general feeling is that it is easier to choose companies which are going to succeed, than to predict short term variations, things which last only weeks or months, which they worry about on Wall Street Week. There is a lot more randomness there and things happen which you cannot predict, which cause people to sell or buy a lot of stock. I think it is very hard to predict short term stock fluctuations. Furthermore when you get into short term fluctuations you are always paying short term capital gains. With a long term stock you may never pay taxes because you keep it forever.

OMNI: How did you get to M.I.T.?

Shannon: When I got my bachelor's from Michigan I wasn't sure what I was going to do. There was this little postcard on the wall saying that M.I.T. was looking for somebody to run the differential analyser, a machine which Vannevar Bush had invented to solve differential equations. They wanted a research assistant to run it, and I applied for the job. I spent the next four years at M.I.T. getting first a Master's degree in electrical engineering, and then a doctorate in mathematics. So throughout my life I have been straddling those two fields.

OMNI: What was the differential analyser made of?

Shannon: The main machine was mechanical with spinning discs and integrators, and there was a complicated control circuit with relays. I had to understand both of these. The relay part got me interested. I knew about symbolic logic at the time from a course at Michigan, and I realized that Boolean algebra was just the thing to take care of relay circuits and switching circuits. I went to the library and got all the books I could on symbolic logic and Boolean algebra, started interplaying the two, and wrote my Master's thesis on it. That was the beginning of my great career! (Laughs.)

OMNI: You saw the connection between a relay circuit and Boolean algebra? It was quite an inspiration?

Shannon: Oh yeah. Trivial, actually, once you make it. The connection was not the main thing. The more important, harder part was working out the details, how to interleave the topology of the switching circuits, the way the contacts are connected up and so on, with the

Boolean algebra expressions. Working that out was a lot of fun. I think I had more fun doing that than anything else in my life, creatively speaking. It worked out so well. When I finished, it was shown to several people there, including Vannevar Bush who was then vice-president and dean of engineering at M.I.T.. He was very impressed and wrote a recommendation to get it published, and to get me into the mathematics department there, instead of electrical engineering. So I did my doctorate in mathematics.

OMNI: Was the basic insight that yes/no can be embodied in on/off switches so trivial?

Shannon: It's not so much that a thing is "open" or "closed," the "yes" or "no" that you mentioned. The real point is that two things in series are described by the word "and" in logic, so you would say this "and" this, while two things in parallel are described by the word "or." The word "not" connects with the back contact of a relay rather than the front contact. There are contacts which close when you operate the relay, and there are other contacts which open, so the word "not" is related to that aspect of relays. All of these things together form a more complex connection between Boolean algebra, if you like, or symbolic logic, and relay circuits.

The people who had worked with relay circuits were, of course, aware of how to make these things. But they didn't have the mathematical apparatus or the Boolean algebra to work with them, and to do them efficiently. A lot of my work has to do with minimizing circuits, trying to get the smallest number of contacts, for example. They had done this to a certain extent, but they hadn't gone deeply into the mathematics, so they hadn't done it nearly as well as you could with the Boolean algebra.

OMNI: But they already had some idea, did they, of translating the words "and," "or," and "not" into a physical embodiment?

Shannon: They all knew the simple fact that if you had two contacts in series both had to be closed to make a connection through. Or if they are in parallel, if either one is closed the connection is made. They knew it in that sense, but they didn't write down equations with plus and times, where plus is like a parallel connection and times is like a series connection.

OMNI: Still, making the connection between relay circuits and Boolean algebra was inspired, wasn't it?

Shannon: Well, I don't know what inspiration is. I think you do have flashes of insight. I may have had an insight one day and then I would spend some time in the library, writing equations and so on, and more insights would come.

OMNI: Most people don't know very much about your Ph.D. thesis, which applied mathematics to biology, I understand – it sounds like DNA coding?

Shannon: Yes, it's related to that. Animals have many pairs of chromosomes, long lines of genes, and when two animals mate they get one of a pair from the mother and one from the father, for each of the pairs. More complicated things can happen too. The chromosomes can have a crossover so that you only get a portion of one half and a portion of the other half.

I tried to get a mathematical description of what goes on when you mix these chromosomes in this kind of a process, and more generally when you have whole populations mixing their chromosomes this way – what goes on in the statistics of the different gene frequencies, which determine if your hair is brown, or what color your eyes are, or how tall you are.

So I set up an algebra which described this complicated process. One could calculate, if one wanted to (although not many people have wanted to in spite of my work), the kind of population you would have after a number of generations.

OMNI: So your scheme would tell us, for example, if Americans will eventually turn into a nation of brunettes?

Shannon: I don't know how many genes are related to hair color, I think probably more than one pair, just as IQ is not just one or two genes but probably a great many.

My theory has to do with what happens when you have all the genetic facts. But people don't know all of them, especially for humans. They are pretty well versed on the fruitfly! There they understand that this gene does this, this gene does that. But with regard to humans, it's hard to perform experiments to get the data. I was at a much more theoretical level, assuming that all the genetic facts were available.

OMNI: Before you wrote your classic paper on *The Mathematical Theory of Communication*, Norbert Wiener went round the offices at Bell Labs announcing "information is entropy." Did that remark provoke you in any way to come up with information theory?

Shannon: No. I hadn't even heard of that remark when I started my work. I don't think Wiener had much to do with information theory. He wasn't a big influence on my ideas there, though I once took a course from him. Don't get me wrong, he was a great mathematician. He was an idol of mine when I was a young student at M.I.T.

OMNI: When *The Mathematical Theory of Communication* was published, there was an indignant review by a certain mathematician, accusing you of mathematical dishonesty because your results weren't proved, he said, with mathematical rigor. Did you think that plain silly, or did you think, Well, maybe I should work hard to meet his criticisms?

Shannon: I didn't like his review. He hadn't read the paper carefully. You can write mathematics line by line with each tiny inference indicated, or you can assume that the reader understands what you are talking about. I was confident I was correct, not only in an intuitive way but in a rigorous way. I knew exactly what I was doing, and it all came out exactly right.

OMNI: How would you explain the impact of your information theory on communications engineering?

Shannon: On the philosophical level, one is able to understand the communication process and measure what is being sent, measure information in so many bits or choices per second. On the actual operational level, it enables you to combat noise and send information efficiently and use the right amount of redundancy to allow you to decode at the receiving end in spite of noisy communication.

OMNI: What about its importance in other fields? In the fifties, you criticized what you called the bandwagon effect, where people in your view over-enthusiastically applied your ideas to fields other than communications. Recently, the book *Grammatical Man* has again suggested that it may be widely applicable. Are you as skeptical as you were in the fifties about there being something more to it?

Shannon: I'd have to say I am interested in information theory and always was in the narrow sense of communication work, on problems of coding and so on. You can broaden the meaning of the term information theory to apply to all kinds of things, like genetics and how the brain works and so on.

Many people now see it in a much broader context than I ever did. They apply it for example to the nervous system of animals or humans, where information is transmitted along nerve networks, and there is redundancy, because the system is not very precise and accurate. This is a noisy system.

A similar thing happens in the social system where we have lots of aids to communication. If you're talking to me I might say "what?" which is a feedback system to overcome some of the noise, and to get correct transmission.

OMNI: Does your theory give a hint of how life might have evolved, seemingly in the face of the second law of thermodynamics, which says that order should slowly disintegrate?

Shannon: The evolution of the universe is certainly a very puzzling thing to me as well as to everybody else. It's fantastic we've ever come to the level of organization we have, starting from a big bang. Nonetheless, I believe in the big bang.

The second law of thermodynamics is not quite so simple as to say that from that big bang you couldn't get anything more than disorganization. There's a lot of energy involved. You could get local organization at the cost of overall increase of entropy. I'm a firm believer in an increase in entropy as time goes on. But you can use some of it to increase order elsewhere. In a steam engine, you can use disorganized heat energy to produce organized mechanical energy but only at a certain cost. So I think it's kind of that way in the universe.

I've puzzled many hours about the gradual organization of life and the structure of knowledge, and all the things we humans have. To me it's the most incredible thing! I don't happen to be a religious man and I don't think it would help if I were!

OMNI: You wouldn't want to say information theory is a substitute for belief in a God?

Shannon: I certainly would not!

OMNI: Marvin Minsky said you stopped working on information theory because you felt all the important theorems were proved. Is that correct?

Shannon: No, I just developed different interests. As life goes on, you change your direction.

OMNI: You have avoided the press over the years, have you?

Betty Shannon: Not deliberately. On the other hand, we haven't sought them either. We live very quietly.

Shannon: I'll tell you this, I'm not too crazy about interviews.

OMNI: Did you feel you were destined for fame?

Shannon: I don't think so. I always thought I was quite sharp scientifically, but scientists by and large don't get the press that politicians or authors or other people do. I thought my paper on switching was quite good, and I got a prize for it, and I thought my information paper was very good, and I got all kinds of acclaim for that – there's a wallful of prizes and stuff in the other room.

OMNI: Do you find fame a burden?

Shannon: Not too much. I have people like you coming and wasting my afternoons, but that isn't too much of a burden!

OMNI: Why is juggling so interesting to you, especially mathematically?

Shannon: I did write a paper for *Scientific American*, as yet unpublished. There is a theorem which relates to how many balls you are juggling, and how long each one is in the air. I talk about a uniform juggle where every time you throw a ball it stays in the air the same amount of time, and when it hits your hand it stays there the same amount of time. We visualize a person not just with two hands but with several hands, or there could be several different people involved. The theorem relates five quantities, the number of hands, the number of balls, the vacant time when your hand has nothing in it, the contact time and the flight time. These five things are all connected by a very simple relationship, which would be exciting to nobody except a few mathematically inclined jugglers!

OMNI: Would it lead to a way of juggling more objects than ever before?

Shannon: You have to throw the balls higher to get more time, and it gives an indication of how much higher you have to throw them, as a function of the number of balls you are juggling.

I've measured jugglers with stopwatches and observed how they do it, and if they're juggling seven balls, which is a very hard thing to do, they have to throw them very high. I even had them put metallic strips on jugglers' hands and had them juggling metal covered balls so they would close a contact when they were holding the balls, and ran this data into electronic clocks.

OMNI: Does it show what the limits of juggling are? Can we say that no one will ever juggle more than fifteen balls, for example?

Shannon: No. All you have to do is throw them higher and be quicker. Indeed a friend of ours holds the world record of twelve rings.

OMNI: It's remarkable that you've never commercialized your delightful juggling clowns.

Betty Shannon: Oh fiddle!

Shannon: Well, I don't think there would be too much of a market.

Betty Shannon: We don't really believe in commercializing fun.

OMNI: You have a nice array of computerized chess machines in your toy room. Do you still play chess?

Shannon: I don't play at all.

Betty Shannon: He used to play very well. Good enough to play Botvinnik in Moscow. Claude at one point got the exchange. Botvinnik was worried. He finally won, but it was close.

OMNI: Do you find it depressing that chess computers are getting so strong?

Shannon: I am not depressed by it. I am rooting for machines. I have always been on the machines' side.

Betty Shannon: Some people get very angry when he says that.

Shannon: I am not depressed by machines getting better. Whether people are going to be replaced by machines, I don't know. That's a hard question. It may be possible within a century or so, that machines are going to be doing almost everything better than we do. They already do a lot of things better than we do. An automobile can go down the street a heck of a lot faster than any person can, for example. They can do factory work of all kinds better than we can. The highly intellectual stuff is going to come later.

But I wouldn't be at all surprised, no.

OMNI: Do you agree with Norbert Wiener, who is reported to have denied any basic distinction between life and non-life, man and machine?

Shannon: That's a heavily loaded question! Let me say this. I am an atheist to begin with. I believe in evolutionary theory and that we are basically machines, but a very complex type, far more so than any machine man has made yet. So in a way that's both a Yes and a No. We are kind of an extreme case of mechanical device – by mechanical I don't mean just metals are involved, of course, gears and so on. A natural device. I see no God involved or anything like that.

OMNI: Will robots be complex enough to be friends of people, do you think?

Shannon: I think so. But it's quite a way away.

OMNI: Could you imagine being friends with a robot?

Shannon: Yes I could. I could imagine that happening very easily. I see no limit to the capability of machines. The microchips are getting smaller and smaller and faster and faster and I can see them getting better than we are. I can visualize sometime in the future we will be to robots as dogs are to humans.

OMNI: Can you imagine a robot President of the United States?

Shannon: Could be! I think by then you wouldn't speak of the United States any more. It would be a totally different organization.

OMNI: Is your famous proof that a reliable circuit can be built using unreliable components relevant to the brain's operations? Could the brain be making use of such design?

Shannon: How the brain manages to work so well with the kinds of elements it has is quite a puzzle. It must make some use of redundancy in its connections. We know the brain can suffer all kinds of damage and in particular neurons can go out of operation and it can still handle things pretty well. So it must use some redundancy to take care of faulty operations. But whether it does it the way we discussed in that paper is a much deeper and harder question.

In a modern desk computer there is generally no redundancy. If one part gets into trouble that will show up in later operation. It seems to me that the way the brain works and how we manage to live in spite of all kinds of internal troubles shows that there must be a great deal of redundancy there, and a design which involves some kind of concept of multiple units or parallelism.

OMNI: But your paper involved more than redundancy – you showed that even if you had relays which closed only 60 per cent of the time when triggered, you could still cleverly design a circuit which would work. Could the brain be using such an approach?

Shannon: The brain has ten billion neurons, or some such huge number, so probably it is cheaper for biology to make more components than to work out sophisticated circuits. But I wouldn't put it past evolution to do some very clever things like that! I am totally astounded by how clever and sophisticated some of the things we see in the human or animal bodies are, due to long evolutionary changes, I presume. This could be happening in the brain, but an easier way would be parallelism. The brain is pretty sophisticated in other directions, as we know. When it really gets going we have all these clever people like Einstein.

OMNI: Why aren't you more involved with computers, personally? One would think you would love playing with them. Aren't they the ultimate gadget?

Shannon: I don't mess around with programming at all. I find that kind of dull, feeding stuff into a computer. Designing computers would be more my taste, but I haven't been feeling much like it lately. I guess I've had a bellyful of that game. There was the differential analyser, then relay circuits, and all those things that were leading up to these computers, and I've written papers on all those subjects.

OMNI: Perhaps you like machines that you can build yourself, rather than computers which you can't build from scratch any more?

Shannon: I do like the physical aspects of these things, but you're oversimplifying to say I don't really like the symbolic things too. Mathematics itself involves symbolics.

OMNI: Where did you find all your chess machines?

Shannon: There's a store in Los Angeles which has all these different chess machines.

Mrs. Shannon: Claude went hog wild.

Shannon: Yes. Bought one of each.

OMNI: Did you make the motorized pogo stick hanging in your garage?

Shannon: No, I bought it, from a guy in New Jersey who made it. I don't think he had much success with it. I may have been one of the few buyers. It's gasoline driven. There's a piston in it which fires each time it comes down, so you go along at great velocity! But I found it very uncomfortable. · It was kind of a shock each time the thing exploded there and so it didn't ever get much use.

OMNI: When you went to Las Vegas equipped with computer and radio to win at roulette, why did you abandon the project?

Shannon: The thing worked very well here in the house. The roulette wheel is up in the attic now. A real professional one you know. The predictor would predict not in which hole the ball was going to fall but which half of the wheel. It was a lot better than a 50-50 prognosis. Two thirds of the time it would pick the right half of the wheel. This improved the odds so that you would win at a very good rate if it kept going.

OMNI: It worked extremely well, then, on that roulette wheel at least. How did it do it?

Shannon: Part of it depended on the fact that wheels in Las Vegas and elsewhere are somewhat tilted, and they don't level them up well. We examined many wheels and we could see some of them were tilted quite strongly. If you pick those out then there is a strong probability that the ball will fall in a certain segment of the outside of the wheel, and you can tell quite well how long it will take for that to happen.

If you time the spinning of the wheel you can see where the wheel is going to be when the ball falls in. The wheel is going around one way and the ball is going around the other, and you find the concurrence of those two things, where the wheel is going to be when the ball falls in. It's a simple dynamical system with very little friction.

OMNI: Why wouldn't you have to take into account the strength of the croupier's throw?

Shannon: The device we used timed both the wheel and the ball. The person standing there would press a button when they gave the wheel a good spin, and the double zero went by a certain point, and also when the ball was thrown and passed a certain point, and came around again to that point. The croupier could throw it at different speeds, true, but this was taken into account in the computation.

OMNI: But you had to see where it started?

Shannon: You had to both time the wheel and get an indication of when the ball left the croupier's hand. Both of those things were involved in this little computer that we made. But we had a lot of practical problems, and we never made any money really.

OMNI: But could you have made money if you had worked hard to solve these purely practical problems?

Shannon: I think so, if we had been willing to spend another month cleaning up details. But we got discouraged after we spent a lot of time and effort.

OMNI: You once wrote that the redundancy of a language determined whether you could have crossword puzzles in that language, and that since English has a redundancy of about half, you couldn't have three dimensional crossword puzzles in English. Is that right?

Shannon: Yes. You can't build big ones in three dimensions. In English there are more constraints among the letters, and it gets harder to find other words which will tie them together in a two dimensional pattern. A fortiori, if I may use another English word, it gets even harder to tie them together in three dimensions.

OMNI: Your interest in balance and controlled instability which shows up in your unicycles and juggling is very relevant to robots and their control systems. Are the robot designers making the pilgrimage to your house to ask about robots?

Shannon: I have built a number of robotic devices and juggling machines. They are more a matter of entertainment for me than practical devices for the rest of the world. I like to show them off to people but I don't expect to sell very many.

OMNI: If you were funded to the full would you build a robot that would ride a bicycle?

Shannon: Oh, I have built little bicycle riders already. I have one four inches high that rides a tiny two wheeled bicycle. That's almost trivial to do, actually. I worked on a little mechanical unicycle rider but I never got that working very well.

OMNI: Is it true you investigated the idea of mirrored rooms?

Shannon: Yes, I tried to work out all the possible mirrored rooms that made sense, in that if you looked everywhere from inside one, space would be divided into a bunch of rooms, and you would be in each room and this would go on to infinity without contradiction. That is, you'd move your head around and everything would look sensible. I think there were seven types of room. I planned to build them all in my extra room here and give people an exciting tour.

The simplest case would be a cube where you would just see an infinite series of yourself receding into the distance. All of space would be divided sensibly into these cubical patterns. But other ones, tetrahedra and so on, yield much more complex and interesting patterns. I will build them if I can finish all my other projects!

At the moment I am working on another juggling machine, which might juggle five balls. I am using an air hockey table, and plan to juggle disks by tilting the table.

OMNI: What's your secret in remaining so carefree?

Shannon: I do what comes naturally, and usefulness is not my main goal. I like to solve new problems all the time. I keep asking myself, *How would you do this? Is it possible to make a machine to do that? Can you prove this theorem?* These are my kind of problems. Not because I am going to do something useful.

Bibliography of Claude Elwood Shannon

[1] "A Symbolic Analysis of Relay and Switching Circuits," *Transactions American Institute of Electrical Engineers*, Vol. 57 (1938), pp. 713-723. (Received March 1, 1938.) Included in Part B.

[2] Letter to Vannevar Bush, Feb. 16, 1939. Printed in F.-W. Hagemeyer, *Die Entstehung von Informationskonzepten in der Nachrichtentechnik: eine Fallstudie zur Theoriebildung in der Technik in Industrie- und Kriegsforschung* [*The Origin of Information Theory Concepts in Communication Technology: Case Study for Engineering Theory-Building in Industrial and Military Research*], Doctoral Dissertation, Free Univ. Berlin, Nov. 8, 1979, 570 pp. Included in Part A.

[3] "An Algebra for Theoretical Genetics," Ph.D. Dissertation, Department of Mathematics, Massachusetts Institute of Technology, April 15, 1940, 69 pp. Included in Part C.

[4] "A Theorem on Color Coding," Memorandum 40-130-153, July 8, 1940, Bell Laboratories. Superseded by "A Theorem on Coloring the Lines of a Network." Not included.

[5] "The Use of the Lakatos-Hickman Relay in a Subscriber Sender," Memorandum MM 40-130-179, August 3, 1940, Bell Laboratories, 7 pp. + 8 figs. Abstract only included in Part B.

[6] "Mathematical Theory of the Differential Analyzer," *Journal of Mathematics and Physics*, Vol. 20 (1941), pp. 337-354. Included in Part B.

[7] "A Study of the Deflection Mechanism and Some Results on Rate Finders," Report to National Defense Research Committee, Div. 7-311-M1, circa April, 1941, 37 pp. + 15 figs. Abstract only included in Part B.

[8] "Backlash in Overdamped Systems," Report to National Defense Research Committee, Princeton Univ., May 14, 1941, 6 pp. Abstract only included in Part B.

[9] "A Height Data Smoothing Mechanism," Report to National Defense Research Committee, Div. 7-313.2-M1, Princeton Univ., May 26, 1941, 9 pp. + 9 figs. Not included.

[10] "The Theory of Linear Differential and Smoothing Operators," Report to National Defense Research Committee, Div. 7-313.1-M1, Princeton Univ., June 8, 1941, 11 pp. Not included.

[11] "Some Experimental Results on the Deflection Mechanism," Report to National Defense Research Committee, Div. 7-311-M1, June 26, 1941, 11 pp. Abstract only included in Part B.

[12] "Criteria for Consistency and Uniqueness in Relay Circuits," Typescript, Sept. 8, 1941, 5 pp. + 3 figs. Not included.

[13] "The Theory and Design of Linear Differential Equation Machines," Report to the Services 20, Div. 7-311-M2, Jan. 1942, Bell Laboratories, 73 pp. + 30 figs. Included in Part B.

[14]   (With John Riordan) "The Number of Two-Terminal Series-Parallel Networks," *Journal of Mathematics and Physics*, Vol. 21 (August, 1942), pp. 83-93. Included in Part B.

[15]   "Analogue of the Vernam System for Continuous Time Series," Memorandum MM 43-110-44, May 10, 1943, Bell Laboratories, 4 pp. + 4 figs. Included in Part A.

[16]   (With W. Feller) "On the Integration of the Ballistic Equations on the Aberdeen Analyzer," Applied Mathematics Panel Report No. 28.1, National Defense Research Committee, July 15, 1943, 9 pp. Not included.

[17]   "Pulse Code Modulation," Memorandum MM 43-110-43, December 1, 1943, Bell Laboratories. Not included.

[18]   "Feedback Systems with Periodic Loop Closure," Memorandum MM 44-110-32, March 16, 1944, Bell Laboratories. Not included.

[19]   "Two New Circuits for Alternate Pulse Counting," Typescript, May 29, 1944, Bell Laboratories, 2 pp. + 3 Figs. Not included.

[20]   "Counting Up or Down With Pulse Counters," Typescript, May 31, 1944, Bell Laboratories, 1 p. + 1 fig. Not included.

[21]   (With B. M. Oliver) "Circuits for a P.C.M. Transmitter and Receiver," Memorandum MM 44-110-37, June 1, 1944, Bell Laboratories, 4 pp., 11 figs. Abstract only included in Part A.

[22]   "The Best Detection of Pulses," Memorandum MM 44-110-28, June 22, 1944, Bell Laboratories, 3 pp. Included in Part A.

[23]   "Pulse Shape to Minimize Bandwidth With Nonoverlapping Pulses," Typescript, August 4, 1944, Bell Laboratories, 4 pp. Not included.

[24]   "A Mathematical Theory of Cryptography," Memorandum MM 45-110-02, Sept. 1, 1945, Bell Laboratories, 114 pp. + 25 figs. Superseded by the following paper. Not included.

[25]   "Communication Theory of Secrecy Systems," *Bell System Technical Journal*, Vol. 28 (1949), pp. 656-715. "The material in this paper appeared originally in a confidential report 'A Mathematical Theory of Cryptography', dated Sept. 1, 1945, which has now been declassified." Included in Part A.

[26]   "Mixed Statistical Determinate Systems," Typescript, Sept. 19, 1945, Bell Laboratories, 17 pp. Not included.

[27]   (With R. B. Blackman and H. W. Bode) "Data Smoothing and Prediction in Fire-Control Systems," Summary Technical Report, Div. 7, National Defense Research Committee, Vol. 1, *Gunfire Control*, Washington, DC, 1946, pp. 71-159 and 166-167. AD 200795. Also in National Military Establishment Research and Development Board, Report #13 MGC 12/1, August 15, 1948. Superseded by [51] and by R. B. Blackman, *Linear Data-Smoothing and Prediction in Theory and Practice*, Addison-Wesley, Reading, Mass., 1965. Not included.

[28]   (With B. M. Oliver) "Communication System Employing Pulse Code Modulation," Patent 2,801,281. Filed Feb. 21, 1946, granted July 30, 1957.

Not included.

[29]   (With B. D. Holbrook) "A Sender Circuit For Panel or Crossbar Telephone Systems," Patent application circa 1946, application dropped April 13, 1948. Not included.

[30]   (With C. L. Dolph) "The Transient Behavior of a Large Number of Four-Terminal Unilateral Linear Networks Connected in Tandem," Memorandum MM 46-110-49, April 10, 1946, Bell Laboratories, 34 pp. + 16 figs. Abstract only included in Part B.

[31]   "Electronic Methods in Telephone Switching," Typescript, October 17, 1946, Bell Laboratories, 5 pp. + 1 fig. Not included.

[32]   "Some Generalizations of the Sampling Theorem," Typescript, March 4, 1948, 5 pp. + 1 fig. Not included.

[33]   (With J. R. Pierce and J. W. Tukey) "Cathode-Ray Device," Patent 2,576,040. Filed March 10, 1948, granted Nov. 20, 1951. Not included.

[34]   "The Normal Ergodic Ensembles of Functions," Typescript, March 15, 1948, 5 pp. Not included.

[35]   "Systems Which Approach the Ideal as P/N $\to$ ∞," Typescript, March 15, 1948, 2 pp. Not included.

[36]   "Theorems on Statistical Sequences," Typescript, March 15, 1948, 8 pp. Not included.

[37]   "A Mathematical Theory of Communication," *Bell System Technical Journal*, Vol. 27 (July and October 1948), pp. 379-423 and 623-656. Reprinted in D. Slepian, editor, *Key Papers in the Development of Information Theory*, IEEE Press, NY, 1974. Included in Part A.

[38]   (With Warren Weaver) *The Mathematical Theory of Communication*, University of Illinois Press, Urbana, IL, 1949, vi + 117 pp. Reprinted (and repaginated) 1963. The section by Shannon is essentially identical to the previous item. Not included.

[39]   (With Warren Weaver) *Mathematische Grundlagen der Informationstheorie*, Scientia Nova, Oldenbourg Verlag, Münich, 1976, pp. 143. German translation of the preceding book. Not included.

[40]   (With B. M. Oliver and J. R. Pierce) "The Philosophy of PCM," *Proceedings Institute of Radio Engineers*, Vol. 36 (1948), pp. 1324-1331. (Received May 24, 1948.) Included in Part A.

[41]   "Samples of Statistical English," Typescript, June 11, 1948, Bell Laboratories, 3 pp. Not included.

[42]   "Network Rings," Typescript, June 11, 1948, Bell Laboratories, 26 pp. + 4 figs. Included in Part B.

[43]   "Communication in the Presence of Noise," *Proceedings Institute of Radio Engineers*, Vol. 37 (1949), pp. 10-21. (Received July 23, 1940 [1948?].) Reprinted in D. Slepian, editor, *Key Papers in the Development of Information Theory*, IEEE Press, NY, 1974. Reprinted in *Proceedings Institute of Electrical and Electronic Engineers*, Vol. 72 (1984), pp. 1192-1201. Included

in Part A.

[44]   "A Theorem on Coloring the Lines of a Network," *Journal of Mathematics and Physics*, Vol. 28 (1949), pp. 148-151. (Received Sept. 14, 1948.) Included in Part B.

[45]   "Significance and Application [of Communication Research]," *Symposium on Communication Research, 11-13 October, 1948*, Research and Development Board, Department of Defense, Washington, DC, pp. 14-23, 1948. Not included.

[46]   "Note on Certain Transcendental Numbers," Typescript, October 27, 1948, Bell Laboratories, 1 p. Not included.

[47]   "A Case of Efficient Coding for a Very Noisy Channel," Typescript, Nov. 18, 1948, Bell Laboratories, 2 pp. Not included.

[48]   "Note on Reversing a Discrete Markhoff Process," Typescript, Dec. 6 1948, Bell Laboratories, 2 pp. + 2 Figs. Not included.

[49]   "Information Theory," Typescript of abstract of talk for American Statistical Society, 1949, 5 pp. Not included.

[50]   "The Synthesis of Two-Terminal Switching Circuits," *Bell System Technical Journal*, Vol. 28 (Jan., 1949), pp. 59-98. Included in Part B.

[51]   (With H. W. Bode) "A Simplified Derivation of Linear Least Squares Smoothing and Prediction Theory," *Proceedings Institute of Radio Engineers*, Vol. 38 (1950), pp. 417-425. (Received July 13, 1949.) Included in Part B.

[52]   "Review of *Transformations on Lattices and Structures of Logic* by Stephen A. Kiss," *Proceedings Institute of Radio Engineers*, Vol. 37 (1949), p. 1163. Included in Part B.

[53]   "Review of *Cybernetics, or Control and Communication in the Animal and the Machine* by Norbert Wiener," *Proceedings Institute of Radio Engineers*, Vol. 37 (1949), p. 1305. Included in Part B.

[54]   "Programming a Computer for Playing Chess," *Philosophical Magazine*, Series 7, Vol. 41 (No. 314, March 1950), pp. 256-275. (Received Nov. 8, 1949.) Reprinted in D. N. L. Levy, editor, *Computer Chess Compendium*, Springer-Verlag, NY, 1988. Included in Part B.

[55]   "A Chess-Playing Machine," *Scientific American*, Vol. 182 (No. 2, February 1950), pp. 48-51. Reprinted in *The World of Mathematics*, edited by James R. Newman, Simon and Schuster, NY, Vol. 4, 1956, pp. 2124-2133. Included in Part B.

[56]   "Memory Requirements in a Telephone Exchange," *Bell System Technical Journal*, Vol. 29 (1950), pp. 343-349. (Received Dec. 7, 1949.) Included in Part B.

[57]   "A Symmetrical Notation for Numbers," *American Mathematical Monthly*, Vol. 57 (Feb., 1950), pp. 90-93. Included in Part B.

[58]   "Proof of an Integration Formula," Typescript, circa 1950, Bell Laboratories, 2 pp. Not included.

[59]   "A Digital Method of Transmitting Information," Typescript, no date, circa
       1950, Bell Laboratories, 3 pp. Not included.

[60]   "Communication Theory — Exposition of Fundamentals," in "Report of
       Proceedings, Symposium on Information Theory, London, Sept., 1950,"
       Institute of Radio Engineers, Transactions on Information Theory, No. 1
       (February, 1953), pp. 44-47. Included in Part A.

[61]   "General Treatment of the Problem of Coding," in "Report of Proceedings,
       Symposium on Information Theory, London, Sept., 1950," *Institute of Radio
       Engineers, Transactions on Information Theory*, No. 1 (February, 1953), pp.
       102-104. Included in Part A.

[62]   "The Lattice Theory of Information," in "Report of Proceedings, Symposium
       on Information Theory, London, Sept., 1950," *Institute of Radio Engineers,
       Transactions on Information Theory*, No. 1 (February, 1953), pp. 105-107.
       Included in Part A.

[63]   (With E. C. Cherry, S. H. Moss, Dr. Uttley, I. J. Good, W. Lawrence and W. P.
       Anderson) "Discussion of Preceding Three Papers," in "Report of
       Proceedings, Symposium on Information Theory, London, Sept., 1950,"
       Institute of Radio Engineers, Transactions on Information Theory, No. 1
       (February, 1953), pp. 169-174. Included in Part A.

[64]   "Review of *Description of a Relay Computer*, by the Staff of the [Harvard]
       Computation Laboratory," *Proceedings Institute of Radio Engineers*, Vol. 38
       (1950), p. 449. Included in Part B.

[65]   "Recent Developments in Communication Theory," *Electronics*, Vol. 23
       (April, 1950), pp. 80-83. Included in Part A

[66]   German translation of [65], in *Tech. Mitt. P.T.T.*, Bern, Vol. 28 (1950), pp.
       337-342. Not included.

[67]   "A Method of Power or Signal Transmission To a Moving Vehicle,"
       Memorandum for Record, July 19, 1950, Bell Laboratories, 2 pp. + 4 figs.
       Included in Part B.

[68]   "Some Topics in Information Theory," in *Proceedings International Congress
       of Mathematicians (Cambridge, Mass., Aug. 30 - Sept. 6, 1950)* , American
       Mathematical Society, Vol. II (1952), pp. 262-263. Included in Part A.

[69]   "Prediction and Entropy of Printed English," *Bell System Technical Journal*,
       Vol. 30 (1951), pp. 50-64. (Received Sept. 15, 1950.) Reprinted in D. Slepian,
       editor, *Key Papers in the Development of Information Theory*, IEEE Press, NY,
       1974. Included in Part A.

[70]   "Presentation of a Maze Solving Machine," in *Cybernetics: Circular, Causal
       and Feedback Mechanisms in Biological and Social Systems, Transactions
       Eighth Conference, March 15-16, 1951, New York, N. Y.*, edited by H. von
       Foerster, M. Mead and H. L. Teuber, Josiah Macy Jr. Foundation, New York,
       1952, pp. 169-181. Included in Part B.

[71]   "Control Apparatus," Patent application Aug. 1951, dropped Jan. 21, 1954.
       Not included.

[72] "Creative Thinking," Typescript, March 20, 1952, Bell Laboratories, 10 pp. Not included.

[73] "A Mind-Reading (?) Machine," Typescript, March 18, 1953, Bell Laboratories, 4 pp. Included in Part B.

[74] (With E. F. Moore) "The Relay Circuit Analyzer," Memorandum MM 53-1400-9, March 31, 1953, Bell Laboratories, 14 pp. + 4 figs. Abstract only included in Part B.

[75] "The Potentialities of Computers," Typescript, April 3, 1953, Bell Laboratories. Included in Part B.

[76] "Throbac I," Typescript, April 9, 1953, Bell Laboratories, 5 pp. Included in Part B.

[77] "Throbac – Circuit Operation," Typescript, April 9, 1953, Bell Laboratories, 7 pp. Not included.

[78] "Tower of Hanoi," Typescript, April 20, 1953, Bell Laboratories, 4 pp. Not included.

[79] (With E. F. Moore) "Electrical Circuit Analyzer," Patent 2,776,405. Filed May 18, 1953, granted Jan. 1, 1957. Not included.

[80] (With E. F. Moore) "Machine Aid for Switching Circuit Design," *Proceedings Institute of Radio Engineers*, Vol. 41 (1953), pp. 1348-1351. (Received May 28, 1953.) Included in Part B.

[81] "Mathmanship or How to Give an Explicit Solution Without Actually Solving the Problem," Typescript, June 3, 1953, Bell Laboratories, 2 pp. Not included.

[82] "Computers and Automata," *Proceedings Institute of Radio Engineers*, Vol. 41 (1953), pp. 1234-1241. (Received July 17, 1953.) Reprinted in *Methodos*, Vol. 6 (1954), pp. 115-130. Included in Part B.

[83] "Realization of All 16 Switching Functions of Two Variables Requires 18 Contacts," Memorandum MM 53-1400-40, November 17, 1953, Bell Laboratories, 4 pp. + 2 figs. Included in Part B.

[84] (With E. F. Moore) "The Relay Circuit Synthesizer," Memorandum MM 53-140-52, November 30, 1953, Bell Laboratories, 26 pp. + 5 figs. Abstract only included in Part B.

[85] (With D. W. Hagelbarger) "A Relay Laboratory Outfit for Colleges," Memorandum MM 54-114-17, January 10, 1954, Bell Laboratories. Included in Part B.

[86] "Efficient Coding of a Binary Source With One Very Infrequent Symbol," Memorandum MM 54-114-7, January 29, 1954, Bell Laboratories. Included in Part A.

[87] "Bounds on the Derivatives and Rise Time of a Band and Amplitude Limited Signal," Typescript, April 8, 1954, Bell Laboratories, 6 pp. + 1 Fig. Not included.

[88] (With Edward F. Moore) "Reliable Circuits Using Crummy Relays," Memorandum 54-114-42, Nov. 29, 1954, Bell Laboratories. Published as the

following two items.

[89] (With Edward F. Moore) "Reliable Circuits Using Less Reliable Relays I," *Journal Franklin Institute*, Vol. 262 (Sept., 1956), pp. 191-208. Included in Part B.

[90] (With Edward F. Moore) "Reliable Circuits Using Less Reliable Relays II," *Journal Franklin Institute*, Vol. 262 (Oct., 1956), pp. 281-297. Included in Part B.

[91] (Edited jointly with John McCarthy) *Automata Studies*, Annals of Mathematics Studies Number 34, Princeton University Press, Princeton, NJ, 1956, ix + 285 pp. The Preface, Table of Contents, and the two papers by Shannon are included in Part B.

[92] (With John McCarthy), *Studien zur Theorie der Automaten*, Münich, 1974. (German translation of the preceding work.)

[93] "A Universal Turing Machine With Two Internal States," Memorandum 54-114-38, May 15, 1954, Bell Laboratories. Published in *Automata Studies*, pp. 157-165. Included in Part B.

[94] (With Karel de Leeuw, Edward F. Moore and N. Shapiro) "Computability by Probabilistic Machines," Memorandum 54-114-37, Oct. 21, 1954, Bell Laboratories. Published in [87], pp. 183-212. Included in Part B.

[95] "Concavity of Transmission Rate as a Function of Input Probabilities," Memorandum MM 55-114-28, June 8, 1955, Bell Laboratories. Abstract only is included in Part A.

[96] "Some Results on Ideal Rectifier Circuits," Memorandum MM 55-114-29, June 8, 1955, Bell Laboratories. Included in Part B.

[97] "The Simultaneous Synthesis of s Switching Functions of n Variables," Memorandum MM 55-114-30, June 8, 1955, Bell Laboratories. Included in Part B.

[98] (With D. W. Hagelbarger) "Concavity of Resistance Functions," *Journal Applied Physics*, Vol. 27 (1956), pp. 42-43. (Received August 1, 1955.) Included in Part B.

[99] "Game Playing Machines," *Journal Franklin Institute*, Vol. 260 (1955), pp. 447-453. (Delivered Oct. 19, 1955.) Included in Part B.

[100] "Information Theory," *Encyclopedia Britannica*, Chicago, IL, 14th Edition, 1968 printing, Vol. 12, pp. 246B-249. (Written circa 1955.) Included in Part A.

[101] "Cybernetics," *Encyclopedia Britannica*, Chicago, IL, 14th Edition, 1968 printing, Vol. 12. (Written circa 1955.) Not included.

[102] "The Rate of Approach to Ideal Coding (Abstract)," *Proceedings Institute of Radio Engineers*, Vol. 43 (1955), p. 356. Included in Part A.

[103] "The Bandwagon (Editorial)," *Institute of Radio Engineers, Transactions on Information Theory*, Vol. IT-2 (March, 1956), p. 3. Included in Part A.

[104]   "Information Theory," Seminar Notes, Massachusetts Institute of Technology, 1956 and succeeding years. Not included. Contains the following sections:

"A skeleton key to the information theory notes," 3 pp. "Bounds on the tails of martingales and related questions," 19 pp. "Some useful inequalities for distribution functions," 3 pp. "A lower bound on the tail of a distribution," 9 pp. "A combinatorial theorem," 1 p. "Some results on determinants," 3 pp. "Upper and lower bounds for powers of a matrix with non-negative elements," 3 pp. "The number of sequences of a given length," 3 pp. "Characteristic for a language with independent letters," 4 pp. "The probability of error in optimal codes," 5 pp. "Zero error codes and the zero error capacity C_0," 10 pp. "Lower bound for P_{ef} for a completely connected channel with feedback," 1 p. "A lower bound for P_e when $R > C$," 2 pp. "A lower bound for P_e," 2 pp. "Lower bound with one type of input and many types of output," 3 pp. "Application of 'sphere-packing' bounds to feedback case," 8 pp. "A result for the memoryless feedback channel," 1 p. "Continuity of $P_{e\,opt}$ as a function of transition probabilities," 1 p. "Codes of a fixed composition," 1 p. "Relation of P_e to ρ," 2 pp. "Bound on P_e for random ode by simple threshold argument," 4 pp. "A bound on P_e for a random code," 3 pp. "The Feinstein bound," 2 pp. "Relations between probability and minimum word separation," 4 pp. "Inequalities for decodable codes," 3 pp. "Convexity of channel capacity as a function of transition probabilities," 1 pp. "A geometric interpretation of channel capacity," 6 pp. "Log moment generating function for the square of a Gaussian variate," 2 pp. "Upper bound on P_e for Gaussian channel by expurgated random code," 2 pp. "Lower bound on P_e in Gaussian channel by minimum distance argument," 2 pp. "The sphere packing bound for the Gaussian power limited channel," 4 pp. "The T-terminal channel," 7 pp. "Conditions for constant mutual information," 2 pp. "The central limit theorem with large deviations," 6 pp. "The Chernoff inequality," 2 pp. "Upper and lower bounds on the tails of distributions," 4 pp. "Asymptotic behavior of the distribution function," 5 pp. "Generalized Chebycheff and Chernoff inequalities," 1 p. "Channels with side information at the transmitter," 13 pp. "Some miscellaneous results in coding theory," 15 pp. "Error probability bounds for noisy channels," 20 pp.

[105]   "Reliable Machines from Unreliable Components," notes of five lectures, Massachusetts Institute of Technology, Spring 1956, 24 pp. Not included.

[106]   "The Portfolio Problem, and How to Pay the Forecaster," lecture notes taken by W. W. Peterson, Massachusetts Institute of Technology, Spring, 1956, 8 pp. Not included.

[107]   "Notes on Relation of Error Probability to Delay in a Noisy Channel," notes of a lecture, Massachusetts Institute of Technology, Aug. 30, 1956, 3 pp. Not included.

[108]   "Notes on the Kelly Betting Theory of Noisy Information," notes of a lecture, Massachusetts Institute of Technology, Aug. 31, 1956, 2 pp. Not included.

[109]   "The Zero Error Capacity of a Noisy Channel," *Institute of Radio Engineers, Transactions on Information Theory*, Vol. IT-2 (September, 1956), pp. S8-S19. Reprinted in D. Slepian, editor, *Key Papers in the Development of Information*

Theory, IEEE Press, NY, 1974. Included in Part A.

[110] (With Peter Elias and Amiel Feinstein) "A Note on the Maximum Flow Through a Network," *Institute of Radio Engineers, Transactions on Information Theory*, Vol. IT-2 (December, 1956), pp. 117-119. (Received July 11, 1956.) Included in Part B.

[111] "Certain Results in Coding Theory for Noisy Channels," *Information and Control*, Vol. 1 (1957), pp. 6-25. (Received April 22, 1957.) Reprinted in D. Slepian, editor, *Key Papers in the Development of Information Theory*, IEEE Press, NY, 1974. Included in Part A.

[112] "Geometrische Deutung einiger Ergebnisse bei die Berechnung der Kanal Capazität" [Geometrical meaning of some results in the calculation of channel capacity], *Nachrichtentechnische Zeit. (N.T.Z.)*, Vol. 10 (No. 1, January 1957), pp. 1-4. Not included, since the English version is included.

[113] "Some Geometrical Results in Channel Capacity," *Verband Deutsche Elektrotechniker Fachber.*, Vol. 19 (II) (1956), pp. 13-15 = *Nachrichtentechnische Fachber. (N.T.F.)*, Vol. 6 (1957). English version of the preceding work. Included in Part A.

[114] "Von Neumann's Contribution to Automata Theory," *Bulletin American Mathematical Society*, Vol. 64 (No. 3, Part 2, 1958), pp. 123-129. (Received Feb. 10, 1958.) Included in Part B.

[115] "A Note on a Partial Ordering for Communication Channels," *Information and Control*, Vol. 1 (1958), pp. 390-397. (Received March 24, 1958.) Reprinted in D. Slepian, editor, *Key Papers in the Development of Information Theory*, IEEE Press, NY, 1974. Included in Part A.

[116] "Channels With Side Information at the Transmitter," *IBM Journal Research and Development*, Vol. 2 (1958), pp. 289-293. (Received Sept. 15, 1958.) Reprinted in D. Slepian, editor, *Key Papers in the Development of Information Theory*, IEEE Press, NY, 1974. Included in Part A.

[117] "Probability of Error for Optimal Codes in a Gaussian Channel," *Bell System Technical Journal*, Vol. 38 (1959), pp. 611-656. (Received Oct. 17, 1958.) Included in Part A.

[118] "Coding Theorems for a Discrete Source With a Fidelity Criterion," *Institute of Radio Engineers, International Convention Record*, Vol. 7 (Part 4, 1959), pp. 142-163. Reprinted with changes in *Information and Decision Processes*, edited by R. E. Machol, McGraw-Hill, NY, 1960, pp. 93-126. Reprinted in D. Slepian, editor, *Key Papers in the Development of Information Theory*, IEEE Press, NY, 1974. Included in Part A.

[119] "Two-Way Communication Channels," in *Proceedings Fourth Berkeley Symposium Probability and Statistics, June 20 - July 30, 1960* , edited by J. Neyman, Univ. Calif. Press, Berkeley, CA, Vol. 1, 1961, pp. 611-644. Reprinted in D. Slepian, editor, *Key Papers in the Development of Information Theory*, IEEE Press, NY, 1974. Included in Part A.

[120] "Computers and Automation — Progress and Promise in the Twentieth Century," *Man, Science, Learning and Education. The Semicentennial Lectures at Rice University* , edited by S. W. Higginbotham, Supplement 2 to

Vol. XLIX, Rice University Studies, Rice Univ., 1963, pp. 201-211. Included in Part B.

[121]   *Papers in Information Theory and Cybernetics* (in Russian), Izd. Inostr. Lit., Moscow, 1963, 824 pp. Edited by R. L. Dobrushin and O. B. Lupanova, preface by A. N. Kolmogorov. Contains Russian translations of [1], [6], [14], [25], [37], [40], [43], [44], [50], [51], [54]-[56], [65], [68]-[70], [80], [82], [89], [90], [93], [94], [99], [103], [109]-[111], [113]-[119].

[122]   (With R. G. Gallager and E. R. Berlekamp) ''Lower Bounds to Error Probability for Coding on Discrete Memoryless Channels I,'' *Information and Control*, Vol. 10 (1967), pp. 65-103. (Received Jan. 18, 1966.) Reprinted in D. Slepian, editor, *Key Papers in the Development of Information Theory*, IEEE Press, NY, 1974. Included in Part A.

[123]   (With R. G. Gallager and E. R. Berlekamp) ''Lower Bounds to Error Probability for Coding on Discrete Memoryless Channels II,'' *Information and Control*, Vol. 10 (1967), pp. 522-552. (Received Jan. 18, 1966.) Reprinted in D. Slepian, editor, *Key Papers in the Development of Information Theory*, IEEE Press, NY, 1974. Included in Part A.

[124]   ''The Fourth-Dimensional Twist, or a Modest Proposal in Aid of the American Driver in England,'' typescript, All Souls College, Oxford, Trinity term, 1978, 7 pp. + 8 figs. Not included.

[125]   ''Claude Shannon's No-Drop Juggling Diorama,'' *Juggler's World*, Vol. 34 (March, 1982), pp. 20-22. Included in Part B.

[126]   ''Scientific Aspects of Juggling,'' Typescript, circa 1980. Included in Part B.

[127]   ''A Rubric on Rubik Cubics,'' Typescript, circa 1982, 6 pp. Not included.

Part A
Communication Theory
Information Theory
Cryptography

Preface to Shannon's Collected Papers (Part A)

Claude Shannon's creation in the 1940's of the subject of information theory is one of the great intellectual achievements of the twentieth century. Information theory has had an important and significant influence on mathematics, particularly on probability theory and ergodic theory, and Shannon's mathematics is in its own right a considerable and profound contribution to pure mathematics. But Shannon did his work primarily in the context of communication engineering, and it is in this area that his remarkably original work stands as a unique monument. In his classical paper of 1948 and its sequels, he formulated a model of a communication system that is distinctive for its generality as well as for its amenability to mathematical analysis. He formulated the central problems of theoretical interest, and gave a brilliant and elegant solution to these problems. We preface this section of his collected works with a very short description of this pioneering work.

Let us look first at his model. Shannon saw the communication process as essentially stochastic in nature. The meaning of information plays no role in the theory. In the Shannon paradigm, information from a "source" (defined as a stochastic process) must be transmitted though a "channel" (defined by a transition probability law relating the channel output to the input). The system designer is allowed to place a device called an "encoder" between the source and channel which can introduce a fixed though finite (coding) delay. A "decoder" can be placed at the output of the channel. The theory seeks to answer questions such as how rapidly or reliably can the information from the source be transmitted over the channel, when one is allowed to optimize with respect to the encoder/decoder?

Shannon gives elegant answers to such questions. His solution has two parts. First, he gives a fundamental limit which, for example, might say that for a given source and channel, it is impossible to achieve a fidelity or reliability or speed better than a certain value. Second, he shows that for large coding delays and complex codes, it is possible to achieve performance that is essentially as good as the fundamental limit. To do this, the encoder might have to make use of a coding scheme that would be too slow or complicated to be used in practice.

One of Shannon's most brilliant insights was the separation of problems like these (where the encoder must take both the source and channel into account) into two coding problems. He showed that with no loss of generality one can study the source and channel separately and assume that they are connected by a digital (say binary) interface. One then finds the (source) encoder/decoder to optimize the source-to-digital performance, and the (channel) encoder/decoder to optimize the performance of the channel as a transmitter of digital data. Solution of the source and channel problems leads immediately to the solution of the original joint source-channel problem. The fact that a digital interface between the source and channel is essentially optimal has profound implications in the modern era of digital storage and communication of all types of information.

Thus the revolutionary elements of Shannon's contribution were the invention of the source-encoder-channel-decoder-destination model, and the elegant and remarkably general solution of the fundamental problems which he was able to pose in terms of this model. Particularly significant is the demonstration of the power of coding with delay in a communication system, the separation of the source and channel coding problems, and the establishment of fundamental natural limits on communication.

In the course of developing the solutions to the basic communication problem outlined above, Shannon created several original mathematical concepts. Primary among these is the

3

notion of the "entropy" of a random variable (and by extension of a random sequence), the "mutual information" between two random variables or sequences, and an algebra that relates these quantities and their derivatives. He also achieved a spectacular success with his technique of random coding, in which he showed that an encoder chosen at random from the universe of possible encoders will, with high probability, give essentially optimal performance.

Shannon's work, as well as that of his legion of disciples, provides a crucial knowledge base for the discipline of communication engineering. The communication model is general enough so that the fundamental limits and general intuition provided by Shannon theory provide an extremely useful "roadmap" to designers of communication and information storage systems. For example, the theory tells us that English text is not compressible to fewer than about 1.5 binary digits per English letter, no matter how complex and clever the encoder/decoder. Most significant is the fact that Shannon's theory indicated how to design more efficient communication and storage systems by demonstrating the enormous gains achievable by coding, and by providing the intuition for the correct design of coding systems. The sophisticated coding schemes used in systems as diverse as "deep-space" communication systems (for example, NASA's planetary probes), and home compact disk audio systems, owe a great deal to the insight provided by Shannon theory. As time goes on, and our ability to implement more and more complex processors increases, the information theoretic concepts introduced by Shannon become correspondingly more relevant to day-to-day communications.

A Mathematical Theory of Communication

By C. E. SHANNON

INTRODUCTION

THE recent development of various methods of modulation such as PCM and PPM which exchange bandwidth for signal-to-noise ratio has intensified the interest in a general theory of communication. A basis for such a theory is contained in the important papers of Nyquist[1] and Hartley[2] on this subject. In the present paper we will extend the theory to include a number of new factors, in particular the effect of noise in the channel, and the savings possible due to the statistical structure of the original message and due to the nature of the final destination of the information.

The fundamental problem of communication is that of reproducing at one point either exactly or approximately a message selected at another point. Frequently the messages have *meaning*; that is they refer to or are correlated according to some system with certain physical or conceptual entities. These semantic aspects of communication are irrelevant to the engineering problem. The significant aspect is that the actual message is one *selected from a set* of possible messages. The system must be designed to operate for each possible selection, not just the one which will actually be chosen since this is unknown at the time of design.

If the number of messages in the set is finite then this number or any monotonic function of this number can be regarded as a measure of the information produced when one message is chosen from the set, all choices being equally likely. As was pointed out by Hartley the most natural choice is the logarithmic function. Although this definition must be generalized considerably when we consider the influence of the statistics of the message and when we have a continuous range of messages, we will in all cases use an essentially logarithmic measure.

The logarithmic measure is more convenient for various reasons:

1. It is practically more useful. Parameters of engineering importance

---

[1] Nyquist, H., "Certain Factors Affecting Telegraph Speed," *Bell System Technical Journal*, April 1924, p. 324; "Certain Topics in Telegraph Transmission Theory," *A. I. E. E. Trans.*, v. 47, April 1928, p. 617.

[2] Hartley, R. V. L., "Transmission of Information," *Bell System Technical Journal*, July 1928, p. 535.

Published in THE BELL SYSTEM TECHNICAL JOURNAL
Vol. 27, pp. 379-423, 623-656, July, October, 1948
Copyright 1948 by AMERICAN TELEPHONE AND TELEGRAPH Co.
Printed in U. S. A.

MONOGRAPH B-1598
Reissued December, 1957

such as time, bandwidth, number of relays, etc., tend to vary linearly with the logarithm of the number of possibilities. For example, adding one relay to a group doubles the number of possible states of the relays. It adds 1 to the base 2 logarithm of this number. Doubling the time roughly squares the number of possible messages, or doubles the logarithm, etc.

2. It is nearer to our intuitive feeling as to the proper measure. This is closely related to (1) since we intuitively measure entities by linear comparison with common standards. One feels, for example, that two punched cards should have twice the capacity of one for information storage, and two identical channels twice the capacity of one for transmitting information.

3. It is mathematically more suitable. Many of the limiting operations are simple in terms of the logarithm but would require clumsy restatement in terms of the number of possibilities.

The choice of a logarithmic base corresponds to the choice of a unit for measuring information. If the base 2 is used the resulting units may be called binary digits, or more briefly *bits*, a word suggested by J. W. Tukey. A device with two stable positions, such as a relay or a flip-flop circuit, can store one bit of information. N such devices can store N bits, since the total number of possible states is 2^N and $\log_2 2^N = N$. If the base 10 is used the units may be called decimal digits. Since

$$\log_2 M = \log_{10} M / \log_{10} 2$$

$$= 3.32 \log_{10} M,$$

a decimal digit is about $3\frac{1}{3}$ bits. A digit wheel on a desk computing machine has ten stable positions and therefore has a storage capacity of one decimal digit. In analytical work where integration and differentiation are involved the base e is sometimes useful. The resulting units of information will be called natural units. Change from the base a to base b merely requires multiplication by $\log_b a$.

By a communication system we will mean a system of the type indicated schematically in Fig. 1. It consists of essentially five parts:

1. An *information source* which produces a message or sequence of messages to be communicated to the receiving terminal. The message may be of various types: e.g. (a) A sequence of letters as in a telegraph or teletype system; (b) A single function of time $f(t)$ as in radio or telephony; (c) A function of time and other variables as in black and white television—here the message may be thought of as a function $f(x, y, t)$ of two space coordinates and time, the light intensity at point (x, y) and time t on a pickup tube plate; (d) Two or more functions of time, say $f(t)$, $g(t)$, $h(t)$—this is the case in "three dimensional" sound transmission or if the system is intended to service several individual channels in multiplex; (e) Several functions of

several variables—in color television the message consists of three functions $f(x, y, t)$, $g(x, y, t)$, $h(x, y, t)$ defined in a three-dimensional continuum—we may also think of these three functions as components of a vector field defined in the region—similarly, several black and white television sources would produce "messages" consisting of a number of functions of three variables; (f) Various combinations also occur, for example in television with an associated audio channel.

2. A *transmitter* which operates on the message in some way to produce a signal suitable for transmission over the channel. In telephony this operation consists merely of changing sound pressure into a proportional electrical current. In telegraphy we have an encoding operation which produces a sequence of dots, dashes and spaces on the channel corresponding to the message. In a multiplex PCM system the different speech functions must be sampled, compressed, quantized and encoded, and finally interleaved

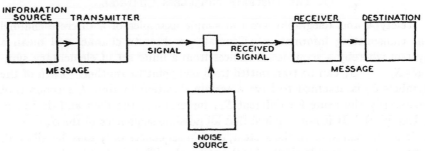

Fig. 1—Schematic diagram of a general communication system.

properly to construct the signal. Vocoder systems, television, and frequency modulation are other examples of complex operations applied to the message to obtain the signal.

3. The *channel* is merely the medium used to transmit the signal from transmitter to receiver. It may be a pair of wires, a coaxial cable, a band of radio frequencies, a beam of light, etc.

4. The *receiver* ordinarily performs the inverse operation of that done by the transmitter, reconstructing the message from the signal.

5. The *destination* is the person (or thing) for whom the message is intended.

We wish to consider certain general problems involving communication systems. To do this it is first necessary to represent the various elements involved as mathematical entities, suitably idealized from their physical counterparts. We may roughly classify communication systems into three main categories: discrete, continuous and mixed. By a discrete system we will mean one in which both the message and the signal are a sequence of discrete symbols. A typical case is telegraphy where the message is a sequence of letters and the signal a sequence of dots, dashes and spaces. A continuous system is one in which the message and signal are both treated as continuous functions, e.g. radio or television. A mixed system is one in which both discrete and continuous variables appear, e.g., PCM transmission of speech.

We first consider the discrete case. This case has applications not only in communication theory, but also in the theory of computing machines, the design of telephone exchanges and other fields. In addition the discrete case forms a foundation for the continuous and mixed cases which will be treated in the second half of the paper.

PART I: DISCRETE NOISELESS SYSTEMS

1. THE DISCRETE NOISELESS CHANNEL

Teletype and telegraphy are two simple examples of a discrete channel for transmitting information. Generally, a discrete channel will mean a system whereby a sequence of choices from a finite set of elementary symbols $S_1 \cdots S_n$ can be transmitted from one point to another. Each of the symbols S_i is assumed to have a certain duration in time t_i seconds (not necessarily the same for different S_i, for example the dots and dashes in telegraphy). It is not required that all possible sequences of the S_i be capable of transmission on the system; certain sequences only may be allowed. These will be possible signals for the channel. Thus in telegraphy suppose the symbols are: (1) A dot, consisting of line closure for a unit of time and then line open for a unit of time; (2) A dash, consisting of three time units of closure and one unit open; (3) A letter space consisting of, say, three units of line open; (4) A word space of six units of line open. We might place the restriction on allowable sequences that no spaces follow each other (for if two letter spaces are adjacent, it is identical with a word space). The question we now consider is how one can measure the capacity of such a channel to transmit information.

In the teletype case where all symbols are of the same duration, and any sequence of the 32 symbols is allowed the answer is easy. Each symbol represents five bits of information. If the system transmits n symbols per second it is natural to say that the channel has a capacity of $5n$ bits per second. This does not mean that the teletype channel will always be transmitting information at this rate—this is the maximum possible rate and whether or not the actual rate reaches this maximum depends on the source of information which feeds the channel, as will appear later.

In the more general case with different lengths of symbols and constraints on the allowed sequences, we make the following definition:

Definition: The capacity C of a discrete channel is given by

$$C = \operatorname*{Lim}_{T \to \infty} \frac{\log N(T)}{T}$$

where $N(T)$ is the number of allowed signals of duration T.

It is easily seen that in the teletype case this reduces to the previous result. It can be shown that the limit in question will exist as a finite number in most cases of interest. Suppose all sequences of the symbols $S_1, \cdots,$ S_n are allowed and these symbols have durations $t_1, \cdots, t_n$. What is the channel capacity? If $N(t)$ represents the number of sequences of duration t we have

$$N(t) = N(t - t_1) + N(t - t_2) + \cdots + N(t - t_n)$$

The total number is equal to the sum of the numbers of sequences ending in $S_1, S_2, \cdots, S_n$ and these are $N(t - t_1), N(t - t_2), \cdots, N(t - t_n)$, respectively. According to a well known result in finite differences, $N(t)$ is then asymptotic for large t to X_0^t where X_0 is the largest real solution of the characteristic equation:

$$X^{-t_1} + X^{-t_2} + \cdots + X^{-t_n} = 1$$

and therefore

$$C = \log X_0$$

In case there are restrictions on allowed sequences we may still often obtain a difference equation of this type and find C from the characteristic equation. In the telegraphy case mentioned above

$$N(t) = N(t - 2) + N(t - 4) + N(t - 5) + N(t - 7) + N(t - 8)$$
$$+ N(t - 10)$$

as we see by counting sequences of symbols according to the last or next to the last symbol occurring. Hence C is $- \log \mu_0$ where μ_0 is the positive root of $1 = \mu^2 + \mu^4 + \mu^5 + \mu^7 + \mu^8 + \mu^{10}$. Solving this we find $C = 0.539$.

A very general type of restriction which may be placed on allowed sequences is the following: We imagine a number of possible states $a_1, a_2, \cdots,$ a_m. For each state only certain symbols from the set $S_1, \cdots, S_n$ can be transmitted (different subsets for the different states). When one of these has been transmitted the state changes to a new state depending both on the old state and the particular symbol transmitted. The telegraph case is a simple example of this. There are two states depending on whether or not

a space was the last symbol transmitted. If so then only a dot or a dash
can be sent next and the state always changes. If not, any symbol can be
transmitted and the state changes if a space is sent, otherwise it remains
the same. The conditions can be indicated in a linear graph as shown in
Fig. 2. The junction points correspond to the states and the lines indicate
the symbols possible in a state and the resulting state. In Appendix I it is
shown that if the conditions on allowed sequences can be described in this
form C will exist and can be calculated in accordance with the following
result:

Theorem 1: Let $b_{ij}^{(s)}$ be the duration of the sth symbol which is allowable in
state i and leads to state j. Then the channel capacity C is equal to log
W where W is the largest real root of the determinant equation:

$$\left|\sum_s W^{-b_{ij}^{(s)}} - \delta_{ij}\right| = 0.$$

where $\delta_{ij} = 1$ if $i = j$ and is zero otherwise.

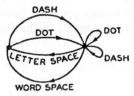

Fig. 2—Graphical representation of the constraints on telegraph symbols.

For example, in the telegraph case (Fig. 2) the determinant is:

$$\left|\begin{matrix} -1 & (W^{-2} + W^{-4}) \\ (W^{-3} + W^{-6}) & (W^{-2} + W^{-4} - 1) \end{matrix}\right| = 0$$

On expansion this leads to the equation given above for this case.

2. The Discrete Source of Information

We have seen that under very general conditions the logarithm of the
number of possible signals in a discrete channel increases linearly with time.
The capacity to transmit information can be specified by giving this rate of
increase, the number of bits per second required to specify the particular
signal used.

We now consider the information source. How is an information source
to be described mathematically, and how much information in bits per second is produced in a given source? The main point at issue is the effect of
statistical knowledge about the source in reducing the required capacity

of the channel, by the use of proper encoding of the information.   In telegraphy, for example, the messages to be transmitted consist of sequences of letters.   These sequences, however, are not completely random.   In general, they form sentences and have the statistical structure of, say, English.   The letter E occurs more frequently than Q, the sequence TH more frequently than XP, etc.   The existence of this structure allows one to make a saving in time (or channel capacity) by properly encoding the message sequences into signal sequences.   This is already done to a limited extent in telegraphy by using the shortest channel symbol, a dot, for the most common English letter E; while the infrequent letters, Q, X, Z are represented by longer sequences of dots and dashes.   This idea is carried still further in certain commercial codes where common words and phrases are represented by four- or five-letter code groups with a considerable saving in average time.   The standardized greeting and anniversary telegrams now in use extend this to the point of encoding a sentence or two into a relatively short sequence of numbers.

We can think of a discrete source as generating the message, symbol by symbol.   It will choose successive symbols according to certain probabilities depending, in general, on preceding choices as well as the particular symbols in question.   A physical system, or a mathematical model of a system which produces such a sequence of symbols governed by a set of probabilities is known as a stochastic process.[3]   We may consider a discrete source, therefore, to be represented by a stochastic process.   Conversely, any stochastic process which produces a discrete sequence of symbols chosen from a finite set may be considered a discrete source.   This will include such cases as:

1. Natural written languages such as English, German, Chinese.
2. Continuous information sources that have been rendered discrete by some quantizing process.   For example, the quantized speech from a PCM transmitter, or a quantized television signal.
3. Mathematical cases where we merely define abstractly a stochastic process which generates a sequence of symbols.   The following are examples of this last type of source.
    (A) Suppose we have five letters A, B, C, D, E which are chosen each with probability .2, successive choices being independent.   This would lead to a sequence of which the following is a typical example.
    B D C B C E C C C A D C B D D A A E C E E A
    A B B D A E E C A C E E B A E E C B C E A D
    This was constructed with the use of a table of random numbers.[4]

---

[3] See, for example, S. Chandrasekhar, "Stochastic Problems in Physics and Astronomy," *Reviews of Modern Physics*, v. 15, No. 1, January 1943, p. 1.
[4] Kendall and Smith, "Tables of Random Sampling Numbers," Cambridge, 1939.

(B) Using the same five letters let the probabilities be .4, .1, .2, .2, .1 respectively, with successive choices independent. A typical message from this source is then:

A A A C D C B D C E A A D A D A C E D A

E A D C A B E D A D D C E C A A A A A D

(C) A more complicated structure is obtained if successive symbols are not chosen independently but their probabilities depend on preceding letters. In the simplest case of this type a choice depends only on the preceding letter and not on ones before that. The statistical structure can then be described by a set of transition probabilities $p_i(j)$, the probability that letter i is followed by letter j. The indices i and j range over all the possible symbols. A second equivalent way of specifying the structure is to give the "digram" probabilities $p(i, j)$, i.e., the relative frequency of the digram $i\,j$. The letter frequencies $p(i)$, (the probability of letter i), the transition probabilities $p_i(j)$ and the digram probabilities $p(i, j)$ are related by the following formulas.

$$p(i) = \sum_j p(i, j) = \sum_j p(j, i) = \sum_j p(j)p_j(i)$$

$$p(i, j) = p(i)p_i(j)$$

$$\sum_j p_i(j) = \sum_i p(i) = \sum_{i,j} p(i, j) = 1.$$

As a specific example suppose there are three letters A, B, C with the probability tables:

$p_i(j)$		j			i	$p(i)$		$p(i, j)$		j	
	A	B	C						A	B	C
A	0	$\frac{4}{5}$	$\frac{1}{5}$		A	$\frac{9}{27}$		A	0	$\frac{4}{15}$	$\frac{1}{15}$
i B	$\frac{1}{2}$	$\frac{1}{2}$	0		B	$\frac{16}{27}$		i B	$\frac{8}{27}$	$\frac{8}{27}$	0
C	$\frac{1}{2}$	$\frac{2}{5}$	$\frac{1}{10}$		C	$\frac{2}{27}$		C	$\frac{1}{27}$	$\frac{4}{135}$	$\frac{1}{135}$

A typical message from this source is the following:

A B B A B A B A B A B A B A B B B A B B B B B A B

A B A B A B A B B B A C A C A B B A B B B B B A B B

A B A C B B B A B A

The next increase in complexity would involve trigram frequencies but no more. The choice of a letter would depend on the preceding two letters but not on the message before that point. A set of trigram frequencies $p(i, j, k)$ or equivalently a set of transition probabilities $p_{ij}(k)$ would be required. Continuing in this way one obtains successively more complicated stochastic processes. In the general n-gram case a set of n-gram probabilities $p(i_1, i_2, \cdots, i_n)$ or of transition probabilities $p_{i_1, i_2, \cdots, i_{n-1}}(i_n)$ is required to specify the statistical structure.

(D) Stochastic processes can also be defined which produce a text consisting of a sequence of "words." Suppose there are five letters A, B, C, D, E and 16 "words" in the language with associated probabilities:

.10 A	.16 BEBE	.11 CABED	.04 DEB
.04 ADEB	.04 BED	.05 CEED	.15 DEED
.05 ADEE	.02 BEED	.08 DAB	.01 EAB
.01 BADD	.05 CA	.04 DAD	.05 EE

Suppose successive "words" are chosen independently and are separated by a space. A typical message might be:

DAB EE A BEBE DEED DEB ADEE ADEE EE DEB BEBE BEBE BEBE ADEE BED DEED DEED CEED ADEE A DEED DEED BEBE CABED BEBE BED DAB DEED ADEB

If all the words are of finite length this process is equivalent to one of the preceding type, but the description may be simpler in terms of the word structure and probabilities. We may also generalize here and introduce transition probabilities between words, etc.

These artificial languages are useful in constructing simple problems and examples to illustrate various possibilities. We can also approximate to a natural language by means of a series of simple artificial languages. The zero-order approximation is obtained by choosing all letters with the same probability and independently. The first-order approximation is obtained by choosing successive letters independently but each letter having the same probability that it does in the natural language.[5] Thus, in the first-order approximation to English, E is chosen with probability .12 (its frequency in normal English) and W with probability .02, but there is no influence between adjacent letters and no tendency to form the preferred digrams such as TH, ED, etc. In the second-order approximation, digram structure is introduced. After a letter is chosen, the next one is chosen in accordance with the frequencies with which the various letters follow the first one. This requires a table of digram frequencies $p_i(j)$. In the third-order approximation, trigram structure is introduced. Each letter is chosen with probabilities which depend on the preceding two letters.

[5] Letter, digram and trigram frequencies are given in "Secret and Urgent" by Fletcher Pratt, Blue Ribbon Books 1939. Word frequencies are tabulated in "Relative Frequency of English Speech Sounds," G. Dewey, Harvard University Press, 1923.

3. The Series of Approximations to English

To give a visual idea of how this series of processes approaches a language, typical sequences in the approximations to English have been constructed and are given below.   In all cases we have assumed a 27-symbol "alphabet," the 26 letters and a space.

1. Zero-order approximation (symbols independent and equi-probable).

    XFOML RXKHRJFFJUJ ZLPWCFWKCYJ
    FFJEYVKCQSGXYD QPAAMKBZAACIBZLHJQD

2. First-order approximation (symbols independent but with frequencies of English text).

    OCRO HLI RGWR NMIELWIS EU LL NBNESEBYA TH EEI
    ALHENHTTPA OOBTTVA NAH BRL

3. Second-order approximation (digram structure as in English).

    ON IE ANTSOUTINYS ARE T INCTORE ST BE S DEAMY
    ACHIN D ILONASIVE TUCOOWE AT TEASONARE FUSO
    TIZIN ANDY TOBE SEACE CTISBE

4. Third-order approximation (trigram structure as in English).

    IN NO IST LAT WHEY CRATICT FROURE BIRS GROCID
    PONDENOME OF DEMONSTURES OF THE REPTAGIN IS
    REGOACTIONA OF CRE

5. First-Order Word Approximation.   Rather than continue with tetra-gram, $\cdots$, n-gram structure it is easier and better to jump at this point to word units.   Here words are chosen independently but with their appropriate frequencies.

    REPRESENTING AND SPEEDILY IS AN GOOD APT OR
    COME CAN DIFFERENT NATURAL HERE HE THE A IN
    CAME THE TO OF TO EXPERT GRAY COME TO FUR-
    NISHES THE LINE MESSAGE HAD BE THESE.

6. Second-Order Word Approximation. The word transition probabil-ities are correct but no further structure is included.

    THE HEAD AND IN FRONTAL ATTACK ON AN ENGLISH
    WRITER THAT THE CHARACTER OF THIS POINT IS
    THEREFORE ANOTHER METHOD FOR THE LETTERS
    THAT THE TIME OF WHO EVER TOLD THE PROBLEM
    FOR AN UNEXPECTED

The resemblance to ordinary English text increases quite noticeably at each of the above steps. Note that these samples have reasonably good structure out to about twice the range that is taken into account in their construction.   Thus in (3) the statistical process insures reasonable text for two-letter sequence, but four-letter sequences from the sample can usually be fitted into good sentences. In (6) sequences of four or more words can easily be placed in sentences without unusual or strained constructions. The particular sequence of ten words "attack on an English writer that the character of this" is not at all unreasonable. It appears then that a sufficiently complex stochastic process will give a satisfactory representation of a discrete source.

The first two samples were constructed by the use of a book of random numbers in conjunction with (for example 2) a table of letter frequencies. This method might have been continued for (3), (4), and (5), since digram, trigram, and word frequency tables are available, but a simpler equivalent method was used. To construct (3) for example, one opens a book at random and selects a letter at random on the page. This letter is recorded. The book is then opened to another page and one reads until this letter is encountered. The succeeding letter is then recorded. Turning to another page this second letter is searched for and the succeeding letter recorded, etc. A similar process was used for (4), (5), and (6). It would be interesting if further approximations could be constructed, but the labor involved becomes enormous at the next stage.

4. GRAPHICAL REPRESENTATION OF A MARKOFF PROCESS

Stochastic processes of the type described above are known mathematically as discrete Markoff processes and have been extensively studied in the literature.[6] The general case can be described as follows: There exist a finite number of possible "states" of a system; $S_1, S_2, \cdots, S_n$. In addition there is a set of transition probabilities; $p_i(j)$ the probability that if the system is in state S_i it will next go to state S_j. To make this Markoff process into an information source we need only assume that a letter is produced for each transition from one state to another. The states will correspond to the "residue of influence" from preceding letters.

The situation can be represented graphically as shown in Figs. 3, 4 and 5. The "states" are the junction points in the graph and the probabilities and letters produced for a transition are given beside the corresponding line. Figure 3 is for the example B in Section 2, while Fig. 4 corresponds to the example C. In Fig. 3 there is only one state since successive letters are independent. In Fig. 4 there are as many states as letters. If a trigram example were constructed there would be at most n^2 states corresponding to the possible pairs of letters preceding the one being chosen. Figure 5 is a graph for the case of word structure in example D. Here S corresponds to the "space" symbol.

[6] For a detailed treatment see M. Frechet, "Methods des fonctions arbitraires. Theorie des énénements en chaine dans le cas d'un nombre fini d'états possibles." Paris, Gauthier-Villars, 1938.

5. Ergodic and Mixed Sources

As we have indicated above a discrete source for our purposes can be considered to be represented by a Markoff process. Among the possible discrete Markoff processes there is a group with special properties of significance in

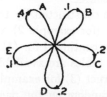

Fig. 3—A graph corresponding to the source in example B.

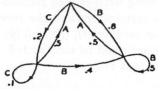

Fig. 4—A graph corresponding to the source in example C.

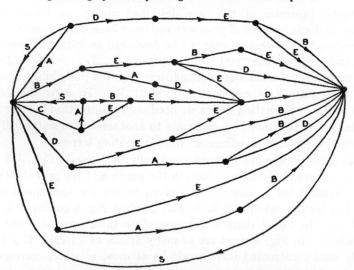

Fig. 5—A graph corresponding to the source in example D.

communication theory. This special class consists of the "ergodic" processes and we shall call the corresponding sources ergodic sources. Although a rigorous definition of an ergodic process is somewhat involved, the general idea is simple. In an ergodic process every sequence produced by the process is the same in statistical properties. Thus the letter frequencies, digram frequencies, etc., obtained from particular sequences will, as the lengths of the sequences increase, approach definite limits independent of the particular sequence. Actually this is not true of every sequence but the set for which it is false has probability zero. Roughly the ergodic property means statistical homogeneity.

All the examples of artificial languages given above are ergodic. This property is related to the structure of the corresponding graph. If the graph has the following two properties[7] the corresponding process will be ergodic:

1. The graph does not consist of two isolated parts A and B such that it is impossible to go from junction points in part A to junction points in part B along lines of the graph in the direction of arrows and also impossible to go from junctions in part B to junctions in part A.

2. A closed series of lines in the graph with all arrows on the lines pointing in the same orientation will be called a "circuit." The "length" of a circuit is the number of lines in it. Thus in Fig. 5 the series BEBES is a circuit of length 5. The second property required is that the greatest common divisor of the lengths of all circuits in the graph be one.

If the first condition is satisfied but the second one violated by having the greatest common divisor equal to $d > 1$, the sequences have a certain type of periodic structure. The various sequences fall into d different classes which are statistically the same apart from a shift of the origin (i.e., which letter in the sequence is called letter 1). By a shift of from 0 up to $d - 1$ any sequence can be made statistically equivalent to any other. A simple example with $d = 2$ is the following: There are three possible letters a, b, c. Letter a is followed with either b or c with probabilities $\frac{1}{3}$ and $\frac{2}{3}$ respectively. Either b or c is always followed by letter a. Thus a typical sequence is

$$a b a c a c a c a b a c a b a b a c a c$$

This type of situation is not of much importance for our work.

If the first condition is violated the graph may be separated into a set of subgraphs each of which satisfies the first condition. We will assume that the second condition is also satisfied for each subgraph. We have in this case what may be called a "mixed" source made up of a number of pure components. The components correspond to the various subgraphs. If L_1, L_2, L_3, $\cdots$ are the component sources we may write

$$L = p_1 L_1 + p_2 L_2 + p_3 L_3 + \cdots$$

where p_i is the probability of the component source L_i.

[7] These are restatements in terms of the graph of conditions given in Frechet.

Physically the situation represented is this: There are several different sources L_1, L_2, L_3, $\cdots$ which are each of homogeneous statistical structure (i.e., they are ergodic). We do not know *a priori* which is to be used, but once the sequence starts in a given pure component L_i it continues indefinitely according to the statistical structure of that component.

As an example one may take two of the processes defined above and assume $p_1 = .2$ and $p_2 = .8$. A sequence from the mixed source

$$L = .2\,L_1 + .8\,L_2$$

would be obtained by choosing first L_1 or L_2 with probabilities .2 and .8 and after this choice generating a sequence from whichever was chosen.

Except when the contrary is stated we shall assume a source to be ergodic. This assumption enables one to identify averages along a sequence with averages over the ensemble of possible sequences (the probability of a discrepancy being zero). For example the relative frequency of the letter A in a particular infinite sequence will be, with probability one, equal to its relative frequency in the ensemble of sequences.

If P_i is the probability of state i and $p_i(j)$ the transition probability to state j, then for the process to be stationary it is clear that the P_i must satisfy equilibrium conditions:

$$P_j = \sum_i P_i\, p_i(j).$$

In the ergodic case it can be shown that with any starting conditions the probabilities $P_j(N)$ of being in state j after N symbols, approach the equilibrium values as $N \to \infty$.

6. Choice, Uncertainty and Entropy

We have represented a discrete information source as a Markoff process. Can we define a quantity which will measure, in some sense, how much information is "produced" by such a process, or better, at what rate information is produced?

Suppose we have a set of possible events whose probabilities of occurrence are p_1, p_2, $\cdots$, p_n. These probabilities are known but that is all we know concerning which event will occur. Can we find a measure of how much "choice" is involved in the selection of the event or of how uncertain we are of the outcome?

If there is such a measure, say $H(p_1, p_2, \cdots, p_n)$, it is reasonable to require of it the following properties:

1. H should be continuous in the p_i.

2. If all the p_i are equal, $p_i = \dfrac{1}{n}$, then H should be a monotonic increasing

function of n.   With equally likely events there is more choice, or uncertainty, when there are more possible events.

3. If a choice be broken down into two successive choices, the original
H should be the weighted sum of the individual values of H.   The
meaning of this is illustrated in Fig. 6.   At the left we have three
possibilities $p_1 = \frac{1}{2}$, $p_2 = \frac{1}{3}$, $p_3 = \frac{1}{6}$.   On the right we first choose between two possibilities each with probability $\frac{1}{2}$, and if the second occurs
make another choice with probabilities $\frac{2}{3}$, $\frac{1}{3}$.   The final results have
the same probabilities as before.   We require, in this special case,
that

$$H(\tfrac{1}{2}, \tfrac{1}{3}, \tfrac{1}{6}) = H(\tfrac{1}{2}, \tfrac{1}{2}) + \tfrac{1}{2}H(\tfrac{2}{3}, \tfrac{1}{3})$$

The coefficient $\frac{1}{2}$ is because this second choice only occurs half the time.

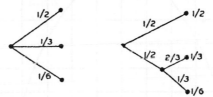

Fig. 6—Decomposition of a choice from three possibilities.

In Appendix II, the following result is established:
Theorem 2: The only H satisfying the three above assumptions is of the
form:

$$H = -K \sum_{i=1}^{n} p_i \log p_i$$

where K is a positive constant.

This theorem, and the assumptions required for its proof, are in no way
necessary for the present theory.   It is given chiefly to lend a certain plausi-
bility to some of our later definitions.   The real justification of these definitions, however, will reside in their implications.

Quantities of the form $H = -\Sigma\, p_i \log p_i$ (the constant K merely amounts
to a choice of a unit of measure) play a central role in information theory as
measures of information, choice and uncertainty.   The form of H will be
recognized as that of entropy as defined in certain formulations of statistical
mechanics[8] where p_i is the probability of a system being in cell i of its phase
space. H is then, for example, the H in Boltzmann's famous H theorem.
We shall call $H = -\Sigma\, p_i \log p_i$ the entropy of the set of probabilities

[8] See, for example, R. C. Tolman, "Principles of Statistical Mechanics," Oxford.
Clarendon, 1938.

$p_1, \cdots, p_n$. If x is a chance variable we will write $H(x)$ for its entropy; thus x is not an argument of a function but a label for a number, to differentiate it from $H(y)$ say, the entropy of the chance variable y.

The entropy in the case of two possibilities with probabilities p and $q = 1 - p$, namely

$$H = -(p \log p + q \log q)$$

is plotted in Fig. 7 as a function of p.

The quantity H has a number of interesting properties which further substantiate it as a reasonable measure of choice or information.

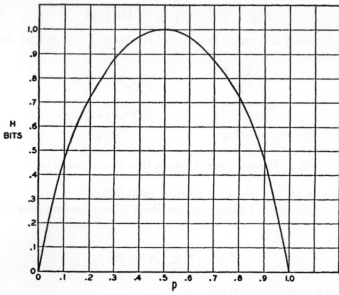

Fig. 7—Entropy in the case of two possibilities with probabilities p and $(1 - p)$.

1. $H = 0$ if and only if all the p_i but one are zero, this one having the value unity. Thus only when we are certain of the outcome does H vanish. Otherwise H is positive.

2. For a given n, H is a maximum and equal to $\log n$ when all the p_i are equal $\left(\text{i.e., } \frac{1}{n} \right)$. This is also intuitively the most uncertain situation.

3. Suppose there are two events, x and y, in question with m possibilities for the first and n for the second. Let $p(i, j)$ be the probability of the joint occurrence of i for the first and j for the second. The entropy of the joint event is

$$H(x, y) = - \sum_{i,j} p(i, j) \log p(i, j)$$

while

$$H(x) = - \sum_{i,j} p(i, j) \log \sum_j p(i, j)$$

$$H(y) = - \sum_{i,j} p(i, j) \log \sum_i p(i, j).$$

It is easily shown that

$$H(x, y) \leq H(x) + H(y)$$

with equality only if the events are independent (i.e., $p(i, j) = p(i) \, p(j)$). The uncertainty of a joint event is less than or equal to the sum of the individual uncertainties.

4. Any change toward equalization of the probabilities $p_1, p_2, \cdots, p_n$ increases H. Thus if $p_1 < p_2$ and we increase p_1, decreasing p_2 an equal amount so that p_1 and p_2 are more nearly equal, then H increases. More generally, if we perform any "averaging" operation on the p_i of the form

$$p'_i = \sum_j a_{ij} p_j$$

where $\sum_i a_{ij} = \sum_j a_{ij} = 1$, and all $a_{ij} \geq 0$, then H increases (except in the special case where this transformation amounts to no more than a permutation of the p_j with H of course remaining the same).

5. Suppose there are two chance events x and y as in 3, not necessarily independent. For any particular value i that x can assume there is a conditional probability $p_i(j)$ that y has the value j. This is given by

$$p_i(j) = \frac{p(i, j)}{\sum_j p(i, j)}.$$

We define the *conditional entropy* of y, $H_x(y)$ as the average of the entropy of y for each value of x, weighted according to the probability of getting that particular x. That is

$$H_x(y) = -\sum_{i,j} p(i, j) \log p_i(j).$$

This quantity measures how uncertain we are of y on the average when we know x. Substituting the value of $p_i(j)$ we obtain

$$H_x(y) = -\sum_{ij} p(i, j) \log p(i, j) + \sum_{ij} p(i, j) \log \sum_j p(i, j)$$

$$= H(x, y) - H(x)$$

or

$$H(x, y) = H(x) + H_x(y)$$

The uncertainty (or entropy) of the joint event x, y is the uncertainty of x plus the uncertainty of y when x is known.

6. From 3 and 5 we have

$$H(x) + H(y) \geq H(x, y) = H(x) + H_x(y)$$

Hence

$$H(y) \geq H_x(y)$$

The uncertainty of y is never increased by knowledge of x. It will be decreased unless x and y are independent events, in which case it is not changed.

7. The Entropy of an Information Source

Consider a discrete source of the finite state type considered above. For each possible state i there will be a set of probabilities $p_i(j)$ of producing the various possible symbols j. Thus there is an entropy H_i for each state. The entropy of the source will be defined as the average of these H_i weighted in accordance with the probability of occurrence of the states in question:

$$H = \sum_i P_i H_i$$

$$= -\sum_{i,j} P_i p_i(j) \log p_i(j)$$

This is the entropy of the source per symbol of text. If the Markoff process is proceeding at a definite time rate there is also an entropy per second

$$H' = \sum_i f_i H_i$$

where f_i is the average frequency (occurrences per second) of state i. Clearly

$$H' = mH$$

where m is the average number of symbols produced per second. H or H' measures the amount of information generated by the source per symbol or per second. If the logarithmic base is 2, they will represent bits per symbol or per second.

If successive symbols are independent then H is simply $-\Sigma\, p_i \log p_i$ where p_i is the probability of symbol i. Suppose in this case we consider a long message of N symbols. It will contain with high probability about $p_1 N$ occurrences of the first symbol, $p_2 N$ occurrences of the second, etc. Hence the probability of this particular message will be roughly

$$p = p_1^{p_1 N} p_2^{p_2 N} \cdots p_n^{p_n N}$$

or

$$\log p \doteq N \sum_i p_i \log p_i$$

$$\log p \doteq -NH$$

$$H \doteq \frac{\log 1/p}{N} .$$

H is thus approximately the logarithm of the reciprocal probability of a typical long sequence divided by the number of symbols in the sequence. The same result holds for any source.   Stated more precisely we have (see Appendix III):

Theorem 3: Given any $\epsilon > 0$ and $\delta > 0$, we can find an N_0 such that the sequences of any length $N \geq N_0$ fall into two classes:

1. A set whose total probability is less than ϵ.

2. The remainder, all of whose members have probabilities satisfying the inequality

$$\left| \frac{\log p^{-1}}{N} - H \right| < \delta$$

In other words we are almost certain to have $\dfrac{\log p^{-1}}{N}$ very close to H when N is large.

A closely related result deals with the number of sequences of various probabilities.   Consider again the sequences of length N and let them be arranged in order of decreasing probability.   We define $n(q)$ to be the number we must take from this set starting with the most probable one in order to accumulate a total probability q for those taken.

Theorem 4:

$$\underset{N \to \infty}{\text{Lim}} \frac{\log n(q)}{N} = H$$

when q does not equal 0 or 1.

We may interpret $\log n(q)$ as the number of bits required to specify the sequence when we consider only the most probable sequences with a total probability q.   Then $\dfrac{\log n(q)}{N}$ is the number of bits per symbol for the specification.   The theorem says that for large N this will be independent of q and equal to H.   The rate of growth of the logarithm of the number of reasonably probable sequences is given by H, regardless of our interpretation of "reasonably probable."   Due to these results, which are proved in appendix III, it is possible for most purposes to treat the long sequences as though there were just 2^{HN} of them, each with a probability 2^{-HN}.

The next two theorems show that H and H' can be determined by limiting operations directly from the statistics of the message sequences, without reference to the states and transition probabilities between states.

Theorem 5: Let $p(B_i)$ be the probability of a sequence B_i of symbols from the source.   Let

$$G_N = -\frac{1}{N} \sum_i p(B_i) \log p(B_i)$$

where the sum is over all sequences B_i containing N symbols.   Then G_N is a monotonic decreasing function of N and

$$\lim_{N \to \infty} G_N = H.$$

Theorem 6: Let $p(B_i, S_j)$ be the probability of sequence B_i followed by symbol S_j and $p_{B_i}(S_j) = p(B_i, S_j)/p(B_i)$ be the conditional probability of S_j after B_i.   Let

$$F_N = -\sum_{i,j} p(B_i, S_j) \log p_{B_i}(S_j)$$

where the sum is over all blocks B_i of $N - 1$ symbols and over all symbols S_j.   Then F_N is a monotonic decreasing function of N,

$$F_N = N G_N - (N - 1) G_{N-1},$$

$$G_N = \frac{1}{N} \sum_1^n F_N,$$

$$F_N \leq G_N,$$

and $\lim_{N \to \infty} F_N = H.$

These results are derived in appendix III.   They show that a series of approximations to H can be obtained by considering only the statistical structure of the sequences extending over 1, 2, $\cdots$ N symbols. F_N is the better approximation.   In fact F_N is the entropy of the Nth order approximation to the source of the type discussed above.   If there are no statistical influences extending over more than N symbols, that is if the conditional probability of the next symbol knowing the preceding $(N - 1)$ is not changed by a knowledge of any before that, then $F_N = H$. F_N of course is the conditional entropy of the next symbol when the $(N - 1)$ preceding ones are known, while G_N is the entropy per symbol of blocks of N symbols.

The ratio of the entropy of a source to the maximum value it could have while still restricted to the same symbols will be called its *relative entropy*. This is the maximum compression possible when we encode into the same alphabet.   One minus the relative entropy is the *redundancy*.   The redundancy of ordinary English, not considering statistical structure over greater distances than about eight letters is roughly 50%. This means that when we write English half of what we write is determined by the structure of the language and half is chosen freely. The figure 50% was found by several independent methods which all gave results in this neighborhood. One is by calculation of the entropy of the approximations to English. A second method is to delete a certain fraction of the letters from a sample of English text and then let someone attempt to restore them. If they can be restored when 50% are deleted the redundancy must be greater than 50%. A third method depends on certain known results in cryptography.

Two extremes of redundancy in English prose are represented by Basic English and by James Joyces' book "Finigans Wake." The Basic English vocabulary is limited to 850 words and the redundancy is very high. This is reflected in the expansion that occurs when a passage is translated into Basic English. Joyce on the other hand enlarges the vocabulary and is alleged to achieve a compression of semantic content.

The redundancy of a language is related to the existence of crossword puzzles. If the redundancy is zero any sequence of letters is a reasonable text in the language and any two dimensional array of letters forms a crossword puzzle. If the redundancy is too high the language imposes too many constraints for large crossword puzzles to be possible. A more detailed analysis shows that if we assume the constraints imposed by the language are of a rather chaotic and random nature, large crossword puzzles are just possible when the redundancy is 50%. If the redundancy is 33%, three dimensional crossword puzzles should be possible, etc.

8. Representation of the Encoding and Decoding Operations

We have yet to represent mathematically the operations performed by the transmitter and receiver in encoding and decoding the information. Either of these will be called a discrete transducer. The input to the transducer is a sequence of input symbols and its output a sequence of output symbols. The transducer may have an internal memory so that its output depends not only on the present input symbol but also on the past history. We assume that the internal memory is finite, i.e. there exists a finite number m of possible states of the transducer and that its output is a function of the present state and the present input symbol. The next state will be a second function of these two quantities. Thus a transducer can be described by two functions:

$$y_n = f(x_n, \alpha_n)$$

$$\alpha_{n+1} = g(x_n, \alpha_n)$$

where: x_n is the nth input symbol,

α_n is the state of the transducer when the nth input symbol is introduced,

y_n is the output symbol (or sequence of output symbols) produced when x_n is introduced if the state is α_n.

If the output symbols of one transducer can be identified with the input symbols of a second, they can be connected in tandem and the result is also a transducer. If there exists a second transducer which operates on the output of the first and recovers the original input, the first transducer will be called non-singular and the second will be called its inverse.

Theorem 7: The output of a finite state transducer driven by a finite state statistical source is a finite state statistical source, with entropy (per unit time) less than or equal to that of the input. If the transducer is non-singular they are equal.

Let α represent the state of the source, which produces a sequence of symbols x_i ; and let β be the state of the transducer, which produces, in its output, blocks of symbols y_j . The combined system can be represented by the "product state space" of pairs (α, β). Two points in the space, (α_1, β_1) and $(\alpha_2 \beta_2)$, are connected by a line if α_1 can produce an x which changes β_1 to β_2 , and this line is given the probability of that x in this case. The line is labeled with the block of y_j symbols produced by the transducer. The entropy of the output can be calculated as the weighted sum over the states. If we sum first on β each resulting term is less than or equal to the corresponding term for α, hence the entropy is not increased. If the transducer is non-singular let its output be connected to the inverse transducer. If H_1' , H_2' and H_3' are the output entropies of the source, the first and second transducers respectively, then $H_1' \geq H_2' \geq H_3' = H_1'$ and therefore $H_1' = H_2'$.

Suppose we have a system of constraints on possible sequences of the type which can be represented by a linear graph as in Fig. 2. If probabilities $p_{ij}^{(s)}$ were assigned to the various lines connecting state i to state j this would become a source. There is one particular assignment which maximizes the resulting entropy (see Appendix IV).

Theorem 8: Let the system of constraints considered as a channel have a capacity C. If we assign

$$p_{ij}^{(s)} = \frac{B_j}{B_i} C^{-\ell_{ij}^{(s)}}$$

where $\ell_{ij}^{(s)}$ is the duration of the sth symbol leading from state i to state j and the B_i satisfy

$$B_i = \sum_{s,j} B_j C^{-\ell_{ij}^{(s)}}$$

then H is maximized and equal to C.

By proper assignment of the transition probabilities the entropy of symbols on a channel can be maximized at the channel capacity.

9. The Fundamental Theorem for a Noiseless Channel.

We will now justify our interpretation of H as the rate of generating information by proving that H determines the channel capacity required with most efficient coding.

Theorem 9: Let a source have entropy H (bits per symbol) and a channel have a capacity C (bits per second). Then it is possible to encode the output of the source in such a way as to transmit at the average rate $\frac{C}{H} - \epsilon$ symbols per second over the channel where ϵ is arbitrarily small. It is not possible to transmit at an average rate greater than $\frac{C}{H}$.

The converse part of the theorem, that $\frac{C}{H}$ cannot be exceeded, may be proved by noting that the entropy of the channel input per second is equal to that of the source, since the transmitter must be non-singular, and also this entropy cannot exceed the channel capacity. Hence $H' \le C$ and the number of symbols per second $= H'/H \le C/H$.

The first part of the theorem will be proved in two different ways. The first method is to consider the set of all sequences of N symbols produced by the source. For N large we can divide these into two groups, one containing less than $2^{(H+\eta)N}$ members and the second containing less than 2^{RN} members (where R is the logarithm of the number of different symbols) and having a total probability less than μ. As N increases η and μ approach zero. The number of signals of duration T in the channel is greater than $2^{(C-\theta)T}$ with θ small when T is large. If we choose

$$T = \left(\frac{H}{C} + \lambda\right) N$$

then there will be a sufficient number of sequences of channel symbols for the high probability group when N and T are sufficiently large (however small λ) and also some additional ones. The high probability group is coded in an arbitrary one to one way into this set. The remaining sequences are represented by larger sequences, starting and ending with one of the sequences not used for the high probability group. This special sequence acts as a start and stop signal for a different code. In between a sufficient time is allowed to give enough different sequences for all the low probability messages. This will require

$$T_1 = \left(\frac{R}{C} + \varphi\right) N$$

where φ is small. The mean rate of transmission in message symbols per second will then be greater than

$$\left[(1 - \delta)\frac{T}{N} + \delta\frac{T_1}{N} \right]^{-1} = \left[(1 - \delta)\left(\frac{H}{C} + \lambda\right) + \delta\left(\frac{R}{C} + \varphi\right) \right]^{-1}$$

As N increases δ, λ and φ approach zero and the rate approaches $\frac{C}{H}$.

Another method of performing this coding and proving the theorem can be described as follows: Arrange the messages of length N in order of decreasing probability and suppose their probabilities are $p_1 \geq p_2 \geq p_3 \ldots \geq p_n$. Let $P_s = \sum_1^{s-1} p_i$; that is P_s is the cumulative probability up to, but not including, p_s. We first encode into a binary system. The binary code for message s is obtained by expanding P_s as a binary number. The expansion is carried out to m_s places, where m_s is the integer satisfying:

$$\log_2 \frac{1}{p_s} \leq m_s < 1 + \log_2 \frac{1}{p_s}$$

Thus the messages of high probability are represented by short codes and those of low probability by long codes. From these inequalities we have

$$\frac{1}{2^{m_s}} \leq p_s < \frac{1}{2^{m_s-1}}.$$

The code for P_s will differ from all succeeding ones in one or more of its m_s places, since all the remaining P_i are at least $\frac{1}{2^{m_s}}$ larger and their binary expansions therefore differ in the first m_s places. Consequently all the codes are different and it is possible to recover the message from its code. If the channel sequences are not already sequences of binary digits, they can be ascribed binary numbers in an arbitrary fashion and the binary code thus translated into signals suitable for the channel.

The average number H' of binary digits used per symbol of original message is easily estimated. We have

$$H' = \frac{1}{N} \Sigma m_s p_s$$

But,

$$\frac{1}{N} \Sigma \left(\log_2 \frac{1}{p_s} \right) p_s \leq \frac{1}{N} \Sigma m_s p_s < \frac{1}{N} \Sigma \left(1 + \log_2 \frac{1}{p_s} \right) p_s$$

and therefore,

$$G_N \leq H' < G_N + \frac{1}{N}$$

As N increases G_N approaches H, the entropy of the source and H' approaches H.

We see from this that the inefficiency in coding, when only a finite delay of N symbols is used, need not be greater than $\frac{1}{N}$ plus the difference between the true entropy H and the entropy G_N calculated for sequences of length N. The per cent excess time needed over the ideal is therefore less than

$$\frac{G_N}{H} + \frac{1}{HN} - 1.$$

This method of encoding is substantially the same as one found independently by R. M. Fano.[9] His method is to arrange the messages of length N in order of decreasing probability. Divide this series into two groups of as nearly equal probability as possible. If the message is in the first group its first binary digit will be 0, otherwise 1. The groups are similarly divided into subsets of nearly equal probability and the particular subset determines the second binary digit. This process is continued until each subset contains only one message. It is easily seen that apart from minor differences (generally in the last digit) this amounts to the same thing as the arithmetic process described above.

10. DISCUSSION AND EXAMPLES

In order to obtain the maximum power transfer from a generator to a load a transformer must in general be introduced so that the generator as seen from the load has the load resistance. The situation here is roughly analogous. The transducer which does the encoding should match the source to the channel in a statistical sense. The source as seen from the channel through the transducer should have the same statistical structure as the source which maximizes the entropy in the channel. The content of Theorem 9 is that, although an exact match is not in general possible, we can approximate it as closely as desired. The ratio of the actual rate of transmission to the capacity C may be called the efficiency of the coding system. This is of course equal to the ratio of the actual entropy of the channel symbols to the maximum possible entropy.

In general, ideal or nearly ideal encoding requires a long delay in the transmitter and receiver. In the noiseless case which we have been considering, the main function of this delay is to allow reasonably good

[9] Technical Report No. 65, The Research Laboratory of Electronics, M. I. T.

matching of probabilities to corresponding lengths of sequences. With a good code the logarithm of the reciprocal probability of a long message must be proportional to the duration of the corresponding signal, in fact

$$\left| \frac{\log p^{-1}}{T} - C \right|$$

must be small for all but a small fraction of the long messages.

If a source can produce only one particular message its entropy is zero, and no channel is required. For example, a computing machine set up to calculate the successive digits of π produces a definite sequence with no chance element. No channel is required to "transmit" this to another point. One could construct a second machine to compute the same sequence at the point. However, this may be impractical. In such a case we can choose to ignore some or all of the statistical knowledge we have of the source. We might consider the digits of π to be a random sequence in that we construct a system capable of sending any sequence of digits. In a similar way we may choose to use some of our statistical knowledge of English in constructing a code, but not all of it. In such a case we consider the source with the maximum entropy subject to the statistical conditions we wish to retain. The entropy of this source determines the channel capacity which is necessary and sufficient. In the π example the only information retained is that all the digits are chosen from the set 0, 1, ..., 9. In the case of English one might wish to use the statistical saving possible due to letter frequencies, but nothing else. The maximum entropy source is then the first approximation to English and its entropy determines the required channel capacity.

As a simple example of some of these results consider a source which produces a sequence of letters chosen from among A, B, C, D with probabilities $\frac{1}{2}$, $\frac{1}{4}$, $\frac{1}{8}$, $\frac{1}{8}$, successive symbols being chosen independently. We have

$$H = -(\tfrac{1}{2} \log \tfrac{1}{2} + \tfrac{1}{4} \log \tfrac{1}{4} + \tfrac{2}{8} \log \tfrac{1}{8})$$

$$= \tfrac{7}{4} \text{ bits per symbol.}$$

Thus we can approximate a coding system to encode messages from this source into binary digits with an average of $\frac{7}{4}$ binary digit per symbol. In this case we can actually achieve the limiting value by the following code (obtained by the method of the second proof of Theorem 9):

$$
\begin{array}{cc}
A & 0 \\
B & 10 \\
C & 110 \\
D & 111
\end{array}
$$

The average number of binary digits used in encoding a sequence of N symbols will be

$$
N(\tfrac{1}{2} \times 1 + \tfrac{1}{4} \times 2 + \tfrac{2}{8} \times 3) = \tfrac{7}{4}N
$$

It is easily seen that the binary digits 0, 1 have probabilities $\tfrac{1}{2}$, $\tfrac{1}{2}$ so the H for the coded sequences is one bit per symbol. Since, on the average, we have $\tfrac{7}{4}$ binary symbols per original letter, the entropies on a time basis are the same. The maximum possible entropy for the original set is $\log 4 = 2$, occurring when A, B, C, D have probabilities $\tfrac{1}{4}, \tfrac{1}{4}, \tfrac{1}{4}, \tfrac{1}{4}$. Hence the relative entropy is $\tfrac{7}{8}$. We can translate the binary sequences into the original set of symbols on a two-to-one basis by the following table:

$$
\begin{array}{cc}
00 & A' \\
01 & B' \\
10 & C' \\
11 & D'
\end{array}
$$

This double process then encodes the original message into the same symbols but with an average compression ratio $\tfrac{7}{8}$.

As a second example consider a source which produces a sequence of A's and B's with probability p for A and q for B. If $p << q$ we have

$$
\begin{aligned}
H &= -\log p^p(1 - p)^{1-p} \\
&= -p \log p \, (1 - p)^{(1-p)/p} \\
&\doteq p \log \frac{e}{p}
\end{aligned}
$$

In such a case one can construct a fairly good coding of the message on a 0, 1 channel by sending a special sequence, say 0000, for the infrequent symbol A and then a sequence indicating the *number* of B's following it. This could be indicated by the binary representation with all numbers containing the special sequence deleted. All numbers up to 16 are represented as usual; 16 is represented by the next binary number after 16 which does not contain four zeros, namely $17 = 10001$, etc.

It can be shown that as $p \to 0$ the coding approaches ideal provided the length of the special sequence is properly adjusted.

PART II: THE DISCRETE CHANNEL WITH NOISE

11. REPRESENTATION OF A NOISY DISCRETE CHANNEL

We now consider the case where the signal is perturbed by noise during transmission or at one or the other of the terminals. This means that the received signal is not necessarily the same as that sent out by the transmitter. Two cases may be distinguished. If a particular transmitted signal always produces the same received signal, i.e. the received signal is a definite function of the transmitted signal, then the effect may be called distortion. If this function has an inverse—no two transmitted signals producing the same received signal—distortion may be corrected, at least in principle, by merely performing the inverse functional operation on the received signal.

The case of interest here is that in which the signal does not always undergo the same change in transmission. In this case we may assume the received signal E to be a function of the transmitted signal S and a second variable, the noise N.

$$E = f(S, N)$$

The noise is considered to be a chance variable just as the message was above. In general it may be represented by a suitable stochastic process. The most general type of noisy discrete channel we shall consider is a generalization of the finite state noise free channel described previously. We assume a finite number of states and a set of probabilities

$$p_{\alpha, i}(\beta, j).$$

This is the probability, if the channel is in state α and symbol i is transmitted, that symbol j will be received and the channel left in state β. Thus α and β range over the possible states, i over the possible transmitted signals and j over the possible received signals. In the case where successive symbols are independently perturbed by the noise there is only one state, and the channel is described by the set of transition probabilities $p_i(j)$, the probability of transmitted symbol i being received as j.

If a noisy channel is fed by a source there are two statistical processes at work: the source and the noise. Thus there are a number of entropies that can be calculated. First there is the entropy $H(x)$ of the source or of the input to the channel (these will be equal if the transmitter is non-singular). The entropy of the output of the channel, i.e. the received signal, will be denoted by $H(y)$. In the noiseless case $H(y) = H(x)$. The joint entropy of input and output will be $H(xy)$. Finally there are two conditional entropies $H_x(y)$ and $H_y(x)$, the entropy of the output when the input is known and conversely. Among these quantities we have the relations

$$H(x, y) = H(x) + H_x(y) = H(y) + H_y(x)$$

All of these entropies can be measured on a per-second or a per-symbol basis.

12. Equivocation and Channel Capacity

If the channel is noisy it is not in general possible to reconstruct the original message or the transmitted signal with *certainty* by any operation on the received signal E. There are, however, ways of transmitting the information which are optimal in combating noise. This is the problem which we now consider.

Suppose there are two possible symbols 0 and 1, and we are transmitting at a rate of 1000 symbols per second with probabilities $p_0 = p_1 = \frac{1}{2}$. Thus our source is producing information at the rate of 1000 bits per second. During transmission the noise introduces errors so that, on the average, 1 in 100 is received incorrectly (a 0 as 1, or 1 as 0). What is the rate of transmission of information? Certainly less than 1000 bits per second since about 1% of the received symbols are incorrect. Our first impulse might be to say the rate is 990 bits per second, merely subtracting the expected number of errors. This is not satisfactory since it fails to take into account the recipient's lack of knowledge of where the errors occur. We may carry it to an extreme case and suppose the noise so great that the received symbols are entirely independent of the transmitted symbols. The probability of receiving 1 is $\frac{1}{2}$ whatever was transmitted and similarly for 0. Then about half of the received symbols are correct due to chance alone, and we would be giving the system credit for transmitting 500 bits per second while actually no information is being transmitted at all. Equally "good" transmission would be obtained by dispensing with the channel entirely and flipping a coin at the receiving point.

Evidently the proper correction to apply to the amount of information transmitted is the amount of this information which is missing in the received signal, or alternatively the uncertainty when we have received a signal of what was actually sent. From our previous discussion of entropy as a measure of uncertainty it seems reasonable to use the conditional entropy of the message, knowing the received signal, as a measure of this missing information. This is indeed the proper definition, as we shall see later. Following this idea the rate of actual transmission, R, would be obtained by subtracting from the rate of production (i.e., the entropy of the source) the average rate of conditional entropy.

$$R = H(x) - H_y(x)$$

The conditional entropy $H_y(x)$ will, for convenience, be called the equivocation. It measures the average ambiguity of the received signal.

In the example considered above, if a 0 is received the *a posteriori* probability that a 0 was transmitted is .99, and that a 1 was transmitted is .01. These figures are reversed if a 1 is received. Hence

$$H_y(x) = - [.99 \log .99 + 0.01 \log 0.01]$$

$$= .081 \text{ bits/symbol}$$

or 81 bits per second. We may say that the system is transmitting at a rate $1000 - 81 = 919$ bits per second. In the extreme case where a 0 is equally likely to be received as a 0 or 1 and similarly for 1, the a posteriori probabilities are $\frac{1}{2}$, $\frac{1}{2}$ and

$$H_y(x) = - [\tfrac{1}{2} \log \tfrac{1}{2} + \tfrac{1}{2} \log \tfrac{1}{2}]$$

$$= 1 \text{ bit per symbol}$$

or 1000 bits per second. The rate of transmission is then 0 as it should be.

The following theorem gives a direct intuitive interpretation of the equivocation and also serves to justify it as the unique appropriate measure. We consider a communication system and an observer (or auxiliary device) who can see both what is sent and what is recovered (with errors due to noise). This observer notes the errors in the recovered message and transmits data to the receiving point over a "correction channel" to enable the receiver to correct the errors. The situation is indicated schematically in Fig. 8.

Theorem 10: If the correction channel has a capacity equal to $H_y(x)$ it is possible to so encode the correction data as to send it over this channel and correct all but an arbitrarily small fraction ϵ of the errors. This is not possible if the channel capacity is less than $H_y(x)$.

Roughly then, $H_y(x)$ is the amount of additional information that must be supplied per second at the receiving point to correct the received message.

To prove the first part, consider long sequences of received message M' and corresponding original message M. There will be logarithmically $TH_y(x)$ of the M's which could reasonably have produced each M'. Thus we have $TH_y(x)$ binary digits to send each T seconds. This can be done with ϵ frequency of errors on a channel of capacity $H_y(x)$.

The second part can be proved by noting, first, that for any discrete chance variables x, y, z

$$H_y(x, z) \geq H_y(x)$$

The left-hand side can be expanded to give

$$H_y(z) + H_{yz}(x) \geq H_y(x)$$

$$H_{yz}(x) \geq H_y(x) - H_y(z) \geq H_y(x) - H(z)$$

If we identify x as the output of the source, y as the received signal and z as the signal sent over the correction channel, then the right-hand side is the equivocation less the rate of transmission over the correction channel. If the capacity of this channel is less than the equivocation the right-hand side will be greater than zero and $H_{yz}(x) \geq 0$. But this is the uncertainty of what was sent, knowing both the received signal and the correction signal. If this is greater than zero the frequency of errors cannot be arbitrarily small.

Example:

Suppose the errors occur at random in a sequence of binary digits: probability p that a digit is wrong and $q = 1 - p$ that it is right. These errors can be corrected if their position is known. Thus the correction channel need only send information as to these positions. This amounts to trans-

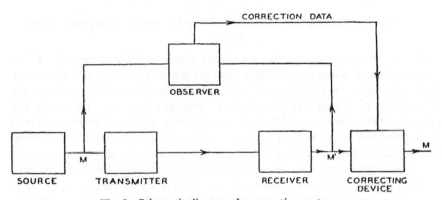

Fig. 8—Schematic diagram of a correction system.

mitting from a source which produces binary digits with probability p for 1 (correct) and q for 0 (incorrect). This requires a channel of capacity

$$-[p \log p + q \log q]$$

which is the equivocation of the original system.

The rate of transmission R can be written in two other forms due to the identities noted above. We have

$$R = H(x) - H_y(x)$$
$$= H(y) - H_x(y)$$
$$= H(x) + H(y) - H(x, y).$$

The first defining expression has already been interpreted as the amount of information sent less the uncertainty of what was sent. The second measures the amount received less the part of this which is due to noise. The third is the sum of the two amounts less the joint entropy and therefore in a sense is the number of bits per second common to the two. Thus all three expressions have a certain intuitive significance.

The capacity C of a noisy channel should be the maximum possible rate of transmission, i.e., the rate when the source is properly matched to the channel. We therefore define the channel capacity by

$$C = \text{Max} \ (H(x) - H_y(x))$$

where the maximum is with respect to all possible information sources used as input to the channel. If the channel is noiseless, $H_y(x) = 0$. The definition is then equivalent to that already given for a noiseless channel since the maximum entropy for the channel is its capacity.

13. The Fundamental Theorem for a Discrete Channel with Noise

It may seem surprising that we should define a definite capacity C for a noisy channel since we can never send certain information in such a case. It is clear, however, that by sending the information in a redundant form the probability of errors can be reduced. For example, by repeating the message many times and by a statistical study of the different received versions of the message the probability of errors could be made very small. One would expect, however, that to make this probability of errors approach zero, the redundancy of the encoding must increase indefinitely, and the rate of transmission therefore approach zero. This is by no means true. If it were, there would not be a very well defined capacity, but only a capacity for a given frequency of errors, or a given equivocation; the capacity going down as the error requirements are made more stringent. Actually the capacity C defined above has a very definite significance. It is possible to send information at the rate C through the channel *with as small a frequency of errors or equivocation as desired* by proper encoding. This statement is not true for any rate greater than C. If an attempt is made to transmit at a higher rate than C, say $C + R_1$, then there will necessarily be an equivocation equal to a greater than the excess R_1. Nature takes payment by requiring just that much uncertainty, so that we are not actually getting any more than C through correctly.

The situation is indicated in Fig. 9. The rate of information into the channel is plotted horizontally and the equivocation vertically. Any point above the heavy line in the shaded region can be attained and those below cannot. The points on the line cannot in general be attained, but there will usually be two points on the line that can.

These results are the main justification for the definition of C and will now be proved.

Theorem 11. Let a discrete channel have the capacity C and a discrete source the entropy per second H. If $H \leq C$ there exists a coding system such that the output of the source can be transmitted over the channel with an arbitrarily small frequency of errors (or an arbitrarily small equivocation). If $H > C$ it is possible to encode the source so that the equivocation is less than $H - C + \epsilon$ where ϵ is arbitrarily small. There is no method of encoding which gives an equivocation less than $H - C$.

The method of proving the first part of this theorem is not by exhibiting a coding method having the desired properties, but by showing that such a code must exist in a certain group of codes. In fact we will average the frequency of errors over this group and show that this average can be made less than ϵ. If the average of a set of numbers is less than ϵ there must exist at least one in the set which is less than ϵ. This will establish the desired result.

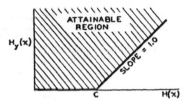

Fig. 9—The equivocation possible for a given input entropy to a channel.

The capacity C of a noisy channel has been defined as

$$C = \text{Max}\ (H(x) - H_y(x))$$

where x is the input and y the output. The maximization is over all sources which might be used as input to the channel.

Let S_0 be a source which achieves the maximum capacity C. If this maximum is not actually achieved by any source let S_0 be a source which approximates to giving the maximum rate. Suppose S_0 is used as input to the channel. We consider the possible transmitted and received sequences of a long duration T. The following will be true:

1. The transmitted sequences fall into two classes, a high probability group with about $2^{TH(x)}$ members and the remaining sequences of small total probability.

2. Similarly the received sequences have a high probability set of about $2^{TH(y)}$ members and a low probability set of remaining sequences.

3. Each high probability output could be produced by about $2^{TH_y(x)}$ inputs. The probability of all other cases has a small total probability.

All the ϵ's and δ's implied by the words "small" and "about" in these statements approach zero as we allow T to increase and S_0 to approach the maximizing source.

The situation is summarized in Fig. 10 where the input sequences are points on the left and output sequences points on the right. The fan of cross lines represents the range of possible causes for a typical output.

Now suppose we have another source producing information at rate R with $R < C$. In the period T this source will have 2^{TR} high probability outputs. We wish to associate these with a selection of the possible channel

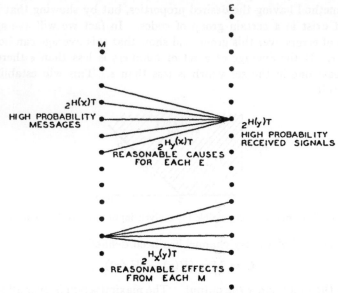

Fig. 10—Schematic representation of the relations between inputs and outputs in a channel.

inputs in such a way as to get a small frequency of errors. We will set up this association in all possible ways (using, however, only the high probability group of inputs as determined by the source S_0) and average the frequency of errors for this large class of possible coding systems. This is the same as calculating the frequency of errors for a random association of the messages and channel inputs of duration T. Suppose a particular output y_1 is observed. What is the probability of more than one message in the set of possible causes of y_1? There are 2^{TR} messages distributed at random in $2^{TH(x)}$ points. The probability of a particular point being a message is thus

$$2^{T(R-H(x))}$$

The probability that none of the points in the fan is a message (apart from the actual originating message) is

$$P = [1 - 2^{T(R-H(x))}]^{2^{TH_y(x)}}$$

Now $R < H(x) - H_y(x)$ so $R - H(x) = -H_y(x) - \eta$ with η positive. Consequently

$$P = [1 - 2^{-TH_y(x)-T\eta}]^{2^{TH_y(x)}}$$

approaches (as $T \to \infty$)

$$1 - 2^{-T\eta}.$$

Hence the probability of an error approaches zero and the first part of the theorem is proved.

The second part of the theorem is easily shown by noting that we could merely send C bits per second from the source, completely neglecting the remainder of the information generated. At the receiver the neglected part gives an equivocation $H(x) - C$ and the part transmitted need only add ϵ. This limit can also be attained in many other ways, as will be shown when we consider the continuous case.

The last statement of the theorem is a simple consequence of our definition of C. Suppose we can encode a source with $R = C + a$ in such a way as to obtain an equivocation $H_y(x) = a - \epsilon$ with ϵ positive. Then $R = H(x) = C + a$ and

$$H(x) - H_y(x) = C + \epsilon$$

with ϵ positive. This contradicts the definition of C as the maximum of $H(x) - H_y(x)$.

Actually more has been proved than was stated in the theorem. If the average of a set of numbers is within ϵ of their maximum, a fraction of at most $\sqrt{\epsilon}$ can be more than $\sqrt{\epsilon}$ below the maximum. Since ϵ is arbitrarily small we can say that almost all the systems are arbitrarily close to the ideal.

14. Discussion

The demonstration of theorem 11, while not a pure existence proof, has some of the deficiencies of such proofs. An attempt to obtain a good approximation to ideal coding by following the method of the proof is generally impractical. In fact, apart from some rather trivial cases and certain limiting situations, no explicit description of a series of approximation to the ideal has been found. Probably this is no accident but is related to the difficulty of giving an explicit construction for a good approximation to a random sequence.

An approximation to the ideal would have the property that if the signal is altered in a reasonable way by the noise, the original can still be recovered. In other words the alteration will not in general bring it closer to another reasonable signal than the original. This is accomplished at the cost of a certain amount of redundancy in the coding. The redundancy must be introduced in the proper way ·to combat the particular noise structure involved. However, any redundancy in the source will usually help if it is utilized at the receiving point. In particular, if the source already has a certain redundancy and no attempt is made to eliminate it in matching to the channel, this redundancy will help combat noise. For example, in a noiseless telegraph channel one could save about 50% in time by proper encoding of the messages. This is not done and most of the redundancy of English remains in the channel symbols. This has the advantage, however, of allowing considerable noise in the channel. A sizable fraction of the letters can be received incorrectly and still reconstructed by the context. In fact this is probably not a bad approximation to the ideal in many cases, since the statistical structure of English is rather involved and the reasonable English sequences are not too far (in the sense required for theorem) from a random selection.

As in the noiseless case a delay is generally required to approach the ideal encoding. It now has the additional function of allowing a large sample of noise to affect the signal before any judgment is made at the receiving point as to the original message. Increasing the sample size always sharpens the possible statistical assertions.

The content of theorem 11 and its proof can be formulated in a somewhat different way which exhibits the connection with the noiseless case more clearly. Consider the possible signals of duration T and suppose a subset of them is selected to be used. Let those in the subset all be used with equal probability, and suppose the receiver is constructed to select, as the original signal, the most probable cause from the subset, when a perturbed signal is received. We define $N(T, q)$ to be the maximum number of signals we can choose for the subset such that the probability of an incorrect interpretation is less than or equal to q.

Theorem 12: $\lim\limits_{T \to \infty} \dfrac{\log N(T, q)}{T} = C$, where C is the channel capacity, provided that q does not equal 0 or 1.

In other words, no matter how we set our limits of reliability, we can distinguish reliably in time T enough messages to correspond to about CT bits, when T is sufficiently large. Theorem 12 can be compared with the definition of the capacity of a noiseless channel given in section 1.

15. Example of a Discrete Channel and Its Capacity

A simple example of a discrete channel is indicated in Fig. 11. There are three possible symbols. The first is never affected by noise. The second and third each have probability p of coming through undisturbed, and q of being changed into the other of the pair. We have (letting $\alpha = -\,[p \log$

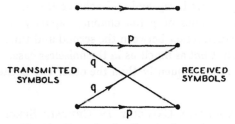

Fig. 11—Example of a discrete channel.

$p + q \log q]$ and P and Q be the probabilities of using the first or second symbols)

$$H(x) = -P \log P - 2Q \log Q$$

$$H_y(x) = 2Q\alpha$$

We wish to choose P and Q in such a way as to maximize $H(x) - H_y(x)$, subject to the constraint $P + 2Q = 1$. Hence we consider

$$U = -P \log P - 2Q \log Q - 2Q\alpha + \lambda(P + 2Q)$$

$$\frac{\partial U}{\partial P} = -1 - \log P + \lambda = 0$$

$$\frac{\partial U}{\partial Q} = -2 - 2 \log Q - 2\alpha + 2\lambda = 0.$$

Eliminating λ

$$\log P = \log Q + \alpha$$

$$P = Qe^{\alpha} = Q\beta$$

$$P = \frac{\beta}{\beta + 2} \qquad Q = \frac{1}{\beta + 2}.$$

The channel capacity is then

$$C = \log \frac{\beta + 2}{\beta}.$$

Note how this checks the obvious values in the cases $p = 1$ and $p = \frac{1}{2}$. In the first, $\beta = 1$ and $C = \log 3$, which is correct since the channel is then noiseless with three possible symbols. If $p = \frac{1}{2}$, $\beta = 2$ and $C = \log 2$. Here the second and third symbols cannot be distinguished at all and act together like one symbol. The first symbol is used with probability $P = \frac{1}{2}$ and the second and third together with probability $\frac{1}{2}$. This may be distributed in any desired way and still achieve the maximum capacity.

For intermediate values of p the channel capacity will lie between $\log 2$ and $\log 3$. The distinction between the second and third symbols conveys some information but not as much as in the noiseless case. The first symbol is used somewhat more frequently than the other two because of its freedom from noise.

16. The Channel Capacity in Certain Special Cases

If the noise affects successive channel symbols independently it can be described by a set of transition probabilities p_{ij}. This is the probability, if symbol i is sent, that j will be received. The maximum channel rate is then given by the maximum of

$$\sum_{i,j} P_i\, p_{ij} \log \sum_i P_i\, p_{ij} - \sum_{i,j} P_i\, p_{ij} \log p_{ij}$$

where we vary the P_i subject to $\Sigma P_i = 1$. This leads by the method of Lagrange to the equations,

$$\sum_j p_{sj} \log \frac{p_{sj}}{\sum_i P_i\, p_{ij}} = \mu \qquad\qquad s = 1, 2, \cdots.$$

Multiplying by P_s and summing on s shows that $\mu = -C$. Let the inverse of p_{sj} (if it exists) be h_{st} so that $\sum_s h_{st} p_{sj} = \delta_{tj}$. Then:

$$\sum_{s,i} h_{st}\, p_{sj} \log p_{sj} - \log \sum_i P_i\, p_{it} = -C \sum_s h_{st}.$$

Hence:

$$\sum_i P_i\, p_{it} = \exp\left[C \sum_s h_{st} + \sum_{s,j} h_{st}\, p_{sj} \log p_{sj}\right]$$

or,

$$P_i = \sum_t h_{it} \exp\left[C \sum_s h_{st} + \sum_{s,j} h_{st}\, p_{sj} \log p_{sj}\right].$$

This is the system of equations for determining the maximizing values of P_i, with C to be determined so that $\Sigma P_i = 1$. When this is done C will be the channel capacity, and the P_i the proper probabilities for the channel symbols to achieve this capacity.

If each input symbol has the same set of probabilities on the lines emerging from it, and the same is true of each output symbol, the capacity can be easily calculated. Examples are shown in Fig. 12. In such a case $H_x(y)$ is independent of the distribution of probabilities on the input symbols, and is given by $-\Sigma\ p_i \log p_i$ where the p_i are the values of the transition probabilities from any input symbol. The channel capacity is

$$\text{Max}\ \ [H(y)\ \ -\ \ H_x(y)]$$
$$= \text{Max}\ H(y) + \Sigma\ p_i \log p_i.$$

The maximum of $H(y)$ is clearly $\log m$ where m is the number of output

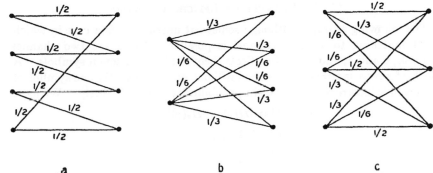

a   b   c

Fig. 12—Examples of discrete channels with the same transition probabilities for each input and for each output.

symbols, since it is possible to make them all equally probable by making the input symbols equally probable. The channel capacity is therefore

$$C = \log m + \Sigma\ p_i \log p_i.$$

In Fig. 12a it would be

$$C = \log 4 - \log 2 = \log 2.$$

This could be achieved by using only the 1st and 3d symbols. In Fig. 12b

$$C = \log 4 - \tfrac{2}{3} \log 3 - \tfrac{1}{3} \log 6$$
$$= \log 4 - \log 3 - \tfrac{1}{3} \log 2$$
$$= \log \tfrac{1}{3}\ 2^{\frac{5}{3}}.$$

In Fig. 12c we have

$$C = \log 3 - \tfrac{1}{2} \log 2 - \tfrac{1}{3} \log 3 - \tfrac{1}{6} \log 6$$
$$= \log \frac{3}{2^{\frac{1}{2}} 3^{\frac{1}{3}} 6^{\frac{1}{6}}}.$$

Suppose the symbols fall into several groups such that the noise never causes a symbol in one group to be mistaken for a symbol in another group. Let the capacity for the nth group be C_n when we use only the symbols in this group. Then it is easily shown that, for best use of the entire set, the total probability P_n of all symbols in the nth group should be

$$P_n = \frac{2^{C_n}}{\Sigma 2^{C_n}}.$$

Within a group the probability is distributed just as it would be if these were the only symbols being used. The channel capacity is

$$C = \log \Sigma 2^{C_n}.$$

17. An Example of Efficient Coding

The following example, although somewhat unrealistic, is a case in which exact matching to a noisy channel is possible. There are two channel symbols, 0 and 1, and the noise affects them in blocks of seven symbols. A block of seven is either transmitted without error, or exactly one symbol of the seven is incorrect. These eight possibilities are equally likely. We have

$$C = \text{Max} \, [H(y) - H_x(y)]$$
$$= \tfrac{1}{7} [7 + \tfrac{8}{8} \log \tfrac{1}{8}]$$
$$= \tfrac{4}{7} \text{ bits/symbol}.$$

An efficient code, allowing complete correction of errors and transmitting at the rate C, is the following (found by a method due to R. Hamming):

Let a block of seven symbols be $X_1, X_2, \ldots X_7$. Of these X_3, X_5, X_6 and X_7 are message symbols and chosen arbitrarily by the source. The other three are redundant and calculated as follows:

X_4 is chosen to make $\alpha = X_4 + X_5 + X_6 + X_7$ even

X_2 " " " " $\beta = X_2 + X_3 + X_6 + X_7$ "

X_1 " " " " $\gamma = X_1 + X_3 + X_5 + X_7$ "

When a block of seven is received α, β and γ are calculated and if even called zero, if odd called one. The binary number $\alpha \beta \gamma$ then gives the subscript of the X_i that is incorrect (if 0 there was no error).

APPENDIX 1

The Growth of the Number of Blocks of Symbols With A Finite State Condition

Let $N_i(L)$ be the number of blocks of symbols of length L ending in state i. Then we have

$$N_j(L) = \sum_{i s} N_i(L - b_{ij}^{(s)})$$

where b_{ij}^1, b_{ij}^2, $\ldots b_{ij}^m$ are the length of the symbols which may be chosen in state i and lead to state j. These are linear difference equations and the behavior as $L \rightarrow \infty$ must be of the type

$$N_j = A_j W^L$$

Substituting in the difference equation

$$A_j W^L = \sum_{i,s} A_i W^{L-b_{ij}^{(s)}}$$

or

$$A_j = \sum_{i s} A_i W^{-b_{ij}^{(s)}}$$

$$\sum_i \left(\sum_s W^{-b_{ij}^{(s)}} - \delta_{ij} \right) A_i = 0.$$

For this to be possible the determinant

$$D(W) = |a_{ij}| = \left| \sum_s W^{-b_{ij}^{(s)}} - \delta_{ij} \right|$$

must vanish and this determines W, which is, of course, the largest real root of $D = 0$.

The quantity C is then given by

$$C = \lim_{L \rightarrow \infty} \frac{\log \Sigma A_j W^L}{L} = \log W$$

and we also note that the same growth properties result if we require that all blocks start in the same (arbitrarily chosen) state.

APPENDIX 2

DERIVATION OF $H - -\Sigma\, p_i \log p_i$

Let $H\left(\dfrac{1}{n}, \dfrac{1}{n}, \cdots, \dfrac{1}{n}\right) = A(n)$. From condition (3) we can decompose a choice from s^m equally likely possibilities into a series of m choices each from s equally likely possibilities and obtain

$$A(s^m) = m\, A(s)$$

Similarly

$$A(t^n) = n\, A(t)$$

We can choose n arbitrarily large and find an m to satisfy

$$s^m \leq t^n < s^{(m+1)}$$

Thus, taking logarithms and dividing by $n \log s$,

$$\frac{m}{n} \leq \frac{\log t}{\log s} \leq \frac{m}{n} + \frac{1}{n} \quad \text{or} \quad \left| \frac{m}{n} - \frac{\log t}{\log s} \right| < \epsilon$$

where ϵ is arbitrarily small.

Now from the monotonic property of $A(n)$,

$$A(s^m) \leq A(t^n) \leq A(s^{m+1})$$

$$m A(s) \leq n A(t) \leq (m+1) A(s)$$

Hence, dividing by $nA(s)$,

$$\frac{m}{n} \leq \frac{A(t)}{A(s)} \leq \frac{m}{n} + \frac{1}{n} \quad \text{or} \quad \left| \frac{m}{n} - \frac{A(t)}{A(s)} \right| < \epsilon$$

$$\left| \frac{A(t)}{A(s)} - \frac{\log t}{\log s} \right| \leq 2\epsilon \qquad A(t) = -K \log t$$

where K must be positive to satisfy (2).

Now suppose we have a choice from n possibilities with commeasurable probabilities $p_i = \frac{n_i}{\Sigma n_i}$ where the n_i are integers. We can break down a choice from Σn_i possibilities into a choice from n possibilities with probabilities $p_i \dots p_n$ and then, if the ith was chosen, a choice from n_i with equal probabilities. Using condition 3 again, we equate the total choice from Σn_i as computed by two methods

$$K \log \Sigma n_i = H(p_1, \dots, p_n) + K \Sigma p_i \log n_i$$

Hence

$$H = K [\Sigma p_i \log \Sigma n_i - \Sigma p_i \log n_i]$$

$$= -K \Sigma p_i \log \frac{n_i}{\Sigma n_i} = -K \Sigma p_i \log p_i .$$

If the p_i are incommeasurable, they may be approximated by rationals and the same expression must hold by our continuity assumption. Thus the expression holds in general. The choice of coefficient K is a matter of convenience and amounts to the choice of a unit of measure.

APPENDIX 3

THEOREMS ON ERGODIC SOURCES

If it is possible to go from any state with $P > 0$ to any other along a path of probability $p > 0$, the system is ergodic and the strong law of large numbers can be applied. Thus the number of times a given path p_{ij} in the network is traversed in a long sequence of length N is about proportional to the probability of being at i and then choosing this path, $P_i p_{ij} N$. If N is large enough the probability of percentage error $\pm \delta$ in this is less than ϵ so that for all but a set of small probability the actual numbers lie within the limits

$$(P_i p_{ij} \pm \delta) N$$

Hence nearly all sequences have a probability p given by

$$p = \Pi p_{ij}^{(P_i p_{ij} \pm \delta) N}$$

and $\dfrac{\log p}{N}$ is limited by

$$\frac{\log p}{N} = \Sigma(P_i p_{ij} \pm \delta) \log p_{ij}$$

or

$$\left| \frac{\log p}{N} - \Sigma P_i p_{ij} \log p_{ij} \right| < \eta.$$

This proves theorem 3.

Theorem 4 follows immediately from this on calculating upper and lower bounds for $n(q)$ based on the possible range of values of p in Theorem 3.

In the mixed (not ergodic) case if

$$L = \Sigma p_i L_i$$

and the entropies of the components are $H_1 \geq H_2 \geq \ldots \geq H_n$ we have the

Theorem: $\underset{N \to \infty}{\text{Lim}} \dfrac{\log n(q)}{N} = \varphi(q)$ is a decreasing step function,

$$\varphi(q) = H_s \quad \text{in the interval} \quad \sum_1^{s-1} \alpha_i < q < \sum_1^{s} \alpha_i.$$

To prove theorems 5 and 6 first note that F_N is monotonic decreasing because increasing N adds a subscript to a conditional entropy. A simple substitution for $p_{B_i}(S_j)$ in the definition of F_N shows that

$$F_N = N G_N - (N - 1) G_{N-1}$$

and summing this for all N gives $G_N = \dfrac{1}{N} \Sigma F_N$. Hence $G_N \geq F_N$ and G_N monotonic decreasing. Also they must approach the same limit. By using theorem 3 we see that $\underset{N \to \infty}{\text{Lim}} G_N = H.$

APPENDIX 4

MAXIMIZING THE RATE FOR A SYSTEM OF CONSTRAINTS

Suppose we have a set of constraints on sequences of symbols that is of the finite state type and can be represented therefore by a linear graph.

Let $\ell_{ij}^{(s)}$ be the lengths of the various symbols that can occur in passing from state i to state j. What distribution of probabilities P_i for the different states and $p_{ij}^{(s)}$ for choosing symbol s in state i and going to state j maximizes the rate of generating information under these constraints? The constraints define a discrete channel and the maximum rate must be less than or equal to the capacity C of this channel, since if all blocks of large length were equally likely, this rate would result, and if possible this would be best. We will show that this rate can be achieved by proper choice of the P_i and $p_{ij}^{(s)}$.

The rate in question is

$$\frac{-\Sigma P_i\, p_{ij}^{(s)} \log p_{ij}^{(s)}}{\Sigma P_{(i)} p_{ij}^{(s)}\, \ell_{ij}^{(s)}} = \frac{N}{M}.$$

Let $\ell_{ij} = \sum_s \ell_{ij}^{(s)}$. Evidently for a maximum $p_{ij}^{(s)} = k \exp \ell_{ij}^{(s)}$. The constraints on maximization are $\Sigma P_i = 1$, $\sum_j p_{ij} = 1$, $\Sigma\, P_i(p_{ij} - \delta_{ij}) = 0$.

Hence we maximize

$$U = \frac{-\Sigma P_i\, p_{ij} \log p_{ij}}{\Sigma P_i\, p_{ij}\, \ell_{ij}} + \lambda \sum_i P_i + \Sigma \mu_i\, p_{ij} + \Sigma \eta_j\, P_i(p_{ij} - \delta_{ij})$$

$$\frac{\partial U}{\partial p_{ij}} = -\frac{M P_i(1 + \log p_{ij}) + N P_i\, \ell_{ij}}{M^2} + \lambda + \mu_i + \eta_i P_i = 0.$$

Solving for p_{ij}

$$p_{ij} = A_i\, B_j\, D^{-\ell_{ij}}.$$

Since

$$\sum_j p_{ij} = 1, \qquad A_i^{-1} = \sum_j B_j\, D^{-\ell_{ij}}$$

$$p_{ij} = \frac{B_j\, D^{-\ell_{ij}}}{\sum_s B_s\, D^{-\ell_{is}}}.$$

The correct value of D is the capacity C and the B_j are solutions of

$$B_i = \Sigma\, B_j\, C^{-\ell_{ij}}$$

for then

$$p_{ij} = \frac{B_j}{B_i}\, C^{-\ell_{ij}}$$

$$\Sigma P_i\, \frac{B_j}{B_i}\, C^{-\ell_{ij}} = P_j$$

or

$$\Sigma \frac{P_i}{B_i} C^{-\ell_{ij}} = \frac{P_j}{B_i}$$

So that if λ_i satisfy

$$\Sigma \gamma_i C^{-\ell_{ij}} = \gamma_j$$

$$P_i = B_i \gamma_i$$

Both of the sets of equations for B_i and γ_i can be satisfied since C is such that

$$|C^{-\ell_{ij}} - \delta_{ij}| = 0$$

In this case the rate is

$$- \frac{\Sigma P_i \, p_{ij} \log \frac{B_j}{B_i} C^{-\ell_{ij}}}{\Sigma P_i \, p_{ij} \ell_{ij}}$$

$$= C - \frac{\Sigma P_i \, p_{ij} \log \frac{B_j}{B_i}}{\Sigma P_i \, p_{ij} \ell_{ij}}$$

but

$$\Sigma P_i \, p_{ij}(\log B_j - \log B_i) = \sum_i P_j \log B_j - \Sigma P_i \log B_i = 0$$

Hence the rate is C and as this could never be exceeded this is the maximum' justifying the assumed solution.

PART III: MATHEMATICAL PRELIMINARIES

In this final installment of the paper we consider the case where the signals or the messages or both are continuously variable, in contrast with the discrete nature assumed until now. To a considerable extent the continuous case can be obtained through a limiting process from the discrete case by dividing the continuum of messages and signals into a large but finite number of small regions and calculating the various parameters involved on a discrete basis. As the size of the regions is decreased these parameters in general approach as limits the proper values for the continuous case. There are, however, a few new effects that appear and also a general change of emphasis in the direction of specialization of the general results to particular cases.

We will not attempt, in the continuous case, to obtain our results with the greatest generality, or with the extreme rigor of pure mathematics, since this would involve a great deal of abstract measure theory and would obscure the main thread of the analysis. A preliminary study, however, indicates that the theory can be formulated in a completely axiomatic and rigorous manner which includes both the continuous and discrete cases and many others. The occasional liberties taken with limiting processes in the present analysis can be justified in all cases of practical interest.

18. SETS AND ENSEMBLES OF FUNCTIONS

We shall have to deal in the continuous case with sets of functions and ensembles of functions. A set of functions, as the name implies, is merely a class or collection of functions, generally of one variable, time. It can be specified by giving an explicit representation of the various functions in the set, or implicitly by giving a property which functions in the set possess and others do not. Some examples are:

1. The set of functions:

$$f_\theta(t) = \sin (t + \theta).$$

Each particular value of θ determines a particular function in the set.

2. The set of all functions of time containing no frequencies over W cycles per second.
3. The set of all functions limited in band to W and in amplitude to A.
4. The set of all English speech signals as functions of time.

An *ensemble* of functions is a set of functions together with a probability measure whereby we may determine the probability of a function in the set having certain properties.[1] For example with the set,

$$f_\theta(t) = \sin(t + \theta),$$

we may give a probability distribution for θ, $P(\theta)$. The set then becomes an ensemble.

Some further examples of ensembles of functions are:
1. A finite set of functions $f_k(t)$ $(k = 1, 2, \cdots, n)$ with the probability of f_k being p_k.
2. A finite dimensional family of functions

$$f(\alpha_1, \alpha_2, \cdots, \alpha_n; t)$$

with a probability distribution for the parameters α_i :

$$p(\alpha_1, \cdots, \alpha_n)$$

For example we could consider the ensemble defined by

$$f(a_1, \cdots, a_n, \theta_1, \cdots, \theta_n; t) = \sum_{n=1}^{n} a_n \sin n(\omega t + \theta_n)$$

with the amplitudes a_i distributed normally and independently, and the phrases θ_i distributed uniformly (from 0 to 2π) and independently.
3. The ensemble

$$f(a_i, t) = \sum_{n=-\infty}^{+\infty} a_n \frac{\sin \pi(2Wt - n)}{\pi(2Wt - n)}$$

with the a_i normal and independent all with the same standard deviation $\sqrt{N}$. This is a representation of "white" noise, band-limited to the band from 0 to W cycles per second and with average power N.[2]

---

[1] In mathematical terminology the functions belong to a measure space whose total measure is unity.

[2] This representation can be used as a definition of band limited white noise. It has certain advantages in that it involves fewer limiting operations than do definitions that have been used in the past. The name "white noise," already firmly intrenched in the literature, is perhaps somewhat unfortunate. In optics white light means either any continuous spectrum as contrasted with a point spectrum, or a spectrum which is flat with *wavelength* (which is not the same as a spectrum flat with frequency).

4. Let points be distributed on the t axis according to a Poisson distribution. At each selected point the function $f(t)$ is placed and the different functions added, giving the ensemble

$$\sum_{k=-\infty}^{\infty} f(t + t_k)$$

where the t_k are the points of the Poisson distribution. This ensemble can be considered as a type of impulse or shot noise where all the impulses are identical.

5. The set of English speech functions with the probability measure given by the frequency of occurrence in ordinary use.

An ensemble of functions $f_\alpha(t)$ is *stationary* if the same ensemble results when all functions are shifted any fixed amount in time. The ensemble

$$f_\theta(t) = \sin (t + \theta)$$

is stationary if θ distributed uniformly from 0 to 2π. If we shift each function by t_1 we obtain

$$f_\theta(t + t_1) = \sin (t + t_1 + \theta)$$
$$= \sin (t + \varphi)$$

with φ distributed uniformly from 0 to 2π. Each function has changed but the ensemble as a whole is invariant under the translation. The other examples given above are also stationary.

An ensemble is *ergodic* if it is stationary, and there is no subset of the functions in the set with a probability different from 0 and 1 which is stationary. The ensemble

$$\sin (t + \theta)$$

is ergodic. No subset of these functions of probability $\neq 0, 1$ is transformed into itself under all time translations. On the other hand the ensemble

$$a \sin (t + \theta)$$

with a distributed normally and θ uniform is stationary but not ergodic. The subset of these functions with a between 0 and 1 for example is stationary.

Of the examples given, 3 and 4 are ergodic, and 5 may perhaps be considered so. If an ensemble is ergodic we may say roughly that each function in the set is typical of the ensemble. More precisely it is known that with an ergodic ensemble an average of any statistic over the ensemble is equal (with probability 1) to an average over all the time translations of a particular function in the set.[3]   Roughly speaking, each function can be expected, as time progresses, to go through, with the proper frequency, all the convolutions of any of the functions in the set.

Just as we may perform various operations on numbers or functions to obtain new numbers or functions, we can perform operations on ensembles to obtain new ensembles.   Suppose, for example, we have an ensemble of functions $f_\alpha(t)$ and an operator T which gives for each function $f_\alpha(t)$ a result $g_\alpha(t)$:

$$g_\alpha(t) = Tf_\alpha(t)$$

Probability measure is defined for the set $g_\alpha(t)$ by means of that for the set $f_\alpha(t)$.   The probability of a certain subset of the $g_\alpha(t)$ functions is equal to that of the subset of the $f_\alpha(t)$ functions which produce members of the given subset of g functions under the operation T.   Physically this corresponds to passing the ensemble through some device, for example, a filter, a rectifier or a modulator.   The output functions of the device form the ensemble $g_\alpha(t)$.

A device or operator T will be called invariant if shifting the input merely shifts the output, i.e., if

$$g_\alpha(t) = Tf_\alpha(t)$$

implies

$$g_\alpha(t + t_1) = Tf_\alpha(t + t_1)$$

for all $f_\alpha(t)$ and all t_1.   It is easily shown (see appendix 1) that if T is invariant and the input ensemble is stationary then the output ensemble is stationary.   Likewise if the input is ergodic the output will also be ergodic.

A filter or a rectifier is invariant under all time translations.   The operation of modulation is not since the carrier phase gives a certain time structure.   However, modulation is invariant under all translations which are multiples of the period of the carrier.

Wiener has pointed out the intimate relation between the invariance of physical devices under time translations and Fourier theory.[4]   He has

---

[3] This is the famous ergodic theorem or rather one aspect of this theorem which was proved is somewhat different formulations by Birkhoff, von Neumann, and Koopman, and subsequently generalized by Wiener, Hopf, Hurewicz and others.   The literature on ergodic theory is quite extensive and the reader is referred to the papers of these writers for precise and general formulations; e.g., E. Hopf "Ergodentheorie" Ergebnisse der Mathematic und ihrer Grenzgebiete, Vol. 5, "On Causality Statistics and Probability" Journal of Mathematics and Physics, Vol. XIII, No. 1, 1934; N. Weiner "The Ergodic Theorem" Duke Mathematical Journal, Vol. 5, 1939.

[4] Communication theory is heavily indebted to Wiener for much of its basic philosophy and theory.   His classic NDRC report "The Interpolation, Extrapolation, and Smoothing of Stationary Time Series," to appear soon in book form, contains the first clear-cut formulation of communication theory as a statistical problem, the study of operations

shown, in fact, that if a device is linear as well as invariant Fourier analysis is then the appropriate mathematical tool for dealing with the problem.

An ensemble of functions is the appropriate mathematical representation of the messages produced by a continuous source (for example speech), of the signals produced by a transmitter, and of the perturbing noise. Communication theory is properly concerned, as has been emphasized by Wiener, not with operations on particular functions, but with operations on ensembles of functions. A communication system is designed not for a particular speech function and still less for a sine wave, but for the ensemble of speech functions.

19. Band Limited Ensembles of Functions

If a function of time $f(t)$ is limited to the band from 0 to W cycles per second it is completely determined by giving its ordinates at a series of discrete points spaced $\dfrac{1}{2W}$ seconds apart in the manner indicated by the following result.[5]

Theorem 13: Let $f(t)$ contain no frequencies over W. Then

$$f(t) = \sum_{-\infty}^{\infty} X_n \frac{\sin \pi(2Wt - n)}{\pi(2Wt - n)}$$

where

$$X_n = f\left(\frac{n}{2W}\right).$$

In this expansion $f(t)$ is represented as a sum of orthogonal functions. The coefficients X_n of the various terms can be considered as coordinates in an infinite dimensional "function space." In this space each function corresponds to precisely one point and each point to one function.

A function can be considered to be substantially limited to a time T if all the ordinates X_n outside this interval of time are zero.   In this case all but $2TW$ of the coordinates will be zero.   Thus functions limited to a band W and duration T correspond to points in a space of $2TW$ dimensions.

A subset of the functions of band W and duration T corresponds to a region in this space.   For example, the functions whose total energy is less

---

on time series. This work, although chiefly concerned with the linear prediction and filtering problem, is an important collateral reference in connection with the present paper. We may also refer here to Wiener's forthcoming book "Cybernetics" dealing with the general problems of communication and control.

[5] For a proof of this theorem and further discussion see the author's paper "Communication in the Presence of Noise" to be published in the *Proceedings of the Institute of Radio Engineers*.

than or equal to E correspond to points in a $2TW$ dimensional sphere with radius $r = \sqrt{2WE}$.

An *ensemble* of functions of limited duration and band will be represented by a probability distribution $p(x_1 \cdots x_n)$ in the corresponding n dimensional space. If the ensemble is not limited in time we can consider the $2TW$ co-ordinates in a given interval T to represent substantially the part of the function in the interval T and the probability distribution $p(x_1, \cdots, x_n)$ to give the statistical structure of the ensemble for intervals of that duration.

20. ENTROPY OF A CONTINUOUS DISTRIBUTION

The entropy of a discrete set of probabilities $p_1, \cdots p_n$ has been defined as:

$$H = -\sum p_i \log p_i .$$

In an analogous manner we define the entropy of a continuous distribution with the density distribution function $p(x)$ by:

$$H = -\int_{-\infty}^{\infty} p(x) \log p(x)\, dx$$

With an n dimensional distribution $p(x_1, \cdots, x_n)$ we have

$$H = -\int \cdots \int f(x_1 \cdots x_n) \log p(x_1, \cdots, x_n)\, dx_1 \cdots dx_n .$$

If we have two arguments x and y (which may themselves be multi-dimensional) the joint and conditional entropies of $p(x, y)$ are given by

$$H(x, y) = -\int\int p(x, y) \log p(x, y)\, dx\, dy$$

and

$$H_x(y) = -\int\int p(x, y) \log \frac{p(x, y)}{p(x)}\, dx\, dy$$

$$H_y(x) = -\int\int p(x, y) \log \frac{p(x, y)}{p(y)}\, dx\, dy$$

where

$$p(x) = \int p(x, y)\, dy$$

$$p(y) = \int p(x, y)\, dx.$$

The entropies of continuous distributions have most (but not all) of the properties of the discrete case. In particular we have the following:

1. If x is limitēd to a certain volume v in its space, then $H(x)$ is a maximum and equal to $\log v$ when $p(x)$ is constant $\left(\dfrac{1}{v}\right)$ in the volume.

2. With any two variables x, y we have

$$H(x, y) \le H(x) + H(y)$$

with equality if (and only if) x and y are independent, i.e., $p(x, y) = p(x)$ $p(y)$ (apart possibly from a set of points of probability zero).

3. Consider a generalized averaging operation of the following type:

$$p'(y) = \int a(x, y)p(x) \, dx$$

with

$$\int a(x, y) \, dx = \int a(x, y) \, dy = 1, \qquad a(x, y) \ge 0.$$

Then the entropy of the averaged distribution $p'(y)$ is equal to or greater than that of the original distribution $p(x)$.

4. We have

$$H(x, y) = H(x) + H_x(y) = H(y) + H_y(x)$$

and

$$H_x(y) \le H(y).$$

5. Let $p(x)$ be a one-dimensional distribution. The form of $p(x)$ giving a maximum entropy subject to the condition that the standard deviation of x be fixed at σ is gaussian. To show this we must maximize

$$H(x) = -\int p(x) \log p(x) \, dx$$

with

$$\sigma^2 = \int p(x)x^2 \, dx \quad \text{and} \quad 1 = \int p(x) \, dx$$

as constraints. This requires, by the calculus of variations, maximizing

$$\int [-p(x) \log p(x) + \lambda p(x)x^2 + \mu p(x)] \, dx.$$

The condition for this is

$$-1 - \log p(x) + \lambda x^2 + \mu = 0$$

and consequently (adjusting the constants to satisfy the constraints)

$$p(x) = \frac{1}{\sqrt{2\pi}\,\sigma} e^{-(x^2/2\sigma^2)}.$$

Similarly in n dimensions, suppose the second order moments of $p(x_1, \cdots, x_n)$ are fixed at A_{ij}:

$$A_{ij} = \int \cdots \int x_i x_j \, p(x_1, \cdots, x_n) \, dx_1 \cdots dx_n.$$

Then the maximum entropy occurs (by a similar calculation) when $p(x_1, \cdots, x_n)$ is the n dimensional gaussian distribution with the second order moments A_{ij}.

6. The entropy of a one-dimensional gaussian distribution whose standard deviation is σ is given by

$$H(x) = \log \sqrt{2\pi e}\,\sigma.$$

This is calculated as follows:

$$p(x) = \frac{1}{\sqrt{2\pi}\,\sigma} e^{-(x^2/2\sigma^2)}$$

$$-\log p(x) = \log \sqrt{2\pi}\,\sigma + \frac{x^2}{2\sigma^2}$$

$$H(x) = -\int p(x) \log p(x) \, dx$$

$$= \int p(x) \log \sqrt{2\pi}\,\sigma \, dx + \int p(x) \frac{x^2}{2\sigma^2} \, dx$$

$$= \log \sqrt{2\pi}\,\sigma + \frac{\sigma^2}{2\sigma^2}$$

$$= \log \sqrt{2\pi}\,\sigma + \log \sqrt{e}$$

$$= \log \sqrt{2\pi e}\,\sigma.$$

Similarly the n dimensional gaussian distribution with associated quadratic form a_{ij} is given by

$$p(x_1, \cdots, x_n) = \frac{|a_{ij}|^{\frac{1}{2}}}{(2\pi)^{n/2}} \exp\left(-\tfrac{1}{2}\Sigma a_{ij} X_i X_j\right)$$

and the entropy can be calculated as

$$H = \log (2\pi e)^{n/2} \, |a_{ij}|^{\frac{1}{2}}$$

where $|a_{ij}|$ is the determinant whose elements are a_{ij}.

7. If x is limited to a half line ($p(x) = 0$ for $x \leq 0$) and the first moment of x is fixed at a:

$$a = \int_0^\infty p(x)x \, dx,$$

then the maximum entropy occurs when

$$p(x) = \frac{1}{a} e^{-(x/a)}$$

and is equal to $\log ea$.

8. There is one important difference between the continuous and discrete entropies. In the discrete case the entropy measures in an *absolute* way the randomness of the chance variable. In the continuous case the measurement is *relative to the coordinate system*. If we change coordinates the entropy will in general change. In fact if we change to coordinates $y_1 \cdots y_n$ the new entropy is given by

$$H(y) = \int \cdots \int p(x_1 \cdots x_n) J\left(\frac{x}{y}\right) \log p(x_1 \cdots x_n) J\left(\frac{x}{y}\right) dy_1 \cdots dy_n$$

where $J\left(\dfrac{x}{y}\right)$ is the Jacobian of the coordinate transformation. On expanding the logarithm and changing variables to $x_1 \cdots x_n$, we obtain:

$$H(y) = H(x) - \int \cdots \int p(x_1, \cdots, x_n) \log J\left(\frac{x}{y}\right) dx_1 \cdots dx_n.$$

Thus the new entropy is the old entropy less the expected logarithm of the Jacobian. In the continuous case the entropy can be considered a measure of randomness *relative to an assumed standard*, namely the co-ordinate system chosen with each small volume element $dx_1 \cdots dx_n$ given equal weight. When we change the coordinate system the entropy in the new system measures the randomness when equal volume elements $dy_1 \cdots dy_n$ in the new system are given equal weight.

In spite of this dependence on the coordinate system the entropy concept is as important in the continuous case as the discrete case. This is due to the fact that the derived concepts of information rate and channel capacity depend on the *difference* of two entropies and this difference *does not* depend on the coordinate frame, each of the two terms being changed by the same amount.

The entropy of a continuous distribution can be negative. The scale of measurements sets an arbitrary zero corresponding to a uniform distribution over a unit volume. A distribution which is more confined than this has less entropy and will be negative. The rates and capacities will, however, always be non-negative.

9. A particular case of changing coordinates is the linear transformation

$$y_j = \sum_i a_{ij} x_i.$$

In this case the Jacobian is simply the determinant $|\, a_{ij}\,|^{-1}$ and

$$H(y) = H(x) + \log |\, a_{ij}\,|.$$

In the case of a rotation of coordinates (or any measure preserving transformation) $J = 1$ and $H(y) = H(x)$.

21. ENTROPY OF AN ENSEMBLE OF FUNCTIONS

Consider an ergodic ensemble of functions limited to a certain band of width W cycles per second. Let

$$p(x_1 \cdots x_n)$$

be the density distribution function for amplitudes $x_1 \cdots x_n$ at n successive sample points. We define the entropy of the ensemble per degree of freedom by

$$H' = -\operatorname*{Lim}_{n \to \infty} \frac{1}{n} \int \cdots \int p(x_1 \cdots x_n) \log p(x_1, \cdots, x_n)\, dx_1 \cdots dx_n.$$

We may also define an entropy H per second by dividing, not by n, but by the time T in seconds for n samples. Since $n = 2TW$, $H' = 2WH$.

With white thermal noise p is gaussian and we have

$$H' = \log \sqrt{2\pi e N},$$

$$H = W \log 2\pi e N.$$

For a given average power N, white noise has the maximum possible entropy. This follows from the maximizing properties of the Gaussian distribution noted above.

The entropy for a continuous stochastic process has many properties analogous to that for discrete processes. In the discrete case the entropy was related to the logarithm of the *probability* of long sequences, and to the *number* of reasonably probable sequences of long length. In the continuous case it is related in a similar fashion to the logarithm of the *probability density* for a long series of samples, and the *volume* of reasonably high probability in the function space.

More precisely, if we assume $p(x_1 \cdots x_n)$ continuous in all the x_i for all n, then for sufficiently large n

$$\left| \frac{\log p}{n} - H' \right| < \epsilon$$

for all choices of $(x_1, \cdots, x_n)$ apart from a set whose total probability is less than δ, with δ and ϵ arbitrarily small. This follows from the ergodic property if we divide the space into a large number of small cells.

The relation of H to volume can be stated as follows: Under the same assumptions consider the n dimensional space corresponding to $p(x_1, \cdots, x_n)$. Let $V_n(q)$ be the smallest volume in this space which includes in its interior a total probability q.   Then

$$\operatorname*{Lim}_{n \to \infty} \frac{\log V_n(q)}{n} = H'$$

provided q does not equal 0 or 1.

These results show that for large n there is a rather well-defined volume (at least in the logarithmic sense) of high probability, and that within this volume the probability density is relatively uniform (again in the logarithmic sense).

In the white noise case the distribution function is given by

$$p(x_1 \cdots x_n) = \frac{1}{(2\pi N)^{n/2}} \exp - \frac{1}{2N} \Sigma x_i^2 .$$

Since this depends only on Σx_i^2 the surfaces of equal probability density are spheres and the entire distribution has spherical symmetry.   The region of high probability is a sphere of radius $\sqrt{nN}$.   As $n \to \infty$ the probability of being outside a sphere of radius $\sqrt{n(N + \epsilon)}$ approaches zero and $\frac{1}{n}$ times the logarithm of the volume of the sphere approaches $\log \sqrt{2\pi eN}$.

In the continuous case it is convenient to work not with the entropy H of an ensemble but with a derived quantity which we will call the entropy power.   This is defined as the power in a white noise limited to the same band as the original ensemble and having the same entropy.   In other words if H' is the entropy of an ensemble its entropy power is

$$N_1 = \frac{1}{2\pi e} \exp 2H'.$$

In the geometrical picture this amounts to measuring the high probability volume by the squared radius of a sphere having the same volume.   Since white noise has the maximum entropy for a given power, the entropy power of any noise is less than or equal to its actual power.

22. Entropy Loss in Linear Filters

Theorem 14: If an ensemble having an entropy H_1 per degree of freedom in band W is passed through a filter with characteristic $Y(f)$ the output ensemble has an entropy

$$H_2 = H_1 + \frac{1}{W} \int_W \log | Y(f) |^2 \, df.$$

The operation of the filter is essentially a linear transformation of co-ordinates. If we think of the different frequency components as the original coordinate system, the new frequency components are merely the old ones multiplied by factors. The coordinate transformation matrix is thus es-

TABLE I

GAIN	ENTROPY POWER FACTOR	ENTROPY POWER GAIN IN DECIBELS	IMPULSE RESPONSE
$1-\omega$	$\dfrac{1}{e^2}$	-8.68	$\dfrac{\sin^2 \pi t}{(\pi t)^2}$
$1-\omega^2$	$\left(\dfrac{2}{e}\right)^4$	-5.32	$2\left[\dfrac{\sin t}{t^3} - \dfrac{\cos t}{t^2}\right]$
$1-\omega^3$	0.384	-4.15	$6\left[\dfrac{\cos t-1}{t^4} - \dfrac{\cos t}{2t^2} + \dfrac{\sin t}{t^3}\right]$
$\sqrt{1-\omega^2}$	$\left(\dfrac{2}{e}\right)^2$	-2.66	$\dfrac{\pi}{2}\dfrac{J_1(t)}{t}$
	$\dfrac{1}{e^{2\alpha}}$	$-8.68\,\alpha$	$\dfrac{1}{\alpha t^2}\left[\cos(1-\alpha)t - \cos t\right]$

sentially diagonalized in terms of these coordinates. The Jacobian of the transformation is (for n sine and n cosine components)

$$J = \prod_{i=1}^{n} |Y(f_i)|^2$$

where the f_i are equally spaced through the band W. This becomes in the limit

$$\exp \frac{1}{W} \int_w \log |Y(f)|^2 \, df.$$

Since J is constant its average value is this same quantity and applying the theorem on the change of entropy with a change of coordinates, the result follows. We may also phrase it in terms of the entropy power. Thus if the entropy power of the first ensemble is N_1 that of the second is

$$N_1 \exp \frac{1}{W} \int_w \log |Y(f)|^2 \, df.$$

The final entropy power is the initial entropy power multiplied by the geometric mean gain of the filter. If the gain is measured in db, then the output entropy power will be increased by the arithmetic mean db gain over W.

In Table I the entropy power loss has been calculated (and also expressed in db) for a number of ideal gain characteristics. The impulsive responses of these filters are also given for $W = 2\pi$, with phase assumed to be 0.

The entropy loss for many other cases can be obtained from these results. For example the entropy power factor $\frac{1}{e^2}$ for the first case also applies to any gain characteristic obtained from $1 - \omega$ by a measure preserving transformation of the ω axis. In particular a linearly increasing gain $G(\omega) = \omega$, or a "saw tooth" characteristic between 0 and 1 have the same entropy loss. The reciprocal gain has the reciprocal factor. Thus $\frac{1}{\omega}$ has the factor e^2. Raising the gain to any power raises the factor to this power.

23. Entropy of the Sum of Two Ensembles

If we have two ensembles of functions $f_\alpha(t)$ and $g_\beta(t)$ we can form a new ensemble by "addition." Suppose the first ensemble has the probability density function $p(x_1, \cdots, x_n)$ and the second $q(x_1, \cdots, x_n)$. Then the density function for the sum is given by the convolution:

$$r(x_1, \cdots, x_n) = \int \cdots \int p(y_1, \cdots, y_n)$$
$$\cdot q(x_1 - y_1, \cdots, x_n - y_n) \, dy_1, dy_2, \cdots, dy_n .$$

Physically this corresponds to adding the noises or signals represented by the original ensembles of functions.

The following result is derived in Appendix 6.

Theorem 15: Let the average power of two ensembles be N_1 and N_2 and let their entropy powers be $\bar{N}_1$ and $\bar{N}_2$. Then the entropy power of the sum, $\bar{N}_3$, is bounded by

$$\bar{N}_1 + \bar{N}_2 \le \bar{N}_3 \le N_1 + N_2.$$

White Gaussian noise has the peculiar property that it can absorb any other noise or signal ensemble which may be added to it with a resultant entropy power approximately equal to the sum of the white noise power and the signal power (measured from the average signal value, which is normally zero), provided the signal power is small, in a certain sense, compared to the noise.

Consider the function space associated with these ensembles having n dimensions. The white noise corresponds to a spherical Gaussian distribution in this space. The signal ensemble corresponds to another probability distribution, not necessarily Gaussian or spherical. Let the second moments of this distribution about its center of gravity be a_{ij}. That is, if $p(x_1, \cdots, x_n)$ is the density distribution function

$$a_{ij} = \int \cdots \int p(x_i - \alpha_i)(x_j - \alpha_j)\, dx_1, \cdots, dx_n$$

where the α_i are the coordinates of the center of gravity. Now a_{ij} is a positive definite quadratic form, and we can rotate our coordinate system to align it with the principal directions of this form. a_{ij} is then reduced to diagonal form b_{ii}. We require that each b_{ii} be small compared to N, the squared radius of the spherical distribution.

In this case the convolution of the noise and signal produce a Gaussian distribution whose corresponding quadratic form is

$$N + b_{ii}.$$

The entropy power of this distribution is

$$[\Pi(N + b_{ii})]^{1/n}$$

or approximately

$$= [(N)^n + \Sigma b_{ii}(N)^{n-1}]^{1/n}$$

$$\doteq N + \frac{1}{n}\Sigma b_{ii}.$$

The last term is the signal power, while the first is the noise power.

PART IV: THE CONTINUOUS CHANNEL

24. THE CAPACITY OF A CONTINUOUS CHANNEL

In a continuous channel the input or transmitted signals will be continuous functions of time $f(t)$ belonging to a certain set, and the output or received signals will be perturbed versions of these. We will consider only the case where both transmitted and received signals are limited to a certain band W. They can then be specified, for a time T, by $2TW$ numbers, and their statistical structure by finite dimensional distribution functions. Thus the statistics of the transmitted signal will be determined by

$$P(x_1, \cdots, x_n) = P(x)$$

and those of the noise by the conditional probability distribution

$$P_{x_1,\cdots,x_n}(y_1, \cdots, y_n) = P_x(y).$$

The rate of transmission of information for a continuous channel is defined in a way analogous to that for a discrete channel, namely

$$R = H(x) - H_y(x)$$

where $H(x)$ is the entropy of the input and $H_y(x)$ the equivocation. The channel capacity C is defined as the maximum of R when we vary the input over all possible ensembles. This means that in a finite dimensional approximation we must vary $P(x) = P(x_1, \cdots, x_n)$ and maximize

$$-\int P(x) \log P(x)\, dx + \iint P(x, y) \log \frac{P(x, y)}{P(y)}\, dx\, dy.$$

This can be written

$$\iint P(x, y) \log \frac{P(x, y)}{P(x)P(y)}\, dx\, dy$$

using the fact that $\iint P(x, y) \log P(x)\, dx\, dy = \int P(x) \log P(x)\, dx$. The channel capacity is thus expressed

$$C = \operatorname*{Lim}_{T \to \infty} \operatorname*{Max}_{P(x)} \frac{1}{T} \iint P(x, y) \log \frac{P(x, y)}{P(x)P(y)}\, dx\, dy.$$

It is obvious in this form that R and C are independent of the coordinate system since the numerator and denominator in $\log \frac{P(x, y)}{P(x)P(y)}$ will be multiplied by the same factors when x and y are transformed in any one to one way. This integral expression for C is more general than $H(x) - H_y(x)$. Properly interpreted (see Appendix 7) it will always exist while $H(x) - H_y(x)$

may assume an indeterminate form $\infty - \infty$ in some cases. This occurs, for example, if x is limited to a surface of fewer dimensions than n in its n dimensional approximation.

If the logarithmic base used in computing $H(x)$ and $H_y(x)$ is two then C is the maximum number of binary digits that can be sent per second over the channel with arbitrarily small equivocation, just as in the discrete case. This can be seen physically by dividing the space of signals into a large number of small cells, sufficiently small so that the probability density $P_x(y)$ of signal x being perturbed to point y is substantially constant over a cell (either of x or y). If the cells are considered as distinct points the situation is essentially the same as a discrete channel and the proofs used there will apply. But it is clear physically that this quantizing of the volume into individual points cannot in any practical situation alter the final answer significantly, provided the regions are sufficiently small. Thus the capacity will be the limit of the capacities for the discrete subdivisions and this is just the continuous capacity defined above.

On the mathematical side it can be shown first (see Appendix 7) that if u is the message, x is the signal, y is the received signal (perturbed by noise) and v the recovered message then

$$H(x) - H_v(x) \geq H(u) - H_v(u)$$

regardless of what operations are performed on u to obtain x or on y to obtain v. Thus no matter how we encode the binary digits to obtain the signal, or how we decode the received signal to recover the message, the discrete rate for the binary digits does not exceed the channel capacity we have defined. On the other hand, it is possible under very general conditions to find a coding system for transmitting binary digits at the rate C with as small an equivocation or frequency of errors as desired. This is true, for example, if, when we take a finite dimensional approximating space for the signal functions, $P(x, y)$ is continuous in both x and y except at a set of points of probability zero.

An important special case occurs when the noise is added to the signal and is independent of it (in the probability sense). Then $P_x(y)$ is a function only of the difference $n = (y - x)$,

$$P_x(y) = Q(y - x)$$

and we can assign a definite entropy to the noise (independent of the statistics of the signal), namely the entropy of the distribution $Q(n)$. This entropy will be denoted by $H(n)$.

Theorem 16: If the signal and noise are independent and the received signal is the sum of the transmitted signal and the noise then the rate of transmission is

$$R = H(y) - H(n)$$

i.e., the entropy of the received signal less the entropy of the noise.   The channel capacity is

$$C = \underset{P(x)}{\text{Max}} \, H(y) - H(n).$$

We have, since $y = x + n$:

$$H(x, y) = H(x, n).$$

Expanding the left side and using the fact that x and n are independent

$$H(y) + H_y(x) = H(x) + H(n).$$

Hence

$$R = H(x) - H_y(x) = H(y) - H(n).$$

Since $H(n)$ is independent of $P(x)$, maximizing R requires maximizing $H(y)$, the entropy of the received signal.   If there are certain constraints on the ensemble of transmitted signals, the entropy of the received signal must be maximized subject to these constraints.

25. Channel Capacity with an Average Power Limitation

A simple application of Theorem 16 is the case where the noise is a white thermal noise and the transmitted signals are limited to a certain average power P.   Then the received signals have an average power $P + N$ where N is the average noise power.   The maximum entropy for the received signals occurs when they also form a white noise ensemble since this is the greatest possible entropy for a power $P + N$ and can be obtained by a suitable choice of the ensemble of transmitted signals, namely if they form a white noise ensemble of power P.   The entropy (per second) of the received ensemble is then

$$H(y) = W \log 2\pi e(P + N),$$

and the noise entropy is

$$H(n) = W \log 2\pi e N.$$

The channel capacity is

$$C = H(y) - H(n) = W \log \frac{P + N}{N}.$$

Summarizing we have the following:

Theorem 17: The capacity of a channel of band W perturbed by white thermal noise of power N when the average transmitter power is P is given by

$$C = W \log \frac{P + N}{N}.$$

This means of course that by sufficiently involved encoding systems we can transmit binary digits at the rate $W \log_2 \frac{P + N}{N}$ bits per second, with arbitrarily small frequency of errors. It is not possible to transmit at a higher rate by any encoding system without a definite positive frequency of errors.

To approximate this limiting rate of transmission the transmitted signals must approximate, in statistical properties, a white noise.[6]   A system which approaches the ideal rate may be described as follows: Let $M = 2^s$ samples of white noise be constructed each of duration T.   These are assigned binary numbers from 0 to $(M - 1)$.   At the transmitter the message sequences are broken up into groups of s and for each group the corresponding noise sample is transmitted as the signal.   At the receiver the M samples are known and the actual received signal (perturbed by noise) is compared with each of them.   The sample which has the least R.M.S. discrepancy from the received signal is chosen as the transmitted signal and the corresponding binary number reconstructed.   This process amounts to choosing the most probable (*a posteriori*) signal.   The number M of noise samples used will depend on the tolerable frequency ϵ of errors, but for almost all selections of samples we have

$$\lim_{\epsilon \to 0} \lim_{T \to \infty} \frac{\log M(\epsilon, T)}{T} = W \log \frac{P + N}{N},$$

so that no matter how small ϵ is chosen, we can, by taking T sufficiently large, transmit as near as we wish to $TW \log \frac{P + N}{N}$ binary digits in the time T.

Formulas similar to $C = W \log \frac{P + N}{N}$ for the white noise case have been developed independently by several other writers, although with somewhat different interpretations.   We may mention the work of N. Wiener,[7] W. G. Tuller,[8] and H. Sullivan in this connection.

In the case of an arbitrary perturbing noise (not necessarily white thermal noise) it does not appear that the maximizing problem involved in deter-

<hr/>

[6] This and other properties of the white noise case are discussed from the geometrical point of view in "Communication in the Presence of Noise," loc. cit.

[7] "Cybernetics," loc. cit.

[8] Sc. D. thesis, Department of Electrical Engineering. M.I.T., 1948

mining the channel capacity C can be solved explicitly. However, upper and lower bounds can be set for C in terms of the average noise power N and the noise entropy power N_1. These bounds are sufficiently close together in most practical cases to furnish a satisfactory solution to the problem.

Theorem 18: The capacity of a channel of band W perturbed by an arbitrary noise is bounded by the inequalities

$$W \log \frac{P + N_1}{N_1} \leq C \leq W \log \frac{P + N}{N_1}$$

where

P = average transmitter power

N = average noise power

N_1 = entropy power of the noise.

Here again the average power of the perturbed signals will be $P + N$. The maximum entropy for this power would occur if the received signal were white noise and would be $W \log 2\pi e(P + N)$. It may not be possible to achieve this; i.e. there may not be any ensemble of transmitted signals which, added to the perturbing noise, produce a white thermal noise at the receiver, but at least this sets an upper bound to $H(y)$. We have, therefore

$$C = \max H(y) - H(n)$$
$$\leq W \log 2\pi e(P + N) - W \log 2\pi e N_1 .$$

This is the upper limit given in the theorem. The lower limit can be obtained by considering the rate if we make the transmitted signal a white noise, of power P. In this case the entropy power of the received signal must be at least as great as that of a white noise of power $P + N_1$ since we have shown in a previous theorem that the entropy power of the sum of two ensembles is greater than or equal to the sum of the individual entropy powers. Hence

$$\max H(y) \geq W \log 2\pi e(P + N_1)$$

and

$$C \geq W \log 2\pi e(P + N_1) - W \log 2\pi e N_1$$
$$= W \log \frac{P + N_1}{N_1} .$$

As P increases, the upper and lower bounds approach each other, so we have as an asymptotic rate

$$W \log \frac{P + N}{N_1}$$

If the noise is itself white, $N = N_1$ and the result reduces to the formula proved previously:

$$C = W \log \left(1 + \frac{P}{N} \right).$$

If the noise is Gaussian but with a spectrum which is not necessarily flat, N_1 is the geometric mean of the noise power over the various frequencies in the band W. Thus

$$N_1 = \exp \frac{1}{W} \int_w \log N(f) \, df$$

where $N(f)$ is the noise power at frequency f.

Theorem 19: If we set the capacity for a given transmitter power P equal to

$$C = W \log \frac{P + N - \eta}{N_1}$$

then η is monotonic decreasing as P increases and approaches 0 as a limit.

Suppose that for a given power P_1 the channel capacity is

$$W \log \frac{P_1 + N - \eta_1}{N_1}$$

This means that the best signal distribution, say $p(x)$, when added to the noise distribution $q(x)$, gives a received distribution $r(y)$ whose entropy power is $(P_1 + N - \eta_1)$. Let us increase the power to $P_1 + \Delta P$ by adding a white noise of power ΔP to the signal. The entropy of the received signal is now at least

$$H(y) = W \log 2\pi e(P_1 + N - \eta_1 + \Delta P)$$

by application of the theorem on the minimum entropy power of a sum. Hence, since we can attain the H indicated, the entropy of the maximizing distribution must be at least as great and η must be monotonic decreasing. To show that $\eta \to 0$ as $P \to \infty$ consider a signal which is a white noise with a large P. Whatever the perturbing noise, the received signal will be approximately a white noise, if P is sufficiently large, in the sense of having an entropy power approaching $P + N$.

26. The Channel Capacity with a Peak Power Limitation

In some applications the transmitter is limited not by the average power output but by the peak instantaneous power. The problem of calculating the channel capacity is then that of maximizing (by variation of the ensemble of transmitted symbols)

$$H(y) - H(n)$$

subject to the constraint that all the functions $f(t)$ in the ensemble be less than or equal to $\sqrt{S}$, say, for all t. A constraint of this type does not work out as well mathematically as the average power limitation. The most we have obtained for this case is a lower bound valid for all $\frac{S}{N}$, an "asymptotic" upper band $\left(\text{valid for large } \frac{S}{N}\right)$ and an asymptotic value of C for $\frac{S}{N}$ small.

Theorem 20: The channel capacity C for a band W perturbed by white thermal noise of power N is bounded by

$$C \geq W \log \frac{2}{\pi e^3} \frac{S}{N},$$

where S is the peak allowed transmitter power. For sufficiently large $\frac{S}{N}$

$$C \leq W \log \frac{\frac{2}{\pi e} S + N}{N} (1 + \epsilon)$$

where ϵ is arbitrarily small. As $\frac{S}{N} \to 0$ (and provided the band W starts at 0)

$$C \to W \log \left(1 + \frac{S}{N}\right).$$

We wish to maximize the entropy of the received signal. If $\frac{S}{N}$ is large this will occur very nearly when we maximize the entropy of the transmitted ensemble.

The asymptotic upper bound is obtained by relaxing the conditions on the ensemble. Let us suppose that the power is limited to S not at every instant of time, but only at the sample points. The maximum entropy of the transmitted ensemble under these weakened conditions is certainly greater than or equal to that under the original conditions. This altered problem can be solved easily. The maximum entropy occurs if the different samples are independent and have a distribution function which is constant from $-\sqrt{S}$ to $+\sqrt{S}$. The entropy can be calculated as

$$W \log 4S.$$

The received signal will then have an entropy less than

$$W \log (4S + 2\pi e N)(1 + \epsilon)$$

with $\epsilon \to 0$ as $\dfrac{S}{N} \to \infty$ and the channel capacity is obtained by subtracting the entropy of the white noise, $W \log 2\pi e N$

$$W \log (4S + 2\pi eN)(1 + \epsilon) - W \log (2\pi eN) = W \log \frac{\dfrac{2}{\pi e} S + N}{N} (1 + \epsilon).$$

This is the desired upper bound to the channel capacity.

To obtain a lower bound consider the same ensemble of functions. Let these functions be passed through an ideal filter with a triangular transfer characteristic. The gain is to be unity at frequency 0 and decline linearly down to gain 0 at frequency W. We first show that the output functions of the filter have a peak power limitation S at all times (not just the sample points). First we note that a pulse $\dfrac{\sin 2\pi Wt}{2\pi Wt}$ going into the filter produces

$$\frac{1}{2} \frac{\sin^2 \pi Wt}{(\pi Wt)^2}$$

in the output. This function is never negative. The input function (in the general case) can be thought of as the sum of a series of shifted functions

$$a \frac{\sin 2\pi Wt}{2\pi Wt}$$

where a, the amplitude of the sample, is not greater than $\sqrt{S}$. Hence the output is the sum of shifted functions of the non-negative form above with the same coefficients. These functions being non-negative, the greatest positive value for any t is obtained when all the coefficients a have their maximum positive values, i.e. $\sqrt{S}$. In this case the input function was a constant of amplitude $\sqrt{S}$ and since the filter has unit gain for D.C., the output is the same. Hence the output ensemble has a peak power S.

The entropy of the output ensemble can be calculated from that of the input ensemble by using the theorem dealing with such a situation. The output entropy is equal to the input entropy plus the geometrical mean gain of the filter;

$$\int_0^W \log G^2 \, df = \int_0^W \log \left(\frac{W - f}{W}\right)^2 df = -2W$$

Hence the output entropy is

$$W \log 4S - 2W = W \log \frac{4S}{e^2}$$

and the channel capacity is greater than

$$W \log \frac{2}{\pi e^3} \frac{S}{N}.$$

We now wish to show that, for small $\frac{S}{N}$ (peak signal power over average white noise power), the channel capacity is approximately

$$C = W \log \left(1 + \frac{S}{N}\right).$$

More precisely $C/W \log \left(1 + \frac{S}{N}\right) \to 1$ as $\frac{S}{N} \to 0$. Since the average signal power P is less than or equal to the peak S, it follows that for all $\frac{S}{N}$

$$C \le W \log \left(1 + \frac{P}{N}\right) \le W \log \left(1 + \frac{S}{N}\right).$$

Therefore, if we can find an ensemble of functions such that they correspond to a rate nearly $W \log \left(1 + \frac{S}{N}\right)$ and are limited to band W and peak S the result will be proved.   Consider the ensemble of functions of the following type.   A series of t samples have the same value, either $+\sqrt{S}$ or $-\sqrt{S}$, then the next t samples have the same value, etc.   The value for a series is chosen at random, probability $\frac{1}{2}$ for $+\sqrt{S}$ and $\frac{1}{2}$ for $-\sqrt{S}$ If this ensemble be passed through a filter with triangular gain characteristic (unit gain at D.C.), the output is peak limited to $\pm S$.   Furthermore the average power is nearly S and can be made to approach this by taking t sufficiently large.   The entropy of the sum of this and the thermal noise can be found by applying the theorem on the sum of a noise and a small signal.   This theorem will apply if

$$\sqrt{t} \frac{S}{N}$$

is sufficiently small.   This can be insured by taking $\frac{S}{N}$ small enough (after t is chosen).   The entropy power will be $S + N$ to as close an approximation as desired, and hence the rate of transmission as near as we wish to

$$W \log \left(\frac{S + N}{N}\right).$$

PART V: THE RATE FOR A CONTINUOUS SOURCE

27. FIDELITY EVALUATION FUNCTIONS

In the case of a discrete source of information we were able to determine a definite rate of generating information, namely the entropy of the underlying stochastic process. With a continuous source the situation is considerably more involved. In the first place a continuously variable quantity can assume an infinite number of values and requires, therefore, an infinite number of binary digits for exact specification. This means that to transmit the output of a continuous source with *exact recovery* at the receiving point requires, in general, a channel of infinite capacity (in bits per second). Since, ordinarily, channels have a certain amount of noise, and therefore a finite capacity, exact transmission is impossible.

This, however, evades the real issue. Practically, we are not interested in exact transmission when we have a continuous source, but only in transmission to within a certain tolerance. The question is, can we assign a definite rate to a continuous source when we require only a certain fidelity of recovery, measured in a suitable way. Of course, as the fidelity requirements are increased the rate will increase. It will be shown that we can, in very general cases, define such a rate, having the property that it is possible, by properly encoding the information, to transmit it over a channel whose capacity is equal to the rate in question, and satisfy the fidelity requirements. A channel of smaller capacity is insufficient.

It is first necessary to give a general mathematical formulation of the idea of fidelity of transmission. Consider the set of messages of a long duration, say T seconds. The source is described by giving the probability density, in the associated space, that the source will select the message in question $P(x)$. A given communication system is described (from the external point of view) by giving the conditional probability $P_x(y)$ that if message x is produced by the source the recovered message at the receiving point will be y. The system as a whole (including source and transmission system) is described by the probability function $P(x, y)$ of having message x and final output y. If this function is known, the complete characteristics of the system from the point of view of fidelity are known. Any evaluation of fidelity must correspond mathematically to an operation applied to $P(x, y)$. This operation must at least have the properties of a simple ordering of systems; i.e. it must be possible to say of two systems represented by $P_1(x, y)$ and $P_2(x, y)$ that, according to our fidelity criterion, either (1) the first has higher fidelity, (2) the second has higher fidelity, or (3) they have equal fidelity.   This means that a criterion of fidelity can be represented by a numerically valued function:

$$v(P(x, y))$$

whose argument ranges over possible probability functions $P(x, y)$.

We will now show that under very general and reasonable assumptions the function $v(P(x, y))$ can be written in a seemingly much more specialized form, namely as an average of a function $\rho(x, y)$ over the set of possible values of x and y:

$$v(P(x, y)) = \int\int P(x, y)\, \rho(x, y)\, dx\, dy$$

To obtain this we need only assume (1) that the source and system are ergodic so that a very long sample will be, with probability nearly 1, typical of the ensemble, and (2) that the evaluation is "reasonable" in the sense that it is possible, by observing a typical input and output x_1 and y_1, to form a tentative evaluation on the basis of these samples; and if these samples are increased in duration the tentative evaluation will, with probability 1, approach the exact evaluation based on a full knowledge of $P(x, y)$. Let the tentative evaluation be $\rho(x, y)$.   Then the function $\rho(x, y)$ approaches (as $T \to \infty$) a constant for almost all (x, y) which are in the high probability region corresponding to the system:

$$\rho(x, y) \to v(P(x, y))$$

and we may also write

$$\rho(x, y) \to \int\int P(x, y)\rho(x, y)\, dx,\, dy$$

since

$$\int\int P(x, y)\, dx\, dy = 1$$

This establishes the desired result.

The function $\rho(x, y)$ has the general nature of a "distance" between x and y.[9]   It measures how bad it is (according to our fidelity criterion) to receive y when x is transmitted.   The general result given above can be restated as follows: Any reasonable evaluation can be represented as an average of a distance function over the set of messages and recovered messages x and y weighted according to the probability $P(x, y)$ of getting the pair in question, provided the duration T of the messages be taken sufficiently large.

---

[9] It is not a "metric" in the strict sense, however, since in general it does not satisfy either $\rho(x, y) = \rho(y, x)$ or $\rho(x, y) + \rho(y, z) \geq \rho(x, z)$.

The following are simple examples of evaluation functions:
1. R.M.S. Criterion.

$$v = \overline{(x(t) - y(t))^2}$$

In this very commonly used criterion of fidelity the distance function $\rho(x, y)$ is (apart from a constant factor) the square of the ordinary euclidean distance between the points x and y in the associated function space.

$$\rho(x, y) = \frac{1}{T} \int_0^T [x(t) - y(t)]^2 \, dt$$

2. Frequency weighted R.M.S. criterion. More generally one can apply different weights to the different frequency components before using an R.M.S. measure of fidelity. This is equivalent to passing the difference $x(t) - y(t)$ through a shaping filter and then determining the average power in the output. Thus let

$$e(t) = x(t) - y(t)$$

and

$$f(t) = \int_{-\infty}^{\infty} e(\tau)k(t - \tau) \, d\tau$$

then

$$\rho(x, y) = \frac{1}{T} \int_0^T f(t)^2 \, dt.$$

3. Absolute error criterion.

$$\rho(x, y) = \frac{1}{T} \int_0^T |\, x(t) - y(t) \,| \, dt$$

4. The structure of the ear and brain determine implicitly an evaluation, or rather a number of evaluations, appropriate in the case of speech or music transmission. There is, for example, an "intelligibility" criterion in which $\rho(x, y)$ is equal to the relative frequency of incorrectly interpreted words when message $x(t)$ is received as $y(t)$. Although we cannot give an explicit representation of $\rho(x, y)$ in these cases it could, in principle, be determined by sufficient experimentation. Some of its properties follow from well-known experimental results in hearing, e.g., the ear is relatively insensitive to phase and the sensitivity to amplitude and frequency is roughly logarithmic.

5. The discrete case can be considered as a specialization in which we have

tacitly assumed an evaluation based on the frequency of errors.   The function $\rho(x, y)$ is then defined as the number of symbols in the sequence y differing from the corresponding symbols in x divided by the total number of symbols in x.

28. THE RATE FOR A SOURCE RELATIVE TO A FIDELITY EVALUATION

We are now in a position to define a rate of generating information for a continuous source.   We are given $P(x)$ for the source and an evaluation v determined by a distance function $\rho(x, y)$ which will be assumed continuous in both x and y.   With a particular system $P(x, y)$ the quality is measured by

$$v = \iint \rho(x, y)\ P(x, y)\ dx\, dy.$$

Furthermore the rate of flow of binary digits corresponding to $P(x, y)$ is

$$R = \iint P(x, y)\ \log \frac{P(x, y)}{P(x)P(y)}\ dx\, dy.$$

We define the rate R_1 of generating information for a given quality v_1 of reproduction to be the minimum of R when we keep v fixed at v_1 and vary $P_x(y)$.   That is:

$$R_1 = \underset{P_x(y)}{\mathrm{Min}} \iint P(x, y)\ \log \frac{P(x, y)}{P(x)P(y)}\ dx\, dy$$

subject to the constraint:

$$v_1 = \iint P(x, y)\rho(x, y)\ dx\, dy.$$

This means that we consider, in effect, all the communication systems that might be used and that transmit with the required fidelity.   The rate of transmission in bits per second is calculated for each one and we choose that having the least rate.   This latter rate is the rate we assign the source for the fidelity in question.

The justification of this definition lies in the following result:

Theorem 21: If a source has a rate R_1 for a valuation v_1 it is possible to encode the output of the source and transmit it over a channel of capacity C with fidelity as near v_1 as desired provided $R_1 \leq C$.   This is not possible if $R_1 > C$.

The last statement in the theorem follows immediately from the definition of R_1 and previous results.   If it were not true we could transmit more than C bits per second over a channel of capacity C.   The first part of the theorem is proved by a method analogous to that used for Theorem 11.   We may, in the first place, divide the (x, y) space into a large number of small cells and represent the situation as a discrete case. This will not change the evaluation function by more than an arbitrarily small amount (when the cells are very small) because of the continuity assumed for $\rho(x, y)$. Suppose that $P_1(x, y)$ is the particular system which minimizes the rate and gives R_1. We choose from the high probability y's a set at random containing

$$2^{(R_1 + \epsilon)T}$$

members where $\epsilon \to 0$ as $T \to \infty$. With large T each chosen point will be connected by a high probability line (as in Fig. 10) to a set of x's. A calculation similar to that used in proving Theorem 11 shows that with large T almost all x's are covered by the fans from the chosen y points for almost all choices of the y's. The communication system to be used operates as follows: The selected points are assigned binary numbers. When a message x is originated it will (with probability approaching 1 as $T \to \infty$) lie within one at least of the fans. The corresponding binary number is transmitted (or one of them chosen arbitrarily if there are several) over the channel by suitable coding means to give a small probability of error. Since $R_1 \leq C$ this is possible. At the receiving point the corresponding y is reconstructed and used as the recovered message.

The evaluation v_1' for this system can be made arbitrarily close to v_1 by taking T sufficiently large. This is due to the fact that for each long sample of message $x(t)$ and recovered message $y(t)$ the evaluation approaches v_1 (with probability 1).

It is interesting to note that, in this system, the noise in the recovered message is actually produced by a kind of general quantizing at the transmitter and is not produced by the noise in the channel. It is more or less analogous to the quantizing noise in P.C.M.

29. THE CALCULATION OF RATES

The definition of the rate is similar in many respects to the definition of channel capacity. In the former

$$R = \underset{P_x(y)}{\text{Min}} \iint P(x, y) \log \frac{P(x, y)}{P(x)P(y)} \, dx \, dy$$

with $P(x)$ and $v_1 = \iint P(x, y)\rho(x, y) \, dx \, dy$ fixed. In the latter

$$C = \underset{P(x)}{\text{Max}} \iint P(x, y) \log \frac{P(x, y)}{P(x)P(y)} \, dx \, dy$$

with $P_x(y)$ fixed and possibly one or more other constraints (e.g., an average power limitation) of the form $K = \iint P(x, y) \lambda(x, y) \, dx \, dy$.

A partial solution of the general maximizing problem for determining the rate of a source can be given. Using Lagrange's method we consider

$$\iint \left[P(x, y) \log \frac{P(x, y)}{P(x)P(y)} + \mu \, P(x, y)\rho(x, y) + \nu(x)P(x, y) \right] dx \, dy$$

The variational equation (when we take the first variation on $P(x, y)$) leads to

$$P_y(x) = B(x) \, e^{-\lambda \rho(x, y)}$$

where λ is determined to give the required fidelity and $B(x)$ is chosen to satisfy

$$\int B(x)e^{-\lambda \rho(x, y)} \, dx = 1$$

This shows that, with best encoding, the conditional probability of a certain cause for various received y, $P_y(x)$ will decline exponentially with the distance function $\rho(x, y)$ between the x and y is question.

In the special case where the distance function $\rho(x, y)$ depends only on the (vector) difference between x and y,

$$\rho(x, y) = \rho(x - y)$$

we have

$$\int B(x)e^{-\lambda \rho(x-y)} \, dx = 1.$$

Hence $B(x)$ is constant, say α, and

$$P_y(x) = \alpha e^{-\lambda \rho(x-y)}$$

Unfortunately these formal solutions are difficult to evaluate in particular cases and seem to be of little value. In fact, the actual calculation of rates has been carried out in only a few very simple cases.

If the distance function $\rho(x, y)$ is the mean square discrepancy between x and y and the message ensemble is white noise, the rate can be determined. In that case we have

$$R = \text{Min} \, [H(x) - H_y(x)] = H(x) - \text{Max} \, H_y(x)$$

with $N = \overline{(x - y)^2}$. But the Max $H_y(x)$ occurs when $y - x$ is a white noise, and is equal to $W_1 \log 2\pi e \, N$ where W_1 is the bandwidth of the message ensemble. Therefore

$$R = W_1 \log 2\pi e Q - W_1 \log 2\pi e N$$

$$= W_1 \log \frac{Q}{N}$$

where Q is the average message power. This proves the following:

Theorem 22: The rate for a white noise source of power Q and band W_1 relative to an R.M.S. measure of fidelity is

$$R = W_1 \log \frac{Q}{N}$$

where N is the allowed mean square error between original and recovered messages.

More generally with any message source we can obtain inequalities bounding the rate relative to a mean square error criterion.

Theorem 23: The rate for any source of band W_1 is bounded by

$$W_1 \log \frac{Q_1}{N} \le R \le W_1 \log \frac{Q}{N}$$

where Q is the average power of the source, Q_1 its entropy power and N the allowed mean square error.

The lower bound follows from the fact that the max $H_y(x)$ for a given $(x - y)^2 = N$ occurs in the white noise case. The upper bound results if we place the points (used in the proof of Theorem 21) not in the best way but at random in a sphere of radius $\sqrt{Q - N}$.

ACKNOWLEDGMENTS

The writer is indebted to his colleagues at the Laboratories, particularly to Dr. H. W. Bode, Dr. J. R. Pierce, Dr. B. McMillan, and Dr. B. M. Oliver for many helpful suggestions and criticisms during the course of this work. Credit should also be given to Professor N. Wiener, whose elegant solution of the problems of filtering and prediction of stationary ensembles has considerably influenced the writer's thinking in this field.

APPENDIX 5

Let S_1 be any measurable subset of the g ensemble, and S_2 the subset of the f ensemble which gives S_1 under the operation T. Then

$$S_1 = TS_2.$$

Let H^λ be the operator which shifts all functions in a set by the time λ. Then

$$H^\lambda S_1 = H^\lambda TS_2 = TH^\lambda S_2$$

since T is invariant and therefore commutes with H^λ. Hence if $m[S]$ is the probability measure of the set S

$$m[H^\lambda S_1] = m[TH^\lambda S_2] = m[H^\lambda S_2]$$

$$= m[S_2] = m[S_1]$$

where the second equality is by definition of measure in the g space the third since the f ensemble is stationary, and the last by definition of g measure again.

To prove that the ergodic property is preserved under invariant operations, let S_1 be a subset of the g ensemble which is invariant under H^λ, and let S_2 be the set of all functions f which transform into S_1. Then

$$H^\lambda S_1 = H^\lambda T S_2 = T H^\lambda S_2 = S_1$$

so that $H^\lambda S_1$ is included in S_1 for all λ. Now, since

$$m[H^\lambda S_2] = m[S_1]$$

·this implies

$$H^\lambda S_2 = S_2$$

for all λ with $m[S_2] \neq 0, 1$. This contradiction shows that S_1 does not exist.

APPENDIX 6

The upper bound, $\bar{N}_3 \leq N_1 + N_2$, is due to the fact that the maximum possible entropy for a power $N_1 + N_2$ occurs when we have a white noise of this power. In this case the entropy power is $N_1 + N_2$.

To obtain the lower bound, suppose we have two distributions in n dimensions $p(x_i)$ and $q(x_i)$ with entropy powers $\bar{N}_1$ and $\bar{N}_2$. What form should p and q have to minimize the entropy power $\bar{N}_3$ of their convolution $r(x_i)$:

$$r(x_i) = \int p(y_i) q(x_i - y_i) \, dy_i \,.$$

The entropy H_3 of r is given by

$$H_3 = -\int r(x_i) \log r(x_i) \, dx_i \,.$$

We wish to minimize this subject to the constraints

$$H_1 = -\int p(x_i) \log p(x_i) \, dx_i$$

$$H_2 = -\int q(x_i) \log q(x_i) \, dx_i \,.$$

We consider then

$$U = -\int [r(x) \log r(x) + \lambda p(x) \log p(x) + \mu q(x) \log q(x)] \, dx$$

$$\delta U = -\int [[1 + \log r(x)] \delta r(x) + \lambda[1 + \log p(x)] \delta p(x)$$

$$+ \mu[1 + \log q(x) \delta q(x)]] \, dx.$$

If $p(x)$ is varied at a particular argument $x_i = s_i$, the variation in $r(x)$ is

$$\delta r(x) = q(x_i - s_i)$$

and

$$\delta U = -\int q(x_i - s_i) \log r(x_i)\, dx_i - \lambda \log p(s_i) = 0$$

and similarly when q is varied. Hence the conditions for a minimum are

$$\int q(x_i - s_i) \log r(x_i) = -\lambda \log p(s_i)$$

$$\int p(x_i - s_i) \log r(x_i) = -\mu \log q(s_i).$$

If we multiply the first by $p(s_i)$ and the second by $q(s_i)$ and integrate with respect to s we obtain

$$H_3 = -\lambda\, H_1$$

$$H_3 = -\mu\, H_2$$

or solving for λ and μ and replacing in the equations

$$H_1 \int q(x_i - s_i) \log r(x_i)\, dx_i = -H_3 \log p(s_i)$$

$$H_2 \int p(x_i - s_i) \log r(x_i)\, dx_i = -H_3 \log p(s_i).$$

Now suppose $p(x_i)$ and $q(x_i)$ are normal

$$p(x_i) = \frac{|A_{ij}|^{n/2}}{(2\pi)^{n/2}} \exp - \tfrac{1}{2}\Sigma A_{ij} x_i x_j$$

$$q(x_i) = \frac{|B_{ij}|^{n/2}}{(2\pi)^{n/2}} \exp - \tfrac{1}{2}\Sigma B_{ij} x_i x_j.$$

Then $r(x_i)$ will also be normal with quadratic form C_{ij}. If the inverses of these forms are a_{ij}, b_{ij}, c_{ij} then

$$c_{ij} = a_{ij} + b_{ij}.$$

We wish to show that these functions satisfy the minimizing conditions if and only if $a_{ij} = K b_{ij}$ and thus give the minimum H_3 under the constraints. First we have

$$\log r(x_i) = \frac{n}{2} \log \frac{1}{2\pi} |C_{ij}| - \tfrac{1}{2}\Sigma C_{ij} x_i x_j$$

$$\int q(x_i - s_i) \log r(x_i) = \frac{n}{2} \log \frac{1}{2\pi} |C_{ij}| - \tfrac{1}{2}\Sigma C_{ij} s_i s_j - \tfrac{1}{2}\Sigma C_{ij} b_{ij}.$$

This should equal

$$\frac{H_3}{H_1}\left[\frac{n}{2}\log\frac{1}{2\pi}\,|A_{ij}|\,-\,\tfrac{1}{2}\Sigma A_{ij}s_is_j\right]$$

which requires $A_{ij} = \dfrac{H_1}{H_3}\,C_{ij}$.

In this case $A_{ij} = \dfrac{H_1}{H_2}\,B_{ij}$ and both equations reduce to identities.

APPENDIX 7

The following will indicate a more general and more rigorous approach to the central definitions of communication theory. Consider a probability measure space whose elements are ordered pairs (x, y). The variables x, y are to be identified as the possible transmitted and received signals of some long duration T. Let us call the set of all points whose x belongs to a subset S_1 of x points the strip over S_1, and similarly the set whose y belongs to S_2 the strip over S_2. We divide x and y into a collection of non-overlapping measurable subsets X_i and Y_i approximate to the rate of transmission R by

$$R_1 = \frac{1}{T}\sum_i P(X_i, Y_i)\log\frac{P(X_i, Y_i)}{P(X_i)P(Y_i)}$$

where

$\quad P(X_i)$ is the probability measure of the strip over X_i
$\quad P(Y_i)$ is the probability measure of the strip over Y_i
$\quad P(X_i, Y_i)$ is the probability measure of the intersection of the strips.

A further subdivision can never decrease R_1. For let X_1 be divided into $X_1 = X_1' + X_1''$ and let

$$P(Y_1) = a \qquad\qquad P(X_1) = b + c$$
$$P(X_1') = b \qquad\qquad P(X_1', Y_1) = d$$
$$P(X_1'') = c \qquad\qquad P(X_1'', Y_1) = e$$
$$P(X_1, Y_1) = d + e$$

Then in the sum we have replaced (for the X_1, Y_1 intersection)

$$(d + e)\log\frac{d + e}{a(b + c)} \quad\text{by}\quad d\log\frac{d}{ab} + e\log\frac{e}{ac}.$$

It is easily shown that with the limitation we have on b, c, d, e,

$$\left[\frac{d + e}{b + c}\right]^{d+e} \leq \frac{d^d\,e^e}{b^d\,c^e}$$

and consequently the sum is increased.   Thus the various possible subdivisions form a directed set, with R monotonic increasing with refinement of the subdivision.   We may define R unambiguously as the least upper bound for the R_1 and write it

$$R = \frac{1}{T} \int\int P(x, y) \log \frac{P(x, y)}{P(x)P(y)} \, dx \, dy.$$

This integral, understood in the above sense, includes both the continuous and discrete cases and of course many others which cannot be represented in either form.   It is trivial in this formulation that if x and u are in one-to-one correspondence, the rate from u to y is equal to that from x to y.   If v is any function of y (not necessarily with an inverse) then the rate from x to y is greater than or equal to that from x to v since, in the calculation of the approximations, the subdivisions of y are essentially a finer subdivision of those for v.   More generally if y and v are related not functionally but statistically, i.e., we have a probability measure space (y, v), then $R(x, v) \leq R(x, y)$.   This means that any operation applied to the received signal, even though it involves statistical elements, does not increase R.

   Another notion which should be defined precisely in an abstract formulation of the theory is that of "dimension rate," that is the average number of dimensions required per second to specify a member of an ensemble.   In the band limited case 2W numbers per second are sufficient.   A general definition can be framed as follows.   Let $f_\alpha(t)$ be an ensemble of functions and let $\rho_T[f_\alpha(t), f_\beta(t)]$ be a metric measuring the "distance" from f_α to f_β over the time T (for example the R.M.S. discrepancy over this interval.) Let $N(\epsilon, \delta, T)$ be the least number of elements f which can be chosen such that all elements of the ensemble apart from a set of measure δ are within the distance ϵ of at least one of those chosen.   Thus we are covering the space to within ϵ apart from a set of small measure δ.   We define the dimension rate λ for the ensemble by the triple limit

$$\lambda = \operatorname*{Lim}_{\delta \to 0} \operatorname*{Lim}_{\epsilon \to 0} \operatorname*{Lim}_{T \to \infty} \frac{\log N(\epsilon, \delta, T)}{T \log \epsilon}.$$

This is a generalization of the measure type definitions of dimension in topology, and agrees with the intuitive dimension rate for simple ensembles where the desired result is obvious.

Communication Theory of Secrecy Systems*

By C. E. SHANNON

1. Introduction and Summary

THE problems of cryptography and secrecy systems furnish an interesting application of communication theory.[1] In this paper a theory of secrecy systems is developed. The approach is on a theoretical level and is intended to complement the treatment found in standard works on cryptography.[2] There, a detailed study is made of the many standard types of codes and ciphers, and of the ways of breaking them. We will be more concerned with the general mathematical structure and properties of secrecy systems.

The treatment is limited in certain ways. First, there are three general types of secrecy system: (1) concealment systems, including such methods as invisible ink, concealing a message in an innocent text, or in a fake covering cryptogram, or other methods in which the existence of the message is concealed from the enemy; (2) privacy systems, for example speech inversion, in which special equipment is required to recover the message; (3) "true" secrecy systems where the meaning of the message is concealed by cipher, code, etc., although its existence is not hidden, and the enemy is assumed to have any special equipment necessary to intercept and record the transmitted signal. We consider only the third type—concealment systems are primarily a psychological problem, and privacy systems a technological one.

Secondly, the treatment is limited to the case of discrete information, where the message to be enciphered consists of a sequence of discrete symbols, each chosen from a finite set. These symbols may be letters in a language, words of a language, amplitude levels of a "quantized" speech or video signal, etc., but the main emphasis and thinking has been concerned with the case of letters.

The paper is divided into three parts. The main results will now be briefly summarized. The first part deals with the basic mathematical structure of secrecy systems. As in communication theory a language is considered to

---

* The material in this paper appeared originally in a confidential report "A Mathematical Theory of Cryptography" dated Sept. 1, 1945, which has now been declassified.

[1] Shannon, C. E., "A Mathematical Theory of Communication," *Bell System Technical Journal*, July 1948, p. 379; Oct. 1948, p. 623.

[2] See, for example, H. F. Gaines, "Elementary Cryptanalysis," or M. Givierge, "Cours de Cryptographie."

be represented by a stochastic process which produces a discrete sequence of symbols in accordance with some system of probabilities. Associated with a language there is a certain parameter D which we call the redundancy of the language. D measures, in a sense, how much a text in the language can be reduced in length without losing any information. As a simple example, since u always follows q in English words, the u may be omitted without loss. Considerable reductions are possible in English due to the statistical structure of the language, the high frequencies of certain letters or words, etc. Redundancy is of central importance in the study of secrecy systems.

A secrecy system is defined abstractly as a set of transformations of one space (the set of possible messages) into a second space (the set of possible cryptograms). Each particular transformation of the set corresponds to enciphering with a particular key. The transformations are supposed reversible (non-singular) so that unique deciphering is possible when the key is known.

Each key and therefore each transformation is assumed to have an *a priori* probability associated with it—the probability of choosing that key. Similarly each possible message is assumed to have an associated *a priori* probability, determined by the underlying stochastic process. These probabilities for the various keys and messages are actually the enemy cryptanalyst's *a priori* probabilities for the choices in question, and represent his *a priori* knowledge of the situation.

To use the system a key is first selected and sent to the receiving point. The choice of a key determines a particular transformation in the set forming the system. Then a message is selected and the particular transformation corresponding to the selected key applied to this message to produce a cryptogram. This cryptogram is transmitted to the receiving point by a channel and may be intercepted by the "enemy*." At the receiving end the inverse of the particular transformation is applied to the cryptogram to recover the original message.

If the enemy intercepts the cryptogram he can calculate from it the *a posteriori* probabilities of the various possible messages and keys which might have produced this cryptogram. This set of *a posteriori* probabilities constitutes his knowledge of the key and message after the interception. "Knowledge" is thus identified with a set of propositions having associated probabilities. The calculation of the *a posteriori* probabilities is the generalized problem of cryptanalysis.

As an example of these notions, in a simple substitution cipher with random key there are 26! transformations, corresponding to the 26! ways we

---

* The word "enemy," stemming from military applications, is commonly used in cryptographic work to denote anyone who may intercept a cryptogram.

can substitute for 26 different letters. These are all equally likely and each therefore has an *a priori* probability 1/26!. If this is applied to "normal English" the cryptanalyst being assumed to have no knowledge of the message source other than that it is producing English text, the *a priori* probabilities of various messages of N letters are merely their relative frequencies in normal English text.

If the enemy intercepts N letters of cryptogram in this system his probabilities change. If N is large enough (say 50 letters) there is usually a single message of *a posteriori* probability nearly unity, while all others have a total probability nearly zero. Thus there is an essentially unique "solution" to the cryptogram. For N smaller (say $N = 15$) there will usually be many messages and keys of comparable probability, with no single one nearly unity. In this case there are multiple "solutions" to the cryptogram.

Considering a secrecy system to be represented in this way, as a set of transformations of one set of elements into another, there are two natural combining operations which produce a third system from two given systems. The first combining operation is called the *product operation* and corresponds to enciphering the message with the first secrecy system R and enciphering the resulting cryptogram with the second system S, the keys for R and S being chosen independently. This total operation is a secrecy system whose transformations consist of all the products (in the usual sense of products of transformations) of transformations in S with transformations in R. The probabilities are the products of the probabilities for the two transformations.

The second combining operation is "*weighted addition*."

$$T = pR + qS \qquad p + q = 1$$

It corresponds to making a preliminary choice as to whether system R or S is to be used with probabilities p and q, respectively. When this is done R or S is used as originally defined.

It is shown that secrecy systems with these two combining operations form essentially a "linear associative algebra" with a unit element, an algebraic variety that has been extensively studied by mathematicians.

Among the many possible secrecy systems there is one type with many special properties. This type we call a "*pure*" *system*. A system is pure if all keys are equally likely and if for any three transformations T_i, T_j, T_k in the set the product

$$T_i T_j{}^{-1} T_k$$

is also a transformation in the set. That is enciphering, deciphering, and enciphering with any three keys must be equivalent to enciphering with some key.

With a pure cipher it is shown that all keys are essentially equivalent—
they all lead to the same set of *a posteriori* probabilities. Furthermore, when
a given cryptogram is intercepted there is a set of messages that might have
produced this cryptogram (a "residue class") and the *a posteriori* prob
abilities of messages in this class are proportional to the *a priori* probabilities.
All the information the enemy has obtained by intercepting the cryptogram
is a specification of the residue class. Many of the common ciphers are pure
systems, including simple substitution with random key. In this case the
residue class consists of all messages with the same pattern of letter repetitions as the intercepted cryptogram.

Two systems R and S are defined to be *"similar"* if there exists a fixed
transformation A with an inverse, A^{-1}, such that

$$R = AS.$$

If R and S are similar, a one-to-one correspondence between the resulting
cryptograms can be set up leading to the same *a posteriori* probabilities.
The two systems are crypt analytically the same.

The second part of the paper deals with the problem of "theoretical
secrecy." How secure is a system against cryptanalysis when the enemy has
unlimited time and manpower available for the analysis of intercepted
cryptograms? The problem is closely related to questions of communication
in the presence of noise, and the concepts of entropy and equivocation
developed for the communication problem find a direct application in this
part of cryptography.

"Perfect Secrecy" is defined by requiring of a system that after a cryptogram is intercepted by the enemy the *a posteriori* probabilities of this cryptogram representing various messages be identically the same as the *a priori*
probabilities of the same messages before the interception. It is shown that
perfect secrecy is possible but requires, if the number of messages is finite,
the same number of possible keys. If the message is thought of as being
constantly generated at a given "rate" R (to be defined later), key must be
generated at the same or a greater rate.

If a secrecy system with a finite key is used, and N letters of cryptogram
intercepted, there will be, for the enemy, a certain set of messages with
certain probabilities, that this cryptogram could represent. As N increases
the field usually narrows down until eventually there is a unique "solution"
to the cryptogram; one message with probability essentially unity while all
others are practically zero. A quantity $H(N)$ is defined, called the *equivocation*, which measures in a statistical way how near the average cryptogram
of N letters is to a unique solution; that is, how uncertain the enemy is of the
original message after intercepting a cryptogram of N letters. Various
properties of the equivocation are deduced—for example, the equivocation

of the key never increases with increasing N. This equivocation is a theoretical secrecy index—theoretical in that it allows the enemy unlimited time to analyse the cryptogram.

The function $H(N)$ for a certain idealized type of cipher called the random cipher is determined. With certain modifications this function can be applied to many cases of practical interest. This gives a way of calculating approximately how much intercepted material is required to obtain a solution to a secrecy system. It appears from this analysis that with ordinary languages and the usual types of ciphers (not codes) this "unicity distance" is approximately $H(K)/D$. Here $H(K)$ is a number measuring the "size" of the key space. If all keys are *a priori* equally likely $H(K)$ is the logarithm of the number of possible keys. D is the redundancy of the language and measures the amount of "statistical constraint" imposed by the language. In simple substitution with random key $H(K)$ is $\log_{10} 26!$ or about 20 and D (in decimal digits per letter) is about .7 for English. Thus unicity occurs at about 30 letters.

It is possible to construct secrecy systems with a finite key for certain "languages" in which the equivocation does not approach zero as $N \rightarrow \infty$. In this case, no matter how much material is intercepted, the enemy still does not obtain a unique solution to the cipher but is left with many alternatives, all of reasonable probability. Such systems we call *ideal* systems. It is possible in any language to approximate such behavior—i.e., to make the approach to zero of $H(N)$ recede out to arbitrarily large N. However, such systems have a number of drawbacks, such as complexity and sensitivity to errors in transmission of the cryptogram.

The third part of the paper is concerned with "practical secrecy." Two systems with the same key size may both be uniquely solvable when N letters have been intercepted, but differ greatly in the amount of labor required to effect this solution. An analysis of the basic weaknesses of secrecy systems is made. This leads to methods for constructing systems which will require a large amount of work to solve. Finally, a certain incompatibility among the various desirable qualities of secrecy systems is discussed.

PART I

MATHEMATICAL STRUCTURE OF SECRECY SYSTEMS

2. Secrecy Systems

As a first step in the mathematical analysis of cryptography, it is necessary to idealize the situation suitably, and to define in a mathematically acceptable way what we shall mean by a secrecy system. A "schematic" diagram of a general secrecy system is shown in Fig. 1. At the transmitting end there are two information sources—a message source and a key source. The key source produces a particular key from among those which are possible in the system. This key is transmitted by some means, supposedly not interceptible, for example by messenger, to the receiving end. The message source produces a message (the "clear") which is enciphered and the resulting cryptogram sent to the receiving end by a possibly interceptible means, for example radio. At the receiving end the cryptogram and key are combined in the decipherer to recover the message.

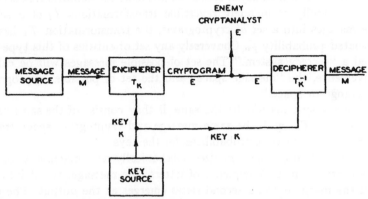

Fig. 1—Schematic of a general secrecy system.

Evidently the encipherer performs a functional operation. If M is the message, K the key, and E the enciphered message, or cryptogram, we have

$$E = f(M, K)$$

that is E is a function of M and K. It is preferable to think of this, however, not as a function of two variables but as a (one parameter) family of operations or transformations, and to write it

$$E = T_i M.$$

The transformation T_i applied to message M produces cryptogram E. The index i corresponds to the particular key being used.

We will assume, in general, that there are only a finite number of possible keys, and that each has an associated probability p_i. Thus the key source is represented by a statistical process or device which chooses one from the set of transformations $T_1, T_2, \cdots, T_m$ with the respective probabilities $p_1, p_2, \cdots, p_m$. Similarly we will generally assume a finite number of possible messages $M_1, M_2, \cdots, M_n$ with associated *a priori* probabilities $q_1, q_2, \cdots, q_n$. The possible messages, for example, might be the possible sequences of English letters all of length N, and the associated probabilities are then the relative frequencies of occurrence of these sequences in normal English text.

At the receiving end it must be possible to recover M, knowing E and K. Thus the transformations T_i in the family must have unique inverses T_i^{-1} such that $T_i T_i^{-1} = I$, the identity transformation. Thus:

$$M = T_i^{-1}E.$$

At any rate this inverse must exist uniquely for every E which can be obtained from an M with key i. Hence we arrive at the definition: A secrecy system is a family of uniquely reversible transformations T_i of a set of possible mssages into a set of cryptograms, the transformation T_i having an associated probability p_i. Conversely any set of entities of this type will be called a "secrecy system." The set of possible messages will be called, for convenience, the "message space" and the set of possible cryptograms the "cryptogram space."

Two secrecy systems will be the same if they consist of the same set of transformations T_i, with the same message and cryptogram space (range and domain) and the same probabilities for the keys.

A secrecy system can be visualized mechanically as a machine with one or more controls on it. A sequence of letters, the message, is fed into the input of the machine and a second series emerges at the output. The particular setting of the controls corresponds to the particular key being used. Some statistical method must be prescribed for choosing the key from all the possible ones.

To make the problem mathematically tractable we shall assume that *the enemy knows the system being used*. That is, he knows the family of transformations T_i, and the probabilities of choosing various keys. It might be objected that this assumption is unrealistic, in that the cryptanalyst often does not know what system was used or the probabilities in question. There are two answers to this objection:

1. The restriction is much weaker than appears at first, due to our broad definition of what constitutes a secrecy system. Suppose a cryptographer intercepts a message and does not know whether a substitution, transposition, or Vigenère type cipher was used. He can consider the message as being enciphered by a system in which part of the key is the specification of which of these types was used, the next part being the particular key for that type. These three different possibilities are assigned probabilities according to his best estimates of the *a priori* probabilities of the encipherer using the respective types of cipher.

2. The assumption is actually the one ordinarily used in cryptographic studies. It is pessimistic and hence safe, but in the long run realistic, since one must expect his system to be found out eventually. Thus,

even when an entirely new system is devised, so that the enemy cannot assign any *a priori* probability to it without discovering it himself, one must still live with the expectation of his eventual knowledge.

The situation is similar to that occurring in the theory of games[3] where it is assumed that the opponent "finds out" the strategy of play being used. In both cases the assumption serves to delineate sharply the opponent's knowledge.

A second possible objection to our definition of secrecy systems is that no account is taken of the common practice of inserting nulls in a message and the use of multiple substitutes. In such cases there is not a unique cryptogram for a given message and key, but the encipherer can choose at will from among a number of different cryptograms. This situation could be handled, but would only add complexity at the present stage, without substantially altering any of the basic results.

If the messages are produced by a Markoff process of the type described in (¹) to represent an information source, the probabilities of various messages are determined by the structure of the Markoff process. For the present, however, we wish to take a more general view of the situation and regard the messages as merely an abstract set of entities with associated probabilities, not necessarily composed of a sequence of letters and not necessarily produced by a Markoff process.

It should be emphasized that throughout the paper a secrecy system means not one, but a set of many transformations. After the key is chosen only one of these transformations is used and one might be led from this to define a secrecy system as a single transformation on a language. The enemy, however, does not know what key was chosen and the "might have been" keys are as important for him as the actual one. Indeed it is only the existence of these other possibilities that gives the system any secrecy. Since the secrecy is our primary interest, we are forced to the rather elaborate concept of a secrecy system defined above. This type of situation, where possibilities are as important as actualities, occurs frequently in games of strategy. The course of a chess game is largely controlled by threats which are *not* carried out. Somewhat similar is the "virtual existence" of unrealized imputations in the theory of games.

It may be noted that a single operation on a language forms a degenerate type of secrecy system under our definition—a system with only one key of unit probability. Such a system has no secrecy—the cryptanalyst finds the message by applying the inverse of this transformation, the only one in the system, to the intercepted cryptogram. The decipherer and cryptanalyst in this case possess the same information. In general, the only difference between the decipherer's knowledge and the enemy cryptanalyst's knowledge

[3] See von Neumann and Morgenstern "The Theory of Games," Princeton 1947.

is that the decipherer knows the particular key being used, while the cryptanalyst knows only the *a priori* probabilities of the various keys in the set.
The process of deciphering is that of applying the inverse of the particular
transformation used in enciphering to the cryptogram. The process of cryptanalysis is that of attempting to determine the message (or the particular
key) given only the cryptogram and the *a priori* probabilities of various
keys and messages.

There are a number of difficult epistemological questions connected with
the theory of secrecy, or in fact with any theory which involves questions of
probability (particularly *a priori* probabilities, Bayes' theorem, etc.) when
applied to a physical situation. Treated abstractly, probability theory can
be put on a rigorous logical basis with the modern measure theory approach.[4,5] As applied to a physical situation, however, especially when
"subjective" probabilities and unrepeatable experiments are concerned,
there are many questions of logical validity. For example, in the approach
to secrecy made here, *a priori* probabilities of various keys and messages
are assumed known by the enemy cryptographer—how can one determine
operationally if his estimates are correct, on the basis of his knowledge of the
situation?

One can construct artificial cryptographic situations of the "urn and die"
type in which the *a priori* probabilities have a definite unambiguous meaning
and the idealization used here is certainly appropriate. In other situations
that one can imagine, for example an intercepted communication between
Martian invaders, the *a priori* probabilities would probably be so uncertain
as to be devoid of significance. Most practical cryptographic situations lie
somewhere between these limits. A cryptanalyst might be willing to classify
the possible messages into the categories "reasonable," "possible but unlikely" and "unreasonable," but feel that finer subdivision was meaningless.

Fortunately, in practical situations, only extreme errors in *a priori* probabilities of keys and messages cause significant errors in the important
parameters. This is because of the exponential behavior of the number of
messages and cryptograms, and the logarithmic measures employed.

3. Representation of Systems

A secrecy system as defined above can be represented in various ways.
One which is convenient for illustrative purposes is a line diagram, as in
Figs. 2 and 4. The possible messages are represented by points at the left
and the possible cryptograms by points at the right. If a certain key, say key
1, transforms message M_2 into cryptogram E_4 then M_2 and E_4 are connected

[4] See J. L. Doob, "Probability as Measure," *Annals of Math. Stat.*, v. 12, 1941, pp. 206–214.
[5] A. Kolmogoroff, "Grundbegriffe der Wahrscheinlichkeits rechnung," *Ergebnisse der Mathematic*, v. 2, No. 3 (Berlin 1933).

by a line labeled 1, etc. From each possible message there must be exactly one line emerging for each different key. If the same is true for each cryptogram, we will say that the system is *closed*.

A more common way of describing a system is by stating the operation one performs on the message for an arbitrary key to obtain the cryptogram. Similarly, one defines implicitly the probabilities for various keys by describing how a key is chosen or what we know of the enemy's habits of key choice. The probabilities for messages are implicitly determined by stating our *a priori* knowledge of the enemy's language habits, the tactical situation (which will influence the probable content of the message) and any special information we may have regarding the cryptogram.

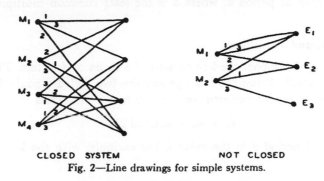

CLOSED SYSTEM   NOT CLOSED

Fig. 2—Line drawings for simple systems.

4. Some Examples of Secrecy Systems

In this section a number of examples of ciphers will be given. These will often be referred to in the remainder of the paper for illustrative purposes.

1. *Simple Substitution Cipher.*

In this cipher each letter of the message is replaced by a fixed substitute, usually also a letter. Thus the message,

$$M = m_1 m_2 m_3 m_4 \cdots$$

where m_1, m_2, $\cdots$ are the successive letters becomes:

$$E = e_1 e_2 e_3 e_4 \cdots$$
$$= f(m_1)f(m_2)f(m_3)f(m_4) \cdots$$

where the function $f(m)$ is a function with an inverse. The key is a permutation of the alphabet (when the substitutes are letters) e.g. $X\ G\ U\ A\ C\ D\ T\ B\ F\ H\ R\ S\ L\ M\ Q\ V\ Y\ Z\ W\ I\ E\ J\ O\ K\ N\ P$. The first letter X is the substitute for A, G is the substitute for B, etc.

2. *Transposition (Fixed Period d).*

The message is divided into groups of length d and a permutation applied to the first group, the same permutation to the second group, etc. The permutation is the key and can be represented by a permutation of the first d integers. Thus, for $d = 5$, we might have 2 3 1 5 4 as the permutation. This means that:

$$m_1\ m_2\ m_3\ m_4\ m_5\ m_6\ m_7\ m_8\ m_9\ m_{10} \cdots \text{ becomes}$$
$$m_2\ m_3\ m_1\ m_5\ m_4\ m_7\ m_8\ m_6\ m_{10}\ m_9 \cdots .$$

Sequential application of two or more transpositions will be called compound transposition. If the periods are d_1, d_2, $\cdots$, d_s it is clear that the result is a transposition of period d, where d is the least common multiple of d_1, d_2, $\cdots$, d_s.

3. *Vigenère, and Variations.*

In the Vigenère cipher the key consists of a series of d letters. These are written repeatedly below the message and the two added modulo 26 (considering the alphabet numbered from $A = 0$ to $Z = 25$. Thus

$$e_i = m_i + k_i \ (\text{mod } 26)$$

where k_i is of period d in the index i. For example, with the key $G\ A\ H$, we obtain

message	$N O W I S T H E \cdots$
repeated key	$G A H G A H G A \cdots$
cryptogram	$T O D O S A N E \cdots$

The Vigenère of period 1 is called the Caesar cipher. It is a simple substitution in which each letter of M is advanced a fixed amount in the alphabet. This amount is the key, which may be any number from 0 to 25. The so-called Beaufort and Variant Beaufort are similar to the Vigenère, and encipher by the equations

$$e_i = k_i - m_i \ (\text{mod } 26)$$

and

$$e_i = m_i - k_i \ (\text{mod } 26)$$

respectively. The Beaufort of period one is called the reversed Caesar cipher.

The application of two or more Vigenères in sequence will be called the compound Vigenère. It has the equation

$$e_i = m_i + k_i + l_i + \cdots + s_i \ (\text{mod } 26)$$

where k_i, l_i, $\cdots$, s_i in general have different periods. The period of their sum,

$$k_i + l_i + \cdots + s_i$$

as in compound transposition, is the least common multiple of the individual periods.

When the Vigenère is used with an unlimited key, never repeating, we have the Vernam system,[6] with

$$e_i = m_i + k_i \pmod{26}$$

the k_i being chosen at random and independently among 0, 1, $\cdots$, 25. If the key is a meaningful text we have the "running key" cipher.

4. *Digram, Trigram, and N-gram substitution.*

Rather than substitute for letters one can substitute for digrams, trigrams, etc. General digram substitution requires a key consisting of a permutation of the 26^2 digrams. It can be represented by a table in which the row corresponds to the first letter of the digram and the column to the second letter, entries in the table being the substitutes (usually also digrams).

5. *Single Mixed Alphabet Vigenère.*

This is a simple substitution followed by a Vigenère.

$$e_i = f(m_i) + k_i$$
$$m_i = f^{-1}(e_i - k_i)$$

The "inverse" of this system is a Vigenère followed by simple substitution

$$e_i = g(m_i + k_i)$$
$$m_i = g^{-1}(e_i) - k_i$$

6. *Matrix System.*[7]

One method of n-gram substitution is to operate on successive n-grams with a matrix having an inverse. The letters are assumed numbered from 0 to 25, making them elements of an algebraic ring. From the n-gram $m_1 m_2 \cdots m_n$ of message, the matrix a_{ij} gives an n-gram of cryptogram

$$e_i = \sum_{j=1}^{n} a_{ij} m_j \qquad i = 1, \cdots, n$$

---

[6] G. S. Vernam, "Cipher Printing Telegraph Systems for Secret Wire and Radio Telegraphic Communications," *Journal American Institute of Electrical Engineers*, v. XLV, pp. 109-115, 1926.
[7] See L. S. Hill, "Cryptography in an Algebraic Alphabet," *American Math. Monthly*, v. 36, No. 6, 1, 1929, pp. 306–312; also "Concerning Certain Linear Transformation Apparatus of Cryptography," v. 38, No. 3, 1931, pp. 135–154.

The matrix a_{ij} is the key, and deciphering is performed with the inverse matrix. The inverse matrix will exist if and only if the determinant $|a_{ij}|$ has an inverse element in the ring.

7. *The Playfair Cipher.*

This is a particular type of digram substitution governed by a mixed 25 letter alphabet written in a 5 x 5 square. (The letter J is often dropped in cryptographic work—it is very infrequent, and when it occurs can be replaced by I.) Suppose the key square is as shown below:

$$L \; Z \; Q \; C \; P$$
$$A \; G \; N \; O \; U$$
$$R \; D \; M \; I \; F$$
$$K \; Y \; H \; V \; S$$
$$X \; B \; T \; E \; W$$

The substitute for a digram AC, for example, is the pair of letters at the other corners of the rectangle defined by A and C, i.e., LO, the L taken first since it is above A. If the digram letters are on a horizontal line as RI, one uses the letters to their right DF; RF becomes DR. If the letters are on a vertical line, the letters below them are used. Thus PS becomes UW. If the letters are the same nulls may be used to separate them or one may be omitted, etc.

8. *Multiple Mixed Alphabet Substitution.*

In this cipher there are a set of d simple substitutions which are used in sequence. If the period d is four

$$m_1 \; m_2 \; m_3 \; m_4 \; m_5 \; m_6 \; \cdots$$

becomes

$$f_1(m_1) \; f_2(m_2) \; f_3(m_3) \; f_4(m_4) \; f_1(m_5) \; f_2(m_6) \; \cdots$$

9. *Autokey Cipher.*

A Vigenère type system in which either the message itself or the resulting cryptogram is used for the "key" is called an autokey cipher. The encipherment is started with a "priming key" (which is the entire key in our sense) and continued with the message or cryptogram displaced by the length of the priming key as indicated below, where the priming key is COMET. The message used as "key":

Message	$S \; E \; N \; D \; S \; U \; P \; P \; L \; I \; E \; S \; \cdots$
Key	$C \; O \; M \; E \; T \; S \; E \; N \; D \; S \; U \; P \; \cdots$
Cryptogram	$U \; S \; Z \; H \; L \; M \; T \; C \; O \; A \; Y \; H$

The cryptogram used as "key":[8]

Message	*S E N D S U P P L I E S* ⋯
Key	*C O M E T U S Z H L O H* ⋯
Cryptogram	*U S Z H L O H O S T S* ⋯

10. *Fractional Ciphers.*

In these, each letter is first enciphered into two or more letters or numbers and these symbols are somehow mixed (e.g. by transposition). The result may then be retranslated into the original alphabet. Thus, using a mixed 25-letter alphabet for the key, we may translate letters into two-digit quinary numbers by the table:

$$
\begin{array}{c c c c c c}
 & 0 & 1 & 2 & 3 & 4 \\
0 & L & Z & Q & C & P \\
1 & A & G & N & O & U \\
2 & R & D & M & I & F \\
3 & K & Y & H & V & S \\
4 & X & B & T & E & W \\
\end{array}
$$

Thus *B* becomes 41. After the resulting series of numbers is transposed in some way they are taken in pairs and translated back into letters.

11. *Codes.*

In codes words (or sometimes syllables) are replaced by substitute letter groups. Sometimes a cipher of one kind or another is applied to the result.

5. VALUATIONS OF SECRECY SYSTEMS

There are a number of different criteria that should be applied in estimating the value of a proposed secrecy system. The most important of these are:

1. *Amount of Secrecy.*

There are some systems that are perfect—the enemy is no better off after intercepting any amount of material than before. Other systems, although giving him some information, do not yield a unique "solution" to intercepted cryptograms. Among the uniquely solvable systems, there are wide variations in the amount of labor required to effect this solution and in the amount of material that must be intercepted to make the solution unique.

---

[8] This system is trivial from the secrecy standpoint since, with the exception of the first *d* letters, the enemy is in possession of the entire "key."

2. *Size of Key.*

The key must be transmitted by non-interceptible means from transmitting to receiving points. Sometimes it must be memorized. It is therefore desirable to have the key as small as possible.

3. *Complexity of Enciphering and Deciphering Operations.*

Enciphering and deciphering should, of course, be as simple as possible. If they are done manually, complexity leads to loss of time, errors, etc. If done mechanically, complexity leads to large expensive machines.

4. *Propagation of Errors.*

In certain types of ciphers an error of one letter in enciphering or transmission leads to a large number of errors in the deciphered text. The errors are spread out by the deciphering operation, causing the loss of much information and frequent need for repetition of the cryptogram. It is naturally desirable to minimize this error expansion.

5. *Expansion of Message.*

In some types of secrecy systems the size of the message is increased by the enciphering process. This undesirable effect may be seen in systems where one attempts to swamp out message statistics by the addition of many nulls, or where multiple substitutes are used. It also occurs in many "concealment" types of systems (which are not usually secrecy systems in the sense of our definition).

6. The Algebra of Secrecy Systems

If we have two secrecy systems T and R we can often combine them in various ways to form a new secrecy system S. If T and R have the same domain (message space) we may form a kind of "weighted sum,"

$$S = pT + qR$$

where $p + q = 1$. This operation consists of first making a preliminary choice with probabilities p and q determining which of T and R is used. This choice is part of the key of S. After this is determined T or R is used as originally defined. The total key of S must specify which of T and R is used and which key of T (or R) is used.

If T consists of the transformations $T_1, \cdots, T_m$ with probabilities $p_1, \cdots, p_m$ and R consists of $R_1, \cdots, R_k$ with probabilities $q_1, \cdots, q_k$ then $S = pT + qR$ consists of the transformations $T_1, T_2, \cdots, T_m, R_1, \cdots, R_k$ with probabilities $pp_1, pp_2, \cdots, pp_m, qq_1, qq_2, \cdots, qq_k$ respectively.

More generally we can form the sum of a number of systems.

$$S = p_1T + p_2R + \cdots + p_mU \qquad \sum p_i = 1$$

We note that any system T can be written as a sum of fixed operations

$$T = p_1T_1 + p_2T_2 + \cdots + p_mT_m$$

T_i being a definite enciphering operation of T corresponding to key choice i, which has probability p_i.

A second way of combining two secrecy systems is by taking the "product," shown schematically in Fig. 3. Suppose T and R are two systems and the domain (language space) of R can be identified with the range (cryptogram space) of T. Then we can apply first T to our language and then R

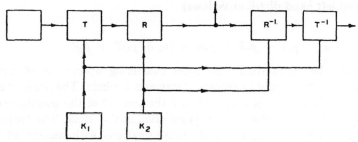

Fig. 3—Product of two systems $S = RT$.

to the result of this enciphering process. This gives a resultant operation S which we write as a product

$$S = RT$$

The key for S consists of both keys of T and R which are assumed chosen according to their original probabilities and independently. Thus, if the m keys of T are chosen with probabilities

$$p_1 \ p_2 \ \cdots \ p_m$$

and the n keys of R have probabilities

$$p_1' \ p_2' \ \cdots \ p_n' \ ,$$

then S has at most mn keys with probabilities $p_i p_j'$. In many cases some of the product transformaions R_iT_j will be the same and can be grouped together, adding their probabilities.

Product encipherment is often used; for example, one follows a substitution by a transposition or a transposition by a Vigenère, or applies a code to the text and enciphers the result by substitution, transposition, fractionation, etc.

It may be noted that multiplication is not in general commutative, (we do not always have $RS = SR$), although in special cases, such as substitution and transposition, it is. Since it represents an operation it is definitionally associative. That is $R(ST) = (RS)T = RST$. Furthermore we have the laws

$$p(p'T + q'R) + qS = pp'T + pq'R + qS$$

(weighted associative law for addition)

$$T(pR + qS) = pTR + qTS$$
$$(pR + qS)T = pRT + qST$$

(right and left hand distributive laws)
and

$$p_1T + p_2T + p_3R = (p_1 + p_2)T + p_3R$$

It should be emphasized that these combining operations of addition and multiplication apply to secrecy systems as a whole. The product of two systems TR should not be confused with the product of the transformations in the systems T_iR_j, which also appears often in this work. The former TR is a secrecy system, i.e., a set of transformations with associated probabilities; the latter is a particular transformation. Further the sum of two systems $pR + qT$ is a system—the sum of two transformations is not defined. The systems T and R may commute without the individual T_i and R_j commuting, e.g., if R is a Beaufort system of a given period, all keys equally likely,

$$R_iR_j \neq R_jR_i$$

in general, but of course RR does not depend on its order; actually

$$RR = V$$

the Vigenère of the same period with random key. On the other hand, if the individual T_i and R_j of two systems T and R commute, then the systems commute.

A system whose M and E spaces can be identified, a very common case as when letter sequences are transformed into letter sequences, may be termed *endomorphic*. An endomorphic system T may be raised to a power T^n.

A secrecy system T whose product with itself is equal to T, i.e., for which

$$TT = T,$$

will be called idempotent. For example, simple substitution, transposition of period p, Vigenère of period p (all with each key equally likely) are idempotent.

The set of all endomorphic secrecy systems defined in a fixed message space constitutes an "algebraic variety," that is, a kind of algebra, using the operations of addition and multiplication. In fact, the properties of addition and multiplication which we have discussed may be summarized as follows:

The set of endomorphic ciphers with the same message space and the two combining operations of weighted addition and multiplication form a linear associative algebra with a unit element, apart from the fact that the coefficients in a weighted addition must be non-negative and sum to unity.

The combining operations give us ways of constructing many new types of secrecy systems from certain ones, such as the examples given. We may also use them to describe the situation facing a cryptanalyst when attempting to solve a cryptogram of unknown type. He is, in fact, solving a secrecy system of the type

$$T = p_1 A + p_2 B + \cdots + p_r S + p' X \qquad \sum p = 1$$

where the A, B, $\cdots$, S are known types of ciphers, with the p_i their *a priori* probabilities in this situation, and $p' X$ corresponds to the possibility of a completely new unknown type of cipher.

7. PURE AND MIXED CIPHERS

Certain types of ciphers, such as the simple substitution, the transposition of a given period, the Vigenère of a given period, the mixed alphabet Vigenère, etc. (all with each key equally likely) have a certain homogeneity with respect to key. Whatever the key, the enciphering, deciphering and decrypting processes are essentially the same. This may be contrasted with the cipher

$$pS + qT$$

where S is a simple substitution and T a transposition of a given period. In this case the entire system changes for enciphering, deciphering and decryptment, depending on whether the substitution or transposition is used.

The cause of the homogeneity in these systems stems from the group property—we notice that, in the above examples of homogeneous ciphers, the product $T_i T_j$ of any two transformations in the set is equal to a third transformation T_k in the set. On the other hand $T_i S_j$ does not equal any transformation in the cipher

$$pS + qT$$

which contains only substitutions and transpositions, no products.

We might define a "pure" cipher, then, as one whose T_i form a group. This, however, would be too restrictive since it requires that the E space be the same as the M space, i.e. that the system be endomorphic. The fractional transposition is as homogeneous as the ordinary transposition without being endomorphic. The proper definition is the following: A cipher T is *pure* if for every T_i, T_j, T_k there is a T_s such that

$$T_i T_j^{-1} T_k = T_s$$

and every key is equally likely. Otherwise the cipher is mixed. The systems of Fig. 2 are mixed. Fig. 4 is pure if all keys are equally likely.

Theorem 1: In a pure cipher the operations $T_i^{-1} T_j$ which transform the message space into itself form a group whose order is m, the number of different keys.

For

$$T_j^{-1} T_k T_k^{-1} T_j = I$$

so that each element has an inverse. The associative law is true since these are operations, and the group property follows from

$$T_i^{-1} T_j T_k^{-1} T_l = T_s^{-1} T_k T_k^{-1} T_l = T_s^{-1} T_l$$

using our assumption that $T_i^{-1} T_j = T_s^{-1} T_k$ for some s.

The operation $T_i^{-1} T_j$ means, of course, enciphering the message with key j and then deciphering with key i which brings us back to the message space. If T is endomorphic, i.e. the T_i themselves transform the space Ω_M into itself (as is the case with most ciphers, where both the message space and the cryptogram space consist of sequences of letters), and the T_i are a group and equally likely, then T is pure, since

$$T_i T_j^{-1} T_k = T_i T_r = T_s .$$

Theorem 2: The product of two pure ciphers which commute is pure.

For if T and R commute $T_i R_j = R_l T_m$ for every i, j with suitable l, m, and

$$\begin{aligned} T_i R_j (T_k R_l)^{-1} T_m R_n &= T_i R_j R_l^{-1} T_k^{-1} T_m R_n \\ &= R_u R_v^{-1} R_w T_r T_s^{-1} T_t \\ &= R_h T_g. \end{aligned}$$

The commutation condition is not necessary, however, for the product to be a pure cipher.

A system with only one key, i.e., a single definite operation T_1, is pure since the only choice of indices is

$$T_1 T_1^{-1} T_1 = T_1 .$$

Thus the expansion of a general cipher into a sum of such simple transformations also exhibits it as a sum of pure ciphers.

An examination of the example of a pure cipher shown in Fig. 4 discloses certain properties. The messages fall into certain subsets which we will call *residue classes*, and the possible cryptograms are divided into corresponding residue classes. There is at least one line from each message in a class to each cryptogram in the corresponding class, and no line between classes which do not correspond. The number of messages in a class is a divisor of the total number of keys. The number of lines "in parallel" from a message M to a cryptogram in the corresponding class is equal to the number of keys divided by the number of messages in the class containing the message (or cryptogram). It is shown in the appendix that these hold in general for pure ciphers. Summarized formally, we have:

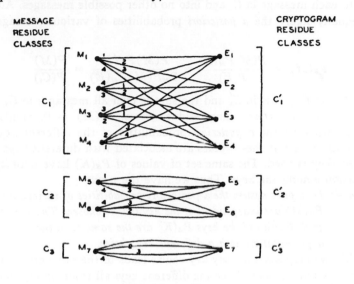

PURE SYSTEM
Fig. 4—Pure system.

Theorem 3: In a pure system the messages can be divided into a set of "residue classes" $C_1, C_2, \cdots, C_s$ and the cryptograms into a corresponding set of residue classes $C_1', C_2', \cdots, C_s'$ with the following properties:

(1) *The message residue classes are mutually exclusive and collectively contain all possible messages. Similarly for the cryptogram residue classes.*

(2) *Enciphering any message in C_i with any key produces a cryptogram in C_i'. Deciphering any cryptogram in C_i' with any key leads to a message in C_i.*

(3) *The number of messages in C_i, say φ_i, is equal to the number of cryptograms in C_i' and is a divisor of k the number of keys.*

(4) *Each message in C_i can be enciphered into each cryptogram in C_i' by exactly k/φ_i different keys. Similarly for decipherment.*

The importance of the concept of a pure cipher (and the reason for the name) lies in the fact that in a pure cipher all keys are essentially the same. Whatever key is used for a particular message, the *a posteriori* probabilities of all messages are identical. To see this, note that two different keys applied to the same message lead to two cryptograms in the same residue class, say C_i'. The two cryptograms therefore could each be deciphered by $\dfrac{k}{\varphi_i}$ keys into each message in C_i and into no other possible messages. All keys being equally likely the *a posteriori* probabilities of various messages are thus

$$P_E(M) = \frac{P(M)P_M(E)}{P(E)} = \frac{P(M)P_M(E)}{\Sigma_M P(M)P_M(E)} = \frac{P(M)}{P(C_i)}$$

where M is in C_i, E is in C_i' and the sum is over all messages in C_i. If E and M are not in corresponding residue classes, $P_E(M) = 0$. Similarly it can be shown that the *a posteriori* probabilities of the different keys are the same in value but these values are associated with different keys when a different key is used. The same set of values of $P_E(K)$ have undergone a permutation among the keys. Thus we have the result

Theorem 4: In a pure system the a posteriori *probabilities of various messages $P_E(M)$ are independent of the key that is chosen. The* a posteriori *probabilities of the keys $P_E(K)$ are the same in value but undergo a permutation with a different key choice.*

Roughly we may say that any key choice leads to the same cryptanalytic problem in a pure cipher. Since the different keys all result in cryptograms in the same residue class this means that all cryptograms in the same residue class are cryptanalytically equivalent—they lead to the same *a posteriori* probabilities of messages and, apart from a permutation, the same probabilities of keys.

As an example of this, simple substitution with all keys equally likely is a pure cipher. The residue class corresponding to a given cryptogram E is the set of all cryptograms that may be obtained from E by operations $T_j T_k^{-1} E$. In this case $T_j T_k^{-1}$ is itself a substitution and hence any substitution on E gives another member of the same residue class. Thus, if the cryptogram is

$$E = X\ C\ P\ P\ G\ C\ F\ Q,$$

then

$$E_1 = R\ D\ H\ H\ G\ D\ S\ N$$
$$E_2 = A\ B\ C\ C\ D\ B\ E\ F$$

etc. are in the same residue class. It is obvious in this case that these cryptograms are essentially equivalent. All that is of importance in a simple substitution with random key is the *pattern* of letter repetitions, the actual letters being dummy variables. Indeed we might dispense with them entirely, indicating the pattern of repetitions in E as follows:

This notation describes the residue class but eliminates all information as to the specific member of the class. Thus it leaves precisely that information which is cryptanalytically pertinent. This is related to one method of attacking simple substitution ciphers—the method of pattern words.

In the Caesar type cipher only the first differences mod 26 of the cryptogram are significant. Two cryptograms with the same Δe_i are in the same residue class. One breaks this cipher by the simple process of writing down the 26 members of the message residue class and picking out the one which makes sense.

The Vigenère of period d with random key is another example of a pure cipher. Here the message residue class consists of all sequences with the same first differences as the cryptogram, for letters separated by distance d. For $d = 3$ the residue class is defined by

$$
\begin{aligned}
m_1 - m_4 &= e_1 - e_4 \\
m_2 - m_5 &= e_2 - e_5 \\
m_3 - m_6 &= e_3 - e_6 \\
m_4 - m_7 &= e_4 - e_7
\end{aligned}
$$

$$\vdots$$

where $E = e_1, e_2, \cdots$ is the cryptogram and $m_1, m_2, \cdots$ is any M in the corresponding residue class.

In the transposition cipher of period d with random key, the residue class consists of all arrangements of the e_i in which no e_i is moved out of its block of length d, and any two e_i at a distance d remain at this distance. This is used in breaking these ciphers as follows: The cryptogram is written in successive blocks of length d, one under another as below ($d = 5$):

$$
\begin{array}{ccccc}
e_1 & e_2 & e_3 & e_4 & e_5 \\
e_6 & e_7 & e_8 & e_9 & e_{10} \\
e_{11} & e_{12} & \cdot & \cdot & \cdot
\end{array}
$$

The columns are then cut apart and rearranged to make meaningful text. When the columns are cut apart, the only information remaining is the residue class of the cryptogram.

Theorem 5: If T is pure then $T_iT_j^{-1}T = T$ where T_iT_j are any two transformations of T. Conversely if this is true for any T_iT_j in a system T then T is pure.

The first part of this theorem is obvious from the definition of a pure system. To prove the second part we note first that, if $T_iT_j^{-1}T = T$, then $T_iT_j^{-1}T_s$ is a transformation of T. It remains to show that all keys are equiprobable. We have $T = \sum_s p_sT_s$ and

$$\sum_s p_sT_iT_j^{-1}T_s = \sum_s p_sT_s.$$

The term in the left hand sum with $s = j$ yields p_jT_i. The only term in T_i on the right is p_iT_i. Since all coefficients are nonnegative it follows that

$$p_j \leq p_i.$$

The same argument holds with i and j interchanged and consequently

$$p_j = p_i$$

and T is pure. Thus the condition that $T_iT_j^{-1}T = T$ might be used as an alternative definition of a pure system.

8. Similar Systems

Two secrecy systems R and S will be said to be *similar* if there exists a transformation A having an inverse A^{-1} such that

$$R = AS$$

This means that enciphering with R is the same as enciphering with S and then operating on the result with the transformation A. If we write $R \approx S$ to mean R is similar to S then it is clear that $R \approx S$ implies $S \approx R$. Also $R \approx S$ and $S \approx T$ imply $R \approx T$ and finally $R \approx R$. These are summarized by saying that similarity is an equivalence relation.

The cryptographic significance of similarity is that if $R \approx S$ then R and S are equivalent from the cryptanalytic point of view. Indeed if a cryptanalyst intercepts a cryptogram in system S he can transform it to one in system R by merely applying the transformation A to it. A cryptogram in system R is transformed to one in S by applying A^{-1}. If R and S are applied to the same language or message space, there is a one-to-one correspondence between the resulting cryptograms. Corresponding cryptograms give the same distribution of *a posteriori* probabilities for all messages.

If one has a method of breaking the system R then any system S similar to R can be broken by reducing to R through application of the operation A. This is a device that is frequently used in practical cryptanalysis.

As a trivial example, simple substitution where the substitutes are not letters but arbitrary symbols is similar to simple substitution using letter substitutes. A second example is the Caesar and the reversed Caesar type ciphers. The latter is sometimes broken by first transforming into a Caesar type. This can be done by reversing the alphabet in the cryptogram. The Vigenère, Beaufort and Variant Beaufort are all similar, when the key is random. The "autokey" cipher (with the message used as "key") primed with the key $K_1 K_2 \cdots K_d$ is similar to a Vigenère type with the key alternately added and subtracted Mod 26. The transformation A in this case is that of "deciphering" the autokey with a series of d A's for the priming key

PART II

THEORETICAL SECRECY

9. INTRODUCTION

We now consider problems connected with the "theoretical secrecy" of a system. How immune is a system to cryptanalysis when the cryptanalyst has unlimited time and manpower available for the analysis of cryptograms? Does a cryptogram *have* a unique solution (even though it may require an impractical amount of work to find it) and if not how many reasonable solutions does it have? How much text in a given system must be intercepted before the solution becomes unique? Are there systems which never become unique in solution no matter how much enciphered text is intercepted? Are there systems for which no information whatever is given to the enemy no matter how much text is intercepted? In the analysis of these problems the concepts of entropy, redundancy and the like developed in "A Mathematical Theory of Communication" (hereafter referred to as MTC) will find a wide application.

10. PERFECT SECRECY

Let us suppose the possible messages are finite in number $M_1, \cdots, M_n$ and have *a priori* probabilities $P(M_1), \cdots, P(M_n)$, and that these are enciphered into the possible cryptograms $E_1, \cdots, E_m$ by

$$E = T_i M.$$

The cryptanalyst intercepts a particular E and can then calculate, in principle at least, the *a posteriori* probabilities for the various messages, $P_E(M)$. It is natural to define *perfect secrecy* by the condition that, for all E the *a posteriori* probabilities are equal to the *a priori* probabilities independently of the values of these. In this case, intercepting the message has given the cryptanalyst no information.[9] Any action of his which depends on the information contained in the cryptogram cannot be altered, for all of his probabilities as to what the cryptogram contains remain unchanged. On the other hand, if the condition is *not* satisfied there will exist situations in which the enemy has certain *a priori* probabilities, and certain key and message choices may occur for which the enemy's probabilities do change. This in turn may affect his actions and thus perfect secrecy has not been obtained. Hence the definition given is necessarily required by our intuitive ideas of what perfect secrecy should mean.

A necessary and sufficient condition for perfect secrecy can be found as follows: We have by Bayes' theorem

$$P_E(M) = \frac{P(M)P_M(E)}{P(E)}$$

in which:

$P(M)$ = *a priori* probability of message M.

$P_M(E)$ = conditional probability of cryptogram E if message M is chosen, i.e. the sum of the probabilities of all keys which produce cryptogram E from message M.

$P(E)$ = probability of obtaining cryptogram E from any cause.

$P_E(M)$ = *a posteriori* probability of message M if cryptogram E is intercepted.

For perfect secrecy $P_E(M)$ must equal $P(M)$ for all E and all M. Hence either $P(M) = 0$, a solution that must be excluded since we demand the equality independent of the values of $P(M)$, or

$$P_M(E) = P(E)$$

for every M and E. Conversely if $P_M(E) = P(E)$ then

$$P_E(M) = P(M)$$

and we have perfect secrecy. Thus we have the result:

Theorem 6: A necessary and sufficient condition for perfect secrecy is that

$$P_M(E) = P(E)$$

for all M and E. That is, $P_M(E)$ must be independent of M.

Stated another way, the total probability of all keys that transform M_i

---

[9] A purist might object that the enemy has obtained some information in that he knows a message was sent. This may be answered by having among the messages a "blank" corresponding to "no message." If no message is originated the blank is enciphered and sent as a cryptogram. Then even this modicum of remaining information is eliminated.

into a given cryptogram E is equal to that of all keys transforming M_j into the same E, for all M_i, M_j and E.

Now there must be as many E's as there are M's since, for a fixed i, T_i gives a one-to-one correspondence between all the M's and some of the E's. For perfect secrecy $P_M(E) = P(E) \neq 0$ for any of these E's and any M. Hence there is at least one key transforming any M into any of these E's. But all the keys from a fixed M to different E's must be different, and therefore *the number of different keys is at least as great as the number of M's.* It is possible to obtain perfect secrecy with only this number of keys, as

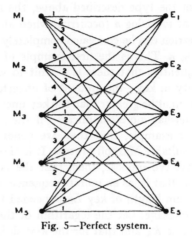

Fig. 5—Perfect system.

one shows by the following example: Let the M_i be numbered 1 to n and the E_i the same, and using n keys let

$$T_i M_j = E_s$$

where $s = i + j$ (Mod n). In this case we see that $P_E(M) = \dfrac{1}{n} = P(E)$ and we have perfect secrecy. An example is shown in Fig. 5 with $s = i + j - 1$ (Mod 5).

Perfect systems in which the number of cryptograms, the number of messages, and the number of keys are all equal are characterized by the properties that (1) each M is connected to each E by exactly one line, (2) all keys are equally likely. Thus the matrix representation of the system is a "Latin square."

In MTC it was shown that information may be conveniently measured by means of entropy. If we have a set of possibilities with probabilities p_1, p_2, $\cdots$, p_n, the entropy H is given by:

$$H = -\sum p_i \log p_i.$$

In a secrecy system there are two statistical choices involved, that of the message and of the key. We may measure the amount of information produced when a message is chosen by $H(M)$:

$$H(M) = - \sum P(M) \log P(M),$$

the summation being over all possible messages. Similarly, there is an uncertainty associated with the choice of key given by:

$$H(K) = - \sum P(K) \log P(K).$$

In perfect systems of the type described above, the amount of information in the message is at most $\log n$ (occurring when all messages are equiprobable). This information can be concealed completely only if the key uncertainty is at least $\log n$. This is the first example of a general principle which will appear frequently: that there is a limit to what we can obtain with a given uncertainty in key—the amount of uncertainty we can introduce into the solution cannot be greater than the key uncertainty.

The situation is somewhat more complicated if the number of messages is infinite. Suppose, for example, that they are generated as infinite sequences of letters by a suitable Markoff process. It is clear that no finite key will give perfect secrecy. We suppose, then, that the key source generates key in the same manner, that is, as an infinite sequence of symbols. Suppose further that only a certain length of key L_K is needed to encipher and decipher a length L_M of message. Let the logarithm of the number of letters in the message alphabet be R_M and that for the key alphabet be R_K. Then, from the finite case, it is evident that perfect secrecy requires

$$R_M L_M \leq R_K L_K.$$

This type of perfect secrecy is realized by the Vernam system.

These results have been deduced on the basis of unknown or arbitrary *a priori* probabilities for the messages. The key required for perfect secrecy depends then on the total number of possible messages.

One would expect that, if the message space has fixed known statistics, so that it has a definite mean rate R of generating information, in the sense of MTC, then the amount of key needed could be reduced on the average in just this ratio $\dfrac{R}{R_M}$, and this is indeed true. In fact the message can be passed through a transducer which eliminates the redundancy and reduces the expected length in just this ratio, and then a Vernam system may be applied to the result. Evidently the amount of key used per letter of message is statistically reduced by a factor $\dfrac{R}{R_M}$ and in this case the key source and information source are just matched—a bit of key completely conceals a bit of message information. It is easily shown also, by the methods used in MTC, that this is the best that can be done.

Perfect secrecy systems have a place in the practical picture—they may be used either where the greatest importance is attached to complete secrecy—e.g., correspondence between the highest levels of command, or in cases where the number of possible messages is small. Thus, to take an extreme example, if only two messages "yes" or "no" were anticipated, a perfect system would be in order, with perhaps the transformation table:

M $\quad$ K	A	B
yes	0	1
no	1	0

The disadvantage of perfect systems for large correspondence systems is, of course, the equivalent amount of key that must be sent. In succeeding sections we consider what can be achieved with smaller key size, in particular with finite keys.

11. EQUIVOCATION

Let us suppose that a simple substitution cipher has been used on English text and that we intercept a certain amount, N letters, of the enciphered text. For N fairly large, more than say 50 letters, there is nearly always a unique solution to the cipher; i.e., a single good English sequence which transforms into the intercepted material by a simple substitution. With a smaller N, however, the chance of more than one solution is greater; with $N = 15$ there will generally be quite a number of possible fragments of text that would fit, while with $N = 8$ a good fraction (of the order of 1/8) of all reasonable English sequences of that length are possible, since there is seldom more than one repeated letter in the 8. With $N = 1$ any letter is clearly possible and has the same *a posteriori* probability as its *a priori* probability. For one letter the system is perfect.

This happens generally with solvable ciphers. Before any material is intercepted we can imagine the *a priori* probabilities attached to the various possible messages, and also to the various keys. As material is intercepted, the cryptanalyst calculates the *a posteriori* probabilities; and as N increases the probabilities of certain messages increase, and, of most, decrease, until finally only one is left, which has a probability nearly one, while the total probability of all others is nearly zero.

This calculation can actually be carried out for very simple systems. Table I shows the *a posteriori* probabilities for a Caesar type cipher applied to English text, with the key chosen at random from the 26 possibilities. To enable the use of standard letter, digram and trigram frequency tables, the text has been started at a random point (by opening a book and putting a pencil down at random on the page). The message selected in this way begins "creases to . . ." starting inside the word increases. If the message were known to start a sentence a different set of probabilities must be used, corresponding to the frequencies of letters, digrams, etc., at the beginning of sentences.

TABLE I

A *Posteriori* Probabilities for a Caesar Type Cryptogram

Decipherments	$N = 1$	$N = 2$	$N = 3$	$N = 4$	$N = 5$
C R E A S	.028	.0377	.1111	.3673	1
D S F B T	.038	.0314			
E T G C U	.131	.0881			
F U H D V	.029	.0189			
G V I E W	.020				
H W J F X	.053	.0063			
I X K G Y	.063	.0126			
J Y L H Z	.001				
K Z M I A	.004				
L A N J B	.034	.1321	.2500		
M B O K C	.025		.0222		
N C P L D	.071	.1195			
O D Q M E	.080	.0377			
P E R N F	.020	.0818	.4389	.6327	
Q F S O G	.001				
R G T P H	.068	.0126			
S H U Q I	.061	.0881	.0056		
T I V R J	.105	.2830	.1667		
U J W S K	.025				
V K X T L	.009				
W L Y U M	.015		.0056		
X M Z V N	.002				
Y N A W O	.020				
Z O B X P	.001				
A P C Y Q	.082	.0503			
B Q D Z R	.014				
H (decimal digits)	1.2425	.9686	.6034	.285	0

The Caesar with random key is a pure cipher and the particular key chosen does not affect the *a posteriori* probabilities. To determine these we need merely list the possible decipherments by all keys and calculate their *a priori* probabilities. The *a posteriori* probabilities are these divided by their sum. These possible decipherments are found by the standard process of "running down the alphabet" from the message and are listed at the left. These form the residue class for the message. For one intercepted letter the *a posteriori* probabilities are equal to the *a priori* probabilities for letters[10] and are shown in the column headed $N = 1$. For two intercepted letters the probabilities are those for digrams adjusted to sum to unity and these are shown in the column $N = 2$.

[10] The probabilities for this table were taken from frequency tables given by Fletcher Pratt in a book "Secret and Urgent" published by Blue Ribbon Books, New York, 1939. Although not complete, they are sufficient for present purposes.

Trigram frequencies have also been tabulated and these are shown in the column $N = 3$. For four- and five-letter sequences probabilities were obtained by multiplication from trigram frequencies since, roughly,

$$p(ijkl) = p(ijk)p_{jk}(l).$$

Note that at three letters the field has narrowed down to four messages of fairly high probability, the others being small in comparison. At four there are two possibilities and at five just one, the correct decipherment.

In principle this could be carried out with any system but, unless the key is very small, the number of possibilities is so large that the work involved prohibits the actual calculation.

This set of *a posteriori* probabilities describes how the cryptanalyst's knowledge of the message and key gradually becomes more precise as enciphered material is obtained. This description, however, is much too involved and difficult to obtain for our purposes. What is desired is a simplified description of this approach to uniqueness of the possible solutions.

A similar situation arises in communication theory when a transmitted signal is perturbed by noise. It is necessary to set up a suitable measure of the uncertainty of what was actually transmitted knowing only the perturbed version given by the received signal. In MTC it was shown that a natural mathematical measure of this uncertainty is the conditional entropy of the transmitted signal when the received signal is known. This conditional entropy was called, for convenience, the equivocation.

From the point of view of the cryptanalyst, a secrecy system is almost identical with a noisy communication system. The message (transmitted signal) is operated on by a statistical element, the enciphering system, with its statistically chosen key. The result of this operation is the cryptogram (analogous to the perturbed signal) which is available for analysis. The chief differences in the two cases are: first, that the operation of the enciphering transformation is generally of a more complex nature than the perturbing noise in a channel; and, second, the key for a secrecy system is usually chosen from a finite set of possibilities while the noise in a channel is more often continually introduced, in effect chosen from an infinite set.

With these considerations in mind it is natural to use the equivocation as a theoretical secrecy index. It may be noted that there are two significant equivocations, that of the key and that of the message. These will be denoted by $H_E(K)$ and $H_E(M)$ respectively. They are given by:

$$H_E(K) = \sum_{E,K} P(E, K) \log P_E(K)$$

$$H_E(M) = \sum_{E,M} P(E, M) \log P_E(K)$$

in which E, M and K are the cryptogram, message and key and

$P(E, K)$ is the probability of key K and cryptogram E

$P_E(K)$ is the *a posteriori* probability of key K if cryptogram E is intercepted

$P(E, M)$ and $P_E(M)$ are the similar probabilities for message instead of key.

The summation in $H_E(K)$ is over all possible cryptograms of a certain length (say N letters) and over all keys. For $H_E(M)$ the summation is over all messages and cryptograms of length N. Thus $H_E(K)$ and $H_E(M)$ are both functions of N, the number of intercepted letters. This will sometimes be indicated explicitly by writing $H_E(K, N)$ and $H_E(M, N)$. Note that these are "total" equivocations; i.e., we do not divide by N to obtain the equivocation rate which was used in *MTC*.

The same general arguments used to justify the equivocation as a measure of uncertainty in communication theory apply here as well. We note that zero equivocation requires that one message (or key) have unit probability, all others zero, corresponding to complete knowledge. Considered as a function of N, the gradual decrease of equivocation corresponds to increasing knowledge of the original key or message. The two equivocation curves, plotted as functions of N, will be called the equivocation characteristics of the secrecy system in question.

The values of $H_E(K, N)$ and $H_E(M, N)$ for the Caesar type cryptogram considered above have been calculated and are given in the last row of Table I. $H_E(K, N)$ and $H_E(M, N)$ are equal in this case and are given in decimal digits (i.e. the logarithmic base 10 is used in the calculation). It should be noted that the equivocation here is for a particular cryptogram, the summation being only over M (or K), not over E. In general the summation would be over all possible intercepted cryptograms of length N and would give the average uncertainty. The computational difficulties are prohibitive for this general calculation.

12. PROPERTIES OF EQUIVOCATION

Equivocation may be shown to have a number of interesting properties, most of which fit into our intuitive picture of how such a quantity should behave. We will first show that the equivocation of key or of a fixed part of a message decreases when more enciphered material is intercepted.

Theorem 7: The equivocation of key $H_E(K, N)$ is a non-increasing function of N. The equivocation of the first A letters of the message is a non-increasing function of the number N which have been intercepted. If N letters have been intercepted, the equivocation of the first N letters of message is less than or equal to that of the key. These may be written:

$$H_E(K, S) \leq H_E(K, N) \qquad S \geq N,$$
$$H_E(M, S) \leq H_E(M, N) \qquad S \geq N \ (H \text{ for first } A \text{ letters of text})$$
$$H_E(M, N) \leq H_E(K, N)$$

The qualification regarding A letters in the second result of the theorem is so that the equivocation will not be calculated with respect to the amount of message that has been intercepted. If it is, the message equivocation may (and usually does) increase for a time, due merely to the fact that more letters stand for a larger possible range of messages. The results of the theorem are what we might hope from a good secrecy index, since we would hardly expect to be worse off on the average after intercepting additional material than before. The fact that they can be proved gives further justification to our use of the equivocation measure.

The results of this theorem are a consequence of certain properties of conditional entropy proved in MTC. Thus, to show the first or second statements of Theorem 7, we have for any chance events A and B

$$H(B) \geq H_A(B).$$

If we identify B with the key (knowing the first S letters of cryptogram) and A with the remaining $N - S$ letters we obtain the first result. Similarly identifying B with the message gives the second result. The last result follows from

$$H_E(M) \leq H_E(K, M) = H_E(K) + H_{E,K}(M)$$

and the fact that $H_{E,K}(M) = 0$ since K and E uniquely determine M.

Since the message and key are chosen independently we have:

$$H(M, K) = H(M) + H(K).$$

Furthermore,

$$H(M, K) = H(E, K) = H(E) + H_E(K),$$

the first equality resulting from the fact that knowledge of M and K or of E and K is equivalent to knowledge of all three. Combining these two we obtain a formula for the equivocation of key:

$$H_E(K) = H(M) + H(K) - H(E).$$

In particular, if $H(M) = H(E)$ then the equivocation of key, $H_E(K)$, is equal to the *a priori* uncertainty of key, $H(K)$. This occurs in the perfect systems described above.

A formula for the equivocation of message can be found by similar means. We have:

$$H(M, E) = H(E) + H_E(M) = H(M) + H_M(E)$$
$$H_E(M) = H(M) + H_M(E) - H(E).$$

If we have a product system $S = TR$, it is to be expected that the second enciphering process will not decrease the equivocation of message. That this is actually true can be shown as follows: Let M, E_1, E_2 be the message and the first and second encipherments, respectively. Then

$$P_{E_1 E_2}(M) = P_{E_1}(M).$$

Consequently

$$H_{E_1 E_2}(M) = H_{E_1}(M).$$

Since, for any chance variables, x, y, z, $H_{xy}(z) \leq H_y(z)$, we have the desired result, $H_{E_2}(M) \geq H_{E_1}(M)$.

Theorem 8: The equivocation in message of a product system $S = TR$ is not less than that when only R is used.

Suppose now we have a system T which can be written as a weighted sum of several systems R, S, $\cdots$, U

$$T = p_1 R + P_2 S + \cdots + p_m U \qquad \sum p_i = 1$$

and that systems R, S, $\cdots$, U have equivocations H_1, H_2, H_3, $\cdots$, H_m.

Theorem 9: The equivocation H of a weighted sum of systems is bounded by the inequalities

$$\sum p_i H_i \leq H \leq \sum p_i H_i - \sum p_i \log p_i.$$

These are best limits possible. The H's may be equivocations either of key or message.

The upper limit is achieved, for example, in strongly ideal systems (to be described later) where the decomposition is into the simple transformations of the system. The lower limit is achieved if all the systems R, S, $\cdots$, U go to completely different cryptogram spaces. This theorem is also proved by the general inequalities governing equivocation,

$$H_A(B) \leq H(B) \leq H(A) + H_A(B).$$

We identify A with the particular system being used and B with the key or message.

There is a similar theorem for weighted sums of languages. For this we identify A with the particular language.

Theorem 10: Suppose a system can be applied to languages L_1, L_2, $\cdots$, L_m and has equivocation characteristics H_1, H_2, $\cdots$, H_m. When applied to the weighted sum $\sum p_i L_i$, the equivocation H is bounded by

$$\sum p_i H_i \leq H \leq \sum p_i H_i - \sum p_i \log p_i.$$

These limits are the best possible and the equivocations in question can be either for key or message.

The total redundancy D_N for N letters of message is defined by

$$D_N = \log G - H(M)$$

where G is the total number of messages of length N and $H(M)$ is the uncertainty in choosing one of these. In a secrecy system where the total number of possible cryptograms is equal to the number of possible messages of length N, $H(E) \leq \log G$. Consequently

$$H_E(K) = H(K) + H(M) - H(E)$$

$$\geq H(K) - [\log G - H(M)].$$

Hence

$$H(K) - H_E(K) \leq D_N.$$

This shows that, in a closed system, for example, the decrease in equivocation of key after N letters have been intercepted is not greater than the redundancy of N letters of the language. In such systems, which comprise the majority of ciphers, it is only the existence of redundancy in the original messages that makes a solution possible.

Now suppose we have a pure system. Let the different residue classes of messages be $C_1, C_2, C_3, \cdots, C_r$, and the corresponding set of residue classes of cryptograms be $C_1', C_2', \cdots, C_r'$. The probability of each E in C_i' is the same:

$$P(E) = \frac{P(C_i)}{\varphi_i} \qquad E \text{ a member of } C_i$$

where φ_i is the number of different messages in C_i. Thus we have

$$H(E) = -\sum_i \varphi_i \frac{P(C_i)}{\varphi_i} \log \frac{P(C_i)}{\varphi_i}$$

$$= -\sum P(C_i) \log \frac{P(C_i)}{\varphi_i}$$

Substituting in our equation for $H_E(K)$ we obtain:

Theorem 11: For a pure cipher

$$H_E(K) = H(K) + H(M) + \sum_i P(C_i) \log \frac{P(C_i)}{\varphi_i}.$$

This result can be used to compute $H_E(K)$ in certain cases of interest.

13. Equivocation for Simple Substitution on a Two Letter Language

We will now calculate the equivocation in key or message when simple substitution is applied to a two letter language, with probabilities p and q for 0 and 1, and successive letters chosen independently. We have

$$H_E(M) \;=\; H_E(K) \;=\; -\sum \; P(E)P_E(K) \log P_E(K)$$

The probability that E contains exactly s 0's in a particular permutation is:

$$\tfrac{1}{2}(p^s q^{N-s} + q^s p^{N-s})$$

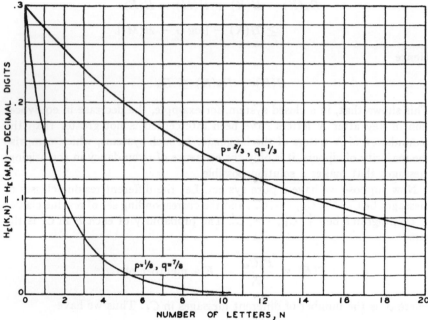

Fig. 6—Equivocation for simple substitution on two-letter language.

and the *a posteriori* probabilities of the identity and inverting substitutions (the only two in the system) are respectively:

$$P_E(0) \;=\; \frac{p^s q^{N-s}}{(p^s q^{N-s} + q^s p^{N-s})} \quad P_E(1) \;=\; \frac{p^{N-s} q^s}{(p^s q^{N-s} + q^s p^{N-s})} \,.$$

There are $\binom{N}{s}$ terms for each s and hence

$$H_E(K, N) \;=\; -\sum_s \binom{N}{s} p^s q^{N-s} \log \frac{p^s q^{N-s}}{(p^s q^{N-s} + q^s p^{N-s})} \,.$$

For $p = \frac{1}{3}$, $q = \frac{2}{3}$, and for $p = \frac{1}{8}$, $q = \frac{7}{8}$, $H_E(K, N)$ has been calculated and is shown in Fig. 6.

14. THE EQUIVOCATION CHARACTERISTIC FOR A "RANDOM" CIPHER

In the preceding section we have calculated the equivocation characteristic for a simple substitution applied to a two-letter language. This is about the simplest type of cipher and the simplest language structure possible, yet already the formulas are so involved as to be nearly useless. What are we to do with cases of practical interest, say the involved transformations of a fractional transposition system applied to English with its extremely complex statistical structure? This complexity itself suggests a method of approach. Sufficiently complicated problems can frequently be solved statistically. To facilitate this we define the notion of a "random" cipher.

We make the following assumptions:

1. The number of possible messages of length N is $T = 2^{R_0 N}$, thus $R_0 = \log_2 G$, where G is the number of letters in the alphabet. The number of possible cryptograms of length N is also assumed to be T.

2. The possible messages of length N can be divided into two groups: one group of high and fairly uniform a priori probability, the second group of negligibly small total probability. The high probability group will contain $S = 2^{RN}$ messages, where $R = H(M)/N$, that is, R is the entropy of the message source per letter.

3. The deciphering operation can be thought of as a series of lines, as in Figs. 2 and 4, leading back from each E to various M's. We assume k different equiprobable keys so there will be k lines leading back from each E. For the random cipher we suppose that the lines from each E go back to a random selection of the possible messages. Actually, then, a random cipher is a whole ensemble of ciphers and the equivocation is the average equivocation for this ensemble.

The equivocation of key is defined by

$$H_E(K) = \sum P(E) P_E(K) \log P_E(K).$$

The probability that exactly m lines go back from a particular E to the high probability group of messages is

$$\binom{k}{m} \left(\frac{S}{T} \right)^m \left(1 - \frac{S}{T} \right)^{k-m}$$

If a cryptogram with m such lines is intercepted the equivocation is $\log m$. The probability of such a cryptogram is $\frac{mT}{SK}$, since it can be produced by

m keys from high probability messages each with probability $\dfrac{T}{S}$. Hence the equivocation is:

$$H_E(K) = \frac{T}{Sk} \sum_{m=1}^{k} \binom{k}{m} \left(\frac{S}{T}\right)^m \left(1 - \frac{S}{T}\right)^{k-m} m \log m$$

We wish to find a simple approximation to this when k is large. If the expected value of m, namely $\overline{m} = Sk/T$, is $\gg 1$, the variation of $\log m$ over the range where the binomial distribution assumes large values will be small, and we can replace $\log m$ by $\log \overline{m}$. This can now be factored out of the summation, which then reduces to $\overline{m}$. Hence, in this condition,

$$H_E(K) \doteq \log \frac{Sk}{T} = \log S - \log T + \log k$$

$$H_E(K) \doteq H(K) - DN,$$

where D is the redundancy per letter of the original language ($D = D_N/N$).

If $\overline{m}$ is small compared to the large k, the binomial distribution can be approximated by a Poisson distribution:

$$\binom{k}{m} p^m q^{k-m} \doteq \frac{e^{-\lambda} \lambda^m}{m!}$$

where $\lambda = \dfrac{Sk}{T}$. Hence

$$H_E(K) \doteq \frac{1}{\lambda} e^{-\lambda} \sum_{2}^{\infty} \frac{\lambda^m}{m!} m \log m.$$

If we replace m by $m + 1$, we obtain:

$$H_E(K) \doteq e^{-\lambda} \sum_{1}^{\infty} \frac{\lambda^m}{m!} \log (m + 1).$$

This may be used in the region where λ is near unity. For $\lambda \ll 1$, the only important term in the series is that for $m = 1$; omitting the others we have:

$$\begin{aligned} H_E(K) &\doteq e^{-\lambda} \lambda \log 2 \\ &\doteq \lambda \log 2 \\ &\doteq 2^{-ND} k \log 2 . \end{aligned}$$

To summarize: $H_E(K)$, considered as a function of N, the number of intercepted letters, starts off at $H(K)$ when $N = 0$. It decreases linearly with a slope $-D$ out to the neighborhood of $N = \dfrac{H(K)}{D}$. After a short transition region, $H_E(K)$ follows an exponential with "half life" distance

$\frac{1}{D}$ if D is measured in bits per letter. This behavior is shown in Fig. 7, together with the approximating curves.

By a similar argument the equivocation of message can be calculated. It is

$$H_E(M) = R_0 N \text{ for } R_0 N \ll H_E(K)$$
$$H_E(M) = H_E(K) \text{ for } R_0 N \gg H_E(K)$$
$$H_E(M) = H_E(K) - \varphi(N) \text{ for } R_0 N \sim H_E(K)$$

where $\varphi(N)$ is the function shown in Fig. 7 with N scale reduced by factor of $\frac{D}{R_0}$. Thus, $H_E(M)$ rises linearly with slope R_0, until it nearly intersects

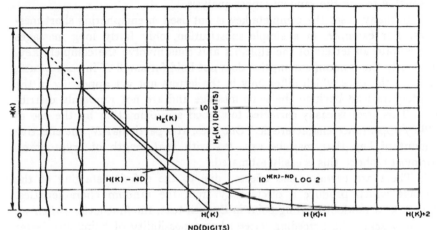

Fig. 7—Equivocation for random cipher.

the $H_E(K)$ line. After a rounded transition it follows the $H_E(K)$ curve down.

It will be seen from Fig. 7 that the equivocation curves approach zero rather sharply. Thus we may, with but little ambiguity, speak of a point at which the solution becomes unique. This number of letters will be called the unicity distance. For the random cipher it is approximately $H(K)/D$.

15. APPLICATION TO STANDARD CIPHERS

Most of the standard ciphers involve rather complicated enciphering and deciphering operations. Furthermore, the statistical structure of natural languages is extremely involved. It is therefore reasonable to assume that the formulas derived for the random cipher may be applied in such cases. It is necessary, however, to apply certain corrections in some cases. The main points to be observed are the following:

1. We assumed for the random cipher that the possible decipherments of a cryptogram are a random selection from the possible messages. While not strictly true in ordinary systems, this becomes more nearly the case as the complexity of the enciphering operations and of the language structure increases. With a transposition cipher it is clear that letter frequencies are preserved under decipherment operations. This means that the possible decipherments are chosen from a more limited group, not the entire message space, and the formula should be changed. In place of R_0 one uses R_1 the entropy rate for a language with independent letters but with the regular letter frequencies. In some other cases a definite tendency toward returning the decipherments to high probability messages can be seen. If there is no clear tendency of this sort, and the system is fairly complicated, then it is reasonable to use the random cipher analysis.

2. In many cases the complete key is not used in enciphering short messages. For example, in a simple substitution, only fairly long messages will contain all letters of the alphabet and thus involve the complete key. Obviously the random assumption does not hold for small N in such a case, since all the keys which differ only in the letters not yet appearing in the cryptogram lead back to the same message and are not randomly distributed. This error is easily corrected to a good approximation by the use of a "key appearance characteristic." One uses, at a particular N, the effective amount of key that may be expected with that length of cryptogram. For most ciphers, this is easily estimated.

3. There are certain "end effects" due to the definite starting of the message which produce a discrepancy from the random characteristics. If we take a random starting point in English text, the first letter (when we do not observe the preceding letters) has a possibility of being any letter with the ordinary letter probabilities. The next letter is more completely specified since we then have digram frequencies. This decrease in choice value continues for some time. The effect of this on the curve is that the straight line part is displaced, and approached by a curve depending on how much the statistical structure of the language is spread out over adjacent letters. As a first approximation the curve can be corrected by shifting the line over to the half redundancy point—i.e., the number of letters where the language redundancy is half its final value.

If account is taken of these three effects, reasonable estimates of the equivocation characteristic and unicity point can be made. The calculation can be done graphically as indicated in Fig. 8. One draws the key appearance characteristic and the total redundancy curve D_N (which is usually sufficiently well represented by the line ND_∞). The difference between these out to the neighborhood of their intersection is $H_E(M)$. With a simple substitution cipher applied to English, this calculation gave the curves shown in Fig. 9. The key appearance characteristic in this case was estimated by counting the number of different letters appearing in typical English passages of N letters. In so far as experimental data on the simple substitution could be found, they agree very well with the curves of Fig. 9, considering the various idealizations and approximations which have been made. For example, the unicity point, at about 27 letters, can be shown experimentally to lie between the limits 20 and 30. With 30 letters there is

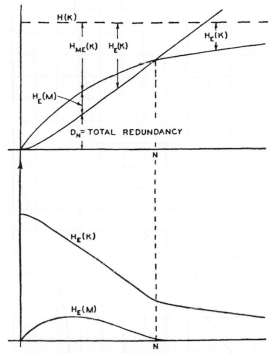

Fig. 8—Graphical calculation of equivocation.

nearly always a unique solution to a cryptogram of this type and with 20 it is usually easy to find a number of solutions.

With transposition of period d (random key), $H(K) = \log d!$, or about $d \log d/e$ (using a Stirling approximation for $d!$). If we take .6 decimal digits per letter as the appropriate redundancy, remembering the preservation of letter frequencies, we obtain about $1.7d \log d/e$ as the unicity distance This also checks fairly well experimentally. Note that in this case $H_E(M)$. is defined only for integral multiples of d.

With the Vigenère the unicity point will occur at about $2d$ letters, and this too is about right. The Vigenère characteristic with the same key size

C. E. Shannon

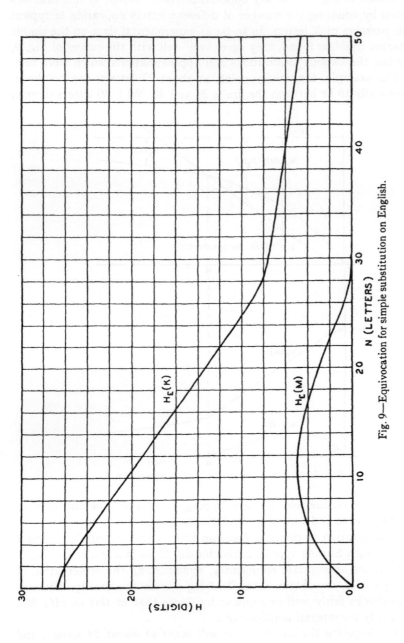

Fig. 9—Equivocation for simple substitution on English.

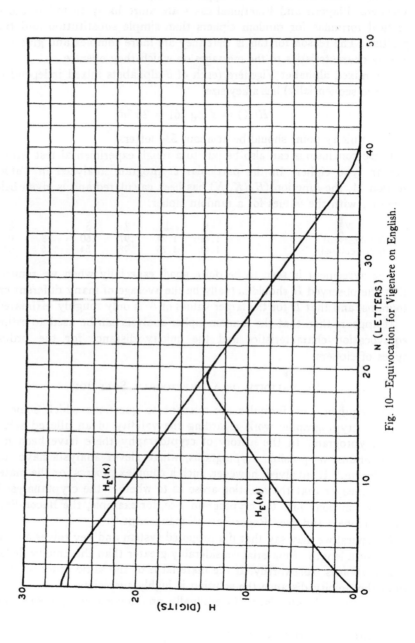

Fig. 10—Equivocation for Vigenère on English.

as simple substitution will be approximately as shown in Fig. 10. The Vigenère, Playfair and Fractional cases are more likely to follow the theoretical formulas for random ciphers than simple substitution and transposition. The reason for this is that they are more complex and give better mixing characteristics to the messages on which they operate.

The mixed alphabet Vigenère (each of d alphabets mixed independently and used sequentially) has a key size,

$$H(K) = d \log 26! = 26.3d$$

and its unicity point should be at about $53d$ letters.

These conclusions can also be put to a rough experimental test with the Caesar type cipher. In the particular cryptogram analyzed in Table I, section 11, the function $(H_E(K, N)$ has been calculated and is given below, together with the values for a random cipher.

N	0	1	2	3	4	5
H (observed)	1.41	1.24	.97	.60	.28	0
H (calculated)	1.41	1.25	.98	.54	.15	.03

The agreement is seen to be quite good, especially when we remember that the observed H should actually be the average of many different cryptograms, and that D for the larger values of N is only roughly estimated.

It appears then that the random cipher analysis can be used to estimate equivocation characteristics and the unicity distance for the ordinary types of ciphers.

16. Validity of a Cryptogram Solution

The equivocation formulas are relevant to questions which sometimes arise in cryptographic work regarding the validity of an alleged solution to a cryptogram. In the history of cryptography there have been many cryptograms, or possible cryptograms, where clever analysts have found a "solution." It involved, however, such a complex process, or the material was so meager that the question arose as to whether the cryptanalyst had "read a solution" into the cryptogram. See, for example, the Bacon-Shakespeare ciphers and the "Roger Bacon" manuscript.[10]

In general we may say that if a proposed system and key solves a cryptogram for a length of material considerably greater than the unicity distance the solution is trustworthy. If the material is of the same order or shorter than the unicity distance the solution is highly suspicious.

This effect of redundancy in gradually producing a unique solution to a cipher can be thought of in another way which is helpful. The redundancy is essentially a series of conditions on the letters of the message, which

[10] See Fletcher Pratt, *loc. cit.*

insure that it be statistically reasonable. These consistency conditions produce corresponding consistency conditions in the cryptogram. The key gives a certain amount of freedom to the cryptogram but, as more and more letters are intercepted, the consistency conditions use up the freedom allowed by the key. Eventually there is only one message and key which satisfies all the conditions and we have a unique solution. In the random cipher the consistency conditions are, in a sense "orthogonal" to the "grain of the key" and have their full effect in eliminating messages and keys as rapidly as possible. This is the usual case. However, by proper design it is possible to "line up" the redundancy of the language with the "grain of the key" in such a way that the consistency conditions are automatically satisfied and $H_E(K)$ does not approach zero. These "ideal" systems, which will be considered in the next section, are of such a nature that the transformations T_i all induce the same probabilities in the E space.

17. Ideal Secrecy Systems.

We have seen that perfect secrecy requires an infinite amount of key if we allow messages of unlimited length. With a finite key size, the equivocation of key and message generally approaches zero, but not necessarily so. In fact it is possible for $H_E(K)$ to remain constant at its initial value $H(K)$. Then, no matter how much material is intercepted, there is not a unique solution but many of comparable probability. We will define an "ideal" system as one in which $H_E(K)$ and $H_E(M)$ do not approach zero as $N \to \infty$. A "strongly ideal" system is one in which $H_E(K)$ remains constant at $H(K)$. .

An example is a simple substitution on an artificial language in which all letters are equiprobable and successive letters independently chosen. It is easily seen that $H_E(K) = H(K)$ and $H_E(M)$ rises linearly along a line of slope $\log G$ (where G is the number of letters in the alphabet) until it strikes the line $H(K)$, after which it remains constant at this value.

With natural languages it is in general possible to approximate the ideal characteristic—the unicity point can be made to occur for as large N as is desired. The complexity of the system needed usually goes up rapidly when we attempt to do this, however. It is not always possible to attain actually the ideal characteristic with any system of finite complexity.

To approximate the ideal equivocation, one may first operate on the message with a transducer which removes all redundancies. After this almost any simple ciphering system—substitution, transposition, Vigenère, etc., is satisfactory. The more elaborate the transducer and the nearer the output is to the desired form, the more closely will the secrecy system approximate the ideal characteristic.

Theorem 12: A necessary and sufficient condition that T be strongly ideal is that, for any two keys, $T_i^{-1}T_j$ is a measure preserving transformation of the message space into itself.

This is true since the *a posteriori* probability of each key is equal to its *a priori* probability if and only if this condition is satisfied.

18. EXAMPLES OF IDEAL SECRECY SYSTEMS

Suppose our language consists of a sequence of letters all chosen independently and with equal probabilities. Then the redundancy is zero, and from a result of section 12, $H_E(K) = H(K)$. We obtain the result

Theorem 13: If all letters are equally likely and independent any closed cipher is strongly ideal.

The equivocation of message will rise along the key appearance characteristic which will usually approach $H(K)$, although in some cases it does not. In the cases of *n*-gram substitution, transposition, Vigenère, and variations, fractional, etc., we have strongly ideal systems for this simple language with $H_E(M) \rightarrow H(K)$ as $N \rightarrow \infty$.

Ideal secrecy systems suffer from a number of disadvantages.

1. The system must be closely matched to the language. This requires an extensive study of the structure of the language by the designer. Also a change in statistical structure or a selection from the set of possible messages, as in the case of probable words (words expected in this particular cryptogram), renders the system vulnerable to analysis.

2. The structure of natural languages is extremely complicated, and this implies a complexity of the transformations required to eliminate redundancy. Thus any machine to perform this operation must necessarily be quite involved, at least in the direction of information storage, since a "dictionary" of magnitude greater than that of an ordinary dictionary is to be expected.

3. In general, the transformations required introduce a bad propagation of error characteristic. Error in transmission of a single letter produces a region of changes near it of size comparable to the length of statistical effects in the original language.

19. FURTHER REMARKS ON EQUIVOCATION AND REDUNDANCY

We have taken the redundancy of "normal English" to be about .7 decimal digits per letter or a redundancy of 50%. This is on the assumption that word divisions were omitted. It is an approximate figure based on statistical structure extending over about 8 letters, and assumes the text to be of an ordinary type, such as newspaper writing, literary work, etc. We may note here a method of roughly estimating this number that is of some cryptographic interest.

A running key cipher is a Vernam type system where, in place of a random sequence of letters, the key is a meaningful text. Now it is known that running key ciphers can usually be solved uniquely. This shows that English can be reduced by a factor of two to one and implies a redundancy of at least 50%. This figure cannot be increased very much, however, for a number of reasons, unless long range "meaning" structure of English is considered.

The running key cipher can be easily improved to lead to ciphering systems which could not be solved without the key. If one uses in place of one English text, about 4 different texts as key, adding them all to the message, a sufficient amount of key has been introduced to produce a high positive equivocation. Another method would be to use, say, every 10th letter of the text as key. The intermediate letters are omitted and cannot be used at any other point of the message. This has much the same effect, since these spaced letters are nearly independent.

The fact that the vowels in a passage can be omitted without essential loss suggests a simple way of greatly improving almost any ciphering system. First delete all vowels, or as much of the message as possible without running the risk of multiple reconstructions, and then encipher the residue. Since this reduces the redundancy by a factor of perhaps 3 or 4 to 1, the unicity point will be moved out by this factor. This is one way of approaching ideal systems—using the decipherer's knowledge of English as part of the deciphering system.

20. Distribution of Equivocation

A more complete description of a secrecy system applied to a language than is afforded by the equivocation characteristics can be found by giving the *distribution of equivocation*. For N intercepted letters we consider the fraction of cryptograms for which the equivocation (for these particular E's, not the mean $H_E(M)$) lies between certain limits. This gives a density distribution function

$$P(H_E(M), N)\ dH_E(M)$$

for the probability that for N letters H lies between the limits H and $H + dH$. The mean equivocation we have previously studied is the mean of this distribution. The function $P(H_E(M), N)$ can be thought of as plotted along a third dimension, normal to the paper, on the $H_E(M)$, N plane. If the language is pure, with a small influence range, and the cipher is pure, the function will usually be a ridge in this plane whose highest point follows approximately the mean $H_E(M)$, at least until near the unicity point. In this case, or when the conditions are nearly verified, the mean curve gives a reasonably complete picture of the system.

On the other hand, if the language is not pure, but made up of a set of pure components

$$L = \sum p_i L_i$$

having different equivocation curves with the system, then the total distribution will usually be made up of a series of ridges. There will be one for each L_i weighted in accordance with its p_i. The mean equivocation characteristic will be a line somewhere in the midst of these ridges and may not give a very complete picture of the situation. This is shown in Fig. 11. A similar effect occurs if the system is not pure but made up of several systems with different H curves.

The effect of mixing pure languages which are near to one another in statistical structure is to increase the width of the ridge. Near the unicity

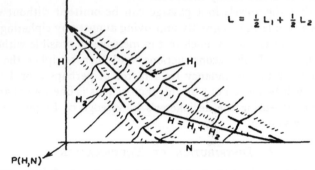

Fig. 11—Distribution of equivocation with a mixed language $L = \frac{1}{2}L_1 + \frac{1}{2}L_2$.

point this tends to raise the mean equivocation, since equivocation cannot become negative and the spreading is chiefly in the positive direction. We expect, therefore, that in this region the calculations based on the random cipher should be somewhat low.

PART III

PRACTICAL SECRECY

21. The Work Characteristic

After the unicity point has been passed in intercepted material there will usually be a unique solution to the cryptogram. The problem of isolating this single solution of high probability is the problem of cryptanalysis. In the region before the unicity point we may say that the problem of cryptanalysis is that of isolating all the possible solutions of high probability (compared to the remainder) and determining their various probabilities.

Although it is always possible in principle to determine these solutions (by trial of each possible key for example), different enciphering systems show a wide variation in the amount of work required. The average amount of work to determine the key for a cryptogram of N letters, $W(N)$, measured say in man hours, may be called the work characteristic of the system. This average is taken over all messages and all keys with their appropriate probabilities. The function $W(N)$ is a measure of the amount of "practical secrecy" afforded by the system.

For a simple substitution on English the work and equivocation characteristics would be somewhat as shown in Fig. 12. The dotted portion of

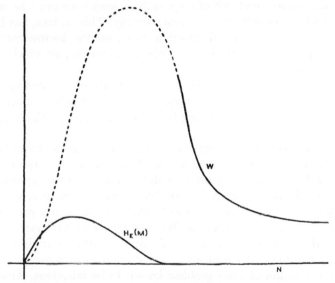

Fig. 12—Typical work and equivocation characteristics.

the curve is in the range where there are numerous possible solutions and these must all be determined. In the solid portion after the unicity point only one solution exists in general, but if only the minimum necessary data are given a great deal of work must be done to isolate it. As more material is available the work rapidly decreases toward some asymptotic value— where the additional data no longer reduces the labor.

Essentially the behavior shown in Fig. 12 can be expected with any type of secrecy system where the equivocation approaches zero. The scale of man hours required, however, will differ greatly with different types of ciphers, even when the $H_E(M)$ curves are about the same. A Vigenère or compound Vigenère, for example, with the same key size would have a much better (i.e., much higher) work characteristic. A good practical secrecy system is one in which the $W(N)$ curve remains sufficiently high, out to the number of letters one expects to transmit with the key, to prevent the enemy from actually carrying out the solution, or to delay it to such an extent that the information is then obsolete.

We will consider in the following sections ways of keeping the function $W(N)$ large, even though $H_E(K)$ may be practically zero. This is essentially a "max min" type of problem as is always the case when we have a battle of wits.[11] In designing a good cipher we must maximize the minimum amount of work the enemy must do to break it. It is not enough merely to be sure none of the standard methods of cryptanalysis work—we must be sure that no method whatever will break the system easily. This, in fact, has been the weakness of many systems; designed to resist all the known methods of solution, they later gave rise to new cryptanalytic techniques which rendered them vulnerable to analysis.

The problem of good cipher design is essentially one of finding difficult problems, subject to certain other conditions. This is a rather unusual situation, since one is ordinarily seeking the simple and easily soluble problems in a field.

How can we ever be sure that a system which is not ideal and therefore *has* a unique solution for sufficiently large N will require a large amount of work to break with *every* method of analysis? There are two approaches to this problem; (1) We can study the possible methods of solution available to the cryptanalyst and attempt to describe them in sufficiently general terms to cover any methods he might use. We then construct our system to resist this "general" method of solution. (2) We may construct our cipher in such a way that breaking it is equivalent to (or requires at some point in the process) the solution of some problem known to be laborious. Thus, if we could show that solving a certain system requires at least as much work as solving a system of simultaneous equations in a large number of unknowns, of a complex type, then we would have a lower bound of sorts for the work characteristic.

The next three sections are aimed at these general problems. It is difficult to define the pertinent ideas involved with sufficient precision to obtain results in the form of mathematical theorems, but it is believed that the conclusions, in the form of general principles, are correct.

[11] See von Neumann and Morgenstern, *loc. cit.* The situation between the cipher designer and cryptanalyst can be thought of as a "game" of a very simple structure; a zero-sum two-person game with complete information, and just two "moves." The cipher designer chooses a system for his "move." Then the cryptanalyst is informed of this choice and chooses a method of analysis. The "value" of the play is the average work required to break a cryptogram in the system by the method chosen.

22. GENERALITIES ON THE SOLUTION OF CRYPTOGRAMS

After the unicity distance has been exceeded in intercepted material, any system can be solved in principle by merely trying each possible key until the unique solution is obtained—i.e., a deciphered message which "makes sense" in the original language. A simple calculation shows that this method of solution (which we may call *complete trial and error*) is totally impractical except when the key is absurdly small.

Suppose, for example, we have a key of 26! possibilities or about 26.3 decimal digits, the same size as in simple substitution on English. This is, by any significant measure, a small key. It can be written on a small slip of paper, or memorized in a few minutes. It could be registered on 27 switches, each having ten positions, or on 88 two-position switches.

Suppose further, to give the cryptanalyst every possible advantage, that he constructs an electronic device to try keys at the rate of one each microsecond (perhaps automatically selecting from the results by a χ^2 test for statistical significance). He may expect to reach the right key about half way through, and after an elapsed time of about $2 \times 10^{26}/2 \times 60^2 \times 24 \times 365 \times 10^6$ or 3×10^{12} years.

In other words, even with a small key complete trial and error will never be used in solving cryptograms, except in the trivial case where the key is extremely small, e.g., the Caesar with only 26 possibilities, or 1.4 digits. The trial and error which is used so commonly in cryptography is of a different sort, or is augmented by other means. If one had a secrecy system which required complete trial and error it would be extremely safe. Such a system would result, it appears, if the meaningful original messages, all say of 1000 letters, were a random selection from the set of all sequences of 1000 letters. If any of the simple ciphers were applied to this type of language it seems that little improvement over complete trial and error would be possible.

The methods of cryptanalysis actually used often involve a great deal of trial and error, but in a different way. First, the trials progress from more probable to less probable hypotheses, and, second, each trial disposes of a large group of keys, not a single one. Thus the key space may be divided into say 10 subsets, each containing about the same number of keys. By at most 10 trials one determines which subset is the correct one. This subset is then divided into several secondary subsets and the process repeated. With the same key size ($26! \doteq 2 \times 10^{26}$) we would expect about 26×5 or 130 trials as compared to 10^{26} by complete trial and error. The possibility of choosing the most likely of the subsets first for test would improve this result even more. If the divisions were into two compartments (the best way to minimize the number of trials) only 88 trials would be required. Whereas complete trial and error requires trials to the order of the number of keys, this subdividing trial and error requires only trials to the order of the key size in bits.

This remains true even when the different keys have different probabilities. The proper procedure, then, to minimize the expected number of trials is to divide the key space into subsets of equiprobability. When the proper subset is determined, this is again subdivided into equiprobability subsets. If this process can be continued the number of trials expected when each division is into two subsets will be

$$h = \frac{H(K)}{\log 2}$$

If each test has S possible results and each of these corresponds to the key being in one of S equiprobability subsets, then

$$h = \frac{H(K)}{\log S}$$

trials will be expected. The intuitive significance of these results should be noted. In the two-compartment test with equiprobability, each test yields one bit of information as to the key. If the subsets have very different probabilities, as in testing a single key in complete trial and error, only a small amount of information is obtained from the test. Thus with 26! equiprobable keys, a test of one yields only

$$-\left[\frac{26! - 1}{26!} \log \frac{26! - 1}{26!} + \frac{1}{26!} \log \frac{1}{26!} \right]$$

or about 10^{-25} bits of information. Dividing into S equiprobability subsets maximizes the information obtained from each trial at $\log S$, and the expected number of trials is the total information to be obtained, that is $H(K)$, divided by this amount.

The question here is similar to various coin weighing problems that have been circulated recently. A typical example is the following: It is known that one coin in 27 is counterfeit, and slightly lighter than the rest. A chemist's balance is available and the counterfeit coin is to be isolated by a series of weighings. What is the least number of weighings required to do this? The correct answer is 3, obtained by first dividing the coins into three groups of 9 each. Two of these are compared on the balance. The three possible results determine the set of 9 containing the counterfeit. This set is then divided into 3 subsets of 3 each and the process continued. The set of coins corresponds to the set of keys, the counterfeit coin to the correct key, and the weighing procedure to a trial or test. The original uncertainty is $\log_2 27$

bits, and each trial yields $\log_2 3$ bits of information; thus, when there is no "diophantine trouble," $\log_2 27/\log_2 3$ or 3 trials are sufficient.

This method of solution is feasible only if the key space can be divided into a small number of subsets, with a simple method of determining the subset to which the correct key belongs. One does not need to assume a complete key in order to apply a consistency test and determine if the assumption is justified—an assumption on a part of the key (or as to whether the key is in some large section of the key space) can be tested. In other words it is possible to solve for the key bit by bit.

The possibility of this method of analysis is the crucial weakness of most ciphering systems. For example, in simple substitution, an assumption on a single letter can be checked against its frequency, variety of contact, doubles or reversals, etc. In determining a single letter the key space is reduced by 1.4 decimal digits from the original 26. The same effect is seen in all the elementary types of ciphers. In the Vigenère, the assumption of two or three letters of the key is easily checked by deciphering at other points with this fragment and noting whether clear emerges. The compound Vigenère is much better from this point of view, if we assume a fairly large number of component periods, producing a repetition rate larger than will be intercepted. In this case as many key letters are used in enciphering each letter as there are periods. Although this is only a fraction of the entire key, at least a fair number of letters must be assumed before a consistency check can be applied.

Our first conclusion then, regarding practical small key cipher design, is that a considerable amount of key should be used in enciphering each small element of the message.

23. Statistical Methods

It is possible to solve many kinds of ciphers by statistical analysis. Consider again simple substitution. The first thing a cryptanalyst does with an intercepted cryptogram is to make a frequency count. If the cryptogram contains, say, 200 letters it is safe to assume that few, if any, of the letters are out of their frequency groups, this being a division into 4 sets of well defined frequency limits. The logarithm of the number of keys within this limitation may be calculated as

$$\log 2! \, 9! \, 9! \, 6! = 14.28$$

and the simple frequency count thus reduces the key uncertainty by 12 decimal digits, a tremendous gain.

In general, a statistical attack proceeds as follows: A certain statistic is measured on the intercepted cryptogram E. This statistic is such that for all reasonable messages M it assumes about the same value, S_K, the value depending only on the particular key K that was used. The value thus obtained serves to limit the possible keys to those which would give values of S in the neighborhood of that observed. A statistic which does not depend on K or which varies as much with M as with K is not of value in limiting K. Thus, in transposition ciphers, the frequency count of letters gives no information about K—every K leaves this statistic the same. Hence one can make no use of a frequency count in breaking transposition ciphers.

More precisely one can ascribe a *"solving power"* to a given statistic S. For each value of S there will be a conditional equivocation of the key $H_S(K)$, the equivocation when S has its particular value, and that is all that is known concerning the key. The weighted mean of these values

$$\sum P(S) \quad H_S(K)$$

gives the mean equivocation of the key when S is known, $P(S)$ being the *a priori* probability of the particular value S. The key size $H(K)$, less this mean equivocation, measures the "solving power" of the statistic S.

In a strongly ideal cipher *all* statistics of the cryptogram are independent of the particular key used. This is the measure preserving property of $T_j T_k^{-1}$ on the E space or $T_j^{-1} T_k$ on the M space mentioned above.

There are good and poor statistics, just as there are good and poor methods of trial and error. Indeed the trial and error testing of an hypothesis *is* is a type of statistic, and what was said above regarding the best types of trials holds generally. A good statistic for solving a system must have the following properties:

1. It must be simple to measure.
2. It must depend more on the key than on the message if it is meant to solve for the key. The variation with M should not mask its variation with K.
3. The values of the statistic that can be "resolved" in spite of the "fuzziness" produced by variation in M should divide the key space into a number of subsets of comparable probability, with the statistic specifying the one in which the correct key lies. The statistic should give us sizeable information about the key, not a tiny fraction of a bit.
4. The information it gives must be simple and usable. Thus the subsets in which the statistic locates the key must be of a simple nature in the key space.

Frequency count for simple substitution is an example of a very good statistic.

Two methods (other than recourse to ideal systems) suggest themselves for frustrating a statistical analysis. These we may call the methods of *diffusion* and *confusion*. In the method of diffusion the statistical structure of M which leads to its redundancy is "dissipated" into long range statistics—i.e., into statistical structure involving long combinations of letters in the cryptogram. The effect here is that the enemy must intercept a tremendous amount of material to tie down this structure, since the structure is evident only in blocks of very small individual probability. Furthermore, even when he has sufficient material, the analytical work required is much greater since the redundancy has been diffused over a large number of individual statistics. An example of diffusion of statistics is operating on a message $M = m_1, m_2, m_3, \cdots$ with an "averaging" operation, e.g.

$$y_n = \sum_{i=1}^{s} m_{n+i} \ (\text{mod } 26),$$

adding s successive letters of the message to get a letter y_n. One can show that the redundacy of the y sequence is the same as that of the m sequence, but the structure has been dissipated. Thus the letter frequencies in y will be more nearly equal than in m, the digram frequencies also more nearly equal, etc. Indeed any reversible operation which produces one letter out for each letter in and does not have an infinite "memory" has an output with the same redundancy as the input. The statistics can never be eliminated without compression, but they can be spread out.

The method of *confusion* is to make the relation between the simple statistics of E and the simple description of K a very complex and involved one. In the case of simple substitution, it is easy to describe the limitation of K imposed by the letter frequencies of E. If the connection is very involved and confused the enemy may still be able to evaluate a statistic S_1, say, which limits the key to a region of the key space. This limitation, however, is to some complex region R in the space, perhaps "folded over" many times, and he has a difficult time making use of it. A second statistic S_2 limits K still further to R_2, hence it lies in the intersection region; but this does not help much because it is so difficult to determine just what the intersection is.

To be more precise let us suppose the key space has certain "natural coordinates" $k_1, k_2, \cdots, k_p$ which he wishes to determine. He measures, let us say, a set of statistics $s_1, s_2, \cdots, s_n$ and these are sufficient to determine the k_i. However, in the method of confusion, the equations connecting these sets of variables are involved and complex. We have, say,

$$f_1(k_1, k_2, \cdots, k_p) = s_1$$
$$f_2(k_1, k_2, \cdots, k_p) = s_2$$
$$\cdot$$
$$\cdot$$
$$\cdot$$
$$f_n(k_1, k_2, \cdots, k_p) = s_n,$$

and all the f_i involve all the k_i. The cryptographer must solve this system simultaneously—a difficult job. In the simple (not confused) cases the functions involve only a small number of the k_i—or at least some of these do. One first solves the simpler equations, evaluating some of the k_i and substitutes these in the more complicated equations.

The conclusion here is that for a good ciphering system steps should be taken either to diffuse or confuse the redundancy (or both).

24. THE PROBABLE WORD METHOD

One of the most powerful tools for breaking ciphers is the use of probable words. The probable words may be words or phrases expected in the particular message due to its source, or they may merely be common words or syllables which occur in any text in the language, such as *the, and, tion, that,* and the like in English.

In general, the probable word method is used as follows: Assuming a probable word to be at some point in the clear, the key or a part of the key is determined. This is used to decipher other parts of the cryptogram and provide a consistency test. If the other parts come out in the clear, the assumption is justified.

There are few of the classical type ciphers that use a small key and can resist long under a probable word analysis. From a consideration of this method we can frame a test of ciphers which might be called the acid test. It applies only to ciphers with a small key (less than, say, 50 decimal digits), applied to natural languages, and not using the ideal method of gaining secrecy. The acid test is this: How difficult is it to determine the key or a part of the key knowing a small sample of message and corresponding cryptogram? Any system in which this is easy cannot be very resistant, for the cryptanalyst can always make use of probable words, combined with trial and error, until a consistent solution is obtained.

The conditions on the size of the key make the amount of trial and error small, and the condition about ideal systems is necessary, since these automatically give consistency checks. The existence of probable words and phrases is implied by the assumption of natural languages.

Note that the requirement of difficult solution under these conditions is not, by itself, contradictory to the requirements that enciphering and deciphering be simple processes. Using functional notation we have for enciphering

$$E = f(K, M)$$

and for deciphering

$$M = g(K, E).$$

Both of these may be simple operations on their arguments without the third equation

$$K = h(M, E)$$

being simple.

We may also point out that in investigating a new type of ciphering system one of the best methods of attack is to consider how the key could be determined if a sufficient amount of M and E were given.

The principle of confusion can be (and must be) used to create difficulties for the cryptanalyst using probable word techniques. Given (or assuming) $M = m_1, m_2, \cdots, m_s$ and $E = e_1, e_2, \cdots, e_s$ the cryptanalyst can set up equations for the different key elements $k_1, k_2, \cdots, k_r$ (namely the enciphering equations).

$$e_1 = f_1(m_1, m_2, \cdots, m_s ; k_1, \cdots, k_r)$$
$$e_2 = f_2(m_1, m_2, \cdots, m_s ; k_1, \cdots, k_r)$$
$$\cdot$$
$$\cdot$$
$$\cdot$$
$$\cdot$$
$$e_s = f_s(m_1, m_2, \cdots, m_s ; k_1, \cdots, k_r)$$

All is known, we assume, except the k_i. Each of these equations should therefore be complex in the k_i, and involve many of them. Otherwise the enemy can solve the simple ones and then the more complex ones by substitution.

From the point of view of increasing confusion, it is desirable to have the f_i involve several m_i, especially if these are not adjacent and hence less correlated. This introduces the undesirable feature of error propagation, however, for then each e_i will generally affect several m_i in deciphering, and an error will spread to all these.

We conclude that much of the key should be used in an involved manner in obtaining any cryptogram letter from the message to keep the work characteristic high. Further a dependence on several uncorrelated m_i is desirable, if some propagation of error can be tolerated. We are led by all three of the arguments of these sections to consider "mixing transformations."

25. Mixing Transformations

A notion that has proved valuable in certain branches of probability theory is the concept of a *mixing transformation*. Suppose we have a probability or measure space Ω and a measure preserving transformation F of the space into itself, that is, a transformation such that the measure of a transformed region FR is equal to the measure of the initial region R. The transformation is called mixing if for any function defined over the space and any region R the integral of the function over the region F^nR approaches, as $n \to \infty$, the integral of the function over the entire space Ω multiplied by the volume of R. This means that any initial region R is mixed with uniform density throughout the entire space if F is applied a large number of times. In general, F^nR becomes a region consisting of a large number of thin filaments spread throughout Ω. As n increases the filaments become finer and their density more constant.

A mixing transformation in this precise sense can occur only in a space with an infinite number of points, for in a finite point space the transformation must be periodic. Speaking loosely, however, we can think of a mixing transformation as one which distributes any reasonably cohesive region in the space fairly uniformly over the entire space. If the first region could be described in simple terms, the second would require very complex ones.

In cryptography we can think of all the possible messages of length N as the space Ω and the high probability messages as the region R. This latter group has a certain fairly simple statistical structure. If a mixing transformation were applied, the high probability messages would be scattered evenly throughout the space.

Good mixing transformations are often formed by repeated products of two simple non-commuting operations. Hopf[12] has shown, for example, that pastry dough can be mixed by such a sequence of operations. The dough is first rolled out into a thin slab, then folded over, then rolled, and then folded again, etc.

In a good mixing transformation of a space with natural coordinates X_1, X_2, $\cdots$, X_S the point X_i is carried by the transformation into a point X_i', with

$$X_i' = f_1(X_1, X_2, \cdots, X_S) \quad i = 1, 2, \cdots, S$$

and the functions f_i are complicated, involving all the variables in a "sensitive" way. A small variation of any one, X_3, say, changes all the X_i' considerably. If X_3 passes through its range of possible variation the point X_i' traces a long winding path around the space.

Various methods of mixing applicable to statistical sequences of the type found in natural languages can be devised. One which looks fairly good is to follow a preliminary transposition by a sequence of alternating substitutions and simple linear operations, adding adjacent letters mod 26 for example. Thus we might take

[12] E. Hopf, "On Causality, Statistics and Probability," *Journal of Math. and Physics.* v. 13, pp. 51-102, 1934.

$$F = LSLSLT$$

where T is a transposition, L is a linear operation, and S is a substitution.

26. Ciphers of the Type $T_k F S_j$

Suppose that F is a good mixing transformation that can be applied to sequences of letters, and that T_k and S_j are any two simple families of transformations, i.e., two simple ciphers, which may be the same. For concreteness we may think of them as both simple substitutions.

It appears that the cipher TFS will be a very good secrecy system from the standpoint of its work characteristic. In the first place it is clear on reviewing our arguments about statistical methods that no simple statistics will give information about the key—any significant statistics derived from E must be of a highly involved and very sensitive type—the redundancy has been both diffused and confused by the mixing transformation F. Also probable words lead to a complex system of equations involving all parts of the key (when the mix is good), which must be solved simultaneously.

It is interesting to note that if the cipher T is omitted the remaining system is similar to S and thus no stronger. The enemy merely "unmixes" the cryptogram by application of F^{-1} and then solves. If S is omitted the remaining system is much stronger than T alone when the mix is good, but still not comparable to TFS.

The basic principle here of simple ciphers separated by a mixing transformation can of course be extended. For example one could use

$$T_k F_1 S_j F_2 R_i$$

with two mixes and three simple ciphers. One can also simplify by using the same ciphers, and even the same keys as well as the same mixing transformations. This might well simplify the mechanization of such systems.

The mixing transformation which separates the two (or more) appearances of the key acts as a kind of barrier for the enemy—it is easy to carry a known element over this barrier but an unknown (the key) does not go easily.

By supplying two sets of unknowns, the key for S and the key for T, and separating them by the mixing transformation F we have "entangled" the unknowns together in a way that makes solution very difficult.

Although systems constructed on this principle would be extremely safe they possess one grave disadvantage. If the mix is good then the propagation of errors is bad. A transmission error of one letter will affect several letters on deciphering.

27. Incompatibility of the Criteria for Good Systems

The five criteria for good secrecy systems given in section 5 appear to have a certain incompatibility when applied to a natural language with its complicated statistical structure. With artificial languages having a simple statistical structure it is possible to satisfy all requirements simultaneously, by means of the ideal type ciphers. In natural languages a compromise must be made and the valuations balanced against one another with a view toward the particular application.

If any one of the five criteria is dropped, the other four can be satisfied fairly well, as the following examples show:

1. If we omit the first requirement (amount of secrecy) any simple cipher such as simple substitution will do. In the extreme case of omitting this condition completely, no cipher at all is required and one sends the clear!
2. If the size of the key is not limited the Vernam system can be used.
3. If complexity of operation is not limited, various extremely complicated types of enciphering process can be used.
4. If we omit the propagation of error condition, systems of the type *TFS* would be very good, although somewhat complicated.
5. If we allow large expansion of message, various systems are easily devised where the "correct" message is mixed with many "incorrect" ones (misinformation). The key determines which of these is correct.

A very rough argument for the incompatibility of the five conditions may be given as follows: From condition 5, secrecy systems essentially as studied in this paper must be used; i.e., no great use of nulls, etc. Perfect and ideal systems are excluded by condition 2 and by 3 and 4, respectively. The high secrecy required by 1 must then come from a high work characteristic, not from a high equivocation characteristic. If the key is small, the system simple, and the errors do not propagate, probable word methods will generally solve the system fairly easily, since we then have a fairly simple system of equations for the key.

This reasoning is too vague to be conclusive, but the general idea seems quite reasonable. Perhaps if the various criteria could be given quantitative significance, some sort of an exchange equation could be found involving them and giving the best physically compatible sets of values. The two most difficult to measure numerically are the complexity of operations, and the complexity of statistical structure of the language.

APPENDIX

Proof of Theorem 3

Select any message M_1 and group together all cryptograms that can be obtained from M_1 by any enciphering operation T_i. Let this class of cryptograms be C_1'. Group with M_1 all messages that can be obtained from M_1 by $T_i^{-1}T_jM_1$, and call this class C_1. The same C_1' would be obtained if we started with any other M in C_1 since

$$T_sT_i^{-1}T_iM_1 = T_lM_1.$$

Similarly the same C_1 would be obtained.

Choosing an M not in C_1 (if any such exist) we construct C_2 and C_2' in the same way. Continuing in this manner we obtain the residue classes with properties (1) and (2). Let M_1 and M_2 be in C_1 and suppose

$$M_2 = T_1T_2^{-1}M_1.$$

If E_1 is in C_1' and can be obtained from M_1 by

$$E_1 = T_\alpha M_1 = T_\beta M_1 = \cdots = T_\eta M_1,$$

then

$$E_1 = T_\alpha T_2^{-1}T_1M_2 = T_\beta T_2^{-1}T_1M_2 = \cdots$$
$$= T_\lambda M_2 = T_\mu M_2 \cdots$$

Thus each M_i in C_1 transforms into E_1 by the same number of keys. Similarly each E_i in C_1' is obtained from any M in C_1 by the same number of keys. It follows that this number of keys is a divisor of the total number of keys and hence we have properties (3) and (4).

Analogue of the Vernam System for Continuous Time Series*

Claude E. Shannon

Abstract

The perfect secrecy of the Vernam system is proved by probability arguments and an analogous secrecy system for continuous functions is described.

The well-known Vernam system for obtaining secrecy in telegraphy, or more generally in any communication system using a discrete sequence of symbols, each being a choice from a finite number of possibilities, operates as follows. Let

$$X_1, X_2, \ldots, X_s$$

be a message, where the X's are symbols chosen from a finite set $a_1, \ldots, a_n$. A random sequence of a's is constructed by some means, each element being chosen with probability $\frac{1}{n}$ from among the a_i, and each element independent of the rest. This sequence, $Y_1, \ldots, Y_s$ (say), which is the key to the code, is carried independently of the communication system to the receiving point, for example by a messenger. The X's and Y's are combined at the transmitter by adding the a's mod n, that is, if $X_i = a_r$ and $Y_i = a_t$ then a_p, where $p \equiv r + t$ mod n, is sent in the ith place. At the receiver the inverse of this operation is performed to give the original sequence $X_1, \ldots, X_s$.

In a certain sense this type of secrecy system can be said to be theoretically perfect. To make this precise, let us assume the following:

1. The enemy has a complete knowledge of the system used in encoding the message including the statistics of the key (i.e., that the Y_i are chosen independently and with equal probabilities of being any of the a_i).

2. The enemy has no further knowledge of the exact key used. The particular key chosen has been kept entirely secret.

3. The enemy has some knowledge of the message statistics. For example, he may know that it is in English, which implies certain statistical properties of the sequence of X's. Or he might know or think it likely that it was addressed to a certain party or dealt with some known thing, etc. This knowledge, whatever it may be, is an *a priori* knowledge of the message, which he had before intercepting the coded message, and can be represented by a probability distribution in the space of all possible sequences $X_1, \ldots, X_s$. Those sequences which are *a priori* likely have relatively large probabilities, those which are unlikely have small probabilities.

4. The encoded message is intercepted by the enemy without error. When the message is intercepted the enemy can compute *a posteriori* probabilities of various sequences of X's in the original message, and this process is essentially all that can be done toward breaking the code. If the coding means used are simple (not the Vernam system), and the message long enough,

---

* Bell Laboratories Memorandum, May 10, 1943.

the *a posteriori* probabilities are distorted in such a way as to make it nearly certain that a particular sequence of X_i was the original message. Thus one particular sequence has an *a posteriori* probability nearly equal to 1, and all others are nearly 0. If the message is short the *a posteriori* probabilities are still distorted when the coding means are simple (as in a substitution cipher), and may not give a clear-cut solution but only reduce the field of possibilities considerably. However, in the Vernam system, no information whatever is gained about the original message apart from the number of symbols it contains. In fact, we have the following:

Theorem. *In the Vernam secrecy system the* a posteriori *probabilities of the original message possibilities are equal to the* a priori *probabilities for messages of the same number of symbols as the intercepted message. This is true independently of the original message statistics and of the partial knowledge of the enemy.*

That is, intercepting the message is of no help to the enemy whatever, other than telling the number of symbols.

This theorem is a simple consequence of Bayes' theorem in inverse probabilities, which states that the *a posteriori* probability of a ''cause'' A when a ''result'' B has been observed is given by

$$P_B(A) = \frac{P(A)P_A(B)}{P(B)} \quad,$$

where $P(A)$ is the *a priori* probability of A, $P_A(B)$ is the probability of B if A is known to have occurred, and $P(B)$ is the probability of B from any cause. In our case A is any particular uncoded message, of the same number of symbols as the intercepted message. $P(A)$ is the enemy's *a priori* probability of the message, $P_A(B)$ is the probability of getting the encoded message B if A actually was the message, and $P(B)$ the probability of getting message B by any cause (i.e. from any original message). Our theorem states that with the Vernam system $P_B(A) = P(A)$. We have $P_A(B) = \dfrac{1}{n^s}$ for any A, B since the Vernam code is equally likely to transform any A into any B by its method of construction. Also $P(B) = \sum_A P(A)P_A(B) = \dfrac{1}{n^s}\sum_A P(A) = \dfrac{1}{n^s}$ since $\sum_A P(A) = 1$. Hence the theorem follows.

Of course the modicum of information contained in the knowledge of the number of symbols can be reduced by similar devices, e.g. adding dummy symbols at the end of the message, the number of dummies being chosen by probability means. The system may also be used continuously, with no gaps between messages, thus concealing the number of symbols in a message.

The question arises as to the continuous analogue of this system of encoding, for use with speech, for example. One might at first think of adding a thermal noise to the signal and subtracting it at the receiver, but theoretically this is not appropriate, and it is known experimentally that it takes a large noise to drown a speech signal; if they are of the same order of magnitude it is possible to understand the speech merely by listening to the combination.

Actually the proper generalization of the Vernam system is as follows. Let us assume that the signal is band- and amplitude-limited, so that it contains no frequencies over f_0 and no amplitudes outside the range -1 to $+1$. Construct a thermal noise with unit RMS value and with flat spectrum out to f_0 and no power at higher frequencies, for example by passing ordinary flat noise through an ideal low-pass filter. Pass this noise through a non-linear device with a characteristic f given by the integrated error curve doubled and with unity subtracted (Figs. 1,3):

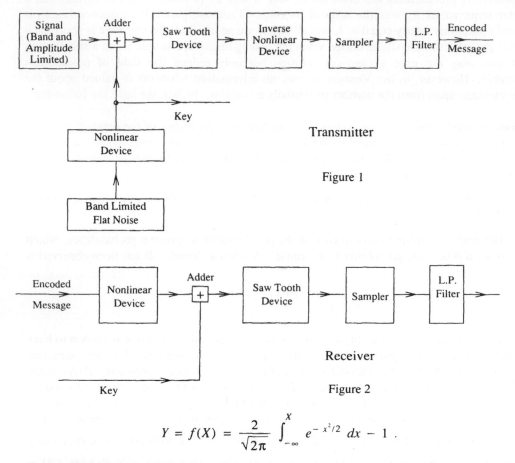

Transmitter

Figure 1

Receiver

Figure 2

$$Y = f(X) = \frac{2}{\sqrt{2\pi}} \int_{-\infty}^{X} e^{-x^2/2} \, dx - 1 \, .$$

The ensemble of functions obtained in this way has the property that the values of the amplitude are uniformly distributed between -1 and $+1$, since before passing through the nonlinear device the amplitudes were distributed normally with unit standard deviation. Also the values at intervals of $1/(2f_0)$ have zero correlation coefficient, since the autocorrelation of flat thermal noise band limited to f_0 is zero for $t = \pm 1/(2f_0), \pm 2/(2f_0), \pm 3/(2f_0), \dots$. Add this output Y to the signal in a circular manner: if $S(t)$ is the signal, form $S(t) + Y(t) \pm 1$ according as $S(t) + Y(t)$ is negative or positive.

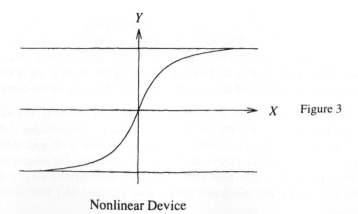

Figure 3

Nonlinear Device

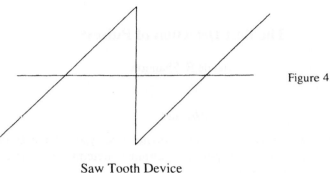

Figure 4

Saw Tooth Device

This circular addition can be performed, as J. R. Pierce has pointed out, by merely adding S and Y and passing the result through a saw tooth non-linear device (with characteristic shown in Fig. 4). Pierce has designed a simple electronic circuit for realizing this saw tooth characteristic. The output of this device can be sampled at periods $1/(2f_0)$ and the resulting impulses passed through a low-pass filter, or first it may be passed through a device with the inverse of characteristic of Fig. 4. In the latter case the output signal is statistically a flat thermal noise. It can be shown that in either case this system gives perfect secrecy in the same sense as the ordinary Vernam system. In fact the original message, being of limited frequency f_0, can be represented by giving its values every $1/(2f_0)$ seconds. The non-linear operation on the thermal noise gives a wave whose values every $1/(2f_0)$ seconds are independent and are uniformly distributed between the values -1 and $+1$. Adding these in a circle is then precisely analogous to the Vernam modulo n addition. The result is thus still uniformly distributed between these limits and successive values are independent. The theorem is then proved in a similar fashion, the discrete probabilities being replaced by distribution functions in a high-dimensional space (of dimension $2f_0T$, where T is the time of transmission), and the summation replaced by an integration over this space, using the continuous generalization of Bayes' theorem.

At the receiver the message is recovered with the inverse operations indicated in Fig. 2.

The Best Detection of Pulses*

Claude E. Shannon

Abstract

The form of pulse detector which best differentiates two types of pulses of known shape distorted by a thermal noise of known power spectrum is determined, where "best" means with least probability of erroneous reading.

In telegraphy, teletype, P.C.M. and other communication systems it is necessary to determine which of two types of pulses was sent at the transmitter when the received signal is distorted by noise. We consider the problem of how best to accomplish this when by the "best" method we mean the one giving the least probability of an erroneous determination.

Suppose the two types of pulses are $\phi(t)$ and $\psi(t)$ and the distorting noise is a "normal" noise; i.e., statistically equivalent to a thermal noise which has passed through a linear filter giving it a power spectrum $P(\omega)$. The problem can be thought of geometrically as follows. The two types of pulses ϕ and ψ represent points in function space, and the noise added to the transmitted signal gives a received signal which is also a point in function space. The ensemble of noise added to the signal gives a probability distribution in function space. The problem in differentiating the two types of pulses is to divide functions space into two regions R_ϕ and R_ψ, such that if the received signal is in R_ϕ the probability that the transmitted signal was ϕ exceeds $\frac{1}{2}$; if it is in R_ψ the probability that it was ψ exceeds $\frac{1}{2}$.

The general problem for infinite dimensional function space can best be approached by analogy with a finite dimensional case. We suppose there are two signals represented by vectors in an n-dimensional vector space; the signals being given in tensor notation by α^i and β^i. These are distorted in transmission by a normal (gaussian) error X^i whose associated quadratic form is a_{ij}, i.e., the probability distribution function for the error is given by

$$\frac{\sqrt{|a_{ij}|}}{(2\pi)^{\frac{n}{2}}} \exp{-\frac{1}{2}a_{ij}X^iX^j},$$

using the Einstein summation convention.

Let the *a priori* probability of α^i be p and of β^i be $q = 1 - p$. The vector space must be divided into two regions R_α and R_β as before, and the dividing surface will be such that on it the *a posteriori* probabilities (when a signal lying on the surface has been received) of the transmitted signal being α or β are equal. Using Bayes' theorem this requires that

$$\frac{P_\alpha(S)P(\alpha)}{P(S)} = \frac{P_\beta(S)P(\beta)}{P(S)},$$

where the vector S lies on the surface and

---

*   Bell Laboratories Memorandum, June 22, 1944.

$P(\alpha) = p = a\ priori$ probability of α,

$P(\beta) = q = 1 - p = a\ priori$ probability of β,

$P_\alpha (S)$ = probability of receiving S if α was sent,

$P_\beta (S)$ = probability of receiving S if β was sent,

$P(S)$ = probability of receiving S.

All these are actually probability densities. Hence we have

$$p\ \frac{\sqrt{|a_{ij}|}}{(2\pi)^{\frac{n}{2}}}\ \exp\ [-\tfrac{1}{2}\ a_{ij}(S^i - \alpha^i)(S^j - \alpha^j)]$$

$$= q\ \frac{\sqrt{|a_{ij}|}}{(2\pi)^{\frac{n}{2}}}\ \exp\ [-\tfrac{1}{2}\ a_{ij}(S^i - \beta^i)(S^j - \beta^j)]\ .$$

Taking logarithms, we have for the equation of the dividing surface

$$a_{ij}[(S^i - \alpha^i)(S^j - \alpha^j) - (S^i - \beta^i)(S^j - \beta^j)] = 2\ \ln\ \frac{q}{p}\ ,$$

or, by collecting terms and manipulating indices,

$$2a_{ij}(\alpha^i - \beta^i)S^j = a_{ij}(\alpha^i\alpha^j - \beta^i\beta^j) + 2\ \ln\ \frac{p}{q}\ .$$

This is the equation of a hyperplane in S^j. If we rotate the axes of our coordinate system to line up with the principal axes of the quadratic form a_{ij} we obtain the equation

$$2\ \Sigma\ \lambda_i(\bar{\alpha}^i - \bar{\beta}^i)\bar{S}^j = \Sigma\ \lambda_i(\bar{\alpha}^{i^2} - \bar{\beta}^{i^2}) + 2\ \ln\ p/q\ ,$$

where the barred letters are transformed coordinates and the λ_i are the eigenvalues of a_{ij}. In case these λ_i are all equal we notice that the dividing plane is normal to the line joining α^i and β^i. Otherwise an affine transformation will make them equal and bring about this orthogonality.

To determine which signal was sent one should therefore perform on the received signal the linear operation

$$a_{ij}(\alpha^i - \beta^i)S^j$$

and if this quantity exceeds a certain threshold value the most probable signal was α, while if it is less than the threshold the most probable signal was β. The threshold is given by the right members of the last two equations. If $p = q = 1/2$ the threshold is proportional to the operator when the noise amplitude varies; thus no change in the operation is required. If we make $\alpha^i = -\beta^i$ the threshold is zero and the operation is independent of both noise and signal amplitudes. This selection is also best from the point of view of signal power for a given frequency of errors.

The case of pulses $\phi\ (t)$ and $\psi\ (t)$ is a direct generalization of these results. The equation of the plane of separation becomes

$$2 \int \sqrt{P(\omega)^{-1}} \; [\Phi(\omega) - \Psi(\omega)] S(\omega) d\omega$$

$$= \int \sqrt{P(\omega)^{-1}} \; [\overline{\Psi(\omega)}^2 - \overline{\psi(\omega)}^2] d\omega + 2 \ln \frac{p}{q} .$$

Here $\Phi(\omega)$ and $\Psi(\omega)$ are the spectra of the two pulses and $S(\omega)$ is the spectrum of the received signal. This means that we must modulate the received signal with a gating pulse whose spectrum is given by

$$\sqrt{P(\omega)^{-1}} \; [\Phi(\omega) - \Psi(\omega)]$$

and integrate this product function. If the integral exceeds the above threshold the most probable pulse is ϕ, otherwise ψ.

These results can be easily generalized to the separation of more than two pulses. In the case of three pulses ϕ, ψ, θ there are three hyperplanes obtained by setting the probabilities equal in pairs. These planes have a hyperline in common and divide the space into six regions. One pair of adjacent regions corresponds to ϕ, another to ψ and the third to θ. To mechanize this system three gating integrating operations can be performed, and the numerical results compared.

The Philosophy of PCM*

B. M. OLIVER†, MEMBER, IRE, J. R. PIERCE†, FELLOW, IRE, AND C. E. SHANNON†

Summary—Recent papers[1,4] describe experiments in transmitting speech by PCM (pulse code modulation). This paper shows in a general way some of the advantages of PCM, and distinguishes between what can be achieved with PCM and with other broadband systems, such as large-index FM. The intent is to explain the various points simply, rather than to elaborate them in detail. The paper is for those who want to find out about PCM rather than for those who want to design a system. Many important factors will arise in the design of a system which are not considered in this paper.

I. PCM AND ITS FEATURES

THERE ARE SEVERAL important elements of a PCM (pulse-code modulation) system. These will be introduced, and the part each plays in PCM will be explained in this section.

Sampling

In general, the object of a transmission system is to reproduce at the output any function of time which appears at the input. In any practical system only a certain class of functions, namely, those limited to a finite frequency band, are admissible inputs. A signal which contains no frequencies greater than W_0 cps cannot assume an infinite number of independent values per second. It can, in fact, assume exactly $2W_0$ *independent* values per second, and the amplitudes at any set of points in time spaced τ_0 seconds apart, where $\tau_0 = 1/2W_0$, specify the signal completely. A simple proof of this is given in Appendix I. Hence, to transmit a band-limited signal of duration T, we do not need to send the entire continuous function of time. It suffices to send the finite set of $2W_0T$ independent values obtained by sampling the instantaneous amplitude of the signal at a regular rate of $2W_0$ samples per second.

If it surprises the reader to find that $2W_0T$ pieces of data will describe a continuous function completely over the interval T, it should be remembered that the $2W_0T$ coefficients of the sine and cosine terms of a Fourier series do just this, if, as we have assumed, the function contains no frequencies higher than W_0.

Reconstruction

Let us now proceed to the receiving end of the system, and assume that, by some means, the sample values representing the signal are there and available in proper time sequence, and can be used at the regular rate $2W_0$. To reconstruct the signal it is merely necessary to generate from each sample a proportional impulse, and to pass this regularly spaced series of impulses through an ideal low-pass filter of cutoff frequency W_0. The output of this filter will then be (except for an over-all time delay and possibly a constant of proportionality) identical to the input signal. Since the response of an ideal low-pass filter to an impulse is a $\sin x/x$ pulse, and since the total output is the linear sum of the responses to all inputs, this method of reconstruction is simply the physical embodiment of the method indicated in Appendix I.

Ideally, then, we could achieve perfect reproduction of a signal if we could transmit information giving us exactly the instantaneous amplitude of the signal at intervals spaced $1/2W_0$ apart in time.

Quantization

It is, of course, impossible to transmit the *exact* amplitude of a sample. The amplitude of a sample is often transmitted as the amplitude of a pulse, or as the time position of a pulse. Noise, distortion, and crosstalk between pulses will disturb the amplitude and position, and hence cause errors in the recovered information concerning the size of the sample. Ordinarily the error becomes greater as the signal is amplified by successive repeaters, and hence the accumulation of noise sets a limit to the distance a signal can be transmitted even with enough amplification.

It is possible, however, to allow only certain discrete levels of amplitude or position of the transmitted pulse. Then, when the signal is sampled, the level nearest the true signal level is sent. When this is received and amplified, it will have a level a little different from any of the specified levels. If the noise and distortion are not too great, we can surely tell which level the signal was supposed to have. Then the signal can be reformed, or a new signal created, which again has the level originally sent.

Representing the signal by certain discrete allowed levels only is called *quantizing*. It inherently introduces an initial error in the amplitude of the samples, giving rise to *quantization noise*. But once the signal is in a quantized state, it can be relayed for any distance without further loss in quality, provided only that the added noise in the signal received at each repeater is not too great to prevent correct recognition of the particular level each given signal is intended to represent. By quantizing we limit our "alphabet." If the received signal lies between a and b, and is closer (say) to b, we guess that b was sent. If the noise is small enough, we shall always be right.

* Decimal classification: R148.6. Original manuscript received by the Institute, May 24, 1948.
† Bell Telephone Laboratories, Inc., New York, N. Y.
[1] W. M. Goodall, "Telephony by pulse code modulation," *Bell Sys. Tech. Jour.*, vol. 26, pp. 395–409; July, 1947.
[1] D. D. Grieg, "Pulse count modulation system," *Tele-Tech.*, vol. 6, pp. 48–52; September, 1947.
[3] D. D. Grieg, "Pulse count modulation," *Elec. Commun.*, vol. 24, pp. 287–296; September, 1947.
[4] H. S. Black and J. O. Edson, "PCM equipment," *Elec. Eng.*, vol. 66, pp. 1123–25; November, 1947.
[5] A. C. Clavier, D. D. Grieg, and P. F. Panter, "PCM distortion analysis," *Elec. Eng.*, vol. 66, pp. 1110–1122; November, 1947.
[6] L. A. Meacham and E. Peterson, "An experimental multi-channel pulse code modulation system of toll quality," *Bell Sys Tech. Jour.*, vol. 27, pp. 1–43; January, 1948.

TABLE I

Amplitude Represented	Code
0	000
1	001
2	010
3	011
4	100
5	101
6	110
7	111

Coding

A quantized sample could be sent as a single pulse which would have certain possible discrete amplitudes, or certain discrete positions with respect to a reference position. However, if many allowed sample amplitudes are required, one hundred, for example, it would be difficult to make circuits to distinguish these one from another. On the other hand, it is very easy to make a circuit which will tell whether or not a pulse is present. Suppose, then, that several pulses are used as a *code group* to describe the amplitude of a single sample. Each pulse can be on (1) or off (0). If we have three pulses, for instance, we can have the combinations representing the amplitudes shown in Table I.

The codes are, in fact, just the numbers (amplitudes) at the left written in binary notation. In this notation, the place-values are 1, 2, 4, 8,—; i.e., a unit in the right-hand column represents 1, a unit in the middle (second) column represents 2, a unit in the left (third) column represents 4, etc. We see that with a code group of n on-off pulses we can represent 2^n amplitudes. For example, 7 pulses yield 128 sample levels.

It is possible, of course, to code the amplitude in terms of a number of pulses which have allowed amplitudes of 0, 1, 2 (base 3 or ternary code), or 0, 1, 2, 3 (base 4 or quaternary code), etc., instead of the pulses with allowed amplitudes 0, 1 (base 2 or binary code). If ten levels were allowed for each pulse, then each pulse in a code group would be simply a digit of an ordinary decimal number expressing the amplitude of the sample. If n is the number of pulses and b is the base, the number of quantizing levels the code can express is b^n.

Decoding

To decode a code group of the type just described, one must generate a pulse which is the linear sum of all the pulses in the group, each multiplied by its place value $(1, b, b^2, b^3, \ldots)$ in the code. This can be done in a number of ways. Perhaps the simplest way which has been used involves sending the code group in "reverse" order, i.e., the "units" pulse first, and the pulse with the highest place value last. The pulses are then stored as charge on a capacitor-resistor combination with a time constant such that the charge decreases by the factor $1/b$ between pulses. After the last pulse, the charge (voltage) is sampled.

A Complete PCM System

A PCM system embodies all the processes just described. The input signal is band-limited to exclude any frequencies greater than W_0. This signal is then sampled at the rate $2W_0$. The samples are then quantized and encoded. Since only certain discrete code groups are possible, the selection of the nearest code group automatically quantizes the sample, and with certain types of devices it is therefore not necessary to quantize as a separate, prior operation. The code groups are then transmitted, either as a time sequence of pulses (time division) over the same channel, or by frequency division, or over separate channels. The code groups are regenerated (i.e., reshaped) at intervals as required. At the receiver the (regenerated) code groups are decoded to form a series of impulses proportional to the original samples (except quantized), and these impulses are sent through a low-pass filter of bandwidth W_0 to recover the signal wave.

II. Transmission Requirements for PCM

Suppose we consider what requirements exist, ideally, on the channel which is to carry the encoded PCM signal; that is, ruling out physically impossible devices, but allowing ideal components such as ideal filters, ideal gates, etc.

Bandwidth

If a channel has a bandwidth W cps, it is possible to send up to $2W$ independent pulses per second over it. We can show this very simply. Let the pulses occur (or not occur) at the time $t = 0, \tau, 2\tau, \cdots, m\tau$ where $\tau = 1/2W$, and let each pulse as received be of the form

$$V = V_0 \frac{\sin \frac{\pi}{\tau}(t - m\tau)}{\frac{\pi}{\tau}(t - m\tau)}. \qquad (1)$$

The shape of this pulse is shown in Fig. 1. It will be seen that the pulse centered at time $m\tau$ will be zero at $t = k\tau$ where $k \neq m$. Thus, if we sample the pulse train at the time $t = m\tau$, we will see only the pulse belonging to that time and none of the others.

TABLE II

Signal to Noise $\dfrac{P_\bullet}{N}$	Probability of Error	This Is About One Error Every	
13.3 db	10^{-2}	10^{-3}	sec
17.4 db	10^{-4}	10^{-1}	sec
19.6 db	10^{-6}	10	sec
21.0 db	10^{-8}	20	min
22.0 db	10^{-10}	1	day
23.0 db	10^{-12}	3	months

Further, the pulse given by (1) contains no frequencies higher than W. It is the pulse one would get out of an ideal low-pass filter of cutoff W, on applying a very short impulse to the input.

Now, to send a signal of bandwidth W_0 by *PCM*, we must send $2W_0$ code groups per second and each code group contains (say) n pulse places. We must be prepared, therefore, to send $2nW_0$ pulses per second, and this requires a bandwidth $W = nW_0$. The pulses may be sent in time sequence over one channel or by frequency division. In either case the total bandwidth will be the same. Of course, if double-sideband transmission is used in the frequency-division case, or if the time-division signal is sent as double-sideband rf pulses, the total bandwidth will be $2nW_0$.

In short, the bandwidth required for PCM is, in the ideal case, n times as great as that required for direct transmission of the signal, where n is the number of pulses per code group.

Threshold Power

To detect the presence or absence of a pulse reliably requires a certain signal-to-noise ratio. If the pulse power is too low compared to the noise, even the best possible detector will make mistakes and indicate an occasional pulse when there is none, or vice versa. Let us assume that we have an ideal detector, i.e., one which makes the fewest possible mistakes. If the received pulses are of the form (1), and if the noise is "white" noise (i.e., noise with a uniform power spectrum and gaussian amplitude distribution as, for example, thermal noise), ideal detection could be achieved by passing the signal through an ideal low-pass filter of bandwidth W ($= nW_0$ in the ideal case) and sampling the output at the pulse times $k\tau$. If the signal when sampled exceeds $V_0/2$, we say a pulse is present; if less than $V_0/2$, we say there is no pulse. The result will be in error if the noise at that instant exceeds $V_0/2$ in the right direction. With gaussian noise, the probability of this happening is proportional to the complementary error function[7] of

$$\frac{V_0}{2\sigma} = \sqrt{\frac{P_\bullet}{4N}}$$

where

σ = rms noise amplitude
$P_\bullet$ = signal (pulse) "power" = V_0^2
N = noise power in bandwidth $W = \sigma^2$.

As the signal power $P_\bullet$ is increased, this function decreases very rapidly, so that if $P_\bullet/N$ is large enough to make the signal intelligible at all, only a small increase will make the transmission nearly perfect. An idea of how rapidly this improvement occurs may be had from Table II. The last column in the table assumes a pulse rate of 10^5 per second.

Clearly, there is a fairly definite *threshold* (at about 20 db, say) below which the interference is serious, and above which the interference is negligible. Comparing this figure of 20 db with the 60- to 70-odd db required for high-quality straight AM transmission of speech, it will be seen that PCM requires much less signal power, even though the noise power is increased by the n-fold increase in bandwidth.

The above discussion has assumed an on-off (base 2) system. In this system pulses will be present half the time, on the average, and the *average* signal power[8] will

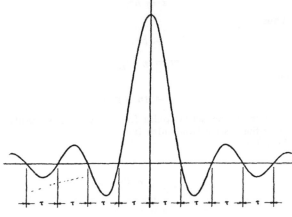

Fig. 1—Pulse of the form $V_\bullet \dfrac{\sin(\pi t/\tau)}{\pi t/\tau}$.

[7] Complementary error function of $x = 1/\sqrt{2\pi} \int_x^\infty e^{-\lambda^2/2} d\lambda$.
[8] See Appendix II.

be $P_0/2$. If a balanced base 2 system were used, i.e., one in which 1 is sent as a + pulse (say) and 0 as a − pulse, the peak-to-peak signal swing would have to be the same as in the on-off system for the same noise margin, and this swing would be provided by pulses of only half the former amplitude. Since either a + or − pulse would always be present, the signal power would be $P_0/4$.

If pulses are used which have b different amplitude levels (i.e., a base b system), then a certain amplitude separation must exist between the adjacent levels to provide adequate noise margin. Call this separation $K\sigma$. where K =a constant. (From the preceding discussion we see that K is about 10.) The total amplitude range is therefore $K\sigma(b-1)$. The signal power will be least if this amplitude range is symmetrical about zero, i.e., from $-K\sigma(b-1)/2$ to $+K\sigma(b-1)/2$. The average signal power S, assuming all levels to be equally likely, is then[8]

$$S = K^2\sigma^2 \frac{b^2-1}{12}$$

$$= K^2 N \frac{b^2-1}{12}. \qquad (2)$$

It will be noticed that the required signal power increases rapidly with the base b.

Regeneration: The Pay-Off

In most transmission systems, the noise and distortion from the individual links cumulate. For a given quality of over-all transmission, the longer the system, the more severe are the requirements on each link. For example, if 100 links are to be used in tandem, the noise power added per link can only be one-hundredth as great as would be permissible in a single link.

Because the signal in a PCM system can be regenerated as often as necessary, the effects of amplitude and phase and nonlinear distortions in one link, if not too great, produce no effect whatever on the regenerated input signal to the next link. If noise in a single link causes a certain fraction p of the pulses to be regenerated incorrectly, then after m links, if $p \ll 1$, the fraction incorrect will be approximately mp. However, to reduce p to a value $p' = p/m$ requires only a slight increase in the power in each link, as we have seen in the section on threshold power. Practically, then, the transmission requirements for a PCM link are almost independent of the total length of the system. The importance of this fact can hardly be overstated.

III. PERFORMANCE OF A PCM SYSTEM

We have seen that PCM requires more bandwidth and less power than is required with direct transmission of the signal itself, or with straight AM. We have, in a sense, exchanged bandwidth for power. Has the exchange been an efficient one? Are good signal-to-noise ratios in the recovered signal feasible in PCM? And

how sensitive to interference is PCM? We shall now try to answer these questions.

Channel Capacity

A good measure of the bandwidth efficiency is the information capacity of the system as compared with the theoretical limit for a channel of the same bandwidth and power. The information capacity of a system may be thought of as the number of independent symbols or characters which can be transmitted without error in unit time. The simplest, most elementary character is a binary digit, and it is convenient to express the information capacity as the equivalent number of binary digits per second, C, which the channel can handle. Shannon and others have shown that an ideal system has the capacity[9]

$$C = W \log_2\left(1 + \frac{P}{N}\right) \qquad (3)$$

where

W =bandwidth
P =average signal power
N =white noise power.

Two channels having the same C have the same capacity for transmitting information, even though the quantities W, P, and N may be different.

In a PCM system, operating over the threshold so that the frequency of errors is negligible,

$$C = sm$$

where

s =sampling rate = $2W_0$
m =equivalent number of binary digits per code group.

If there are l quantizing levels, the number of binary digits required per code group is given by $l = 2^m$, while the actual number of (base b) digits n will be given by

$$l = b^n.$$

Thus,

$$2^m = b^n$$

$$m = n \log_2 b$$

and

$$C = sn \log_2 b.$$

Now sn is the actual pulse frequency, and is ideally twice the system bandwidth W.
Therefore,

$$C = 2W \log_2 b$$

$$= W \log_2 b^2.$$

[9] C. E. Shannon, "A mathematical theory of communication," *Bell Sys. Tech. Jour.*, vol. 27, July, October, 1948.

Substituting for b the power required for this base (from (2)), we have

$$C = W \log_2 \left(1 + \frac{12S}{K^2 N}\right). \qquad (4)$$

Comparing (4) with (3), we see they are identical if $S = (K^2/12)P$. In other words, PCM requires $K^2/12$ (or about 8) times the power theoretically required to realize a given channel capacity for a given bandwidth.

Perhaps the most important thing to notice about (4) is that the form is right. Power and bandwidth are exchanged on a logarithmic basis, and the channel capacity is proportional[10] to W. In most broadband systems, which improve signal-to-noise ratio at the expense of bandwidth, C is proportional only to log W.

Signal-to-Noise Ratio

There are two types of noise introduced by a PCM system. One of these is the quantizing noise mentioned in the section on quantization. This is a noise introduced at the transmitting end of the system and nowhere else. The other is *false pulse* noise caused by the incorrect interpretation of the intended amplitude of a pulse by the receiver or by any repeater. This noise may arise anywhere along the system, and is cumulative. However, as we have seen earlier, this noise decreases so rapidly as the signal power is increased above threshold that in any practical system it would be made negligible by design. As a result, the signal-to-noise ratio in PCM systems is set by the quantizing noise alone.

If the signal is large compared with a single quantizing step, the errors introduced in successive samples by quantizing will be substantially uncorrelated. The maximum error which can be introduced is one-half of one quantizing step in either direction. All values of error up to this maximum value are equally likely. The rms error introduced is, therefore, $1/2\sqrt{3}$ times the height of a single quantizing step.[8] When the signal is reconstructed from the decoded samples (containing this quantizing error), what is obtained is the original signal plus a noise having a uniform frequency spectrum out to W_0 and an rms amplitude of $1/2\sqrt{3}$ times a quantizing step height. The ratio of peak-to-peak signal to rms noise is, therefore,

$$R = 2\sqrt{3}\, b^n,$$

since b^n is the number of levels. Expressing this ratio in db, we have

$$20 \log_{10} R = 20 \log_{10} 2\sqrt{3} + n(20 \log_{10} b)$$
$$= 10.8 + n(20 \log_{10} b). \qquad (5)$$

In a binary system, $b = 2$, and

$$20 \log_{10} R \cong 10.8 + 6n.$$

[10] Provided S is increased in proportion to W to compensate for the similar increase in N.

In examining (5) let us remember that n, the number of digits, is a factor relating the *total bandwidth used in transmission* to the *bandwidth of the signal to be transmitted*, i.e., $W = nW_0$. It is something like the index of modulation in FM. Now, for every increment of W_0 added to the bandwidth used for transmission, n may be increased by one, and this increases the signal-to-noise ratio by a constant number of db. In other words, in PCM, *the signal-to-noise ratio in db varies linearly with* the number of digits per code group, and hence with the *bandwidth*. Of course, as the bandwidth is increased the noise power increases, and a proportional increase in signal power is required to stay adequately above threshold.

A binary PCM system using ten times the bandwidth of the original signal will give a 70-db signal-to-noise ratio. Higher base systems will require less bandwidth.

Ruggedness

One important characteristic of a transmission system is its susceptibility to interference. We have seen that noise in a PCM circuit produces no effect unless the peak amplitude is greater than half the separation between pulse levels. In a binary (on-off) system, this is half the pulse height. Similarly, interference such as stray impulses, or pulse crosstalk from a near-by channel, will produce no effect unless the peak amplitude of this interference plus the peak noise is half the pulse height. The presence of interference thus increases the threshold required for satisfactory operation. But, if an adequate margin over threshold is provided, comparatively large amounts of interference can be present without affecting the performance of the circuit at all. A PCM system, particularly an on-off (binary) system, is therefore quite "rugged."

When a number of radio communication routes must converge on a single terminal, or follow similar routes between cities, the ruggedness of the channels is a particularly important consideration. If the susceptibility of the channels to mutual interference is high, many separate frequency bands will be required, and the total bandwidth required for the service will be large. Although PCM requires an initial increase of bandwidth for each channel, the resulting ruggedness permits many routes originating from, or converging toward, a single terminal to occupy the same frequency band. Different planes of polarization for two channels over the same path can often be used, and the directivities of practical antennas are such that only a small difference in direction of arrival will separate two routes on the same frequency. As a result, the frequency occupancy of PCM is exceptionally good, and its other transmission advantages are then obtained with little, if any, increase in *total* bandwidth.

IV. COMPARISON OF PCM AND FM

One feature of PCM is that the signal-to-noise ratio can be substantially improved by increasing the transmission bandwidth. This is an advantage shared with certain other pulse systems and with FM. As FM is the best known of these other systems, it is interesting to compare PCM and FM.

Broadband Gain

In going to high-deviation FM, the gain in signal-to-noise voltage ratio over AM (with the same power and the same noise per unit bandwidth) is proportional to the deviation ratio, or to the ratio of half the bandwidth actually used in transmission to the bandwidth of the signal to be transmitted. This ratio corresponds to n in our notation. If noise power is uniformly distributed with respect to frequency, and if one desires to provide the same margin over threshold in FM with various bandwidths, the transmitter power must be proportional to bandwidth (to n). If we so vary the power in varying the bandwidth of wide-deviation FM, the signal-to-noise voltage ratio will vary as $n(n^{1/2})$, where the factor $n^{1/2}$ comes about through the increased signal voltage. Thus the signal-to-noise ratio R will be given by

$$R = (\text{const})n^{3/2}$$

$$20 \log_{10} R = 30 \log_{10} n + \text{const.} \qquad (6)$$

For binary (on-off) PCM we have, from (5), for the same simultaneous variation of bandwidth and power

$$20 \log_{10} R = 6n + 10.8.$$

Or, for ternary (base 3) PCM,

$$20 \log_{10} R = 9.54n + 10.8.$$

We see that, as the bandwidth (proportional to n) is increased in FM, the signal-to-noise ratio varies as $\log n$, while in PCM it varies as n. Thus, as bandwidth is increased, PCM is bound to exhibit more improvement in the end. Further, a more elaborate analysis shows that, ideally at least, PCM can provide, for any bandwidth, nearly as high a signal-to-noise ratio as is possible with any system of modulation.

Why is PCM so good in utilizing bandwidth to increase the signal-to-noise ratio? A very clear picture of the reason can be had by considering a simple PCM system in which four binary digits are transmitted on four adjacent frequency bands with powers just sufficient to over-ride noise. In Fig. 2(a) the signals in these four channels B_1, B_2, B_3, B_4 are shown versus time. A black rectangle represents a pulse; a white rectangle, the absence of a pulse. The rectangles are $\tau_0 = (1/2W_0)$ long. The particular sequence of code groups shown in the figure represents a quantized approximation to a linear change of amplitude with time, as shown in Fig. 2(b).

Now suppose, instead, that we confine ourselves to sending a pulse in only one channel at a time, as shown in Fig. 2(c). The best quantized representation of the signal we can get is shown in Fig. 2(d). Here the number of levels is four, while in Fig. 2(b) there are sixteen. In other words, Fig. 2(b) represents four times as good a signal-to-noise amplitude ratio as Fig. 2(d).

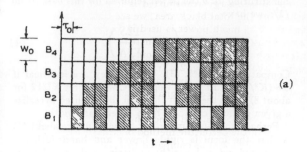

(a)

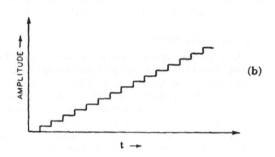

(b)

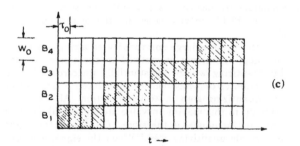

(c)

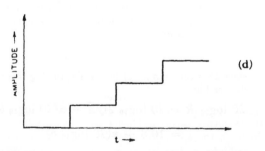

(d)

Fig. 2—The signals in channels B_1, B_2, B_3, and B_4. (a) Signal in a frequency-division PCM system. (b) Amplitudes corresponding to (a). (c) Signal in a quantized FM system. (d) Amplitudes corresponding to (c).

The total energy transmitted is in each case represented by the total black area; we see that on the average twice as much power is used in Fig. 2(a) as in Fig. 2(c). Thus we obtain a 12-db increase in signal-to-noise ratio with a power increase of only 3 db by sending the signal according to Fig. 2(a) rather than Fig. 2(c). If we had started out with six channels instead of four, we would have obtained a signal-to-noise improvement of 21 db for 4.77 db more average power. The greater the number of channels, and hence the wider the frequency band used, the better the method of transmission represented by Fig. 2(a) as compared to that represented by Fig. 2(c).

Now Fig. 2(a) represents PCM, while Fig. 2(c) represents what is essentially quantized FM with sampling. The signal in Fig. 2(c) varies with frequency according to the amplitude of the signal. Hence, we have compared PCM and a sort of FM, to the obvious advantage of PCM.

The trouble with the FM type of signal of Fig. 2(c) is that only a few of the possible signals which might be sent in the four bands B_1–B_4 are ever produced; all the others, those for which there is a signal in more than one band at a time, are wasted. Ideally, PCM takes advantage of every possible signal which can be transmitted over a given band of frequencies with pulses having discrete amplitudes.[11]

The relation between FM and PCM is closely analogous to the relation between the two types of computing machines: the so-called analogue machines and the digital machines. In analogue machines the numbers involved are represented as proportional to some physical quantity capable of continuous variation. Typical examples are the slide rule, network analyzers, and the differential analyzer. An increase in precision requires, in general, a proportional increase in the range of physical variables used to represent the numbers. Furthermore, small errors tend to accumulate and cannot be eliminated. In digital machines the numbers are expressed in digital form, and the digits are represented by the states of certain physical parts of the machine which can assume one of a finite set of possible states. Typical digital machines are the abacus, ordinary desk computers, and the Eniac. In this type of machine the precision increases exponentially with the number of digits, and hence with the size of the machine. Small errors, which are not large enough to carry any part from one state to another state, have no effect and do not cumulate.

In FM (analogue), the amplitude of the audio signal is measured by the radio frequency. To improve the precision by 2 to 1 requires roughly a 2 to 1 increase in the frequency swing, and hence the bandwidth. In PCM doubling the bandwidth permits twice the number of

digits, and therefore *squares* rather than doubles the number of distinguishable levels.

Other Factors

There are other considerations in a comparison between PCM and ordinary, unquantized FM, however. For instance, PCM allows the use of regenerative repeaters, and FM does not. PCM lends itself, like other pulse systems, to time division multiplex. On the other hand, when the received signal rises considerably above threshold during good reception, the signal-to-noise ratio improves with FM but not with PCM. When we come to consider transmitters and receivers, we find that, for high signal-to-noise ratios at least, an FM transmitter and receiver will be somewhat less complicated than those for PCM are at present.

V. Conclusions

PCM offers a greater improvement in signal-to-noise than other systems, such as FM, which also depend upon the use of wide bands.

By using binary (on-off) PCM, a high quality signal can be obtained under conditions of noise and interference so bad that it is just possible to recognize the presence of each pulse. Further, by using regenerative repeaters which detect the presence or absence of pulses and then emit reshaped, respaced pulses, the initial signal-to-noise ratio can be maintained through a long chain of repeaters.

PCM lends itself to time-division multiplex.

PCM offers no improvement in signal-to-noise ratio during periods of high signal or low noise.

PCM transmitters and receivers are somewhat more complex than are those used for some other forms of modulation.

In all, PCM seems ideally suited for multiplex message circuits, where a standard quality and high reliability are required.

Appendix I

We wish to show that a function of time $f(t)$ which contains no frequency components greater than W_0 cps is uniquely determined by the values of $f(t)$ at any set of sampling points spaced $1/2W_0$ seconds apart. Let $F(\omega)$ be the complex spectrum of the function, i.e.,

$$ F(\omega) = \int_{-\infty}^{\infty} e^{-i\omega t} f(t)dt. $$

By assumption, $F(\omega) = 0$ for $|\omega| > 2\pi W_0$. $F(\omega)$ can be expanded in the interval $-2\pi W_0$ to $+2\pi W_0$ in a Fourier series having the coefficients

$$ a_n = \frac{1}{4\pi W_0} \int_{-2\pi W_0}^{2\pi W_0} F(\omega) e^{-i(\omega n/2W_0)} d\omega. \quad (1) $$

---

[11] It might be objected that one could have signals with a finer structure in the frequency direction than those shown in Fig. 2(a). This is possible only if τ is made larger, so that the pulses representing samples occur less frequently, are broader, and have narrower spectra. This means reducing W_0.

Now, since $F(\omega)$ is the Fourier transform of $f(t)$, $f(t)$ is the inverse transform of $F(\omega)$.

$$f(t) = \frac{1}{2\pi} \int_{-\infty}^{\infty} F(\omega) e^{i\omega t} d\omega$$

$$= \frac{1}{2\pi} \int_{-2\pi W_0}^{2\pi W_0} F(\omega) e^{i\omega t} d\omega,$$

since $F(\omega)$ is zero outside these limits.

If we let $t = n/2W_0$, we have

$$f\left(\frac{n}{2W_0}\right) = \frac{1}{2\pi} \int_{-2\pi W_0}^{2\pi W_0} F(\omega) e^{i(\omega n/2W_0)} d\omega. \quad (2)$$

Comparing (1) and (2), we see that

$$a_n = \frac{1}{2W_0} f\left(\frac{-n}{2W_0}\right).$$

Thus, if the function $f(t)$ is known at the sampling points, $\cdots -(2/2W_0)$, $1/2W_0$, 0, $1/2W_0$, $2/2W_0 \cdots$, then the coefficients a_n are determined. These coefficients determine the spectrum $F(\omega)$ and $F(\omega)$ determines $f(t)$ for all values of t. This shows that there is exactly one function containing no frequencies over W_0 and passing through a given set of amplitudes at sampling points $1/2W_0$ apart.

To reconstruct the function, given these amplitudes, we note that

$$F(\omega) = \sum_n a_n e^{i(\omega n/2W_0)} \text{ for } |\omega| < 2\pi W_0$$

$$F(\omega) = 0 \qquad\qquad \text{ for } |\omega| > 2\pi W_0.$$

Taking the inverse transform, we have

$$f(t) = 2W_0 \sum_n a_n \frac{\sin \pi(2W_0 t + n)}{\pi(2W_0 t + n)}$$

$$= \sum_n f\left(-\frac{n}{2W_0}\right) \frac{\sin \pi(2W_0 t + n)}{\pi(2W_0 t + n)}$$

$$= \sum_n f\left(\frac{n}{2W_0}\right) \frac{\sin \pi(2W_0 t - n)}{\pi(2W_0 t - n)}.$$

In other words, the function $f(t)$ may be thought of as the sum of a series of elementary functions of the form $\sin x/x$ centered at the sampling points, and each having a peak value equal to $f(t)$ at the corresponding sampling point. To reconstruct the function $f(t)$, then, we merely need to generate a series of $\sin x/x$ pulses proportional to the samples and add the ensemble.

APPENDIX II

We wish to find the average power in a series of pulses of the form

$$f(t) = \frac{\sin \pi \dfrac{t}{\tau}}{\pi \dfrac{t}{\tau}}$$

occurring at the regular rate $1/\tau$.

The signal wave may then be written

$$v(t) = \sum_{k=1}^{n} V_k f(t - k\tau)$$

where V_k = peak amplitude of pulse occurring at the time $t = k\tau$. The average "power" (i.e., mean-square amplitude) S of the signal will then be

$$S = \overline{v^2} = \lim_{n \to \infty} \frac{1}{n\tau} \int_{-\infty}^{\infty} v^2(t) dt$$

$$= \lim_{n \to \infty} \frac{1}{n\tau} \left[\sum_{k=1}^{n} V_k^2 \int_{-\infty}^{\infty} f^2(t - k\tau) dt \right.$$

$$\left. + \sum_{j=1}^{n} \sum_{k=1}^{n} V_j V_k \int_{-\infty}^{\infty} f(t - j\tau) f(t - k\tau) dt \right]_{j \neq k}$$

For the assumed pulse shape, the first integral is equal to τ, while the second integral is equal to zero. Thus

$$S = \lim_{n \to \infty} \frac{1}{n} \sum_{k=1}^{n} V_k^2.$$

S is simply the mean-square value of the individual pulse peak amplitudes, and may also be written

$$S = \int_{-\infty}^{\infty} V^2 p(V) dV$$

where

$p(V)dV$ = probability that pulse amplitude lies between V and $V + dV$.

Suppose the pulses have b discrete amplitude levels $K\sigma$ apart, ranging from 0 to $(b-1)K\sigma$. Each pulse then has an amplitude $aK\sigma$ where a is an integer. The average power will be

$$S = K^2 \sigma^2 \sum_{a=0}^{a=b-1} p(a) a^2$$

where $p(a)$ = probability of level a. If all levels are

equally likely, $p(a) = 1/b$, and

$$S = K^2\sigma^2 \frac{1}{b} \sum_0^{b-1} a^2$$

$$S = K^2\sigma^2 \frac{(b-1)(2b-1)}{6} \, .$$

The quantity

$$\frac{1}{b} \sum_0^{b-1} a^2$$

is the square of the radius of gyration (i.e., the mean-square radius) about one end of a linear array of b points separated by unit distance. The average power of any amplitude distribution is the average of the squares of the amplitudes and is therefore proportional to the square of the radius of gyration of the distribution. The radius of gyration about any point is

$$r^2 = r_0{}^2 + d^2$$

where

r = radius of gyration about chosen point
r_0 = radius of gyration about center of gravity
d = distance to center of gravity from chosen point.

Obviously, $r_0 < r$, so that the average power will be least if the average amplitude is zero. S will be least if the pulse amplitude range is from $-K\sigma(b-1)/2$ to $+K\sigma(b-1)/2$, and will then be given by

$$S = K^2\sigma^2 \left[\frac{(b-1)(2b-1)}{6} - \left(\frac{b-1}{2} \right)^2 \right]$$

$$S = K^2\sigma^2 \frac{b^2-1}{12} \, .$$

This may also be written

$$S = \frac{A^2}{12} \frac{(b+1)}{(b-1)}$$

where A = total amplitude range = $(b-1)K\sigma$. As $b \to \infty$,

$$S \to \frac{A^2}{12} \, .$$

Thus, if all amplitude levels in a range A are possible and equally likely, the rms amplitude of the distribution will be $\sqrt{S} = (A/2\sqrt{3})$.

Communication in the Presence of Noise*

CLAUDE E. SHANNON†, MEMBER, IRE

Summary—A method is developed for representing any communication system geometrically. Messages and the corresponding signals are points in two "function spaces," and the modulation process is a mapping of one space into the other. Using this representation, a number of results in communication theory are deduced concerning expansion and compression of bandwidth and the threshold effect. Formulas are found for the maximum rate of transmission of binary digits over a system when the signal is perturbed by various types of noise. Some of the properties of "ideal" systems which transmit at this maximum rate are discussed. The equivalent number of binary digits per second for certain information sources is calculated.

I. INTRODUCTION

A GENERAL COMMUNICATIONS system is shown schematically in Fig. 1. It consists essentially of five elements.

1. *An information source.* The source selects one message from a set of possible messages to be transmitted to the receiving terminal. The message may be of various types; for example, a sequence of letters or numbers, as in telegraphy or teletype, or a continuous function of time $f(t)$, as in radio or telephony.

2. *The transmitter.* This operates on the message in some way and produces a signal suitable for transmission to the receiving point over the channel. In telephony, this operation consists of merely changing sound pressure into a proportional electrical current. In telegraphy, we have an encoding operation which produces a sequence of dots, dashes, and spaces corresponding to the letters of the message. To take a more complex example, in the case of multiplex PCM telephony the different speech functions must be sampled, compressed, quantized and encoded, and finally interleaved properly to construct the signal.

3. *The channel.* This is merely the medium used to transmit the signal from the transmitting to the receiving point. It may be a pair of wires, a coaxial cable, a band of radio frequencies, etc. During transmission, or at the receiving terminal, the signal may be perturbed by noise or distortion. Noise and distortion may be differentiated on the basis that distortion is a fixed operation applied to the signal, while noise involves statistical and unpredictable perturbations. Distortion can, in principle, be corrected by applying the inverse operation, while a perturbation due to noise cannot always be removed, since the signal does not always undergo the same change during transmission.

4. *The receiver.* This operates on the received signal and attempts to reproduce, from it, the original message. Ordinarily it will perform approximately the mathematical inverse of the operations of the transmitter, although they may differ somewhat with best design in order to combat noise.

5. *The destination.* This is the person or thing for whom the message is intended.

Following Nyquist[1] and Hartley[2] it is convenient to use a logarithmic measure of information. If a device has n possible positions it can, by definition, store $\log_b n$ units of information. The choice of the base b amounts to a choice of unit, since $\log_b n = \log_b c \log_c n$. We will use the base 2 and call the resulting units binary digits or bits. A group of m relays or flip-flop circuits has 2^m possible sets of positions, and can therefore store $\log_2 2^m = m$ bits.

If it is possible to distinguish reliably M different signal functions of duration T on a channel, we can say that the channel can transmit $\log_2 M$ bits in time T. The *rate* of transmission is then $\log_2 M/T$. More precisely the *channel capacity* may be defined as

$$C = \lim_{T \to \infty} \frac{\log_2 M}{T} . \qquad (1)$$

* Decimal classification: 621.38. Original manuscript received by the Institute, July 23, 1940. Presented, 1948 IRE National Convention, New York, N. Y., March 24, 1948; and IRE New York Section, New York, N. Y., November 12, 1947.

† Bell Telephone Laboratories, Murray Hill, N. J.

[1] H. Nyquist, "Certain factors affecting telegraph speed," *Bell Syst. Tech. Jour.*, vol. 3, p. 324; April, 1924.

[2] R. V. L. Hartley, "The transmission of information," *Bell Sys. Tech. Jour.*, vol. 3, p. 535–564; July, 1928.

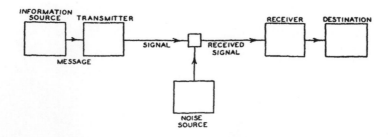

Fig. 1—General communications system.

A precise meaning will be given later to the requirement of reliable resolution of the M signals.

II. The Sampling Theorem

Let us suppose that the channel has a certain bandwidth W in cps starting at zero frequency, and that we are allowed to use this channel for a certain period of time T. Without any further restrictions this would mean that we can use as signal functions any functions of time whose spectra lie entirely within the band W, and whose time functions lie within the interval T. Although it is not possible to fulfill both of these conditions exactly, it is possible to keep the spectrum within the band W, and to have the time function very small outside the interval T. Can we describe in a more useful way the functions which satisfy these conditions? One answer is the following:

THEOREM 1: *If a function $f(t)$ contains no frequencies higher than W cps, it is completely determined by giving its ordinates at a series of points spaced $1/2W$ seconds apart.*

This is a fact which is common knowledge in the communication art. The intuitive justification is that, if $f(t)$ contains no frequencies higher than W, it cannot change to a substantially new value in a time less than one-half cycle of the highest frequency, that is, $1/2W$. A mathematical proof showing that this is not only approximately, but exactly, true can be given as follows. Let $F(\omega)$ be the spectrum of $f(t)$. Then

$$f(t) = \frac{1}{2\pi} \int_{-\infty}^{\infty} F(\omega)e^{i\omega t}d\omega \qquad (2)$$

$$= \frac{1}{2\pi} \int_{-2\pi W}^{+2\pi W} F(\omega)e^{i\omega t}d\omega, \qquad (3)$$

since $F(\omega)$ is assumed zero outside the band W. If we let

$$t = \frac{n}{2W} \qquad (4)$$

where n is any positive or negative integer, we obtain

$$f\left(\frac{n}{2W}\right) = \frac{1}{2\pi} \int_{-2\pi W}^{+2\pi W} F(\omega)e^{i\omega \frac{n}{2W}}\, d\omega. \qquad (5)$$

On the left are the values of $f(t)$ at the sampling points. The integral on the right will be recognized as essentially the nth coefficient in a Fourier-series expansion of the function $F(\omega)$, taking the interval $-W$ to $+W$ as a fundamental period. This means that the values of the samples $f(n/2W)$ determine the Fourier coefficients in the series expansion of $F(\omega)$. Thus they determine $F(\omega)$, since $F(\omega)$ is zero for frequencies greater than W, and for lower frequencies $F(\omega)$ is determined if its Fourier coefficients are determined. But $F(\omega)$ determines the origi-

nal function $f(t)$ completely, since a function is determined if its spectrum is known. Therefore the original samples determine the function $f(t)$ completely. There is one and only one function whose spectrum is limited to a band W, and which passes through given values at sampling points separated $1/2W$ seconds apart. The function can be simply reconstructed from the samples by using a pulse of the type

$$\frac{\sin 2\pi Wt}{2\pi Wt}. \qquad (6)$$

This function is unity at $t=0$ and zero at $t=n/2W$, i.e., at all other sample points. Furthermore, its spectrum is constant in the band W and zero outside. At each sample point a pulse of this type is placed whose amplitude is adjusted to equal that of the sample. The sum of these pulses is the required function, since it satisfies the conditions on the spectrum and passes through the sampled values.

Mathematically, this process can be described as follows. Let x_n be the nth sample. Then the function $f(t)$ is represented by

$$f(t) = \sum_{n=-\infty}^{\infty} x_n \frac{\sin \pi(2Wt - n)}{\pi(2Wt - n)}. \qquad (7)$$

A similar result is true if the band W does not start at zero frequency but at some higher value, and can be proved by a linear translation (corresponding physically to single-sideband modulation) of the zero-frequency case. In this case the elementary pulse is obtained from $\sin x/x$ by single-side-band modulation.

If the function is limited to the time interval T and the samples are spaced $1/2W$ seconds apart, there will be a total of $2TW$ samples in the interval. All samples outside will be substantially zero. To be more precise, we can define a function to be limited to the time interval T if, and only if, all the samples outside this interval are exactly zero. Then we can say that any function limited to the bandwidth W and the time interval T can be specified by giving $2TW$ numbers.

Theorem 1 has been given previously in other forms by mathematicians[3] but in spite of its evident importance seems not to have appeared explicitly in the literature of communication theory. Nyquist,[4,5] however, and more recently Gabor,[6] have pointed out that approximately $2TW$ numbers are sufficient, basing their argu-

[3] J. M. Whittaker, "Interpolatory Function Theory," Cambridge Tracts in Mathematics and Mathematical Physics, No. 33, Cambridge University Press, Chapt. IV; 1935.
[4] H. Nyquist, "Certain topics in telegraph transmission theory," *A.I.E.E. Transactions*, p. 617; April, 1928.
[5] W. R. Bennett, "Time division multiplex systems," *Bell Sys. Tech. Jour.*, vol. 20, p. 199; April, 1941, where a result similar to Theorem 1 is established, but on a steady-state basis.
[6] D. Gabor, "Theory of communication," *Jour. I.E.E.* (London), vol. 93; part 3, no. 26, p. 429; 1946.

ments on a Fourier series expansion of the function over the time interval T. This gives TW sine and $(TW+1)$ cosine terms up to frequency W. The slight discrepancy is due to the fact that the functions obtained in this way will not be strictly limited to the band W but, because of the sudden starting and stopping of the sine and cosine components, contain some frequency content outside the band. Nyquist pointed out the fundamental importance of the time interval $1/2W$ seconds in connection with telegraphy, and we will call this the Nyquist interval corresponding to the band W.

The $2TW$ numbers used to specify the function need not be the equally spaced samples used above. For example, the samples can be unevenly spaced, although, if there is considerable bunching, the samples must be known very accurately to give a good reconstruction of the function. The reconstruction process is also more involved with unequal spacing. One can further show that the value of the function and its derivative at every other sample point are sufficient. The value and first and second derivatives at every third sample point give a still different set of parameters which uniquely determine the function. Generally speaking, any set of $2TW$ independent numbers associated with the function can be used to describe it.

III. Geometrical Representation of the Signals

A set of three numbers x_1, x_2, x_3, regardless of their source, can always be thought of as co-ordinates of a point in three-dimensional space. Similarly, the $2TW$ evenly spaced samples of a signal can be thought of as co-ordinates of a point in a space of $2TW$ dimensions. Each particular selection of these numbers corresponds to a particular point in this space. Thus there is exactly one point corresponding to each signal in the band W and with duration T.

The number of dimensions $2TW$ will be, in general, very high. A 5-Mc television signal lasting for an hour would be represented by a point in a space with $2 \times 5 \times 10^6 \times 60^2 = 3.6 \times 10^{10}$ dimensions. Needless to say, such a space cannot be visualized. It is possible, however, to study analytically the properties of n-dimensional space. To a considerable extent, these properties are a simple generalization of the properties of two- and three-dimensional space, and can often be arrived at by inductive reasoning from these cases. The advantage of this geometrical representation of the signals is that we can use the vocabulary and the results of geometry in the communication problem. Essentially, we have replaced a complex entity (say, a television signal) in a simple environment (the signal requires only a plane for its representation as $f(t)$) by a simple entity (a point) in a complex environment ($2TW$ dimensional space).

If we imagine the $2TW$ co-ordinate axes to be at right angles to each other, then distances in the space have a simple interpretation. The distance from the origin to a point is analogous to the two- and three-dimensional cases

$$d = \sqrt{\sum_{n=1}^{2TW} x_n^2} \qquad (8)$$

where x_n is the nth sample. Now, since

$$f(t) = \sum_{n=1}^{2TW} x_n \frac{\sin \pi(2Wt - n)}{\pi(2Wt - n)}, \qquad (9)$$

we have

$$\int_{-\infty}^{\infty} f(t)^2 dt = \frac{1}{2W} \sum x_n^2, \qquad (10)$$

using the fact that

$$\int_{-\infty}^{\infty} \frac{\sin \pi(2Wt - m)}{\pi(2Wt - m)} \frac{\sin \pi(2Wt - n)}{\pi(Wt - n)} dt$$

$$= \begin{cases} 0 & m \neq n \\ \frac{1}{2W} & m = n. \end{cases} \qquad (11)$$

Hence, the square of the distance to a point is $2W$ times the energy (more precisely, the energy into a unit resistance) of the corresponding signal

$$d^2 = 2WE$$
$$= 2WTP \qquad (12)$$

where P is the average power over the time T. Similarly, the distance between two points is $\sqrt{2WT}$ times the rms discrepancy between the two corresponding signals.

If we consider only signals whose average power is less than P, these will correspond to points within a sphere of radius

$$r = \sqrt{2WTP}. \qquad (13)$$

If noise is added to the signal in transmission, it means that the point corresponding to the signal has been moved a certain distance in the space proportional to the rms value of the noise. Thus noise produces a small region of uncertainty about each point in the space. A fixed distortion in the channel corresponds to a warping of the space, so that each point is moved, but in a definite fixed way.

In ordinary three-dimensional space it is possible to set up many different co-ordinate systems. This is also possible in the signal space of $2TW$ dimensions that we are considering. A different co-ordinate system corresponds to a different way of describing the same signal function. The various ways of specifying a function given above are special cases of this. One other way of particular importance in communication is in terms of frequency components. The function $f(t)$ can be expanded as a sum of sines and cosines of frequencies $1/T$ apart, and the coefficients used as a different set of co-ordinates. It can be shown that these co-ordinates are all perpendicular to each other and are obtained by what is essentially a rotation of the original co-ordinate system.

Passing a signal through an ideal filter corresponds to projecting the corresponding point onto a certain region in the space. In fact, in the frequency-co-ordinate system those components lying in the pass band of the filter are retained and those outside are eliminated, so that the projection is on one of the co-ordinate lines, planes, or hyperplanes. Any filter performs a linear operation on the vectors of the space, producing a new vector linearly related to the old one.

IV. Geometrical Representation of Messages

We have associated a space of $2TW$ dimensions with the set of possible signals. In a similar way one can associate a space with the set of possible messages. Suppose we are considering a speech system and that the messages consist of all possible sounds which contain no frequencies over a certain limit W_1 and last for a time T_1.

Just as for the case of the signals, these messages can be represented in a one-to-one way in a space of $2T_1W_1$ dimensions. There are several points to be noted, however. In the first place, various different points may represent the same message, insofar as the final destination is concerned. For example, in the case of speech, the ear is insensitive to a certain amount of phase distortion. Messages differing only in the phases of their components (to a limited extent) sound the same. This may have the effect of reducing the number of essential dimensions in the message space. All the points which are equivalent for the destination can be grouped together and treated as one point. It may then require fewer numbers to specify one of these "equivalence classes" than to specify an arbitrary point. For example, in Fig. 2 we have a two-dimensional space, the set of points in a square. If all points on a circle are regarded as equivalent, it reduces to a one-dimensional space—a point can now be specified by one number, the radius of the circle. In the case of sounds, if the ear were completely insensitive to

phase, then the number of dimensions would be reduced by one-half due to this cause alone. The sine and cosine components a_n and b_n for a given frequency would not need to be specified independently, but only $\sqrt{a_n^2 + b_n^2}$; that is, the total amplitude for this frequency. The reduction in frequency discrimination of the ear as frequency increases indicates that a further reduction in dimensionality occurs. The vocoder makes use to a considerable extent of these equivalences among speech sounds, in the first place by eliminating, to a large degree, phase information, and in the second place by lumping groups of frequencies together, particularly at the higher frequencies.

In other types of communication there may not be any equivalence classes of this type. The final destination is sensitive to any change in the message within the full message space of $2T_1W_1$ dimensions. This appears to be the case in television transmission.

A second point to be noted is that the information source may put certain restrictions on the actual messages. The space of $2T_1W_1$ dimensions contains a point for *every* function of time $f(t)$ limited to the band W_1 and of duration T_1. The class of messages we wish to transmit may be only a small subset of these functions. For example, speech sounds must be produced by the human vocal system. If we are willing to forego the transmission of any other sounds, the effective dimensionality may be considerably decreased. A similar effect can occur through probability considerations. Certain messages may be possible, but so improbable relative to the others that we can, in a certain sense, neglect them. In a television image, for example, successive frames are likely to be very nearly identical. There is a fair probability of a particular picture element having the same light intensity in successive frames. If this is analyzed mathematically, it results in an effective reduction of dimensionality of the message space when T_1 is large.

We will not go further into these two effects at present, but let us suppose that, when they are taken into account, the resulting message space has a dimensionality D, which will, of course, be less than or equal to $2T_1W_1$. In many cases, even though the effects are present, their utilization involves too much complication in the way of equipment. The system is then designed on the basis that all functions are different and that there are no limitations on the information source. In this case, the message space is considered to have the full $2T_1W_1$ dimensions.

V. Geometrical Representation of the Transmitter and Receiver

We now consider the function of the transmitter from this geometrical standpoint. The input to the transmitter is a message; that is, one point in the message space. Its output is a signal—one point in the signal space. Whatever form of encoding or modulation is performed, the transmitter must establish some correspondence between the points in the two spaces. Every point in the message space must correspond to a point in the signal

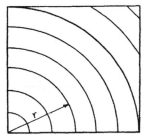

Fig. 2—Reduction of dimensionality through equivalence classes.

TABLE I

Communication System	Geometrical Entity
The set of possible signals	A space of $2TW$ dimensions
A particular signal	A point in the space
Distortion in the channel	A warping of the space
Noise in the channel	A region of uncertainty about each point
The average power of the signal	$(2TW)^{-1}$ times the square of the distance from the origin to the point
The set of signals of power P	The set of points in a sphere of radius $\sqrt{2TW\,P}$
The set of possible messages	A space of $2T_1W_1$ dimensions
The set of actual messages distinguishable by the destination	A space of D dimensions obtained by regarding all equivalent messages as one point, and deleting messages which the source could not produce
A message	A point in this space
The transmitter	A mapping of the message space into the signal space
The receiver	A mapping of the signal space into the message space

space, and no two messages can correspond to the same signal. If they did, there would be no way to determine at the receiver which of the two messages was intended. The geometrical name for such a correspondence is a mapping. The transmitter maps the message space into the signal space.

In a similar way, the receiver maps the signal space back into the message space. Here, however, it is possible to have more than one point mapped into the same point. This means that several different signals are demodulated or decoded into the same message. In AM, for example, the phase of the carrier is lost in demodulation. Different signals which differ only in the phase of the carrier are demodulated into the same message. In FM the shape of the signal wave above the limiting value of the limiter does not affect the recovered message. In PCM considerable distortion of the received pulses is possible, with no effect on the output of the receiver.

We have so far established a correspondence between a communication system and certain geometrical ideas. The correspondence is summarized in Table I.

VI. MAPPING CONSIDERATIONS

It is possible to draw certain conclusions of a general nature regarding modulation methods from the geometrical picture alone. Mathematically, the simplest types of mappings are those in which the two spaces have the same number of dimensions. Single-sideband amplitude modulation is an example of this type and an especially simple one, since the co-ordinates in the signal space are proportional to the corresponding co-ordinates in the message space. In double-sideband transmission the signal space has twice the number of co-ordinates, but they occur in pairs with equal values. If there were only one dimension in the message space and two in the signal space, it would correspond to mapping

a line onto a square so that the point x on the line is represented by (x, x) in the square. Thus no significant use is made of the extra dimensions. All the messages go into a subspace having only $2T_1W_1$ dimensions.

In frequency modulation the mapping is more involved. The signal space has a much larger dimensionality than the message space. The type of mapping can be suggested by Fig. 3, where a line is mapped into a three-dimensional space. The line starts at unit distance from the origin on the first co-ordinate axis, stays at this distance from the origin on a circle to the next co-ordinate axis, and then goes to the third. It can be seen that the line is lengthened in this mapping in proportion to the total number of co-ordinates. It is not, however, nearly as long as it could be if it wound back and forth through the space, filling up the internal volume of the sphere it traverses.

This expansion of the line is related to the improved signal-to-noise ratio obtainable with increased bandwidth. Since the noise produces a small region of uncertainty about each point, the effect of this on the recovered message will be less if the map is in a large scale. To obtain as large a scale as possible requires that the line

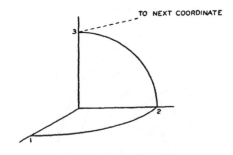

Fig. 3—Mapping similar to frequency modulation.

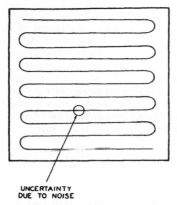

UNCERTAINTY
DUE TO NOISE

Fig. 4—Efficient mapping of a line into a square.

wander back and forth through the higher-dimensional region as indicated in Fig. 4, where we have mapped a line into a square. It will be noticed that when this is done the effect of noise is small relative to the length of the line, provided the noise is less than a certain critical value. At this value it becomes uncertain at the receiver as to which portion of the line contains the message. This holds generally, and it shows that *any system which attempts to use the capacities of a wider band to the full extent possible will suffer from a threshold effect when there is noise*. If the noise is small, very little distortion will occur, but at some critical noise amplitude the message will become very badly distorted. This effect is well known in PCM.

Suppose, on the other hand, we wish to reduce dimensionality, i.e., to compress bandwidth or time or both. That is, we wish to send messages of band W_1 and duration T_1 over a channel with $TW < T_1W_1$. It has already been indicated that the effective dimensionality D of the message space may be less than $2T_1W_1$ due to the properties of the source and of the destination. Hence we certainly need no more than D dimension in the signal space for a good mapping. To make this saving it is necessary, of course, to isolate the effective co-ordinates in the message space, and to send these only. The reduced bandwidth transmission of speech by the vocoder is a case of this kind.

The question arises, however, as to whether further reduction is possible. In our geometrical analogy, is it possible to map a space of high dimensionality onto one of lower dimensionality? The answer is that it is possible, with certain reservations. For example, the points of a square can be described by their two co-ordinates which could be written in decimal notation

$$x = .a_1a_2a_3 \cdots$$
$$y = .b_1b_2b_3 \cdots . \tag{14}$$

From these two numbers we can construct one number by taking digits alternately from x and y:

$$z = .a_1b_1a_2b_2a_3b_3 \cdots . \tag{15}$$

A knowledge of x and y determines z, and z determines both x and y. Thus there is a one-to-one correspondence between the points of a square and the points of a line.

This type of mapping, due to the mathematician Cantor, can easily be extended as far as we wish in the direction of reducing dimensionality. A space of n dimensions can be mapped in a one-to-one way into a space of one dimension. Physically, this means that the frequency-time product can be reduced as far as we wish when there is no noise, with exact recovery of the original messages.

In a less exact sense, a mapping of the type shown in Fig. 4 maps a square into a line, provided we are not too particular about recovering exactly the starting point, but are satisfied with a near-by one. The sensitivity we noticed before when increasing dimensionality now takes a different form. In such a mapping, to reduce TW, there will be a certain threshold effect when we perturb the message. As we change the message a small amount, the corresponding signal will change a small amount, until some critical value is reached. At this point the signal will undergo a considerable change. In topology it is shown[7] that it is not possible to map a region of higher dimension into a region of lower dimension *continuously*. It is the necessary discontinuity which produces the threshold effects we have been describing for communication systems.

This discussion is relevant to the well-known "Hartley Law," which states that " . . . an upper limit to the amount of information which may be transmitted is set by the sum for the various available lines of the product of the line-frequency range of each by the time during which it is available for use."[2] There is a sense in which this statement is true, and another sense in which it is false. It is not possible to map the message space into the signal space in a one-to-one, continuous manner (this is known mathematically as a *topological* mapping) unless the two spaces have the same dimensionality; i.e., unless $D = 2TW$. Hence, if we limit the transmitter and receiver to continuous one-to-one operations, there is a lower bound to the product TW in the channel. This lower bound is determined, not by the product W_1T_1 of message bandwidth and time, but by the number of *essential* dimension D, as indicated in Section IV. There is, however, no good reason for limiting the transmitter and receiver to topological mappings. In fact, PCM and similar modulation systems are highly discontinuous and come very close to the type of mapping given by (14) and (15). It is desirable, then, to find limits for what can be done with no restrictions on the type of transmitter and receiver operations. These limits, which will be derived in the following sections, depend on the amount and nature of the noise in the channel, and on the transmitter power, as well as on the bandwidth-time product.

It is evident that any system, either to compress TW,

[7] W. Hurewitz and H. Wallman, "Dimension Theory," Princeton University Press, Princeton, N. J.; 1941.

or to expand it and make full use of the additional volume, must be highly nonlinear in character and fairly complex because of the peculiar nature of the mappings involved.

VII. The Capacity of a Channel in the Presence of White Thermal Noise

It is not difficult to set up certain quantitative relations that must hold when we change the product TW. Let us assume, for the present, that the noise in the system is a white thermal-noise band limited to the band W, and that it is added to the transmitted signal to produce the received signal. A white thermal noise has the property that each sample is perturbed independently of all the others, and the distribution of each amplitude is Gaussian with standard deviation $\sigma = \sqrt{N}$ where N is the average noise power. How many different signals can be distinguished at the receiving point in spite of the perturbations due to noise? A crude estimate can be obtained as follows. If the signal has a power P, then the perturbed signal will have a power $P+N$. The number of amplitudes that can be reasonably well distinguished is

$$K \sqrt{\frac{P+N}{N}} \qquad (16)$$

where K is a small constant in the neighborhood of unity depending on how the phrase "reasonably well" is interpreted. If we require very good separation, K will be small, while toleration of occasional errors allows K to be larger. Since in time T there are $2TW$ independent amplitudes, the total number of reasonably distinct signals is

$$M = \left[K \sqrt{\frac{P+N}{N}} \right]^{2TW}. \qquad (17)$$

The number of bits that can be sent in this time is $\log_2 M$, and the rate of transmission is

$$\frac{\log_2 M}{T} = W \log_2 K^2 \frac{P+N}{N} \text{ (bits per second).} \qquad (18)$$

The difficulty with this argument, apart from its general approximate character, lies in the tacit assumption that for two signals to be distinguishable they must differ at some sampling point by more than the expected noise. The argument presupposes that PCM, or something very similar to PCM, is the best method of encoding binary digits into signals. Actually, two signals can be reliably distinguished if they differ by only a small amount, provided this difference is sustained over a long period of time. Each sample of the received signal then gives a small amount of statistical information concerning the transmitted signal; in combination,

these statistical indications result in near certainty. This possibility allows an improvement of about 8 db in power over (18) with a reasonable definition of reliable resolution of signals, as will appear later. We will now make use of the geometrical representation to determine the exact capacity of a noisy channel.

THEOREM 2: *Let P be the average transmitter power, and suppose the noise is white thermal noise of power N in the band W. By sufficiently complicated encoding systems it is possible to transmit binary digits at a rate*

$$C = W \log_2 \frac{P+N}{N} \qquad (19)$$

with as small a frequency of errors as desired. It is not possible by any encoding method to send at a higher rate and have an arbitrarily low frequency of errors.

This shows that the rate $W \log (P+N)/N$ measures in a sharply defined way the capacity of the channel for transmitting information. It is a rather surprising result, since one would expect that reducing the frequency of errors would require reducing the rate of transmission, and that the rate must approach zero as the error frequency does. Actually, we can send at the rate C but reduce errors by using more involved encoding and longer delays at the transmitter and receiver. The transmitter will take long sequences of binary digits and represent this entire sequence by a particular signal function of long duration. The delay is required because the transmitter must wait for the full sequence before the signal is determined. Similarly, the receiver must wait for the full signal function before decoding into binary digits.

We now prove Theorem 2. In the geometrical representation each signal point is surrounded by a small region of uncertainty due to noise. With white thermal noise, the perturbations of the different samples (or coordinates) are all Gaussian and independent. Thus the probability of a perturbation having co-ordinates $x_1, x_2, \cdots, x_n$ (these are the differences between the original and received signal co-ordinates) is the product of the individual probabilities for the different co-ordinates:

$$\prod_{n=1}^{2TW} \frac{1}{\sqrt{2\pi 2TWN}} \exp - \frac{x_n^2}{2TWN}$$
$$= \frac{1}{(2\pi 2TWN)^{TW}} \exp \frac{-1}{2TW} \sum_1^{2TW} x_n^2.$$

Since this depends only on

$$\sum_1^{2TW} x_n^2,$$

the probability of a given perturbation depends only on the *distance* from the original signal and not on the direction. In other words, the region of uncertainty is spherical in nature. Although the limits of this region are not sharply defined for a small number of dimensions ($2TW$), the limits become more and more definite as the dimensionality increases. This is because the square of the distance a signal is perturbed is equal to $2TW$ times the average noise power during the time T. As T increases, this average noise power must approach N. Thus, for large T, the perturbation will almost certainly be to some point near the surface of a sphere of radius $\sqrt{2TWN}$ centered at the original signal point. More precisely, by taking T sufficiently large we can insure (with probability as near to 1 as we wish) that the perturbation will lie within a sphere of radius $\sqrt{2TW(N+\epsilon)}$ where ϵ is arbitrarily small. The noise regions can therefore be thought of roughly as sharply defined billiard balls, when $2TW$ is very large. The received signals have an average power $P+N$, and in the same sense must almost all lie on the surface of a sphere of radius $\sqrt{2TW(P+N)}$. How many different transmitted signals can be found which will be distinguishable? Certainly not more than the volume of the sphere of radius $\sqrt{2TW(P+N)}$ divided by the volume of a sphere of radius $\sqrt{2TWN}$, since overlap of the noise spheres results in confusion as to the message at the receiving point. The volume of an n-dimensional sphere[8] of radius r is

$$V = \frac{\pi^{n/2}}{\Gamma\left(\dfrac{n}{2}+1\right)}\, r^n \cdot \qquad (20)$$

Hence, an upper limit for the number M of distinguishable signals is

$$M \leqq \left(\sqrt{\frac{P+N}{N}}\right)^{2TW} \cdot \qquad (21)$$

Consequently, the channel capacity is bounded by:

$$C = \frac{\log_2 M}{T} \leqq W \log_2 \frac{P+N}{N} \cdot \qquad (22)$$

This proves the last statement in the theorem.

To prove the first part of the theorem, we must show that there exists a system of encoding which transmits $W \log_2 (P+N)/N$ binary digits per second with a frequency of errors less than ϵ when ϵ is arbitrarily small. The system to be considered operates as follows. A long sequence of, say, m binary digits is taken in at the transmitter. There are 2^m such sequences, and each corresponds to a particular signal function of duration T. Thus there are $M=2^m$ different signal functions. When the sequence of m is completed, the transmitter starts sending the corresponding signal. At the receiver a per-

turbed signal is received. The receiver compares this signal with each of the M possible transmitted signals and selects the one which is nearest the perturbed signal (in the sense of rms error) as the one actually sent. The receiver then constructs, as its output, the corresponding sequence of binary digits. There will be, therefore, an over-all delay of $2T$ seconds.

To insure a frequency of errors less than ϵ, the M signal functions must be reasonably well separated from each other. In fact, we must choose them in such a way that, when a perturbed signal is received, the nearest signal point (in the geometrical representation) is, with probability greater than $1-\epsilon$, the actual original signal.

It turns out, rather surprisingly, that it is possible to choose our M signal functions at random from the points inside the sphere of radius $\sqrt{2TWP}$, and achieve the most that is possible. Physically, this corresponds very nearly to using M different samples of band-limited white noise with power P as signal functions.

A particular selection of M points in the sphere corresponds to a particular encoding system. The general scheme of the proof is to consider all such selections, and to show that the frequency of errors averaged over all the particular selections is less than ϵ. This will show that there are particular selections in the set with frequency of errors less than ϵ. Of course, there will be other particular selections with a high frequency of errors.

The geometry is shown in Fig. 5. This is a plane cross section through the high-dimensional sphere defined by a typical transmitted signal B, received signal A, and the origin 0. The transmitted signal will lie very close to the surface of the sphere of radius $\sqrt{2TWP}$, since in a high-dimensional sphere nearly all the volume is very close to the surface. The received signal similarly will lie on the surface of the sphere of radius $\sqrt{2TW(P+N)}$. The high-dimensional lens-shaped region L is the region of possible signals that might have caused A, since the distance between the transmitted and received signal is almost certainly very close to $\sqrt{2TWN}$. L is of smaller volume than a sphere of radius

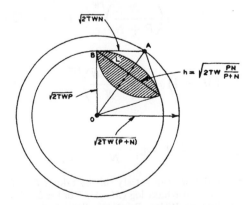

Fig. 5—The geometry involved in Theorem 2.

[8] D. M. Y. Sommerville, "An Introduction to the Geometry of N Dimensions," E. P. Dutton, Inc., New York, N. Y., 1929; p. 135.

h. We can determine h by equating the area of the triangle OAB, calculated two different ways:

$$\tfrac{1}{2}h\sqrt{2TW(P+N)} = \tfrac{1}{2}\sqrt{2TWP}\sqrt{2TWN}$$

$$h = \sqrt{2TW\frac{PN}{P+N}}\,.$$

The probability of any particular signal point (other than the actual cause of A) lying in L is, therefore, less than the ratio of the volumes of spheres of radii $\sqrt{2TW\,PN/P+N}$ and $\sqrt{2TWP}$, since in our ensemble of coding systems we chose the signal points at random from the points in the sphere of radius $\sqrt{2TWP}$. This ratio is

$$\left(\frac{\sqrt{2TW\dfrac{PN}{P+N}}}{\sqrt{2TWP}}\right)^{2TW} = \left(\frac{N}{P+N}\right)^{TW}. \quad (23)$$

We have M signal points. Hence the probability p that all except the actual cause of A are *outside* L is greater than

$$\left[1 - \left(\frac{N}{P+N}\right)^{TW}\right]^{M-1}. \quad (24)$$

When these points are outside L, the signal is interpreted correctly. Therefore, if we make P greater than $1-\epsilon$, the frequency of errors will be less than ϵ. This will be true if

$$\left[1 - \left(\frac{N}{P+N}\right)^{TW}\right]^{(M-1)} > 1 - \epsilon. \quad (25)$$

Now $(1-x)^n$ is always greater than $1-nx$ when n is positive. Consequently, (25) will be true if

$$1 - (M-1)\left(\frac{N}{P+N}\right)^{TW} > 1 - \epsilon \quad (26)$$

or if

$$(M-1) < \epsilon\left(\frac{P+N}{N}\right)^{TW} \quad (27)$$

or

$$\frac{\log(M-1)}{T} < W\log\frac{P+N}{N} + \frac{\log\epsilon}{T}. \quad (28)$$

For any fixed ϵ, we can satisfy this by taking T sufficiently large, and also have $\log(M-1)/T$ or $\log M/T$ as close as desired to $W\log P+N/N$. This shows that,

with a random selection of points for signals, we can obtain an arbitrarily small frequency of errors and transmit at a rate arbitrarily close to the rate C. We can also send *at* the rate C with arbitrarily small ϵ, since the extra binary digits need not be sent at all, but can be filled in at random at the receiver. This only adds another arbitrarily small quantity to ϵ. This completes the proof.

VIII. Discussion

We will call a system that transmits without errors at the rate C an ideal system. Such a system cannot be achieved with any finite encoding process but can be approximated as closely as desired. As we approximate more closely to the ideal, the following effects occur: (1) The rate of transmission of binary digits approaches $C = W\log_2(1+P/N)$. (2) The frequency of errors approaches zero. (3) The transmitted signal approaches a white noise in statistical properties. This is true, roughly speaking, because the various signal functions used must be distributed at random in the sphere of radius $\sqrt{2TWP}$. (4) The threshold effect becomes very sharp. If the noise is increased over the value for which the system was designed, the frequency of errors increases very rapidly. (5) The required delays at transmitter and receiver increase indefinitely. Of course, in a wide-band system a millisecond may be substantially an infinite delay.

In Fig. 6 the function $C/W = \log(1+P/N)$ is plotted with P/N in db horizontal and C/W the number of bits per cycle of band vertical. The circles represent PCM systems of the binary, ternary, etc., types, using positive and negative pulses and adjusted to give one error

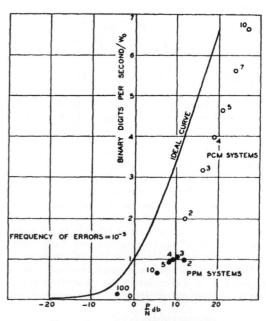

Fig. 6—Comparison of PCM and PPM
with ideal performance.

in about 10^6 binary digits. The dots are for a PPM system with two, three, etc., discrete positions for the pulse.[9] The difference between the series of points and the ideal curve corresponds to the gain that could be obtained by more involved coding systems. It amounts to about 8 db in power over most of the practical range. The series of points and circles is about the best that can be done without delay. Whether it is worth while to use more complex types of modulation to obtain some of this possible saving is, of course, a question of relative costs and valuations.

The quantity $TW \log (1+P/N)$ is, for large T, the number of bits that can be transmitted in time T. It can be regarded as an exchange relation between the different parameters. The individual quantities T, W, P, and N can be altered at will without changing the amount of information we can transmit, provided $TW \log (1+P/N)$ is held constant. If TW is reduced, P/N must be increased, etc.

Ordinarily, as we increase W, the noise power N in the band will increase proportionally; $N = N_0 W$ where N_0 is the noise power per cycle. In this case, we have

$$C = W \log \left(1 + \frac{P}{N_0 W}\right). \qquad (29)$$

If we let $W_0 = P/N_0$, i.e., W_0 is the band for which the noise power is equal to the signal power, this can be written

$$\frac{C}{W_0} = \frac{W}{W_0} \log \left(1 + \frac{W_0}{W}\right). \qquad (30)$$

In Fig. 7, C/W_0 is plotted as a function of W/W_0. As we increase the band, the capacity increases rapidly until the total noise power accepted is about equal to the signal power; after this, the increase is slow, and it approaches an asymptotic value $\log_2 e$ times the capacity for $W = W_0$.

IX. ARBITRARY GAUSSIAN NOISE

If a white thermal noise is passed through a filter whose transfer function is $Y(f)$, the resulting noise has a power spectrum $N(f) = K|Y(f)|^2$ and is known as Gaussian noise. We can calculate the capacity of a channel perturbed by any Gaussian noise from the white-noise result. Suppose our total transmitter power is P and it is distributed among the various frequencies according to $P(f)$. Then

$$\int_0^W P(f)df = P. \qquad (31)$$

[9] The PCM points are calculated from formulas given in "The philosophy of PCM," by B. M. Oliver, J. R. Pierce, and C. E. Shannon, PROC. I.R.E., vol. 36, pp. 1324–1332; November, 1948. The PPM points are from unpublished calculations of B. McMillan, who points out that, for very small P/N, the points approach to within 3 db of the ideal curve.

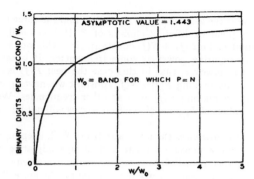

Fig. 7—Channel capacity as a function of bandwidth.

We can divide the band into a large number of small bands, with $N(f)$ approximately constant in each. The total capacity for a given distribution $P(f)$ will then be given by

$$C_1 = \int_0^W \log \left(1 + \frac{P(f)}{N(f)}\right) df, \qquad (32)$$

since, for each elementary band, the white-noise result applies. The maximum rate of transmission will be found by maximizing C_1 subject to condition (31). This requires that we maximize

$$\int_0^W \left[\log \left(1 + \frac{P(f)}{N(f)}\right) + \lambda P(f)\right] df. \qquad (33)$$

The condition for this is, by the calculus of variations, or merely from the convex nature of the curve $\log (1+x)$,

$$\frac{1}{N(f) + P(f)} + \lambda = 0, \qquad (34)$$

or $N(f) + P(f)$ must be constant. The constant is adjusted to make the total signal power equal to P. For frequencies where the noise power is low, the signal power should be high, and vice versa, as we would expect.

The situation is shown graphically in Fig. 8. The

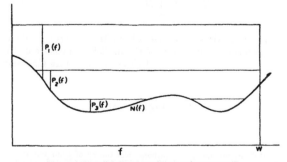

Fig. 8—Best distribution of transmitter power.

curve is the assumed noise spectrum, and the three lines correspond to different choices of P. If P is small, we cannot make $P(f) + N(f)$ constant, since this would require negative power at some frequencies. It is easily shown, however, that in this case the best $P(f)$ is obtained by making $P(f) + N(f)$ constant whenever possible, and making $P(f)$ zero at other frequencies. With low values of P, some of the frequencies will not be used at all.

If we now vary the noise spectrum $N(f)$, keeping the total noise power constant and always adjusting the signal spectrum $P(f)$ to give the maximum transmission, we can determine the worst spectrum for the noise. This turns out to be the white-noise case. Although this only shows it to be worst among the Gaussian noises, it will be shown later to be the worst among all possible noises with the given power N in the band.

X. The Channel Capacity with an Arbitrary Type of Noise

Of course, there are many kinds of noise which are not Gaussian; for example, impulse noise, or white noise that has passed through a nonlinear device. If the signal is perturbed by one of these types of noise, there will still be a definite channel capacity C, the maximum rate of transmission of binary digits. We will merely outline the general theory here.[10]

Let $x_1, x_2, \cdots, x_n$ be the amplitudes of the noise at successive sample points, and let

$$p(x_1, x_2, \cdots, x_n)dx_1 \cdots dx_n \qquad (35)$$

be the probability that these amplitudes lie between x_1 and $x_1 + dx_1$, x_2 and $x_2 + dx_2$, etc. Then the function p describes the statistical structure of the noise, insofar as n successive samples are concerned. The *entropy*, H, of the noise is defined as follows. Let

$$H_n = -\frac{1}{n} \int \cdots \int p(x_1, \cdots, x_n)$$

$$\log_e p(x_1, \cdots, x_n)dx_1, \cdots, dx_n. \qquad (36)$$

Then

$$H = \lim_{n \to \infty} H_n. \qquad (37)$$

This limit exists in all cases of practical interest, and can be determined in many of them. H is a measure of the randomness of the noise. In the case of white Gaussian noise of power N, the entropy is

$$H = \log_e \sqrt{2\pi e N}. \qquad (38)$$

[10] C. E. Shannon, "A mathematical theory of communication," *Bell Sys. Tech. Jour.*, vol. 27, pp. 379–424 and 623–657; July and October, 1948.

It is convenient to measure the randomness of an arbitrary type of noise not directly by its entropy, but by comparison with white Gaussian noise. We can calculate the power in a white noise having the same entropy as the given noise. This power, namely,

$$\overline{N} = \frac{1}{2\pi e} \exp 2H \qquad (39)$$

where H is the entropy of the given noise, will be called the *entropy power* of the noise.

A noise of entropy power $\overline{N}$ acts very much like a white noise of power $\overline{N}$, insofar as perturbing the message is concerned. It can be shown that the region of uncertainty about each signal point will have the same volume as the region associated with the white noise. Of course, it will no longer be a spherical region. In proving Theorem 1 this volume of uncertainty was the chief property of the noise used. Essentially the same argument may be applied for any kind of noise with minor modifications. The result is summarized in the following:

THEOREM 3: *Let a noise limited to the band W have power N and entropy power N_1. The capacity C is then bounded by*

$$W \log_2 \frac{P + N_1}{N_1} \leqq C \leqq W \log_2 \frac{P + N}{N_1} \qquad (40)$$

where P is the average signal power and W the bandwidth.

If the noise is a white Gaussian noise, $N_1 = N$, and the two limits are equal. The result then reduces to the theorem in Section VII.

For any noise, $N_1 < N$. This is why white Gaussian noise is the worst among all possible noises. If the noise is Gaussian with spectrum $N(f)$, then

$$N_1 = W \exp \frac{1}{W} \int_0^W \log N(f)df. \qquad (41)$$

The upper limit in Theorem 3 is then reached when we are above the highest noise power in Fig. 8. This is easily verified by substitution.

In the cases of most interest, P/N is fairly large. The two limits are then nearly the same, and we can use $W \log (P+N)/N_1$ as the capacity. The upper limit is the best choice, since it can be shown that as P/N increases, C approaches the upper limit.

XI. Discrete Sources of Information

Up to now we have been chiefly concerned with the channel. The capacity C measures the maximum rate at which a random series of binary digits can be transmitted when they are encoded in the best possible way. In general, the information to be transmitted will not be in this form. It may, for example, be a sequence of letters as in telegraphy, a speech wave, or a television signal. Can we find an equivalent number of bits per second for information sources of this type? Consider first the discrete case; i.e., the message consists of a sequence of discrete symbols. In general, there may be correlation of various sorts between the different symbols. If the message is English text, the letter E is the most frequent, T is often followed by H, etc. These correlations allow a certain compression of the text by proper encoding. We may define the entropy of a discrete source in a way analogous to that for a noise; namely, let

$$H_n = -\frac{1}{n} \sum_{i,j,\cdots,s} p(i, j, \cdots, s)$$

$$\log_2 p(i, j, \cdots, s) \quad (42)$$

where $p(i, j, \cdots, s)$ is the probability of the sequence of symbols $i, j, \cdots, s$, and the sum is over all sequences of n symbols. Then the entropy is

$$H = \lim_{n \to \infty} H_n. \quad (43)$$

It turns out that H is the number of bits produced by the source for each symbol of message. In fact, the following result is proved in the Appendix.

THEOREM 4. *It is possible to encode all sequences of n message symbols into sequences of binary digits in such a way that the average number of binary digits per message symbol is approximately H, the approximation approaching equality as n increases.*

It follows that, if we have a channel of capacity C and a discrete source of entropy H, it is possible to encode the messages via binary digits into signals and transmit at the rate C/H of the original message symbols per second.

For example, if the source produces a sequence of letters A, B, or C with probabilities $p_A = 0.6$, $p_B = 0.3$, $p_C = 0.1$, and successive letters are chosen independently, then $H_n = H_1 = -[0.6 \log_2 0.6 + 0.3 \log_2 0.3 + 0.1 \log_2 0.1] = 1.294$ and the information produced is equivalent to 1.294 bits for each letter of the message. A channel with a capacity of 100 bits per second could transmit with best encoding $100/1.294 = 77.3$ message letters per second.

XII. CONTINUOUS SOURCES

If the source is producing a continuous function of time, then without further data we must ascribe it an infinite rate of generating information. In fact, merely to specify exactly one quantity which has a continuous range of possibilities requires an infinite number of binary digits. We cannot send continuous information *exactly* over a channel of finite capacity.

Fortunately, we do not need to send continuous messages exactly. A certain amount of discrepancy be-

tween the original and the recovered messages can always be tolerated. If a certain tolerance is allowed, then a definite finite rate in binary digits per second can be assigned to a continuous source. It must be remembered that this rate depends on the nature and magnitude of the allowed error between original and final messages. The rate may be described as the rate of generating information *relative to the criterion of fidelity*.

Suppose the criterion of fidelity is the rms discrepancy between the original and recovered signals, and that we can tolerate a value $\sqrt{N_1}$. Then each point in the message space is surrounded by a small sphere of radius $\sqrt{2I_1 W_1 N_1}$. If the system is such that the recovered message lies within this sphere, the transmission will be satisfactory. Hence, the number of different messages which must be capable of distinct transmission is of the order of the volume V_1 of the region of possible messages divided by the volume of the small spheres. Carrying out this argument in detail along lines similar to those used in Sections VII and IX leads to the following result:

THEOREM 5: *If the message source has power Q, entropy power $\overline{Q}$, and bandwidth W_1, the rate R of generating information in bits per second is bounded by*

$$W_1 \log_2 \frac{\overline{Q}}{N_1} \leq R \leq W_1 \log_2 \frac{Q}{N_1} \quad (44)$$

where N_1 is the maximum tolerable mean square error in reproduction. If we have a channel with capacity C and a source whose rate of generating information R is less than or equal to C, it is possible to encode the source in such a way as to transmit over this channel with the fidelity measured by N_1. If $R > C$, this is impossible.

In the case where the message source is producing white thermal noise, $\overline{Q} = Q$. Hence the two bounds are equal and $R = W_1 \log Q/N_1$. We can, therefore, transmit white noise of power Q and band W_1 over a channel of band W perturbed by a white noise of power N and recover the original message with mean square error N_1 if, and only if,

$$W_1 \log \frac{Q}{N_1} \leq W \log \frac{P+N}{N}. \quad (45)$$

APPENDIX

Consider the possible sequences of n symbols. Let them be arranged in order of decreasing probability, $p_1 \geq p_2 \geq p_3 \cdots \geq p_s$. Let $P_i = \sum_1^{i-1} p_j$. The ith message is encoded by expanding P_i as a binary fraction and using only the first t_i places where t_i is determined from

$$\log_2 \frac{1}{p_i} \leq t_i < 1 + \log_2 \frac{1}{p_i}. \quad (46)$$

Probable sequences have short codes and improbable ones long codes. We have

$$\frac{1}{2^{t_i}} \leq p_i \leq \frac{1}{2^{t_i-1}} \cdot \qquad (47)$$

The codes for different sequences will all be different. P_{i+1}, for example, differs by p_i from P_i, and therefore its binary expansion will differ in one or more of the first t_i places, and similarly for all others. The average length of the encoded message will be $\sum p_i t_i$. Using (46),

$$-\sum p_i \log p_i \leq \sum p_i t_i < \sum p_i (1 - \log p_i) \qquad (48)$$

or

$$nH_n \leq \sum p_i t_i < 1 + nH_n. \qquad (49)$$

The average number of binary digits used per message symbol is $1/n \sum p_i t_i$ and

$$H_n \leq \frac{1}{n} \sum p_i t_i < \frac{1}{n} + H_n. \qquad (50)$$

As $n \to \infty$, $H_n \to H$ and $1/n \to 0$, so the average number of bits per message symbol approaches H.

Communication Theory — Exposition of Fundamentals*

Claude E. Shannon

In any branch of applied mathematics, the vague and ambiguous concepts of a physical problem are given a more refined and idealized meaning. In information theory, one of the basic notions is that of the amount of information associated with a given situation. "Information" here, although related to the everyday meaning of the word, should not be confused with it. In everyday usage, information usually implies something about the semantic content of a message. For the purposes of communication theory, the "meaning" of a message is generally irrelevant; what is significant is the difficulty in transmitting the message from one point to another.

From this point of view, information exists only when there is a choice of possible messages. If there were only one possible message there would be no information; no transmission system would be required in such a case, for this message could be on a record at the receiving point. Information is closely associated with uncertainty. The information I obtain when you say something to me corresponds to the amount of uncertainty I had, previous to your speaking, of what you were going to say. If I was certain of what you were going to say, I obtain no information by your saying it.

In general, when there are a number of possible events or messages that may occur, there will also be a set of *a priori* probabilities for these messages and the amount of information, still arguing heuristically, should depend upon these probabilities. If one particular message is overwhelmingly probable, the amount of information or the *a priori* uncertainty will be small.

It turns out that the appropriate measure for the amount of information when a choice is made from a set of possibilities with the probabilities $p_1, p_2, \ldots, p_n$ is given by the formula

$$H = - \sum_{i=1}^{n} p_i \log p_i .$$ (1)

Some of the reasons justifying this formula are (1) $H = 0$ if and only if all the p_i are zero except one which is unity, i.e., a situation with no choice, no information, no uncertainty. (2) With a fixed n, the maximum H occurs when all the p_i are equal, $p_i = \dfrac{1}{n}$. This is also, intuitively, the most uncertain situation. H then reduces to $\log n$. (3) H is always positive or zero. (4) If there are two events x and y, we can consider the information H_c in the composite event consisting of a choice of both x and y:

$$H_c(x, y) = - \sum p(x, y) \log p(x, y) .$$ (2)

It can be shown that this composite information is greatest when the two events, x and y, are statistically independent. It is then the sum of the individual amounts of information.

Equation (1) is identical in form with certain formulas for entropy used in statistical mechanics, in particular in the formulation due to Boltzmann. It is to be noted that both here and in thermodynamics $- \sum p_i \log p_i$ is a measure of randomness: in thermodynamics, the

---

* IRE Transactions Information Theory, No. 1, Feb. 1950.

random position of a representative point in a dynamical phase-space; in information theory, the randomness in the choice of the particular message to be transmitted from an ensemble of possible messages. We shall frequently speak of quantities having the form $-\Sigma p_i \log p_i$ as *entropies* because of this identity in form.

The formula (1) measures the amount of information when a single choice is made from a finite set of possible events. In a communication system we frequently must consider messages which are produced by a sequence of such choices. Thus the English text to be transmitted over a telegraph system consists of a sequence of letters, spaces and punctuation. In such a case we are concerned with the amount of information produced per symbol of text. The formula (1) must be generalized to take account of influences between letters and the general statistical structure of the language. We think of a language, then, as being produced by a stochastic (i.e., statistical) process which chooses the letters of a text one by one in accordance with certain probabilities depending in general on previous choices that have been made.

Samples of statistical English based on such a representation of the English language have been constructed. The following are some examples with varying amounts of the statistics of English introduced.

1. Letter approximation (letter probabilities the same as in English)
    OCRO HLI RGWR NMIELWIS EU LL NBNESEBYA TH EEI

2. Trigram approximation (probabilities for triplets of letters the same as in English)
    IN NO IST LAT WHEY CRATICT FROURE BIRS GROCID

3. Word-digram approximation (probabilities for word-pairs as in English)
    THE HEAD AND IN FRONTAL ATTACK ON AN ENGLISH WRITER THAT THE CHARACTER OF THIS POINT IS THEREFORE

4. Word-tetragram approximation
    THIS WAS THE FIRST. THE SECOND TIME IT HAPPENED WITHOUT HIS APPROVAL. NEVERTHELESS IT CANNOT BE DONE. IT COULD HARDLY HAVE BEEN THE ONLY LIVING VETERAN OF THE FOREIGN POWER HAD STATED THAT NEVER MORE COULD HAPPEN.

The amount of information produced by a stochastic process per letter of message is defined by formulas similar to (1). For example, one method is to calculate the amount of information for a choice of N letters of text, divide by N to put it on a per letter basis, and then allow N to increase indefinitely.

The fundamental reason why the entropy per letter obtained in this way forms the appropriate measure of the amount of information is contained in what may be called the "coding theorem." This states that if a language has an entropy H bits per letter (i.e., $\log_2$ was used in the calculation) then it is possible to approximate as closely as desired to a coding system which translates the original messages into binary digits (0 to 1) in a reversible way and uses, on the average, H binary digits in the encoded version per letter of the original language. Furthermore there is no such system of encoding which uses less than H binary digits on the average. In other words, speaking roughly, H measures the equivalent number of binary digits for each letter produced in the language in question. H measures all languages by the common yardstick of binary digits.

A closely related aspect of a language is its redundancy. This is defined as follows. Suppose all the letters in the language were independent and equiprobable. Then the entropy per letter would be the logarithm of the number of letters in the alphabet. The relative entropy is the ratio of the actual entropy to this maximum possible entropy for the same alphabet. The redundancy is one minus the relative entropy. The redundancy determines how much a language can be compressed when properly encoded into the same alphabet. Thus, if the redundancy were 70 per cent, a suitable encoding of the language would reduce its length on the average by this amount.

A number of methods have been developed for estimating the entropy and redundancy of various stochastic processes. In the case of printed English, the most direct approach is to make use of tables of letter, digram, trigram, etc., probabilities and to calculate from them the entropy of the various approximations to English. Unfortunately, with the tables actually available it is not possible to go farther than approximations including about six or eight letters. At this point, figures of the order of 50 per cent for redundancy are obtained. They of course do not include long range statistical influences extending over groups of words, phrases and sentences.

Another more delicate method of estimating these parameters has recently been devised. It is based on the fact that anyone speaking a language possesses implicitly an enormous knowledge of the statistical structure of that language. By a relatively simple experiment, it is possible to translate this knowledge into numerical data which give upper and lower bounds for the entropy and redundancy. The experiment is to ask a subject to guess an unknown text in the language letter by letter. At each letter he guesses first what he considers the most probable next letter in view of the preceding text. If he is wrong he is required to guess again, and so on until he finally arrives at the correct next letter. In a typical experiment of this type with a text containing 102 letters, the subject guessed right on his first guess 79 times. Eight times he was right on the second guess, three times on the third, twice each on the fourth and fifth, and only eight times required more than five guesses. These figures clearly indicate the great redundancy of English. Furthermore from them one can estimate upper and lower numerical bounds for the redundancy which take into account rather long-range structure, inasmuch as the subject made considerable use of this structure in formulating his guesses. From the results of this work it appears that the redundancy of printed English at 100 letters is of the order of 75 per cent, and may well exceed this figure for still longer range structure.

So far we have been considering information only in the discrete cases. In generalizing to the continuous case, for example a speech wave or a television signal, a number of new features emerge. The generalization is by no means trivial. In the first place, a continuously variable quantity is capable of assuming an infinite number of possible values, and if there were no other considerations this would imply an infinite amount of information. Actually in practical cases there are always features which prevent this and enable one to effectively reduce the continuous case to a discrete case. The two facts which produce this result are the presence of perturbing noise in the signal and the finite resolving power of any physical receiving apparatus.

One important mathematical result which expedites the analysis of continuous information is the "sampling theorem." This states that a function of time limited in frequency components to a band W cycles wide is determined by giving its values at a series of sample points equally spaced in time and separated by $\frac{1}{2W}$ seconds. The knowledge of such a function is equivalent to knowledge of a sequence of numbers, the numbers occurring at the rate of $2W$ per second. If a message consists of such a band-limited function of time which persists for substantially T seconds, it is determined by giving $2TW$ numbers. Geometrically, such a function can be represented by a point in a space with $2TW$ dimensions. Certain aspects of communication theory can be analyzed by a consideration of the properties of mappings (which correspond to systems of modulation) in such spaces.

The problem of measuring the amount of information in a continuous message is more involved than a simple generalization of the entropy formula. It is necessary at this point to introduce a measure of the fidelity of reception of the message when it is perturbed by noise. When a suitable measure of fidelity has been set up, it is possible to define the amount of information (in bits per second) for a given continuous source and for a given fidelity of transmission. As the fidelity requirements are made more stringent, the amount of information increases. For example, in transmitting English speech, if we are satisfied with an intelligible reproduction the amount of information per second is small; if a high fidelity reproduction is required, preserving personal accents, etc., the information is greater.

REFERENCES

1. Shannon, C. E. and Weaver, W. "The Mathematical Theory of Communication", University of Illinois Press, Urbana, 1949.

2. Shannon, C. E. "Communication in the Presence of Noise", Proc. Inst. of Radio Engineers, *37*, pp. 10-21, January 1949.

3. Shannon, C. E. "The Prediction and Entropy of Printed English", Bell System Technical Journal, *30*, pp. 50-64, January 1951.

General Treatment of the Problem of Coding*

Claude E. Shannon

A typical communication system consists of the following five elements:

(1) An information *source*. This can be considered to be represented mathematically by a suitable stochastic process which chooses one message from a set of possible messages. The *rate R* of producing information is measured by the entropy per symbol of the process.

(2) An encoding or transmitting element. Mathematically this amounts to a transformation applied to the message to produce the *signal*, i.e. the encoded message.

(3) A *channel* on which the signal is transmitted from transmitter to receiver. During transmission the signal may be perturbed by noise.

(4) A receiving and decoding (or demodulating) device which recovers the original message from the received signal.

(5) The destination of the information, e.g. the human ear (for telephony) or the eye (for television). The characteristics of the destination may determine the significant elements of the information to be transmitted. For example, with sound transmission, precise recovery of the phases of components is not required because of the insensitivity of the ear to this type of distortion.

The central problems to be considered are how one can measure the capacity of a channel for transmitting information; how this capacity depends on various parameters such as bandwidth, available transmitter power and type of noise; and what is the best encoding system for a given information source to utilize a channel most efficiently.

Since the output of any information source can be encoded into binary digits using, statistically, R binary digits per symbol, the problem of defining a channel capacity can be reduced to the problem of determining the maximum number of binary digits that can be transmitted per second over the channel.

When there is no noise in the channel, it is generally possible to set up a difference equation whose asymptotic solution gives essentially the number of different signals of duration T when T is large. From this, it is possible to calculate the number of binary digits that can be transmitted in time T and, consequently, the channel capacity.

In a noisy system, the problem is mathematically considerably more difficult. Nevertheless, a definite channel capacity C exists in the following sense. It is possible by proper encoding of binary digits into allowable signal functions to transmit as closely as desired to the rate C binary digits per second with arbitrarily small frequency of errors. There is no method of encoding which transmits a larger number. In general, the ideal rate C can only be approached by using more and more complex encoding systems and longer and longer delays at both transmitter and receiver.

---

* IRE Transactions Information Theory, No. 1, Feb. 1950.

The channel capacity C is given by an expression involving the difference of two entropies. This expression must be maximized over all possible stochastic processes which might be used to generate signal functions. The actual numerical evaluation of C is difficult and has been carried out in only a few cases. Even when C is known, the construction of coding systems which approach the ideal rate of transmission is often infeasible.

A simple example of a noisy channel in which the capacity and an explicit ideal code can be found is the following. Assume the elementary signals are binary digits and that the noise produces at most one error in a group of seven of these. The channel capacity can be calculated as 4/7 bits per elementary signal. A code which transmits at this rate on the average is as follows. Let a block of seven symbols be $x_1, x_2, x_3, x_4, x_5, x_6, x_7$ (each x_i either 0 or 1). x_3, x_5, x_6 and x_7 are used as message symbols, and x_1, x_2 and x_4 are used redundantly for checking purposes. These are chosen by the following rules:

(1) x_4 is chosen so that $\alpha = (x_4 + x_5 + x_6 + x_7) \equiv 0 \mod 2$

(2) x_2 is chosen so that $\beta = (x_2 + x_3 + x_6 + x_7) \equiv 0 \mod 2$

(3) x_1 is chosen so that $\gamma = (x_1 + x_3 + x_5 + x_7) \equiv 0 \mod 2$.

The binary number $\alpha\beta\gamma$ calculated by these same expressions from the received signal gives the location of the error. (If zero, there was no error.) This forms a completely self-correcting code for the assumed type of noise.

If the signal functions are capable of continuous variation we have a *continuous channel*. If there were no noise whatever, a continuous channel would have an infinite capacity. Physically, there is always some noise. With white Gaussian noise the capacity is given by

$$C = W \log (1 + \frac{P}{N}) \tag{1}$$

in which

    W = bandwidth in cycles per second,

    P = available average transmitter power,

    N = average noise power within the band W.

The equation (1) is an exchange relation among the quantities W, P, N and C. Thus the transmitter power can be reduced by increasing the bandwidth, retaining the same channel capacity. Conversely a smaller bandwidth can be used at the expense of a greater signal-to-noise ratio.

If, as is usually the case, the noise power increases proportionally with bandwidth, $N = N_0 W$, we have

$$C = W \log (1 + \frac{P}{N_0 W}) . \tag{2}$$

As W increases, C approaches the asymptotic value

$$C_\infty = \frac{P}{N_0} \log e . \tag{3}$$

If the perturbing noise is Gaussian but does not have a flat spectrum, the most efficient use of the band occurs when the sum of the transmitter power and the noise power at each frequency is constant,

$$P(\omega) + N(\omega) = K . \qquad (4)$$

When the noise is Gaussian, it turns out that most efficient coding requires that the transmitted signal have the same statistical structure as Gaussian noise.

If the perturbing noise is not Gaussian, the mathematical problems of calculating channel capacity and ideal codes are formidable. The most that is known for the general case are upper and lower bounds for the channel capacity, given by the following inequalities

$$W \log \left(\frac{P + N_1}{N_1} \right) \le C \le W \log \left(\frac{P + N}{N_1} \right) ,$$

where P, N and C are as before, and N_1 is the average power in a thermal noise having the same entropy as the actual noise. N_1 is a measure of the amount of randomness in the noise. It is intuitively reasonable that this should be a controlling term in the channel capacity since the more predictable the noise the more it can be compensated for.

Among communication systems in actual use PCM (Pulse Code Modulation) and PPM (Pulse Position Modulation) come reasonably close to the ideal limits of channel capacity with white Gaussian noise. For high signal-to-noise ratios PCM is most appropriate. When the number of quantized amplitude levels is suitably adjusted, this method of modulation requires some eight to ten db greater power than the theoretical minimum. With low signal-to-noise ratios, PPM requires about the same extra signal power except for extremely low P/N values, in which case it is still closer to the ideal. Other more involved codes have been investigated, although not yet put into practice, which are about two db closer than PCM to the ideal. Rice has shown that certain types of codes approach the ideal roughly according to $1/\sqrt{\tau}$ where τ is the delay involved in the encoding process.

The general principles of communication theory and coding have an application in the study of secrecy systems. A secrecy system can be considered to be a communication system in which the noise is the arbitrariness introduced by the encoding process. It can be shown under certain assumptions that the redundancy of the original language is the fundamental factor governing the amount of material that must be intercepted in order to solve a cipher. These results check reasonably well against experimentally known results for certain simple secrecy systems.

REFERENCES

1. Shannon, C. E. and Weaver, W. "The Mathematical Theory of Communication," University of Illinois Press, Urbana, 1949.

2. Shannon, C. E. "Communication Theory of Secrecy Systems," Bell System Technical Journal, vol. 28, pp. 656-715, October 1949.

The Lattice Theory of Information*

Claude E. Shannon

The word "information" has been given many different meanings by various writers in the general field of information theory. It is likely that at least a number of these will prove sufficiently useful in certain applications to deserve further study and permanent recognition. It is hardly to be expected that a single concept of information would satisfactorily account for the numerous possible applications of this general field. The present note outlines a new approach to information theory which is aimed specifically at the analysis of certain communication problems in which there exist a number of information sources simultaneously in operation. A typical example is that of a simple communication channel with a feedback path from the receiving point to the transmitting point. The problem is to make use of the feedback information for improving forward transmission, and to determine the forward channel capacity when the best possible use is made of this feedback information. Another more general problem is that of a communication system consisting of a large number of transmitting and receiving points with some type of interconnecting network between the various points. The problem here is to formulate the best systems design whereby, in some sense, the best overall use of the available facilities is made. While the analysis sketched here has not yet proceeded to the point of a complete solution of these problems, partial answers have been found and it is believed that a complete solution may be possible.

1. The Nature of Information

In communication theory we consider information to be produced by a suitable stochastic process. We consider here only the discrete case; the successive symbols of the message are chosen from a finite "alphabet", and it is assumed for mathematical simplicity that the stochastic process producing the message has only a finite number of possible internal states. The message itself is then a discrete time series which is one sample from the ensemble of possible messages that might have been produced by the information source. The entropy $H(x)$ of such a source is a measure of the *amount* of information produced by the source per letter of message. However, $H(x)$ can hardly be said to represent the actual information. Thus two entirely different sources might produce information at the same rate (same H) but certainly they are not producing the same information.

To define a concept of actual information, consider the following situation. Suppose a source is producing, say, English text. This may be translated or encoded into many other forms (e.g. Morse code) in such a way that it is possible to decode and recover the original. For most purposes of communication, any of these forms is equally good and may be considered to contain the same information. Given any particular encoded form, any of the others may be obtained (although of course it may require an involved computation to do so). Thus we are led to define the actual information of a stochastic process as that which is common to all stochastic processes which may be obtained from the original by reversible encoding operations. It is desirable from a practical standpoint and mathematically convenient to limit the kind of allowed encoding operations in certain ways. In particular, it is desirable to require that the encoding be done by a transducer with a finite number of possible internal

---

* IRE Transactions Information Theory, No. 1, Feb. 1950.

states. This finite memory condition prevents paradoxical situations in which information goes into a transducer more rapidly on the average than it comes out.

Each coded version of the original process may be called a *translation* of the original language. These translations may be viewed as different ways of describing the same information, in about the same way that a vector may be described by its components in various coordinate systems. The information itself may be regarded as the equivalence class of all translations or ways of describing the same information.

2. The Metric, Topology and Convergent Sequences

With this definition of information, it is possible to set up a metric satisfying the usual requirements. The metric $\rho\,(x, y)$ measures the distance between two information elements x and y, and is given in terms of conditional entropies. We define

$$\rho\,(x, y) = H_x(y) + H_y(x) = 2\,H(x, y) - H(x) - H(y)\ .$$

The symmetry property $\rho\,(x, y) = \rho(y, x)$ is obvious from the definition. If $\rho\,(x, y) = 0$, both $H_x(y)$ and $H_y(x)$ must be zero (since both are necessarily non-negative), and this requires that the x sequence be calculable with probability 1 from the y sequence and vice versa. The triangle law for a metric,

$$\rho(x, y) + \rho(y, z) \geq \rho(x, z)\ ,$$

is readily shown by expanding these terms into the various entropies and making use of known inequalities for entropies. It may be noted that $\rho\,(x, y)$ is independent of the particular translations of x and y used in its calculation. This is due to the fact that $H_x(y)$ and $H_y(x)$ are invariant under finite state encoding operations applied to x and y.

The existence of a natural metric enables us to define a topology for a set of information elements and in particular the notion of sequences of such elements which approach a limit. A set of information elements $x_1, x_2, \ldots, x_n, \ldots$ will be said to be Cauchy convergent if

$$\lim_{\substack{m \to \infty \\ n \to \infty}} \rho(x_m, x_n) = 0\ .$$

The introduction of these sequences as new elements (analogous to irrational numbers) completes the space in a satisfactory way and enables one to simplify the statement of various results.

3. The Information Lattice

A relation of inclusion, $x \geq y$, between two information elements x and y can be defined by

$$x \geq y \equiv H_x(y) = 0\ .$$

This essentially requires that y can be obtained by a suitable finite state operation (or limit of such operations) on x. If $x \geq y$ we call y an *abstraction* of x. If $x \geq y$, $y \geq z$, then $x \geq z$. If $x \geq y$, then $H(x) \geq H(y)$. Also $x > y$ means $x \geq y$, $x \neq y$. The information element, one of whose translations is the process which always produces the same symbol, is the 0 element, and $x \geq 0$ for any x.

The *sum* of two information elements, $z = x + y$, is the process one of whose translations consists of the ordered pairs (x_n, y_n), where x_n is the nth symbol produced by the x sequence and similarly for y_n. We have $z \geq x$, $z \geq y$ and there is no $\mu < z$ with these properties; z is the least upper bound of x and y. The element z represents the total information of both x and y.

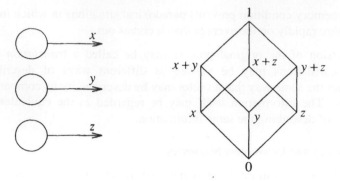

Fig. 1

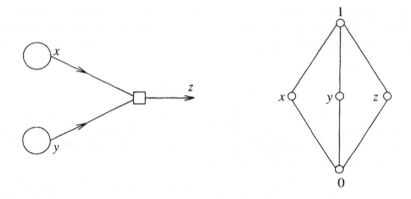

Fig. 2

The *product* $z = x\,y$ is defined as the largest z such that $z \leq x$, $z \leq y$; that is, there is no $\mu > z$ which is an abstraction of both x and y. The product is unique. Here z is the common information of x and y.

With these definitions a set of information elements with all their sums and products form a metric lattice. The lattices obtained in this way are not, in general, distributive, nor even modular. However they can be made to be relatively complemented by the addition of suitable elements. For $x \leq y$ it is possible to construct an element z with

$$z + x = y \,,$$

$$z\,x = 0 \,.$$

The element z is not in general unique.

The lattices obtained from a finite set of information sources are of a rather general type; they are at least as general as the class of finite partition lattices. With any finite partition lattice it is possible to construct an information lattice which is abstractly isomorphic to it by a simple procedure.

Some examples of simple information lattices are shown in Figs. 1 and 2.

In Fig. 1 there are three independent sources. The product of any two of these elements is zero, and the conventional lattice diagram is that shown at the right. In Fig. 2 there are two independent sources of binary digits, x and y. The sequence z is the sum mod 2 of corresponding symbols from x and y. In this case again the product of any two of x, y and z is zero, but the sum of any two represents the total information in the system. In this case the lattice is non-distributive, since $z\,y + z\,x = 0 + 0 = 0$, while $z(x + y) = z \neq 0$.

4. The Delay Free Group G_1

The definition of equality for information based on the group G of all reversible encoding operations allows $x = y$ when y is for example a delayed version of x: $y_n = x_{n+a}$. In some situations, when one must act on information at a certain time, a delay is not permissible. In such a case we may consider the more restricted group G_1 of *instantaneously reversible* translations. One may define inclusion, sum, product, etc., in an analogous way, and this also leads to a lattice but of much greater complexity and with many different invariants.

Discussion of Preceding Three Papers*

Mr. E. C. Cherry

There is a well-known elementary way of interpreting the "selective entropy" expression for the information conveyed by a symbol-sequence, which serves as an introduction to the subject, and which should perhaps be recorded. Consider one symbol, having a known probability of occurrence P_i, in a code of n such symbols. It is reasonable to assume that the "information" conveyed by this one symbol is the least number of selections, H, needed to identify it amongst the n in the code. Arrange the symbols in order of decreasing probability $P_1 P_2 \dots P_i \dots P_n$ (total probability = 1.0); divide into two groups $(P_1 P_2 \dots)$ and $(\dots P_i \dots P_n)$ of equal total probability $\frac{1}{2}$; again divide the group containing P_i into two, of probabilities $\frac{1}{4}$. Continue such bisection H times until two groups remain, each of probability P_i, one being the wanted symbol. Then

$$P_i \cdot 2^H = \text{total probability of the symbols in the code} = 1.0 ,$$

or

$$H = -\log_2 P_i . \tag{1}$$

The average number of selections required for a complete message is then the mean of H, or

$$H_{\text{average}} = -\sum_i P_i \log_2 P_i . \tag{2}$$

This argument assumes of course that the symbols may always be divided into two groups of equal probability; it perhaps has the merit of emphasizing the reasonable nature of the expression (2) as representing information.

Mr. S. H. Moss

During the discussion following Dr. Shannon's second talk, Professor Van Der Pol raised the question of what is meant by the delay imposed on a transient waveform by a process which at the same time distorts it.

If the process is linear, and has a finite zero-frequency response, the time lag between the (temporal) centroid of the output transient and the centroid of the input transient is a constant, which is a characteristic only of the system, and is independent of the wave-form of the input transient. It is thus an appropriate measure of delay. Its value is the slope of the phase-shift versus frequency curve at zero frequency.

For a wave-packet, considered as a sinusoidal wave of reference frequency, modulated in amplitude and phase by a transient complex envelope, there is an acceptable sense in which the centroid of the envelope is delayed by a constant time interval, independent of its waveform, if the amplitude versus frequency characteristic of the system is finite and stationary at the reference frequency. Here again its value is the slope of the phase-shift curve at the reference frequency, the well-known expression for the group-delay. In the general case, when the

---

* IRE Transactions Information Theory, No. 1, Feb. 1950.

amplitude characteristic of the process is not stationary at the reference frequency, the situation is more complex.

Each of these results is a special case of a class of additive invariants associated with linear systems. They are closely analogous to the cumulant statistics used to describe the properties of a univariate statistical distribution and of its characteristic function (i.e. its Fourier transform) in sampling theory.

Dr. Uttley

Concerning the mistakes made by an automatic computer, it is the principle of redundancy which can contribute to a solution.

Firstly one can incorporate redundant equipment, checking-circuits for example, and in the limit by employing two computers as mentioned by Prof. A. V. Hill. At present, however, the designers of large computers quite reasonably are loath to take this step. As a result present machines possess the property of a nonredundant code that a single error or change produces a quite different result; this is intolerable.

Redundancy can be incorporated in a second way. When a number is fed into a machine, additional redundant digits can be introduced with it; their function can be to indicate the presence and location of errors in the number. This redundancy can be obtained at the expense of speed of operation of the computer.

Dr. Shannon pointed out that the specialized theory of coding called by him "time reserving theory" is far more important with practical aims in mind. But would he not agree that from this practical point of view, it should be still better to deal with an unfortunately much more difficult case — I mean the case of a *given definite time* of coding operation?

Dr. I. J. Good

I would like to mention very briefly a mathematical curiosity which may be of some significance.

Consider a source of information which produces digits of N types with independent probabilities $p_0, p_1, \ldots, p_{N-1}$. Imagine an infinite sequence of such digits produced and prefixed by a decimal point (or rather an N-imal point). Then the resulting point will almost certainly belong to a set of points of Hausdorff-Besicovitch fractional dimensional number equal to the relative entropy of the source.

Mr. W. Lawrence

In consideration of the block schematic of Fig. 1, it has commonly been assumed that the only function of the decoder was to restore the message to the form presented to the encoder, in order that the message might be "understood." Alternatively, the message might be restored to some other understandable form, as when a message originally spoken is transmitted as a telegram and presented to the receiving mind in writing. In either case the decoder operates to increase the redundancy of the message, and it is this increase in redundancy that I wish to talk about.

The mind can only accept as information, material that is presented to the senses with a considerable degree of redundancy. Random acoustical noise, or random scintillations on a television receiver mean nothing. The more highly redundant the material presented to the senses, the more effortlessly does the mind receive it, provided of course, that the redundancy conforms to an agreed convention that the mind has been educated to accept.

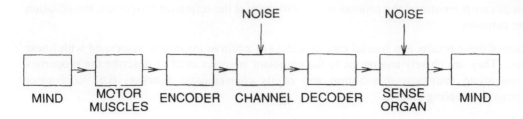

We can just apprehend speech presented with a 1000 c.p.s. bandwidth and a 15 db signal to noise ratio, though to do so requires considerable mental effort. Speech with a bandwidth of 3000 c.p.s. and a 40 db noise ratio can be apprehended without appreciable conscious mental effort. With a bandwidth of 15,000 c.p.s. and a noise ratio of 60 db we feel a marked improvement which is especially appreciated when we are listening to something difficult to understand, such as a philosophical lecture.

We can express the channel capacity required for these presentations in bits/sec. by considering the P.C.M. channel that will just handle them.

The inherent information rate of spoken English is, say, 100 bits/sec. The channel capacities required for the three presentations considered above are roughly 5000 bits/sec., 50,000 bits/sec. and 500,000 bits/sec., representing "minimum tolerable," "good commercial" and "near perfect" presentations.

It is also interesting to consider telegraphy, presented to the senses and the mind as written matter. The channel capacity required for the material presented to the eyes of the recipient can be assessed by considering a P.C.M. television channel just adequate for the presentation considered. The number of digits in the Pulse Code is controlled by the extent to which the blacks and whites of the writing stand out from the random specularity of the background. The number of elements in the picture is controlled by faithfulness of the reproduction of the latter forms and the number of letters or words simultaneously visible. The number of frames per second is controlled by the desired steadiness of the picture.

A "minimum tolerable" presentation might be 3 digit P.C.M., 50 elements per letter, 5 letters simultaneously visible and 10 frames per second, which requires a channel capacity of 7500 bits/sec. A "good commercial" presentation, as good as a ticker tape, requires a channel of about 10^5 bits/sec. and a "near perfect" presentation, such as first class printing with a whole page simultaneously visible, requires about 10^8 bits/sec. This again is the condition we would like to have when trying to understand something really difficult.

The higher channel capacities required for the written presentation are consistent with the fact that we can read language faster than we can listen to it, and also with the fact that we prefer a written presentation when the subject matter is really difficult.

I believe that the habit of only attending to redundant material is a defense mechanism that the mind adopts to sort out information worth attending to, from the inconceivably vast volume of information with which the senses continually bombard it.

This also clears up a paradox that used to worry me and may have worried others. Instinctively we feel that a "random" sequence contains no information, whereas an orderly sequence "means something." Communication Theory, however, says that a random sequence contains maximum information and that a completely ordered pattern contains no information at all. I would explain this by saying that the more nearly a sequence is random the harder it is for the mind to comprehend, and in the limit it contains maximum information which is, however, totally incomprehensible.

Even a machine requires some redundancy in the signal, such as the synchronization digit in P.C.M., before it can "comprehend" or "decode it. It can work with very little because it knows just what to look for, and its attention is not distracted. Our mind and senses, which have been evolved in a highly competitive environment, demand much more.

Mr. W. P. Anderson

1. The proposal to investigate a system in which the interference takes the form of a random binary signal added to the wanted signal is an interesting one but such a system is a very long way from the noisy communication channel with which the engineer is concerned. The errors in such a system are absolute, as the errors are assumed to be in the error correcting code described in the paper, that is to say a single element of the code is received either correctly or incorrectly.

In a physical communication system however there are no absolute errors. From the amplitude of the received signal element the probability that the transmitted element was a "mark" can be computed. If the signal to noise ratio is large, this probability will almost always either be nearly unity or nearly zero, depending on whether the transmitted element was in fact a "mark" or a "space", but if the signal to noise ratio is small it may have any value. This probability contains all the information obtained as a result of the reception of the element, and if the system at some stage distinguishes between only two classes of elements, those having the greater probability of being "mark" and those having the lesser probability of being "mark," information is being discarded. Error detecting codes necessarily operate in this way, hence it would appear that they must be less effective than integrating systems in which the amplitudes of individual elements are preserved.

This conclusion is of some interest, apart from its application to error detecting codes, as integration is equivalent to narrowing the band, and it suggests that no advantage is to be gained by increasing the baud speed of a telegraph transmission and introducing a code containing more than the minimum number of elements per character. It is believed that this conclusion is correct for double current working where the energy required to transmit a character is simply proportional to its length, but not for single current working, where the energy required to transmit a character of given length varies over a wide range. In the latter case increasing the speed increases the number of possible characters and the number actually required can be selected from those requiring least power to transmit. In the limit of course as the bandwidth is increased such a system reduces to Pulse Position Modulation, with one mark element per character.

2. A somewhat similar loss of information arises in the process of "quantization" in pulse code modulation systems and it would appear that it must always be better in principle to send the residual amplitude or "error signal" instead of the least significant digit.

3. Information theory has so far dealt with signals and noise superimposed in linear systems. In a system of great practical importance, however, long distance radio communication involving ionospheric propagation, the transmission path itself fluctuates in a manner which is only definable in a statistical sense. It would appear that the existence of such fluctuations must reduce the rate at which information can be passed over the link and that the extent of the reduction should be determinable by the methods of Information Theory. It is hoped that some attention will be given to this problem in the further development of the theory of information.

Dr. C. E. Shannon (In reply)

The point raised by Dr. Uttley regarding the use of redundancy for error detection and error correction in computing machines is certainly an important one, and will become more so as the machines become larger and more complex. In addition to the two methods pointed out by Dr. Uttley, redundancy in equipment and redundancy in encoding, a third may be added, redundancy in programming (as, for example, in redoing the calculation a second time on the same computer). The first two methods require additional equipment and the last additional time.

The present Bell Laboratories Relay Computer as well as some of the previous designs use both of the first two methods, the third of course being optional in any computer. All the relays are furnished with twin contacts. In effect, this amounts to a second at least partially independent computer, paralleled with the first one at the most critical points, the relay contacts. Furthermore, the numbers are represented in a two-out-of-five code; each decimal digit is represented by a group of five relays, and the code is such that exactly two of the relays must be operated to represent a digit. If this check fails at any stage the machine is automatically stopped. The circuit is such that any single error will be detected.

This is an example of an error-detecting scheme, which works exceptionally well. If errors were more frequent, it might be advisable to introduce an error-correction system in such a way that any single error would be corrected automatically by the machine, while two simultaneous errors would be detected and cause the machine to stop. It is possible to encode a decimal digit into seven binary digits and obtain single error correction. With eight binary digits, a code can be found which gives single error correction and double error detection.

Concerning the points brought up by Mr. Anderson, the error-correcting system suggested in the paper was meant particularly for applications such as computing machines where the information is encoded into a binary system with a definite reading of zero or one. In a pulse communication system with additive Gaussian noise a preliminary integration process followed by a threshold device gives a binary indication of whether the pulse was there or not, and in fact it can be shown that by proper choice of the weighting function in the integration such a detection system divides all possible received signals properly into two classes, those for which the *a posteriori* probability is in favor of a pulse and those for which it is not. Thus such a detection system is ideal in such a case in the sense of making the fewest possible errors for individual pulses. However, if this error frequency is still too high, it may be desirable to introduce redundant encoding and error correction.

Information theory has by no means been limited to linear systems, although some of the special results apply only in these cases. Statistical variations in path length, etc., must of course be considered as a form of perturbing noise, and the channel capacity and proper encoding systems, can in principle be calculated from the usual expressions, although such calculations are, because of their complexity, usually impractical.

M. Indjoudjian has raised the question of what might be called a finite delay theory of information. Such a theory would indeed be of great practical importance, but the mathematical difficulties are quite formidable. The class of coding operations with a delay $\leq T$ is not *closed* in the mathematical sense, for if two such operations or transducers are used in sequence the overall delay may be as much as $2T$. Thus we lose the important group theoretical property of closure which is so useful in the "infinite delay" and "time-preserving" theories. Nevertheless, any results in a finite delay theory would be highly interesting, even if they were restricted to the solution of a few special cases. Some work along this line appears in a recent paper by S. O. Rice (*Bell System Technical Journal*, Vol. 29, January 1950, pp. 60-93), where estimates are made of the probability of errors with various delays when attempting to transmit binary digits through white thermal noise.

Mr. Lawrence has pointed out that the brain can generally accept information only in a highly redundant form. It seems likely that the reason for this lies in the fact that our environments present us with highly redundant information. The scenes we view are well organized and change relatively slowly, and the significant sounds we hear tend to be localized in pitch and to persist much longer than this localization required. Nature, then, would design the nervous system in such a way as to be an efficient receptor for this type of information and to make use of the redundancy to achieve higher resolving power and better discrimination against noise. Experiments in psychological optics have, indeed, shown that the eye can determine if two line segments lie in a straight line much more closely than the width of a rod or cone, or of the diffraction pattern of the lines in question, thus showing that the eye makes use of this redundancy to improve discrimination.

The number of nerve cells in the optic nerve is only about one per cent of the number of rods and cones in the retina. If the time constants of both elements are about the same, this implies that the capacity of the optic nerve for transmitting information to the brain can be only about one per cent of the information that would be received by the retina. Thus only if this information is highly redundant could it all be encoded into a signal to be transmitted via the optic nerve to the occipital lobe. At that point further abstraction of the basic information, i.e., elimination of redundancy, probably occurs in the connections with the related association areas.

Mr. Good has pointed out an interesting relation which I had also noticed between entropy and the Hausdorff-Besicovitch dimension number. While it is easy to see the reason for this from the basic definition of Hausdorff-Besicovitch dimension number and certain properties of entropy, I believe the root of the relation springs from the following consideration. A dimension number to be reasonable should have the property that it is additive for product-spaces, that is, the set of ordered pairs (λ, ν) should have dimension number $d_1 + d_2$, where d_1 is the dimension number of the set (λ) and d_2 that for (ν). Similarly, a measure of information should be additive when we combine two independent information sources, i.e., a stochastic process producing ordered pairs, one from each of two independent sources. These *desiderata* result in the logarithmic measures which appear in both fields.

Recent Developments in Communication Theory

Nonmathematical analysis of present-day and possible future communications systems. Author cites feasibility of a system for transmitting the English language at speaking rate over a channel with 20-to-1 signal-to-noise ratio and a bandwidth of only 2.3 cycles per second

By CLAUDE E. SHANNON

Bell Telephone Laboratories, Inc.
Murray Hill, New Jersey

THE NEWER SYSTEMS of modulation, such as f-m, ppm (pulse position modulation), and pcm (pulse code modulation), have the interesting property that it is possible to exchange bandwidth for signal-to-noise ratio; that is, we can transmit the same information with a smaller transmitter power provided we are willing to use a larger bandwidth. Conversely, in pcm it is possible to use a smaller bandwidth at the expense of an increased signal power. The discovery of these systems has prompted a re-examination of the foundations of communication theory. A number of workers have contributed to this field, among them Gabor, Wiener, Tuller, Sullivan and the writer.

The basic ideas of communication theory are not new. Important pioneering work was done by Nyquist and Hartley in the 1920's and some of the roots can even be traced back to the nineteenth century physicist Boltzmann. The more recent developments, however, include factors that were ignored in earlier treatments; in particular, we now have a much better understanding of the effect of noise in the channel and of the importance of statistical properties of the messages to be transmitted.

In this paper the highlights of this recent work will be described with as little mathematics as possible. Since the subject is essentially a mathematical one, this necessitates a sacrifice of rigor; for more precise treatments the reader may consult the bibliography.

The type of communication system that has been most extensively investigated is shown in Fig. 1. It consists of an information source which produces the raw information or message to be transmitted, a transmitter which encodes or modulates this information into a form suitable for the channel, and the channel on which the encoded information or signal is transmitted to the receiving point. During transmission the signal may be perturbed by noise as indicated schematically by the noise source. The received signal goes to the receiver, which decodes or demodulates to recover the original message, and then to the final destination of the information.

It will be seen that this system is sufficiently general to include the majority of communication problems if the various elements are suitably interpreted. In television, for example, the information source is the scene being televised, the message is the output of the pick-up tube and the signal is the output of the transmitter.

A basic idea in communication theory is that information can be treated very much like a physical quantity such as mass or energy. The system in Fig. 1 is roughly analogous to a transportation system; for example, we can imagine a lumber mill producing lumber at a certain point and a conveyor system for transporting the lumber to a second point. In such a situation there are two important quantities, the rate R (in cubic feet per second) at which lumber is produced at the mill and the capacity C (cubic feet per second) of the conveyor. If R is greater than C

it will certainly be impossible to transport the full output of the lumber mill. If R is less than or equal to C, it may or may not be possible, depending on whether the lumber can be packed efficiently in the conveyor. Suppose, however, that we allow ourselves a saw-mill at the source. Then the lumber can be cut up into small pieces in such a way as to fill out the available capacity of the conveyor with 100-percent efficiency. Naturally in this case we should provide a carpenter shop at the receiving point to glue the pieces back together in their original form before passing them on to the consumer.

If this analogy is sound, we should be able to set up a measure R in suitable units telling how much information is produced per second by a given information source, and a second measure C which determines the capacity of a channel for transmitting information. Furthermore, it should be possible, by using a suitable coding or modulation system, to transmit the information over the channel if and only if the rate of production R is not greater than the capacity C. That this is actually possible is a key result of recent research and we will indicate briefly how this is accomplished.

Measurement of Information

Before we can consider how information is to be measured it is necessary to clarify the precise meaning of information from the point of view of the communication engineer. In general, the messages to be transmitted have meaning. This, however, is quite irrelevant to the problem of transmitting the information. It is as difficult (more so, in fact) to transmit a series of nonsense syllables as straight English text. A little thought on the subject will convince one that the significant aspect of information from the transmission standpoint is the fact that one particular message is chosen from a set of possible messages. The thing that must be transmitted is a specification of the particular message which was chosen by the information source. If and only if such an unambiguous specification is transmitted, the original message can be reconstructed at the receiving point. Thus information in our sense must be correlated with the notion of a choice from a set of possibilities.

The simplest type of choice is a choice from two possibilities, each with probability $\frac{1}{2}$. This is the situation, for example, when one tosses a coin which is equally likely to come up heads or tails. It is convenient to use the amount of information produced by such a choice as the basic unit, called a binary digit or, more briefly, a bit. The choice involved with one bit of information can be indicated schematically as in Fig. 2A. At point b we may choose either the upper or lower line with probability $\frac{1}{2}$ for each possibility. If there are N possibilities, all equally likely, the amount of information is given by $\log_2 N$. The reason for this can be seen from Fig. 2B, where we have eight possibilities each with probability $\frac{1}{8}$. The choice can be imagined to occur in three stages, each involving one bit. The first bit corresponds to a choice of either the first four or the second four of the eight possibilities, the second bit corresponds to the first or second pair of the four chosen, and the final bit determines the first or second member of the pair. It will be seen that the number of bits required is $\log_2 N$, in this case $\log_2 8$ or 3.

If the probabilities are not equal,

the formula is a little more complicated. A simple case is shown in Fig. 2C. There are four possible choices with probabilities $\frac{1}{2}$, $\frac{1}{4}$, $\frac{1}{8}$ and $\frac{1}{8}$. This can be broken down into a sequence of binary choices as indicated. The information produced is given by $(1 + \frac{1}{2} + \frac{1}{4})$; the 1 is from the first choice (at point p) which always occurs, the $\frac{1}{2}$ is from the choice at point q, which occurs only half the time (when the lower line is chosen at point p), and so on. In general, by a similar decomposition, the information, when the choices have probabilities $p_1, p_2, \cdots, p_n$, is given by:

$$H = -(p_1 \log_2 p_1 + p_2 \log_2 p_2 + \cdots + p_n \log_2 p_n) \qquad (1)$$

This formula, then, gives the amount of information produced by a single choice. An information source produces a message which consists of a sequence of choices, for example, the letters of printed text or the elementary words or sounds of speech. In these cases, by an application of Eq. 1, the amount of information produced per second or per symbol can be calculated. It is interesting that this information rate for printed English text is about two bits per letter, when we consider statistical

structure only out to word lengths. Long-range meaning structure may reduce this figure considerably.

Encoding Information

The importance of the measure of information, H, is that it determines the saving in transmission time that is possible, by proper encoding, due to the statistics of the message source. To illustrate this, consider a language in which there are only four letters: A, B, C and D. Suppose these letters have the probabilities $\frac{1}{2}$, $\frac{1}{4}$, $\frac{1}{8}$ and $\frac{1}{8}$, as in Fig. 2C.

In a long text in this language, A will occur half the time, B one-quarter of the time, and so on. Suppose we wish to encode this language into binary digits, 0 or 1. Thus we might wish to transmit on a pulse system with two types of pulse. The most direct code is the following: $A = 00$, $B = 01$, $C = 10$, $D = 11$. This code requires two binary digits per letter of message. By using the statistics, a better code can be constructed as follows: $A = 0$, $B = 10$, $C = 110$, $D = 111$. It is readily verified that the original message can be recovered from its encoded form. Furthermore, the number of binary digits used is smaller on the average. It will be,

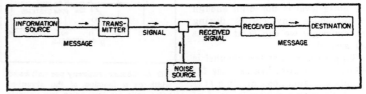

FIG. 1—Generalized communication system is roughly analogous to a transportation system

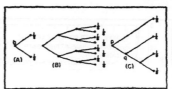

FIG. 2—Schematic representation of equal and unequal probabilities. The choice involved with one bit (binary digit) of information is comparable to tossing a coin heads or tails

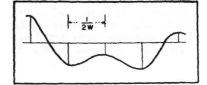

FIG. 3—Signals represented by functions of time which lie within a band of frequencies W cps wide can be specified by the values of a series of equally spaced samples 1/2W seconds apart

in fact calculated as follows:

$$\tfrac{1}{2}(1) + \tfrac{1}{4}(2) + \tfrac{1}{8}(3) + \tfrac{1}{8}(3) = 1\tfrac{3}{4}$$

where the first term is due to the letter A, which occurs half the time and is one binary digit long, and similarly for the others. It will be noted that $1\tfrac{3}{4}$ is just the value of H calculated for Fig. 2C.

The result we have verified for this special case holds generally. If the information rate of the message is H bits per letter, it is possible to encode it into binary digits using, on the average, only H binary digits per letter of text. There is no method of encoding which uses less than this amount.

Capacity of a Channel

Now consider the problem of defining the capacity C of a channel for transmitting information. Since the rate of production for an information source has been measured in bits per second, we would naturally like to measure C in the same units. The question then becomes "What is the maximum number of binary digits per second that can be transmitted over a given channel?"

In some cases the answer is simple. With a teletype channel there are 32 possible symbols. Each symbol therefore represents 5 bits, provided the possible symbols are used with equal probability. If we can send n symbols per second, and the noise level is not high enough to introduce any errors during transmission, we can send $5n$ bits per second.

Suppose now that the channel is defined as follows: We can use for signals any functions of time $f(t)$ which lie within a certain band of frequencies, W cycles per second wide. It is known that a function of this type can be specified by giving its values at a series of equally spaced sampling points $1/2W$ seconds apart as shown in Fig. 3. Thus we may say that such a function has $2W$ degrees of freedom, or dimensions, per second.

If there is no noise whatever on such a channel we can distinguish an infinite number of different amplitude levels for each sample. Consequently we could, in principle, transmit an infinite number of binary digits per second, and the capacity C would be infinite.

Even when there is noise, if we place no limitations on the transmitter power, the capacity will be infinite, for we may still distinguish at each sample point an unlimited number of different amplitude levels. Only when noise is present and the transmitter power is limited in some way do we obtain a finite capacity C. The capacity depends, of course, on the statistical structure of the noise as well as the nature of the power limitation.

The simplest type of noise is white thermal noise or resistance noise. The probability distribution of amplitudes follows a Gaussian curve and the spectrum is flat with frequency over the band in question and may be assumed to be zero outside the band. This type of noise is completely specified by giving its mean square amplitude N, which is the power it would deliver into

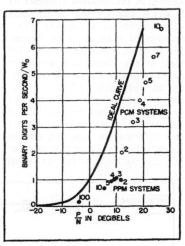

FIG. 4—Channel capacity per unit bandwidth as a function of the signal-to-noise ratio for two pulse transmission systems

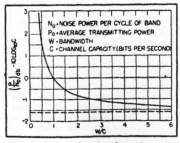

FIG. 5—Where the signal-to-noise ratio is large, halving the bandwidth roughly doubles the signal-to-noise ratio required for a given channel capacity

a standard unit of resistance. The simplest limitation on transmitter power is to assume that the average power delivered by the transmitter (or more precisely the mean square amplitude of the signal) is not greater than P. If we define our channel by these three parameters W, P and N, the capacity C can be calculated. It turns out to be

$$C = W \log_2 \frac{P + N}{N} \qquad (2)$$

bits per second. It is easy to see that this formula is approximately right when P/N is large. The received signal will have a power $P + N$ and we can distinguish something of the order of

$$\sqrt{(P + N)/N}$$

different amplitudes at each sample point. The reason for this is that the range of amplitude of the received signal is proportional to $\sqrt{P + N}$, while the noise introduces an uncertainty proportional to $\sqrt{N}$. The amount of information that can be transmitted with one sample will therefore be $\log_2 [(P + N)/N]$. Since there are $2W$ independent samples per second, the capacity is given by Eq. 2. This formula has a much deeper and more precise significance than the above argument would indicate. In fact it can be shown that it is possible, by properly choosing our signal functions, to transmit $W \log_2 [(P+N)/N]$ bits per second with as small a frequency of errors as desired. It is not possible to transmit at any higher rate with an arbitrarily small frequency of errors. This means that the capacity is a sharply defined quantity in spite of the noise.

The formula for C applies for all values of P/N. Even when P/N is very small, the average noise power being much greater than the average transmitter power, it is possible to transmit binary digits at the rate $W \log_2 [(P + N)/N]$ with as small a frequency of errors as desired. In this case $\log_2 (1 + P/N)$ is very nearly $(P/N) \log_2 e$ or $1.443 \, P/N$ and we have, approximately, $C = 1.443 \, PW/N$.

It should be emphasized that it is possible to transmit at a rate C over a channel only by properly encoding the information. In general the rate C cannot be actually attained but only approached as a limit by using more and more complex encoding and longer and longer delays at both transmitter and receiver. In the white noise case the best encoding turns out to be such that the transmitted signals themselves have the structure of a resistance noise of power P.

Ideal and Practical Systems

In Fig. 4 the curve is the function $C/W = \log (1 + P/N)$ plotted against P/N measured in db. It represents, therefore, the channel capacity per unit of band with white noise. The circles and points correspond to pcm and ppm systems used to send a sequence of binary digits, adjusted to give about one error in 10^5 binary digits. In the pcm case the number adjacent to a point represents the number of amplitude levels; 3 for example is a ternary pcm system. In all cases positive and negative amplitudes are used. The ppm systems are quantized with a discrete set of possible positions for the pulse, the spacing is $1/2W$ and the number adjacent to a point is the number of possible positions for a pulse.

The series of points follows a curve of the same shape as the ideal but displaced horizontally about 8 db. This means that with more involved encoding or modulation systems a gain of 8 db in power could be achieved over the systems indicated.

Unfortunately, as one attempts to approach the ideal, the transmitter and receiver required become more complicated and the delays increase. For these reasons there will be some point where an economic balance is established between the various factors. It is possible, however, that even at the present time more complex systems would be justified.

A curious fact illustrating the general misanthropic behavior of nature is that at both extremes of P/N (when we are well outside the practical range) the series of points in Fig. 4 approaches more closely the ideal curve.

The relation $C = W \log (1 + P/N)$ can be regarded as an exchange relation between the parameters W and P/N. Keeping the

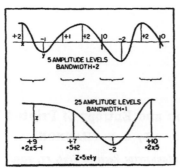

FIG. 6—Graphic representation of a typical system for conserving bandwidth at the cost of increasing transmitted power

channel capacity fixed we can decrease the bandwidth W provided we increase P/N sufficiently. Conversely, an increase in band allows a lower signal-to-noise ratio in the channel. The required P/N in db is shown in Fig. 5 as a function of the band W. It is assumed here that as we increase the band W, the noise power N increases proportionally, $N = W N_o$ where N_o is the noise power per cycle of band. It will be noticed that if P/N is large a reduction of band is very expensive in power. Halving the band roughly doubles the signal-to-noise ratio in db that is required.

One method of exchanging bandwidth for signal-to-noise ratio is shown in Fig. 6. The upper curve represents a signal function whose bandwidth is such that it can be specified by giving the samples shown. Each sample has five amplitude levels. The lower curve is obtained by combining pairs of samples from the first curve as shown. There are now 25 amplitude levels that must be distinguished but the samples occur only half as frequently; consequently the band is reduced by half, at the cost of doubling the signal-to-noise ratio in db. Operating this in reverse doubles the band but reduces the required signal-to-noise ratio.

To summarize, there are three essentially different ways in which bandwidth can be reduced in a system such as television or speech transmission. The first is the straightforward exchange of bandwidth for signal-to-noise ratio just discussed. The second method is utilization of the statistical correla-

tions existing in the message. This capitalizes on particular properties of the information source, and can be regarded as a type of matching of the source to the channel. Finally, particular properties of the destination can be used. Thus, in speech transmission the ear is relatively insensitive to phase distortion. Consequently, phase information is not as important as amplitude information, and need not be sent so accurately. This can be translated into a bandwidth saving, and in fact part of the reduction attained in the vocoder is due to this effect. In general, the exploitation of particular sensitivities or blindnesses in the destination requires a proper matching of channel to the destination.

Many present-day communication systems are extremely inefficient in that they fail to make use of the statistical properties of the information source. To illustrate this, suppose we are interested in a system to transmit English speech (no music or other sounds) and the quality requirements on reproduction are only that it be intelligible as to meaning. Personal accents, inflections and the like can be lost in the process of transmission. In such a case we could, at least in principle, transmit by the following scheme. A device is constructed at the transmitter which prints the English text corresponding to the spoken words. This can be encoded into binary digits using, on the average, not more than two binary digits per letter or nine per word. Taking 100 words per minute as a reasonable rate of speaking, we obtain 15 bits per second as an estimate of the rate of producing information in English speech when intelligibility is the only fidelity requirement. From Fig. 4 this information could be transmitted over a channel with 20 db signal-to-noise ratio and a bandwith of only 2.3 cps!

BIBLIOGRAPHY

R. V. L. Hartley, Transmission of Information, *B.S.T.J.*, p 535, July 1928.
C. E. Shannon, A Mathematical Theory of Communication, *B.S.T.J.*, p 379, July 1948, and p 623, Oct. 1948.
C. E. Shannon, Communication in the Presence of Noise, *Proc. IRE*, p 10, Jan. 1949.
C. B. Feldman and W. R. Bennett, Bandwidth and Transmission Performance, *B.S.T.J.*, p 490, July 1949.
D. G. Fink, Bandwidth vs Noise in Communication Systems, ELECTRONICS, Jan. 1948.

Prediction and Entropy of Printed English

By C. E. SHANNON

(Manuscript Received Sept. 15, 1950)

A new method of estimating the entropy and redundancy of a language is described. This method exploits the knowledge of the language statistics possessed by those who speak the language, and depends on experimental results in prediction of the next letter when the preceding text is known. Results of experiments in prediction are given, and some properties of an ideal predictor are developed.

1 INTRODUCTION

IN A previous paper[1] the entropy and redundancy of a language have been defined. The entropy is a statistical parameter which measures, in a certain sense, how much information is produced on the average for each letter of a text in the language. If the language is translated into binary digits (0 or 1) in the most efficient way, the entropy H is the average number of binary digits required per letter of the original language. The redundancy, on the other hand, measures the amount of constraint imposed on a text in the language due to its statistical structure, e.g., in English the high frequency of the letter E, the strong tendency of H to follow T or of U to follow Q. It was estimated that when statistical effects extending over not more than eight letters are considered the entropy is roughly 2.3 bits per letter, the redundancy about 50 per cent.

Since then a new method has been found for estimating these quantities, which is more sensitive and takes account of long range statistics, influences extending over phrases, sentences, etc. This method is based on a study of the predictability of English; how well can the next letter of a text be predicted when the preceding N letters are known. The results of some experiments in prediction will be given, and a theoretical analysis of some of the properties of ideal prediction. By combining the experimental and theoretical results it is possible to estimate upper and lower bounds for the entropy and redundancy. From this analysis it appears that, in ordinary literary English, the long range statistical effects (up to 100 letters) reduce the entropy to something of the order of one bit per letter, with a corresponding redundancy of roughly 75%. The redundancy may be still higher when structure extending over paragraphs, chapters, etc. is included. However, as the lengths involved are increased, the parameters in question become more

---

[1] C. E. Shannon, "A Mathematical Theory of Communication," *Bell System Technical Journal*, v. 27, pp. 379–423, 623–656, July, October, 1948.

erratic and uncertain, and they depend more critically on the type of text involved.

2. Entropy Calculation from the Statistics of English

One method of calculating the entropy H is by a series of approximations F_0, F_1, F_2, $\cdots$, which successively take more and more of the statistics of the language into account and approach H as a limit. F_N may be called the N-gram entropy; it measures the amount of information or entropy due to statistics extending over N adjacent letters of text. F_N is given by[1]

$$
\begin{aligned}
F_N &= -\sum_{i,j} p(b_i, j) \log_2 p_{b_i}(j) \\
&= -\sum_{i,j} p(b_i, j) \log_2 p(b_i, j) + \sum_i p(b_i) \log p(b_i)
\end{aligned}
\tag{1}
$$

in which: b_i is a block of N-1 letters [$(N\text{-}1)$-gram]

j is an arbitrary letter following b_i

$p(b_i, j)$ is the probability of the N-gram b_i, j

$p_{b_i}(j)$ is the conditional probability of letter j after the block b_i

and is given by $p(b_i, j)/p(b_i)$.

The equation (1) can be interpreted as measuring the average uncertainty (conditional entropy) of the next letter j when the preceding N-1 letters are known. As N is increased, F_N includes longer and longer range statistics and the entropy, H, is given by the limiting value of F_N as $N \rightarrow \infty$:

$$
H = \operatorname*{Lim}_{N \to \infty} F_N .
\tag{2}
$$

The N-gram entropies F_N for small values of N can be calculated from standard tables of letter, digram and trigram frequencies.[2] If spaces and punctuation are ignored we have a twenty-six letter alphabet and F_0 may be taken (by definition) to be $\log_2 26$, or 4.7 bits per letter. F_1 involves letter frequencies and is given by

$$
F_1 = -\sum_{i=1}^{26} p(i) \log_2 p(i) = 4.14 \text{ bits per letter.}
\tag{3}
$$

The digram approximation F_2 gives the result

$$
\begin{aligned}
F_2 &= -\sum_{i,j} p(i, j) \log_2 p_i(j) \\
&= -\sum_{i,j} p(i, j) \log_2 p(i, j) + \sum_i p(i) \log_2 p(i)
\end{aligned}
\tag{4}
$$

$$
= 7.70 - 4.14 = 3.56 \text{ bits per letter.}
$$

[2] Fletcher Pratt, "Secret and Urgent," Blue Ribbon Books, 1942.

The trigram entropy is given by

$$F_3 = - \sum_{i,j,k} p(i, j, k) \log_2 p_{ij}(k)$$

$$= - \sum_{i,j,k} p(i, j, k) \log_2 p(i, j, k) + \sum_{i,j} p(i, j) \log_2 p(i, j) \tag{5}$$

$$\doteq 11.0 - 7.7 = 3.3$$

In this calculation the trigram table[2] used did not take into account trigrams bridging two words, such as WOW and OWO in TWO WORDS. To compensate partially for this omission, corrected trigram probabilities $p(i, j, k)$ were obtained from the probabilities $p'(i, j, k)$ of the table by the following rough formula:

$$p(i, j, k) = \frac{2.5}{4.5} p'(i, j, k) + \frac{1}{4.5} r(i) p(j, k) + \frac{1}{4.5} p(i, j) s(k)$$

where $r(i)$ is the probability of letter i as the terminal letter of a word and $s(k)$ is the probability of k as an initial letter. Thus the trigrams within words (an average of 2.5 per word) are counted according to the table; the bridging trigrams (one of each type per word) are counted approximately by assuming independence of the terminal letter of one word and the initial digram in the next or vice versa. Because of the approximations involved here, and also because of the fact that the sampling error in identifying probability with sample frequency is more serious, the value of F_3 is less reliable than the previous numbers.

Since tables of N-gram frequencies were not available for $N > 3$, F_4, F_5, etc. could not be calculated in the same way. However, word frequencies have been tabulated[3] and can be used to obtain a further approximation. Figure 1 is a plot on log-log paper of the probabilities of words against frequency rank. The most frequent English word "the" has a probability .071 and this is plotted against 1. The next most frequent word "of" has a probability of .034 and is plotted against 2, etc. Using logarithmic scales both for probability and rank, the curve is approximately a straight line with slope -1; thus, if p_n is the probability of the nth most frequent word, we have, roughly

$$p_n = \frac{.1}{n}. \tag{6}$$

Zipf[4] has pointed out that this type of formula, $p_n = k/n$, gives a rather good approximation to the word probabilities in many different languages. The

[3] G. Dewey, "Relative Frequency of English Speech Sounds," Harvard University Press, 1923.

[4] G. K. Zipf, "Human Behavior and the Principle of Least Effort," Addison-Wesley Press, 1949.

formula (6) clearly cannot hold indefinitely since the total probability Σp_n must be unity, while $\sum_{1}^{\infty} .1/n$ is infinite. If we assume (in the absence of any better estimate) that the formula $p_n = .1/n$ holds out to the n at which the

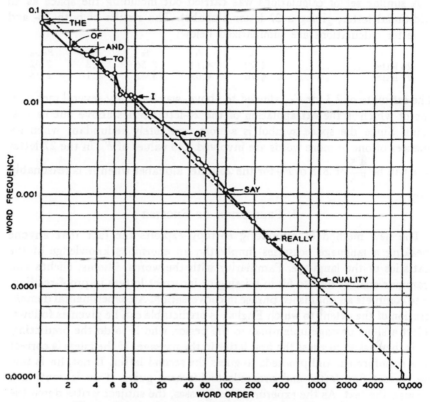

Fig. 1—Relative frequency against rank for English words.

total probability is unity, and that $p_n = 0$ for larger n, we find that the critical n is the word of rank 8,727. The entropy is then:

$$-\sum_{1}^{8727} p_n \log_2 p_n = 11.82 \text{ bits per word,} \qquad (7)$$

or $11.82/4.5 = 2.62$ bits per letter since the average word length in English is 4.5 letters. One might be tempted to identify this value with $F_{4.5}$, but actually the ordinate of the F_N curve at $N = 4.5$ will be above this value. The reason is that F_4 or F_5 involves groups of four or five letters regardless of word division. A word is a cohesive group of letters with strong internal statistical influences, and consequently the N-grams within words are more restricted than those which bridge words. The effect of this is that we have obtained, in 2.62 bits per letter, an estimate which corresponds more nearly to, say, F_5 or F_6.

A similar set of calculations was carried out including the space as an additional letter, giving a 27 letter alphabet. The results of both 26- and 27-letter calculations are summarized below:

	F_0	F_1	F_2	F_3	F_{word}
26 letter............ ..	4.70	4.14	3.56	3.3	2.62
27 letter............ ..	4.76	4.03	3.32	3.1	2.14

The estimate of 2.3 for F_8, alluded to above, was found by several methods, one of which is the extrapolation of the 26-letter series above out to that point. Since the space symbol is almost completely redundant when sequences of one or more words are involved, the values of F_N in the 27-letter case will be $\frac{4.5}{5.5}$ or .818 of F_N for the 26-letter alphabet when N is reasonably large.

3. Prediction of English

The new method of estimating entropy exploits the fact that anyone speaking a language possesses, implicitly, an enormous knowledge of the statistics of the language. Familiarity with the words, idioms, clichés and grammar enables him to fill in missing or incorrect letters in proof-reading, or to complete an unfinished phrase in conversation. An experimental demonstration of the extent to which English is predictable can be given as follows: Select a short passage unfamiliar to the person who is to do the predicting. He is then asked to guess the first letter in the passage. If the guess is correct he is so informed, and proceeds to guess the second letter. If not, he is told the correct first letter and proceeds to his next guess. This is continued through the text. As the experiment progresses, the subject writes down the correct text up to the current point for use in predicting future letters. The result of a typical experiment of this type is given below. Spaces were included as an additional letter, making a 27 letter alphabet. The first line is the original text; the second line contains a dash for each letter correctly guessed. In the case of incorrect guesses the correct letter is copied in the second line.

```
(1) THE ROOM WAS NOT VERY LIGHT A SMALL OBLONG
(2) ----ROO------NOT-V-----I------SM----OBL----
(1) READING LAMP ON THE DESK SHED GLOW ON
(2) REA----------0------D----SHED-GLO--0--
(1) POLISHED WOOD BUT LESS ON THE SHABBY RED CARPET
(2) P-L-S-----0---BU--L-S--0-------SH-----RE--C------
```
                                                                            (8)

Of a total of 129 letters, 89 or 69% were guessed correctly. The errors, as would be expected, occur most frequently at the beginning of words and syllables where the line of thought has more possibility of branching out. It might be thought that the second line in (8), which we will call the *reduced text*, contains much less information than the first. Actually, both lines contain the same information in the sense that it is possible, at least in principle, to recover the first line from the second. To accomplish this we need an identical twin of the individual who produced the sequence. The twin (who must be mathematically, not just biologically identical) will respond in the same way when faced with the same problem. Suppose, now, we have only the reduced text of (8). We ask the twin to guess the passage. At each point we will know whether his guess is correct, since he is guessing the same as the first twin and the presence of a dash in the reduced text corresponds to a correct guess. The letters he guesses wrong are also available, so that at each stage he can be supplied with precisely the same information the first twin had available.

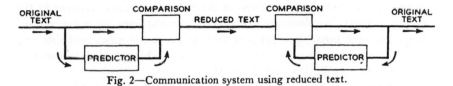

Fig. 2—Communication system using reduced text.

The need for an identical twin in this conceptual experiment can be eliminated as follows. In general, good prediction does not require knowledge of more than N preceding letters of text, with N fairly small. There are only a finite number of possible sequences of N letters. We could ask the subject to guess the next letter for each of these possible N-grams. The complete list of these predictions could then be used both for obtaining the reduced text from the original and for the inverse reconstruction process.

To put this another way, the reduced text can be considered to be an encoded form of the original, the result of passing the original text through a reversible transducer. In fact, a communication system could be constructed in which only the reduced text is transmitted from one point to the other. This could be set up as shown in Fig. 2, with two identical prediction devices.

An extension of the above experiment yields further information concerning the predictability of English. As before, the subject knows the text up to the current point and is asked to guess the next letter. If he is wrong, he is told so and asked to guess again. This is continued until he finds the correct letter. A typical result with this experiment is shown below. The first line is the original text and the numbers in the second line indicate the guess at which the correct letter was obtained.

```
(1) T H E R E   I S   N O   R E V E R S E   O N   A   M O T O R C Y C L E   A
(2) 1 1 1 5 1 1 2 1 1 2 1 1 1 5 1 1 7 1 1 1 2 1 3 2 1 2 2 7 1 1 1 1 4 1 1 1 1 1 3  1
(1) F R I E N D   O F   M I N E   F O U N D   T H I S   O U T
(2) 8 6 1 3 1 1 1 1 1 1 1 1 1 1 1 6 2 1 1 1 1 1 1 2 1 1 1 1 1 1
(1) R A T H E R   D R A M A T I C A L L Y   T H E   O T H E R   D A Y
(2) 4 1 1 1 1 1 1 1 1 5 1 1 1 1 1 1 1 1 1 1 1 6 1 1 1 1 1 1 1 1 1 1 1 1 1      (9)
```

Out of 102 symbols the subject guessed right on the first guess 79 times, on the second guess 8 times, on the third guess 3 times, the fourth and fifth guesses 2 each and only eight times required more than five guesses. Results of this order are typical of prediction by a good subject with ordinary literary English. Newspaper writing, scientific work and poetry generally lead to somewhat poorer scores.

The reduced text in this case also contains the same information as the original. Again utilizing the identical twin we ask him at each stage to guess as many times as the number given in the reduced text and recover in this way the original. To eliminate the human element here we must ask our subject, for each possible N-gram of text, to guess the most probable next letter, the second most probable next letter, etc. This set of data can then serve both for prediction and recovery.

Just as before, the reduced text can be considered an encoded version of the original. The original language, with an alphabet of 27 symbols, A, B, $\cdots$, Z, space, has been translated into a new language with the alphabet 1, 2, $\cdots$, 27. The translating has been such that the symbol 1 now has an extremely high frequency. The symbols 2, 3, 4 have successively smaller frequencies and the final symbols 20, 21, $\cdots$, 27 occur very rarely. Thus the translating has simplified to a considerable extent the nature of the statistical structure involved. The redundancy which originally appeared in complicated constraints among groups of letters, has, by the translating process, been made explicit to a large extent in the very unequal probabilities of the new symbols. It is this, as will appear later, which enables one to estimate the entropy from these experiments.

In order to determine how predictability depends on the number N of preceding letters known to the subject, a more involved experiment was carried out. One hundred samples of English text were selected at random from a book, each fifteen letters in length. The subject was required to guess the text, letter by letter, for each sample as in the preceding experiment. Thus one hundred samples were obtained in which the subject had available 0, 1, 2, 3, $\cdots$, 14 preceding letters. To aid in prediction the subject made such use as he wished of various statistical tables, letter, digram and trigram tables, a table of the frequencies of initial letters in words, a list of the frequencies of common words and a dictionary. The samples in this experiment were from *"Jefferson the Virginian"* by Dumas Malone. These results, together with a similar test in which 100 letters were known to the subject, are summarized in Table I. The column corresponds to the number of preceding letters known to the subject plus one; the row is the number of the guess. The entry in column N at row S is the number of times the subject guessed the right letter at the Sth guess when $(N-1)$ letters were known. For example,

TABLE I

	1	2	3	4	5	6	7	8	9	10	11	12	13	14	15	100
1	18.2	29.2	36	47	51	58	48	66	66	67	62	58	66	72	60	80
2	10.7	14.8	20	18	13	19	17	15	13	10	9	14	9	6	18	7
3	8.6	10.0	12	14	8	5	3	5	9	4	7	7	4	9	5	
4	6.7	8.6	7	3	4	1	4	4	4	4	5	6	4	3	5	3
5	6.5	7.1	1	1	3	4	3	6	1	6	5	2	3			4
6	5.8	5.5	4	5	2	3	2			1	4	2	3	4	1	2
7	5.6	4.5	3	3	2	2	8		1	1	1	4	1		4	1
8	5.2	3.6	2	2	1	1	2	1	1	1	1		2	1	3	
9	5.0	3.0	4		5	1	4		2	1	1	2		1		1
10	4.3	2.6	2	1	3		3	1					2			
11	3.1	2.2	2	2	2	1			1	3		1	1	2	1	
12	2.8	1.9	4		2	1	1	1			2	1	1		1	1
13	2.4	1.5	1	1	1	1	1	1	1	1		1	1			
14	2.3	1.2		1			1						1			1
15	2.1	1.0	1	1							1	1	1			
16	2.0	.9					1				1			1		
17	1.6	.7	1		2	1	1				1		2	2		
18	1.6	.5													1	
19	1.6	.4			1	1			1		1					
20	1.3	.3		1		1	1									
21	1.2	.2														
22	.8	.1														
23	.3	.1														
24	.1	.0														
25	.1															
26	.1															
27	.1															

the entry 19 in column 6, row 2, means that with five letters known the correct letter was obtained on the second guess nineteen times out of the hundred. The first two columns of this table were not obtained by the experimental procedure outlined above but were calculated directly from the known letter and digram frequencies. Thus with no known letters the most probable symbol is the space (probability .182); the next guess, if this is wrong, should be E (probability .107), etc. These probabilities are the frequencies with which the right guess would occur at the first, second, etc., trials with best prediction. Similarly, a simple calculation from the digram table gives the entries in column 1 when the subject uses the table to best advantage. Since the frequency tables are determined from long samples of English, these two columns are subject to less sampling error than the others.

It will be seen that the prediction gradually improves, apart from some statistical fluctuation, with increasing knowledge of the past as indicated by the larger numbers of correct first guesses and the smaller numbers of high rank guesses.

One experiment was carried out with "reverse" prediction, in which the subject guessed the letter preceding those already known. Although the task is subjectively much more difficult, the scores were only slightly poorer. Thus, with two 101 letter samples from the same source, the subject obtained the following results:

No. of guess	1	2	3	4	5	6	7	8	>8
Forward	70	10	7	2	2	3	3	0	4
Reverse	66	7	4	4	6	2	1	2	9

Incidentally, the N-gram entropy F_N for a reversed language is equal to that for the forward language as may be seen from the second form in equation (1). Both terms have the same value in the forward and reversed cases.

4. IDEAL N-GRAM PREDICTION

The data of Table I can be used to obtain upper and lower bounds to the N-gram entropies F_N. In order to do this, it is necessary first to develop some general results concerning the best possible prediction of a language when the preceding N letters are known. There will be for the language a set of conditional probabilities $p_{i_1, i_2, \cdots, i_{N-1}}(j)$. This is the probability when the $(N\text{-}1)$ gram $i_1, i_2, \cdots, i_{N-1}$ occurs that the next letter will be j. The best guess for the next letter, when this $(N\text{-}1)$ gram is known to have occurred, will be that letter having the highest conditional probability. The second guess should be that with the second highest probability, etc. A machine or person guessing in the best way would guess letters in the order of decreasing conditional probability. Thus the process of reducing a text with such an ideal predictor consists of a mapping of the letters into the numbers from 1 to 27 in such a way that the most probable next letter [conditional on the known preceding $(N\text{-}1)$ gram] is mapped into 1, etc. The frequency of 1's in the reduced text will then be given by

$$q_1^N = \Sigma p(i_1, i_2, \cdots, i_{N-1}, j) \tag{10}$$

where the sum is taken over all $(N\text{-}1)$ grams $i_1, i_2, \cdots, i_{N-1}$ the j being the one which maximizes p for that particular $(N\text{-}1)$ gram. Similarly, the frequency of 2's, q_2^N, is given by the same formula with j chosen to be that letter having the second highest value of p, etc.

On the basis of N-grams, a different set of probabilities for the symbols in the reduced text, q_1^{N+1}, q_2^{N+1}, $\cdots$, q_{27}^{N+1}, would normally result. Since this prediction is on the basis of a greater knowledge of the past, one would expect the probabilities of low numbers to be greater, and in fact one can prove the following inequalities:

$$\sum_{i=1}^{S} q_i^{N+1} \geq \sum_{i=1}^{S} q_i^{N} \qquad S = 1, 2, \cdots . \tag{11}$$

This means that the probability of being right in the first S guesses when the preceding N letters are known is greater than or equal to that when only $(N\text{-}1)$ are known, for all S. To prove this, imagine the probabilities $p(i_1, i_2, \cdots, i_N, j)$ arranged in a table with j running horizontally and all the N-grams vertically. The table will therefore have 27 columns and 27^N rows. The term on the left of (11) is the sum of the S largest entries in each row, summed over all the rows. The right-hand member of (11) is also a sum of entries from this table in which S entries are taken from each row but not necessarily the S largest. This follows from the fact that the right-hand member would be calculated from a similar table with $(N\text{-}1)$ grams rather than N-grams listed vertically. Each row in the N-1 gram table is the sum of 27 rows of the N-gram table, since:

$$p(i_2, i_3, \cdots, i_N, j) = \sum_{i_1=1}^{27} p(i_1, i_2, \cdots, i_N, j). \tag{12}$$

The sum of the S largest entries in a row of the N-1 gram table will equal the sum of the $27.S$ selected entries from the corresponding 27 rows of the N-gram table only if the latter fall into S columns. For the equality in (11) to hold for a particular S, this must be true of every row of the N-1 gram table. In this case, the first letter of the N-gram does not affect the set of the S most probable choices for the next letter, although the ordering within the set may be affected. However, if the equality in (11) holds for all S, it follows that the ordering as well will be unaffected by the first letter of the N-gram. The reduced text obtained from an ideal N-1 gram predictor is then identical with that obtained from an ideal N-gram predictor.

Since the partial sums

$$Q_S^N = \sum_{i=1}^{S} q_i^N \qquad S = 1, 2, \cdots \tag{13}$$

are monotonic increasing functions of N, <1 for all N, they must all approach limits as $N \rightarrow \infty$. Their first differences must therefore approach limits as $N \rightarrow \infty$, i.e., the q_i^N approach limits, q_i^∞. These may be interpreted as the relative frequency of correct first, second, $\cdots$, guesses with knowledge of the entire (infinite) past history of the text.

The ideal N-gram predictor can be considered, as has been pointed out, to be a transducer which operates on the language translating it into a sequence of numbers running from 1 to 27. As such it has the following two properties:

1. The output symbol is a function of the present input (the predicted next letter when we think of it as a predicting device) and the preceding (N-1) letters.

2. It is *instantaneously* reversible. The original input can be recovered by a suitable operation on the reduced text without loss of time. In fact, the inverse operation also operates on only the (N-1) preceding symbols of the reduced text together with the present output.

The above proof that the frequencies of output symbols with an N-1 gram predictor satisfy the inequalities:

$$\sum_1^S q_i^N \geq \sum_1^S q_i^{N-1} \qquad S = 1, 2, \cdots, 27 \tag{14}$$

can be applied to any transducer having the two properties listed above· In fact we can imagine again an array with the various (N-1) grams listed vertically and the present input letter horizontally. Since the present output is a function of only these quantities there will be a definite output symbol which may be entered at the corresponding intersection of row and column. Furthermore, the instantaneous reversibility requires that no two entries in the same row be the same. Otherwise, there would be ambiguity between the two or more possible present input letters when reversing the translation. The total probability of the S most probable symbols in the output, say $\sum_1^S r_i$, will be the sum of the probabilities for S entries in each row, summed over the rows, and consequently is certainly not greater than the sum of the S largest entries in each row. Thus we will have

$$\sum_1^S q_i^N \geq \sum_1^S r_i \qquad S = 1, 2, \cdots, 27 \tag{15}$$

In other words ideal prediction as defined above enjoys a preferred position among all translating operations that may be applied to a language and which satisfy the two properties above. Roughly speaking, ideal prediction collapses the probabilities of various symbols to a small group more than any other translating operation involving the same number of letters which is instantaneously reversible.

Sets of numbers satisfying the inequalities (15) have been studied by Muirhead in connection with the theory of algebraic inequalities.[5] If (15) holds when the q_i^N and r_i are arranged in decreasing order of magnitude, and

---

[5] Hardy, Littlewood and Polya, "Inequalities," Cambridge University Press, 1934.

also $\sum_{1}^{27} q_i^{N} = \sum_{1}^{27} r_i$, (this is true here since the total probability in each case is 1), then the first set, q_i^{N}, is said to *majorize* the second set, r_i. It is known that the majorizing property is equivalent to either of the following properties:

1. The r_i can be obtained from the q_i^{N} by a finite series of "flows." By a flow is understood a transfer of probability from a larger q to a smaller one, as heat flows from hotter to cooler bodies but not in the reverse direction.

2. The r_i can be obtained from the q_i^{N} by a generalized "averaging" operation. There exists a set of non-negative real numbers, a_{ij}, with $\sum_{j} a_{ij} = \sum_{i} a_{ij} = 1$ and such that

$$r_i = \sum_{j} a_{ij}(q_j^{N}).$$ (16)

5. Entropy Bounds from Prediction Frequencies

If we know the frequencies of symbols in the reduced text with the ideal N-gram predictor, q_i^{N}, it is possible to set both upper and lower bounds to the N-gram entropy, F_N, of the original language. These bounds are as follows:

$$\sum_{i=1}^{27} i(q_i^{N} - q_{i+1}^{N}) \log i \leq F_N \leq - \sum_{i=1}^{27} q_i^{N} \log q_i^{N}.$$ (17)

The upper bound follows immediately from the fact that the maximum possible entropy in a language with letter frequencies q_i^{N} is $-\sum q_i^{N} \log q_i^{N}$. Thus the entropy per symbol of the reduced text is not greater than this. The N-gram entropy of the reduced text is equal to that for the original language, as may be seen by an inspection of the definition (1) of F_N. The sums involved will contain precisely the same terms although, perhaps, in a different order. This upper bound is clearly valid, whether or not the prediction is ideal.

The lower bound is more difficult to establish. It is necessary to show that with any selection of N-gram probabilities $p(i_1, i_2, \ldots, i_N)$, we will have

$$\sum_{i=1}^{27} i(q_i^{N} - q_{i+1}^{N}) \log i \leq \sum_{i_1, \ldots, i_N} p(i, \cdots i_N) \log p_{i, \cdots i_{N-1}}(i_N)$$ (18)

The left-hand member of the inequality can be interpreted as follows: Imagine the q_i^{N} arranged as a sequence of lines of decreasing height (Fig. 3). The actual q_i^{N} can be considered as the sum of a set of rectangular distributions as shown. The left member of (18) is the entropy of this set of distributions. Thus, the ith rectangular distribution has a total probability of

$i(q_i^N - q_{i+1}^N)$. The entropy of the distribution is $\log i$. The total entropy is then

$$\sum_{i=1}^{27} i(q_i^N - q_{i+1}^N) \log i. \tag{19}$$

The problem, then, is to show that any system of probabilities $p(i_1, \dots, i_N)$, with best prediction frequencies q_i has an entropy F_N greater than or equal to that of this rectangular system, derived from the same set of q_i.

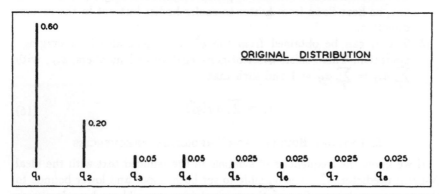

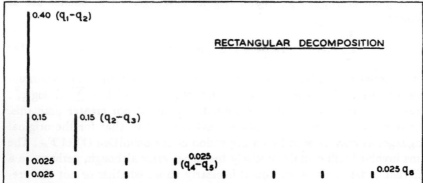

Fig. 3—Rectangular decomposition of a monotonic distribution.

The q_i as we have said are obtained from the $p(i_1, \dots, i_N)$ by arranging each row of the table in decreasing order of magnitude and adding vertically. Thus the q_i are the sum of a set of monotonic decreasing distributions. Replace each of these distributions by its rectangular decomposition. Each one is replaced then (in general) by 27 rectangular distributions; the q_i are the sum of 27×27^N rectangular distributions, of from 1 to 27 elements, and all starting at the left column. The entropy for this set is less than or equal to that of the original set of distributions since a termwise addition of two or more distributions always increases entropy. This is actually an application of the general theorem that $H_y(x) \leq H(x)$ for any chance variables x and y. The equality holds only if the distributions being added are proportional. Now we may add the different components of the same width without changing the entropy (since in this case the distributions *are* proportional). The result is that we have arrived at the rectangular decomposition of the q_i, by a series of processes which decrease or leave constant the entropy, starting with the original N-gram probabilities. Consequently the entropy of the original system F_N is greater than or equal to that of the rectangular decomposition of the q_i. This proves the desired result.

It will be noted that the lower bound is definitely less than F_N unless each row of the table has a rectangular distribution. This requires that for each

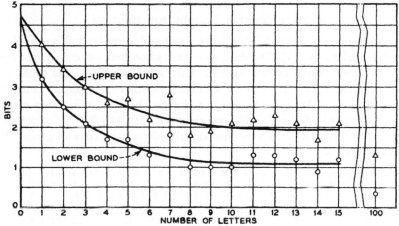

Fig. 4—Upper and lower experimental bounds for the entropy of 27-letter English.

possible $(N\text{-}1)$ gram there is a set of possible next letters each with equal probability, while all other next letters have zero probability.

It will now be shown that the upper and lower bounds for F_N given by (17) are monotonic decreasing functions of N. This is true of the upper bound since the q_i^{N+1} majorize the q_i^{N} and any equalizing flow in a set of probabilities increases the entropy. To prove that the lower bound is also monotonic decreasing we will show that the quantity

$$U = \sum_i i(q_i - q_{i+1}) \log i \qquad (20)$$

is increased by an equalizing flow among the q_i. Suppose a flow occurs from q_i to q_{i+1}, the first decreased by Δq and the latter increased by the same amount. Then three terms in the sum change and the change in U is given by

$$\Delta U = [-(i - 1) \log (i - 1) + 2i \log i - (i + 1) \log (i + 1)]\Delta q \qquad (21)$$

The term in brackets has the form $-f(x-1) + 2f(x) - f(x+1)$ where $f(x) = x \log x$. Now $f(x)$ is a function which is concave upward for positive x, since $f''(x) = 1/x > 0$. The bracketed term is twice the difference between the ordinate of the curve at $x = i$ and the ordinate of the midpoint of the chord joining $i-1$ and $i+1$, and consequently is negative. Since Δq also is negative, the change in U brought about by the flow is positive. An even simpler calculation shows that this is also true for a flow from q_1 to q_2 or from q_{26} to q_{27} (where only two terms of the sum are affected). It follows that the lower bound based on the N-gram prediction frequencies q_i^N is greater than or equal to that calculated from the $N+1$ gram frequencies q_i^{N+1}.

6. Experimental Bounds for English

Working from the data of Table I, the upper and lower bounds were calculated from relations (17). The data were first smoothed somewhat to overcome the worst sampling fluctuations. The low numbers in this table are the least reliable and these were averaged together in groups. Thus, in column 4, the 47, 18 and 14 were not changed but the remaining group totaling 21 was divided uniformly over the rows from 4 to 20. The upper and lower bounds given by (17) were then calculated for each column giving the following results:

Column	1	2	3	4	5	6	7	8	9	10	11	12	13	14	15	100
Upper	4.03	3.42	3.0	2.6	2.7	2.2	2.8	1.8	1.9	2.1	2.2	2.3	2.1	1.7	2.1	1.3
Lower	3.19	2.50	2.1	1.7	1.7	1.3	1.8	1.0	1.0	1.0	1.3	1.3	1.2	.9	1.2	.6

It is evident that there is still considerable sampling error in these figures due to identifying the observed sample frequencies with the prediction probabilities. It must also be remembered that the lower bound was proved only for the ideal predictor, while the frequencies used here are from human prediction. Some rough calculations, however, indicate that the discrepancy between the actual F_N and the lower bound with ideal prediction (due to the failure to have rectangular distributions of conditional probability) more than compensates for the failure of human subjects to predict in the ideal manner. Thus we feel reasonably confident of both bounds apart from sampling errors. The values given above are plotted against N in Fig. 4.

Acknowledgment

The writer is indebted to Mrs. Mary E. Shannon and to Dr. B. M. Oliver for help with the experimental work and for a number of suggestions and criticisms concerning the theoretical aspects of this paper.

Efficient Coding of a Binary Source with One Very Infrequent Symbol*

Claude E. Shannon

Abstract

Details are given of a coding system for a binary source of information with one highly infrequent symbol. This code approaches the ideal compression ratio as the probability p of the infrequent symbol approaches zero.

In the paper ''A Mathematical Theory of Communication,'' an information source was considered which produces a sequence of A's and B's, successive choices independent, with probability p for A, $q = 1 - p$ for B, and with p much less than q. A simple and reasonably efficient coding into 0's and 1's was mentioned which approaches ideal encoding as $p \to 0$. That is, the ratio of the expected length of the encoded text to the length of original text asymptotically approaches the entropy of this source:

$$H = - p \log p - q \log q \ .$$

When p is small H is approximately $p \log\ ep^{-1}$.

Several people have requested details of this analysis. This note proves this result for a coding system similar to that described in the communication paper, but simplified slightly to facilitate calculation.

The infrequent letter A with probability p is represented in the code by l 0's (000...0). The series of B's following each A is represented by giving a binary number telling the number of B's. This binary number is filled out at the beginning with additional 0's (if necessary) to give an even multiple of $l - 1$ binary digits. At positions $l + 1, 2l + 1$, etc., 1's are inserted both as markers and to prevent the possibility of l 0's appearing in the code associated with the B's. The following example shows how this would work when $l = 5$, so that $A = 00000$. Suppose the original message is

$$A, \quad 15 \ B's, \quad A, \quad 1024 \ B's, \quad A, 45 \ B's, \quad A, \quad A, \text{one } B, \ ...$$

Then the encoded form is

00000	11111	00000	10100	10000	10000
A	no. of B's	A			
	15 in binary form		$\leftarrow$ 1024 in binary form $\rightarrow$		

00000	10010	11101	00000	00000	10001
A	$\longleftarrow 45 \longrightarrow$		A	A	1

It is clear that this code can be uniquely decoded to recover the original text.

---

*   Bell Laboratories Memorandum, Jan. 29, 1954.

A sequence of n B's will require not more than

$$[\log_2(n + 1) + 1 + (l - 1)] \frac{l}{l - 1}$$

binary digits in its encoded form. The term $\log_2(n + 1) + 1$ is a pessimistic estimate of the number of digits in the binary expression for n, $(l - 1)$ is the worst possible number of added digits to give a multiple of $l - 1$ and the factor $l/(l - 1)$ accounts for the number of added 1's used as markers.

The A preceding a sequence of n B's adds l more binary digits, giving a total of less than

$$\frac{l}{l - 1} \log_2(n + 1) + 2l + 2 .$$

The probability (or relative frequency) of a sequence consisting of A followed by n B's is $p\,q^n$. Therefore the expected number of binary digits in the corresponding encoded form, averaged over all n, is less than

$$\sum_{n=0}^{\infty} p\,q^n \left[\frac{l}{l - 1} \log_2(n + 1) + 2l + 2 \right]. \tag{1}$$

We now prove that this sum is less than $\frac{l}{l - 1} \log_2 p^{-1} + (2l + 2)$. We have

$$\log_2 (n + 1) = \int_1^{n+1} \frac{dx}{x} = \int_1^2 \frac{dx}{x} + \int_2^3 \frac{dx}{x} + \cdots + \int_n^{n+1} \frac{dx}{x}$$

$$< 1 + \frac{1}{2} + \frac{1}{3} + \cdots + \frac{1}{n} .$$

Hence the term $\frac{l}{l - 1} p \sum_{n=1}^{\infty} q^n \log_2(n + 1)$ is less than

$$\frac{l}{l - 1} p \left[q + q^2(1 + \frac{1}{2}) + q^3(1 + \frac{1}{2} + \frac{1}{3}) + \cdots \right] .$$

By rearranging terms in the sum (the series is absolutely convergent) we obtain

$$\frac{l}{l - 1} p \left[(q + \frac{q^2}{2} + \frac{q^3}{3} + \cdots) + (q^2 + \frac{q^3}{2} + \frac{q^4}{3} + \cdots) + \cdots \right]$$

$$= -\frac{l}{l - 1} p \left[\log_2 (1 - q) + q \log_2 (1 - q) + q^2 \log_2 (1 - q) \right.$$

$$\left. + q^3 \log_2 (1 - q) + \cdots \right]$$

$$= -\frac{l}{l - 1} p \left[1 + q + q^2 + \cdots \right] \log_2 (1 - q)$$

$$= \frac{l}{l - 1} p \frac{1}{1 - q} \log_2 p^{-1}$$

$$= \frac{l}{l - 1} \log_2 p^{-1} .$$

The entire expression (1) is therefore less than

$$\frac{l}{l-1} \log p^{-1} + (2l + 2) .$$

If we let $l = (\frac{1}{2} \log_2 p^{-1})^{1/2}$ this is approximated, when p is small, by

$$\log p^{-1} + 2(\sqrt{2} \log p^{-1} + 1) , \tag{2}$$

ignoring terms whose ratio to those given approaches zero as $p \to 0$.

Expression (2) is therefore an approximation to the *average encoded length* of a sequence consisting of A followed by a group of B's. In the original message A occurs p^{-1} of the time, on the average. Therefore in the original the average length of the subgroups of this type is p^{-1}. The message has been reduced in length, on the average (or for a very long message), in the ratio

$$\frac{\log p^{-1} + 2(\sqrt{2} \log p^{-1} + 1)}{p^{-1}} .$$

As p approaches zero this approaches the value

$$p \log e \, p^{-1} .$$

Hence the code approaches the ideal compression ratio as p goes to zero.

Information Theory*

Claude E. Shannon

One of the most prominent features of 20th-century technology is the development and exploitation of new communication mediums. Concurrent with the growth of devices for transmitting and processing information, a unifying theory was developed and became the subject of intensive research.

This theory, known as communication theory, or, in its broader applications, information theory, is concerned with the discovery of mathematical laws governing systems designed to communicate or manipulate information. It sets up quantitative measures of information and of the capacity of various systems to transmit, store and otherwise process information.

Some of the problems treated relate to finding the best methods of utilizing various available communication systems, the best methods of separating signals from noise and the problem of setting upper bounds on what it is possible to do with a given channel. While the central results are chiefly of interest to communication engineers, some of the concepts have been adopted and found useful in such fields as psychology and linguistics.

Information is interpreted in its broadest sense to include the messages occurring in any of the standard communication mediums such as telegraphy, radio or television, the signals involved in electronic computing machines, servomechanisms systems and other data-processing devices, and even the signals appearing in the nerve networks of animals and man. The signals or messages need not be meaningful in any ordinary sense. This theory, then, is quite different from classical communication engineering theory which deals with the devices employed but not with that which is communicated.

Central Problems of Communication Theory. The type of communication system that has been most extensively investigated is shown in Fig. 1. It consists of the following:

1. An information source which produces the raw information or "message" to be transmitted.

2. A transmitter which transforms or encodes this information into a form suitable for the channel. This transformed message is called the signal.

3. The channel on which the encoded information or signal is transmitted to the receiving point. During transmission the signal may be changed or distorted. In radio, for example, there often is static, and in television transmission so-called "snow." These disturbing effects are known generally as noise, and are indicated schematically in Fig. 1 by the noise source.

4. The receiver, which decodes or translates the received signal back into the original message or an approximation of it.

5. The destination or intended recipient of the information.

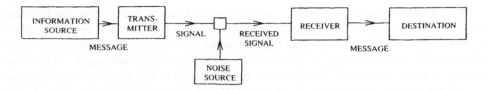

Figure 1. Diagram of general communication system

It will be seen that this system is sufficiently general to include a wide variety of communication problems if the various elements are suitably interpreted. In radio, for example, the information source may be a person speaking into a microphone. The message is then the sound that he produces, and the transmitter is the microphone and associated electronic equipment which changes this sound into an electromagnetic wave, the signal. The channel is the space between the transmitting and receiving antennas, and any static or noise disturbing the signal corresponds to the noise source in the schematic diagram. The home radio is the receiver in the system and its sound output the recovered message. The destination is a person listening to the message.

A basic idea in communication theory is that information can be treated very much like a physical quantity such as mass or energy. A homely analogy may be drawn between the system in Fig. 1 and a transportation system; for example, we can imagine an information source to be like a lumber mill producing lumber at a certain point. The channel in Fig. 1 might correspond to a conveyor system for transporting the lumber to a second point. In such a situation there are two important quantities: the rate R (in cubic feet per second) at which lumber is produced at the mill, and the capacity (in cubic feet per second) of the conveyor. These two quantities determine whether or not the conveyor system will be adequate for the lumber mill. If the rate of production R is greater than the conveyor capacity C, it will certainly be impossible to transport the full output of the mill; there will not be sufficient space available. If R is less than or equal to C, it may or may not be possible, depending on whether the lumber can be packed efficiently in the conveyor. Suppose, however, that we allow ourselves a sawmill at the source. This corresponds in our analogy to the encoder or transmitter. Then the lumber can be cut up into small pieces in such a way as to fill out the available capacity of the conveyor with 100% efficiency. Naturally in this case we should provide a carpenter shop at the receiving point to fasten the pieces back together in their original form before passing them on to the consumer.

If this analogy is sound, we should be able to set up a measure R in suitable units telling the rate at which information is produced by a given information source, and a second measure C which determines the capacity of a channel for transmitting information. Furthermore, the analogy would suggest that by a suitable coding or modulation system, the information can be transmitted over the channel if and only if the rate of production R is not greater than the capacity C. A key result of information theory is that it is indeed possible to set up measures R and C having this property.

Measurement of Information. Before we can consider how information is to be measured it is necessary to clarify the precise meaning of "information" from the point of view of the communication engineer. Often the messages to be transmitted have meaning: they describe or relate to real or conceivable events. However, this is not always the case. In transmitting music, the meaning, if any, is much more subtle than in the case of a verbal message. In some situations the engineer is faced with transmitting a totally meaningless sequence of numbers or letters. In any case, meaning is quite irrelevant to the problem of transmitting the information. It is as difficult to transmit a series of nonsense syllables as it is to transmit straight English text (more so, in fact). The significant aspect of information from the transmission standpoint is the fact that one particular message is chosen from a set of possible messages. What must be transmitted is a specification of the particular message which was chosen by the information source. The original message can be reconstructed at the receiving point only if such an unambiguous specification is transmitted. Thus in information theory, information is thought of as a choice of one message from a set of possible messages. Furthermore, these choices occur with certain probabilities; some messages are more frequent than others.

The simplest type of choice is a choice from two equally likely possibilities; that is, each has a probability 1/2. This is the situation, for example, when a coin is tossed which is equally likely to come up heads or tails. It is convenient to use the amount of information produced by such a choice as the basic unit and this basic unit is called a binary digit or, more briefly, a "bit." The choice involved with one bit of information can be indicated schematically as in Fig. 2(A). At point b either the upper or lower line may be chosen with probability 1/2 for each possibility.

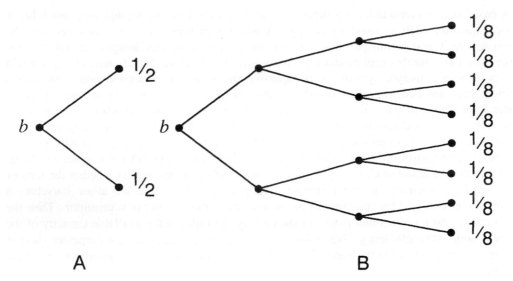

Figure 2. A choice from (A) two possibilities; (B) eight possibilities.

If there are N possibilities, all equally likely, the amount of information is given by $\log_2 N$. The reason for this can be seen from Fig. 2(B), where there are eight possibilities each with probability 1/8. The choice can be imagined to occur in three stages, each involving one bit. The first bit corresponds to a choice of either the first four or the second four of the eight possibilities, the second bit corresponds to the first or second pair of the four chosen, and the final bit determines the first or second member of the pair. It will be seen that the number of bits required is $\log_2 N$, in this case $\log_2 8 = 3$.

If the probabilities are not equal, the formula is more complicated. When the choices have probabilities $p_1, p_2, \ldots, p_n$, the amount of information H is given by

$$H = -(p_1 \log_2 p_1 + p_2 \log_2 p_2 + \cdots + p_n \log_2 p_n) .$$

This formula for the amount of information gives values ranging from zero — when one of the two events is certain to occur (i.e. has a probability of 1) and all others are certain not to occur (i.e. have probability 0) — to a maximum value of $\log_2 N$ when all events are equally probable (i.e. have probability $1/N$). These situations correspond intuitively to the minimum information produced by a particular event (when it is already certain what will occur) and the greatest information or the greatest prior uncertainty of the event.

The parlor game "Twenty Questions" illustrates some of these ideas. In this game, one person thinks of an object and the other players attempt to determine what it is by asking not more than twenty questions that can be answered "yes" or "no." According to information theory each question can, by its answer, yield anywhere from no information to $\log_2 2$ or one bit of information, depending upon whether the probabilities of "yes" and "no" answers are very unequal or approximately equal. To obtain the greatest amount of information, the players should ask questions that subdivide the set of possible objects, as nearly as possible, into two equally likely groups. For example, if they have established by previous questions that the object is a town in the United States, a good question would be, "Is it east of the Mississippi?" This divides the possible towns into two roughly equal sets. The next question then might be, "Is it north of the Mason-Dixon line?" If it were possible to choose questions which always had the effect of subdividing into two equal groups, it would be possible to isolate, in twenty questions, one object from approximately 1,000,000 possibilities. This corresponds to twenty bits.

The formula for the amount of information is identical in form with equations representing entropy in statistical mechanics, and suggests that there may be deep-lying connections between thermodynamics and information theory. Some scientists believe that a proper statement of the second law of thermodynamics requires a term relating to information. These connections with physics, however, do not have to be considered in the engineering and other applications of information theory.

Most information sources produce a message which consists not of a single choice but of a sequence of choices; for example, the letters of printed text or the elementary words or sounds of speech. The writing of English sentences can be thought of as a process of choice: choosing a first word from possible first words with various probabilities; then a second, with probabilities depending on the first; etc. This kind of statistical process is called a stochastic process, and information sources are thought of, in information theory, as stochastic processes. A more general formula for H can be given which determines the rate at which information is produced by a stochastic process or an information source.

Printed English is a type of information source that has been studied considerably. By playing a kind of "Twenty Questions" game, suitably modified, with subjects trying to guess the next letter in an English sentence, it can be shown that the information rate of written English is not more than about one bit per letter. This is a result of the very unequal frequencies of occurrence of different letters (for example, E is very common in English while Z, Q and X are very infrequent), of pairs of letters (TH is very common and QZ very rare), and the existence of frequently recurring words, phrases and so on. This body of statistical data relating to a language is called the statistical structure of the language. If all 26 letters and the space in English had equal frequencies of occurrence (i.e. each had probability $1/27$) and the occurrence of each letter of text was independent of previous letters, the information rate would be $\log_2 27$, or about 4.76 bits per letter. Since only one bit actually is produced, English is said to be about 80% redundant.

The redundancy of English is also exhibited by the fact that a great many letters can be deleted from a sentence without making it impossible for a reader to fill the gaps and determine the original meaning. For example, in the following sentence the vowels have been deleted:

MST PPL HV LTTL DFFCLTY N RDNG THS SNTNC.

As might easily be deduced, redundancy in a language plays an important role in the science of cryptography.

Encoding Information. An important feature of the measure of information, H, is that it determines the saving in transmission time that is possible, by proper encoding, due to the statistics of the message source. To illustrate this, consider a model language in which there are only four letters — A, B, C and D. Suppose these letters have the probabilities $1/2$, $1/4$, $1/8$ and $1/8$. In a long text in this language, A will occur one-half the time, B one-quarter of the time and C and D each one-eighth of the time. Suppose this language is to be encoded into binary digits, 0 or 1, as for example in a pulse system with two types of pulse. The most direct code is the following:

$$A = 00; \quad B = 01; \quad C = 10; \quad D = 11 .$$

This code requires two binary digits per letter of message. By proper use of the statistics, a better code can be constructed as follows:

$$A = 0; \quad B = 10; \quad C = 110; \quad D = 111 .$$

It is readily verified that the original message can be recovered from its encoded form. Furthermore, the number of binary digits used is smaller on the average. It will be, in fact,

$$\frac{1}{2}(1) + \frac{1}{4}(2) + \frac{1}{8}(3) + \frac{1}{8}(3) = 1\frac{3}{4} ,$$

where the first term is due to the letter A, which occurs half the time and is one binary digit long, and similarly for the others. It may be found by a simple calculation that $1\frac{3}{4}$ is just the value of H, calculated for the probabilities $1/2$, $1/4$, $1/8$, $1/8$.

The result verified for this special case holds generally — if the information rate of the message is H bits per letter, it is possible to encode it into binary digits using, on the average, only H binary digits per letter of text. There is no method of encoding which uses less than this amount.

This important result in information theory gives a direct meaning to the quantity H which measures the information rate for a source or a language. It says, in fact, that H can be interpreted as the equivalent number of binary digits when the language or source is encoded in 0 and 1 in the most efficient way. For instance, if the estimate of one bit per letter, mentioned above as the rate for printed English, is correct, then it is possible to encode printed English into binary digits using, on the average, one for each letter of text; and, furthermore, no encoding method would average less than this.

Capacity of a Channel. Now consider the problem of defining the capacity C of a channel for transmitting information. Since the rate of production for an information source has been measured in bits per second, we would naturally like to measure C in the same units. The question then becomes, what is the maximum number of binary digits per second that can be transmitted over a given channel? In some cases the answer is simple. With a teletype channel there are 32 possible symbols. By calculating $\log_2 32$ it is found that each symbol represents 5 bits, provided the possible symbols are used with equal probability. Therefore, if we can send n symbols per second, and the noise level is not high enough to introduce any errors during transmission, we can send $5n$ bits per second.

The problem of calculating the capacity of a channel is usually more complex than this example because of disturbing noise. As an example, suppose there are two possible kinds of pulse that can be transmitted in a system, a 0 pulse and a 1 pulse. Suppose further than when 0 is transmitted it is received as 0 nine-tenths of the time, but one-tenth of the time noise causes it to be received as 1. Conversely, suppose a transmitted 1 is received as 1 nine-tenths of the time but distorted into a 0 pulse one-tenth of the time. This type of channel is called a binary symmetric channel. It and other noisy channels have definite capacities that can be calculated by appropriate formulas. In this particular case, the capacity is about 0.53 bits per pulse.

The meaning of the capacity of such a noisy channel may be roughly described as follows. It is possible to construct codes that will transmit a series of binary digits at a rate equal to the capacity. This can be done in such a way that they can be decoded at the receiving point with a very small probability of error. These codes are called error-correcting codes, and are so constructed that the type of transmission errors likely to occur in the channel can be corrected at the receiving point. Finally, it is not possible to transmit at a higher rate than the channel capacity and retain this error-correcting property.

The functioning of error-correcting codes can be likened to the ability of a person to correct a reasonable number of typographical errors in a manuscript because of his knowledge of the structure and context of the language. Much of the work in information theory centers around the theory and construction of such error-correcting codes.

Band-limited Channels. A frequently occurring restriction on communication channels is that the signals must lie within a certain band of frequencies W cycles per second wide. A result known as the sampling theorem states that a signal of this type can be specified by giving its values at a series of equally spaced sampling points $1/2W$ seconds apart. Thus it may be said that such a function has $2W$ degrees of freedom, or dimensions, per second.

If there were no noise whatever on such a channel it would be possible to distinguish an infinite number of different amplitude levels for each sample. Consequently, in principle, an infinite number of binary digits per second could be transmitted, and the capacity C would be infinite. In practice, there is always some noise, but even so if no limitations are placed on the transmitter power P, the capacity will be infinite, since at each sample point an unlimited number of different amplitude levels may be distinguished. Only when noise is present and the transmitter power is limited in some way does the capacity C become finite. This capacity depends on the statistical structure of the noise as well as the nature of the power limitation.

The simplest type of noise is resistance noise, produced in an electrical resistor by thermal effects. This type of noise is completely specified by giving its average power N.

The simplest limitation on transmitter power is the assumption that the average power delivered by the transmitter is not greater than P. If a channel is defined by these three parameters W, P and N, the capacity C can be shown to be

$$C = W \log_2 \frac{P + N}{N} \text{ (bits per second)}$$

The implication of this formula is that it is possible, by properly choosing the signal functions, to transmit $W \log_2 \dfrac{P + N}{N}$ binary digits per second and to recover them at the receiving point *with as small a frequency of errors as desired.* It is not possible to transmit binary digits at any higher rate with an arbitrarily small frequency of errors.

Encoding systems in current use, pulse-code modulation and pulse-position modulation, use about four times the power predicted by the ideal formula. Unfortunately, as one attempts to approach more closely this ideal, the transmitter and receiver required become more complicated and the delays increase.

The relation

$$C = W \log_2 (1 + \frac{P}{N})$$

can be regarded as an exchange relation between the bandwidth W and the signal-to-noise ratio P/N. Keeping the channel capacity fixed, the bandwidth can be decreased provided the signal-to-noise ratio is sufficiently increased. Conversely, an increase in bandwidth allows a lower signal-to-noise ratio in the channel.

One method of exchanging bandwidth for signal-to-noise ratio is shown in Fig. 3. The upper curve represents a signal function whose bandwidth is such that it can be specified by giving the samples shown. Each sample has five amplitude levels. The lower curve is obtained by combining pairs of samples from the first curve as shown. If the pair of samples from the upper curve have amplitudes x and y, a single amplitude z for the lower curve is computed from the formula

$$z = 5x + y .$$

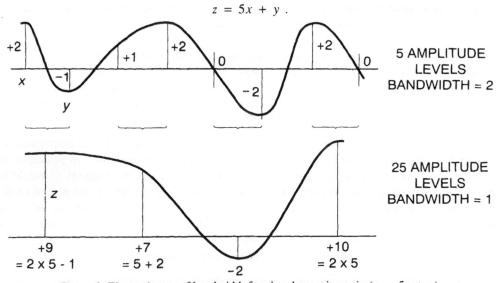

Figure 3. The exchange of bandwidth for signal-to-noise ratio ($z = 5x + y$).

The five possible values of x combined with the five possible values of y produce 25 possible values of z which must be distinguished. However, the samples now occur only half as frequently; consequently the band is reduced by half, at the cost of increasing the signal-to-noise ratio. Operating this in reverse doubles the band but reduces the required signal-to-noise ratio.

To summarize, there are three essentially different ways in which bandwidth can be reduced in a system such as television or speech transmission. The first is the straightforward exchange of bandwidth for signal-to-noise ratio just discussed. The second method is utilization of the statistical correlations existing in the message. This capitalizes on particular properties of the information source feeding the channel. Finally, particular properties of the ultimate destination of the messages can be used. Thus in speech transmission the ear is relatively insensitive to phase distortion. Consequently, phase information is not as important as amplitude information, and need not be sent so accurately, resulting in a saving of bandwidth or of power. In general, the exploitation of particular "sensitivities" or "blindness" in the destination requires a proper matching of the channel to the destination.

Filtering and Prediction Problem. Another type of problem that has been studied extensively in the field of information theory is that of determining the best devices for eliminating noise from a signal and predicting the future value of the signal. These are known as the filtering and prediction problems. The two problems may also occur in combination if it is desired to predict the future value of a noisy signal. Possible applications of the filtering problem occur in the detection of various types of communication signals which have been corrupted by noise or in the smoothing of data subject to observational error. The prediction problem, with or without filtering, may arise, for example, in weather or economic forecasting or in the control of gun directors, where it is desired to predict the future position of a moving target.

The most successful work in this general field has been carried out under the following two assumptions. First, the best prediction or filtering is interpreted to be that which minimizes the mean-square error between the computed value and the true value. Second, the devices performing these operations are assumed to perform linear operations on the signals which they filter or predict. Under these conditions, substantially complete solutions have been found specifying the characteristics of predicting or filtering device in terms of the power spectra of the signal and of the noise.

Cryptography, Linguistics and Other Applications. Some applications have been made in the fields of cryptography and linguistics. It is possible to formulate a theory of cryptography or secrecy systems in terms of the concepts occurring in information theory. When this is done, it appears that the information rate R of a language is intimately related to the possibility of solving cryptograms in that language. The smaller this rate, the easier such a solution becomes and the less material is necessary to render such a solution unique. Indeed, within limits, the theory becomes quantitative and predictive, giving means of calculating how much material must be intercepted in a given language and with a given cipher in order to ensure the existence of a unique solution.

A study has been made of the distribution of lengths and frequency of occurrence of the different words in a language such as English. It has been found, for example, that the relative frequency of the nth most frequent word may be expressed quite closely by a formula of the type $P(n + m)^{-b}$, with suitable constants for P, m and b. Experimental data of this type can be explained as consequences of the assumption that a language gradually evolves under continued use into an efficient communication code.

Psychologists have discovered interesting relationships between the amount of information in a stimulus and reaction time to the stimulus. For example, an experiment can be set up in which there are four lights and four associated push buttons. The lights go on in a random order and the subject is required to press the corresponding button as quickly as possible after a light goes on. It develops that the average time required for this reaction increases linearly with an increase in the amount of information conveyed by the lights. This experimental result holds true under a wide variety of changes in the experiment: the number of lights, the probabilities of different lights, and even varying correlations between successive lights.

These results suggest that under certain conditions the human being, in manipulating information, may adopt codes and methods akin to those used in information theory.

Bibliography. C. E. Shannon and W. Weaver, *The Mathematical Theory of Communication* (1949); W. Jackson (ed.), *Communication Theory* (1953); A. Feinstein, *Foundations of Information Theory* (1958); N. Wiener, *Extrapolation, Interpolation, and Smoothing of Stationary Time Series* (1949); C. E. Shannon, ''Communication Theory of Secrecy Systems,'' *Bell System Technical Journal* (Oct. 1949); *Bibliography on Communication Theory*, Union Internationale des Télécommunications (1953).

The Zero Error Capacity of a Noisy Channel

Claude E. Shannon

Abstract

The zero error capacity C_0 of a noisy channel is defined to be the least upper bound of rates at which it is possible to transmit information with zero probability of error. Various properties of C_0 are studied; upper and lower bounds and methods of evaluation of C_0 are given. Inequalities are obtained for the C_0 relating to the "sum" and "product" of two given channels. The analogous problem of zero error capacity C_{0F} for a channel with a feedback link is considered. It is shown that while the ordinary capacity of a memoryless channel with feedback is equal to that of the same channel without feedback, the zero error capacity may be greater. A solution is given to the problem of evaluating C_{0F}.

Introduction

The ordinary capacity C of a noisy channel may be thought of as follows. There exists a sequence of codes for the channel of increasing block length such that the input rate of transmission approaches C and the probability of error in decoding at the receiving point approaches zero. Furthermore, this is not true for any value higher than C. In some situations it may be of interest to consider, rather than codes with probability of error *approaching* zero, codes for which the probability *is* zero and to investigate the highest possible rate of transmission (or the least upper bound of these rates) for such codes. This rate, C_0, is the main object of investigation of the present paper. It is interesting that while C_0 would appear to be a simpler property of a channel than C, it is in fact more difficult to calculate and leads to a number of as yet unsolved problems.

We shall consider only finite discrete memoryless channels. Such a channel is specified by a finite transition matrix $[p_i(j)]$, where $p_i(j)$ is the probability of input letter i being received as output letter j ($i = 1, 2, \ldots, a$; $j = 1, 2, \ldots, b$) and $\sum_j p_i(j) = 1$. Equivalently, such a channel may be represented by a line diagram such as that shown in Fig. 1.

The channel being *memoryless* means that successive operations are independent. If the input letters i and j are used, the probability of output letters k and l will be $p_i(k)p_j(l)$. A sequence of input letters will be called an *input word,* a sequence of output letters an *output word.* A mapping of M messages (which we may take to be the integers $1, 2, \ldots, M$) into a subset of input words of length n will be called a block code of length n. $R = \dfrac{1}{n} \log M$ will be called the *input rate* for this code. Unless otherwise specified, a code will mean such a block code. We will, throughout, use natural logarithms and natural (rather than binary) units of information, since this simplifies the analytical processes that will be employed.

A *decoding system* for a block code of length n is a method of associating a unique input message (integer from 1 to M) with each possible output word of length n, that is, a function from output words of length n to the integers 1 to M. The *probability of error* for a code is the probability when the M input messages are each used with probability $1/M$ that the noise and the decoding system will lead to an input message different from the one that actually occurred.

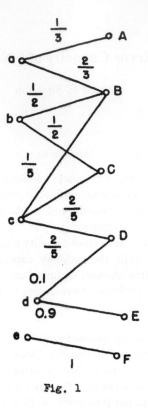

Fig. 1

If we have two given channels, it is possible to form a single channel from them in two natural ways which we call the sum and product of the two channels. The *sum* of two channels is the channel formed by using inputs from either of the two given channels with the same transition probabilities to the set of output letters consisting of the logical sum of the two output alphabets. Thus the sum channel is defined by a transition matrix formed by placing the matrix of one channel below and to the right of that for the other channel and filling the remaining two rectangles with zeros. If $[p_i(j)]$ and $[p_i'(j)]$ are the individual matrices, the sum has the following matrix:

$$\begin{bmatrix} p_1(1) & \ldots & p_1(r) & 0 & \ldots & 0 \\ \vdots & & \vdots & \vdots & & \vdots \\ p_t(t) & \ldots & p_t(r) & 0 & \ldots & 0 \\ 0 & \ldots & 0 & p_1'(1) & \ldots & p_1'(r') \\ \vdots & & \vdots & \vdots & & \vdots \\ 0 & \ldots & 0 & p_{t'}''(1) & \ldots & p_{t'}'(r') \end{bmatrix}.$$

The *product* of two channels is the channel whose input alphabet consists of all ordered pairs (i,i') where i is a letter from the first channel alphabet and i' from the second, whose output alphabet is the similar set of ordered pairs of letters from the two individual output alphabets and whose transition probability from (i,i') to (j,j') is $p_i(j)p_{i'}'(j')$.

The sum of channels corresponds physically to a situation where either of two channels may be used (but not both), a new choice being made for each transmitted letter. The product channel corresponds to a situation where both channels are used each unit of time. It is interesting to note that multiplication and addition of channels are both associative and commutative, and that the product distributes over a sum. Thus one can develop a kind of algebra for channels in which it is possible to write, for example, a polynomial $\Sigma a_n K^n$, where the a_n are non-negative integers and K is a channel. We shall not, however, investigate here the algebraic properties of this system.

The Zero Error Capacity

In a discrete channel we will say that two input letters are *adjacent* if there is an output letter which can be caused by either of them. Thus i and j are adjacent if there exists a t such that both $p_i(t)$ and $p_j(t)$ do not vanish. In Fig. 1, a and c are adjacent, while a and d are not.

If all input letters are adjacent to each other, any code with more than one word has a probability of error at the receiving point greater than zero. In fact, the probability of error in decoding words satisfies

$$P_e \geq \frac{M-1}{M} p_{\min}^n ,$$

where $p_{\min}$ is the smallest (nonzero) number among the $p_i(j)$, n is the length of the code and M is the number of words in the code. To prove this, note that any two words have a possible output word in common, namely the word consisting of the sequence of common output letters when the two input words are compared letter by letter. Each of the two input words has a probability at least $p_{\min}^n$ of producing this common output word. In using the code, the two particular input words will each occur $\frac{1}{M}$ of the time and will cause the common output $\frac{1}{M} p_{\min}^n$ of the time. This output can be decoded in only one way. Hence at least one of these situations leads to an error. This error probability, $\frac{1}{M} p_{\min}^n$, is assigned to this code word, and from the remaining $M-1$ code words another pair is chosen. A source of error to the amount $\frac{1}{M} p_{\min}^n$ is assigned in similar fashion to one of these, and this is a disjoint event. Continuing in this matter, we obtain a total of at least $\frac{M-1}{M} p_{\min}^n$ as probability of error.

If it is not true that the input letters are all adjacent to each other, it is possible to transmit at a positive rate with zero probability of error. The least upper bound of all rates which can be achieved with zero probability of error will be called the *zero error capacity* of the channel and denoted by C_0. If we let $M_0(n)$ be the largest number of words in a code of length n, no two of which are adjacent, then C_0 is the least upper bound of the numbers $\frac{1}{n} \log M_0(n)$ when n varies through all positive integers.

One might expect that C_0 would be equal to $\log M_0(1)$, that is, that if we choose the largest possible set of non-adjacent letters and form all sequences of these of length n, then this would be the best error-free code of length n. This is not, in general, true, although it holds in many cases, particularly when the number of input letters is small. The first failure occurs with five input letters with the channel in Fig. 2. In this channel, it is possible to choose at most two nonadjacent letters, for example 0 and 2. Using sequences of these, 00, 02, 20, and 22 we obtain four words in a code of length two. However, it is possible to construct a code of length

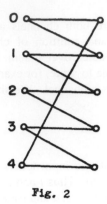

Fig. 2

two with five members no two of which are adjacent as follows: 00, 12, 24, 31, 43. It is readily verified that no two of these are adjacent. Thus C_0 for this channel is at least ½ log 5.

No method has been found for determining C_0 for the general discrete channel, and this we propose as an interesting unsolved problem in coding theory. We shall develop a number of results which enable one to determine C_0 in many special cases, for example, in all channels with five or fewer input letters with the single exception of the channel of Fig. 2 (or channels equivalent in adjacency structure to it). We will also develop some general inequalities enabling one to estimate C_0 quite closely in most cases.

It may be seen, in the first place, that the value of C_0 depends only on which input letters are adjacent to each other. Let us define the *adjacency matrix* $[A_{ij}]$ for a channel, as follows:

$$A_{ij} = \begin{cases} 1 & \text{if input letter } i \text{ is adjacent to } j \text{ or if } i = j, \\ 0 & \text{otherwise} . \end{cases}$$

Suppose two channels have the same adjacency matrix (possibly after renumbering the input letters of one of them). Then it is obvious that a zero error code for one will be a zero error code for the other and, hence, that the zero error capacity C_0 for one will also apply to the other.

The adjacency structure contained in the adjacency matrix can also be represented as a linear graph. Construct a graph with as many vertices as there are input letters, and connect two distinct vertices with a line or branch of the graph if the corresponding input letters are adjacent. Two examples are shown in Fig. 3, corresponding to the channels of Figs. 1 and 2.

Theorem 1: The zero error capacity C_0 of a discrete memoryless channel is bounded by the inequalities

$$-\log \min_{P_i} \sum_{ij} A_{ij} P_i P_j \leq C_0 \leq \min_{p_i(j)} C ,$$

where

$$\sum_i P_i = 1, P_i \geq 0, \sum_j p_i(j) = 1, p_i(j) \geq 0 ,$$

and C is the capacity of any channel with transition probabilities $p_i(j)$ and having the adjacency matrix A_{ij}.

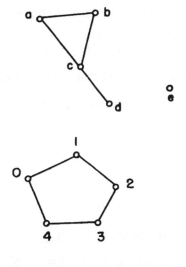

Fig. 3

The upper bound is fairly obvious. The zero error capacity is certainly less than or equal to the ordinary capacity for any channel with the same adjacency matrix since the former requires codes with zero probability of error while the latter requires only codes approaching zero probability of error. By minimizing the capacity through variation of the $p_i(j)$ we find the lowest upper bound available through this argument. Since the capacity is a continuous function of the $p_i(j)$ in the closed region defined by $p_i(j) \geq 0$, $\sum_j p_i(j) = 1$, we may write min instead of greatest lower bound.

It is worth noting that it is only necessary to consider a particular channel in performing this minimization, although there are an infinite number with the same adjacency matrix. This one particular channel is obtained as follows from the adjacency matrix. If $A_{ik} = 1$ for a pair $i\,k$, define an output letter j with $p_i(j)$ and $p_k(j)$ both differing from zero. Now if there are any three input letters, say $i\,k\,l$, all adjacent to each other, define an output letter, say m, with $p_i(m)p_k(m)p_l(m)$ all different from zero. In the adjacency graph this corresponds to a complete subgraph with three vertices. Next, subsets of four letters or complete subgraphs with four vertices, say $i\,k\,l\,m$, are given an output letter, each being connected to it, and so on. It is evident that any channel with the same adjacency matrix differs from that just described only by variation in the number of output symbols for some of the pairs, triplets, etc., of adjacent input letters. If a channel has more than one output symbol for an adjacent subset of input letters, then its capacity is reduced by identifying these. If a channel contains no element, say for a triplet $i\,k\,l$ of adjacent input letters, this will occur as a special case of our canonical channel which has output letter m for this triplet when $p_i(m)$, $p_k(m)$ and $p_l(m)$ all vanish.

The lower bound of the theorem will now be proved. We use the procedure of random codes based on probabilities for the letters P_i, these being chosen to minimize the quadratic form $\sum_{ij} A_{ij} P_i P_j$. Construct an ensemble of codes each containing M words, each word n letters long. The words in a code are chosen by the following stochastic method. Each letter of each word is chosen independently of all others and is the letter i with probability P_i. We now compute the probability in the ensemble that any particular word is not adjacent to any other word in its code. The probability that the first letter of one word is adjacent to the first letter of a second word is $\sum_{ij} A_{ij} P_i P_j$, since this sums the case of adjacency with coefficient 1 and those of non-adjacency with coefficient 0. The probability that two words are adjacent in all letters, and therefore adjacent as words, is $(\sum_{ij} A_{ij} P_i P_j)^n$. The probability of non-adjacency is therefore $1 - (\sum_{ij} A_{ij} P_i P_j)^n$. The probability that all $M - 1$ other words in a code are not adjacent to a given word is, since they are chosen independently,

$$\left[1 - (\sum_{ij} A_{ij} P_i P_j)^n \right]^{M-1}$$

which is, by a well known inequality, greater than $1 - (M-1)(\sum_{ij} A_{ij} P_i P_j)^n$, which in turn is greater than $1 - M(\sum_{ij} A_{ij} P_i P_j)^n$. If we set $M = (1 - \varepsilon)^n (\sum_{ij} A_{ij} P_i P_j)^{-n}$, we then have, by taking ε small, a rate as close as desired to $-\log \sum_{ij} A_{ij} P_i P_j$. Furthermore, once ε is chosen, by taking n sufficiently large we can insure that $M(\sum_{ij} A_{ij} P_i P_j)^n = (1 - \varepsilon)^n$ is as small as desired, say, less than δ. The probability in the ensemble of codes of a particular word being adjacent to any other in its own code is now less than δ. This implies that there are codes in the ensemble for which the ratio of the number of such undesired words to the total number in the code is less than or equal to δ. For, if not, the ensemble average would be worse than δ. Select such a code and delete from it the words having this property. We have reduced our rate only by at most $\log(1 - \delta)^{-1}$; since ε and δ were both arbitrarily small, we obtain error-free codes arbitrarily close to the rate $-\log \min_{P_i} \sum_{ij} A_{ij} P_i P_j$ as stated in the theorem.

In connection with the upper bound of Theorem 1, the following result is useful in evaluating the minimum C. It is also interesting in its own right and will prove useful later in connection with channels having a feedback link.

Theorem 2: In a discrete memoryless channel with transition probabilities $p_i(j)$ and input letter probabilities P_i the following three statements are equivalent.

1) The rate of transmission

$$R = \sum_{i,j} P_i p_i(j) \log (p_i(j)/ \sum_k P_k p_k(j))$$

is stationary under variation of all non-vanishing P_i subject to $\sum_i P_i = 1$ and under variation of $p_i(j)$ for those $p_i(j)$ such that $P_i p_i(j) > 0$ and subject to $\sum_j p_i(j) = 1$.

2) The mutual information between input-output pairs $I_{ij} = \log(p_i(j)/ \sum_k P_k p_k(j))$ is constant, $I_{ij} = I$, for all ij pairs of non-vanishing probability (i.e. pairs for which $P_i p_i(j) > 0$).

3) We have $p_i(j) = r_j$, a function of j only, whenever $P_i p_i(j) > 0$; and also $\sum_{i \in S_j} P_i = h$, a constant independent of j where S_j is the set of input letters that can produce output letter j with probability greater than zero. We also have $I = \log h^{-1}$.

The $p_i(j)$ and P_i corresponding to the maximum and minimum capacity when the $p_i(j)$ are varied (keeping, however, any $p_i(j)$ that are zero fixed at zero) satisfy 1), 2) and 3).

Proof: We will show first that 1) and 2) are equivalent and then that 2) and 3) are equivalent.

R is a bounded continuous function of its arguments P_i and $p_i(j)$ in the (bounded) region of allowed values defined by $\Sigma\, P_i = 1, P_i \geq 0, \Sigma\, p_i(j) = 1, p_i(i) > 0$. R has a finite partial derivative with respect to any $p_i(j) > 0$. In fact, we readily calculate

$$\frac{\partial R}{\partial p_i(j)} = P_i \log\left(p_i(j) / \sum_k P_k p_k(j)\right) .$$

A necessary and sufficient condition that R be stationary for small variation of the non-vanishing $p_i(j)$ subject to the conditions given is that

$$\frac{\partial R}{\partial p_i(j)} = \frac{\partial R}{\partial p_i(k)} ,$$

for all i, j, k such that P_i, $p_i(j)$, $p_i(k)$ do not vanish. This requires that

$$P_i \log p_i(j) / \sum_m P_m p_m(j) = P_i \log p_i(k) / \sum_m P_m p_m(k) .$$

If we let $Q_j = \sum_m P_m p_m(j)$, the probability of output letter j, then this is equivalent to

$$\frac{p_i(j)}{Q_j} = \frac{p_i(k)}{Q_k} .$$

In other words, $p_i(j)/Q_j$ is independent of j, a function of i only, whenever $P_i > 0$ and $p_i(j) > 0$. This function of i we call α_i. Thus

$$p_i(j) = \alpha_i Q_j$$

unless $P_i p_i(j) = 0$.

Now, taking the partial derivative of R with respect to P_i we obtain:

$$\frac{\partial R}{\partial P_i} = \sum_j p_i(j) \log \frac{p_i(j)}{Q_j} - 1 .$$

For R to be stationary subject to $\Sigma\, P_i = 1$ we must have $\partial R/\partial P_i = \partial R/\partial P_k$. Thus

$$\sum_j p_i(j) \log \frac{p_i(j)}{Q_j} = \sum_j p_k(j) \log \frac{p_k(j)}{Q_j} .$$

Since for $P_i p_i(j) > 0$ we have $p_i(j)/Q_j = \alpha_i$, this becomes

$$\sum_j p_i(j) \log \alpha_i = \sum_j p_k(j) \log \alpha_k$$

$$\log \alpha_i = \log \alpha_k .$$

Thus α_i is independent of i and may be written as α. Consequently

$$\frac{p_i(j)}{Q_j} = \alpha \,,$$

$$\log\frac{p_i(j)}{Q_j} = \log \alpha = I$$

whenever $P_i p_i(j) > 0$.

The converse result is an easy reversal of the above argument. If

$$\log\frac{p_i(j)}{Q_j} = I \,,$$

then $\partial R/\partial P_i = I - 1$, by a simple substitution in the $\partial R/\partial P_i$ formula. Hence R is stationary under variation of P_i constrained by $\Sigma P_i = 1$. Further, $\partial R/\partial p_i(j) = P_i I = \partial R/\partial p_i(k)$, and hence the variation of R also vanishes subject to $\sum\limits_j p_i(j) = 1$.

We now prove that 2) implies 3). Suppose $\log\dfrac{p_i(j)}{Q_j} = I$ whenever $P_i p_i(j) > 0$. Then $p_i(j) = e^I Q_j$, a function of j only under this same condition. Also, if $q_j(i)$ is the conditional probability of i given j, then

$$\frac{Q_j q_j(i)}{P_i Q_j} = e^I \,,$$

$$q_j(i) = e^I P_i \,,$$

$$1 = \sum_{i \in S_j} q_j(i) = e^I \sum_{i \in S_j} P_i \,.$$

To prove that 3) implies 2), we assume $p_i(j) = r_j$ when $P_i p_i(j) > 0$. Then

$$\frac{P_i p_i(j)}{P_i Q_j} = \frac{r_j}{Q_j} = \lambda_j (\text{say}) = \frac{Q_j q_j(i)}{P_i Q_j} = \frac{q_j(i)}{P_i} \,.$$

Now, summing the equation $P_i \lambda_j = q_j(i)$ over $i \in S_j$ and using the assumption from 3) that $\sum\limits_{S_j} P_i = h$, we obtain

$$h \lambda_j = 1 \,,$$

so λ_j is h^{-1} and independent of j. Hence $I_{ij} = I = \log h^{-1}$.

The last statement of the theorem concerning minimum and maximum capacity under variation of $p_i(j)$ follows from the fact that R at these points must be stationary under variation of all non-vanishing P_i and $p_i(j)$, and hence the corresponding P_i and $p_i(j)$ satisfy condition 1) of the theorem.

For simple channels it is usually more convenient to apply particular tricks in trying to evaluate C_0 instead of the bounds given in Theorem 1, which involve maximizing and minimizing processes. The simplest lower bound, as mentioned before, is obtained by merely finding the logarithm of the maximum number of non-adjacent input letters.

A very useful device for determining C_0 which works in many cases may be described using the notion of an *adjacency-reducing mapping*. By this we mean a mapping of letters into other letters, $i \rightarrow \alpha(i)$, with the property that if i and j are not adjacent in the channel (or graph) then $\alpha(i)$ and $\alpha(j)$ are not adjacent. If we have a zero-error code, then we may apply such a mapping letter by letter to the code and obtain a new code which will also be of the zero-error type, since no adjacencies can be produced by the mapping.

Theorem 3: If all the input letters i can be mapped by an adjacency-reducing mapping $i \rightarrow \alpha(i)$ into a subset of the letters no two of which are adjacent, then the zero-error capacity C_0 of the channel is equal to the logarithm of the number of letters in this subset.

For, in the first place, by forming all sequences of these letters we obtain a zero-error code at this rate. Secondly, any zero error code for the channel can be mapped into a code using only these letters and containing, therefore, at most e^{nC_0} non-adjacent words.

The zero error capacities, or, more exactly, the equivalent numbers of input letters for all adjacency graphs up to five vertices are shown in Fig. 4. These can all be found readily by the method of Theorem 3, except for the channel of Fig. 2 mentioned previously, for which we know only that the zero-error capacity lies in the range $\frac{1}{2} \log 5 \le C_0 \le \log \frac{5}{2}$.

All graphs with six vertices have been examined and the capacities of all of these can also be found by this theorem, with the exception of four. These four can be given in terms of the capacity of Fig. 2, so that this case is essentially the only unsolved problem up to seven vertices. Graphs with seven vertices have not been completely examined but at least one new situation arises, the analog of Fig. 2 with seven input letters.

As examples of how the N_0 values were computed by the method of adjacency-reducing mappings, several of the graphs in Fig. 4 have been labelled to show a suitable mapping. The scheme is as follows. All nodes labelled a are mapped into node α as well as α itself. All nodes labelled b and also β are mapped into node β. All nodes labelled c and γ are mapped into node γ. It is readily verified that no new adjacencies are produced by the mappings indicated and that the α, β, γ nodes are non-adjacent.

C_0 for Sum and Product Channels

Theorem 4: If two memoryless channels have zero-error capacities $C'_0 = \log A$ and $C''_0 = \log B$, their sum has a zero error capacity greater than or equal to $\log(A + B)$ and their product has a zero error capacity greater than or equal to $C'_0 + C''_0$. If the graph of either of the two channels can be reduced to non-adjacent points by the mapping method (Theorem 3), then these inequalities can be replaced by equalities.

Proof: It is clear that in the case of the product, the zero error capacity is at least $C'_0 + C''_0$, since we may form a product code from two codes with rates close to C'_0 and C''_0. If these codes are not of the same length, we use for the new code length the least common multiple of the individual lengths and form all sequences of the code words of each of the codes up to this length. To prove equality in case one of the graphs, say that for the first channel, can be mapped into A non-adjacent points, suppose we have a code for the product channel. The letters for the product code, of course, are ordered pairs of letters corresponding to the original channels. Replace the first letter in each pair in all code words by the letter corresponding to reduction by the mapping method. This reduces or preserves adjacency between words in the code. Now sort the code words into A^n subsets according to the sequences of first letters in the

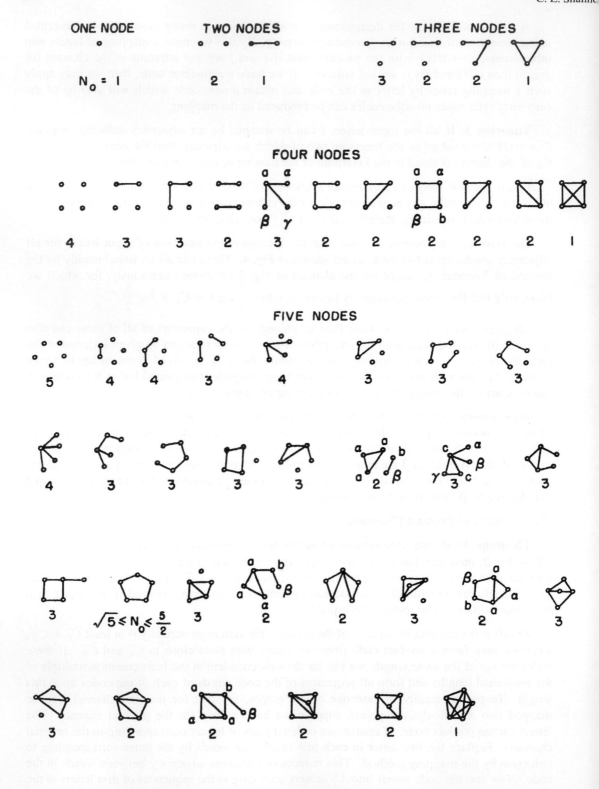

Fig. 4 – All graphs with 1, 2, 3, 4, 5 nodes and the corresponding N_0 for channels with these as adjacency graphs (note $C_0 = \log N_0$)

ordered pairs. Each of these subsets can contain at most B^n members, since this is the largest possible number of codes for the second channel of this length. Thus, in total, there are at most $A^n B^n$ words in the code, giving the desired result.

In the case of the sum of the two channels, we first show how, from two given codes for the two channels, to construct a code for the sum channel with equivalent number of letters equal to $A^{1-\delta} + B^{1-\delta}$, where δ is arbitrarily small and A and B are the equivalent number of letters for the two codes. Let the two codes have lengths n_1 and n_2. The new code will have length n where n is the smallest integer greater than both $\frac{n_1}{\delta}$ and $\frac{n_2}{\delta}$. Now form codes for the first channel and for the second channel for all lengths k from zero to n as follows. Let k equal $an_1 + b$, where a and b are integers and $b < n_1$. We form all sequences of a words from the given code for the first channel and fill in the remaining b letters arbitrarily, say all with the first letter in the code alphabet. We achieve at least $A^{k-\delta n}$ different words of length k none of which is adjacent to any other. In the same way we form codes for the second channel and achieve $B^{k-\delta n}$ words in this code of length k. We now intermingle the k code for the first channel with the $n - k$ code for the second channel in all $\binom{n}{k}$ possible ways and do this for each value of k. This produces a code n letters long with at least

$$\sum_{k=0}^{n} \binom{n}{k} A^{k-n\delta} B^{n-k-n\delta} = (AB)^{-\delta n} (A + B)^n$$

different words. It is readily seen that no two of these different words are adjacent. The rate is at least $\log(A + B) - \delta \log AB$, and since δ was arbitrarily small, we can achieve a rate arbitrarily close to $\log(A + B)$.

To show that it is not possible, when one of the graphs reduces by mapping to non-adjacent points, to exceed the rate corresponding to the number of letters $A + B$, consider any given code of length n for the sum channel. The words in this consist of sequences of letters, each letter corresponding to one or the other of the two channels. The words may be subdivided into classes corresponding to the pattern of the choices of letters between the two channels. There are 2^n such classes with $\binom{n}{k}$ classes in which exactly k of the letters are from the first channel and $n - k$ from the second. Consider now a particular class of words of this type. Replace the letters from the first channel alphabet by the corresponding non-adjacent letters. This does not harm the adjacency relations between words in the code. Now, as in the product case, partition the code words according to the sequence of letters involved from the first channel. This produces at most A^k subsets. Each of these subsets contains at most B^{n-k} members, since this is the greatest possible number of nonadjacent words for the second channel of length $n - k$. In total, then, summing over all values of k and taking account of the $\binom{n}{k}$ classes for each k, there are at most

$$\sum_{k} \binom{n}{k} A^k B^{n-k} = (A + B)^n$$

words in the code for the sum channel. This proves the desired result.

Theorem 4, of course, is analogous to known results for the ordinary capacity C, where the product channel has the sum of the ordinary capacities and the sum channel has an equivalent number of letters equal to the sum of the equivalent numbers of letters for the individual channels. We conjecture but have not been able to prove that the equalities in Theorem 4 hold in general, not just under the conditions given. We now prove a lower bound for the probability of error when transmitting at a rate greater than C_0.

Theorem 5: In any code of length n and rate $R > C_0$, $C_0 > 0$, the probability of error P_e will satisfy $P_e \geq (1 - e^{-n(C_0 - R)}) p_{\min}^n$, where $p_{\min}$ is the minimum non-vanishing $p_i(j)$.

Proof: By definition of C_0 there are not more than e^{nC_0} non-adjacent words of length n. With $R > C_0$, among e^{nR} words there must, therefore, be an adjacent pair. The adjacent pair has a common output word which either can cause with a probability at least $p_{\min}^n$. This output word cannot be decoded into both inputs. At least one, therefore, must cause an error when it leads to this output word. This gives a contribution at least $e^{-nR} p_{\min}^n$ to the probability of error P_e. Now omit this word from consideration and apply the same argument to the remaining $e^{nR} - 1$ words of the code. This will give another adjacent pair and another contribution of error of at least $e^{-nR} p_{\min}^n$. The process may be continued until the number of code points remaining is just e^{nC_0}. At this time, the computed probability of error must be at least

$$(e^{nR} - e^{nC_0}) e^{-nR} p_{\min}^n = (1 - e^{n(C_0 - R)}) p_{\min}^n .$$

Channels with a Feedback Link

We now consider the corresponding problem for channels with complete feedback. By this we mean that there exists a return channel sending back from the receiving point to the transmitting point, without error, the letters actually received. It is assumed that this information is received at the transmitting point before the next letter is transmitted, and can be used, therefore, if desired, in choosing the next transmitted letter.

It is interesting that for a memoryless channel the ordinary forward capacity is the same with or without feedback. This will be shown in Theorem 6. On the other hand, the zero error capacity may, in some cases, be greater with feedback than without. In the channel shown in Fig. 5, for example, $C_0 = \log 2$. However, we will see as a result of Theorem 7 that with feedback the zero error capacity $C_{0F} = \log 2.5$.

We first define a block code of length n for a feedback system. This means that at the transmitting point there is a device with two inputs, or, mathematically, a function with two

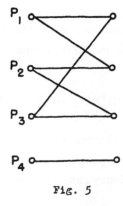

Fig. 5

arguments. One argument is the message to be transmitted, the other, the past received letters (which have come in over the feedback link). The value of the function is the next letter to be transmitted. Thus the function may be thought of as $x_{j+1} = f(k, v_j)$, where x_{j+1} is the $(j + 1)$st transmitted letter in a block, k is an index ranging from 1 to M and represents the specific message, and v_j is a received word of length j. Thus j ranges from 0 to $n - 1$ and v_j ranges over all received words of these lengths.

In operation, if message m_k is to be sent, f is evaluated for $f(k-)$ where the $-$ means "no word" and this is sent as the first transmitted letter. If the feedback link sends back α, say, as the first received letter, the next transmitted letter will be $f(k, \alpha)$. If this is received as β, the next transmitted letter will be $f(k, \alpha\beta)$, etc.

Theorem 6: In a memoryless discrete channel with feedback, the forward capacity is equal to the ordinary capacity C (without feedback). The average change in mutual information I_{vm} between received sequence v and message m for a letter of text is not greater than C.

Proof: Let v be the received sequence to date of a block, m the message, x the next transmitted letter and y the next received letter. These are all random variables and, also, x is a function of m and v. This function, namely, is the one which defines the encoding procedure with feedback whereby the next transmitted letter x is determined by the message m and the feedback information v from the previous received signals. The channel being memoryless implies that the next operation is independent of the past, and in particular that $Pr[y/x] = Pr[y/x,v]$.

The average change in mutual information, when a particular v has been received, due to the x,y pair is given by (we are averaging over messages m and next received letters y, for a given v):

$$\overline{\Delta I} = \overline{I_{m,vy}} - \overline{I_{m,v}}$$

$$= \sum_{y,m} Pr[y,m/v] \log \frac{Pr[v,y,m]}{Pr[v,y]Pr[m]} - \sum_{m} Pr[m/v] \log \frac{Pr[v,m]}{Pr[v]Pr[m]} .$$

Since $Pr[m/v] = \sum_y Pr[y,m/v]$, the second sum may be rewritten as $\sum_{y,m} Pr[y,m/v] \log \frac{Pr[v,m]}{Pr[v]Pr[m]}$. The two sums then combine to give

$$\overline{\Delta I} = \sum_{y,m} Pr[y,m/v] \log \frac{Pr[v,y,m]Pr[v]}{Pr[v,m]Pr[v,y]}$$

$$= \sum_{y,m} Pr[y,m/v] \log \frac{Pr[y/v,m]Pr[v]}{Pr[v,y]} .$$

The sum on m may be thought of as summed first on the m's which result in the same x (for the given v), recalling that x is a function of m and v, and then summing on the different x's. In the first summation, the term $Pr[y/v,m]$ is constant at $Pr[y/x]$ and the coefficient of the logarithm sums to $Pr[x,y/v]$. Thus we can write

$$\Delta I = \sum_{x,y} Pr[x,y/v] \log \frac{Pr[y/x]}{Pr[y/v]} .$$

Now consider the rate for the channel (in the ordinary sense without feedback) if we should assign to the x's the probabilities $q(x) = Pr[x/v]$. The probabilities for pairs, $r(x,y)$, and for the y's alone, $w(y)$, in this situation would then be

$$r(x,y) = q(x)Pr[y/x] = Pr[x/v]Pr[y/x] = Pr[x,y/v] ,$$

$$w(y) = \sum_x r(x,y) = \sum_x Pr[x,y/v] = Pr[y/v] .$$

Hence the rate would be

$$R = \sum_{x,y} r(x,y) \log \frac{Pr[y/x]}{w(y)}$$

$$= \sum_{x,y} Pr[x,y/v] \log \frac{Pr[y/x]}{Pr[y/v]}$$

$$= \Delta I .$$

Since $R \leq C$, the channel capacity (which is the maximum possible R for all $q(x)$ assignments), we conclude that

$$\Delta I \leq C .$$

Since the average change in I per letter is not greater than C, the average change in n letters is not greater than nC. Hence, in a block code of length n with input rate R, if $R > C$ then the equivocation at the end of a block will be at least $R - C$, just as in the non-feedback case. In other words, it is not possible to approach zero equivocation (or, as easily follows, zero probability of error) at a rate exceeding the channel capacity. It is, of course, possible to do this at rates less than C, since certainly anything that can be done without feedback can be done with feedback.

It is interesting that the first sentence of Theorem 6 can be generalized readily to channels with memory provided they are of such a nature that the internal state of the channel can be calculated at the transmitting point from the initial state and the sequence of letters that have been transmitted. If this is not the case, the conclusion of the theorem will not always be true, that is, there exist channels of a more complex sort for which the forward capacity with feedback exceeds that without feedback. We shall not, however, give the details of these generalizations here.

Returning now to the zero-error problem, we define a zero error capacity C_{0F} for a channel with feedback in the obvious way – the least upper bound of rates for block codes with no errors. The next theorem solves the problem of evaluating C_{0F} for memoryless channels with feedback, and indicates how rapidly C_{0F} may be approached as the block length n increases.

Theorem 7: In a memoryless discrete channel with complete feedback of received letters to the transmitting point, the zero error capacity C_{0F} is zero if all pairs of input letters are adjacent. Otherwise $C_{0F} = \log P_0^{-1}$, where

$$P_0 = \min_{P_i} \max_j \sum_{i \in S_j} P_i ,$$

P_i being a probability assigned to input letter i ($\sum_i P_i = 1$) and S_j the set of input letters which can cause output letter j with probability greater than zero. A zero error block code of length n can be found for such a feedback channel which transmits at a rate $R \geq C_{0F}(1 - \dfrac{2}{n}\log_2 2t)$ where t is the number of input letters.

The P_0 occurring in this theorem has the following meaning. For any given assignment of probabilities P_i to the input letters one may calculate, for each output letter j, the total probability of all input letters that can (with positive probability) cause j. This is $\sum\limits_{i \varepsilon S_j} P_i$. Output letters for which this is large may be thought of as "bad" in that when received there is a large uncertainty as to the cause. To obtain P_0 one adjusts the P_i so that the worst output letter in this sense is as good as possible.

We first show that, if all letters are adjacent to each other, $C_{0F} = 0$. In fact, in any coding system, any two messages, say m_1 and m_2, can lead to the same received sequence with positive probability. Namely, the first transmitted letters corresponding to m_1 and m_2 have a possible received letter in common. Assuming this occurs, calculate the next transmitted letters in the coding system for m_1 and m_2. These also have a possible received letter in common. Continuing in this manner we establish a received word which could be produced by either m_1 and m_2 and therefore they cannot be distinguished with certainty.

Now consider the case where not all pairs are adjacent. We will first prove, by induction on the block length n, that the rate $\log P_0^{-1}$ cannot be exceeded with a zero error code. For $n = 0$ the result is certainly true. The inductive hypothesis will be that no block code of length $n - 1$ transmits at a rate greater than $\log P_0^{-1}$, or, in other words, can resolve with certainty more than

$$e^{(n-1)\log P_0^{-1}} = P_0^{-(n-1)}$$

different messages. Now suppose (in contradiction to the desired result) we have a block code of length n resolving M messages with $M > P_0^{-n}$. The first transmitted letter for the code partitions these M messages among the input letters for the channel. Let F_i be the fraction of the messages assigned to letter i (that is, for which i is the first transmitted letter). Now these F_i are like probability assignments to the different letters and therefore, by definition of P_0, there is some output letter, say letter k, such that $\sum\limits_{i \varepsilon S_k} F_i \geq P_0$. Consider the set of messages for which the first transmitted letter belongs to S_k. The number of messages in this set is at least $P_0 M$. Any of these can cause output letter k to be the first received letter. When this happens there are $n - 1$ letters yet to be transmitted and since $M > P_0^{-n}$ we have $P_0 M > P_0^{-(n-1)}$. Thus we have a zero error code of block length $n - 1$ transmitting at a rate greater than $\log P_0^{-1}$, contradicting the inductive assumption. Note that the coding function for this code of length $n - 1$ is formally defined from the original coding function by fixing the first received letter at k.

We must now show that the rate $\log P_0^{-1}$ can actually be approached as closely as desired with zero error codes. Let P_i be the set of probabilities which, when assigned to the input letters, give P_0 for $\min\limits_{P_i} \max\limits_{j} \sum\limits_{i \varepsilon S_j} P_i$. The general scheme of the code will be to divide the M original messages into t different groups corresponding to the first transmitted letter. The number of messages in these groups will be approximately proportional to $P_1, P_2, \ldots, P_t$. The first transmitted letter, then, will correspond to the group containing the message to be transmitted. Whatever letter is received, the number of possible messages compatible with this received letter will be approximately $P_0 M$. This subset of possible messages is known both at the receiver and (after the received letter is sent back to the transmitter) at the transmitting point.

The code system next subdivides this subset of messages into t groups, again approximately in proportion to the probabilities P_i. The second letter transmitted is that corresponding to the group containing the actual message. Whatever letter is received, the number of messages compatible with the two received letters is now, roughly, $P_0^2 M$.

This process is continued until only a few messages (less than t^2) are compatible with all the received letters. The ambiguity among these is then resolved by using a pair of non-adjacent letters in a simple binary code. The code thus constructed will be a zero error code for the channel.

Our first concern is to estimate carefully the approximation involved in subdividing the messages into the t groups. We will show that for any M and any set of P_i with $\sum P_i = 1$, it is possible to subdivide the M messages into groups of $m_1, m_2, \ldots, m_t$ such that $m_i = 0$ whenever $P_i = 0$ and

$$\left| \frac{m_i}{M} - P_i \right| \le \frac{1}{M}, \quad i = 1, \ldots, t .$$

We assume without loss of generality that $P_1, P_2, \ldots, P_s$ are the non-vanishing P_i. Choose m_1 to be the largest integer such that $\frac{m_1}{M} \le P_1$. Let $P_1 - \frac{m_1}{M} = \delta_1$. Clearly $|\delta_1| \le \frac{1}{M}$. Next choose m_2 to be the smallest integer such that $\frac{m_2}{M} \ge P_2$ and let $P_2 - \frac{m_2}{M} = \delta_2$. We have $|\delta_2| \le \frac{1}{M}$. Also $|\delta_1 + \delta_2| \le \frac{1}{M}$, since δ_1 and δ_2 are opposite in sign and each less than $\frac{1}{M}$ in absolute value. Next, m_3 is chosen so that $\frac{m_3}{M}$ approximates, to within $\frac{1}{M}$, to P_3. If $\delta_1 + \delta_2 \ge 0$, then $\frac{m_3}{M}$ is chosen less than or equal to P_3. If $\delta_1 = \delta_2 < 0$, then $\frac{m_3}{M}$ is chosen greater than or equal to P_3. Thus again $P_3 - \frac{m_3}{M} = \delta_3 \le \frac{1}{M}$ and $|\delta_1 + \delta_2 + \delta_3| \le \frac{1}{M}$. Continuing in this manner through P_{s-1} we obtain approximations for $P_1, P_2, \ldots, P_{s-1}$ with the property that $|\delta_1 + \delta_2 + \ldots + \delta_{s-1}| \le \frac{1}{M}$, or $|M(P_1 + P_2 + \ldots + P_{s-1}) - (m_1 + m_2 + \ldots + m_{s-1})| \le 1$. If we now define m_s to be $M - \sum_1^{s-1} m_i$ then this inequality can be written $|M(1 - P_s) - (M - m_s)| \le 1$. Hence $\left| \frac{m_s}{M} - P_s \right| \le \frac{1}{M}$. Thus we have achieved the objective of keeping all approximations $\frac{m_i}{M}$ to within $\frac{1}{M}$ of P_i and satisfying $\Sigma m_i = M$.

Returning now to our main problem, note first that if $P_0 = 1$ then $C_{0F} = 0$ and the theorem is trivially true. We assume, then, that $P_0 < 1$. We wish to show that $P_0 \le (1 - \frac{1}{t})$. Consider the set of input letters which have the maximum value of P_i. This maximum is certainly greater than or equal to the average $\frac{1}{t}$. Furthermore, we can arrange to have at least one of these input letters not connected to some output letter. For suppose this is not the case. Then either there are no other input letters beside this set and we contradict the assumption that $P_0 < 1$, or there are other input letters with smaller values of P_i. In this case, by reducing the P_i for one input letter in the maximum set and increasing correspondingly that for some input letter which does not connect to all output letters, we do not increase the value of P_0 (for any S_j) and create an input letter of the desired type. By consideration of an output letter to which this input letter does not connect we see that $P_0 \leq 1 - \frac{1}{t}$.

Now suppose we start with M messages and subdivide into groups approximating proportionality to the P_i as described above. Then when a letter has been received, the set of possible messages (compatible with this received letter) will be reduced to those in the groups corresponding to letters which connect to the actual received letter. Each output letter connects to not more than $t - 1$ input letters (otherwise we would have $P_0 = 1$). For each of the connecting groups, the error in approximating P_i has been less than or equal to $\frac{1}{M}$. Hence the total relative number in all connecting groups for any output letter is less than or equal to $P_0 + \frac{t - 1}{M}$. The total number of possible messages after receiving the first letter consequently drops from M to a number less than or equal to $P_0 M + t - 1$.

In the coding system to be used, this remaining possible subset of messages is subdivided again among the input letters to approximate in the same fashion the probabilities P_i. This subdivision can be carried out both at the receiving point and the transmitting point using the same standard procedure (say, exactly the one described above) since with the feedback both terminals have available the required data, namely the first received letter.

The second transmitted letter obtained by this procedure will again reduce at the receiving point the number of possible messages to a value not greater than $P_0(P_0 M + t - 1) + t - 1$. This same process continues with each transmitted letter. If the upper bound on the number of possible remaining messages after k letters is M_k, then $M_{k+1} = P_0 M_k + t - 1$. The solution of this difference equation is

$$M_k = A P_0^k + \frac{t - 1}{1 - P_0} \ .$$

This may be readily verified by substitution in the difference equation. To satisfy the initial conditions $M_0 = M$ requires $A = M - \frac{t - 1}{1 - P_0}$. Thus the solution becomes

$$M_k = (M - \frac{t - 1}{1 - P_0}) P_0^k + \frac{t - 1}{1 - P_0}$$

$$= M P_0^k + \frac{t - 1}{1 - P_0}(1 - P_0^k)$$

$$\leq M P_0^k + t(t - 1) \ ,$$

since we have seen above that $1 - P_0 \geq \frac{1}{t}$.

If the process described is carried out for n_1 steps, where n_1 is the smallest integer $\geq d$ and d is the solution of $MP_0^d = 1$, then the number of possible messages left consistent with the received sequence will be not greater than $1 + t(t - 1) \leq t^2$ (since $t > 1$, otherwise we should have $C_{0F} = 0$). Now the pair of nonadjacent letters assumed in the theorem may be used to resolve the ambiguity among these t^2 or fewer messages. This will require not more than $1 + \log_2 t^2 = \log_2 2t^2$ additional letters. Thus, in total, we have used not more than $d + 1 + \log_2 2t^2 + d + \log_2 4t^2 = n$ (say) as block length. We have transmitted in this block length a choice from $M = P_0^{-d}$ messages. Thus the zero error rate we have achieved is

$$R = \frac{1}{n}\log M \geq \frac{d\log P_0^{-1}}{d + \log_2 4t^2}$$

$$= (1 - \frac{1}{n}\log 4t^2)\log P_0^{-1}$$

$$= (1 - \frac{1}{n}\log 4t^2)C_{0F} .$$

Thus we can approximate to C_{0F} as closely as desired with zero error codes.

As an example of Theorem 7 consider the channel in Fig. 5. We wish to evaluate P_0. It is easily seen that we may take $P_1 = P_2 = P_3$ in forming the min max of Theorem 7, for if they are unequal the maximum $\sum_{i \in S_j} P_i$ for the corresponding three output letters would be reduced by equalizing. Also it is evident, then, that $P_4 = P_1 + P_2$, since otherwise a shift of probability one way or the other would reduce the maximum. We conclude, then, that $P_1 = P_2 = P_3 = 1/5$ and $P_4 = 2/5$. Finally, the zero error capacity with feedback is $\log P_0^{-1} = \log 5/2$.

There is a close connection between the min max process of Theorem 7 and the process of finding the minimum capacity for the channel under variation of the non-vanishing transition probabilities $p_i(j)$ as in Theorem 2. It was noted there that at the minimum capacity each output letter can be caused by the same total probability of input letters. Indeed, it seems very likely that the probabilities of input letters to attain the minimum capacity are exactly those which solve the min max problem of Theorem 7, and, if this is so, the $C_{\min} = \log P_0^{-1}$.

Acknowledgment

I am indebted to Peter Elias for first pointing out that a feedback link could increase the zero error capacity, as well as for several suggestions that were helpful in the proof of Theorem 7.

Certain Results in Coding Theory for Noisy Channels[*]

CLAUDE E. SHANNON

Massachusetts Institute of Technology, Cambridge, Massachusetts

In this paper we will develop certain extensions and refinements of coding theory for noisy communication channels. First, a refinement of the argument based on "random" coding will be used to obtain an upper bound on the probability of error for an optimal code in the memoryless finite discrete channel. Next, an equation is obtained for the capacity of a finite state channel when the state can be calculated at both transmitting and receiving terminals. An analysis is also made of the more complex case where the state is calculable at the transmitting point but not necessarily at the receiving point.

PROBABILITY OF ERROR BOUND FOR THE DISCRETE FINITE MEMORYLESS CHANNEL

A discrete finite memoryless channel with finite input and output alphabets is defined by a set of transition probabilities $p_i(j)$,

$$i = 1, 2, \cdots, a; \qquad j = 1, 2, \cdots, b,$$

with $\sum_j p_i(j) = 1$ $(i = 1, 2, \cdots, a)$ and all $p_i(j) \geqq 0$. Here $p_i(j)$ is the probability, if input letter i is used, that output letter j will be received. A *code word* of length n is a sequence of n input letters (that is, n integers each chosen from $1, 2, \cdots, a$). A *block code of length n* with M words is a mapping of the integers from 1 to M (messages) into a set of code words each of length n. A *decoding system* for such a code is a mapping of all sequences of output words of length n into the integers from 1 to M (that is, a procedure for deciding on an original integer or message when any particular output word is received). We will be considering situa-

[*] This work was carried out at the Research Laboratory of Electronics, Massachusetts Institute of Technology, and was supported in part by the United States Army (Signal Corps), the United States Air Force (Office of Scientific Research, Air Research and Development Command), and the United States Navy (Office of Naval Research); and in part by Bell Telephone Laboratories, Inc.

tions in which all integers from 1 to M are used with the same probability $1/M$. The probability of error P_e for a code and decoding system is the probability of an integer being transmitted and received as a word which is mapped into a different integer (that is, decoded as another message).

Thus:

$$P_e = \sum_u \sum_{v \in S_u} \frac{1}{M} Pr(v \mid u)$$

where u ranges over all input integers $1, 2, \cdots, M$; v ranges over the received words of length n; and S_u is the set of received words that are not decoded as u. $Pr(v \mid u)$ is of course the probability of receiving v if the message is u. Thus if u is mapped into input word $(i_1, i_2, \cdots, i_n)$ and v is word $(j_1, j_2, \cdots, j_n)$, then

$$Pr(v \mid u) = p_{i_1}(j_1)\, p_{i_2}(j_2) \cdots p_{i_n}(j_n).$$

While we assume all messages in a code to be used with equal probabilities $1/M$, it is useful, in studying a channel, to consider the assignment of different probabilities to input words. Suppose, in fact, that in a given channel we assign arbitrary probabilities to the different input words u of length n, probability $P(u)$ for word u. We then have probabilities for all input-output word pairs of length n,

$$Pr(u, v) = P(u)\, Pr(v \mid u),$$

where u and v are input and output words of length n and $Pr(v \mid u)$ is the probability of output word v if input word u is used. (This is the product of the transition probabilities for corresponding letters of u and v). Given $P(u)$ then, any numerical function of u and v becomes a random variable. In particular, the mutual information (per letter), $I(u, v)$ is a random variable

$$I(u, v) = \frac{1}{n} \log \frac{Pr(u, v)}{P(u)Pr(v)} = \frac{1}{n} \log \frac{Pr(v \mid u)}{\sum_u P(u)Pr(v \mid u)}$$

The distribution function for this random variable will be denoted by $\rho(x)$. Thus

$$\rho(x) = Pr[I(u, v) \leq x]$$

The function $\rho(x)$ of course depends on the arbitrary assignment of probabilities $P(u)$. We will now prove a theorem bounding the probability of error for a possible code in terms of the function $\rho(x)$.

THEOREM 1: *Suppose some $P(u)$ for input words u of length n gives rise to a distribution of information per letter $\rho(I)$. Then given any integer M and any $\theta > 0$ there exists a block code with M messages and a decoding system such that if these messages are used with equal probability, the probability of error P_e is bounded by*

$$P_e \leqq \rho(R + \theta) + e^{-n\theta}$$

where $R = (1/n)\log M$.

PROOF: For a given M and θ consider the pairs (u, v) of input and output words and define the set T to consist of those pairs for which $\log Pr(u, v)/P(u)Pr(v) > n(R + \theta)$. When the u's are chosen with probabilities $P(u)$, then the probability that the (u, v) pair will belong to the set T is, by definition of ρ, equal to $1 - \rho(R + \theta)$.

Now consider the ensemble of codes obtained in the following manner. The integers $1, 2, 3, \cdots, M = e^{nR}$ are associated independently with the different possible input words $u_1, u_2, \cdots, u_B$ with probabilities $P(u_1), P(u_2), \cdots P(u_B)$. This produces an ensemble of codes each using M (or less) input words. If there are B different input words u_i, there will be exactly B^M different codes in this ensemble corresponding to the B^M different ways we can associate M integers with B input words. These codes have different probabilities. Thus the (highly degenerate) code in which all integers are mapped into input word u_1 has probability $P(u_1)^M$. A code in which d_k of the integers are mapped into u_k has probability $\prod_k P(u_k)^{d_k}$. We will be concerned with the average probability of error for this ensemble of codes. By this we mean the average probability of error when these codes are weighted according to the probabilities we have just defined. We imagine that in using any one of these codes, each integer is used with probability $1/M$. Note that, for some particular selections, several integers may fall on the same input word. This input word is then used with higher probability than the others.

In any particular code of the ensemble, our decoding procedure will be defined as follows. Any received v is decoded as the integer with greatest probability conditional on the received v. If several integers have the same conditional probability we decode (conventionally) as the smallest such integer. Since all integers have unconditional probability $1/M$, this decoding procedure chooses one of those having the greatest probability of causing the received v.

We now wish to compute the average probability of error or "ambiguity" P_a in this ensemble of codes where we pessimistically include with the errors all cases where there are several equally probable causes of the received v.

In any particular code of the ensemble an input word u or a pair (u, v) will not, in general, occur with the probabilities $P(u)$ or $Pr(u, v)$. In the ensemble average, however, each word u has probability $P(u)$ and each (u, v) pair probability $Pr(u, v)$, since integers are mapped into u with just this probability. Indeed, a particular message, say the integer 1, will be mapped into u with probability $P(u)$. A particular case of integer 1, say, mapped into u and resulting in received v will result in an error or ambiguity if there are, in the code in question, one or more integers mapped into the set $S_v(u)$ of input words which have a probability of causing v higher than are equal to that of u. Because of the independence in placing the other integers, it is easy to calculate the fraction of codes in which this occurs. In fact, let

$$Q_v(u) = \sum_{u' \epsilon S_v(u)} P(u')$$

Thus $Q_v(u)$ is the probability associated with all words which can cause v with as high or higher a probability than u causes v. The fraction of codes in which integer 2 is not in $S_v(u)$ is (because of the independence of placing of the integers) equal to $1 - Q_v(u)$. The fraction of codes in which $S_v(u)$ is free of *all* other integers is $(1 - Q_v(u))^{M-1}$. A similar argument applies to any other integer as well as 1. Thus, in the ensemble, the probability of error or ambiguity due to cases where the message is mapped into input word u and received as v is given exactly by

$$Pr(u, v)[1 - (1 - Q_v(u))^{M-1}].$$

The average probability of error or ambiguity, then, is given by

$$P_a = \sum_{u,v} Pr(u, v)[1 - (1 - Q_v(u))^{M-1}]. \tag{1}$$

We now wish to place a bound on this in terms of the information distribution ρ. First, break the sum into two parts, a sum over the (u, v) set T defined above where $\log Pr(u, v)/P(u)Pr(v) > n(R + \theta)$ and over the complementary set $\overline{T}$.

$$P_a = \sum_{\overline{T}} Pr(u, v)[1 - (1 - Qv(u))^{M-1}]$$
$$+ \sum_T Pr(u, v)[1 - (1 - Q_v(u))^{M-1}].$$

Since $[1 - (1 - Q_r(u))]^{M-1}$ is a probability, we may replace it by 1 in the first sum, increasing the quantity. This term becomes, then, $\sum_{T} Pr(u, v)$ which by definition is $\rho(R + \theta)$. In the second sum, note first that $(1 - Q_v(u))^{M-1} \geq 1 - (M - 1)Q_v(u)$ by a well-known inequality. Hence, the second sum is increased by replacing

$$[1 - (1 - Q_v(u))^{M-1}]$$

by $(M - 1)Q_v(u)$ and even more so by $MQ_v(u)$.

$$P_e \leq P_a \leq \rho(R + \theta) + M \sum_T Pr(u, v)Q_v(u).$$

We now show that for u, v in T, $Q_v(u) \leq e^{-n(R+\theta)}$. In fact, with u, v in T

$$\log \frac{Pr(v|u)}{Pr(v)} > n(R + \theta),$$

$$Pr(v \mid u) > Pr(v)e^{n(R+\theta)}.$$

If $u' \epsilon S_v(u)$,

$$Pr(v \mid u') \geq Pr(v \mid u) > Pr(v)e^{n(R+\theta)}$$

$$Pr(u', v) > Pr(u')Pr(v)e^{n(R+\theta)}$$

$$Pr(u' \mid v) > Pr(u')e^{n(R+\theta)}$$

Summing each side over $u' \epsilon S_v(u)$ gives

$$1 \geq \sum_{u' \epsilon S_v(u)} P_r(u' \mid v) > e^{n(R+\theta)} Q_v(u)$$

The left inequality holds because the sum of a set of disjoint probabilities cannot exceed 1. We obtain

$$Q_v(u) < e^{-n(R+\theta)} \qquad\qquad (u, v) \epsilon T$$

Using this in our estimate of P_e we have

$$P_e < \rho(R + \theta) + e^{nR}e^{-n(R+\theta)}\sum_T Pr(u, v)$$

$$\leq \rho(R + \theta) + e^{-n\theta}$$

using again the fact that the sum of a set of disjoint probabilities cannot exceed one. Since the average P_e over the ensemble of codes satisfies $P_e \leq \rho(R + \theta) + e^{-n\theta}$, there must exist a particular code satisfying the same inequality. This concludes the proof.

Theorem 1 is one of a number of results which show a close relation between the probability of error in codes for noisy channels and the distribution of mutual information $\rho(x)$. Theorem 1 shows that if, by associating probabilities $P(u)$ with input words, a certain $\rho(x)$ can be obtained, then codes can be constructed with a probability of error bounded in terms of this $\rho(x)$. We now develop a kind of converse relation: given a code, there will be a related $\rho(x)$. It will be shown that the probability of error for the code (with optimal decoding) is closely related to this $\rho(x)$.

THEOREM 2: *Suppose a particular code has $M = e^{nR}$ messages and the distribution function for the mutual information I (per letter) between messages and received words is $\rho(x)$ (the messages being used with equal probability). Then the optimal detection system for this code gives a probability of error P_e satisfying the inequalities*

$$ \tfrac{1}{2}\rho\left(R - \frac{1}{n}\log 2 \right) \leqq P_e \leqq \rho\left(R - \frac{1}{n}\log 2 \right) $$

It should be noted that ρ has a slightly different meaning here than in Theorem 1. Here it relates to mutual information between messages and received words—in Theorem 1, between *input words* and received words. If, as would usually be the case, all messages of a code are mapped into distinct input words, these reduce to the same quantity.

PROOF: We first prove the lower bound. By definition of the function ρ, the probability is equal to $\rho(R - (1/n)\log 2)$, that

$$ \frac{1}{n}\log\frac{Pr(u, v)}{Pr(u)Pr(v)} \leq R - \frac{1}{n}\log 2, $$

where u is a message and v a received word. Equivalently,

$$ Pr(u \mid v) \leq Pr(u)e^{Rn\frac{1}{2}} $$

or (using the fact that $Pr(u) = e^{-nR}$)

$$ Pr(u \mid v) \leqq \tfrac{1}{2} $$

Now fix attention on these pairs (u, v) for which this inequality

$$ Pr(u \mid v) \leqq \tfrac{1}{2} $$

is true, and imagine the corresponding (u, v) lines to be marked in black and all other (u, v) connecting lines marked in red. We divide the v points into two classes: C_1 consists of those v's which are decoded into u's connected by a red line (and also any v's which are decoded into u's not connected to the v's): C_2 consists of v's which are decoded into u's connected by a black line. We have established that with probability $\rho(R - (1/n) \log 2)$ the (u, v) pair will be connected by a black line. The v's involved will fall into the two classes C_1 and C_2 with probability ρ_1, say and $\rho_2 = \rho(R - (1/n) \log 2) - \rho_1$. Whenever the v is in C_1 an error is produced since the actual u was one connected by a black line and the decoding is to a u connected by a red line (or to a disconnected u). Thus these cases give rise to a probability ρ_1 of error. When the v in question is in class C_2, we have $Pr(u \mid v) \leqq \frac{1}{2}$. This means that with at least an equal probability these v's can be obtained through other u's than the one in question. If we sum for these v's the probabilities of all pairs $Pr(u, v)$ except that corresponding to the decoding system, then we will have a probability at least $\rho_2/2$ and all of these cases correspond to incorrect decoding. In total, then, we have a probability of error given by

$$P_e \geqq \rho_1 + \rho_2/2 \geqq \tfrac{1}{2}\rho(R - (1/n) \log 2)$$

We now prove the upper bound. Consider the decoding system defined as follows. If for any received v there exists a u such that $Pr(u \mid v) > \frac{1}{2}$, then the v is decoded into that u. Obviously there cannot be more than one such u for a given v, since, if there were, the sum of these would imply a probability greater than one. If there is no such u for a given v, the decoding is irrelevant to our argument. We may, for example, let such u's all be decoded into the first message in the input code. The probability of error, with this decoding, is then less than or equal to the probability of all (u, v) pairs for which $Pr(u \mid v) \leqq \frac{1}{2}$. That is,

$$P_e \leqq \sum_S Pr(u, v) \quad \text{(where S is the set of pairs (u, v) with $Pr(u \mid v) \leqq \frac{1}{2}$).}$$

The condition $Pr(u \mid v) \leqq \frac{1}{2}$ is equivalent to $Pr(u, v)/Pr(v) \leqq \frac{1}{2}$, or, again, to $Pr(u, v)/Pr(u) Pr(v) \leqq \frac{1}{2} P_r(u)^{-1} = \frac{1}{2} e^{nR}$. This is equivalent to the condition

$$(1/n) \log Pr(u, v)/Pr(u)Pr(v) \leqq R - (1/n) \log 2.$$

The sum $\sum_S Pr(u, v)$ where this is true is, by definition, the distribution function of $(1/n) \log Pr(u, v)/Pr(u)Pr(v)$ evaluated at $R - (1/n) \log 2$, that is,

$$P_e \leqq \sum_S Pr(u, v) = \rho(R - (1/n) \log 2).$$

PROBABILITY OF ERROR BOUND IN TERMS OF MOMENT GENERATING FUNCTION

We will now develop from the bound of Theorem 1 another expression that can be more easily evaluated in terms of the channel parameters. Suppose first that the probabilities $P(u)$ assigned to words in Theorem 1 are equal to the product of probabilities for letters making up the words. Thus, suppose u consists of the sequence of letters i_1, i_2, $\cdots$, i_n and $P(u)$ is then $P_{i_1} \cdot P_{i_2} \cdot P_{i_3} \cdots P_{i_n}$. If v consists of letters j_1, j_2, $\cdots$, j_n then $Pr(v) = Pr(j_1) \cdot Pr(j_2) \cdots Pr(j_n)$ and $Pr(u, v) = Pr(i_1, j_1) \cdot Pr(i_2, j_2) \cdots Pr(i_n, j_n)$. Also

$$I(u, v) = \frac{1}{n} \left[\log \frac{Pr(i_1 j_2)}{Pr(i_1)Pr(j_2)} + \log \frac{Pr(i_2 j_2)}{Pr(i_2)Pr(j_2)} + \cdots \right]$$

$$= \frac{1}{n} [I_1 + I_2 + \cdots + I_n]$$

where I_k is the mutual information between the kth letters of u and v.

The different I's are here independent random variables all with the same distribution. We therefore have a central limit theorem type of situation; $nI(u, v)$ is the sum of n independent random variables with identical distributions. $\rho(x)$ can be bounded by any of the inequalities which are known for the distribution of such a sum. In particular, we may use an inequality due to Chernov on the "tail" of such a distribution (Chernov, 1952). He has shown, by a simple argument using the generalized Chebycheff inequality, that the distribution of such sums can be bounded in terms of the moment generating function for a single one of the random variables, say $\varphi(s)$. Thus let

$$\varphi(s) = E[e^{sI}]$$

$$= \sum_{ij} P_i p_i(j) \exp \left[s \log \frac{p_i(j)}{\sum_k P_k p_k(j)} \right]$$

$$= \sum_{ij} P_i p_i(j) \left[\frac{p_i(j)}{\sum_k P_k p_k(j)} \right]^s$$

It is convenient for our purposes to use the log of the moment generating function $\mu(s) = \log \varphi(s)$, (sometimes called the semi-invariant generating function). Chernov's result translated into our notation states that

$$\rho(\mu'(s)) \leq e^{[\mu(s) - s\mu'(s)]n} \qquad\qquad s \leq 0$$

Thus by choosing the parameter s at any negative value we obtain a bound on the information distribution ρ of exponential form in n. It is easily shown, also, that if the variance of the original distribution is positive then $\mu'(s)$ is a strictly monotone increasing function of s and so also is the coefficient of n in the exponent, $\mu(s) - s\mu'(s)$ (for negative s). Indeed the derivatives of these quantities exist and are $\mu''(s)$ and $- s\mu''(s)$, respectively. $\mu''(s)$ is readily shown to be positive by a Schwartz inequality.

THEOREM 3: *In a memoryless channel with finite input and output alphabets, let $\mu(s)$ be the semi-invariant generating function for mutual information with some assignment of input letter probabilities, P_i for letter i, and with channel transition probabilities $p_i(j)$, that is:*

$$\mu(s) = \log \sum_{i,j} P_i p_i(j) \left[\frac{p_i(j)}{\sum_i P_i p_i(j)} \right]^s$$

Then there exists a code and decoding system of length n, rate R and probability of error P_e satisfying the inequalities

$$R \geqq \mu(s) - (s - 1)\mu'(s)$$

$$P_e \leqq 2c^{(\mu(s)-s\mu'(s))n} \qquad\qquad s \leqq 0$$

If as $s \to -\infty$, $\mu(s) - (s-1)\mu'(s) \to R^* > 0$ then for $R \leqq R^*$

$$P_e \leqq c^{(E^*+R-R^*)n}$$

where $E^* = \lim (\mu(s) - s\mu'(s))$ as $s \to -\infty$.

PROOF: We have, from *Theorem 1*, that

$$P_e \leqq \rho(R + \theta) + c^{-n\theta}$$

$$\leqq c^{[\mu(s)-s\mu'(s)]n} + c^{-n\theta} \qquad\qquad s \leqq 0$$

where s is chosen so that $\mu'(s) = R + \theta$. This will hold when θ is such that the resulting s is negative. We choose θ (which is otherwise arbitrary) to make the coefficients of n in the exponents equal. (Since the first term is monotone increasing in θ and the second monotone decreasing, it is easily seen that this choice of θ is quite good to minimize the bound. In fact, the bound can never be less than half its value for this particular θ.) This relation requires that

$$\mu(s) - s\mu'(s) = -\theta$$

$$= R - \mu'(s)$$

$$R = \mu(s) + (1 - s)\mu'(s)$$

Since the exponents are now equal, the probability of error is bounded by twice the first term:

$$P_e \leqq 2e^{[\mu(s)-s\mu'(s)]\,n}$$

These relations are true for all negative s and give the first results of the theorem.

However, in some cases, as $s \rightarrow -\infty$ the rate R approaches a positive limiting value. In fact, $R \rightarrow I_{min} + \log Pr[I_{min}]$ and the exponent in the P_e bound approaches $\log Pr[I_{min}]$. For rates R lower than this limiting value the exponents cannot be made equal by any choice of s. We may, however, now choose θ in such a way that $R + \theta$ is just smaller than I_{min}, say $I_{min} - \epsilon$. Since $\rho(I_{min} - \epsilon) = 0$ the probability of error is now bounded by $P_e \leqq e^{-n\theta} = e^{-n(I_{min}-R-\epsilon)}$. This being true for any $\epsilon > 0$, we can construct codes for which it is true with $\epsilon = 0$. That is

$$P_e \leqq e^{-n(I_{min}-R)}$$

for $R < R^*$. Notice that as R approaches its limiting value in the first bound, $I_{min} + \log Pr[I_{min}]$, the exponents in both bounds approach the same value, namely $\log Pr[I_{min}]$. The coefficient, however, improves from 2 to 1.

These bounds can be written in another form that is perhaps more revealing. Define a set of "tilted" probabilities $Q_s(I)$ for different values of information I by the following:

$$Q_s(I) = \frac{Pr(I)e^{sI}}{\sum_I Pr(I)e^{sI}}$$

In other words the original probability of a value I is increased or decreased by a factor e^{sI} and the resulting values normalized to sum to unity. For large positive values of s, this tilted set of probabilities $Q_s(I)$ tend to emphasize the probabilities $Pr(I)$ for positive I and reduce those for negative I. At $s = 0$ $Q_0(I) = Pr(I)$. At negative s the negative I values have enhanced probabilities at the expense of positive I values. As $s \rightarrow \infty$, $Q_s(I) \rightarrow 0$ except for $I = I_{max}$ the largest value of I with positive probability (since the set of u, v pairs is finite, I_{max} exists), and $Q_s(I_{max}) \rightarrow 1$. These tilted probabilities are convenient in evaluating the "tails" of distribution that are sums of other distributions. In terms of $Q_s(I)$ we may write

$$\mu(s) = \log \sum Pr(I)e^{sI}$$

$$= \sum_{I'} Q_s(I') \log \sum_I Pr(I)e^{sI}$$

$$\mu'(s) = \sum_I Pr(I)e^{sI}I / \sum_I Pr(I)e^{sI}$$

$$= \sum_I Q_s(I)I$$

$$\mu(s) - s\mu'(s) = \sum_I Q_s(I) \log (Pr(I)/Q_s(I))$$

$$\mu - (s - 1)\mu'(s) = \sum_I Q_s(I)[I + \log Pr(I)/Q_s(I)]$$

The coefficients of n in the exponents of Theorem 3 are of some interest. They relate to the rapidity of approach of P_e to zero as n increases. Plotted as a function of R, the behavior is typically as shown in Fig. 1. Here we have assumed the P_i for the letters to be the P_i which give channel capacity. The coefficient E of $-n$ for the first bound in the theorem is a curve tangent to the axis at C (here $s = 0$), convex downward and ending ($s = -\infty$) at $R = I_{\min} + \log Pr[I_{\min}]$ and $E = -\log Pr[I_{\min}]$. The second bound in the theorem gives an E curve which is a straight line of slope -1 passing through this point and intersecting the axes at $I_{\min}, 0$ and $0, I_{\min}$. In the neighborhood of $R = C$ the curve behaves as

$$E \doteq \frac{(C - R)^2}{2\mu''(0)}$$

Here $\mu''(0)$ is the variance of I. These properties all follow directly from the formulas for the curves.
We have

$$\frac{dE}{dR} = \frac{dE}{ds} \bigg/ \frac{dR}{ds}$$

$$= \frac{s}{1 - s}$$

so the slope of the ER curve is monotone decreasing as s ranges from 0 to $-\infty$, the slope going from 0 to -1. Since the second bound corresponds to a straight line of slope -1 in the ER plot, the two bounds not only join in value but have the same slope as shown in Fig. 1.

The curve would be as indicated if the P_i are those which maximize the rate at the channel capacity, for then

$$R(0) = \mu(0) - (0 - 1)\mu'(0) = \mu'(0) = C.$$

The bound, however, of the theorem applies for any set of P_i when the corresponding $\mu(s)$ is used. To obtain the strongest result the bound should be optimized for each value of R under variation of P_i. The same applies to the straight line portion where we maximize $I_{\min}$. If this were done a curve would be obtained which is the envelope of all possible curves of this type with different values of P_i. Since each individual curve is convex downward the envelope is also convex downward. The equations for this envelope may be found by the Lagrange method maximizing $R + \lambda E + \eta \sum_i P_i$. It must be remembered, of course, that the P_i must be non-negative. The problem is similar to that involved in calculating the channel capacity. The equations for the envelope will be

$$E = \mu(s) - s\mu'(s)$$

$$R = \mu(s) - (s - 1)\mu'(s)$$

$$(1 + \lambda)\frac{\partial \mu}{\partial P_i} - (1 + \lambda)s\frac{\partial \mu'}{\partial P_i} + \frac{\partial \mu'}{\partial P_i} + \eta = 0 \quad \text{for all } i \text{ except a set for}$$

$$\text{which } P_i = 0.$$

and subject to:

$$\sum P_i = 1$$

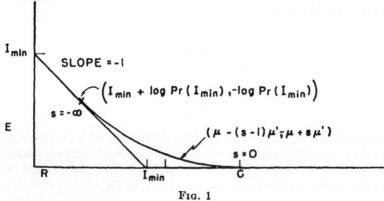

Fig. 1

The bound here should be maximized by choosing different subsets of the P_i for the nonvanishing set.

The upper bound obtained in Theorem 3 is by no means the strongest that can be found. As $n \to \infty$ even the coefficients of n in the exponent can be, in general, improved by more refined arguments. We hope in another paper to develop these further results, and also to give corresponding *lower* bounds on the probability of error of the same exponential type. The upper bound in Theorem 3 is, however, both simple and useful. It has a universality lacking in some of the stronger results (which only assume simple form when n is large).

CAPACITY OF THE FINITE STATE CHANNEL WITH STATE CALCULABLE AT BOTH TERMINALS

In certain channels with memory, the internal state of the channel can be calculated from the initial state (assumed known) at the beginning of transmission and the sequence of transmitted letters. It may also be possible to determine the state at any time at the receiving terminal from the initial state and the sequence of received letters. For such channels we shall say the state is *calculable at both terminals*.

To satisfy the first requirement it is clearly necessary that for any (attainable) internal state s, the next state t must be a function of s and x, $t = f(s, x)$, where x is the transmitted letter.

For the state to be calculable at the receiving point it is necessary that, for all attainable states s, the next stage t must be a function of s and the received letter y, $t = g(s, y)$.

For each possible s, t pair we may find the subset $A(s, t)$ of x's leading from s to t and the subset $B(s, t)$ of y's which correspond to a state transition from s to t. For each input letter x in the set $A(s, t)$ the output letter y will necessarily be in the set $B(s, t)$ and there will be a transition probability, the probability (in state s), if x is transmitted, that y will be received. For a particular s, t pair, the sets of letters $A(s, t)$ and $B(s, t)$ and the corresponding transition probabilities can be thought of as defining a memoryless discrete channel corresponding to the s, t pair. Namely, we consider the memoryless channel with input alphabet the letters from $A(s, t)$, output letters from $B(s, t)$ and the corresponding transition probabilities.

This channel would be physically realized from the given channel as follows. The given channel is first placed in state s, one letter is transmitted from set $A(s, t)$ (resulting in state t), the channel is then returned to state s and a second letter from set $A(s, t)$ transmitted, etc. The capacity of such a discrete memoryless channel can be found by the standard methods. Let the capacity from state s to state t be C_{st} (in natural units) and let $N_{st} = e^{C_{st}}$. Thus N_{st} is the number of equivalent noiseless letters for the s, t sub-channel. If the set $A(s, t)$ is empty, we set $N_{st} = 0$.

The states of such a channel can be grouped into equivalence classes as follows. States s and s' are in the same class if there is a sequence of input letters which, starting with state s, ends in s', and conversely a sequence leading from s' to s. The equivalence classes can be partially ordered as follows. If there is a sequence leading from a member of one class to a member of a second class, the first class is higher in the ordering than the second class.

Within an equivalence class one may consider various possible closed sequences of states; various possible ways, starting with a state, to choose a sequence of input letters which return to this state. The number of states around such a cycle will be called the cycle length. The greatest common divisor of all cycle lengths in a particular equivalence class will be called the basic period of that class. These structural properties are analogous to those of finite state markoff processes, in which "transition with positive probability" takes the place of a "possible transition for some input letter."

We shall consider only channels in which there is just one equivalence class. That is, it is possible to go from any state s to any state t by some sequence of input letters (i.e., any state is accessible from any other). The more general case of several equivalence classes is more complex without being significantly more difficult.

THEOREM 4: *Let K be a finite state channel with finite alphabets, with state calculable at both terminals, and any state accessible from any other state. Let N_{st} be the number of equivalent letters for the sub-channel relating to transitions from state s to state t. Let N be the (unique) positive real eigenvalue of the matrix N_{st}, that is, the positive real root of*

$$| N_{st} - N\delta_{st} | = 0.$$

Then N is the equivalent number of letters for the given channel K; its capacity is $C = \log N$.

PROOF: We will first show that there exist block codes which transmit at any rate $R < C$ and with probability of error arbitrarily small. Consider the matrix N_{st}. If this is raised to the nth power we obtain a matrix with elements, say, $N_{st}^{(n)}$. The element $N_{st}^{(n)}$ can be thought of as a sum of products, each product corresponding to some path n steps long from state s to state t, the product being the product of the original matrix elements along this path, and the sum being the sum of such products for all such possible paths. This follows immediately by mathematical induction and the definition of matrix multiplication.

Furthermore, $N_{st}^{(n)}$ can be interpreted as the equivalent number of letters for the memoryless channel defined as follows. Imagine starting the original channel in state s and using as input "letters" sequences of length n of the original letters allowing just those sequences which will end in state t after the sequence of n. The output "letters" are sequences of received letters of length n that could be produced under these conditions. This channel can be thought of as a "sum" of channels (corresponding to the different state sequences from s to t in n steps) each of which is a "product" of channels (corresponding to simple transitions from one state to another). (The sum of two channels is a channel in which a letter from either of the two channels may be used; the product is the channel in which a letter from both given channels is used, this ordered pair being an input letter of the product channel). The equivalent number of noise free letters for the sum of channels is additive, and for the product, multiplicative. Consequently the channel we have just described, corresponding to sequences from state s to state t in n steps, has an equivalent number of letters equal to the matrix element $N_{st}^{(n)}$.

The original matrix N_{st} is a matrix with non-negative elements. Consequently it has a positive real eigenvalue which is greater than or equal to all other eigenvalues in absolute value. Furthermore, under our assumption that it be possible to pass from any state to any other state by some sequence of letters, there is only one positive real eigenvalue. If d is the greatest common divisor of closed path lengths (through sequences of states), then there will be d eigenvalues equal to the positive real root multiplied by the different dth roots of unity. When the matrix N_{st} is raised to the nth power, a term $N_{st}^{(n)}$ is either zero (if it is impossible to go from s to t in exactly n steps) or is asymptotic to a constant times $N^{(n)}$.

In particular, for n congruent to zero, mod d, the diagonal terms $N_{tt}^{(n)}$ are asymptotic to a constant times N^n, while if this congruence is not satisfied the terms are zero. These statements are all well known results in the Frobenius theory of matrices with non-negative elements, and will not be justified here (Frobenius, 1912).

If we take n a sufficiently large multiple of d we will have, then,

$N_{11}{}^{(n)} > k \, N^n$ with k positive. By taking n sufficiently large, then, the capacity of the channel whose input "letters" are from state 1 to state 1 in n steps can be made greater than $(1/n)\log kN^n = \log N + (1/n)\log k$. Since the latter term can be made arbitrarily small we obtain a capacity as close as we wish to $\log N$. Since we may certainly use the original channel in this restricted way (going from state 1 to state 1 in blocks of n) the original channel has a capacity at least equal to $\log N$.

To show that this capacity cannot be exceeded, consider the channel K_n defined as follows for sequences of length n. At the beginning of a block of length n the channel K_n can be put into an arbitrary state chosen from a set of states corresponding to the states of K. This is done by choice of a "state letter" at the transmitting point and this "state letter" is transmitted noiselessly to the receiving point. For the next n symbols the channel behaves as the given channel K with the same constraints and probabilities. At the end of this block a new state can be freely chosen at the transmitter for the next block. Considering a block of length n (including its initial state information) as a single letter and the corresponding y block including the received "state letter," as a received letter we have a memoryless channel K_n.

For any particular initial-final state pair s, t, the corresponding capacity is equal to $\log N_{st}{}^{(n)}$. Since we have the "sum" of these channels available, the capacity of K_n is equal to $\log \sum_{s,t} N_{st}{}^{(n)}$. Each term in this sum is bounded by a constant times N^n, and since there are only a finite number of terms (because there are only a finite number of states) we may assume one constant for all the terms, that is $N_{st}{}^{(n)} < kN^n$ (all n, s, t). By taking n sufficiently large we clearly have the capacity of K_n per letter, bounded by $\log N + \epsilon$ for any positive ϵ. But now any code that can be used in the original channel can also be used in the K_n channel for any n since the latter has identical constraints except at the ends of n blocks at which point all constraints are eliminated. Consequently the capacity of the original channel is less than or equal to that of K_n for all n and therefore is less than or equal to $\log N$. This completes the proof of the theorem.

This result can be generalized in a number of directions. In the first place, the finiteness of the alphabets is not essential to the argument. In effect, the channel from state s to t can be a general memoryless channel rather than a discrete finite alphabet channel.

A second slight generalization is that it is not necessary that the state be calculable at the receiver after each received letter, provided it is eventually possible at the receiver to determine all previous states. Thus, in place of requiring that the next state be a function of the preceding state and the received letter, we need only require that there should not be two different sequences of states from any state s to any state t compatible with the same sequence of received letters.

THE CAPACITY OF A FINITE STATE CHANNEL WITH STATE CALCULABLE AT TRANSMITTER BUT NOT NECESSARILY AT RECEIVER

Consider now a channel with a finite input alphabet, a finite output alphabet, and a finite number of internal states with the further property that the state is known at the beginning and can be calculated at the transmitter for each possible sequence of input letters. That is, the next state is a function of the current state and the current input letter. Such a channel is defined by this state transition function $s_{n+1} = f(s_n, x_n)$, (the $n + 1$ state as a function of state s_n and nth input symbol), and the conditional probabilities in state s, if letter x is transmitted, that the output letter will be y, $p_{sx}(y)$. We do not assume that the state is calculable at the receiving point.

As before, the states of such a channel can be grouped into a partially ordered set of equivalence classes. We shall consider again only channels in which there is just one equivalence class. That is, it is possible to go from any state s to any state t by some sequence of input letters.

We first define a capacity for a particular state s. Let the channel be in state s and let $X_1 = (x_1, x_2, \cdots, x_n)$ be a sequence of n input letters which cause the channel to end in the same state s. If the channel is in state s and the sequence X_1 is used, we can calculate the conditional probabilities of the various possible output sequences Y of length n. Thus, if the sequence X_1 leads through states $s, s_2, s_3, \cdots, s_n, s$ the conditional probability of $Y_1 = (y_1, y_2, \cdots, y_n)$ will be $Pr(Y_1/X_1) = Psx_1(y_1)Ps_2x_2(y_2) \cdots Ps_nx_n(y_n)$. Consider the X's (leading from s to s in n steps) as individual input letters in a memoryless channel with the y sequences Y as output letters and the conditional probabilities as the transition probabilities. Let $C(n, s)$ be the capacity of this channel. Let $C(s)$ be the least upper bound of $(1/n)C(n, s)$ when n varies over the positive integers. We note the following properties:

1. $C(kn, s) \geqq kC(n, s)$. This follows since in choosing probabilities to assign the X letters of length kn to achieve channel capacity one may at least do as well as the product probabilities for a sequence of kX's each of length n. It follows that if we approximate to $C(s)$

within ϵ at some particular n (i.e. $|\,C(s) - - C(n,\, s)\,| < \epsilon$) we will approximate equally well along the infinite sequence $2n,\, 3n,\, 4n,\, \cdots$.

2. $C(s) = C$ is independent of the state s. This is proved as follows. Select a sequence of input letters U leading from state s' to state s and a second sequence V leading from s to s'. Neither of these need contain more than m letters where m is the (finite) number of states in the channel. Select an n_1 for which $C(n_1,\, s) > C(s) - \epsilon/2$ and with n_1 large enough so that:

$$(C(s) - \epsilon/2)\, \frac{n_1}{n_1 + 2m} \geq C(s) - \epsilon$$

This is possible since by the remark 1 above $C(s)$ is approximated as closely as desired with arbitrarily large n_1. A set of X sequences for the s' state is constructed by using the sequences for the s state and annexing the U sequence at the beginning and the V sequence at the end. If each of these is given a probability equal to that used for the X sequences in the s state to achieve $C(n,\, s)$, then this gives a rate for the s' sequences of exactly $C(n,\, s)$ but with sequences of length at most $n_1 + 2m$ rather than n_1. It follows that $C(s') \geq (C(s) - \epsilon/2)(n_1/n_1 + 2m) \geq C(s) - \epsilon$. Of course, interchanging s and s' gives the reverse result $C(s) \geq C(s') - \epsilon$ and consequently $C(s) = C(s')$. (Note that, if there were several equivalence classes, we would have a C for each class, not necessarily equal).

3. Let $C(n,\, s,\, s')$ be the capacity calculated for sequences starting at s and ending at s' after n steps. Let $C(s, s') = \overline{\lim}_{n\to\infty}(1/n)C(n,\, s,\, s')$. Then $C(s,\, s') = C(s) = C$. This is true since we can change sequences from s to s' into sequences from s to s by a sequence of length at most m added at the end. By taking n sufficiently large in the lim the effect of an added m can be made arbitrarily small, (as in the above remark 2) so that $C(s,\, s') \geq C(s) - \epsilon$. Likewise, the s to s sequences which approximate $C(s)$ and can be made arbitrarily long can be translated into s to s' sequences with at most m added letters. This implies $C(s) \geq C(s,\, s') - \epsilon$. Hence $C(s) = C(s,\, s')$.

We wish to show first that starting in state s_1 it is possible to signal with arbitrarily small probability of error at any rate $R < C$ where C is the quantity above in remark 3. More strongly, we will prove the following.

THEOREM 5: *Given any $R < C$ there exists $E(R) > 0$ such that for any* *n = k d (an integer multiple of d, the basic cycle length) there are block codes of length n having M words with $(1/n) \log M \geq R$ and with probability of error $P_e \leqq e^{-E(R)n}$. There does not exist a sequence of codes of increasing block length with probability of error approaching zero and rate greater than C.*

PROOF: The affirmative part of the result is proved as follows. Let $R_1 = (R + C)/2$. Let s_1 be the initial state of the channel and consider sequences of letters which take the state from s_1 to s_1 in n_1 steps. Choose n_1 so that $C(n_1 , s_1) > (3C + R)/4$. Use these sequences as input letters and construct codes for the rate R_1. By Theorem 3 the probability of error will go down exponentially in the length of the code. The codes here are of length $n_1 , 2n_1 , 3n_1 , \cdots$ in terms of the original letters, but this merely changes the coefficient of n by a factor $1/n_1$. Thus, for multiples of n_1 the affirmative part of the theorem is proved. To prove it for all multiples of d, first note that it is true for all sufficiently large multiples of d, since by going out to a sufficiently large multiple of n_1 the effect of a suffix on the code words bringing the state back to s_1 after multiples of d, can be made small (so that the rate is not substantially altered). But now for smaller multiples of d one may use any desired code with a probability of error less than 1 (e.g., interpret any received word as message 1, with $P_e = 1 - 1/M < 1$). We have then a finite set of codes up to some multiple of d at which a uniform exponential bound takes over. Thus, one may choose a coefficient $E(R)$ such that $P_e < e^{-E(R)n}$ for n *any* integer multiple of d.

The negative part of our result, that the capacity C cannot be exceeded, is proved by an argument similar to that used for the case where the state was calculable at the receiver. Namely, consider the channel K_n defined as follows. The given channel K may be put at the beginning into any state and the name of this state transmitted noiselessly to the receiving point. Then n letters are transmitted with the constraints and probabilities of the given channel K. The final state is then also transmitted to the receiver point. This process is then repeated in blocks of n. We have here a memoryless channel which for any n "includes" the given channel. Any code for the given channel K could be used if desired in K_n with equally good probability of error. Hence the capacity of the given channel K must be less than or equal to that of K_n for every n. On the other hand K_n is actually the "sum" of a set of channels corresponding to sequences from state s to state t in n steps; channels with capacities previously denoted by $C(n, s, t)$. For all sufficiently large n, and for all s, t, we have $(1/n)C(n, s, t) < C + \epsilon$ as we have seen above. Hence for all $n > n_0$, say, the capacity of K_n is bounded by $C + \epsilon + (1/n) \log m^2$ where m is the number of states. It follows that the capacity of K is not greater than C.

It is interesting to compare the results of this section where the state is calculable at the transmitter only with those of the preceding section where the state is calculable at both terminals. In the latter case, a fairly explicit formula is given for the capacity, involving only the calculation of capacities of memoryless channels and the solution of an algebraic equation. In the former case, the solution is far less explicit, involving as it does the evaluation of certain limits of a rather complex type.

RECEIVED: April 22, 1957.

REFERENCES

CHERNOV, H., (1952). A Measure of Asymptotic Efficiency for Tests of a Hypothesis Based on the Sum of Observations. *Ann. Math. Stat.* **23**, 493–507.

ELIAS, P. (1956). *In* "Information Theory" (C. Cherry, ed.). Academic Press, New York.

FEINSTEIN, A. (1955). Error Bounds in Noisy Channels Without Memory. *IRE Trans. on Inform. Theory* **IT-1**, 13–14 (Sept.).

FROBENIUS, G. (1912). Über Matrizen aus nichtnegativen Elementen. *Akad. Wiss. Sitzber. Berlin*, pp. 456–477.

SHANNON, C. E. (1948). Mathematical Theory of Communication. *Bell System Tech. J.* **27**, 379–423.

SHANNON, C. E. (1956). The Zero Error Capacity of a Noisy Channel. *IRE Trans. on Inform. Theory* **IT-2**, 8–19 (Sept.).

Some Geometrical Results in Channel Capacity*

Claude E. Shannon**

Abstract

A memoryless discrete channel is defined by a set of transition probabilities $p_i(j)$. The rate R of information flow per symbol can be represented as a line segment inside a certain convex body, when the source symbols occur with given probabilities. With the help of this geometric picture one can easily obtain a number of interesting properties of channel capacity and rate of information flow. We show for example that the rate is an upward convex function of the source probabilities, and a strictly convex function of the probabilities of the output symbols. Therefore a local maximum of R is necessarily equal to the absolute maximum C. If ρ is the rank of the matrix $\|p_i(j)\|$, then one needs only ρ (suitably chosen) input symbols to achieve capacity; one has $C \leq \log \rho$. Other results of a similar nature are developed, including a simple geometric construction of the channel capacity in the case of only two output characters.

The calculations involved in determining the rate R and channel capacity C for a discrete memoryless channel [1] can be given an interesting geometric formulation that leads to new results and insights into the properties of these quantities. Our results extend and to some extent overlap from a different viewpoint the interesting paper of S. Muroga [2]. The method of analysis, however, is quite different, using a geometrical approach depending on results in the theory of convex bodies [3] rather than the algebraic approach of Muroga.

Let a channel be defined by the matrix $\|p_i(j)\|$ of transition probabilities from input letter i to output letter j ($i = 1, 2, \cdots, a; j = 1, 2, \cdots, b$). We can think of each row of this matrix as defining a vector or a point in a $(b - 1)$-dimensional equilateral simplex (the $b - 1$ dimensional analog of line segment, triangle, tetrahedron, etc.). The coordinates of the point are the distances from the faces and they sum to one, $\sum_j p_i(j) = 1$. They are known as barycentric coordinates. They correspond, for example, to the coordinates often used by chemists in describing an alloy in terms of the fraction of various components.

We thus associate a point or vector $\underline{A}_i$ with input i. Its components are equal to the probabilities of various output letters if only the input i were used. If all the inputs are used, with probability P_i for input i, the probabilities of the output letters are given by the components of the vector sum

$$\underline{Q} = \sum_i P_i \underline{A}_i .$$

$\underline{Q}$ is a vector or point in the simplex corresponding to the output letter probabilities. Its jth component is $\sum_i P_i p_i(j)$. Since the P_i are non-negative and sum to unity, the point $\underline{Q}$ is in the convex hull (or barycentric hull) of the points $\underline{A}_i$. Furthermore, any point in this convex

---

* *Nachrichtentechnische Zeit*, vol. 10, 1957.

** Mr. Shannon was unfortunately prevented by university commitments from giving his report in person. In his stead, Mr. Kretzmer delivered his report in German in a free-form interpretation, and was kind enough to take the responsibility of answering questions afterwards.

hull can be obtained by suitable choice of the P_i.

Now, for notational convenience, we define the *entropy* of a point or a vector in a simplex to be the entropy of the barycentric coordinates of the point interpreted as probabilities. Thus we write

$$H(\underline{A}_i) = - \sum_j p_i(j) \log p_i(j) , \quad i = 1, 2, \cdots, a ,$$

$$H(\underline{Q}) = - \sum_j \sum_i P_i \, p_i(j) \log \sum_i P_i p_i(j)$$

$$= \text{entropy of received distribution.}$$

In this notation, the rate of transmission R for a given set of input probabilities P_i is given by

$$R = H(\sum_i P_i \underline{A}_i) - \sum_i P_i H(\underline{A}_i)$$

$$= H(\underline{Q}) - \sum_i P_i H(\underline{A}_i) .$$

The function $H(\underline{Q})$, where $\underline{Q}$ is a point in the simplex, is a convex upward function. For if the components of $\underline{Q}$ are x_i, we have

$$H = - \sum x_i \log x_i ,$$

$$\frac{\partial H}{\partial x_i} = - (1 + \log x_i) ,$$

$$H_{ij} = \frac{\partial^2 H}{\partial x_i \partial x_j} = \begin{matrix} 0 & i \neq j \\ 1/x_i & i = j . \end{matrix}$$

Hence $\sum_{ij} H_{ij} \, \Delta x_i \, \Delta x_j = - \sum_i (\Delta x_i^2)/x_i$ is a negative definite form. This is true in the space of all non-negative x_i and, hence, certainly in the sub-space where $\sum x_i = 1$. It follows that the rate R above is always non-negative and, indeed, since H is *strictly* convex (no flat regions), that R is positive unless $\underline{A}_i = \underline{Q}$, whenever $P_i > 0$.

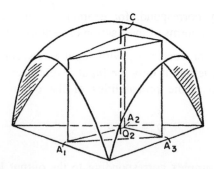

Fig. 1   Construction for channel capacity with three input and three output letters

The process of calculating R can be visualized readily in the cases of two or three output letters. With three output letters, imagine an equilateral triangle on the floor. This is the simplex containing the points $\underline{A}_i$ and $\underline{Q}$. Above this triangle is a rounded dome as in Fig. 1. The height of the dome over any point $\underline{A}$ is $H(\underline{A})$. If there were three input letters with corresponding vectors $\underline{A}_1, \underline{A}_2, \underline{A}_3$ these correspond to three points in the triangle and, straight up from these, to three points on the dome. Any received vector $Q = \sum P_i \underline{A}_i$ is a point within the triangle on the floor defined by $\underline{A}_1, \underline{A}_2, \underline{A}_3$. $H(Q)$ is the height of the dome above the point Q and $\sum (P_i H \underline{A}_i)$ is the height above Q of the plane defined by the three dome points over $\underline{A}_1, \underline{A}_2, \underline{A}_3$. In other words, R is the vertical distance over Q from the dome down to the plane defined by these three points.

The capacity C is the maximum R. Consequently in this particular case it is the maximum vertical distance from the dome to the plane interior to the triangle defined by $\underline{A}_1, \underline{A}_2, \underline{A}_3$. This clearly occurs at the point of tangency of a plane tangent to the dome and parallel to the plane defined by the input letters, provided this point is interior to the triangle. If not, the maximum R will occur on an edge of the triangle.

If there were four input letters, they would define a triangle or a quadrilateral on the floor depending on their positions, and their vertical points in the dome would in general define a tetrahedron. Using them with different probabilities would give any point in the tetrahedron as the subtracted value $\sum P_i H(\underline{A}_i)$. Clearly, the maximum R would occur by choosing probabilities which place this subtracted part somewhere on the lower surface of the tetrahedron.

These remarks also apply if there are still more input letters. If there are $\underline{a}$ input letters they define an $\underline{a}$-gon or less in the floor and the vertically overhead points in the dome produce a polyhedron. Any point in the convex hull of the points obtained in the dome can be reached with suitable choice of the P_i and corresponds to some subtracted term in R. It is clear that to maximize R and thus obtain C one need only consider the lower surface of this convex hull.

It is also clear geometrically, from the fact that the lower surface of the polyhedron is convex downward and the dome is *strictly* convex upward, that there is a unique point at which the maximum R, that is, C, occurs. For if there were two such points, the point halfway between would be even better since the dome would go up above the line connecting the points at the top and the lower surface of the convex hull would be at least as low at the midpoint of the lower connecting line. The rate R is therefore a strictly convex upward function of the received vector Q.

It is also true that the rate R is a convex upward function of the *input* probability vector (this vector has a barycentric coordinates $P_1, P_2, \cdots, P_a$ rather than the $\underline{b}$ coordinates of our other vectors). This is true since the $\underline{Q}$ vectors $\underline{Q}'$ and $\underline{Q}''$ corresponding to the input probabilities P_i' and P_i'' are given by

$$\underline{Q}' = \sum P_i' \underline{A}_i \, ,$$

$$\underline{Q}'' = \sum P_i'' \underline{A}_i \, .$$

The $\underline{Q}$ corresponding to $\alpha P_i' + \beta P_i''$ (where $\alpha + \beta = 1$ and both are positive) is $\alpha \underline{Q}' + \beta \underline{Q}''$ and consequently the corresponding $R \geq \alpha R' + \beta R''$, the desired result. Equality can occur when $\underline{Q}' = \underline{Q}''$, so in this case we cannot say that we have a *strictly* convex function.

These last remarks also imply that the set S of P vectors which maximize the rate at the capacity C form a convex set in its a dimensional simplex. If the maximum is obtained at two different points it is also attained at all points on the line segment joining these points. Furthermore, any local maximum of R is the absolute maximum C, for if not, join the points corresponding to the local maximum and the absolute maximum. The value of R must lie on or above this line by the convexity property, but must lie below it when sufficiently close to the local maximum to make it a local maximum. This contradiction proves our statement.

While we have described these results in terms of three output letters for geometrical clarity, it is easy to generalize them to the case of b output letters using well known results from the theory of convex bodies.

Another property we may deduce easily is that the capacity C can always be attained using not more than ρ of the input letters, where ρ is the rank of the matrix $\|p_i(j)\|$. This is because $\rho - 1$ is the dimensionality of the set of Q points. Any point on the surface of a $\rho - 1$ dimensional polyhedron is in some face. This face may be subdivided into $\rho - 1$ dimensional simplexes (if it is not already a simplex). The point is then in one of these. The vertices of the simplex are ρ input letters, and the desired point can be expressed in terms of these. A result of Muroga, that the capacity is not greater than $\log \rho$, now follows easily. In fact if only ρ letters are used, the entropy of the input is necessarily not greater than $\log \rho$, and the equivocation can only decrease this value.

The geometric picture gives considerable information concerning which input letters should be used to achieve channel capacity. If the vector $\underline{A}_t$, say, corresponding to input letter t, is in the convex hull of the remaining letters, it need not be used. Thus, suppose $\underline{A}_t = \sum_{i \neq t} a_i \underline{A}_i$ where $\sum_i a_i = 1, a_i \geq 0$. Then by the convexity properties $H(\underline{A}_t) \geq \sum_{i \neq t} a_i H(\underline{A}_i)$. If by using the $\underline{A}_i$ with probabilities P_i we obtain a rate $R = H(\sum P_i \underline{A}_i) - \sum P_i H(\underline{A}_i)$, then a rate greater than or equal to R can be obtained by expressing $\underline{A}_t$ in terms of the other $\underline{A}_i$, for this leaves unaltered the first term of R and decreases or leaves constant the sum.

In the case of only two output letters the situation is extremely simple. Whatever the number of input letters, only two of them need be used to achieve channel capacity. These two will be those with the maximum and minimum transition probabilities to one of the output letters. These values, p_1 and p_2 say, are then located in the one-dimensional simplex, a line segment of unit length, and projected upward to the H-curve as shown in Fig. 2. The secant line is drawn and the capacity is the largest vertical distance from the secant to the curve. The probabilities to achieve this capacity are in proportion to the distances from this point to the two ends of the secant.

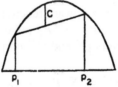

Fig. 2 Construction for channel capacity with two output letters

In the case of three output letters, the positions of all vectors corresponding to input letters may be plotted in an equilateral triangle. The circumscribing polygon (convex hull) of these points may now be taken and any points interior to this polygon (including those on edges) may be deleted. What is desired is the lower surface of the polyhedron determined by the points in the H-surface above these points. This lower surface, in general, will consist of triangles and the problem is to determine which vertices are connected by edges. A method of doing this is to consider a line joining a pair of vertices and then to calculate for other lines whose projections on the floor cross this line, whether they are above it or below it in space. If there is no line below the first line, this line is an edge on the lower surface of the polyhedron. If a second line is found below the first line this one may be tested in a similar fashion, and eventually an edge is isolated. This edge divides the projection into two smaller polygons and these may now be studied individually by the same means. Eventually, the original polygon will be divided by edges into a set of polygons corresponding to faces of the polyhedron. Each of these polygons may then be examined to determine whether or not the point of tangency of the parallel plane which is tangent to the H-surface lies over the polyhedron. This will happen in exactly one of the polygons and corresponds to the Q for maximum R.

We now prove another convexity property of discrete channels, namely that the channel capacity for transition probabilities $p_i(j)$ is a convex downward function of these probabilities. That is, the capacity C for the transition probabilities $r_i(j) = \frac{1}{2}(p_i(j) + q_i(j))$ satisfies the inequality

$$C \leq \frac{1}{2} C_1 + \frac{1}{2} C_2 ,$$

where C_1 is the capacity with probabilities $p_i(j)$ and C_2 that with probabilities $q_i(j)$.

To prove this let the capacity of the $r_i(j)$ channel be achieved by the input probabilities P_i. Now consider the following channel. There are as many inputs as in the given channels but twice as many outputs, a set j and a set j'. Each input has transitions $\frac{1}{2} p_i(j)$ and $\frac{1}{2} q_i(j')$. This is the channel we would obtain by halving all probabilities in the $p_i(j)$ and the $q_i(j)$ channels and identifying the corresponding inputs but leaving the outputs distinct. We note that if the corresponding outputs are identified, the channel reduces to the $r_i(j)$ channel. We note also that without this identification the channel looks like one which half the time acts like the $p_i(j)$ channel and half the time the $q_i(j)$ channel. An identification of certain outputs always reduces (or leaves equal) the rate of transmission. Let this channel be used with probabilities P_i for the input symbols. Then this inequality in rates may be written

$$H(x) - \left[\frac{1}{2} H_{y1}(x) + \frac{1}{2} H_{y2}(x) \right] \geq H(x) - H_y(x) = C ,$$

where $H_{y1}(x)$ is the conditional entropy of x when y is in the j group and $H_{y2}(x)$ that when y is in the j' group. Splitting $H(x)$ into two parts to combine with the $H_{y1}(x)$ and $H_{y2}(x)$, we obtain

$$\frac{1}{2} R_1 + \frac{1}{2} R_2 \geq C ,$$

where R_1 is the rate for the $p_i(j)$ channel when the inputs have probabilities P_i and R_2 is the similar quantity for the $q_i(j)$ channel. These rates, of course, are less, respectively, than C_1 or C_2, since the capacities are the maximum possible rates. Hence we get the desired result that

$$\frac{1}{2} C_1 + \frac{1}{2} C_2 \geq C .$$

The various results we have found may be summarized as follows.

Theorem: In a finite discrete memoryless channel we have the following properties.

(1)   The rate of transmission R is a strictly convex upward function of the received letter probabilities Q_i.

(2)   The rate R is a convex upward function of the input letter probabilities P_i.

(3)   The region in the space of input letter probabilities where channel capacity is achieved is a convex set of points.

(4)   There is no local maximum of R which is not the absolute maximum C.

(5)   Any input letter interior to the convex hull defined by the other input letters can be deleted without affecting channel capacity.

(6)   Only ρ (suitably chosen) input letters need be used to achieve channel capacity where ρ is the rank of $\|p_i(j)\|$. Furthermore $C \geq \log \rho$ (Muroga).

(7)   The channel capacity is a convex downward function of the transition probabilities $p_i(j)$.

References

[1]   Shannon, C. E., and Weaver, W.: *The Mathematical Theory of Communication*, University of Illinois Press (1949).

[2]   Muroga, Saburo: "On the Capacity of a Discrete Channel", *Research and Development Data No. 5*, Nippon Telegraph and Telephone Public Corporation, Tokyo (1953).

[3]   Alexandroff, P., and Hopf, H.: *Topologie I*, Berlin (1935).

Discussion

Mr. P. Neidhardt: I would like to make a remark concerning the properties of the geometric representation of the quantity defined as the average information, per information element, that is lost in transmission.

It is known that the information flow rate R which reaches the receiver is the difference between the information content of the signal $H(X)$ and the equivocation $H(X|Y)$, when X is the ensemble of the information sent and Y that which is received. Thus one has

$$ - \sum_X p(x)^2 \log p(x) - \sum_Y \sum_X p(x,y)^2 \log p(x|y) = R \, , $$

where x and y denote elements of the ensembles X and Y. Shannon has shown that one can also define the channel capacity of a transmission channel, without referring to information content or information flow, indeed solely on the basis of the probabilities $p(y|x)$. [See also Amiel Feinstein, *IRE Transactions on Information Theory*, September 1954, pp. 2-22].

There now arises the question, when considering the geometric representation of the information rate R described in the report, the convexity properties of this function and the transparent calculation of the channel capacity C, whether there are not also convexity properties of the function

$$ - \sum_Y \sum_X p(x,y)^2 \log p(x|y) \, , $$

which alas always absorbs a certain part of the $- \sum_X p(x)^2 \log p(x)$ in the quantity R. This would reveal interesting geometric properties of the entropy relation defined by myself as the information-theoretic efficiency. [See NTF, vol. 3, 1956].

Mr. E. R. Kretzmer: In the geometric representation just described it is not the equivocation that enters, but another related quantity, which I have called the "dispersion loss." Convexity properties of functions almost always occur with these quantities. Probably this is also the case for equivocation. This would require further research.

A Note on a Partial Ordering for Communication Channels

Claude E. Shannon*

Center for Advanced Study in the Behavioral Sciences, Stanford, California

A partial ordering is defined for discrete memoryless channels. It is transitive and is preserved under channel operations of addition and multiplication. The main result proved is that if K_1 and K_2 are such channels, and $K_1 \supseteq K_2$, then if a code exists for K_2, there exists at least as good a code for K_1, in the sense of probability of error.

Consider the three discrete memoryless channels shown in Fig. 1. The first may be said to include the second, since by the use at the input of only the letters A, B, and C, the channel reduces to the second channel. Anything that could be done in the way of signaling with the second channel could be done with the first channel by this artificial restriction (and of course, in general, more, by using the full alphabet). The second channel in a sense includes the third, since if at the receiving point we ignore the difference between received letters A' and B' the third channel results. We could imagine a device added to the output which produces letter A' if either A' or B' goes in, and lets C' go through without change.

These are examples of a concept of channel inclusion we wish to define and study. Another example is the pair of binary symmetric channels in Fig. 2. Here we can reduce the first channel to the second one not by identification of letters in the input or output alphabets but by addition of a statistical device at either input or output; namely, if we place before (or after) the first channel a binary symmetric channel, as shown in Fig. 3, with value p_2 such that $\{p_1 = p p_2 + q q_2\}$, then this over-all arrangement acts like the second channel of Fig. 2. Physically this could be done by a suitable device involving a random element. We might be inclined, therefore, to define a channel K_1 with transition probability matrix $\| p_i(j) \|$ to include

---

* On leave of absence from Massachusetts Institute of Technology.

INFORMATION AND CONTROL 1, 390–397 (1958)

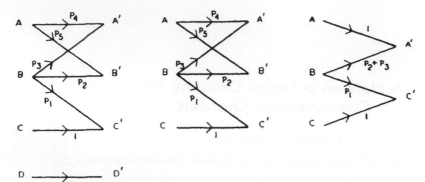

FIG. 1. Examples of channels illustrating inclusion relation.

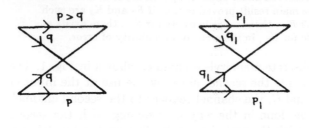

$$q \leq P_i \leq P$$

FIG. 2. A further example of inclusion.

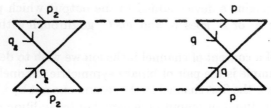

FIG. 3. Reduction of the left channel of Fig. 2 to the right, by a preceding channel.

channel K_2 with matrix $\|q_i(j)\|$ if there exist stochastic matrices A and B such that

$$A \, \| \, p_i(j) \, \| \, B = \| \, q_i(j) \, \|.$$

This is a possible definition, but actually we can generalize this somewhat and still obtain the properties we would like for channel inclusion. Namely, we may consider fore and aft stochastic operations which are correlated. Physically one can imagine devices placed at the transmitting end and at the receiving end which involve random but not necessarily independent elements. For example, they may obtain their random choices from tapes which were prepared together with certain correlations. Physically this would be a perfectly feasible process. Mathematically this corresponds, in the simplest case, to the following.

DEFINITION. Let $p_i(j)$ $(i = 1, \cdots, a; j = 1, \cdots, b)$ be the transition probabilities for a discrete memoryless channel K_1 and $q_k(l)$ $(k = 1, \cdots, c; l = 1, \cdots, d)$ be those for K_2. We shall say that K_1 includes K_2, $K_1 \supseteq K_2$, if and only if there exist two sets of transition probabilities, $r_{\alpha k}(i)$ and $t_{\alpha j}(l)$, with

$$r_{\alpha k}(i) \geqq 0, \qquad \sum_i r_{\alpha k}(i) = 1,$$

and

$$t_{\alpha j}(l) \geqq 0, \qquad \sum_l t_{\alpha j}(l) = 1,$$

and there exists

$$g_\alpha \geqq 0, \qquad \sum_\alpha g_\alpha = 1$$

with

$$\sum_{\alpha, i, j} g_\alpha r_{\alpha k}(i) \, p_i(j) \, t_{\alpha j}(l) = q_k(l). \tag{1}$$

Roughly speaking, this requires a set of pre- and post-channels R_α and T_α, say, which are used in pairs, g_α being the probability for the pair with subscript α. When this sort of operation is applied the channel K_1 looks like K_2.

Let us define a *pure channel* as one in which all the transitions have probability either 0 or 1; thus each input letter is carried with certainty into some output letter. Any particular pre- and post-channel R_α and T_α in (1) can be thought of as a weighted sum of pure pre- and post-channels operating on K_1. Namely, consider all ways of mapping the input letters of R_α into its output letters and associate probabilities with these to give the equilavent of R_α. The mapping where letter k is mapped into m_k is given probability $\prod_k r_{\alpha k}(m_k)$. A similar reduction can be carried out for the post-channel T_α and combinations of the pre- and post-pure channels are given the corresponding product probabilities.

This reduction to pure components can be carried out for each α and the probabilities added for the same components with different α. In this way, the entire operation in (1) can be expressed as the same sort of operation, where the R_α and T_α are now pure channels. In other words, channel inclusion can be defined equivalently to the above definition but with the added condition that the $r_{\alpha k}(i)$ and $t_{\alpha j}(l)$ correspond to pure channels.

The relation of channel inclusion is transitive. If $K_1 \supseteq K_2$ and $K_2 \supseteq K_3$, then $K_1 \supseteq K_3$. Indeed, if g_α, R_α, T_α are the probabilities and pre- and post-channels for the first inclusion relation, and g'_β, R'_β, T'_β those for the second, then the probabilities $g_\alpha g'_\beta$ with channels $R'_\beta \cup R_\alpha$ for premultiplier and $T_\alpha \cup T'_\beta$ for postmultiplier (the $\cup$ means tandem connection or matrix product) will produce K_3 from K_1. If $K_1 \supseteq K_2$ and $K_2 \supseteq K_1$, we will say these are equivalent channels and write $K_1 \equiv K_2$. Note that always $K_1 \equiv K_1$. Grouping channels into these equivalence classes we have, then, a partial ordering of discrete memoryless channels. There is a universal lower bound of all channels, namely, the channel with one input letter and one output letter with probability 1 for the transition. There is no (finite) universal upper bound of all channels. However, if we restrict ourselves to channels with at most n input and n output letters (or channels equivalent to these) we can give an upper bound to this subset, namely, the pure channel with n inputs and n outputs, the inputs mapped one-to-one into the outputs.

The ordering relation is preserved under channel operations of addition and multiplication. If K_1, K'_1, K_2, and K'_2 are channels and $K_1 \supseteq K'_1$ and $K_2 \supseteq K'_2$, then

$$K_1 + K_2 \supseteq K'_1 + K'_2$$

$$K_1 K_2 \supseteq K'_1 K'_2.$$

The sum and product of channels as defined in an earlier paper (Shannon, 1956) correspond to a channel in which either K_1 or K_2 may be used (for the sum) or to a channel where both K_1 and K_2 are used (for the product). To prove the product relationship suppose $(g_\alpha, R_\alpha, T_\alpha)$ produce K'_1 from K_1 and $(g'_\beta, R'_\beta, T'_\beta)$ produce K'_2 from K_2. Then $(g_\alpha g'_\beta, R_\alpha R'_\beta, T_\alpha T')'_\beta$ produces $K'_1 K'_2$ from $K_1 K_2$, where the product $R_\alpha R'_\beta$ means the product of the channels. The sum case works similarly. The sum $K'_1 + K'_2$ can be produced from $K_1 + K_2$ by $(g_\alpha g'_\beta, R_\alpha + R'_\beta, T_\alpha + T'_\beta)$ where the plus means sum of channels and α and β range over all pairs.

If in a memoryless discrete channel K we consider blocks of n letters, then we have another memoryless discrete channel, one in which the input "letters" are input words of length n for the original channel and the output "letters" are output words of length n for the original channel. This channel is clearly equivalent to K^n. Consequently, if $K_1 \supseteq K_2$ the channel K_1^n for words of length n from K_1 includes K_2^n, the channel for words of length n from K_2.

Suppose $K_1 \supseteq K_2$ and $K_1 \supseteq K_3$ and that K_1 and K_3 have matrices $\| p_i(j) \|$ and $\| q_i(j) \|$, respectively. Then K_1 also includes the channel whose matrix is

$$\lambda \| p_i(j) \| + (1 - \lambda) \| q_i(j) \| \qquad (0 \leq \lambda \leq 1).$$

Thus, in the transition probability space the set of channels included in K_1 form a convex body. The $\lambda \| p_i(j) \| + (1 - \lambda) \| q_i(j) \|$ channel can in fact be obtained from K_1 by the union of $(\lambda g_\alpha, R_\alpha, T_\alpha)$ and

$$((1 - \lambda)g_\beta', R_\beta', T_\beta').$$

Our most important result and the chief reason for considering the relation of channel inclusion connects this concept with coding theory. We shall show, in fact, that if a code exists for K_2 and $K_1 \supseteq K_2$, at least as good a code exists for K_1 in the sense of low probability of error.

THEOREM. Suppose $K_1 \supseteq K_2$ and there is a set of code words of length n for K_2, W_1, W_2, $\cdots$, W_m, and a decoding system such that if the W_i are used with probabilities P_i then the average probability of error in decoding is P_e. Then there exists for channel K_1 a set of m code words of length n and a decoding system which if used with the same probabilities P_i given an average probability of error $P_e' \leq P_e$. Consequently, the capacity of K_1 is greater than or equal to that of K_2.

PROOF. If $K_1 \supseteq K_2$ a set $(g_\alpha, R_\alpha, T_\alpha)$ makes K_1 like K_2, where R_α and T_α are *pure* channels. For any particular α, R_α defines a mapping of input words from the K_2^n code into input words from the K_1^n dictionary (namely, the words into which the R_α transforms the code). Furthermore, T_α definies a mapping of K_1 output words into K_2 output words. From a code and decoding system for K_2 we can obtain, for any particular α, a code and decoding system for K_1. Take as the code the set of words obtained by the mapping R_α from the code words for K_2. For the decoding system, decode a K_1 word as the given system decodes the word into which a K_1 word is transformed by T_α. Such a code will have a probability of error for K_1 of, say, $P_{e\alpha}$. Now it is clear that

$$P_e = \sum_\alpha g_\alpha P_{e\alpha} \qquad (2)$$

since the channel K_2 acts like these different codes with probability g_α.
Since this equation says that a (weighted) average of the $P_{e\alpha}$ is equal to
P_e, there must be at least one particular $P_{e\alpha}$ that is equal to or greater
than P_e. (If all the $P_{e\alpha}$ were less than P_e the right-hand side would necessarily be less than P_e.) The code and decoding system defined above for
this particular α then give the main result for the theorem. It follows,
then, that $P_{e\ \text{opt}}(M, n)$, the minimum probability of error for M equally
probable words of length n, will be at least as good for K_1 as for K_2.
Similarly, the channel capacity, the greatest lower bound of rates such
that P_e can be made to approach zero, will be at least as high for K_1 as
for K_2.

It is interesting to examine geometrically the relation of channel inclusion in the simple case of channels with two inputs and two outputs
(the general binary channel). Such a channel is defined by two probabilities p_1 and p_2 (Fig. 4) and can be represented by a point in the unit
square. In this connection, see Silverman (1955) where channel capacity
and other parameters are plotted as contour lines in such a square. In
Fig. 5 the channel with $p_1 = \frac{1}{4}$, $p_2 = \frac{1}{2}$ is plotted together with the
three other equivalent channels with probabilities p_2, p_1 ; $1 - p_2$,
$1 - p_1$; and $1 - p_1$, $1 - p_2$. Adding the two points $(0,0)$ and $(1,1)$

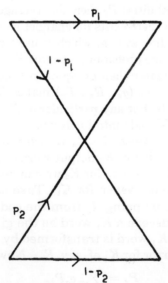

Fig. 4. The general binary channel.

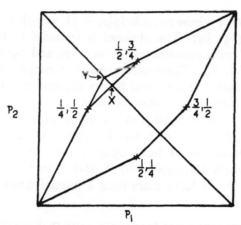

FIG. 5. The hexagon of binary channels included in a typical binary channel.

gives a total of six points. The hexagon defined by these—i.e., their convex hull—includes all the points which correspond to channels included in the given channel. This is clear since all pairs of pure pre- and postchannels produce from the given channel one of these six. This is readily verified by examination of cases. Hence any mixture with probabilities g_α will correspond to a point within the convex hull.

In Fig. 5, binary symmetric channels lie on the square diagonal from $(1,0)$ to $(0,1)$. Thus the given channel includes in particular the binary

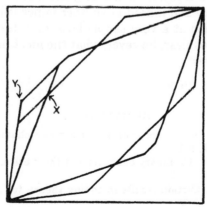

FIG. 6. The greatest lower bound X and the least upper bound Y of two comparable binary channels.

symmetric channel X whose point is $\frac{1}{2}[p_1 + (1 - p_2)]$, $\frac{1}{2}[p_2 + (1 - p_1)]$, in our example $(\frac{3}{8}, \frac{5}{8})$. The channel is *included* in the binary symmetric channel Y with coordinates $(p_1/p_1 + p_2$ and $p_2/p_1 + p_2)$, in our particular case $(\frac{1}{3}, \frac{2}{3})$. These inclusions give simple upper and lower bounds on the capacity of a general binary channel in terms of the more easily calculated binary symmetric channel.

If we have two channels neither of which includes the other, the situation will be that of Fig. 6, with two hexagons. In this case there is a greatest lower bound and a least upper bound of the two channels, namely, the channels represented by X and Y in Fig. 6. Thus, in the binary channel case we have more than a partial ordering; we have a *lattice*.

FURTHER GENERALIZATIONS AND CONJECTURES

We have not been able to determine whether or not the partial ordering defines a lattice in the case of channels with n letters. The set of points included in a given channel can be found by a construction quite similar to Fig. 5, namely, the convex hull of points obtained from the channel by pure pre- and post-channels; but it is not clear, for example, that the intersection of two such convex bodies corresponds to a channel.

Another question relates to a converse of the coding theorem above. Can one show that in some sense the ordering we have defined is the most general for which such a coding theorem will hold?

The notion of channel inclusion can be generalized in various ways to channels with memory and indeed in another paper (Shannon, 1957) we used this sort of notion at a very simple level to obtain some results in coding theory. It is not clear, however, what the most natural generalization will be in all cases.

RECEIVED: March 24, 1958.

REFERENCES

SHANNON, C. E. (1956). Zero error capacity of a noisy channel. *IRE Trans. on Inform. Theory* **IT-2,** 8–19.

SILVERMAN, R. A. (1955). On binary channels and their cascades. *IRE Trans. on Inform. Theory,* **IT-1,** 19–27.

SHANNON, C. E. (1957). Certain results in coding theory for noisy channels. *Inform. and Control* **1,** 6–25.

Channels with Side Information at the Transmitter

C. E. Shannon

Abstract: In certain communication systems where information is to be transmitted from one point to another, additional side information is available at the transmitting point. This side information relates to the state of the transmission channel and can be used to aid in the coding and transmission of information. In this paper a type of channel with side information is studied and its capacity determined.

Introduction

Channels with feedback[1] from the receiving to the transmitting point are a special case of a situation in which there is additional information available at the transmitter which may be used as an aid in the forward transmission system. In Fig. 1 the channel has an input x and an output y.

There is a second output from the channel, u, available at the transmitting point, which may be used in the coding process. Thus the encoder has as inputs the message to be transmitted, m, and the side information u. The sequence of input letters x to the channel will be a function of the available part (that is, the past up to the current time) of these signals.

The signal u might be the received signal y, it might be a noisy version of this signal, or it might not relate to y but be statistically correlated with the general state of the channel. As a practical example, a transmitting station might have available a receiver for testing the current noise conditions at different frequencies. These results would be used to choose the frequency for transmission.

A simple discrete channel with side information is shown in Fig. 2. In this channel, x, y and u are all binary variables; they can be either zero or one. The channel can be used once each second. Immediately after it is used the random device chooses a zero or one independently of previous choices and with probabilities 1/2, 1/2. This value of u then appears at the transmitting point. The next x that is sent is added in the channel modulo 2 to this value of u to give the received y. If the side information u were *not* available at the transmitter, the channel would be that of Fig. 3, a channel in which input 0 has probabilities 1/2 of being received as 0 and 1/2 as 1 and similarly for input 1.

Such a channel has capacity zero. However, with the side information *available*, it is possible to send one bit per second through the channel. The u information is used to compensate for the noise inside by a preliminary reversal of zero and one, as in Fig. 4.

Figure 1

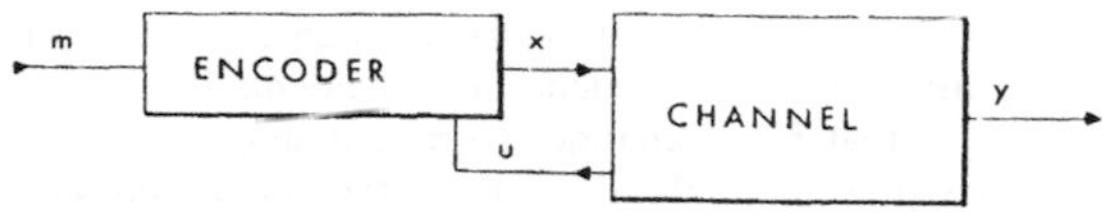

Figure 2

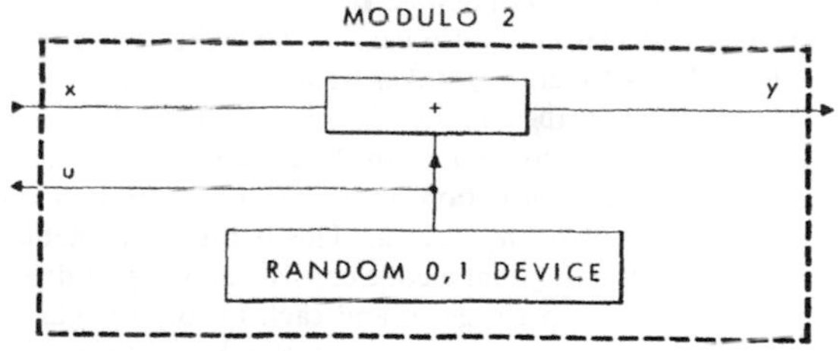

MODULO 2

Figure 3

Figure 4

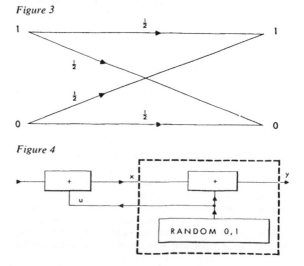

Without studying the problem of side information in its fullest generality, which would involve possible historical effects in the channel, possibly infinite input and output alphabets, et cetera, we shall consider a moderately general case for which a simple solution has been found.

The memoryless discrete channel with side state information

Consider a channel which has a finite number of possible states, s_1, s_2, ..., s_h. At each use of the channel a new state is chosen, probability g_t for state s_t. This choice is statistically independent of previous states and previous input or output letters in the channel. The state is available as side information u at the transmitting point. When in state s_t the channel acts like a particular discrete channel K_t. Thus, its operation is defined by a set of transition probabilities $P_{ti}(j)$, $t = 1, 2, ..., h$, $i = 1, 2, ..., a$, $j = 1, 2, ..., b$, where a is the number of input letters and b the number of output letters. Thus, abstractly, the channel is described by the set of state probabilities g_t and transition probabilities $p_{ti}(j)$, with g_t the probability of state t and $p_{ti}(j)$ the conditional probability, if in state t and i is transmitted, that j will be received.

A *block code* with M messages (the integers 1, 2, ..., M) may be defined as follows for such a channel with side information. This definition, incidentally, is analogous to that for a channel with feedback given previously.[1] If n is the block length of the code, there are n functions $f_1(m; u_1)$, $f_2(m; u_1, u_2)$, $f_3(m; u_1, u_2, u_3)$, ..., $f_n(m; u_1, u_2, ..., u_n)$. In these functions m ranges over the set of possible messages. Thus $m = 1, 2, ..., M$. The u_i all range over the possible side information alphabet. In the particular case here each u_i can take values from 1 to g. Each function f_i takes values in the alphabet of input letters x of the channel. The value $f_i(m; u_1, u_2, ..., u_i)$ is the input x_i to be used in the code if the message is m and the side information up to the time corresponding to i consisted of $u_1, u_2, ..., u_i$. This is the mathematical equivalent of saying that a code consists of a way of determining, for each message m and each history of side information from the beginning of the block up to the present, the next transmitted letter. The important feature here is that only the data available at the time i, namely $m; u_1, u_2, ..., u_i$, may be used in deciding the next transmitted letter x_i, not the side information $u_{i+1}, ..., u_n$ yet to appear.

A decoding system for such a code consists of a mapping or function $h(y_1, y_2, ..., y_n)$ of received blocks of length n into messages m; thus h takes values from 1 to M. It is a way of deciding on a transmitted message given a complete received block $y_1, y_2, ..., y_n$.

For a given set of probabilities of the messages, and for a given channel and coding and decoding system, there will exist a calculable probability of error P_e; the probability of a message being encoded and received in such a way that the function h leads to deciding on a different message. We shall be concerned particularly with cases where the messages are equiprobable, each having probability $1/M$. The *rate* for such a code is $(1/n) \log M$. We are interested in the channel capacity C, that is, the largest rate R such that it is possible to construct codes

arbitrarily close to rate R and with probability of error P_e arbitrarily small.

It may be noted that if the state information were *not* available at the transmitting point, the channel would act like a memoryless channel with transition probabilities given by

$$p'_i(j) = \sum_t g_t p_{ti}(j).$$

Thus, the capacity C_1 under this condition could be calculated by the ordinary means for memoryless channels. On the other hand, if the state information were available *both* at transmitting and receiving points, it is easily shown that the capacity is then given by $C_2 = \sum_t g_t C_t$, where C_t is the capacity of the memoryless channel with transmission probabilities $p_{ti}(j)$. The situation we are interested in here is intermediate—the state information is available at the transmitting point but not at the receiving point.

Theorem: *The capacity of a memoryless discrete channel K with side state information, defined by g_t and $p_{ti}(j)$, is equal to the capacity of the memoryless channel K' (without side information) with the same output alphabet and an input alphabet with a^h input letters $X = (x_1, x_2, ..., x_h)$ where each $x_i = 1, 2, ..., a$. The transition probabilities $r_X(y)$ for the channel K' are given by*

$$r_X(y) = r_{x_1, x_2, ..., x_h}(y) = \sum_t g_t p_{tx_t}(y).$$

Any code and decoding system for K' can be translated into an equivalent code and decoding system for K with the same probability of error. Any code for K has an equivocation of message (conditional entropy per letter of the message given the received sequence) at least $R - C$, where C is the capacity of K'. Any code with rate $R > C$ has a probability of error bounded away from zero (whatever the block length n)

$$P_e \geq \frac{R - C}{6 \left(R + \dfrac{1}{n} \ln \dfrac{R}{R - C} \right)}.$$

It may be noted that this theorem reduces the analysis of the given channel K *with* side information to that for a memoryless channel K' with more input letters but *without* side information. One uses known methods to determine the capacity of this derived channel K' and this gives the capacity of the original channel. Furthermore, codes for the derived channel may be translated into codes for the original channel with identical probability of error. (Indeed, all statistical properties of the codes are identical.)

We first show how codes for K' may be translated into codes for K. A code word for the derived channel K' consists of a sequence of n letters X from the X input alphabet of K'. A particular input *letter* X of this channel may be recognized as a particular *function* from the state alphabet to the input alphabet x of channel K. The full possible alphabet of X consists of the full set of a^h different possible functions from the state alphabet with h

values to the input value with a values. Thus, each letter $X = (x_1, x_2, \ldots, x_h)$ of a code word for K' may be interpreted as a function from state u to input alphabet x. The translation of codes consists merely of using the input x given by this function of the state variable. Thus if the state variable u has the value 1, then x_1 is used in channel K; if it were state k, then x_k. In other words, the translation is a simple letter-by-letter translation without memory effects depending on previous states.

The codes for K' are really just another way of describing certain of the codes for K—namely those where the next input letter x is a function only of the message m and the current state u, and does not depend on the previous states.

It might be pointed out also that a simple physical device could be constructed which, placed ahead of the channel K, makes it look like K'. This device would have the X alphabet for one input and the state alphabet for another (this input connected to the u line of Fig. 1). Its output would range over the x alphabet and be connected to the x line of Fig. 1. Its operation would be to give an x output corresponding to the X function of the state u. It is clear that the statistical situations for K and K' with the translated code are identical. The probability of an input word for K' being received as a particular output word is the same as that for the corresponding operation with K. This gives the first part of the theorem.

To prove the second part of the theorem, we will show that in the original channel K, the change in conditional entropy (equivocation) of the message m at the receiving point when a letter is received cannot exceed C (the capacity of the derived channel K'). In Fig. 1, we let m be the message; x, y, u be the next input letter, output letter and state letter. Let U be the past sequence of u states from the beginning of the block code to the present (just before u), and Y the past sequence of output letters up to the current y. We are assuming here a given block code for encoding messages. The messages are chosen from a set with certain probabilities (not necessarily equal). Given the statistics of the message source, the coding system, and the statistics of the channel, these various entities m, x, y, U, Y all belong to a probability space and the various probabilities involved in the following calculation are meaningful. Thus the equivocation of message when Y has been received, $H(m|Y)$, is given by

$$H(m|Y) = - \sum_{m,Y} P(m, Y) \log P(m|Y)$$

$$= -E\left(\log P(m|Y) \right).$$

(The symbol $E(G)$ here and later means the expectation or average of G over the probability space.) The *change* in equivocation when the next letter y is received is

$$H(m|Y) - H(m|Y, y) = -E\left(\log P(m|Y) \right)$$

$$+ E\left(\log P(m|Y, y) \right)$$

$$= E\left(\log \frac{P(m|Y, y)}{P(m|Y)} \right)$$

$$= E\left(\log \frac{P(m, Y, y) P(Y)}{P(Y, y) P(m, Y)} \right)$$

$$= E\left(\log \frac{P(y|m, Y) P(Y)}{P(Y, y)} \right)$$

$$= E\left(\log \frac{P(y|m, Y)}{P(y)} \right) - E\left(\log \frac{P(Y, y)}{P(Y) P(y)} \right)$$

$$H(m|Y) - H(m|Y, y) \leq E\left(\log \frac{P(y|m, Y)}{P(y)} \right).$$

$$(1)$$

The last reduction is true since the term $E\left(\log \frac{P(Y, y)}{P(Y) P(y)} \right)$ is an average mutual information and therefore nonnegative. Now note that by the independence requirements of our original system

$$P(y|x) = P(y|x, m, u, U) = P(y|x, m, u, U, Y).$$

Now since x is a strict function of m, u, and U (by the coding system function) we may omit this in the conditioning variables

$$P(y|m, u, U) = P(y|m, u, U, Y),$$

$$\frac{P(y, m, u, U)}{P(m, u, U)} = \frac{P(y, m, u, U, Y)}{P(m, u, U, Y)}.$$

Since the new state u is independent of the past $P(m, u, U) = P(u) P(m, U)$ and $P(m, u, U, Y) = P(u) P(m, U, Y)$. Substituting and simplifying,

$$P(y, u|m, U) = P(y, u|m, U, Y).$$

Summing on u gives

$$P(y|m, U) = P(y|m, U, Y).$$

Hence:

$$H(y|m, U) = H(y|m, U, Y) \leq H(y|m, Y)$$

$$-E\left(\log P(y|m, U) \right) \leq -E\left(\log P(y|m, Y) \right).$$

Using this in (1),

$$H(m|Y) - H(m|Y, y) \leq E\left(\log \frac{P(y|m, U)}{P(y)} \right).$$

$$(2)$$

We now wish to show that $P(y|m, U) = P(y|X)$. Here X is a random variable specifying the *function* from u to x imposed by the encoding operation for the next input x to the channel. Equivalently, X corresponds to an input letter in the derived channel K'. We have $P(y|x, u) = P(y|x, u, m, U)$. Furthermore, the coding system used implies a functional relation for determining the next input letter x, given m, U and u. Thus $x = f(m, U, u)$. If $f(m, U, u) = f(m', U', u)$ for two particular pairs (m, U)

and (m', U') but for all u, then it follows that $P(y|m, U, u) = P(y|m', U', u)$ for all u and y; since m, U and u lead to the same x as m', U'. and u. From this we obtain $P(y|m, U) = \sum_u P(u)P(y|m, U, u) =$

$\sum_u P(u)P(y|m', U', u) = P(y|m', U')$. In other words, (m, U) pairs which give the same function $f(m, U, u)$ give the same value of $P(y|m, U)$ or, said another way, $P(y|m, U) = P(y|X)$.

Returning now to our inequality (2), we have

$$H(m|Y) - H(m|Y, y) \leq E\left(\log \frac{P(y|X)}{P(y)} \right)$$

$$\leq \max_{P(X)} E\left(\log \frac{P(y|X)}{P(y)} \right)$$

$$H(m|Y) - H(m|Y, y) \leq C.$$

This is the desired inequality on the equivocation. The equivocation cannot be reduced by more than C, the capacity of the derived channel K', for each received letter. In particular in a block code with M equiprobable messages, $R = 1/n \log M$. If $R > C$, then at the end of the block the equivocation must still be at least $nR - nC$, since it starts at nR and can only reduce at most C for each of the n letters.

It is shown in the Appendix that if the equivocation per letter is at least $R - C$ then the probability of error in decoding is bounded by

$$P_e \geq \frac{R - C}{6\left(R + \dfrac{1}{n} \ln \dfrac{R}{R - C} \right)}.$$

Thus the probability of error is bounded away from zero regardless of the block length n, if the code attempts to send at a rate $R > C$. This concludes the proof of the theorem.

As an example of this theorem, consider a channel with two output letters, any number a of input letters and any number h of states. Then the derived channel K' has two output letters and a^h input letters. However, in a channel with just two output letters, only two of the input letters need be used to achieve channel capacity, as shown in (2). Namely, we should use in K' only the two letters with maximum and minimum transition probabilities to one of the output letters. These two may be found as follows. The transition probabilities for a particular letter of K' are averages of the corresponding transitions for a set of letters for K, one for each state. To maximize the transition probability to one of the output letters, it is clear that we should choose in each state the letter with the maximum transition to that output letter. Similarly, to minimize, one chooses in each state the letter with the minimum transition probability to that letter. These two resulting letters in K' are the only ones used, and the corresponding channel gives the desired channel capacity. Formally, then, if the given channel has probabilities $p_{ti}(1)$ in state t for input letter i to output letter 1, and $p_{ti}(2) = 1 - p_{ti}(1)$ to the other output letter 2, we calculate:

$$p_1 = \sum_t g_t \max_i p_{ti}(1),$$

$$p_2 = \sum_t g_t \min_i p_{ti}(1).$$

The channel K' with two input letters having transition probabilities p_1 and $1 - p_1$ and p_2, $1 - p_2$ to the two output letters respectively, has the channel capacity of the original channel K.

Another example, with three output letters, two input letters and three states, is the following. With the states assumed to each have probability $1/3$, the probability matrices for the three states are:

State 1			State 2			State 3		
1	0	0	0	1	0	0	0	1
0	1/2	1/2	1/2	0	1/2	1/2	1/2	0

In this case there are $2^3 = 8$ input letters in the derived channel K'. The matrix of these is as follows:

1/2	1/2	0
0	1/2	1/2
1/2	0	1/2
2/3	1/6	1/6
1/6	2/3	1/6
1/6	1/6	2/3
1/3	1/3	1/3
1/3	1/3	1/3

If there are only three output letters, one need use only three input letters to achieve channel capacity, and in this case it is readily shown that the first three can (and in fact must) be used. Because of the symmetry, these three letters must be used with equal probability and the resulting channel capacity is $\log (3/2)$.

In the original channel, it is easily seen that, if the state information were *not* available, the channel would act like one with the transition matrix

1/3	1/3	1/3
1/3	1/3	1/3

This channel clearly has zero capacity. On the other hand, if the state information were available at the *receiving* point or at *both* the receiving point and the transmitting point, the two input letters can be perfectly distinguished and the channel capacity is $\log 2$.

Appendix

Lemma: Suppose there are M possible events with probabilities $p_i (i = 1, 2, \ldots, M)$. Given that the entropy H satisfies

$$H = -\sum p_i \ln p_i \geq \Delta,$$

then the total probability P_e for all possibilities except the most probable satisfies

$$P_e \geq \frac{\Delta}{6 \ln \left(\dfrac{M \ln M}{\Delta} \right)}.$$

Proof: For a given H, the minimum P_e will occur if all the probabilities except the largest one are equal. This follows from the convexity properties of entropy; equalizing two probabilities increases the entropy. Consequently, we may assume as the worst case a situation where there are $M-1$ possibilities, each with probability q, and one possibility with probability $1-(M-1)q$. Our given condition is then

$$-(M-1)q\ln q-[1-(M-1)q]\ln[1-(M-1)q]\geqslant\Delta.$$

Since $f(x)=-(1-x)\ln(1-x)$ is concave downward with slope 1 at $x=0$, $(f'(x)=1+\ln(1-x); f''(x)=-\dfrac{1}{1-x}\leqslant0$ for $0\leqslant x\leqslant1)$, it follows that $f(x)\leqslant x$ and the second term above is dominated by $(M-1)q$. The given condition then implies

$-(M-1)q\ln q+(M-1)q\geqslant\Delta$

or

$$(M-1)q\ln\frac{e}{q}\geqslant\Delta.$$

Now assume in contradiction to the conclusion of the lemma that

$$P_e=(M-1)q<\frac{\Delta}{6\left(\ln M+\ln\dfrac{\ln M}{\Delta}\right)}.$$

Since $q\ln\dfrac{e}{q}$ is monotone increasing in q, this would imply that

$$(M-1)q\ln\frac{e}{q}<\frac{\Delta}{6\left(\ln M+\ln\dfrac{\ln M}{\Delta}\right)}\log\frac{6e(M-1)\left(\ln M+\ln\dfrac{\ln M}{\Delta}\right)}{\Delta}$$

$$=\frac{\Delta}{6}\left[\frac{\ln\dfrac{M-1}{\Delta}}{\ln M+\ln\dfrac{\ln M}{\Delta}}+\frac{\ln 6e}{\ln M+\ln\dfrac{\ln M}{\Delta}}+\frac{\ln\left(\ln M+\ln\dfrac{\ln M}{\Delta}\right)}{\ln M+\ln\dfrac{\ln M}{\Delta}}\right]$$

$$\leqslant\frac{\Delta}{6}\left[1+3+\frac{1}{e}\right]<\Delta\qquad\qquad(M>1).$$

The first dominating constant is obtained by writing the corresponding term as $(\ln\ln M-\ln\Delta+\ln(M-1)-\ln\ln M)/(\ln\ln M-\ln\Delta+\ln M)$. Since $\ln M\geqslant\Delta$, this is easily seen to be dominated by 1 for $M\geqslant2$. (For $M=1$, the lemma is trivially true since then $\Delta=0$.) The term dominated by 3 is obvious. The last term is of the form $\ln Z/Z$. By differentiation we find this takes its maximum at $Z=e$ and the maximum is $1/e$. Since our conclusion contradicts the hypothesis of the lemma, we have proved the desired result.

The chief application of this lemma is in placing a lower bound on probability of error in coding systems. If it is known that in a certain situation the "equivocation," that is, the conditional entropy of the message given a received signal, exceeds Δ, the lemma leads to a lower bound on the probability of error. Actually, the equivocation is an average over a set of received signals. Thus, the $\Delta=\sum P_i\Delta_i$ where P_i is the probability of receiving signal i and Δ_i is the corresponding entropy of message. If $f(\Delta)$ is the lower bound in the lemma, that is,

$$f(\Delta)=\frac{\Delta}{6\ln\left(\dfrac{M\ln M}{\Delta}\right)},$$

then the lower bound on P_e would be $P_e\geqslant\sum P_if(\Delta_i)$. Now the function $f(\Delta)$ is convex downward (its second derivative is non-negative in the possible range). Consequently $\sum P_if(\Delta_i)\geqslant f(\sum P_i\Delta_i)=f(\Delta)$ and we conclude that *the bound of the lemma remains valid even in this more general case by merely substituting the averaged value of* Δ.

A common situation for use of this result is in signaling with a code at a rate R greater than channel capacity C. In many types of situation this results in an equivocation of $\Delta=n(R-C)$ after n letters have been sent. In this case we may say that the probability of error for the block sent is bounded by (substituting these values in the lemma)

$$P_e\geqslant\frac{R-C}{6\left(R+\dfrac{1}{n}\ln\dfrac{R}{(R-C)}\right)}$$

$$=\frac{R-C}{6\left(R-\ln\left(1-\dfrac{C}{R}\right)\right)}.$$

This then is a lower bound on probability of error for rates greater than capacity under these conditions.

References

1. C. E. Shannon, "Zero Error Capacity of a Noisy Channel," *IRE Transactions on Information Theory, 1956 Symposium,* **IT-2,** No. 3.
2. C. E. Shannon, "Geometrische Deutung einiger Ergebnisse bei der Berechnung der Kanalkapazität," *Nachrichtentechnische Zeitschrift,* **10,** Heft 1, January 1957.
3. C. E. Shannon, "Certain Results in Coding Theory for Noisy Channels," *Information and Control,* **1,** No. 1, September 1957.

Revised manuscript received September 15, 1958

Probability of Error for Optimal Codes in a Gaussian Channel

By CLAUDE E. SHANNON

(Manuscript received October 17, 1958)

A study is made of coding and decoding systems for a continuous channel with an additive gaussian noise and subject to an average power limitation at the transmitter. Upper and lower bounds are found for the error probability in decoding with optimal codes and decoding systems. These bounds are close together for signaling rates near channel capacity and also for signaling rates near zero, but diverge between. Curves exhibiting these bounds are given.

I. INTRODUCTION

Consider a communication channel of the following type: Once each second a real number may be chosen at the transmitting point. This number is transmitted to the receiving point but is perturbed by an additive gaussian noise, so that the ith real number, s_i, is received as $s_i + x_i$. The x_i are assumed independent gaussian random variables all with the same variance N.

A *code word* of length n for such a channel is a sequence of n real numbers $(s_1, s_2, \cdots, s_n)$. This may be thought of geometrically as a point in n-dimensional Euclidean space. The effect of noise is then to move this point to a nearby point according to a spherical gaussian distribution.

A *block code* of length n with M words is a mapping of the integers 1, 2, $\cdots$, M into a set of M code words $w_1, w_2, \cdots, w_M$ (not necessarily all distinct). Thus, geometrically, a block code consists of a collection of M (or less) points with associated integers. It may be thought of as a way of transmitting an integer from 1 to M to the receiving point (by sending the corresponding code word). A *decoding system* for such a code is a partitioning of the n-dimensional space into M subsets corresponding to the integers from 1 to M. This is a way of deciding, at the receiving point, on the transmitted integer. If the received signal is in subset S_i, the transmitted message is taken to be integer i.

We shall assume throughout that all integers from 1 to M occur as messages with equal probability $1/M$. There is, then, for a given code and decoding system, a definite probability of error for transmitting a message. This is given by

$$P_e = \frac{1}{M} \sum_{i=1}^{M} P_{ei},$$

where P_{ei} is the probability, if code word w_i is sent, that it will be decoded as an integer other than i. P_{ei} is, of course, the total probability under the gaussian distribution, centered on w_i in the region complementary to S_i.

An *optimal decoding system* for a code is one which minimizes the probability of error for the code. Since the gaussian density is monotone decreasing with distance, an optimal decoding system for a given code is one which decodes any received signal as the integer corresponding to the geometrically nearest code word. If there are several code words at the same minimal distance, any of these may be used without affecting the probability of error. A decoding system of this sort is called *minimum distance* decoding or *maximum likelihood* decoding. It results in a partitioning of the n-dimensional space into n-dimensional polyhedra, or polytopes, around the different signal points, each polyhedron bounded by a finite number (not more than $M - 1$) of $(n - 1)$-dimensional hyperplanes.

We are interested in the problem of finding good codes, that is, placing M points in such a way as to minimize the probability of error P_e. If there were no conditions on the code words, it is evident that the probability of error could be made as small as desired for any M, n and N by placing the code words at sufficiently widely separated points in the n space. In normal applications, however, there will be limitations on the choice of code words that prevent this type of solution. An interesting case that has been considered in the past is that of placing some kind of *average power limitation* on the code words; the distance of the points from the origin should not be too great. We may define three different possible limitations of this sort:

i. All code words are required to have *exactly the same power P* or the same distance from the origin. Thus, we are required to choose for code words points lying on the surface of a sphere of radius $\sqrt{nP}$.

ii. All code words have power *P or less*. Here all code words are required to lie interior to or on the surface of a sphere of radius $\sqrt{nP}$.

iii. The *average power* of all code words is *P* or less. Here, individual code words may have a greater squared distance than nP but the average of the set of squared distances cannot exceed nP.

These three cases lead to quite similar results, as we shall see. The first condition is simpler and leads to somewhat sharper conclusions — we shall first analyze this case and use these results for the other two conditions. *Therefore, until the contrary is stated, we assume all code words to lie on the sphere of radius* $\sqrt{nP}$.

Our first problem is to estimate, as well as possible, the probability of error $P_e(M, n, \sqrt{P/N})$ for the best code of length n containing M words each of power P and perturbed by noise of variance N. This minimal or *optimal probability* of error we denote by $P_{e\,\mathrm{opt}}(M, n, \sqrt{P/N})$. It is clear that, for fixed M, n, $P_{e\,\mathrm{opt}}$ will be a function only of the quotient $A = \sqrt{P/N}$ by change of scale in the geometrical picture. We shall obtain upper and lower bounds on $P_{e\,\mathrm{opt}}$ of several different types. Over an important range of values these bounds are reasonably close together, giving good estimates of $P_{e\,\mathrm{opt}}$. Some calculated values and curves are given and the bounds are used to develop other bounds for the second and third type conditions on the code words.

The geometrical approach we use is akin to that previously used by the author[1] but carried here to a numerical conclusion. The problem is also close to that studied by Rice,[2] who obtained an estimate similar to but not as sharp as one of our upper bounds. The work here is also analogous to bounds given by Elias[3] for the binary symmetric and binary erasure channels, and related to bounds for the general discrete memoryless channel given by the author.[4]

In a general way, our bounds, both upper and lower, vary exponentially with n for a fixed signaling rate, R, and fixed P/N. In fact, they all can be put [letting $R = (1/n) \log M$, so that R is the transmitting rate for the code] in the form

$$e^{-E(R)n + o(n)}, \tag{1}$$

where $E(R)$ is a suitable function of R (and of P/N, which we think of as a fixed parameter). [In (1), $o(n)$ is a term of order less than n; as $n \to \infty$ it becomes small relative to $E(R)n$.]

Thus, for large n, the logarithm of the bound increases linearly with n or, more precisely, the ratio of this logarithm to n approaches a constant $E(R)$. This quantity $E(R)$ gives a crude measure of how rapidly the probability of error approaches zero. We will call this type of quantity a *reliability*. More precisely, we may define the reliability for a channel as follows:

$$E(R) = \lim_{n \to \infty} \sup - \frac{1}{n} \log P_{e \, \text{opt}}(R, n), \qquad (2)$$

where $P_{e \, \text{opt}}(R, n)$ is the optimal probability of error for codes of rate R and length n. We will find that our bounds determine $E(R)$ *exactly* over an important range of rates, from a certain critical rate R_c up to channel capacity. Between zero and R_c, E is not exactly determined by our bounds, but lies within a not too wide range.

In connection with the reliability E, it may be noted that, in (1) above, knowledge of $E(R)$ and n does not closely determine the probability of error, even when n is large; the term $o(n)$ can cause a large and, in fact, increasing multiplier. On the other hand, given a desired probability of error and $E(R)$, the necessary value of the code length n *will* be sharply determined when n is large; in fact, n will be asymptotic to $-(1/E) \log P_e$. This inverse problem is perhaps the more natural one in applications: given a required level of probability of error, how long must the code be?

The type of channel we are studying here is, of course, closely related to a band-limited channel (W cycles per second wide) perturbed by white gaussian noise. In a sense, such a band-limited channel can be thought of as having $2W$ coordinates per second, each independently perturbed by a gaussian variable. However, such an identification must be treated with care, since to control these degrees of freedom physically and stay strictly within the bandwidth would require an infinite delay.

It is possible to stay very closely within a bandwidth W with a large but finite delay T, for example, by using $(\sin x)/x$ pulses with one tail deleted T from the maximum point. This deletion causes a spill-over outside the band of not more than the energy of the deleted part, an amount less than $1/T$ for the unit $(\sin x)/x$ case. By making T large, we can approach the situation of staying within the allotted bandwidth and also, for example, approach zero probability of error at signaling rates close to channel capacity.

However, for the problems we are studying here, delay as related to probability of error is of fundamental importance and, in applications of our results to such band-limited channels, the additional delay involved in staying closely within the allotted channel must be remembered. This is the reason for defining the channel as we have above.

II. SUMMARY

In this section we summarize briefly the main results obtained in the paper, both for easy reference and for readers who may be interested in the results without wishing to work through the detailed analysis. It might be said that the algebra involved is in several places unusually tedious.

We use the following notations:

P = signal power (each code word is on the surface of a sphere of radius $\sqrt{nP}$);

N = noise power (variance N in each dimension);

$A = \sqrt{P/N}$ = signal-to-noise "amplitude" ratio;

n = number of dimensions or block length of code;

M = number of code words;

$R = (1/n) \log M$ = signaling rate for a code (natural units);

$C = \frac{1}{2} \log (P + N)/N = \frac{1}{2} \log (A^2 + 1)$ = channel capacity (per degree of freedom);

θ = variable for half-angle of cones appearing in the geometrical problem which follows;

$\Omega(\theta)$ = solid angle in n space of a cone of half-angle θ, or area of unit n sphere cut out by the cone;

$\theta_0 = \cot^{-1}A$ = cone angle relating to channel capacity;

θ_1 = cone angle such that the solid angle $\Omega(\theta_1)$ of this cone is $(1/M)\Omega(\pi)$, [the solid angle of a sphere is $\Omega(\pi)$]; thus, θ_1 is a cone angle related to the rate R;

$G = G(\theta) = \frac{1}{2}(A \cos \theta + \sqrt{A^2 \cos^2 \theta + 4})$, a quantity which appears often in the formulas;

θ_c = the solution of $2 \cos \theta_c - AG(\theta_c) \sin^2 \theta_c = 0$ (this critical angle is important in that the nature of the bounds change according as $\theta_1 > \theta_c$ or $\theta_1 < \theta_c$);

$Q(\theta) = Q(\theta, A, n)$ = probability of a point X in n space, at distance $A\sqrt{n}$ from the origin, being moved outside a circular cone of half-angle θ with vertex at the origin O and axis OX (the perturbation is assumed spherical gaussian with unit variance in all dimensions);

$E_L(\theta) = A^2/2 - \frac{1}{2}AG \cos \theta - \log (G \sin \theta)$, an exponent appearing in our bounds;

$P_{e \, opt}(n, R, A)$ = Probability of error for the best code of length n, signal-to-noise ratio A and rate R;

$\Phi(X)$ = normal distribution with zero mean and unit variance.

The results of the paper will now be summarized. $P_{e\,\text{opt}}$ can be bounded as follows:

$$Q(\theta_1) \leqq P_{e\,\text{opt}} \leqq Q(\theta_1) - \int_0^{\theta_1} \frac{\Omega(\theta)}{\Omega(\theta_1)}\, dQ(\theta). \qquad (3)$$

[Here $dQ(\theta)$ is negative, so the right additional term is positive.] These bounds can be written in terms of rather complex integrals. To obtain more insight into their behavior, we obtain, in the first place, asymptotic expressions for these bounds when n is large and, in the second place, cruder bounds which, however, are expressed in terms of elementary functions without integrals.

The asymptotic lower bound is (asymptotically correct as $n \to \infty$)

$$Q(\theta_1) \sim \frac{1}{\sqrt{n\pi}\, G\, \sqrt{1 + G^2}\, \sin\theta_1\, (\cos\theta_1 - AG\sin^2\theta_1)}\, e^{-E_L(\theta_1)n}$$

$$= \frac{\alpha(\theta_1)}{\sqrt{n}}\, e^{-E_L(\theta_1)n} \qquad\qquad (\theta_1 > \theta_0). \qquad (4)$$

The asymptotic upper bound is

$$Q(\theta_1) - \int_0^{\theta_1} \frac{\Omega(\theta)}{\Omega(\theta_1)}\, dQ(\theta) \sim \frac{\alpha(\theta_1)}{\sqrt{n}}\, e^{-E_L(\theta_1)n} \left(1 - \frac{\cos\theta_1 - AG\sin^2\theta_1}{2\cos\theta_1 - AG\sin^2\theta_1} \right). \quad (5)$$

This formula is valid for $\theta_0 < \theta_1 < \theta_c$. In this range the upper and lower asymptotic bounds differ only by the factor in parentheses independent of n. Thus, asymptotically, the probability of error is determined by these relations to within a multiplying factor depending on the rate. For rates near channel capacity (θ_1 near θ_0) the factor is just a little over unity; the bounds are close together. For lower rates near R_c (corresponding to θ_c), the factor becomes large. For $\theta_1 > \theta_c$ the upper bound asymptote is

$$\frac{1}{\cos\theta_c\, \sin^3\theta_c\, G(\theta_c)\, \sqrt{\pi E''(\theta_c)[1 + G(\theta_c)]^2}}\, e^{-n[E_L(\theta_c) - R]}. \qquad (6)$$

In addition to the asymptotic bound, we also obtain firm bounds, valid for all n, but poorer than the asymptotic bounds when n is large. The firm lower bound is

$$P_e \geq \frac{1}{6}\, \frac{\sqrt{n-1}\, e^{3/2}}{n(A+1)^3 e^{(A+1)^2/2}}\, e^{-E_L(\theta_1)n}. \qquad (7)$$

It may be seen that this is equal to the asymptotic bound multiplied by a factor essentially independent of n. The firm upper bound {valid if the maximum of $G^n (\sin \theta)^{2n-3} \exp [- (n/2)(A^2 - AG \cos \theta)]$ in the range 0 to θ_1 occurs at θ_1} is

$$P_{e \text{ opt}} \leqq \theta_1 \sqrt{2n}\, e^{3/2} G^n(\theta_1) \sin {\theta_1}^{n-2} \exp \left[\frac{n}{2} \left(-A^2 + AG \cos \theta_1 \right) \right]$$
$$\cdot \left\{ 1 + \frac{1}{n \theta_1 \min [A, AG(\theta_1) \sin \theta_1 - \cot \theta_1]} \right\}. \tag{8}$$

For rates near channel capacity, the upper and lower asymptotic bounds are both approximately the same, giving, where n is large and $C - R$ small (but positive):

$$P_{e \text{ opt}} \doteq \Phi \left[\sqrt{n}\, \sqrt{\frac{2P(P + N)}{N(P + 2N)}}\, (R - C) \right], \tag{9}$$

where Φ is the normal distribution with unit variance.

To relate the angle θ_1 in the above formulas to the rate R, inequalities are found:

$$\frac{\Gamma \left(\frac{n}{2} + 1 \right) (\sin \theta_1)^{n-1}}{n \Gamma \left(\frac{n+1}{2} \right) \pi^{1/2} \cos \theta_1} \left(1 - \frac{1}{n} \tan^2 \theta_1 \right) \leqq e^{-nR}$$

$$\leqq \frac{\Gamma \left(\frac{n}{2} + 1 \right) (\sin \theta_1)^{n-1}}{n \Gamma \left(\frac{(n+1)}{2} \right) \pi^{1/2} \cos \theta_1} . \tag{10}$$

Asymptotically, it follows that:

$$e^{-nR} \sim \frac{\sin^n \theta_1}{\sqrt{2\pi n}\, \sin \theta_1 \cos \theta_1} . \tag{11}$$

For low rates (particularly $R < R_c$), the above bounds diverge and give less information. Two different arguments lead to other bounds useful at low rates. The *low rate upper bound* is:

$$P_{e \text{ opt}} \leqq \frac{1}{\lambda A \sqrt{\pi n}}\, e^{n[R - (\lambda^2 A^2)/4]}, \tag{12}$$

where λ satisfies $R = [1 - (1/n)] \log (\sin 2 \sin^{-1} \lambda/\sqrt{2})$. Note that as $R \to 0$, $\lambda \to 1$ and the upper bound is approximately

$$\frac{1}{A\sqrt{\pi n}} e^{-nA^2/4}.$$

The *low rate lower bound* may be written

$$P_{e\,\text{opt}} \geq \frac{1}{2}\,\Phi\left[-A\left(\frac{2M}{2M-1}\,\frac{n}{2}\right)^{1/2}\right]. \tag{13}$$

For M large, this bound is close to $\frac{1}{2}\Phi(-A\sqrt{n/2})$ and, if n is large, this is asymptotic to $1/(A\sqrt{\pi n})\,e^{-nA^2/4}$. Thus, for rates close to zero and large n we again have a situation where the bounds are close together and give a sharp evaluation of $P_{e\,\text{opt}}$.

With codes of rate $R \geq C + \epsilon$, where ϵ is fixed and positive, $P_{e\,\text{opt}}$ approaches unity as the code length n increases.

III. THE LOWER BOUND BY THE "SPHERE-PACKING" ARGUMENT

Suppose we have a code with M points each at distance $\sqrt{nP}$ from the origin in n space. Since any two words are at equal distance from the origin, the $n-1$ hyperplane which bisects the connecting line passes through the origin. Thus, all of the hyperplanes which determine the polyhedra surrounding these points (for the optimal decoding system) pass through the origin. These polyhedra, therefore, are pyramids with apexes at the origin. The probability of error for the code is

$$\frac{1}{M}\sum_{i=1}^{M} P_{ei},$$

where P_{ei} is the probability, if code word i is used, that it will be carried by the noise outside the pyramid around the ith word. The probability of being *correct* is

$$1 - \frac{1}{M}\sum_{i=1}^{M} P_{ei} = \frac{1}{M}\sum_{i=1}^{M}(1 - P_{ei}) \, ;$$

that is, the average probability of a code word being moved to a point *within* its own pyramid.

Let the ith pyramid have a solid angle Ω_i (that is, Ω_i is the area cut out by the pyramid on the unit n-dimensional spherical surface). Consider, for comparison, a right circular n-dimensional cone with the same solid angle Ω_i and having a code word on its axis at distance $\sqrt{nP}$. We assert that *the probability of this comparison point being moved to within its cone is greater than that of w_i being moved to within its pyramid.* This is because of the monotone decreasing probability density with distance from the code word. The pyramid can be deformed into the cone by moving small conical elements from far distances to nearer distances, this movement continually increasing probability. This is suggested for a three-dimensional case in Fig. 1. Moving small conical elements from outside the cone to inside it increases probability, since the probability density is greater inside the cone than outside. Formally, this follows by integrating the probability density over the region R_1 in the cone but not in the pyramid, and in the region R_2 in the pyramid but not in the cone. The first is greater than the solid angle Ω of R_1 times the density at the edge of the cone. The value for the pyramid is less than the same quantity.

We have, then, a bound on the probability of error P_e for a given code:

$$P_e \geqq \frac{1}{M} \sum_{i=1}^{M} Q^*(\Omega_i),\qquad(14)$$

where Ω_i is the solid angle for the ith pyramid, and $Q^*(\Omega)$ is the probability of a point being carried outside a surrounding cone of solid angle Ω. It is also true that

$$\sum_{i=1}^{M} \Omega_i = \Omega_0,$$

the solid angle of an n sphere, since the original pyramids corresponded to a partitioning of the sphere. Now, using again the property that the density decreases with distance, it follows that $Q^*(\Omega)$ is a convex function of Ω. Then we may further simplify this bound by replacing each Ω_i by

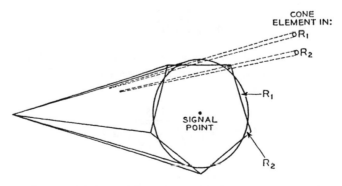

Fig. 1 — Pyramid deformed into cone by moving small conical elements from far to nearer distances.

the average Ω_0/M. In fact,

$$\frac{1}{M} \sum_{i=1}^{M} Q^*(\Omega_i) \geqq Q^*\left(\frac{\Omega_0}{M}\right),$$

and hence

$$P_e \geqq Q^*\left(\frac{\Omega_0}{M}\right).$$

It is more convenient to work in terms of the half-cone angle θ rather than solid angles Ω. We define $Q(\theta)$ to be the probability of being carried outside a cone of half-angle θ. Then, if θ_1 corresponds to the cone of solid angle Ω_0/M, the bound above may be written

$$P_e \geqq Q(\theta_1). \tag{15}$$

This is our fundamental lower bound for P_e. It still needs translation into terms of P, N, M and n, and estimation in terms of simple functions.

It may be noted that this bound is exactly the probability of error that would occur if it were possible to subdivide the space into M congruent cones, one for each code word, and place the code words on the axes of these cones. It is, of course, very plausible intuitively that any actual code would have a higher probability of error than would that with such a conical partitioning. Such a partitioning clearly is possible only for $n = 1$ or 2, if $M > 2$.

The lower bound $Q(\theta_1)$ can be evaluated in terms of a distribution familiar to statisticians as the noncentral t-distribution.[5] The noncentral t may be thought of as the probability that the ratio of a random variable $(z + \delta)$ to the root mean square of f other random variables

$$\sqrt{\frac{1}{f} \sum x_i^2}$$

does not exceed t, where all variates x_i and z are gaussian and independent with mean zero and unit variance and δ is a constant. Thus, denoting it by $P(f, \delta, t)$, we have

$$P(f, \delta, t) = \Pr\left\{ \frac{z + \delta}{\sqrt{\dfrac{1}{f} \sum_{1}^{f} x_i^2}} \leqq t \right\}. \tag{16}$$

In terms of our geometrical picture, this amounts to a spherical gaussian distribution with unit variance about a point δ from the origin in $f + 1$ space. The probability $P(f, \delta, t)$ is the probability of being outside a cone from the origin having the line segment to the center of the distribution as axis. The cotangent of the half-cone angle θ is $t/\sqrt{f}$. Thus the probability $Q(\theta)$ is seen to be given by

$$Q(\theta) = P\left(n - 1, \sqrt{\frac{nP}{N}}, \sqrt{n - 1}\cot\theta\right). \tag{17}$$

The noncentral t-distribution does not appear to have been very extensively tabled. Johnson and Welch[5] give some tables, but they are aimed at other types of application and are inconvenient for the purpose at hand. Further, they do not go to large values of n. We therefore will estimate this lower bound by developing an asymptotic formula for the cumulative distribution $Q(\theta)$ and also the density distribution $dQ/d\theta$. First, however, we will find an *upper* bound on $P_{e\,\mathrm{opt}}$ in terms of the same distribution $Q(\theta)$.

IV. UPPER BOUND BY A RANDOM CODE METHOD

The upper bound for $P_{e\,\mathrm{opt}}$ will be found by using an argument based on random codes. Consider the ensemble of codes obtained by placing M points randomly on the surface of a sphere of radius $\sqrt{nP}$. More precisely, each point is placed independently of all others with probability measure proportional to surface area or, equivalently, to solid angle. Each of the codes in the ensemble is to be decoded by the minimum distance process. We wish to compute the *average probability of error* for this *ensemble of codes*.

Because of the symmetry of the code points, the probability of error averaged over the ensemble will be equal to M times the average probability of error due to any particular code point, for example, code point 1. This may be computed as follows. The probability of message number 1 being transmitted is $1/M$. The differential probability that it will be displaced by the noise into the region between a cone of half-angle θ and one of half-angle $\theta + d\theta$ (these cones having vertex at the origin and axis out to code word 1) is $-dQ(\theta)$. [Recall that $Q(\theta)$ was defined as the probability that noise would carry a point outside the cone of angle θ with axis through the signal point.] Now consider the cone of half-angle θ surrounding such a *received point* (not the cone about the message point just described). If this cone is empty of signal points, the received word will be decoded correctly as message 1. If it is not empty, other points will be nearer and the received signal will be incorrectly decoded. (The probability of two or more points at exactly the same distance is readily seen to be zero and may be ignored.)

The probability in the ensemble of codes of the cone of half-angle θ being empty is easily calculated. The probability that any particular code word, say code word 2 or code word 3, etc. is in the cone is given by $\Omega(\theta)/\Omega(\pi)$, the ratio of the solid angle in the cone to the total solid angle. The probability a particular word is *not* in the cone is $1 - \Omega(\theta)/\Omega(\pi)$. The probability that all $M - 1$ other words are not in the cone is $[1 - \Omega(\theta)/\Omega(\pi)]^{M-1}$ since these are, in the ensemble of codes, placed independently. The probability of error, then, contributed by situations where the point 1 is displaced by an angle from θ to $\theta + d\theta$ is given by $-(1/M)\{1 - [1 - \Omega(\theta)/\Omega(\pi)]^{M-1}\}dQ(\theta)$. The total average probability of error for all code words and all noise displacements is then given by

$$P_{er} = - \int_{\theta=0}^{\pi} \left\{ 1 - \left[1 - \frac{\Omega(\theta)}{\Omega(\pi)} \right]^{M-1} \right\} dQ(\theta). \tag{18}$$

This is an exact formula for the average probability of error P_{er} for our random ensemble of codes. Since this is an average of P_e for particular codes, there must exist particular codes in the ensemble with at least this good a probability of error, and certainly then $P_{e\,opt} \leq P_{er}$.

We may weaken this bound slightly but obtain a simpler formula for calculation as follows. Note first that $\{1 - [\Omega(\theta)/\Omega(\pi)]^{M-1}\} \leq 1$ and also, using the well-known inequality $(1 - x)^n \geq 1 - nx$, we have $\{1 - [1 - \Omega(\theta)/\Omega(\pi)]^{M-1}\} \leq (M - 1)[\Omega(\theta)/\Omega(\pi)] \leq M[\Omega(\theta)/\Omega(\pi)]$. Now, break the integral into two parts, $0 \leq \theta \leq \theta_1$ and $\theta_1 \leq \theta \leq \pi$. In the first range, use the inequality just given and, in the second range, bound the expression in braces by 1. Thus,

$$P_{er} \leq - \int_0^{\theta_1} M \left[\frac{\Omega(\theta)}{\Omega(\pi)} \right] dQ(\theta) - \int_{\theta_1}^{\pi} dQ(\theta),$$
$$P_{er} \leq - \frac{M}{\Omega(\pi)} \int_0^{\theta_1} \Omega(\theta) dQ(\theta) + Q(\theta_1). \tag{19}$$

It is convenient to choose for θ_1 the same value as appeared in the lower bound; that is, the θ_1 such that $\Omega(\theta_1)/\Omega(\pi) = 1/M$ — in other words, the θ_1 for which one expects one point within the θ_1 cone. The second term in (19) is then the same as the lower bound on $P_{e\,opt}$ obtained previously. In fact, collecting these results, we have

$$Q(\theta_1) \leq P_{e\,opt} \leq Q(\theta_1) - \frac{M}{\Omega(\pi)} \int_0^{\theta_1} \Omega(\theta) dQ(\theta), \tag{20}$$

where $M\Omega(\theta_1) = \Omega(\pi)$. *These are our fundamental lower and upper bounds on $P_{e\,opt}$.*

We now wish to evaluate and estimate $\Omega(\theta)$ and $Q(\theta)$.

V. FORMULAS FOR RATE R AS A FUNCTION OF THE CONE ANGLE θ

Our bounds on probability of error involve the code angle θ_1 such that the solid angle of the cone is $1/M = e^{-nR}$ times the full solid angle of a sphere. To relate these quantities more explicitly we calculate the solid angle of a cone in n dimensions with half-angle θ. In Fig. 2 this means calculating the $(n-1)$-dimensional area of the cap cut out by the cone on the unit sphere. This is obtained by summing the contributions due to ring-shaped elements of area (spherical surfaces in $n-1$ dimensions

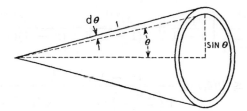

Fig. 2 — Cap cut out by the cone on the unit sphere.

of radius $\sin \theta$ and of incremental width $d\theta$). Thus, the total area of the cap is given by

$$\Omega(\theta_1) = \frac{(n-1)\pi^{(n-1)/2}}{\Gamma\left(\dfrac{n+1}{2}\right)} \int_0^{\theta_1} (\sin \theta)^{n-2} d\theta. \qquad (21)$$

Here we used the formula for the surface $S_n(r)$ of a sphere of radius r in n dimensions, $S_n(r) = n\pi^{n/2}r^{n-1}/\Gamma(n/2 + 1)$.

To obtain simple inequalities and asymptotic expressions for $\Omega(\theta_1)$, make the change of variable in the integral $x = \sin \theta$, $d\theta = (1 - x^2)^{-1/2}dx$. Let $x_1 = \sin \theta_1$ and assume $\theta_1 < \pi/2$, so that $x_1 < 1$. Using the mean value theorem we obtain

$$(1 - x^2)^{-1/2} = (1 - x_1^2)^{-1/2} + \frac{\alpha}{(1 - \alpha^2)^{3/2}} (x - x_1), \qquad (22)$$

where $0 \leq \alpha \leq x_1$. The term $\alpha(1 - \alpha^2)^{-3/2}$ must lie in the range from 0 to $x_1(1 - x_1^2)^{-3/2}$ since this is a monotone increasing function. Hence we have the inequalities

$$(1 - x_1^2)^{-1/2} + \frac{(x - x_1)x_1}{(1 - x_1^2)^{3/2}} \leq (1 - x^2)^{-1/2} \leq (1 - x_1^2)^{-1/2} \qquad (23)$$

$$0 \leq x \leq x_1.$$

Note that $x - x_1$ is negative, so the correction term on the left is of the right sign. If we use these in the integral for $\Omega(\theta_1)$ we obtain

$$
\frac{(n-1)\pi^{(n-1)/2}}{\Gamma\left(\dfrac{n+1}{2}\right)} \int_0^{x_1} x^{n-2}\left[(1-x_1^2)^{-1/2} + \frac{(x-x_1)x_1}{(1-x_1^2)^{3/2}}\right] dx
$$

$$
\leq \Omega(\theta_1) \leq \frac{(n-1)\pi^{(n-1)/2}}{\Gamma\left(\dfrac{n+1}{2}\right)} \int_0^{x_1} x^{n-2}\frac{dx}{\sqrt{1-x_1^2}},
$$

(24)

$$
\frac{(n-1)\pi^{(n-1)/2}}{\Gamma\left(\dfrac{n+1}{2}\right)\sqrt{1-x_1^2}}\left[\frac{x_1^{n-1}}{n-1} + \frac{x_1^{n+1}}{n(1-x_1^2)} - \frac{x_1^{n+1}}{(n-1)(1-x_1^2)}\right]
$$

$$
\leq \Omega(\theta_1) \leq \frac{(n-1)\pi^{(n-1)/2}x_1^{n-1}}{\Gamma\left(\dfrac{n+1}{2}\right)(n-1)\sqrt{1-x_1^2}},
$$

(25)

$$
\frac{\pi^{(n-1)/2}(\sin\theta_1)^{n-1}}{\Gamma\left(\dfrac{n+1}{2}\right)\cos\theta_1}\left(1-\frac{1}{n}\tan^2\theta_1\right)
$$

$$
\leq \Omega(\theta_1) \leq \frac{\pi^{(n-1)/2}(\sin\theta_1)^{n-1}}{\Gamma\left(\dfrac{n+1}{2}\right)\cos\theta_1}.
$$

(26)

Therefore, as $n \to \infty$, $\Omega(\theta_1)$ is asymptotic to the expression on the right. The surface of the unit n sphere is $n\pi^{n/2}/\Gamma(n/2+1)$, hence,

$$
\frac{\Gamma\left(\dfrac{n}{2}+1\right)(\sin\theta_1)^{n-1}}{n\Gamma\left(\dfrac{n+1}{2}\right)\pi^{1/2}\cos\theta_1}\left(1-\frac{1}{n}\tan^2\theta_1\right) \leq e^{-nR}
$$

(27)

$$
= \frac{\Omega(\theta_1)}{\Omega(\pi)} \leq \frac{\Gamma\left(\dfrac{n}{2}+1\right)(\sin\theta_1)^{n-1}}{n\Gamma\left(\dfrac{n+1}{2}\right)\pi^{1/2}\cos\theta_1}.
$$

Replacing the gamma functions by their asymptotic expressions, we obtain

$$
e^{-nR} = \frac{\sin^n\theta_1}{\sqrt{2\pi n}\,\sin\theta_1\cos\theta_1}\left[1+O\!\left(\frac{1}{n}\right)\right].
$$

(28)

Thus $e^{-nR} \sim \sin^n \theta_1 / \sqrt{2\pi n} \sin \theta_1 \cos \theta_1$ and $e^{-R} \sim \sin \theta_1$. The somewhat sharper expression for e^{-nR} must be used when attempting asymptotic evaluations of P_e, since P_e is changed by a factor when θ_1 is changed by, for example, k/n. However, when only the reliability E is of interest, the simpler $R \sim -\log \sin \theta_1$ may be used.

VI. ASYMPTOTIC FORMULAS FOR $Q(\theta)$ AND $Q'(\theta)$

In Fig. 3, O is the origin, S is a signal point and the plane of the figure is a plane section in the n-dimensional space. The lines OA and OB represent a (circular) cone of angle θ about OS (that is, the intersection of this cone with the plane of the drawing.) The lines OA' and OB' correspond to a slightly larger cone of angle $\theta + d\theta$. We wish to estimate the probability $-dQ_n(\theta)$ of the signal point S being carried by noise into the region between these cones. From this, we will further calculate the probability $Q_n(\theta)$ of S being carried outside the θ cone. What is desired in both cases is an asymptotic estimate — a simple formula whose

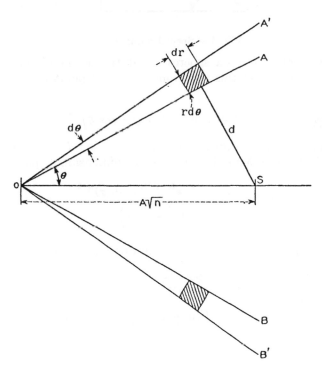

Fig. 3 — Plane of cone of half-angle θ.

ratio to the true value approaches 1 as n, the number of dimensions, increases.

The noise perturbs all coordinates normally and independently with variance 1. It produces a spherical gaussian distribution in the n-dimensional space. The probability density of its moving the signal point a distance d is given by

$$\frac{1}{(2\pi)^{n/2}}\, e^{-d^2/2}\, dV\,, \tag{29}$$

where dV is the element of volume. In Fig. 4 we wish to first calculate the probability density for the crosshatched ring-shaped region between

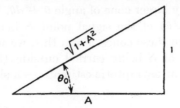

Fig. 4 — Special value θ_0.

the two cones and between spheres about the origin of radius r and $r + dr$. The distance of this ring from the signal point is given by the cosine law as

$$d = (r^2 + A^2 n - 2rA\sqrt{n}\,\cos\theta)^{1/2}. \tag{30}$$

The differential volume of the ring-shaped region is $r\, dr\, d\theta$ times the surface of a sphere of radius $r\sin\theta$ in $(n-1)$-dimensional space; that is

$$r\, dr\, d\theta\, \frac{(n-1)\pi^{(n-1)/2}(r\sin\theta)^{n-2}}{\Gamma\left(\dfrac{n+1}{2}\right)}\,. \tag{31}$$

Hence, the differential probability for the ring-shaped region is

$$\frac{1}{(\sqrt{2\pi})^n}\exp\left[\frac{-(r^2 + A^2 n - 2rA\sqrt{n}\,\cos\theta)}{2}\right]$$
$$\cdot\left[\frac{(n-1)\pi^{(n-1)/2}(r\sin\theta)^{n-2}}{\Gamma\left(\dfrac{n+1}{2}\right)}\right] r\, dr\, d\theta \tag{32}$$

The differential probability $-dQ$ of being carried between the two cones is the integral of this expression from zero to infinity on dr:

$$-dQ = \frac{1}{2^{n/2}} \frac{(n-1)\,d\theta}{\sqrt{\pi}\,\Gamma\left(\dfrac{n+1}{2}\right)}$$

$$\cdot \int_0^\infty \exp\left[\frac{-(r^2 + A^2 n - 2rA\sqrt{n}\cos\theta)}{2}\right](r\sin\theta)^{n-2}r\,dr. \qquad (33)$$

In the exponent we can think of $A^2 n$ as $A^2 n(\sin^2\theta + \cos^2\theta)$. The $\cos^2$ part then combines with the other terms to give a perfect square

$$(r - A\sqrt{n}\cos\theta)^2$$

and the $\sin^2$ term can be taken outside the integral. Thus

$$-dQ = \frac{(n-1)\exp\left[-\dfrac{A^2 n \sin^2\theta}{2}\right](\sin\theta)^{n-2}\,d\theta}{2^{n/2}\sqrt{\pi}\,\Gamma\left(\dfrac{n+1}{2}\right)}$$

$$\cdot \int_0^\infty \exp\left[\frac{-(r - A\sqrt{n}\cos\theta)^2}{2}\right]r^{n-1}\,dr. \qquad (34)$$

We can now direct our attention to estimating the integral, which we call K. The integral can be expressed exactly as a finite, but complicated, sum involving normal distribution functions by a process of continued integration by parts. We are, however, interested in a simple formula giving the asymptotic behavior of the integral as n becomes infinite. This problem was essentially solved by David and Kruskal,[6] who prove the following asymptotic formula as a lemma:

$$\int_0^\infty z^\nu \exp\left(-\tfrac{1}{2}z^2 + z\sqrt{\nu+1}\,w\right)dz \sim \sqrt{2\pi}\left(\frac{\bar{z}}{e}\right)^\nu \exp\left(\tfrac{1}{2}\bar{z}^2\right)T, \quad (35)$$

as $\nu \to \infty$, w is fixed, $T = [1 + \tfrac{1}{4}(\sqrt{w^2 + 4} - w)^2]^{-1/2}$ and

$$\bar{z} = \tfrac{1}{2}\sqrt{\nu+1}\,w + \sqrt{\tfrac{1}{4}(\nu+1)w^2 + \nu}.$$

This is proved by showing that the main contribution to the integral is essentially in the neighborhood of the point $\bar{z}$ where the integral is a maximum. Near this point, when ν is large, the function behaves about as a normal distribution.

The integral K in (34) that we wish to evaluate is, except for a multiplying factor, of the form appearing in the lemma, with

$$z = r, \qquad w = A\cos\theta, \qquad \nu = n - 1.$$

The integral then becomes

$$K = \exp\left(-\frac{A^2 n \cos^2 \theta}{2}\right) \int_0^\infty z^{n-1} \exp -\left(\frac{z^2}{2} + zA\sqrt{n}\cos\theta\right) dz$$

$$\sim \exp\left(-\frac{A^2 n \cos^2 \theta}{2}\right) \sqrt{2\pi} \left(\frac{\bar{z}}{e}\right)^{n-1} T \exp\left(\frac{\bar{z}^2}{2}\right). \tag{36}$$

We have

$$\bar{z} = \tfrac{1}{2}\sqrt{n}\, A\cos\theta + \sqrt{\tfrac{1}{4}nA^2\cos^2\theta + n - 1}$$

$$= \sqrt{n}\left[\tfrac{1}{2}A\cos\theta + \sqrt{\frac{A^2}{4}\cos^2\theta + 1 - \frac{1}{n}}\right]$$

$$= \sqrt{n}\left[\tfrac{1}{2}A\cos\theta + \sqrt{\frac{A^2}{4}\cos^2\theta + 1}\right. \tag{37}$$

$$\left. - \frac{1}{2n\sqrt{\dfrac{A^2}{4}\cos^2\theta + 1}} + O\left(\frac{1}{n^2}\right)\right].$$

Letting

$$G = \tfrac{1}{2}[A\cos\theta + \sqrt{A^2\cos^2\theta + 4}],$$

we have

$$\bar{z} = \sqrt{n}\, G\left[1 - \frac{1}{nG\sqrt{A^2\cos^2\theta + 4}} + O\left(\frac{1}{n^2}\right)\right],$$

so

$$\left(\frac{\bar{z}}{e}\right)^{n-1} = \left(\frac{\sqrt{n}\, G}{e}\right)^{n-1}\left[1 - \frac{1}{nG\sqrt{A^2\cos^2\theta + 4}} + O\left(\frac{1}{n^2}\right)\right]^{n-1}$$

$$\sim \left(\frac{\sqrt{n}\, G}{e}\right)^{n-1} \exp\left(-\frac{1}{G\sqrt{A^2\cos^2\theta + 4}}\right). \tag{38}$$

Also,

$$\exp\frac{\bar{z}^2}{2} = \exp\tfrac{1}{2}nG^2\left[1 - \frac{1}{nG\sqrt{A^2\cos^2\theta + 4}} + O\left(\frac{1}{n^2}\right)\right]^2$$

$$\sim \exp\left(\tfrac{1}{2}nG^2 - \frac{2G}{2\sqrt{A^2\cos^2\theta + 4}}\right) \tag{39}$$

$$= \exp\left[\tfrac{1}{2}n(1 + AG\cos\theta) - \frac{G}{\sqrt{A^2\cos^2\theta + 4}}\right],$$

since, on squaring G, we find $G^2 = 1 + AG \cos \theta$. Collecting terms:

$$K \sim T \sqrt{2\pi} \left(\frac{\sqrt{n}G}{e} \right)^{n-1} e^{n/2} \exp \left(- \frac{1}{G \sqrt{A^2 \cos^2 \theta + 4}} \right.$$

$$\left. - \frac{G}{\sqrt{A^2 \cos^2 \theta + 4}} - \frac{A^2 n}{2} \cos^2 \theta + \frac{n}{2} AG \cos \theta \right) \qquad (40)$$

$$= T \sqrt{2\pi}\, n^{(n-1)/2} G^{n-1} e^{-n/2} \exp \left(- \frac{n}{2} A^2 \cos^2 \theta + \frac{n}{2} AG \cos \theta \right)$$

since a little algebra shows that the terms

$$1 - \frac{1}{G\sqrt{A^2 \cos^2 \theta + 4}} - \frac{G}{\sqrt{A^2 \cos^2 \theta + 4}}$$

in the exponential cancel to zero. The coefficient of the integral (34), using the asymptotic expression for $\Gamma[(n+1)/2]$, is asymptotic to

$$\frac{(n-1)e^{-(\sin^2 \theta)(A^2 n)/2} \sin \theta^{n-2} e^{(n+1)/2}}{2^{n/2} \sqrt{\pi} \left(\frac{n+1}{2} \right)^{n/2} \sqrt{2\pi}} . \qquad (41)$$

Combining with the above and collecting terms (we find that $T = G/\sqrt{1 + G^2}$):

$$-\frac{dQ}{d\theta} \sim$$

$$\frac{n-1}{\sqrt{\pi n}} \frac{1}{\sqrt{1 + G^2 \sin^2 \theta}} \left[G \sin \theta \exp \left(-\frac{A^2}{2} + \tfrac{1}{2} AG \cos \theta \right) \right]^n . \qquad (42)$$

This is our desired asymptotic expression for the density $dQ/d\theta$.

As we have arranged it, the coefficient increases essentially as $\sqrt{n}$ and there is another term of the form $e^{-E_L(\theta)n}$, where

$$E_L(\theta) = \frac{A^2}{2} - \tfrac{1}{2} AG \cos \theta - \log (G \sin \theta).$$

It can be shown that if we use for θ the special value $\theta_0 = \cot^{-1} A$ (see Fig. 4) then $E_L(\theta_0) = 0$ and also $E'_L(\theta_0) = 0$. In fact, for this value

$$G(\theta_0) = \tfrac{1}{2}(A \cos \theta_0 + \sqrt{A^2 \cos^2 \theta_0 + 4}) = \frac{1}{2} \left(\frac{A^2}{\sqrt{A^2 + 1}} \right.$$

$$\left. + \sqrt{\frac{A^4}{A^2 + 1} + 4} \right) = \frac{1}{2} \left(\frac{A^2}{\sqrt{A^2 + 1}} + \frac{A^2 + 2}{\sqrt{A^2 + 1}} \right) = \csc \theta_0.$$

Hence the two terms in the logarithm cancel. Also

$$\frac{A^2}{2} - \tfrac{1}{2}AG \cos \theta_0 = \frac{A^2}{2} - \tfrac{1}{2}A \sqrt{A^2 + 1} \; \frac{A}{\sqrt{A^2 + 1}} = 0.$$

So $E_L(\theta_0) = 0$. We also have

$$E'_L(\theta) = \tfrac{1}{2}AG \sin \theta - \tfrac{1}{2}AG' \cos \theta - \frac{G'}{G} - \cot \theta. \tag{43}$$

When evaluated, the term $-G'/G$ simplifies, after considerable algebra, to

$$\frac{A \sin \theta}{\sqrt{A^2 \cos^2 \theta + 4}}.$$

Substituting this and the other terms we obtain

$$\begin{aligned}
E'_L(\theta) = {} & \frac{A^2}{2} \sin \theta \cos \theta + \frac{A^3 \cos^2 \theta \sin \theta}{4\sqrt{A^2 \cos^2 \theta + 4}} \\
& + \frac{A}{4} \frac{(A^2 \cos^2 \theta + 4)}{\sqrt{A^2 \cos^2 \theta + 4}} \sin \theta + \frac{A \sin \theta}{\sqrt{A^2 \cos^2 \theta + 4}} - \cot \theta.
\end{aligned} \tag{44}$$

Adding and collecting terms, this simplifies to

$$\begin{aligned}
E'_L(\theta) &= \frac{A}{2} \left(A \cos \theta + \sqrt{A^2 \cos^2 \theta + 4} \right) \sin \theta - \cot \theta \\
&= AG \sin \theta - \cot \theta \tag{45} \\
&= \cot \theta \left[\frac{A^2}{2} \sin^2 \theta + \frac{A}{2} \sin^2 \theta \sqrt{A^2 + \frac{4}{\cos^2 \theta}} - 1 \right].
\end{aligned}$$

Notice that the bracketed expression is a monotone increasing function of θ ($0 \leqq \theta \leqq \pi/2$) ranging from -1 at $\theta = 0$ to ∞ at $\theta = \pi/2$. Also, as mentioned above, at θ_0, $G = \csc \theta_0$ and $A = \cot \theta_0$, so $E'_L(\theta_0) = 0$. It follows that $E'_L(\theta) < 0$ for $0 \leqq \theta < \theta_0$ and $E'_L(\theta) > 0$ for $\theta_0 \leqq \theta < \pi/2$.

From this, it follows that, in the range from some θ_1 to $\pi/2$ with $\theta_1 > \theta_0$, the minimum $E_L(\theta)$ will occur at the smallest value of θ in the range, that is, at θ_1. The exponential appearing in our estimate of $Q(\theta)$, namely, $e^{-E_L(\theta)n}$, will have its *maximum* at θ_1, for such a range. Indeed, for sufficiently large n, the maximum of the entire expression (45) must occur at θ_1, since the effect of the n in the exponent will eventually dominate anything due to the coefficient. For, if the coefficient is called $\alpha(\theta)$ with $y(\theta) = \alpha(\theta) e^{-nE_L(\theta)}$, then

$$y'(\theta) = e^{-nE_L(\theta)}[-\alpha(\theta)nE'_L(\theta) + \alpha'(\theta)], \tag{46}$$

and, since $\alpha(\theta) > 0$, when n is sufficiently large $y'(\theta)$ will be negative and the only maximum will occur at θ_1. In the neighborhood of θ_1 the function goes down exponentially.

We may now find an asymptotic formula for the integral

$$Q(\theta) = \int_{\theta_1}^{\pi/2} \alpha(\theta) e^{-nE_L(\theta)} d\theta + Q(\pi/2) \tag{47}$$

by breaking the integral into two parts,

$$Q(\theta) = \int_{\theta_1}^{\theta_1 + n^{-2/3}} + \int_{\theta_1 + n^{-2/3}}^{\pi/2} + Q(\pi/2). \tag{48}$$

In the range of the first integral, $(1 - \epsilon)\alpha(\theta_1) \leq \alpha(\theta) \leq \alpha(\theta_1)(1 + \epsilon)$, and ϵ can be made as small as desired by taking n sufficiently large. This is because $\alpha(\theta)$ is continuous and nonvanishing in the range. Also, using a Taylor's series expansion with remainder,

$$e^{-nE_L(\theta)} = \exp\left[-nE_L(\theta_1) - n(\theta - \theta_1)E'_L(\theta_1)\right. \\ \left. - n\frac{(\theta - \theta_1)^2}{2} E''_L(\theta^*)\right], \tag{49}$$

where θ^* is the interval θ_1 to θ. As n increases the maximum value of the remainder term is bounded by $n(n/2)^{-4/3} E''_{max}$, and consequently approaches zero. Hence, our first integral is asymptotic to

$$\alpha(\theta_1) \int_{\theta_1}^{\theta_1 + n^{-2/3}} \exp\left[-nE_L(\theta_1) - n(\theta - \theta_1)E'_L(\theta_1)\right] d\theta$$

$$= -\alpha(\theta_1) \exp\left[-nE_L(\theta_1)\right] \frac{\exp\left[-n(\theta - \theta_1)E'_L(\theta_1)\right]}{nE'_L(\theta_1)}\Bigg]_{\theta_1}^{\theta_1 + n^{-2/3}} \tag{50}$$

$$\sim \frac{\alpha(\theta_1)e^{-nE_L(\theta_1)}}{nE'_L(\theta_1)}.$$

since, at large n, the upper limit term becomes small by comparison. The second integral from $\theta_1 + n^{-2/3}$ to $\pi/2$ can be dominated by the value of the integrand at $\theta_1 + n^{-2/3}$ multiplied by the range

$$\pi/2 - (\theta_1 + n^{-2/3}),$$

(since the integrand is monotone decreasing for large n). The value at $\theta_1 + n^{-2/3}$ is asymptotic, by the argument just given, to

$$\alpha(\theta_1) \exp\left[-nE_L(\theta_1) - n(n^{-2/3}) E'_L(\theta_1)\right].$$

This becomes small compared to the first integral [as does $Q(\pi/2) =$

$\Phi(-A)$ in (47)] and, consequently, on substituting for $\alpha(\theta_1)$ its value and writing θ for θ_1, *we obtain as an asymptotic expression for $Q(\theta)$*:

$$Q(\theta) \sim \frac{1}{\sqrt{n\pi}} \frac{1}{\sqrt{1 + G^2 \sin \theta}} \frac{\left[G \sin \theta \exp \left(-\frac{A^2}{2} + \frac{1}{2}AG \cos \theta \right) \right]^n}{(AG \sin^2 \theta - \cos \theta)} \quad (51)$$

$$\left(\frac{\pi}{2} \geqq \theta > \theta_0 = \cot^{-1} A \right).$$

This expression gives an asymptotic lower bound for $P_{e \text{ opt}}$, obtained by evaluating $Q(\theta)$ for the θ_1 such that $M\Omega(\theta_1) = \Omega(\pi)$.

Incidentally, the asymptotic expression (51) can be translated into an asymptotic expression for the noncentral t cumulative distribution by substitution of variables $\theta = \cot^{-1}(t/\sqrt{f})$ and $n - 1 = f$. This may be useful in other applications of the noncentral t-distribution.

VII. ASYMPTOTIC EXPRESSIONS FOR THE RANDOM CODE BOUND

We now wish to find similar asymptotic expressions for the *upper bound* on $P_{e \text{ opt}}$ of (20) found by the random code method. Substituting the asymptotic expressions for $dQ(\theta)d\theta$ and for $\Omega(\theta)/\Omega(\pi)$ gives for an asymptotic upper bound the following:

$$Q(\theta_1) + e^{nR} \int_0^{\theta_1} \frac{\Gamma\left(\frac{n}{2} + 1 \right) (\sin \theta)^{n-1}}{n\Gamma\left(\frac{n+1}{2} \right) \pi^{1/2} \cos \theta} \sqrt{\frac{n}{\pi}}$$

$$\cdot \frac{\left[G \sin \theta \exp \left(-\frac{P}{2N} + \frac{1}{2} \sqrt{\frac{P}{N}} G \cos \theta \right) \right]^n}{\sqrt{1 + G^2 \sin^2 \theta}} \, d\theta. \quad (52)$$

Thus we need to estimate the integral

$$W = \int_0^{\theta_1} \frac{1}{\cos \theta \sin^3 \theta \sqrt{1 + G^2}}$$

$$\cdot \exp\left\{ n\left(-\frac{P}{2N} + \frac{1}{2} \sqrt{\frac{P}{N}} G \cos \theta + \log G + 2 \log \sin \theta \right) \right\} d\theta. \quad (53)$$

The situation is very similar to that in estimating $Q(\theta)$. Let the coefficient of n in the exponent be D. Note that $D = -E_L(\theta) + \log \sin \theta$. Hence its derivative reduces to

$$\frac{dD}{d\theta} = -AG \sin \theta + 2 \cot \theta. \quad (54)$$

$dD/d\theta = 0$ has a unique root θ_c, $0 \leq \theta_c \leq \pi/2$ for any fixed $A > 0$. This follows from the same argument used in connection with (45), the only difference being a factor of 2 in the right member. Thus, for $\theta < \theta_c$, $dD/d\theta$ is positive and D is an increasing function of θ. Beyond this maximum, D is a decreasing function.

We may now divide the problem of estimating the integral W into cases according to the relative size of θ_c and θ_1.

Case 1: $\theta_1 < \theta_c$.

In this case the maximum of the exponent within the range of integration occurs at θ_1. Consequently, when n is sufficiently large, the maximum of the entire integrand occurs at θ_1. The asymptotic value can be estimated exactly as we estimated $Q(\theta)$ in a similar situation. The integral is divided into two parts, a part from $\theta_1 - n^{-2/3}$ to θ_1 and a second part from 0 to $\theta_1 - n^{-2/3}$. In the first part the integrand behaves asymptotically like:

$$\frac{1}{\cos \theta_1 \sin^3 \theta_1 \sqrt{1 + G^2(\theta_1)}} \exp\left(n\left\{-\frac{P}{2N} + \frac{1}{2}\sqrt{\frac{P}{N}} G(\theta_1) \cos \theta_1 \right.\right.$$
$$+ \log G(\theta_1) + 2 \log \sin \theta_1 \qquad (55)$$
$$\left.\left. - (\theta - \theta_1)[AG(\theta_1) \sin \theta_1 - 2 \cot \theta_1]\right\}\right).$$

This integrates asymptotically to

$$\frac{\exp\left\{n\left[-\frac{P}{2N} + \frac{1}{2}\sqrt{\frac{P}{N}} G(\theta_1) \cos \theta_1 + \log G(\theta_1) + 2 \log \sin \theta_1\right]\right\}}{\cos \theta_1 \sin^3 \theta_1 \sqrt{1 + G^2(\theta_1)}\, [-AG(\theta_1) \sin \theta_1 + 2 \cot \theta_1]n}. \qquad (56)$$

The second integral becomes small in comparison to this, being dominated by an exponential with a larger negative exponent multiplied by the range $\theta_1 - n^{-2/3}$. With the coefficient

$$\frac{1}{\pi\sqrt{n}}\left[\frac{\Gamma\left(\frac{n}{2}+1\right)}{\Gamma\left(\frac{n+1}{2}\right)}\right] e^{nR},$$

and using the fact that

$$\frac{\Gamma\left(\frac{n}{2}+1\right)}{\Gamma\left(\frac{n+1}{2}\right)} \sim \sqrt{\frac{n}{2}},$$

our dominant term approaches

$$\frac{\left[G \sin \theta_1 \exp \left(-\frac{A^2}{2} + \frac{1}{2} AG \cos \theta_1 \right) \right]^n}{\sqrt{n\pi} \sqrt{1 + G^2} \sin \theta_1 (2 \cos \theta_1 - AG \sin^2 \theta_1)}. \tag{57}$$

Combining this with the previously obtained asymptotic expression (51) for $Q(\theta_1)$ we obtain the following *asymptotic expression for the upper bound on* $P_{e \, \text{opt}}$ *for* $\theta_1 < \theta_c$:

$$\left(1 - \frac{\cos \theta_1 - AG \sin^2 \theta_1}{2 \cos \theta_1 - AG \sin^2 \theta_1} \right)$$

$$\cdot \frac{\left[G \sin \theta_1 \exp \left(-\frac{A^2}{2} + \frac{1}{2} AG \cos \theta_1 \right) \right]^n}{\sqrt{n\pi} \sqrt{1 + G^2} \sin \theta_1 (AG \sin^2 \theta_1 - \cos \theta_1)}. \tag{58}$$

Since our lower bound was asymptotic to the same expression without the parenthesis in front, *the two asymptotes differ only by the factor*

$$\left(1 - \frac{\cos \theta_1 - AG \sin^2 \theta_1}{2 \cos \theta_1 - AG \sin^2 \theta_1} \right)$$

independent of n. This factor increases as θ_1 increases from the value θ_0, corresponding to channel capacity, to the critical value θ_c, for which the denominator vanishes. Over this range the factor increases from 1 to ∞. In other words, for large n, $P_{e \, \text{opt}}$ is determined to within a factor. Furthermore, the percentage uncertainty due to this factor is smaller at rates closer to channel capacity, approaching zero as the rate approaches capacity. It is quite interesting that these seemingly weak bounds can work out to give such sharp information for certain ranges of the variables.

Case 2: $\theta_1 > \theta_c$.

For θ_1 in this range the previous argument does not hold, since the maximum of the exponent is not at the end of the range of integration but rather interior to it. This unique maximum occurs at θ_c, the root of $2 \cos \theta_c - AG \sin^2 \theta_c = 0$. We divide the range of integration into three parts: 0 to $\theta_c - n^{-2/5}$, $\theta_c - n^{-2/5}$ to $\theta_c + n^{-2/5}$ and $\theta_c + n^{-2/5}$ to θ. Proceeding by very similar means, in the neighborhood of θ_c the exponential behaves as

$$\exp \left(-n \left\{ E_L(\theta_c) + \frac{(\theta - \theta_c)^2}{2} E''_L(\theta_c) + O[(\theta - \theta_c)^3] \right\} \right).$$

The coefficient of the exponential approaches constancy in the small interval surrounding θ_c. Thus the integral (53) for this part is asymptotic to

$$\frac{1}{\cos\theta_c \sin^3\theta_c \sqrt{1+G^2}}$$

$$\cdot \int \exp\left\{-n\left[E_L(\theta_c) + \frac{(\theta-\theta_c)^2}{2}E''_L(\theta_c)\right]\right\}d\theta \qquad (59)$$

$$\sim \frac{1}{\cos\theta_c \sin^3\theta_c \sqrt{1+G^2}}\exp[-nE_L(\theta_c)]\frac{\sqrt{2\pi}}{\sqrt{nE''_L(\theta_c)}}.$$

The other two integrals become small by comparison when n is large, by essentially the same arguments as before. They may be dominated by the value of the integrand at the end of the range near θ_c multiplied by the range of integration. Altogether, then, the integral (52) is asymptotic to

$$\frac{1}{\sqrt{\pi n}\,\cos\theta_c \sin^3\theta_c \sqrt{1+G^2}\,\sqrt{E''_L(\theta_c)}}\,e^{-n[E_L(\theta_c)-R]}. \qquad (60)$$

The other term in (52), namely, $Q(\theta_1)$, is asymptotically small compared to this, under the present case $\theta > \theta_c$, since the coefficient of n in the exponent for $Q(\theta)$ in (51) will be smaller. Thus, all told, *the random code bound is asymptotic to*

$$\frac{1}{\cos\theta_c \sin^3\theta_c\sqrt{n\pi E''_L(\theta_c)[1+G(\theta_c)^2]}}\,e^{-n[E_L(\theta_c)-R]} \qquad (61)$$

for $\theta > \theta_c$ or for rates $R < R_c$ the rate corresponds to θ_c.

Incidentally, the rate R_c is very closely one-half bit less than channel capacity when $A \geqq 4$, and approaches this exactly as $A \to \infty$. For lower values of A the difference $C - R_c$ becomes smaller but the ratio $C/R_c \to 4$ as $A \to 0$.

VIII. THE FIRM UPPER BOUND ON $P_{s\,\mathrm{opt}}$

In this section we will find an upper bound, valid for all n, on the probability of error by manipulation of the upper bound (20). We first find an upper bound on $Q'(\theta)$. In Ref. 6 the integral (35) is transformed into $\bar{z}^r \exp(-\frac{1}{2}\bar{z}^2 + \bar{z}\sqrt{\nu+1}\,w)$ times the following integral (in their notation):

$$U = \int_{-\infty}^{\infty} \varphi_{\bar{z}}(y)\exp\left\{-\frac{1}{2}y^2 + \nu\left[\ln\left(1+\frac{y}{\bar{z}}\right) - \frac{y}{\bar{z}}\right]\right\}dy.$$

It is pointed out that the integrand here can be dominated by $e^{-v^2/2}$. This occurs in the paragraph in Ref. 6 containing Equation 2.6. Therefore, this integral can be dominated by $\sqrt{2\pi}$, and our integral in (34) involved in $dQ/d\theta$ is dominated as follows:

$$\int_0^\infty \exp\left[-\frac{(r - A\sqrt{n}\cos\theta)^2}{2}\right] r^{n-1}\,dr$$

$$= \left(\frac{\bar{z}}{e}\right)^{n-1} \exp\left(\frac{\bar{z}}{2}\right)^2 \exp\frac{-A^2 n}{2}\cos^2\theta\, U$$

$$\leq \left(\frac{\bar{z}}{e}\right)^{n-1} \exp\left(\frac{\bar{z}}{2}\right)^2 \exp\frac{-A^2 n}{2}\cos^2\theta\,\sqrt{2\pi}.$$

We have

$$\bar{z} = \tfrac{1}{2}\sqrt{n}\,(A\cos\theta + \sqrt{A^2\cos^2\theta + 4 - 4/n}) \leq \sqrt{n}\,G.$$

Replacing $\bar{z}$ by this larger quantity gives

$$\left(\frac{\sqrt{n}G}{e}\right)^{n-1} \exp\left(\frac{nG^2}{2} - \frac{A^2 n}{2}\cos^2\theta\right)\sqrt{2\pi}.$$

We have, then,

$$-\frac{dQ}{d\theta} \leq \frac{(n-1)\exp\left(\frac{-A^2 n}{2}\sin^2\theta\right)(\sin\theta)^{n-2}}{2^{n/2}\sqrt{\pi}\,\Gamma\frac{n+1}{2}}\left(\frac{\sqrt{n}G}{e}\right)^{n-1}$$

$$\cdot\exp\left(\frac{nG^2}{2} - \frac{A^2 n}{2}\cos^2\theta\right)\sqrt{2\pi}. \tag{62}$$

Replacing the gamma function by its Stirling expression

$$\left(\frac{n+1}{2}\right)^{n/2}\exp\left(\frac{n+1}{2}\right)\sqrt{2\pi}$$

(which is always too small), and replacing $[1 + (1/n)]^{n/2}$ by $\sqrt{2}$ (which is also too small) again increases the right member. After simplification, we get

$$-\frac{dQ}{d\theta} \leq \frac{(n-1)(G\sin\theta)^n \exp\left[\left(\frac{n}{2}\right)(-A^2 + 1 + AG\cos\theta)\right]}{\sqrt{n}\,G\sin^2\theta\,\sqrt{2\pi}\exp\left(\frac{n-3}{2}\right)} \tag{63}$$

$$\leq \frac{(n-1)e^{3/2}e^{-E_L(\theta)n}}{\sqrt{2\pi n}\,G\sin^2\theta}.$$

Notice that this differs from the asymptotic expression (42) only by a factor

$$\frac{e^{3/2}\sqrt{1 + G^2}}{\sqrt{2}\,G} \leqq e^{3/2}$$

(since $G \geqq 1$). A firm upper bound can now be placed on $Q(\theta)$:

$$Q(\theta_1) = \int_{\theta_1}^{\pi/2} \frac{dQ}{d\theta}\,d\theta + Q\left(\frac{\pi}{2}\right).$$

We use the upper bound above for $dQ/d\theta$ in the integral. The coefficient of $-n$ in the exponent of e

$$E_L(\theta) = \tfrac{1}{2}(A^2 - AG\cos\theta) - \log G\sin\theta$$

is positive and monotone increasing with θ for $\theta > \theta_0$, as we have seen previously. Its derivative is

$$E'_L(\theta) = AG\sin\theta - \cot\theta.$$

As a function of θ this curve is as shown in Fig. 5, either rising monotonically from $-\infty$ at $\theta = 0$ to A at $\theta = \pi/2$, or with a single maximum. In any case, the curve is concave downward. To show this analytically, take the second derivative of E'_L. This consists of a sum of negative terms.

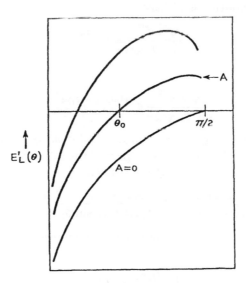

Fig. 5 — $E_L'(\theta)$ as a function of θ.

Returning to our upper bound on Q, the coefficient in (63) does not exceed

$$\frac{\frac{\sqrt{n}}{\sqrt{2\pi}} e^{3/2}}{\sin^2 \theta_1},$$

replacing $\sin \theta$ and G by $\sin \theta_1$ and 1, their minimum values in the range. We now wish to replace $e^{-nE_L(\theta)}$ by

$$\exp - n[E_L(\theta_1) + (\theta - \theta_1)h].$$

If h is chosen equal to the minimum $E'_L(\theta)$, this replacement will increase the integral and therefore give an upper bound. From the behavior of $E'_L(\theta)$ this minimum occurs at either θ_1 or $\pi/2$. Thus, we may take $h = \min [A, AG(\theta_1) \sin \theta_1 - \cot \theta_1]$. With this replacement the integral becomes a simple exponential and can be immediately integrated.

The term $Q(\pi/2)$ is, of course,

$$\Phi(-A \sqrt{n}) \leqq \frac{1}{\sqrt{2\pi n} \, A} e^{-A^2 n/2}.$$

If we continue the integral out to infinity instead of stopping at $\pi/2$, the extra part added will more than cover $Q(\pi/2)$. In fact, $E_L(\pi/2) = A^2/2$, so the extra contribution is at least

$$\frac{\sqrt{n} \, e^{3/2}}{An \sin^2 \theta_1 \sqrt{2\pi}} e^{-A^2 n/2},$$

if we integrate

$$\frac{\sqrt{n} \, e^{3/2}}{\sin^2 \theta_1 \sqrt{2\pi}} e^{-A^2 n/2 - n(\theta - \theta_1)A}$$

to ∞ instead of stopping at $\pi/2$. Since $e^{3/2}/\sin^2 \theta_1 \geqq 1$, we may omit the $Q(\pi/2)$ term in place of the extra part of the integral.

Consequently, we can *bound* $Q(\theta_1)$ *as follows:*

$$Q(\theta_1) \leqq \frac{e^{3/2} \exp \{(n/2) [AG(\theta_1) \cos \theta_1 - A^2 + 2 \log G \sin \theta_1]\}}{\sqrt{2\pi n} \sin^2 \theta_1 \min (A, AG(\theta_1) \sin \theta_1 - \cot \theta_1)}. \quad (64)$$

In order to overbound $P_{e \, opt}$ by (3) it is now necessary to overbound the term

$$\int_0^{\theta_1} \frac{\Omega(\theta)}{\Omega(\theta_1)} \, dQ(\theta).$$

This can be done by a process very similar to that just carried out for $\int dQ(\theta)$. First, we overbound $\Omega(\theta)/\Omega(\theta_1)$ using (21). We have

$$\frac{\Omega(\theta)}{\Omega(\theta_1)} = \frac{\int_0^\theta (\sin x)^{n-2}\, dx}{\int_0^{\theta_1} (\sin x)^{n-2}\, dx}$$

$$= \frac{\int_0^\theta (\sin x)^{n-2}\, dx}{\int_0^\theta (\sin x)^{n-2}\, dx + \int_\theta^{\theta_1} (\sin x)^{n-2}\, dx}$$

$$\leqq \frac{\int_0^\theta (\sin x)^{n-2} \cos x\, dx}{\int_0^\theta (\sin x)^{n-2} \cos x\, dx + \cos \theta \int_\theta^{\theta_1} (\sin x)^{n-2}\, dx}$$

$$\leqq \frac{\int_0^\theta (\sin x)^{n-2} \cos x\, dx}{\int_0^\theta (\sin x)^{n-2} \cos x\, dx + \int_\theta^{\theta_1} (\sin x)^{n-2} \cos x\, dx},$$

and, finally,

$$\frac{\Omega(\theta)}{\Omega(\theta_1)} \leqq \frac{(\sin \theta)^{n-1}}{(\sin \theta_1)^{n-1}}. \tag{65}$$

Here the third line follows since the first integral in the denominator is reduced by the same factor as the numerator and the second integral is reduced more, since $\cos \theta$ is decreasing. In the next line, the denominator is reduced still more by taking the cosine inside.

Using this inequality and also the upper bound (63) on $dQ/d\theta$, we have

$$\int_0^{\theta_1} \frac{\Omega(\theta)}{\Omega(\theta_1)}\, dQ(\theta) \leqq$$

$$\int_0^{\theta_1} \frac{(\sin \theta)^{n-1}}{(\sin \theta_1)^{n-1}} \frac{(n-1)e^{3/2}(G \sin \theta)^n e^{(n/2)(-A^2 + A\cos\theta G)}}{\sqrt{2\pi n G} \sin^2 \theta}\, d\theta \tag{66}$$

$$= \frac{(n-1)e^{3/2}}{\sqrt{2\pi n}\, (\sin \theta_1)^{n-1}} \int_0^{\theta_1} G^n (\sin \theta)^{2n-3} e^{(n/2)(-A^2 + A\cos\theta G)}\, d\theta.$$

Near the point θ_1 the integrand here behaves like an exponential when n is large (provided $\theta_1 < \theta_c$), and it should be possible to find a firm upper bound of the form

$$\frac{k}{\sqrt{n}}\, e^{-E_L(\theta_1)n},$$

where k would not depend on n. This, however, leads to considerable complexity and we have settled for a cruder formulation as follows:

The integrand may be bounded by its maximum values. If $\theta_1 < \theta_c$, the maximum of the integrand will occur at θ_1, at least when n is large enough. In this case, the integral will certainly be bounded by

$$\theta_1 G^n(\theta_1)(\sin \theta_1)^{2n-3}\, e^{(n/2)\{-A^2 + A \cos \theta_1\, G(\theta_1)\}}.$$

The entire expression for $P_{e\,\mathrm{opt}}$ may then be bounded by [adding in the bound (64) on $Q(\theta_1)$]

$$P_{e\,\mathrm{opt}} \leqq \frac{\sqrt{n}\, c^{3/2}\, \theta_1 c^{-E_L(\theta_1)}}{\sqrt{2\pi}\, \sin^2 \theta_1}\left\{1 + \frac{1}{n\theta_1 \min\,[A,\, AG(\theta_1)\, \sin \theta_1 - \cot \theta_1]}\right\}, \quad (67)$$

It must be remembered that (67) is valid only for $\theta_1 < \theta_c$ and if n is large enough to make the maximum of the integrand above occur at θ. For $\theta_1 > \theta_c$, bounds could also be constructed based on the maximum value of the integrand.

IX. A FIRM LOWER BOUND ON $P_{e\,\mathrm{opt}}$

In this section we wish to find a lower bound on $P_{e\,\mathrm{opt}}$ that is valid for all n. To do this we first find a lower bound on $Q'(\theta)$ and from this find a lower bound on $Q(\theta)$. The procedure is quite similar to that involved in finding the firm upper bound.

In Ref. 6, the integral (35) above was reduced to the evaluation of the following integral (Equation 2.5 of Ref. 6):

$$\int_{-z}^{\infty}\left(1 + \frac{y}{z}\right)^{\nu}\exp\left(-\tfrac{1}{2}y^2 - y\frac{\nu}{z}\right)dy$$

$$\geqq \int_{0}^{\infty}\exp\left\{-\tfrac{1}{2}y^2 + \nu\left[\ln\left(1 + \frac{y}{z}\right) - \frac{y}{z}\right]\right\}dy$$

$$\geqq \int_{0}^{\infty}\exp\left[-\tfrac{1}{2}y^2 + \nu\left(\frac{-y^2}{2z^2}\right)\right]dy$$

$$= \int_{0}^{\infty}\exp\left[\frac{-y^2}{2}\left(1 + \frac{\nu}{z^2}\right)\right]dy = \frac{1}{2}\frac{\sqrt{2\pi}}{\sqrt{1 + \frac{\nu}{z^2}}}$$

$$\geqq \frac{\sqrt{2\pi}}{2\sqrt{2}} = \frac{\sqrt{\pi}}{2}$$

Here we used the inequality

$$\ln\left(1 + \frac{y}{\bar{z}}\right) - \frac{y}{\bar{z}} \geqq -\frac{y^2}{2\bar{z}^2} \qquad \text{for} \qquad \frac{y}{\bar{z}} > 0,$$

and also the fact that $\nu/\bar{z}^2 \leqq 1$. This latter follows from Equation 2.3 of Ref. 6 on dividing through by $\bar{z}^2$.

Using this lower bound, we obtain from (34)

$$\frac{dQ}{d\theta} \geqq \frac{(n-1)\ \sin^{n-2}\theta\ \exp\left(\dfrac{-A^2 n}{2}\right)}{2^{n/2}\sqrt{\pi}\ \Gamma\left(\dfrac{n+1}{2}\right)}\left(\frac{\bar{z}}{c}\right)^{n-1}\exp\left(\frac{\bar{z}^2}{2}\right)\frac{\sqrt{\pi}}{2}. \qquad (68)$$

Now $\bar{z} \geqq \sqrt{n-1}\ G$ and

$$\Gamma\left(\frac{n+1}{2}\right) < \left(\frac{n+1}{2}\right)^{n/2} e^{-(n+1)/2}\ \sqrt{2\pi}\ \exp\left[\frac{1}{6(n+1)}\right]$$

and, using the fact that

$$\left(\frac{n-1}{n+1}\right)^{n/2} \geqq \frac{1}{3} \qquad \text{for} \qquad n \geqq 2,$$

we obtain

$$\frac{dQ}{d\theta} \geqq \frac{1}{6\sqrt{2\pi}}\ \frac{\sqrt{n-1}\ e^{3/2}\ e^{-nE_L(\theta)}}{G\ \exp\left[\dfrac{G^2}{2} + \dfrac{1}{6(n+1)}\right]\sin^2\theta} \qquad \text{for } n \geqq 2. \qquad (69)$$

This is our lower bound on $dQ/d\theta$.

To obtain a lower bound on $Q(\theta)$ we may use the same device as before—here, however, replacing the coefficient by its minimum value in the range and the exponent by $-nE_L(\theta_1) - n(\theta - \theta_1)E'_{L\ \max}$:

$$E'_L = AG\sin\theta - \cot\theta$$

$$\leqq AG$$

$$\leqq A(A+1).$$

Similarly, in the coefficient, G can be dominated by $A + 1$ and $\sin^2\theta$ by 1. Thus,

$$Q(\theta_1) \geqq$$

$$\int_{\theta_1}^{\pi/2}\frac{\sqrt{n-1}\ e^{3/2}e^{-nE_L(\theta_1)}e^{-n(\theta-\theta_1)A(A+1)}}{6\ \sqrt{2\pi}(A+1)\ \exp\left[\dfrac{(A+1)^2}{2} + \dfrac{1}{6(n+1)}\right]}\ d\theta + Q\left(\frac{\pi}{2}\right). \qquad (70)$$

Integrating and observing that the term due to the $\pi/2$ limit can be absorbed into the $Q(\pi/2) - $ erf A, we arrive at the lower bound:

$$Q(\theta_1) \geqq \frac{\sqrt{n-1}\, e^{3/2} e^{-nEL(\theta_1)}}{6\sqrt{2\pi n}\,(A+1)^3 \exp\left[\dfrac{(A+1)^2}{2} + \dfrac{1}{6(n+1)}\right]}. \qquad (71)$$

X. BEHAVIOR NEAR CHANNEL CAPACITY

As we have seen, near channel capacity the upper and lower asymptotic bounds are substantially the same. If in the asymptotic lower bound (42) we form a Taylor expansion for θ near θ_0, retaining terms up to $(\theta - \theta_0)^2$, we will obtain an expression applying to the neighborhood of channel capacity. Another approach is to return to the original noncentral t-distribution and use its normal approximation which will be good near the mean (see Ref. 5). Either approach gives, in this neighborhood, the approximations [since $E(\theta_0) = E'(\theta_0) = 0$]:

$$-\frac{dQ}{d\theta} \doteq \frac{\sqrt{n}\,(1+A^2)}{\sqrt{\pi}\,\sqrt{2+A^2}} \exp\left[-n\frac{(A^2+1)^2}{A^2+2}(\theta-\theta_0)^2\right]$$

$$Q(\theta) \doteq \Phi\left[(\theta_0-\theta)\frac{A^2+1}{\sqrt{A^2+2}}\sqrt{2n}\right], \qquad (72)$$

or, since near channel capacity, using $e^{-R} \doteq \sin\theta$,

$$\theta - \theta_0 \doteq A^{-1}(C-R)$$

$$P_{e\,\text{opt}}\left(n, R, \sqrt{\frac{P}{N}}\right) \doteq \Phi\left[\sqrt{2n}\,A^{-1}\frac{A^2+1}{\sqrt{A^2+2}}(R-C)\right] \qquad (73)$$

$$= \Phi\left[\frac{P+N}{\sqrt{P(P+2N)}}\sqrt{2n}\,(R-C)\right].$$

The reliability curve is approximated near C by

$$E(R) \doteq \frac{(P+N)^2}{P(P+2N)}(C-R)^2. \qquad (74)$$

It is interesting that Rice[2] makes estimates of the behavior of what amounts to a lower bound on the exponent E near channel capacity. His exponent, translated into our notation, is

$$E^*(R) \doteq \frac{P+N}{2P}(C-R)^2,$$

a poorer value than (74); that is, it will take a larger block length to achieve the same probability of error. This difference is evidently due to the slight difference in the manner of construction of the random codes. Rice's codes are obtained by placing points according to an n-dimensional gaussian distribution, each coordinate having variance P. In our codes the points are placed at random on a sphere of precisely fixed radius $\sqrt{nP}$. These are very close to the same thing when n is large, since in Rice's situation the points will, with probability approaching 1, lie between the spheres of radii $\sqrt{nP}\,(1 - \epsilon)$ and $\sqrt{nP}\,(1 + \epsilon)$, (any $\epsilon > 0$). However, we are dealing with very small probability events in any case when we are estimating probability of error, and the points within the sphere are sufficiently important to affect the exponent E. In other words, the Rice type of code is sufficient to give codes that will have a probability of error approaching zero at rates arbitrarily near channel capacity. However, they will not do so at as rapid a rate (even in the exponent) as can be achieved. To achieve the best possible E it is evidently necessary to avoid having too many of the code points interior to the $\sqrt{nP}$ sphere.

At rates R greater than channel capacity we have $\theta_1 < \theta_0$. Since the Q distribution approaches normality with mean at θ_0 and variance $2n(A^2 + 1)^2/(A^2 + 2)$, we will have $Q(\theta_1)$ approaching 1 with increasing n for any fixed rate greater than C. Indeed, even if the rate R varies but remains always greater than C (perhaps approaching it from above with increasing n), we will still have $P_{e\,\mathrm{opt}} > \frac{1}{2} - \epsilon$ for any $\epsilon > 0$ and sufficiently large n.

XI. UPPER BOUND ON $P_{e\,\mathrm{opt}}$ BY METHOD OF EXHAUSTION

For low rates of transmission, where the upper and lower bounds diverge widely, we may obtain better estimates by other methods. For very low rates of transmission, the main contribution to the probability of error can be shown to be due to the code points that are nearest together and thus often confused with each other, rather than to the general average structure of the code. The important thing, at low rates, is to maximize the minimum distance between neighbors. Both the upper and lower bounds which we will derive for low rates are based on these considerations.

We will first show that, for $D \leqq \sqrt{2\,nP}$, it is possible to find at least

$$M_D = \left(\sin 2 \sin^{-1} \frac{D}{2\,\sqrt{nP}} \right)^{1-n}$$

points on the surface of an n sphere of radius $\sqrt{nP}$ such that no pair of them is separated by a distance less than D. (If M_D is not an integer, take the next larger integer.) The method used will be similar to one used by E. N. Gilbert for the binary symmetric channel.

Select any point on the sphere's surface for the first point. Delete from the surface all points within D of the selected point. In Fig. 6, x is the selected point and the area to be deleted is that cut out by the cone. This area is certainly less (if $D \leqq \sqrt{2nP}$) than the area of the hemisphere of radius H shown and, even more so, less than the area of the sphere of radius H. If this deletion does not exhaust the original sphere, select any point from those remaining and delete the points within D of this new point. This again will not take away more area than that of a sphere of radius H. Continue in this manner until no points remain. Note that each point chosen is at least D from each preceding point. Hence all interpoint distances are at least D. Furthermore, this can be continued at least as many times as the ratio of the surface of a sphere of radius $\sqrt{nP}$ to that of a sphere of radius H, since each deletion takes away not more than this much surface area. This ratio is clearly

$$(\sqrt{nP}/H)^{n-1}.$$

By simple geometry in Fig. 6, we see that H and D are related as follows:

$$\sin \theta = \frac{H}{\sqrt{nP}},$$

$$\sin \frac{\theta}{2} = \frac{D}{2\sqrt{nP}}.$$

Hence

$$H = \sqrt{nP} \sin 2 \sin^{-1} \frac{D}{2\sqrt{nP}}. \qquad (75)$$

Substituting, *we can place at least*

$$M_D = \left(\sin 2 \sin^{-1} \frac{D}{2\sqrt{nP}} \right)^{-(n-1)}$$

points at distances at least D from each other, for any $D \leqq \sqrt{2nP}$.

If we have M_D points with minimum distance at least D, then the probability of error with optimal decoding will be less than or equal to

$$M_D \Phi \left(\frac{-D}{2\sqrt{N}} \right).$$

To show this we may add up pessimistically the probabilities of each point being received as each other point. Thus the probability of point 1 being moved closer to point 2 than to the original point 1 is not greater than $\Phi[-D/(2\sqrt{N})]$, that is, the probability of the point being moved in a certain direction at least $D/2$ (half the minimum separation). The contribution to errors due to this cause cannot, therefore, exceed $(1/M_D)\Phi[-D/(2\sqrt{N})]$, (the $1/M_D$ factor being the probability of message 1 being transmitted). A similar argument occurs for each (ordered) pair of points, a total of $M_D(M_D - 1)$ contributions of this kind. Consequently, the probability of error cannot exceed $(M_D - 1)\Phi[-D/(2\sqrt{N})]$ or, more simply, $M_D\Phi[-D/(2\sqrt{N})]$.

If we set

$$e^{nR} = M_D = \left(\sin 2 \sin^{-1} \frac{D}{2\sqrt{nP}}\right)^{-(n-1)}$$

then the rate R (in natural units) is

$$R = \left(1 - \frac{1}{n}\right) \log \left(\sin 2 \sin^{-1} \frac{D}{2\sqrt{nP}}\right)^{-1}$$

with

$$P_e \leqq e^{nR}\Phi\left(\frac{-D}{2\sqrt{N}}\right) \leqq e^{nR} \frac{\sqrt{2N}}{D\sqrt{\pi}} e^{-(D^2/8N)}, \tag{76}$$

using the well-known upper bound $\Phi(-x) \leqq (1/x\sqrt{2\pi})e^{-x^2/2}$. These are

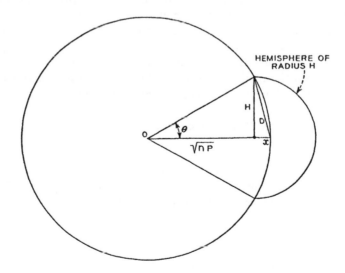

HEMISPHERE OF
RADIUS H

Fig. 6 — Geometry of sphere of radius $\sqrt{nP}$.

parametric equations in terms of D. It is more convenient to let

$$D = \lambda \sqrt{2nP}.$$

We then have

$$R = \left(1 - \frac{1}{n}\right) \log \left(\sin 2 \sin^{-1} \frac{\lambda}{\sqrt{2}}\right)^{-1},$$

$$P_e \leq \frac{1}{\lambda \sqrt{\pi n \frac{P}{N}}} e^{n[R-(\lambda^2 P)/(4N)]}. \tag{77}$$

The asymptotic reliability, that is, the coefficient of $-n$ in the exponent of P_e, is given by $(\lambda^2 P/4N) - R$. This approaches

$$(\sin \tfrac{1}{2} \sin^{-1} e^R)^2 \frac{P}{2N} - R \qquad \text{as} \qquad n \to \infty.$$

Thus our asymptotic *lower* bound for reliability is (eliminating λ):

$$E \geq (\sin \tfrac{1}{2} \sin^{-1} e^R)^2 \frac{P}{2N} - R. \tag{78}$$

As $R \to 0$ the right-hand expression approaches $P/(4N)$.

This lower bound on the exponent is plotted in the curves in Section XIV and it may be seen to give more information at low rates than the random code bound. It is possible, however, to improve the random coding procedure by what we have called an "expurgating" process. It then becomes the equal of the bound just derived and, in fact, is somewhat stronger over part of the range. We shall not go into this process in detail but only mention that the expurgating process consists of eliminating from the random code ensemble points which have too close neighbors, and working with the codes that then remain.

XII. LOWER BOUND ON P_e IN GAUSSIAN CHANNEL BY MINIMUM DISTANCE ARGUMENT

In a code of length n with M code words, let $m_{is}(i = 1, 2, \cdots, M;$ $s = 1, 2, \cdots, n)$ be the sth coordinate of code word i. We are here assuming an average power limitation P, so that

$$\frac{1}{nM} \sum_{i,s} m_{is}^2 \leq P. \tag{79}$$

We also assume an independent gaussian noise of power N added to each coordinate.

We now calculate the average squared distance between all the $M(M-1)/2$ pairs of points in n-space corresponding to the M code words. The squared distance from word i to word j is

$$\sum_s (m_{is} - m_{js})^2.$$

The average $\overline{D^2}$ between all pairs will then be

$$\overline{D^2} = \frac{1}{M(M-1)} \sum_{s,i,j} (m_{is} - m_{js})^2.$$

Note that each distance is counted twice in the sum and also that the extraneous terms included in the sum, where $i = j$, contribute zero to it. Squaring the terms in the sum,

$$\overline{D^2} = \frac{1}{M(M-1)} \left(\sum_{i,j,s} m_{is}^2 - 2 \sum_s \sum_{i,j} m_{is}m_{js} + \sum_{i,j,s} m_{js}^2 \right)$$

$$= \frac{1}{M(M-1)} \left[2M \sum_{i,s} m_{is}^2 - 2 \sum_s \left(\sum_i m_{is} \right)^2 \right] \tag{80}$$

$$\leqq \frac{1}{M(M-1)} 2MPnM$$

$$\overline{D^2} \leqq \frac{2nMP}{M-1},$$

where we obtain the third line by using the inequality on the average power (79) and by noting that the second term is necessarily nonpositive.

If the *average* squared distance between pairs of points it

$$\leqq (2nMP)/(M-1),$$

there must exist a pair of points for whose distance this inequality holds. Each point in this pair is used $1/M$ of the time. The best detection for separating this pair (if no other points were present) would be by a hyperplane normal to and bisecting the joining line segment. Either point would then give rise to a probability of error equal to that of the noise carrying a point half this distance or more in a specified direction. We obtain, then, a contribution to the probability of error at least

$$\frac{1}{M} \cdot \mathrm{Pr} \left\{ \text{noise in a certain direction} \geqq \frac{1}{2} \sqrt{\frac{2nMP}{M-1}} \right\}$$

$$= \frac{1}{M} \Phi \left[-\sqrt{\frac{nMP}{(M-1)2N}} \right].$$

This we may assign to the first of the two points in question, and the errors we have counted are those when this message is sent and is received closer to the second message (and should therefore be detected as the second or some other message).

Now delete this first message from the set of code points and consider the remaining $M - 1$ points. By the same argument there must exist among these a pair whose distance is less than or equal to

$$\sqrt{\frac{2nP(M - 1)}{(M - 2)}}$$

This pair leads to a contribution to probability of error, due to the first of these being displaced until nearer the second, of an amount

$$\frac{1}{M}\Phi\left[-\sqrt{\frac{(M - 1)nP}{(M - 2)2N}}\right].$$

This same argument is continued, deleting points and adding contributions to the error, until only two points are left. Thus we obtain a lower bound on $P_{e\,\text{opt}}$ as follows:

$$P_{e\,\text{opt}} \geqq \frac{1}{M}\left[\Phi\left(-\sqrt{\frac{nP}{2N}\frac{M}{M - 1}}\right) + \Phi\left(-\sqrt{\frac{nP}{2N}\frac{M - 1}{M - 2}}\right) \right.$$
$$\left. + \cdots + \Phi\left(-\sqrt{\frac{nP}{2N}\frac{2}{1}}\right)\right]. \tag{81}$$

To simplify this bound somewhat, one may take only the first $M/2$ terms [or $(M + 1)/2$ if M is odd]. Since they are decreasing, each term would be reduced by replacing it with the last term taken. Thus we may reduce the bound by these operations and obtain

$$P_{e\,\text{opt}} \geqq \frac{1}{2}\Phi\left(-\sqrt{\frac{M}{M - 2}\frac{nP}{2N}}\right). \tag{82}$$

For any rate $R > 0$, as n increases the term $M/(M - 2)$ approaches 1 and the bound, then, behaves about as

$$\frac{1}{2}\Phi\left(-\sqrt{\frac{nP}{2N}}\right).$$

This is asymptotic to

$$\frac{1}{2\sqrt{\dfrac{\pi nP}{N}}}e^{-(nP)/(4N)}.$$

It follows that the reliability $E \leqq P/(4N) = A^2/4$. This is the same value as the lower bound for E when $R \to 0$.

XIII. ERROR BOUNDS AND OTHER CONDITIONS ON THE SIGNAL POINTS

Up to now we have (except in the last section) assumed that all signal points were required to lie on the surface of the sphere, i.e., have a mean square value $\sqrt{nP}$. Consider now the problem of estimating $P'_{e\,\text{opt}}(M, n, \sqrt{P/N})$, where the signal points are only required to lie on or within the spherical surface. Clearly, since this relaxes the conditions on the code, it can only improve, i.e., decrease the probability of error for the best code. Thus $P'_{e\,\text{opt}} \leq P_{e\,\text{opt}}$.

On the other hand, we will show that

$$P'_{e\,\text{opt}}\left(M, n, \sqrt{\frac{P}{N}}\right) \geq P_{e\,\text{opt}}\left(M, n+1, \sqrt{\frac{P}{N}}\right). \qquad (83)$$

In fact, suppose we have a code of length n, all points on or within the

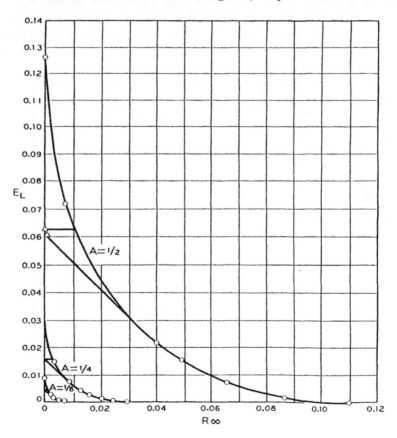

Fig. 7 — Curves showing E_L vs. R for $A = \frac{1}{8}, \frac{1}{4}$ and $\frac{1}{2}$.

n sphere. To each code word add a further coordinate of such value that in the $n + 1$ space the point thus formed lies *exactly on* the $n + 1$ sphere surface. If the first n coordinates of a point have values $x_1, x_2, \cdots, x_n$ with

$$\sum_{i=1}^{n} x_i^2 \leqq nP,$$

the added coordinate will have the value

$$x_{n+1} = \sqrt{(n + 1)P - \sum_{i=1}^{n} x_i^2}.$$

This gives a derived code of the first type (all points *on* the $n + 1$ sphere surface) with M words of length $n + 1$ at signal-to-noise ratio P/N. The probability of error for the given code is at least as great as that of the derived code, since the added coordinate can only improve

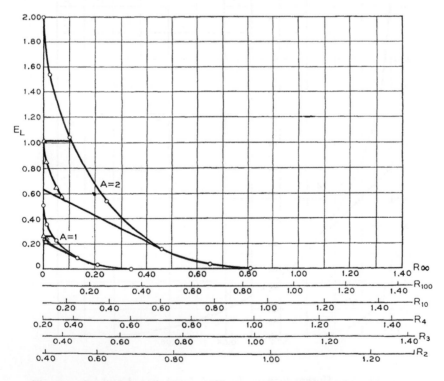

Fig. 8 — Curves showing E_L vs. different values of R for $A = 1$ and 2.

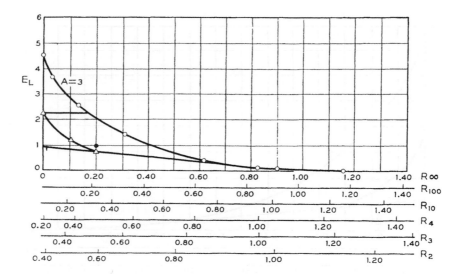

Fig. 9 — Curves showing E_L vs. different values of R for $A = 3$.

the decoding process. One might, for example, decode ignoring the last coordinate and then have the same probability of error. Using it in the best way would, in general, improve the situation.

The probability of error for the derived code of length $n + 1$ must be greater than or equal to that of the optimal code of the length $n + 1$ with all points on the surface. Consequently we have (83). Since $P_{e\,\text{opt}}(M, n, \sqrt{P/N})$ varies essentially exponentially with n when n is large, the effect of replacing n by $n + 1$ is essentially that of a constant multiplier. Thus, our upper bounds on $P_{e\,\text{opt}}$ are not changed and our lower bounds are multiplied by a quantity which does not depend much on n when n is large. The asymptotic reliability curves consequently will be the same. Thus the E curves we have plotted may be applied in either case.

Now consider the third type of condition on the points, namely, that the *average* squared distance from the origin of the set of points be less than or equal to nP. This again is a weakening of the previous conditions and hence the optimal probability of error, $P''_{e\,\text{opt}}$, is less than or equal to that of the previous cases:

$$P''_{e\,\text{opt}}\left(M, n, \frac{P}{N}\right) \leqq P'_{e\,\text{opt}}\left(M, n, \frac{P}{N}\right) \leqq P_{e\,\text{opt}}\left(M, n, \frac{P}{N}\right). \quad (84)$$

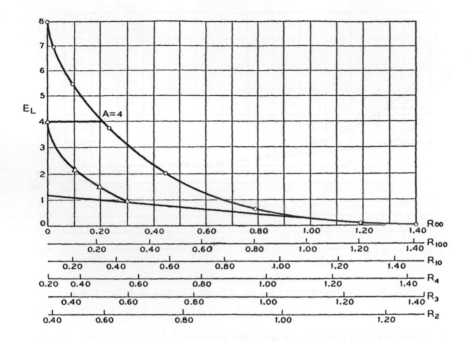

Fig. 10 — Curves showing E_L vs. different values of R for $A = 4$.

Our upper bounds on probability of error (and, consequently, lower bounds on reliability) can be used as they stand.

Lower bounds on $P''_{e \, opt}$ may be obtained as follows. If we have M points whose mean square distance from the origin does not exceed nP, then for any $\alpha(0 < \alpha \leq 1)$ at least αM of the points are within a sphere of squared radius $nP/(1 - \alpha)$. [For, if more than $(1 - \alpha)M$ of them were outside the sphere, these alone would contribute more than

$$(1 - \alpha)MnP/(1 - \alpha)$$

to the total squared distance, and the mean would then necessarily be greater than nP.] Given an optimal code under the third condition, we can construct from it, by taking αM points within the sphere of radius $\sqrt{nP/1 - \alpha}$, a code satisfying the second condition with this smaller number of points and larger radius. The probability of error for the new code cannot exceed $1/\alpha$ times that of the original code. (Each new code word is used $1/\alpha$ times as much; when used, its probability of error is at least as good as previously.) Thus:

$$P''_{e \, opt} \left(M, n, \sqrt{\frac{P}{N}} \right) \geqq \frac{1}{\alpha} P'_{e \, opt} \left(\alpha M, n, \sqrt{\frac{P}{(1 - \alpha)N}} \right)$$

$$\geqq \frac{1}{\alpha} P_{e \, opt} \left(\alpha M, n + 1, \sqrt{\frac{P}{(1 - \alpha)N}} \right).$$

XIV. CURVES FOR ASYMPTOTIC BOUNDS

Curves have been calculated to facilitate evaluation of the exponents in these asymptotic bounds. The basic curves range over values of

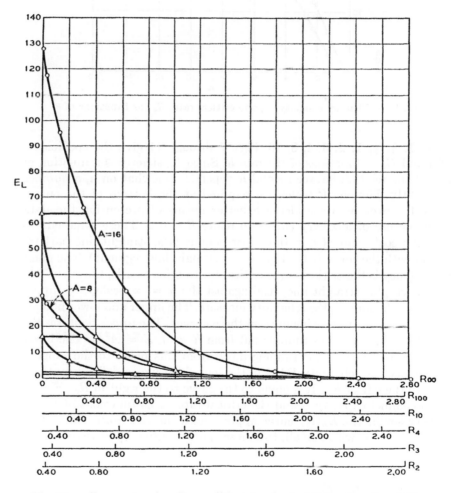

Fig. 11 — Curves showing E_L vs. different values of R for $A = 8$ and 16.

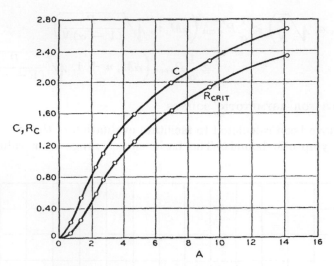

Fig. 12 — Channel capacity, C, and critical rate, R_c, as functions of θ.

$A = \frac{1}{8}, \frac{1}{4}, \frac{1}{2}, 1, 2, 3, 4, 8, 16$. Figs. 7 through 11 give the coefficients of n and E_L as functions of the rate R. Since E_L strictly is a function of θ, and the relation between θ and R depends somewhat on n, a number of slightly different R scales are required at the bottom of the curve. This, however, was considered a better means of presenting the data than the use of auxiliary curves to relate R and θ. These same curves give the coefficient of n in the upper bounds (the straight line part together with the curve to the right of the straight line segment). The point of tangency is the critical R (or critical θ). In other words, the curve and the curve plus straight line, read against the $n = \infty$ scale, give upper and lower bounds on the reliability measure. The upper and lower bounds on E for low R are also included in these curves. The upper bound is the horizontal line segment running out from $R = 0$, $E = A^2/4$. The lower bound is the curved line running down from this point to the tangent line. Thus, the reliability E lies in the four-sided figure defined by these lines to the left of R_c. It is equal to the curve to the right of R_c. Fig. 12 gives channel capacity C and the critical rate R_c as functions of θ. For A very small, the $E_L(R)$ curve approaches a limiting form. In fact, if $\theta = (\pi/2) - \epsilon$, with ϵ small, to a close approximation by obvious expansions we find

$$E_L(R) \doteq \frac{A^2}{2} - A\epsilon + \frac{\epsilon^2}{2} \quad \text{and} \quad R \doteq \frac{\epsilon^2}{2}.$$

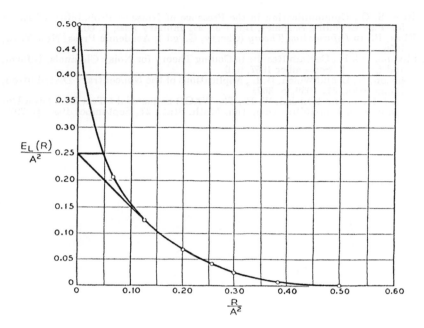

Fig. 13 — Plots of $E_L(R)/A^2$ against R/A^2.

Eliminating ϵ, we obtain

$$\frac{E_L(R)}{A^2} \doteq \frac{1}{2} - \sqrt{\frac{2R}{A^2}}.$$

Fig. 13 plots $E_L(R)/A^2$ against R/A^2.

XV. ACKNOWLEDGMENTS

I am grateful to several people for help in preparing this paper. Mrs. Judy Frankman computed the curves of E_L and other members of the Center for Advanced Study in the Behavioral Sciences were helpful in many ways. The referee made several valuable suggestions which have been incorporated in the paper. Finally, I am particularly indebted to my wife Betty for checking much of the algebra involved in the asymptotic bounds.

REFERENCES

1. Shannon, C. E., Communication in the Presence of Noise, Proc. I.R.E., **37**, January 1949, p. 10.

2. Rice, S. O., Communication in the Presence of Noise — Probability of Error for Two Encoding Schemes, B.S.T.J., **29**, January 1950, p. 60.
3. Elias, P., in *Information Theory* (Cherry, C., ed.), Academic Press, New York, 1956.
4. Shannon, C. E., Certain Results in Coding Theory for Noisy Channels, Inform. and Cont., **1**, September 1957, p. 6.
5. Johnson, N. L. and Welch, B. L., Applications of the Noncentral t-Distribution, Biometrika, **31**, 1939, p. 362.
6. David, H. T. and Kruskal, W. H., The WAGR Sequential t-Test Reaches a Decision with Probability One, Ann. Math. Stat., **27**, September 1956, p. 797.

Coding Theorems for a Discrete Source
With a Fidelity Criterion*

Claude E. Shannon**

Abstract

Consider a discrete source producing a sequence of message letters from a finite alphabet. A single-letter distortion measure is given by a non-negative matrix (d_{ij}). The entry d_{ij} measures the "cost" or "distortion" if letter i is reproduced at the receiver as letter j. The average distortion of a communications system (source-coder-noisy channel-decoder) is taken to be $d = \sum_{i,j} P_{ij} d_{ij}$ where P_{ij} is the probability of i being reproduced as j. It is shown that there is a function $R(d)$ that measures the "equivalent rate" of the source for a given level of distortion. For coding purposes where a level d of distortion can be tolerated, the source acts like one with information rate $R(d)$. Methods are given for calculating $R(d)$, and various properties discussed. Finally, generalizations to ergodic sources, to continuous sources, and to distortion measures involving blocks of letters are developed.

In this paper a study is made of the problem of coding a discrete source of information, given a *fidelity criterion* or a *measure of the distortion* of the final recovered message at the receiving point relative to the actual transmitted message. In a particular case there might be a certain tolerable level of distortion as determined by this measure. It is desired to so encode the information that the maximum possible signaling rate is obtained without exceeding the tolerable distortion level. This work is an expansion and detailed elaboration of ideas presented earlier [1], with particular reference to the discrete case.

We shall show that for a wide class of distortion measures and discrete sources of information there exists a function $R(d)$ (depending on the particular distortion measure and source) which measures, in a sense, the equivalent rate R of the source (in bits per letter produced) when d is the allowed distortion level. Methods will be given for evaluating $R(d)$ explicitly in certain simple cases and for evaluating $R(d)$ by a limiting process in more complex cases. The basic results are roughly that it is impossible to signal at a rate faster than $C / R(d)$ (source letters per second) over a memoryless channel of capacity C (bits per second) with a distortion measure less than or equal to d. On the other hand, by sufficiently long block codes it is possible to approach as closely as desired the rate $C / R(d)$ with distortion level d.

Finally, some particular examples, using error probability per letter of message and other simple distortion measures, are worked out in detail.

The Single-Letter Distortion Measure. Suppose that we have a discrete information source producing a sequence of letters or "word" $m = m_1, m_2, m_3, \ldots, m_t$, each chosen from a finite alphabet. These are to be transmitted over a channel and reproduced, at least

---

* Institute of Radio Engineers, *International Convention Record*, vol. 7, 1959.

** This work was supported in part by the U.S. Army (Signal Corps), the U.S. Air Force (Office of Scientific Research, Air Reserve and Development Command), and the U.S. Navy (Office of Naval Research).

approximately, at a receiving point. Let the reproduced word be $Z = z_1, z_2, \ldots, z_t$. The z_i letters may be from the same alphabet as the m_i letters or from an enlarged alphabet including, perhaps, special symbols for unknown or semi-unknown letters. In a noisy telegraph situation m and Z might be as follows:

m = I HAVE HEARD THE MERMAIDS SINGING...

$\qquad$? $\qquad\qquad\qquad\qquad\qquad$?

Z = I H?VT HEA?D TSE B?RMAIDZ ??NGING...

In this case, the Z alphabet consists of the ordinary letters and space of the m alphabet, together

$\qquad\qquad\qquad\qquad\qquad\qquad$? $\qquad$?

with additional symbols "?", "A", "B", etc., indicating less certain identification. Even more generally, the Z alphabet might be entirely different from the m alphabet.

Consider a situation in which there is a measure of the fidelity of transmission or the "distortion" between the original and final words. We shall assume first that this distortion measure is of a very simple and special type, and later we shall generalize considerably on the basis of the special case.

A *single-letter distortion measure* is defined as follows. There is given a matrix d_{ij} with $d_{ij} \geq 0$. Here i ranges over the letters of the m alphabet of, say, a letters (assumed given a numerical ordering), while j ranges over the Z alphabet. The quantity d_{ij} may be thought of as a "cost" if letter i is reproduced as letter j.

If the Z alphabet includes the m alphabet, we will assume the distortion between an m letter and its correct reproduction to be zero and all incorrect reproductions to have positive distortion. It is convenient in this case to assume that the alphabets are arranged in the same indexing order so that $d_{ii} = 0, d_{ij} > 0 \ (i \neq j)$.

The distortion d, if *word m* is reproduced as word Z, is to be measured by

$$d(m, Z) = \frac{1}{t} \sum_{k=1}^{t} d_{m_k z_k} .$$

If, in a communication system, word m occurs with probability $P(m)$ and the conditional probability, if m is transmitted, that word Z will be reproduced, is $P(Z|m)$, then we assume that the *over-all distortion of the system* is given by

$$d = \sum_{m,Z} P(m) \, P(Z|m) \, d(m, Z) .$$

Here we are supposing that all messages and reproduced words are of the same length t. In variable-length coding systems the analogous measure is merely the over-all probability that letter i reproduced as j, multiplied by d_{ij} and summed on i and j. Note that $d = 0$ if and only if each word is correctly reproduced with probability 1, otherwise $d > 0$ (in cases where the Z alphabet includes the m alphabet).

Some Simple Examples. A distortion measure may be represented by giving the matrix of its elements, all terms of which are non-negative. An alternative representation is in terms of a line diagram similar to those used for representing a memoryless noisy channel. The lines are now labeled, however, with the values d_{ij} rather than probabilities.

A simple example of a distortion measure, with identical m and Z alphabets, is the error probability per letter. In this case, if the alphabets are ordered similarly, $d_{ij} = 1 - \delta_{ij}$. If there were three letters in the m and and Z alphabets, the line diagram would be that shown in Fig. 1(a). Such a distortion measure might be appropriate in measuring the fidelity of a teletype or a remote typesetting system.

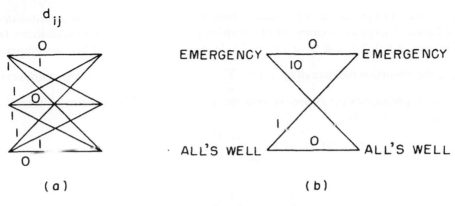

Fig. 1.

Another example is that of transmitting the quantized position of a wheel or shaft. Suppose that the circumference is divided into five equal arcs. It might be only half as costly to have an error of plus or minus one segment as larger errors. Thus the distortion measure might be

$$d_{ij} = \begin{cases} 0 & i = j \\ \tfrac{1}{2} & |i - j| = 1 \quad (\text{mod } 5), \\ 1 & |i - j| > 1 \quad (\text{mod } 5). \end{cases}$$

A third example might be a binary system sending information each second, either "all's well" or "emergency," for some situation. Generally, it would be considerably more important that the "emergency" signal be correctly received than that the "all's well" signal be correctly received. Thus if these were weighted 10 to 1, the diagram would be as shown in Fig. 1(b).

A fourth example with entirely distinct m and Z alphabets is a case in which the m alphabet consists of three possible readings, -1, 0 and $+1$. Perhaps, for some reasons of economy, it is desired to work with a reproduced alphabet of two letters, $-\tfrac{1}{2}$ and $+\tfrac{1}{2}$. One might then have the matrix that is shown in Fig. 2.

	$-\tfrac{1}{2}$	$+\tfrac{1}{2}$
-1	1	2
0	1	1
1	2	1

Fig. 2.

The Rate-Distortion Function R(d). Now suppose that successive letters of the message are statistically independent but chosen with the same probabilities, P_i being the probability of letter i from the alphabet. This type of source we call an *independent letter source.*

Given such a set of probabilities P_i and a distortion measure d_{ij}, we define a *rate-distortion curve* as follows. Assign an arbitrary set of transition probabilities $q_i(j)$ for transitions from i to j. (Of course, $q_i(j) \geq 0$ and $\sum_j q_i(j) = 1$.) One could calculate for this assignment two things: first, the distortion measure $d(q_i(j)) = \sum_{ij} P_i\, q_i(j)\, d_{ij}$ if letter i were reproduced as j with conditional probability $q_i(j)$, and, second, the average mutual information between i and j if this were the case, namely

$$R(q_i(j)) = E \log \frac{q_i(j)}{\sum_k P_k\, q_k(j)}$$

$$= \sum_{i,j} P_i\, q_i(j) \log \frac{q_i(j)}{\sum_k P_k\, q_k(j)}\ .$$

The rate-distortion function $R(d^*)$ is defined as the greatest lower bound of $R(q_i(j))$ when the $q_i(j)$ are varied subject to their probability limitations and subject to the average distortion d being less than or equal to d^*.

Note that $R(q_i(j))$ is a continuous function of the $q_i(j)$ in the allowed region of variation of $q_i(j)$ which is closed. Consequently, *the greatest lower bound of R is actually attained as a minimum* for each value of R that can occur at all. Further, from its definition it is clear that $R(d)$ is a monotonically decreasing function of d.

Convexity of the $R(d)$ Curve. Suppose that two points on the $R(d)$ curve are (R, d) obtained with assignment $q_i(j)$ and (R', d') attained with assignment $q_i'(j)$. Consider a mixture of these assignments $\lambda q_i(j) + (1 - \lambda)\, q_i'(j)$. This produces a d'' (because of the linearity of d) not greater than $\lambda d + (1 - \lambda)\, d'$. On the other hand, $R(q_i(j))$ is known to be a convex downward function (the rate for a channel as a function of its transition probabilities). Hence $R'' \leq \lambda R + (1 - \lambda)\, R'$. The minimizing $q_i''(j)$ for d'' must give at least this low a value of R''. *Hence the curve R as a function of d (or conversely) is convex downward.*

The minimum possible d value clearly occurs if, for each i, $q_i(j)$ is assigned the value 1 for the j having the minimum d_{ij}. Thus the lowest possible d is given by

$$d_{\min} = \sum_i P_i \min_j d_{ij}\ .$$

If the m alphabet is imaged in the Z alphabet, then $d_{\min} = 0$, and the corresponding R value is the ordinary entropy or rate for the source. In the more general situation, $R(d_{\min})$ may be readily evaluated if there is a unique $\min_j d_{ij}$ by evaluating R for the assignment mentioned. Otherwise the evaluation of $R(d_{\min})$ is a bit more complex.

On the other hand, $R = 0$ is obtained if and only if $q_i(j) = Q_j$, a function of j only. This is because an average mutual information is positive unless the events are independent. For a given Q_j giving $R = 0$, the d is then $\sum_{ij} P_i\, Q_j\, d_{ij} = \sum_j Q_j \sum_i P_i\, d_{ij}$. The inner sum is non-negative. If we wish the minimum d for $R = 0$, this would result by finding a j that gives a minimum $\sum_i P_i\, d_{ij}$ (say j^*) and making $Q_{j^*} = 1$. This can be done by assigning $q_i(j^*) = 1$ (all other $q_i(j)$ are made 0).

Summarizing, then, $R(d)$ is a convex downward function as shown in Fig. 3 running from $R(d_{\min})$ at $d_{\min} = \sum_i P_i \min_j d_{ij}$ to zero at $d_{\max} = \min_j \sum_i P_i\, d_{ij}$. It is continuous both ways (R as a function of d or d as a function of R) in the interior of this interval because of its convexity. For $d \geq d_{max}$, we have $R = 0$. The curve is strictly monotonically decreasing from d_{min} to d_{max}. Also it is easily seen that in this interval the assignment of $q_i(j)$ to obtain any point $R(d^*)$ must give a d satisfying the equality $d = d^*$ (not the inequality $d < d^*$). For $d^* > d_{max}$ the inequality will occur for the minimizing $q_i(j)$. Thus the minimizing problem can be limited to a consideration of minima in the subspace where $d = d^*$, except in the range $d^* > d_{max}$ (where $R(d^*) = 0$).

The convex downward nature of R as a function of the assigned $q_i(j)$ is helpful in evaluating the $R(d)$ in specific cases. It implies that any local minimum (in the subspace for a fixed d) is the absolute minimum in this subspace. For otherwise we could connect the local and absolute minima by a straight line and find a continuous series of points lower than the local minimum along this line. This would contradict its being a local minimum.

Furthermore, the functions $R(q_i(j))$ and $d(q_i(j))$ have continuous derivatives interior to the allowed $q_i(j)$ set. Hence ordinary calculus methods (e.g., Lagrangian multipliers) may be used to locate the minimum. In general, however, this still involves the solution of a set of simultaneous equations.

Solution for $R(d)$ in Certain Simple Cases. One special type of situation leads to a simple explicit solution for the $R(d)$ curve. Suppose that all a input letters are equiprobable: $P_i = 1/a$. Suppose further that the d_{ij} matrix is square and is such that each row has the same set of entries and each column also has the same set of entries, although, of course, in different order.

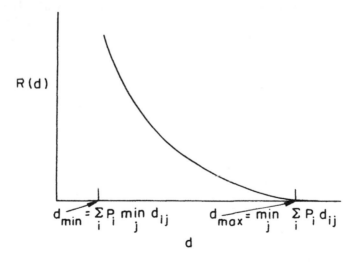

Fig. 3.

An example of this type is the positioning of a wheel mentioned earlier if all positions are equally likely. Another example is the simple error probability distortion measure if all letters are equally likely.

In general, let the entries in any row or column be $d_1, d_2, d_3, \ldots, d_a$. Then we shall show that the minimizing R for a given d occurs when all lines with distortion assignment d_k are given the probability assignment

$$q_k = \frac{e^{-\lambda d_k}}{\sum_i e^{-\lambda d_i}} .$$

Here λ is a parameter ranging from 0 to ∞ which determines the value of d. With this minimizing assignment, d and R are given parametrically in terms of λ:

$$d = \frac{\sum_i d_i e^{-\lambda d_i}}{\sum_i e^{-\lambda d_i}} ,$$

$$R = \log \frac{a}{\sum_i e^{-\lambda d_i}} - \lambda d .$$

When $\lambda = 0$ it can be seen that $d = \frac{1}{a} \sum_i d_i$ and $R = 0$. When $\lambda \to \infty$, $d \to d_{\min}$ and $R \to \log \frac{a}{k}$ where k is the number of d_i with value $d_{\min}$.

This solution is proved as follows. Suppose that we have an assignment $q_i(j)$ giving a certain d^* and a certain R^*. Consider now a new assignment where each line with d_{ij} value d_1 is assigned the average of the assignments for these lines in the original assignment. Similarly, each line labeled d_2 is given the average of all the d_2 original assignments, and so on. Because of the linearity of d, this new assignment has the same d value, namely d^*. The new R is the same as or smaller than R^*. This is shown as follows. R may be written $H(m) - H(m|Z)$. $H(m)$ is not changed, and $H(m|Z)$ can only be increased by this averaging. The latter fact can be seen by observing that because of the convexity of $- \sum_i x_i \log x_i$ we have

$$- \sum_j \alpha_j \sum_t x_j^{(t)} \log x_j^{(t)} \geq - \sum_t \left[\sum_j \alpha_j x_j^{(t)} \right] \log \sum_j \alpha_j x_j^{(t)} ,$$

where for a given t, $x_j^{(t)}$ is a set of probabilities, and α_j is a set of weighting factors. In particular

$$- \sum_j \frac{\sum_s q_j^{(s)}}{\sum_{s,i} q_i^{(s)}} \sum_t \frac{q_j^{(t)}}{\sum_s q_j^{(s)}} \log \frac{q_j^{(t)}}{\sum_s q_j^{(s)}}$$

$$\geq - \sum_t \frac{\sum_j q_j^{(t)}}{\sum_{s,i} q_i^{(s)}} \log \frac{\sum_j q_j^{(t)}}{\sum_{s,i} q_i^{(s)}} ,$$

where $q_j^{(s)}$ is the original assignment to the line of value d_j from letter s. But this inequality can be interpreted on the left as $H(m|Z)$ after the averaging process, while the right-hand side is $H(m|Z)$ before the averaging. The desired result then follows.

Hence, for the minimizing assignment, all lines with the same d value will have equal probability assignments. We denote these by q_i corresponding to a line labeled d_i. The rate R and distortion d can now be written

$$d = \sum_i q_i \, d_i \, ,$$

$$R = \log a + \sum_i q_i \log q_i \, ,$$

since all z's are now equiprobable, and $H(m) = \log a, H(m|Z) = - \sum_i q_i \log q_i$. We wish, by proper choice of the q_i, to minimize R for a given d and subject to $\sum_i q_i = 1$. Consider then, using Lagrange multipliers,

$$U = \log a + \sum_i q_i \log q_i + \lambda \sum_i q_i \, d_i + \mu \sum_i q_i \, ,$$

$$\frac{\partial U}{\partial q_i} = 1 + \log q_i + \lambda d_i + \mu = 0 \, ,$$

$$q_i = A \, e^{-\lambda d_i} \, .$$

If we choose $A = \dfrac{1}{\sum_i e^{-\lambda d_i}}$ we satisfy $\sum_i q_i = 1$. This then gives a stationary point and by the convexity properties mentioned above it must be the absolute minimum for the corresponding value of d. By substituting this probability assignment in the formulas for d and R we obtain the results stated above.

Rate for a Product Source with a Sum Distortion Measure. Suppose that we have two independent sources each with its own distortion measure, d_{ij} and $d'_{i'j'}$, and resulting in rate distortion functions $R_1(d_1)$ and $R_2(d_2)$. Suppose that each source produces one letter each second. Considering ordered pairs of letters as single letters the combined system may be called the *product source*. If the total distortion is to be measured by the sum of the individual distortions, $d = d_1 + d_2$, then there is a simple method of determining the function $R(d)$ for the product source. In fact, we shall show that $R(d)$ is obtained by adding both coordinates of the curves $R_1(d_1)$ and $R_2(d_2)$ at points on the two curves having the same slope. The set of points obtained in this manner is the curve $R(d)$. Furthermore, a probability assignment to obtain any point of $R(d)$ is the product of the assignments for the component points.

We shall first show that given any assignment $q_{i,i'}(j, j')$ for the product source, we can do at least as well in the minimizing process using an assignment of the form $q_i(j) \, q'_{i'}(j')$ where q and q' are derived from the given $q_{i,i'}(j, j')$. Namely, let

$$q_i(j) = \sum_{i',j'} P'_{i'} \, q_{i,i'}(j,j') \, ,$$

$$q'_{i'}(j') = \sum_{i,j} P_i \, q_{i,i'}(j, j') \, .$$

We see that these are non-negative and, summed on j and j' respectively, give 1, so they are satisfactory transition probabilities. Also the assignment $q_i(j) \, q'_{i'}(j')$ gives the same total distortion as the assignment $q_{i,i'}(j,j')$. The former is

$$\sum_{i,i',j,j'} P_i \, P'_{i'} \, q_i(j) \, q'_{i'}(j')[d_{ij} + d'_{i'j'}]$$

$$= \sum_{i,j} P_i q_i(j) d_{ij} + \sum_{i',j'} P'_i \, q'_i(j') \, d'_{i'j'}$$

$$= \sum_{\substack{i,i' \\ j,j'}} P_i \, P'_{i'} \, q_{i,i'}(j,j')[d_{ij} + d'_{i',j'}] \; .$$

This last may be recognized as the distortion with $q_{i,i'}(j,j')$.

On the other hand, the mutual information R is decreased or left constant if we use $q_i(j) \, q'_{i'}(j)$ instead of $q_{i,i'}(j,j')$. In fact, this average mutual information can be written in terms of entropies as follows (using asterisks for entropies with the assignment $q_i(j) \, q'_{i'}(j')$ and none for the assignment $q_{i,i'}(j,j')$). We have

$$r = H(i, i') - H(i, i' | j, j')$$

$$\geq H(i,i') - H(i|j) - H(i'|j')$$

$$= H(i,i') - H^*(i|j) - H^*(i'|j') \; .$$

Here we use the fact that with our definition of $q_i(j)$ and $q'_{i'}(j')$ we have $Pr^*(i|j) = Pr(i|j)$ and $Pr^*(i'|j') = pr(i'|j')$. (This follows immediately on writing out these probabilities.) Now, using the fact that the sources are independent, $H(i,i') = H(i) + H(i') = H^*(i) + H^*(I')$. Hence our last reduction above is equal to R^*. This is the desired conclusion.

It follows that any point on the $R(d)$ curve for the product source is obtained by an independent or product assignment $q_i(j) \, q'_{i'}(j')$, and consequently is the sum in both coordinates of a pair of points on the two curves. The best choice for a given distortion d is clearly given by

$$R(d) = \min_t [R_1(t) + R_2(d - t)] \; ,$$

and this minimum will occur when

$$\frac{d}{dt} R_1(t) = \frac{d}{dt} R_2(d - t) \; .$$

Thus the component points to be added are points where the component curves have the same slope. The convexity of these curves insures the uniqueness of this pair for any particular d.

The Lower Bound on Distortion for a Given Channel Capacity. The importance of the $R(d)$ function is that it determines the channel capacity required to send at a certain rate and with a certain minimum distortion. Consider the following situation. We have given an independent letter source with probabilities P_i for the different possible letters. We have given a single-letter distortion measure d_{ij} which leads to the rate distortion function $R(d)$. Finally, there is a memoryless discrete channel K of capacity C bits per second (we assume that this channel may be used once each second). We wish to transmit words of length t from the source over the channel with a block code. The length of the code words in the channel is n. What is the lowest distortion d that might be obtained with a code and a decoding system of this sort?

Theorem 1. Under the assumptions given above it is not possible to have a code with distortion d smaller than the (minimum) d^* satisfying

$$R(d^*) = \frac{n}{t} C \,,$$

or, equivalently, in any code, $d \geq \phi\left[\dfrac{n}{t} C\right]$, where ϕ is the function inverse to $R(d)$.

This theorem, and a converse positive result to be given later, show that $R(d)$ may be thought of as the equivalent *rate of the source for a given distortion d*. Theorem 1 asserts that for the distortion d and t letters of text, one must supply in the channel at least $t R(d)$ total bits of capacity spread over the n uses of the channel in the code. The converse theorem will show that by taking n and t sufficiently large and with suitable codes it is possible to approach this limiting curve.

To prove Theorem 1, suppose that we have given a block code which encodes all message words of length t into channel words of length n and a decoding procedure for interpreting channel output words of length n into Z words of length t. Let a message word be represented by $m = m_1, m_2, \ldots, m_t$. A channel input word is $X = x_1, x_2, \ldots, x_n$. A channel output word is $Y = y_1, y_2, \ldots, y_n$ and a reproduced, or Z, word is $Z = z_1, z_2, \ldots, z_t$. By the given code and decoding system, X is a function of m and Z is a function of Y. The m_i are chosen independently according to the letter probabilities, and the channel transition probabilities give a set of conditional probabilities $P(y|x)$ applying to each x_i, y_i pair. Finally, the source and channel are independent in the sense that $P(Y|m, X) = P(Y|X)$.

We wish first to show that $H(m|Z) \geq H(m) - nC$. We have that $H(m|Z) \geq H(m|Y)$ (since Z is a function of Y) and also that $H(m|Y) \geq H(X|Y) - H(X) + H(m)$. This last is because, from the independence condition above, $H(Y|m, X) = H(Y|X)$, so $H(Y, m, X) - H(m, X) = H(X, Y) - H(X)$. But $H(m, X) = H(m)$, since X is a function of m, and for the same reason $H(m, X, Y) = H(m, Y)$. Hence, rearranging, we have

$$H(X, Y) = H(m, Y) + H(X) - H(m, X)$$

$$= H(m, Y) + H(X) - H(m) \,,$$

$$H(X|Y) \leq H(m|Y) + H(X) - H(m) \,.$$

Here we used $H(m, x) = H(m)$ and then subtracted $H(Y)$ from each side. Hence $H(m|Z) \geq H(X|Y) - H(X) + H(m)$.

Now we show that $H(X|Y) \geq nC$. This follows from a method we have used in other similar situations, by considering the *change* in $H(X|Y)$ with each received letter. Thus (using Y_k for the first k of the y letters, etc.),

$$\Delta H(X|Y) = H(X|y_1, y_2, \ldots, y_k) - H(X|y_1, y_2, \ldots, y_{k+1})$$

$$= H(X, X_k) - H(Y_k) - H(X, Y_k, y_{k+1}) + H(Y_k, y_{k+1})$$

$$= H(y_{k+1}|Y_k) - H(y_{k+1}|X, Y_k)$$

$$= H(y_{k+1}|Y_k) - H(y_{k+1}|x_{k+1})$$

$$\leq H(y_{k+1}) - H(y_{k+1}|x_{k+1})$$

$$\leq C \,.$$

Here we used the fact that the channel is memoryless, so $P(y_{k+1}|X, Y_k) = P(y_{k+1}|x_{k+1})$ and therefore $H(y_{k+1}|X, Y_k) = H(y_{k+1}|x_{k+1})$. Finally, C is the maximum possible $H(y) - H(y|X)$, giving the last inequality.

Since the incremental change in $H(X|Y_k)$ is bounded by C, the total change after n steps is bounded by nC. Consequently, the final $H(X|Y)$ is at least the initial value $H(X)$ less nC. Therefore

$$H(m|Z) \geq H(X|Y) - H(X) + H(m)$$

$$\geq H(X) - nC - H(X) + H(m) \ ,$$

$$H(m|Z) \geq H(m) - nC \ . \tag{1}$$

We now wish to *overbound* $H(m|Z)$ in terms of the distortion d. We have

$$H(m|Z) = H(m_1 \ m_2 \ ... \ m_t | z_1 \ z_2 \ ... \ z_t)$$

$$\leq \sum_i H(m_i|z_i)$$

$$= \sum_i H(m_i) - \sum_i (H(m_i) - H(m_i|z_i)) \ .$$

The quantity $H(m_i) - H(m_i|z_i)$ is the average mutual information between original message letter m_i and the reproduced letter z_i. If we let d_i be the distortion between these letters, then $R(d_i)$ (the rate-distortion function evaluated for this d_i) satisfies

$$R(d_i) \leq H(m_i) - H(m_i|z_i) \ ,$$

since $R(d_i)$ is the minimum mutual information for the distortion d_i. Hence our inequality may be written

$$H(m|Z) \leq \sum_{i=1}^{t} H(m_i) - \sum_{i=1}^{t} R(d_i) \ .$$

Using now the fact that $R(d)$ is a convex downward function, we have

$$H(m|Z) \leq \sum_i H(m_i) - t \, R\left[\sum_i \frac{d_i}{t} \right] \ .$$

But $\sum_i \dfrac{d_i}{t} = d$, the overall distortion of the system, so

$$H(m|Z) \leq \sum_i H(m_i) - t \, R(d) \ .$$

Combining this with our previous inequality (1) and using the independent letter assumption, we have $H(m) = \sum_i H(m_i)$, so

$$H(m) - nC \leq H(m) - t \, R(d) \ ,$$

$$nC \geq t \, R(d) \ .$$

This is essentially the result stated in Theorem 1.

It should be noted that the result in the theorem is an assertion about the minimum distortion after any finite number n of uses of the channel. It is not an asymptotic result for large n. Also, as seen by the method of proof, it applies to any code, block or variable length, provided only that after n uses of the channel, t (or more) letters are reproduced at the receiving point, whatever the received sequence may be.

The Coding Theorem for a Single-Letter Distortion Measure. We now prove a positive coding theorem corresponding to the negative statements of Theorem 1; namely, that it is possible to approach the lower bound of distortion for a given ratio of number n of channel letters to t message letters. We consider then a source of message letters and single-letter distortion measure d_{ij}. More generally than Theorem 1, however, this source may be ergodic; it is not necessarily an independent letter source. This more general situation will be helpful in a later generalization of the theorem. For an ergodic source there will still, of course, be letter probabilities P_i, and we could determine the rate distortion function $R(d)$ based on these probabilities as though it were an independent letter source.

We first establish the following result.

Lemma 1. Suppose that we have an ergodic source with letter probabilities P_i, a single-letter distortion measure d_{ij}, and a set of assigned transition probabilities $q_i(j)$ such that

$$\sum_{i,j} P_i \, q_i(j) \, d_{ij} = d^* \, ,$$

$$\sum_{i,j} P_i \, q_i(j) \log \frac{q_i(j)}{\sum_k P_k \, q_k(j)} = R \, .$$

Let $Q(Z)$ be the probability measure of a sequence Z in the space of reproduced sequences if successive source letters had independent transition probabilities $q_i(j)$ into the Z alphabet. Then, given $\varepsilon > 0$, for all sufficiently large block lengths t, there exists a set α of messages of length t from the source with total source probability $P(\alpha) \geq 1 - \varepsilon$, and for each m belonging to α a set of Z blocks of length t, say β_m, such that

1) $d(m, Z) \leq d^* + \varepsilon$ for $m \in \alpha$ and $Z \in \beta_m$,

2) $Q(\beta_m) \geq e^{-t(R + \varepsilon)}$ for any $m \in \alpha$.

In other words, and somewhat roughly, long messages will, with high probability, fall in a certain subset α. Each member m of this subset has an associated set of Z sequences β_m. The members of β_m have only (at most) slightly more than d^* distortion with m and the logarithm of the total probability of β_m in the Q measure is underbounded by $e^{-t(R + \varepsilon)}$.

To prove the lemma, consider source blocks of length t and the Z blocks of length t. Consider the two random variables, the distortion d between an m block and a Z block and the (unaveraged) mutual information type of expression below:

$$d = \frac{1}{t} \sum_i d_{m, z_i} \, ,$$

$$I(m; Z) = \frac{1}{t} \log \frac{Pr(Z|m)}{Q(Z)} = \frac{1}{t} \sum_i \log \frac{Pr(z_i|m_i)}{Q(z_i)} \, .$$

Here m_i is the ith letter of a source block m, and z_i is the ith letter of a Z block. Both R and d are random variables, taking on different values corresponding to different choices of m and Z. They are both the sum of t random variables which are identical functions of the joint (m, Z) process except for shifting along over t positions.

Since the joint process is ergodic, we may apply the ergodic theorem and assert that when t is large, d and R will, with probability nearly 1, be close to their expected values. In particular, for any given ε_1 and δ, if t is sufficiently large, we will have with probability $\geq 1 - \delta^2/2$ that

$$d \le \sum_{i,j} P_i \, q_i(j) \, d_{ij} + \varepsilon_1 = d^* + \varepsilon_1 \; .$$

Also, with probability at least $1 - \delta^2/2$ we will have

$$I \le \sum_{i,j} P_i \, q_i(j) \log \frac{q_i(j)}{Q_j} + \varepsilon_1 = R(d^*) + \varepsilon_1 \; .$$

Let γ be the set of (m, Z) pairs for which *both* inequalities hold. Then $Pr(\gamma) \ge 1 - \delta^2$ because each of the conditions can exclude, at most, a set of probability $\delta^2/2$. Now for any m_1 define β_{m_1} as the set of Z such that (m_1, Z) belongs to γ.

We have

$$Pr(\beta_m \mid m) \ge 1 - \delta$$

on a set of α of m whose total probability satisfies $Pr(\alpha) \ge 1 - \delta$. This is true, since if it were not we would have a total probability in the set complementary to γ of at least $\delta \cdot \delta = \delta^2$, a contradiction. The first δ would be the probability of m not being in α, and the second δ the conditional probability for such m's of Z not being in β_m. The product gives a lower bound on the probability of the complementary set to γ.

If $Z \in \beta_{m_1}$, then

$$\frac{1}{t} \log \frac{Pr(Z \mid m_1)}{Q(Z)} \le R(d^*) + \varepsilon_1 \; ,$$

$$Pr(Z \mid m_1) \le Q(Z) \, e^{t(R(d^*) + \varepsilon_1)} \; ,$$

$$Q(Z) \ge Pr(Z \mid m_1) e^{-t(R(d^*) + \varepsilon_1)} \; .$$

Sum this inequality over all $Z \in \beta_{m_1}$:

$$Q(\beta_m) = \sum_{Z \in \beta_{m_1}} Q(Z)$$

$$\ge e^{-t(R + \varepsilon_1)} \sum_{Z \in \beta_{m_1}} Pr(Z \mid m_1) \; .$$

If $m_1 \in \alpha$ then $\displaystyle\sum_{Z \in \beta_{m_1}} Pr(Z \mid m_1) \ge 1 - \delta$ as seen above. Hence the inequality can be continued to give

$$Q(\beta_{m_1}) \ge (1 - \delta) e^{-t(R + \varepsilon_1)} \; , \quad m_1 \in \alpha \; .$$

We have now established that for any $\varepsilon_1 > 0$ and $\delta > 0$ there exists a set α of m's and sets β_m of Z's defined for each m with the three properties

1) $Pr(\alpha) \ge 1 - \delta$,

2) $d(Z, m) \le d^* + \varepsilon_1$,   if $Z \in \beta_m$,

3) $Q(\beta_m) \ge (1 - \delta) \, e^{-t(R + \varepsilon_1)}$,   if $m \in \alpha$,

provided that the block length t is sufficiently large. Clearly, this implies that for any $\varepsilon > 0$ and sufficiently large t we will have

1) $Pr(\alpha) \geq 1 - \varepsilon$,

2) $d(Z, m) \leq d^* + \varepsilon$,   if $Z \in \beta_m$,

3) $Q(\beta_m) \geq e^{-t(R + \varepsilon)}$,

since we may take the ε_1 and δ sufficiently small to satisfy these simplified conditions in which we use the same ε. This concludes the proof of the lemma.

Before attacking the general coding problem, we consider the problem indicated schematically in Fig. 4. We have an ergodic source and a single-letter distortion measure that gives the rate distortion function $R(d)$. It is desired to encode this by a coder into sequences u in such a way that the original messages can be reproduced by the reproducer with an average distortion that does not exceed d^* (d^* being some fixed tolerable distortion level). We are considering here block coding devices for both boxes. Thus the coder takes as input successive blocks of length t produced by the source and has, as output, corresponding to each possible m block, a block from a u alphabet.

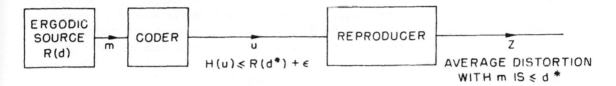

Fig. 4.

The aim is to do the coding in such a way as to keep the entropy of the u sequences as low as possible, subject to this requirement of reproducibility with distortion d^* or less. Here the entropy to which we are referring is the entropy per letter of the original source. Alternatively, we might think of the source as producing one letter per second and we are then interested in the u entropy per second.

We shall show that, for any d^* and any $\varepsilon > 0$, coders and reproducers can be found that are such that $H(u) \leq R(d^*) + \varepsilon$. As $\varepsilon \to 0$ the block length involved in the code in general increases. This result, of course, is closely related to our interpretation of $R(d^*)$ as the equivalent rate of the source for distortion d^*. It will follow readily from the following theorem.

Theorem 2. Given an ergodic source, a distortion measure d_{ij}, and rate distortion function $R(d)$ (based on the single-letter frequencies of the source), given $d^* \geq d_{min}$ and $\delta > 0$, for any sufficiently large t there exists a set Λ containing M words of length t in the Z alphabet with the following properties:

1) $\dfrac{1}{t} \log M \leq R(d^*) + \delta$,

2) the average distortion between an m word of length t and its nearest (i.e., least distortion) word in the set Λ is less than or equal to $d^* + \delta$.

This theorem implies (except for the δ in property (2) which will later be eliminated) the results mentioned above. Namely, for the coder, one merely uses a device that maps any m word into its nearest member of Λ. The reproducer is then merely an identity transformation.

The entropy per source letter of the coded sequence cannot exceed $R(d^*) + \delta$, since this would be maximized at $\frac{1}{t} \log M$ if all of the M members of Λ were equally probable and $\frac{1}{t} \log M$ is, by the theorem, less than or equal to $R(d^*) + \delta$.

This theorem will be proved by a random coding argument. We shall consider an ensemble of ways of selecting the members of Λ and estimate the average distortion for this ensemble. From the bounds on the average it will follow that at least one code exists in the ensemble with the desired properties.

The ensemble of codes is defined as follows. For the given d^* there will be a set of transition probabilities $q_i(j)$ that result in the minimum R, that is, $R(d^*)$. The set of letter probabilities, together with these transition probabilities, induce a measure $Q(Z)$ in the space of reproduced words. The Q measure for a single Z letter, say letter j, is $\sum_i P_i \, q_i(j)$. The Q measure for a Z word consisting of letters $j_1, j_2, \ldots, j_t$ is $Q(Z) = \prod_{k=1}^{t} \left[\sum_i P_i q_i(j_k) \right]$.

In the ensemble of codes of length t, the integers from 1 to M are mapped into Z words of length t in all possible ways. An integer is mapped into a particular word Z_1, say, with probability $Q(Z_1)$, and the probabilities for different integers are statistically independent. This is exactly the same process as that of constructing a random code ensemble for a memoryless channel, except that here the integers are mapped into the Z space by using the $Q(Z)$ measure. Thus we arrive at a set of codes (if there are f letters in the Z alphabet there will be f^{tM} different codes in the ensemble) and each code will have an associated probability. The code in which integer i is mapped into Z_i has probability $\prod_{i=1}^{M} Q(Z_i)$.

We now use Lemma 1 to bound the average distortion for this ensemble of codes (using the probabilities associated with the codes in calculating the average). Note, first, that in the ensemble of codes if $Q(\beta)$ is the Q measure of a set β of Z words, then the probability that this set contains no code words is $[1 - Q(\beta)]^M$, that is, the product of the probability that code word 1 is not in β, that for code word 2, etc. Hence the probability that β contains at least one code word is $1 - [1 - Q(\beta)]^M$. Now, referring to Lemma 1, the average distortion may be bounded by

$$\bar{d} \leq \varepsilon \, d_{\max} + [1 - Q(\beta_m)]^M \, d_{\max} + (d^* + \varepsilon) \ .$$

Here $d_{\max}$ is the largest possible distortion between an M letter and a Z letter. The first term, $\varepsilon d_{\max}$, arises from message words m which are not in the set α. These have total probability less than or equal to ε and, when they occur, average distortion less than or equal to $d_{\max}$. The second term overbounds the contribution that is due to cases in which the set β_m for the message m does not contain at least one code word. The probability in the ensemble of this is certainly bounded by $[1 - Q(\beta_m)]^M$, and the distortion is necessarily bounded by $d_{\max}$. Finally, if the message is in α and there is at least one code word in β_m, the distortion is bounded by $d^* + \varepsilon$, according to Lemma 1. Now, $Q(\beta_m) \geq e^{-t(R(d^*) + \varepsilon)}$. Also, for $0 < x \leq 1$,

$$(1 - x)^{\frac{1}{x}} = e^{\frac{1}{x} \log(1 - x)} \leq e^{\frac{1}{x}\left[-x + \frac{x^2}{2}\right]}$$

$$= e^{-1 + \frac{x}{2}} \leq e^{-\frac{1}{2}}.$$

(using the alternating and monotonically decreasing nature of the terms of the logarithmic expansion). Hence

$$[1 - Q(\beta_m)]^M \leq (1 - e^{-t(R(d^\cdot) + \varepsilon)})^M ,$$

and replacing the exponent by

$$M\, e^{t(R(d^\cdot) + \varepsilon)}\, e^{-t(R(d^\cdot) + \varepsilon)}$$

we see that this is

$$\leq \exp \{-\tfrac{1}{2}\, e^{-t(R(d^\cdot) + \varepsilon)}\, M\} .$$

If we choose for M, the number of points, the value $e^{t(R(d^\cdot) + 2\varepsilon)}$ (or, if this is not an integer, the smallest integer exceeding this quantity), then the expression given above is bounded by $\exp \{-\tfrac{1}{2}\, e^{t\varepsilon}\}$. Thus the average distortion is bounded with this choice of M by

$$\bar{d} \leq \varepsilon d_{max} + \exp \{-\tfrac{1}{2}\, e^{t\varepsilon}\}\, d_{max} + d^* + \varepsilon$$

$$\leq d^* + \delta ,$$

provided that ε in Lemma 1 is chosen small enough to make $(\varepsilon d_{max} + 1) \leq \delta/2$ and then t is chosen large enough to make $\exp \{-\tfrac{1}{2}e^{t\varepsilon}\}\, d_{max} \leq \delta/2$. We also require that ε be small enough and t large enough to make M, the integer just greater than or equal to $e^{t(R(d^\cdot) + 2\varepsilon)}$, less than or equal to $e^{t(R(d^\cdot) + \delta)}$. Since Lemma 1 holds for all sufficiently large t and any positive ε, these can all be simultaneously satisfied.

We have shown, then, that the conditions of the theorem are satisfied by the average distortion of the ensemble of codes. It follows that there exists at least one specific code in the ensemble whose average distortion is bounded by $d^* + \varepsilon$. This concludes the proof.

Corollary: Theorem 2 remains true if δ is replaced by 0 in property (1). It also remains true if the δ in property (1) is retained and the δ in property (2) is replaced by 0, provided in this case that $d^* > d_{min}$, the smallest d for which $R(d)$ is defined.

This corollary asserts that we can attain (or do better than) one coordinate of the $R(d)$ curve and approximate, as closely as desired, the other, except possibly for the d_{min} point. To prove the first statement of the corollary, note first that it is true for $d^* \geq d_1$, the value for which $R(d_1) = 0$. Indeed, we may achieve the point $\bar{d} = d_1$ with $M = 1$ and a code of length 1, using only the Z word consisting of the single Z letter which gives this point of the curve. For $d_{min} \leq d^* < d_1$, apply Theorem 2 to approximate $d^{**} = d^* + \delta/2$. Since the curve is strictly decreasing, this approximation will lead to codes with $\bar{d} \leq d^* + \delta$ and $\frac{1}{t} \log M \leq R(d^*)$), if the δ in Theorem 2 is made sufficiently small.

The second simplification in the corollary is carried out in a similar fashion, by choosing a d^{**} slightly smaller than the desired d^* that is such that $R(d^{**}) = R(d^*) + \delta/2$, and by using Theorem 2 to approximate this point of the curve.

Now suppose we have a memoryless channel of capacity C. By the coding theorem for such channels it is possible to construct codes and decoding systems with rate approximating C (per use of the channel) and error probability $\leq \varepsilon_1$ for any $\varepsilon_1 > 0$. We may combine such a code for a channel with a code of the type mentioned above for a source at a given distortion level d^* and obtain the following result.

Theorem 3. Given a source characterized by $R(d)$ and a memoryless channel with capacity $C > 0$, given $\varepsilon > 0$ and $d^* > d_{min}$, there exists, for sufficiently large t and n, a block code that maps source words of length t into channel words of length n and a decoding system that maps channel output words of length n into reproduced words of length t which satisfy

$$1)\ \bar{d} \le d^* \ ,$$

$$2)\ \frac{nC}{t} \le R(d^*) + \varepsilon \ .$$

Thus we may attain a desired distortion level d^* (greater than $d_{\min}$) and at the same time approximate using the channel at a rate corresponding to $R(d^*)$. This is done, as in the corollary stated above, by approximating the $R(d)$ curve slightly to the left of d^*, say, at $R(d^*) - \delta$. Such a code will have $M = e^{t(R(d^* - \delta) + \delta_1)}$ words, where δ_1 can be made small by taking t large. A code for the channel is constructed with M words and of length n, the largest integer satisfying $\frac{nC}{t} \le R(d^* - \delta) + \delta_1$. By choosing t sufficiently large, this will approach zero error probability, since it corresponds to a rate less than channel capacity. If these two codes are combined, it produces an over-all code with average distortion at most d^*.

Numerical Results for Some Simple Channels. In this section some numerical results will be given for certain simple channels and sources. Consider, first, the binary independent letter source with equiprobable letters and suppose that the distortion measure is the error probability (per digit). This falls into the class for which a simple explicit solution can be given. The $R(d)$ curve, in fact, is

$$R(d) = 1 + d \log_2 d + (1 - d) \log_2 (1 - d) \ .$$

This, of course, is the capacity of a symmetric binary channel with probabilities d and $(1 - d)$, the reason being that this is the probability assignment $q_i(j)$ which solves the minimizing problem.

This $R(d)$ curve is shown in Fig. 5. Also plotted are a number of points corresponding to specific simple codes, with the assumption of a noiseless binary channel. These will give some idea of how well the lower bound may be approximated by simple means. One point, $d = 0$, is obtained at rate $R = 1$ simply by sending the binary digits through the channel. Other simple codes which encode 2, 3, 4 and 5 message letters into one channel letter are the following. For the ratio 3 or 5, encode message sequences of three or five digits into 0 or 1 accordingly as the sequence contains more than half zeros or more than half ones. For the ratios 2 and 4, the same procedure is followed, while sequences with half zeros and half ones are encoded into 0.

At the receiving point, a 0 is decoded into a sequence of zeros of the appropriate length and a 1 into a sequence of ones. These rather degenerate codes are plotted in Fig. 5 with crosses. Simple though they are, with block length of the channel sequences only one, they still approximate to some extent the lower bound.

Plotted on the same curve are square points corresponding to the well-known single-error correcting codes with block lengths 3, 7, 15 and 31. These codes are used backwards here – any message in the 15-dimensional cube, for example, is transmitted over the channel as the *eleven message* digits of its nearest code point. At the receiving point, the corresponding fifteen-digit message is reconstructed. This can differ at most in one place from the original message. Thus for this case the ratio of channel to message letters is $\frac{11}{15}$, and the error probability is easily found to be $\frac{1}{16}$. This series of points gives a closer approximation to the lower bound.

It is possible to fill in densely between points of these discrete series by a technique of *mixing codes*. For example, one may alternate in using two codes. More generally, one may mix them in proportions λ and $1 - \lambda$, where λ is any rational number. Such a mixture gives a code with a new ratio R of message to channel letters, given by $\dfrac{1}{R} = \dfrac{\lambda}{R_1} + \dfrac{(1 - \lambda)}{R_2}$, where R_1 and R_2 are the ratios for the given codes, and with new error probability

$$P_e = \frac{\lambda R_1 P_{e1} + (1 - \lambda) R_2 P_{e2}}{\lambda R_1 + (1 - \lambda) R_2} \ .$$

This interpolation gives a convex upward curve between any two code points. When applied to the series of simple codes and single-error correcting codes in Fig. 5, it produces the dotted-line interpolations indicated.

Another channel was also considered in this connection, namely, the binary symmetric channel of capacity $C = \frac{1}{2}$. This has probabilities 0.89 that a digit is received correctly and 0.11 incorrectly. Here the series of points (Fig. 6) for simple codes actually touches the lower bound at the point $R = \frac{1}{2}$. This is because the channel itself, without coding, produces just this error probability. Any symmetric binary channel will have one point that can be attained exactly by means of straight transmission.

Figure 7 shows the $R(d)$ curve for another simple situation, a binary independent letter source but with the reproduced Z alphabet consisting of three letters, 0, 1, and ?. The distortion measure is zero for a correct digit, one for an incorrect digit, and 0.25 for ?. In the same figure is shown, for comparison, the $R(d)$ curve without the ? option.

Figure 8 shows the $R(d)$ curves for independent letter sources with various numbers of equiprobable letters in the alphabet (2, 3, 4, 5, 10, 100). Here again the distortion measure is taken to be error probability (per digit). With b letters in the alphabet the $R(d, b)$ curve is given by

$$R(d, b) = \log_2 b + d \log_2 d + (1 - d) \log_2 \frac{1 - d}{b - 1} \ .$$

Generalization to Continuous Cases. We will now sketch briefly a generalization of the single-letter distortion measure to cases where the input and output alphabets are not restricted to finite sets but vary over arbitrary spaces.

Assume a message alphabet $A = \{m\}$ and a reproduced letter alphabet $B = \{z\}$. For each pair (m, z) in these alphabets let $d(m, z)$ be a non-negative number, the distortion if m is reproduced as z. Further, we assume a probability measure P defined over a Borel field of subsets of the A space. Finally, we require that, for each z belonging to B, $d(m, z)$ is a measurable function with finite expectation.

Consider a finite selection of points z_i $(i = 1, 2, \ldots, l)$ from the B space, and a measurable assignment of transition probabilities $q(z_i|m)$. (That is, for each i, $q(z_i|m)$ is a measurable function in the A space.) For such a choice of z_i and assignment $q(z_i|m)$, a mutual information and an average distortion are determined:

$$R = \sum_i \int q(z_i|m) \log \frac{q(z_i|m)}{\int q(z_i|m) dP(m)} dP(m) \ ,$$

$$d = \sum_i \int d(m, z_i) \, q(z_i|m) \, dP(m) \ .$$

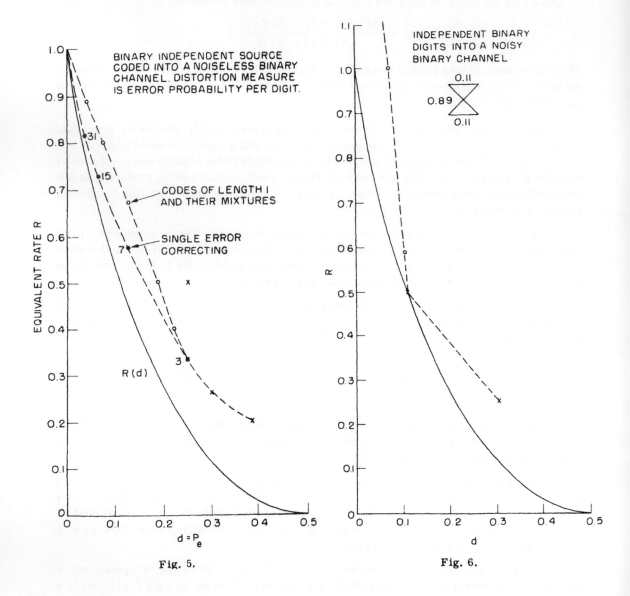

Fig. 5.

Fig. 6.

We define the rate distortion function $R(d^*)$ for such a case as the greatest lower bound of R when the set of points z_i is varied (both in choice and number) and the $q(z_i|m)$ is varied over measurable transition probabilities, subject to keeping the distortion at the level d^* or less.

Most of the results we have found for the finite alphabet case carry through easily under this generalization. In particular, the convexity property of the $R(d)$ curve still holds. In fact, if $R(d)$ can be approximated to within ε by a choice z_i and $q(z_i|m,)$ and $R(d')$ by a choice of z_i' and $q'(z_i'|m)$, then one considers the choice z_i'' consisting of the union of the points z_i and z_i', together with $q''(z_i''|m) = \frac{1}{2}[q(z_i''|m) + q'(z_i''|m)]$ (using zero if $q(z''|m)$ or $q'(z''|m)$ is undefined). This leads, by the convexity of R and by the linearity of d, to an assignment for $d'' = \frac{1}{2} d + \frac{1}{2} d'$, giving an R'' within ε of the midpoint of the line joining $d R(d)$ and $d' R(d')$. It follows, since ε can be made arbitrarily small, that the greatest lower bound of $R(d'')$ is on or below this midpoint.

In the general case it is, however, not necessarily true that the $R(d)$ curve approaches a finite end-point when d decreases toward its minimum possible value. The behavior may be as indicated in Fig. 9 with $R(d)$ going to infinity as d goes to $d_{\min}$. On the other hand, under the conditions we have stated, there is a finite $d_{\max}$ for which $R(d_{\max}) = 0$. This value of d is given by

$$d_{\max} = \underset{z}{g.l.b.} \ E[d(m, z)] \ .$$

The negative part of the coding theorem goes through in a manner essentially the same as the finite alphabet case, it being assumed that the only allowed coding functions from the source sequences to channel inputs correspond to measurable subsets of the source space. (If this assumption were not made, the average distortion would not, in general, even be defined.) The various inequalities may be followed through, changing the appropriate sums in the A space to integrals and resulting in the corresponding negative theorem.

For the positive coding theorem also, substantially the same argument may be used with an additional ε involved to account for the approximation to the greatest lower bound of $R(d)$ with a finite selection of z_i points. Thus one chooses a set of z_i to approximate the $R(d)$ curve to within ε, and then proceeds with the random coding method. The only point to be noted is that the $d_{\max}$ term must now be handled in a slightly different fashion. To each code in the ensemble one may add a particular point, say z_0, and replace $d_{\max}$ by $E(d(m, z_0))$, a finite quantity. The results of the theorem then follow.

Difference Distortion Measure. A special class of distortion measures for certain continuous cases of some importance and for which more explicit results can be obtained will now be considered. For these the m and z spaces are both the sets of all real numbers. The distortion measure $d(m, z)$ will be called a *difference distortion measure* if it is a function only of the difference $m - z$, thus $d(m, z) = d(m - z)$. A common example is the squared error measure, $d(m, z) = (m - z)^2$ or, again, the absolute error criterion $d(m, z) = |m - z|$.

We will develop a lower bound on $R(d)$ for a difference distortion measure. First we define a function $\phi(d)$ for a given difference measure $d(u)$ as follows. Consider an arbitrary distribution function $G(u)$ and let H be its entropy and d the average distortion between a random variable with a given distribution and zero. Thus

$$H = - \int_{-\infty}^{\infty} \log dG(u) \ dG(u) \ ,$$

$$d = \int_{-\infty}^{\infty} d(u) \ dG(u) \ .$$

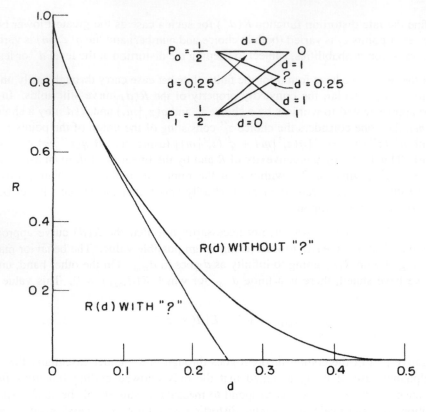

Fig. 7.

We wish to vary the distribution $G(u)$, keeping $d \le d^*$, and seek the maximum H. The least upper bound, if finite, is clearly actually attained as a maximum for some distribution. This maximum H for a given d^* we call $\phi(d^*)$, and a corresponding distribution function is called a maximizing distribution for this d^*.

Now suppose we have a distribution function for the m space (generalized letter probabilities) $P(m)$, with entropy $H(m)$. We wish to show that

$$R(d) \ge H(m) - \phi(d) .$$

Let z_i be a set of z points and $q(z_i|m)$ an assignment of transition probabilities. Then the mutual information between m and z may be written

$$R = H(m) - \sum_i Q_i H(m|z_i) ,$$

where Q_i is the resulting probability of z_i. If we let d_i be the average distortion between m and z_i, then

$$H(m|z_i) \le \phi(d_i) .$$

This is because $\phi(d)$ was the maximum H for a given average distortion and also because the distortion is a function only of the difference between m and z, so that this maximizing value applies for any z_i. Thus

$$R \ge H(m) - \sum_i Q_i \phi(d_i) .$$

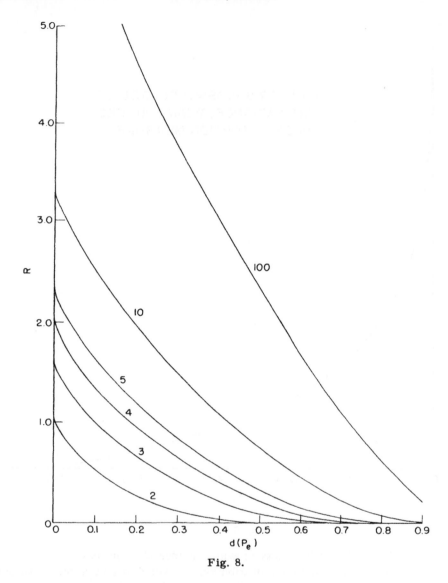

Fig. 8.

Now $\phi(d)$ is a concave function. This is a consequence of the concavity of entropy considered as a function of a distribution function and the linearity of d in the same space of distribution functions, by an argument identical with that used previously. Hence $\sum_i Q_i \phi(d_i) \leq \phi(\sum_i Q_i d_i) = \phi(d)$, where d is the average distortion with the choice z_i and the assigned transition probabilities. It follows that

$$r \geq H(m) - \phi(d) \ .$$

This is true for any assignment z_i and $q(z_i|m)$, and proves the desired result.

If, for a particular $P(m)$ and $d(u)$, assignments can be made which approach this lower bound, then, of course, this is the $R(d)$ function. Such is the case, for example, if $P(m)$ is Gaussian and $d(u) = u^2$ (mean square error measure of distortion). Suppose that the message has variance σ^2, and consider a Gaussian distribution of mean zero and variance $\sigma^2 - d$ in the z space. (If this is zero or negative, clearly $R(d) = 0$ by using only the z point zero.) Let the

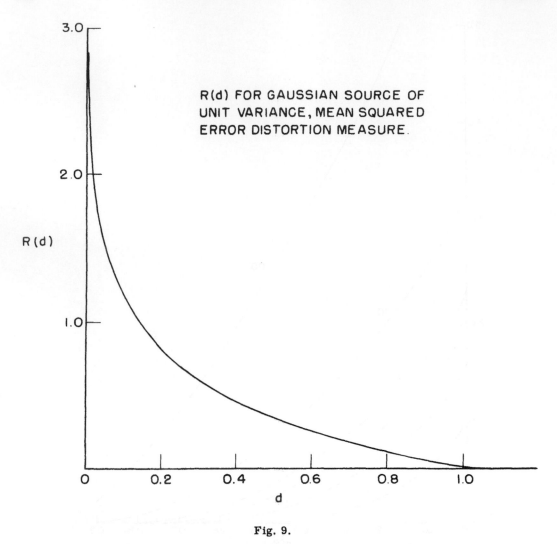

R(d) FOR GAUSSIAN SOURCE OF
UNIT VARIANCE, MEAN SQUARED
ERROR DISTORTION MEASURE.

Fig. 9.

conditional probabilities $q(m|z)$ be Gaussian with variance d. This is consistent with the Gaussian character of $P(m)$, since normal distributions convolve to give normal distributions with the sum of the individual variances. These assignments determine the conditional probability measure $q(z|m)$, also then normal.

A simple calculation shows that this assignment attains the lower bound given above. The resulting $R(d)$ curve is

$$R(d) = \begin{cases} \log \dfrac{\sigma}{\sqrt{d}} & d \le \sigma^2, \\ 0 & d > \sigma^2. \end{cases}$$

This is shown for $\sigma^2 = 1$ in Fig. 9.

Definition of a Local Distortion Measure. Thus far we have considered only a distortion measure d_{ij} (or $d(m, z)$) which depends upon comparison of a message letter with the corresponding reproduced letter, this letter-to-letter distortion to be averaged over the length of message and over the set of possible messages and possible reproduced messages. In many practical cases, however, this type of measure is not sufficiently general. The seriousness of a particular type of error often depends on the context.

Thus in transmitting a stock market quotation, say: "A.T.&T. 5900 shares, closing 194," an error in the 9 of 5900 shares would normally be much less serious than an error in the 9 of the closing price.

We shall now consider a distortion measure that depends upon local context and, in fact, compares blocks of g message letters with the corresponding blocks of g letters of the reproduced message.

A *local distortion measure of span g* is a function $d(m_1, m_2, \ldots, m_g; z_1, z_2, \ldots, z_g)$ of message sequences of length g and reproduced message sequences of length g (from a possibly different or larger alphabet) with the property that $d \geq 0$. The distortion between $m = m_1, m_2, \ldots, m_t$ and $z = z_1, z_2, \ldots, z_t$ $(t \geq g)$ is defined by

$$d(m, Z) = \frac{1}{t-g} \sum_{k=1}^{t-g+1} d(m_k, m_{k+1}, \ldots, m_{k+g-1}; z_k, z_{k+1}, \ldots, z_{k+g-1}) .$$

The distortion of a *block code* in which message m and reproduced version Z occur with probability $P(m, Z)$ is defined by

$$d = \sum_{m,Z} P(m, Z) \, d(m, Z) .$$

In other words, we assume, with a local distortion measure, that the evaluation of an entire system is obtained by averaging the distortions for all block comparisons of length g each with its probability of occurrence a weighting factor.

The Functions $R_n(d)$ and $R(d)$ for a Local Distortion Measure and Ergodic Source. Assume that we have given an ergodic message source and a local distortion measure. Consider blocks of m message letters with their associated probabilities (as determined by the source) together with possible blocks Z of reproduced message of length n. Let an arbitrary assignment of transition probabilities from the m blocks to the Z blocks, $q(Z|m)$, be made. For this assignment we can calculate two quantities: 1) the average mutual information per letter

$$R = \frac{1}{n} E\left[\log \frac{q(Z|m)}{Q(z)}\right]$$ and 2) the average distortion if the m's were reproduced as Z's with

the probabilities $q(Z|m)$. This is $d = \sum_{m,Z} P(m, Z) \, d(m, Z)$. By variation of $q(Z|m)$, while holding $d \leq d^*$, we can, in principle, find the minimum R for each d^*. This we call $R_n(d^*)$.

The minimizing problem here is identical with that discussed previously if we think of m and Z as individual letters in a (large) alphabet, and various results relating to this minimum can be applied. In particular, $R_n(d)$ is a convex downward function.

We now define the *rate distortion function* for the given source relative to the distortion measure as

$$R(d) = \liminf_{n \to \infty} R_n(d) .$$

It can be shown, by a direct but tedious argument that we shall omit, that the "inf" may be deleted from this definition. In other words, $R_n(d)$ approaches a limit as $n \to \infty$.

We are now in a position to prove coding theorems for a general ergodic source with a local distortion measure.

The Positive Coding Theorem for a Local Distortion Measure.

Theorem 4. Suppose that we are given an ergodic source and a local distortion measure with rate distortion function $R(d)$. Let K be a memoryless discrete channel with capacity C, let d^* be a value of distortion, and let ε be a positive number. Then there exists a block code with distortion less than or equal to $d^* + \varepsilon$, and a signaling rate at least $\left[\dfrac{C}{R} - \varepsilon\right]$ message letters per channel letter.

Proof. Choose an n_1 so that $R_{n_1}(d^*) - R(d^*) < \dfrac{\varepsilon}{3}$ and, also, so large that $\dfrac{g}{n_1} d_{\max} < \dfrac{\varepsilon}{3}$. Now consider blocks of length n_1 and "letters" of an enlarged alphabet. Using Theorem 3 we can construct a block code using sufficiently long sequences of these "letters" signaling at a rate close to (say within $\varepsilon/3$ of) $R_{n_1}(d^*)/C$ (in terms of original message letters) and with distortion less than $d^* + \dfrac{\varepsilon}{3}$. It must be remembered that this distortion is based on a single "letter" comparison. However, the distortion by the given local distortion measure will differ from this only because of overlap comparisons (g for each n_1 letters of message) and hence the discrepancy is, at most, $\dfrac{g}{n_1} d_{\max} < \dfrac{\varepsilon}{3}$. It follows that this code signals at a rate within ε of $R(d^*)$ and at a distortion within ε of d^*.

The Converse Coding Theorem.

Theorem 5. Suppose that we are given an ergodic source and a local distortion measure with rate distortion function $R(d)$. Let K be a memoryless discrete channel with capacity C, let d^* be a value of distortion, and let ε be a positive number. Then there exists t_0 which is such that any code transmitting $t \geq t_0$ message letters with n uses of the channel at distortion d^*, or less, satisfies

$$\frac{n}{t} C \geq R(d^*) - \varepsilon .$$

That is, the channel capacity bits used per message letter must be nearly $R(d^*)$ for long transmissions.

Proof. Choose t_0 so that for $t \geq t_0$ we have $R_t(d) \geq R(d) - \varepsilon$. Since $R(d)$ was defined as $\lim_{t \to \infty} \inf R_t(d)$, this is possible. Suppose that we have a code for such a $t \geq t_0$ which maps sequences m consisting of t message letters into sequences X of n channel letters and decodes sequences Y of n channel output letters into sequences Z of reproduced messages. The channel will have, from its transition probabilities, some $P(Y|X)$. Furthermore, from the encoding and decoding functions, we shall have $X = f(m)$ and $Z = g(Y)$. Finally there will be, from the source, probabilities for the message sequences $P(m)$. By the encoding function $f(m)$ this will induce a set of probabilities $P(X)$ for input sequences. If the channel capacity is C, the average mutual information $R(X, Y)$ between input and output sequences must satisfy

$$R(X, Y) = E \log \frac{P(X|Y)}{P(X)} \leq nC ,$$

since nC is the maximum possible value of this quantity when $P(X)$ is varied. Also, since X is a function of m and Z is a function of Y, we have

$$R(m, Z) = E \log \frac{P(m|Z)}{P(m)} \leq R(X, Y) \leq nC .$$

The coding system in question amounts, overall, to a set of conditional probabilities from m sequences to Z sequences as determined by the two coding functions and the transition probabilities. If the distortion of the overall system is less than or equal to d^*, then $t R_t(d^*) = \min_{P(Z|m)} R(m, Z)$ is certainly less than or equal to the particular $R(m, Z)$ obtained with the probabilities given by the channel and coding system. (The t factor is present because $R_t(d)$ is measured on a per message letter basis, while the $R(m, Z)$ quantities are for sequences of length t.) Thus

$$tR_t(d^*) \leq R(m, Z) \leq nC ,$$

$$t(R(d^*) - \varepsilon) \leq nC ,$$

$$\frac{n}{t} C \geq R(d^*) - \varepsilon .$$

This is the conclusion of the theorem.

Notice from the method of proof that again the code used need not be a block code, provided only that, after n uses of the channel, t recovered letters are written down. If one has some kind of variable-length code and, starting at time zero, uses this code continually, the inequality of the theorem will hold for any finite time after t_0 message letters have been recovered; and of course as longer and longer blocks are compared, $\varepsilon \to 0$. It is even possible to generalize this to variable-length codes in which, after n uses of the channel, the number of recovered message letters is a random variable depending, perhaps, on the particular message and the particular chance operation of the channel. If, as is usually the case in such codes, there exists an average signaling rate with the properties that after n uses of the channel then, with probability nearly one, t letters will be written down, with t lying between $t_1(1 - \delta)$ and $t_1(1 + \delta)$ (the $\delta \to 0$ as $n \to \infty$), then essentially the same theorem applies, using the mean t_1 for t.

Channels with Memory. Finally we mention that while we have, in the above discussion, assumed the channel to be memoryless, very similar results, both of positive and negative type, can be obtained for channels with memory.

For a channel with memory one may define a capacity C_n for the first n use of the channel starting at state s_0. This C_n is $\frac{1}{n}$ times the maximum average mutual information between input sequences of length n and resulting output sequences when the probabilities assigned the input sequences of length n are varied. The lower bound on distortion after n uses of the channel is that given by Theorem 1 using C_n for C.

We can also define the capacity C for such a channel as $C = \lim\sup_{n \to \infty} C_n$. The positive parts of the theorem then state that one can find arbitrarily long block codes satisfying Theorem 3. In most channels of interest, of course, historical influences die out in such a way as to make $C_n \to C$ as $n \to \infty$. For memoryless channels, $C_n = C$ for all n.

Duality of a Source and a Channel. There is a curious and provocative duality between the properties of a source with a distortion measure and those of a channel. This duality is enhanced if we consider channels in which there is a "cost" associated with the different input letters, and it is desired to find the capacity subject to the constraint that the expected cost not exceed a certain quantity. Thus input letter i might have cost a_i and we wish to find the capacity with the side condition $\sum_i P_i a_i \leq a$, say, where P_i is the probability of using input letter i. This problem amounts, mathematically, to *maximizing* a mutual information under variation of the P_i with a linear inequality as constraint. The solution of this problem leads to a capacity cost function $C(a)$ for the channel. It can be shown readily that this function is *concave* downward. Solving this problem corresponds, in a sense, to finding a source that is just right for the channel and the desired cost.

In a somewhat dual way, evaluating the rate distortion function $R(d)$ for a source amounts, mathematically, to *minimizing* a mutual information under variation of the $q_i(j)$, again with a linear inequality as constraint. The solution leads to a function $R(d)$ which is *convex* downward. Solving this problem corresponds to finding a channel that is just right for the source and allowed distortion level. This duality can be pursued further and is related to a duality between past and future and the notions of control and knowledge. Thus we may have knowledge of the past but cannot control it; we may control the future but have no knowledge of it.

BIBLIOGRAPHY

[1]   C. E. Shannon and W. Weaver, *The Mathematical Theory of Communication*, University of Illinois Press, 1949.

[2]   R. W. Hamming, "Error-Detecting and Error-Correcting Codes," *Bell System Technical Journal,* Vol. 29, 1950, p. 147.

TWO-WAY COMMUNICATION CHANNELS

CLAUDE E. SHANNON

MASSACHUSETTS INSTITUTE OF TECHNOLOGY

CAMBRIDGE, MASSACHUSETTS

1. Introduction

A two-way communication channel is shown schematically in figure 1. Here x_1 is an input letter to the channel at terminal 1 and y_1 an output while x_2 is an

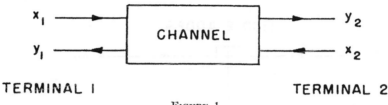

TERMINAL 1   TERMINAL 2

FIGURE 1

input at terminal 2 and y_2 the corresponding output. Once each second, say, new inputs x_1 and x_2 may be chosen from corresponding input alphabets and put into the channel; outputs y_1 and y_2 may then be observed. These outputs will be related statistically to the inputs and perhaps historically to previous inputs and outputs if the channel has memory. The problem is to communicate in both directions through the channel as effectively as possible. Particularly, we wish to determine what pairs of signalling rates R_1 and R_2 for the two directions can be approached with arbitrarily small error probabilities.

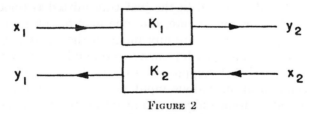

FIGURE 2

Before making these notions precise, we give some simple examples. In figure 2 the two-way channel decomposes into two independent one-way noiseless binary

This work was supported in part by the U.S. Army (Signal Corps), the U.S. Air Force (Office of Scientific Research, Air Research and Development Command), and the U.S. Navy (Office of Naval Research).

channels K_1 and K_2. Thus x_1, x_2, y_1 and y_2 are all binary variables and the operation of the channel is defined by $y_2 = x_1$ and $y_1 = x_2$. We can here transmit in each direction at rates up to one bit per second. Thus we can find codes whose

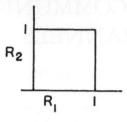

FIGURE 3

rates (R_1, R_2) approximate as closely as desired any point in the square, figure 3, with arbitrarily small (in this case, zero) error probability.

In figure 4 all inputs and outputs are again binary and the operation is defined

MOD. 2 ADDER

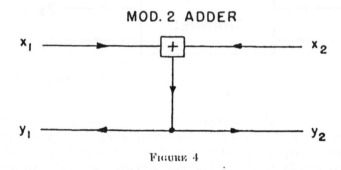

FIGURE 4

by $y_1 = y_2 = x_1 + x_2$ (mod 2). Here again it is possible to transmit one bit per second in each direction simultaneously, but the method is a bit more sophisticated. Arbitrary binary digits may be fed in at x_1 and x_2 but, to decode, the observed y must be corrected to compensate for the influence of the transmitted x. Thus an observed y_1 should be added to the just transmitted x_1 (mod 2) to determine the transmitted x_2. Of course here, too, one may obtain lower rates than the (1, 1) pair and again approximate any point in the square, figure 3.

A third example has inputs x_1 and x_2 each from a *ternary* alphabet and outputs y_1 and y_2 each from a binary alphabet. Suppose that the probabilities of different output pairs (y_1, y_2), conditional on various input pairs (x_1, x_2), are given by table I. It may be seen that by using only $x_1 = 0$ at terminal 1 it is possible to send one bit per second in the $2 - 1$ direction using only the input letters 1 and 2 at terminal 2, which then result with certainty in a and b respectively at terminal 1. Similarly, if x_2 is held at 0, transmission in the $1 - 2$ direction is possible at one bit per second. By dividing the time for use of these two strategies in the ratio λ to $1 - \lambda$ it is possible to transmit in the two directions with

TABLE I

$x_1 x_2$ \\ $y_1 y_2$		Output Pair			
		aa	ab	ba	bb
Input Pair	00	1/4	1/4	1/4	1/4
	01	1/2	1/2	0	0
	02	0	0	1/2	1/2
	10	1/2	0	1/2	0
	11	1/4	1/4	1/4	1/4
	12	1/4	1/4	1/4	1/4
	20	0	1/2	0	1/2
	21	1/4	1/4	1/4	1/4
	22	1/4	1/4	1/4	1/4

average rates $R_1 = 1 - \lambda$, $R_2 = \lambda$. Thus we can find codes approaching any point in the triangular region, figure 5. It is not difficult to see, and will follow

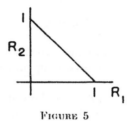

FIGURE 5

from later results, that no point outside this triangle can be approached with codes of arbitrarily low error probability.

In this channel, communication in the two directions might be called incompatible. Forward communication is possible only if x_2 is held at zero. Otherwise, all x_1 letters are completely noisy. Conversely, backward communication is possible only if x_1 is held at zero. The situation is a kind of discrete analogue to a common physical two-way system; a pair of radio telephone stations with "push-to-talk" buttons so arranged that when the button is pushed the local receiver is turned off.

A fourth simple example of a two-way channel, suggested by Blackwell, is the binary multiplying channel. Here all inputs and outputs are binary and the operation is defined $y_1 = y_2 = x_1 x_2$. The region of approachable rate pairs for this channel is not known exactly, but we shall later find bounds on it.

In this paper we will study the coding properties of two-way channels. In particular, inner and outer bounds on the region of approachable rate pairs (R_1, R_2) will be found, together with bounds relating to the rate at which zero error probability can be approached. Certain topological properties of these bounds will be discussed and, finally, we will develop an expression describing the region of approachable rates in terms of a limiting process.

2. Summary of results

We will summarize here, briefly and somewhat roughly, the main results of the paper. It will be shown that for a memoryless discrete channel there exists a convex region G of approachable rates. For any point in G, say (R_1, R_2), there exist codes signalling with rates arbitrarily close to the point and with arbitrarily small error probability. This region is of the form shown typically in figure 6,

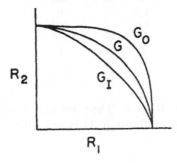

Figure 6

bounded by the middle curve G and the two axis segments. This curve can be described by a limiting expression involving mutual informations for long sequences of inputs and outputs.

In addition, we find an inner and outer bound, G_I and G_O, which are more easily evaluated, involving, as they do, only a maximizing process over single letters in the channel. G_O is the set of points (R_{12}, R_{21}) that may be obtained by assigning probabilities $P\{x_1, x_2\}$ to the input letters of the channel (an arbitrary joint distribution) and then evaluating

$$
\begin{aligned}
R_{12} &= E\left(\log \frac{P\{x_1|x_2, y_2\}}{P\{x_1|x_2\}}\right) = \sum_{x_1 x_2 y_2} P\{x_1 x_2 y_2\} \log \frac{P\{x_1|x_2, y_2\}}{P\{x_1|x_2\}} \\
R_{21} &= E\left(\log \frac{P\{x_2|x_1, y_1\}}{P\{x_2|x_1\}}\right),
\end{aligned}
$$

(1)

where $E(\mu)$ means expectation of μ. The inner bound G_I is found in a similar way but restricting the distribution to an independent one $P\{x_1, x_2\} = P\{x_1\}P\{x_2\}$. Then G_I is the *convex hull* of (R_{12}, R_{21}) points found under this restriction.

It is shown that in certain important cases these bounds are identical so the capacity region is then completely determined from the bounds. An example is also given (the binary multiplying channel) where there is a discrepancy between the bounds.

The three regions G_I, G and G_O are all convex and have the same intercepts on the axes. These intercepts are the capacities in the two directions when the other input letter is fixed at its best value [for example, x_1 is held at the value which maximizes R_{21} under variation of $P\{x_2\}$]. For any point inside G the error probabilities approach zero exponentially with the block length n. For any point outside G at least one of the error probabilities for the two codes will be bounded away from zero by a bound independent of the block length.

Finally, these results may be partially generalized to channels with certain types of memory. If there exists an internal state of the channel such that it is possible to return to this state in a bounded number of steps (regardless of previous transmission) then there will exist again a capacity region G with similar properties. A limiting expression is given determining this region.

3. Basic definitions

A *discrete memoryless two-way channel* consists of a set of transition probabilities $P\{y_1, y_2|x_1, x_2\}$ where x_1, x_2, y_1, y_2 all range over finite alphabets (not necessarily the same).

A *block code pair* of length n for such a channel with M_1 messages in the forward direction and M_2 in the reverse direction consists of two sets of n functions

$$(2) \quad \begin{aligned} &f_0(m_1), f_1(m_1, y_{11}), f_2(m_1, y_{11}, y_{12}), \cdots, f_{n-1}(m_1, y_{11}, \cdots, y_{1,n-1}) \\ &g_0(m_2), g_1(m_2, y_{21}), g_2(m_2, y_{21}, y_{22}), \cdots, g_{n-1}(m_2, y_{21}, \cdots, y_{2,n-1}). \end{aligned}$$

Here the f functions all take values in the x_1 alphabet and the g functions in the x_2 alphabet, while m_1 takes values from 1 to M_1 (the forward messages) and m_2 takes values from 1 to M_2 (the backward messages). Finally y_{1i}, for $i = 1, 2, \cdots, n-1$, takes values from the y_1 alphabet and similarly for y_{2i}. The f functions specify how the next input letter at terminal 1 should be chosen as determined by the message m_1 to be transmitted and the observed outputs $y_{11}, y_{12}, \cdots$ at terminal 1 up to the current time. Similarly the g functions determine how message m_2 is encoded as a function of the information available at each time in the process.

A *decoding system* for a block code pair of length n consists of a pair of functions $\phi(m_1, y_{11}, y_{12}, \cdots, y_{1n})$ and $\psi(m_2, y_{21}, y_{22}, \cdots, y_{2n})$. These functions take values from 1 to M_2 and 1 to M_1 respectively.

The decoding function φ represents a way of deciding on the original transmitted message from terminal 2 given the information available at terminal 1 at the end of a block of n received letters, namely, $y_{11}, y_{12}, \cdots, y_{1n}$ together with the transmitted message m_1 at terminal 1. Notice that the transmitted sequence $x_{11}, x_{12}, \cdots, x_{1n}$ although known at terminal 1 need not enter as an argument in the decoding function since it is determined (via the encoding functions) by m_1 and the received sequence.

We will assume, except when the contrary is stated, that all messages m_1 are equiprobable (probability $1/M_1$), that all messages m_2 are equiprobable (probability $1/M_2$), and that these events are statistically independent. We also assume that the successive operations of the channel are independent,

$$(3) \quad P\{y_{11}, y_{12}, \cdots, y_{1n}, y_{21}, y_{22}, \cdots, y_{2n}|x_{11}, x_{12}, \cdots, x_{1n}, x_{21}, x_{22}, \cdots, x_{2n}\}$$

$$= \prod_{i=1}^{n} P\{y_{1i}, y_{2i}|x_{1i}, x_{2i}\}.$$

This is the meaning of the memoryless condition. This implies that the probability of a set of outputs from the channel, conditional on the corresponding inputs, is the same as this probability conditional on these inputs and any previous inputs.

The *signalling rates* R_1 and R_2 for a block code pair with M_1 and M_2 messages for the two directions are defined by

(4)
$$R_1 = \frac{1}{n} \log M_1$$

$$R_2 = \frac{1}{n} \log M_2.$$

Given a code pair and a decoding system, together with the conditional probabilities defining a channel and our assumptions concerning message probability, it is possible, in principle, to compute error probabilities for a code. Thus one could compute for each message pair the probabilities of the various possible received sequences, if these messages were transmitted by the given coding functions. Applying the decoding functions, the probability of an incorrect decoding could be computed. This could be averaged over all messages for each direction to arrive at final error probabilities P_{e1} and P_{e2} for the two directions.

We will say that a point (R_1, R_2) belongs to the *capacity region G* of a given memoryless channel K if, given any $\epsilon > 0$, there exists a block code and decoding system for the channel with signalling rates R_1^* and R_2^* satisfying $|R_1 - R_1^*| < \epsilon$ and $|R_2 - R_2^*| < \epsilon$ and such that the error probabilities satisfy $P_{e1} < \epsilon$ and $P_{e2} < \epsilon$.

4. Average mutual information rates

The two-way discrete memoryless channel with finite alphabets has been defined by a set of transition probabilities $P\{y_1, y_2|x_1, x_2\}$. Here x_1 and x_2 are the input letters at terminals 1 and 2 and y_1 and y_2 are the output letters. Each of these ranges over its corresponding finite alphabet.

If a set of probabilities $P\{x_1\}$ is assigned (arbitrarily) to the different letters of the input alphabet for x_1 and another set of probabilities $P\{x_2\}$ to the alphabet for x_2 (these two taken statistically independent) then there will be definite corresponding probabilities for y_1 and y_2 and, in fact, for the set of four random variables x_1, x_2, y_1, y_2, namely,

(5)
$$P\{x_1, x_2, y_1, y_2\} = P\{x_1\} P\{x_2\} P\{y_1, y_2|x_1, x_2\}$$
$$P\{y_1\} = \sum_{x_1, x_2, y_2} P\{x_1, x_2, y_1, y_2\},$$

and so forth.

Thinking first intuitively, and in analogue to the one-way channel, we might think of the rate of transmission from x_1 to the terminal 2 as given by $H(x_1) - H(x_1|x_2, y_2)$, that is, the uncertainty or entropy of x_1 less its entropy conditional on what is available at terminal 2, namely, y_2 and x_2. Thus, we might write

$$(6) \qquad R_{12} = H(x_1) - H(x_1|x_2, y_2)$$

$$= E\left[\log \frac{P\{x_1, x_2, y_2\}}{P\{x_1\} P\{x_2, y_2\}}\right]$$

$$= E\left[\log \frac{P\{x_1|x_2, y_2\}}{P\{x_1\}}\right]$$

$$(7) \qquad R_{21} = H(x_2) - H(x_2|x_1, y_1)$$

$$= E\left[\log \frac{P\{x_1, x_2, y_1\}}{P\{x_2\} P\{x_1, y_1\}}\right]$$

$$= E\left[\log \frac{P\{x_2|x_1, y_1\}}{P\{x_2\}}\right].$$

These are the average mutual informations with the assigned input probabilities between the input at one terminal and the input-output pair at the other terminal. We might expect, then, that by suitable coding it should be possible to send in the two directions *simultaneously* with arbitrarily small error probabilities and at rates arbitrarily close to R_{12} and R_{21}. The codes would be based on these probabilities $P\{x_1\}$ and $P\{x_2\}$ in generalization of the one-way channel. We will show that in fact it is possible to find codes based on the probabilities $P\{x_1\}$ and $P\{x_2\}$ which do this.

However the capacity region may be larger than the set of rates available by this means. Roughly speaking, the difference comes about because of the probability of having x_1 and x_2 dependent random variables. In this case the appropriate mutual informations are given by $H(x_2|x_1) - H(x_2|x_1, y_1)$ and $H(x_1|x_2) - H(x_1|x_2, y_2)$. The above expressions for R_{21} and R_{12} of course reduce to these when x_1 and x_2 are independent.

5. The distribution of information

The method we follow is based on random codes using techniques similar to those used in [1] for the one-way channel. Consider a sequence of n uses of the channel or, mathematically, the product probability space. The inputs are $X_1 = (x_{11}, x_{12}, \cdots, x_{1n})$ and $X_2 = (x_{21}, x_{22}, \cdots, x_{2n})$ and the outputs $Y_1 = (y_{11}, y_{12}, \cdots, y_{1n})$ and $Y_2 = (y_{21}, y_{22}, \cdots, y_{2n})$, that is, sequences of n choices from the corresponding alphabets.

The conditional probabilities for these blocks are given by

$$(8) \qquad P\{Y_1, Y_2|X_1, X_2\} = \prod_k P\{y_{1k}, y_{2k}|x_{1k}, x_{2k}\}.$$

This uses the assumption that the channel is memoryless, or successive operations independent. We also associate a probability measure with input blocks X_1 and X_2 given by the product measure of that taken for x_1, x_2. Thus

$$P\{X_1\} = \prod_k P\{x_{1k}\}$$

(9)

$$P\{X_2\} = \prod_k P\{x_{2k}\}.$$

It then follows that other probabilities are also the products of those for the individual letters. Thus, for example,

$$P\{X_1, X_2, Y_1, Y_2\} = \prod_k P\{x_{1k}, x_{2k}, y_{1k}, y_{2k}\}$$

(10)

$$P\{X_2|X_1, Y_1\} = \prod_k P\{x_{2k}|x_{1k}, y_{1k}\}.$$

The (unaveraged) mutual information between, say, X_1 and the pair X_2, Y_2 may be written as a sum, as follows:

$$I(X_1; X_2, Y_2) = \log \frac{P\{X_1, X_2, Y_2\}}{P\{X_1\}P\{X_2, Y_2\}} = \log \frac{\prod_k P\{x_{1k}, x_{2k}, y_{2k}\}}{\prod_k P\{x_{1k}\} \prod_k P\{x_{2k}, y_{2k}\}}$$

(11)

$$= \sum_k \log \frac{P\{x_{1k}, x_{2k}, y_{2k}\}}{P\{x_{1k}\}P\{x_{2k}, y_{2k}\}}$$

$$I(X_1; X_2, Y_2) = \sum_k I(x_{1k}; x_{2k}, y_{2k}).$$

Thus, the mutual information is, as usual in such independent situations, the sum of the individual mutual informations. Also, as usual, we may think of the mutual information as a random variable. Here $I(X_1; X_2, Y_2)$ takes on different values with probabilities given by $P\{X_1, X_2, Y_2\}$. The *distribution function* for $I(X_1; X_2, Y_2)$ will be denoted by $\rho_{12}(Z)$ and similarly for $I(X_2; X_1, Y_1)$

$$\rho_{12}(Z) = P\{I(X_1; X_2, Y_2) \leqq Z\}$$

(12)

$$\rho_{21}(Z) = P\{I(X_2; X_1, Y_1) \leqq Z\}.$$

Since each of the random variables $I(X_1; X_2, Y_2)$ and $I(X_2; X_1, Y_1)$ is the sum of n independent random variables, each with the same distribution, we have the familiar statistical situation to which one may apply various central limit theorems and laws of large numbers. The mean of the distributions ρ_{12} and ρ_{21} will be nR_{12} and nR_{21} respectively and the variances n times the corresponding variances for one letter. As $n \to \infty$, $\rho_{12}[n(R_{12} - \epsilon)] \to 0$ for any fixed $\epsilon > 0$, and similarly for ρ_{21}. In fact, this approach is exponential in n; $\rho_{12}[n(R_{12} - \epsilon)] \leqq \exp[-A(\epsilon)n]$.

6. Random codes for the two-way channel

After these preliminaries we now wish to prove the existence of codes with certain error probabilities bounded by expressions involving the distribution functions ρ_{12} and ρ_{21}.

We will construct an ensemble of codes or, more precisely, of *code pairs*, one code for the $1 - 2$ direction and another for the $2 - 1$ direction. Bounds will be established on the error probabilities P_{e1} and P_{e2} *averaged over the ensemble,* and from these will be shown the existence of *particular* codes in the ensemble with related bounds on their error probabilities.

The random ensemble of code pairs for such a two-way channel with M_1 words in the $1 - 2$ code and M_2 words in the $2 - 1$ code is constructed as follows. The M_1 integers $1, 2, \cdots, M_1$ (the messages of the first code) are mapped in all possible ways into the set of input words X_1 of length n. Similarly the integers $1, 2, \cdots, M_2$ (the messages of the second code) are mapped in all possible ways into the set of input words X_2 of length n.

If there were a_1 possible input *letters* at terminal 1 and a_2 input *letters* at terminal 2, there will be a_1^n and a_2^n input *words* of length n and $a_1^{nM_1}$ *mappings* in the first code and $a_2^{nM_1}$ in the second code. We consider all pairs of these codes, a total of $a_1^{nM_1} a_2^{nM_1}$ pairs.

Each code pair is given a weighting, or probability, equal to the probability of occurrence of that pair if the two mappings were done independently and an integer is mapped into a word with the assigned probability of that word. Thus, a code pair is given a weighting equal to the product of the probabilities associated with all the input words that the integers are mapped into for both codes. This set of code pairs with these associated probabilities we call the *random ensemble of code pairs* based on the assigned probabilities $P\{X_1\}$ and $P\{X_2\}$.

Any particular code pair of the ensemble could be used to transmit information, if we agreed upon a method of decoding. The method of decoding will here consist of two functions $\phi(X_1, Y_1)$ and $\psi(X_2, Y_2)$, a special case of that defined above. Here X_1 varies over the input words of length n at terminal 1, and Y_1 over the possible received blocks of length n. The function ϕ takes values from 1 to M_2 and represents the decoded message for a received Y_1 if X_1 was transmitted. (Of course, X_1 is used in the decoding procedure in general since it may influence Y_1 and is, therefore, pertinent information for best decoding.)

Similarly, $\psi(X_2, Y_2)$ takes values from 1 to M_1 and is a way of deciding on the transmitted message m_1 on the basis of information available at terminal 2. It should be noted here that the decoding functions, ϕ and ψ, need not be the same for all code pairs in the ensemble.

We also point out that the encoding functions for our random ensemble are more specialized than the general case described above. The sequence of input letters X_1 for a given message m_1 do not depend on the received letters at terminal 1. In any particular code of the ensemble there is a strict mapping from messages to input sequences.

Given an ensemble of code pairs as described above and decoding functions, one could compute for each particular code pair two error probabilities for the two codes: P_{e1}, the probability of error in decoding the first code, and P_{e2} that for the second. Here we are assuming that the different messages in the first code occur with equal probability $1/M_1$, and similarly for the second.

By the *average error probabilities for the ensemble* of code pairs we mean the averages $E(P_{e1})$ and $E(P_{e2})$ where each probability of error for a particular code is weighted according to the weighting factor or probability associated with the code pair. We wish to describe a particular method of decoding, that is, a choice of ϕ and ψ, and then place upper bounds on these average error probabilities for the ensemble.

7. Error probability for the ensemble of codes

THEOREM 1.   *Suppose probability assignments $P\{X_1\}$ and $P\{X_2\}$ in a discrete memoryless two-way channel produce information distribution functions $\rho_{12}(Z)$ and $\rho_{21}(Z)$. Let $M_1 = \exp(R_1 n)$ and $M_2 = \exp(R_2 n)$ be arbitrary integers and θ_1 and θ_2 be arbitrary positive numbers. Then the random ensemble of code pairs with M_1 and M_2 messages has (with appropriate decoding functions) average error probabilities bounded as follows:*

$$(13) \qquad \begin{aligned} E(P_{e1}) &\leqq \rho_{12}[n(R_1 + \theta_1)] + e^{-n\theta_1} \\ E(P_{e2}) &\leqq \rho_{21}[n(R_2 + \theta_2)] + e^{-n\theta_2}. \end{aligned}$$

There will exist in the ensemble at least one code pair whose individual *error probabilities are bounded by two times these expressions, that is, satisfying*

$$(14) \qquad \begin{aligned} P_{e1} &\leqq 2\rho_{12}[n(R_1 + \theta_1)] + 2e^{-n\theta_1} \\ P_{e2} &\leqq 2\rho_{21}[n(R_2 + \theta_2)] + 2e^{-n\theta_2}. \end{aligned}$$

This theorem is a generalization of theorem 1 in [1] which gives a similar bound on P_e for a one-way channel. The proof for the two-way channel is a generalization of that proof.

The statistical situation here is quite complex. There are several statistical events involved: the choice of messages m_1 and m_2, the choice of code pair in the ensemble of code pairs, and finally the statistics of the channel itself which produces the output words Y_1 and Y_2 according to $P\{Y_1, Y_2 | X_1, X_2\}$. The ensemble error probabilities we are calculating are averages over *all* these statistical events.

We first define decoding systems for the various codes in the ensemble. For a given θ_2, define for each pair X_1, Y_1 a corresponding set of words in the X_2 space denoted by $S(X_1, Y_1)$ as follows:

$$(15) \qquad S(X_1, Y_1) = \left\{ X_2 \middle| \log \frac{P\{X_1, X_2, Y_1\}}{P\{X_2\}P\{X_1, Y_1\}} > n(R_2 + \theta_2) \right\}.$$

That is, $S(X_1, Y_1)$ is the set of X_2 words whose mutual information with the particular pair (X_1, Y_1) exceeds a certain level, $n(R_2 + \theta_2)$. In a similar way, we define a set $S'(X_2, Y_2)$ of X_1 words for each X_2, Y_2 pair as follows:

$$(16) \qquad S'(X_2, Y_2) = \left\{ X_1 \middle| \log \frac{P\{X_1, X_2, Y_2\}}{P\{X_1\}P\{X_2, Y_2\}} > n(R_1 + \theta_1) \right\}.$$

We will use these sets S and S' to define the decoding procedure and to aid in overbounding the error probabilities. The decoding process will be as follows. In any particular code pair in the random ensemble, suppose message m_1 is sent and this is mapped into input word X_1. Suppose that Y_1 is received at terminal 1 in the corresponding block of n letters. Consider the subset of X_2 words, $S(X_1, Y_1)$. Several situations may occur. (1) There is no message m_2 mapped into the subset $S(X_1, Y_1)$ for the code pair in question. In this case, X_1, Y_1 is decoded (conventionally) as message number one. (2) There is exactly one message mapped into the subset. In this case, we decode as this particular message. (3) There are more than one such messages. In this case, we decode as the smallest numbered such message.

The error probabilities that we are estimating would normally be thought of as calculated in the following manner. For each code pair one would calculate the error probabilities for all messages m_1 and m_2, and from their averages get the error probabilities for that code pair. Then these error probabilities are averaged over the ensemble of code pairs, using the appropriate weights or probabilities. We may, however, interchange this order of averaging. We may consider the cases where a particular $\overline{m}_1$ and $\overline{m}_2$ are the messages and these are mapped into particular $\overline{X}_1$ and $\overline{X}_2$, and the received words are $\overline{Y}_1$ and $\overline{Y}_2$. There is still, in the statistical picture, the range of possible code pairs, that is, mappings of the other $M_1 - 1$ messages for one code and $M_2 - 1$ for the other. We wish to show that, averaged over this subset of codes, the probabilities of any of these messages being mapped into subsets $S'(\overline{X}_2, \overline{Y}_2)$ and $S(\overline{X}_1, \overline{Y}_1)$ respectively do not exceed $\exp(-n\theta_1)$ and $\exp(-n\theta_2)$.

Note first that if X_1 belongs to the set $S'(\overline{X}_2, \overline{Y}_2)$ then by the definition of this set

$$\log \frac{P\{X_1, \overline{X}_2, \overline{Y}_2\}}{P\{X_1\} P\{\overline{X}_2, \overline{Y}_2\}} > n(R_1 + \theta_1)$$

(17)

$$P\{X_1 | \overline{X}_2, \overline{Y}_2\} > P\{X_1\} e^{n(R_1 + \theta_1)}.$$

Now sum each side over the set of X_1 belonging to $S'(\overline{X}_2, \overline{Y}_2)$ to obtain

$$(18) \qquad 1 \geqq \sum_{X_1 \in S'(\overline{X}_2, \overline{Y}_2)} P\{X_1 | \overline{X}_2, \overline{Y}_2\} > e^{n(R_1 + \theta_1)} \sum_{X_1 \in S'(\overline{X}_2, \overline{Y}_2)} P\{X_1\}.$$

The left inequality here holds since a sum of disjoint probabilities cannot exceed one. The sum on the right we may denote by $P\{S'(\overline{X}_2, \overline{Y}_2)\}$. Combining the first and last members of this relation

$$(19) \qquad\qquad P\{S'(\overline{X}_2, \overline{Y}_2)\} < e^{-n(R_1 + \theta_1)}.$$

That is, the total probability associated with any set $S'(\overline{X}_2, \overline{Y}_2)$ is bounded by an expression involving n, R_1 and θ_1 but *independent* of the particular $\overline{X}_2$, $\overline{Y}_2$.

Now recall that the messages were mapped independently into the input words using the probabilities $P\{X_1\}$ and $P\{X_2\}$. The probability of a particular message being mapped into $S'(\overline{X}_2, \overline{Y}_2)$ in the ensemble of code pairs is just $P\{S'(\overline{X}_2, \overline{Y}_2)\}$. The probability of being in the complementary set is $1 -$

$P\{S'(\overline{X}_2, \overline{Y}_2)\}$. The probability that *all* messages other than $\overline{m}_1$ will be mapped into this complementary set is

$$(20) \qquad [1 - P\{S'(\overline{X}_2, \overline{Y}_2)\}]^{M_1-1} \geqq 1 - (M_1 - 1)P\{S'(\overline{X}_2, \overline{Y}_2)\}$$
$$\geqq 1 - M_1 P\{S'(\overline{X}_2, \overline{Y}_2)\}$$
$$\geqq 1 - M_1 e^{-n(R_1+\theta_1)}$$
$$= 1 - e^{-n\theta_1}.$$

Here we used the inequality $(1 - x)^p \geqq 1 - px$, the relation (19) and finally the fact that $M_1 = \exp(nR_1)$.

We have established, then, that in the subset of cases being considered ($\overline{m}_1$ and $\overline{m}_2$ mapped into $\overline{X}_1$ and $\overline{X}_2$ and received as $\overline{Y}_1$ and $\overline{Y}_2$), with probability at least $1 - \exp(-n\theta_1)$, there will be no other messages mapped into $S'(\overline{X}_2, \overline{Y}_2)$. A similar calculation shows that with probability exceeding $1 - \exp(-n\theta_2)$ there will be no other messages mapped into $S(\overline{X}_1, \overline{Y}_1)$. These bounds, as noted, are independent of the particular $\overline{X}_1, \overline{Y}_1$ and $\overline{X}_2, \overline{Y}_2$.

We now bound the probability of the actual message $\overline{m}_1$ being within the subset $S'(\overline{X}_2, \overline{Y}_2)$. Recall that from the definition of $\rho_{12}(Z)$

$$(21) \qquad \rho_{12}[n(R_1 + \theta_1)] = P\left\{\log \frac{P\{X_1, X_2, Y_2\}}{P\{X_1\}P\{X_2, Y_2\}} \leqq n(R_1 + \theta_1)\right\}.$$

In the ensemble of code pairs a message $\overline{m}_1$, say, is mapped into words X_1 with probabilities just equal to $P\{X_1\}$. Consequently, the probability in the full ensemble of code pairs, message choices and channel statistics, that the actual message is mapped into $S'(\overline{X}_2, \overline{Y}_2)$ is precisely $1 - \rho_{12}[n(R_1 + \theta_1)]$.

The probability that the actual message is mapped *outside* $S'(\overline{X}_2, \overline{Y}_2)$ is therefore given by $\rho_{12}[n(R_1 + \theta_1)]$ and the probability that there are any other messages mapped into $S'(\overline{X}_2, \overline{Y}_2)$ is bounded as shown before by $\exp(-n\theta_1)$. The probability that *either* of these events is true is then certainly bounded by $\rho_{12}[n(R_1 + \theta_1)] + \exp(-n\theta_1)$; but this is then a bound on $E(P_{e1})$, since if neither event occurs the decoding process will correctly decode.

Of course, the same argument with interchanged indices gives the corresponding bound for $E(P_{e2})$. This proves the first part of the theorem.

With regard to the last statement of the theorem, we will first prove a simple combinatorial lemma which is useful not only here but in other situations in coding theory.

LEMMA. *Suppose we have a set of objects $B_1, B_2, \cdots, B_n$ with associated probabilities $P_1, P_2, \cdots, P_n$, and a number of numerically valued properties (functions) of the objects $f_1, f_2, \cdots, f_d$. These are all nonnegative, $f_i(B_j) \geqq 0$, and we know the averages A_i of these properties over the objects,*

$$(22) \qquad \sum_j P_j f_i(B_j) = A_i, \qquad\qquad i = 1, 2, \cdots, d.$$

Then there exists an object B_p for which

$$(23) \qquad f_i(B_p) \leqq dA_i, \qquad\qquad i = 1, 2, \cdots, d.$$

More generally, given any set of $K_i > 0$ satisfying $\sum_{i=1}^{d} (1/K_i) \leqq 1$, then there exists an object B_p with

$$(24) \qquad\qquad f_i(B_p) \leqq K_i A_i, \qquad\qquad i = 1, 2, \cdots, d.$$

PROOF. The second part implies the first by taking $K_i = d$. To prove the second part let Q_i be the total probability of objects B for which $f_i(B) > K_i A_i$. Now the average $A_i > Q_i K_i A_i$ since $Q_i K_i A_i$ is contributed by the B_i with $f(B) > K_i A_i$ and all the remaining B have f_i values $\geqq 0$. Hence

$$(25) \qquad\qquad Q_i < \frac{1}{K_i}, \qquad\qquad i = 1, 2, \cdots, d.$$

The total probability Q of objects violating *any* of the conditions is less than or equal to the sum of the individual Q_i, so that

$$(26) \qquad\qquad Q < \sum_{i=1}^{d} \frac{1}{K_i} \leqq 1.$$

Hence there is at least one object not violating any of the conditions, concluding the proof.

For example, suppose we know that a room is occupied by a number of people whose average age is 40 and average height 5 feet. Here $d = 2$, and using the simpler form of the theorem we can assert that there is someone in the room not over 80 years old and not over ten feet tall, even though the room might contain aged midgets and youthful basketball players. Again, using $K_1 = 8/3$, $K_2 = 8/5$, we can assert the existence of an individual not over 8 feet tall and not over 106 2/3 years old.

Returning to the proof of theorem 1, we can now establish the last sentence. We have a set of objects, the code pairs, and two properties of each object, its error probability P_{e1} for the code from 1 to 2 and its error probability P_{e2} for the code from 2 to 1. These are nonnegative and their averages are bounded as in the first part of theorem 1. It follows from the combinatorial result that there exists at least one particular code pair for which simultaneously

$$(27) \qquad \begin{aligned} P_{e1} &\leqq 2\{\rho_{12}[n(R_1 + \theta_1)] + e^{-n\theta_1}\} \\ P_{e2} &\leqq 2\{\rho_{21}[n(R_2 + \theta_2)] + e^{-n\theta_2}\}. \end{aligned}$$

This concludes the proof of theorem 1.

It is easily seen that this theorem proves the possibility of code pairs arbitrarily close in rates R_1 and R_2 to the mean mutual information per letter R_{12} and R_{21} for any assigned $P\{x_1\}$ and $P\{x_2\}$ and with arbitrarily small probability of error. In fact, let $R_{12} - R_1 = R_{21} - R_2 = \epsilon > 0$ and in the theorem take $\theta_1 = \theta_2 = \epsilon/2$. Since $\rho_{12}[n(R_{12} - \epsilon/2)] \to 0$ and, in fact, exponentially fast with n (the distribution function $\epsilon n/2$ to the left of the mean, of a sum of n random variables) the bound on P_{e1} approaches zero with increasing n exponentially fast. In a similar way, so does the bound on P_{e2}. By choosing, then, a sequence of the M_1 and M_2 for increasing n which approach the desired rates R_1 and R_2 from below, we obtain the desired result, which may be stated as follows.

THEOREM 2.   *Suppose in a two-way memoryless channel K an assignment of probabilities to the input letters $P\{x_1\}$ and $P\{x_2\}$ gives average mutual informations in the two directions*

$$R_{12} = E\left(\log \frac{P\{x_1|x_2, y_2\}}{P\{x_1\}}\right)$$

(28)

$$R_{21} = E\left(\log \frac{P\{x_2|x_1, y_1\}}{P\{x_2\}}\right).$$

Then given $\epsilon > 0$ there exists a code pair for all sufficiently large block length n with signalling rates in the two directions greater than $R_{12} - \epsilon$ and $R_{21} - \epsilon$ respectively, and with error probabilities $P_{e1} \leq \exp\left[-A(\epsilon)n\right]$, $P_{e2} \leq \exp\left[-A(\epsilon)n\right]$ where $A(\epsilon)$ is positive and independent of n.

By trying different assignments of letter probabilities and using this result, one obtains various points in the capacity region. Of course, to obtain the best rates available from this theorem we should seek to maximize these rates. This is most naturally done à la Lagrange by maximizing $R_{12} + \lambda R_{21}$ for various positive λ.

8. The convex hull G_1 as an inner bound of the capacity region

In addition to the rates obtained this way we may construct codes which are *mixtures* of codes obtained by this process. Suppose one assignment $P\{x_1\}$, $P\{x_2\}$ gives mean mutual informations R_{12}, R_{21} and a second assignment $P'\{x_1\}$, $P'\{x_2\}$ gives R'_{12}, R'_{21}. Then we may find a code of (sufficiently large) length n for the first assignment with error probabilities $< \delta$ and rate discrepancy less than or equal to ϵ and a second code of length n' based on $P'\{x_1\}$, $P'\{x_2\}$ with the same δ and ϵ. We now consider the code of length $n + n'$ with $M_1 M_1'$ words in the forward direction, and $M_2 M_2'$ in the reverse, consisting of all words of the first code followed by all words for the same direction in the second code. This has signalling rates R_1^* and R_2^* equal to the weighted average of rates for the original codes $[R_1^* = nR_1/(n + n') + n'R_1'/(n + n'); R_2^* = nR_2/(n + n') + n'R_2'/(n + n')]$ and consequently its rates are within ϵ of the weighted averages, $|R_1^* - nR_{12}/(n + n') - n'R_{12}'/(n + n')| < \epsilon$ and similarly. Furthermore, its error probability is bounded by 2δ, since the probability of either of two events (an error in either of the two parts of the code) is bounded by the sum of the original probabilities. We can construct such a mixed code for *any* sufficiently large n and n'. Hence by taking these large enough we can approach any weighted average of the given rates and simultaneously approach zero error probability exponentially fast. It follows that *we can annex to the set of points found by the assignment of letter probabilities all points in the convex hull of this set*. This actually does add new points in some cases as our example, of a channel (table I) with incompatible transmission in the two directions, shows. By mixing the codes for assignments which give the points (0, 1) and (1, 0) in equal proportions, we obtain the point $(1/2, 1/2)$. There is no single letter assignment giving this pair of rates. We may summarize as follows.

THEOREM 3.   *Let G_I be the convex hull of points (R_{12}, R_{21})*

(29)
$$R_{12} = E\left(\log \frac{P\{x_1|x_2, y_2\}}{P\{x_1\}}\right)$$

$$R_{21} = E\left(\log \frac{P\{x_2|x_1, y_1\}}{P\{x_2\}}\right)$$

when $P\{x_1\}$ and $P\{x_2\}$ are given various probability assignments. All points of G_I are in the capacity region. For any point (R_1, R_2) in G_I and any $\epsilon > 0$ we can find codes whose signalling rates are within ϵ of R_1 and R_2 and whose error probabilities in both directions are less than $\exp[-\Lambda(\epsilon)n]$ for all sufficiently large n, and some positive $\Lambda(\epsilon)$.

It may be noted that the convex hull G_I in this theorem is a closed set (contains all its limit points). This follows from the continuity of R_{12} and R_{21} as functions of the probability assignments $P\{x_1\}$ and $P\{x_2\}$. Furthermore if G_I contains a point (R_1, R_2) it contains the projections $(R_1, 0)$ and $(0, R_2)$. This will now be proved.

It will clearly follow if we can show that the projection of any point obtained by a letter probability assignment is also in G_I. To show this, suppose $P\{x_1\}$ and $P\{x_2\}$ give the point (R_{12}, R_{21}). Now R_{12} is the average of the various particular R_{12} when x_2 is given various particular values. Thus

(30)
$$R_{12} = \sum_{x_2} P\{x_2\} \sum_{x_1, y_2} P\{x_1, y_2|x_2\} \log \frac{P\{x_1|x_2, y_2\}}{P\{x_1\}}.$$

There must exist, then, a particular x_2, say x_2^*, for which the inner sum is at least as great as the average, that is, for which

(31)
$$\sum_{x_1, y_2} P\{x_1, y_2|x_2^*\} \log \frac{P\{x_1|x_2^*, y_2\}}{P\{x_1\}}$$

$$\geq \sum_{x_2} P\{x_2\} \sum_{x_1, y_2} P\{x_1, y_2|x_2\} \log \frac{P\{x_1|x_2, y_2\}}{P\{x_1\}}.$$

The assignment $P\{x_1|x_2^*\}$ for letter probabilities x_1 and the assignment $P\{x_2\} = 1$ if $x_2 = x_2^*$ and 0 otherwise, now gives a point on the horizontal axis below or to the right of the projection of the given point R_{12}, R_{21}. Similarly, we can find an x_1^* such that the assignment $P\{x_2|x_1^*\}$ for x_2 and $P\{x_1^*\} = 1$ gives a point on the vertical axis equal to or above the projection of R_{12}, R_{21}. Note also that the assignment $P\{x_1^\dagger\} = 1, P\{x_2^\dagger\} = 1$ gives the point $(0, 0)$. By suitable mixing of codes obtained for these four assignments one can approach any point of the quadrilateral defined by the corresponding pairs of rates, and in particular any point in the rectangle subtended by R_{12}, R_{21}. It follows from these remarks that the convex hull G_I is a region of the form shown typically in figure 7 bounded by a horizontal segment, a convex curve, a vertical segment, and two segments of the axes. Of course, any of these parts may be of zero length.

The convex hull G_I is, as we have seen, inside the capacity region and we will refer to it as the *inner bound*.

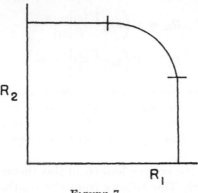

$$R_2$$

$$R_1$$

FIGURE 7

It is of some interest to attempt a sharper evaluation of the rate of improvement of error probability with increasing code length n. This is done in the appendix and leads to a generalization of theorem 2 in [1]. The bound we arrive at is based on logarithms of moment generating functions.

9. An outer bound on the capacity region

While in some cases the convex hull G_I, the inner bound defined above, is actually the capacity region this is not always the case. By an involved calculation R. G. Gallager has shown that in the binary multiplying channel the inner bound is strictly interior to the capacity region. However a *partial* converse to theorem 3 and an *outer* bound on the capacity region can be given. Suppose we have a code starting at time zero with messages m_1 and m_2 at the two terminals. After n operations of the channel, let Y_1 and Y_2 be the received blocks at the two terminals (sequences of n letters), and let x_1, x_2, y_1, y_2 be the next transmitted and received letters. Consider the change in "equivocation" of message at the two terminals due to the next received letter. At terminal 2, for example, this change is (making some obvious reductions)

$$(32) \qquad \Delta = H(m_1|m_2, Y_2) - H(m_1|m_2, Y_2, y_2)$$

$$= E\left[\log \frac{P\{m_2, Y_2\}}{P\{m_1, m_2, Y_2\}}\right] - E\left[\log \frac{P\{m_2, Y_2, y_2\}}{P\{m_1, m_2, Y_2, y_2\}}\right]$$

$$= E\left[\log \frac{P\{y_2|m_1, m_2, Y_2\}}{P\{y_2|x_2\}} \frac{P\{y_2|x_2\}}{P\{y_2|Y_2, m_2\}}\right].$$

Now $H(y_2|m_1, m_2, Y_2) \geqq H(y_2|m_1, m_2, Y_1, Y_2) = H(y_2|x_1, x_2)$ since adding a conditioning variable cannot increase an entropy and since $P\{y_2|m_1, m_2, Y_1, Y_2\} = P\{y_2|x_1, x_2\}$.

Also $H(y_2|x_2) \geqq H(y_2|Y_2, m_2)$ since x_2 is a function of Y_2 and m_2 by the coding function. Therefore

$$(33) \qquad \Delta \leqq E\left(\log \frac{P\{y_2|x_1, x_2\}}{P\{y_2|x_2\}}\right) + H(y_2|Y_2, m_2) - H(y_2|x_2)$$

$$(34) \qquad \Delta \leqq E\left(\log \frac{P\{y_2|x_1, x_2\}}{P\{y_2|x_2\}}\right) = E\left(\log \frac{P\{y_2, x_1, x_2\} P\{x_2\}}{P\{x_2, y_2\} P\{x_1, x_2\}}\right)$$

$$\qquad\qquad = E\left(\log \frac{P\{x_1|x_2, y_2\}}{P\{x_1|x_2\}}\right).$$

This would actually lead to a converse of theorem 1 if we had independence of the random variables x_1 and x_2. This last expression would then reduce to $E[\log (P\{x_1|x_2, y_2\}/P\{x_1\})]$. Unfortunately in a general code they are not necessarily independent. In fact, the next x_1 and x_2 may be functionally related to received X and Y and hence dependent.

We may, however, at least obtain an outer bound on the capacity surface. Namely, the above inequality together with the similar inequality for the second terminal imply that the vector change in equivocation due to receiving another letter must be a vector with components bounded by

$$(35) \qquad E\left(\log \frac{P\{x_1|x_2, y_2\}}{P\{x_1|x_2\}}\right), \; E\left(\log \frac{P\{x_2|x_1, y_1\}}{P\{x_2|x_1\}}\right)$$

for some $P\{x_1, x_2\}$. Thus the vector change is included in the convex hull of all such vectors G_O (when $P\{x_1, x_2\}$ is varied).

In a code of length n, the *total* change in equivocation from beginning to end of the block cannot exceed the sum of n vectors from this convex hull. Thus this sum will lie in the convex hull nG_O, that is, G_O expanded by a factor n.

Suppose now our given code has signalling rates $R_1 = (1/n) \log M_1$ and $R_2 = (1/n) \log M_2$. Then the initial equivocations of message are nR_1 and nR_2. Suppose the point (nR_1, nR_2) is outside the convex hull nG_O with nearest distance $n\epsilon_1$, figure 8. Construct a line L passing through the nearest point of nG_O and

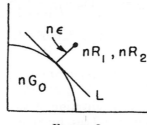

FIGURE 8

perpendicular to the nearest approach segment with nG_O on one side (using the fact that nG_O is a convex region). It is clear that for any point (nR_1^*, nR_2^*) on the nG_O side of L and particularly for any point of nG_O, that we have $|nR_1 - nR_1^*| + |nR_2 - nR_2^*| \geqq n\epsilon$ (since the shortest distance is $n\epsilon$) and furthermore at least one of the $nR_1 - nR_1^*$ and $nR_2 - nR_2^*$ is at least $n\epsilon/\sqrt{2}$. (In a right triangle at least one leg is as great as the hypotenuse divided by $\sqrt{2}$.)

Thus after n uses of the channel, if the signalling rate pair R_1, R_2 is distance ϵ outside the convex hull G_0, at least one of the two final equivocations is at least $\epsilon/\sqrt{2}$, where all equivocations are on a per second basis. Thus for signalling rates ϵ outside of G_0 the equivocations per second are bounded from below independent of the code length n. This implies that the error probability is also bounded from below, that is, at least one of the two codes will have error probability $\geqq f(\epsilon) > 0$ independent of n, as shown in [2], appendix.

To summarize, the capacity region G is included in the convex hull G_0 of all points R_{12}, R_{21}

(36)
$$R_{12} = E\left[\log \frac{P\{x_1|x_2, y_2\}}{P\{x_1|x_2\}}\right]$$
$$R_{21} = E\left[\log \frac{P\{x_2|x_1, y_1\}}{P\{x_2|x_1\}}\right]$$

when arbitrary joint probability assignments $P\{x_1, x_2\}$ are made.

Thus the inner bound G_I and the outer bound G_0 are both found by the same process, assigning input probabilities, calculating the resulting average mutual informations R_{12} and R_{21} and then taking the convex hull. The only difference is that for the outer bound a general joint assignment $P\{x_1, x_2\}$ is made, while for the inner bound the assignments are restricted to independent $P\{x_1\}P\{x_2\}$.

We now develop some properties of the outer bound.

10. The concavity of R_{12} and R_{21} as functions of $P(x_1, x_2)$

THEOREM 4.   *Given the transition probabilities $P\{y_1, y_2|x_1, x_2\}$ for a channel K, the rates*

(37)
$$R_{12} = E\left[\log \frac{P\{y_2|x_1, x_2\}}{P\{y_2|x_2\}}\right]$$
$$R_{21} = E\left[\log \frac{P\{y_1|x_1, x_2\}}{P\{y_1|x_1\}}\right]$$

are concave downward functions of the assigned input probabilities $P\{x_1, x_2\}$. For example, $R_{12}(P_1\{x_1, x_2\}/2 + P_2\{x_1, x_2\}/2) \geqq R_{12}(P_1\{x_1, x_2\})/2 + R_{12}(P_2\{x_1, x_2\})/2$.

This concave property is a generalization of that given in [3] for a one-way channel. To prove the theorem it suffices, by known results in convex functions, to show that

(38)
$$R_{12}\left(\frac{1}{2}P_1\{x_1, x_2\} + \frac{1}{2}P_2\{x_1, x_2\}\right) \geqq \frac{1}{2}R_{12}(P_1\{x_1, x_2\}) + \frac{1}{2}R_{12}(P_2\{x_1, x_2\}).$$

But $R_{12}(P_1\{x_1, x_2\})$ and $R_{12}(P_2\{x_1, x_2\})$ may be written

(39) $\qquad R_{12}(P_1\{x_1, x_2\}) = \sum_{x_2} P_1\{x_2\} \sum_{x_1,y_2} P_1\{x_1, y_2|x_2\} \log \dfrac{P_2\{y_2|x_1, x_2\}}{P_1\{y_2|x_2\}}$

(40) $\qquad R_{12}(P_2\{x_1, x_2\}) = \sum_{x_2} P_2\{x_2\} \sum_{x_1,y_2} P_2\{x_1, y_2|x_2\} \log \dfrac{P_2\{y_2|x_1, x_2\}}{P_2\{y_2|x_2\}}.$

Here the subscripts 1 on probabilities correspond to those produced with the probability assignment $P_1\{x_1, x_2\}$ to the inputs, and similarly for the subscript 2. The inner sum $\sum_{x_1,y_2} P_1\{x_1, y_2|x_2\} \log (P_1\{y_2|x_1, x_2\}/P_1\{y_2|x_2\})$ may be recognized as the rate for the channel from x_1 to y_2 conditional on x_2 having a particular value and with the x_1 assigned probabilities corresponding to its conditional probability according to $P_1\{x_1, x_2\}$.

The corresponding inner sum with assigned probabilities $P_2\{x_1, x_2\}$ is $\sum_{x_1,y_2} P_2\{x_1, y_2|x_2\} \log (P_2\{y_2|x_1, x_2\}/P_2\{y_2|x_2\})$, which may be viewed as the rate conditional on x_2 for the same one-way channel but with the assignment $P_2\{x_1|x_2\}$ for the input letters.

Viewed this way, we may apply the concavity result of [2]. In particular, the weighted average of these rates with weight assignments $P_1\{x_2\}/(P_1\{x_2\} + P_2\{x_2\})$ and $P_2\{x_2\}/(P_1\{x_2\} + P_2\{x_2\})$ is dominated by the rate for this one-way channel when the probability assignments are the weighted average of the two given assignments. This weighted average of the given assignment is

(41) $\qquad P_3\{x_1, x_2\} = \dfrac{P_1\{x_2\}}{P_1\{x_2\} + P_2\{x_2\}} P_1\{x_1|x_2\} + \dfrac{P_2\{x_2\}}{P_1\{x_2\} + P_2\{x_2\}} P_2\{x_1|x_2\}$

$\qquad\qquad\qquad = \dfrac{1}{2} \dfrac{1}{(P_1\{x_2\} + P_2\{x_2\})} 2 (P_1\{x_1, x_2\} + P_2\{x_1, x_2\}).$

Thus the sum of two corresponding terms (the same x_2) from (38) above is dominated by $P_1\{x_2\} + P_2\{x_2\}$ multiplied by the rate for this one-way channel with these averaged probabilities. This latter rate, on substituting the averaged probabilities, is seen to be

(42) $\qquad\qquad \sum_{x_1,y_2} P_3\{x_1, y_2|x_2\} \log \dfrac{P_3\{y_2|x_1, x_2\}}{P_3\{y_2|x_2\}}$

where the subscript 3 corresponds to probabilities produced by using $P_3\{x_1, x_2\} = (P_1\{x_1, x_2\} + P_2\{x_1, x_2\}/2)/2$. In other words, the sum of (39) and (40) (including the first summation on x_2) is dominated by

(43) $\qquad \sum_{x_2} (P_1\{x_2\} + P_2\{x_2\}) \sum_{x_1,y_2} P_3\{x_1, y_2|x_2\} \log \dfrac{P_3\{y_2|x_1, x_2\}}{P_3\{y_2|x_2\}}$

$\qquad\qquad\qquad\qquad = 2 \sum_{x_1,x_2,y_2} P_3\{x_1, y_2, x_2\} \log \dfrac{P_3\{y_2|x_1, x_2\}}{P_3\{y_2|x_2\}}.$

This is the desired result for the theorem.

11. Applications of the concavity property; channels with symmetric structure

Theorem 4 is useful in a number of ways in evaluating the outer bound for particular channels. In the first place, we note that $R_{12} + \lambda R_{21}$ as a function of $P\{x_1, x_2\}$ and for positive λ is also a concave downward function. Consequently any local maximum is the absolute maximum and numerical investigation in locating such maxima by the Lagrange multiplier method is thereby simplified.

In addition, this concavity result is very powerful in helping locate the maxima when "symmetries" exist in a channel. Suppose, for example, that in a given channel the transition probability array $P\{y_1, y_2|x_1, x_2\}$ has the following property. There exists a relabelling of the input letters x_1 and of the output letters y_1 and y_2 which interchanges, say, the first two letters of the x_1 alphabet but leaves the set of probabilities $P\{y_1, y_2|x_1, x_2\}$ the same. Now if some particular assignment $P\{x_1, x_2\}$ gives outer bound rates R_{12} and R_{21}, then if we apply the same permutation to the x alphabet in $P\{x_1, x_2\}$ we obtain a new probability assignment which, however, will give exactly the same outer bound rates R_{12} and R_{21}. By our concavity property, if we average these two probability assignments we obtain a new probability assignment which will give at least as large values of R_{12} and R_{21}. In this averaged assignment for any particular x_2 the first two letters in the x_1 alphabet are assigned equal probability. In other words, in such a case an assignment for maximizing $R_{12} + \lambda R_{21}$, say $P\{x_1, x_2\}$ viewed as a matrix, will have its first two rows identical.

If the channel had sufficiently symmetric structure that *any* pair of x_1 letters might be interchanged by relabelling the x_1 alphabet and the y_1 and y_2 alphabets while preserving $P\{y_1, y_2|x_1, x_2\}$, then a maximizing assignment $P\{x_1, x_2\}$ would exist in which *all* rows are identical. In this case the entries are functions of x_2 only: $P\{x_1, x_2\} = P\{x_2\}/\alpha$ where α is the number of letters in the x_1 alphabet. Thus the maximum for a dependent assignment of $P\{x_1, x_2\}$ is actually obtained with x_1 and x_2 independent. *In other words, in this case of a full set of symmetric interchanges on the x_1 alphabet, the inner and outer bounds are identical.* This gives an important class of channels for which the capacity region can be determined with comparative ease.

An example of this type is the channel with transition probabilities as follows. All inputs and outputs are binary, $y_1 = x_2$ (that is, there is a noiseless binary channel from terminal 2 to terminal 1). If $x_2 = 0$, then $y_2 = x_1$, while if $x_2 = 1$, y_2 has probability .5 of being 0 and .5 of being 1. In other words, if x_2 is 0 the binary channel in the forward direction is noiseless, while if x_2 is 1 it is completely noisy. We note here that if the labels on the x_1 alphabet are interchanged while we simultaneously interchange the y_2 labels, the channel remains unaltered, all conditional probabilities being unaffected. Following the analysis above, then, the inner and outer bounds will be the same and give the capacity region. Furthermore, the surface will be attained with equal rows in the $P\{x_1, x_2\}$ matrix as shown in table II.

TABLE II

		x_2	
		0	1
x_1	0	$p/2$	$q/2$
	1	$p/2$	$q/2$

For a particular p this assignment gives the rates

$$(44) \qquad R_{12} = p, \qquad R_{21} = -(p \log p + q \log q).$$

These come from substituting in the formulas or by noting that in the $1-2$ direction the channel is acting like an erasure channel, while in the $2-1$ direction it is operating like a binary noiseless channel with unequal probabilities assigned to the letters. This gives the capacity region of figure 9.

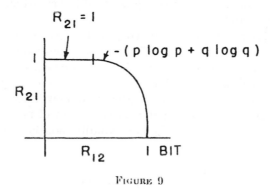

FIGURE 9

There are many variants and applications of these interchange and symmetry tricks for aid in the evaluation of capacity surfaces. For example, if *both* the x_1 and x_2 alphabets have a full set of interchanges leaving the transition probabilities the same, then the maximizing distribution must be identical both in rows and columns and hence all entries are the same, $P\{x_1, x_2\} = 1/ac$ where a and c are the number of letters in the x_1 and x_2 alphabets. In this case, then, all attainable $R_{12}R_{21}$ points are dominated by the particular point obtained from this uniform probability assignment. *In other words, the capacity region is a rectangle in the case of a full set of symmetric interchanges for both x_1 and x_2.*

An example of this type is the channel of figure 2 defined by $y_1 = y_2 = x_1 \oplus x_2$ where $\oplus$ means mod 2 addition.

12. Nature of the region attainable in the outer bound

We now will use the concavity property to establish some results concerning the set Γ of points (R_{12}, R_{21}) that can be obtained by all possible assignments of probabilities $P\{x_1, x_2\}$ in a given channel K, and whose convex hull is G_0. We will show that the set Γ is in fact already convex and therefore identical with G_0 and that it consists of all points in or on the boundary of a region of the type shown in figure 10 bounded by a horizontal segment L_1, an outward convex seg-

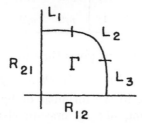

FIGURE 10

ment L_2, a vertical segment L_3 and two segments of the coordinate axes. Thus G_0 has a structure similar to G_I.

Suppose some $P\{x_1, x_2\}$ gives a point (R_{12}, R_{21}). Here R_{12} is, as we have observed previously, an average of the different R_{12} which would be obtained by fixing x_2 at different values, that is, using these with probability 1 and applying the conditional probabilities $P\{x_1|x_2\}$ to the x_1 letters. The weighting is according to factors $P\{x_2\}$. It follows that some particular x_2 will do as well at least as this weighted average. If this particular x_2 is x_2^*, the set of probabilities $P\{x_1|x_2^*\}$ gives at least as large a value of R_{12} and simultaneously makes $R_{21} = 0$. In

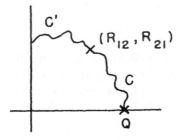

FIGURE 11

figure 11 this means we can find a point in Γ below or to the right of the projection of the given point as indicated (point Q).

Now consider mixtures of these two probability assignments, that is, assignments of the form $\lambda P\{x_1x_2\} + (1 - \lambda)P\{x_1|x_2^*\}$. Here λ is to vary continuously from 0 to 1. Since R_{12} and R_{21} are continuous functions of the assigned probability, this produces a continuous curve C running from the given point to the point Q. Furthermore, this curve lies entirely to the upper right of the connecting line segment. This is because of the concavity property for the R_{12} and R_{21} expressions. In a similar way, we construct a curve C', as indicated, of points belonging to Γ and lying on or above the horizontal straight line through the given point.

Now take all points on the curves C and C' and consider mixing the corresponding probability assignments with the assignment $P\{x_1^*, x_2^*\} = 1$ (all other pairs given zero probability). This last assignment gives the point $(0, 0)$. The fraction of this $(0, 0)$ assignment is gradually increased for 0 up to 1. As this is done the curve of resulting points changes continuously starting at the CC' curve and collapsing into the point $(0, 0)$. The end points stay on the axes during this operation. Consequently by known topological results the curve sweeps through the entire area bounded by C, C' and the axes and in particular *covers the rectangle subtended by the original point* (R_{12}, R_{21}).

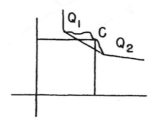

FIGURE 12

We will show that the set of points Γ is a convex set. Suppose Q_1 and Q_2, figure 12, are two points which can be obtained by assignments $P_1\{x_1, x_2\}$ and $P_2\{x_1, x_2\}$.

By taking mixtures of varying proportions one obtains a continuous curve C connecting them, lying, by the concavity property, to the upper right of the connecting line segment. Since these are points of Γ all of their subtended rectangles are, as just shown, points of Γ. It follows that all points of the connecting line segment are points of Γ. Note that if Q_1 and Q_2 are in the first and third quadrants relative to each other the result is trivially true, since then the connecting line segment lies in the rectangle of one of the points.

These results are sufficient to imply the statements at the beginning of this section, namely the set Γ is convex, identical with G_0, and if we take the largest attainable R_{12} and for this R_{12} the largest R_{21}, then points in the subtended rectangle are attainable. Similarly for the largest R_{21}.

It may be recalled here that the set of points attainable by *independent* assignments, $P\{x_1, x_2\} = P\{x_1\}P\{x_2\}$, is not necessarily a convex set. This is shown by the example of table I.

It follows also from the results of this section that *the end points of the outer bound curve* (where it reaches the coordinate axes) *are the same as the end points of the inner bound curve*. This is because, as we have seen, the largest R_{12} can be achieved using only one particular x_2 with probability 1. When this is done, $P\{x_1, x_2\}$ reduces to a product of independent probabilities.

13. An example where the inner and outer bounds differ

The inner and outer bounds on the capacity surface that we have derived above are not always the same. This was shown by David Blackwell for the binary multiplying channel defined by $y_1 = y_2 = x_1 x_2$. The inner and outer bounds for this channel have been computed numerically and are plotted in figure 13. It may be seen that they differ considerably, particularly in the middle

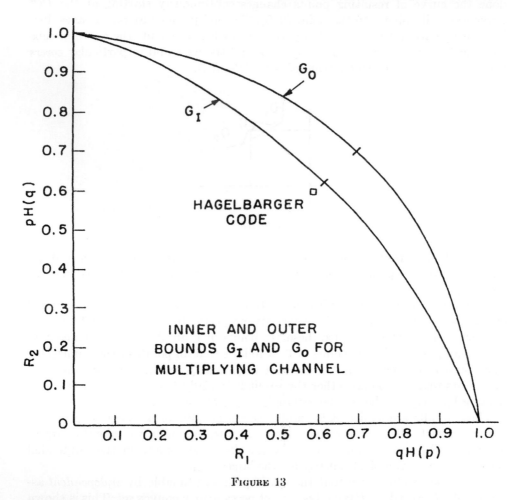

FIGURE 13

of the range. The calculation of the inner bound, in this case, amounts to finding the envelope of points

(45)
$$R_{12} = -p_2[p_1 \log p_1 + (1 - p_1) \log (1 - p_1)]$$
$$R_{21} = -p_1[p_2 \log p_2 + (1 - p_2) \log (1 - p_2)].$$

These are the rates with independent probability assignments at the two ends:

probability p_1 for using letter 1 at terminal 1 and probability p_2 for using letter 1 at terminal 2. By evaluating these rates for different p_1 and p_2 the envelope shown in the figure was obtained.

For the outer bounds, the envelope of rates for a general dependent assignment of probabilities is required. However it is easily seen that any assignment in which $P\{0, 0\}$ is positive can be improved by transferring this probability to one of the other possible pairs. Hence we again have a two parameter family of points (since the sum of the three other probabilities must be unity). If the probabilities are denoted by $p_1 = P\{1, 0\}$, $p_2 = P\{0, 1\}$, $1 - p_1 - p_2 = P\{1, 1\}$, we find the rates are

(46)
$$R_{12} = -(1 - p_1)\left[\frac{p_2}{1 - p_1}\log\frac{p_2}{1 - p_1} + \left(1 - \frac{p_2}{1 - p_1}\right)\log\left(1 - \frac{p_2}{1 - p_1}\right)\right]$$
$$R_{21} = -(1 - p_2)\left[\frac{p_1}{1 - p_2}\log\frac{p_1}{1 - p_2} + \left(1 - \frac{p_1}{1 - p_2}\right)\log\left(1 - \frac{p_1}{1 - p_2}\right)\right].$$

Here again a numerical evaluation for various values of p_1 and p_2 led to the envelope shown in the figure.

In connection with this channel, D. W. Hagelbarger has devised an interesting and simple code (not a block code however) which is error free and transmits at average rates $R_{12} = R_{21} = .571$, slightly less than our lower bound. His code operates as follows. A 0 or 1 is sent from each end with independent probabilities $1/2, 1/2$. If a 0 is received then the next digit transmitted is the complement of what was just sent. This procedure is followed at both ends. If a 1 is received, both ends progress to the next binary digit of the message. It may be seen that three-fourths of the time on the average the complement procedure is followed and one-fourth of the time a new digit is sent. Thus the average number of channel uses per message digit is $(3/4)(2) + (1/4)(1) = 7/4$. The average rate is $4/7 = .571$ in both directions. Furthermore it is readily seen that the message digits can be calculated without error for each communication direction.

By using message sources at each end with biased probabilities it is possible to improve the Hagelbarger scheme slightly. Thus, if 1's occur as message digits with probability .63 and 0's with probability .37, we obtain rates in both directions

(47)
$$R_{12} = R_{21} = \frac{-.63\log.63 - .37\log.37}{1 - (.63)^2} = .593.$$

We will, in a later section, develop a result which in principle gives for any channel the exact capacity region. However, the result involves a limiting process over words of increasing length and consequently is difficult to evaluate in most cases. In contrast, the upper and lower bounds involve only maximizing operations relating to a single transmitted letter in each direction. Although sometimes involving considerable calculation, it is possible to actually evaluate them when the channel is not too complex.

14. Attainment of the outer bound with dependent sources

With regard to the outer bound there is an interesting interpretation relating to a somewhat more general communication system. Suppose that the message sources at the two ends of our channel are not independent but statistically dependent. Thus, one might be sending weather information from Boston to New York and from New York to Boston. The weather at these cities is of course not statistically independent. If the dependence were of just the right type for the channel or if the messages could be transformed so that this were the case, then it may be possible to attain transmission at the rates given by the outer bound. For example, in the multiplying channel just discussed, suppose that the messages at the two ends consist of streams of binary digits which occur with the dependent probabilities given by table III. Successive x_1, x_2 pairs

TABLE III

		x_2	
		0	1
x_1	0	0	.275
	1	.275	.45

are assumed independent. Then by merely sending these streams into the channel (without processing) the outer bound curve is achieved at its midpoint.

It is not known whether this is possible in general. Does there always exist a suitable pair of dependent sources that can be coded to give rates R_1, R_2 within ϵ of any point in the outer bound? This is at least often possible in the noiseless, memoryless case, that is, when y_1 and y_2 are strict functions of x_1 and x_2 (no channel noise). The source pair defined by the assignment $P\{x_1, x_2\}$ that produces the point in question is often suitable in such a case without coding as in the above example.

The inner bound also has an interesting interpretation. If we artificially limit the codes to those where the transmitted sequence at each terminal depends only on the message and not on the received sequence at that terminal, then the inner bound is indeed the capacity region. This results since in this case we have at each stage of the transmission (that is, given the index of the letter being transmitted) independence between the two next transmitted letters. It follows that the total vector change in equivocation is bounded by the sum of n vectors, each corresponding to an independent probability assignment. Details of this proof are left to the reader. The independence required would also occur if the transmission and reception points at each end were at different places with no direct cross communication.

15. General solution for the capacity region in the two-way channel

For a given memoryless two-way channel K we define a series of *derived channels* $K_1, K_2, \cdots$. These will also be memoryless channels and the capacity region for K will be evaluated as a limit in terms of the inner bounds for the series K_n.

The channel K_1 is identical with K. The derived channel K_2 is one whose input letters are actually strategies for working with K for a block of two input letters. Thus the input letters at terminal 1 for K_2 consist of pairs $[x_1^1, f(x_1^1, y_1^1)]$. Here x_1^1 is the first transmitted letter of the pair and ranges therefore over the a possible input letters of K. Now $f(x_1^1, y_1^1)$ represents any function from the first input letter x_1^1 and output letter y_1^1 to the second input letter x_1^2. Thus this function may be thought of as a rule for choosing a second input letter at terminal 1 depending on the first input letter and the observed first output letter. If x_1^1 can assume a values and y_1^1 can assume b values, then the (x_1^1, y_1^1) pair can assume ab values, and since the function f takes values from a possibilities there are a^{ab} possible functions. Hence there are $a \cdot a^{ab}$ possible pairs $[x_1^1, f(x_1^1, y_1^1)]$, or possible input letters to K_2 at terminal 1.

In a similar way, at terminal 2 consider pairs $[x_2^1, g(x_2^1, y_2^1)]$. Here g ranges over functions from the first received and transmitted letters at terminal 2 and takes values from the x_2 alphabet. Thus these pairs have $c \cdot c^{cd}$ values, where c and d are the sizes of the input and output alphabets at terminal 2.

The pairs $[x_1^1, f(x_1^1, y_1^1)]$ and $[x_2^1, g(x_2^1, y_2^1)]$ may be thought of as strategies for using the channel K in two letter sequences, the second letter to be dependent on the first letter sent and the first letter received. The technique here is very similar to that occurring in the theory of games. There one replaces a sequence of moves by a player (whose available information for making a choice is increasing through the series) by a single move in which he chooses a strategy. The strategy describes what the player will do at each stage in each possible contingency. Thus a game with many moves is reduced to a game with a single move chosen from a larger set.

The *output* letters for K_2 are, at terminal 1, pairs (y_1^1, y_1^2) and, at terminal 2, pairs (y_2^1, y_2^2); that is, the pairs of received letters at the two terminals. The transition probabilities for K_2 are the probabilities, if these strategies for introducing a particular pair of letters were used in K, that the output pairs would occur. Thus

$$(48) \quad P_{K_2}\{(y_1^1, y_1^2), (y_2^1, y_2^2) | [x_1^1, f(x_1^1, y_1^1)], [x_2^1, g(x_2^1, y_2^1)]\}$$

$$= P_K\{y_1^1, y_2^1 | x_1^1, x_2^1\} P_K\{y_1^2, y_2^2 | f(x_1^1, y_1^1), g(x_2^1, y_2^1)\}.$$

In a similar way the channels $K_3, K_4, \cdots$ are defined. Thus K_n may be thought of as a channel corresponding to n uses of K with successive input letters at a terminal functions of previous input and output letters at that terminal. Therefore the input letters at terminal 1 are n-tuples

(49) $[x_1^1, f(x_1^1, y_1^1), \cdots, f_{n-1}(x_1^1, x_1^2, \cdots, x_1^{n-1}, y_1^1, y_1^2, \cdots, y_1^{n-1})],$

a possible alphabet of

(50) $aa^{ab}a^{(ab)^2} \cdots a^{(ab)^{n-1}} = a^{[(ab)^n - 1]/(ab-1)}$

possibilities. The output letters at terminal 1 consist of n-tuples

(51) $(y_1^1, y_1^2, \cdots, y_1^n)$

and range therefore over an alphabet of b^n generalized letters. The transition probabilities are defined for K_n in terms of those for K by the generalization of equation (39)

(52) $P_{K_n}\{y_1^1, y_1^2, \cdots, y_1^n|(x_1^1, f_1, f_2, \cdots, f_{n-1}), (x_2^1, g_1, g_2, \cdots, g_{n-1})\}$

$$= \prod_{i=1}^{n} P_K\{y_1^i|f_{i-1}, g_{i-1}\}.$$

The channel K_n may be thought of, then, as a memoryless channel whose properties are identical with using channel K in blocks of n, allowing transmitted and received letters within a block to influence succeeding choices.

For each of the channels K_n one could, in principle, calculate the lower bound on its capacity region. The lower bound for K_n is to be multiplied by a factor $1/n$ to compare with K, since K_n corresponds to n uses of K.

THEOREM 5. *Let B_n be the lower bound of the capacity region for the derived channel K_n reduced in scale by a factor $1/n$. Then as $n \to \infty$ the regions B_n approach a limit B which includes all the particular regions and is the capacity region of K.*

PROOF.   We first show the positive assertion that if (R_{12}, R_{21}) is any point in some B_n and ϵ is any positive number, then we can construct block codes with error probabilities $P_e < \epsilon$ and rates in the two directions at least $R_{12} - \epsilon$ and $R_{21} - \epsilon$. This follows readily from previous results if the derived channel K_n and its associated inner bound B_n are properly understood. K_n is a memoryless channel, and by theorem 3 we can find codes for it transmitting arbitrarily close to the rates R_{12}, R_{21} in B_n with arbitrarily small error probability. These codes are sequences of letters from the K_n alphabet. They correspond, then, to sequences of *strategies* for blocks of n for the original channel K.

Thus these codes can be directly translated into codes for K n times as long, preserving all statistical properties, in particular the error probability. These codes, then, can be interpreted as codes signalling at rates $1/n$ as large for the K channel with the same error probability. In fact, from theorem 3, it follows that for any pair of rates strictly inside B_n we can find codes whose error probability decreases at least exponentially with the code length.

We will now show that the regions B_n approach a limit B as n increases and that B includes all the individual B_n. By a limiting region we mean a set of points B such that for any point P of B, and $\epsilon > 0$, there exists n_0 such that for $n > n_0$ there are points of B_n within ϵ of P, while for any P not in B there exist ϵ and n_0 such that for $n > n_0$ no points of B_n are within ϵ of P. In the first place B_n is included in B_{kn} for any integer k. This is because the strategies for B_{kn} include as special cases strategies where the functional influence only involves subblocks of n. Hence all points obtainable by independent probability assignments with K_n are also obtainable with K_{kn} and the convex hull of the latter set must include the convex hull of the former set.

It follows that the set B_{kn} approaches a limit B, the union of all the B_{kn} plus limit points of this set. Also B includes B_{n_1} for any n_1. For n and n_1 have a common multiple, for example nn_1, and B includes B_{nn_1} while B_{nn_1} includes B_{n_1}.

Furthermore, any point obtainable with K_{kn} can be obtained with $K_{kn+\alpha}$, for $0 \leqq \alpha \leqq n$, reduced in both coordinates by a factor of not more than $k/(k+1)$. This is because we may use the strategies for K_{kn} followed by a series of α of the first letters in the x_1 and x_2 alphabets. (That is, fill out the assignments to the length $kn + \alpha$ with essentially dummy transmitted letters.) The only difference then will be in the normalizing factor, $1/(\text{block length})$. By making k sufficiently large, this discrepancy from a factor of 1, namely $1/(k+1)$, can be made as small as desired. Thus for any $\epsilon > 0$ and any point P of B there is a point of B_{n_1} within ϵ of P for *all* sufficiently large n_1.

With regard to the converse part of the theorem, suppose we have a block code of length n with signalling rates (R_1, R_2) corresponding to a point outside B, closest distance to B equal to ϵ. Then since B includes B_n, the closest distance to B_n is at least ϵ. We may think of this code as a block code of length 1 for the channel K_n. As such, the messages m_1 and m_2 are mapped directly into "input letters" of K_n without functional dependence on the received letters. We have then since m_1 and m_2 are independent the independence of probabilities associated with these input letters sufficient to make the inner bound and outer bound the same. Hence the code in question has error probability bounded away from zero by a quantity dependent on ϵ but not on n.

16. Two-way channels with memory

The general discrete two-way channel with memory is defined by a set of conditional probabilities

(53) $P\{y_{1n}, y_{2n}|x_{11}, x_{12}, \cdots, x_{1n}; x_{21}, x_{22}, \cdots, x_{2n};$

$$y_{11}, y_{12}, \cdots, y_{1n-1}; y_{21}, y_{22}, \cdots, y_{2n-1}\}.$$

This is the probability of the nth output pair y_{1n}, y_{2n} conditional on the preceding history from time $t = 0$, that is, the input and output sequences from the starting time in using the channel. In such a general case, the probabilities might change in completely arbitrary fashion as n increases. Without further limitation, it is too general to be either useful or interesting. What is needed is some condition of reasonable generality which, however, ensures a certain stability in behavior and allows, thereby, significant coding theorems. For example, one might require finite historical influence so that probabilities of letters depend only on a bounded past history. (Knowing the past d inputs and outputs, earlier inputs and outputs do not influence the conditional probabilities.) We shall, however, use a condition which is, by and large, more general and also more realistic for actual applications.

We will say that a two-way channel has the *recoverable state property* if it satisfies the following condition. There exists an integer d such that for any input and output sequences of length n, X_{1n}, X_{2n}, Y_{1n}, Y_{2n}, there exist two functions $f(X_{1n}, Y_{1n})$, $g(X_{2n}, Y_{2n})$ whose values are sequences of input letters of the same length less than d and such that if these sequences f and g are now sent over the channel it is returned to its original state. Thus, conditional probabilities after this are the same as if the channel were started again at time zero.

The recoverable state property is common in actual physical communication systems where there is often a "zero" input which, if applied for a sufficient period, allows historical influences to die out. Note also that the recoverable state property may hold even in channels with an infinite set of internal states, provided it is possible to return to a "ground" state in a bounded number of steps.

The point of the recoverable state condition is that if we have a block code for such a channel, we may annex to the input words of this code the functions f and g at the two terminals and then repeat the use of the code. Thus, if such a code is of length n and has, for one use of the code, signalling rates R_1 and R_2 and error probabilities P_{e1} and P_{e2}, we may *continuously* signal at rates $R_1' \geqq nR_1/(n + d)$ and $R_2' \geqq nR_2/(n + d)$ with error probabilities $P_{e1}' \leqq P_{e1}$ and $P_{e2}' \leqq P_{e2}$.

For a recoverable state channel we may consider strategies for the first n letters just as we did in the memoryless case, and find the corresponding inner bound B_n on the capacity region (with scale reduced by $1/n$). We define the region B which might be called the limit supremum of the regions B_n. Namely, B consists of all points which belong to an infinite number of B_n together with limit points of this set.

THEOREM 6.   *Let (R_1, R_2) be any point in the region B. Let n_0 be any integer and let ϵ_1 and ϵ_2 be any positive numbers. Then there exists a block code of length $n > n_0$ with signalling rates R_1', R_2' satisfying $|R_1 - R_1'| < \epsilon_1$, $|R_2 - R_2'| < \epsilon_1$ and error probabilities satisfying $P_{e1} < \epsilon_2$, $P_{e2} < \epsilon_2$. Conversely, if (R_1, R_2) is not in B then there exist n_0 and $\delta > 0$ such that any block code of length exceeding n_0 has either $P_{e1} > \delta$ or $P_{e2} > \delta$ (or both).*

PROOF.   To show the first part of the theorem choose an $n_1 > n_0$ and also large enough to make both $dR_1/(d + n)$ and $dR_2/(d + n)$ less than $\epsilon_1/2$. Since the point (R_1, R_2) is in an infinite sequence of B_n, this is possible. Now construct a block code based on n_1 uses of the channel as individual "letters," within $\epsilon_1/2$ of the rate pair (R_1, R_2) and with error probabilities less than ϵ_2. To each of the "letters" of this code annex the functions which return the channel to its original state. We thus obtain codes with arbitrarily small error probability $< \epsilon_2$ approaching the rates R_1, R_2 and with arbitrarily large block length.

To show the converse statement, suppose (R_1, R_2) is *not* in B. Then for some

n_0 every B_n, where $n > n_0$, is outside a circle of some radius, say ϵ_2, centered on (R_1, R_2). Otherwise (R_1, R_2) would be in a limit point of the B_n. Suppose we have a code of length $n_1 > n_0$. Then its error probability is bounded away from zero since we again have a situation where the independence of "letters" obtains.

The region B may be called the capacity region for such a recoverable state channel. It is readily shown that B has the same convexity properties as had the capacity region G for a memoryless channel. Of course, the actual evaluation of B in specific channels is even more impractical than in the memoryless case.

17. Generalization to T-terminal channels

Many of the tricks and techniques used above may be generalized to channels with three or more terminals. However, some definitely new phenomena appear in these more complex cases. In another paper we will discuss the case of a channel with two or more terminals having inputs only and one terminal with an output only, a case for which a complete and simple solution of the capacity region has been found.

APPENDIX. ERROR PROBABILITY BOUNDS IN TERMS OF MOMENT GENERATING FUNCTIONS

Suppose we assign probabilities $P\{x_1\}$ to input letters at terminal 1 and $P\{x_2\}$ to input letters at terminal 2. (Notice that we are here working with letters, not with words as in theorem 2.) We can then calculate the log of the moment generating functions of the mutual information between input letters at terminal 1 and input letter-output letter pairs at terminal 2. (This is the log of the moment generating function of the distribution ρ_{12} when $n = 1$.) The expressions for this and the similar quantity in the other direction are

$$
(54) \qquad \mu_1(s) = \log \sum_{x_1, x_2, y_2} P\{x_1, x_2, y_2\} \exp\left(s \log \frac{P\{x_1, x_2, y_2\}}{P\{x_1\} P\{x_2, y_2\}} \right)
$$

$$
= \log \sum_{x_1, x_2, y_2} \frac{P\{x_1, x_2, y_2\}^{s+1}}{P\{x_1\}^s P\{x_2, y_2\}^s},
$$

$$
(55) \qquad \mu_2(s) = \log \sum_{x_1, x_2, y_1} \frac{P\{x_1, x_2, y_1\}^{s+1}}{P\{x_2\}^s P\{x_1, y_1\}^s}.
$$

These functions μ_1 and μ_2 may be used to bound the tails on the distributions ρ_{12} and ρ_{21} obtained by adding n identically distributed samples together. In fact, Chernoff [4] has shown that the tail to the left of a mean may be bounded as follows:

$$
(56) \qquad
\begin{aligned}
\rho_{12}[n\mu_1'(s_1)] &\leq \exp\{n[\mu_1(s_1) - s_1\mu_1'(s_1)]\}, & s_1 &\leq 0, \\
\rho_{21}[n\mu_2'(s_2)] &\leq \exp\{n[\mu_2(s_2) - s_2\mu_2'(s_2)]\}, & s_2 &\leq 0.
\end{aligned}
$$

Thus, choosing an arbitrary negative s_1, this gives a bound on the distribution function at the value $n\mu_1'(s_1)$. It can be shown that $\mu'(s)$ is a monotone increasing function and that $\mu'(0)$ is the mean of the distribution. The minimum $\mu'(s)$ corresponds to the minimum possible value of the random variable in question, in this case, the minimum $I(x_1; x_2, y_2)$. Thus, an s_1 may be found to place $\mu_1(s_1)$ anywhere between $I_{\min}(x_1; x_2, y_2)$ and $E(I)$. Of course, to the left of $I_{\min}$ the distribution is identically zero and to the right of $E(I)$ the distribution approaches one with increasing n.

We wish to use these results to obtain more explicit bounds on P_{e1} and P_{e2}, using theorem 2. Recalling that in that theorem θ_1 and θ_2 are arbitrary, we attempt to choose them so that the exponentials bounding the two terms are equal. This is a good choice of θ_1 and θ_2 to keep the total bound as small as possible. The first term is bounded by $\exp\{n[\mu_1(s_1) - s_1\mu_1'(s_1)]\}$ where s_1 is such that $\mu_1'(s_1) = R_1 + \theta_1$, and the second term is equal to $\exp(-n\theta_1)$. Setting these equal, we have

$$(57) \qquad \mu_1(s_1) - s_1\mu_1'(s_1) = -\theta_1, \qquad R_1 + \theta_1 = \mu_1'(s_1).$$

Eliminating θ_1, we have

$$(58) \qquad\qquad R_1 = \mu_1(s_1) - (s_1 - 1)\mu_1'(s_1)$$

and

$$(59) \qquad\qquad E(P_{e1}) \leqq 2 \exp\{n[\mu_1(s_1) - s_1\mu_1'(s_1)]\}.$$

This is because the two terms are now equal and each dominated by $\exp\{n[\mu_1(s_1) - s_1\mu_1'(s_1)]\}$. Similarly, for

$$(60) \qquad\qquad R_2 = \mu_2(s_2) - (s_2 - 1)\mu_2'(s_2)$$

we have

$$(61) \qquad\qquad E(P_{e2}) \leqq 2 \exp\{n[\mu_2(s_2) - s_2\mu_2'(s_2)]\}.$$

These might be called parametric bounds in terms of the parameters s_1 and s_2. One must choose s_1 and s_2 such as to make the rates R_1 and R_2 have the desired values. These s_1 and s_2 values, when substituted in the other formulas, give bounds on the error probabilities.

The derivative of R_1 with respect to s_1 is $-(s_1 - 1)\mu_1''(s_1)$, a quantity always positive when s_1 is negative except for the special case where $\mu''(0) = 0$. Thus, R_1 is a monotone increasing function of s_1 as s_1 goes from $-\infty$ to 0, with R_1 going from $-I_{\min} - \log P\{I_{\min}\}$ to $E(I)$. The bracketed term in the exponent of $E(P_{e1})$, namely $\mu_1(s_1) - s_1\mu_1(s_1)$, meanwhile varies from $\log P\{I_{\min}\}$ up to zero. The rate corresponding to $s_1 = -\infty$, that is, $-I_{\min} - \log P\{I_{\min}\}$, may be positive or negative. If negative (or zero) the entire range of rates is covered from zero up to $E(I)$. However, if it is positive, there is a gap from rate $R_1 = 0$ up to this end point. This means that there is no way to solve the equation for rates in this interval to make the exponents of the two terms equal. The best course here to give a good bound is to choose θ_1 in such a way that $n(R_1 + \theta_1)$ is just smaller than $I_{\min}$, say $I_{\min} - \epsilon$. Then $p_{12}[n(R_1 + \theta_1)] = 0$ and only the second term, $\exp(\theta_1 n)$, is left in the bound. Thus $\exp[-n(I_{\min} - R_1 - \epsilon)]$ is a bound on P_e. This is true for any $\epsilon > 0$. Since we can construct such codes for any positive ϵ and since there are only a finite number of codes, this implies that we can construct a code satisfying this inequality with $\epsilon = 0$. Thus, we may say that

$$(62) \qquad E(P_{e1}) \leqq \exp[-n(I_{\min} - R_1)], \qquad\qquad R_1 \leqq I_{\min}.$$

Of course, exactly similar statements hold for the second code working in the reverse direction. Combining and summarizing these results we have the following.

THEOREM 7. *In a two-way memoryless channel K with finite alphabets, let $P\{x_1\}$ and $P\{x_2\}$ be assignments of probabilities to the input alphabets, and suppose these lead to the logarithms of moment generating functions for mutual information $\mu_1(s_1)$ and $\mu_2(s_2)$,*

$$(63) \qquad \begin{aligned} \mu_1(s_1) &= \log \sum_{x_1,x_2,y_2} \frac{P\{x_1, x_2, y_2\}^{s+1}}{P\{x_1\}^s P\{x_2, y_2\}^s} \\[1em] \mu_2(s_2) &= \log \sum_{x_1,x_2,y_1} \frac{P\{x_1, x_2, y_1\}^{s+1}}{P\{x_2\}^s P\{x_1, y_1\}^s}. \end{aligned}$$

Let $M_1 = \exp(R_1 n)$, $M_2 = \exp(R_2 n)$ be integers, and let s_1, s_2 be the solutions (when they exist) of

$$(64) \qquad \begin{aligned} R_1 &= \mu_1(s_1) - (s_1 + 1)\mu_1'(s_1) \\ R_2 &= \mu_2(s_2) - (s_2 + 1)\mu_2'(s_2). \end{aligned}$$

The solution s_1 will exist if

$$(65) \qquad -I_{\min}(x_1; x_2, y_2) - \log P\{I_{\min}(x_1; x_2, y_2)\} \leqq R_1 \leqq E[I(x_1; x_2, y_2)],$$

and similarly for s_2. If both s_1 and s_2 exist, then there is a code pair for the channel K of length n with M_1 and M_2 messages and error probabilities satisfying

$$(66) \qquad \begin{aligned} P_{e1} &\leqq 4 \exp\{+n[\mu_1(s_1) - s_1\mu_1'(s_1)]\} \\ P_{e2} &\leqq 4 \exp\{+n[\mu_2(s_2) - s_2\mu_2'(s_2)]\}. \end{aligned}$$

If either (or both) of the R is so small that the corresponding s does not exist, a code pair exists with the corresponding error probability bounded by

$$(67) \qquad P_{e1} \leqq 2 \exp\{-n[I(x_1; x_2, y_2) - R_1]\}$$

or

$$(68) \qquad P_{e2} \leqq 2 \exp\{-n[I(x_2; x_1, y_1) - R_2]\}.$$

Thus, if s_1 exists and not s_2, then inequalities (66) would be used. If neither exists, (67) and (68) hold.

REFERENCES

[1] C. E. SHANNON, "Certain results in coding theory for noisy channels," *Information and Control*, Vol. 1 (1957), pp. 6–25.

[2] ———, "Channels with side information at the transmitter," *IBM J. Res. Develop.*, Vol. 2 (1958), pp. 289–293.

[3] ———, "Geometrische Deutung einiger Ergebnisse bei der Berechnung der Kanal-kapazitat," *Nachrtech. Z.*, Vol. 10 (1957).

[4] H. CHERNOFF, "A measure of asymptotic efficiency for tests of a hypothesis based on the sum of observations," *Ann. Math. Statist.*, Vol. 23 (1952), pp. 493–507.

Lower Bounds to Error Probability for Coding on Discrete Memoryless Channels. I

C. E. SHANNON* AND R. G. GALLAGER*

*Departments of Electrical Engineering and Mathematics, Research
Laboratory of Electronics, Massachusetts Institute of Technology,
Cambridge, Massachusetts*

AND

E. R. BERLEKAMP†

Department of Electrical Engineering, University of California, Berkeley, California

New lower bounds are presented for the minimum error probability that can be achieved through the use of block coding on noisy discrete memoryless channels. Like previous upper bounds, these lower bounds decrease exponentially with the block length N. The coefficient of N in the exponent is a convex function of the rate. From a certain rate of transmission up to channel capacity, the exponents of the upper and lower bounds coincide. Below this particular rate, the exponents of the upper and lower bounds differ, although they approach the same limit as the rate approaches zero. Examples are given and various incidental results and techniques relating to coding theory are developed. The paper is presented in two parts: the first, appearing here, summarizes the major results and treats the case of high transmission rates in detail; the second, to appear in the subsequent issue, treats the case of low transmission rates.

I. INTRODUCTION AND SUMMARY OF RESULTS

The noisy channel coding theorem (Shannon, 1948) states that for a broad class of communication channels, data can be transmitted over the channel in appropriately coded form at any rate less than channel

* The work of these authors was supported by the National Aeronautics and Space Administration (Grants NsG-334 and NsG-496), the Joint Services Electronics Program (contract DA-36-039-AMC-03200 (EE)), and the National Science Foundation (Grant GP-2495).

† The work of this author is supported by the Air Force Office of Scientific Research (Grant, AF-AFOSR-639-65).

Reprinted from INFORMATION AND CONTROL, Volume 10, No. 1, February 1967
Copyright © by Academic Press Inc.   *Printed in U.S.A.*

INFORMATION AND CONTROL **10**, 65–103 (1967)

capacity with arbitrarily small error probability. Naturally there is a rub in such a delightful sounding theorem, and the rub here is that the error probability can, in general, be made small only by making the coding constraint length large; this, in turn, introduces complexity into the encoder and decoder. Thus, if one wishes to employ coding on a particular channel, it is of interest to know not only the capacity but also how quickly the error probability can be made to approach zero with increasing constraint length. Feinstein (1955), Shannon (1958), Fano (1961), and Gallager (1965) have shown that for discrete memoryless channels, block coding and decoding schemes exist for which the error probability approaches zero exponentially with increasing block length for any given data rate less than channel capacity.

This paper is concerned primarily with the magnitude of this exponential dependence. We derive some lower bounds on achievable error probability, summarized in Theorems 1 to 4 below, and compare these bounds with the tightest known general upper bounds on error probability.

A *discrete channel* is a channel for which the input and output are sequences of letters from finite alphabets. Without loss of generality, we can take the input alphabet to be the set of integers $(1, \cdots, K)$ and the output alphabet to be the set of integers $(1, \cdots, J)$. A *discrete memoryless channel* is a discrete channel in which each letter of the output sequence is statistically dependent only on the corresponding letter of the input sequence. A discrete memoryless channel is specified by its set of transition probabilities $P(j \mid k)$, $1 \leqq j \leqq J$, $1 \leqq k \leqq K$, where $P(j \mid k)$ is the probability of receiving digit j given that digit k was transmitted. If $\mathbf{x} = (k_1, k_2, \cdots, k_N)$ is a sequence of N input letters and $\mathbf{y} = (j_1, \cdots, j_N)$ is a corresponding sequence of N output letters, then for a memoryless channel

$$\Pr(\mathbf{y} \mid \mathbf{x}) = \prod_{n=1}^{N} P(j_n \mid k_n) \qquad (1.1)$$

A *block code* with M code words of length N is a mapping from a set of M *source messages*, denoted by the integers 1 to M, onto a set of M *code words*, $\mathbf{x}_1, \cdots, \mathbf{x}_M$, where each code word is a sequence of N letters from the channel input alphabet. A *decoding scheme* for such a code is a mapping from the set of output sequences of length N into the integers 1 to M. If the source attempts to transmit message m over the channel via this coding and decoding scheme, message m is encoded into sequence $\mathbf{x}_m$;

after transmitting $\mathbf{x}_m$, some sequence $\mathbf{y}$ is received which is mapped into an integer m'. If $m' \neq m$, we say that a decoding error has occurred.

It is convenient here to consider a somewhat more general problem, *list decoding*, where the decoder, rather than mapping the received sequence into a single integer, maps it into a list of integers each between 1 and M. If the transmitted source message is not on the list of decoded integers, we say that a *list decoding error* has occurred.

List decoding was first considered by Elias (1955) for the Binary Symmetric Channel. Most of the known bounds on error probability extend readily with simple alterations to list decoding and the concept has been very useful both in providing additional insight about ordinary decoding and as a tool in proving theorems (see, for example, Jacobs and Berlekamp (1967)).

For a given code and list decoding scheme, let Y_m be the set of received sequences for which message m is on the list of decoded integers and let $Y_m{}^c$ be the complement of the set Y_m . Then the probability of a list decoding error, given that the source message is m, is the conditional probability that $\mathbf{y}$ is in $Y_m{}^c$, or

$$P_{e,m} = \sum_{\mathbf{y} \in Y_m{}^c} \mathrm{Pr}\,(\mathbf{y} \mid \mathbf{x}_m) \tag{1.2}$$

The error probability for a given code and list decoding scheme is then defined as the average $P_{e,m}$ over m assuming that the messages are equally likely,

$$P_e = \frac{1}{M} \sum_{m=1}^{M} P_{e,m} \tag{1.3}$$

We define $P_e(N, M, L)$ as the minimum error probability for the given channel minimized over all codes with M code words of length N and all list decoding schemes where the size of the list is limited to L. $P_e(N, M, 1)$ is thus the minimum error probability using ordinary decoding. Finally the *rate R* of a code with list decoding is defined as

$$R = \frac{\ln M/L}{N} = \frac{\ln M}{N} - \frac{\ln L}{N} \tag{1.4}$$

For ordinary decoding where $L = 1$, this is the usual definition of rate and is the source entropy per channel digit for equally likely messages. For larger L, we may think of $(\ln L)/N$ as a correction term to account for the fact that the receiver is only asserting the message to be one of a list of L. For example, if $M = L$, (1.4) asserts that $R = 0$, and indeed no channel is required.

With these definitions, we can proceed to summarize the major results of the paper. The major result of Section II is Theorem 1 below, which lower bounds the error probability of a code in terms of the minimum achievable error probability at 2 shorter blocklengths.

THEOREM 1. *Let N_1, N_2 be arbitrary blocklengths and let M, L_1, and L_2 be arbitrary positive integers. Then the minimum error probability achievable for a code of M code words of length $N_1 + N_2$ is bounded by*

$$P_e(N_1 + N_2, M, L_2) \geqq P_e(N_1, M, L_1)P_e(N_2, L_1 + 1, L_2) \quad (1.5)$$

In Section VI this theorem leads directly to an exponential type lower bound on error probability which for low transmission rates is considerably tighter than any previously known bound.

In Section III, codes containing only two code words are analyzed in detail. We find the trade-offs between the error probability when the first word is sent and the error probability when the second word is sent. The results, which are used in Sections IV and V, are summarized in Section III by Theorem 5 and Fig. 3.1.

The major result of Section IV is the "sphere packing" bound on error probability, given below as Theorem 2. This theorem, in slightly different form, was discovered by Fano (1961) but has not been rigorously proven before.

THEOREM 2. *Given a discrete memoryless channel with transition probabilities $P(j \mid k)$; $1 \leqq k \leqq K$, $1 \leqq j \leqq J$; $P_e(N, M, L)$ is lower bounded by*

$$P_e(N, M, L) \geqq \exp - N\{E_{sp}[R - o_1(N)] + o_2(N)\} \quad (1.6)$$

where the function E_{sp} is defined by

$$E_{sp}(R) = \underset{\rho \geqq 0}{\text{L.U.B.}} [E_0(\rho) - \rho R] \quad (1.7)$$

$$E_0(\rho) = \max_{\mathbf{q}} E_0(\rho, \mathbf{q}) \quad (1.8)$$

$$E_0(\rho, \mathbf{q}) = -\ln \sum_{j=1}^{J} \left[\sum_{k=1}^{K} q_k P(j \mid k)^{1/(1+\rho)} \right]^{1+\rho} \quad (1.9)$$

The maximum in (1.8) is over all probability vectors $\mathbf{q} = (q_1, \cdots, q_K)$; that is, over all $\mathbf{q}$ with nonnegative components summing to 1. The quantities $o(N)$ go to 0 with increasing N and can be taken as

$$o_1(N) = \frac{\ln 8}{N} + \frac{K \ln N}{N} \quad \text{and} \quad o_2(N)$$

$$= \sqrt{\frac{8}{N}} \ln \frac{e}{\sqrt{P_{\min}}} + \frac{\ln 8}{N} \qquad (1.10)$$

where $P_{\min}$ is the smallest nonzero $P(j \mid k)$ for the channel and K and J are the sizes of the input and output alphabets respectively.

The quantity in braces in (1.6) can be found graphically from $E_{sp}(R)$ by taking each point on the $E_{sp}(R)$ curve, moving to the right $o_1(N)$ and moving upward $o_2(N)$. Thus the major problem in understanding the implication of the theorem is understanding the behavior of $E_{sp}(R)$. Figure 1 sketches $E_{sp}(R)$ for a number of channels. Figure 1(a) is the typical behavior; the other sketches are examples of the rather peculiar curves that can occur if some of the $P(j \mid k)$ are zero.

For a given ρ, $E_0(\rho) - \rho R$ is a linear function of R with slope $-\rho$. Thus, as shown in Fig. 2, $E_{sp}(R)$ is the least upper bound of this family of straight lines. It is obvious geometrically, and easy to prove analytically, that $E_{sp}(R)$ is nonincreasing in R and is convex $\cup$[1] (see Fig. 2). It is shown in the appendix that $E_{sp}(R) = 0$ for $R \geq C$ where C is channel capacity and that $E_{sp}(R) > 0$ for $0 \leq R < C$. It sometimes happens that $E_{sp}(R) = \infty$ for sufficiently small values of R (see Fig. 1(b), (c), (d), (e)). To investigate this, we observe that for fixed ρ, $E_0(\rho) - \rho R$ intercepts the R axis at $E_0(\rho)/\rho$. As $\rho \to \infty$ this line will approach a vertical line at $R = \lim_{\rho \to \infty} E_0(\rho)/\rho$ (see Fig. 2(b)). This limiting rate is called R_∞ and $E_{sp}(R)$ is finite for $R \geq R_\infty$ and infinite for $R < R_\infty$.

$$R_\infty = \lim_{\rho \to \infty} \max_q \frac{-\ln \sum_j [\sum_k q_k P(j \mid k)^{1/(1+\rho)}]^{1+\rho}}{\rho}$$

Finding the limit either by expanding in a Taylor series in $1/(1 + \rho)$ or by using L'Hospitals rule,

$$R_\infty = \max_q - \ln \max_{1 \leq j \leq J} \sum_k q_k \varphi(j \mid k) \qquad (1.11)$$

$$\varphi(j \mid k) = \begin{cases} 1; & P(j \mid k) \neq 0 \\ 0; & P(j \mid k) = 0 \end{cases}$$

---

[1] We will use convex $\cup$ (read convex cup) and concave $\cap$ (concave cap) as mnemonic aids to the reader for convex and concave functions. It seems as difficult for the nonspecialist to remember which is which as to remember the difference between stalagmites and stalactites.

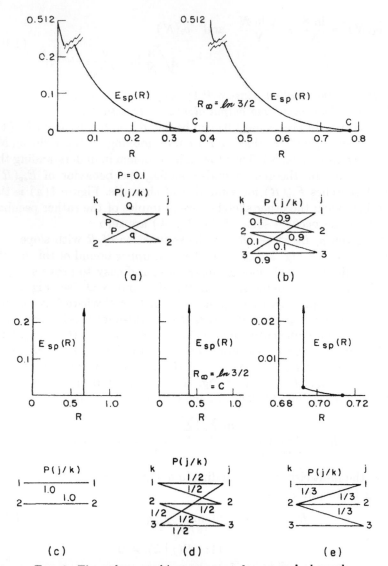

Fɪɢ. 1. The sphere packing exponent for several channels.

That is, for each output, we sum the input probabilities q_k that lead to that output. We then adjust the q_k to minimize the largest of these sums; R_∞ is minus the logarithm of that min-max sum. It can be seen from this that $R_\infty > 0$ iff each output is unreachable from at least one input.

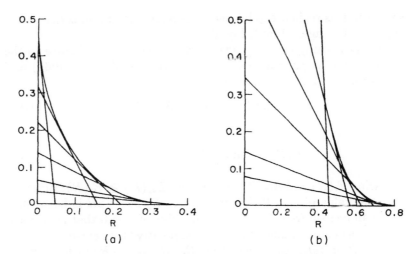

FIG. 2. $E_{sp}(R)$ as convex hull of straight lines (same channels as Fig. 1).

R_{∞} is an upper bound to the zero error capacity of the channel, C_0. Shannon (1956) has defined C_0 as the least upper bound of rates at which information can be transmitted with no possibility of errors. C_0 is greater than 0 iff there are two or more inputs from which no common output can be reached and thus it is possible to have $R_{\infty} > 0$ and $C_0 = 0$ (see Fig. 1(b) for such a channel). Shannon (1956) has shown that if $C_0 > 0$, then the expression in (1.11) for R_{∞} is equal to the zero error capacity of the channel with noiseless feedback.

If it happens that R_{∞} equals channel capacity C, then the sphere packing bound merely states the true but uninteresting result that $P_e \geqq 0$ for $R < C$. It is shown in the appendix that this occurs iff the following relations are satisfied for the input probability assignment $\mathbf{q} = (q_1, \cdots, q_K)$ that yields capacity.

(a) All transition probabilities that lead to a given output with non-zero probability are the same (i.e., $P(j \mid k)$ is independent of k for those j, k such that $q_k P(j \mid k) \neq 0$).

(b) The sum of the q_k over inputs leading to a given output j is independent of the output j.

These conditions are satisfied by all noiseless channels and also a few noisy channels such as that in Fig. 1(c). For all other channels, $R_{\infty} < C$. It is shown in the appendix that $E_{sp}(R)$ is strictly convex $\cup$ and strictly decreasing in this region. $E_{sp}(R)$ need not have a continuous derivative however (see Gallager (1965), Fig. 6).

The sphere packing bound above bears a striking resemblance to the "random coding" *upper* bound on error probability of Fano (1961) and Gallager (1965). That bound, as stated by Gallager, is

$$P_e(N, M, 1) \leqq \exp - N E_r(R) \qquad (1.12)$$

where

$$E_r(R) = \max_{0 \leqq \rho \leqq 1} [E_0(\rho) - \rho R] \qquad (1.13)$$

Comparing $E_r(R)$ and $E_{sp}(R)$, we see that $E_{sp}(R) \geqq E_r(R)$. Equality holds iff the value of $\rho \geqq 0$ that maximizes $E_0(\rho) - \rho R$ is between 0 and 1. It can be seen from Fig. 2 that the value of $\rho \geqq 0$ that maximizes $E_0(\rho) - \rho R$ is nonincreasing with R. Consequently there exists a number called the *critical rate*, R_{crit}, such that $E_{sp}(R) = E_r(R)$ iff $R \geqq R_{\text{crit}}$. R_{crit} lies between R_∞ and C and it is shown in the appendix that $R_{\text{crit}} = C$ iff $R_\infty = C$ (i.e., if conditions (a) and (b) above are satisfied). For all other channels there is a nonzero range of rates, $R_{\text{crit}} \leqq R \leqq C$, where the upper and lower bounds on error probability agree except for the $o(N)$ terms (see Fig. 3).

This completes our discussion of Theorem 2. For a more complete discussion of how to calculate $E_{sp}(R)$ and $E_r(R)$ see Gallager (1965). One additional result needed here, however, is the following (Gallager (1965), Theorem 4): any local maximum of (1.8) over the probability vector **q** is a global maximum, and necessary and sufficient conditions on **q** to maximize (1.8) for a given ρ are

$$\sum_j [P(j \mid k)]^{1/(1+\rho)} \alpha_j{}^\rho \geqq \sum_j \alpha_j^{1+\rho} \quad \text{for all} \quad k, 1 \leqq k \leqq K \quad (1.14)$$

where

$$\alpha_j = \sum_k q_k [P(j \mid k)]^{1/(1+\rho)} \qquad (1.15)$$

Equation (1.14) must be satisfied with equality except for those k for which $q_k = 0$; this can be seen by multiplying both sides of (1.14) by q_k and summing over k.

In Section V (contained in Part II) we find bounds on error probability for codes with a fixed number of code words in the limit as the block length becomes large. The exponent E_M for a code with M code

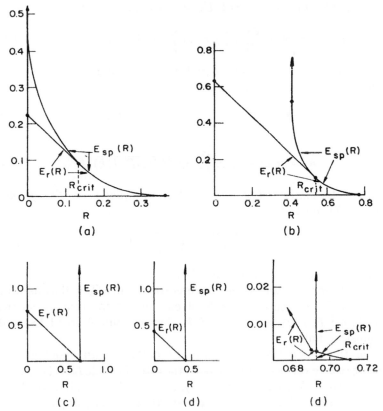

FIG. 3. Comparison of sphere packing exponent with random coding exponent (same channels as Fig. 1).

words is defined as

$$E_M = \limsup_{N \to \infty} \frac{-\ln P_e(N, M, 1)}{N} \qquad (1.16)$$

The major result of the section is the following theorem concerning the exponents, E_M.

THEOREM 3. *Given a discrete memoryless channel with transition probabilities* $P(j \mid k);\ 1 \leq k \leq K,\ 1 \leq j \leq J$, *and given that the zero error capacity is zero,* $P_e(N, M, 1)$ *is lower bounded by*

$$P_e(N, M, 1) \geq \exp - N[E_M + o_3(N)] \qquad (1.17)$$

The exponents approach a limit, $E_\infty = \lim_{M\to\infty} E_M$, given by

$$E_\infty = \max_{\mathbf{q}} - \sum_{i=1}^{K} \sum_{k=1}^{K} q_i\, q_k \ln \sum_{j=1}^{J} \sqrt{P(j\,|\,i)P(j\,|\,k)} \qquad (1.18)$$

The maximum in (1.18) is over all probability vectors $\mathbf{q} = (q_1, \cdots, q_K)$. The exponents E_M are bounded by

$$E_\infty \leqq E_M \leqq E_\infty + 2\sqrt{K}A/\sqrt{[\log_2 (\log_2 M)]^-} \qquad (1.19)$$

where

$$A = \max_{i,k} - 2\ln \sum_{j=1}^{J} \sqrt{P(j\,|\,i)P(j\,|\,k)} \qquad (1.20)$$

and $[x]^-$ denotes the largest integer less than or equal to x. The quantity $o_3(N)$ in (1.17) can be taken as

$$o_3(N) = \frac{\ln 4M}{N} - \sqrt{\frac{2}{N}} \ln P_{\min} \qquad (1.21)$$

where $P_{\min}$ is the smallest nonzero $P(j\,|\,k)$.

Theorem 3 again requires some interpretation. Since $C_0 = 0$ by assumption, every pair of inputs has at least one output in common so that $\sum_{j=1}^{J} \sqrt{P(j\,|\,i)P(j\,|\,k)} > 0$ for all i, k; thus E_∞ and A in (1.18) and (1.20) must be finite.

Each of the exponents E_M can be interpreted as an exponent corresponding to zero rate since for fixed M, the rate of a code $R = (\ln M)/N$ approaches zero as N approaches infinity. On the other hand, if we choose M as a function of N in such a way that $\lim_{N\to\infty} M(N) = \infty$; $\lim_{N\to\infty} (\ln M(N))/N = 0$, then (1.17) becomes

$$P_e(N, M(N), 1) \geqq \exp - N[E_\infty + o_4(N)] \qquad (1.22)$$

where $o_4(N)$ approaches zero as N approaches infinity.

For channels with a symmetry condition called pairwise reversibility, the exponents E_M can be uniquely determined. A channel is defined to be pairwise reversible iff for each pair of inputs, i and k,

$$\sum_{j=1}^{J} \sqrt{P(j\,|\,k)P(j\,|\,i)} \ln P(j\,|\,k)$$
$$= \sum_{j=1}^{J} \sqrt{P(j\,|\,k)P(j\,|\,i)} \ln P(j\,|\,i) \qquad (1.23)$$

This condition will be discussed more fully in Section V, but it is satisfied by such common channels as the binary symmetric channel and the binary symmetric erasure channel. For any channel satisfying (1.23), it is shown that

$$E_M = \frac{M}{M-1} \max_{M_1, \cdots, M_K} - \sum_i \sum_k \frac{M_i}{M} \frac{M_k}{M} \ln \sum_j \sqrt{P(j \mid i) P(j \mid k)} \quad (1.24)$$

where the $M_k \geqq 0$ are integers summing to M.

In Section VI, Theorems 1, 2, and 3 are combined to yield a new lower bound on error probability. The sphere packing bound is applied to $P_e(N_1, M, L)$ in (1.5) and the zero rate bound is applied to $P_e(N_2, L + 1, 1)$. The result is given by the following theorem.

THEOREM 4. *Let $E_{sp}(R)$ and E_∞ be given by (1.7) and (1.18) for an arbitrary discrete memoryless channel for which $C_0 = 0$. Let $E_{sl}(R)$ be the smallest linear function of R which touches the curve $E_{sp}(R)$ and which satisfies $E_{sl}(0) = E_\infty$. Let R_1 be the point where $E_{sl}(R)$ touches $E_{sp}(R)$. Then for any code with a rate $R < R_1$,*

$$P_e(N, M, 1) \geqq \exp - N[E_{sl}(R - o_5(N)) + o_6(N)] \quad (1.25)$$

where $o_5(N)$ and $o_6(N)$ are given by (6.6) and (6.7) and approach zero as N approaches infinity.

The function $E_{sl}(R)$ is sketched for a number of channels in Fig. 4. E_∞ is always strictly less than $E_{sp}(0^+)$ unless channel capacity C is zero. Thus the straight line bound of Theorem 4 is always tighter than the sphere packing bound at low rates for sufficiently large block lengths whenever $C > 0$, $C_0 = 0$.

Theorem 4 can be compared with an upper bound to error probability derived by Gallager (1965, Theorem 6) using expurgated randomly chosen codes. That result states that for any N, M,

$$P_e(N, M, 1) \leqq \exp - N\left[E_{ex}\left(R + \frac{\ln 4}{N}\right)\right] \quad (1.26)$$

where the function E_{ex} is given by

$$E_{ex}(R) = \text{L.U.B.} \, [E_x(\rho) - \rho R] \quad (1.27)$$
$$\,_{\rho \geqq 1}$$

$$E_x(\rho) = \max_q - \rho \ln \sum_{k=1}^{K} \sum_{i=1}^{K} q_k q_i \left[\sum_{j=1}^{J} \sqrt{P(j \mid k) P(j \mid i)} \right]^{1/\rho} \quad (1.28)$$

The maximization in (1.28) is again over probability vectors **q**.

The function $E_{ex}(R)$ is sketched for several channels in Fig. 4. It can

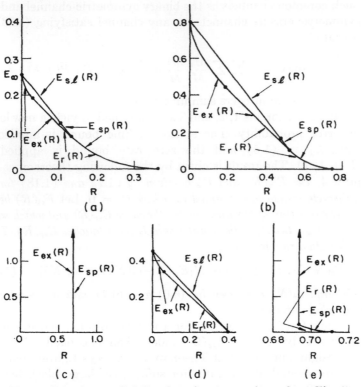

Fɪɢ. 4. Bounds on reliability function (same channels as Fig. 1)

be interpreted as the least upper bound of a set of straight lines where the lines have slope $-\rho$ and zero intercept $E_x(\rho)$. The function $E_x(\rho)$ is increasing with ρ and if $C_0 = 0$, we can calculate $\lim_{\rho \to \infty} E_x(\rho)$ as

$$\lim_{\rho \to \infty} E_x(\rho) = \max_q \sum_{k=1}^{K} \sum_{i=1}^{K} q_k q_i \ln \sum_{j=1}^{J} \sqrt{P(j \mid k) P(j \mid i)} \qquad (1.29)$$

Also it can be seen from (1.27) that

$$\lim_{R \to 0} E_{ex}(R) = \lim_{\rho \to \infty} E_x(\rho) \qquad (1.30)$$

Combining (1.18), (1.29), and (1.30), we see that

$$\lim_{R \to 0} E_{ex}(R) = E_\infty \qquad (1.31)$$

Thus, in the limit as $R \to 0$ our upper and lower bounds on P_e have the same exponential dependence on the block length.

It is to be observed that all the upper and lower bounds to error probability discussed so far have an exponential dependence on block length for fixed rate. The correct value of this exponential dependence, as a function of rate, is of fundamental importance in coding theory and is defined as the *reliability function*, $E(R)$, of the channel. More precisely,

$$E(R) = \lim_{N \to \infty} \sup \frac{-\ln P_e(N, [e^{NR}]^+, 1)}{N} \tag{1.32}$$

where $[x]^+$ is the smallest integer greater than or equal to x. We see that $E_{sp}(R)$ and $E_{sl}(R)$ are upper bounds to $E(R)$, and $E_r(R)$ and $E_{ex}(R)$ are lower bounds. The bounds are identical for the rather uninteresting case of noiseless channels and for some rather peculiar channels such as Fig. 1(e), but for typical channels there is a region of uncertainty for rates between 0 and R_{crit}. Although the bounds are close enough to give considerable insight into the behavior of a channel with coding, it is still interesting to speculate on the value of $E(R)$ in this region of uncertainty, $0 < R \leq R_{\text{crit}}$. For the binary symmetric channel, we improve on $E_{sl}(R)$ in Section VI by using a bound on minimum distance derived by Elias, but the technique does not generalize to arbitrary discrete memoryless channels. The authors would all tend to conjecture that $E(R)$ is equal to $E_{ex}(R)$ for $R \leq R_{\text{crit}}$ if the maximization in (1.29) is performed on a block basis rather than a letter basis (i.e., using $\text{Pr}(\mathbf{y} \mid \mathbf{x})$ in place of $P(j \mid k)$ and $q(\mathbf{x})$ in place of q) (see Gallager (1965)). As yet there is little concrete evidence for this conjecture.

II. PROOF OF THEOREM 1

Theorem 1 establishes a lower bound on error probability for a code in terms of the error probabilities for two codes of shorter block lengths. Let N_1 and N_2 be arbitrary block lengths and consider a code with M code words of block length $N_1 + N_2$. We shall be interested in considering each code word as consisting of two subsequences, the first of length N_1 and the second of length N_2. Let $\mathbf{x}_m$ be the mth code word and let the *prefix* $\mathbf{x}_{m,1}$ be the first N_1 letters of $\mathbf{x}_m$ and let the *suffix* $\mathbf{x}_{m,2}$ be the final N_2 letters of $\mathbf{x}_m$. Likewise, we separate the received sequence $\mathbf{y}$ into the prefix $\mathbf{y}_1$ and the suffix $\mathbf{y}_2$, consisting of N_1 and N_2 letters respectively.

We can visualize a list decoder of size L_2 as first observing $\mathbf{y}_1$, then $\mathbf{y}_2$, and decoding on the basis of these observations. Suppose that on the basis of $\mathbf{y}_1$ alone, there is a given number, say L_1, of messages that are more likely at the decoder than the actual transmitted message. If L_2 of these L_1 messages are also more likely than the transmitted message on the basis of $\mathbf{y}_2$ above, then a list decoding error should surely be made. Reasoning heuristically, it appears that the probability of the first event above is the probability of a list decoding error for a code of M code words of length N_1 with a list size of L_1. Similarly, given the first event, the probability of the second event should be lower bounded by the probability of a list decoding error for a code of block length N_2 consisting of the L_1 most likely messages plus the actual transmitted message. We thus conclude heuristically that

$$P_e(N_1 + N_2, M, L_2) \geq P_e(N_1, M, L_1)P_e(N_2, L_1 + 1, L_2) \quad (2.1)$$

This is the result of Theorem 1, and we now turn to a rigorous proof.

For a given code with M code words of length $N_1 + N_2$, and a list decoding scheme of size L_2, let Y_m be the set of received sequences $\mathbf{y}$ for which message m is on the decoding list. Also, for any given received prefix, $\mathbf{y}_1$, let $Y_{m,2}(\mathbf{y}_1)$ be the set of suffixes $\mathbf{y}_2$ for which m is on the list when $\mathbf{y}_1\mathbf{y}_2$ is received. Using (1.2) and (1.3) the error probability for the code is given by

$$P_e = \frac{1}{M} \sum_{m=1}^{M} \sum_{\mathbf{y} \in Y_m{}^c} \Pr(\mathbf{y} \mid \mathbf{x}_m) \quad (2.2)$$

For a discrete memoryless channel, $\Pr(\mathbf{y} \mid \mathbf{x}_m) = \Pr(\mathbf{y}_1 \mid \mathbf{x}_{m,1}) \Pr(\mathbf{y}_2 \mid \mathbf{x}_{m,2})$ and we can rewrite (2.2) as

$$P_e = \frac{1}{M} \sum_{m=1}^{M} \sum_{\mathbf{y}_1} \Pr(\mathbf{y}_1 \mid \mathbf{x}_{m,1}) \sum_{\mathbf{y}_2 \in Y_{m,2}^c(\mathbf{y}_1)} \Pr(\mathbf{y}_2 \mid \mathbf{x}_{m,2}) \quad (2.3)$$

Now consider the set of code word suffixes, $\mathbf{x}_{1,2}, \cdots, \mathbf{x}_{m,2}, \cdots, \mathbf{x}_{M,2}$. Pick any subset of $L_1 + 1$ of the messages and consider the associated $L_1 + 1$ suffixes as a set of $L_1 + 1$ code words of block length N_2. For any given $\mathbf{y}_1$, the associated $L_1 + 1$ decoding regions $Y_{m,2}(\mathbf{y}_1)$ form a list decoding rule of size L_2. Presumably some suffixes $\mathbf{y}_2$ are mapped into fewer than L_2 messages from the given subset, so that this is not the best set of decoding regions, but it is certainly a valid set. Now $P_e(N_2, L_1 + 1, L_2)$ is a lower bound to the error probability for any set of $L_1 + 1$ code words of length N_2 with any list decoding scheme of size L_2, and at least one code word in any such code must have an error probability that large. Thus, for at least one value of m in any given subset of $L_1 + 1$ suffixes, we have

$$\sum_{\mathbf{y}_2 \in Y_{m,2}^c(\mathbf{y}_1)} \Pr\left(\mathbf{y}_2 \mid \mathbf{x}_{m,2}\right) \geqq P_e(N_2, L_1 + 1, L_2) \qquad (2.4)$$

For any given $\mathbf{y}_1$, consider the entire set of M messages again. Let $m_1(\mathbf{y}_1), m_2(\mathbf{y}_1), \cdots, m_l(\mathbf{y}_1)$ be the set of messages for which (2.4) is *not* satisfied. This set must contain at most L_1 messages since otherwise we would have a subset of $L_1 + 1$ messages for which no member satisfied (2.4). We can then lower bound the left hand side of (2.4) for any m by

$$\sum_{\mathbf{y}_2 \in Y_{m,2}^c(\mathbf{y}_1)} \Pr\left(\mathbf{y}_2 \mid \mathbf{x}_{m,2}\right)$$

$$\geqq \begin{cases} 0; & m = m_1(\mathbf{y}_1), \cdots, m_l(\mathbf{y}_1) \\ P_e(N_2, L_1 + 1, L_2); & m \neq m_1(\mathbf{y}_1), \cdots, m_l(\mathbf{y}_1) \end{cases} \qquad (2.5)$$

where l depends on $\mathbf{y}_1$ but always satisfies $l \leqq L_1$.

Interchanging the order of summation between m and $\mathbf{y}_1$ in (2.3) and substituting (2.5) into (2.3), we obtain

$$P_e \geqq \frac{1}{M} \sum_{\mathbf{y}_1} \sum_{\substack{m \neq m_i(\mathbf{y}_1) \\ i=1,\cdots,l}} \Pr\left(\mathbf{y}_1 \mid \mathbf{x}_{m,1}\right) P_e(N_2, L_1 + 1, L_2) \qquad (2.6)$$

$$P_e \geqq P_e(N_2, L_1 + 1, L_2) \left[\frac{1}{M} \sum_{\mathbf{y}_1} \sum_{\substack{m \neq m_i(\mathbf{y}_1) \\ i=1,\cdots,l}} \Pr\left(\mathbf{y}_1 \mid \mathbf{x}_{m,1}\right) \right] \qquad (2.7)$$

Finally, to complete the proof, we can consider the set of prefixes $\mathbf{x}_{1,1}, \cdots, \mathbf{x}_{M,1}$ as a set of M code words of length N_1, and the sets $m_1(\mathbf{y}_1), \cdots, m_l(\mathbf{y}_1)$ as a list decoding rule of size L_1 (recall that $l \leqq L_1$ for all $\mathbf{y}_1$). Let $Y_{m,1}$ be the set of $\mathbf{y}_1$ for which m is on the list $m_1(\mathbf{y}_1), \cdots, m_l(\mathbf{y}_1)$. Interchanging the sum over m and $\mathbf{y}_1$ in (2.7), we obtain

$$P_e \geqq P_e(N_2, L_1 + 1, L_2) \left[\frac{1}{M} \sum_{m=1}^{M} \sum_{\mathbf{y}_1 \in Y_{m,1}^c} \Pr\left(\mathbf{y}_1 \mid \mathbf{x}_{m,1}\right) \right] \qquad (2.8)$$

The quantity in brackets is the probability of list decoding error for this code of length N_1 and is lower bounded by $P_e(N_1, M, L_1)$

$$P_e \geqq P_e(N_2, L_1 + 1, L_2) P_e(N_1, M, L_1) \qquad (2.9)$$

Thus any code with M code words of length $N_1 + N_2$ and any list decoding scheme of size L_2 has an error probability satisfying (2.9) and this establishes (2.1).

The above theorem can be generalized considerably. First we note that the assumption of a discrete channel was used only in writing sums over the output sequences. For continuous channels, these sums are replaced by integrals. The theorem can also be modified to apply to a broad class of channels with memory. Also, if there is feedback from the receiver to transmitter, the theorem is still valid. The encoder can then change the code word suffixes depending on which $\mathbf{y}_1$ is received, but (2.5) is valid independent of the choice of the set $\{\mathbf{x}_{m,2}\}$. Finally the theorem can be extended to the case where two independent channels are available and $\mathbf{x}_{m,1}$ is sent over one channel and $\mathbf{x}_{m,2}$ is sent over the other channel.

III. ERROR PROBABILITY FOR TWO CODE WORDS

In this section we shall derive both upper and lower bounds to the probability of decoding error for a block code with two code words of length N. Surprisingly enough, the results are fundamental to both Sections IV and V.

Let $P_m(\mathbf{y})$, $m = 1, 2$, be the probability of receiving sequence $\mathbf{y}$ when message m is transmitted. If Y_m is the set of sequences decoded into message m, then from (1.2), the probability of decoding error when message m is transmitted is

$$P_{e,m} = \sum_{\mathbf{y} \in Y_m{}^c} P_m(\mathbf{y}); \qquad m = 1, 2 \qquad (3.1)$$

For initial motivation, suppose that the decoder adopts a maximum likelihood decision rule: decode $\mathbf{y}$ into message 1 if $P_1(\mathbf{y}) > P_2(\mathbf{y})$ and decode into message 2 otherwise. Under these circumstances $P_m(\mathbf{y})$ in (3.1) is equal to $\min_{m'=1,2} P_{m'}(\mathbf{y})$. Summing (3.1) over m, we then get

$$P_{e,1} + P_{e,2} = \sum_{\mathbf{y}} \min_{m=1,2} P_m(\mathbf{y}) \qquad (3.2)$$

For any s in the interval $0 < s < 1$, a simple bound on $\min P_m(\mathbf{y})$ is given by

$$\min_{m=1,2} P_m(\mathbf{y}) \leqq P_1(\mathbf{y})^{1-s} P_2(\mathbf{y})^s \leqq \max_{m=1,2} P_m(\mathbf{y}) \qquad (3.3)$$

Thus,

$$P_{e,1} + P_{e,2} \leqq \sum_{\mathbf{y}} P_1(\mathbf{y})^{1-s} P_2(\mathbf{y})^s; \qquad 0 < s < 1 \qquad (3.4)$$

We shall see later that when the right hand side of (3.4) is minimized over s, the bound is quite tight despite its apparent simplicity.

The logarithm of the right side of (3.4) is a fundamental quantity in most of the remainder of this paper; we denote it by

$$\mu(s) \triangleq \ln \sum_{\mathbf{y}} P_1(\mathbf{y})^{1-s} P_2(\mathbf{y})^{s}; \qquad 0 < s < 1 \qquad (3.5)$$

It is convenient to extend this definition to cover $s = 0$ and $s = 1$.

$$\mu(0) \triangleq \lim_{s \to 0^+} \mu(s); \qquad \mu(1) \triangleq \lim_{s \to 1^-} \mu(s) \qquad (3.6)$$

Then we can rewrite (3.4), minimized over s, as

$$P_{e,1} + P_{e,2} \leq \min_{0 \leq s \leq 1} \exp \mu(s) \qquad (3.7)$$

Some typical modes of behavior of $\mu(s)$ are shown in Fig. 5. The block length in these figures is one and the first code word is the input letter 1 and the second is the input letter 2. It is shown later that $\mu(s)$ is always nonpositive and convex $\cup$.

We next show that when the block length is greater than one, $\mu(s)$ can be written as a sum over the individual letters in the block. Let the code words be denoted by $\mathbf{x}_m = (k_{m,1}, \cdots, k_{m,N})$, $m = 1, 2$, and let the received sequence be $\mathbf{y} = (j_1, \cdots, j_N)$. Then, using (1.1), we have $P_m(\mathbf{y}) = \prod_n P(j_n \mid k_{m,n})$, and $\mu(s)$ becomes

$$\mu(s) = \ln \sum_{j_1=1}^{J} \cdots \sum_{j_N=1}^{J} \prod_{n=1}^{N} P(j_n \mid k_{1,n})^{1-s} P(j_n \mid k_{2,n})^{s} \qquad (3.8)$$

$$\mu(s) = \ln \sum_{j_1=1}^{J} P(j_1 \mid k_{1,1})^{1-s} P(j_1 \mid k_{2,1})^{s} \sum_{j_2=1}^{J} P(j_2 \mid k_{1,2})^{1-s}$$

$$\cdot P(j_2 \mid k_{2,2})^{s} \cdots \sum_{j_N=1}^{J} P(j_N \mid k_{1,N})^{1-s} P(j_N \mid k_{2,N})^{s} \qquad (3.9)$$

$$\mu(s) = \sum_{n=1}^{N} \mu_n(s); \qquad \mu_n(s) = \ln \sum_{j=1}^{J} P(j \mid k_{1,n})^{1-s} P(j \mid k_{2,n})^{s} \qquad (3.10)$$

We now generalize the bound in (3.7) in two directions. First we want both upper and lower bounds on $P_{e,1}$ and $P_{e,2}$. Second, for reasons that will be clear in Section IV, we want to allow ourselves the flexibility of making $P_{e,1}$ very much larger than $P_{e,2}$ or vice versa. The following theorem achieves both of these objectives.

THEOREM 5. *Let $P_1(\mathbf{y})$ and $P_2(\mathbf{y})$ be two probability assignments on a*

C. E. Shannon, R. G. Gallager, and E. R. Berlekamp

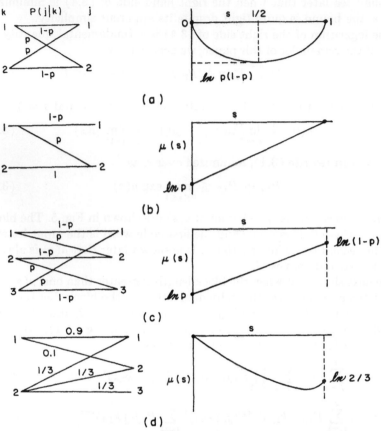

FIG. 5. The functions $\mu(s) = \ln \sum_j P(j \mid 1)^{1-s} P(j \mid 2)^s$ for several channels.

discrete set of sequences, let Y_1 and Y_2 be disjoint decision regions for these sequences, let $P_{e,1}$ and $P_{e,2}$ be given by (3.1) and assume that $P_1(\mathbf{y})P_2(\mathbf{y}) \neq 0$ for at least one sequence $\mathbf{y}$. Then, for any s, $0 < s < 1$, either

$$P_{e,1} > \tfrac{1}{4} \exp\left[\mu(s) - s\mu'(s) - s\sqrt{2\mu''(s)}\right] \qquad (3.11)$$

or

$$P_{e,2} > \tfrac{1}{4} \exp\left[\mu(s) + (1 - s)\mu'(s) - (1 - s)\sqrt{2\mu''(s)}\right] \qquad (3.12)$$

Furthermore, for an appropriate choice of Y_1, Y_2,

$$P_{e,1} \leqq \exp\left[\mu(s) - s\mu'(s)\right] \qquad and \qquad (3.13)$$

$$P_{e,2} \leqq \exp\left[\mu(s) + (1 - s)\mu'(s)\right] \qquad (3.14)$$

Finally $\mu(s)$ *is nonpositive and convex* $\cup$ *for* $0 < s < 1$. *The convexity is strict unless* $P_1(\mathbf{y})/P_2(\mathbf{y})$ *is constant over all* $\mathbf{y}$ *for which* $P_1(\mathbf{y})P_2(\mathbf{y}) \neq 0$. *Also* $\mu(s)$ *is strictly negative for* $0 < s < 1$ *unless* $P_1(\mathbf{y}) = P_2(\mathbf{y})$ *for all* $\mathbf{y}$.

Remarks: The probabilities $P_1(\mathbf{y})$ and $P_2(\mathbf{y})$ do not have to correspond to two code words and in Section IV the theorem will be used where $P_2(\mathbf{y})$ does not correspond to a code word. For interpretation, however, we shall consider only the problem of two code words on a memoryless channel, in which case (3.10) is valid. Taking the derivatives of (3.10), we have

$$\mu'(s) = \sum_{n=1}^{N} \mu_n'(s); \qquad \mu''(s) = \sum_{n=1}^{N} \mu_n''(s) \qquad (3.15)$$

Therefore, for any s, $0 < s < 1$, the first part of the theorem states that either

$$P_{e,1} > \tfrac{1}{4} \exp\left\{\sum_{n=1}^{N} [\mu_n(s) - s\mu_n'(s)] - s\sqrt{\sum_n 2\mu_n''(s)}\right\} \qquad (3.16)$$

or

$$P_{e,2} > \tfrac{1}{4} \exp\left\{\sum_{n=1}^{N} [\mu_n(s) + (1 - s)\mu_n'(s)] - (1 - s)\right.$$
$$\left. \cdot \sqrt{\sum_n \mu_n''(s)}\right\} \qquad (3.17)$$

We see from this that in some sense the terms involving $\mu(s)$ and $\mu'(s)$ are proportional to the block length N and that the term involving $\sqrt{\mu''(s)}$ is proportional to $\sqrt{N}$. It follows that for large N we should focus our attention primarily on $\mu(s)$ and $\mu'(s)$.

Figure 6 gives a graphical interpretation of the terms $\mu(s) - \mu'(s)$ and $\mu(s) + (1 - s)\mu'(s)$. It is seen that they are the endpoints, at 0 and 1, of the tangent at s to the curve $\mu(s)$. As s increases, the tangent see-saws around, decreasing $\mu(s) - s\mu'(s)$ and increasing $\mu(s) + (1 - s)\mu'(s)$. In the special case where $\mu(s)$ is a straight line, of course, this see-sawing does not occur and $\mu(s) - s\mu'(s)$ and $\mu(s) + (1 - s)\mu'(s)$ do not vary with s.

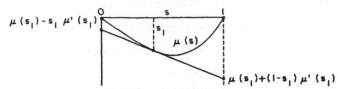

FIG. 6. Geometric interpretation of the exponents $\mu(s) - s\mu'(s)$ and
$$\mu(s) + (1 - s)\mu'(s).$$

Since $\mu(s)$ is convex $\cup$ over $0 < s < 1$, any tangent to μ in this range will lie on or beneath μ. Furthermore, since $\mu(s) \leqq 0$ in this range, we have in general, for $0 < s < 1$,

$$\mu(s) - s\mu'(s) \leqq 0 \tag{3.18}$$

$$\mu(s) + (1 - s)\mu'(s) \leqq 0 \tag{3.19}$$

A particularly important special case of the theorem is that in which s is chosen to minimize $\mu(s)$. In that case we get the following corollary.

COROLLARY. *Let s^* minimize $\mu(s)$ over $0 \leqq s \leqq 1$. Then either*

$$P_{e,1} \geqq \tfrac{1}{4} \exp\left[\mu(s^*) - s^*\sqrt{2\mu''(s^*)}\right] \tag{3.20}$$

or

$$P_{e,2} \geqq \tfrac{1}{4} \exp\left[\mu(s^*) - (1 - s^*)\sqrt{2\mu''(s^*)}\right] \tag{3.21}$$

where if $s^* = 0$ or 1, $\mu''(s^*)$ is the limit of $\mu''(s)$ from the interior of the interval.

Proof of Corollary: If s^* is within the interval $0 < s^* < 1$, then $\mu'(s^*) = 0$ and (3.20) and (3.21) follow immediately from (3.11) and (3.12). If $s^* = 0$, then $\mu'(0^+) \geqq 0$, and

$$\lim_{s \to 0^+} \mu(s) - s\mu'(s) = \mu(0^+) = \mu(s^*)$$
$$\lim_{s \to 0^+} \mu(s) + (1 - s)\mu'(s) \geqq \mu(0^+) = \mu(s^*) \tag{3.22}$$

Likewise if $s^* = 1$, *then $\mu'(1^-) \leqq 0$, and*

$$\lim_{s \to 1^-} \mu(s) - s\mu'(s) \geqq \mu(1^-) = \mu(s^*)$$
$$\lim_{s \to 1^-} \mu(s) + (1 - s)\mu'(s) = \mu(1^-) = \mu(s^*) \tag{3.23}$$

Substituting these relations into (3.11) and (3.12) completes the proof.

Notice that the exponent $\mu(s^*)$ appearing in (3.20) and (3.21) is the same as the exponent in the upper bound to $P_{e,1} + P_{e,2}$ of (3.7).

Proof of Theorem 5: The sum over $\mathbf{y}$ in $\mu(s)$ as given by (3.5) can either be considered to be over all output sequences $\mathbf{y}$ or over only those sequences in the overlap region where $P_1(\mathbf{y})$ and $P_2(\mathbf{y})$ are both nonzero. For the remainder of the proof, we consider all sums over $\mathbf{y}$ to be over only the overlap region.

Taking the derivatives of $\mu(s)$, we get

$$\mu'(s) = \left\{ \sum_{\mathbf{y}} \frac{P_1(\mathbf{y})^{1-s} P_2(\mathbf{y})^s}{\sum_{\mathbf{y}'} P_1(\mathbf{y}')^{1-s} P_2(\mathbf{y}')^s} \ln \frac{P_2(\mathbf{y})}{P_1(\mathbf{y})} \right\} \tag{3.24}$$

$$\mu''(s) = \left\{ \sum_{\mathbf{y}} \frac{P_1(\mathbf{y})^{1-s} P_2(\mathbf{y})^s}{\sum_{\mathbf{y}'} P_1(\mathbf{y}')^{1-s} P_2(\mathbf{y}')^s} \left[\ln \frac{P_2(\mathbf{y})}{P_1(\mathbf{y})} \right]^2 \right\} - [\mu'(s)]^2 \tag{3.25}$$

Let $D(\mathbf{y})$ be the log likelihood ratio,

$$D(\mathbf{y}) = \ln \frac{P_2(\mathbf{y})}{P_1(\mathbf{y})} \tag{3.26}$$

and for $0 < s < 1$, define

$$Q_s(\mathbf{y}) = \frac{P_1(\mathbf{y})^{1-s} P_2(\mathbf{y})^s}{\sum_{\mathbf{y}'} P_1(\mathbf{y}')^{1-s} P_2(\mathbf{y}')^s} \tag{3.27}$$

It will be seen later that $Q_s(\mathbf{y})$ is large for those $\mathbf{y}$ that are likely to cause errors; thus this probability assignment allows us to focus our attention on the region of interest.

If we consider $D(\mathbf{y})$ to be a random variable with probability assignment $Q_s(\mathbf{y})$, then we see from (3.24) and (3.25) that $\mu'(s)$ and $\mu''(s)$ are the mean and variance of $D(\mathbf{y})$ respectively. Since $\mu''(s)$ is a variance, it is nonnegative and therefore $\mu(s)$ is convex $\cup$. It can also be seen from this that $\mu(s)$ will be strictly convex $\cup$ unless $P_2(\mathbf{y})/P_1(\mathbf{y})$ is a constant for all $\mathbf{y}$ in the overlap region. Since $\mu(0)$ and $\mu(1)$ are nonpositive (see (3.5) and (3.6)), it follows from convexity that μ is nonpositive for all $s, 0 \leq s \leq 1$. Furthermore, for $\mu(s)$ to be 0 at any point within the interval $(0, 1)$ it is necessary for $\mu(0), \mu(1)$, and $\mu''(s)$ all to be zero. It is easy to see that this can happen only if $P_1(\mathbf{y}) = P_2(\mathbf{y})$ for all $\mathbf{y}$.

It can be verified easily by substituting (3.26) and (3.5) into (3.27) that

$$P_1(\mathbf{y}) = \{\exp [\mu(s) - sD(\mathbf{y})]\} Q_s(\mathbf{y}) \tag{3.28}$$

$$P_2(\mathbf{y}) = \{\exp\left[\mu(s) + (1 - s)D(\mathbf{y})\right]\}Q_s(\mathbf{y}) \qquad (3.29)$$

We shall now establish the second part of the theorem, (3.13) and (3.14). For a given s, define the decision region Y_1 to be

$$Y_1 = \{\mathbf{y}\!:\!D(\mathbf{y}) < \mu'(s)\} \qquad (3.30)$$

Then for $\mathbf{y} \in Y_1^c$, we have $-sD(\mathbf{y}) \leqq -s\mu'(s)$, and (3.28) is bounded by

$$P_1(\mathbf{y}) \leqq \{\exp\left[\mu(s) - s\mu'(s)\right]\}Q_s(\mathbf{y}); \qquad \mathbf{y} \in Y_1^c \qquad (3.31)$$

Substituting (3.31) into (3.1), we have

$$P_{e,1} \leqq \{\exp\left[\mu(s) - s\mu'(s)\right]\} \sum_{\mathbf{y} \in Y_1^c} Q_s(\mathbf{y}) \qquad (3.32)$$

Equation (3.13) follows upon upper bounding the sum of probabilities in (3.32) by 1. Equation (3.14) follows in the same way upon recognizing that $(1 - s)D(\mathbf{y}) \leqq (1 - s)\mu'(s)$ for $\mathbf{y} \in Y_2^c$.

We now turn to the proof of the first part of the theorem. Define Y_s as the set of sequences for which $D(\mathbf{y})$ is within $\sqrt{2}$ standard deviations of its mean according to $Q_s(\mathbf{y})$.

$$Y_s = \{\mathbf{y}\!:\!\mid D(\mathbf{y}) - \mu'(s) \mid \leqq \sqrt{2\mu''(s)}\} \qquad (3.33)$$

From the Chebychev inequality,

$$\sum_{\mathbf{y} \in Y_s} Q_s(\mathbf{y}) > \tfrac{1}{2} \qquad (3.34)$$

We now lower bound $P_{e,1}$ and $P_{e,2}$ by considering only those $\mathbf{y}$ in the set Y_s. This is motivated by the fact that for the decision rule (3.30), most of the errors presumably occur when $\mid D(\mathbf{y}) - \mu'(s)\mid$ is small.

$$P_{e,1} = \sum_{\mathbf{y} \in Y_1^c} P_1(\mathbf{y}) \geqq \sum_{\mathbf{y} \in Y_1^c \cap Y_s} P_1(\mathbf{y}) \qquad (3.35)$$

$$P_{e,2} = \sum_{\mathbf{y} \in Y_2^c} P_2(\mathbf{y}) \geqq \sum_{\mathbf{y} \in Y_2^c \cap Y_s} P_2(\mathbf{y}) \qquad (3.36)$$

For $\mathbf{y} \, \epsilon \, Y_s$, (3.33) gives us

$$\mu'(s) - \sqrt{2\mu''(s)} \leqq D(\mathbf{y}) \leqq \mu'(s) + \sqrt{2\mu''(s)} \qquad (3.37)$$

Thus, for $\mathbf{y} \in Y_s$, (3.28) and (3.29) are bounded by

$$P_1(\mathbf{y}) \geqq \{\exp\left[\mu(s) - s\mu'(s) - s\sqrt{2\mu''(s)}\right]\}Q_s(\mathbf{y}) \qquad (3.38)$$

$$P_2(\mathbf{y}) \geqq \{\exp\left[\mu(s) - (1 - s)\mu'(s) - (1 - s)\sqrt{2\mu''(s)}\right]\}$$
$$\cdot Q_s(\mathbf{y}) \qquad (3.39)$$

Substituting (3.38) into (3.35) and (3.39) into (3.36) leaves only $Q_s(\mathbf{y})$ under the summation signs.

$$P_{e,1} \geq \{\exp \left[\mu(s) - s\mu'(s) - s\sqrt{2\mu''(s)}\right]\} \sum_{\mathbf{y} \in Y_1{}^c \cap Y_s} Q_s(\mathbf{y}) \qquad (3.40)$$

$$P_{e,2} \geq \{\exp \left[\mu(s) + (1 - s)\mu'(s) - (1 - s)\sqrt{2\mu''(s)}\right]\}$$
$$\cdot \sum_{\mathbf{y} \in Y_2{}^c \cap Y_s} Q_s(\mathbf{y}) \qquad (3.41)$$

Since Y_1 and Y_2 are disjoint, (3.34) yields

$$\sum_{\mathbf{y} \in Y_1{}^c \cap Y_s} Q_s(\mathbf{y}) + \sum_{\mathbf{y} \in Y_2{}^c \cap Y_s} Q_s(\mathbf{y}) > \tfrac{1}{2} \qquad (3.42)$$

Thus, either

$$\sum_{\mathbf{y} \in Y_1{}^c \cap Y_s} Q_s(\mathbf{y}) > \tfrac{1}{4} \qquad (3.43)$$

or

$$\sum_{\mathbf{y} \in Y_2{}^c \cap Y_s} Q_s(\mathbf{y}) > \tfrac{1}{4} \qquad (3.44)$$

Substituting these inequalities into (3.40) and (3.41) completes the proof of the theorem.

There are a number of other approaches that could have been taken to prove theorems essentially equivalent to Theorem 3. The theorem treats a simple statistical decision theory problem with 2 hypotheses. According to the Neyman-Pearson (1928) theorem, we can minimize $P_{e,1}$ for a given value of $P_{e,2}$ by letting Y_1 be the set of $\mathbf{y}$ for which $D(\mathbf{y})$ is less than a constant chosen to give $P_{e,2}$ its given value. Then $P_{e,1}$ is the probability according to $P_1(\mathbf{y})$ that $D(\mathbf{y})$, which is the sum of N independent random variables, is greater than or equal to that constant. Likewise, $P_{e,2}$ is the probability according to $P_2(\mathbf{y})$ that $D(\mathbf{y})$ is less than the constant. A number of estimates and bounds on the probability that a sum of independent random variables will be far from the mean are given by Feller (1943), Chernoff (1952), Chapter 8 of Fano (1961), and Gallager (1965b). The particular theorem chosen here was selected primarily for the simplicity of the result and for its generality. Observe that Theorem 5 is applicable whenever $\mu(s)$ and its first two derivatives exist. For example $\mathbf{y}$ may be a sequence of real numbers and $P_1(\mathbf{y})$ and $P_2(\mathbf{y})$ may be replaced with probability densities.

IV. THE SPHERE PACKING BOUND

Let $\mathbf{x}_1$, $\mathbf{x}_2$, $\cdots$, $\mathbf{x}_M$ be a set of M code words each of length N for use on a discrete memoryless channel with transition probabilities $P(j \mid k)$. Assume a list decoding scheme in which for each received sequence $\mathbf{y}$, the decoder produces a list of at most L integers from 1 to M. If Y_m is the set of output sequences $\mathbf{y}$ for which message m is on the decoding list, then, as in (1.2), the probability of list decoding error when message m is sent is

$$P_{e,m} = \sum_{\mathbf{y} \in Y_m^c} \Pr(\mathbf{y} \mid \mathbf{x}_m) \tag{4.1}$$

Let $P_{e,\max}$ be the maximum over m of $P_{e,m}$ for the code and list decoding scheme under consideration. In this section we first find a lower bound on $P_{e,\max}$ for a special class of codes called fixed composition codes. We then generalize the results to arbitrary codes, and prove Theorem 2 of the introduction.

For any given m, $P_{e,m}$ can generally be reduced by enlarging the size of the decoding set Y_m this will decrease the size of $Y_{m'}$, for some $m' \neq m$, however, and thus generally increase $P_{e,m'}$. In order to keep some control over the size of Y_m without specifically considering the other code words, we define an arbitrary product probability measure on the output sequences $\mathbf{y} = (j_1, \cdots, j_N)$,

$$f_N(\mathbf{y}) = \prod_{n=1}^{N} f(j_n) \tag{4.2}$$

where $\mathbf{f} = \{f(1), \cdots, f(J)\}$ is an arbitrary probability assignment on the output letters 1 to J. The size of Y_m is now defined as

$$F(Y_m) = \sum_{\mathbf{y} \in Y_m} f_N(\mathbf{y}) \tag{4.3}$$

Theorem 5 can be used to relate $P_{e,m}$ and $F(Y_m)$ if we let $\Pr(\mathbf{y} \mid \mathbf{x}_m)$ correspond to $P_1(\mathbf{y})$ in the theorem and let $f_N(\mathbf{y})$ correspond to $P_2(\mathbf{y})$. The function $\mu(s)$ of Theorem 5 corresponding to $\Pr(\mathbf{y} \mid \mathbf{x}_m)$ and $f_N(\mathbf{y})$ is given by

$$\mu(s) = \ln \sum_{\mathbf{y}} \Pr(\mathbf{y} \mid \mathbf{x}_m)^{1-s} f_N(\mathbf{y})^s \tag{4.4}$$

Assume that $\Pr(\mathbf{y}/\mathbf{x}_m) f_N(\mathbf{y}) \neq 0$ for at least one $\mathbf{y}$. Theorem 5 then states that for each s, $0 < s < 1$, either

$$P_{e,m} > \tfrac{1}{4} \exp[\mu(s) - s\mu'(s) - s\sqrt{2\mu''(s)}] \tag{4.5}$$

or

$$F(Y_m) > \tfrac{1}{4} \exp \left[\mu(s) + (1 - s)\, \mu'(s) - (1 - s)\, \sqrt{2\mu''(s)} \right] \quad (4.6)$$

Since $f_N(\mathbf{y}) = \prod_n f(j_n)$, $\mu(s)$ can be broken up into a sum of terms as in (3.10). If $\mathbf{x}_m = (k_{m,1}, \cdots, k_{m,N})$, we have

$$\mu(s) = \sum_{n=1}^{N} \mu_{k_{m,n}}(s, \mathbf{f}) \quad (4.7)$$

$$\mu_k(s, \mathbf{f}) = \ln \sum_{j} P(j/k)^{1-s} f(j)^s \quad (4.8)$$

The function $\mu(s)$ depends on $\mathbf{x}_m$ only through the number of appearances of each alphabet letter in $\mathbf{x}_m$. Let

$$q_k(m) = \frac{\text{Number of times input letter } k \text{ appears in } \mathbf{x}_m}{N} \quad (4.9)$$

The vector $\mathbf{q}(m) = (q_1(m), \cdots, q_K(m))$ is called the composition of the mth code word. In terms of $\mathbf{q}(m)$, $\mu(s)$ becomes

$$\mu(s) = N \sum_{k=1}^{K} q_k(m) \mu_k(s, \mathbf{f}) \quad (4.10)$$

Let us restrict our attention temporarily to codes in which all code words have the same composition. Then the m can be dropped from $q_k(m)$ in (4.10), and (4.5) and (4.6) become: for each s, $0 < s < 1$, either

$$P_{e,m} > \tfrac{1}{4} \exp N \left\{ \sum_{k} q_k \left[\mu_k(s, \mathbf{f}) - s\mu_k'(s, \mathbf{f}) \right] \right.$$
$$\left. - \frac{s}{\sqrt{N}} \sqrt{2 \sum_{k} q_k \mu_k''(s, \mathbf{f})} \right\} \quad (4.11)$$

or

$$F(Y_m) > \tfrac{1}{4} \exp N \left\{ \sum_{k} q_k [\mu_k(s, \mathbf{f}) + (1 - s)\mu_k'(s, \mathbf{f})] \right.$$
$$\left. - \frac{(1 - s)}{\sqrt{N}} \sqrt{2 \sum_{k} q_k \mu_k''(s, \mathbf{f})} \right\} \quad (4.12)$$

The square root terms in (4.11) and (4.12) turn out to be unimportant for large N. Thus we simplify the expressions by the following loose but general bound on μ_k'' (see appendix).

$$s\sqrt{\mu_k{}''(s, \mathbf{f})} \leqq \ln \frac{e}{\sqrt{P_{\min}}} \tag{4.13}$$

$P_{\min}$ is the smallest nonzero transition probability on the channel.

We can now relate $F(Y_m)$ to the number of code words M and the list size L by observing that

$$\sum_{m=1}^{M} F(Y_m) = \sum_{m=1}^{M} \sum_{\mathbf{y} \in Y_m} f_N(\mathbf{y}) \leqq L \tag{4.14}$$

Equation (4.14) follows from the facts that each $\mathbf{y}$ appears in at most L decoding subsets and that $\sum_{\mathbf{y}} f_N(\mathbf{y}) = 1$. As a consequence of (4.14), there must be some m for which

$$F(Y_m) \leqq L/M \tag{4.15}$$

For this m, we can substitute (4.13) and (4.15) into (4.11) and (4.12). Bringing the factors of $\frac{1}{4}$ inside the exponents and upper bounding $P_{e,m}$ by $P_{e,\max}$, (4.11) and (4.12) become: either

$$P_{e,\max} > \exp N \left\{ \sum_{k=1}^{K} q_k[\mu_k(s, \mathbf{f}) - s\mu_k{}'(s, \mathbf{f})] \right.$$
$$\left. - \sqrt{\frac{2}{N}} \ln \frac{e}{\sqrt{P_{\min}}} - \frac{\ln 4}{N} \right\} \tag{4.16}$$

or

$$\frac{L}{M} > \exp N \left\{ \sum_{k=1}^{K} q_k[\mu_k(s, \mathbf{f}) + (1 - s)\mu_k{}'(s, \mathbf{f})] \right.$$
$$\left. - \frac{1 - s}{s} \sqrt{\frac{2}{N}} \ln \frac{e}{\sqrt{P_{\min}}} - \frac{\ln 4}{N} \right\} \tag{4.17}$$

Equations (4.16) and (4.17) provide a parametric lower bound on $P_{e,\max}$ for a given L/M in terms of the parameter s in the same way that Theorem 5 provided a parametric lower bound on $P_{e,1}$ for a given $P_{e,2}$. The bound is valid for any fixed composition code of composition $\mathbf{q}$ with M code words of length N and for any list decoding scheme with lists of size L.

The reason for calling this a sphere packing bound is somewhat historical, but also adds some insight into what we have done. From the discussion following Theorem 5, we see that $P_{e,m}$ can be minimized for a decoding subset of given size by picking the set Y_m to be those $\mathbf{y}$ for which $\ln [f_N(\mathbf{y})/\Pr(\mathbf{y} \mid \mathbf{x}_m)]$ is less than a constant. If we think of

$\ln [f_N(\mathbf{y})/\Pr(\mathbf{y} \mid \mathbf{x}_m)]$ as a generalized type of distance from $\mathbf{x}_m$ to $\mathbf{y}$, then we can think of the Y_m that minimizes $P_{e,m}$ as being a sphere around $\mathbf{x}_m$. Thus our bound on $P_{e,\max}$ in terms of M would be a very tight bound if we could pick the Y_m as a set of spheres, each sphere around one code word, with spheres packed into the space of output sequences.

The bound of (4.16) and (4.17) is a function of the arbitrary probability assignment $\mathbf{f}$. The straightforward approach now would be to find that $\mathbf{f}$ which yields the tightest bound on $P_{e,\max}$, i.e., that *maximizes* the lower bound for a given composition. We could then look for the best composition, i.e., the $\mathbf{q}$ that *minimizes* the lower bound on $P_{e,\max}$. Such a procedure turns out to be both tedious and unenlightening. We shall instead simply state the resulting $\mathbf{f}$ and $\mathbf{q}$ as functions of the parameter s and then show that this choice gives us the bound of Theorem 2.

For a given s, $0 < s < 1$, let $\mathbf{q}_s = (q_{1,s}, \cdots, q_{K,s})$ satisfy the equations

$$\sum_j P(j \mid k)^{1-s} \alpha_{j,s}^{s/(1-s)} \geqq \sum_j \alpha_{j,s}^{1/(1-s)}; \qquad \text{all } k \qquad (4.18)$$

where

$$\alpha_{j,s} = \sum_{k=1}^{K} q_{k,s} P(j \mid k)^{1-s} \qquad (4.19)$$

Let $\mathbf{f}_s = (f_s(1), \cdots, f_s(J))$ be given by

$$f_s(j) = \frac{\alpha_{j,s}^{1/(1-s)}}{\sum_{j'=1}^{J} \alpha_{j',s}^{1/(1-s)}} \qquad (4.20)$$

This is a rather formidable looking set of equations, but the solutions have some remarkable properties. If we set $\rho = s/(1-s)$, (4.18) and (4.19) are identical to the necessary and sufficient conditions (1.14) and (1.15) on $\mathbf{q}$ to maximize the function $E_0(\rho, \mathbf{q})$ discussed in Section I. Thus (4.18) is satisfied with equality for those k with $q_{k,s} > 0$. Since $E_0(\rho, \mathbf{q})$ must have a maximum over the probability vectors $\mathbf{q}$, (4.18) and (4.19) must have a solution (though it need not be unique).

The fact that $\mathbf{f}$ is chosen here as a function of s in no way changes the validity of the lower bound to $P_{e,\max}$ given by (4.16) and (4.17). We must remember, however, that $\mu_k{}'(s, \mathbf{f}_s)$ is the partial derivative of μ_k

with respect to s holding $\mathbf{f}_s$ fixed. The condition that for each $k, f(j)P(j \mid k) \neq 0$ for some j is clearly met by $\mathbf{f}_s$, since the left side of (4.18) must be strictly positive.

Next we show that $\mathbf{f}_s$ has the property that $\mu_k(s, \mathbf{f}_s)$ is independent of k for those inputs with $q_{k,s} \neq 0$. Substituting (4.20) into the expression (4.8) for μ_k, we have

$$\mu_k(s, \mathbf{f}_s) = \ln \sum_{j=1}^{J} P(j \mid k)^{1-s} \alpha_{j,s}^{s/(1-s)} - s \ln \sum_{j=1}^{J} \alpha_{j,s}^{1/(1-s)} \quad (4.21)$$

Using (4.18) in (4.21),

$$\mu_k(s, \mathbf{f}_s) \geq (1 - s) \ln \sum_{j=1}^{J} \alpha_{j,s}^{1/(1-s)}$$

with equality if $q_{k,s} \neq 0$. Finally, using (4.19) for $\alpha_{j,s}$, we have the expression for $E_0(\rho)$ in (1.8) and (1.9). Thus

$$\mu_k(s, \mathbf{f}_s) \geq -(1 - s)E_0\left(\frac{s}{1 - s}\right); \qquad \text{equality if } q_{k,s} \neq 0 \quad (4.22)$$

One final property of $\mathbf{q}_s$ and $\mathbf{f}_s$, which we shall not need but which gives some insight into why $\mathbf{f}_s$ yields the tightest bound on $P_{e,\max}$ for the "best" composition $\mathbf{q}_s$, is that $\mathbf{q}_s$, $\mathbf{f}_s$ yields a min-max point for the function $\sum_k q_k \mu_k(s, \mathbf{f})$. That is, for all $\mathbf{q}, \mathbf{f}$,

$$\sum_k q_{k,s} \mu_k(s, \mathbf{f}) \leq \sum_k q_{k,s} \mu_k(s, \mathbf{f}_s) \leq \sum_k q_k \mu_k(s, \mathbf{f}_s) \quad (4.23)$$

This relation is established in the appendix.

We can now state a theorem that is equivalent to Theorem 2 in the introduction, with the exception that the theorem here applies only to fixed composition codes.

THEOREM 6. *Let $P(j \mid k)$ be the transition probabilities for a discrete memoryless channel and let a fixed composition code for the channel have M code words of length N with a list decoding scheme of list size L. Then at least one code word will have a probability of list decoding error bounded by*

$$P_{e,\max} \geq \exp$$

$$- N\left\{E_{sp}\left(R - \frac{\ln 4}{N} - \epsilon\right) + \sqrt{\frac{8}{N}} \ln \frac{e}{\sqrt{P_{\min}}} + \frac{\ln 4}{N}\right\} \quad (4.24)$$

where $R = (1/N) \ln (M/L)$, the function E_{sp} is given by (1.7), and ϵ is an arbitrarily small positive number.

Proof: We shall first express the parametric lower bound on $P_{e,\max}$ of (4.16) and (4.17) in a more convenient way. Define $R(s, \mathbf{q})$ as minus the quantity in braces in (4.17), using $\mathbf{f}_s$ for $\mathbf{f}$.

$$R(s, \mathbf{q}) = \sum_k - q_k[\mu_k(s, \mathbf{f}_s) + (1 - s)\mu_k'(s, \mathbf{f}_s)]$$
$$+ \frac{1 - s}{s} \sqrt{\frac{2}{N}} \ln \frac{e}{\sqrt{P_{\min}}} + \frac{\ln 4}{N} \quad (4.25)$$

Then (4.17) can be rewritten

$$R = \frac{\ln M/L}{N} < R(s, \mathbf{q}) \quad (4.26)$$

Also we can use (4.25) to eliminate the μ_k' term in (4.16), getting

$$P_{e,\max} > \exp N \left\{ \sum_k q_k \left(1 + \frac{s}{1 - s} \right) \mu_k(s, \mathbf{f}_s) + \frac{s}{1 - s} R(s, \mathbf{q}) \right.$$
$$\left. - \sqrt{\frac{8}{N}} \ln \frac{e}{\sqrt{P_{\min}}} - \left(1 + \frac{s}{1 - s} \right) \frac{\ln 4}{N} \right\} \quad (4.27)$$

Thus, for every s, $0 < s < 1$, either (4.26) or (4.27) is satisfied.

We now consider two separate cases

(a) $\qquad\qquad R = R(s, \mathbf{q}) \quad$ for some s, $\quad 0 < s < 1 \qquad\qquad$ (4.28)

(b) $\qquad\qquad R < R(s, \mathbf{q}) \quad$ for all s, $\qquad 0 < s < 1 \qquad\qquad$ (4.29)

It is shown in the appendix that $R(s, \mathbf{q})$ is a continuous function of s for $0 < s < 1$, and it can be seen from the term containing $(1 - s)/s$ in (4.25) that $\lim_{s \to 0} R(s, \mathbf{q}) = \infty$. Thus either (a) or (b) above must be satisfied. If (a) is satisfied for some s, then (4.26) is unsatisfied and (4.27) must be satisfied for that s; substituting (4.22) and (4.28) into (4.27), we have

$$P_{e,\max} > \exp N \left\{ -E_0 \left(\frac{s}{1 - s} \right) + \frac{s}{1 - s} \left(R - \frac{\ln 4}{N} \right) \right.$$
$$\left. - \sqrt{\frac{8}{N}} \ln \frac{e}{\sqrt{P_{\min}}} - \frac{\ln 4}{N} \right\} \quad (4.30)$$

Using ρ for $s/(1 - s)$ and further lower bounding by taking the lowest upper bound of the negative exponent over ρ, we have

$$
P_{e,\max} > \exp - N \left\{ \underset{\rho \geq 0}{\text{L.U.B.}} \left[E_0(\rho) - \rho \left(R - \frac{\ln 4}{N} \right) \right] \right.
$$
$$
\left. + \sqrt{\frac{8}{N}} \ln \frac{e}{\sqrt{P_{\min}}} + \frac{\ln 4}{N} \right\} \tag{4.31}
$$

$$
> \exp - N \left\{ \underset{\rho \geq 0}{\text{L.U.B.}} \left[E_0(\rho) - \rho \left(R - \frac{\ln 4}{N} - \epsilon \right) \right] \right.
$$
$$
\left. + \sqrt{\frac{8}{N}} \ln \frac{e}{\sqrt{P_{\min}}} + \frac{\ln 4}{N} \right\} \tag{4.32}
$$

Using the definition of E_{sp} in (1.7), this is equivalent to (4.24) and proves the theorem for case (a).

Next we show that for case (b), (4.24) reduces to $P_{e,\max} \geq 0$ which is trivially true. From (3.18),

$$
\mu_k(s, \mathbf{f}_s) - s\mu_k'(s, \mathbf{f}_s) \leq 0; \quad -\mu_k'(s, \mathbf{f}_s) \leq \frac{-\mu_k(s, \mathbf{f}_s)}{s} \tag{4.33}
$$

Substituting (4.33) into (4.25), we obtain for all s, $0 < s < 1$,

$$
R < R(s, \mathbf{q}) \leq - \sum_{k=1}^{K} q_k \left(1 + \frac{1-s}{s} \right) \mu_k(s, \mathbf{f}_s)
$$
$$
+ \frac{1-s}{s} \sqrt{\frac{2}{N}} \ln \frac{e}{\sqrt{P_{\min}}} + \frac{\ln 4}{N}
$$

Using (4.22) again and letting $\rho = s/(1-s)$, this becomes

$$
R < \frac{E_0(\rho)}{\rho} + \frac{1}{\rho} \sqrt{\frac{2}{N}} \ln \frac{e}{\sqrt{P_{\min}}} + \frac{\ln 4}{N}; \qquad \text{all } \rho > 0 \tag{4.34}
$$

Using (1.7) and (4.34), we have

$$
E_{sp} \left(R - \frac{\ln 4}{N} - \epsilon \right) = \underset{\rho \geq 0}{\text{L.U.B.}} \left[E_0(\rho) - \rho \left(R - \frac{\ln 4}{N} - \epsilon \right) \right]
$$
$$
\geq \underset{\rho \geq 0}{\text{L.U.B.}} - \sqrt{\frac{2}{N}} \ln \frac{e}{\sqrt{P_{\min}}} + \rho\epsilon \tag{4.35}
$$

Thus E_{sp} is infinite here and (4.24) reduces to $P_{e,\max} \geq 0$, completing the proof.

The theorem will now be generalized to lower bound the error probability for an arbitrary set of code words rather than a fixed composition set. The number of different ways to choose the composition of a code word is the number of ways of picking K nonnegative integers, N_1, N_2, $\cdots$, N_K such that $\sum_k N_k = N$, where K is the input alphabet size and N is the block length. Thus there are $\binom{N + K - 1}{K - 1}$ different compositions, and it follows that in any code of M code words, there must be some composition containing a number of code words M' bounded by

$$M' \geqq M \bigg/ \binom{N + K - 1}{K - 1} \qquad (4.36)$$

Consider the messages corresponding to this set of M' words as a fixed composition code and assume that the same list decoding scheme is used as for the original code. Thus for each m in the fixed composition set, Y_m is the same as for the original code and $P_{e,m}$ is the same. This is presumably a rather foolish decoding scheme for the fixed composition code since the decoding lists might contain fewer than L integers from the fixed composition set. None the less, Theorem 6 applies here, and using $\ln (M'/L)/N$ for R, there is some m in the fixed composition set for which $P_{e,m}$ satisfies

$$P_{e,m} > \exp - N \left\{ E_{sp} \left[\frac{\ln (M'/L)}{N} - \frac{\ln 4}{N} - \epsilon \right] \right. $$
$$\left. + \sqrt{\frac{8}{N}} \ln \frac{e}{\sqrt{P_{\min}}} + \frac{\ln 4}{N} \right\} \qquad (4.37)$$

Since E_{sp} is a decreasing function of its argument, we can substitute (4.36) into (4.37). Also $P_{e,m} \leqq P_{e,\max}$ for the original code, so that

$$P_{e,\max} > \exp - N \left\{ E_{sp} \left[\frac{\ln (M/L) - \ln \binom{N + K - 1}{K - 1}}{N} \right. \right.$$
$$\left. \left. - \frac{\ln 4}{N} - \epsilon \right] + \sqrt{\frac{8}{N}} \ln \frac{e}{\sqrt{P_{\min}}} + \frac{\ln 4}{N} \right\} \qquad (4.38)$$

For the given channel, define $P_{e,\max}(N, M, L)$ as the minimum $P_{e,\max}$ over all codes of M code words of length N and all list decoding schemes of list size L. Equation (4.38) clearly applies to the code and decoding scheme that achieves $P_{e,\max}(N, M, L)$. Finally, since

$$\binom{N + K - 1}{K - 1} < N^K \tag{4.39}$$

We can rewrite (4.38) as

$$
\begin{aligned}
P_{e,\max}(N, M, L) > \exp -N \Bigg\{ E_{sp} &\left[\frac{\ln (M/L)}{N} - \frac{K \ln N}{N} - \frac{\ln 4}{N} \right] \\
&+ \sqrt{\frac{8}{N}} \ln \frac{e}{\sqrt{P_{min}}} + \frac{\ln 4}{N} \Bigg\}
\end{aligned} \tag{4.40}
$$

We have chosen $\epsilon > 0$ to absorb the inequality in (4.39).

One more step will now complete the proof of Theorem 2. We show that, in general,

$$P_e(N, M, L) \geqq \tfrac{1}{2} P_{e,\max}(N, [M/2]^+, L) \tag{4.41}$$

To see this, consider the code that achieves the minimum average error probability $P_e(N, M, L)$. At least $M/2$ of these words must have $P_{e,m} \leqq 2P_e(N, M, L)$. This set of $[M/2]^+$ code words with the original decoding scheme then has $P_{e,\max} \leqq 2P_e(N, M, L)$. By definition, however, this $P_{e,\max}$ is greater than or equal to $P_{e,\max}(N, [M/2]^+, L)$, thus establishing (4.41).

Substituting (4.40) into (4.41), we obtain (1.6), thus completing the proof of Theorem 2.

In the proof of Theorem 2, it was not made quite clear why the artifice of fixed composition codes had to be introduced. We started the derivation of the bound by relating the error probability for a given message, m, to the size of the decoding subset $F(Y_m)$, and then observing that at least one $F(Y_m)$ must be at most L/M. This last observation, however, required that all Y_m be measured with the same probability assignment $\mathbf{f}$. Unfortunately, a good choice of $\mathbf{f}$ for one code word composition is often a very poor choice for some other composition, and in general, no choice of $\mathbf{f}$ is uniformly good. We eventually chose $\mathbf{f}$ as a function of the parameter s, but the appropriate value of s (i.e., that which satisfies (4.28) with equality) is a function of the code word composition $\mathbf{q}$, making $\mathbf{f}_s$ also implicitly dependent upon $\mathbf{q}$.

The reliance of the bound on fixed composition codes is particularly unfortunate in that it prevents us from extending the bound to continuous channels, channels with memory, and channels with feedback.

In the first case the size of the input alphabet K becomes infinite, and in the other cases $\mu(s)$ in (4.4) depends on more than just the composition of a code word. One way to avoid these difficulties is to classify code words by the value of s for which (4.28) is satisfied with equality but, so far, no *general* theorem has been proved using this approach. These extensions to more general channels are possible, however, if the channel has sufficient symmetry and we conjecture that the exponential bound $E_{sp}(R)$ is valid under much broader conditions than we have assumed here.

APPENDIX

PROPERTIES OF $E_{sp}(R)$

Using (1.7) and (1.8) we can rewrite $E_{sp}(R)$ as

$$E_{sp}(R) = \max_{\mathbf{q}} E(R, \mathbf{q}) \qquad (A.1)$$

$$E(R, \mathbf{q}) = \underset{\rho \geq 0}{\text{L.U.B.}} [E_0(\rho, \mathbf{q}) - \rho R] \qquad (A.2)$$

Define $I(\mathbf{q})$ as the average mutual information on the channel using the input probabilities $(q_1, \cdots, q_K)$,

$$I(\mathbf{q}) = \sum_{k=1}^{K} \sum_{j=1}^{J} q_k P(j \mid k) \ln \frac{P(j \mid k)}{\sum_{i=1}^{K} q_i P(j \mid i)} \qquad (A.3)$$

It has been shown by Gallager (1965, Theorem 2), that if $I(\mathbf{q}) \neq 0$, then

$$E_0(\rho, \mathbf{q}) \geq 0 \qquad (A.4)$$

$$0 < \frac{\partial E_0(\rho, \mathbf{q})}{\partial \rho} \leq I(\mathbf{q}) \qquad (A.5)$$

$$\frac{\partial^2 E_0(\rho, \mathbf{q})}{\partial \rho^2} \leq 0 \qquad (A.6)$$

with equality in (A.4) iff $\rho = 0$; in (A.5) if $\rho = 0$; and in (A.6) iff the following conditions are satisfied:

(a) $P(j \mid k)$ is independent of k for those j, k such that $q_k P(j \mid k) \neq 0$.

(b) The sum of the q_k over inputs leading to output j with nonzero probability is independent of j. It follows trivially from the same proof that $E_0(\rho, \mathbf{q}) = 0$ for all $\rho \geq 0$ if $I(\mathbf{q}) = 0$.

Using these results, we can give $E(R, \mathbf{q})$ parametrically as

$$E(R, \mathbf{q}) = E_0(\rho, \mathbf{q}) - \rho \frac{\partial E_0(\rho, \mathbf{q})}{\partial \rho} \qquad (A.7)$$

$$R = \frac{\partial E_0(\rho, \mathbf{q})}{\partial \rho} \qquad (A.8)$$

Equations (A.7) and (A.8) are valid for

$$\lim_{\rho \to \infty} \frac{\partial E_0(\rho, \mathbf{q})}{\partial \rho} < R < \frac{\partial E_0(\rho, \mathbf{q})}{\partial \rho}\bigg|_{\rho=0} = I(\mathbf{q}) \qquad (A.9)$$

also,

$$E(R, \mathbf{q}) = 0 \quad \text{if} \quad R \geqq I(\mathbf{q}) \qquad (A.10)$$

$$E(R, \mathbf{q}) = \infty \quad \text{if} \quad R < \lim_{\rho \to \infty} \frac{\partial E_0(\rho, \mathbf{q})}{\partial \rho} \qquad (A.11)$$

From (A.7) and (A.8), we have

$$\frac{\partial E(R, \mathbf{q})}{\partial R} = -\rho; \qquad R = \frac{\partial E_0(\rho, \mathbf{q})}{\partial \rho} \qquad (A.12)$$

If (A.6) is satisfied with strict inequality, then R in (A.8) is strictly decreasing with ρ and from (A.12), $E(R, \mathbf{q})$ is strictly decreasing with R and is strictly convex $\cup$ over the range of R given by (A.9).

We now observe from (A.10) that if $R \geqq C = \max_{\mathbf{q}} I(\mathbf{q})$, then $E(R, \mathbf{q}) = 0$ for all $\mathbf{q}$ and $E_{sp}(R) = 0$. Also if $R < C$, then for the $\mathbf{q}$ that yields capacity, $E(R, \mathbf{q}) > 0$ and thus $E_{sp}(R) > 0$. Finally, for a given R in the range $R_\infty < R < C$ the $\mathbf{q}$ that maximizes $E(R, \mathbf{q})$ satisfies (A.9), and thus $E_{sp}(R)$ is strictly decreasing and strictly convex $\cup$ in this range.

Next suppose that $R_{\text{crit}} = C$. Then for some $\rho^* \geqq 1$, $E_0(\rho^*)/\rho^* = C$, and thus for some $\mathbf{q}$, $E_0(\rho^*, \mathbf{q})/\rho^* = C$. But since $\partial E_0(\rho, \mathbf{q})/\partial \rho \leqq C$, this implies that $\partial E_0(\rho, \mathbf{q})/\partial \rho = C$ for $0 \leqq \rho \leqq \rho^*$ and $\partial^2 E_0(\rho, \mathbf{q})/\partial \rho^2 = 0$ for $0 \leqq \rho \leqq \rho^*$. From (A.6) this implies that conditions (a) and (b) above are satisfied for $\mathbf{q}$ yielding capacity. This in turn implies that $\partial E_0(\rho, \mathbf{q})/\partial \rho = C$ for all ρ and thus $R_\infty = C$. The same argument shows that if $R_\infty = C$, conditions (a) and (b) above must be satisfied.

A Bound on μ_k''

From (3.25), $\mu_k''(s)$ is the variance of the random variable $D_k(j) = \ln [f(j)/P(j/k)]$ with the probability assignment

$$Q_{sk}(j) = \frac{P(j/k)^{1-s}f(j)^s}{\sum\limits_i P(i/k)^{1-s}f(i)^s} \tag{A.13}$$

If follows that $s^2\mu_k''(s)$ is the variance of $sD_k(j)$ with the same probability assignment. From (A.13), however, we see that

$$sD_k(j) = \ln \frac{Q_{sk}(j)}{P(j/k)} + \mu_k(s) \tag{A.14}$$

Thus $s^2\mu_k''(s)$ is also the variance of the random variable $\ln [Q_{sk}(j)/P(j/k)]$ with the probability assignment $Q_{sk}(j)$. Since a variance can be upper bounded by a second moment around any point, we have

$$s^2\mu_k''(s) \leqq \sum_j Q_{sk}(j)\left[\ln \frac{Q_{sk}(j)}{P(j/k)} - \ln \frac{e}{\sqrt{P_{\min}}}\right]^2 \tag{A.15}$$

where $P_{\min}$ is the smallest nonzero transition probability on the channel and the sum is over those j for which $P(j/k) > 0$.

We next upper bound the right hand side of (A.15) by maximizing over all choices of the probability vector $Q_{sk}(j)$. There must be a maximum since the function is continuous and the region is closed and bounded. The function cannot be maximized when any of the $Q_{sk}(j) = 0$, for the derivative with respect to such a $Q_{sk}(j)$ is infinite. Thus the maximum must be at a stationary point within the region, and any stationary point can be found by the LaGrange multiplier technique. This gives us, for each j,

$$\left[\ln \frac{Q_{sk}(j)\sqrt{P_{\min}}}{P(j/k)e}\right]^2 + 2\ln \frac{Q_{sk}(j)\sqrt{P_{\min}}}{P(j/k)e} + \lambda = 0 \tag{A.16}$$

Solving for the logarithmic term, we obtain

$$\ln \frac{Q_{sk}(j)\sqrt{P_{\min}}}{P(j/k)e} = -1 \pm \sqrt{1-\lambda}; \quad \text{each} \quad j \tag{A.17}$$

There are two cases to consider: first where the same sign is used for the square root for each j; and second when the positive square root is used for some j and the negative for others. In the first case, all terms on the left are equal, and $Q_{sk}(j) = P(j/k)$ to satisfy the constraint that $Q_{sk}(j)$ is a probability vector. Then (A.15) reduces to

$$s^2 \mu_k''(s) \leq \left[\ln \frac{e}{\sqrt{P_{\min}}} \right]^2 \qquad (A.18)$$

In the second case, the left hand side of (A.17) is upper bounded by $Q_{sk}(j) = 1$, $P(j/k) = P_{\min}$, yielding $-\ln e\sqrt{P_{\min}}$. From the right hand side of (A.17), the terms using the negative square root can have a magnitude at most 2 larger than the positive term. Thus

$$\left| \ln \frac{Q_{sk}(j)\sqrt{P_{\min}}}{P(j/k)e} \right| \leq 2 - \ln e\sqrt{P_{\min}} = \ln \frac{e}{\sqrt{P_{\min}}} \qquad (A.19)$$

Substituting (A.19) into (A.15) again yields (A.18) completing the proof.

Proof that q_s, f_s Yields a Saddle Point for $q_k \mu_k(s, f)$ (see (4.23))

From (4.22), we see that the right side of (4.23) is valid and also that

$$\sum_k q_{ks} \mu_k(s, f_s) = (1 - s) \ln \sum_j \alpha_{js}^{1/(1-s)}. \qquad (A.20)$$

In order to establish the left side of (4.23) we must show that

$$\sum_k q_{ks} \ln \left[\sum_j P(j \mid k)^{1-s} f(j)^s \right] - (1 - s) \ln \sum_j \alpha_{js}^{1/(1-s)} \leq 0 \quad (A.21)$$

Combining the logarithm terms, and using the inequality $\ln z \leq z - 1$ for $z \geq 0$ (taking $\ln 0$ as $-\infty$), the left side of (A.21) becomes

$$\sum_k q_{ks} \ln \frac{\sum_j P(j \mid k)^{1-s} f(j)^s}{(\sum_j \alpha_{js}^{1/(1-s)})^{1-s}} \leq \frac{\sum_{k,j} q_{ks} P(j \mid k)^{1-s} f(j)^s}{(\sum_j \alpha_{js}^{1/(1-s)})^{1-s}} - 1 \quad (A.22)$$

$$\leq \sum_j f_s(j)^{1-s} f(j)^s - 1 \qquad (A.23)$$

$$\leq 0 \qquad (A.24)$$

when we have used (4.19) and then (4.20) to go from (A.22) to (A.23), and used Holder's inequality to go from (A.23) to (A.24). This completes the proof.

Proof that $R(s, q)$ (see (4.25)) is Continuous in s, $0 < s < 1$

The problem here is to show that f_s is a continuous vector function of s. It will then follow immediately that $\mu_k(s, f_s)$ and $\mu_k'(s, f_s)$ are continuous functions of s, and then from (4.25) that $R(s, q)$ is a continuous function of s for fixed q.

$E_0(\rho, \mathbf{q})$ as given by (1.9) can be rewritten as

$$E_0\left(\frac{s}{1-s}, \mathbf{q}\right) = -\ln \sum_j \alpha_j(s, \mathbf{q})^{1/(1-s)} \qquad (A.25)$$

$$\alpha_j(s, \mathbf{q}) = \sum_k q_k P(j \mid k)^{1-s} \qquad (A.26)$$

Let $\mathbf{q}_s$ be a choice of probability vector $\mathbf{q}$ that maximizes $E_0(s/(1-s), \mathbf{q})$. We show that $\alpha_j(s, \mathbf{q}_s)$, which is α_{js} as defined in (4.19), is a continuous function of s, and it then follows from (4.20) that $\mathbf{f}_s$ is a continuous function of s. Since $\mathbf{q}_s$ maximizes $E_0(s/(1-s), \mathbf{q})$, we have

$$E_0\left(\frac{s}{1-s}, \mathbf{q}_s\right) = -\ln \min_{\alpha(s,\mathbf{q})} \sum_j \alpha_j(s, \mathbf{q})^{1/(1-s)} \qquad (A.27)$$

where the minimization is over the set of vectors α whose components satisfy (A.26) for some choice of probability vector $\mathbf{q}$. Since this is a convex set of vectors and since $\sum_j \alpha_j^{1/(1-s)}$ is a *strictly* convex $\cup$ function of α for $0 < s < 1$, the minimizing α in (A.27) is unique and the strict convexity tells us that for any s, $0 < s < 1$ and for any $\epsilon > 0$ there exists a $\delta > 0$ such that if

$$\mid \alpha_j(s, \mathbf{q}) - \alpha_j(s, \mathbf{q}_s) \mid \geqq \epsilon/2; \qquad \text{any } j \qquad (A.28)$$

then

$$\sum_j \alpha_j(s, \mathbf{q})^{1/(1-s)} \geqq \sum_j \alpha_j(s, \mathbf{q}_s)^{1/(1-s)} + \delta \qquad (A.29)$$

Next we observe that $E_0(s/(1-s), \mathbf{q})$ is a continuous function of s with the continuity being uniform in $\mathbf{q}$. It follows from this that $E_0(s/(1-s), \mathbf{q}_s)$ is also continuous in s. Also $\alpha_j(s, \mathbf{q})$ is continuous in s, uniformly in $\mathbf{q}$. It follows from these three statements that for a given s, $0 < s < 1$, and for the given ϵ, δ above, there exists a $\delta_1 > 0$ such that for $\mid s_1 - s \mid < \delta_1$,

$$\left| \sum_j \alpha_j(s_1, \mathbf{q}_{s_1})^{1/(1-s_1)} - \sum_j \alpha_j(s, \mathbf{q}_{s_1})^{1/(1-s)} \right| < \delta/2 \quad (A.30)$$

$$\left| \sum_j \alpha_j(s_1, \mathbf{q}_{s_1})^{1/(1-s_1)} - \sum_j \alpha_j(s, \mathbf{q}_s)^{1/(1-s)} \right| < \delta/2 \quad (A.31)$$

$$\mid \alpha_j(s_1, \mathbf{q}_{s_1}) - \alpha_j(s, \mathbf{q}_{s_1}) \mid < \epsilon/2; \qquad \text{all } j \qquad (A.32)$$

Combining (A.30) and (A.31), we see that (A.29) is unsatisfied for $\mathbf{q} = \mathbf{q}_{s_1}$; thus (A.28) must be unsatisfied for all j and

$$\mid \alpha_j(s, \mathbf{q}_{s_1}) - \alpha_j(s, \mathbf{q}_s) \mid < \epsilon/2; \qquad \text{all } j, \mid s - s_1 \mid < \delta_1 \quad (A.33)$$

Combining (A.32) and (A.33), we then have for all j

$$| \alpha_j(s_1, \mathbf{q}_{s_1}) - \alpha_j(s, \mathbf{q}_s) | < \epsilon; \qquad | s - s_1 | < \delta_1 \qquad (A.34)$$

Thus $\alpha_j(s, \mathbf{q}_s)$ is continuous in s, completing the proof. Using other methods, it can be shown that $\alpha_j(s, \mathbf{q}_s)$ is a piecewise analytic function of s.

RECEIVED: January 18, 1966

REFERENCES

ASH, R. B. (1965), "Information Theory." Interscience, New York.

BERLEKAMP, E. R. (1964), "Block Coding with Noiseless Feedback." Ph.D. Thesis, Department of Electrical Engineering, M.I.T.

BHATTACHARYYA, A. (1943), On a measure of divergence between two statistical populations defined by their probability distributions. *Bull. Calcutta Math. Soc.* **35**, No. 3, 99–110.

CHERNOFF, H. (1952), A measure of asymptotic efficiency for tests of an hypothesis based on the sum of observations. *Ann. Math. Statist.* **23**, 493.

ELIAS, P. (1955), "List Decoding for Noisy Channels." Tech. Rept. 335, Research Laboratory of Electronics, M.I.T.

FANO, R. M. (1961), "Transmission of Information." M.I.T. Press, and Wiley, New York.

FEINSTEIN, A. (1955), Error bounds in noisy channels without memory. *IEEE Trans. Inform. Theory* **IT-1**, 13–14.

FELLER, W. (1943), Generalizations of a probability limit theorem of Cramer. *Trans. Am. Math. Soc.* **54**, 361.

GALLAGER, R. (1963), "Low Density Parity Check Codes." M.I.T. Press.

GALLAGER, R. (1965a), A simple derivation of the coding theorem and some applications. *IEEE Trans. Inform. Theory* **IT-11**, 3–18.

GALLAGER, R. (1965), "Lower Bounds on the Tails of Probability Distributions." M.I.T. Research Laboratory of Electronics. OPR **77**, pp. 277–291.

GILBERT, E. N. (1952), A comparison of signalling alphabets. *Bell System Tech. J.* **3**, 504–522.

HAMMING, R. W. (1950), Error detecting and error correcting codes. *Bell System Tech. J.* **29**, 47–160.

HELLIGER, E. (1909), Neue Begrundung der Theorie quadratischer Formen von unendlichvielen Veranderlichen. *J. reine angew. Math.* **136**, 210–271.

JACOBS, I. M., AND BERLEKAMP, E. R. (1967), A lower bound to the distribution of computation for sequential decoding. *IEEE Trans. Inform. Theory* **IT-13**, in press.

NEYMAN, J. AND PEARSON, E. S. (1928), On the use and interpretation of certain test criterion for purposes of statistical inference, *Biometrica* **20A**, 175, 263.

PETERSON, W. W. (1961), "Error-Correcting Codes." M.I.T. Press, and Wiley, New York.

PLOTKIN, M. (1960), Research Division Report 51-20, University of Pennsylvania.

Published in 1960 as: Binary codes with specified minimum distance. *IEEE Trans. Inform. Theory* **IT-6**, 445–450.

REIFFEN, B. (1963), A note on "very noisy" channels. *Inform. and Control* **6**, 120–130.

SHANNON, C. E. (1948), A mathematical theory of communication. *Bell System Tech. J.* **27**, 379, 623. Also in book form with postscript by W. Weaver, Univ. of Illinois Press, Urbana, Illinois.

SHANNON, C. E. (1956), Zero error capacity of noisy channels. *IEEE Trans. Inform. Theory* **IT-2**, 8.

SHANNON, C. E. (1958), Certain results in coding theory for noisy channels. *Inform. Control* **1**, 6.

SUN, M. (1965), Asymptotic bounds on the probability of error for the optimal transmission of information in the channel without memory which is symmetric in pairs of input symbols for small rates of transmission. *Theory Probab. Appl.* (Russian) **10**, no. 1, 167–175.

Lower Bounds to Error Probability for Coding on Discrete Memoryless Channels. II

C. E. SHANNON* AND R. G. GALLAGER*

*Departments of Electrical Engineering and Mathematics, Research Laboratory of
Electronics, Massachusetts Institute of Technology, Cambridge,
Massachusetts 02139*

AND

E. R. BERLEKAMP†

Department of Electrical Engineering, University of California, Berkeley, California

New lower bounds are presented for the minimum error probability that can be achieved through the use of block coding on noisy discrete memoryless channels. Like previous upper bounds, these lower bounds decrease exponentially with the block length N. The coefficient of N in the exponent is a convex function of the rate. From a certain rate of transmission up to channel capacity, the exponents of the upper and lower bounds coincide. Below this particular rate, the exponents of the upper and lower bounds differ, although they approach the same limit as the rate approaches zero. Examples are given and various incidental results and techniques relating to coding theory are developed. The paper is presented in two parts: the first, appearing in the January issue, summarizes the major results and treats the case of high transmission rates in detail; the second, appearing here, treats the case of low transmission rates.

1. ZERO RATE EXPONENTS

In this section we shall investigate the error probability for codes whose block length is much larger than the number of codewords, $N \gg M$. We assume throughout this section that the zero error capacity of the chan-

* The work of these authors is supported by the National Aeronautics and Space Administration (Grants NsG-334 and NsG-496), the Joint Services Electronics Program (contract DA-36-039-AMC-03200 (EE)), and the National Science Foundation (Grant GP-2495).

† The work of this author is supported by the Air Force Office of Scientific Research (Grant AF-AFOSR-639-65).

Reprinted from INFORMATION AND CONTROL, Volume 10, No. 5, May 1967

INFORMATION AND CONTROL 10, 522–552 (1967)

nel, C_0, is zero. We also assume that ordinary decoding is to be used rather than list decoding, i.e., that the list size L is one.

Our basic technique will be to bound the error probability for a given set of code words in terms of the error probability between any pair of the words, say x_m and $x_{m'}$. We can apply the corollary to Theorem I-5, given by (I-3.20) and (I-3.21), as follows.[1] Let $P_1(y)$ and $P_2(y)$ in Theorem I-5 correspond to $\Pr(y \mid x_m)$ and $\Pr(y \mid x_{m'})$ here, and let Y_1 and Y_2 in Theorem I-5 correspond to the decoding regions Y_m and $Y_{m'}$ for the given decoding scheme here. The fact that some output sequences are decoded into messages other than m or m' in no way effects the validity of Theorem 5 or its corollary. From (I-3.20) and (I-3.21), the error probabilities $P_{e,m}$ and $P_{e,m'}$ for the given decoding scheme are bounded by either

$$P_{e,m} \geqq \tfrac{1}{4} \exp\left[\mu(s^*) - s^* \sqrt{2\mu''(s^*)}\right] \tag{1.01}$$

or

$$P_{e,m'} \geqq \tfrac{1}{4} \exp\left[\mu(s^*) \pm (1 - s^*) \sqrt{2\mu''(s^*)}\right], \tag{1.02}$$

where

$$\mu(s) = \ln \sum_y \Pr(y \mid x_m)^{1-s} \Pr(y \mid x_{m'})^s \tag{1.03}$$

and s^* minimizes $\mu(s)$ over $0 \leqq s \leqq 1$.

This result can be put into a more convenient form with the aid of the following definitions.

The joint composition of x_m and $x_{m'}$, $q_{i,k}(m, m')$ is the fraction of the positions in the block in which the ith channel input occurs in codeword x_m and the kth channel input occurs in $x_{m'}$.

The function $\mu_{i,k}(s)$ is defined for $0 < s < 1$ by

$$\mu_{i,k}(s) \triangleq \ln \sum_j P(j \mid i)^{1-s} P(j \mid k)^s. \tag{1.04}$$

As before,

$$\mu_{i,k}(0) = \lim_{s \to 0^+} \mu_{i,k}(s)$$

and

$$\mu_{i,k}(1) = \lim_{s \to 1^-} \mu_{i,k}(s).$$

---

[1] References to equations, sections and theorems of the first part of this paper will be prefixed by I.

Using (I-3.10), $\mu(s)$ in (1.03) can be expressed in terms of these definitions by

$$\mu(s) = N \sum_i \sum_k q_{i,k}(m, m')\mu_{i,k}(s). \qquad (1.05)$$

The *discrepancy* between x_m and $x_{m'}$, $D(m, m')$, is defined by

$$D(m, m') \overset{\triangle}{=} - \min_{0 \leq s \leq 1} \sum_i \sum_k q_{i,k}(m, m')\mu_{i,k}(s). \qquad (1.06)$$

It can be seen that the quantity $\mu(s^*)$ appearing in (1.01) and (1.02) is given by $-ND(m, m')$. The discrepancy plays a role similar to that of the conventional Hamming distance for binary symmetric channels.

The *minimum discrepancy* for a code $D_{\min}$ is the minimum value of $D(m, m')$ over all pairs of code words of a particular code.

The *maximum minimum discrepancy*, $D_{\min}(N, M)$ is the maximum value of $D_{\min}$ over all codes containing M code words of block-length N.

THEOREM 1. *If x_m and $x_{m'}$ are a pair of code words in a code of block-length N, then either*

$$P_{e,m} \geq \frac{1}{4} \exp - N\left[D(m, m') + \sqrt{\frac{2}{N}} \ln \left(1/P_{\min}\right) \right] \qquad (1.07)$$

or

$$P_{e,m'} \geq \frac{1}{4} \exp - N\left[D(m, m') + \sqrt{\frac{2}{N}} \ln \left(1/P_{\min}\right) \right], \qquad (1.08)$$

where $P_{\min}$ is the smallest nonzero transition probability for the channel.

Proof. We shall show that $\mu''(s)$ is bounded by

$$\mu''(s) \leq N\left[\ln \frac{1}{P_{\min}} \right]^2. \qquad (1.09)$$

Then the theorem will follow from (1.01) and (1.02) by upper bounding s^* and $(1 - s^*)$ by 1. To establish (1.09), we use (I-3.25), obtaining

$$\mu''_{i,k}(s) = \sum_j Q_s(j) \left[\ln \frac{P(j\,|\,k)}{P(j\,|\,i)} \right]^2 - [\mu'_{i,k}(s)]^2, \qquad (1.10)$$

where $Q_s(j)$ is a probability assignment over the outputs for which $P(j\,|\,k)$ and $P(j\,|\,i)$ are nonzero. Observing that

$$|\ln P(j\,|\,k)/P(j\,|\,i)| \leq \ln \left(1/P_{\min}\right),$$

we can ignore the last term in (1.10), getting

$$\mu''_{i,k}(s) \le \sum_j Q_s(j)[\ln(1/P_{\min})]^2 = [\ln(1/P_{\min})]^2. \qquad (1.11)$$

Combining (1.11) with (1.05), we have (1.09), completing the proof.

Since the probability of error for the entire code of M code words is lower bounded by $P_e \ge P_{e,m}/M$ for any m, it follows from the theorem that

$$P_e \ge \frac{1}{4M} \exp - N\left[D_{\min} + \sqrt{\frac{2}{N} \ln \frac{1}{P_{\min}}} \right]. \qquad (1.12)$$

Conversely, we now show that there exist decoding regions such that

$$P_{e,m} \le (M-1) \exp -ND_{\min} \quad \text{for all} \quad m. \qquad (1.13)$$

These regions may be chosen as follows: From Theorem I-5, there exist decoding regions $Y_m(m, m')$ and $Y_{m'}(m, m')$ for the code containing only the codewords m and m' such that both $P_{e,m}$ and $P_{e,m'}$ are no greater than $\exp -ND_{\min}$. To decode the larger code, set $Y_m = \bigcap_{m'} Y_m(m, m')$. Since the sets Y_m are not overlapping, they are legitimate decoding sets. Also, $Y_m{}^c = \bigcup_{m'} Y_m{}^c(m, m')$, and since the probability of a union of events cannot exceed the sum of their probabilities, we have

$$P_{e,m} \le \sum_{y \in Y_m{}^c} \Pr(y \mid \underline{x}_m) \le \sum_{m' \ne m} \sum_{y \in Y_m{}^c(m,m')} \Pr(y \mid \underline{x}_m) \qquad (1.14)$$

$$\le (M-1) \exp - ND_{\min}. \qquad (1.15)$$

Combining (1.12) and (1.15) yields the first part of the following theorem:

THEOREM 2. *Let* E_M *be defined by*

$$\limsup_{N \to \infty} - \frac{1}{N} \ln P_e(N, M, 1).$$

Then

$$E_M = \limsup_{N \to \infty} D_{\min}(N, M) = \text{l.u.b.}_N \, D_{\min}(N, M)$$

$$= \lim_{N \to \infty} D_{\min}(N, M). \qquad (1.16)$$

The second part of the theorem follows from the observation that we can construct a code of block length AN from a code of blocklength N by repeating every word of the original code A times. The two codes have equal $q_{i,k}(m, m')$ for all i, k, m, m', and hence they have equal $D_{\min}$.

Thus

$$D_{\min}(AN, M) \geqq D_{\min}(N, M). \qquad (1.17)$$

This implies the second part of the theorem. The third part follows from (1.17) and the fact that $P_e(N, M, 1)$ is nonincreasing with N.

Theorem 2 reduces the problem of computing E_M to the problem of computing $D_{\min}(N, M)$. This computation is always easy for $M = 2$, so we treat that case first. Recall from (1.06) that $-D(m, m')$ is the minimum over s of a weighted sum of the $\mu_{i,k}(s)$. This can be lower bounded by the weighted sum of the minimums, yielding

$$-D(m, m') \geqq \sum_i \sum_k q_{i,k}(m, m') \min_{0 \leq s \leq 1} \mu_{i,k}(s). \qquad (1.18)$$

with equality iff the same value of s simultaneously minimizes all $\mu_{i,k}(s)$ for which $q_{i,k}(m, m') > 0$. If we, set $q_{i,k}(m, m') = 1$ for the i, k pair that minimizes $\min_{0 \leq s \leq 1} \mu_{i,k}(s)$, then (1.18) is satisfied with equality and at the same time the right-hand side is minimized. We thus have

$$E_2 = D_{\min}(N, 2) = \max_{i,k} [-\min_{0 \leq s \leq 1} \mu_{i,k}(s)]. \qquad (1.19)$$

It is interesting to compare this expression with the sphere packing exponent $E_{sp}(R)$ in the limit as $R \to 0$. If $R_\infty = 0$, some manipulation on (I-1.7), (I-1.8), and (I-1.9) yields

$$E_{sp}(0^+) = \lim_{\rho \to \infty} E_0(\rho) = \max_q - \ln \sum_j \prod_k P(j \mid k)^{q_k} \qquad (1.20)$$

Comparing (1.20) with the definition of $\mu_{i,k}(s)$ in (1.04), we see that $E_2 \leq E_{sp}(0^+)$ with equality iff the probability vector q that maximizes (1.20) has only 2 nonzero components.

Having found the pair of input letters i, k that yield E_2, it clearly does not matter whether we set $q_{i,k}(1, 2) = 1$ or $q_{k,i}(1, 2) = 1$. However, we must *not* attempt to form some linear combination of these two optimum solutions, for by making both $q_{i,k}(1, 2)$ and $q_{k,i}(1, 2)$ nonzero we may violate the condition for equality in (1.18). For example, suppose we compare the following two codes of block length N for the completely asymmetric binary channel of Fig. I-56. The disastrous result is depicted below:

Code 1: $x_1 = 1\ 1\ 1\ 1\ 1\quad 1\ 1\ 1\ 1\ 1$

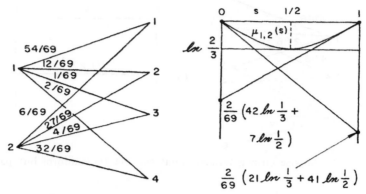

FIG. 1. A pairwise reversible binary input channel.

$$x_2 = 2\ 2\ 2\ 2\ 2 \quad 2\ 2\ 2\ 2\ 2$$

$$\leftarrow N/2 \rightarrow \quad \leftarrow N/2 \rightarrow$$

Code 2:
$$x_1 = 1\ 1\ 1\ 1\ 1 \quad 2\ 2\ 2\ 2\ 2$$

$$x_2 = 2\ 2\ 2\ 2\ 2 \quad 1\ 1\ 1\ 1\ 1.$$

Using either code, an error will occur only if the received sequence consists entirely of output letter 2. For Code 1, $P_e = \frac{1}{2}p^N$; for Code 2, $P_e = \frac{1}{2}p^{N/2}$.

For a class of channels to be defined as pairwise reversible channels, this sensitivity to interchanging letters does not occur, and for these channels we shall soon see that the calculation of E_M is relatively straightforward. A channel is pairwise reversible iff, for each i, k, $\mu'_{i,k}(\frac{1}{2}) = 0$. Differentiating (1.04), this is equivalent to

$$\sum_j \sqrt{P(j \mid i)P(j \mid k)} \ln P(j \mid i)$$

$$= \sum_j \sqrt{P(j \mid i)P(j \mid k)} \ln P(j \mid k); \quad \text{all} \quad i, k. \tag{1.21}$$

Equation (1.21) is equivalent to $\mu_{i,k}(s)$ being minimized at $s = \frac{1}{2}$ for all i, k. This guarantees that (1.18) is satisfied with equality and that a pair of inputs in the same position in a pair of code words, x_m and $x_{m'}$, can be reversed without changing $D(m, m')$.

The class of pairwise reversible channels includes all of the symmetric binary input channels considered by Sun (1965) and Dobrushin (1962) (which are defined in a manner that guarantees that $\mu_{i,k}(s) = \mu_{k,i}(s)$

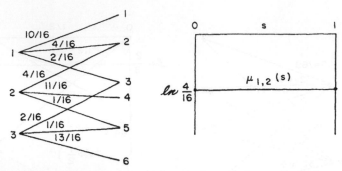

FIG. 2. A pairwise erasing ternary input channel (nonuniform but pairwise reversible).

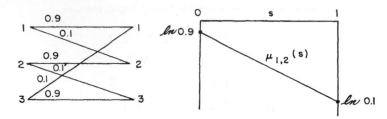

FIG. 3. A ternary unilateral channel (TUC) (uniform but not pairwise reversible).

for all s), and many other binary input channels, such as the one in Fig. 1 (as the reader is invited to verify). For multi-input channels, there is no relationship between the class of pairwise reversible channels and the uniform channels discussed by Fano (1961, p. 126). The channel of Fig. 2 is pairwise reversible but nonuniform; from any pair of inputs it looks like a binary erasure channel. The channel of Fig. 3 is not pairwise reversible even though it is uniform; from any pair of inputs it looks like an asymmetric binary erasure channel.

For pairwise reversible channels, we may compute an exact expression for E_M. To do this, we obtain a lower bound on $D_{\min}(N, M)$ which can be attained for certain values of N. The bound is derived by a method first introduced by Plotkin (1951). For any pair of code words for a pairwise reversible channel, we have[2]

[2] Readers who are familiar with the statistical literature will recognize the expression for $\mu_{i,k}(\tfrac{1}{2})$ as the measure of the difference between the distributions $P(j/i)$ and $P(j/k)$ which was first suggested by Helliger (1909) and later developed by Bhattacharyya (1943).

$$D(m, m') = -\sum_i \sum_k q_{i,k}(m, m')\mu_{i,k}(\tfrac{1}{2}). \qquad (1.22)$$

Since the minimum discrepancy cannot exceed the average discrepancy,

$$D_{\min}(N, M) \leqq \frac{1}{M(M-1)} \sum_{n \neq m'} \sum D(m, m'). \qquad (1.23)$$

The total discrepancy can be computed on a column by column basis.

$$\sum_{n=1}^{M} \sum_{n'=1}^{M} D(m, m') = -\sum_{n=1}^{N} \sum_{i=1}^{K} \sum_{k=1}^{K} M_i(n)M_k(n)\mu_{i,k}(\tfrac{1}{2}), \qquad (1.24)$$

where $M_k(n)$ is the number of times the kth channel input occurs in the nth column. Let M_k^* denote the number of times the kth channel input occurs in the best possible column,

$$\max_{\Sigma M_k = M} [-\sum_i \sum_k M_i M_k \mu_{i,k}(\tfrac{1}{2})] = -\sum_i \sum_k M_i^* M_k^* \mu_{i,k}(\tfrac{1}{2}) \quad (1.25)$$

Combining (1.23) through (1.25) results in a bound for pairwise reversible channels.

$$D_{\min}(N, M) \leqq -1/(M(M-1)) \sum_i \sum_k M_i^* M_k^* \mu_{i,k}(\tfrac{1}{2}) \qquad (1.26)$$

We now show that this bound can be achieved when $N = M!/\prod_k M_k^*!$ To do this, we select the first column of the code so that it has the prescribed composition, the kth channel input occurring M_k^* times. Then we choose as subsequent columns of the code all possible permutations of the first column. In the constructed code, every column contributes the same maximum amount to the total discrepancy, assuring equality between (1.24) and (1.25). Every pair of codewords is the same distance apart, assuring equality in (1.23). Because of these two facts, (1.26) holds with equality when $N = M!/(\prod_k M_k^*!)$.

This construction can likewise be used for channels that are not pairwise reversible. The constructed code has the property that $q_{i,k}(m, m') = q_{k,i}(m, m') = q_{i,k}$ independent of m and m'. This guarantees that, for this code, (1.06) is optimized by setting $s = \tfrac{1}{2}$, for $\mu_{i,k}(s) + \mu_{k,i}(s)$ always attains its minimum at $s = \tfrac{1}{2}$, even when $\mu_{i,k}(s)$ does not.

However, it may be possible to improve upon this construction for channels which are not pairwise reversible. We summarize these results in a theorem, whose proof follows directly from Theorem 2, (1.26), and the construction discussed in the preceding two paragraphs.

THEOREM 3.

$$E_M \geqq 1/(M(M-1)) \max_{\Sigma M_k = M} \sum_i \sum_k M_i M_k \left(-\ln \sum_j \sqrt{P(j/i)\ P(j/k)} \right)$$

with equality for channels which are pairwise reversible.

We next compare this result with $E_{ex}(0^+)$, Gallager's (1965) lower bound to $E(0^+)$, the error exponent at infinitesimal rates. $E_{ex}(0^+)$ is given by (I-1.29) and (I-1.30) as

$$E_{ex}(0^+) = \max_q \sum_i \sum_k q_i q_k \left(-\ln \sum_j \sqrt{P(j/i)P(j/k)} \right), \qquad (1.27)$$

where q is the probability vector specifying the composition of the code. The vector q is unrestricted by the Diophantine constraints placed on the vector $\underline{M}^*/M$. (Here $M_k{}^*$ is the kth component of $\underline{M}^*$). This additional freedom can only increase $E_{ex}(0^+)$. This proves the first of the three corollaries.

COROLLARY 3.1. *For pairwise reversible channels,*

$$E_M \leqq (M/(M-1))E_{ex}(0^+)$$

The evaluation of the expression on the right of Theorem 3 is complicated by the Diophantine constraints on the components of the vector M. To first order in M, however, these constraints may be ignored, as indicated by the following corollary.

COROLLARY 3.2. *For any channel,*

$$E_M \geqq M/(M-1)E_{ex}(0^+) - 0(1/M^2)$$

where

$$0(1/M^2) \leqq \frac{-K\mu_{\max} - \sum_{i \neq k} \sum (\mu_{i,k}(\tfrac{1}{2}) - \mu_{\max})}{4M(M-1)}.$$

Here K is the number of channel inputs and $\mu_{\max} = \max_{i \neq k} \mu_{i,k}(\tfrac{1}{2})$.

Since this corollary is not essential to the proof of Theorem 4, we omit its proof. The details of the straightforward but tedious calculation are given by Berlekamp (1964).

For the remainder of this section, we shall be primarily concerned with the behavior of E_M for very large M. We are especially interested in the limit of E_M as M goes to infinity, which we denote by the symbol E_∞.

Since E_M is a monotonic nonincreasing function of M, it is clear that the limit exists. As a consequence of Corollaries 3.1 and 3.2, we have

COROLLARY 3.3. $E_\infty \geqq E_{ex}(0^+)$ *with equality for channels which are pairwise reversible.*

This general inequality also follows directly from the definitions of E_x and $E_{ex}(0^+)$ without invoking Corollary 3.2.

We now proceed to show that Corollary 3.3 holds with equality even for channels which are not pairwise reversible.

THEOREM 4. *For any discrete memoryless channel* $E_x = E_{ex}(0^+)$.

Remarks. The natural approach in attempting to prove Theorem 4 would be to attempt to calculate the average discrepancy on a column by column basis as in (1.24). This direct approach does not work for channels that are not pairwise reversible, however, the difficulty being that the value of s that determines $D(m, m')$ in (1.06) is not the same as the value of s that minimizes $\mu_{i,k}(s)$ for the pairs of letters in the two code words.

We shall circumvent this difficulty by going through some manipulations on a particular subset of the code words in a code. The argument is rather lengthy and will be carried out as a sequence of 5 Lemmas. For motivation, the reader is advised to keep the ternary unilateral channel (TUC) of Figure 3 in mind throughout the proof. We begin by defining a relation of dominance between code words.

DEFINITION. x_m dominates $x_{m'}$ iff

$$-\sum_i \sum_k q_{i,k}(m, m')\mu'_{i,k}(\tfrac{1}{2}) \geqq 0. \qquad (1.28)$$

Notice that either x_m dominates $x_{m'}$, or $x_{m'}$ dominates x_m, or both. This follows because

$$\mu'_{i,k}(\tfrac{1}{2}) = -\mu'_{k,i}(\tfrac{1}{2}); \qquad q_{i,k}(m, m') = q_{k,i}(m', m) \qquad (1.29)$$

$$\sum_i \sum_k q_{i,k}(m', m)\mu'_{i,k}(\tfrac{1}{2}) = -\sum_i \sum_k q_{i,k}(m, m')\mu'_{i,k}(\tfrac{1}{2}). \qquad (1.30)$$

For the TUC the codeword consisting of all 1's dominates any other codeword which contains at least as many 2's as 3's, but it is dominated by any other codeword which contains at least as many 3's as 2's.

Notice that dominance is *not* necessarily transitive except when the input alphabet is binary. In general, we may have x dominate x' and x' dominate x'' without having x dominate x''.

LEMMA 4.1. *If* x_m *dominates* $x_{m'}$, *then*

$$D(m, m') \leqq \sum_i \sum_k q_{i,k}(m, m')[-\mu_{i,k}(\tfrac{1}{2}) - \tfrac{1}{2}\mu'_{i,k}(\tfrac{1}{2})].$$

Proof. Recall from (1.06) that

$$D(m, m') = -\min_{0 \leqq s \leqq 1} \sum_i \sum_k q_{i,k}(m, m')\mu_{i,k}(s). \qquad (1.06)$$

The tangent line to a convex U function is a lower bound to the function. Taking this tangent to $\mu_{i,k}(s)$ at $s = \frac{1}{2}$ yields

$$\min_{0 \leq s \leq 1} \sum_i \sum_k q_{i,k}(m, m')\mu_{i,k}(s)$$

$$\geq \min_{0 \leq s \leq 1} \sum_i \sum_k q_{i,k}(m, m')[\mu_{i,k}(\tfrac{1}{2}) + (s - \tfrac{1}{2})\mu'_{i,k}(\tfrac{1}{2})]. \quad (1.31)$$

From the definition of dominance, (1.28), this linear function of s is minimized at $s^* = 1$.

q.e.d.

LEMMA 4.2. *From an original code containing M codewords, we may extract a subset of at least $\log_2 M$ codewords which form an "ordered" code, in which each word dominates every subsequent word.*

Proof. We first select the word in the original code which dominates the most others. According to the remarks following (1.28), this word must dominate at least half of the other words in the original code. We select this word as x_1 in the ordered code. All words in the original code which are not dominated by x_1 are then discarded. From the remaining words in the original code, we select the word which dominates the most others and choose it as x_2 in the ordered code. The words which are not dominated by x_2 are then discarded from the original code. This process is continued until all words of the original code are either placed in the ordered code or discarded. Since no more than half of the remaining words in the original code are discarded as each new word is placed in the ordered code, the ordered code contains at least $\log_2 M$ codewords.

q.e.d.

Within an ordered code, every word dominates each succeeding word. In particular, every word in the top half of the code dominates every word in the bottom half of the code. This fact enables us to bound the average discrepancy between words in the top half of the code and words in the bottom half of the code on a column by column basis. Using this technique, Lemma 4.3 gives us a bound to the minimum discrepancy of any ordered code in terms of $E_{ex}(0^+)$ and another term which must be investigated further in subsequent lemmas.

LEMMA 4.3. *Consider any ordered code having $2M$ words of block length N. The minimum discrepancy of this code is bounded by*

$$D_{\min} \leq \sum_{n=1}^{M} \sum_{m'=M+1}^{2M} D(m, m')/M^2$$

$$\leq E_{ex}(0^+) + 2d_{\max} \sqrt{K} \sqrt{\frac{1}{4N} \sum_{n=1}^{N} \sum_{k=1}^{K} (q_k{}^t(n) - q_k{}^b(n))^2},$$

where

$$d_{\max} \triangleq \max_{i,k} | \mu_{i,k}(\tfrac{1}{2}) + \tfrac{1}{2}\mu'_{i,k}(\tfrac{1}{2})| \qquad (1.32)$$

and $q^t(n) = [q_1{}^t(n), \cdots, q_K{}^t(n)]$ *is the composition of the nth column of the top half of the code (i.e., the kth channel input letter occurs $M q_k{}^t(n)$ times in the nth column of the first M codewords). Similarly, $q^b(n) = [q_1{}^b(n), \cdots, q_K{}^b(n)]$ is the composition of the nth column of the bottom half of the code.*

Proof.

$$D_{\min} \leq \sum_{m=1}^{M} \sum_{m'=M+1}^{2M} \frac{D(m, m')}{M^2} \qquad (1.33)$$

$$\leq \sum_{m=1}^{M} \sum_{m'=M+1}^{2M} \sum_{i=1}^{K} \sum_{k=1}^{K} \frac{q_{i,k}(m, m')}{M^2} \left[- u_{i,k}(1/2) - \frac{1}{2} u'_{i,k}(1/2) \right]. \quad (1.34)$$

Now for any values of i and k,

$$\sum_{m=1}^{M} \sum_{m'=M+1}^{2M} \frac{q_{i,k}(m, m')}{M^2} = \sum_{n=1}^{N} \frac{q_i{}^t(n) q_k{}^b(n)}{N} \qquad (1.35)$$

because both sides represent the average number of occurrences of the ith letter in the top half of the code opposite the kth letter in the same column of the bottom half of the code. Using this fact gives

$$D_{\min} \leq \frac{1}{N} \sum_{n=1}^{N} \sum_{i=1}^{K} \sum_{k=1}^{K} q_i{}^t(n) q_k{}^b(n) \left[- u_{i,k}\left(\frac{1}{2}\right) - \frac{1}{2} u'_{i,k}\left(\frac{1}{2}\right) \right]. \quad (1.36)$$

This bounds $D_{\min}$ in terms of the vectors $q^t(n)$ and $q^b(n)$. We now introduce the vectors $q(n)$ and $r(n)$ defined by

$$q(n) \triangleq \tfrac{1}{2}[q^t(n) + q^b(n)]$$
$$r(n) \triangleq \tfrac{1}{2}[q^t(n) - q^b(n)]. \qquad (1.37)$$

$$q^t(n) = q(n) + r(n)$$
$$q^b(n) = q(n) - r(n) \qquad (1.38)$$

$$q_i{}^t(n) q_k{}^b(n) = [q_i(n) + r_i(n)][q_k(n) - r_k(n)]$$
$$= q_i(n) q_k(n) + r_i(n) q_k(n) - q_i{}^t(n) r_k(n). \qquad (1.39)$$

Since $q(n)$ is an average of the probability vectors $q^t(n)$ and $q^b(n)$, $q(n)$ is itself a probability vector. In fact, $q(n)$ is just the composition vector for the nth column of the whole code. Since $q(n)$ is a probability vector.

$$-\sum_i \sum_k q_i(n)q_k(n)\mu_{i,k}(\tfrac{1}{2}) \leqq \max_q -\sum_i \sum_k q_i q_k \mu_{i,k}(\tfrac{1}{2})$$

$$= E_{ex}(0^+). \tag{1.40}$$

Equation (1.40) follows from (1.27) and the definition of $\mu_{i,k}$ in (1.06). Furthermore, since $\mu'_{i,k}(\tfrac{1}{2}) = -\mu'_{k,i}(\tfrac{1}{2})$, we have

$$\sum_i \sum_k q_i(n)q_k(n)\mu'_{i,k}(\tfrac{1}{2}) = 0. \tag{1.41}$$

Substituting (1.39), (1.40), and (1.41) into (1.36) gives

$$D_{\min} \leqq E_{ex}(0^+) + \frac{1}{N}\sum_{n=1}^{N} \sum_i \sum_k \left| r_i(n)q_k(n) - q_i{}^t(n)r_k(n) \right|$$

$$\cdot \left| \mu_{i,k}\left(\frac{1}{2}\right) + \frac{1}{2}\mu'_{i,k}\left(\frac{1}{2}\right) \right| \tag{1.42}$$

$$\leqq E_{ex}(0^+) + \frac{d_{\max}}{N}\sum_{n=1}^{N} \sum_i \sum_k \mid r_i(n)q_k(n) - q_i{}^t(n)r_k(n) \mid , \tag{1.43}$$

where we have used the definition of $d_{\max}$ in (1.32). The remainder term is bounded as follows:

$$\sum_i \sum_k \mid r_i(n)q_k(n) - q_i{}^t(n)r_k(n) \mid$$

$$\leqq \sum_i \sum_k \mid r_i(n)q_k(n) \mid + \mid q_i{}^t(n)r_k(n) \mid$$

$$= \sum_k \mid r_k(n) \mid \sum_i \mid q_i(n) \mid + \mid q_i{}^t(n) \mid$$

$$= 2 \sum_k \mid r_k(n) \mid \tag{1.44}$$

$$\leqq 2 \sqrt{K \sum_k r_k{}^2(n)}. \tag{1.45}$$

Equation (1.45) follows from Cauchy's inequality which states that

$$\sum_k a_k b_k \leqq \sqrt{\sum_k a_k{}^2 \sum_k b_k{}^2}.$$

We have used $a_k = 1, b_k = \mid r_k(n) \mid$. Averaging (1.45) over all N columns gives

$$1/N \sum_{n=1}^{N} \sum_i \sum_k \mid r_i(n)q_k(n) - q_i{}^t(n)r_k(n) \mid$$

$$\leqq \frac{2\sqrt{K}}{N}\sum_{n=1}^{N} \sqrt{\sum_{k=1}^{K} r_k{}^2(n)} \tag{1.46}$$

$$\le 2\sqrt{K}\ \sqrt{\frac{1}{N}\sum_{n=1}^{N}\sum_{k=1}^{K}r_k^{\,2}(n)}$$

by Cauchy. Substituting (1.37) into (1.46) completes the proof of Lemma 4.3.

Lemma 4.3 bounds the minimum discrepancy in terms of the quantity

$$\frac{1}{4N}\sum_{n=1}^{N}\sum_{k=1}^{K}(q_k^{\,t}(n)-q_k^{\,b}(n))^2 = 1/N\sum_{n,k}r_k(n)^2 = 1/N\sum_{n=1}^{N}\underline{r}(n)^2,$$

where we let $\underline{r}(n)^2$ denote the dot product of the K-dimensional vector $\underline{r}(n)$ with itself.

To complete the proof of Theorem 4, we would like to show that $1/N\sum_{n=1}^{N}\underline{r}(n)^2$ can be made arbitrarily small. Unfortunately, however, the direct approach fails, because many columns may have substantially different compositions in their top halves and their bottom halves. Nor can this difficulty be resolved by merely tightening the bound in the latter half of Lemma 4.3, for columns which are very inhomogeneous may actually make undeservedly large contributions to the total discrepancy between the two halves of the code. For example, consider a code for the TUC of Fig. 3. A column whose top fourth contains ones, whose middle half contains twos, and whose bottom fourth contains threes contributes $-\frac{1}{2}\ln\frac{1}{10}-\frac{1}{8}\ln\frac{9}{10}$ to the average discrepancy. We wish to show that the minimum discrepancy for this channel is actually not much better than $-\frac{1}{3}\ln\frac{1}{10}-\frac{1}{3}\ln\frac{9}{10}$. This cannot be done directly because of columns of the type just mentioned. We note, however, that this column which contributes so heavily to the average discrepancy between the top and bottom halves of the code contributes nothing to discrepancies between words in the same quarter of the block. It happens that all abnormally good columns have some fatal weakness of this sort, which we exploit by the following construction.

LEMMA 4.4. *Given an ordered code with $2M$ words of block length N, we can form a new code with M words of block length $2N$ by annexing the*

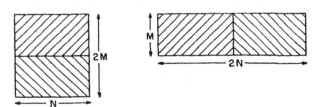

FIG. 4. Halving an ordered code.

$(M + i)$th *word to the ith word for all* $i = 1, \cdots, M$ *as shown in Fig.* 4. *The new code has the following properties.*

(1) *The new code is ordered.*

(2) *The minimum discrepancy of the new code is no smaller than the minimum discrepancy of the original code.*

$$(3) \quad \text{Var}\,(q') - \text{Var}\,(q) = \left(\frac{1}{4N}\right) \sum_{n=1}^{N} (q'(n) - q'(n + N))^2$$

$$(4) \qquad\qquad\qquad \text{Var}\,(q) \leqq \text{Var}\,(q') < 1$$

where:

$q(n)$ *is the composition of the nth column of the original code,* $n = 1, 2, \cdots, N$.

$q'(n)$ *is the composition of the nth column of the new code,* $n = 1, 2, \cdots, 2N$.

$$\bar{q} = 1/N \sum_{n=1}^{N} q(n)$$

$$\bar{q}' = 1/2N \sum_{n=1}^{2N} q'(n)$$

$$\text{Var}\,(q) = 1/N \sum_{n=1}^{N} (q(n) - \bar{q})^2 = \left[\frac{1}{N} \sum_{n=1}^{N} q(n)^2\right] - \bar{q}^2$$

$$\text{Var}\,(q') = 1/2N \sum_{n=1}^{2N} (q'(n) - \bar{q}')^2 = \left[\frac{1}{2N} \sum_{n=1}^{2N} q'(n)^2\right] - \bar{q}'^2.$$

Proof of Property 1. Let $q'_{i,k}(m, m')$ be the joint composition of the mth and m'th words in the new code, i.e., the fraction of times that the ith channel input letter occurs in the mth word of the new code opposite the kth channel input letter in the m'th word. By the halving construction which generated the new code (Fig. 4),

$$q'_{i,k}(m, m') = \tfrac{1}{2}[q_{i,k}(m, m') + q_{i,k}(m + M, m' + M)]. \quad (1.47)$$

If $m < m'$, then, in the original code

$$-\sum_i \sum_k q_{i,k}(m, m')\mu'_{i,k}(\tfrac{1}{2}) \geqq 0$$

$$-\sum_i \sum_k q_{i,k}(m + M, m' + M)\mu'_{i,k}(\tfrac{1}{2}) \geqq 0$$

Consequently, in the new code

$$-\sum_i \sum_k q'_{i,k}(m, m')\mu'_{i,k}(\tfrac{1}{2}) \geqq 0. \qquad\qquad (1.48)$$

Proof of Property 2. In the new code,

$$D'(m, m') = \tfrac{1}{2}[D(m, m') + D(m + M, m' + M)].$$

Thus $D'(m, m')$ can not be smaller than both $D(m, m')$ and $D(m + M, m' + M)$.

Proof of Property 3. $q(n) = \tfrac{1}{2}[\underline{q}'(n) + \underline{q}'(n + N)]$

$$\bar{q} = \frac{1}{2N} \sum_{n=1}^{N} [\underline{q}'(n) + \underline{q}'(n + N)] = \bar{\underline{q}}' \tag{1.49}$$

$$\mathrm{Var}\,(\underline{q}') - \mathrm{Var}\,(\underline{q}) = \left(\frac{1}{2N} \sum_{n=1}^{2N} \underline{q}'(n)^2 \right) - \left(\frac{1}{N} \sum_{n=1}^{N} \underline{q}(n)^2 \right)$$

$$= \frac{1}{4N} \sum_{n=1}^{N} \{ 2[\underline{q}'(n)^2 + \underline{q}'(n + N)^2] - (\underline{q}'(n)$$

$$+ \underline{q}'(n + N))^2 \} \tag{1.50}$$

$$= \frac{1}{4N} \sum_{n=1}^{N} (\underline{q}'(n) - \underline{q}'(n + N))^2.$$

Proof of Property 4. From Property 3, $\mathrm{Var}\,(\underline{q}) \leq \mathrm{Var}\,(\underline{q}')$. Also, for every n,

$$[\underline{q}'(n)]^2 = \sum_{k} [q_k'(n)]^2 \leq 1 \tag{1.51}$$

$$\mathrm{Var}\,(\underline{q}') \leq \frac{1}{2N} \sum_{n=1}^{2N} [\underline{q}'(n)]^2 \leq 1. \tag{1.52}$$

We may now complete the proof of the theorem by iterating the halving construction to prove Lemma 4.5.

LEMMA 4.5.

$$D_{\min}(N, M) < E_{ez}(0^+) + \frac{2d_{\max} \sqrt{K}}{\sqrt{[\log (\log M)]^-}} \tag{1.53}$$

Proof. Starting from any original code containing M codewords of block length N, we may extract a subset of $2^{[\log(\log M)]^-}$ code words which form an ordered code. This follows from Lemma 4.2 and the observation that $2^{[\log(\log M)]^-} \leq \log M$. (Here $[\log (\log M)]^-$ is the largest integer less than or equal to $\log (\log M)$.)

We next halve the ordered code $[\log (\log M)]^-$ times. This gives us a sequence of $[\log (\log M)]^- + 1$ codes, starting with the original ordered code and terminating with a degenerate code containing only one codeword of block length $N2^{[\log(\log M)]^-}$. Since the properties of Lemma 4.4

are hereditary, every code in the sequence is ordered and each code has a minimum discrepancy no smaller than any of its ancestors (except the final degenerate code, for which the minimum discrepancy is undefined). The average variance of the column compositions of each of these codes is at least as great as the average variance of the column compositions of the preceding codes; yet the average variance of each code in the sequence must be between zero and one. Consequently, this sequence of $[\log{(\log M)}]^- + 1$ codes must contain two consecutive codes for which the difference in the variance of column compositions is less than $1/[\log{(\log M)}]^-$. The former of these two consecutive codes is non-degenerate, and Lemma 4.3 applies, with

$$\frac{1}{4N} \sum_{n=1}^{N} \sum_{k=1}^{K} (q_k{}^t(n) - q_k{}^b(n))^2 = \frac{1}{4N} \sum_{n=1}^{N} (q'(n) - q'(n+N))^2 \tag{1.54}$$

$$= \mathrm{Var}\,(q') - \mathrm{Var}\,(q) < 1/[\log{(\log M)}]^-$$

q.e.d.

Theorem 4 follows directly from Lemma 4.5 and Theorem 2.

q.e.d.

Combining (1.53) and (1.12), we obtain an explicit bound on $P_e(N, M, 1)$.

$$P_e(N, M, 1) \geq \exp - N\left[E_{ex}(0^+) + \frac{2d_{\max}\sqrt{K}}{\sqrt{[\log{(\log M)}]^-}} + \sqrt{\frac{2}{N}\ln\frac{1}{P_{\min}}} + \frac{\ln 4M}{N} \right] \tag{1.55}$$

If we upper bound $d_{\max}$, as given by (1.32) by

$$d_{\max} \leq 2 \max_{i,k} |\mu_{i,k}(\tfrac{1}{2})|,$$

then (1.55) becomes equivalent to (I-1.17) and we have completed the proof of Theorem I-3.

Equation (1.55) has a rather peculiar behavior with M. On the other hand, $P_e(N, M, 1)$ must be a monotone nondecreasing function of M, and thus for any M greater than some given value, we can use (1.55) evaluated at that given M. It is convenient to choose this given M as $2^{\sqrt{N}}$, yielding

$$P_e(N, M, 1) \geq \exp - N[E_{ex}(0^+) + o_4(N)]; \qquad M \geq 2^{\sqrt{N}} \tag{1.56}$$

where

$$o_4(N) = \frac{2d_{\max} \sqrt{K}}{\sqrt{|\log N|}} + \sqrt{\frac{2}{N} \ln \frac{1}{P_{\min}}} + \frac{\ln 2}{\sqrt{N}} + \frac{2 \ln 2}{N}. \quad (1.57)$$

These equations can now be restated in a form similar to our other bounds on $P_e(N, M, 1)$.

THEOREM 5.

$$P_e(N, M, 1) \geqq \exp -N[E_{lr}(R - o_3(N)) + o_4(N)], \quad (1.58)$$

where

$$E_{lr}(R) = \begin{cases} E_{ex}(0^+); & R \geqq 0 \\ \infty; & R < 0 \end{cases} \quad (1.59)$$

$$o_3(N) = \frac{\ln 2}{\sqrt{N}}. \quad (1.60)$$

Proof. Observe that when $M \geqq 2^{\sqrt{N}}$ we have $R = (\ln M)/N \geqq (\ln 2)/\sqrt{N}$ and (1.58) reduces to (1.56). For $M < 2^{\sqrt{N}}$, (1.58) simply states that $P_e(N, M, 1) \geqq 0$.

2. THE STRAIGHT LINE BOUND

We have seen that the sphere packing bound (Theorem I-2) specifies the reliability of a channel at rates above R_{crit} and that the zero rate bound (Theorem I-3 or Theorem 5) specifies the reliability in the limit as the rate approaches zero. In this section, we shall couple these results with Theorem I-1 to establish the straight line bound on reliability given in Theorem I-4. Actually we shall prove a somewhat stronger theorem here which allows us to upper bound the reliability of a channel by a straight line between the sphere packing exponent and any low rate, exponential bound on error probability.

THEOREM 6. *Let $E_{lr}(R)$ be a nonincreasing function of R (not necessarily that given by (1.59)), let $o_3(N)$ and $o_4(N)$ be nonincreasing with N and let $No_3(N)$ and $No_4(N)$ be nondecreasing with N. Let $R_2 < R_1$ be nonnegative numbers and define the linear function*

$$E_{sl}(R_0) = \lambda E_{sp}(R_1) + (1 - \lambda)E_{lr}(R_2), \quad (2.01)$$

where E_{sp} is given by (I-1.07) and λ is given by

$$R_0 = \lambda R_1 + (1 - \lambda)R_2. \quad (2.02)$$

If

$$P_e(N, M, 1) \geqq \exp - N[E_{lr}(R - o_3(N)) + o_4(N)] \qquad (2.03)$$

is valid for arbitrary positive M, N, *then*

$$P_e(N, M, 1) \geqq \exp - N\{E_{sl}[R - o_5(N)] + o_6(N)\} \qquad (2.04)$$

is valid for

$$R_2 \leqq R - o_5(N) \leqq R_1, \qquad (2.05)$$

where

$$o_5(N) = o_1(N) + o_3(N) + R_2/N \qquad (2.06)$$

$$o_6(N) = o_2(N) + o_4(N) + \frac{1}{N} E_{lr}(R_2) \qquad (2.07)$$

and $o_1(N)$ *and* $o_2(N)$ *are given by* (I-1.10) *and* $R = (\ln M)/N$.

Remarks. As shown in Figs. 5–8, $E_{sl}(R)$ is a straight line joining $E_{lr}(R_2)$ at R_2 to $E_{sp}(R_1)$ at R_1. It is clearly desirable, in achieving the best bound, to choose R_1 and R_2 so as to minimize $E_{sl}(R)$. If $E_{lr}(R)$ is not convex ∪, it may happen, as in Fig. 8 that the best choice of R_1, R_2 depends on R.

Theorem I-4 of the introduction is an immediate consequence of Theorem 6, obtained by choosing $E_{lr}(R)$ as in Theorem 5 and choosing

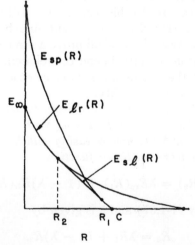

FIGS. 5-8. Geometric construction for $E_{sl}(R)$.

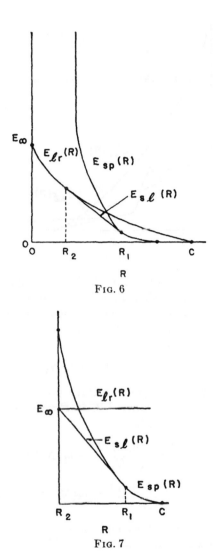

FIG. 6

FIG. 7

$R_2 = 0$. The increased generality of Theorem 6 over Theorem I-4 is non-empty, however. In Theorem 8 we shall give an example of a low rate bound for the binary symmetric channel in which $E_{lr}(R)$ behaves as in Fig. 5.

The restriction in the theorem that $E_{lr}(R)$ be nonincreasing with R is no real restriction. Since $P_e(N, M, 1)$ is nonincreasing with M, any

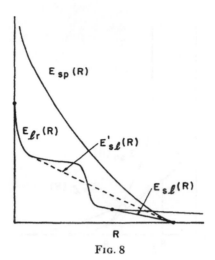

$$\text{F}_{\text{IG. }} 8$$

bound in which $E_{lr}(R)$ is increasing with R can be tightened to a bound in which $E_{lr}(R)$ is not increasing. Likewise the restriction that $No_3(N)$ and $No_4(N)$ be increasing with N is not serious since any bound can be weakened slightly to satisfy this restriction.

Proof. By Theorem I-1, we have

$$P_e(N, M, 1) \geqq P_e(N_1, M, L) P_e(N_2, L + 1, 1), \qquad (2.08)$$

where $N_1 + N_2 = N$ and L is an arbitrary positive integer. Applying the sphere packing bound, Theorem I-2, to $P_e(N_1, M, L)$ and applying (2.03) to $P_e(N_2, L + 1, 1)$, we have

$$P_e(N, M, 1) \geqq \exp\left\{ -N_1\left[E_{sp}\left(\frac{\ln M/L}{N_1} - o_1(N_1)\right) + o_2(N_1) \right]\right.$$
$$\left. - N_2\left[E_{lr}\left(\frac{\ln (L + 1)}{N_2} - o_3(N_2)\right) + o_4(N_2) \right]\right\}. \qquad (2.09)$$

Using the expressions for $o_1(N)$ and $o_2(N)$ in (I-1.10), we see that $No_i(N)$ is increasing with N for $i = 1, 2, 3, 4$. Thus we can lower bound (2.09) by

$$P_e(N, M, 1) \geqq \exp\left\{ -N_1 E_{sp}\left(\frac{\ln M/L}{N_1} - \frac{No_1(N)}{N_1}\right) - No_2(N) \right.$$
$$\left. - N_2 E_{lr}\left(\frac{\ln (L + 1)}{N_2} - \frac{No_3(N)}{N_2}\right) - No_4(N) \right\} \qquad (2.10)$$

This is valid for any positive integers N_1 and N_2 summing to N, and we observe that it is trivially valid if either N_1 or N_2 is 0.

We next get rid of the restrictions that L, N_1, and N_2 be integers. Let $\tilde{L}$ be an arbitrary real number between L and $L + 1$. We can lower bound the right-hand side of (2.10) by replacing $\ln M/L$ with $\ln M/\tilde{L}$ and $\ln (L + 1)$ with $\ln \tilde{L}$. Similarly, let $\tilde{N}_1$ be an arbitrary real number between N_1 and $N_1 + 1$. The right-hand side of (2.10) can be lower bounded by replacing N_1 with $\tilde{N}_1$. Finally, since $N_2 \leq N - \tilde{N}_1 + 1$, we can lower bound (2.10) by replacing N_2 with $N - \tilde{N}_1 + 1$. Making these changes, we have

$$
P_e(N, M, 1) \geq \exp\left\{-\tilde{N}_1 E_{sp}\left(\frac{\ln (M/\tilde{L}) - No_1(N)}{\tilde{N}_1}\right)\right.
$$
$$
\left. - N[o_2(N) + o_4(N)] - (N - \tilde{N}_1 + 1)E_{lr}\left(\frac{\ln \tilde{L} - No_3(N)}{N - \tilde{N}_1 + 1}\right)\right\}
$$
(2.11)

Define λ to satisfy

$$
R - o_5(N) = \lambda R_1 + (1 - \lambda)R_2 \tag{2.12}
$$

From the restriction (2.05), λ satisfies $0 \leq \lambda \leq 1$. Now choose $\tilde{N}_1$ and $\tilde{L}$ by

$$
\tilde{N}_1 = \lambda N \tag{2.13}
$$
$$
\ln \tilde{L} = R_2(N - \tilde{N}_1 + 1) + No_3(N). \tag{2.14}
$$

By rearranging (2.14), we see that the argument of E_{lr} in (2.11) satisfies

$$
\frac{\ln \tilde{L} - No_3(N)}{N - \tilde{N}_1 + 1} = R_2 \tag{2.15}
$$

Likewise, using (2.12), (2.13), (2.14), and (2.06), the argument of E_{sp} in (2.11) is given by

$$
\frac{\ln(M/\tilde{L}) - No_1(N)}{\tilde{N}_1} = \frac{1}{\lambda}\left[\frac{\ln M}{N} - \frac{\ln \tilde{L}}{N} - o_1(N)\right]
$$
$$
= \frac{1}{\lambda}\left[R - R_2\left(1 - \lambda + \frac{1}{N}\right) - o_1(N) - o_2(N)\right]
$$
$$
= \frac{1}{\lambda}[R - R_2(1 - \lambda) - o_5(N)] = R_1. \tag{2.16}
$$

Substituting (2.15) and (2.16) into (2.11), we have

$$P_e(N, M, 1) \geqq \exp - N\left\{\lambda E_{sp}(R_1) + \left(1 - \lambda + \frac{1}{N}\right) E_{lr}(R_2)\right.$$
$$\left. + o_2(N) + o_4(N)\right\} \qquad (2.17)$$

Combining (2.12), (2.02), and (2.01), we have

$$E_{sl}(R - o_5(N)) = \lambda E_{sp}(R_1) + (1 - \lambda)E_{lr}(R_2) \qquad (2.18)$$

Finally, substituting (2.18) and (2.07) into (2.17), we have (2.04), completing the proof.

The straight line bound $E_{sl}(R)$ depends critically on the low rate bound $E_{lr}(R)$ to which it is joined. If the low rate bound is chosen as E_∞, then the resulting straight line bound $E_{sl}(R)$ is given by Theorem I-4. Plots of this bound for several channels are shown in Figure I-4.

From the discussion following (1.20), we see that if $C \neq 0$ and $C_0 = 0$, then E_∞ is strictly less than $E_{sp}(0^+)$, and the straight line bound $E_{sl}(R)$ of Theorem 4 exists over a nonzero range of rates. Also it follows from Theorem 7 of Gallager (1965) that $E_{ex}(R)$ is strictly convex $\cup$ and therefore is strictly less than $E_{sl}(R)$ in the interior of this range of rates.

There is an interesting limiting situation, however, in which $E_{sl}(R)$ and $E_{ex}(R)$ virtually coincide. These are the very noisy channels, first introduced by Reiffen (1963) and extended by Gallager (1965). A very noisy channel is a channel whose transition probabilities may be expressed by

$$P(j \mid k) = r_j(1 + \epsilon_{j,k}), \qquad (2.19)$$

where r_j is an appropriate probability distribution defined on the channel outputs and $|\epsilon_{j,k}| \ll 1$ for all j and k. The function $E_0(\rho)$ for such a channel can be expanded as a power series in $\epsilon_{j,k}$. By neglecting all terms of higher than second order, Gallager (1965) obtained

$$E_0(\rho) = \frac{\rho}{1 + \rho} C, \qquad (2.20)$$

where the capacity C is given by

$$C = \max_{\underline{q}} \frac{1}{2} \sum_j r_j \left[\sum_k q_k \epsilon_{j,k}^2 - \left(\sum_k q_k \epsilon_{j,k}\right)^2\right] \qquad (2.21)$$

$$= \max_{\underline{q}} \frac{1}{4} \sum_i \sum_k q_i q_k \sum_j r_j(\epsilon_{j,i}^2 + \epsilon_{j,k}^2 - 2\epsilon_{j,i}\epsilon_{j,k}). \qquad (2.22)$$

The resulting random coding exponent is given by

$$E_r(R) = (\sqrt{C} - \sqrt{R})^2 \quad \text{for} \quad C/4 \leqq R \leqq C \qquad (2.23)$$

$$= C/2 - R \qquad \text{for} \quad R < C/4. \qquad (2.24)$$

We can calculate E_∞ in the same way

$$E_\infty = \max_{\underline{q}} - \sum_i \sum_k q_i q_k \ln \sum_j \sqrt{P(j \mid i)P(j \mid k)}. \qquad (\text{I-1.18})$$

Using (2.19) and expanding to second order in ϵ, gives

$$\sum_j \sqrt{P(j \mid i)P(j \mid k)} = \sum_j r_j(1 + \epsilon_{j,i}/2 - \epsilon_{j,i}^2/8)$$
$$\cdot(1 + \epsilon_{j,k}/2 - \epsilon_{j,k}^2/8). \qquad (2.25)$$

From (2.19) we observe that

$$\sum_j r_j \epsilon_{j,k} = 0 \quad \text{for all} \quad k \qquad (2.26)$$

$$\sum_j \sqrt{P(j \mid i)P(j \mid k)} = 1 - \tfrac{1}{8} \sum_j r_j(\epsilon_{j,i}^2 + \epsilon_{j,k}^2 - 2\epsilon_{j,i}\,\epsilon_{j,k}). \qquad (2.27)$$

From (2.27), (I-1.18), and (2.22), we conclude that

$$E_\infty = C/2 = E_r(0). \qquad (2.28)$$

Thus in the limit as the $\epsilon_{j,k}$ approach 0, the upper and lower bounds to the reliability $E(R)$ come together at all rates and (2.23) and (2.24) give the reliability function of a very noisy channel.

For channels which are not very noisy, the actual reliability may lie well below the straight line bound from E_∞ to the sphere packing bound. As a specific case in which these bounds may be improved, we consider the binary symmetric channel.

This channel has received a great deal of attention in the literature, primarily because it provides the simplest context within which most coding problems can be considered. The minimum distance of a code, $d_{\min}$, is defined as the least number of positions in which any two code words differ. We further define $d(N, M)$ as the maximum value of $d_{\min}$ over all codes with M code words of length N. Here we are interested primarily in the asymptotic behavior of $d(N, M)$ for large N and M and fixed $R = (\ln M)/N$. The *asymptotic distance ratio* is defined as

$$\delta(R) \triangleq \limsup_{N \to \infty} \frac{1}{N} d(N, [e^{RN}]^+). \qquad (2.29)$$

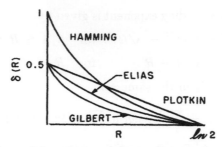

FIG. 9. Comparison of bounds on minimum distance for a binary symmetric channel.

There are two well known upper bounds to $\delta(R)$, due to Hamming (1950) and Plotkin (1951), and one well known lower bound due to Gilbert (1952). These are given implicitly by

$$\ln 2 - H(\delta(R)/2) \geq R \qquad \text{(Hamming)} \qquad (2.30)$$

$$\ln 2 - 2\delta(R) \ln 2 \geq R \qquad \text{(Plotkin)} \qquad (2.31)$$

$$\ln 2 - H(\delta(R)) \leq R \qquad \text{(Gilbert)}, \qquad (2.32)$$

where

$$H(\delta) = -\delta \ln \delta - (1 - \delta) \ln (1 - \delta). \qquad (2.33)$$

See Peterson (1961) for an excellent discussion of these bounds.

Here we shall derive a third upper bound to $\delta(R)$, derived by Elias in 1960 but as yet unpublished. As shown in Fig. 9 the Elias bound is stronger than either the Hamming or Plotkin bounds for $0 < R < \ln 2$. It should be observed, however, that this superiority applies only to the asymptotic quantity, $\delta(R)$. For sufficiently small values of N, M there are a number of bounds on $d(N, M)$ which are stronger than the Elias bound.

THEOREM 7 (Elias).

$$\delta(R) \leq 2\lambda_R(1 - \lambda_R), \qquad (2.34)$$

where λ_R is given by

$$\ln 2 - H(\lambda_R) = R; \qquad 0 \leq \lambda_R \leq \tfrac{1}{2}. \qquad (2.35)$$

Before proving this theorem, we shall discuss the relationship between $\delta(R)$ and the reliability function $E(R)$. Suppose that a code contains two code words at a distance d apart. From I-3.10, $\mu(s)$ for these two words is given by $d \ln [p^s q^{1-s} + q^s p^{1-s}]$, where p is the cross-over probability of the channel (see Fig. I-5a) and $q = 1 - p$. This is minimized at $s = \frac{1}{2}$, and from (I-3.20) and (I-3.21), one of the code words has an error probability bounded by

$$P_{e,m} \geq \frac{1}{4} \exp \left[d \ln 2\sqrt{pq} - \sqrt{\frac{d}{2} \ln \frac{1}{p}} \right], \qquad (2.36)$$

where we have used (1.11) in bounding $\mu''(\frac{1}{2})$.

Next, for a code with $2M$ code words of block length N, we see by expurgating M of the worst words that at least M code words have a distance at most $d(N, M)$ from some other code word. For such a code

$$P_e \geq \frac{1}{8} \exp \left[-d(N, M) \ln 2 \sqrt{pq} - \sqrt{d(N, M)/2} \ln \frac{1}{p} \right]. \qquad (2.37)$$

Combining (2.37) with (2.29), we obtain

$$P_e(N, M, 1) \geq \exp -N[\delta(R) \ln 2 \sqrt{pq} + o(N)] \qquad (2.38)$$

$$E(R) \leq \frac{\delta(R)}{2} \ln 4pq. \qquad (2.39)$$

Conversely, if a code of block length N has minimum distance $\delta(R)N$, then it is always possible to decode correctly when fewer than $\frac{1}{2}\delta(R)N$ errors occur. By using the Chernov (1952) bound, if $p < \frac{1}{2}\delta(R)$, the probability of $\frac{1}{2}\delta(R)N$ or more errors is bounded by

$$P_e \leq \exp - N \left[-\frac{\delta(R)}{2} \ln p - \left(1 - \frac{\delta(R)}{2} \right) \ln q - H\left(\frac{\delta(R)}{2} \right) \right] \qquad (2.40)$$

$$E(R) \geq -\frac{\delta(R)}{2} \ln p - \left(1 - \frac{\delta(R)}{2} \right) \ln q - H\left(\frac{\delta(R)}{2} \right). \qquad (2.41)$$

For more complete discussions of techniques for bounding the error probability on a binary symmetric channel, see Fano (1961), Chap. 7 or Gallager (1963), Chap. 3. The bounds on reliability given by (2.39) and (2.41) are quite different, primarily because it is usually possible to decode correctly when many more than $\frac{1}{2}\delta(R)N$ errors occur. As p becomes very small, however, the minimum distance of the code becomes increasingly important, and dividing (2.39) and (2.41) by $-\ln p$, we see that

$$\frac{\delta(R)}{2} = \lim_{p \to 0} \frac{E(R)}{-\ln p} . \qquad (2.42)$$

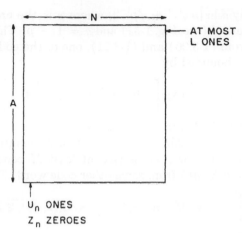

FIG. 10. Construction for Elias bound.

Along with (2.42), there are several other interesting connections be-tween $E(R)$ and $\delta(R)$. For example, if one could show that $\delta(R)$ was given by the Gilbert bound (2.32) with equality, then upon substituting (2.32) into (2.39) one would find an *upper* bound for reliability which is equal to the lower bound $E_{ex}(R)$ over the range of rates for which $E_{ex}(R) > E_r(R)$. By combining this with Theorem 6, $E(R)$ would be determined for all rates and would be equal to the known lower bound to $E(R)$. Thus the question of determining $E(R)$ for the *BSC* hinges around the problem of determining $\delta(R)$.

Proof of Theorem 7. The proof of the Elias bound combines the argu-ments of Plotkin and Hamming in an ingenious way. For any integer L, $0 \leq L \leq N/2$, there are $\sum_{i=0}^{L} \binom{N}{i}$ binary N-tuples within a sphere of radius L around any given code word (i.e., N-tuples that have a distance L or less from the code word). For M code words, these spheres contain $M \sum_{i=0}^{L} \binom{N}{i}$ N-tuples, counting an N-tuple once for each appearance in a sphere. Since there are only 2^N different binary N-tuples, some criti-cal N-tuple must appear in at least A spheres where

$$A \triangleq \left[2^{-N} M \sum_{i=0}^{L} \binom{N}{i} \right]^{+}. \qquad (2.43)$$

Thus this critical N-tuple contains at least A code words within a sphere of radius L around itself.

For the remainder of the proof, we consider only these A code words and we assume that L is chosen so that $A \geqq 2$. For convenience we translate these code words by subtracting the critical word from each of them. Each of the A translated code words then has at most L ones.

We next list the A translated code words as in Fig. 10. Let U_n denote the number of ones in the nth column Z_n, the number of zeroes. The total number of ones in the $A \times N$ matrix of Fig. 10 may be computed either by summing along the columns or along the rows. This gives

$$\sum_n U_n \leqq AL.$$

(2.44)

We now compute the total distance among the $\binom{A}{2}$ pairs of translated code words. The contribution to the total distance from the nth column is $U_n Z_n$. Consequently,

$$d_{\text{tot}} = \sum_n U_n Z_n.$$

(2.45)

Since the minimum distance cannot exceed the average distance, we have

$$d_{\min} \leqq d_{\text{tot}} \Big/ \binom{A}{2} = \sum_{n=1}^{N} U_n(A - U_n) \Big/ \binom{A}{2}.$$

(2.46)

The function $\sum_{n=1}^{N} U_n(A - U_n)$ is a concave function of the U_n, and is therefore maximized, subject to the constraint (2.44), by making the partial derivation with respect to U_n a constant. Thus the maximum occurs with $U_n = AL/N$ for all n:

$$d_{\min} \leqq \frac{2NA^2 \left(\dfrac{L}{N}\right)\left(1 - \dfrac{L}{N}\right)}{A(A - 1)} = 2N(L/N)(1 - L/N)$$

$$\left(1 + \frac{1}{A - 1}\right)$$

(2.47)

$$\frac{d_{\min}}{N} \leqq 2(L/N)(1 - L/N) + \frac{1}{2(A - 1)}.$$

(2.48)

Since (2.48) is valid for any L such that $A \geqq 2$, L can be chosen so as to optimize the bound. In the theorem, however, we are interested in asymptotic results for fixed R, large N, and $M = [e^{NR}]^+$. First we lower bound A.

Shannon[3] has shown that

$$\binom{N}{L} \geqq [8L(N - L)/N]^{-1/2} \exp NH(L/N). \qquad (2.49)$$

The first term is lower bounded by taking $L = N/2$, yielding

$$\sum_{i=0}^{L} \binom{N}{i} > \binom{N}{L} \geqq \frac{1}{\sqrt{2N}} \exp NH(L/N). \qquad (2.50)$$

Next, choose L to satisfy

$$H\left(\frac{L-1}{N}\right) < \ln 2 - \frac{\ln M}{N} + \frac{3}{2}\frac{\ln N}{N} \leqq H\left(\frac{L}{N}\right). \qquad (2.51)$$

Observe that for any fixed $R > 0$, this will have a solution for large enough N. Combining (2.43), (2.50), and (2.51) we obtain

$$A > \sqrt{\frac{1}{2N}} \exp\left[\frac{3}{2}\ln N\right] = \frac{N}{\sqrt{2}} \qquad (2.52)$$

Next recalling the definition of λ_R in (2.35), the left-hand side of (2.51) becomes

$$H\left(\frac{L-1}{N}\right) < H(\lambda_R) + \frac{3}{2}\frac{\ln N}{N}. \qquad (2.53)$$

Since H is a concave $\cap$ function, we can combine (2.53) with the result that $H(\frac{1}{2}) = \ln 2$ to obtain

$$\frac{L-1}{N} < \lambda_R + \left(\frac{3}{2}\frac{\ln N}{N}\right)\left[\frac{\ln 2 - H(\lambda_R)}{\frac{1}{2} - \lambda_R}\right] \qquad (2.54)$$

Substituting (2.52) and (2.54) into (2.48), we have

$$\frac{d(N, M)}{N} \leqq 2\lambda_R(1 - \lambda_R) + o(N), \qquad (2.55)$$

where $o(N)$ can be taken as

$$o(N) = 3\frac{\ln N}{N}\left(\frac{\ln 2 - H(\lambda_R)}{\frac{1}{2} - \lambda_R}\right) + \frac{2}{N} + \frac{1}{\sqrt{2N} - 2}. \qquad (2.56)$$

If we now substitute the Elias bound (2.34) into (2.39), we get a new upper bound on reliability given by:

THEOREM 8. *For a binary symmetric channel, an upper bound on relia-*

[3] C. E. Shannon, unpublished seminar notes, M. I. T., 1956. For a published derivation, see Ash (1965), p. 113.

bility is given by

$$E(R) \leq E_{tr}(R) = -\lambda_R(1 - \lambda_R) \ln 4pq, \qquad (2.57)$$

where λ_R is given by (2.35).

RECEIVED: January 18, 1966

REFERENCES

ASH, R. B. (1965), "Information Theory." Wiley (Interscience), New York.

BERLEKAMP, E. R. (1964), Block coding with noiseless feedback. Ph.D. Thesis. Department of Electrical Engineering. M.I.T.

BHATTACHARYYA, A. (1943), On a measure of divergence between two statistical populations defined by their probability distributions. *Bull. Calcutta Math. Soc.* **35**(3), 99–110.

CHERNOFF, H. (1952), A measure of asymptotic efficiency for tests of an hypothesis based on the sum of observations. *Ann. Math. Stat.* **23**, 493.

DOBRUSHIN, (1962), "Optimal binary codes for small rates of transmission of information," *Theory of Probability and its Applications*, Vol. 7, p. 199–204.

ELIAS, P. (1955), List decoding for noisy channels. *Tech. Report 335.* Research Laboratory of Electronics, M.I.T., Cambridge.

FANO, R. M. (1961), "Transmission of Information." M.I.T. Press, Cambridge, and Wiley, New York.

FEINSTEIN, A. (1955), Error bounds in noisy channels without memory. *IEEE Trans.* IT-1, 13–14.

FELLER, W. (1943), Generalizations of a probability limit theorem of Cramer. *Trans. Am. Math. Soc.* **54**, 361.

GALLAGER, R. (1963), "Low Density Parity Check Codes." M.I.T. Press, Cambridge.

GALLAGER, R. (1965), A simple derivation of the coding theorem and some applications. *IEEE Trans.* IT-11, 3–18.

GALLAGER, R. (1965), Lower bounds on the tails of probability distributions. M.I.T. Research Laboratory of Electronics, OPR 77, 277–291.

GILBERT, E. N. (1952), A comparison of signalling alphabets. *BSTJ* **3**, 504–522.

HAMMING, R. W. (1950), Error detecting and error correcting codes. *BSTJ* **29**, 47–160.

HELLIGER, E. (1909), Neue Begrundung der Theorie quadratischer Formen von unendlichvielen Veranderlichen. *J. Reine Angew. Math.* **136**, 210–271.

JACOBS, I. M., AND BERLEKAMP, E. R. (1967), A lower bound to the distribution of computation for sequential decoding. *IEEE Trans.* IT-13 (to appear).

NEYMAN, J., AND PEARSON, E. S. (1928), On the use and interpretation of certain test criterion for purposes of statistical inference. *Biometrica* **20A**, 175, 263.

PETERSON, W. W. (1961), "Error-Correcting Codes." M.I.T. Press, Cambridge, and Wiley, New York.

PLOTKIN, M. (1960), Research Division Report 51-20, University of Pennsylvania. Eventually published in 1960 as: Binary codes with specified minimum distance. *PGIT* IT6, 445–450.

REIFFEN, B. (1963), A note on 'very noisy' channels. *Inform. Control* **6,** 126–130.

SHANNON, C. E. (1948), A mathematical theory of communication. *BSTJ* **27,** 379, 623. Also in book form with postscript by W. Weaver, University of Illinois Press, Urbane, Illinois.

SHANNON, C. E. (1956), Zero error capacity of noisy channels. *IEEE Trans.* **IT-2,** 8.

SHANNON, C. E. (1958), Certain results in coding theory for noisy channels. *Inform. Control* **1,** 6.

SHANNON, C. E., GALLAGER, R. G., AND BERLEKAMP, E. R. (1967), Lower bounds to error probability for coding on discrete memoryless channels. I. *Inform. Control.* **10,** 65–103.

SUN, M. (1965), Asymptotic bounds on the probability of error for the optimal transmission of information in the channel without memory which is symmetric in pairs of input symbols for small rates of transmission. *Theory Prob. Appl.* (Russian) **10** (1), 167–175.

Letter to Vannevar Bush, February 16, 1939

Claude E. Shannon

Dear Dr. Bush,

Off and on I have been working on an analysis of some of the fundamental properties of general systems for the transmission of intelligence, including telephony, radio, television, telegraphy, etc. Practically all systems of communication may be thrown into the following form:

$$f_1(t) \rightarrow \boxed{T} \rightarrow F(t) \rightarrow \boxed{R} \rightarrow f_2(t)$$

$f_1(t)$ is a general function of time (arbitrary except for certain frequency limitations) representing the intelligence to be transmitted. It represents, for example, the pressure-time function in radio and telephony, or the voltage-time curve output of an iconoscope in television.

T is a transmission element which operates on $f_1(t)$ through modulation, distortion, etc. to give a new function of time $F(t)$, which is actually transmitted. $F(t)$ in radio and television is the electromagnetic wave sent out by the transmitter, and in general need not be at all similar to $f_1(t)$, although, of course, they are closely related. I consider T to be a mathematical operator which transforms f_1 into F, thus $F(t) = T[f_1(t)]$.

$F(t)$ enters the receiving element R and is there transformed into a third function of time $f_2(t)$ which should be as closely similar to $f_1(t)$ as possible. In an ideal system it would be an exact replica. A fundamental theorem on the subject, which so far as I can determine has not been rigorously proved before, is that there is no system of communication of this type which will transmit an arbitrary f_1 with absolute fidelity without using an infinite frequency spectrum for the intermediate function F. This fact necessitates the mathematical definition of what we should call the "distortion" between two functions f_1 and f_2 that can be applied to any functions, for since we never can reach perfection we must have some measure of how far away we are. Previous definitions are entirely inadequate, for example percent harmonic distortion can only be applied when f_1 is a pure sine wave lasting forever, and entirely neglects other types of distortion.

I propose the following as a definition of "distortion": $D(f_1, f_2)$ between any two functions of time f_1 and f_2

$$D(f_1, f_2) = \sqrt{\int_{-\infty}^{\infty} \left[\frac{f_1(t)}{A} - \frac{f_2(t)}{B} \right]^2 dt}$$

where $A = \sqrt{\int_{-\infty}^{\infty} [f_a(t)]^2 \, dt}$ and $B = \sqrt{\int_{-\infty}^{\infty} [f_2(t)]^2 \, dt}$. This rather wicked looking formula is really a kind of root-mean-square error between the functions after they have been reduced by the factors A and B, so that they contain the same energy. It possesses several useful properties: if the only distortion is harmonic distortion of a small amount this formula gives the percent harmonic distortion according to the usual formula.

Also, if f_2 is exactly like f_1 except for a small amount of random noise (e.g. static) the formula gives the percent of the random noise, which has been found experimentally to measure the psychological distortion. In speech transmission we might think that a better measure of distortion would be found by taking the root-mean-square error in the frequency spectrum of f_1 and f_2. Actually it can be shown that the two results will always be the same, that although the ear operates on a frequency basis and the eye (television or facsimile) on an absolute value basis we can use the same measure for distortion.

With this definition I have been trying to prove the following theorem: for any operators T,R the length of an arbitrary message f_1 multiplied by its essential spectrum and divided by the distortion of the system is less than a certain constant times the time of transmission of F multiplied by its essential spectrum width or – roughly speaking – it is impossible to reduce bandwidth times transmission time for a given distortion.

This seems to be true although I do not have a general proof as yet (I can prove it for certain types of operators T).

The idea is quite old: both Hartley and Carson have made statements of this type without rigid mathematical specifications or proof. It is by no means obvious, however. You might think of a transmitting element T which made a Fourier spectrum analysis of the input wave f_1, divided each frequency component by ten, combined these new frequencies to give a function F using a band only one tenth as wide, and transmitted the function. R would perform the reverse operation.

Such a system would be used to reduce the bandwidth of television signals, for instance. This particular system has a theoretical fallacy, but I am not sure that all such systems do.

There are several other theorems at the foundations of communication engineering which have not been thoroughly investigated.

Of course, my main project is still the machine for performing symbolic mathematical operations; although I have made some progress in various outskirts of the problem I am still pretty much in the woods, so far as actual results are concerned and so can't tell you much about it. I have a set of circuits drawn up which actually will perform symbolic differentiation and integration on most functions, but the method is not quite general or natural enough to be perfectly satisfactory. Some of the general philosophy underlying the machine seems to evade me completely...

Claude Shannon

Circuits for a P.C.M. Transmitter and Receiver*

Claude E. Shannon and B. M. Oliver

Abstract

Circuits are described for a P.C.M. transmitter and receiver. The transmitter operates on the principle of counting in the binary system the number of quanta of charge required to nullify the sampled voltage.

---

* Bell Laboratories Memorandum, June 1, 1944.

SOME TOPICS IN INFORMATION THEORY

C. E. Shannon

Previous work in communication theory [2] has shown that *amount* of information for purposes of communication has a natural measure in terms of entropy type formulas $H = - \Sigma p \log p$. This has led to theorems giving the most efficient encoding of the messages produced by a stochastic process into a standard form, say a random sequence of binary digits, and for the most efficient use of an available communication channel. However, no concept of information itself was defined. It is possible to formulate an approach to the theory in which the information sources in a communication network appear as elements of a lattice.

The leading idea is that any reversible translation of the messages produced by a stochastic process, say by a non-singular finite state transducer, should be regarded as containing the same information as the original messages. From the communications point of view, knowledge of the Morse code translation of the text originating at a telegraph office is equivalent to knowledge of the text itself. Thus we consider the information of a source to be the equivalence class of all reversible translations of the messages produced by the source. Each particular translation is a representative of the class, analogous to describing a tensor by giving its components in a particular coordinate system.

Various theories may be obtained depending on the set of translation operations allowed for equivalence. Two choices lead to interesting and applicable developments: (1) the group of all finite state transducers (allowing effectively positive or negative delays), (2) the group of *delay free* finite state transducers, in which it is required that the present output symbol be a function of the present and past history of the input, and similarly for the reverse transducer.

The first case is the simplest and relates most closely to previous work in which unlimited encoding delays at transmitter and receiver were allowed. A transitive inclusion relation between information elements, $x \geqq y$, (inducing a partial ordering) means that y can be obtained by operating on x with some finite state transducer (not necessarily reversible). The entropy of a source (which is invariant under the group of reversible transducers) appears as a norm monotone with the ordering. The least upper bound for two elements is the total information in both sources, a representation being the sequence of ordered pairs of letters from the two sources. A greatest lower bound can also be defined, thus resulting in an information lattice. There will always be a universal lower bound, and if the set of sources considered is finite, a universal upper bound. The lattices obtained in this way are, in general, non-modular. In fact, an information lattice can be constructed isomorphic to any finite partition lattice.

A metric can be defined by $\rho(x, y) = H_x(y) + H_y(x)$ satisfying the usual requirements. This introduces a topology and the notion of Cauchy convergent sequences of information elements and of limit points. If convergent sequences are annexed to the lattice as new points, with corresponding modifications of the definition of equality, etc., there result continuous lattices, for example tho set of all the abstractions of the total information in the system by finite state transducers, or limiting sequences of such transducers.

The delay free theory leads also to a lattice but the problems, while perhaps more important in the applications, are less well understood. The entropy of a source is no longer sufficient to characterize the source for purposes of encoding, and in fact an infinite number of independent invariants have been found. Certain of them are related to the problem of best prediction of the next symbol to be produced, knowing the entire past history. The delay free theory has an application to the problem of communication over a channel where there is a second channel available for sending information in the reverse direction. The second channel can, in certain cases, be used to improve forward transmission. Upper bounds have been found for the forward capacity in such a case. The delay free theory also has an application to the problem of linear least square smoothing and prediction [1]. A minimum phase filter has an inverse (without delay) and therefore belongs to the delay free group of translations for continuous time series. The least square prediction problem can be solved by translating the time series in question to a canonical form and finding the best prediction operator for this form.

REFERENCES

1. H. W. BODE and C. E. SHANNON, *A simplified derivation of linear least square smoothing and prediction theory*, Proceedings of the Institute of Radio Engineers vol. 38 (1950) pp. 417–425.

2. C. E. SHANNON and W. WEAVER, *A mathematical theory of communication*, University of Illinois Press, 1949.

BELL TELEPHONE LABORATORIES, INC.,
MURRAY HILL, N. J., U. S. A.

Concavity of Transmission Rate as a Function of Input Probabilities*

Claude E. Shannon

Abstract

In a discrete noisy channel without memory, the rate of transmission R is a concave downward function of the probabilities P_i of the input symbols. Hence any local maximum of R will be the absolute maximum or channel capacity C.

* Bell Laboratories Memorandum, June 8, 1955.

The Rate of Approach to Ideal Coding*

Claude E. Shannon

Abstract

Let C be the capacity of a noisy discrete channel without memory. Consider codes for the channel consisting of 2^{Hn} sequences, each sequence being n symbols long. The basic coding theorem for a noisy channel states that by taking n sufficiently large it is possible to find codes such that both $\Delta = C - H$ and the probability of error after reception, P_E, are arbitrarily small. This paper is concerned with the problem of estimating the necessary value of n as a function of P_E and Δ. Both upper and lower bounds are found in fairly general cases. The upper and lower bounds for n approach each other percentage-wise as Δ and P_E approach zero, giving an asymptotic formula for n. Various special cases are investigated in detail, such as the symmetric binary channel and the flat gaussian channel.

* *Proceedings Institute of Radio Engineers*, volume 43, 1955.

The Bandwagon*

Claude E. Shannon

Information theory has, in the last few years, become something of a scientific bandwagon. Starting as a technical tool for the communication engineer, it has received an extraordinary amount of publicity in the popular as well as the scientific press. In part, this has been due to connections with such fashionable fields as computing machines, cybernetics, and automation; and in part, to the novelty of its subject matter. As a consequence, it has perhaps been ballooned to an importance beyond its actual accomplishments. Our fellow scientists in many different fields, attracted by the fanfare and by the new avenues opened to scientific analysis, are using these ideas in their own problems. Applications are being made to biology, psychology, linguistics, fundamental physics, economics, the theory of organization, and many others. In short, information theory is currently partaking of a somewhat heady draught of general popularity.

Although this wave of popularity is certainly pleasant and exciting for those of us working in the field, it carries at the same time an element of danger. While we feel that information theory is indeed a valuable tool in providing fundamental insights into the nature of communication problems and will continue to grow in importance, it is certainly no panacea for the communication engineer or, *a fortiori*, for anyone else. Seldom do more than a few of nature's secrets give way at one time. It will be all too easy for our somewhat artificial prosperity to collapse overnight when it is realized that the use of a few exciting words like *information, entropy, redundancy*, do not solve all our problems.

What can be done to inject a note of moderation in this situation? In the first place, workers in other fields should realize that the basic results of the subject are aimed in a very specific direction, a direction that is not necessarily relevant to such fields as psychology, economics, and other social sciences. Indeed, the hard core of information theory is, essentially, a branch of mathematics, a strictly deductive system. A thorough understanding of the mathematical foundation and its communication application is surely a prerequisite to other applications. I personally believe that many of the concepts of information theory will prove useful in these other fields – and, indeed, some results are already quite promising – but the establishing of such applications is not a trivial matter of translating words to a new domain, but rather the slow tedious process of hypothesis and experimental verification. If, for example, the human being acts in some situations like an ideal decoder, this is an experimental and not a mathematical fact, and as such must be tested under a wide variety of experimental situations.

Secondly, we must keep our own house in first class order. The subject of information theory has certainly been sold, if not oversold. We should now turn our attention to the business of research and development at the highest scientific plane we can maintain. Research rather than exposition is the keynote, and our critical thresholds should be raised. Authors should submit only their best efforts, and these only after careful criticism by themselves and their colleagues. A few first rate research papers are preferable to a large number that are poorly conceived or half-finished. The latter are no credit to their writers and a waste of time to their readers. Only by maintaining a thoroughly scientific attitude can we achieve real progress in communication theory and consolidate our present position.

---

* *IEEE Transactions Information Theory*, volume 2, March 1956.

Notes to Part A

The first paper, [37], is Shannon's classic paper, by far his greatest, and one of the cornerstones of twentieth-century science (see the remarks in the Preface to Part A). It appeared in 1948 in two parts in the *Bell System Technical Journal*. In this remarkable paper Shannon presented the world with a new and exciting discipline which would be known as "information theory" and sometimes as "Shannon theory." The theory and results that were presented here were the culmination of nearly a decade of research and refinement, the publication having been delayed by Shannon's participation in the war effort.

In this paper Shannon formulated his paradigm for the communication problem which is represented by the famous block diagram:

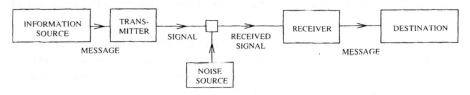

Diagram of general communication system

He then introduces the tools and techniques that enable him to establish his fundamental theorems. Although these theorems are quite general and powerful, this paper was hardly the end of the matter. There remained many interesting and important questions to be answered. Furthermore the subject of information theory turned out to be especially rich. As questions were answered, many more questions and problems appeared to take their place. Almost immediately, scholarly groups organized meetings to discuss research issues in information theory. Within a few years of the publication of Shannon's paper, the Institute of Radio Engineers (now the Institute of Electrical and Electronic Engineers — the "IEEE") formed a "professional group" on information theory, most of the work of which was inspired directly or indirectly by Shannon's theory. The group is today the 6000-member IEEE Information Theory Society, and its 40 years of "Transactions" contain thousands of research papers, with the rate of publication still increasing. In addition there are many national information theory societies, each with its journal and meetings. Among the many books that have been written on Shannon theory are Berger [Berg71], Blahut [Blah87], Cover and Thomas [CoTh91], Csiszár and Körner [CsKo81], Gallager [Gall68], Gray [Gray90], Jelinek [Jeli68], McEliece [McEl77] and Wolfowitz [Wolf78].

In the decade following 1948, Shannon himself was the research leader in the field that he had founded. Most of the remaining papers in Part A represent either Shannon's information theory research or his efforts to explain and publicize the theory. In what follows we will enumerate the areas that he studied in his 1948 paper. As we shall point out, Shannon's later research papers developed certain of these areas more fully. We will also give a brief (and of course highly abridged and subjective) indication of some of the research by others that bears strongly and directly on issues discussed by Shannon.

The 1948 paper [37] begins with a discussion of what are now called "constrained-input noiseless channels," and the main result is an expression for the capacity of such channels in terms of the largest eigenvalues of a matrix that defines the input constraints. Shannon himself did not publish anything further on this issue. Such channels occur in the study of magnetic recording, and Shannon's influence was heavily felt in research in this area — see [Blah87], Chap. 2.

463

In the next several sections of the paper, Shannon gets down to business with a discussion of information sources and the concept of entropy. He obtains his entropy measure of uncertainty using an axiomatic approach. For a detailed treatment of subsequent work in this direction, see Aczél and Daróczy [AcDa75]. He discusses the English language as an information source, and gives an estimate of its entropy as no more than about 2.3 bits/per letter. In paper [69], Shannon gave a better upper bound of about 1 bit/letter. For later work on this subject, see Cover and King [CoKi72] and Savchuk [Savc64], and the references therein. In these sections, Shannon establishes what we now call the asymptotic equipartition property (AEP), which was extended by McMillan [McMi53] and Breiman [Brei57]. The concept of entropy continues to play an important role in the development of ergodic theory (see Shields [Shie73] and Gray [Gray90]). The AEP establishes that the entropy of an information source is the minimum binary rate at which the source can be represented in an error-free manner. Hundreds of research papers have since been published concerning both the theoretical and practical aspects of so-called "entropy coding". See Blahut [Blah39] and Cover and Thomas [Coth91] for references.

The final sections of the first installment of the paper are devoted to discrete noisy channels, the notion of channel capacity, and the celebrated theorem that transmission at any rate less than capacity is possible with negligible error probability (and conversely that reliable transmission at rates greater than capacity is not possible). It is this aspect of the Shannon theory which inspired the greatest amount of research during tha next forty years. One direction that was explored by many researchers was to obtain estimates of the rate of approach to error-free coding as the coding-delay grows to infinity. Early results were obtained by Rice [Rice50], Elias [Elia55], Shannon himself [111], [117], [122], [123] and Gallager [Gall65]. See also Blahut [Blah87] and references therein.

Another direction was attempts to construct explicit and practical coding schemes. This was and is a vast research area in which Shannon himself never participated. See MacWilliams and Sloane [MaSl77] and references therein.

Shannon himself wrote two papers which would later set off another large body of research. The first is his paper on "zero-error capacity" [109]. Here he formulated the notion of zero-error capacity, and obtained bounds on this quantity. In this paper he left open a challenging question concerning the zero-error capacity of a certain channel with five inputs and outputs, or equivalently of the graph consisting of a single pentagon. This problem was finally solved by Lovász ([Lova79]; see also [Haem79]) who showed that the zero error capacity of the pentagon is $\sqrt{5}$, and gave a method for obtaining an upper bound on the capacity of an arbitrary graph. Lovász's method turns out to be closely related to the Delsarte linear programming bound for subsets of an association scheme (see [McEl79], [McRR78], [Schr79]).

The "zero-error capacity" paper [109] also contains one of Shannon's most celebrated results, that the capacity of a discrete memoryless channel is not increased by feedback. The notion of two-way communication is further elaborated on in Shannon's paper [119], and a host of papers by many other researchers. In fact these papers are the precursors of the entire area that we call today multiple-user information theory. See Blahut [Blah87], Cover and Thomas [CoTh91], Csiszár and Körner [CsKo81], McEliece [McEl77], Wyner [Wyne74] and Section III of Slepian [Slep74].

The second installment of [37] is concerned with continuous sources and channels, especially Gaussian channels and sources. He introduces the notion of differential entropy and gives the "entropy-power" inequality (a correct proof of which was later given by Stam [Stam59]).

The "sampling theorem" given in §19 of [37] has often been referred to in the literature as the Shannon sampling theorem (or the Whittaker-Kotel'nikov-Shannon sampling theorem), although as Shannon himself indicates, immediately following the theorem, this was already a well-known result. In fact, the theorem, and the formula that expresses a function in terms of its sample values (usually called the "cardinal series") have a very long history — see for example Higgins [Higg85], Jerri [Jerr77].

As a consequence of the sampling theorem it is possible to represent a signal of bandwidth W and with almost all of its energy confined to a time interval of T seconds by a single point in $2WT$-dimensional Euclidean space (§19 of [37]). This leads naturally to the question of how many $2WT$-dimensional billiard balls can be packed into a large sphere in that space [40]. For a current account of such packing problems see Conway and Sloane [CoS188].

At the end of [37], Shannon gives a very brief treatment of what we now call rate-distortion theory. Shannon himself wrote several subsequent papers that relate to this part. Paper [43] is a detailed treatment of the continuous Gaussian channel, and includes a geometric proof of the coding theorem and the famous "water-filling" solution for the capacity of the colored-noise channel. Paper [117] is a very detailed study of the error probability for optimal codes on the Gaussian channel. Finally, in paper [118], Shannon returned to rate-distortion theory, giving this subject a firm theoretical basis.

The third paper in this section, [14], is a hitherto unpublished and originally secret Bell Labs memorandum, which gives a mathematical proof that the Vernam encryption scheme is perfectly secure, and then describes an analogous scheme for continuous functions (speech, for example). Today, nearly fifty years later, speech encryption is a flourishing business. For descriptions of current techniques see Beker [Beke85], Gersho and Steele [GeSt84], Wyner [Wyne79, Wyne79a], or any of the annual CRYPTO conference proceedings, for example Menezes and Vanstone [MeVa91].

References

[AcDa75]   J. Aczél and Z. Daróoczy, *On Measures of Information and Their Characterization*, Academic Press, N.Y., 1975.

[Beke85]   H. Beker, *Secure Speech Communications*, Academic Press, London, 1985.

[Berg71]   T. Berger, *Rate Distortion Theory: A Mathematical Basis for Data Compression*, Prentice-Hall, Englewood Cliffs, N.J., 1971.

[Blah87]   R. E. Blahut, *Principles and Practices of Information Theory*, Addison-Wesley, Reading, MA, 1987.

[Brei57]   L. Breiman, "The individual ergodic theorems of information theory," *Ann. Math. Stat.*, **28** (1957), 809-811.

[CoS188]   J. H. Conway and N. J. A. Sloane, *Sphere-Packings, Lattices and Groups*, Springer-Verlag, New York, 1988.

[CoKi78]   T. M. Cover and R. King, "A convergent gambling estimate of the entropy of English," *IEEE Trans. Inform. Theory*, **24** (1978), 413-421.

[CoTh91]   T. M. Cover and J. A. Thomas, *Elements of Information Theory*, Wiley, New York, 1991.

[CsKo81]   I. Csiszár and J. Körner, *Information Theory*, Academic Press, New York, 1981.

[Elia55]   P. Elias, "Coding for noisy channels," *IRE Convention Record* (Pt. 4, 1955), 37-46.

[Gall65]   R. G. Gallager, "A simple derivation of the coding theorem and some applications," *IEEE Trans. Inform. Theory*, **11** (1965), 3-18.

[Gall68]   R. G. Gallager, *Information Theory and Reliable Communication*, Wiley, New York, 1968.

[GeSt84]   A. Gersho and R. Steele, editors, "Special Section on the Encryption of Analog Signal," *IEEE J. Selected Areas in Commun.* **2** (1984), pp. 423-466.

[Gray90]   R. M. Gray, *Entropy and Information Theory*, Springer-Verlag, New York, 1990.

[Haem79]   W. Haemers, "On some problems of Lovász concerning the Shannon capacity of a graph," *IEEE Trans. Inform. Theory*, **25** (1979), 231-232.

[Higg85]   J. R. Higgins, "Five short stories about the cardinal series," *Bull. Amer. Math. Soc.* **12** (1985), 45-89.

[Jeli68]   F. Jelinek, *Probabilistic Information Theory*, McGraw-Hill, New York, 1968.

[Jerr77]   A. J. Jerri, "The Shannon sampling theorem — its various extensions and applications: a tutorial review," *Proc. IEEE*, **65** (1977), 1565-1596.

[Lova79]   L. Lovász, "On the Shannon capacity of a graph," *IEEE Trans. Inform. Theory*, **25** (1979), 1-7.

[MaSl77]   F. J. MacWilliams and N. J. A. Sloane, *The Theory of Error-Correcting Codes*, North-Holland, Amsterdam, 1977.

[McEl77]   R. J. McEliece, *The Theory of Information and Coding*, Addison-Wesley, Reading, MA, 1977.

[McEl79]   R. J. McEliece, "The bounds of Delsarte and Lovász, and their application to coding theory," in *Algebraic Coding Theory and Applications*, ed. G. Longo, CISM Courses and Lectures No. 258, Springer-Verlag, N.Y., 1979, pp. 107-178.

[McRR78]   R. J. McEliece, E. R. Rodemich and H. C. Rumsey, Jr., "The Lovász bound and some generalizations," *J. Combinatorics, Inform. Syst. Sci.*, **3** (1978), 134-152.

[McMi53]   B. McMillan, "The basic theorems of information theory," *Ann. Math. Stat.*, **24** (1952), 196-219.

[MeVa91]   A. J. Menezes and S. A. Vanstone, editors, *Advances in Cryptography — CRYPTO '90*, Springer-Verlag, New York, 1991.

[Rice50]   S. O. Rice, "Communication in the presence of noise — Probability of error for two encoding schemes," *Bell Sys. Tech. Journal*, **29** (1950), 60-93.

[Savc64]   A. P. Savchuk, "On estimates for the entropy of a language according to Shannon," *Teor. Veroyatnost. i Primenen.*, **9** (1964), 154-157; English translation in *Theory Prob. Appl.* **9** (1964), 138-141.

[Schr79]   A. Schrijver, "A comparison of the Delsarte and Lovász bounds," *IEEE Trans. Inform. Theory*, **25** (1979), 425-429.

[Shie73]   P. Shields, *Theory of Bernoulli Shifts*, Univ. of Chicago Press, Chicago, Ill., 1973.

[Slep74]   D. Slepian, *Key Papers in the Development of Information Theory*, IEEE Press, New York, 1974.

[Stam59]   A. Stam, "Some inequalities satisfied by the quantities of information of Fisher and Shannon," *Inform. Contr.*, **2** (1959), 101-112.

[Wolf78]   J. Wolfowitz, *Coding Theorems of Information Theory*, Springer-Verlag, Berlin, 1978.

[Wyne74]   A. D. Wyner, "Recent results in the Shannon theory," *IEEE Trans. Inform. Theory*, **20** (1974), 2-10.

[Wyne79]   A. D. Wyner, "An analog scrambling scheme which does not expand bandwidth — I: discrete-time," *IEEE Trans. Info. Theory* **25** (1979), 261-274.

[Wyne79a]   A. D. Wyner "An analog scrambling scheme which does not expand bandwidth — II: continuous-time," *IEEE Trans. Info. Theory*, **25** (1979), 415-424.

Part B

Computers

Circuits

Games

Preface to Shannon's Collected Papers (Part B)

Besides creating the subject of information theory (see Preface to Part A), Shannon also started the whole subject of logical circuit design and wrote the seminal paper on computer chess, as well as several other fundamental papers on computers.

The papers in this section deal with switching circuits, analog and digital computers, automata theory, graph theory and game-playing machines.

The central theme in many of these papers is the problem of constructing an efficient switching circuit to perform a given task. The first paper, Shannon's Master's thesis at M.I.T., won the Alfred Noble Prize, and launched Shannon on his career. As mentioned in the Biography at the beginning of this collection, H. H. Goldstine called this "one of the most important master's theses ever written. . . a landmark in that it helped to change digital circuit design from an art to a science."

The knowledgeable reader may notice that there is no mention of Shannon's switching game in any of these papers. Apparently he did not publish an account of this game. However, it is described in [BeCG82], Chap. 22; [Brua74]; [Edmo65]; [HamV88]; [Lehm64]; and [Wels76], Chap. 19. The Pollak-Shannon strategy for drawing at the game of nine-in-a-row is described in [BeCG82], p. 676.

A Symbolic Analysis of Relay and Switching Circuits[*]

Claude E. Shannon[**]

I. Introduction

In the control and protective circuits of complex electrical systems it is frequently necessary to make intricate interconnections of relay contacts and switches. Examples of these circuits occur in automatic telephone exchanges, industrial motor-control equipment, and in almost any circuits designed to perform complex operations automatically. In this paper a mathematical analysis of certain of the properties of such networks will be made. Particular attention will be given to the problem of network synthesis. Given certain characteristics, it is required to find a circuit incorporating these characteristics. The solution of this type of problem is not unique and methods of finding those particular circuits requiring the least number of relay contacts and switch blades will be studied. Methods will also be described for finding any number of circuits equivalent to a given circuit in all operating characteristics. It will be shown that several of the well-known theorems on impedance networks have roughly analogous theorems in relay circuits. Notable among these are the delta-wye and star-mesh transformations, and the duality theorem.

The method of attack on these problems may be described briefly as follows: any circuit is represented by a set of equations, the terms of the equations corresponding to the various relays and switches in the circuit. A calculus is developed for manipulating these equations by simple mathematical processes, most of which are similar to ordinary algebraic algorisms. This calculus is shown to be exactly analogous to the calculus of propositions used in the symbolic study of logic. For the synthesis problem the desired characteristics are first written as a system of equations, and the equations are then manipulated into the form representing the simplest circuit. The circuit may then be immediately drawn from the equations. By this method it is always possible to find the simplest circuit containing only series and parallel connections, and in some cases the simplest circuit containing any type of connection.

Our notation is taken chiefly from symbolic logic. Of the many systems in common use we have chosen the one which seems simplest and most suggestive for our interpretation. Some of our phraseology, such as node, mesh, delta, wye, etc., is borrowed from ordinary network theory for simple concepts in switching circuits.

---

[*] *Transactions American Institute of Electrical Engineers,* vol. 57, 1938. (Paper number **38-80,** recommended by the AIEE committees on communication and basic sciences and presented at the AIEE summer convention, Washington, D.C., June 20-24, 1938. Manuscript submitted March 1, 1938; made available for preprinting May 27, 1938.)

[**] Claude E. Shannon is a research assistant in the department of electrical engineering at Massachusetts Institute of Technology, Cambridge. This paper is an abstract of a thesis presented at MIT for the degree of master of science. The author is indebted to Doctor F. L. Hitchcock, Doctor Vannevar Bush, and Doctor S. H. Caldwell, all of MIT, for helpful encouragement and criticism.

II. Series-Parallel Two-Terminal Circuits

Fundamental Definitions and Postulates

We shall limit our treatment of circuits containing only relay contacts and switches, and therefore at any given time the circuit between any two terminals must be either open (infinite impedance) or closed (zero impedance). Let us associate a symbol X_{ab} or more simply X, with the terminals a and b. This variable, a function of time, will be called the hindrance of the two-terminal circuit $a-b$. The symbol 0 (zero) will be used to represent the hindrance of a closed circuit, and the symbol 1 (unity) to represent the hindrance of an open circuit. Thus when the circuit $a-b$ is open $X_{ab} = 1$ and when closed $X_{ab} = 0$. Two hindrances X_{ab} and X_{cd} will be said to be equal if whenever the circuit $a-b$ is open, the circuit $c-d$ is open, and whenever $a-b$ is closed, $c-d$ is closed. Now let the symbol + (plus) be defined to mean the series connection of the two-terminal circuits whose hindrances are added together. Thus $X_{ab} + X_{cd}$ is the hindrance of the circuit $a-d$ when b and c are connected together. Similarly the product of two hindrances $X_{ab} \cdot X_{cd}$ or more briefly $X_{ab}X_{cd}$ will be defined to mean the hindrance of the circuit formed by connecting the circuits $a-b$ and $c-d$ in parallel. A relay contact or switch will be represented in a circuit by the symbol in Figure 1, the letter being the corresponding hindrance function. Figure 2 shows the interpretation of the plus sign and Figure 3 the multiplication sign. This choice of symbols makes the manipulation of hindrances very similar to ordinary numerical algebra.

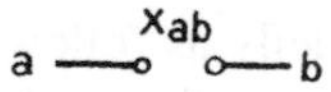

Figure   1   (left).   Symbol   for   hindrance
                 function

Figure 2 (right).   Interpretation of addition

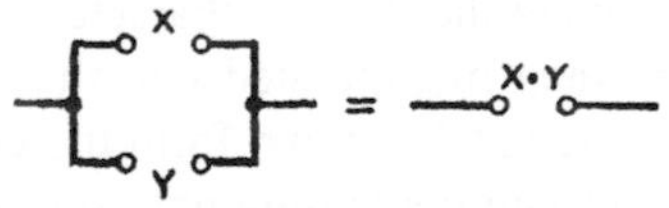

Figure 3   (middle).   Interpretation   of   multipli-
                        cation

It is evident that with the above definitions the following postulates will hold:

Postulates

1. *a.* $0 \cdot 0 = 0$ A closed circuit in parallel with a closed circuit is a closed circuit.

   b. $1 + 1 = 1$ An open circuit in series with an open circuit is an open circuit.

2. *a.* $1 + 0 = 0 + 1 = 1$ An open circuit in series with a closed circuit in either order (i.e., whether the open circuit is to the right or left of the closed circuit) is an open circuit.

   b. $0 \cdot 1 = 1 \cdot 0 = 0$ A closed circuit in parallel with an open circuit in either order is a closed circuit.

3. *a.* $0 + 0 = 0$ A closed circuit in series with a closed circuit is a closed circuit.

   b. $1 \cdot 1 = 1$ An open circuit in parallel with an open circuit is an open circuit.

4. At any given time either $X = 0$ or $X = 1$.

These are sufficient to develop all the theorems which will be used in connection with circuits containing only series and parallel connections. The postulates are arranged in pairs to emphasize a duality relationship between the operations of addition and multiplication and the quantities zero and one. Thus if in any of the a postulates the zero's are replaced by one's and the multiplications by additions and vice versa, the corresponding b postulate will result. This fact is of great importance. It gives each theorem a dual theorem, it being necessary to prove only one to establish both. The only one of these postulates which differs from ordinary algebra is 1b. However, this enables great simplifications in the manipulation of these symbols.

Theorems

In this section a number of theorems governing the combination of hindrances will be given. Inasmuch as any of the theorems may be proved by a very simple process, the proofs will not be given except for an illustrative example. The method of proof is that of "perfect induction," i.e., the verification of the theorem for all possible cases. Since by Postulate 4 each variable is limited to the values 0 and 1, this is a simple matter. Some of the theorems may be proved more elegantly by recourse to previous theorems, but the method of perfect induction is so universal that it is probably to be preferred.

$$X + Y = Y + X , \tag{1a}$$

$$XY = YX , \tag{1b}$$

$$X + (Y + Z) = (X + Y) + Z , \tag{2a}$$

$$X(YZ) = (XY)Z , \tag{2b}$$

$$X(Y + Z) = XY + XZ , \tag{3a}$$

$$X + YZ = (X + Y)(X + Z) , \tag{3b}$$

$$1 \cdot X = X , \tag{4a}$$

$$0 + X = X , \tag{4b}$$

$$1 + X = 1 , \tag{5a}$$

$$0 \cdot X = 0 . \tag{5b}$$

For example, to prove Theorem 4a, note that X is either 0 or 1. If it is 0, the theorem follows from Postulate 2b; if 1, it follows from Postulate 3b. Theorem 4b now follows by the duality principle, replacing the 1 by 0 and the $\cdot$ by $+$.

Due to the associative laws (2a and 2b) parentheses may be omitted in a sum or product of several terms without ambiguity. The Σ and Π symbols will be used as in ordinary algebra.

The distributive law (3a) makes it possible to "multiply out" products and to factor sums. The dual of this theorem, (3b), however, is not true in numerical algebra.

We shall now define a new operation to be called negation. The negative of a hindrance X will be written X' and is defined to be a variable which is equal to 1 when X equals 0 and equal to 0 when X equals 1. If X is the hindrance of the make contacts of a relay, then X' is the hindrance of the break contacts of the same relay. The definition of the negative of a hindrance gives the following theorems:

$$X + X' = 1 , \tag{6a}$$

$$XX' = 0 , \tag{6b}$$

$$0' = 1 , \tag{7a}$$

$$1' = 0 , \tag{7b}$$

$$(X')' = X . \tag{8}$$

Analogue With the Calculus of Propositions

We are now in a position to demonstrate the equivalence of this calculus with certain elementary parts of the calculus of propositions. The algebra of logic[1-3], originated by George Boole, is a symbolic method of investigating logical relationships. The symbols of Boolean algebra admit of two logical interpretations. If interpreted in terms of classes, the variables are not limited to the two possible values 0 and 1. This interpretation is known as the algebra of classes. If, however, the terms are taken to represent propositions, we have the calculus of propositions in which variables are limited to the values 0 and 1,[*] as are the hindrance functions above. Usually the two subjects are developed simultaneously from the same set of postulates, except for the addition in the case of the calculus of propositions of a postulate equivalent to Postulate 4 above. E. V. Huntington[4] gives the following set of postulates for symbolic logic:

1. The class K contains at least two distinct elements.

2. If a and b are in the class K then $a + b$ is in the class K.

3. $a + b = b + a$.

4. $(a + b) + c = a + (b + c)$.

5. $a + a = a$.

6. $ab + ab' = a$ where ab is defined as $(a' + b')'$.

If we let the class K be the class consisting of the two elements 0 and 1, then these postulates follow from those given in the first section. Also Postulates 1, 2, and 3 given there can be deduced from Huntington's postulates. Adding 4 and restricting our discussion to the calculus of propositions, it is evident that a perfect analogy exists between the calculus for switching circuits and this branch of symbolic logic.[**] The two interpretations of the symbols are shown in Table I.

Due to this analogy any theorem of the calculus of propositions is also a true theorem if interpreted in terms of relay circuits. The remaining theorems in this section are taken directly from this field.

De Morgan's theorem:

$$(X + Y + Z...)' = X' \cdot Y' \cdot Z'... , \tag{9a}$$

$$(X \cdot Y \cdot Z...)' = X' + Y' + Z' +... . \tag{9b}$$

---

[*] This refers only to the classical theory of the calculus of propositions. Recently some work has been done with logical systems in which propositions may have more than two "truth values."

[**] This analogy may also be seen from a slightly different viewpoint. Instead of associating X_{ab} directly with the circuit $a - b$ let X_{ab} represent the *proposition* that the circuit $a - b$ is open. Then all the symbols are directly interpreted as propositions and the operations of addition and multiplication will be seen to represent series and parallel connections.

This theorem gives the negative of a sum or product in terms of the negatives of the summands or factors. It may be easily verified for two terms by substituting all possible values and then extended to any number n of variables by mathematical induction.

A function of certain variables $X_1, X_2 .... X_n$ is any expression formed from the variables with the operations of addition, multiplication, and negation. The notation $f(X_1, X_2, ... X_n)$ will be used to represent a function. Thus we might have $f(X,Y,Z) = XY + X'(Y' + Z')$. In infinitesimal calculus it is shown that any function (providing it is continuous and all derivatives are continuous) may be expanded in a Taylor series. A somewhat similar expansion is possible in the calculus of propositions. To develop the series expansion of functions first note the following equations:

$$f(X_1, X_2, ... X_n) = X_1 \cdot f(1, X_2 ... X_n) + X_1' \cdot f(0, X_2 ... X_n) , \tag{10a}$$

$$f(X_1, ..., X_n) = [f(0, X_2 ... X_n) + X_1] \cdot [f(1, X_2 ... X_n) + X_1'] . \tag{10b}$$

These reduce to identities if we let X_1 equal either 0 or 1. In these equations the function f is said to be expanded about X_1. The coefficients of X_1 and X_1' in 10a are functions of the $(n-1)$ variables $X_2 ... X_n$ and may thus be expanded about any of these variables in the same manner. The additive terms in 10b also may be expanded in this manner. Expanding about X_2 we have:

$$f(X_1 ... X_n) = X_1 X_2 f(1,1, X_3 ... X_n) + X_1 X_1' f(1,0, X_3 ... X_n) +$$
$$X_1' X_2 f(0,1, X_3 ... X_n) + X_1' X_2' f(0,0, X_3 ... X_n) , \tag{11a}$$

$$f(X_1 ... X_n) = [X_1 + X_2 + f(0,0, X_3 ... X_n)] \cdot [X_1 + X_2' + f(0,1, X_3 ... X_n)] \cdot$$
$$[X_1' + X_2 + f(1,0, X_3 ... X_n)] \cdot [X_1' + X_2' + f(1,1, X_3 ... X_n)] . \tag{11b}$$

Continuing this process n times we will arrive at the complete series expansion having the form:

$$f(X_1 ... X_n) = f(1,1,1 ... 1) X_1 X_2 ... X_n + f(0,1,1 ... 1) X_1' X_2 ... X_n + \cdots \tag{12a}$$
$$+ f(0,0,0 ... 0) X_1' X_2' ... X_n' ,$$

$$f(X_1 ... X_n) = [X_1 + X_2 + \cdots X_n + f(0,0,0 ... 0)] \cdot ... \tag{12b}$$
$$\cdot [X_1' + X_2' \cdots + X_n' + f(1,1 ... 1)] .$$

Table I. Analogue Between the Calculus of Propositions and the Symbolic Relay Analysis

Symbol	Interpretation in Relay Circuits	Interpretation in the Calculus of Propositions
X	The circuit X	The proposition X
0	The circuit is closed	The proposition is false
1	The circuit is open	The proposition is true
$X + Y$	The series connection of circuits X and Y	The proposition which is true if either X or Y is true
$X Y$	The parallel connection of circuits X and Y	The proposition which is true if both X and Y are true
X'	The circuit which is open when X is closed and closed when X is open	The contradictory of proposition X
$=$	The circuits open and close simultaneously	Each proposition implies the other

By 12a, f is equal to the sum of the products formed by permuting primes on the terms of $X_1 X_2 ... X_n$ in all possible ways and giving each product a coefficient equal to the value of the function when that product is 1. Similarly for 12b.

As an application of the series expansion it should be noted that if we wish to find a circuit representing any given function we can always expand the function by either 10a or 10b in such a way that any given variable appears at most twice, once as a make contact and once as a break contact. This is shown in Figure 4. Similarly by 11 any other variable need appear no more than four times (two make and two break contacts), etc.

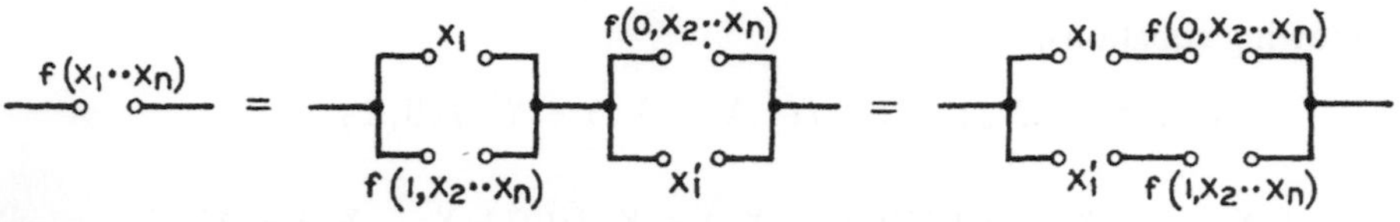

Figure 4. Expansion about one variable

A generalization of De Morgan's theorem is represented symbolically in the following equation:

$$f(X_1, X_2 ... X_n, +, \cdot)' = f(X_1', X_2' ... X_n', \cdot, +) . \tag{13}$$

By this we mean that the negative of any function may be obtained by replacing each variable by its negative and interchanging the $+$ and $\cdot$ symbols. Explicit and implicit parentheses will, of course, remain in the same places. For example, the negative of $X + Y \cdot (Z + WX')$ will be $X'[Y' + Z'(W' + X)]$.

Some other theorems useful in simplifying expressions are given below:

$$X = X + X = X + X + X = \text{etc.} , \tag{14a}$$

$$X = X \cdot X = X \cdot X \cdot X = \text{etc.} , \tag{14b}$$

$$X + XY = X , \tag{15a}$$

$$X(X + Y) + X , \tag{15b}$$

$$XY + X'Z = XY + X'Z + YZ , \tag{16a}$$

$$(X + Y)(X' + Z) = (X + Y)(X' + Z)(Y + Z) , \tag{16b}$$

$$Xf(X,Y,Z,...) = Xf(1,Y,Z,...) , \tag{17a}$$

$$X + f(X,Y,Z,...) = X + f(0,Y,Z,...) , \tag{17b}$$

$$X'f(X,Y,Z,...) = X'f(0,Y,Z,...) , \tag{18a}$$

$$X' + f(X,Y,Z,...) = X' + f(1,Y,Z,...) . \tag{18b}$$

All of these theorems may be proved by the method of perfect induction.

Any expression formed with the operations of addition, multiplication, and negation represents explicitly a circuit containing only series and parallel connections. Such a circuit will be called a series-parallel circuit. Each letter in an expression of this sort represents a make or break relay contact, or a switch blade and contact. To find the circuit requiring the least number of contacts, it is therefore necessary to manipulate the expression into the form in which the least number of letters appear. The theorems given above are always sufficient to do this. A little practice in the manipulation of these symbols is all that is required. Fortunately most of the theorems are exactly the same as those of numerical algebra – the associative, commutative, and distributive laws of algebra hold here. The writer has found Theorems 3, 6, 9, 14, 15, 16a, 17, and 18 to be especially useful in the simplification of complex expressions.

Frequently a function may be written in several ways, each requiring the same minimum number of elements. In such a case the choice of circuit may be made arbitrarily from among these, or from other considerations.

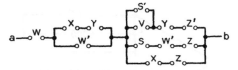

Figure 5.   Circuit to be simplified

As an example of the simplification of expressions consider the circuit shown in Figure 5. The hindrance function X_{ab} for this circuit will be:

$$X_{ab} = W + W'(X + Y) + (X + Z)(S + W' + Z)(Z' + Y + S'V)$$

$$= W + X + Y + (X + Z)(S + 1 + Z)(Z' + Y + S'V)$$

$$= W + X + Y + Z(Z' + S'V) \, .$$

These reductions were made with 17b using first W, then X and Y as the "X" of 17b. Now multiplying out:

$$X_{ab} = W + X + Y + ZZ' + ZS'V$$

$$= W + X + Y + ZS'V \, .$$

The circuit corresponding to this expression is shown in Figure 6. Note the large reduction in the number of elements.

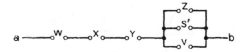

Figure 6.   Simplification of figure 5

It is convenient in drawing circuits to label a relay with the same letter as the hindrance of make contacts of the relay. Thus if a relay is connected to a source of voltage through a network whose hindrance function is X, the relay and any make contacts on it would be labeled X. Break contacts would be labeled X'. This assumes that the relay operates instantly and that the make contacts close and the break contacts open simultaneously. Cases in which there is a time delay will be treated later.

III. Multi-Terminal and Non-Series-Parallel Circuits

Equivalence of n-Terminal Networks

The usual relay control circuit will take the form of Figure 7, where $X_1, X_2, ...X_n$ are relays or other devices controlled by the circuit and N is a network of relay contacts and switches. It is desirable to find transformations that may be applied to N which will keep the operation of *all* the relays $X_1, \ldots X_n$ the same. So far we have only considered transformations which may be applied to a two-terminal network keeping the operation of one relay in series with this network the same. To this end we define equivalence of n-terminal networks as follows. Definition: Two n-terminal networks M and N will be said to be equivalent with respect to these n terminals if and only if $X_{jk} = Y_{jk}$; $j,k = 1,2,3 \ldots .n$, where X_{jk} is the hindrance of N (considered as a two-terminal network) between terminals j and k, and Y_{jk} is that for M between the corresponding terminals. Under this definition the equivalences of the preceding sections were with respect to two terminals.

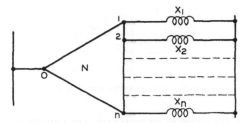

Figure 7. General constant-voltage relay circuit

Star-Mesh and Delta-Wye Transformations

As in ordinary network theory there exist star-to-mesh and delta-to-wye transformations. In impedance circuits these transformations, if they exist, are unique. In hindrance networks the transformations always exist and are not unique. Those given here are the simplest in that they require the least number of elements. The delta-to-wye transformation is shown in Figure 8. These two networks are equivalent with respect to the three terminals a,b, and c, since by distributive law $X_{ab} = R(S + T) = RS + RT$ and similarly for the other pairs of terminals $a-c$ and $b-c$.

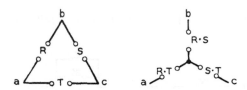

Figure 8. Delta-wye transformation

The wye-to-delta transformation is shown in Figure 9. This follows from the fact that $X_{ab} = R + S = (R + S) \cdot (R + T + T + S)$, etc. An n-point star also has a mesh equivalent with the central junction point eliminated. This is formed exactly as in the simple three-point star, by connecting each pair of terminals of the mesh through a hindrance which is the sum of the corresponding arms of the star. This may be proved by mathematical induction. We have shown it to be true for $n = 3$. Now assuming it true for $n - 1$, we shall prove it for n. Suppose we construct a mesh circuit from the given n-point star according to this method. Each corner of the mesh will be an $(n - 1)$-point star and since we have assumed the theorem true for $n - 1$ we may replace the nth corner by its mesh equivalent. If Y_{0j} was the hindrance of the original star from the central node 0 to the point j, then the reduced mesh will have the hindrance $(Y_{0s} + Y_{or}) \cdot (Y_{0s} + Y_{on} + Y_{0r} + Y_{0n})$ connecting nodes r and s. But this reduces to $Y_{0s} Y_{0r}$ which is the correct value, since the original n-point star with the nth arm deleted becomes an $(n - 1)$-point star and by our assumption may be replaced by a mesh having this hindrance connecting nodes r and s. Therefore the two networks are equivalent with respect to the first $n - 1$ terminals. By eliminating other nodes than the nth, or by symmetry, the equivalence with respect to all n terminals is demonstrated.

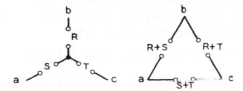

Figure 9. Wye-delta transformation

Hindrance Function of a Non-Series-Parallel Network

The methods of Part II were not sufficient to handle circuits which contained connections other than those of a series-parallel type. The "bridge" of Figure 10, for example, is a non-series-parallel network. These networks will be treated by first reducing to an equivalent series-parallel circuit. Three methods have been developed for finding the equivalent of a network such as the bridge.

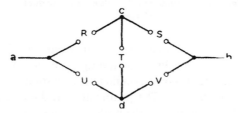

Figure 10.   Non-series-parallel circuit

The first is the obvious method of applying the transformations until the network is of the series parallel type and then writing the hindrance function by inspection. This process is exactly the same as is used in simplifying the complex impedance networks. To apply this to the circuit of Figure 10, first we may eliminate the node c, by applying the star-to-mesh transformation to the star $a-c$, $b-c$, $d-c$. This gives the network of Figure 11. The hindrance function may be written down from inspection for this network:

$$X_{ab} = (R + S)[U(R + T) + V(T + S)] .$$

This may be written as

$$X_{ab} = RU + SV + RTV + STU = R(U + TV) + S(V + TU) .$$

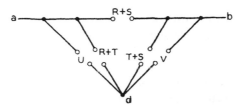

Figure 11.   Hindrance function by means of transformations

The second method of analysis is to draw all possible paths through the network between the points under consideration. These paths are drawn along the lines representing the component hindrance elements of the circuit. If any one of these paths has zero hindrance, the required function must be zero. Hence if the result is written as a product, the hindrance of each path will be a factor of this product. The required result may therefore be written as the product of the hindrances of all possible paths between the two points. Paths which touch the same point more than once need not be considered. In Figure 12 this method is applied to the bridge. The paths are shown dotted. The function is therefore given by

$$X_{ab} = (R + S)(U + V)(R + T + V)(U + T + S)$$

$$= RU + SV + RTV + UTS = R(U + TV) + S(V + TU) \ .$$

The same result is thus obtained as with the first method.

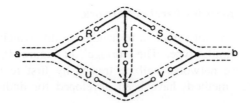

Figure 12.   Hindrance function as a product of sums

The third method is to draw all possible lines which would break the circuit between the points under consideration, making the lines go through the hindrances of the circuit. The result is written as a sum, each term corresponding to a certain line. These terms are the products of all the hindrances on the line. The justification of the method is similar to that for the second method. This method is applied to the bridge in Figure 13.

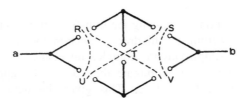

Figure 13.   Hindrance function as a sum of products

This again gives for the hindrance of the network:

$$X_{ab} = RU + SV + RTV + STU = R(U + TV) + S(V + TU) \ .$$

The third method is usually the most convenient and rapid, for it gives the result directly as a sum. It seems much easier to handle sums than products due, no doubt, to the fact that in ordinary algebra we have the distributive law $X(Y + Z) = XY + XZ$, but not its dual $X + YZ = (X + Y)(X + Z)$. It is, however, sometimes difficult to apply the third method to nonplanar networks (networks which cannot be drawn on a plane without crossing lines) and in this case one of the other two methods may be used.

Simultaneous Equations

In analyzing a given circuit it is convenient to divide the various variables into two classes. Hindrance elements which are directly controlled by a source external to the circuit under consideration will be called independent variables. These will include hand-operated switches, contacts on external relays, etc. Relays and other devices controlled by the network will be called dependent variables. We shall, in general, use the earlier letters of the alphabet to represent independent variables and the later letters for dependent variables. In Figure 7 the dependent variables are $X_1, X_2 \ldots X_n$. X_k will evidently be operated if and only if $X_{0k} = 0$, where X_{0k} is the hindrance function of N between terminals 0 and k. That is,

$$X_k = X_{0k}, \quad k = 1, 2, \ldots n .$$

This is a system of equations which completely define the operation of the system. The right-hand members will be known functions involving the various dependent and independent variables and given the starting conditions and the values of the independent variables the dependent variables may be computed.

A transformation will now be described for reducing the number of elements required to realize a set of simultaneous equations. This transformation keeps X_{0k} ($k = 1, 2 \ldots n$) invariant, but X_{jk} ($j, k = 1, 2 \ldots n$) may be changed, so that the new network may not be equivalent in the strict sense defined to the old one. The operation of all the relays will be the same, however, This simplification is only applicable if the X_{0k} functions are written as sums and certain terms are common to two or more equations. For example, suppose the set of equations is as follows:

$$W = A + B + CW ,$$

$$X = A + B + WX ,$$

$$Y = A + CY ,$$

$$Z = EZ + F .$$

This may be realized with the circuit of Figure 14, using only one A element for the three places where A occurs and only one B element for its two appearances. The justification is quite obvious. This may be indicated symbolically by drawing a vertical line after the terms common to the various equations, as shown below.

$$
\begin{array}{cccc}
W = & & B + & CW \\
X = & A + & & WX \\
Y = & & CY & \\
Z = & F + EZ & &
\end{array}
$$

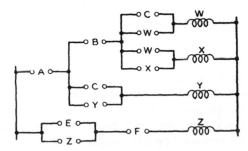

Figure 14. Example of reduction of simultaneous equations

It follows from the principle of duality that if we had defined multiplication to represent series connection, and addition for parallel connection, exactly the same theorems of manipulation would be obtained. There were two reasons for choosing the definitions given. First, as has been mentioned, it is easier to manipulate sums than products and the transformation just described can only be applied to sums (for constant-current relay circuits this condition is exactly reversed), and second, this choice makes the hindrance functions closely analogous to impedances. Under the alternative definitions they would be more similar to admittances, which are less commonly used.

Sometimes the relation $XY' = 0$ obtains between two relays X and Y. This is true if Y can operate only if X is operated. This frequently occurs in what is known as a sequential system. In a circuit of this type the relays can only operate in a certain order or sequence, the operation of one relay in general "preparing" the circuit so that the next in order can operate. If X precedes Y in the sequence and both are constrained to remain operated until the sequence is finished then this condition will be fulfilled. In such a case the following equations hold and may sometimes be used for simplification of expressions. If $XY' = 0$, then

$$X'Y' = Y',$$

$$XY = X,$$

$$X' + Y = 1,$$

$$X' + Y' = X',$$

$$X + Y = Y.$$

These may be proved by adding $XY' = 0$ to the left-hand member or multiplying it by $X' + Y = 1$, thus not changing the value. For example, to prove the first one, add XY' to $X'Y'$ and factor.

Special Types of Relays and Switches

In certain types of circuits it is necessary to preserve a definite sequential relation in the operation of the contacts of a relay. This is done with make-before-break (or continuity) and break-make (or transfer) contacts. In handling this type of circuit the simplest method seems to be to assume in setting up the equations that the make and break contacts operate simultaneously, and after all simplifications of the equations have been made and the resulting circuit drawn, the required type of contact sequence is found from inspection.

Relays having a time delay in operating or deoperating may be treated similarly or by shifting the time axis. Thus if a relay coil is connected to a battery through a hindrance X, and the relay has a delay of p seconds in operating and releasing, then the hindrance function of the contacts of the relay will also be X, but at a time p seconds later. This may be indicated by writing $X(t)$ for the hindrance in series with the relay, and $X(t - p)$ for that of the relay contacts.

There are many special types of relays and switches for particular purposes, such as the stepping switches and selector switches of various sorts, multiwinding relays, cross-bar switches, etc. The operation of all these types may be described with the words "or," "and," "if," "operated," and "not operated." This is a sufficient condition that they may be described in terms of hindrance functions with the operations of addition, multiplication, negation, and equality. Thus a two-winding relay might be so constructed that it is operated if the first *or* the second winding is operated (activated) and the first *and* the second windings are not operated. If the first winding is X and the second Y, the hindrance function of make contacts on the relay will then be $XY + X'Y'$. Usually, however, these special relays occur only at the end of a complex circuit and may be omitted entirely from the calculations to be added after the rest of the circuit is designed.

Sometimes a relay X is to operate when a circuit R closes and to remain closed independent of R until a circuit S opens. Such a circuit is known as a lock-in circuit. Its equation is:

$$X = RX + S .$$

Replacing X by X' gives:

$$X' = RX' + S$$

or

$$X = (R' + X)S' .$$

In this case X is *opened* when R closes and remains open until S opens.

IV. Synthesis of Networks

Some General Theorems on Networks and Functions

It has been shown that any function may be expanded in a series consisting of a sum of products, each product being of the form $X_1 X_2 ... X_n$ with some permutation of primes on the letters, and each product having the coefficient 0 or 1. Now since each of the n variables may or may not have a prime, there is a total of 2^n different products of this form. Similarly each product may have the coefficient 0 or the coefficient 1 so there are 2^{2^n} possible sums of this sort. Hence we have the theorem: The number of functions obtainable from n variables is 2^{2^n}.

Each of these sums will represent a different function, but some of the functions may actually involve fewer than n variables (that is, they are of such a form that for one or more of the n variables, say X_k, we have identically $f|_{X_k=0} = f|_{X_k=1}$ so that under no conditions does the value of the function depend on the value X_k). Thus for two variables, X and Y, among the 16 functions obtained will be $X, Y, X', Y', 0$, and 1 which do not involve both X and Y. To find the number of functions which actually involve all of the n variables we proceed as follows. Let $\phi(n)$ be the number. Then by the theorem just given:

$$2^{2^n} = \sum_{k=0}^{n} \binom{n}{k} \phi(k) ,$$

where $\binom{n}{k} = n!/k!(n-k)!$ is the number of combinations of n things taken k at a time. That is, the total number of functions obtainable from n variables is equal to the sum of the numbers of those functions obtainable from each possible selection of variables from these n which actually involve all the variables in the selection. Solving for $\phi(n)$ gives

$$\phi(n) = 2^{2^n} - \sum_{k=0}^{n-1} \binom{n}{k} \phi(k) .$$

By substituting for $\phi(n-1)$ on the right the similar expression found by replacing n by $n-1$ in this equation, then similarly substituting for $\phi(n-2)$ in the expression thus obtained, etc., an equation may be obtained involving only $\phi(n)$. This equation may then be simplified to the form

$$\phi(n) = \sum_{k=0}^{n} \binom{n}{k} 2^{2^k} (-1)^{n-k} .$$

As n increases this expression approaches its leading term 2^{2^n} asymptotically. The error in using only this term for $n = 5$ is less than 0.01 percent.

We shall now determine those functions of n variables which require the most relay contacts to realize, and find the number of contacts required. In order to do this, it is necessary to define a function of two variables known as the sum modulo two or disjunct of the variables. This function is written $X_1 \oplus X_2$ and is defined by the equation:

$$X_1 \oplus X_2 = X_1 X_2' + X_1' X_2 .$$

It is easy to show that the sum modulo two obeys the commutative, associative, and the distributive law with respect to multiplication, that is,

$$X_1 \oplus X_2 = X_2 \oplus X_1 ,$$

$$(X_1 \oplus X_2) \oplus X_3 = X_1 \oplus (X_2 \oplus X_3) ,$$

$$X_1 (X_2 \oplus X_3) = X_1 X_2 \oplus X_1 X_3 .$$

Also

$$(X_1 \oplus X_2)' = X_1 \oplus X_2' = X_1' \oplus X_2 ,$$

$$X_1 \oplus 0 = X_1 ,$$

$$X_1 \oplus 1 = X_1' .$$

Since the sum modulo two obeys the associative law, we may omit parentheses in a sum of several terms without ambiguity. The sum modulo two of the n variables $X_1, X_2 \ldots X_n$ will for convenience be written:

$$X_1 \oplus X_2 \oplus X_3 \ldots \oplus X_n = \overset{n}{\underset{k=1}{\Xi}} X_k .$$

Theorem:[*] The two functions of n variables which require the most elements (relay contacts) in a series-parallel realization are $\overset{n}{\underset{1}{\Xi}} X_k$ and $(\overset{n}{\underset{1}{\Xi}} X_k)'$, each of which requires $(3 \cdot 2^{n-1} - 2)$ elements.

This will be proved by mathematical induction. First note that it is true for $n = 2$. There are ten functions involving two variables, namely, XY, $X + Y$, $X'Y$, $X' + Y$, XY', $X + Y'$, $X'Y'$, $X' + Y'$, $XY' + X'Y$, $XY + X'Y'$. All of these but the last two require two elements; the last two require four elements and are $X \oplus Y$ and $(X \oplus Y)'$, respectively. Thus the theorem is true for $n = 2$. Now assuming it true for $n - 1$, we shall prove it true for n and thus complete the induction. Any function of n variables may be expanded about the nth variable as follows:

$$f(X_1, X_2 \ldots X_n) = f = X_n f(X_1 \ldots X_{n-1}, 1) + X_n' f(X_1 \ldots X_{n-1}, 0) . \tag{19}$$

Now the terms $f(X_1 \ldots X_{n-1}, 1)$ and $f(X_1 \ldots X_{n-1}, 0)$ are functions of $n - 1$ variables and if they individually require the most elements for $n - 1$ variables, then f will require the most elements for n variables, providing there is no other method of writing f so that fewer elements are required. We have assumed that the most elements for $n - 1$ variables are required by $\overset{n-1}{\underset{1}{\Xi}} X_k$ and its negative. If we, therefore, substitute for $f(X_1 \ldots X_{n-1}, 1)$ the function $\overset{n-1}{\underset{1}{\Xi}} X_k$ and for $f(X_1 \ldots X_{n-1}, 0)$ the function $(\overset{n-1}{\underset{1}{\Xi}} X_k)'$ we find

---

[*] See the Notes to this paper.

$$f = X_n \overset{n-1}{\underset{1}{\Xi}} X_k + X_n'(\overset{n-1}{\underset{1}{\Xi}} X_k)' = (\overset{n}{\underset{1}{\Xi}}X_k)' .$$

From the symmetry of this function there is no other way of expanding which will reduce the number of elements. If the functions are substituted in the other order we get

$$f = X_n(\overset{n-1}{\underset{1}{\Xi}} X_k)' + X_n' \overset{n-1}{\underset{1}{\Xi}} X_k = \overset{n}{\underset{1}{\Xi}}X_k .$$

This completes the proof that these functions require the most elements.

To show that each requires $(3 \cdot 2^{n-1} - 2)$ elements, let the number of elements required be denoted by $s(n)$. Then from (19) we get the difference equation

$$s(n) = 2s(n-1) + 2 ,$$

with $s(2) = 4$. This is linear, with constant coefficients, and may be solved by the usual methods. The solution is

$$s(n) = 3 \cdot 2^{n-1} - 2 ,$$

as may easily be verified by substituting in the difference equation and boundary condition.

Note that the above only applies to a series-parallel realization. In a later section it will be shown that the function $\overset{n}{\underset{1}{\Xi}}X_k$ and its negative may be realized with $4(n-1)$ elements using a more general type of circuit. The function requiring the most elements using any type of circuit has not as yet been determined.

Dual Networks

The negative of any network may be found by De Morgan's theorem, but the network must first be transformed into an equivalent series-parallel circuit (unless it is already of this type). A theorem will be developed with which the negative of any planar two-terminal circuit may be found directly. As a corollary a method of finding a constant-current circuit equivalent to a given constant-voltage circuit and vice versa will be given.

Let N represent a planar network of hindrances, with the function X_{ab} between the terminals a and b which are on the outer edge of the network. For definiteness consider the network of Figure 15 (here the hindrances are shown merely as lines).

Now let M represent the dual of N as found by the following process; for each contour or mesh of N assign a node or junction point of M. For each element of N, say X_k, separating the contours r and s there corresponds an element X_k' connecting the nodes r and s of M. The area exterior to N is to be considered as two meshes, c and d, corresponding to nodes c and d of M. Thus the dual of Figure 15 is the network of Figure 16.

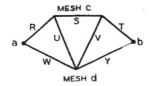

Figure 15 (left). Planar network for illustration of duality theorem

Figure 16 (right). Dual of figure 15

Theorem: If M and N bear this duality relationship, then $X_{ab} = X'_{cd}$. To prove this, let the network M be superimposed upon N, the nodes of M within the corresponding meshes of N and corresponding elements crossing. For the network of Figure 15, this is shown in Figure 17 with N solid and M dotted. Incidentally, the easiest method of finding the dual of a network (whether of this type or an impedance network) is to draw the required network superimposed on the given network. Now, if $X_{ab} = 0$, then there must be some path from a to b along the lines of N such that every element on this path equals zero. But this path represents a path *across* M dividing the circuit from c to d along which every element of M is one. Hence $X_{cd} = 1$. Similarly, if $X_{cd} = 0$, then $X_{ab} = 1$, and it follows that $X_{ab} = X'_{cd}$.

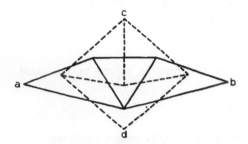

Figure 17. Superposition of a network and its dual

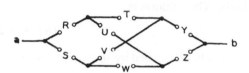

Figure 18. Nonplanar network

It is evident from this theorem that a negative for any planar network may be realized with the same number of elements as the given network.[†]

In a constant-voltage relay system all the relays are in parallel across the line. To open a relay a series connection is opened. The general constant-voltage system is shown in Figure 19. In a constant-current system the relays are all in series in the line. To de-operate a relay it is short-circuited. The general constant-current circuit corresponding to Figure 19 is shown in Figure 20. If the relay Y_k of Figure 20 is to be operated whenever the relay X_k of Figure 19 is operated and not otherwise, then evidently the hindrance in parallel with Y_k which short-circuits it must be the negative of the hindrance in series with X_k which connects it across the voltage source. If this is true for all the relays, we shall say that the constant-current and constant-voltage systems are equivalent. The above theorem may be used to find equivalent circuits of this sort, for if we make the networks N and M of Figures 19 and 20 duals in the sense described, with X_k and Y_k as corresponding elements, then the condition will be satisfied. A simple example of this is shown in Figures 21 and 22.

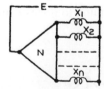

Figure 19 (left). General constant-voltage relay circuit

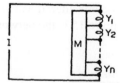

Figure 20 (right). General constant-current relay circuit

[†] This is not in general true if the word "planar" is omitted. The nonplanar network X_{ab}, of Figure 18, for example, has no negative containing only eight elements.

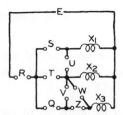

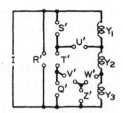

Figure 21 (left). Simple constant-voltage system

Figure 22 (right). Constant-current system equivalent to figure 21

Synthesis of the General Symmetric Function

It has been shown that any function represents explicitly a series-parallel circuit. The series-parallel realization may require more elements, however, than some other network representing the same function. In this section a method will be given for finding a circuit representing a certain type of function which in general is much more economical of elements than the best series-parallel circuit. This type of function is known as a symmetric function and appears frequently in relay circuits.

Definition: A function of the n variables $X_1, X_2 \ldots X_n$ is said to be symmetric in these variables if any interchange of the variables leaves the function identically the same. Thus $XY + XZ + YZ$ is symmetric in the variables X, Y, and Z. Since any permutation of variables may be obtained by successive interchanges of two variables, a necessary and sufficient condition that a function be symmetric is that any interchange of two variables leaves the function unaltered.

By proper selection of the variables many apparently unsymmetric functions may be made symmetric. For example, $XY'Z + X'YZ + X'Y'Z'$ although not symmetric in X, Y, and Z is symmetric in X, Y, and Z'. It is also sometimes possible to write an unsymmetric function as a symmetric function multiplied by a simple term or added to a simple term. In such a case the symmetric part may be realized with the methods to be described, and the additional term supplied as a series or parallel connection.

The following theorem forms the basis of the method of design which has been developed.

Theorem: A necessary and sufficient condition that a function be symmetric is that it may be specified by stating a set of numbers $a_1, a_2 \ldots a_k$ such that if exactly $a_j (j = 1,2,3 \ldots,)$ of the variables are zero, then the function is zero and not otherwise. This follows easily from the definition. The set of numbers $a_1, a_2 \ldots a_k$ may be any set of numbers selected from the numbers 0 to n inclusive, where n is the number of variables in the symmetric function. For convenience, they will be called the a-numbers of the function. The symmetric function $XY + XZ + YZ$ has the a-numbers 2 and 3, since the function is zero if just two of the variables are zero or if three are zero, but not if none or if one is zero. To find the a-numbers of a given symmetric function it is merely necessary to evaluate the function with $0, 1 \ldots n$ of the variables zero. Those numbers for which the result is zero are the a-numbers of the function.

Theorem: There are 2^{n+1} symmetric functions of n variables. This follows from the fact that there are $n + 1$ numbers, each of which may be taken or not in our selection of a-numbers. Two of the functions are trivial, however, namely, those in which all and one of the numbers are taken. These give the "functions" 0 and 1, respectively. The symmetric function of the n variables $X_1, X_2 \ldots X_n$ with the a-numbers $a_1, a_2 \ldots a_k$ will be written $S_{a_1 a_2 \ldots a_k}$ $(X_1, X_2, \ldots, X_n)$. Thus the example given would be $S_{23}(X,Y,Z)$. The circuit which has been developed for realizing the general symmetric function is based on the a-numbers of the function and we shall now assume that they are known.

Theorem: The sum of two given symmetric functions of the same set of variables is a symmetric function of these variables having for a-numbers those numbers common to the two given functions. Thus $S_{1,2,3}(X_1...X_6) + S_{2,3,5}(X_1...X_6) = S_{2,3}(X_1...X_6)$.

Theorem: The product of two given symmetric functions of the same set of variables is a symmetric function of these variables with all the numbers appearing in either or both of the given functions for a-numbers. Thus $S_{1,2,3}(X_1...X_6) \cdot S_{2,3,5}(X_1...X_6) = S_{1,2,3,5}(X_1...X_6)$.

To prove these theorems, note that a product is zero if either factor is zero, while a sum is zero only if both terms are zero.

Theorem: The negative of a symmetric function of n variables is a symmetric function of these variables having for a-numbers all the numbers from 0 to n inclusive which are not in the a-numbers of the given function. Thus $S'_{2,3,5}(X_1...X_6) = S_{0,1,4,6}(X_1...X_6)$.

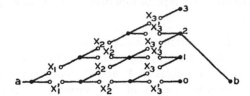

Figure 23.   Circuit for realizing $S_2(X_1, X_2, X_3)$

Before considering the synthesis of the general symmetric function $S_{a_1 a_2 ... a_k}$ $(X_1, X_2, \ldots, X_n)$ a simple example will be given. Suppose the function $S_2(X_1, X_2, X_3)$ is to be realized. This means that we must construct a circuit which will be closed when any two of the variables X_1, X_2, X_3 are zero, but open if none, or one or three are zero. A circuit for this purpose is shown in Figure 23. This circuit may be divided into three bays, one for each variable, and four levels marked 0, 1, 2 and 3 at the right. The terminal b is connected to the levels corresponding to the a-numbers of the required function, in this case to the level marked 2. The line coming in at a first encounters a pair of hindrances X_1 and X'_1. If $X_1 = 0$, the line is switched up to the level marked 1, meaning that one of the variables is zero; if not it stays at the same level. Next we come to hindrances X_2 and X'_2. If $X_2 = 0$, the line is switched up a level; if not, it stays at the same level. X_3 has a similar effect. Finally reaching the right-hand set of terminals, the line has been switched up to a level equal to the total number of variables which are zero. Since terminal b is connected to the level marked 2, the circuit $a - b$ will be completed if and only if 2 of the variables are zero. If $S_{0,3}(X_1, X_2, X_3)$ had been desired, terminal b would be connected to both levels 0 and 3. In Figure 23 certain of the elements are evidently superfluous. The circuit may be simplified to the form of Figure 24.

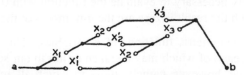

Figure 24.   Simplification of figure 23

For the general function exactly the same method is followed. Using the general circuit for n variables of Figure 25, the terminal b is connected to the levels corresponding to the a-

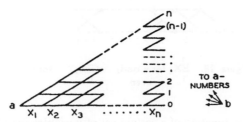

Figure 25. Circuit for realizing the general symmetric function $S_{a_1 a_2 \ldots a_k}(X_1, X_2, \ldots X_n)$

numbers of the desired symmetric function. In Figure 25 the hindrances are respected merely by lines, and the letters are omitted from the circuit, but the hindrance of each line may easily be seen by generalizing Figure 23. After terminal b is connected, all superfluous elements may be deleted.

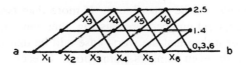

Figure 26. Circuit for $S_{0,3,6}(X_1 \ldots X_n)$ using the "shifting down" process

In certain cases it is possible to greatly simplify the circuit by shifting the levels down. Suppose the function $S_{0,3,6}(X_1 \ldots X_6)$ is desired. Instead of continuing the circuit up to the sixth level, we connect the second level back down to the zero level as shown in Figure 26. The zero level then also becomes the third level and the sixth level. With terminal b connected to this level, we have realized the function with a great savings of elements. Eliminating unnecessary elements the circuit of Figure 27 is obtained. This device is especially useful if the a-numbers form an arithmetic progression, although it can sometimes be applied in other cases.

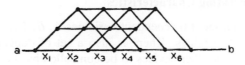

Figure 27. Simplification of figure 26

The functions $\overset{n}{\underset{1}{\Xi}} X_k$ and $(\overset{n}{\underset{1}{\Xi}} X_k)'$ which were shown to require the most elements for a series parallel realization have very simple circuits when developed in this manner. It can be easily shown that if n is even, then $\overset{n}{\underset{1}{\Xi}} X_k$ is the symmetric function with all the even numbers for a-numbers, if n is odd it has all the odd numbers for a-numbers. The function $(\overset{n}{\underset{1}{\Xi}} X_k)'$ is, of course, just the opposite. Using the shifting-down process the circuits are as shown in Figures 28 and 29. These circuits each require $4(n-1)$ elements. They will be recognized as the familiar circuit for controlling a light from n points, using $(n-2)$ double-pole double-throw switches and two single-pole double-throw switches. If at any one of the points the position of the switch is changed, the total number of variables which equal zero is changed by one, so that if the light is on, it will be turned off and if already off, it will be turned on.

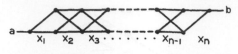

Figure 28. $\displaystyle\mathop{\Xi}_{1}^{n}X_k$ for n odd; $\displaystyle\left(\mathop{\Xi}_{1}^{n}X_k\right)'$ for n even

More than one symmetric function of a certain set of variables may be realized with just one circuit of the form of Figure 25, providing the different functions have no a-numbers in common. If there are common a-numbers the levels may be shifted down, or an extra relay may be added so that one circuit is still sufficient.

The general network of Figure 25 contains $n(n+1)$ elements. We will show that for any given selection of a-numbers, at least n of the elements will be superfluous. Each number from 1 to $n-1$ inclusive which is not in the set of a-numbers produces two unnecessary elements; 0 or n missing will produce one unnecessary element. However, if two of the a-numbers differ by only one, then two elements will be superfluous. If more than two of the a-numbers are adjacent, or if two or more adjacent numbers are missing, then more than one element apiece will be superfluous. It is evident then that the worst case will be that in which the a-numbers are all the odd numbers or all the even numbers from 0 to n. In each of these cases it is easily seen that n of the elements will be superfluous. In these cases the shifting down process may be used if $n > 2$ so that the maximum of n^2 elements will be needed only for the four particular functions X, X', $X \oplus Y$, and $(X \oplus Y)'$.

Figure 29. $\displaystyle\left(\mathop{\Xi}_{1}^{n}X_k\right)$ for n even; $\displaystyle\left(\mathop{\Xi}_{1}^{n}X_k\right)'$ for n odd

Equations From Given Operating Characteristics

In general, there is a certain set of independent variables A, B, C... which may be switches, externally operated or protective relays. There is also a set of dependent variables x, y, z... which represent relays, motors or other devices to be controlled by the circuit. It is required to find a network which gives, for each possible combination of values of the independent variables, the correct values for all the dependent variables. The following principles give the general method of solution.

1.   Additional dependent variables must be introduced for each added phase of operation of a sequential system. Thus if it is desired to construct a system which operates in three steps, two additional variables must be introduced to represent the beginning of the last two steps. These additional variables may represent contacts on a stepping switch or relays which lock in sequentially. Similarly each required time delay will require a new variable, representing a time delay relay of some sort. Other forms of relays which may be necessary will usually be obvious from the nature of the problem.

2.   The hindrance equations for each of the dependent variables should now be written down. These functions may involve any of the variables, dependent or independent, including the variable whose function is being determined (as, for example, in a lock-in circuit). The

Table II.   Relation of Operating Characteristics and Equations

Symbol	In Terms of Operation	In Terms of Nonoperation
X	The switch or relay X is operated	The switch or relay X is not operated
$=$	If	If
X'	The switch or relay X is not operated	The switch or relay X is operated
$\cdot$	Or	And
$+$	And	Or
$(--)'$	The circuit $(--)$ is not closed, or apply De Morgan's theorem	The circuit $(--)$ is closed, or apply De Morgan's theorem
$X(t-p)$	X has been operated for at least p seconds	X has been open for at least p seconds

If the dependent variable appears in its own defining function (as in a lock-in circuit) strict adherence to the above leads to confusing sentences.   In such cases the following equivalents should be used.

$X = RX + S$	X is operated when R is closed (providing S is closed) and remains so independent of R until S opens	
$X = (R' + X)S'$		X is opened when R is closed (providing S is closed) and remains so independent of R until S opens

In using this table it is usually best to write the function under consideration either as a sum of pure products or as a product of pure sums.   In the case of a sum of products the characteristics should be defined in terms of nonoperation; for a product of sums in terms of operation.   If this is not done it is difficult to give implicit and explicit parentheses the proper significance.

conditions may be either conditions for operation or for nonoperation.   Equations are written from operating characteristics according to Table II.   To illustrate the use of this table suppose a relay U is to operate if x is operated and y or z is operated and v or w or z is not operated.   The expression for A will be

$$U = x + yz + v'w'z' \;.$$

Lock-in relay equations have already been discussed.   It does not, of course, matter if the same conditions are put in the expression more than once — all superfluous material will disappear in the final simplification.

3.   The expressions for the various dependent variables should next be simplified as much as possible by means of the theorems on manipulation of these quantities.   Just how much this can be done depends somewhat on the ingenuity of the designer.

4.   The resulting circuit should now be drawn.   Any necessary additions dictated by practical considerations such as current-carrying ability, sequence of contact operation, etc., should be made.

V.   Illustrative Examples

In this section several problems will be solved with the methods which have been developed.   The examples are intended more to illustrate the use of the calculus in actual problems and to show the versatility of relay and switching circuits than to describe practical devices.

It is possible to perform complex mathematical operations by means of relay circuits. Numbers may be represented by the positions of relays or stepping switches, and interconnections between sets of relays can be made to represent various mathematical operations. In fact, any operation that can be completely described in a finite number of steps using the words "if," "or," "and," etc. (see Table II), can be done automatically with relays. The last example is an illustration of a mathematical operation accomplished with relays.

A Selective Circuit

A relay U is to operate when any one, any three or when all four of the relays w, x, y and z are operated but not when none or two are operated. The hindrance function for U will evidently be:

$$U = wxyz + w'x'yz + w'xy'z + w'xyz' + wx'y'z + wx'yz' + wxy'z' \; .$$

Reducing to the simplest series-parallel form:

$$U = w[x(yz + y'z') + x'(y'z + yz')] + w'[x(y'z + yz') + x'yz] \; .$$

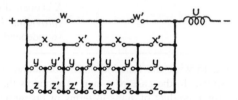

**Figure 30. Series-parallel realization of
selective circuit**

This circuit is shown in Figure 30. It requires 20 elements. However, using the symmetric-function method, we may write for U:

$$U = S_{1,3,4}(w,x,y,z) \; .$$

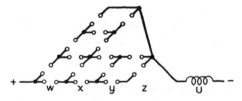

**Figure 31. Selective circuit from symmetric-
function method**

This circuit (Figure 31) contains only 15 elements. A still further reduction may be made with the following device. First write

$$U' = S_{0,2}(w,x,y,z) \; .$$

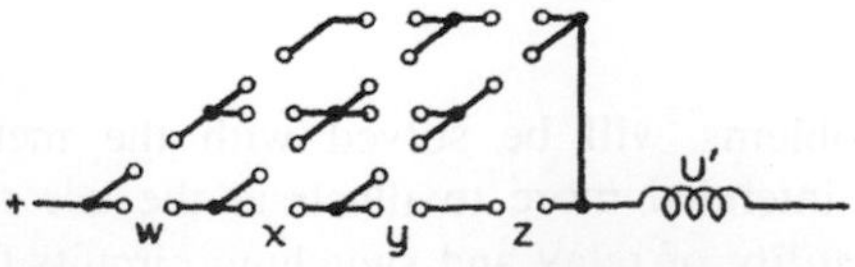

**Figure 32. Negative of selective circuit from
symmetric-function method**

This has the circuit of Figure 32. What is required is the negative of this function. This is a planar network and we may apply the theorem on the dual of a network, thus obtaining the circuit shown in Figure 33. This contains 14 elements and is probably the most economical circuit of any sort.

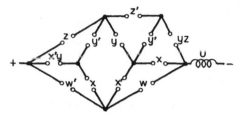

Figure 33.   Dual of figure 32

Design of an Electric Combination Lock

An electric lock is to be constructed with the following characteristics. There are to be five pushbutton switches available on the front of the lock. These will be labeled a, b, c, d, e. To operate the lock the buttons must be pressed in the following order: c, b, a and c simultaneously, d. When operated in this sequence the lock is to unlock, but if any button is pressed incorrectly an alarm U is to operate. To relock the system a switch g must be operated. To release the alarm once it has started a switch h must be operated. This being a sequential system either a stepping switch or additional sequential relays are required. Using sequential relays let them be denoted by w, x, y and z corresponding respectively to the correct sequence of operating the push buttons. An additional time-delay relay is also required due to the third step in the operation. Obviously, even in correct operation a and c cannot be pressed at exactly the same time, but if only one is pressed and held down the alarm should operate. Therefore assume an auxiliary time delay relay v which will operate if either a or c alone is pressed at the end of step 2 and held down longer than time s, the delay of the relay.

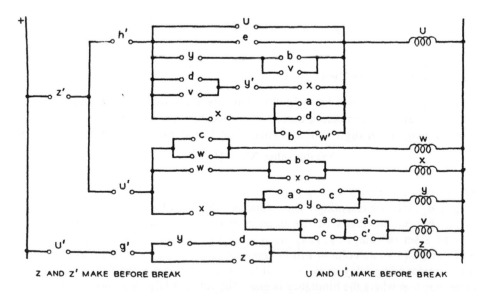

Z AND Z′ MAKE BEFORE BREAK   U AND U′ MAKE BEFORE BREAK

Figure 34.   Combination-lock circuit

When z has operated the lock unlocks and at this point let all the other relays drop out of the circuit. The equations of the system may be written down immediately:

$$w = cw + z' + U' ,$$

$$x = bx + w + z' + U' ,$$

$$y = (a + c)y + x + z' + U' ,$$

$$z = z(d + y) + g' + U' ,$$

$$v = x + ac + a'c' + z' + U' ,$$

$$U = e(w' + abd)(w + x' + ad)[x + y' + dv(t - s)][y + bv(t - s)]U + h' + z' .$$

These expressions can be simplified considerably, first by combining the second and third factors in the first term of U, and then by factoring out the common terms of the several functions. The final simplified form is as below: This corresponds to the circuit of Figure 34.

$$
\begin{aligned}
U = &\quad h' + e[ad(b + w') + x'] \cdot \\
&\quad (x + y' + dv)(y + vb)U \\
w = &\quad cw \\
x = Z' + &\quad bx + w \\
y = \quad U' + &\quad (a + c)y \\
&\quad x + \\
v = &\quad ac + a'c'
\end{aligned}
$$

$$z = g' + (y + d)z + U'$$

Electric Adder to the Base Two

A circuit is to be designed that will automatically add two numbers, using only relays and switches. Although any numbering base could be used the circuit is greatly simplified by using the scale of two. Each digit is thus either 0 or 1; the number whose digits in order are $a_k, a_{k-1}, a_{k-2}, \ldots a_2, a_1, a_0$ has the value $\sum_{j=0}^{k} a_j 2^j$.

Let the two numbers which are to be added be represented by a series of switches: $a_k, a_{k-1}, \ldots a_1, a_0$ representing the various digits of one of the numbers and $b_k, b_{k-1}, \ldots b_1, b_0$ the digits of the other number. The sum will be represented by the positions of a set of relays $s_{k+1}, s_k, s_{k-1} \ldots s_1, s_0$. A number which is carried to the jth column from the $(j-1)$th column will be represented by a relay c_j. If the value of any digit is zero, the corresponding relay or switch will be taken to be in the position of zero hindrance; if one, in the position where the hindrance is one. The actual addition is shown below:

c_{k+1}	c_k	$c_{j+1}c_j$	c_2c_1	Carried numbers
	a_k---$a_{j+1}a_j$---$a_2a_1a_0$			First number
	b_k $b_{j+1}b_j$ $b_2b_1b_0$			Second number

| c_{k+1} | s_k---$s_{j+1}s_j$---s_2,s_1s_0 | | | Sum |

or

s_{k+1}

Starting from the right, s_0 is one if a_0 is one and b_0 is zero or if a_0 is zero and b_0 one but not otherwise. Hence

$$s_0 = a_0 b_0' + a_0' b_0 = a_0 \oplus b_0 \ .$$

c_1 is one if both a_0 and b_0 are one but not otherwise:

$$c_1 = a_0 \cdot b_0 \ .$$

s_j is one if just one of a_j, b_j, c_j is one, or if all three are one:

$$s_j = S_{1,3}(a_j, b_j, c_j) \ , \quad j = 1, 2, ...k \ .$$

c_{j+1} is one if two or if three of these variables are one:

$$c_{j+1} = S_{2,3}(a_j, b_j, c_j) \ , \quad j = 1, 2, ...k \ .$$

Using the method of symmetric functions, and shifting down for s_j gives the circuits of Figure 35. Eliminating superfluous elements we arrive at Figure 36.

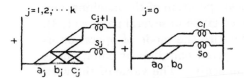

Figure 35.   Circuits for electric adder

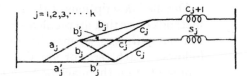

Figure 36.   Simplification of figure 35

References

1. A complete bibliography of the literature of symbolic logic is given in the *Journal of Symbolic Logic*, volume 1, number 4, December 1936. Those elementary parts of the theory that are useful in connection with relay circuits are well treated in the two following references.

2. The Algebra of Logic, **Louis Cauturat.** The Open Court Publishing Company.

3. Universal Algebra, **A. N. Whitehead.** Cambridge, at the University Press, volume I, book III, chapters I and II, pages 35-42.

4. **E. V. Huntington,** *Transactions* of the American Mathematical Society, volume 35, 1933, pages 274-304. The postulates referred to are the fourth set, given on page 280.

MATHEMATICAL THEORY OF THE DIFFERENTIAL ANALYZER

By Claude E. Shannon

Introduction

The Differential Analyzer is a machine developed at the Massachusetts Institute of Technology under the direction of Dr. V. Bush for the purpose of obtaining numerical solutions to ordinary differential equations. The fundamental principles underlying the Differential Analyzer were first conceived by Lord Kelvin, but at the time it was impossible, due to mechanical difficulties, to construct a machine of the type he contemplated. The same principles were discovered independently by Dr. Bush and his associates, and the first Differential Analyzer was completed in 1931. The inherent mechanical difficulties were overcome by means of several ingenious devices such as the torque amplifiers, and backlash correcting units, and through improved machine working technique. Since that time, several other machines have been built in various parts of the world, and have been used in solving many problems arising in engineering, physics and other branches of science.

Detailed descriptions of the mechanical operation of the machine, and methods of setting up problems have been given in several papers (1, 3). For our purposes we may briefly summarize the mode of operation as follows. Each term or variable in the given equation or equations is represented on the machine by a certain shaft. The value of the variable at any instant is proportional to the number of revolutions of the corresponding shaft from some fixed position. These shafts are interconnected by means of mechanical units which enforce certain mathematical relations between the number of turns of the interconnected shafts. The most important mechanical units are of four types;[1] gear boxes, adders, integrators and input tables. With these units, each

---

[1] Some other special units have been developed. The Differential Analyzer at M.I.T. has a multiplying table for obtaining the product of two terms, and the one at Manchester has a unit useful in solving mixed difference differential equations. These, however, are much less important than those mentioned above; the multiplying table, in fact, can always be replaced by two integrators and an adder as will be shown later.

Reprinted from JOURNAL OF MATHEMATICS AND PHYSICS
Vol. XX, No. 4, December, 1941

relation implied by the given equations is forced to hold between the corresponding shafts. For example, if in the differential equation the sum of two terms is equal to a third term, the corresponding shafts on the Analyzer are connected by an adding unit. If the terms x, y and dy/dx appear in the equation, the corresponding shafts would be interconnected through an integrator to enforce the relation $y = \int dy/dx\, dx$, etc. When the shaft representing the independent variable is turned, all other shafts are therefore constrained to turn in accordance with the equation. Thus, a numerical solution may be obtained by counting the number of turns of the dependent variable shaft corresponding to equal increments of the independent variable and plotting the result as a curve, or the machine may be set up to plot its own curves automatically by means of a special output table.

When the Differential Analyzer was first built it was thought that all functional relationships between terms of the equation being solved would have to be introduced into the machine by means of input tables. However, in connection with a problem in ballistics in which the function x^2 was desired, it was noted that by connecting an integrator to perform the operation $2\int_0^x x\, dx$, the function could be obtained without an input table. Soon it was found that practically all the important simple functions could be "generated" using only integrators and adders. This is done by setting up an auxiliary equation on the Analyzer whose solution is the desired function. In a thesis written in 1932, J. Guerrieri (2) describes interconnections for generating most of the elementary functions.

In this paper the mathematical aspects of the Differential Analyzer will be considered. The most important results deal with conditions under which functions of one or more variables can be generated, and conditions under which ordinary differential equations can be solved. Some attention will also be given to approximation of functions (which cannot be generated exactly), approximation of gear ratios, and automatic speed control.

We shall assume throughout that all ordinary differential equations considered have unique solutions and that formal processes of differentiation, integration, etc. are valid in the region of interest. For total differential equations it is not necessary that the equations be integrable but we assume that a solution exists along any curve in the region. The reason for this will appear later.

The Differential Analyzer will be idealized by assuming that we have available an unlimited number of each of the following perfect units.

1. *Integrators.* Given two shafts u and v, the integrator constrains a third shaft w to rotate in accordance with $w = \int_{v_0}^{v} (u + a)\, dv$, where a is an arbitrary constant, for all variations of u and v. In actual integrators the maximum value of $|u + a|$ is limited, but by changing scale factors it can be made as great as desired so that except for poles of u the integration can be performed. The constant a is the initial setting of the integrator.

2. *Adders.* Given two shafts u and v, an adder constrains a third shaft w to turn as $(u + v)$, for all variations of u and v. Except for backlash and tooth ripple, the actual differential adder units fulfill these conditions. It is easily seen that any interconnection of adders with free shafts $X_1 \cdots X_n$, Y, will enforce a relation $Y = \sum_{k=1}^{w} a_k X_k$ where the a's are real constants, and for convenience we will speak of such an interconnection as an adder. By connecting simple adders in series we can make all the a's unity and get $Y = \sum_{k=1}^{n} X_k$.

3. *Input Tables or Function Units.* Given a shaft x, an input table constrains a second shaft y to rotate as $y = f(x)$, where $f(x)$ is an arbitrary given function with only a finite number of finite discontinuities.

4. *Gear Boxes.* Given a shaft x, a gear box of ratio k forces a second shaft to rotate as kx. Since by making the integrand u identically zero in the integrator we get $w = av$, the gear boxes are theoretically superfluous, being used for purposes of economy. Therefore, we will not consider gear boxes, except to show that any ratio k may be approximated using only two sizes of gear pairs.

Finally, we assume that each of the above elements is capable of performing its particular constraint if and only if there is not more than one source of drive to each shaft. By a source of drive is meant any one of the following: the independent variable shaft, the w shaft of an integrator, the w shaft of an adder (or Y in the general sense), the $f(x)$ shaft of an input table, or the kx shaft of a gear box. This condition is extremely important in making Differential Analyzer setups. It places a restriction on possible interconnections of units, and forms the basis of the present analysis.

We shall say that we can solve a system of ordinary differential equati ns with independent variable x and dependent variables $y_1 \cdots y_n$ if and only if a setup can be found using the above elements and satisfying the source of drive assumption, such that when the independent variable shaft x is turned, shafts $y_1 \cdots y_n$ are constrained to turn in accordance with the equations for any given initial conditions. We shall say a system of total differential equations can be solved if a set of connections can be found such that when a set of independent variable shafts $x_1 \cdots x_m$ are turned in any manner whatever, dependent variable shafts $y_1 \cdots y_n$ are constrained to turn in accordance with the equations for arbitrary given initial conditions. In most of the theorems we shall consider setups containing only integrators and adders.

Fundamental Solvability Condition

THEOREM I. A necessary and sufficient condition that a system of ordinary differential equations can be solved using only integrators and adders is that they can be written in the form

$$\frac{dy_k}{dy_1} = \sum_{i,j=0}^{n} a_{ijk} y_i \frac{dy_j}{dy_1} \qquad k = 2, 3 \cdots n \qquad (1)$$

where $y_0 = 1$ (introduced to make notation compact), y_1 is the inde pendent variable, and $y_2 \cdots y_n$ are dependent variables, among which are the dependent variables of the original system.

Proof. The condition is necessary. Suppose the original system can be solved using only integrators and adders. The dependent variable must appear either as the output of adders or integrators. They may all be considered as the outputs of integrators by making those from adders the variables of integration of integrators with constant unit integrand. Now let there be $(n - 1)$ integrators and let the outputs be labeled $y_2 \cdots y_n$. Each displacement (integrand) must be driven by one of three possible sources: the independent variable y_1, the output of an integrator, or the output of an adder (general sense). An adder must be driven by the sum of certain of the y's including possibly y_1. These are all special cases of a source of drive of the form $\sum_{i=1}^{N} b_{ik} y_i$ for the kth integrator, where the b's are constants. The b's can obviously represent gear ratios or complex adder interconnections, or without loss of generality we may take them equal to 0 or 1. The kth integrator may have an initial displacement in addition to its source of drive value. Let this be b_{0k}. Then the kth integrator will have an integrand $\sum_{i=0}^{n} b_{ik} y_i$ where for convenience we introduce $y_0 = 1$. By exactly the same argument the variables of integration of the integrators will be of the form $\sum_{j=1}^{n} c_{jk}y_j$. The integrators place the following constraints on the system:

$$y_k = \int \sum_i b_{ik}y_i \, d \sum_j c_{jk}y_j \qquad\qquad k = 2, 3 \cdots n \qquad (2)$$

$$= \int \sum_i b_{ik}y_i \sum_j c_{jk} \, dy_j \qquad\qquad k = 2, 3 \cdots n \qquad (3)$$

$$= \int \sum_{i,j} a_{ijk}y_i \, dy_j \qquad\qquad k = 2, 3 \cdots n \qquad (4)$$

where $a_{ijk} = b_{ik}c_{jk}$. Now differentiating both sides with respect to y_1:

$$\frac{dy_k}{dy_1} = \sum_{i,j} a_{ijk}y_i \frac{dy_j}{dy_1} \qquad\qquad k = 2, 3 \cdots n \qquad (1)$$

These are the equations (1).

The condition is sufficient. This is true since the system (1) can be integrated to the form (4) and these represent a setup using only integrators and adders with not more than one source of drive to each shaft.

Generation of Functions

We will say that a function of a single variable $y = f(x)$ can be generated if there is a setup using only integrators and adders such that a shaft may be turned independently as x and a second shaft is forced to turn as y. It follows from Theorem I that if $f(x)$ can be generated there must exist a set of equations (1) such that if $y_1 = x$, then y_2 (say) is equal to $f(x)$. A function of n variables $F(x_1 \cdots x_n)$ can be generated if there is a setup such that n shafts $x_1 \cdots x_n$ can be turned independently and another will turn as F.

Functions of a single variable have been classified in the following way. If there is a relation of the form:

$$y = a_0 + a_1x + a_2x^2 + \cdots a_mx^m \qquad (5)$$

where m is a positive integer and the a's are real constants then y is called a polynomial in x, or a rational integral function of x. If

$$y = \frac{F_1(x)}{F_2(x)} \qquad (1)$$

where F_1 and F_2 are polynomials in x, then we say y is a rational function of x. If we have:

$$R_0(x) + yR_1(x) + y^2R_2(x) + \cdots + y^nR_n(x) = 0 \qquad (7)$$

where $R_1 \cdots R_n$ are rational functions of x, then y is said to be an algebraic function of x. If there is no relation of this form then y is called a transcendental function of x. Transcendental functions may be divided into two classes. If there is a differential equation of the form:

$$\sum_j A_j x^{n_j} y^{n_{0j}} (y')^{n_{1j}} (y'')^{n_{2j}} \cdots (y^{(m)})^{n_{mj}} = 0 \qquad (8)$$

where $y^{(k)} = d^k y/dx^k$, the A's are constants, and the powers are integral, (i.e., if a polynomial in x, y, $y' \cdots y^{(m)}$ vanishes identically) then y is said to be an algebraic transcendental function of x. If no relation of this type exists the function is called hypertranscendental, or trans-

TABLE I

Functions of One Variable

Transcendental		Algebraic	
Hypertran-scendental	Algebraic-transcendental	Irrational Algebraic	Rational	
Gamma function. Zeta function.	Exponential and logarithmic. Trigonometric and hyperbolic and inverses. Bessel functions. Elliptic functions and integrals. Probability function.	x^m, m a rational fraction. Solutions of an algebraic equation in terms of a parameter.	Quotients of poly-nomials.	Integral a, x, X^2 etc. poly-nomials.

cendentally-transcendental. Obviously all algebraic functions are non-hypertranscendental, since by multiplying (7) by all denominators and differentiating we obtain an expression of the form (8). In fact only a very few of the common analytic functions are hypertranscendental, the best known being the Gamma function and Riemann's Zeta function. $\left(\Gamma(n) = \int_0^\infty x^{n-1} e^{-x} \, dx; \; \xi(s) = \sum_{k=0}^\infty \frac{1}{k^s} \right)$. The first was shown to be hypertranscendental by Holden, and the last by Hilbert. The classification of some of the common functions is given in Table I.

THEOREM II. A function of one variable can be generated if and only if the function is not hypertranscendental.

Proof. First we will show that if a function can be generated, it is not hypertranscendental. Any function $f(x)$ that can be generated must satisfy a set of equations of the form (1), with $y_1 = x$ and $y_2 = f(x)$. If we differentiate (1) $(n - 2)$ times we will have a total of $(n - 1)^2$ equations, from which we may eliminate the $n^2 - 2n$ variables

$$y_3, y_3', \cdots y_3^{(n-1)}; y_4, y_4', \cdots y_4^{(n-1)}; \cdots; y_n, y_n', \cdots y_n^{(n-1)}$$

for example by Sylvester's method, involving only multiplication and addition and therefore resulting in a relation of the form (8), with $x = y_1$, $y = y_2$, and $1 = y_0$.

To prove that any non-hypertranscendental function can be generated, we will show that (8) can be written in the form (1). Let the left member of (8) be ϕ. Differentiating both sides with respect to x we obtain:

$$\frac{\partial \phi}{\partial x} + \frac{\partial \phi}{\partial y} y' + \frac{\partial \phi}{\partial y'} y'' + \cdots + \frac{\partial \phi}{\partial y^{(m)}} y^{(m+1)} = 0$$

And except for points where $\frac{\partial \phi}{\partial y^{(m)}} = 0$ we have:

$$y^{(m+1)} = \frac{\dfrac{\partial \phi}{\partial x} + \dfrac{\partial \phi}{\partial y} y' + \cdots + \dfrac{\partial \phi}{\partial y^{(m-1)}} y^{(m)}}{\dfrac{\partial \phi}{\partial y^{(m)}}} = \frac{P_1(x, y, y' \cdots y^{(m)})}{P_2(x, y, y' \cdots y^{(m)})}$$

where P_1 and P_2 are polynomials in x, y, y', $y'' \cdots y^{(m)}$. Let $y_1 = x$, $y_2 = y$, $y_3 = y'$, $\cdots y_{m+3} = y^{(m+1)}$. Then we have

$$\frac{dy_k}{dy_1} = y_{k+1} \qquad k = 2, 3, \cdots (m + 2)$$

with the additional condition that

$$y_{(m+3)} = \frac{P_1(y_1, y_2 \cdots y_{(m+2)})}{P_2(y_1, y_2 \cdots y_{m+2})}$$

The problem now is to reduce this relation to the form of equations (1). First consider the function P_1. This is a sum of products of the variables $y_1 \cdots y_{m+3}$. (Since the powers are integral they may be considered as products of a repeated factor). Let the first term of the numerator be $u_1 u_2 \cdots u_s$, where the u's are certain of the y's. Now let

$$\frac{dy_{m+4}}{dy_1} = u_1 \frac{du_2}{dy_1} + u_2 \frac{du_1}{dy_1}$$

so that $y_{m+4} = u_1 u_2$. Next let:

$$\frac{dy_{m+5}}{dy_1} = u_3 \frac{dy_{m+4}}{dy_1} + y_{m+4} \frac{du_3}{dy_1}$$

Hence $y_{m+5} = y_{m+4} \cdot u_3 = u_1 u_2 u_3$. Continuing in this manner we finally get $y_{m+s+2} = u_1 u_2 \cdots u_s$. Each term in the numerator and denominator is treated in exactly the same way, continuing the series of equations until there is a y for each product of P_1 and P_2. Let the y's corresponding to the terms of P_1 be v_1, $v_2 \cdots v_r$ and those corresponding to the terms of P_2 be w_1, $w_2 \cdots w_t$. Then we have reduced the equation (12) to the condition that:

$$y_{m+3} = \sum_1^r v_k / \sum_1^t w_k.$$

Our final step is to reduce this relation to the form of the equations (1). Suppose the last y, w_t, was $y_{\varrho-1}$. Let:

$$\frac{dy_\varrho}{dy_1} = - y_{\varrho+1} \frac{d \sum w}{dy_1}$$

$$\frac{dy_{\varrho+1}}{dy_1} = 2y_\varrho \frac{dy_\varrho}{dy_1}$$

Consequently $y_\varrho = 1/\sum w$. Now by making:

$$\frac{dy_{m+3}}{dy_1} = y_\varrho \frac{d \sum v}{dy_1} + \sum v \frac{dy_\varrho}{dy_1}$$

we get $y_{m+3} = \sum v / \sum w$ and have reduced (8) to the form (1).

THEOREM III. If a function of one variable $y = f(x)$ can be generated, then its derivative $z = f'(x)$, its integral $w = \int_a^x f(x)\, dx$, and its inverse $x = f^{-1}(y)$ can be generated.

Proof. To prove the first part, take the derivative of (8). This gives two equations between which we may eliminate y with processes involving only multiplication and addition, thus resulting in a relation of the form (8) with y missing. Replacing y' by z, y'' by z' etc., shows that z is non-hypertranscendental if y is.

To show the second part, merely replace y by w', y' by w'' etc. in (8), thus obtaining another relation of this form. Therefore if y is non-hypertranscendental, then w is.

For the third part replace y' by $1/x'$ (where $x' = dx/dy$) y'' by

$-x''/(x')^3$ etc. Since all the derivatives of y may be expressed as quotients of polynomials in the derivatives of x, we may reduce the resulting expression to the form (8) with x and y interchanged by multiplying by all denominators. That is, the inverse of a non-hypertranscendental function is non-hypertranscendental.

THEOREM IV. If two functions f and g can both be generated, then the functional product $y = f(g(x))$ can be generated.

Proof. This will be shown by writing two systems of equations, each of the form (1) as a single larger system of the same form. Suppose g satisfies a set of this type with $y_1 = x$ and $y_2 = g$, k running from 2 to n. Now f also satisfies a system of this type and since the argument of f is g we replace y_1 in this system by y_2 and let the y subscripts in the f system run from $n + 1$ to $n + m$ (m being the number of equations in the f system.) Thus we have a group of equations of the form (1) with $y_1 = x$ and $y_{m+2} = f(g(x))$.

Although, as Theorem II shows, the only functions which can be generated exactly are non-hypertranscendental, we can approximate a much broader class of functions, using only integrators.

THEOREM V. Any function $f(x)$, which is continuous in a closed interval $a \leq x \leq b$, can be generated in this interval to within any prescribed allowable error $\epsilon > 0$ using only a finite number of integrators. That is, a setup can be found generating a function $F(x)$ such that

$$| F(x) - f(x) | < \epsilon$$

for $a \leq x \leq b$.

Proof. We base our demonstration on Weierstrass' famous theorem which states that any such function $f(x)$ can be approximated by a polynomial $F(x)$ of degree n

$$F(x) = \sum_{k=0}^{n} a_k x^k$$

by taking n sufficiently large. Now let:

$$\frac{dy_j}{dy_1} = a_j j! + y_{j+1} \qquad \begin{matrix} j = 2, 3 \cdots n \\ y_{m+1} = 0 \end{matrix}$$

Then this system, of the form (1), satisfies (19) if we let $y_1 = x$ and $y_2 = F(x)$. Moreover, this setup requires only integrators, the additive constants being merely initial integrator settings. Hence the theorem. If we allow stopping the machine and turning shafts ahead by hand, we can obviously broaden the conditions of Theorem V to all functions continuous except for a finite number of finite discontinuities.

We now proceed to generalize some of these concepts and theorems to functions of more than one variable.

THEOREM VI. A function of m variables $y_{m+1} = f(y_1 \cdots y_m)$ can be generated if and only if it satisfies a set of total differential equations of the form:

$$dy_k = \sum_{i,j=0}^{n} a_{ijk} y_i dy_j \qquad k = (m+1), (m+2) \cdots {}^n \qquad (10)$$

where $y_0 = 1$ and the a's are real constants.

The proof follows exactly the same plan as was used in proving Theorem I, both for necessity and sufficiency. A solution of equations (1) has been shown to be a non-hypertranscendental function of one variable. Now (21) can be considered as a generalization of (1), and we will say that a function of m variables satisfying a set of equations (1) is a non-hypertranscendental function of these m variables. With this definition we have, as a generalization of Theorem II, the proposition that a function of m variables can be generated if and only if it is not hypertranscendental in these variables. Obviously a necessary condition for a function of m variables to be non-hypertranscendental is that it be non-hypertranscendental in each single variable when all the others are replaced by arbitrary constants. Thus $x + \Gamma(y)$ is a hypertranscendental function of x and y since replacing x by 0 gives the hypertranscendental function of one variable $\Gamma(y)$. Some functions of more than one variable that are not-hypertranscendental are $x + y$, $x \cdot y$, x^y, $\log_x y$, and combinations of these and non-hypertranscendental functions of one variable.

As a generalization of Theorem IV we state the proposition:

THEOREM VII. If two functions of several variables, $f(x_1 \cdots x_n)$ and $g(y_1 \cdots y_m)$ can both be generated, then it is possible to generate any functional product, for example $\phi(x_2, x_3 \cdots x_n, y_1, y_2 \cdots y_m) = f(g, x_2, \cdots x_n)$.

This may be proved by the same method as Theorem IV, combining the two systems of equations into a single larger system of the type (10).

Theorem V may also be generalized for functions of more than one variable, but integrators alone are no longer sufficient:

THEOREM VIII. Given any function of n variables $f(x_1 \cdots x_n)$, continuous in all variables in a closed region of n-space $a_k \leqq x_k \leqq b_k$, $k = 1, 2 \cdots n$, we can generate a function $F(x_1 \cdots x_n)$ using only a finite

number of integrators and adders such that within the region
$a_k \leqq x_k \leqq b_k$

$$|f - F| < \epsilon$$

where ϵ is an arbitrarily small prescribed positive number.

Proof. A generalization of Weierstrass' theorem states that we may approximate f in the manner described with a polynomial F in the variables $x_1, \cdots x_n$. Since a polynomial is a non-hypertranscendental function according to our definition, it can be generated with integrators and adders and hence we have the theorem.

The first part of Theorem III can be generalized for functions of more than one variable as follows.

THEOREM IX. If a function of m variables $f(x_1 \cdots x_n)$ can be generated its partial derivative with respect to any one variable, say x_1 can be generated.

Proof. From theorem VI, if a function can be generated it satisfies a set of equations of the form

$$dy_1 = \sum_{j=1}^{m} A_{ij} dx_i + \sum_{j=1}^{m} B_{ij} dy_j \qquad i = 1, 2 \cdots s$$

where $x_1 \cdots x_m$ are the independent variables, $y_1 \cdots y_s$ are dependent variables, the A's and B's are linear forms in the variables, and y_1 (say) is equal to f. Dividing these equations by dx_1 and setting $0 = dx_2 = dx_3 = \cdots = dx_m$ we have:

$$\frac{\partial y_1}{\partial x_1} = A_{i1} + \sum_{j=1}^{s} B_{ij} \frac{\partial y_j}{\partial x_1} \qquad i = 1, 2 \cdots s$$

or

$$\sum_{j=1}^{s} (B_{ij} - \delta_{ij}) \frac{\partial y_j}{\partial x_1} = A_{i1} \qquad i = 1, 2 \cdots s.$$

Solving for $\dfrac{\partial y_1}{\partial x_1}$ by Cramer's rule:

$$\frac{\partial y_1}{\partial x_1} = \frac{\begin{vmatrix} A_{11} & B_{12} & \cdots & B_{1s} \\ A_{21} & B_{22} & \cdots & B_{2s} \\ \cdots & \cdots & \cdots & \cdots \\ A_{31} & B_{32} & & B_{ss} \end{vmatrix}}{|B_{ij} - \delta_{ij}|} = \frac{P_1}{P_2}$$

where P_1 and P_2 are polynomials in the variables. This equation may be reduced to the form of equations (10) by exactly the same method as was used in reducing equation (9) which was of the same form.

The last part of Theorem III can also be generalized as follows:

THEOREM X. If a function of n variables $y = f(x_1 \cdots x_n)$ can be generated, its inverse with respect to any one variable $x_1 = F(y, x_2 \cdots x_n)$ can be generated.

Proof. Taking the total differential of y we have:

$$dy = \sum_{i=1}^{s} f'_{x_i} \, dx_i .$$

Hence:

$$dx_1 = 1/f'_{x_1} \left(dy - \sum_{i=2}^{s} f'_{x_i} \, dx_i \right).$$

Or:

$$x_1 = \int 1/f'_{x_1} \, dy = \sum_{i=1}^{s} \int f'_{x_i}/f'_{x_1} \, dx_i$$

Now since f could be generated the terms f'_{x_i} $(i = 1, 2, \cdots n)$ can be generated by the preceding theorem. Reciprocals and quotients are not hypertranscendental and therefore the terms $1/f_{x_1}$ and $-f_{x_i}/f_{x_1}$ can be generated. It follows then that x_1 can be obtained by generating these integrands, integrating with respect to the proper variables and adding the results.

Systems of Equations

We are now in a position to prove the following general theorem on the differential analyzer:

THEOREM XI. The most general system of ordinary differential equations:

$$f_k(x; y_1, y'_1 \cdots y_1^{(m)}; \quad y_2, y'_2 \cdots y_2^{(m)} \cdots y_n, y'_n \cdots y_n^{(n)}) = 0$$
$$k = 1, 2, \cdots n \tag{11}$$

of the mth order in n dependent variables can be solved on a differential analyzer using only a finite number of integrators and adders providing the functions f_k are combinations of non-hypertranscendental functions of the variables.

Before proving this it is necessary to demonstrate a preliminary lemma. The natural procedure would be to solve the equation $f_1 = 0$ for $y_1^{(m)}$, $f_2 = 0$ for $y_2^{(m)}$ etc:

$$y_k^{(m)} = \phi_k(x; y_1, y_1' \cdots y_1^m; y_2 y_2' \cdots y_2^{(n)} \cdots y_n y_n' \cdots y_n^{(m)}).$$

It may happen, however, that $y_1^{(m)}$ does not appear in f_m but does appear in some other of the functions. We will first show that by taking derivatives of the equations (11) and rearranging the order, an equivalent system can be found in which the highest ordered derivative of y_1 appearing in the first equation is not exceeded in any of the other equations, the highest ordered derivative of y_2 appearing in the second equation is not exceeded in any of the others, etc.

First note that if f_k be considered a function of the independent variables $(x, y_1, y_1', \cdots y_1^{(m)}, y_2, y_2', \cdots y_2^{(m)}, \cdots y_n, y_n', \cdots y_n^m)$ then taking the derivative of $f_k = 0$ gives an equivalent equation (providing the boundary conditions are adjusted in accord with the original equation) in which the highest ordered derivative of each variable appearing has been increased by one. Also, if the original function f_k involved no hypertranscendental functions, then by Theorem IX the derived function will not, and can be generated.

For our present purposes the essential part of equations (11) is the set of values of the highest ordered derivatives of the different variables appearing in these equations. These may be tabulated in a square array as follows:

	y_1	y_2	$\cdots$	y_n
f_1	a_{11}	a_{12}	$\cdots$	a_{1n}
f_2	a_{21}	a_{22}	$\cdots$	a_{2n}
f_3	a_{31}	a_{32}	$\cdots$	a_{3n}
$\cdots$	$\cdots$	$\cdots$	$\cdots$	$\cdots$
$\cdots$	$\cdots$	$\cdots$	$\cdots$	$\cdots$
f_n	a_{n1}	a_{n2}	$\cdots$	a_{nn}

where a_{jk} is the order of the highest ordered derivative of y_k appearing in function f_j. These a's are integers which may have values from 0 to m, or if the variable does not appear at all, we may give the a a special symbol λ. Taking the derivative of f_k has the effect of adding unity to each element of the kth row except for λ's which remain the same. Two rows of the array may be interchanged since this merely means renumbering the functions. We propose to show that by rearrangement and taking derivatives we can always find a new system where a_{11} is not exceeded in the first column, a_{22} is not exceeded in the second column, and in general a_{kk} is not exceeded in the kth column.

This will be shown by mathematical induction. We will first show it to be true for $n = 2$. For two variables we have the array:

	y_1	y_2
f_1	a_{11}	a_{12}
f_2	a_{21}	a_{22}

If more than one of the letters is λ the system is degenerate. If one of the letters, say a_{11} is λ we may interchange the rows and then differentiate the second row until the new $a_{22} \geqq a_{12}$. If none of the letters are λ then either $a_{22} = a_{12}$ or one is smaller. If they are equal the rows may be interchanged if necessary to make $a_{11} \geqq a_{21}$. If one is smaller, let this row be differentiated until they are equal and proceed as before. Thus, the theorem is true for $n = 2$.

Now, assuming it true for n, we will show that it must then be true for $n + 1$, and thus complete the induction. By hypothesis then, given any $(n + 1)^2$ array, we can find an equivalent system by differentiating and rearranging the first n rows:

	y_1	y_2	$\cdots$	y_n	y_{n+1}
f_1	a_{11}	a_{12}	$\cdots$	a_{1n}	a_{1n+1}
f_2	a_{21}	a_{22}	$\cdots$	a_{2n}	a_{2n+1}
	$\cdots$	$\cdots$	$\cdots$	$\cdots$	$\cdots$
f_n	a_{n1}	a_{n2}	$\cdots$	a_{nn}	a_{nn+1}
f_{n+1}	a_{n+11}	a_{n+12}	$\cdots$	a_{n+1n}	$a_{n+1}a_{n+1}$

such that $a_{kk} \geqq a_{jk}$, $k, j = 1, 2 \cdots n$. We may also assume that $a_{kk} > a_{kn+1}$ for every $k \leqq n$, since, if not, we can make it so by differentiating all the first n functions simultaneously. Now two possibilities arise: (1) $a_{n+1,n+1} \geqq a_{j,n+1}$, $j = 1, 2 \cdots n$. In this case the system is satisfactory as it stands. (2) If this condition does not obtain there must be some $a_{jn+1} > a_{n+1n+1}$. Suppose this is a_{1n}. Now let the last row be differentiated until one of the following three possibilities obtains: (1) $a_{n+1n+1} = a_{1n+1}$. In this case the system is satisfactory. (2) $a_{n+1,1} = a_{11}$. In this case interchange rows 1 and n and the system is satisfactory. (3) $a_{n+1s} = a_{ss}$ for one or more values of s between 1 and $n + 1$. In this case continue differentiating both equations s and $n + 1$ until one of the following three occurs: (1) $a_{n+1,n+1} =$

a_{1n+1} or $a_{n+11} = a_{11}$. Proceed as in (1) and (2) above. (2) $a_{s1} = a_{11}$ or $a_{sn+1} = a_{1n+1}$. Interchange rows s and $n + 1$ and proceed as in (1). (3) The maximum in some other column is reached by the corresponding elements in the rows being differentiated. In this case annex this row or rows to those already being differentiated and continue by the same method. It is easy to see that the process must converge after a finite number of steps since all the elements in the first and last columns except a_{11} and a_{1n+1} cannot be λ. This completes the induction.

It is now comparatively simple to prove Theorem XI. First find, by the method just described, a system equivalent to (11) in which the highest ordered derivative of y_k appearing in equation k is not exceeded in any of the other equations. Let this order be p_k. Now it has been shown that any combinations of non-hypertranscendental functions can be generated (Theorems IV and VII), and therefore the functions f_k can be generated. Hence by the theorem on inverse functions, (Theorem X) we can generate the functions

$$y_k^{(p_k)} = \psi_k(x, y_1, y_1' \cdots y_2, y_2' \cdots \cdots y_n, y_n' \cdots)$$

The variables $y_k^{(v)}$, $v < p_k$ may be obtained by integration of $y_k^{(p_k)}$ and it follows that the system may be solved using only integrators and adders.

Approximation of Factors with Gear Ratios

In setting up problems on a Differential Analyzer it is frequently necessary to introduce constant multiplying factors. This may be done in several ways. As was pointed out, an integrator set with a constant integrand k gives $w = \int_0^v k \, dv = kv$. A second method is to get a rough approximation to k by means of gears whose overall ratio is say k'. Another set of gears is used to get a rough approximation k'' to $(k - k')$ and the variable $k'x$ combined with $k''x$ through an adder to give a second order approximation to k. It is easy to show that proceeding in this way we can obtain a ratio t such that $|t - k| < \epsilon$ where ϵ is an arbitrarily small prescribed positive number, assuming only that we have an unlimited number of adders and of one size of gear pairs with ratio $a \neq 0, 1$. A third way to obtain the ratio k is by the use of gears only. We will now show that any ratio can be approximated using only a finite number of two sizes of gear pairs. More precisely we have

THEOREM XII. Given two gear ratios a and b, neither of which is zero or one, and such that b is not a rational power of a, we can find positive or negative integers u and v such that $0 \leq |a^u b^v - k| < \epsilon$ where ϵ is an arbitrarily small prescribed number.

Without loss of generality we take $a > 1$; for if not inverting the direction of the gears gives a ratio $1/a > 1$. It will first be shown that a ratio U may be obtained such that

$$1 < U < 1 + \delta$$

with δ arbitrarily small. To do this integers x and y must be found such that

$$1 < a^x b^y < 1 + \delta$$

Since $a > 1$, we may take logarithms to the base a leaving the inequalities in the same direction.

$$0 < x + y \log_a b < \log_a (1 + \delta) = \mu$$

Since $\log_a b$ is irrational we can satisfy this by well known theorems in diophantine approximation. Thus we can obtain the gear ratio U. If U is connected in tandem with itself r times with r so chosen that

$$U^{r-1} < k \leq U^r$$

then the difference between U^r and k will be less than δk and is therefore arbitrarily small.

If b is a rational power of a, say $a^{m/n} = b$ where m/n is rational in its lowest terms, then a necessary and sufficient condition that a ratio be obtainable is that it be of the form $a^{k/n}$ where k is any integer. First any ratio will be of the type $a^x b^y = a^{(xn+ym)/n}$ which is of this form. The sufficiency of the condition follows from the fact that the diophantine equation $xn + ym = k$ has a solution in integers for every integer k, if n and m are relatively prime.

Automatic Speed Control

An important part of the Differential Analyzer control circuit is the automatic speed control. The integrator outputs have a maximum speed s, beyond which slippage or vibration is apt to occur. To prevent exceeding this speed, the independent variable shaft might be turned at such a speed that only when the integrators are at maximum displacement is this speed attained. However, with such a system the solution would take a longer time than necessary, for during most of the solution none of the integrators would be at maximum displacement. The automatic speed control is a device which makes the independent variable turn at such a speed that the integrator which is turning fastest is going at the speed s. By the use of some rather broad assumptions it is possible to get a rough estimate of the time saved by this method. The results of this theorem were compared with several experimental solutions and the error was in all cases less than 7%.

THEOREM XIII. If the displacements of n integrators driven by the independent variable with maximum speed s and integrating factor b are assumed random with respect to the independent variable between limits of $-a$ and $+a$, and if the speed is limited only by these and the independent variable x with a maximum speed of r, then the expected average speed of the independent variable will be:

$$\bar{\dot{x}} = \frac{1}{[nab/x(n+1)s] + [1/r(n+1)] \cdot [(s/abr)^n]}$$

Proof:

$$\bar{\dot{x}} = \frac{\displaystyle\int_{x=0}^{x=u} dx}{\displaystyle\int_{x=0}^{x=u} dt}$$

Where u is the maximum value of x and t the time. Now since $dt = \dfrac{dx}{dx/dt}$ we have:

$$\bar{\dot{x}} = \frac{u}{\displaystyle\int_0^u dt/dx \cdot dx}$$

If we let y be the displacement of the integrator with the largest displacement, then the probability that this is between y and $y + dy$ is:

$$n(y/a)^{n-1} \, dy/a$$

The expected number of revolutions of x in this condition will then be:

$$dx = n(y/a)^{n-1} u \, dy/a$$

If $y \leqq s/br$, the speed will be limited by the independent variable, and dx/dt will be r. If $y > s/br$ the speed will be limited by the integrators and dx/dt will be x/yb. For the first case:

$$dt = un/r(y/a)^{n-1} \, dy/a.$$

For the second case:

$$dt = yb/snu(y/a)^{n-1}\, dy/a.$$

Therefore:

$$\bar{\dot{x}} = \frac{u}{\displaystyle\int_{y=0}^{y=\frac{s}{br}} \frac{un}{a\bar{r}} \left(\frac{y}{a}\right)^{n-1} dy + \int_{y=\frac{s}{br}}^{y=a} \frac{bnu}{s} \left(\frac{y}{a}\right)^{h} dy}$$

Or

$$\bar{\dot{x}} = \frac{1}{\dfrac{nab}{(n+1)s} + \dfrac{1}{r(n+1)} \left(\dfrac{s}{abr}\right)^{n}}$$

COROLLARY. If the maximum speed of the independent variable be made infinite, the solution time will be reduced in the ratio of $n/(n+1)$ to what it would be if x were given a fixed speed $v = s/ab$ so that at maximum displacement the integrators just reached the maximum allowable speed.

This follows from the general expression by allowing r to approach infinity.

REFERENCES

(1) Bush, V., "The Differential Analyzer, A New Machine for Solving Differential Equations," *Journal of the Franklin Institute*, v. 212, p. 447, (1931).
(2) Guerrieri, J., "Methods of Introducing Functional Relations Automatically on the Differential Analyzer," S. M. Thesis, M.I.T., (1932).
(3) Hartree, D. R., "The Mechanical Integration of Differential Equations," *The Mathematical Gazette*, v. XXII, p. 342, (1938).

The Theory and Design of
Linear Differential Equation Machines*

Claude E. Shannon

Table of Contents

1. Introduction

This report deals with the general theory of machines constructed from the following five types of mechanical elements.

(1) Integrators. An integrator has three emergent shafts w, x, and y and is so constructed that if x and y are turned in any manner whatever, the w shaft turns according to

---

*   Report to National Defense Research Council, January, 1942.

$$w = A \int_0^x (y+\alpha)\,dx$$

or

$$\frac{dw}{dx} = A(y+\alpha) \tag{1}$$

where α is the displacement of the integrator at $x=0$, and A is the "integrating factor" of the integrator. We idealize the integrators by assuming that unlimited displacements are possible; actually for (1) it is necessary that $|y| \le R$, the radius of the disk. We further only consider machines in which all integrator disks turn at a constant speed, so that (1) reduces to

$$\frac{d}{dt}\,w = pw = y+\alpha, \tag{2}$$

in which p is the Heaviside operator,[1,2] and we have assumed without loss of generality that t is measured in such units as to make the coefficient A unity. Another way of eliminating the coefficient is to replace an integrator with the coefficient A by one with coefficient 1 (i.e., satisfying (2)) having a gear of ratio A in the output. For our purposes, then, we can consider an integrator as having two shafts, w and y; with y, except for a constant, the time derivative of w. Integrators, as ordinarily constructed, cannot be operated backwards. If we attempt to turn the w shaft arbitrarily, the integrator will slip or break down in some way, and y will not turn in such a manner as to satisfy (2).

(2) Adders or differential gears. An adder has three shafts x, y, and z and enforces the relation

$$x + y + z = 0 \tag{3}$$

to obtain between the numbers of revolutions of the shafts from the starting positions. If n adders are connected in series with (-1) gears in between we have what may be called a "compound" adder with $n+2$ emergent shafts constrained by

$$x_1 + x_2 + \cdots + x_{n+2} = 0. \tag{4}$$

The word "adder" alone always means a simple three-shaft adder.

(3) Gear boxes. A gear box has two emergent shafts related by

$$x = ky \tag{5}$$

with k real and non-vanishing. With ordinary gears k must of course be rational, but with rack and pinion gears or lead screws, as are often used on the input to integrators, this is not necessary; and for engineering purposes we waive this condition completely and assume any real non-vanishing ratio is possible since any ratio can be approximated as closely as desired.

(4) Shaft Junctions. Junctions have three emergent shafts related by

$$x = y = z. \tag{6}$$

Compound junctions are also used, equating the positions of n shafts.

----

[1] For all numbered references see the Bibliography.

(5) Shafts.

A machine hereafter means any interconnection of a finite number of the first four types of elements by means of the fifth. Symbols for the different elements are shown in Figure 1.[*]

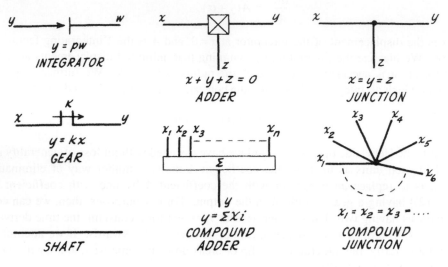

FIG 1 SYMBOLS FOR ELEMENTS

We will consider the following basic problems in connection with these machines:

1. The problem of analysis. Given a certain machine, what are its characteristics? An arbitrary interconnection of machine elements will not, in general, operate satisfactorily. We shall classify the various types of "degeneracies" that can occur and find a method for determining easily whether or not a given machine is degenerate. Any non-degenerate machine is characterized by a set of transfer admittances and a method will be given for rapidly determining these.

2. The problem of synthesis. Given a possible transfer admittance, methods will be developed for designing machines which realize this function, and which require the minimum number of elements.

3. General network theory. The basic mathematical properties of machines will be studied, leading to a network theory not unlike some parts of electrical circuit theory. The two most important results in this direction are the orientation theorem and the duality theorems (Theorems V, XXII and XXIII).

Particular attention will be given to "two-shaft" machines, that is machines having one input shaft e and one output shaft y, these being the only types of machines that have as yet found much use.

---

[*] The adder, shaft and junction symbols are more or less standard in fire control work; the others are slight modifications of a notation developed at the Massachusetts Institute of Technology for use with the differential analyzer.[3]

In another paper[4] the writer has considered a more general problem of this type, namely what can be done if the constant disk speed restriction is removed. The results obtained there, however, were chiefly in the form of existence theorems, and throw no light on questions of the most economical design. We may mention in passing that under the weaker conditions of the former study, it was shown that any system of ordinary or total differential equations not involving hypertranscendental functions can be realized.

Limiting our treatment to machines constructed of the five elements listed has much the same effect as limiting electric circuit theory to inductance, resistance, and capacitance networks and can be justified on the same grounds in the two cases. Only by such a limitation is it possible to achieve anything like a complete mathematical treatment. If we allow the integrator disks to be driven at variable rates (e.g., by the outputs of other integrators) or allow the use of cams and non-circular gears, linearity disappears and we must be satisfied with little more than existence theorems, or solutions in the neighborhood of a point. Furthermore, machines actually in use usually satisfy our conditions, except for elements which may be segregated from the remainder of the device and analyzed separately.

Machines of the type we are considering find constant application in fire control equipment as rate finders, predictors, smoothers, etc., and are also used in other types of control systems and calculating devices.

For precision of statement and easy reference, our results are given mainly in the form of mathematical theorems. The proofs, however, have been placed in the appendix, except for a few which contain methods of procedure essential for the use of the theorems. Examples are given to illustrate almost all general results, and if these are carefully studied the significance and application of the theorems should be clear.

2. Machines without Integrators

In this section we will study the properties of machines containing no integrators; and in the next section apply this analysis to machines containing integrators, by separating the integrators from the remainder of the machines. The reason behind this procedure is that the integrators are essentially unilateral* – we cannot turn the output and expect the input to be its time derivative, and this fact necessitates a special treatment.

A general machine without integrators is indicated in Fig. 2. On the left are P "driving" or "power" shafts and on the right D "driven" shafts. The difference is so far purely subjective; we are considering the possibilities of the machine, with the idea of turning $X_1, X_2, ..., X_P$ arbitrarily and determining if $X_{P+H+1}, ..., X_{P+H+D}$ turn satisfactorily. Inside the machine let us assume that there are A adders and J junctions and let there be H "internal" shafts (i.e., shafts not directly connected through gear boxes to the power or driven shafts), labeled X_{P+1}, $X_{P+2}, ..., X_{P+H}$. The scheme of labeling is indicated in Fig. 3; if two shafts are connected by a gear box of ratio K, they are assigned the same variable but one is K times the other, while all shafts not connected by gears are assigned different variables, except that all power and driven shafts are given different variables even if two are connected directly or through a gear box. These variables represent the positions in revolutions or radians of the shafts as measured from the starting position.

---

* In practice high ratios are also unilateral, but we idealize the situation here for mathematical reasons and assume all gears to be bilateral.

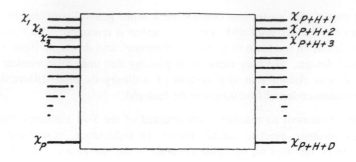

$$FIG\ 2$$

Let us suppose that there are T "through" shafts, such as $X_1 - X_7$, $X_4 - X_{11}$ and $X_{12} - X_{13}$ (Fig. 3) in the machine, connecting one external (power or driven) shaft to another without any intermediate adders or junctions. Each of these places a linear constraint on two of the X's. We may write the set of T constraints as follows:

$$\sum_{i=1}^{P+H+D} a_{ij} X_i = 0 \qquad j = 1, 2, ..., T \tag{7}$$

where all the a_{ij} in any one equation (j fixed) vanish except two.

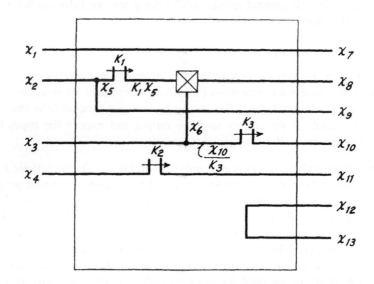

$$FIG.\ 3$$

The adders furnish a set of A constraints

$$\sum_{i=1}^{P+H+D} a_{ij} X_i = 0 \quad j=T+1,\, T+2,\, ...,\, T+A \tag{8}$$

with all but at most three of the a_{ij} in any one equation (j fixed) vanishing (actually less than three could be non-vanishing by having both ends of a single shaft connect to the same adder as in Fig. 4g).

Finally each of the J junctions provides two constraints giving a set of $2J$ equations.

$$\sum_{i=1}^{P+H+D} a_{ij} X_i = 0 \quad j=T+A+1,\, T+A+2,\, ...,\, T+A+2J \tag{9}$$

with at most two coefficients in each equation different from zero. Thus we have a total of $T+A+2J$ linear homogeneous equations relating the $P+H+D$ variables $X_1,\, X_2,\, ...,\, X_{P+H+D}$. The homogeneity of the system of equations follows from the assumption that we measure revolutions from the starting position. As these are the only constraints, the system of equations

$$\sum_{i=1}^{P+H+D} a_{ij} X_i = 0 \quad j=1,\, 2,\, ...,\, T+A+2J \tag{10}$$

completely describes the machine.

For the machine of Fig. 3, the equations are as follows:

$$
\begin{array}{l}
T \text{ eqns} \left[
\begin{array}{l}
X_1 \qquad\qquad\qquad\qquad -X_7 \qquad\qquad\qquad\qquad\qquad = 0 \\[2mm]
\qquad -K_2 X_4 \qquad\qquad\qquad\qquad +X_{11} \qquad\qquad\qquad = 0 \\[2mm]
\qquad\qquad\qquad\qquad\qquad\qquad\qquad\qquad X_{12} - X_{13} \ = 0
\end{array}
\right. \\[10mm]
A \text{ eqns} \left[
\begin{array}{l}
\qquad\qquad\qquad K_1 X_5 + X_6 \quad +X_8 \qquad\qquad\qquad\qquad = 0
\end{array}
\right. \\[10mm]
2J \text{ eqns} \left[
\begin{array}{l}
X_2 \qquad\qquad -X_5 \qquad\qquad\qquad\qquad\qquad\qquad = 0 \\[3mm]
X_2 \qquad\qquad\qquad\qquad\qquad -X_9 \qquad\qquad\qquad = 0 \\[3mm]
\qquad X_3 \qquad\qquad -X_6 \qquad\qquad\qquad\qquad\qquad = 0 \\[3mm]
\qquad X_3 \qquad\qquad\qquad\qquad\qquad -\dfrac{X_{10}}{K_3} \qquad = 0
\end{array}
\right.
\end{array} \tag{11}
$$

$$
\underbrace{\qquad\qquad}_{\substack{P=4 \\ \text{variables}}} \quad \underbrace{\qquad\qquad}_{\substack{H=2 \\ \text{variables}}} \quad \underbrace{\qquad\qquad\qquad}_{\substack{D=7 \\ \text{variables}}}
$$

Now suppose we try to operate the machine, i.e., to turn the P shafts arbitrarily and see if the D shafts turn satisfactorily. A number of possibilities may arise.

1. It may not be possible to turn the P shafts arbitrarily, that is, the machine may enforce a functional relation between these shafts. In this case we will say that the machine is "locked."

2. The positions of the D shafts may not be uniquely determined by the positions of the P shafts; one or more of them can be turned freely while the P shafts are held stationary. In this case we will say that the machine has "free driven shafts."

3. There may be internal shafts that can be turned freely while the P and D shafts are held stationary. These will be called "free internal shafts."

4. There may be shafts in the machine which are unnecessary in the sense that if broken the two ends are constrained by the machine to turn at the same speed when the P and D shafts are allowed to turn freely. Such a shaft will be called "redundant."

A machine with any of these four characteristics will be called "degenerate." Any of the four degeneracies may occur separately and all combinations are possible in a machine. The first two types of degeneracy are obviously unsatisfactory in a machine. The last two are undesirable on economic grounds, for we will show that any machine containing free internal shafts or redundant shafts has superfluous adders or junctions.

A number of examples of degenerate machines are shown in Fig. 4. The possible machine degeneracies are of course closely connected with degeneracies in the system of linear equations (10) describing the machine constraints; in locked machines the system (10) is inconsistent for certain sets of values of $X_1, ..., X_P$; in machines with redundant shafts, certain of the equations are superfluous; and in machines with free shafts, certain of the variables $X_{P+1}, ..., X_{P+H+D}$ are not uniquely determined by $X_1, ..., X_P$. Using the notation M_{H+D} for the matrix of the coefficients of $X_{P+1}, ..., X_{P+H+D}$; M_{P+H+D} for that of $X_1, ..., X_{P+H+D}$; and R_{H+D}, R_{P+H+D}, for the ranks of these matrices, the following theorem can be easily proved.*

Theorem I. A necessary and sufficient condition for non-degeneracy in a machine is that M_{H+D} be square and non-singular, or that

$$R_{P+H+D} = R_{H+D} = H + D = T + A + 2J, \tag{12}$$

the first two equalities being necessary and sufficient for no locked power shafts and no free shafts respectively; while if the first two are satisfied, the third equality is necessary and sufficient for no redundant shafts.

For example, the machine (a), Fig. 4, has the system of equations

$$X_1 \quad - X_3 = 0$$

$$X_2 - X_3 = 0 \tag{13}$$

so that

$$M_{H+D} = \left\| \begin{matrix} -1 \\ -1 \end{matrix} \right\| \tag{14}$$

which is not square, and the machine is degenerate. Also we note that

$$M_{P+H+D} = \left\| \begin{matrix} 1 & 0 & -1 \\ 0 & 1 & -1 \end{matrix} \right\| \tag{15}$$

whose rank is 2 while $R_{H+D} = 1$ so the machine is locked.

---

* See Appendix for proofs of this and succeeding theorems.

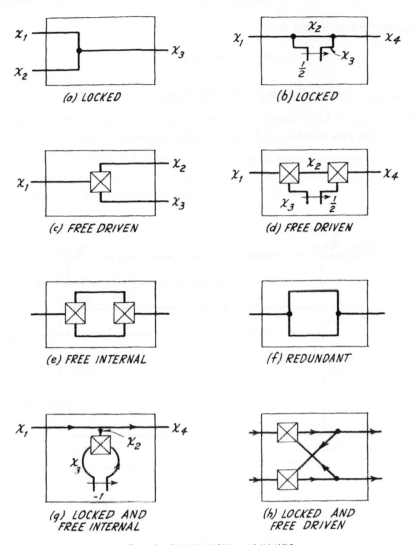

FIG. 4   DEGENERATE MACHINES

Theorem I is given more for mathematical background and for completeness than as a practical test of degeneracy. Later we will develop a rapid and simple method for determining whether or not a machine is degenerate.

The machine of Fig. 3 is easily seen to have the free driven shafts X_{12} and X_{13}. If these shafts are eliminated the machine is non-degenerate.

The first part of the following theorem is a simple consequence of Theorem I.

Theorem II. In a non-degenerate machine without integrators the driven and internal shafts are uniquely determined as linear homogeneous functions of the power shafts:

$$X_i = \sum_{j=1}^{P} b_{ij} X_j \qquad i = P+1, \ldots, P+H+D \tag{16}$$

with real coefficients b_{ij}. Conversely, it is possible to construct a machine realizing any system of D equations defining the *driven* shafts

$$X_i = \sum_{j=1}^{P} b_{ij} X_j \qquad i = P+H+1, \ldots, P+H+D \qquad (17)$$

as linear homogeneous functions of the power shafts with real coefficients.

This realization is, in fact, obtained with the network of Fig. 5, the long boxes being compound adders with gear ratios b_{ij} at the inputs to the adders as indicated.

Theorem II is the important result of this section; it states that in a non-degenerate machine the driven shafts are linear functions of the power shafts, and conversely given any set of such functions we can design a machine in which the power and driven shafts are related by these functions.

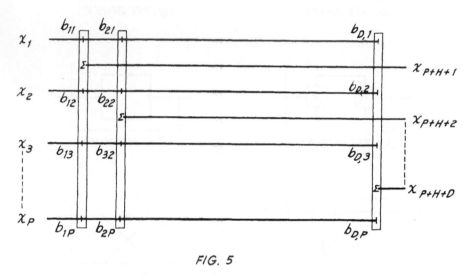

FIG. 5

3. Machines with Integrators

Now consider a machine with just n integrators, an input shaft e and output y, and any number of gears, adders and junctions. Separating the integrators from the remainder the machine will be as in Fig. 6, the box containing all adders, junctions and gears. This part in the box will be called the "integratorless" part of the machine. We will say that the machine is degenerate, contains redundant shafts, etc., if these statements are true of its integratorless part. It is clear that the power shafts of Fig. 6 being locked is unsatisfactory; at worst the machine would break down at some point (e.g., the integrators would be forced to slip), while at best (if the integrators happen to turn at such speeds as to satisfy the locking constraint) at least one integrator is superfluous. Similar considerations hold for the case of free driven shafts, justifying this extended use of the word degenerate.

Since the integrator displacements are the time derivatives of the corresponding outputs, and using the relations (16) we obtain for the equations of the system, assuming that at $t=0$ we suddenly start turning the e shaft according to $e(t)$:

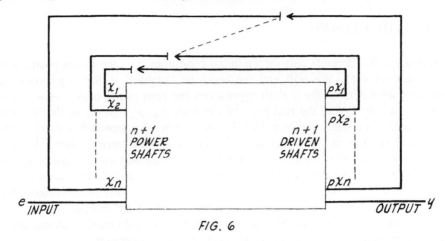

FIG. 6

$$p X_i = \sum_{j=1}^{n} b_{ij} X_j + b_{i,n+1} e + \alpha_i \, l(t), \quad i = 1, 2, ..., n \,,$$

$$y = \sum_{j=1}^{n} b_{n+1,j} X_j + b_{n+1,n+1} e \,, \tag{18}$$

where $\alpha_i = \dfrac{d}{dt} X_i \Big|_{t=0}$ is the initial displacement of integrator i, $l(t)$ is the Heaviside unit function, and $p = \dfrac{d}{dt}$ is the Heaviside operator.

Any non-degenerate machine with n integrators solves a system of equations of this type, and any system of equations of this type can be realized in a machine with n integrators, that is, given a set of equations of the form (18) we can design a machine placing these constraints and these only on the variables $X_1, X_2, ..., X_n, e, y$. The system (18) can be written

$$
\begin{aligned}
(b_{11}-p)X_1 + b_{12} X_2 &+ \cdots + b_{1n} X_n + b_{1,n+1} e + \alpha_1 l = 0 \\
b_{21} X_1 + (b_{22}-p)X_2 &+ \cdots + b_{2n} X_n + b_{2,n+1} e + \alpha_2 l = 0 \\
\cdots \quad\quad \cdots &\quad\quad \cdots \\
b_{n1} X_1 + b_{n2} X_2 &+ \cdots + (b_{n,n}-p)X_n + b_{n,n+1} e + \alpha_n l = 0 \\
b_{n+1,1} X_1 + b_{n+1,2} X_2 &+ \cdots + b_{n+1,n} X_n + b_{n+1,n+1} e + 0 = y \,.
\end{aligned}
\tag{19}
$$

Hence, by Cramer's rule, splitting the numerator determinant into a sum

$$
y(t) = \frac{
\begin{vmatrix}
(b_{11}-p) & b_{12} & \cdots & b_{1n} & b_{1,n+1} \\
b_{21} & (b_{22}-p) & \cdots & b_{2n} & b_{2,n+1} \\
\cdots & \cdots & \cdots\;\cdots & & \cdots \\
\cdots & \cdots & \cdots\;\cdots & & \cdots \\
b_{n,1} & b_{n2} & \cdots & (b_{nn}-p) & b_{n,n+1} \\
b_{n+1,1} & b_{n+1,2} & \cdots & b_{n+1,n} & b_{n+1,n+1}
\end{vmatrix} e(t) +
\begin{vmatrix}
b_{11}-p & \cdots & b_{1n} & \alpha_1 \\
b_{21} & \cdots & b_{2n} & \alpha_2 \\
\cdots & \cdots\;\cdots & & \cdots \\
\cdots & \cdots\;\cdots & & \cdots \\
b_{n1} & \cdots & b_{nn}-p & \alpha_n \\
b_{n+1,1} & \cdots & b_{n+1,n} & 0
\end{vmatrix} l(t)
}{
\begin{vmatrix}
b_{11}-p & b_{12} & \cdots & b_{1n} \\
b_{21} & b_{22}-p & \cdots & b_{2n} \\
\cdots & \cdots & \cdots\;\cdots \\
\cdots & \cdots & \cdots\;\cdots \\
b_{n1} & b_{n2} & \cdots & b_{nn}-p
\end{vmatrix}
}
\tag{20}
$$

$$= Y(p)\, e(t) + L(p)\, l(t) \ . \tag{21}$$

The term $L(p)\,l(t)$ depends only on the initial conditions, i.e., the initial positions α_i of the integrators, not on $e(t)$. We will call the machine "stable" if for any system of initial conditions and with $e(t)=0$ the y shaft approaches the zero position as $t \to \infty$. A sufficient condition for stability is that the real parts of the roots $p_1, p_2, ..., p_n$ of the denominator of (20) be negative.* In a stable machine the solution y eventually approaches $Y(p)\,e(t)$ no matter what the initial settings of the integrators. By analogy with electric circuit theory we call $L(p)\,l(t)$ the transient, $Y(p)\,e(t)$ the steady state and $Y(p)$ the admittance. Since we are chiefly concerned with stable machines in which the term $L(p)\,l(t)$ eventually disappears, we hereafter neglect this transient and consider only the function $Y(p)\,e(t)$. This is equivalent to assuming that the machine starts with all integrators set at the center of the disk, $\alpha_i =0$ ($i=1,2, ..., n$), for in that case the second term of (20) has a column of zeros and vanishes identically. In other words, from now on we consider an integrator as placing the constraint

$$y = p\, w$$

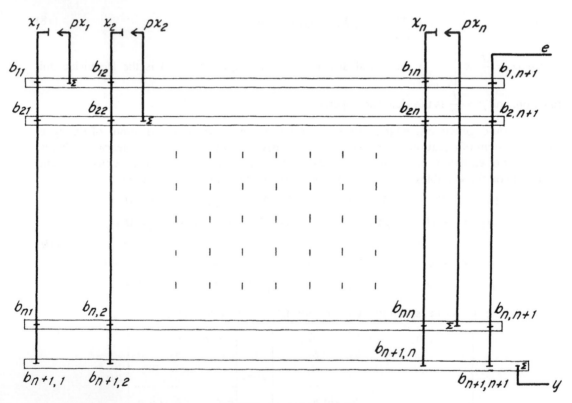

FIG. 7

---

* This is for practical purposes also a necessary condition. It only fails when parts of the machine are isolated in the sense that they cannot affect the y shaft. Such an isolated part would be of no use and might well be eliminated.

on its output w and input y. One design for realizing the admittance $Y(p)$ is shown in Fig. 7. This will be called the *matrix design*. The gear ratios come out directly as the elements of the coefficient matrix of (19) and, as we have drawn the circuit, in the same geometric positions. This design is chiefly of academic interest; it is not recommended for actual machines as it is very uneconomical of adders and gear boxes.

If we expand the first term of (20) in power of p we obtain

$$Y(p) = \frac{A_n p^n + A_{n-1} p^{n-1} + \cdots + A_0}{p^n + B_{n-1} p^{n-1} + \cdots + B_0}. \tag{22}$$

This proves the first part of:

Theorem III. Any non-degenerate machine with n integrators has an admittance of the form

$$Y(p) = \frac{A_n p^n + A_{n-1} p^{n-1} + \cdots + A_0}{p^n + B_{n-1} p^{n-1} + \cdots + B_0} \tag{23}$$

with the A_i and B_i real. Conversely, any such admittance can be realized in a machine with n integrators.

The final statement of this theorem can be demonstrated by actually exhibiting such a machine. Figure 8, for example, realizes (23) with just n integrators. The compound adders place the constraints

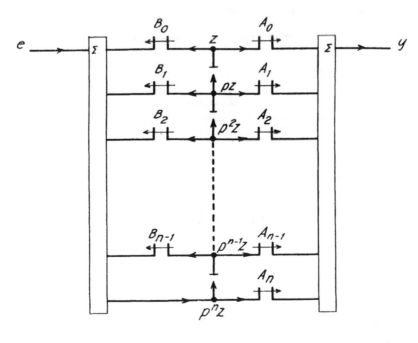

FIG. 8

$$e = -(p^n + B_{n-1}p^{n-1} + \cdots + B_0)z$$

$$ \tag{24}$$

$$y = -(A_n p^n + A_{n-1}p^{n-1} + \cdots + A_0)z$$

on the machine. Eliminating z we obtain

$$y = \frac{A_n p^n + A_{n-1}p^{n-1} + \cdots + A_0}{p^n + B_{n-1}p^{n-1} + \cdots + B_0} e \tag{25}$$

with the A_i and B_i arbitrary real numbers. If any of the A_i or B_i are zero the corresponding shaft of the machine is eliminated. The design of Fig. 7 will be called the "polynomial design" for the rational function (25). The design parameters, namely the gear ratios, come out directly as the coefficients of the polynomials. This design also has other important properties. It is evident from Theorem III that it minimizes the number of integrators required for the general rational function (25). In addition it minimizes the number of adders, or separate gear boxes, and even the number of shaft junctions. Such minimization is of course important not only for reasons of economy but also for reasons of precision in operation.

Note from Theorem III that for a rational $Y(p)$ to be realizable the degree of the numerator must not exceed that of the denominator. This is a direct consequence of the unilateral property of integrators. If mechanical time differentiators were available instead, we could obtain any rational function with denominator degree not exceeding numerator degree, while if bilateral integrator-differentiators were available any rational function could be realized.

If in place of one input shaft e in Fig. 6, there are I of them, $e_1, e_2, ..., e_I$, and O output shafts not driving integrators, $y_1, y_2, ..., y_O$, we have:

Theorem IV. The inputs and outputs are related by

$$y_j = \sum_{j=1}^{I} Y_{ij}(p)e_i < \quad j = 1, ..., O \tag{26}$$

in an n integrator machine, with

$$Y_{ij} = \frac{\sum_{k=1}^{n} A_{ijk}p^k}{p_n + B_{n-1}p^{n-1} + \cdots + B_0} \tag{27}$$

where the A's and B's are real.

Y_{ij} is the "transfer admittance" from input i to output j. The denominator in (27) is the same as in (20),

$$\Delta = |b_{ij} - p\,\delta_{ij}|, \quad i, j = 1, 2, ..., n, \tag{28}$$

where

$$\delta_{ij} = 0, \ i \neq j; \ \delta_{ii} = 1.$$

This will be called the "machine determinant." Stability is governed by the positions of its roots.

4. Theory of Orientation

It is common when drawing machines of this sort to "orient" the shafts; that is, to draw an arrow on each shaft called variously the direction of "drive," of "power flow," or of "constraint." It is sometimes assumed that a necessary and sufficient condition for satisfactory operation of a machine is that such an orientation be possible. The rules for.drawing the arrows are as follows:

1. The arrows on input shafts must point toward the machine.

2. The arrows on output shafts must point away from the machine.

3. Exactly two arrows on the three shafts of an adder must point toward the adder.

4. Exactly two arrows on the shafts of a junction must point away from the junction.

5. One arrow must point away from and one toward a gear box.

6. The arrow on the output shaft of an integrator must point away from the integrator; the arrow on the input shaft, toward the integrator.

If it is possible to draw a set of arrows on the shafts of a machine satisfying these requirements we will say that the machine is "orientable." If this is possible in only one way the machine is "uniquely orientable." Figures 9, 10 and 11, for example, are orientable, the last two uniquely. Note that for a machine to be orientable it is necessary and sufficient that the integratorless part be orientable, considering the outputs of integrators as input shafts to the integratorless part, and the inputs to integrators as outputs of the integratorless part (Fig. 6).

It is easy to determine whether or not a machine can be oriented. First orient all input, output and integrator shafts. Next orient all shafts whose orientation is uniquely determined by those already oriented, etc. If this process terminates without all shafts being oriented continue by trial and error. For an ordinary machine this can be done in a few seconds.

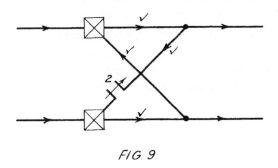

FIG. 9

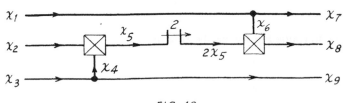

FIG. 10

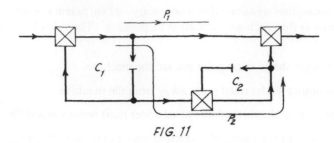

FIG. 11

Before studying the orientation problem mathematically, we will prove by examples some purely negative statements.

1. If by "satisfactory" operation it is meant that a machine is not locked and gives unique results on the output shafts, then orientability is neither necessary nor sufficient for satisfactory operation. Figures 4g and 4h show two orientable machines which are nevertheless locked, and Figs. 4e and 4f show two machines which are not orientable but are "satisfactory."

2. The direction of arrows in an orientable machine (even if uniquely orientable) do not necessarily give the direction of power flow. Operators of input tables on the differential analyzer have often found situations where the crank had to be held back; if left free it would turn faster than the proper speed. This phenomenon will occur when two shafts turning in opposite directions are feeding the same heavily loaded adder. If one of the shafts is turning rapidly and the other slowly, the load on the adder causes a large torque on the slow shaft in such a direction as to tend to increase its speed.

3. The direction of arrows can hardly be called *the* direction of constraint, since with perfectly good machines the orientation may not be unique, as in Fig. 9, where there are two possible orientations, the second one with the arrows reversed on the checked shafts.

In spite of these remarks, the question of orientability will be shown to be highly significant. For the purposes of the next theorem we assume that, in setting up the system of equations (10), if both ends of a single shaft enter the same adder or junction the two coefficients are not added, but retained as a sum. Thus in the machine Fig. 4g, the equation of the adder would be written

$$x_2 + (1-1)x_3 = 0 \tag{29}$$

not as

$$x_2 = 0 . \tag{30}$$

Theorem V. Consider the matrix M_{H+D} of the coefficients of the internal and driven shafts in (10). If this is not square the system is degenerate, and the machine cannot be oriented. If square, let the determinant $|M_{H+D}|$ be expanded in full. The number of different orientations of the machine is exactly equal to the number of non-vanishing terms in this expansion.

For example, the machine Fig. 4g has the equations

$$
\begin{aligned}
x_1 - x_2 \quad\quad\quad\quad &= 0 \\
x_2 \quad\quad\quad - x_4 &= 0 \\
x_2 + (1-1)x_3 \quad\quad &= 0
\end{aligned}
\tag{31}
$$

so that

$$|M_{H+D}| = \begin{vmatrix} -1 & 0 & 0 \\ 1 & 0 & -1 \\ 1 & (1-1) & 0 \end{vmatrix} = -(-1)(-1)(1-1) \tag{32}$$

$$= -1 + 1$$

and the machine can be oriented in two different ways, one as indicated in Fig. 4g; the other is obtained by reversing the arrow on the loop.

From this basic result the next four theorems are easily deduced.

Theorem VI. Any non-degenerate machine can be oriented.

Theorem VII. Any machine that can be oriented is non-degenerate or will become so if gears are inserted in the proper places.

As an example of this we see that by changing the -1 gear in Fig. 4g to any other value the machine becomes non-degenerate. The same is true of Fig. 4h if a gear of any value $\neq 1$ is inserted in one of the internal shafts, as in Fig. 9.

Theorem VIII. If a machine is uniquely orientable M_{H+D} is non-singular and can be made triangular by a proper interchange of rows and columns. In this case, furthermore, the machine is not degenerate.

Theorem IX. If M_{H+D} is non-singular and can be made triangular by interchanges the machine is not degenerate and is uniquely orientable.

The machine of Fig. 10 illustrates these last two theorems. It is uniquely orientable and its equations can be arranged in the form

$$
\begin{aligned}
X_8 + X_6 \qquad\quad + 2X_5 \qquad\qquad\qquad &= 0 \\
X_1 \qquad\qquad - X_6 \qquad\qquad\qquad\qquad\quad &= 0 \\
X_1 \qquad\qquad\qquad - X_7 \qquad\qquad\qquad &= 0 \\
X_2 \qquad\qquad\qquad + X_5 + X_4 \quad &= 0 \\
X_3 \qquad\qquad\qquad\qquad - X_4 \quad &= 0 \\
X_3 \qquad\qquad\qquad\qquad\qquad - X_9 \ &= 0
\end{aligned}
\tag{33}
$$

Displaying $|M_{H+D}|$ as triangular and non-singular:

$$|M_{H+D}| = \begin{vmatrix} 1 & 1 & 0 & 2 & 0 & 0 \\ 0 & -1 & 0 & 0 & 0 & 0 \\ 0 & 0 & -1 & 0 & 0 & 0 \\ 0 & 0 & 0 & 1 & 1 & 0 \\ 0 & 0 & 0 & 0 & -1 & 0 \\ 0 & 0 & 0 & 0 & 0 & -1 \end{vmatrix} = +1 . \tag{34}$$

Since almost all machines actually used are uniquely orientable, Theorem VIII furnishes a useful proof of non-degeneracy.

The interconnection between orientability and degeneracy is now clear. If a machine cannot be oriented, no matter what the gear ratios are, the machine is degenerate. On the other hand, if it is orientable it may or may not be degenerate, depending on the gear ratios. For most ratios it is not degenerate, but for the special ones which made $|M_{H+D}| = 0$ it is. In the particular case of unique orientability there are no such special ratios – the machine is never degenerate. Theorems V to IX also explain the success of the orientation method of determining whether machines are satisfactory; for apart from special gear ratios, orientability is equivalent to non-degeneracy.

The following two theorems are of some theoretical interest in connection with orientation theory. We define a directed path in an oriented machine as a path along shafts of the machine with all the arrows pointing in the same direction. A directed circuit is a closed directed path. Thus the checked shafts in Fig. 9 form a directed circuit.

Theorem X. Suppose a machine can be oriented in one way. This is a unique orientation if and only if the integratorless part contains no directed circuits, that is, if and only if all directed circuits pass through integrators.

In Figs. 4g and 9, directed circuits exist so the orientation is not unique. In Fig. 10 there are no circuits, so the orientation must be unique.

A set of directed circuits will be called independent if no pair has any element in common.

Theorem XI. Two different orientations of the same machine differ only in the reversal of the directions of arrows on a set of independent directed circuits in the integratorless part; and conversely any reversal of such circuits in an oriented machine gives a new orientation.

It is worth noting that in an orientable machine (and hence certainly in any non-degenerate machine)

$$P + A = D + J \tag{35}$$

the letters being the number of power shafts, adders, driven shafts and junctions respectively. In particular in a two shaft orientable machine the number of adders equals the number of junctions.

5. Sufficient Gearing for an Ungeared Machine

It sometimes happens that we have a design for a machine which does not include any gears, and we wish to place gears in the shafts in such a way as to realize the full potentialities of the design, i.e. in such a way that by proper assignment of the gear ratios any transfer admittance realizable with the design can be obtained. For example, Fig. 11 is an ungeared machine; we wish to place a sufficient number of arbitrary gears in the shafts to realize the full generality of the design. This can be done, of course, by placing an arbitrary gear in each shaft; but such a procedure would be inefficient, as a much smaller number will suffice. In this section we state a theorem giving methods of finding a suitable set of shafts to choose for gears so as to realize the maximum possible generality.

The network of interconnected lines obtained from the drawing of a two-shaft machine by connecting the input and output shafts together with a line, eliminating integrators and gears (by drawing lines through them) and drawing junctions and adders both as junctions will be called the network of the machine. Thus the network of Fig. 11 is Fig. 12a.

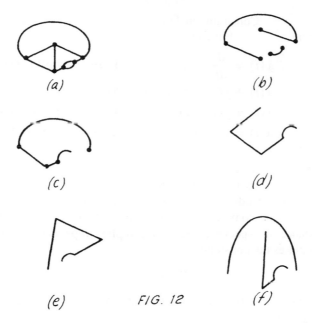

(a)

(b)

(c)

(d)

(e)   FIG. 12   (f)

In topology a set of lines S of a network N is called a fundamental system if when the lines S are deleted from the network, all closed circuits in N are broken, while if any line of S is left in N there is at least one circuit.

Theorem XII. If arbitrary gears are placed in the shafts of a fundamental system of a machine, the full generality of the design is achieved. This requires $A + 1$ gears in a non-degenerate machine, where A is the number of adders.

Figs. 12b-f show some fundamental systems for the network of Fig. 12a. If gears are placed in the shafts of Fig. 11 corresponding to any one of these the machine will be fully geared. Fig. 11 contains 3 adders and $3 + 1 = 4$ gears are sufficient. If the input-output line forms a part of the fundamental system chosen, the gear may be placed either in the output or input shaft of the machine. If an integrator appears in any of the corresponding shafts, the gear may be placed either in its input or output.

To find a fundamental system of a given network N delete any line appearing in a closed circuit of N. Then delete any line appearing in a circuit in the reduced network. Proceed in this way until no circuits remain. The deleted lines form a fundamental system.

6. Integrators as Gears with Complex Ratio

We have up to now always described the motion of shafts in terms of their variation with respect to time. That is, we associate with each shaft a function of time $x(t)$ whose value at $t = t_1$ is the position of the shaft at t_1. We may also describe the motion of a shaft by giving the Fourier transform of its position, a function of frequency. If we denote the time functions by small letters and the corresponding frequency functions by capitals (e.g., the transform of $x(t)$ is $X(j\omega)$) then it is easily shown that different machine elements place the following constraints on the frequency functions:

Machine Element	Constraint on Time Functions	Constraint on Frequency Functions
Integrator	$y(t) = \dfrac{d}{dt}\, w(t)$	$Y(j\omega) = j\omega W(j\omega)$
Adder	$x(t) + y(t) + z(t) = 0$	$X(j\omega) + Y(j\omega) + Z(j\omega) = 0$
Junction	$x(t) = y(t) = z(t)$	$X(j\omega) = Y(j\omega) = Z(j\omega)$
Gear	$x(t) = K\, y(t)$	$X(j\omega) = K\, Y(j\omega)$

The only constraint which has a different form in terms of frequency functions is that of the integrator, which acts like a gear, except that the ratio is complex, $j\omega$, and depends on frequency. We can thus consider integrators and gears both as special instances of a generalized kind of gear where complex ratios are admissible, in the same way that inductance, capacitance and resistance are special cases of a complex impedance. A two-shaft machine with admittance $Y(p)$ places the constraint

$$x(t) = Y(p)\, e(t) \tag{36}$$

on the input e and output x in terms of time functions, while the corresponding constraint in terms of frequency functions is

$$X(j\omega) = Y(j\omega)\, E(j\omega) . \tag{37}$$

Thus the machine is equivalent to a "complex gear" of ratio $Y(j\omega)$.

Of course this interpretation, or something equivalent to it (e.g., Laplace transforms or the indicial admittance), was implied in our algebraic manipulation of the Heaviside operator p.

7. Reversible Machines

It is possible to operate some non-degenerate two-shaft machines backwards – i.e., to turn the output and have the input driven by the machine. If it is also non-degenerate in this direction we will call the machine "reversible."

Theorem XIII. A non-degenerate two-shaft machine with admittance $Y(p)$ is reversible if and only if $Y(\infty) \neq 0$. In this case the admittance of the reversed machine is $[Y(p)]^{-1}$.

The polynomial design, Fig. 8, is reversible if the gear A_n is actually in the machine, since $Y(\infty) = A_n$.

Theorem XIV. If there is exactly one directed path passing through no integrators from the e to the y shaft of a non-degenerate machine it is reversible. At least one such path is necessary for a machine to be reversible.

Note that an orientation for the reversed machine can be obtained by reversing the arrows along such a path, leaving other arrows the same.

8. Interconnections of Two-Shaft Machines

If we have a pair of two-shaft machines with admittances Y_1 and Y_2, we can, in general, connect them together in four different ways to get a new satisfactory two-shaft machine. These four ways are shown in Fig. 13. Figure 13a will be called the series connection of Y_1 and Y_2; Fig. 13b the parallel connection; Fig. 13c will be described as Y_2 in skew parallel with

Y_1, and Fig. 13d is Y_1 in skew parallel with Y_2. It is of interest to know the resultant admittance Y of the machines constructed in these four ways from two given machines.

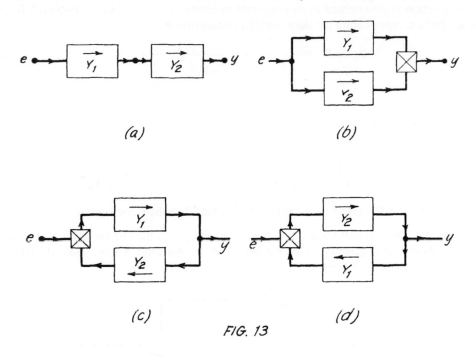

(a)   (b)

(c)   (d)

FIG. 13

Theorem XV. The series connection of two machines is non-degenerate if and only if both are non-degenerate, and has the admittance

$$Y(p) = Y_1(p) \cdot Y_2(p) .$$

(38)

Theorem XVI. The parallel connection of two machines is non-degenerate if and only if both are non-degenerate, and has the admittance

$$- Y(p) = Y_1(p) + Y_2(p) .$$

(39)

Theorem XVII. $Y_2(p)$ in skew parallel with $Y_1(p)$ is non-degenerate if both are non-degenerate and

$$Y_1(\infty) \cdot Y_2(\infty) \neq - 1$$

(40)

and the admittance is then

$$Y(p) = \frac{-1}{[Y_1(p)]^{-1} + Y_2(p)} .$$

(41)

The series, parallel and skew parallel connections play a part in this theory analogous to series and parallel connections in electric circuit theory. They are sufficient to describe all non-degenerate connections of four or fewer two-shaft machines. Five or more machines can be connected in various types of bridge circuits.

The easy realization of the basic mathematical operations, multiplication and addition by series and parallel connections is remarkable and useful in the design of machines. The skew parallel connection is also related to an important mathematical operation – continued fraction expansion. In fact, representing the skew parallel connection by $\oplus$:

$$Y_1 \oplus Y_2 = \cfrac{1}{-Y_1^{-1} - Y_2} \; \cfrac{1}{-Y_1^{-1} - \cfrac{1}{Y_2^{-1}}} \, , \tag{42}$$

we easily see that

$$Y_1 \oplus [Y_2 \oplus [Y_3 [\cdots \oplus Y_n] \cdots]] \tag{43}$$

$$= \cfrac{1}{-Y_1^{-1} +} \; \cfrac{1}{Y_2^{-1} +} \; \cfrac{1}{-Y_3^{-1} +} \; \cfrac{1}{Y_4^{-1} +} \cdots + \cfrac{1}{\pm Y_n^{-1}}$$

where the signs on the Y_i^{-1} alternate except for Y_n^{-1}, which has the same sign as Y_{n-1}^{-1}.

It is interesting to note that for a single fixed frequency ω_0, the simple parallel connection of Fig. 14 gives the most general complex admittance or gear ratio $A + jB$. Both A and B can assume positive or negative values.

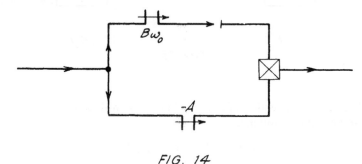

FIG. 14

9. The Analysis Theorem

In this and the next section we will exploit the interconnection between orientation and machine properties by giving a rapid method for evaluating transfer admittances, and testing for stability and degeneracy. We must first define a few preliminary notions. Directed circuits and paths have already been defined in Section 4. The value of a directed path or circuit will be taken as the product of the values of elements along the path (or around the circuit) in the direction of the arrows, giving elements the following values:

(1)   gears have a value equal to their ratio in the direction of the arrow on the path or circuit (not the arrow on the gear),

(2)   adders have a value -1,

(3)   junctions have a value $+1$,

(4)   integrators have a value $\dfrac{1}{p}$.

In Fig. 15 the directed path from e_1 to y_1 has a value

$$P_1 = (-1)(K_1)\left[\frac{1}{p}\right]\left[\frac{1}{K_4}\right] = \frac{-K_1}{K_4 p} . \tag{44}$$

The circuit C_4 has a value (starting at the left-hand adder)

$$C_4 = (-1)\frac{1}{K_2}\frac{1}{p}(-1)K_3(-1)(-1) - \frac{K_3}{K_2 p} . \tag{45}$$

The machine discriminant will be defined as the expression

$$D = 1 - \sum C_i + \sum C_i C_j - \sum C_i C_j C_k + \cdots \tag{46}$$

the first sum $\sum C_i$ being taken over all directed circuits in the machine, the second $\sum C_i C_j$ over all pairs of independent circuits, the third over all triplets of independent circuits, etc.

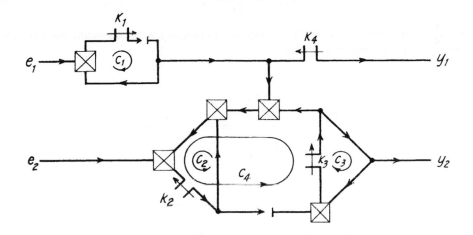

FIG. 15

In Fig. 15 the circuits have values

$$C_1 = \frac{-K_1}{p}, \quad C_2 = \frac{1}{K_2}, \quad C_3 = -K_3, \quad C_4 = \frac{K_3}{K_2 p} .$$

Hence

$$D = 1 - C_1 - C_2 - C_3 - C_4 + C_1 C_2 + C_1 C_3 + C_1 C_4 + C_2 C_3 - C_1 C_2 C_3$$

$$= 1 + \frac{K_1}{p} - \frac{1}{K_2} + K_3 - \frac{K_3}{K_2 p} - \frac{K_1}{K_2 p} + \frac{K_1 K_3}{p} - \frac{K_1 K_3}{K_2 p^2}$$

$$- \frac{K_3}{K_2} - \frac{K_1 K_3}{K_2 p} . \tag{47}$$

In case the circuits can be divided into independent groups as in Fig. 15, where we have C_1 and the independent group C_2, C_3, C_4 the discriminant for each part may be found from (46) by summing only over the circuits in that part and the results multiplied, shortening the work considerably. Thus in Fig. 15 we have:

$$D = (1-C_1)(1-C_2-C_3-C_4+C_2C_3)$$

$$= \left[1+\frac{K_1}{p}\right]\left[1-\frac{1}{K_2}+K_3-\frac{K_3}{K_2p}-\frac{K_3}{K_2}\right] . \tag{48}$$

The discriminant D_i of a machine complementary to a path P_i is the expression (46) summed over those circuits which do not touch the path P_i.

Theorem XVIII. In any non-degenerate machine

$$Y_{ij} = \frac{\Sigma P_k D_k}{D} , \tag{49}$$

where the sum is taken over all paths P_k from input i to output j with complementary D_k and D is the discriminant for the entire machine.

In Fig. 15

$$Y_{11} = \frac{P_1 D_1}{D} = \frac{\dfrac{-K_1}{K_4 p}}{1+\dfrac{K_1}{p}} = -\frac{K_1}{K_4(p+K_1)} . \tag{50}$$

Note that the D_1 cancels.

$$Y_{12} = \frac{(-1)^5 \dfrac{K_1 K_3}{K_2 p^2}}{D} = \frac{-K_1 K_3}{(p+K_1)[(K_2+K_2K_3-K_3-1)p-K_3]} .$$

$$Y_{21} = 0 \quad \text{(no paths)} \tag{51}$$

$$Y_{22} = \frac{(-1)^2 \dfrac{K_3}{K_2 p} D_1}{D} = \frac{K_3}{[(K_2+K_2K_3-K_3-1)p-K_3]} .$$

Here again the D_1 cancels. Hence

$$y_1 = \frac{-K_1 e_1}{K_4(p+K_1)}$$

$$y_2 = \frac{-K_1 K_3 e_1}{(p+K_1)[(K_2+K_2K_3-K_3-1)p-K_3]} \tag{52}$$

$$+ \frac{K_3 e_2}{[(K_2+K_2K_3-K_3-1)p-K_3]} .$$

It simplifies the expression if the direction of gears is taken in the direction of orientation when assigning gears to a machine. The reader is urged to try this method on a few examples. After a little practice it is possible to write down the admittances for ordinary machines almost by inspection. We give another illustration in Fig. 11.

We have

$$C_1 - C_2 = -\frac{1}{p} \qquad P_1 = +1 \qquad P_2 = -\frac{1}{p}$$

$$Y = \frac{P_1(1-C_2)+P_2}{(1-C_1)(1-C_2)} = \frac{\left(1+\dfrac{1}{p}\right)-\dfrac{1}{p}}{\left(1+\dfrac{1}{p}\right)^2} = \frac{p^2}{(p+1)^2} \ . \tag{53}$$

10. Degeneracy Test and Evaluation of the Machine Determinant

We now give two theorems which are easy but useful corollaries of the analysis theorem given in the last section.

Theorem XIX. A machine is non-degenerate if and only if

(1) it is orientable, and

(2) $D^* \neq 0$, where $D^* = D_{p=\infty}$ is the discriminant of circuits not touching integrators, i.e., the discriminant of the integratorless part of the machine.

In Fig. 4h the discriminant D^* is

$$1 - (-1)(-1) = 0 \tag{54}$$

so the machine is degenerate. In Fig. 15 we have

$$D^* = (1-C_2)(1-C_3) = \left(1-\frac{1}{K_2}\right)(1+K_3)$$

and the machine is degenerate if $K_2 = 1$ or $K_3 = -1$, or both, but not otherwise,

Theorem XX. In any oriented machine with n integrators the machine discriminant D and determinant Δ are related by

$$(-p)^n D = \Delta D^* \ .$$

This theorem may be used to test for stability, since stability depends on the location of the roots of Δ. In Fig. 15

$$(-p)^2 D = \Delta D^* = \frac{(p+K_1)}{K_2}[(K_2K_3+K_2-K_3+1)p-K_3]D^* \tag{55}$$

with roots

$$p = -K_1, \qquad \frac{K_3}{K_2 K_3 + K_2 - K_3 + 1}$$

and the machine is stable if these are both negative.

The methods of analysis given in the last three theorems are really no more than simple methods of evaluation of the numerator and denominator determinants in (20). The rapidity of the method is due to the fact that by a simple graphical device we can pick out the non-vanishing terms of these determinants without even writing out the equations of the system. Actually in almost all cases the majority of the terms of the determinants vanish, as may be seen by an inspection of (11).

11. The Duality Theorems

Duality theorems are important in many branches of mathematics – projective geometry, abstract algebra, electric circuit theory, etc. In this section we shall establish a duality relation for linear differential equation machines leading to a number of results in the design and philosophy of these devices.

We will define the dual of a given machine M as the machine M' constructed as follows:

1.   Adders and junctions in M are interchanged.

2.   The direction of each integrator in M is reversed.

3.   The direction of each gear in M is reversed.

4.   A reversing gear (ratio -1) is placed in each internal and through shaft of M.

Thus, for example, the dual of Fig. 15 is Fig. 16. Although in topology only planar networks have duals, every machine has a dual – we do not even limit ourselves to non-degenerate machines. Clearly the dual of the dual of a machine M is M itself, $(M')' = M$. There is an intimate relation between the properties of M and M' which may be stated as follows.

Theorem XXI. If we can divide the external shafts of M into two groups $e_1, e_2, ..., e_r$ and $y_1, y_2, ..., y_s$ such that the e_i can be turned arbitrarily and the y_i are uniquely determined,

$$y_i = \sum_{j=1}^{r} Y_{ij} e_j \qquad i = 1, ..., s, \tag{56}$$

then in the dual machine with corresponding shafts $e_1', e_2', ..., e_r'$ and $y_1', y_2', ..., y_s'$ the y_i' can be turned arbitrarily and the e_i' are uniquely determined by

$$e_j' = - \sum_{i=1}^{s} Y_{ij} y_i' \qquad j = 1, 2, ..., r. \tag{57}$$

In other words replacing a machine by its dual interchanges output and input shafts, transposes the admittance matrix $\|Y_{ij}\|$ and changes the sign of each admittance. The class of machines to which this theorem applies is very broad – the only cases excluded by the conditions of the theorem are certain machines in which the outputs of the integrators are locked, or the inputs of the integrators free.

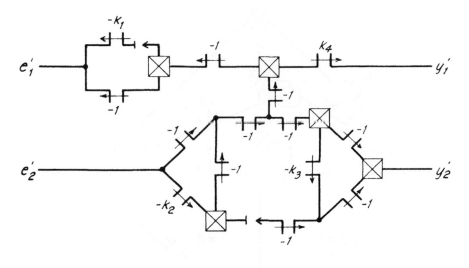

FIG. 16

A two shaft machine has only one admittance

$$y = Y(p)e \tag{58}$$

so its dual gives

$$e' = -Y(p) \, y' \, . \tag{59}$$

Hence we have the

Corollary. If a (-1) gear is introduced in the output of the dual M' of a non-degenerate two-shaft machine its admittance is the same as that of M, with input and output interchanged.

Thus given any machine realizing $Y(p)$ we can construct another with the same admittance which may be superior for mechanical reasons. For example, the dual of the polynomial design (Fig. 8) is Fig. 17, which seems to offer some advantages from the backlash point of view. In Fig. 8 the adders are in a series connection from input to output so that the backlash effects during a reversal of the e shaft add together, while in Fig. 17 they are essentially in parallel and the amount of backlash would be about that of one adder.

Most of the (-1) gears appearing in the dual of a machine can usually be eliminated by a device explained in the proof of Theorem XII, without altering its external behavior. This was done in Fig. 17.

Many machines are of such a nature that the dual machine is essentially the same as the given machine (except for (-1) gears that can be eliminated); and such cases do not give an essentially new design under the corollary. In particular we mention that the series, parallel, and skew parallel connections are essentially self dual, and hence any machine containing only these connections is self dual.

Theorem XXI can also be stated in geometrical terms, throwing the duality into a more natural perspective. Any machine whatever with external shafts x_1, x_2, ..., x_n places on these shafts a set of homogeneous linear constraints

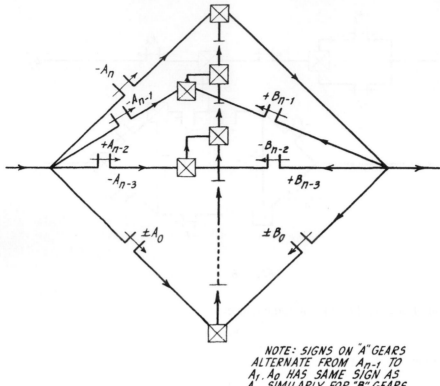

NOTE: SIGNS ON "A" GEARS
ALTERNATE FROM A_{n-1} TO
A_1. A_0 HAS SAME SIGN AS
A_1. SIMILARLY FOR "B" GEARS.

FIG. 17

$$\sum_{i=1}^{n} A_{ij} x_i = 0 \qquad j = 1, ..., s \tag{60}$$

when the A_{ij} are functions of p. Thinking of p as a fixed number and the x_i as coordinates of a point in Euclidean n-space, (60) represents a linear manifold R in this space, i.e., a region such that if $(a_1, a_2, ..., a_n)$ and $(b_1, b_2, ..., b_n)$ are points in the region then

$$\alpha(a_1, ..., a_n) + \beta(b_1, ..., b_n) = (\alpha a_1 + \beta b_1, ..., \alpha a_n + \beta b_n) \tag{61}$$

is also in R for any real numbers α, β. The orthogonal complement R' to such a region is the linear manifold of all points $(y_1, y_2, ..., y_n)$ such that the scalar product

$$(y_1, y_2, ..., y_n)(x_1, x_2, ..., x_n) = x_1 y_1 + x_2 y_2 + \cdots + x_n y_n = 0 \tag{62}$$

for any x_i in R and y_i in R'.

Theorem XXII. The region R of a machine M and the region R' of its dual M' are orthogonal complements.

A simple example is the machine M consisting of a single adder with gears a, b, c in its shafts and its dual M', a single junction with gears $\frac{1}{a}$, $\frac{1}{b}$, $\frac{1}{c}$ in the corresponding shafts. For

M

$$ax + by + cz = 0 \, , \tag{63}$$

the equation of a plane in three-space. For M'

$$\frac{x}{a} = \frac{y}{b} = \frac{z}{c} \, , \tag{64}$$

the perpendicular straight line.

Another aspect of this duality relation is the existence of dual propositions. Many statements have a dual statement which may be found by replacing each term by its dual. Table I gives the most important dual terms and phrases.

Table I: Duality Table

Adder	Junction
Gear	Gear
Integrator	Integrator
Gear of ratio K	Gear of ratio $1/K$
Integrator input	Integrator output
Internal shaft	Internal shaft
External shaft	External shaft
Power shaft	Driven shaft
Input shaft	Output shaft
A particular machine M	The dual machine M'
Any machine	Any machine
Degenerate	Degenerate
Locked power shaft	Free driven shaft
Redundant shaft	Free internal shaft
Orientable	Orientable
Arrow toward	Arrow away from
Circuit product C	Circuit product C
Path product P	Path product $-P$
Machine discriminant D	Machine discriminant D
To hold a set of external shafts at zero	To allow a set of external shafts to turn freely
To be able to turn a set of external shafts arbitrarily	For a set of external shafts to be uniquely determined
To connect the ends of two shafts together	To connect the ends of two-shafts through a (-1) gear
To hold an internal shaft	To break an internal shaft
The linear region R	The orthogonal complement R'

The logical terms of implication, class inclusion, negation, etc. are self duals. We may state our third form of the duality relation as follows.

Theorem XXIII. If dual terms from the duality table are substituted in a true proposition, it remains true.

The proposition in question may apply to a specific machine, a class of machines, or to all machines. Some examples of dual propositions follow.

If there is a path in a machine from one power shaft to another passing through gears and junctions only, the power shafts are locked.	If there is a path in a machine from one driven shaft to another passing through gears and adders only, the driven shafts are free.
If an internal shaft is redundant all elements that can be reached from this shaft passing through only gears and adders may be eliminated, the other shafts of junctions so reached being connected together (Fig. 18).	If an internal shaft is free all elements that can be reached from this shaft passing through only gears and junctions may be eliminated, the other shafts of adders so reached being connected together with a (-1) gear. (Fig. 19).
The machine of Fig. 4e is degenerate. It contains a free internal shaft.	The dual machine (Fig. 4f except for non-essential (-1) gears) is degenerate. It contains a redundant shaft.

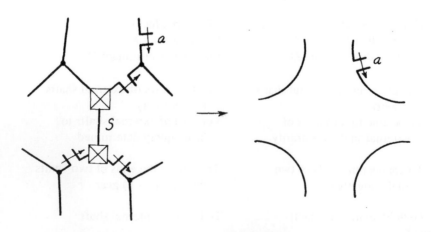

FIG. 18   S REDUNDANT

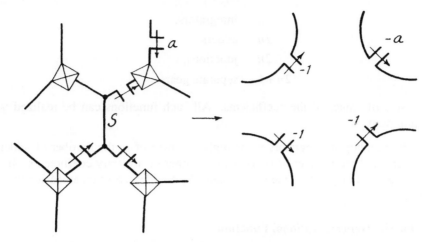

FIG. 19 S FREE INTERNAL

12. Minimal Design Theory

We now consider the problem of minimal designs – how many elements are required for a given admittance or class of admittances. We first state some results dealing with particular elements. As a corollary to Theorem III we note that the admittance

$$Y(p) = \frac{A_n p^n + A_{n-1} p^{n-1} + \cdots + A_0}{p^n + B_{n-1} p^{n-1} + \cdots + B_0} \qquad (65)$$

can be realized with n integrators, and requires this many if the numerator and denominator have no common roots. For gears we have:

Theorem XXIV. Almost all* admittances (65) require G gears if G of the $(2n+1)$ coefficients $A_n, ..., A_0, B_{n-1}, ..., B_0$ are independent.

If all are independent, $2n + 1$ gears are almost always necessary. If we consider the class of functions with $A_n = 0$ and the others independent, $2n$ are almost always required, etc.

For adders it appears likely that for A adders to suffice for (65) it must be possible to write Y using only rational operations with no more than A plus signs, but no proof has been found.

These results together with the polynomial design entail:

Theorem XXV. The function

$$Y(p) = \frac{A_n p^n + \cdots + A_0}{p^n + \cdots + B_0} \qquad (66)$$

requires

---

* Precisely we mean that the set of points in the G space whose G coordinates are an independent set of the A, and B, where fewer gears suffice is of measure zero.

$$n \quad \text{integrators,}$$
$$2n \quad \text{adders,}$$
$$2n \quad \text{junctions,}$$
$$2n+1 \quad \text{separate gears,}$$

for almost all sets of values of the coefficients. All such functions can be realized with this amount of equipment.

Note that the number of integrators is the highest power of p, the number of adders is the number of + signs and the number of gears is the number of arbitrary coefficients. If S of the coefficients are zero we may reduce the requirements by S adders, S gears and S junctions. This is obvious from Fig. 8.

13. Designs for the General Rational Function

We have seen that the rational function

$$Y(p) = \frac{A_n p^n + A_{n-1} p^{n-1} + \cdots + A_0}{p^n + B_{n-1} p^{n-1} + \cdots + B_0} \tag{67}$$

requires in general n integrators, $2n$ adders, $2n$ junctions and $2n+1$ gears and we have given two designs based on the polynomial representation for realizing $Y(p)$ with this minimal number of elements. These designs are shown in Figs. 8 and 17. A rational $Y(p)$ can also be written in three other standard forms and designs have been found based on these representations. These other representations are:

(1)   The partial fraction expansion

$$Y(p) = \sum Y_i(p) \tag{68}$$

where each $Y_i(p)$ is a rational function with real coefficients. To realize a general $Y(p)$ we may expand in partial fractions $Y_i(p)$ and design a machine for each of these by any method, then connect the resulting machines in parallel. It is easily seen that the design is minimal on all types of elements, if the Y_i are minimal.

(2)   In the factored from

$$Y(p) = \frac{\Pi \, P_i(p)}{\Pi \, Q_i(p)} = \Pi \, R_i(p) \, , \tag{69}$$

where the P_i and Q_i are at most second degree polynomials with real coefficients and the R_i pair off the P_i and Q_i into realizable admittances. Each R_i may be designed separately and the resulting machines connected in series.

(3)   In a continued fraction expansion. The function

$$Y(p) = \frac{A_n \, p^n + A_{n-1} \, p^{n-1} + \cdots + A_0}{p^n + B_{n-1} \, p^{n-1} + \cdots + B_0} \tag{70}$$

can be expanded in numerous ways as a continued fraction. Four of these are fairly simple, namely:

(a) Dividing the numerator of (70) by the denominator and inverting at each division

$$Y(p) = \alpha_0 + \cfrac{1}{\alpha_1^{-1}p +} \ \cfrac{1}{\alpha_2^{-1} +} \ \cfrac{1}{\alpha_3^{-1}p +} \ \cfrac{1}{\alpha_4^{-1} +} \ \cdots$$

(71)

$$= - (-\alpha_0) - \left[\frac{\alpha_1}{p} \oplus \left[-\alpha_2 \oplus \left[\frac{\alpha_3}{p} \oplus \left[-\alpha_4 \oplus \ \cdots \ \right] \right] \right] \right]$$

where the $\oplus$ denotes the skew parallel connection. The network is shown in Fig. 20a

(b) Dividing denominator by numerator and inverting at each division

$$Y(p) = \cfrac{1}{\beta_1^{-1} +} \ \cfrac{1}{\beta_2^{-1}p +} \ \cfrac{1}{\beta_3^{-1} +} \ \cfrac{1}{\beta_4^{-1}p +} \ \cdots$$

(72)

$$= - \beta_1 \oplus \left[\frac{\beta_2}{p} \oplus \left[-\beta_3 \oplus \left[\frac{\beta_4}{p} \oplus \left[\ \cdots \ \right] \right] \right] \right]$$

This network is shown in Fig. 20b.

(c) Dividing at each stage until we obtain a proper rational function, starting with the denominator into the numerator.

$$Y(p) = \gamma_o + \cfrac{1}{\gamma_1^{-1}p + \gamma_2 +} \ \cfrac{1}{\gamma_3^{-1}p + \gamma_4 +} \ \cdots$$

(73)

$$= - (-\gamma_0) - \left[\frac{\gamma_1}{p} \oplus \left[-\gamma_2 - \left[\frac{\gamma_3}{p} \oplus \left[-\gamma_4 \ \cdots \ \right] \right] \right] \right].$$

This is realized in Fig. 20c.

(d) The same process, but starting with the numerator into the denominator

$$Y(p) = \cfrac{1}{\delta_1^{-1} +} \ \cfrac{1}{\delta_2^{-1}p + \delta_3 +} \ \cfrac{1}{\delta_4^{-1} + \delta_5 +} \ \cdots$$

(74)

$$= - (-\delta_1) \oplus \left[\frac{\delta_2}{p} \oplus \left[\delta_3 - \left[\frac{\delta_4}{p} \oplus \left[\delta_5 + \ \cdots \ \right] \right] \right] \right].$$

This connection is shown in Fig. 20d.

Using combinations of these basic designs many other minimal networks can be constructed. For example we can combine some of the factors of the product design and realize this part with a partial fraction design in series with the other factors, or we may stop the continued fraction expansion at some realizable admittance and use the polynomial design or its dual, etc. It may happen that in some such expansion one or more of the coefficients that normally appears vanishes, and this allows us in general to reduce the adder, junction and gear requirements.

One particular case of considerable practical importance is when a set of numerator coefficients in (70) is proportional to a set of denominator coefficients, shifted over by a power s of p (s may be positive or negative):

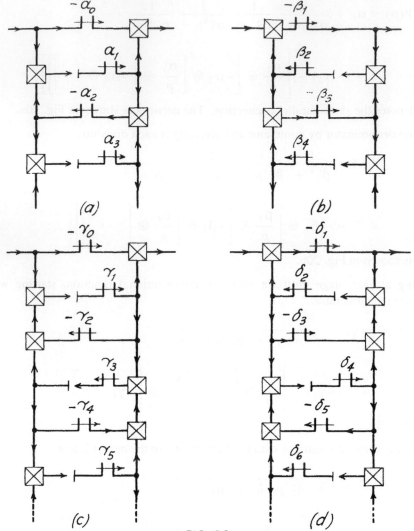

$$\frac{A_\alpha}{B_{\alpha+s}} = \frac{A_\beta}{B_{\beta+s}} = \frac{A_\gamma}{B_{\gamma+s}} = \cdots \tag{75}$$

The requirements of Theorem **XXV** can then be reduced by the number of these equalities. This is accomplished by a continued fraction expansion. For example

$$Y = \frac{2p^2 + 4p + 3}{p^3 + 2p^2 + p + 1} \tag{76}$$

$$= \cfrac{1}{\frac{1}{2}p + \cfrac{1}{(-4)p - 16 + \cfrac{1}{\frac{p}{24} - \frac{1}{12}}}} \tag{77}$$

using only 4 adders, 4 junctions and 5 gears.

14. General Design Method

The following general procedure is recommended for the design of smoothers, rate finders, etc.

1. Determine as well as possible the form of the admittance function $Y_1(p)$ desired. If expected power spectra of the true input $\phi(j\omega)$ and the error function $\psi(j\omega)$ can be obtained the desired $Y_1(p)$ is (under a least square error assumption)[5]

$$Y_1(p) = Y_1(j\omega) = \frac{S(j\omega)\phi(j\omega)}{\phi(j\omega)+\psi(j\omega)} \tag{78}$$

where $S(j\omega)$ is the transform of the operation we wish to perform, e.g. for smoothing we take $S = 1$, for rate finding $S = j\omega$, or for prediction by a time t_p we take $S = e^{j\omega t_p}$.

2. Approximate this admittance Y_1 by a rational function $Y(p)$ having no poles in the positive half plane and with degree of numerator not exceeding that of denominator. This can be done by standard methods of filter design.[6]

3. Construct a machine for this $Y(p)$ by the methods given above. Various different expansions should be tried to reduce if possible the number of elements, particularly if the coefficients in $Y(p)$ have simple relations to one another.

APPENDIX. PROOFS OF THEOREM AND ADDITIONAL REMARKS

SECTION 2

The method of setting up the equations (10) is of course, rather inefficient – a much smaller number of variables would suffice, for example by assigning the same variable to all shafts connected through junctions or gears. The method given, however, is uniform, and leads easily to the results on orientation in Section 4. Since the equations (10) are not used for actual computation, but only theoretical investigations this canonical system seems preferable.

The choice of the four characteristics listed as "degeneracies" may seem arbitrary. For example in Fig. 4g if the (-1) gear is changed to another value, the machine is not degenerate by our definition, but contains unnecessary elements. The real reason for our definition is that we wish to keep our results as general as possible, but must place enough restrictions on machines to obtain the orientation and analysis theorems (V and XVIII).

Theorem I. It is known from the theory of linear homogeneous equations[7] that a necessary and sufficient condition that $X_1, ..., X_P$ in (10) may be ascribed arbitrary values is that

$$R_{P+H+D} = R_{H+D} . \tag{80}$$

Otherwise there is a linear relation between $X_1, ..., X_P$ and the machine is locked. Now if and only if

$$R_{H+D} < H+D , \tag{81}$$

the existence of one solution for the variables $X_{P+1}, ..., X_{P+H+D}$ implies the existence of an infinite number. But there is always one solution even if the power shafts are locked, namely the initial solution. Hence (81) is a necessary and sufficient condition that there exist "free shafts" in the machine, either internally or in the output. If there are more than $H+D$ equations in system (10), we may keep a set having this rank and reject the remainder as superfluous. The existence of superfluous equations in (10) always implies one or more redundant shafts in the machine, assuming that

$$R_{P+H+D} = R_{H+D} = H+D .\qquad(82)$$

This condition makes through shafts from one power shaft to another impossible, for then the machine would be locked; also through shafts from one driven shaft to another would be free. Through shafts from a power shaft to a driven shaft clearly cannot yield a superfluous equation; hence we consider only equations arising from adders and junctions. If an adder equation is superfluous, one of the shafts leading to the adder can be broken thus removing this equation from the system without affecting the other equations. This is a redundant shaft. If a junction equation is redundant the shaft not appearing in the other junction equation of the pair can be broken without affecting the other equations. Reversing this argument gives the converse, that if $R_{P+H+D}=R_{H+D}=H+D$, the existence of a redundant shaft implies a superfluous equation in (10).

Theorem II. M_{H+D} being square and non-singular is sufficient for the solubility of (10). The converse is proved by Fig. 5.

SECTION 3

The transfer admittance of the general n integrator two shaft machine can be written in several other forms (besides (20) and (22)). Adding and subtracting p from $b_{n+1,n+1}$ the first term of the numerator of (20) becomes the sum of two determinants:

$$\begin{vmatrix} b_{11}-p & b_{12} & \cdots & b_{1,n+1} \\ b_{21} & b_{22}-p & \cdots & b_{2,n+1} \\ \cdots & \cdots & \cdots\cdots \\ \cdots & \cdots & \cdots\cdots \\ b_{n+1,1} & b_{n+1,2} & \cdots & (b_{n+1,n+1}-p) \end{vmatrix} + \begin{vmatrix} b_{11}-p & \cdots & b_{1n} & 0 \\ \cdots & \cdots\cdots & 0 \\ \cdots & \cdots\cdots & \\ b_{n1} & \cdots & b_{nn}-p & 0 \\ b_{n+1,1} & \cdots & b_{n+1,n} & p \end{vmatrix}. \qquad(83)$$

The second term is p times the denominator of (20) so that in the steady state

$$y = \left[\frac{\begin{vmatrix} b_{11}-p & \cdots & b_{1,n+1} \\ \cdots & \cdots\cdots \\ \cdots & \cdots\cdots \\ b_{n+1,1} & \cdots & b_{n+1,n+1}-p \end{vmatrix}}{\begin{vmatrix} b_{11}-p & \cdots & b_{n1} \\ \cdots & \cdots\cdots \\ \cdots & \cdots\cdots \\ b_{n1} & \cdots & b_{nn}-p \end{vmatrix}} + p \right] e \qquad(84)$$

or

$$y = \left[\frac{|M_{n+1}-pI_{n+1}|}{|M_n-pI_n|} + p \right] e \qquad(85)$$

where M_n and M_{n+1} are coefficient matrices and I denotes a unit matrix. In terms of the latent roots of M_n and M_{n+1}, say $\alpha_1, ..., \alpha_n; \beta_1, ..., \beta_{n+1}$:

$$Y(p) = \frac{\prod_{1}^{n+1} (p - \beta_i)}{\prod_{1}^{n} (p - \alpha_i)} - p .$$

Theorem III. Proved in text.

Theorem IV. This can be proved by a method identical with that used for Theorem III. The coefficients A_{ijk} here are not all independent, but sufficient conditions for a converse part of this theorem have not been investigated.

SECTION 4

Theorem V. Theorem I shows that M_{H+D} must be square for non-degeneracy. If a machine can be oriented M_{H+D} must be square. For the number of arrows pointing away from points must equal the number of arrows pointing toward points (counting adders, junctions, and ends of P and D shafts as "points"). Thus

$$2J + A + P = 2A + J + D \tag{87}$$

or

$$A + 2J + T = \tfrac{1}{2}[3A + 3J + P + D + 2T] - P . \tag{88}$$

The left member is the number of equations in (10), i.e. the number of rows in M_{H+D}. If we consider a through shaft as two shafts connected together, one for each of the two variables, then the bracketed term counts the number of ends of shafts, three for each adder and junction, one for each external end of a P or D shaft, and two for the connections of the through shafts. Half this is the total number of variables $P + H + D$ since each variable has one shaft with two ends. Subtracting P, the left member is $H + D$, the number of columns of M_{H+D}. Hence in an orientable machine M_{H+D} is square. Incidentally (87) entails equation (35) given later in the section.

Now assuming M_{H+D} square let the determinant $|M_{H+D}|$ be expanded, and consider a non-vanishing term. Such a term is a product of $H + D$ non-vanishing elements of M_{H+D}, one from each row and column. Such a selection of elements describes an orientation of the machine. Each column corresponds to an internal or a driven shaft and each row to a node (junction, adder or center of through shaft) at one end of the shaft (namely the node which gave rise to the row or equation M_{H+D}). Draw the arrow on the shaft away from the associated node. Draw arrows on the power shafts toward the machine. This constitutes a complete orientation since all shafts are oriented and

1. the P and T shafts are obviously oriented correctly,

2. the D shafts connect only to nodes in the machine, hence their arrows point away from the machine,

3. each adder corresponds to exactly one equation (or row in M_{H+D}). Hence there is exactly one arrow pointing away from each adder,

4. each junction corresponds to just two rows in M_{H+D} so there are exactly two arrows pointing away from each junction.

Furthermore, each different term in the expansion of $|M_{H+D}|$ gives a different orientation, for consider two terms differing, say in the selection of an element from column one, the first using a_{11}, the second a_{21}. If row one is an adder equation, in the a_{11} case the arrow on shaft one is away from the adder, in the a_{21} case toward it. In case row one is a junction equation the same holds unless both rows one and two represent the same junction. In this case we have a situation as follows:

$$a_{11} \quad 0 \quad 0 \quad \cdots \quad 0 \quad a_{1k} \quad 0 \quad \cdots \quad 0 \quad \cdots \quad 0$$
$$a_{11} \quad 0 \quad 0 \quad \cdots \quad 0 \quad 0 \quad 0 \quad \cdots \quad a_{2j} \quad \cdots \quad 0$$
$$\cdots \quad \cdots \quad \cdots \quad \cdots \quad \cdots \quad \cdots \quad \cdots \quad \cdots \quad \cdots \cdots \quad \cdots$$

and since there are at most two non-vanishing elements in each row, a_{11} must have a_{2j} in its product and a_{21} has a_{1k}. Thus the two cases have different orientations as shown in Fig. 21. If row one is a T equation any other selection is impossible since only one of the H and D variables appears here.

a_{11} CASE $\qquad\qquad\qquad\qquad$ a_{21} CASE

FIG 21

Conversely we can show that no orientation is possible which does not correspond to a non-vanishing term in $|M_{H+D}|$, for assume we have an orientation. Throwing the previous argument into reverse, this corresponds to an association of a different equation with each different internal or driven variable. The adder equations are obvious, and it is not difficult to see that the junction equations are fixed unambiguously. As the gear ratios are non-vanishing, the corresponding term of the determinant expansion is also.

Theorem VI. This now follows immediately from the fact that for a machine to be non-degenerate $|M_{H+D}| \neq 0$.

Theorem VII. We note that in an orientable machine, at least one term of the determinant expansion does not vanish. By proper choice of gear ratios we can clearly make this term dominate the others, so that $|M_{H+D}| \neq 0$, and the machine is not degenerate.

Theorems VIII and IX. Unique orientation is equivalent to just one term of $|M_{H+D}|$ not vanishing. But this is equivalent to M_{H+D} being non-singular and triangulatable by row and column interchanges.

Theorem X. A direct consequences of Theorem XI.

Theorem XI. Imagine the two orientations superimposed. The orientations can only differ on internal shafts. Consider a shaft where they differ. This must end in an adder or junction and clearly exactly one other shaft entering this adder or junction must differ in orientation. Following along the path of different orientations we must eventually come back to the original shaft since the path cannot end. Also it cannot branch out so the different circuits where the orientations differ are independent. The converse is trivial.

SECTION 5

Theorem XII. The lines remaining after a fundamental system is deleted from a network is called a "gerust." It is easily shown[8] that the gerust of a connected network is a connected tree touching every node of the original network. Hence it contains as many lines as there are nodes less one, or $A + J - 1 = 2A - 1$ lines, using the last sentence in Section 4.

We will assume an arbitrary (but fixed) gear in each shaft of a given machine and show that by transformations which keep the external behavior the same we can eliminate the gears on any chosen gerust, that is, make them all $+ 1$. The transformations are:

1.   a gear may be moved from the input to the output of an integrator.

2.   a gear may be moved from the e shaft to the y shaft of any machine.

3.   we can insert gears of any ratio $a \neq 0$ in the three shafts of a node (either adder or junction).

These transformations are shown in Fig. 22, and it is obvious that they leave external behavior invariant. Due to the first we may omit integrators for present purposes, and due to the second we connect output to input and consider only one gear in this shaft. The third transformation contains the crux of the proof. Draw the network of the machine, Fig. 23 for example, with the gerust in question heavy and the fundamental system dotted, and assume a gear in each line. Start at the end of one branch (node 0) of the gerust and move along the branch to the first node 1. Using the third transformation insert gears of proper ratio about node 1 to make the resulting gear in the line just passed over unity. Now move along the gerust to another node 2. Perform the same transformation making the gear in the line passed over unity. Continue this process until a line is given unity gear ratio for each node of the gerust, i.e. each node of the network. At each stage we go from a node already used to one not used along a line of the gerust and adjust the line passed over. Each node can be reached since the gerust is connected, and at no point is an already adjusted line altered, since the gerust is a tree. Gears will be left only on the $A + 1$ lines of the fundamental system, proving the theorem.

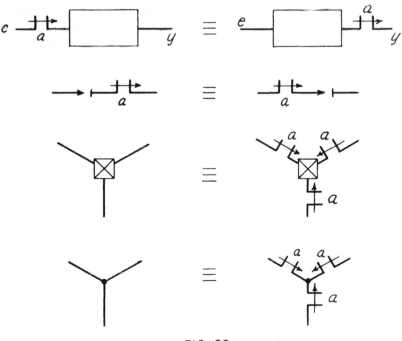

FIG 22

We can generalize this result for machines with more than one input and output shaft as follows.

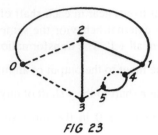

FIG 23

Theorem XIIA. Connecting the ends of all E external shafts to a common node, any fundamental system of this network gives sufficient gearing for the machine. This requires $(E + A - 1)$ gears.

The proof follows the same scheme, using a more general transformation which includes 1, 2, 3 above. Imagine a simple closed Jordan surface S in space cutting through the shafts of a machine. Such a surface divides space into two parts, an inside and an outside. We can insert gears into each shaft cut by the surface, all of the same arbitrary ratio $K \neq 0$, and all pointing from the inside to the outside, without affecting the behavior of the machine. This theorem, whose proof is left to the reader, is useful in eliminating the (-1) gears resulting when we take the dual of a machine (Section 11).

SECTION 7

Theorem XIII. Referring to Fig. 6, $Y(\infty) = b_{n+1,n+1}$ is the admittance from e to y with $X_1 = X_2 = \cdots = X_n = 0$ i.e. held stationary, and the pX_i free to turn. This can be seen from (19) and (20). If $Y(\infty) = 0$ the shaft y is held at 0 under these conditions for any e and the reversed machine must be locked. If $Y(\infty) \neq 0$, y can assume any value with $X_1 = X_2 = \cdots = X_n = 0$ and the reversed machine is not locked. Also e is uniquely determined by y and the X_i so the machine does not have free driven shafts (the pX_i are uniquely determined by e and the X_i, hence by y and the X_i). Finally the reversed machine contains no internal degeneracies, since their definition does not differentiate power and driven shafts. The reversed admittance must obviously be

$$[Y(p)]^{-1} \ .$$

Theorem XIV. If there is no such path $Y(p) \equiv 0$ by Theorem XVIII. If there is exactly one path then reversing the arrows in this path orients the reversed machine and with this orientation there can be no directed circuits touching the path. The result now follows easily from Theorem XIX.

SECTION 8

Theorem XV. The degeneracy part is easily seen from the definitions of the various types of degeneracy. Also, since $y_1 = e_2$,

$$y_2 = Y_2(p)e_2 = Y_2(p)Y_1(p)e_1 \ . \tag{89}$$

Theorem XVI. The degeneracy part is also obvious here and, since $e = e_1 = e_2$,

$$y = - y_1 - y_2 = - Y_1(p)e_1 - Y_2(p)e_2$$

$$= - [Y_1(p) + Y_2(p)]e .$$

(90)

Theorem XVII. Assuming that both machines are non-degenerate,

$$e = e_1 + y_2 = e_1 + Y_2(p)e_2 = (1 + Y_1(p)Y_2(p))e_1 ,$$

$$y = y_1 = Y_1(p)e_1 .$$

e is locked if and only if $1 + Y_1(\infty)Y_2(\infty) = 0$ and if this is not true, by eliminating e_2 we get

$$y = \frac{1}{Y_1^{-1} + Y_2} e .$$

(91)

The conditions of the theorem are also necessary for non-degeneracy with the trivial exception that both machines can be degenerate if they are not degenerate in the reverse direction.

SECTION 9

Theorem XVIII. We will prove this theorem by an induction on the number of adders and junctions in the machine. First the theorem is obvious for any machine with no adders or junctions since in this case there are no circuits and each power shaft is connected to exactly one driven shaft through only gears and integrators. $D = 1$ and the single path product is the transfer admittance. We will now make the theorem for any given machine M depend on the truth of the theorem for a simpler machine M' with one fewer adder or junction. Since the machine M is connected and contains at least one adder or junction it must be possible to reach a junction or adder from one of the input shafts. In Fig. 24 suppose this is possible from e_1 and when we enter the machine at e_1 suppose the first node we reach is a junction (after possibly passing over integrators and gears of admittance $A(p)$). Consider the reduced machine Fig. 25, with one fewer junction. The orientation must be as shown. M' is not degenerate unless M is, for the only possibility is that x_1, x_2 are locked, and in that case they are redundant in M. Assuming the theorem for M' the transfer admittance from e_1 to y_1 (say) in M is the sum of the admittances in M' from x_1 and x_2 to y_1,

$$Y_{12} = \frac{\Sigma A P_k' D_k' + \Sigma A P_k'' D_k''}{D} ,$$

where the P_k' are the paths through the upper x_1 line and P_k'' those through the lower x_2 line. But this is clearly the proper expression from the theorem for Y_{12} since the complementary discriminants must be the same (no circuits being introducing by the junction) and the $A P_k'$ combined with the $A P_k''$ give the path products in M. D of course is the same for M and M'.

In case the first node reached from e_1 is an adder the situation is as shown in Fig. 26. Consider the reduced machine M' in Fig. 27. Again it is clear that M' is not degenerate unless M is. We assume the theorem true for M' so that when $e_2 = e_3 = \cdots = e_n = 0$ then

$$y_1 = Y_1 x ,$$

$$z = Y_2 x ,$$

Y_1 and Y_2 being given by the theorem. In the machine M

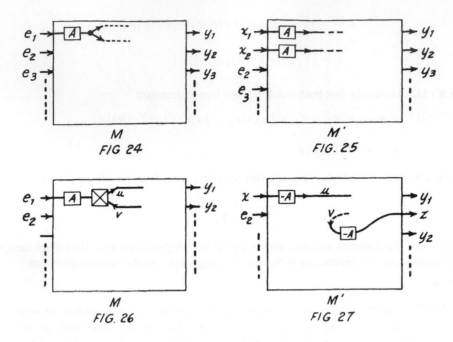

$$Ae_1 + u + v = 0$$

or

$$e_1 - x - z = 0 .$$

Eliminating x and z we obtain the admittance of M in terms of the admittances Y_1 and Y_2 of M':

$$y_1 = \frac{Y_1}{1+Y_2} \, e_1 . \tag{92}$$

We must show that $Y_1/(1+Y_2)$ is the expression for Y_{12} found by applying the theorem to M. By an inspection of Figs. 26 and 27 we note the following facts.

1. The directed circuits in M can be divided into two groups, a set C_i' not passing through the adder in question and a set C_i'' passing through the adder.

2. The circuits of M' are C_i'. Hence the discriminant of M', which we denote D', is given by

$$D' = 1 - \sum C_i' + \sum C_i' C_j' - \cdots \tag{93}$$

3. The circuits in M passing through the adder are the negatives of the path products P_i'' in M' from x to z (note that the A's cancel). Let C_j'' range over circuits in M (or M') not touching P_i''. Then the discriminant for M may be written

$$D = 1 - \sum C_i' + \sum C_i' C_j' - \cdots$$

$$+ \sum P_i'' - \sum P_i'' C_j'' + \sum P_i'' C_j'' C_k'' - \cdots$$

The first series is D' and the second is the numerator of Y_2 since we assume the theorem for M'. Hence

$$D = D' + D'Y_2 = D'(1+Y_2)$$ (94)

and using (92).

$$Y_{12} = \frac{Y_1 D'}{D}.$$ (95)

We have obtained the desired denominator D. Now we show that

$$Y_1 D' = \sum P_k D_k,$$ (96)

where the sum is over paths P_k in M from e_1 to y_1 with complementary D_k. These paths in M are the same as those in M' from x to y_1 (the $-$ sign on the A corresponds to the (-1) introduced by the adder) and the complementary D_k in M are also the same as the D_k in M'. Hence by our inductive assumption $\sum P_k D_k$ is equal to the numerator of Y_1 and

$$Y_1 D' = \sum P_k D_k$$

proving the theorem for M.

SECTION 10

Theorem XIX. An immediate consequence of Theorem XX.

Theorem XX. By its definition D is a polynomial in negative powers of p with constant term D^*:

$$D = D^* + a_1 p^{-1} + a_2 p^{-2} + \cdots + a_n p^{-n}.$$ (97)

Hence $p^n D$ is a polynomial of degree n and must be a constant times the machine determinant (the denominator of (27)). As the coefficient of p^n in (28) is $(-1)^n$,

$$D^* \Delta = (-p)^n D.$$ (98)

SECTION 11

Theorem XXI. We can remove the internal degeneracies by the method of the second pair of dual statements following Theorem XXIII. These are true since:

1. By definition a redundant shaft can be broken, without affecting external behavior. Clearly each other shaft of an adder connected to such a broken shaft can also be broken, etc. A junction with one shaft broken can be jumpered across.

2. By definition a free internal shaft can be held stationary without affecting external behavior. Any shaft connected by junctions and gears to a stationary shaft is held stationary, and if one shaft of an adder is held stationary the other two act as if connected by a (-1) gear. Note that these eliminations retain duality. We may eliminate the degeneracies in our given machine M one by one, arriving at an undegenerate machine M_1 and by performing the corresponding reductions on M' arrive at M_1'.

Since M_1 is not degenerate it can be oriented, and reversing the arrows on corresponding shafts orients M_1'. The directed circuit products in M_1 are the same as in M_1' and the path products change sign. For in the case of circuits the numerical value of a circuit in M_1' is the same as the corresponding circuit in M_1 and has a sign factor

$$(-1)^J (-1)^A (-1)^{J+A} = +1,$$ (99)

the first term for junctions that become adders, the second for adders that become junctions, and the third for the (-1) gears in internal shafts. Similarly for paths where the third exponent is $J + A + 1$. Consequently the discriminant of M_1' is the same as that of M_1, and M_1' is not degenerate. Using Theorem XVIII we see that in M_1'

$$e_j' = - \sum_{i=1}^{s} Y_{ij}\, y_i' , \quad j = 1, 2, ..., r , \tag{100}$$

proving the theorem.

It is well known[9] that the matrices of the coefficients of (57) and (56) (after transposing to the same member)

$$A = \left\| \begin{array}{ccccccc} 1 & 0 & \cdots & 0 & Y_{11} & \cdots & Y_{s1} \\ 0 & 1 & \cdots & 0 & \cdots & \cdots & \cdots \\ \cdots & \cdots & \cdots & \cdots & \cdots & \cdots & \cdots \\ 0 & 0 & \cdots & 1 & Y_{1r} & \cdots & Y_{sr} \end{array} \right\| \tag{101}$$

and

$$B = \left\| \begin{array}{ccccccc} Y_{11} & \cdots & Y_{1r} & -1 & 0 & \cdots & 0 \\ \cdots & \cdots & \cdots & & 0 & -1 & \cdots & 0 \\ \cdots & \cdots & \cdots & & \cdots & \cdots & \cdots & \cdots \\ Y_{s1} & \cdots & Y_{sr} & 0 & 0 & \cdots & -1 \end{array} \right\| , \tag{102}$$

are orthogonal, i.e. represent completely orthogonal regions in $r + s$ space.* This gives a partial proof of Theorem XXII, namely a proof for machines which satisfy the conditions stated in the beginning of Theorem XXI. Theorem XXII is true, however, for any machine in the sense that the equations of the machines place the stated constraints on the regions. We will sketch an inductive proof of this.

Theorem XXII. Another definition of orthogonal complements[10] is that the dot product of any vector in R with any vector in R' vanishes:

$$X \cdot Y = 0 , \quad X \in R, \ Y \in R' , \tag{103}$$

and any vector Z is decomposable into a part in R and a part in R'.

$$Z = X + Y , \quad X \in R, \ Y \in R' . \tag{104}$$

First we show that the theorem is true for any machine with no internal shafts, for example Fig. 28, with the dual machine of Fig. 29. We verify easily that the theorem is true for any single isolated part, such as the adder in Fig. 28. Now suppose it true for a machine with n separate parts. Adding another part the theorem remains true, for suppose the enlarged machine has coordinates

$$(x_1, x_2, ..., x_s, x_{s+1}, ..., x_t) \tag{105}$$

and the dual machine has coordinates

$$(y_1, y_2, ..., y_s, y_{s+1}, ..., y_t) , \tag{106}$$

---

* For this it is necessary and sufficient that $AB' = 0$ and rank A + rank $B = r + S$, B' denoting the transpose of B. These are easily verified for A, B above.

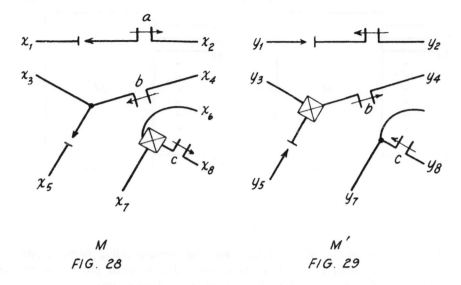

M

FIG. 28

M'

FIG. 29

the first s being present before the addition. Then the dot product of X and Y is

$$x_1 y_1 + x_2 y_2 + \cdots + x_s y_s + x_{s+1} y_{s+1} + \cdots + x_t y_t = 0 + 0,$$

since the first s terms vanish by the inductive hypothesis and the rest since we added a single isolated part for which the theorem was verified. It is also evident that we can decompose any vector since we can decompose the two groups of coordinates independently.

We now perform another induction, this time on the number of internal shafts. We will show that the theorem is true for any machine with m internal shafts if it is true for any machine with $m - 1$ internal shafts. In the given machine break one of the m internal shafts bringing the ends out as external shafts. Suppose that after this breaking the machine is as shown in Fig. 30a with dual 30b, and that the new external shafts of M are x_1 and x_2. By assumption the regions of M and M' are orthogonal complements. Reconnect x_1 to x_2 and y_1 to y_2 with a (-1) gear, thus retaining duality and yielding the original machine and its dual. The external shafts are $x_3, \ldots, x_n$ and $y_3, \ldots, y_n$ and their dot product is

$$x_3 y_3 + x_4 y_4 + \cdots + x_n y_n$$

$$= x_1 y_1 + x_2 y_2 + x_3 y_3 + \cdots + x_n y_n = 0 \tag{107}$$

by assumption and since $x_1 = x_2$, $y_1 = -y_2$. Also since we can decompose any

$$(a_1, \ldots, a_n) = (x_1, \ldots, x_n) + (y_1, \ldots, y_n), \tag{108}$$

it is easy to show by decomposing $(0, 0, b_3, \ldots, b_n)$, $(0, 1, 0, \ldots, 0)$, $(1, 0, 0, \ldots, 0)$ and $(1, 1, 0, \ldots, 0)$ and taking a suitable linear combination that we can decompose

$$(b_3 \ldots b_n) = (x_3 \ldots x_n) + (y_3 \ldots y_n) \tag{109}$$

with

$$x_1 = x_2, \quad y_1 = -y_2 \, .$$

Theorem XXIII. The duality table is, of course, merely a mapping or isomorphism between

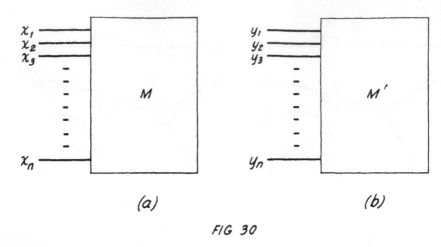

FIG 30

parts, properties, or operations of a machine and the corresponding parts, properties, or operations in the dual machine. Most of these have already been proved in developing Theorems XXI and XXII. The remainder follows easily from these results.

SECTION 12

Theorem XXIV. In (65) the A_i and B_i are polynomials in the b_{ij} and hence rational functions of the a_{ij} (the gear ratios) from their genesis in (20) and (10). If in a certain machine M there are only $G-1$ gears $g_1 \ldots g_{G-1}$ the G independent A_i and B_i are rational functions of these. Hence it is known that a polynomial (not identically zero) in these A_i and B_i must vanish identically in the g_i, namely the eliminant of these G equations. Hence we can solve for one of the A_i or B_i which appears in the polynomial and this coefficient can only assume a finite number of values when the others are fixed. If only a bounded number of adders are used there are only a finite number of different machines, so almost all sets of coefficients cannot be realized. Although the last statement remains true even if the number of adders is unbounded, we could then *approximate* to any set of coefficients, for an unlimited set of adders can approximate an arbitrary gear ratio by expansion in the base two.

SECTION 13

Theorem XXV. n integrators and $2n+1$ gears are necessary as noted. Suppose $2n-1$ adders were sufficient. Then by Theorem XII $2n$ gears are sufficient, a contradiction. Also the number of junctions is equal to the number of adders by (35).

Bibliography

1. V. Bush, "Operational Circuit Analysis," John Wiley.

2. John R. Carson, "Electric Circuit Theory and the Operational Calculus," McGraw Hill, 1926.

3. V. Bush, "The Differential Analyzer, a New Machine for Solving Differential Equations," Journal of the Franklin Institute, v. 212, p. 447 (1931).

4. C. E. Shannon, "Mathematical Theory of the Differential Analyzer," Journal of Mathematics and Physics, v. XX, No. 4, p. 337 (1941).

5. C. E. Shannon, "The Theory of Linear Differential and Smoothing Operators," N.D.R.C. report.

6. E. A. Guillemin, "Communication Networks," Vol. II, John Wiley, 1935.

7. M. Bôcher, "Introduction to Higher Algebra," Macmillan, 1933, Chapter 4.

8. Dénes König, "Theorie der Endlichen and Unendlichen Graphen," Leipzig, 1936, pp. 56-62.

9. C. E. Cullis, "Matrices and Determinoids," Vol. 2, Cambridge, 1918, Chapter XVIII.

10. Birkhoff and MacLane, "A Survey of Modern Algebra," Macmillan, 1941, pp. 186-189.

THE NUMBER OF TWO-TERMINAL SERIES-PARALLEL NETWORKS

By John Riordan and C. E. Shannon

One of the first attempts to list all electrical networks meeting certain specified conditions was made in 1892 by P. A. MacMahon[1] who investigated combinations of resistances in series and in parallel, giving without proof a generating function from which the number of such combinations could be determined and a table of the numbers for combinations with 10 or less elements.[2]

The series-parallel combinations do not exhaust the possible networks since they exclude all bridge arrangements like the Wheatstone net,[3] but they are an important subclass because of their simplicity. When the number of elements is less than 5, all networks are series-parallel; at 5 there is one bridge-type network, the Wheatstone net; as the number of elements rises, bridge type networks increase faster than series-parallel until at 9 e.g. bridge-type are about 40% of the total. It appears from this (and it is known to be true) that for a large number of elements, series parallel networks are a relatively small part of the total; nevertheless the problem of enumerating all networks is so difficult that an extended study of the series-parallel networks is welcome on the principle that a little light is better than none.

Apart from this, the series-parallel networks are interesting in themselves in another setting, namely the design of switching circuits.[4] Here it becomes important to know how many elements are required to realize any switching function $f(x_1, \cdots, x_n)$ of n variables—that is, a number $N(n)$ such that every one of the 2^{2^n} different functions f can be realized with N elements and at least one with no less. An upper bound for the number of two terminal networks with B branches determines a lower bound for N since the number of different networks we can construct with N branches, taking account of different assignments of variables to the branches, can not be exceeded by 2^{2^n}; there must be enough networks to go around. This general fact is equally true if we limit the networks to the series-parallel type, and since switching networks are particularly easy to design in this form, the number of elements necessary for series-parallel realization of a function is of immediate interest.

These considerations have led us to work out a proof of MacMahon's generating function, which is given in full below; to develop recurrences and schemes of computation from this with which to extend MacMahon's table; to investigate

---

[1] "The Combination of Resistances," The Electrician, April 8, 1892; cf. also Cayley, Collected Works, III, **203**, pp. 242–6 for development of the generating function in another problem.

[2] It may be noted here that the number for 10 elements is given incorrectly as 4984; the correct value, 4624, is shown in Table I below.

[3] Complete enumerations of all possible circuits of n elements with n small classified in various ways are given by R. M. Foster, "The Geometrical Circuits of Electrical Networks," Trans. A. I. E. E., **51** (1932), pp. 309–317.

[4] C. E. Shannon, "A Symbolic Analysis of Relay and Switching Circuits," Trans. A. I. E. E., **57** (1938), pp. 713–723.

Reprinted from Journal of Mathematics and Physics
Vol. XXI, No. 2, August, 1942

the behavior of the series-parallel numbers when the number of elements is large, and finally to make the application to switching functions mentioned above.   These subjects are treated in separate sections.

For brevity in what follows we use the initials s.p. for series-parallel, e.s. for essentially series, and e.p. for essentially parallel.[5]

1. Derivation of Generating Function

For a single element, obviously only one network, the element itself, is possible. For 2, 3 and 4 elements, Fig. 1 shows all the s.p. networks obtainable divided into e.s. and e.p. classes for reasons which will appear.

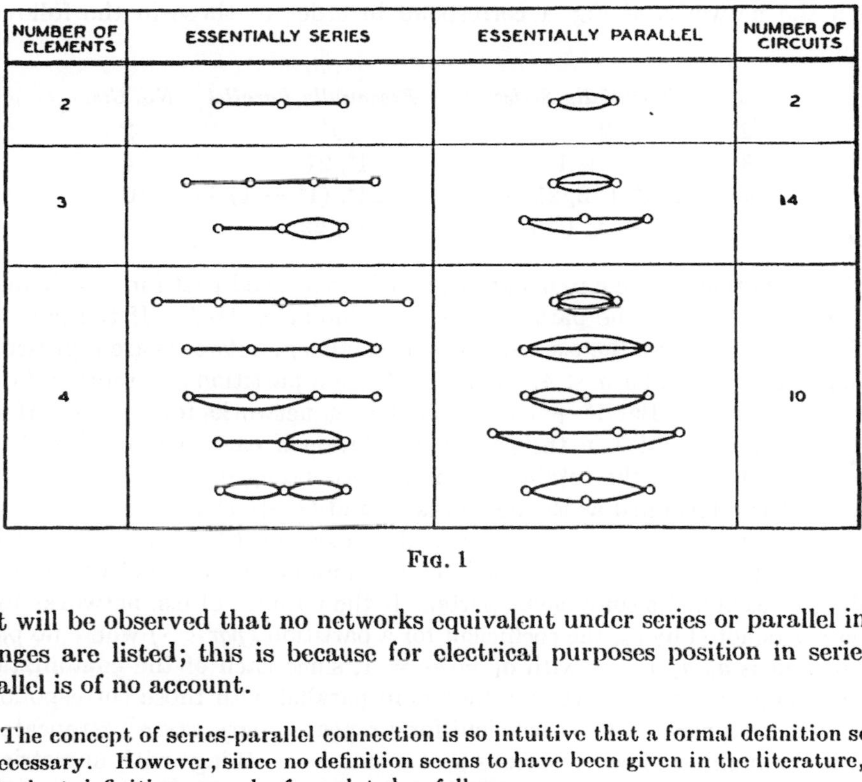

NUMBER OF ELEMENTS	ESSENTIALLY SERIES	ESSENTIALLY PARALLEL	NUMBER OF CIRCUITS
2			2
3			14
4			10

FIG. 1

It will be observed that no networks equivalent under series or parallel interchanges are listed; this is because for electrical purposes position in series or parallel is of no account.

[5] The concept of series-parallel connection is so intuitive that a formal definition seems unnecessary.   However, since no definition seems to have been given in the literature, two equivalent definitions may be formulated as follows:

Definition I—A network N is series-parallel with respect to two terminals a and b if through each element of N there is at least one path from a to b not touching any junction twice, and no two of these paths pass through any element in opposite directions.

Definition II—A network is series-parallel if it is either a series or a parallel connection of two series-parallel networks.   A single element is a series-parallel network.

Definition II is an inductive definition.   Note that it serves to define equivalence under series-parallel interchanges directly; thus:

Two series-parallel networks are the same under series-parallel interchanges if they are series or parallel connections of the same two networks.

Note also the following:

A network is essentially series (essentially parallel) if it is the series (parallel) connection of two s.p. networks.

The classification exhibits a duality: e.s. and e.p. networks are equinumerous and in $1 - 1$ correspondence. The rule of correspondence is that an e.s. network becomes e.p. when the words series and parallel in the description of the network are interchanged.

For enumerative purposes it is convenient to have a numerical representation of the networks. This may be done by using the sign $+$ to denote elements in series, the dot or simple adjunction to denote elements in parallel, 1 to denote a circuit element, and abbreviating $1 + 1 + \cdot \cdot \cdot + 1$ (n elements in series) to n and $1 \cdot 1 \cdot \cdot \cdot \cdot \cdot 1$ (n elements in parallel) to 1^n; e.g. the symbol 21 represents a parallel connection of two elements in series and a single element.

Then the networks of Fig. 1 correspond in order to those in the following table:

n	Essentially Series	Essentially Parallel	No. Cls.
2	2	1^2	2
3	$3, 1^2 + 1$	$1^3, 21$	4
4	$4, 1^2 + 2, 21 + 1$	$1^4, 21^2, (1^2 + 1)\,1$	10
	$1^3 + 1, 1^2 + 1^2$	$31, 22$	

Fixing attention on the e.p. networks, it will be noticed that for $n = 2$ and 3, the representations are the partitions of n, excluding n itself. If the partition n itself is taken to mean the e.s. networks, then all s.p. networks are represented by the partitions of n, for $n < 4$. For $n = 4$ a non-partition e.p. representation $(1^2 + 1)\,1$ appears. But $1^2 + 1$ is one of the e.s. networks for $n = 3$. Hence all networks are included in the partition notation if each part of a partition is interpreted to mean the totality of the corresponding e.s. networks; e.g. the partition 31 is interpreted as the networks 31 and $(1^2 + 1)\,1$.

For enumerative purposes this means that each partition has a numerical coefficient attached to it determined by the number of e.s. networks corresponding to each of its component parts. If the number of e.s. networks for p elements is denoted by a_p, the coefficient for a partition $(pqr \cdot \cdot \cdot)$ where no parts are repeated is $a_p\, a_q\, a_r \cdot \cdot \cdot$ with $a_1 = a_2 = 1$, since each of the combinations corresponding to a given part may be put in parallel with those corresponding to the remaining parts. The coefficient for a repeated part, say p^π, p repeated π times, is the number of combinations π at a time of a_p things with unrestricted repetition, which is the binomial coefficient:[6]

$$\binom{a_p + \pi - 1}{\pi}$$

Hence the total number of s.p. networks s_n for n elements may be written as:

$$s_n = 2a_n = \sum \binom{a_p + \pi_1 - 1}{\pi_1}\binom{a_q + \pi_2 - 1}{\pi_2} \cdots \tag{1}$$

[6] Netto, *Lehrbuch der Combinatorik*, Leipzig, 1901, p. 21 or Chrystal, *Algebra* II, London, 1926, p. 11.

where the sum is over all integral non-negative $p, q \cdots , \pi_1, \pi_2 \cdots$ such that

$$p\pi_1 + q\pi_2 + r\pi_3 + \cdots = n$$

and $a_1 = a_2 = 1$. That is, the sum is over all partitions of n.

Thus for $n = 5$ the partitions are:

$$5, 41, 32, 31^2, 2^21, 21^3, 1^5;$$

and

$$s_5 = a_5 + a_4 + a_3 + a_3 + 1 + 1 + 1,$$

or since $s_n = 2a_n$

$$s_5 = s_4 + 2s_3 + 6 = 24.$$

Similarly:

$$s_6 = s_5 + 2s_4 + 2\binom{a_3 + 1}{2} + 2s_3 + 8 = 66.$$

The generating function[7] given by MacMahon, namely:

$$\prod_1^\infty (1 - x^i)^{-a_i} = 1 + \sum_1^\infty s_n x^n \qquad (2)$$

where $\prod$ signifies a product, may be derived from (1) by an argument not essentially different from that used for the Euler generating-function[8] for the partitions of n, which is

$$\prod_1^\infty (1 - x^i)^{-1} = 1 + \sum_1^\infty p_n x^n$$

2. Numerical Calculation

Direct computation from the generating identity (2) or its equivalent, equation (1), becomes cumbersome for relatively small values of n, since the number of terms is equal to the number of partitions. Moreover, the computation is serial, each number depending on its predecessors, involving cumulation of errors; hence independent schemes of computation are desirable.

The three schemes used in computing the series-parallel numbers shown in Table I[9] follow closely schemes for computing the number of partitions, namely those due respectively to Euler and Gupta, and that implicit in the recurrence formula.

---

[7] It should be observed that this is not a generating function in the sense that the coefficients of the power series are completely determined by expansion, but rather a generating identity determining coefficients by equating terms of like powers.

[8] Cf., for example, Hardy and Wright "An Introduction to the Theory of Numbers," Oxford, 1938, p. 272.

[9] We are indebted to our associate Miss J. D. Goeltz for the actual computation.

TABLE I
Series-Parallel and Associated Numbers

n	s_n	σ_n
1	1	1
2	2	1
3	4	1
4	10	3
5	24	5
6	66	17
7	180	41
8	522	127
9	1,532	365
10	4,624	1,119
11	14,136	3,413
12	43,930	10,685
13	137,908	33,561
14	437,502	106,827
15	1,399,068	342,129
16	4,507,352	1,104,347
17	14,611,576	3,584,649
18	47,633,486	11,701,369
19	156,047,204	38,374,065
20	513,477,502	126,395,259
21	1,696,305,720	
22	5,623,993,944	
23	18,706,733,128	
24	62,408,176,762	
25	208,769,240,140	
26	700,129,713,630	
27	2,353,386,723,912	
28	7,927,504,004,640	
29	26,757,247,573,360	
30	90,479,177,302,242	

The first depends essentially on the computation of an allied set of numbers $s_n(k)$ defined by:

$$\prod_{1}^{k} (1 - x^i)^{-a_i} = 1 + \sum_{n=1}^{\infty} s_n(k)x^n, \tag{3}$$

with $s_n = s_n(N)$, $N \geq n$.

A recurrence formula for these numbers follows directly from the definition and reads as follows:

$$s_n(k) = \sum_{i=0}^{q} \binom{a_k + i - 1}{i} s_{n-ik}(k - 1), \tag{4}$$

with q the integral part of n/k and $s_0(k-1) = s_0(k) = 1$. Clearly $s_n(1) = 1$, $s_n(2) = 1 + [\frac{1}{2}n]$, where the brackets indicate "integral part of."

Note that $s_n(k)$ enumerates the number of c.p. (or c.s.) networks with n elements that can be formed from parts no one of which contains more than k elements; e.g., the c.p. networks enumerated by $s_4(2)$ are 2^2, 21^2, and 1^4. This remark, coupled with the interpretation of the binomial coefficients given in Section 1, gives a ready network interpretation of the recurrence (4).

Although, as indicated, the numbers $s_n(k)$ may be used directly for computation of s_n, they are more efficiently used in the following formula:

$$s_n = s_{n-1} + s_{n-2}s_2 + \cdots + s_{n-m-1}s_{m+1} + 2s_n(m) \qquad (5)$$

where $m = [\frac{1}{2}n]$.

The network interpretation of this is seen more readily in the equivalent form:

$$s_n = a_n + a_{n-1}a_1 + a_{n-2}s_2 + \cdots + a_{n-m-1}s_{m+1} + s_n(m) \qquad (5.1)$$

Thus the total number of networks with n elements is made up of c.s. networks with n elements enumerated by a_n, plus c.p. networks formed by combining all c.s. networks of $n - i$ elements with all networks of i elements, $i = 1$ to the smaller of $m + 1$ and $n - m - 1$, plus finally the networks enumerated by $s_n(m)$ as described above.

This is essentially all that is used in what may be called the Euler computation.

The Gupta computation rests upon division of partitions into classes according to size of the lowest part; e.g. if the partitions of n with lowest part k are designated by $p_{n,k}$, then the classes for $n = 4$ are:

$$p_{4,1} = (31, 21^2, 1^4)$$

$$p_{4,2} = (2^2)$$

$$p_{4,3} = \text{None}$$

$$p_{4,4} = (4)$$

Recurrence formulae for the corresponding network classes $s_{n,k}$ are derived by appropriate modification of a procedure given by Gupta; thus e.g. if a unit is deleted from each of the partitions in $p_{n,1}$, the result is exactly p_{n-1}, hence:

$$s_{n,1} = s_{n-1}.$$

Similarly:

$$s_{n,2} = a_2[s_{n-2,2} + s_{n-2,3} + \cdots s_{n-2,n-2}]$$

$$= s_{n-2} - s_{n-2,1} = s_{n-2} - s_{n-3}.$$

In general:

$$s_{n,k} = \sum_{i=1}^{q} \binom{a_k + i - 1}{i} A_{n-ik,k}, \qquad (6)$$

with

$$q = [n/k]$$
$$A_{0,\,k} = 1,$$
$$A_{r,\,k} = 0, \qquad r = 1, 2 \cdots k,$$
$$A_{r,\,k} = s_r - s_{r,\,1} - \cdots - s_{r,\,k}, \qquad r > k.$$

Another form of (6), derived by iteration and simpler than (6) for small values of k and large values of n, is as follows:

$$s_{n,k} = \sum_{i=1}^{q} \binom{a_k}{i} A_{n-ik,\,k-1}. \tag{6.1}$$

It should be noted that vacuous terms appear in the sum if $q > a_k$.

The third scheme of computation consists in determining a third set of numbers, σ_n, defined by:

$$\prod_{1}^{\infty} (1 - x^i)^{a_i} = 1 - \sum_{1}^{\infty} \sigma_n x^n \tag{7}$$

Coupling this definition with the MacMahon generating identity, equation (2), it follows that:

$$s_n = \sum_{i=1}^{n} \sigma_i s_{n-i}, \tag{8}$$

with s_0 taken by convention as unity.

The recurrence formula for these numbers is as follows:

$$\sigma_n = a_n - \sum_{i=1}^{n-m-1} \sigma_i a_{n-i} + \sigma_n(m) \tag{9}$$

where, as above $m = [\tfrac{1}{2}n]$ and $\sigma_n(k)$ is defined in a manner similar to $s_n(k)$. Note that $\sigma_1 = \sigma_2 = \sigma_3 = 1$. These numbers are included in Table I ($n < 20$).

3. Asymptotic Behavior

The behavior of s_n for large n is ideally specified by an exact formula or, failing that, an asymptotic formula. It is a remarkable fact that the asymptotic formula for the partition function is an "exact" formula, that is, can be used to calculate values for large n with perfect accuracy. We have not been able to find either for s_n; we give instead comparison functions bounding it from above and below.

It is apparent, first of all, that $s_n \geq p_n$ for all values of n. This is very poor. Somewhat better is

$$s_n \geq \pi_n \tag{10}$$

where $\pi_n = 2^{n-1}$ is the number of compositions of n, that is, partitions of n in which the order of occurrence of the parts is essential.

This is proved as follows. From equation (5), $s_n > q_n$ if

$$q_n \leq s_n \qquad n \leq 4$$

$$q_n = q_{n-1} + s_2 q_{n-2}, \qquad n > 4$$

The solution of the last, taking $q_3 = 4$, $q_4 = 8$, is:

$$q_n = 2^{n-1} = \pi_n$$

More terms of equation (5) push the lower bound up but at a relatively slow rate and the analysis increases rapidly in difficulty; the best we have been able to show in this way is:

$$s_n \geq A3^n \tag{11}$$

with A a fixed constant.

An alternative, more intuitive, way, however, is much better. First, notice that the networks for n elements are certainly greater in number than those obtained by connecting a single element in series or in parallel with the networks for $n - 1$ elements, a doubling operation; hence, $s_n \geq \pi_n$ where

$$\pi_n = 2\pi_{n-1} = 2^2\pi_{n-2} = 2^{n-1}\pi_1 = 2^{n-1},$$

which is the result reached above.

The networks of n elements with a single element in series or in parallel are exactly those enumerated by $s_{n,1}$ in the Gupta classification. Hence the approximation may be bettered by considering more terms in the expansion:

$$s_n = 2 \sum_{i=1}^{m} s_{n,i}, \qquad m = [\tfrac{1}{2}n].$$

The term $s_{n,i}$ enumerates the e.s. networks in which the smallest c.p. part has exactly i elements. If this part is removed from each of these networks, the networks left are certainly not less than the e.s. networks with $n - i$ elements if $i < m$; that is

$$s_{n,i} \geq a_i a_{n-i} \qquad i < m$$

For n even, say $2m$;

$$s_{2m,m} = \binom{a_m + 1}{2} = \tfrac{1}{2}(a_m^2 + a_m) = \tfrac{1}{8}(s_m^2 + 2s_m);$$

for n odd;

$$s_{2m+1,m} = a_{m+1}a_m = \tfrac{1}{4}s_{m+1}s_m.$$

Hence:

$$s_{2m} \geq 2 s_{n-1} + \frac{1}{2}\sum_{2}^{m-1} s_i s_{n-i} + \frac{1}{4}(s_m^2 + 2s_m)$$

$$s_{2m+1} \geq 2 s_{n-1} + \frac{1}{2}\sum_{2}^{m} s_i s_{n-i} \tag{12}$$

Then, in general, $s_n > r_n$ if $r_1 = 1, r_2 = 2$ and

$$r_n = \frac{3}{2}r_{n-1} + \frac{1}{4}\sum_1^{n-1} r_i r_{n-i}, \qquad n > 2 \tag{13}$$

Writing the generating function for the r_n as:

$$R(x) = \sum_1^{\infty} r_n x^n,$$

the recurrence (13) together with the initial conditions entail:

$$[R(x)]^2 - (4 - 6x)R(x) + 4x - x^2 = 0;$$

that is:

$$R(x) = 2 - 3x - 2\sqrt{1 - 4x + 2x^2} \tag{14}$$

The asymptotic behavior of the r_n may be determined from $R(x)$ by the method of Darboux[10] with the following result:

$$r_n \sim A\lambda^n n^{-3/2} \tag{15}$$

with A a fixed constant and $\lambda = 2 + \sqrt{2} = 3.414 \cdots$.

An upper bound follows by the same process on remarking that:

$$s_{n, i} \leq a_i s_{n-i}.$$

Hence, $s_n \leq t_n$ if $t_1 = 1, t_2 = 2$ and

$$t_n = t_{n-1} + \frac{1}{2}\sum_1^{n-1} t_i t_{n-i} \tag{16}$$

By the procedure followed above:

$$T(x) = \sum_{n=0}^{\infty} t_n x^n = 1 - x - \sqrt{1 - 4x} \tag{17}$$

and

$$t_n = \frac{4(2n - 3)!}{n!(n - 2)!}, n > 1$$

$$\sim \frac{2}{\sqrt{\pi}} 4^{n-1} n^{-3/2}$$

A comparison of r_n, s_n and t_n for $n \leq 10$, taking for convenience the integral part only of r_n (denoted by $[r_n]$) is as follows:

n	1	2	3	4	5	6	7	8	9	10
$[r_n]$	1	2	4	9	22	57	154	429	1225	3565
s_n	1	2	4	10	24	66	180	522	1532	4624
t_n	1	2	4	10	28	84	264	858	2860	9724

[10] Hilbert-Courant: Methoden der Mathematischen Physik I, pp. 460-2 (Springer, 1931, 2nd ed.).

Note that the lower bound is closer to the true value for the larger values of n.

A third, semi-empirical, bound is worth noting. From table I note that for $n > 2$, $4\sigma_n$ is approximately equal to s_n. Taking this as an equality and using equation (8) and the known values $\sigma_1 = \sigma_2 = 1$ the equation for the generating function $U(x)$ of the approximation u_n turns out to be:

$$U(x) = \tfrac{1}{2}[5 - 3x - 2x^2 - \sqrt{9 - 30x - 11x^2 + 12x^3 + 4x^4}] \qquad (18)$$

A comparison of s_n and the integral part of u_n is shown in Table II for $n \leq 20$. The approximation is remarkably close; the worst percentage difference is 10% for $n = 4$, but from $n = 7$ to 20 the agreement is within 3%.

TABLE II

Approximation to Series-Parallel Numbers

n	$[u_n]$	s_n
1	1	1
2	2	2
3	4	4
4	9	10
5	23	24
6	63	66
7	177	180
8	514	522
9	1,527	1,532
10	4,625	4,624
11	14,230	14,136
12	44,357	43,930
13	139,779	137,908
14	444,558	437,502
15	1,425,151	1,399,068
16	4,600,339	4,507,352
17	14,939,849	14,611,576
18	48,778,197	47,633,486
19	160,019,885	156,047,204
20	527,200,711	513,477,502

The asymptotic behavior of u_n is found to be:

$$u_n \sim A\lambda^n n^{-3/2}$$

with A about 3/7, λ about 3.56.

4. Series-Parallel Realization of Switching Functions

As an application of these results it will be shown now that almost all switching functions of n variables require at least

$$(1 - \epsilon)\,\frac{2^n}{\log_2 n} \qquad\qquad \epsilon > 0$$

switching elements (make or break contacts) for their realization in an s.p. network.

The number of functions that can be realized with h elements is certainly less than the number of s.p. networks s_h multiplied by the number of different ways that the elements in each network may be labeled. This latter number is $(2n)^h$ since each element has a choice of $2n$ labels corresponding to each variable and its negative. Hence, not more than

$$(2n)^h s_h \leq (2n)^h 4^h = (8n)^h$$

different functions can be realized with h elements. If

$$h = \frac{2^n}{\log_2 n} (1 - \epsilon) \qquad\qquad \epsilon > 0$$

the fraction of all 2^{2^n} functions of n variables that can be realized is less than.

$$\frac{(8n)^{\frac{2^n}{\log_2 n}(1-\epsilon)}}{2^{2^n}} = \frac{2^{3(1-\epsilon)2^n \log_n 2 + (1-\epsilon)2^n}}{2^{2^n}}$$

$$< 2^{3 \cdot 2^n \log_n 2 - \epsilon \cdot 2^n}$$

and since this approaches zero as $n \to \infty$ for any positive ϵ, the result is proved

BELL TELEPHONE LABORATORIES.

NETWORK RINGS*

Claude E. Shannon

1. INTRODUCTION

A method developed by a group of Chinese scientists[1,2,3,4] for finding the admittance determinant $|Y_{ij}|$ of a linear electrical network proceeds as follows. Label each admittance of the network with a different letter, say $a_1, a_2, \ldots, a_m$. Choose a set of independent nodes or junction points, i.e., a set of all but one from each separate part of the network. Form the symbolic "sums" of the letters corresponding to the branches which are connected to each selected node and "multiply" these "sums" out by the ordinary rules of algebra, simplifying with the two additional rules

$$a + a = 0 , \tag{1}$$

$$a \cdot a = 0 , \tag{2}$$

where a is any letter or expression. The resulting polynomial is $|Y_{ij}|$ when we substitute the values of the admittances for the corresponding letters, and interpret addition and multiplication in the ordinary arithmetic sense. For example, in Fig. 1 the expression is

$$(a + b + c)(a + b + d) = ad + bd + ac + bc + cd ,$$

and if a, b, c, d are interpreted as the corresponding admittances we have the admittance determinant.

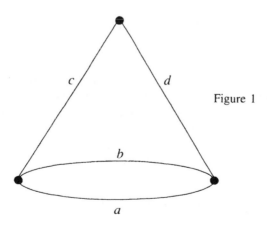

Figure 1

Similar methods give impedance determinants and the numerator determinants in the fractions representing driving point and transfer admittances and impedances. These rules have been treated only as short cut methods of obtaining these determinants. In a conversation with the writer about these results R. M. Foster pointed out that the algebraic system suggested by the two rules (1) and (2) might be worth studying for its own properties. The present paper is an attempt to exploit this idea. This has led to a method of treating the topological properties of

---

* Bell Laboratories Memorandum, June 11, 1948.

linear graphs algebraically, much as analytic geometry studies Euclidean geometry algebraically. A linear graph is represented by an algebraic expression in a certain type of ring, and topological properties of the graph correspond to algebraic properties of the expression. The algebra as developed here is particularly adapted to the study of properties of networks of importance in electrical work, since two network expressions are equal if and only if the corresponding linear graphs are "two-isomorphic" in the sense of H. Whitney[5]. Two graphs are said to be two-isomorphic if one can be obtained from the other by a sequence of the following operations: (1) separating two parts which are connected through a single junction, (2) joining two separate parts at a single junction, (3) inverting a part connected at two junctions only to a second part. This means that two-isomorphic networks have equivalent electrical properties (self and transfer impedances, etc.) and conversely[6].

The correspondence between graphs and network expressions in the ring is not, however, perfect. Every graph has a unique network expression (in the two-isomorphic sense) but there are some network expressions which do not correspond to ordinary graphs. Restricting the study to those expressions corresponding to graphs introduces very unnatural and artificial restrictions. All basic theorems hold equally well for the more general class of expressions. This suggests that we consider the set of graphs as a subclass of the general set of networks defined abstractly by the algebraic methods. Many of the peculiarities of linear graph theory then become more understandable. For example, duality theory becomes much more complete – every network has a dual (not just planar networks) and the whole duality concept can be defined and treated in a unified abstract manner.

The network expressions studied here are isomorphic to a subclass of the "matroids" of H. Whitney[7], being in fact isomorphic to the set of matrices with integer elements reduced modulo 2, when row addition is allowed as an equivalence operation. Many of the theorems in the ring hold for the more general class of matroids, but the proofs given here are of a more "algebraic" character.

The terminology chosen is taken from linear graph theory[8].

2. THE COVERING RING

Consider a finite commutative ring in which each element is nilpotent of index 2 for both addition and multiplication. Let $a_1, \ldots, a_n$ be a polynomial basis for the ring, i.e., every element is a polynomial in the a_i, but this property is lost if any a_i is omitted from the set. The ring will be called a *network ring* if there exists such a basis with $a_1 a_2 \cdots a_n \neq 0$. Thinking of a fixed basis, the elements of this basis will be called "branches". The number of branches in the basis (which turns out to be independent of the basis chosen) will be called the order of the ring. A polynomial in the basis a_i,

$$P = a_r \cdots a_t + \cdots + a_p \cdots a_q ,$$

will be called reduced if it contains no repeated a's in a term and no repeated terms.

Theorem 1. In a network ring there is a unique (apart from order of terms or of factors in a term) reduced expression for each element $X \neq 0$ in terms of a given basis a_i, $\Pi a_i \neq 0$.

By definition of the basis there must be one such expression. To prove uniqueness assume two reduced representations of some element

$$X = P_1(a_i) = P_2(a_i) .$$

Then

$$P = P_1 + P_2 = 0$$

and after P is reduced it still contains some terms since P_1 and P_2 were reduced and different. Let $a_r \cdots a_t$ be the term (or one of the terms) in P with the least number of factors. Multiply by all a_i not among $a_r, \ldots, a_t$. We obtain

$$a_1 \cdots a_n = 0 ,$$

since all other terms contain repeated factors, and this contradicts our hypothesis.

Theorem 2. The number of elements in a network ring of order n is $2^{(2^n - 1)}$.

For we have $2^n - 1$ possible products of the a_i without repeated factors, and may form $2^{(2^n - 1)}$ different selections from these, all of which lead to different elements by Theorem 1. The case where no products are taken corresponds to the element 0.

Suppose now we have a second set of elements forming a basis $b_1, \ldots, b_m$. Evidently $m \geq n$ since there are at most $2^{(2^m - 1)}$ irreducible polynomials in the b_i and there are $2^{(2^n - 1)}$ elements in the ring. If $m > n$ then $\Pi\, b_i = 0$ since each b_i is a polynomial in the a_i, and each term in the product contains at least one repeated a. But then there is a subset of at least n of the b_i with non-vanishing product, as we see by considering $\Pi\, a_i \neq 0$ with the a_i expressed in terms of the b_i. This subset forms a basis and therefore the original b_i did not. Hence $m = n$, and $\Pi\, b_i \neq 0$. Conversely if we have n elements b_i with $\Pi\, b_i \neq 0$ they form a basis since the $2^{(2^n - 1)}$ polynomials in them are all different and must then be the same as the elements in the ring. Thus we have:

Theorem 3. A necessary and sufficient condition that a set of b_i be a basis for a network ring of order n is that there be n of them and that $\Pi\, b_i \neq 0$.

We can now characterize any basis $b_1, \ldots, b_n$ in terms of a given basis $a_1, \ldots, a_n$. Since the a_i form a basis any set of elements can be written as polynomials in the a_i:

$$b_1 = L_1 + \alpha_1 ,$$
$$b_2 = L_2 + \alpha_2 ,$$
$$\ldots\ldots\ldots\ldots\ldots \tag{3}$$
$$b_n = L_n + \alpha_n ,$$

where the L_i are linear in the a_i, while the α_i contain no first degree terms. We have

$$\Pi\, b_i = \Pi\, L_i + [\text{terms with more than } n \text{ factors } a_i]$$
$$= \Pi\, L_i + 0 ,$$

since all products of more than n a_i contain repeated a's and vanish.

Theorem 4. A necessary and sufficient condition that b_i $(i = 1, \ldots, n)$ be a basis is that the b_i can be written in the form (3) in terms of a given basis with $\Pi\, L_i \neq 0$.

Theorem 5. For any n, there exists a unique abstract network ring of order n.

That two network rings of order n are isomorphic follows immediately from Theorem 1 on setting the branches $a_1, \ldots, a_n$ of the one ring in correspondence with the branches $b_1, \ldots, b_n$ of the other, and corresponding polynomials in correspondence.

We now prove by induction that a network ring exists for any n. For $n = 1$ we have the network ring consisting of a single a with:

+	0	a		·	0	a
0	0	a		0	0	0
a	a	0		a	0	0

Now suppose we have exhibited a network ring N_n of order n. Consider the set of ordered triplets

$$(\alpha, \beta, \gamma)$$

where α and β are any elements of N_n and γ is 0 or 1. We define equality, addition and multiplication by

$$(\alpha_1, \beta_1, \gamma_1) = (\alpha_2, \beta_2, \gamma_2) \text{ if } \alpha_1 = \alpha_2, \beta_1 = \beta_2, \gamma_1 = \gamma_2 ,$$

$$(\alpha_1, \beta_1, \gamma_1) + (\alpha_2, \beta_2, \gamma_2) = (\alpha_1 + \alpha_2, \beta_1 + \beta_2, \gamma_1 + \gamma_2)$$

(the γ's are added mod 2),

$$(\alpha_1, \beta_1, \gamma_1)(\alpha_2, \beta_2, \gamma_2) = (\alpha_1\alpha_2, \alpha_1\beta_2 + \alpha_2\beta_1 + \gamma_2\alpha_1 + \gamma_1\alpha_2, \gamma_1\gamma_2) , \qquad (4)$$

where $1 \alpha = \alpha$. These are clearly well defined and closed.

It is readily verified that these elements (α,β,γ) form a commutative ring with the desired nilpotency properties, and that the elements

$$b_i = (a_i, 0,0) , \quad i = 1,2,\ldots,n ,$$
$$b_{n+1} = (0,0,1)$$

form a polynomial basis. Finally

$$\Pi b_i = (a_1 a_2 \ldots a_n,0,0)(0,0,1)$$
$$= (0,a_1 \ldots a_n,0) \neq 0$$

and the definition is nonvacuous for every n.

If each term of a polynomial contains the same number of terms r we say it is homogeneous of rank r.

Theorem 6. There are $2^{\binom{n}{r}}$ homogeneous reduced expressions of rank r.

For the number of different products of r factor is $\binom{n}{r}$, etc.

3. NETWORKS

Thinking of a fixed basis we will define a *network* as an element that can be written as a product of linear terms in the branches. Thus $0 = a \cdot a$, $ab + ac + bc = (a + b)(a + c)$, etc., are networks; $ab + cd$ is not.

The set of branches in any term of the polynomial of a network will be called a frame ("gerust") of the network. For example, the network $ab + ac + bc$ has three frames; the set a, b, the set a, c and the set b, c.

Theorem 7. Suppose $a_1, a_2, \ldots, a_r$ is a frame of the network f. We can write f as

$$f = (a_1 + L_1)(a_2 + L_2) \cdots (a_r + L_r) ,$$

where $L_1, \ldots, L_r$ are linear terms not involving $a_1, \ldots, a_4$. This representation is unique, given the frame $a_1, \ldots, a_r$. Finally, if f can be represented in this form, $a_1, \ldots, a_r$ is a frame.

To prove this note that since f is a network we have

$$f = M_1 M_2 \cdots M_r ,$$

with the M's linear. a_1 must appear in one of these terms since otherwise it could not appear in the polynomial expression for f. Suppose it appears in M_1. Using the fact that $XY = XY + YY = (X + Y)Y$, add M_1 to all other M's in which a_1 appears, thus cancelling it. Hence

$$f = M_1 N_2 \cdots N_r ,$$

where the N's do not involve a_1. Now a_2 must appear in one of the N's since otherwise it could not appear in a product with a_1 in the polynomial. Suppose it appears in N_2. Add N_2 to all other terms in which a_2 appears (including possibly M_1) thus cancelling it. Hence we get

$$f = M_1' N_2 S_3 \cdots S_r$$

where now only M_1' contains a_1 and only N_2 contains a_2. Continuing in this way we obtain the desired expansion. Now assume the expansion is not unique:

$$f = (a_1 + L_1) \cdots (a_r + L_r) = (a_1 + M_1) \cdots (a_r + M_r) ,$$

with $L_1 \neq M_1$. Suppose L_1 contains a_p and M_1 not. Then the expansion of the left side contains the term

$$a_p a_2 a_3 \cdots a_r$$

and the right side does not. As this term could not be cancelled we have a contradiction. The last part of the theorem is obvious on multiplying out the "frame expansion" of f. The frame expansion is of fundamental importance in this theory.

Theorem 8. Given one factorization of a network

$$f = L_1 L_2 \cdots L_r ,$$

any other factorization may be obtained by a sequence of operations, each operation consisting of adding one factor to another (as in the proof of Theorem 7).

The inverse operation is also of this type, e.g.,

$$L_1 L_2 \cdots L_r = (L_1 + L_2) L_2 \cdots L_r$$

has the inverse

$$(L_1 + L_2)L_2 \cdots L_r = (L_1 + L_2 + L_2)L_2 \cdots L_r = L_1 \cdots L_r .$$

Now by the proof of Theorem 7 we can go from any factorization of f to a given frame expansion by a sequence of adding operations. Thus we go from any one factorization $L_1 \cdots L_r$ to a frame expansion $M_1 \cdots M_r$, and then to any other factorization $N_1 \cdots N_r$.

Theorem 9. If a network $f = L_1 L_2 \cdots L_r \neq 0$, the L_i are linearly independent. Conversely, if the L_i are linearly independent, $f = L_1 \cdots L_r \neq 0$.

Suppose a relation $L_r + L_s + \cdots + L_t = 0$. Adding $L_s \cdots L_t$ to L_r, this term then vanishes. Hence $f = 0$, contradicting the hypothesis. Now assume no relation. We may apply the frame expansion method and never arrive at a 0, since if we did the series of adding operations would define a linear relation. The frame expansion does not vanish since it contains a frame term on multiplying out.

Any factor of a network $f \neq 0$ will be called a *cut set* of f. The network 0 is considered to be of rank 0 and to have no cut sets.

Theorem 10. A necessary and sufficient condition that $L \neq 0$ be a cut set of $f \neq 0$ is that

$$Lf = 0 .$$

If L is a cut set of f then $f = Lg$, hence $Lf = LLg = 0$. If $Lf = 0$, $f \neq 0$, there is a relation among the factors of f and L, actually involving L, so that L is a sum of certain factors of f, hence a cut set of f.

Theorem 11. Let $f = L_1 L_2 \cdots L_r$ be any factorization of $f \neq 0$. Then any cut set M can be written as a linear combination of the L_i, and conversely any linear combination of the L_i not identically 0 is a cut set of f.

This is obvious from Theorems 9 and 10. Thus one set of factors of a network f forms a basis for cut sets – any may be expressed as linear combinations of these factors. There are $2^r - 1$ linear combinations of r factors. These must all be different since equality of two would imply a relation among the L_i. Hence:

Theorem 12. A network $f \neq 0$ of rank r has $2^r - 1$ different cut sets.

Theorem 13. Any network of rank r can be factored in exactly

$$N(r) = \frac{\prod\limits_{p=0}^{r-1} (2^r - 2^p)}{r!} \quad \text{different ways} .$$

From the $(2^r - 1)$ factors of f we may choose the first in $(2^r - 1)$ ways, the second in $(2^r - 2)$ ways since it must be different from the first; the third in $(2^r - 4)$ since it must be independent of the first 2, the pth in $(2^r - 2^{p-1})$. As we want combinations, not permutations, we divide by $r!$.

Theorem 14. There are exactly

$$P_r^n = \prod\limits_{k=0}^{r-1} \frac{(2^n - 2^k)}{(2^r - 2^k)}$$

networks of rank r with n branches.

There are $2^n - 1$ linear expressions in the a_i. We may choose the first in $2^n - 1$ ways; the kth in $2^n - 2^{k-1}$ ways to be independent of the first $k - 1$. Thus we can get

$$\frac{1}{r!} \prod\limits_{k=0}^{r-1} (2^n - 2^k)$$

combinations of factors. Since each network can be factored in $\dfrac{1}{r!} \prod\limits_{k=0}^{r-1} (2^r - 2^k)$ ways the result follows.

Theorem 15. If a homogeneous f can be factored, a set of factors is given by the following processes. Pick a frame, say $a_1, a_2, \ldots, a_r$. The factoring is

$$g = (a_1 + L_1)(a_2 + L_2) \cdots (a_r + L_r) ,$$

where L_i is the sum of the other branches in all frames containing branches $a_1, \ldots, a_{i-1}, a_{i+1}, \ldots, a_r$. To determine if the expression f can be factored construct g and multiply out. If $g = f$, g is a factoring of f, if not f is not a network.

If f can be factored it can be factored uniquely about the frame $a_1, \ldots, a_r$. Suppose this factoring is

$$(a_1 + M_1)(a_2 + M_2) \cdots (a_r + M_r) .$$

Then $M_1 = L_1$, since on multiplying out we get terms

$$M_1 a_2 \cdots a_r$$

which cannot be cancelled, and appear in the polynomial expansion. Also these are clearly the only terms of this type. The rest of the theorem is obvious.

4. DUALITY

We now define the dual f' of a network f as follows. Let f be written in its polynomial expansion. Then f' is the sum of products of branches not appearing in the terms of f. Thus with branches a, b, c and d, the dual of $ab + ac$ is $cd + bd$.

Theorem 16. If f is a network then f' is a network. If a frame expansion of f is

$$f = (a_1 + L_1)(a_2 + L_2) \cdots (a_r + L_r)$$

then a frame expansion of f' is

$$g = f' = (b_1 + M_1)(b_2 + M_2) \cdots (b_n + M_n)$$

where $b_1, \ldots, b_n$ are the branches not appearing among $a_1, \ldots, a_r$, and M_j is the sum of the a_i of the factors of f in which b_j appears in the L part.

Thus the dual of $f = (\underline{b} + a) (\underline{c} + a)$ with a, b, c, d the branches is

$$f' = (\underline{d} + c) (\underline{a} + b + c)$$

where we have underlined the frame terms in f and f'. Let us construct the g of Theorem 16. If we multiply f out we get a sum of terms each consisting partly of a's from the frame part of f and partly of b's from the L_i. Those terms containing two equal b's necessarily vanish. All others correspond to a dual term in the expansion of a g found by taking the b's in g factors which do not appear among the b's of the f term in question and a's from the M_i corresponding to the b's which were taken in the f term. These a's actually are available in the proper M_i due to the method of constructing f. Conversely each term of g corresponds to a term of f and hence they are duals in our sense.

The rank of f' will be called the "nullity" of f, the cut sets of f' are "circuits" of f and the frames of f' are "fundamental systems" of f. These are examples of dual concepts. In general, the dual of any operation on, or concept associated with, a network f is the same operation on, or concept associated with, f'. Any theorem we may derive concerning networks has a dual theorem which may be found by replacing "network" by "dual of network" and simplifying through the use of the dual definitions – e.g., "rank of the network" becomes "rank of the dual of the network" and hence "nullity of the network." The dual theorem must be true since "networks" and the "duals of networks" are two descriptions of the same class.

A network f will be called inseparable if it cannot be written as a product

$$f = g_1 g_2$$

with g_1, g_2 involving mutually exclusive sets of branches. Otherwise f is separable.

Theorem 17. Any network f can be written uniquely apart from order of factors as

$$f = g_1 g_2 \cdots g_s ,$$

where the g_i are inseparable and involve mutually exclusive sets of branches.

The g_i together with the branches not appearing in f will be called the inseparable components of f. Obviously there exists at least one such resolution. To prove uniqueness suppose we have two resolutions

$$g_1 g_2 \cdots = h_1 h_2 \cdots .$$

Choose a frame of f and expand each side about this frame, using the method used in proving Theorem 7. This will clearly not disturb the separation. Suppose the frame terms in g_1 are $a_s, \ldots, a_t$. These frame terms on the h side must appear in the same h_i for, if not, g_1 is separable. Conversely all terms appearing in this h_i appear in g_1 otherwise this h_i is separable. Continuing this method with g_2, $g_3 \cdots$ we obtain the theorem. Incidentally we also obtain:

Theorem 18. To resolve a network into separable components, factor f about a frame:

$$f = (a_1 + L_1)(a_2 + L_2) \cdots (a_r + L_r) .$$

To the term $(a_1 + L_1)$ annex all terms containing branches appearing in L_1, say $(a_2 + L_2) \cdots (a_s + L_s)$, also all terms containing branches appearing in $L_2 \cdots L_s$, etc. When this process terminates we have grouped the factors of an inseparable component. If any factors of f remain, use the same process on these, abstracting components until all factors of f are used.

If a branch a does not appear in the polynomial expansion of a network f we will say that a is a *circuit* of f. If a appears in every term of f, a is an *open branch* of f. It is easily seen that these are dual concepts. If neither of these obtains a is *essentially involved* in f.

We now define an operation on networks which will be called extraction. If f is of rank greater than one and a is not a circuit, we can write $f = a\,g + h$ with h possibly 0. We define $E_a f = g$. In case f is of rank 1 and a not a circuit we define $E_a f = 0$. $E_a f$ is not defined when a is a circuit of f.

Theorem 19. $E_a f$ is a network if f is a network. Also

$$E_a(f + g) = E_a f + E_a g ,$$

$$E_a E_b f = E_b E_a f \quad \text{(we write this as } E_{ab} f) ,$$

$$E_a(f\,g) = f E_a g + g E_a f, \quad \text{rank of } f, g > 1 ,$$

whenever all expressions have a meaning.

Note the similarity of E_a with $\dfrac{\partial}{\partial a}$. Indeed if f is expressed in polynomial form and is of rank > 1 , and if $+$ and $\cdot$ be interpreted arithmetically then

$$E_a f = \frac{\partial}{\partial a} f \ .$$

The inverse of this operation is not unique. We will call the inverse operation insertion, and denote it by I_a. $I_a g$ exists only for networks g not involving a.

Theorem 20. The most general f such that

$$E_a f = g \ ,$$

g being a given network with a as a circuit, is

$$f = I_a g = (a + L) \ g$$

when $g \neq 0$, and $I_a g$ when $g = 0$, where L is an arbitrary linear expression in the branches other than a.

An operation similar to $E_a f$ is $(E_a f')'$. It is defined only in case f' involves a. We may denote this operation by $E_a{}'$ and it obeys the same laws as E_a. Its general inverse is (g must be $\underline{a}$ times a network)

$$I_a{}' g = [(a + L) \ g']' \ .$$

Theorem 21.

$$f = a \, E_a f + f|_{a=0} \ .$$

These last three theorems follow easily from the definitions, as does the next one.

Theorem 22. If $a_1 \cdots a_r$ is a frame of f then

$$E_{a_1} E_{a_2} \cdots E_{a_r} f = 0 \ .$$

Further if this equation is meaningful and true then $a_1 \cdots a_r$ is a frame of f.

Two elements a and b will be said to be in parallel in f if $E_a f = E_b f$. They will be said to be in series if $E_a{}' f = E_b{}' f$.

We define a ''simple'' cut set as one such that no proper subset of its branches is also a cut set. A simple circuit is defined similarly.

Theorem 23. Any factor of a frame expansion is a simple cut set. Conversely any simple cut set is a factor in some frame expansion. Furthermore, any branch in the simple cut set may be used as the frame term in the factor.

To prove the first part assume in contradiction that

$$f = (a_1 + A + B)(a_2 + L_2) \cdots (a_r + L_r)$$

is a frame expansion with B a cut set. Obviously if $a_1 + A$ is the part of the first term which is a cut set then B also is, for $B = (a_1 + A + B) + (a_1 + A)$ and the sum of two cut sets is a cut set. Then by Theorem 13, B is a linear combination of the other terms

$$B = (a_p + L_p) + (a_q + L_q) + \cdots \ ,$$

which is manifestly impossible since the frame terms $a_p, a_q, \ldots$ do not appear in B and could not cancel out. The second part may be proved as follows. Let

$$f = L_1 L_2 \cdots L_r \,,$$

L_1 being the given simple cut set. Choose any branch in L_1, say a_1, and add L_1 to other L's in which a_1 appears, as in the regular frame expansion:

$$f = (a_1 + M_1)\, M_2 \cdots M_r \,.$$

We continue as in the proof of Theorem 9 but choose from M_2 a letter *not* appearing in M_1. This is possible, for otherwise a subset of M_1 is a cut set. Continue with the expansion, always choosing for the next frame term a letter not appearing in M_1. We need never then add any terms to the first one, which is left intact.

Thus we see that the set of simple cut sets is identical with the set of frame cut sets and we may construct the former in this way. We may also use these results to determine if a given cut set is simple.

5. RELATION TO LINEAR GRAPHS AND ELECTRICAL NETWORK THEORY

We will say that a network is real if it can be factored in such a way that no branch appears in more than two factors, otherwise it is ideal. Thus $(a + b)(a + c)$ is real and

$$(a + d + e + g)(b + d + f + g)(c + e + f + g)$$

is ideal. This last is true since adding any two terms leaves the distribution of appearances of branches the same, a branch in each term, in each pair of terms and in all three terms. As any factoring can be reached by a sequence of such additions, any factoring has a letter appearing in three terms.

We will now set up a correspondence between real networks and linear graphs. Let any real network f be factored in such a way that no branch appears in more than two factors. Associate a junction point with each factor and add one additional junction point. To each branch appearing in two factors we make correspond a branch of the graph connecting the corresponding junctions. For each branch appearing in one factor only we draw a branch connecting the associated junction with the additional junction. For each branch appearing in no factors we draw a closed loop. It is easily seen that the original factors form a cut set basis for the graph. Furthermore, the cut sets of our network are cut sets of the graph since they are linear combinations of the basis cut sets modulo 2. Two graphs corresponding to the same network are two-isomorphic since they have the same cut sets and it has been shown by Whitney that these properties are equivalent. With this as a basis it is not difficult to show that the other terms we have defined correspond in the case of real networks to similarly named concepts in graph theory. Hence there is a one-to-one correspondence between real networks and the linear graphs under two-isomorphism that can be constructed from a set of labeled branches.

Ignoring interchanges of letters, the possible graphs with three branches[9] are shown in Fig. 2, together with the corresponding network expressions in the network ring of order three.

It is known that the network admittance discriminant $|Y_{ij}|$ of an electrical network is equal to a sum of products, each product having for factors admittances making up a frame. Hence we have the Wang result that the admittance discriminant

$$D_1 = |Y_{ij}| = f|_{a, = Y,}$$

by which we mean that f (written as a polynomial) is evaluated as though $+$ and $\cdot$ were the arithmetic operations, the admittances of branches being substituted for the branches. Similarly the impedance determinant is given by

$$D_2 = |Z_{ij}| = f'|_{a, = z,} .$$

Also the driving point admittances Y_{11} looking across branch a_1 is

$$Y_{11} = \frac{D_y}{\dfrac{\partial D_y}{\partial Y_1}} .$$

Hence for f not of rank 1,

$$Y_{11} = \frac{f}{E_{a_1} f}\Big|_{a, = y,} .$$

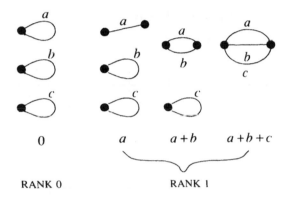

RANK 0   RANK 1

Figure 2

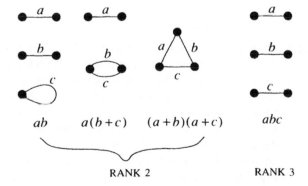

RANK 2   RANK 3

6. SOLUTION OF CAMPBELL'S PROBLEM

A problem proposed by G. A. Campbell is that of determining whether or not a given homogeneous expression in certain admittances (or impedances) is the determinant of an electrical network, and if so to find the network. Theorem 15 solves half of this problem, for it gives a method of determining whether the given expression represents a network – we must now find a method for determining whether a network is real or ideal. Theoretically, Theorem 8 is a solution of this, for we may use it to factor a network in all possible ways, and inspect the various factorings to determine if any occur in which all branches appear at most twice. However, this process is very long and impractical even for quite simple networks. We will now describe a very rapid method of determining whether a given network is real. It is based on the dual of Theorem 23: all circuits of a fundamental system expansion of f are simple. Let us expand f about a fundamental system:

$$f = [(a_1 + L_1)(a_2 + L_2) \cdots (a_n + L_n)]' .$$

Each of these factors is a simple circuit of the network f. If f is a graph and we omit $a_1, \ldots, a_n$, leaving the sets $L_1, L_2, \ldots, L_n$, we have a tree. We proceed step-by-step to construct this tree, using the sets $L_1, L_2, \ldots$ sequentially. The process is best described by an example. Suppose

$$A \quad L_1 = a + b + c + d$$
$$B \quad L_2 = a + b$$
$$C \quad L_3 = b + c + d$$
$$D \quad L_4 = a + b + c$$
$$E \quad L_5 = b + d$$

3a

3b

3c

3d

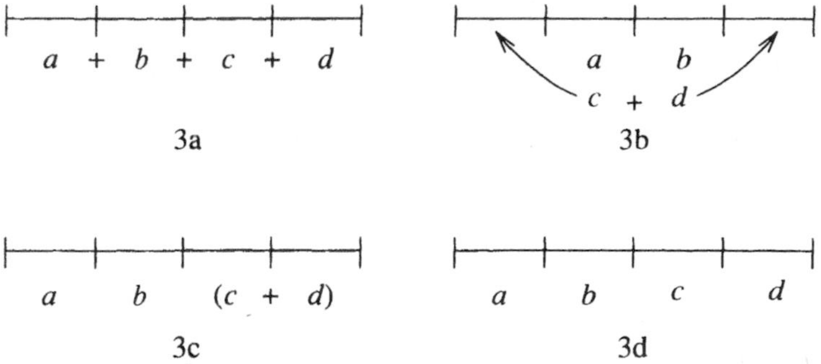

Figure 3

where $A, B, \ldots, E$ are the corresponding fundamental system branches. The first term L_1 tells us that a, b, c, d occur in a sequence, since adding one more branch completes a simple circuit. The first approximation to the tree is shown in Fig. 3a. The + sign between the letters indicates commutativity – nothing is yet known of the order of these branches in the sequence. Now consider $L_2 = a + b$. a and b must be adjacent, hence the second approximation to the tree is given in Fig. 3b. The arrows on $c + d$ indicate that c and d can be distributed in any way on the tails of the tree, both at one or the other end in any order, or one at each end. Now consider $L_3 = b + c + d$. c and d must be in sequence with b, hence we get the third approximation of Fig. 3c. $L_4 = a + b + c$ gives Fig. 3d, and $L_5 = b + d$ is impossible so the network is ideal. The dual of this network is real, however. The dual has

$$a: \quad L_1 = A + B + D$$
$$b: \quad L_2 = A + B + C + D + E$$
$$c: \quad L_3 = A + C + D$$
$$d: \quad L_4 = A + C + E .$$

The successive approximations are shown in Fig. 4 with the network shown in Fig. 4e. This method is very rapid – with a little practice it is possible to construct a network of rank 20 or 30 in a few minutes, starting with a frame or fundamental system expansion. It is usually best, however, to take the L_i in such an order that each one taken involves as many letters previously written down as possible and to start with a large L. With these precautions the process described will converge rapidly to the proper solution for any ordinary network.

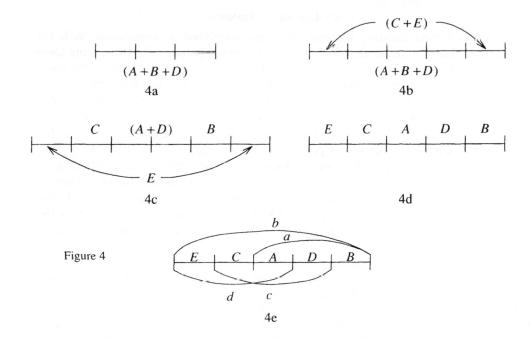

Figure 4

REFERENCES

1. K. T. Wang, *On a New Method for the Analysis of Electric Networks,* Memoir of the National Research Institute of Engineering, Academia Sinica, April 1934.

2. S. L. Ting, *On the General Properties of Electric Network Determinants and the Rules for Finding the Denominator and the Numerators,* Scientific Papers, National Research Institute of Physics, Academia Sinica, v. 1, No. 7, October 1935.

3. Chin-Tao Tsai, *Short Cut Methods for Expanding the Determinants Involved in Network Problems,* Chinese Journal of Physics, v. 3, No. 2, October 1939, p. 148.

4. Wei-Liang Chow, *On Electric Networks,* Journal of the Chinese Mathematical Society, v. 2, 1940.

5. H. Whitney, *On the Classification of Graphs,* American Journal of Mathematics, v. LV, No. 2, April 1933.

6. H. Whitney, *2-Isomorphic Graphs,* American Journal of Mathematics, v. LV, No. 2, April 1933.

7. H. Whitney, *On the Abstract Properties of Linear Dependence,* American Journal of Mathematics, v. LVII, No. 3, July 1935.

8. D. König, *Theorie der Endlichen und Unendlichen Graphen,* Leipzig, 1936.

9. R. M. Foster, *Geometrical Circuits of Electrical Networks,* Trans. AIEE, v. 51, June 1932, p. 309.

A THEOREM ON COLORING THE LINES OF A NETWORK

By Claude E. Shannon

A topological coloring problem has been suggested in connection with the color coding of wires in electrical units such as relay panels. In these units there are a number of relays, switches, and other devices $A, B, \cdots, E$ to be inter-connected. The connecting wires are first formed in a cable with the wires to be connected to A coming out at one point, those to B at another, etc., and it is necessary, in order to distinguish the different wires, that all those coming out of the cable at the same point be differently colored. There may be any number of wires joining the same two points but no wire joins more than two points. Assuming that not more than m wires end at any one point, the question arises as to the least number of different color codings that is sufficient for any network.

Theorem: The lines of any network can be colored so that no two lines with a common junction have the same color using at most $[\frac{3}{2}m]$ colors, where m is the maximum number of lines touching one junction. This number of colors is necessary for some networks.

Simple networks requiring $[\frac{3}{2}m]$ colors can be constructed as follows. For $m = 2n$, let each pair of the three junctions A, B, C be connected with n lines. Since all the lines must obviously be different, $3n = [\frac{3}{2}m]$ colors are necessary. For $m = 2n + 1$, connect AB with n lines, BC with n lines and AC with $n + 1$ lines. Here again all lines must be different and there are $3n + 1 = [\frac{3}{2}(2n + 1)] = [\frac{3}{2}m]$ lines. Another example for $m = 3$ is furnished by the cross connection of two pentagons $abcde$ and $ABCDE$ by lines aA, bD, cB, dE, eC.

For the sufficiency proof let us first suppose m even. Now if N is our given network it is well known that we may add lines and junction points to get a regular network N' of degree m, i.e., one in which exactly m lines end at each junction point. If we can color N' we can surely color N. A theorem due to Peterson states that any regular network of even degree $m = 2n$ can be factored into n regular second degree graphs. In our case let the factors of N' be $N_1, N_2, \cdots, N_n$. Each of these is merely a collection of polygons which do not touch each other, and each N_i, therefore, can be colored with at most three colors. This gives a total of $3n = \frac{3}{2}m$ colors.*

Peterson has conjectured that any regular bridgeless network of odd degree $2n + 1$ can be factored into one first and n second degree graphs, and if this is true the theorem follows easily in the odd case. However this conjecture has never been proved for $m > 3$ and we will use a different attack.

The theorem will be proved by induction, making the coloring of N depend on coloring a network with one less junction point. Let us eliminate from N one junction point P and the $m = 2n + 1$ lines coming to it and assume the remaining network to be satisfactorily colored with $3n + 1$ colors. Let the junctions that were connected to P in the original network be numbered $1, 2, \cdots, s$, and

---

* This proof for m even was suggested by R. M. Foster.

suppose there were p_1 parallel lines in the first group G_1 connecting P to junction 1, etc.   Now after coloring the reduced network we have left available at junction 1 at least $[(3n + 1) - (2n + 1 - p_1)] = n + p_1$ colors, at junction 2, at least $(n + p_2)$ colors, etc.   By choosing properly from these available colors and by suitable interchanges of certain colors in the part of the network already colored we will show that the lines from P can be satisfactorily colored.

Let us arrange the data in a table as follows.

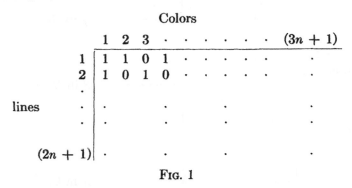

Fig. 1

In this array the $2n + 1$ lines from P are listed vertically, the $3n + 1$ colors horizontally.   If a certain color is available for a certain line a 1 is placed at the intersection of the corresponding row and column, otherwise a 0.   In a row corresponding to a line in G_i there will be $(n + p_i)$ 1's.   By the use of three operations on this array we will arrange to obtain a series of 1's along the main diagonal and this will represent a coloring scheme for the network.   These operations are:

1. Interchange of columns.   This corresponds to merely renumbering the colors.

2. Interchange of rows.   This corresponds to renumbering the lines from P.

3. Interchange of colors in a chain of two colors.   Two junctions will be said to be chained together for two colors if we can go from one junction to the other along lines which alternate these colors.   If we have a satisfactorily colored network and interchange the two colors in a chain of that network over its entire length (note that in a correctly colored network a chain cannot branch out) then it is clear that the network will still be satisfactorily colored.   We will also use the fact that if only one of the two colors in question appears at each of three distinct junctions then only one pair of the junctions (at most) can be chained together for these two colors, since a chain can only have two ends.   Now consider the array of Fig. 1.   Suppose that in the first row there is a 0 in one column and a 1 in another.   Interchanging these two colors in the chain starting from the junction that line one is connected to will be seen to be equivalent to interchanging these two columns for this row and all other rows that are chained to it.

Let us suppose that we have arranged to get 1's on the main diagonal D down to a certain point.   We will show that we can get another 1 on the diagonal.

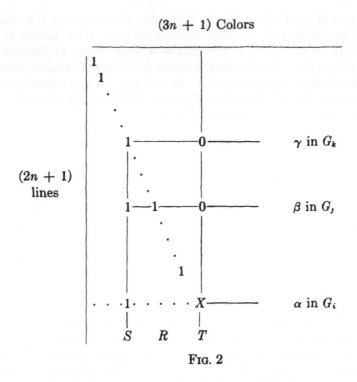

$$(3n + 1) \text{ Colors}$$

$(2n + 1)$ lines

γ in G_k

β in G_j

α in G_i

Fɪɢ. 2

Referring to Fig. 2, if there are any 1's in the next line α, on or to the right of T, one of these may be brought by an interchange of columns, to position X. Assuming this is not true there will be $n + p_i$ 1's to the left of column T in α (assuming α is in G_i). Hence there are $n + p_i$ rows above α having a 1 in D in the same column as a 1 in α. At least $n + 1$ of these rows are not in G_i, since G_i has p_i members and we have accounted for one already, namely α. Let β be one of these, belonging, say, to G_j. If β has a 1 on or to the right of T, by an interchange first of columns, then of α and β this may be moved to X without affecting the 1's along D. Assuming this is not true, there are $n + p_j$ 1's on β to the left of T and hence $n + p_j$ rows above α have a 1 in D in the same column as a 1 in β, and of these at least n do not belong to G_j (as it only has p_j members). Now there are not more than $2n$ rows above α and therefore the n rows we have associated with β and the $n + 1$ we have associated with α must have at least one in common, i.e., there exists a row not belonging to G_i or G_j and having a 1 in D in the same column that α and β also have a 1. Call this row γ, and suppose it belongs to G_k. If γ has a 1 on or to the right of T it may be moved to X by first interchanging columns and then rows α and γ as before. Assuming this is not true, there are 0's and 1's at the intersections of α, β, γ, and T, S, as shown in Fig. 2 and X is 0. Hence at least one of α, β, γ is not chained to either of the others by the two colors of T and S. If it is α, interchange the chain starting at i and the 1 at the αS intersection moves to X without affecting D. If it is β, interchange the chain starting at j and then rows α and β.   This moves the 1 at the βS intersection to X and its place is taken by the 1 at αS.   If it is γ, interchange the chain starting at k and then the rows α and γ so that the 1 at γS moves to X and the 1 at αR takes its place.

BELL TELEPHONE LABORATORIES, INC., NEW YORK CITY.

(Received September 14, 1948)

The Synthesis of Two-Terminal Switching Circuits

By CLAUDE. E. SHANNON

PART I: GENERAL THEORY

1. INTRODUCTION

THE theory of switching circuits may be divided into two major divisions, analysis and synthesis. The problem of analysis, determining the manner of operation of a given switching circuit, is comparatively simple. The inverse problem of finding a circuit satisfying certain given operating conditions, and in particular the *best* circuit is, in general, more difficult and more important from the practical standpoint. A basic part of the general synthesis problem is the design of a two-terminal network with given operating characteristics, and we shall consider some aspects of this problem.

Switching circuits can be studied by means of Boolean algebra.[1,2] This is a branch of mathematics that was first investigated by George Boole in connection with the study of logic, and has since been applied in various other fields, such as an axiomatic formulation of biology,[3] the study of neural networks in the nervous system,[4] the analysis of insurance policies,[5] probability and set theory, etc.

Perhaps the simplest interpretation of Boolean Algebra and the one closest to the application to switching circuits is in terms of propositions. A letter X, say, in the algebra corresponds to a logical proposition. The sum of two letters $X + Y$ represents the proposition "X or Y" and the product XY represents the proposition "X and Y". The symbol X' is used to represent the negation of proposition X, i.e. the proposition "not X". The constants 1 and 0 represent truth and falsity respectively. Thus $X + Y = 1$ means X or Y is true, while $X + YZ' = 0$ means X or (Y and the contradiction of Z) is false.

The interpretation of Boolean Algebra in terms of switching circuits[6,8,9,10] is very similar. The symbol X in the algebra is interpreted to mean a make (front) contact on a relay or switch. The negation of X, written X', represents a break (back) contact on the relay or switch. The constants 0 and 1 represent closed and open circuits respectively and the combining operations of addition and multiplication correspond to series and parallel connections of the switching elements involved. These conventions are shown in Fig. 1. With this identification it is possible to write an algebraic

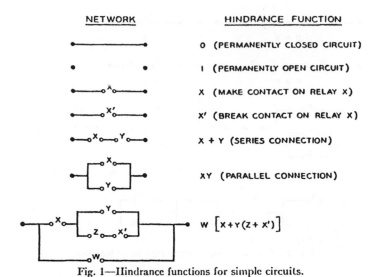

NETWORK   HINDRANCE FUNCTION

0 (PERMANENTLY CLOSED CIRCUIT)

1 (PERMANENTLY OPEN CIRCUIT)

X (MAKE CONTACT ON RELAY X)

X' (BREAK CONTACT ON RELAY X)

X + Y (SERIES CONNECTION)

XY (PARALLEL CONNECTION)

$W \left[X + Y(Z + X') \right]$

Fig. 1—Hindrance functions for simple circuits.

expression corresponding to a two-terminal network. This expression will involve the various relays whose contacts appear in the network and will be called the hindrance or hindrance function of the network. The last network in Fig. 1 is a simple example.

Boolean expressions can be manipulated in a manner very similar to ordinary algebraic expressions. Terms can be rearranged, multiplied out, factored and combined according to all the standard rules of numerical algebra. We have, for example, in Boolean algebra the following identities:

$$0 + X = X$$

$$0 \cdot X = 0$$

$$1 \cdot X = X$$

$$X + Y = Y + X$$

$$XY = YX$$

$$X + (Y + Z) = (X + Y) + Z$$

$$X(YZ) = (XY)Z$$

$$X(Y + Z) = XY + XZ$$

The interpretation of some of these in terms of switching circuits is shown in Fig. 2.

There are a number of further rules in Boolean Algebra which allow

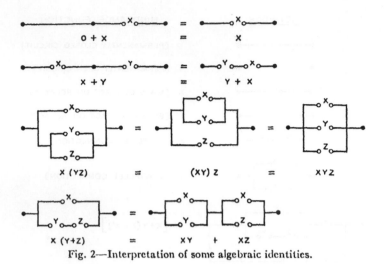

$$X \ (YZ) \qquad = \qquad (XY) \ Z \qquad = \qquad XYZ$$

$$X \ (Y+Z) \qquad = \qquad XY \quad + \quad XZ$$

Fig. 2—Interpretation of some algebraic identities.

simplifications of expressions that are not possible in ordinary algebra. The more important of these are:

$$X = X + X = X + X + X = \text{etc.}$$

$$X = X \cdot X = X \cdot X \cdot X = \text{etc.}$$

$$X + 1 = 1$$

$$X + YZ = (X + Y)(X + Z)$$

$$X + X' = 1$$

$$X \cdot X' = 0$$

$$(X + Y)' = X'Y'$$

$$(XY)' = X' + Y'$$

The circuit interpretation of some of these is shown in Fig. 3. These rules make the manipulation of Boolean expressions considerably simpler than ordinary algebra. There is no need, for example, for numerical coefficients or for exponents, since $nX = X^n = X$.

By means of Boolean Algebra it is possible to find many circuits equivalent in operating characteristics to a given circuit. The hindrance of the given circuit is written down and manipulated according to the rules. Each different resulting expression represents a new circuit equivalent to the given one. In particular, expressions may be manipulated to eliminate elements which are unnecessary, resulting in simple circuits.

Any expression involving a number of variables $X_1, X_2, \cdots, X_n$ is called a *function* of these variables and written in ordinary function notation, $f(X_1, X_2, \cdots, X_n)$. Thus we might have $f(X, Y, Z) = X + Y'Z + XZ'$. In Boolean Algebra there are a number of important general theorems which hold for any function. It is possible to *expand* a function about one or more of its arguments as follows:

$$f(X_1, X_2, \cdots, X_n) = X_1 f(1, X_2, \cdots, X_n) + X' f(0, X_2, \cdots, X_n)$$

This is an expansion about X_1. The term $f(1, X_2, \cdots, X_n)$ is the function

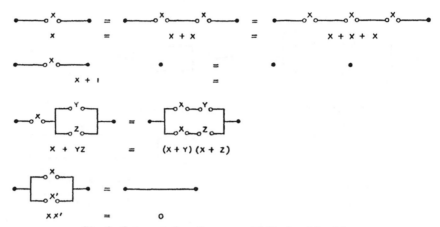

Fig. 3—Interpretation of some special Boolean identities.

$f(X_1, X_2, \cdots, X_n)$ with 1 substituted for X, and 0 for X', and conversely for the term $f(0, X_2, \cdots, X_n)$. An expansion about X_1 and X_2 is:

$$f(X_1, X_2, \cdots, X_n) = X_1 X_2 f(1, 1, X_3, \cdots, X_n) + X_1 X_2' f(1, 0, X_3, \cdots, X_n)$$
$$+ X_1' X_2 f(0, 1, X_3, \cdots, X_n) + X_1' X_2' f(1, 1, X_3, \cdots, X_n)$$

This may be continued to give expansions about any number of variables. When carried out for all n variables, f is written as a sum of 2^n products each with a coefficient which does not depend on any of the variables. Each coefficient is therefore a constant, either 0 or 1.

There is a similar expansion whereby f is expanded as a product:

$$f(X_1, X_2, \cdots, X_2)$$
$$= [X_1 + f(0, X_2, \cdots, X_n)][X_1' + f(1, X_2, \cdots, X_n)]$$
$$= [X_1 + X_2 + f(0, 0, \cdots, X_n)][X_1 + X_2' + f(0, 1, \cdots, X_n)]$$
$$[X_1' + X_2 + f(1, 0, \cdots, X_n)][X_1' + X_2' + f(1, 1, \cdots, X_n)]$$
$$= \text{etc.}$$

The following are some further identities for general functions:

$$X + f(X, Y, Z, \cdots) = X + f(0, Y, Z, \cdots)$$

$$X' + f(X, Y, Z, \cdots) = X' + f(1, Y, Z, \cdots)$$

$$Xf(X, Y, Z, \cdots) = Xf(1, Y, Z, \cdots)$$

$$X'f(X, Y, Z, \cdots) = X'f(0, Y, Z, \cdots)$$

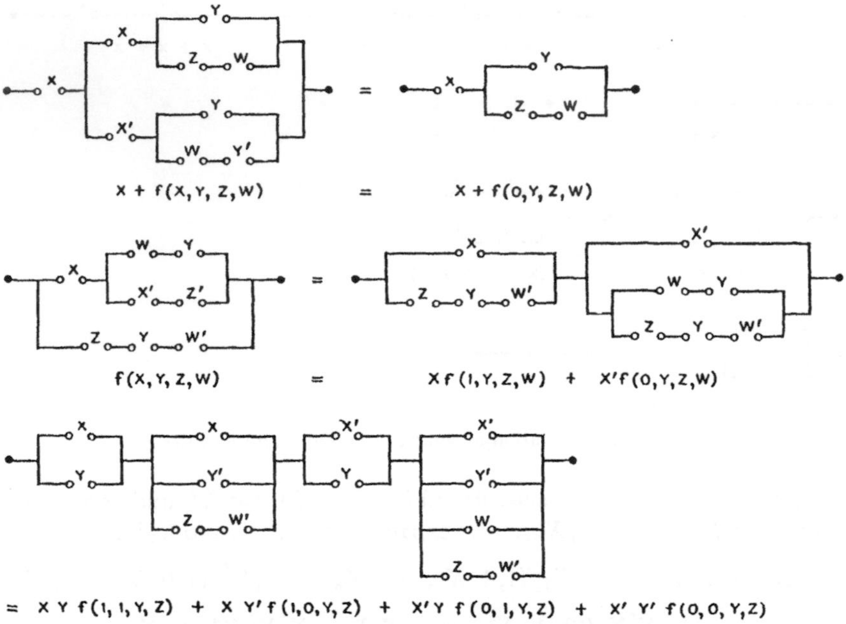

$$X + f(X, Y, Z, W) \qquad = \qquad X + f(0, Y, Z, W)$$

$$f(X, Y, Z, W) \qquad = \qquad Xf(1, Y, Z, W) \quad + \quad X'f(0, Y, Z, W)$$

$$= \quad X\, Y\, f(1, 1, Y, Z) \;+\; X\, Y'\, f(1, 0, Y, Z) \;+\; X'\, Y\, f(0, 1, Y, Z) \;+\; X'\, Y'\, f(0, 0, Y, Z)$$

Fig. 4—Examples of some functional identities.

The network interpretations of some of these identities are shown in Fig. 4. A little thought will show that they are true, in general, for switching circuits.

The hindrance function associated with a two-terminal network describes the network completely from the external point of view. We can determine from it whether the circuit will be open or closed for any particular position of the relays. This is done by giving the variables corresponding to operated relays the value 0 (since the make contacts of these are then closed and the break contacts open) and unoperated relays the value 1. For example, with the function $f = W[X + Y(Z + X')]$ suppose relays X and Y operated and Z and W not operated. Then $f = 1[0 + 0(1 + 1)] = 0$ and in this condition the circuit is closed.

A hindrance function corresponds explicitly to a series-parallel type of circuit, i.e. a circuit containing only series and parallel connections. This is because the expression is made up of sum and product operations. There is however, a hindrance function representing the operating characteristics (conditions for open or closed circuits between the two terminals) for any network, series-parallel or not. The hindrance for non-series-parallel networks can be found by several methods of which one is indicated in Fig. 5 for a simple bridge circuit. The hindrance is written as the product of a set of factors. Each factor is the series hindrance of a possible path between the two terminals. Further details concerning the Boolean method for switching circuits may be found in the references cited above.

This paper is concerned with the problem of synthesizing a two-terminal circuit which represents a given hindrance function $f(X_1, \cdots, X_n)$. Since any given function f can be realized in an unlimited number of different

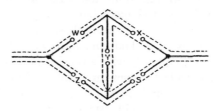

$$f = (w+x)(z+s)(w+y+s)(z+y+x)$$

Fig. 5—Hindrance of a bridge circuit.

ways, the particular design chosen must depend upon other considerations. The most common of these determining criteria is that of economy of elements, which may be of several types, for example:

(1) We may wish to realize our function with the least total number of switching elements, regardless of which variables they represent.

(2) We may wish to find the circuit using the least total number of relay springs. This requirement sometimes leads to a solution different from (1), since contiguous make and break elements may be combined into transfer elements so that circuits which tend to group make and break contacts on the same relay into pairs will be advantageous for (2) but not necessarily for (1).

(3) We may wish to distribute the spring loading on all the relays or on some subset of the relays as evenly as possible. Thus, we might try to find the circuit in which the most heavily loaded relay was as lightly loaded as possible. More generally, we might desire a circuit in which the loading on the relays is of some specified sort, or as near as possible to this given distribution. For example, if the relay X_1

must operate very quickly, while X_2 and X_3 have no essential time
limitations but are ordinary U-type relays, and X_4 is a multicontact
relay on which many contacts are available, we would probably try
to design a circuit for $f(X_1, X_2, X_3, X_4)$ in such a way as, first of all,
to minimize the loading on X_1, next to equalize the loading on X_2
and X_3 keeping it at the same time as low as possible, and finally
not to load X_4 any more than necessary.   Problems of this sort may
be called *problems in spring-load distribution*.

Although all equivalent circuits representing a given function f which
contain only series and parallel connections can be found with the aid of
Boolean Algebra, the most economical circuit in any of the above senses will
often not be of this type.   The problem of synthesizing non-series-parallel
circuits is exceedingly difficult.   It is even more difficult to show that a
circuit found in some way is the *most* economical one to realize a given
function.   The difficulty springs from the large number of essentially
different networks available and more particularly from the lack of a
simple mathematical idiom for representing these circuits.

We will describe a new design method whereby any function $f(X_1, X_2, \cdots,$
$X_n)$ may be realized, and frequently with a considerable saving of elements
over other methods, particularly when the number of variables n is large.
The circuits obtained by this method will not, in general, be of the series-
parallel type, and, in fact, they will usually not even be planar.   This
method is of interest theoretically as well as for practical design purposes,
for it allows us to set new upper limits for certain numerical functions associated with relay circuits.   Let us make the following definitions:

$\lambda(n)$ is defined as the least number such that any function of n variables
can be realized with not more than $\lambda(n)$ elements.*   Thus, any function of
n variables can be realized with $\lambda(n)$ elements and at least one function with
no less.

$\mu(n)$ is defined as the least number such that given any function f of n
variables, there is a two-terminal network having the hindrance f and using
not more than $\mu(n)$ elements on the most heavily loaded relay.

The first part of this paper deals with the general design method and the
behaviour of $\lambda(n)$.   The second part is concerned with the possibility of
various types of spring load distribution, and in the third part we will study
certain classes of functions that are especially easy to synthesize, and give
some miscellaneous theorems on switching networks and functions.

2. Fundamental Design Theorem

The method of design referred to above is based on a simple theorem dealing with the interconnection of two switching networks.   We shall first

---

* An *element* means a make or break contact on one relay.   A *transfer element* means
a make-and-break with a common spring, and contains two *elements*.

state and prove this theorem. Suppose that M and N (Fig. 6) are two $(n + 1)$ terminal networks, M having the hindrance functions U_k ($k = 1, 2, \cdots n$) between terminals a and k, and N having the functions V_k between b and k. Further, let M be such that $U_{jk} = 1 (j, k = 1, 2, \cdots, n)$. We will say, in this case, that M is a *disjunctive* network. Under these conditions we shall prove the following:

Theorem 1: If the corresponding terminals $1, 2, \cdots, n$ of M and N are connected together, then

$$U_{ab} = \prod_{k=1}^{n} (U_k + V_k) \tag{1}$$

where U_{ab} is the hindrance from terminal a to terminal b.

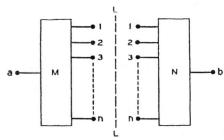

Fig. 6—Network for general design theorem.

Proof: It is known that the hindrance U_{ab} may be found by taking the product of the hindrances of all possible paths from a to b along the elements of the network.[6] We may divide these paths into those which cross the line L once, those which cross it three times, those which cross it five times, etc. Let the product of the hindrances in the first class be W_1, in the second class W_3, etc. Thus

$$U_{ab} = W_1 \cdot W_3 \cdot W_5 \cdots \tag{2}$$

Now clearly

$$W_1 = \prod_{1}^{n} (U_k + V_k)$$

and also

$$W_3 = W_5 = \cdots = 1$$

since each term in any of these must contain a summand of the type U_{jk} which we have assumed to be 1. Substituting in (2) we have the desired result.

The method of using this theorem to synthesize networks may be roughly described as follows: The function to be realized is written in the form of a product of the type (1) in such a way that the functions U_k are the same for a large class of functions, the V_k determining the particular one under consideration. A basic disjunctive network M is constructed having the functions U_k between terminals a and k. A network N for obtaining the functions V_k is then found by inspection or according to certain general rules. We will now consider just how this can be done in various cases.

3. Design of Networks for General Functions—Behavior of $\lambda(n)$.

a. Functions of One, Two and Three Variables:

Functions of one or two variables may be dismissed easily since the number of such functions is so small. Thus, with one variable X, the possible functions are only:

$$0, 1, X, X'$$

and obviously $\lambda(1) = 1$, $\mu(1) = 1$.

With two variables X and Y there are 16 possible functions:

$$0 \ X \ Y \qquad XY \qquad XY' \qquad X'Y \qquad X'Y' \qquad XY' + X'Y$$

$$1 \ X' \ Y' \quad X + Y \quad X + Y' \quad X' + Y \quad X' + Y' \quad XY + X'Y'$$

so that $\lambda(2) = 4$, $\mu(2) = 2$.

We will next show that any function of three variables $f(X, Y, Z)$ can be realized with not more than eight elements and with not more than four from any one relay. Any function of three variables can be expanded in a product as follows:

$$f(X, Y, Z) = [X + Y + f(0, 0, Z)][X + Y' + f(0, 1, Z)]$$
$$[X' + Y + f(1, 0, Z)][X' + Y' + f(1, 1, Z)].$$

In the terminology of Theorem 1 we let

$$U_1 = X + Y \qquad V_1 = f(0, 0, Z)$$
$$U_2 = X + Y' \qquad V_2 = f(0, 1, Z)$$
$$U_3 = X' + Y \qquad V_3 = f(1, 0, Z)$$
$$U_4 = X' + Y' \qquad V_4 = f(1, 1, Z)$$

so that

$$U_{ab} = f(X, Y, Z) = \prod_{k=1}^{4} (U_k + V_k)$$

The above U_k functions are realized with the network M of Fig. 7 and it is easily seen that $U_{jk} = 1\ (j, k = 1, 2, 3, 4)$.   The problem now is to construct a second network N having the V_k functions V_1, V_2, V_3, V_4.   Each of these is a function of the one variable Z and must, therefore, be one of the four possible functions of one variable:

$$0, 1, Z, Z'.$$

Consider the network N of Fig. 8.   If any of the V's are equal to 0, connect the corresponding terminals of M to the terminal of N marked 0; if any are equal to Z, connect these terminals of M to the terminal of N marked Z, etc.   Those which are 1 are, of course, not connected to anything.   It is clear from Theorem 1 that the network thus obtained will realize the function $f(X, Y, Z)$.   In many cases some of the elements will be superfluous, e.g., if one of the V_i is equal to 1, the element of M connected to terminal i can

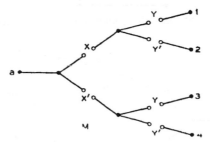

Fig. 7—Disjunctive tree with two bays.

be eliminated.   At worst M contains six elements and N contains two. The variable X appears twice, Y four times and Z twice.   Of course, it is completely arbitrary which variables we call X, Y, and Z.   We have thus proved somewhat more than we stated above, namely,

Theorem 2: Any function of three variables may be realized using not more than 2, 2, and 4 elements from the three variables in any desired order.   Thus $\lambda(3) \leq 8$, $\mu(3) \leq 4$.   Further, since make and break elements appear in adjacent pairs we can obtain the distribution 1, 1, 2, in terms of transfer elements.

The theorem gives only upper limits for $\lambda(3)$ and $\mu(3)$.   The question immediately arises as to whether by some other design method these limits could be lowered, i.e., can the $\leq$ signs be replaced by $<$ signs.   It can be shown by a study of special cases that $\lambda(3) = 8$, the function

$$X \oplus Y \oplus Z = X(YZ + Y'Z') + X'\ (YZ' + Y'Z)$$

requiring eight elements in its most economical realization. $\mu(3)$, however, is actually 3.

It seems probable that, in general, the function

$$X_1 \oplus X_2 \oplus \cdots \oplus X_n$$

requires $4(n-1)$ elements, but no proof has been found.   Proving that a certain function cannot be realized with a small number of elements is somewhat like proving a number transcendental; we will show later that almost all* functions require a large number of elements, but it is difficult to show that a particular one does.

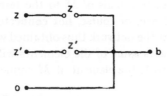

Fig. 8—Network giving all functions of one variable.

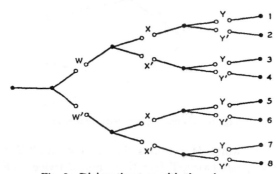

Fig. 9—Disjunctive tree with three bays.

b. Functions of Four Variables:

In synthesizing functions of four variables by the same method, two courses are open.   First, we may expand the function as follows:

$$f(W, X, Y, Z) = [W + X + Y + V_1(Z)] \cdot [W + X + Y' + V_2(Z)].$$
$$[W + X' + Y + V_3(Z)] \cdot [W + X' + Y' + V_4(Z)].$$
$$[W' + X + Y + V_5(Z)] \cdot [W' + X + Y' + V_6(Z)].$$
$$[W' + X' + Y + V_7(Z)] \cdot [W' + X' + Y' + V_8(Z)].$$

By this expansion we would let $U_1 = W + X + Y, U_2 = W + X + Y', \cdots,$ $U_8 = W' + X' + Y'$ and construct the M network in Fig. 9. N would

---

* We use the expression "almost all" in the arithmetic sense: e.g., a property is true of almost all functions of n variables if the fraction of all functions of n variables for which it is not true $\to 0$ as $n \to \infty$.

again be as in Fig. 8, and by the same type of reasoning it can be seen that $\lambda(4) \leq 16$.

Using a slightly more complicated method, however, it is possible to reduce this limit. Let the function be expanded in the following way:

$$f(W, X, Y, Z) = [W + X + V_1(Y, Z)] \cdot [W + X' + V_2(Y, Z)]$$
$$[W' + X + V_3(Y, Z)] \cdot [W' + X' + V_4(Y, Z)].$$

We may use a network of the type of Fig. 7 for M. The V functions are now functions of two variables Y and Z and may be any of the 16 functions:

$$A\begin{cases}0 \\ 1\end{cases} \qquad B\begin{cases}Y \\ Y' \\ Z \\ Z'\end{cases} \qquad C\begin{cases}YZ \\ Y'Z \\ YZ' \\ Y'Z'\end{cases} \qquad D\begin{cases}Y + Z \\ Y + Z' \\ Y' + Z \\ Y' + Z'\end{cases} \qquad E\begin{cases}Y'Z + YZ' \\ YZ + Y'Z'\end{cases}$$

We have divided the functions into five groups, A, B, C, D and E for later reference. We are going to show that any function of four variables can

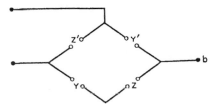

Fig. 10—Simplifying network.

be realized with not more than 14 elements. This means that we must construct a network N using not more than eight elements (since there are six in the M network) for any selection of four functions from those listed above. To prove this, a number of special cases must be considered and dealt with separately:

(1) If all four functions are from the groups, A, B, C, and D, N will certainly not contain more than eight elements, since eight letters at most can appear in the four functions.

(2) We assume now that just one of the functions is from group E; without loss of generality we may take it to be $YZ' + Y'Z$, for it is the other, replacing Y by Y' transforms it into this. If one or more of the remaining functions are from groups A or B the situation is satisfactory, for this function need require no elements. Obviously 0 and 1 require no elements and Y, Y', Z or Z' may be "tapped off" from the circuit for $YZ' + Y'Z$ by writing it as $(Y + Z)(Y' + Z')$. For example, Y' may be obtained with the circuit of Fig. 10. This leaves four elements, certainly a sufficient number for any two functions from A, B, C, or D.

(3) Now, still assuming we have one function, $YZ' + Y'Z$, from E, suppose at least two of the remaining are from D. Using a similar "tapping off" process we can save an element on each of these. For instance, if the functions are $Y + Z$ and $Y' + Z'$ the circuit would be as shown in Fig. 11.

(4) Under the same assumption, then, our worst case is when two of the functions are from C and one from D, or all three from C. This latter case is satisfactory since, then, at least one of the three must be a term of $YZ' + Y'Z$ and can be "tapped off." The former case is bad only when the two functions from C are YZ and $Y'Z'$. It may be seen that the only

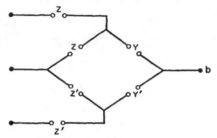

Fig. 11—Simplifying network.

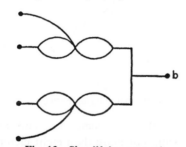

Fig. 12—Simplifying network.

essentially different choices for the function from D are $Y + Z$ and $Y' + Z$. That the four types of functions f resulting may be realized with 14 elements can be shown by writing out typical functions and reducing by Boolean Algebra.

(5) We now consider the cases where two of the functions are from E. Using the circuit of Fig. 12, we can tap off functions or parts of functions from A, B or D, and it will be seen that the only difficult cases are the following: (a) Two functions from C. In this case either the function f is symmetric in Y and Z or else both of the two functions may be obtained from the circuits for the E functions of Fig. 12. The symmetric case is handled in a later section. (b) One is from C, the other from D. There is only one unsymmetric case. We assume the four functions are $Y \oplus Z$, $Y \oplus Z'$, YZ and $Y + Z'$. This gives rise to four types of functions f, which can all be reduced by algebraic methods. This completes the proof.

Theorem 3: Any function of four variables can be realized with not more than 14 *elements.*

c. Functions of More Than Four Variables:

Any function of five variables may be written

$$f(X_1, \cdots, X_5) = [X_5 + f_1(X_1, \cdots, X_4)] \cdot [X_5' + f_2(X_1, \cdots, X_4)]$$

and since, as we have just shown, the two functions of four variables can be realized with 14 elements each, $f(X_1, \cdots X_5)$ can be realized with 30

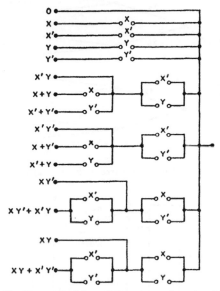

Fig. 13—Network giving all functions of two variables.

Now consider a function $f(X_1, X_2, \cdots, X_n)$ of n variables. For $5 < n \leq 13$ we get the best limit by expanding about all but two variables.

$$f(X_1, X_2, \cdots, X_n) = [X_1 + X_2 + \cdots + X_{n-2} + V_1(X_{n-1}, X_n)]$$
$$\cdot \cdots \cdot [X_1' + X_2' + \cdots + X_{n-2}' + V_8(X_{n-1}, V_n)] \qquad (4)$$

The V's are all functions of the variables X_{n-1}, X_n and may be obtained from the general N network of Fig. 13, in which *every* function of two variables appears. This network contains 20 elements which are grouped into five transfer elements for one variable and five for the other.* The M network for (4), shown in Fig. 14, requires in general $2^{n-1} - 2$ elements. Thus we have:

---

* Several other networks with the same property as Fig. 13 have been found, but they all require 20 elements.

Theorem 4. $\lambda(n) \leq 2^{n-1} + 18$

d. Upper Limits for $\lambda(n)$ with Large n.

Of course, it is not often necessary to synthesize a function of more than say 10 variables, but it is of considerable theoretical interest to determine as closely as possible the behavior of $\lambda(n)$ for large n.

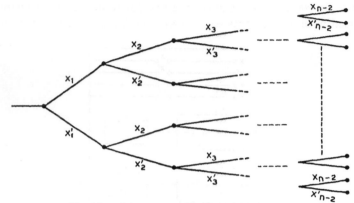

Fig. 14—Disjunctive tree with $(n - 2)$ bays.

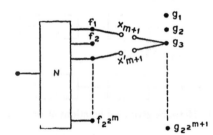

Fig. 15—Network giving all functions of $(m + 1)$ variables constructed from one giving all functions of m variables.

We will first prove a theorem placing limits on the number of elements required in a network analogous to Fig. 13 but generalized for m variables.

Theorem 5. *An N network realizing all 2^{2^m} functions of m variables can be constructed using not more than $2 \cdot 2^{2^m}$ elements, i.e., not more than two elements per function. Any network with this property uses at least $(\frac{3}{2} - \epsilon)$ elements per function for any $\epsilon > 0$ with n sufficiently large.*

The first part will be proved by induction. We have seen it to be true for $m = 1, 2$. Suppose it is true for some m with the network N of Fig. 15. Any function of $m + 1$ variables can be written

$$g = [X_{m+1} + f_a][X'_{m+1} + f_b]$$

where f_a and f_b involve only m variables. By connecting from g to the corresponding f_a and f_b terminals of the smaller network, as shown typically for g_3, we see from Theorem 1 that all the g functions can be obtained. Among these will be the 2^{2^m} f functions and these can be obtained simply by connecting across to the f functions in question without any additional elements. Thus the entire network uses less than

$$(2^{2^{m+1}} - 2^{2^m})2 + 2 \cdot 2^{2^m}$$

elements, since the N network by assumption uses less than $2 \cdot 2^{2^m}$ and the first term in this expression is the number of added elements.

The second statement of Theorem 7 can be proved as follows. Suppose we have a network, Fig. 16, with the required property. The terminals can be divided into three classes, those that have one or less elements di-

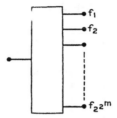

Fig. 16—Network giving all functions of m variables.

rectly connected, those with two, and those with three or more. The first set consists of the functions 0 and 1 and functions of the type

$$(X + f) = X + f_{x=0}$$

where X is some variable or primed variable. The number of such functions is not greater than $2m \cdot 2^{2^{m-1}}$ for there are $2m$ ways of selecting an "X" and then $2^{2^{m-1}}$ different functions $f_{x=0}$ of the remaining $m - 1$ variables. Hence the terminals in this class as a fraction of the total $\rightarrow 0$ as $m \rightarrow \infty$. Functions of the second class have the form

$$g = (X + f_1)(Y + f_2)$$

In case $X \neq Y'$ this may be written

$$XY + XY'g_{x=1,y=0} + X'Yg_{x=0,y=1} + X'Y'g_{x=0,y=0}$$

and there are not more than $(2m)(2m - 2)[2^{2^{m-2}}]^3$ such functions, again a vanishingly small fraction. In case $X = Y'$ we have the situation shown in Fig. 17 and the XX' connection can never carry ground to another terminal since it is always open as a series combination. The inner ends of these elements can therefore be removed and connected to terminals corresponding to functions of less than m variables according to the equation

$$g = (X + f_1)(X' + f_2) = (X + f_{1X=0})(X' + f_{2X=1})$$

if they are not already so connected. This means that all terminals of the second class are then connected to a vanishingly small fraction of the total terminals. We can then attribute two elements each to these terminals and at least one and one-half each to the terminals of the third group. As these two groups exhaust the terminals except for a fraction which $\rightarrow 0$ as $n \rightarrow \infty$, the theorem follows.

If, in synthesizing a function of n variables, we break off the tree at the $(n - m)$th bay, the tree will contain $2^{n-m+1} - 2$ elements, and we can find an N network with not more than $2^{2^m} \cdot 2$ elements exhibiting every function of the remaining m variables. Hence

$$\lambda(n) \leq 2^{n-m+1} - 2 + 2\ 2^{2^m} < 2^{n-m+1} + 2\ 2^{2^m}$$

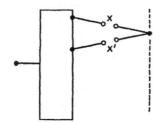

Fig. 17—Possible situation in Fig. 16.

for every integer m. We wish to find the integer $M = M(n)$ minimizing this upper bound.

Considering m as a continuous variable and n fixed, the function

$$f(m) = 2^{n-m+1} + 2^{2^m} \cdot 2$$

clearly has just one minimum. This minimum must therefore lie between m_1 and $m_1 + 1$, where

$$f(m_1) = f(m_1 + 1)$$

i.e., $$2^{n-m_1+1} + 2^{2^{m_1}} \cdot 2 = 2^{n-m_1} + 2^{2^{m_1+1}} \cdot 2$$

or $$2^n = 2^{m_1+1}(2^{2^{m_1+1}} - 2^{2^{m_1}})$$

Now m_1 cannot be an integer since the right-hand side is a power of two and the second term is less than half the first. It follows that to find the *integer* M making $f(M)$ a minimum we must take for M the least integer satisfying

$$2^n \leq 2^{M+1}2^{2^{M+1}}$$

Thus M satisfies:

$$M + 1 + 2^{M+1} \geq n > M + 2^M \qquad (5)$$

This gives:

$$
\begin{array}{ll}
n \leq 11 & M = 2 \\
11 < n \leq 20 & M = 3 \\
20 < n \leq 37 & M = 4 \\
37 < n \leq 70 & M = 5 \\
70 < n \leq 135 & M = 6 \\
\text{etc.}
\end{array}
$$

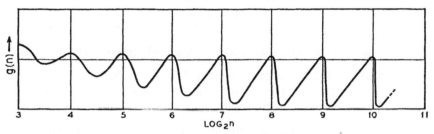

Fig. 18—Behaviour of $g(n)$.

Our upper bound for $\lambda(n)$ behaves something like $\dfrac{2^{n+1}}{n}$ with a superimposed saw-tooth oscillation as n varies between powers of two, due to the fact that m must be an integer. If we define $g(n)$ by

$$2^{n-M+1} + 2^{2^M}2 = g(n)\,\frac{2^{n+1}}{n} ,$$

M being determined to minimize the function (i.e., M satisfying (5)), then $g(n)$ varies somewhat as shown in Fig. 18 when plotted against $\log_2 n$. The maxima occur just beyond powers of two, and closer and closer to them as $n \to \infty$. Also, the saw-tooth shape becomes more and more exact. The sudden drops occur just after we change from one value of M to the next. These facts lead to the following:

Theorem 6. (a) For all n

$$\lambda(n) < \frac{2^{n+3}}{n} .$$

(b) For almost all n

$$\lambda(n) < \frac{2^{n+2}}{n}$$

(c) *There is an infinite sequence of n_i for which*

$$\lambda(n_i) < \frac{2^{n+1}}{n} (1 + \epsilon) \qquad\qquad \epsilon > 0.$$

These results can be proved rigorously without much difficulty.

e. A Lower Limit for $\lambda(n)$ with Large n.

Up to now most of our work has been toward the determination of upper limits for $\lambda(n)$. We have seen that for all n

$$\lambda(n) < B \frac{2^n}{n}.$$

We now ask whether this function $B \frac{2^n}{n}$ is anywhere near the true value of $\lambda(n)$, or may $\lambda(n)$ be perhaps dominated by a smaller order of infinity, e.g., n^p. It was thought for a time, in fact, that $\lambda(n)$ might be limited by n^2 for all n, arguing from the first few values: 1, 4, 8, 14. We will show that this is far from the truth, for actually $\frac{2^n}{n}$ is the correct order of magnitude of $\lambda(n)$:

$$A \frac{2^n}{n} < \lambda(n) < B \frac{2^n}{n}$$

for all n. A closely associated question to which a partial answer will be given is the following: Suppose we define the "complexity" of a given function f of n variables as the ratio of the number of elements in the most economical realization of f to $\lambda(n)$. Then any function has a complexity lying between 0 and 1. Are most functions simple or complex?

Theorem 7: For all sufficiently large n, all functions of n variables excepting a fraction δ require at least $(1 - \epsilon) \frac{2^n}{n}$ elements, where ϵ and δ are arbitrarily small positive numbers. Hence for large n

$$\lambda(n) > (1 - \epsilon) \frac{2^n}{n}$$

and almost all functions have a complexity $> \frac{1}{4}(1 - \epsilon)$. For a certain sequence n_i almost all functions have a complexity $> \frac{1}{2}(1 - \epsilon)$.

The proof of this theorem is rather interesting, for it is a pure existence proof. We do not show that any particular function or set of functions requires $(1 - \epsilon) \frac{2^n}{n}$ elements, but rather that it is impossible for all functions to require less. This will be done by showing that there are not enough networks with less than $(1 - \epsilon)\dfrac{2^n}{n}$ branches to go around, i.e., to represent all the 2^{2^n} functions of n variables, taking account, of course, of the different assignments of the variables to the branches of each network. This is only possible due to the extremely rapid increase of the function 2^{2^n}. We require the following:

Lemma: The number of two-terminal networks with K or less branches is less than $(6K)^K$.

Any two-terminal network with K or less branches can be constructed as follows: First line up the K branches as below with the two terminals a and b.

$$
\begin{aligned}
&\text{a.} &&1\text{---}1' \\
& &&2\text{---}2' \\
& &&3\text{---}3' \\
& &&\cdot\;4\text{---}4' \\
& &&\quad\cdot \\
& &&\quad\cdot \\
& &&\quad\cdot \\
&\text{b.} &&K\text{---}K'
\end{aligned}
$$

We first connect the terminals $a, b, 1, 2, \cdots , K$ together in the desired way. The number of *different* ways we can do this is certainly limited by the number of partitions of $K + 2$ which, in turn, is less than

$$2^{K+1}$$

for this is the number of ways we can put one or more division marks between the symbols $a, 1, \cdots , K, b$. Now, assuming $a, 1, 2, \cdots , K, b$, interconnected in the desired manner, we can connect $1'$ either to one of these terminals or to an additional junction point, i.e., $1'$ has a choice of at most

$$K + 3$$

terminals, $2'$ has a choice of at most $K + 4$, etc. Hence the number of networks is certainly less than

$$2^{K+1}(K + 3)\,(K + 4)\,(K + 5)\, \cdots \,(2K + 3)$$

$$< (6K)^K \qquad\qquad K \geq 3$$

and the theorem is readily verified for $K = 1, 2$.

We now return to the proof of Theorem 7. The number of functions of n variables that can be realized with $\dfrac{(1 - \epsilon)2^n}{n}$ elements is certainly less than the number of networks we can construct with this many branches multiplied by the number of assignments of the variables to the branches, i.e., it is less than

$$H = (2n)^{(1-\epsilon)(2^n/n)} \left[6(1 - \epsilon)\, \frac{2^n}{n} \right]^{(1-\epsilon)(2^n/n)}$$

Hence

$$\log_2 H = (1 - \epsilon)\, \frac{2^n}{n} \log 2n + (1 - \epsilon)\, \frac{2^n}{n} \log (1 - \epsilon)\, \frac{2^n}{n} \cdot 6$$

$$= (1 - \epsilon)\, 2^n + \text{terms dominated by this term for large } n.$$

By choosing n so large that $\frac{\epsilon}{2} 2^n$ dominates the other terms of $\log H$ we arrive at the inequality

$$\log_2 H < (1 - \epsilon_1)\, 2^n$$

$$H < 2^{(1-\epsilon_1)2^n}$$

But there are $S = 2^{2^n}$ functions of n variables and

$$\frac{H}{S} = \frac{2^{(1-\epsilon_1)2^n}}{2^{2^n}} \to 0 \quad \text{as} \quad n \to \infty.$$

Hence almost all functions require more than $(1 - \epsilon_1)2^n$ elements.

Now, since for all $n > N$ there is at least one function requiring more than (say) $\frac{1}{2}\frac{2^n}{n}$ elements and since $\lambda(n) > 0$ for $n > 0$, we can say that for *all* n,

$$\lambda(n) > A\, \frac{2^n}{n}$$

for some constant $A > 0$, for we need only choose A to be the minimum number in the finite set:

$$\frac{1}{2}, \quad \frac{\lambda(1)}{\dfrac{2^1}{1}}, \quad \frac{\lambda(2)}{\dfrac{2^2}{2}}, \quad \frac{\lambda(3)}{\dfrac{2^3}{3}}, \quad \cdots, \quad \frac{\lambda(N)}{\dfrac{2^N}{N}}$$

Thus $\lambda(n)$ is of the order of magnitude of $\frac{2^n}{n}$. The other parts of Theorem 8 follow easily from what we have already shown.

The writer is of the opinion that almost all functions have a complexity nearly 1, i.e., $> 1 - \epsilon$. This could be shown at least for an infinite sequence n_i if the Lemma could be improved to show that the number of networks is less than $(6K)^{K/2}$ for large K. Although several methods have been used in counting the networks with K branches they all give the result $(6K)^K$.

It may be of interest to show that for large K the number of networks is greater than

$$(6K)^{K/4}$$

This may be done by an inversion of the above argument. Let $f(K)$ be the number of networks with K branches. Now, since there are 2^{2^n} functions of n variables and each can be realized with $(1 + \epsilon) \dfrac{2^{n+2}}{n}$ elements (n sufficiently large),

$$f\left((1 + \epsilon)\, \frac{2^{n+2}}{n}\right)(2n)^{(1+\epsilon)(2^{n+2}/n)} > 2^{2^n}$$

for n large. But assuming $f(K) < (6K)^{K/4}$ reverses the inequality, as is readily verified. Also, for an infinite sequence of K,

$$f(K) > (6K)^{K/2}$$

Since there is no obvious reason why $f(K)$ should be connected with powers of 2 it seems likely that this is true for all large K.

We may summarize what we have proved concerning the behavior of $\lambda(n)$ for large n as follows. $\lambda(n)$ varies somewhat as $\dfrac{2^{n+1}}{n}$; if we let

$$\lambda(n) = A_n \frac{2^{n+1}}{n}$$

then, for large n, A_n lies between $\frac{1}{2} - \epsilon$ and $(2 + \epsilon)$, while, for an infinite sequence of n, $\frac{1}{2} - \epsilon < A_n < 1 + \epsilon$.

We have proved, incidentally, that the new design method cannot, in a sense, be improved very much. With series-parallel circuits the best known limit* for $\lambda(n)$ is

$$\lambda(n) < 3.2^{n-1} + 2$$

and almost all functions require $(1 - \epsilon) \dfrac{2^n}{\log_2 n}$ elements.[7] We have lowered the order of infinity, dividing by at least $\dfrac{n}{\log_2 n}$ and possibly by n. The best that can be done now is to divide by a constant factor ≤ 4, and for some n, ≤ 2. The possibility of a design method which does this seems, however, quite unlikely. Of course, these remarks apply only to a perfectly general design method, i.e., one applicable to *any* function. Many special *classes* of functions can be realized by special methods with a great saving.

---

* Mr. J. Riordan has pointed out an error in my reasoning in (6) leading to the statement that this limit is actually reached by the function $X_1 \oplus X_2 \oplus \ldots \oplus X_n$, and has shown that this function and its negative can be realized with about n^2 elements. The error occurs in Part IV after equation 19 and lies in the assumption that the factorization given is the best.

PART II: CONTACT LOAD DISTRIBUTION

4. FUNDAMENTAL PRINCIPLES

We now consider the question of distributing the spring load on the relays as evenly as possible or, more generally, according to some preassigned scheme. It might be thought that an attempt to do this would usually result in an increase in the total number of elements over the most economical circuit. This is by no means true; we will show that in many cases (in fact, for almost all functions) a great many load distributions may be obtained (including a nearly uniform distribution) while keeping the total number of elements at the same minimum value. Incidentally this result has a bearing on the behavior of $\mu(n)$, for we may combine this result with

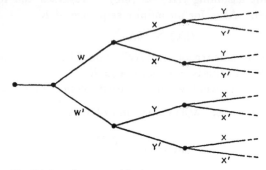

Fig. 19—Disjunctive tree with the contact distribution 1, 3, 3.

preceding theorems to show that $\mu(n)$ is of the order of magnitude of $\dfrac{2^{n+1}}{n^2}$ as $n \to \infty$ and also to get a good evaluation of $\mu(n)$ for small n.

The problem is rather interesting mathematically, for it involves additive number theory, a subject with few if any previous applications. Let us first consider a few simple cases. Suppose we are realizing a function with the tree of Fig. 9. The three variables appear as follows:

$$W, X, Y \qquad\qquad \text{appear}$$

$$2, 4, 8 \qquad\qquad \text{times, respectively.}$$

or, in terms of transfer elements*

$$1, 2, 4.$$

Now, W, X, and Y may be interchanged in any way without altering the operation of the tree. Also we can interchange X and Y in the lower branch of the tree only without altering its operation. This would give the distribution (Fig. 19)

$$1, 3, 3$$

---

* In this section we shall always speak in terms of transfer elements.

A tree with four bays can be constructed with any of the following distributions

$$
\begin{array}{llll}
\text{W} & \text{X} & \text{Y} & \text{Z} \\
1, & 2, & 4, & 8 = 1, 2, 4, + 1, 2, 4 \\
1, & 2, & 5, & 7 = 1, 2, 4 + 1, 3, 3 \\
1, & 2, & 6, & 6 = 1, 2, 4 + 1, 4, 2 \\
1, & 3, & 3, & 8 = 1, 2, 4 + 2, 1, 4 \\
1, & 3, & 4, & 7 = 1, 3, 3 + 2, 1, 4 \\
1, & 3, & 5, & 6 = 1, 4, 2 + 2, 1, 4 \\
1, & 4, & 4, & 6 = 1, 3, 3 + 3, 1, 3 \\
1, & 4, & 5, & 5 = 1, 4, 2 + 3, 1, 3
\end{array}
$$

and the variables may be interchanged in any manner. The "sums" on the right show how these distributions are obtained. The first set of numbers represents the upper half of the tree and the second set the lower half. They are all reduced to the sum of sets 1, 2, 4 or 1, 3, 3 in some order, and these sets are obtainable for trees with 3 bays as we already noted. In general it is clear that if we can obtain the distributions

$$a_1, a_2, a_3, \cdots, a_n$$

$$b_1, b_2, b_3, \cdots, b_n$$

for a tree with n bays then we can obtain the distribution

$$1, a_1 + b_1, a_2 + b_2, \cdots, a_n + b_n$$

for a tree with $n + 1$ bays.

Now note that all the distributions shown have the following property: any one may be obtained from the first, 1, 2, 4, 8, by moving one or more units from a larger number to a smaller number, or by a succession of such operations, without moving any units to the number 1. Thus 1, 3, 3, 8 is obtained by moving a unit from 4 to 2. The set 1, 4, 5, 5 is obtained by first moving two units from the 8 to the 2, then one unit to the 4. Furthermore, every set that may be obtained from the set 1, 2, 4, 8 by this process appears as a possible distribution. This operation is somewhat analogous to heat flow—heat can only flow from a hotter body to a cooler one just as units can only be transferred from higher numbers to lower ones in the above.

These considerations suggest that a disjunctive tree with n bays can be constructed with any load distribution obtained by such a flow from the initial distribution

$$1, 2, 4, 8, \cdots, 2^{n-1}$$

We will now show that this is actually the case.

First let us make the following definition: The symbol $(a_1, a_2, \cdots, a_n)$ represents any set of numbers $b_1, b_2, \cdots, b_n$ that may be obtained from the set $a_1, a_2, \cdots, a_n$ by the following operations:

1. Interchange of letters.

2. A flow from a larger number to a smaller one, no flow, however, being allowed to the number 1. Thus we would write

$$1, 2, 4, 8 = (1, 2, 4, 8)$$

$$4, 4, 1, 6 = (1, 2, 4, 8)$$

$$1, 3, 10, 3, 10 = (1, 2, 4, 8, 12)$$

but $2, 2 \neq (1, 3)$. It is possible to put the conditions that

$$b_1, b_2, \cdots, b_n = (a_1, a_2, \cdots, a_n) \tag{6}$$

into a more mathematical form. Let the a_i and the b_i be arranged as non-decreasing sequences. Then a necessary and sufficient condition for the relation (6) is that

(1)
$$\sum_{i=1}^{s} b_i \geq \sum_{1}^{s} a_i \qquad s = 1, 2, \cdots, n,$$

(2)
$$\sum_{1}^{n} b_i = \sum_{1}^{n} a_i, \quad \text{and}$$

(3) There are the same number of 1's among the a_i as among the b_i. The necessity of (2) and (3) is obvious. (1) follows from the fact that if a_i is non-decreasing, flow can only occur toward the left in the sequence

$$a_1, a_2, a_3, \cdots, a_n$$

and the sum $\sum_{1}^{s} a_i$ can only increase. Also it is easy to see the sufficiency of the condition, for if $b_1, b_2, \cdots, b_n$ satisfies (1), (2), and (3) we can get the b_i by first bringing a_1 up to b_1 by a flow from the a_i as close as possible to a_1 (keeping the "entropy" low by a flow between elements of nearly the same value), then bringing a_2 up to b_2 (if necessary) etc. The details are fairly obvious.

Additive number theory, or the problem of decomposing a number into the sum of numbers satisfying certain conditions, (in our case this definition is generalized to "sets of numbers") enters through the following lemma:

Lemma: If $a_1, a_2, \cdots, a_n = (2, 4, 8, \cdots, 2^n)$
then we can decompose the a_i into the sum of two sets

$$a_i = b_i + c_i$$

such that

$$b_1, b_2, \cdots, b_n = (1, 2, 4, \cdots, 2^{n-1})$$

and

$$c_1, c_2, \cdots, c_n = (1, 2, 4, \cdots, 2^{n-1})$$

We may assume the a_i arranged in a non-decreasing sequence, $a_1 \leq a_2 \leq a_3 \leq \cdots \leq a_n$. In case $a_1 = 2$ the proof is easy. We have

$1, 2, 4, \cdots, 2^{n-1}$	B
$1, 2, 4, \cdots, 2^{n-1}$	C
$2, 4, 8, \cdots, 2^n$	A

and a flow has occurred in the set

$$4, 8, 16, \cdots, 2^n$$

to give $a_2, a_3, \cdots, a_n$. Now any permissible flow in C corresponds to a permissible flow in either A or B since if

$$c_j = a_j + b_j > c_i = a_i + b_i$$

then either $\qquad a_j > a_i \qquad \text{or} \qquad b_j > b_i$

Thus at each flow in the sum we can make a corresponding flow in one or the other of the summands to keep the addition true.

Now suppose $a_1 > 2$. Since the a_i are non-decreasing

$$(n - 1) a_2 \leq (2^{n+1} - 2) - a_1 \leq 2^{n+1} - 2 - 3$$

Hence

$$a_2 - 1 \leq \frac{2^{n+1} - 5}{n - 1} - 1 \leq 2^{n-1}$$

the last inequality being obvious for $n \geq 5$ and readily verified for $n < 5$. This shows that $(a_1 - 1)$ and $(a_2 - 1)$ lie between some powers of two in the set

$$1, 2, 4, \cdots, 2^{n-1}$$

Suppose

$$2^{q-1} < (a_1 - 1) \leq 2^q$$

$$2^{p-1} < (a_2 - 1) \leq a^p \qquad q \leq p \leq (n - 1).$$

Allow a flow between 2^q and 2^{q-1} until one of them reaches $(a_1 - 1)$, the other (say) R; similarly for $(a_2 - 1)$ the other reaching S. As the start toward our decomposition, then, we have the sets (after interchanges)

$(a_1 - 1)$	1	$2, 4 \cdots 2^{q-2}$	R		$2^{q+1} \cdots 2^{p-1} 2^p$		$2^{p+1} \cdots 2^{n-1}$		
1	$a_2 - 1$	$2, 4 \cdots 2^{q-2}$	2^{q-1}	2^q	$\cdots$	$2^{p-2} S$	$2^{p+1} \cdots 2^{n-1}$		
a_1	a_2	$4, 8 \cdots 2^{q-1}$	$\cdots$				$2^{p+2} \cdots 2^n$		

We must now adjust the values to the right of $L - L$ to the values $a_3, a_4, \cdots, a_n$. Let us denote the sequence

$$4, 8, \cdots, 2^{q-1}, (2^{q-1} + R), 3 \cdot 2^q, 3 \cdot 2^{q+1}, \cdots (2^p + S), 2^{p+2}, \cdots, 2^n$$

by $\mu_1, \mu_2, \cdots, \mu_{n-2}$. Now since all the rows in the above addition are non-decreasing to the right of $L - L$, and no 1's appear, we will have proved the lemma if we can show that

$$\sum_{i=1}^{i} \mu_i \leq \sum_{i=3}^{i+3} a_i \qquad i = 1, 2, \cdots, (n-2)$$

since we have shown this to be a sufficient condition that

$$a_3, a_4, \cdots, a_n = (\mu_1, \mu_n, \cdots, \mu_{n-2})$$

and the decomposition proof we used for the first part will work. For $i \leq q - 2$, i.e., before the term $(2^{q-1} + R)$

$$\sum_{i=1}^{i} \mu_i = 4(2^i - 1)$$

and

$$\sum_{3}^{i+3} a_i \geq i a_2 \geq i 2^{p-1} \geq i 2^{q-1}$$

since

$$q \leq p$$

Hence

$$\sum_{1}^{i} \mu_i \leq \sum_{3}^{i+3} a_i \qquad\qquad i \leq q - 2$$

Next, for $(q - 1) \leq i \leq (p - 3)$, i.e., before the term $(2^p + S)$

$$\sum_{1}^{i} \mu_i = 4(2^{q-1} - 1) + R + 3 \cdot 2^q(2^{i-q+1} - 1)$$

$$< 3 \cdot 2^{i+1} - 4 \leq 3 \cdot 2^{i+1} - 5$$

since

$$R < 2^q$$

also again

$$\sum_{3}^{i+3} a_i \geq i 2^{p-1}$$

so that in this interval we also have the desired inequality. Finally for the last interval,

$$\sum_1^i \mu_i = 2^{i-1} - a_1 - a_2 \leq 2^{i+3} - a_1 - a_2 - 2$$

and

$$\sum_3^{i+3} a_i = \sum_1^{i+3} a_i - a_1 - a_2 \geq 2^{i+3} - a_1 - a_2 - 2$$

since

$$a_1, a_2, \cdots, a_n = (2, 4, 8, \cdots, 2^n)$$

This proves the lemma.

5. The Disjunctive Tree

It is now easy to prove the following:

Theorem 8: A disjunctive tree of n bays can be constructed with any distribution

$$a_1, a_2, \cdots, a_n = (1, 2, 4, \cdots, 2^{n-1}).$$

We may prove this by induction. We have seen it to be true for $n = 2, 3, 4$. Assuming it for n, it must be true for $n + 1$ since the lemma shows that any

$$a_1, a_2, \cdots, a_n = (2, 4, 8, \cdots, 2^n)$$

can be decomposed into a sum which, by assumption, can be realized for the two branches of the tree.

It is clear that among the possible distributions

$$(1, 2, 4, \cdots, 2^{n-1})$$

for the tree, an "almost uniform" one can be found for all the variables but one. That is, we can distribute the load on $(n - 1)$ of them uniformly except at worst for one element. We get, in fact, for

$$
\begin{array}{ll}
n = 1 & 1 \\
n = 2 & 1, 2 \\
n = 3 & 1, 3, 3 \\
n = 4 & 1, 4, 5, 5, \\
n = 5 & 1, 7, 7, 8, 8, \\
n = 6 & 1, 12, 12, 12, 13, 13 \\
n = 7 & 1, 21, 21, 21, 21, 21, 21 \\
\text{etc.}
\end{array}
$$

as nearly uniform distributions.

6. Other Distribution Problems

Now let us consider the problem of load distribution in series-parallel circuits. We shall prove the following:

Theorem 9: Any function $f(X_1, X_2, \cdots, X_n)$ may be realized with a series-parallel circuit with the following distribution:

$$(1, 2, 4, \cdots, 2^{n-2}), 2^{n-2}$$

in terms of transfer elements.

This we prove by induction. It is true for $n = 3$, since any function of three variables can be realized as follows:

$$f(X, Y, Z) = [X + f_1(Y, Z)][X' + f_2(Y, Z)]$$

and $f_1(Y, Z)$ and $f_2(Y, Z)$ can each be realized with one transfer on Y and one on Z. Thus $f(X, Y, Z)$ can be realized with the distribution 1, 2, 2. Now assuming the theorem true for $(n - 1)$ we have

$$f(X_1, X_2, \cdots, X_n) = [X_n + f_1(X_1, X_2, \cdots, X_{n-1})]$$
$$[X'_n + f_2(X_1, X_2, \cdots, X_{n-1})]$$

and

$$
\begin{array}{l}
2, 4, 8, \cdots, 2^{n-3} \\
2, 4, 8, \cdots, 2^{n-3} \\
\hline
4, 8, 16, \cdots, 2^{n-2}
\end{array}
$$

A simple application of the lemma thus gives the desired result. Many distributions beside those given by Theorem 9 are possible but no simple criterion has yet been found for describing them. We cannot say any distribution

$$(1, 2, 4, 8, \cdots, 2^{n-2}, 2^{n-2})$$

(at least from our analysis) since for example

$$3, 6, 6, 7 = (2, 4, 8, 8)$$

cannot be decomposed into two sets

$$a_1, a_2, a_3, a_4 = (1, 2, 4, 4)$$

and

$$b_1, b_2, b_3, b_4 = (1, 2, 4, 4)$$

It appears, however, that the almost uniform case is admissible.

As a final example in load distribution we will consider the case of a network in which a number of trees in the same variables are to be realized. A large number of such cases will be found later. The following is fairly obvious from what we have already proved.

Theorem 10: It is possible to construct m different trees in the same n variables with the following distribution:

$$a_1, a_2, \cdots, a_n = (m, 2m, 4m, \cdots, 2^{n-1}m)$$

It is interesting to note that under these conditions the bothersome 1 disappears for $m > 1$.   We can equalize the load on all n of the variables, not just $n - 1$ of them, to within, at worst, one transfer element.

7. THE FUNCTION $\mu(n)$

We are now in a position to study the behavior of the function $\mu(n)$. This will be done in conjunction with a treatment of the load distributions possible for the general function of n variables.   We have already shown that any function of three variables can be realized with the distribution

$$1, 1, 2$$

n terms of transfer elements, and, consequently $\mu(3) \leq 4$.

Any function of four variables can be realized with the distribution

$$1, 1, (2, 4)$$

Hence $\mu(4) \leq 6$.   For five variables we can get the distribution

$$1, 1, (2, 4, 8)$$

or alternatively

$$1, 5, 5, (2, 4)$$

so that $\mu(5) \leq 10$.   With six variables we can get

$$1, 5, 5, (2, 4, 8) \text{ and } \mu(6) \leq 10$$

for seven,

$$1, 5, 5, (2, 4, 8, 16) \text{ and } \mu(7) \leq 16$$

etc.   Also, since we can distribute uniformly on all the variables in a tree except one, it is possible to give a theorem analogous to Theorem 7 for the function $\mu(n)$:

Theorem 11: For all n

$$\mu(n) \leq \frac{2^{n+3}}{n^2}$$

For almost all n

$$\mu(n) \leq \frac{2^{n+2}}{n^2}$$

For an infinite number of n_i ,

$$\mu(n) \leq (1 + \epsilon) \frac{2^{n+1}}{n^2}$$

The proof is direct and will be omitted.

PART III: SPECIAL FUNCTIONS

8. FUNCTIONAL RELATIONS

We have seen that almost all functions require the order of

$$\frac{2^{n+1}}{n^2}$$

elements per relay for their realization. Yet a little experience with the circuits encountered in practice shows that this figure is much too large. In a sender, for example, where many functions are realized, some of them involving a large number of variables, the relays carry an average of perhaps 7 or 8 contacts. In fact, almost all relays encountered in practice have less than 20 elements. What is the reason for this paradox? The answer, of course, is that the functions encountered in practice are far from being a random selection. Again we have an analogue with transcendental numbers —although almost all numbers are transcendental, the chance of first encountering a transcendental number on opening a mathematics book at random is certainly much less than 1. The functions actually encountered are simpler than the general run of Boolean functions for at least two major reasons:

(1) A circuit designer has considerable freedom in the choice of functions to be realized in a given design problem, and can often choose fairly simple ones. For example, in designing translation circuits for telephone work it is common to use additive codes and also codes in which the same number of relays are operated for each possible digit. The fundamental logical simplicity of these codes reflects in a simplicity of the circuits necessary to handle them.

(2) Most of the things required of relay circuits are of a logically simple nature. The most important aspect of this simplicity is that most circuits can be broken down into a large number of small circuits. In place of realizing a function of a large number of variables, we realize many functions, each of a small number of variables, and then perhaps some function of these functions. To get an idea of the effectiveness of this consider the following example: Suppose we are to realize a function

$$f(X_1 , X_2 , \cdots , X_{2n})$$

of $2n$ variables. The best limit we can put on the total number of elements necessary is about $\dfrac{2^{2n+1}}{2n}$. However, if we know that f is a function of two functions f_1 and f_2, each involving only n of the variables, i.e. if

$$f = g(f_1, f_2)$$

$$f_1 = f_1(X_1, X_2, \cdots, X_n)$$

$$f_2 = f_2(X_{n+1}, X_{n+2}, \cdots, X_{2n})$$

then we can realize f with about

$$4 \cdot \frac{2^{n+1}}{n}$$

elements, a much lower order of infinity than $\dfrac{2^{2n+1}}{2n}$. If g is one of the simpler functions of two variables; for example if $g(f_1, f_2) = f_1 + f_2'$, or in any case at the cost of two additional relays, we can do still better and realize f with about $2\dfrac{2^{n+1}}{n}$ elements. In general, the more we can decompose a synthesis problem into a combination of simple problems, the simpler the final circuits. The significant point here is that, due to the fact that f satisfies a certain functional relation

$$f = g(f_1, f_2),$$

we can find a simple circuit for it compared to the average function of the same number of variables.

This type of functional relation may be called functional separability. It is often easily detected in the circuit requirements and can always be used to reduce the limits on the number of elements required. We will now show that most functions are not functionally separable.

Theorem 12: The fraction of all functions of n variables that can be written in the form

$$f = g(h(X_1 \cdots X_s), X_{s+1}, \cdots, X_n)$$

where $1 < s < n - 1$ approaches zero as n approaches ∞.

We can select the s variables to appear in h in $\binom{n}{s}$ ways; the function h then has 2^{2^s} possibilities and g has $2^{2^{n-s+1}}$ possibilities, since it has $n - s + 1$ arguments. The total number of functionally separable functions is therefore dominated by

$$\sum_{s=2}^{n-2} \binom{n}{s} 2^{2^s} 2^{2^{n-s}+1}$$

$$\leq (n-3) \frac{n^2}{2} 2^{2^2} 2^{2^{n-1}}$$

and the ratio of this to $2^{2^n} \to 0$ as $n \to \infty$.

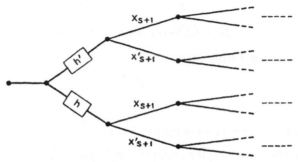

Fig. 20—Use of separability to reduce number of elements.

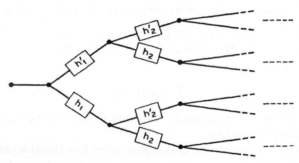

Fig. 21—Use of separability of two sets of variables.

In case such a functional separability occurs, the general design method described above can be used to advantage in many cases. This is typified by the circuit of Fig. 20. If the separability is more extensive, e.g.

$$f = g(h_1(X_1 \cdots X_s), h_2(X_{s+1} \cdots X_t), X_{t+1}, \cdots, X_n)$$

the circuit of Fig. 21 can be used, using for "h_2" either h_1 or h_2, whichever requires the least number of elements for realization together with its negative.

We will now consider a second type of functional relation which often occurs in practice and aids in economical realization. This type of relation may be called group invariance and a special case of it, functions symmetric in all variables, has been considered in (6). A function $f(X_1, \cdots, X_n)$ will be said to be symmetric in X_1, X_2 if it satisfies the relation

$$f(X_1, X_2, \cdots, X_n) = f(X_2, X_1, \cdots, X_n).$$

It is symmetric in X_1 and X'_2 if it satisfies the equation

$$f(X_1, X_2, \cdots, X_n) = f(X'_2, X'_1, X_3, \cdots, X_n)$$

These also are special cases of the type of functional relationships we will consider. Let us denote by

$N_{oo \cdots o} = I$ the operation of leaving the variables in a function as they are,

$N_{1oo \cdots o}$ the operation of negating the first variable (i.e. the one occupying the first position),

$N_{o1o \cdots o}$ that of negating the second variable,

$N_{11o \cdots o}$ that of negating the first two, etc.

So that $N_{1o1}f(X, Y, Z) = f(X'YZ')$ etc.

The symbols Ni form an abelian group, with the important property that each element is its own inverse; $NiNi = I$ The product of two elements may be easily found — if $N_i N_j = N_k$, k is the number found by adding i and j as though they were numbers in the base two but *without carrying*.

Note that there are 2^n elements to this "negating" group. Now let

$S_{1,2,3,\ldots,n} = I =$ the operation of leaving the variables of a function in the same order

$S_{2,1,3,\ldots,n} =$ be that of interchanging the first two variables

$S_{3,2,1,4,\ldots,n} =$ that of inverting the order of the first three, etc.

Thus

$$S_{312}f(X, Y, Z) = f(Z, X, Y)$$

$$S_{312}f(Z, X, Y) = S_{312}^2 f(X, Y, Z) = f(Y, Z, X)$$

etc. The S_i also form a group, the famous "substitution" or "symmetric" group. It is of order $n!$. It does not, however, have the simple properties of the negating group—it is not abelian ($n > 2$) nor does it have the self inverse property.[*] The negating group is not cyclic if $n > 2$, the symmetric group is not if $n > 3$.

The outer product of these two groups forms a group G whose general element is of the form $N_i S_j$ and since i may assume 2^n values and j, $n!$ values, the order of G is $2^n n!$

It is easily seen that $S_j N_i = N_k S_j$, where k may be obtained by per-

_____

[*] This is redundant; the self inverse property implies commutativity for if $XX = I$ then $XY = (XY)^{-1} = Y^{-1}X^{-1} = YX$.

forming on i, considered as an ordered sequence of zero's and one's, the permutation S_j. Thus

$$S_{2314} N_{1100} = N_{1010} S_{2314}.$$

By this rule any product such as $N_i S_j N_k N_l S_m N_n S_p$ can be reduced to the form

$$N_i N_j \cdots N_n S_p S_q \cdots S_r,$$

and this can then be reduced to the standard form $N_i S_j$.

A function f will be said to have a non-trivial group invariance if there are elements $N_i S_j$ of G other than I such that identically in all variables

$$N_i S_j f = f.$$

It is evident that the set of all such elements, $N_i S_j$, for a given function, forms a subgroup G_1 of G, since the product of two such elements is an element, the inverse of such an element is an element, and all functions are invariant under I.

A group operator leaving a function f invariant implies certain equalities among the terms appearing in the expanded form of f. To show this, consider a fixed $N_i S_j$, which changes in some way the variables (say) $X_1, X_2, \cdots, X_r$. Let the function $f(X_1, \cdots, X_n)$ be expanded about $X_1, \cdots, X_r$:

$$= [X_1 + X_2 + \cdots + X_r + f_1(X_{r+1}, \cdots, X_n)]$$
$$[X_1' + X_2 + \cdots + X_r + f_2(X_{r+1}, \cdots, X_n)]$$
$$\cdots\cdots\cdots\cdots\cdots\cdots\cdots\cdots\cdots\cdots\cdots\cdots$$
$$[X_1' + X_2' + \cdots + X_r' + f_{2^r}(X_{r+1}, \cdots, X_n)]$$

If f satisfies $N_i S_j f = f$ we will show that there are at least $\frac{1}{4} 2^r$ equalities between the functions $f_1, f_2, \cdots, f_{2^r}$. Thus the number of functions satisfying this relation is

$$\leq (2^{2^{n-r}})^{\frac{3}{4} 2^r} = 2^{\frac{3}{4} 2^n}$$

since each independent f_i can be any of just $2^{2^{n-r}}$ functions, and there are at most $\frac{3}{4} 2^r$ independent ones. Suppose $N_i S_j$ changes

$$X_1, X_2, \cdots, X_r \qquad\qquad\qquad\qquad\qquad \text{A}$$

into

$$X_{a_1}^*, X_{a_2}^*, \cdots, X_{a_r}^* \qquad\qquad\qquad\qquad\qquad \text{B}$$

where the *'s may be either primes or non primes, but no $X_{a_i}^* = X_i$. Give

X_1 the value 0. This fixes some element in B namely, X_{a_i} where $a_i = 1$. There are two cases:

(1) If this element is the first term, $a_1 = 1$, then we have

$$0 X_2, \cdots, X_r$$

$$1 X_{a_1}, \cdots, X_{a_r}$$

Letting $X_2, \cdots, X_r$ range through their 2^{r-1} possible sets of values gives 2^{r-1} equalities between different functions of the set f_i since these are really

$$f(X_1, X_2, \cdots, X_r, X_{r+1}, \cdots, X_n)$$

with $X_1, X_2, \cdots, X_r$ fixed at a definite set of values.

(2) If the element in question is another term, say X_{a_2}, we then give X_2 in line A the opposite value, $X_2 = (X_{a_2}^*)' = (X_2^*)'$. Now proceeding as before with the remaining $r - 2$ variables we establish 2^{r-2} equalities between the f_i.

Now there are not more* than $2^n n!$ relations

$$N_i S_j f = f$$

of the group invariant type that a function could satisfy, so that the number of functions satisfying *any* non-trivial relation

$$\leq 2^n n! \, 2^{\frac{1}{2} 2^n}.$$

Since

$$2^n n! \, 2^{\frac{1}{2} 2^n} / 2^{2^n} \to 0 \qquad \text{as } n \to \infty$$

we have:

Theorem 13: Almost all functions have no non-trivial group invariance.

It appears from Theorems 12 and 13 and from other results that almost all functions are of an extremely chaotic nature, exhibiting no symmetries or functional relations of any kind. This result might be anticipated from the fact that such relations generally lead to a considerable reduction in the number of elements required, and we have seen that almost all functions are fairly high in "complexity".

If we are synthesizing a function by the disjunctive tree method and the function has a group invariance involving the variables

$$X_1, X_2, \cdots, X_r$$

at least 2^{r-2} of the terminals in the corresponding tree can be connected to

---

* Our factor is really less than this because, first, we must exclude $N_i S_j = I$; and second, except for self inverse elements, one relation of this type implies others, viz. the powers $(N_i S_j)^p f = f$.

other ones, since at least this many equalities exist between the functions to
be joined to these terminals. This will, in general, produce a considerable
reduction in the contact requirements on the remaining variables. Also an
economy can usually be achieved in the M network. In order to apply this

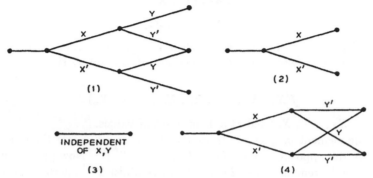

Fig. 22—Networks for group invariance in two variables.

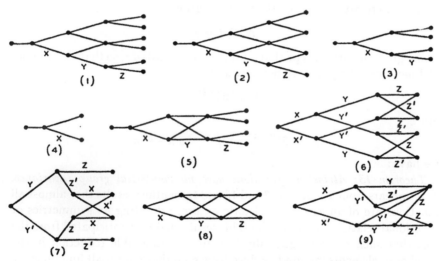

Fig. 23—Networks for group invariance in three variables.

method of design, however, it is essential that we have a method of determining which, if any, of the $N_i S_j$ leave a function unchanged. The
following theorem, although not all that might be hoped for, shows that we
don't need to evaluate $N_i S_j f$ for all $N_i S_j$ but only the $N_i f$ and $S_j f$.

   Theorem 14: A necessary and sufficient condition that $N_i S_j f = f$ is that
$N_i f = S_j f$.

   This follows immediately from the self inverse property of the N_i. Of course, group invariance can often be recognized directly from circuit requirements in a design problem.

Tables I and II have been constructed for cases where a relation exists involving two or three variables. To illustrate their use, suppose we have a function such that

$$N_{111} S_{312} f = f$$

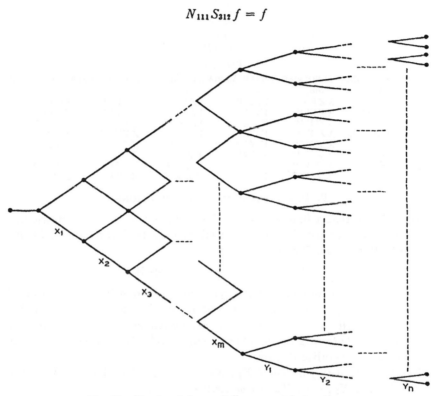

Fig. 24—*M* network for partially symmetric functions.

The corresponding entry $Z'Y'X$ in the group table refers us to circuit 9 of Fig. 23. The asterisk shows that the circuit may be used directly; if there is no asterisk an interchange of variables is required. We expand f about X, Y, Z and only two different functions will appear in the factors. These two functions are realized with two trees extending from the terminals of the network 9. Any such function f can be realized with (using just one variable in the N network)

$$9 + 2(2^{n-4} - 2) + 2$$

$$= 2^{n-3} + 7 \qquad \text{elements,}$$

a much better limit than the corresponding

$$2^{n-1} + 18$$

for the general function.

TABLE I
GROUP INVARIANCE INVOLVING TWO VARIABLES (SUPERSCRIPTS REFER TO FIG. 22)

	S_{12}	S_{21}
N_{oo}	$(x\,y)$	$(y\,x)$[1*]
N_{o1}	$(x\,y')$[2*]	$(y\,x')$[3*]
N_{10}	$(x'y)$[2]	$(y'x)$[3*]
N_{11}	$(x'y')$[4]	$(y'x')$[1]

TABLE II
GROUP INVARIANCE INVOLVING THREE VARIABLES (SUPERSCRIPTS REFER TO FIG. 23)

	S_{123}	S_{132}	S_{213}	S_{231}	S_{312}	S_{321}
N_{ooo}	XYZ	XZY[1]	YXZ[1*]	YZX[2*]	ZXY[2*]	ZYX:
N_{oo1}	XYZ'[3*]	XZY'[4*]	YXZ'[7]	YZX'[9]	ZXY'[9]	ZYX'[4]
N_{o1o}	$XY'Z$[3]	$XZ'Y$[4*]	$YX'Z$[4]	$YZ'X$[9]	$ZX'Y$[9]	$ZY'X$[7]
N_{o11}	$XY'Z'$[5]	$XZ'Y'$[1]	$YX'Z'$[8]	$YZ'X'$[2]	$ZX'Y'$[2]	$ZY'X'$[8]
N_{1oo}	$X'YZ$[3]	$X'ZY$[7*]	$Y'XZ$[4]	$Y'ZX$[9]	$Z'XY$[9]	$Z'YX$[4]
N_{101}	$X'YZ'$[5]	$X'ZY'$[8*]	$Y'XZ'$[8*]	$Y'ZX'$[2]	$Z'XY'$[2]	$Z'YX'$[1]
N_{110}	$X'Y'Z$[5*]	$X'Z'Y$[8*]	$Y'X'Z$[1]	$Y'Z'X$[2]	$Z'X'Y$[2]	$Z'Y'X$[8*]
N_{111}	$X'Y'Z'$[6]	$X'Z'Y'$[7]	$Y'X'Z'$[7]	$Y'Z'X'$[9]	$Z'X'Y'$[9]	$Z'Y'X'$[7]

9. PARTIALLY SYMMETRIC FUNCTIONS

We will say that a function is "partially symmetric" or "symmetric in a certain set of variables" if these variables may be interchanged at will without altering the function.   Thus

$$XYZW + (XY' + X'Y)W + WZ'$$

is symmetric in X and Y.   Partial symmetry is evidently a special case of the general group invariance we have been considering.   It is known that any function symmetric in all variables can be realized with not more than n^2 elements, where n is the number of variables.[6]   In this section we will improve and generalize this result.

Theorem 15: Any function $f(X_1, X_2, \cdots, X_m, Y_1, Y_2, \cdots Y_n)$ *symmetric in* $X_1, X_2, \cdots, X_m$ *can be written*

$$f(X_1, X_2, \cdots, X_m, Y_1, Y_2, \cdots, Y_n)$$

$$= [S_o(X_1, X_2, \cdots, X_m) + f_o(Y_1, Y_2, \cdots, Y_n)].$$

$$[S_1(X_1, X_2, \cdots, X_m) + f_1(Y_1, Y_2, \cdots, Y_n)].$$

$$\cdots\cdots\cdots\cdots\cdots\cdots\cdots\cdots\cdots\cdots\cdots\cdots\cdots\cdots\cdots$$

$$[S_m(X_1, X_2, \cdots, X_m) + f_m(Y_1, Y_2, \cdots, Y_n)] \qquad (6)$$

where

$$f_K(Y_1, Y_2, \cdots, Y_n)$$

$$= f(\underbrace{0, 0, \cdots, 0}_{k\ 0\text{'s}}, \underbrace{1, 1, \cdots, 1}_{(m-k)\ 1\text{'s}}, Y_1, Y_2, \cdots, Y_n)$$

and $S_k(X_1, X_2, \cdots, X_m)$ is the symmetric function of $X_1, X_2, \cdots, X_n$ with k for its only a-number.

This theorem follows from the fact that since f is symmetric in $X_1, X_2, \cdots, X_m$ the value of f depends only on the *number* of X's that are zero and the values of the Y's. If exactly K of the X's are zero the value of f is therefore f_K, but the right-hand side of (6) reduces to f_K in this case, since then $S_j(X_1, X_2, \cdots, X_m) = 1, j \neq K$, and $S_K = 0$.

The expansion (6) is of a form suitable for our design method. We can realize the disjunctive functions $S_K(X_1, X_2, \cdots, X_n)$ with the symmetric function lattice and continue with the general tree network as in Fig. 24, one tree from each level of the symmetric function network. Stopping the trees at Y_{n-1}, it is clear that the entire network is disjunctive and a second application of Theorem 1 allows us to complete the function f with two elements from Y_n. Thus we have

Theorem 16. Any function of $m + n$ variables symmetric in m of them can be realized with not more than the smaller of

$$(m + 1)(\lambda(n) + m) \text{ or } (m + 1)(2^n + m - 2) + 2$$

elements. In particular a function of n variables symmetric in $n - 2$ or more of them can be realized with not more than

$$n^2 - n + 2$$

elements.

If the function is symmetric in $X_1, X_2, \cdots, X_m$, and also in $Y_1, Y_2, \cdots, Y_r$, and not in $Z_1, Z_2, \cdots, Z_n$ it may be realized by the same method, using symmetric function networks in place of trees for the Y variables. It should be expanded first about the X's (assuming $m < r$) then about the Y's and finally the Z's. The Z part will be a set of $(m + 1)(r + 1)$ trees.

REFERENCES

1. G. Birkhoff and S. MacLane, "A Survey of Modern Algebra," Macmillan, 1941.
2. L. Couturat, "The Algebra of Logic," Open Court, 1914.
3. J. H. Woodger, "The Axiomatic Method in Biology," Cambridge, 1937.
4. W. S. McCulloch and W. Pitts, "A Logical Calculus of the Ideas Immanent in Nervous Activity," *Bull. Math. Biophysics,* V. 5, p. 115, 1943.
5. E. C. Berkeley, "Boolean Algebra and Applications to Insurance," *Record (American Institute of Actuaries),* V. 26, p. 373, 1947.
6. C. E. Shannon, "A Symbolic Analysis of Relay and Switching Circuits," *Trans. A. I. E. E.,* V. 57, p. 713, 1938.
7. J. Riordan and C. E. Shannon, "The Number of Two-Terminal Series Parallel Networks," *Journal of Mathematics and Physics,* V. 21, No. 2, p. 83, 1942.
8. A. Nakashima, Various papers in *Nippon Electrical Communication Engineering,* April, Sept., Nov., Dec., 1938.
9. H. Piesch, Papers in Archiv. from *Electrotechnik* XXXIII, p. 692 and p. 733, 1939.
10. G. A. Montgomerie, "Sketch for an Algebra of Relay and Contactor Circuits," *Jour. I. of E. E.,* V. 95, Part III, No. 36, July 1948, p. 303.
11. G. Pólya, "Sur Les Types des Propositions Composées," *Journal of Symbolic Logic,* V. 5, No. 3, p. 98, 1940.

A Simplified Derivation of Linear Least Square Smoothing and Prediction Theory*

H. W. BODE†, SENIOR MEMBER, IRE, AND C. E. SHANNON†, FELLOW, IRE

Summary—The central results of the Wiener-Kolmogoroff smoothing and prediction theory for stationary time series are developed by a new method. The approach is motivated by physical considerations based on electric circuit theory and does not involve integral equations or the autocorrelation function. The cases treated are the "infinite lag" smoothing problem, the case of pure prediction (without noise), and the general smoothing prediction problem. Finally, the basic assumptions of the theory are discussed in order to clarify the question of when the theory will be appropriate, and to avoid possible misapplication.

I. INTRODUCTION

IN A CLASSIC REPORT written for the National Defense Research Council,[1] Wiener has developed a mathematical theory of smoothing and prediction of considerable importance in communication theory. A similar theory was independently developed by Kolmogoroff[2] at about the same time. Unfortunately the work of Kolmogoroff and Wiener involves some rather formidable mathematics—Wiener's yellow-bound report soon came to be known among bewildered engineers as "The Yellow Peril"—and this has prevented the wide circulation and use that the theory deserves. In this paper the chief results of smoothing theory will be developed by a new method which, while not as rigorous or general as the methods of Wiener and Kolmogoroff, has the advantage of greater simplicity, particularly for readers with a background of electric circuit theory. The mathematical steps in the present derivation have, for the most part, a direct physical interpretation, which enables one to see intuitively what the mathematics is doing.

II. THE PROBLEM AND BASIC ASSUMPTIONS

The main problem to be considered may be formulated as follows. We are given a perturbed signal $f(t)$ which is the sum of a true signal $s(t)$, and a perturbing noise $n(t)$

$$f(t) = s(t) + n(t).$$

It is desired to operate on $f(t)$ in such a way as to obtain, as well as possible, the true signal $s(t)$. More generally, one may wish to combine this smoothing operation with prediction, i.e., to operate on $f(t)$ in such a way as to obtain a good approximation to what $s(t)$ will be in the future, say α seconds from now, or to what it was in the past, α seconds ago. In these cases we wish to approximate $s(t+\alpha)$ with α positive or negative, respectively. The situation is indicated schematically in Fig. 1; the problem is that of filling the box marked "?."

It will be seen that this problem and its generalizations are of wide application, not only in communication theory, but also in such diverse fields as economic prediction, weather forecasting, gunnery, statistics, and the like.

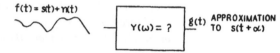

Fig. 1—The smoothing and prediction problem.

The Wiener-Kolmogoroff theory rests on three main assumptions which determine the range of application of the results. These assumptions are:

1. The time series represented by the signal $s(t)$ and the noise $n(t)$ are *stationary*. This means essentially that the statistical properties of the signal and of the noise do not change with time. The theory cannot properly be applied, for example, to *long-term* economic effects since the statistics of, say, the stock market were not the same in 1850 as they are today.

2. The criterion of error of approximation is taken to be the *mean-square discrepancy* between the actual output and the desired output. In Fig. 1 this means that we fill the box "?" in such a way as to minimize the mean square error $\overline{[g(t)-s(t+\alpha)]^2}$, the average being taken over all possible signal and noise functions with each weighted according to its probability of occurrence. This is called the *ensemble* average.

3. The operation to be used for prediction and smoothing is assumed to be a *linear* operation on the available information, or, in communication terms, the box is to be filled with a linear, physically realizable, filter. The available information consists of the past history of the perturbed signal, i.e., the function $f(t)$ with $t \leq t_1$, where t_1 is the present time. A linear, physically realizable filter performs a linear operation on $f(t)$ over just this range as we will see later in connection with equations (3) and (4).

The theory may therefore be described as *linear least square prediction and smoothing of stationary time series.* It should be clearly realized that the theory applies only when these three assumptions are satisfied, or at least are approximately satisfied. If any one of the conditions is changed or eliminated, the prediction and smoothing problem becomes very difficult mathematically, and little

* Decimal classification: 510. Original manuscript received by the Institute, July 13, 1949; revised manuscript received, January 17, 1950.
† Bell Telephone Laboratories, Inc., Murray Hill, N. J.

[1] N. Wiener, "The Interpolation, Extrapolation, and Smoothing of Stationary Time Series," National Defense Research Committee; reprinted as a book, together with two expository papers by N. Levinson, published by John Wiley and Sons, Inc., New York, N. Y., 1949.
[2] A. Kolmogoroff, "Interpolation und Extrapolation von Stationären Zufälligen Folgen," *Bull. Acad. Sci.* (URSS) Sér. Math. 5, pp. 3–14; 1941.

tle is known about usable explicit solutions. Some of the limitations imposed by these assumptions will be discussed later.

How is it possible to predict at all the future behavior of a function when all that is known is a perturbed version of its past history? This question is closely associated with the problems of causality and induction in philosophy and with the significance of physical laws. In general, physical prediction depends basically on an *assumption* that regularities which have been observed in the past will obtain in the future. This assumption can never be proved deductively, i.e., by purely mathematical argument, since we can easily conceive mathematical universes in which the assumption fails. Neither can it be established inductively, i.e., by a generalization from experiments, for this very generalization would assume the proposition we were attempting to establish. The assumption can be regarded only as a central postulate of physics.

Classical physics attempted to reduce the physical world to a set of strict causal laws. The future behavior of a physical system is then exactly predictable from a knowledge of its past history, and in fact all that is required is a knowledge of the present state of the system. Modern quantum physics has forced us to abandon this view as untenable. The laws of physics are now believed to be only statistical laws, and the only predictions are statistical predictions. The "exact" laws of classical physics are subject to uncertainties which are small when the objects involved are large, but are relatively large for objects on the atomic scale.

Linear least square smoothing and prediction theory is based on statistical prediction. The basic assumption that statistical regularities of the past will hold in the future appears in the mathematics as the assumption that the signal and noise are *stationary* time series. This implies, for example, that a statistical parameter of the signal averaged over the past will give the same value as this parameter averaged over the future.

The prediction depends essentially on the existence of correlations between the future value of the signal $s(t_1+\alpha)$ where t_1 is the present time, and the known data $f(t) = s(t) + n(t)$ for $t \leq t_1$. The assumption that the prediction is to be done by a *linear* operation implies that the only type of correlation that can be used is *linear* correlation, i.e., $\overline{s(t_1+\alpha) f(t)}$. If this correlation were zero for all $t \leq t_1$, no significant linear prediction would be possible, as will appear later. The best mean-square estimate of $s(t_1+\alpha)$ would then be zero.

III. PROPERTIES OF LINEAR FILTERS

In this section, a number of well-known results concerning filters will be summarized for easy reference. A linear filter can be characterized in two different but equivalent ways. The first and most common description is in terms of the complex transfer function $Y(\omega)$. If a pure sine wave of angular frequency ω_1 and amplitude E is used as input to the filter, the output is also a

pure sine wave of frequency ω_1 and amplitude $|Y(\omega_1)| E$. The phase of the output is advanced by the angle of $Y(\omega_1)$, the phase of the filter at this frequency. It is frequently convenient to write the complex transfer function $Y(\omega)$ in the form $Y(\omega) = e^{A(\omega)} e^{iB(\omega)}$ where $A(\omega) = \log |Y(\omega)|$ is the gain, and $B(\omega) = $ angle $[Y(\omega)]$ is the phase. Since we will assume that the filter can contain an ideal amplifier as well as passive elements, we can add any constant to A to make the absolute level of the gain as high as we please.

The second characterization of a filter is in terms of time functions. Let $K(t)$ be the inverse Fourier transform of $Y(\omega)$

$$K(t) = \frac{1}{2\pi} \int_{-\infty}^{\infty} Y(\omega) e^{i\omega t} d\omega. \tag{1}$$

Then $Y(\omega)$ is the direct Fourier transform of $K(t)$

$$Y(\omega) = \int_{-\infty}^{\infty} K(t) e^{-i\omega t} dt. \tag{2}$$

Knowledge of $K(t)$ is completely equivalent to knowledge of $Y(\omega)$; either of these may be calculated if the other is known.

The time function $K(t)$ is equal to the output obtained from the filter in response to a unit impulse impressed upon its input at time $t = 0$, as illustrated by Fig. 2. From this relation we can readily obtain the response

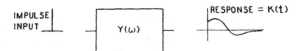

Fig. 2—Impulsive response of a network.

of the filter to any arbitrary input $f(t)$. It is merely necessary to divide the input wave into a large number of thin vertical slices, as shown by Fig. 3. Each slice can be regarded as an impulse of strength $f(t)dt$, which will pro-

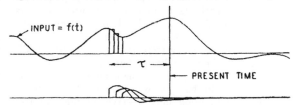

Fig. 3—Response to an arbitrary input as a sum of impulsive responses.

duce a response $f(t)dt\, K(t_1-t)$ at any subsequent time t_1. Upon adding together the contributions of all the slices we have the well-known formula

$$g(t_1) = \int_{-\infty}^{t_1} f(t) K(t_1 - t) dt \tag{3}$$

for the total response at t_1.

For the study of smoothing theory, (3) can conveniently be replaced by a slightly different expression. Setting $\tau = t_1 - t$, we have

$$g(t_1) = \int_0^\infty f(t_1 - \tau) K(\tau) d\tau. \qquad (4)$$

In this formulation, τ stands for the age of the data, so that $f(t_1 - \tau)$ represents the value of the input wave τ seconds ago. $K(\tau)$ is a function like the impulsive admittance, but projecting into the past rather than the future, as shown by Fig. 4. It is evidently a weighting function by which the voltage inputs in the past must be multiplied to determine their contributions to the present output.

Criteria for physical realizability can be given in terms of either the K function or Y. In terms of the impulsive response $K(t)$, it is necessary that $K(t)$ be zero for $t < 0$; that is, the network cannot respond to an impulse before the impulse arrives. Furthermore, $K(t)$ must approach zero (with reasonable rapidity) as $t \rightarrow + \infty$. Thus the effect of an impulse at the present time should eventually die out.

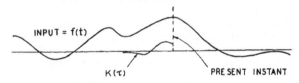

INPUT = f(t)

K(τ)   PRESENT INSTANT

Fig. 4—Response as a weighted average of the past input.

These requirements are also meaningful in terms of the interpretation of K as a weighting function. Thus, the filter cannot apply a weighting to parts of the input that have yet to occur; hence, $K(\tau) = 0$ for $\tau < 0$. Also the effect of the very remote past should gradually die out, so that $K(\tau)$ should approach zero as $\tau \rightarrow \infty$. It may also be noted that these conditions are also sufficient for physical realizability in the sense that any impulsive response $K(t)$ satisfying them can be approximated as closely as desired with a passive lumped element network, together with a single amplifier.

In terms of frequency response, the principal condition for physical realizability is that $Y(\omega)$, considered as a function of the complex variable ω, must be an analytic function in the half plane defined by $Im(\omega) < 0$. In addition, the function must behave on the real frequency axis[3] in such a way that

$$\int_0^\infty \frac{\log |Y(\omega)|}{1 + \omega^2} d\omega \qquad (5)$$

is a finite number.

[3] Including the point at infinity. Actual physical networks will, of course, always have zero gain at infinite frequency, and the above requirement shows that the approach to zero cannot be too rapid. An approach of the type ω^{-n} ($6n$ db per octave) is possible but $e^{-|\omega|}$ or $e^{-\omega^2}$ causes the integral in (5) to diverge and is physically unrealizable.

The requirements of physical realizability lead to the well-known loss-phase relations. For a given gain $A = \log |Y(\omega)|$ satisfying (5), there is a minimum possible phase characteristic. This phase is given by

$$B(\omega_0) = \frac{2\omega_0}{\pi} \int_0^\infty \frac{A(\omega) - A(\omega_0)}{\omega^2 - \omega_0^2} d\omega. \qquad (6)$$

If the square of the prescribed gain $|Y(\omega)|^2 = Y(\omega) \bar{Y}(\omega)$ is a rational function of ω, say, $P_1(\omega)/P_2(\omega)$ where $P_1(\omega)$ and $P_2(\omega)$ are polynomials, the minimum phase characteristic can be found as follows: Calculate the roots of $P_1(\omega)$ and $P_2(\omega)$ and write $|Y(\omega)|^2$ as

$$
|Y(\omega)|^2 \\
= k^2 \frac{(\omega - \alpha_1)(\omega - \bar{\alpha}_1)(\omega - \alpha_2)(\omega - \bar{\alpha}_2) \cdots}{(\omega - \beta_1)(\omega - \bar{\beta}_1)(\omega - \beta_2)(\omega - \bar{\beta}_2) \cdots}
$$
$$(7)$$

where $\alpha_1, \alpha_2 \cdots \beta_1, \beta_2 \cdots$ all have imaginary parts > 0. That is, these are the roots and poles of $|Y(\omega)|^2$ in the upper-half plane and the conjugate terms are the corresponding roots and poles in the lower-half plane. The minimum phase network then has the transfer function

$$Y(\omega) = k \frac{(\omega - \alpha_1)(\omega - \alpha_2) \cdots}{(\omega - \beta_1)(\omega - \beta_2) \cdots}. \qquad (8)$$

A minimum phase network has the important property that its inverse, with the transfer function $Y^{-1}(\omega)$, is also physically realizable.[4] If we pass a signal $f(t)$ through the filter $Y(\omega)$, we can recover it in its original form by passing it through the inverse filter. Moreover, the recovery takes place *without loss of time*. On the other hand, there is no physically realizable exact inverse for a nonminimum phase network. The best we can do is to provide a structure which has all the properties of the theoretical inverse, except for an extra phase lag. The extra phase lag can be equalized to give a constant delay by the addition of a suitable phase equalizer, but it cannot be eliminated. Thus, if we transmit a signal through a nonminimum network, we can recover it only after a delay; that is, we obtain $f(t - \alpha)$ for some positive α.

IV. General Expression for the Mean-Square Error

Suppose we use for the predicting-smoothing filter in Fig. 1 a filter with transfer characteristic $Y(\omega)$. What is the mean-square error in the prediction? Since different frequencies are incoherent, we can calculate the average power in the error function

$$e(t) = s(t + \alpha) - g(t) \qquad (9)$$

[4] If the original function has a zero at infinity, so that the required inverse has a pole there, there are complications, but an adequate approximation can be obtained in physical cases.

by adding the contributions due to different frequencies. Consider the components of the signal and noise of a particular frequency ω_1. It will be assumed that the signal and noise are incoherent at all frequencies. Then, at frequency ω_1 there will be a contribution to the error due to noise equal to $N(\omega_1)|Y(\omega_1)|^2$, where $N(\omega_1)$ is the average noise power at that frequency ω_1.

There is also a contribution to the error due to the failure of components of the signal, after passing through the filter, to be correct. A component of frequency ω_1 should be advanced in phase by $\alpha\omega_1$, and the amplitude of the output should be that of the input. Hence there will be a power error

$$|Y(\omega_1) - e^{i\alpha\omega_1}|^2 P(\omega_1) \qquad (10)$$

where $P(\omega_1)$ is the power in the signal at frequency ω_1.

The total mean-square error due to components of frequency ω_1 is the sum of these two errors, or

$$E_{\omega_1} = |Y(\omega_1)|^2 N(\omega_1) + |Y(\omega_1) - e^{i\alpha\omega_1}|^2 P(\omega_1), \qquad (11)$$

and the total mean-square error for all frequencies is

$$E = \int_{-\infty}^{\infty} [|Y(\omega)|^2 N(\omega) + |Y(\omega) - e^{i\alpha\omega}|^2 P(\omega)]d\omega. \qquad (12)$$

The problem is to minimize E by proper choice of $Y(\omega)$, remembering that $Y(\omega)$ must be physically realizable.

Several important conclusions can be drawn merely from an inspection of (12). The only way in which the signal and noise enter this equation is through their power spectra. Hence, the only statistics of the signal and noise that are needed to solve the problem are these spectra. Two different types of signal with the same spectrum will lead to the same optimal prediction filter and to the same mean-square error. For example, if the signal is speech it will be predicted by the same filter as would be used for prediction of a thermal noise which has been passed through a filter to give it the same power spectrum as speech.

Speaking somewhat loosely, this means that a linear filter can make use only of statistical data pertaining to the *amplitudes* of the different frequency components; the statistics of the relative phase angles of these components cannot be used. Only by going to nonlinear prediction can such statistical effects be used to improve the prediction.

It is also clear that in the linear least square problem we can, if we choose, replace the signal and noise by any desired time series which have the same power spectra. This will not change the optimal filter or the mean square error in any way.

V. THE PURE SMOOTHING PROBLEM

The chief difficulty in minimizing (12) for the mean-square error lies in properly introducing the condition

that $Y(\omega)$ must be a physically realizable transfer function. We will first solve the problem with this constraint waived and then from this solution construct the best physically realizable filter.

Waiving the condition of physical realizability is equivalent to admitting any $Y(\omega)$, or, equivalently, any impulsive response $K(t)$. Thus, $K(t)$ is not necessarily zero for $t < 0$, and we are allowing a weighting function to be applied to both the past and future of $f(t)$. In other words, we assume that the entire function $f(t) = s(t) + n(t)$ from $t = -\infty$ to $t = +\infty$ is available for use in prediction.

In (12), suppose

$$Y(\omega) = C(\omega)e^{iB(\omega)} \qquad (13)$$

with $C(\omega)$ and $B(\omega)$ real. Then (12) becomes

$$E = \int_{-\infty}^{\infty} [C^2 N + P(C^2 + 1 - 2C\cos(\alpha\omega - B))]d\omega \qquad (14)$$

where $C(\omega)$, $N(\omega)$, and the like are written as C, N, and so forth, for short. Clearly, the best choice of $B(\omega)$ is $B(\omega) = \alpha\omega$ since this maximizes $\cos(\alpha\omega - B(\omega))$. Then (14) becomes

$$E = \int_{-\infty}^{\infty} [C^2(P + N) - 2PC + P]d\omega. \qquad (15)$$

Completing the square in C by adding and subtracting $P^2/(P+N)$ we obtain

$$E = \int_{-\infty}^{\infty} \left[C^2(P + N) - 2PC + \frac{P^2}{P + N} - \frac{P^2}{P + N} + P \right] d\omega \qquad (16)$$

or

$$E = \int_{-\infty}^{\infty} \left(\left[\sqrt{P+N}\, C - \frac{P}{\sqrt{P+N}} \right]^2 + \frac{PN}{P+N} \right) d\omega. \qquad (17)$$

The bracketed term is the square of a real number, and therefore positive or zero. Clearly, to minimize E we choose C to make this term everywhere zero, thus

$$C(\omega) = \frac{P(\omega)}{P(\omega) + N(\omega)}$$

and

$$Y(\omega) = \frac{P(\omega)}{P(\omega) + N(\omega)} e^{i\alpha\omega}. \qquad (18)$$

With this choice of $Y(\omega)$ the mean square error will be, from (17),

$$E = \int_{-\infty}^{\infty} \frac{P(\omega)N(\omega)}{P(\omega) + N(\omega)} \, d\omega. \qquad (19)$$

The best weighting function is given by the inverse Fourier transform of (18)

$$K(t) = \frac{1}{2\pi} \int_{-\infty}^{\infty} \frac{P(\omega)}{P(\omega) + N(\omega)} e^{i\omega(t+\alpha)} d\omega. \qquad (20)$$

This $K(t)$ will, in general, extend from $t = -\infty$ to $t = +\infty$. It does not represent the impulsive response of a physical filter. However, it is a perfectly good weighting function. If we could wait until all the function $s(t) + n(t)$ is available, it would be the proper one to apply in estimating $s(t+\alpha)$.

To put the question in another way, the weighting $K(\tau)$ can be obtained in a physical filter if sufficient delay is allowed so that $K(\tau)$ is substantially zero for the future. Thus we have solved here the "infinite lag" smoothing problem. Although $Y(\omega)$ in (18) is nonphysical, $Y(\omega)e^{-i\beta\omega}$ will be physical, or nearly so, if β is taken sufficiently large.

VI. The Pure Prediction Problem

We will now consider another special case, that in which there is no perturbing noise. The problem is then one of pure prediction. What is the best estimate of $s(t+\alpha)$ when we know $s(t)$ from $t = -\infty$ up to $t = 0$?

We have seen that the solution will depend only on the power spectra of the signal and noise, and since we are now assuming the noise to be identically zero, the solution depends only on the power spectrum $P(\omega)$ of the signal. This being the case, we may replace the actual signal by any other having the same spectrum. The solution of the best predicting filter will be the same for the altered problem as for the original problem.

Any desired spectrum $P(\omega)$ can be obtained by passing wide-band resistance noise or "white" noise through a shaping filter whose gain characteristic is $\sqrt{P(\omega)}$. The spectrum of resistance noise is flat (at least out to frequencies higher than any of importance in communication work), and the filter merely multiplies this constant spectrum by the square of the filter gain $P(\omega)$. The phase characteristic of the filter can be chosen in any way consistent with the conditions of physical realizability. Let us choose the phase characteristic so that the filter is minimum phase for the gain $\sqrt{P(\omega)}$. Then the filter has a phase characteristic given by

$$B(\omega_0) = \frac{-\omega_0}{\pi} \int_0^\infty \frac{\log P(\omega) - \log P(\omega_0)}{\omega^2 - \omega_0^2} \, d\omega. \qquad (21)$$

Furthermore, this minimum phase network has a physically realizable inverse.

We have now reduced the problem to the form shown

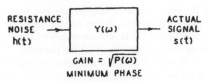

Fig. 5—Construction of actual signal spectrum from resistance noise.

in Fig. 5. What is actually available is the function $s(t)$ up to $t = 0$. However, this is equivalent to a knowledge of the resistance noise $h(t)$ up to $t = 0$, since the filter Y has a physically realizable inverse and we can pass the available function $s(t)$ through the inverse Y^{-1} to obtain $h(t)$.

The problem, therefore, is equivalent to asking what is the best operation to apply to $h(t)$ in order to approximate $s(t+\alpha)$ in the least square sense? The question is easily answered. A resistance noise can be thought of as made up of a large number of closely spaced and very short impulses, as indicated in Fig. 6. The impulses have a Gaussian distribution of amplitudes and are statistically independent of each other. Each of these impulses entering the filter Y produces an output corresponding to the impulsive response of the filter, as shown at the right of Fig. 6, and the signal $s(t)$ is the sum of these elementary responses.

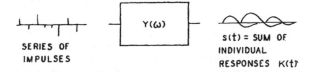

Fig. 6—Result of resistance noise input.

What is known is $h(t)$ up to the present; that is, we know effectively the impulses up to $t = 0$ and nothing about those after $t = 0$; these have not yet occurred. The future signal $s(t+\alpha)$ is thus made up of two parts; the tails of responses due to impulses that have already occurred, and a part due to impulses which will occur between the present time and time $t = \alpha$. The first part is completely predictable, while the second part is entirely unpredictable, being statistically independent of our available information at the present time.

The total result of the first part can be obtained by constructing a filter whose impulsive response is the tail of the impulsive response of filter Y moved ahead α seconds. This is shown in Fig. 7 where $K_1(t)$ is the new impulsive response and $K(t)$ the old one. The new filter responds to an impulse entering *now* as the filter Y will respond in α seconds. It responds to an impulse that entered one second ago as Y will respond in α seconds to one that entered it one second ago. In short, if $h(t)$ is used as input to this new filter Y_1, the output now will be the predictable part of the future response of Y to the same input α seconds from now.

The second, or unpredictable part of the future response, corresponding to impulses yet to occur, cannot,

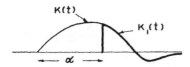

Fig. 7—Construction of the physical response
$K_1(t)$ from $K(t)$.

of course, be constructed. We know, however, that the mean value of this part must be zero, since future impulses are as likely to be of one sign as the other. Thus the arithmetic average, or center of gravity, of the possible future responses is the predictable part given by the output of Y_1. But it is well known that the arithmetic mean of any distribution is the point about which the mean-square error is the least. The output of Y_1 is thus the desired prediction of $s(t+\alpha)$.

In constructing Y_1 we assumed that we had available the white noise $h(t)$. Actually, however, our given data is the signal $s(t)$. Consequently, the best operation on the given data is $Y_1(\omega)\ Y^{-1}(\omega)$, the factor $Y^{-1}(\omega)$ reducing the function $s(t)$ to the white noise $h(t)$, and the second operation $Y_1(\omega)$ performing the best prediction based on $h(t)$.

The solution may be summarized as follows:

1. Determine the minimum phase network having the gain characteristic $\sqrt{P(\omega)}$. Let the complex transfer characteristic of this filter be $Y(\omega)$, and its impulsive response $K(t)$.

2. Construct a filter whose impulsive response is

$$K_1(t) = K(t + \alpha) \quad \text{for} \quad t \geq 0$$
$$= 0 \qquad\qquad \text{for} \quad\;\; < 0. \tag{22}$$

Let the transfer characteristic of this network be $Y_1(\omega)$.

3. The optimal least square predicting filter then has a characteristic

$$Y_1(\omega)Y^{-1}(\omega). \tag{23}$$

The mean square error E in the prediction is easily calculated. The error is due to impulses occurring from time $t=0$ to $t=\alpha$. Since these impulses are uncorrelated, the mean-square sum of the errors is the sum of the individual mean-square errors. The individual pulses are effective in causing mean-square error in proportion to the square of $K(\alpha-t)$. Hence, the total mean-square error will be given by

$$E^2 = \rho \int_0^\alpha K^2(\alpha - t)dt$$
$$\tag{24}$$
$$= \rho \int_0^\alpha K^2(t)dt$$

where $\rho = \int p(\omega)d\omega$ is the mean-square signal. By a similar argument the mean-square value of $s(t+\alpha)$ will be

$$U^2 = \rho \int_0^\infty K^2(t)dt, \tag{25}$$

and the relative error of the prediction may be measured by the ratio of the root-mean-square error to the root-mean-square value of $s(t+\alpha)$, i.e.,

$$\frac{E}{U} = \left[\frac{\int_0^\alpha K^2(t)dt}{\int_0^\infty K^2(t)dt}\right]^{1/2}. \tag{26}$$

The prediction will be relatively poor if the area under the curve $K(t)^2$ out to α is large compared to the total area, good if it is small compared to the total. It is evident from (26) that the relative error starts at zero for $\alpha=0$ and is a monotonic increasing function of α which approaches unity as $\alpha \to \infty$.

There is an important special case in which a great deal more can be shown by the argument just given. In our analysis, the actual problem was replaced by one in which the signal was a Gaussian type of time series, derived from a resistance noise by passing it through a filter with a gain $\sqrt{P(\omega)}$. Suppose the signal is already a time series of this type. Then the error in prediction, due to the tails of impulses occurring between $t=0$ and $t=\alpha$, will have a Gaussian distribution. This follows from the fact that each impulse has a Gaussian distribution of amplitudes and the sum of any number of effects, each Gaussian, will also be Gaussian. The standard deviation of this distribution of errors is just the root-mean-square error E obtained from (24).

Stated another way, on the basis of the available data, that is, $s(t)$ for $t<0$, the future value of the signal $s(t+\alpha)$ is distributed according to a Gaussian distribution. The best linear predictor selects the center of this distribution for the predicted value. The actual future value will differ from this as indicated in Fig. 8, where the future value is plotted horizontally, and the probability density for various values of $s(t+\alpha)$ is plotted vertically.

It is clear that in this special case the linear prediction method is in a sense the best possible. The center of the Gaussian distribution remains the natural point to choose if we replace the least square criterion of the

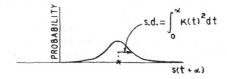

Fig. 8—Distribution of prediction errors in the
Gaussian case.

best prediction by almost any other reasonable criterion, such as the median value or the most probable value. Thus in this case a nonlinear computation would offer nothing which the linear process does not already provide. In the general case, on the other hand, the distribution of future values will not be Gaussian, and the shape of the distribution curve may vary from point to point depending upon the particular past history of the curve. Under these circumstances, a nonlinear scheme may offer improvements upon the linear process and the exact characteristics of the optimal procedure will depend critically upon the criterion adopted for the best prediction.

VII. Prediction in the Presence of Noise

Now consider the general prediction and smoothing problem with noise present. The best estimate of $s(t+\alpha)$ is required when the function $s(t)+n(t)$ is known from $t=-\infty$ to the present. If $s(t)+n(t)$ is passed through a filter whose gain is $[P(\omega)+N(\omega)]^{-1/2}$, the result will be a flat spectrum which we can identify with white noise. Let $Y_1(\omega)$ be the transfer function of a filter having this gain characteristic and the associated minimum phase. Then both $Y_1(\omega)$ and the inverse $Y_1^{-1}(\omega)$ are physically realizable networks. Evidently, knowledge of the input of Y_1 and knowledge of its output are equivalent. The best linear operation on the output will give the same prediction as the corresponding best linear operation on the input.

If we knew the entire function $s(t)+n(t)$ from $t=-\infty$ to $t=+\infty$ the best operation to apply to the input of $Y_1(\omega)$ would be that specified by (18). If we let $B(\omega)$ be the phase component of Y_1, this corresponds to the equivalent operation

$$Y_2(\omega) = \frac{P(\omega)}{[P(\omega) + N(\omega)]^{1/2}} e^{i[\alpha\omega - B(\omega)]} \quad (27)$$

on the "white noise" output of Y_1.

Let the impulse response obtained from (27) be $K_2(t)$. As illustrated by Fig. 9, $K_2(t)$ will, in general, contain tails extending to both $t=+\infty$ and $t=-\infty$, the junction between the two halves of the curve being displaced from the origin by the prediction time α. The associated $K_2(\tau)$ of Fig. 10 is, of course, the ideal weighting function to be applied to the "white noise" output of Y_1. But the only data actually available at $\tau=0$ are the impulses which may be thought of as occurring during the past history of this output. What weights should be given these data to obtain the best prediction? It seems natural to weight these as one would if all data were available, and to weight the future values zero (as we must to keep the filter physical). The fact that this is actually correct weighting when the various input impulses are statistically independent will

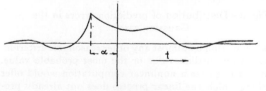

Fig. 9—Possible function $K_2(t)$.

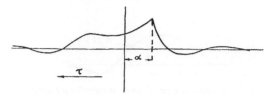

Fig. 10—Weighting function $K_2(\tau)$, corresponding to Fig. 9.

now be shown as a consequence of a general statistical principle.

Suppose we have a number of chance variables, $x_1, x_2, \cdots, x_n$ which are statistically independent, or at least have the property that the mean product of any two, $\overline{x_m x_n}$, is equal to zero. These variables are to be interpreted as the amplitudes of the individual white noise impulses to which we are attempting to apply the weighting function of Fig. 10.

Let y be another chance variable, correlated with $x_1, \cdots, x_n$, which we wish to estimate in the least square sense by performing a linear operation on $x_1 \cdots x_n$. In the problem at hand y is the actual signal $s(t)$ at the time α seconds from now.

The predicted value will be

$$y_1 = \sum_{i=1}^{n} a_i x_i$$

and the mean-square error is

$$
\begin{aligned}
E &= \overline{(y - y_1)^2} = \overline{\left(y - \sum a_i x_i\right)^2} \\
&= \overline{y^2} - 2 \sum_{i=1}^{n} a_i \overline{x_i y} + \sum_{i,j=1}^{n} a_i a_j \overline{x_i x_j} \\
&= \overline{y^2} - 2 \sum a_i \overline{x_i y} + \sum_{i=1}^{n} a_i^2 \overline{x_i^2}, \quad (28)
\end{aligned}
$$

since all terms in the double sum vanish except those for which $i=j$. We seek to minimize E by proper choice of the a_i. Setting the partial derivatives with respect to a_i equal to zero, we have

$$\frac{\partial E}{\partial a_i} = -2\overline{x_i y} + 2a_i \overline{x_i^2} = 0$$

or

$$a_i = \frac{\overline{x_i y}}{\overline{x_i^2}}. \quad (29)$$

The important fact about this calculation is that each of the n minimizing equations involves only the a_i in question; $\partial E/\partial a_1$ involves only a_1, etc. In other words, minimizing E on all the a_i is equivalent to minimizing separately on the individual a_i; a_1 should have the value $\overline{x_1 y}/\overline{x_1^2}$ whatever values are assigned to the other a's.

Returning now to the prediction and smoothing problem, the function $K_2(\tau)$ gives the proper weighting to be attached to the impulses if we could use them all. Requirements of physical realizability demand that future impulses corresponding to $\tau < 0$ be given weight zero. From the above statistical principle those occurring in the past should still be given the weighting $K_2(\tau)$. In other words, the proper filter to apply to the input white noise has an impulse response zero for $t < 0$ and $K_2(t)$ for $t > 0$.

To summarize, the solution consists of the following steps:

1. Calculate the minimum phase transfer function for the gain $(P+N)^{-1/2}$. Let this be $Y_1(\omega)$.

2. Let

$$Y_2(\omega) = Y_1^{-1}(\omega) \frac{P}{P + N}.$$

This is a nonphysical transfer function. Let its Fourier transform be $K_2(t)$.

3. Set $K_3(t) = K_2(t+\alpha)$ for $t \geqq 0$ and $K_3(t) = 0$ for $t < 0$. That is, cut off the first α seconds of $K_2(t)$ and shift the remaining tail over to $t = 0$. This is the impulse response of a physical network, and is the optimal operation on the past history of the white noise input. Let the corresponding transfer function be $Y_3(\omega)$.

4. Construct $Y_4(\omega) = Y_3(\omega) Y_1(\omega)$. This is the optimal smoothing and prediction filter, as applied to the actual given $s(t) + n(t)$.

As in the pure prediction problem, if the signal and noise happen to be Gaussian time series, the linear prediction is an absolute optimum among all prediction operations, linear or not. Furthermore, the distribution of values of $s(t+\alpha)$, when $f(t)$ is known for $t < 0$, is a Gaussian distribution.

VIII. Generalizations

This theory is capable of generalization in several directions. These generalizations will be mentioned only briefly, but can all be obtained by methods similar to those used above.

In the first place, we assumed the true signal and the noise to be uncorrelated. A relatively simple extension of the argument used in Section IV allows one to account for correlation between these time series.

A second generalization is to the case where there are several correlated time series, say $f_1(t), f_2(t), \cdots, f_n(t)$. It is desired to predict, say, $s_1(t+\alpha)$ from a knowledge of $f_1, f_2, \cdots, f_n$.

Finally the desired quantity may not be $s(t+\alpha)$ but, for example, $s'(t+\alpha)$, the future derivative of the true signal. In such a case, one may effectively reduce the problem to that already solved by taking derivatives throughout. The function $f(t)$ is passed through a differentiator to produce $g(t) = f'(t)$. The best linear prediction for $g(t)$ is then determined.

IX. Discussion of the Basic Assumptions

A result in applied mathematics is only as reliable as the assumptions from which it is derived. The theory developed above is especially subject to misapplication because of the difficulty in deciding, in any particular instance, whether the basic assumptions are a reasonable description of the physical situation. Anyone using the theory should carefully consider each of the three main assumptions with regard to the particular smoothing or prediction problem involved.

The assumption that the signal and noise are stationary is perhaps the most innocuous of the three, for it is usually evident from the general nature of the problem when this assumption is violated. The determination of the required power spectra $P(\omega)$ and $N(\omega)$ will often disclose any time variation of the statistical structure of the time series. If the variation is slow compared to the other time constants involved, such nonstationary problems may still be solvable on a quasi-stationary basis. A linear predictor may be designed whose transfer function varies slowly in such a way as to be optimal for the "local" statistics.

The least square assumption is more troublesome, for it involves questions of values rather than questions of fact. When we minimize the mean-square error we are, in effect, paying principal attention to the very large errors. The prediction chosen is one which, on the whole, makes these errors as small as possible, without much regard to relatively minor errors. In many circumstances, however, it is more important to make as many very accurate predictions as possible, even if we make occasional gross errors as a consequence. When the distribution of future events is Gaussian, it does not matter which criterion is used since the most probable event is also the one with respect to which the mean-square error is the least. With lopsided or multimodal distributions, however, a real question is involved.

As a simple example, consider the problem of predicting whether tomorrow will be a clear day. Since clear days are in the majority, and there are no days with negative precipitation to balance days when it rains, we are concerned here with a very lopsided distribution. With such a curve, the average point, which is the one given by a prediction minimizing the mean-square error, might be represented by a day with a light drizzle. To a man planning a picnic, however, such a prediction would have no value. He is interested in the probability that the weather will really be clear. If the picnic must be called off because it in fact rains, the actual amount of precipitation is of comparatively little consequence.

As a second example, consider the problem of intercepting a bandit car attempting to flee down a network of roads. If the road on which the bandit car happens to be forks just ahead, it is clear that a would-be interceptor should station himself on one fork or the other, making the choice at random if necessary. The mean-square error in the interception would be least, however, if he placed himself in the fields beyond the fork.

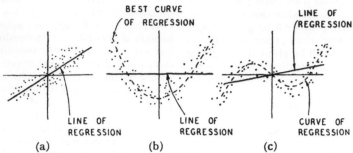

Fig. 11—Some scatter diagrams with lines and curves of regression.

Problems similar to these may also arise in gunnery, where, in general, we are usually interested in the number of actual hits and "a miss is as good as a mile."

The third assumption, that of linearity, is neither a question of fact, nor of evaluation, but a self-imposed limitation on the types of operations or devices to be used in prediction. The mathematical reason for this assumption is clear; linear problems are always much simpler than their nonlinear generalizations. In certain applications the linear assumption may be justified for one or another of the following reasons:

1. The linear predictor may be an absolute optimal method, as in the Gaussian time series mentioned above.

2. Linear prediction may be dictated by the simplicity of mechanization. Linear filters are easy to synthesize and there is an extensive relevant theory, with no corresponding theory for nonlinear systems.

3. One may use the linear theory merely because of the lack of any better approach. An incomplete solution is better than none at all.

How much is lost by restricting ourselves to linear prediction? The fact that nonlinear effects may be important in a prediction can be illustrated by returning to the problem of forecasting tomorrow's weather. We are all familiar with the fact that the pattern of events over a period of time may be more important than the happenings taken individually in determining what will come. For example, the sequence of events in the passage of a cold or warm front is characteristic. Moreover, the significance of a given happening may depend largely upon the intensity with which it occurs. Thus, a sharp dip in the barometer may mean that moderately unpleasant weather is coming. Twice as great a drop in the same time, on the other hand, may not indicate that the weather will be merely twice as unpleasant; it may indicate a hurricane.

As a final point, we may notice that the requirement that the prediction be obtained from a linear device and the objective of minimizing the mean-square error are not, in all problems, quite compatible with one another. The absolute best mean-square prediction (ignoring the assumption of linearity) would, of course, always pick the mean of the future distribution, i.e., the "center of gravity," since in any case this minimizes the mean-square error. In general, however, the position of this center of gravity will be a nonlinear function of the past history. When we require that the prediction be a *linear* operation on the past history, the mathematics is forced to compromise among the conflicting demands of various possible past histories. The compromise amounts essentially to averaging over-all relative phases of the various components of the signal; any pertinent information contained in the relative phases cannot be used properly.

This can be illustrated by the familiar statistical problem of calculating a line or plane of regression to provide a linear least square estimation of one variable y from the knowledge of a set of variables correlated with y.[5] The simplest such problem occurs when there is just one known variable x, and one unknown variable y to be estimated from x. Fig. 11 shows three of the "scatter diagrams" used in statistics. The variable x may be, for example, a man's weight and y his height. A large population is sampled and plotted. It is then desired to estimate, or predict, a man's height, knowing only his weight. If we agree to use only linear operations y must be calculated in the form $y = ax$. The best choice of a for least square prediction is $\overline{xy}/\overline{x^2}$ and the corresponding straight line is known as the line of regression. The case of a normal distribution corresponds to the Gaussian type noise in which the linear prediction is an absolute optimum.

Figs. 11(b) and 11(c) are scatter diagrams for other distributions of two variables. The lines of regression are now not nearly as good in predicting y as they were in Fig. 11(a). The requirement that the predicted value be a *linear* function of the known data requires a compromise which may be very serious. It is obvious in Figs. 11(b) and 11(c) that a much better estimate of y could be formed if we allowed nonlinear operations on x. In particular, functions of the form $ax^2 + b$ and $cx^3 + dx$ would be more suitable.

In predicting y from two known variables x_1 and x_2 we can construct a scatter diagram in three dimensions. The linear prediction requires fitting the points with a plane of regression. If there are n known quantities $x_1, x_2, \cdots, x_n$ we need $(n+1)$ dimensional space and the linear theory corresponds to a hyperplane of n dimensions.

The problem of smoothing and prediction for time series is analogous. What we are now dealing with, however, is the function space defined by all the values of $f(t)$ for $t < 0$. The optimal linear predictor corresponds to a hyperplane in this function space.

[5] P. G. Hoel, "Introduction to Mathematical Statistics," John Wiley and Sons, Inc., New York, N. Y.; 1947.

Programming a Computer for Playing Chess*.

By Claude E. Shannon,
Bell Telephone Laboratories, Inc., Murray Hill, N.J.

1. Introduction.

This paper is concerned with the problem of constructing a computing routine or " program " for a modern general purpose computer which will enable it to play chess. Although perhaps of no practical importance, the question is of theoretical interest, and it is hoped that a satisfactory solution of this problem will act as a wedge in attacking other problems of a similar nature and of greater significance. Some possibilities in this direction are :—

(1) Machines for designing filters, equalizers, etc.

(2) Machines for designing relay and switching circuits.

(3) Machines which will handle routing of telephone calls based on the individual circumstances rather than by fixed patterns.

(4) Machines for performing symbolic (non-numerical) mathematical operations.

(5) Machines capable of translating from one language to another.

(6) Machines for making strategic decisions in simplified military operations.

(7) Machines capable of orchestrating a melody.

(8) Machines capable of logical deduction.

It is believed that all of these and many other devices of a similar nature are possible developments in the immediate future. The techniques developed for modern electronic and relay type computers make them not only theoretical possibilities, but in several cases worthy of serious consideration from the economic point of view.

Machines of this general type are an extension over the ordinary use of numerical computers in several ways. First, the entities dealt with are not primarily numbers, but rather chess positions, circuits, mathematical expressions, words, etc. Second, the proper procedure involves general principles, something of the nature of judgment, and considerable trial and error, rather than a strict, unalterable computing process. Finally, the solutions of these problems are not merely right or wrong but have a continuous range of " quality " from the best down to the worst. We might be satisfied with a machine that designed good filters even though they were not always the best possible.

* First presented at the National IRE Convention, March 9, 1949, New York, U.S.A.

The chess machine is an ideal one to start with, since : (1) the problem is sharply defined both in allowed operations (the moves) and in the ultimate goal (checkmate) ; (2) it is neither so simple as to be trivial nor too difficult for satisfactory solution ; (3) chess is generally considered to require " thinking " for skilful play ; a solution of this problem will force us either to admit the possibility of mechanized thinking or to further restrict our concept of " thinking " ; (4) the discrete structure of chess fits well into the digital nature of modern computers.

There is already a considerable literature on the subject of chess-playing machines. During the late 18th and early 19th centuries, the Maelzel Chess Automaton, a device invented by von Kempelen, was exhibited widely as a chess-playing machine. A number of papers appeared at the time, including an analytical essay by Edgar Allan Poe (entitled Maelzel's Chess Player) purporting to explain its operation. Most of these writers concluded, quite correctly, that the Automaton was operated by a concealed human chess-master ; the arguments leading to this conclusion, however, were frequently fallacious. Poe assumes, for example, that it is as easy to design a machine which will invariably win as one which wins occasionally, and argues that since the Automaton was not invincible it was therefore operated by a human, a clear *non sequitur*. For a complete account of the history and method of operation of the Automaton, the reader is referred to a series of articles by Harkness and Battell in *Chess Review*, 1947.

A more honest attempt to design a chess-playing machine was made in 1914 by Torrès y Quévedo, who constructed a device which played an end game of king and rook against king (Vigneron, 1914). The machine played the side with king and rook and would force checkmate in a few moves however its human opponent played. Since an explicit set of rules can be given for making satisfactory moves in such an end game, the problem is relatively simple, but the idea was quite advanced for that period.

The thesis we will develop is that modern general purpose computers can be used to play a tolerably good game of chess by the use of a suitable computing routine or " program ". While the approach given here is believed fundamentally sound, it will be evident that much further experimental and theoretical work remains to be done.

2. General Considerations.

A chess " position " may be defined to include the following data :—

(1) A statement of the positions of all pieces on the board.

(2) A statement of which side, White or Black, has the move.

(3) A statement as to whether the kings and rooks have moved. This is important since by moving a rook, for example, the right to castle on that side is forfeited.

(4) A statement of, say, the last move. This will determine whether a possible *en passant* capture is legal, since this privilege is forfeited after one move.

(5) A statement of the number of moves made since the last pawn move or capture. This is important because of the 50 move drawing rule. For simplicity, we will ignore the rule of draw after three repetitions of a position.

In chess there is no chance element apart from the original choice of which player has the first move. This is in contrast with card games, backgammon, etc. Furthermore, in chess each of the two opponents has " perfect information " at each move as to all previous moves (in contrast with Kriegspiel, for example). These two facts imply (von Neumann and Morgenstern, 1944) that any given position of the chess pieces must be either :—

(1) A won position for White. That is, White can force a win, however Black defends.

(2) A draw position. White can force at least a draw, however Black plays, and likewise Black can force at least a draw, however White plays. If both sides play correctly the game will end in a draw.

(3) A won position for Black. Black can force a win, however White plays.

This is, for practical purposes, of the nature of an existence theorem. No practical method is known for determining to which of the three categories a general position belongs. If there were chess would lose most of its interest as a game. One could determine whether the initial position is won, drawn, or lost for White and the outcome of a game between opponents knowing the method would be fully determined at the choice of the first move. Supposing the initial position a draw (as suggested by empirical evidence from master games*) every game would end in a draw.

It is interesting that a slight change in the rules of chess gives a game for which it is provable that White has at least a draw in the initial position. Suppose the rules the same as those of chess except that a player is not forced to move a piece at his turn to play, but may, if he chooses, " pass ". Then we can prove as a theorem that White can at least draw by proper play. For in the initial position either he has a winning move or not. If so, let him make this move. If not, let him pass. Black is now faced with essentially the same position that White had before, because of the mirror symmetry of the initial position †. Since White had no winning move before, Black has none now. Hence, Black at best can draw. Therefore, in either case White can at least draw.

---

* The world championship match between Capablanca and Alekhine ended with the score Alekhine 6, Capablanca 3, drawn 25.

† The fact that the number of moves remaining before a draw is called by the 50-move rule has decreased does not affect this argument.

In some games there is a simple *evaluation function* $f(P)$ which can be applied to a position P and whose value determines to which category (won, lost, etc.) the position P belongs. In the game of Nim (Hardy and Wright, 1938), for example, this can be determined by writing the number of matches in each pile in binary notation. These numbers are arranged in a column (as though to add them). If the number of ones in each column is even, the position is lost for the player about to move, otherwise won.

If such an evaluation function $f(P)$ can be found for a game it is easy to design a machine capable of perfect play. It would never lose or draw a won position and never lose a drawn position and if the opponent ever made a mistake the machine would capitalize on it. This could be done as follows : Suppose

$$f(P)=1 \text{ for a won position,}$$
$$f(P)=0 \text{ for a drawn position,}$$
$$f(P)=-1 \text{ for a lost position.}$$

At the machine's turn to move it calculates $f(P)$ for the various positions obtained from the present position by each possible move that can be made. It chooses that move (or one of the set) giving the maximum value to f. In the case of Nim where such a function $f(P)$ is known, a machine has actually been constructed which plays a perfect game *.

With chess it is possible, *in principle*, to play a perfect game or construct a machine to do so as follows : One considers in a given position all possible moves, then all moves for the opponent, etc., to the end of the game (in each variation). The end must occur, by the rules of the game, after a finite number of moves† (remembering the 50 move drawing rule). Each of these variations ends in win, loss or draw. By working backward from the end one can determine whether there is a forced win, the position is a draw or is lost. It is easy to show, however, that even with the high computing speeds available in electronic calculators this computation is impractical. In typical chess positions there will be of the order of 30 legal moves. The number holds fairly constant until the game is nearly finished as shown in Fig. 1. This graph was constructed from data given by De Groot, who averaged the number of legal moves in a large number of master games (De Groot, 1946, *a*). Thus a move for White and then one for Black gives about 10^3 possibilities. A typical game lasts about 40 moves to resignation of one party. This is conservative for our calculation since the machine should calculate out to checkmate, not resignation. However, even at this figure there will be

---

* Condon, Tawney and Derr, U.S. Patent 2,215,544. The "Nimotron" based on this patent was built and exhibited by Westinghouse at the 1938 New York World's Fair.

† The longest possible chess game is 6350 moves, allowing 50 moves between each pawn move or capture. The longest tournament game on record between masters lasted 168 moves, and the shortest four moves. (Chernev, *Curious Chess Facts*, The Black Knight Press, 1937.)

10^{120} variations to be calculated from the initial position. A machine operating at the rate of one variation per micro-microsecond would require over 10^{90} years to calculate its first move !

Another (equally impractical) method is to have a " dictionary " of all possible positions of the chess pieces. For each possible position there is an entry giving the correct move (either calculated by the above process or supplied by a chess master). At the machine's turn to move it merely looks up the position and makes the indicated move. The number of possible positions, of the general order of $64 \,! \mid 32 \,! \, 8 \,!^2 \, 2 \,!^6$, or roughly 10^{43}, naturally makes such a design unfeasible.

It is clear then that the problem is not that of designing a machine to play perfect chess (which is quite impractical) nor one which merely plays legal chess (which is trivial). We would like it to play a skilful game, perhaps comparable to that of a good human player.

A *strategy* for chess may be described as a process for choosing a move in any given position. If the process always chooses the same move in

Fig. 1.

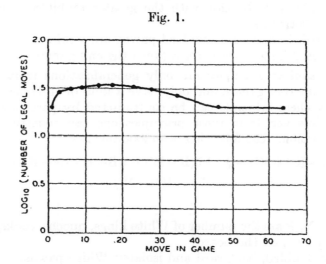

the same position the strategy is known in the theory of games as a " pure " strategy. If the process involves statistical elements and does not always result in the same choice it is a " mixed " strategy. The following are simple examples of strategies :—

(1) Number the possible legal moves in the position P, according to some standard procedure. Choose the first on the list. This is a pure strategy.

(2) Number the legal moves and choose one at random from the list. This is a mixed strategy.

Both of these, of course, are extremely poor strategies, making no attempt to select good moves. Our problem is to develop a tolerably good strategy for selecting the move to be made.

3. Approximate Evaluating Functions.

Although in chess there is no known simple and exact evaluating function $f(P)$, and probably never will be because of the arbitrary and complicated nature of the rules of the game, it is still possible to perform an approximate evaluation of a position. Any good chess player must, in fact, be able to perform such a position evaluation. Evaluations are based on the general structure of the position, the number and kind of Black and White pieces, pawn formation, mobility, etc. These evaluations are not perfect, but the stronger the player the better his evaluations. Most of the maxims and principles of correct play are really assertions about evaluating positions, for example :—

(1) The relative values of queen, rook, bishop, knight and pawn are about 9, 5, 3, 3, 1, respectively. Thus other things being equal (!) if we add the numbers of pieces for the two sides with these coefficients, the side with the largest total has the better position.

(2) Rooks should be placed on open files. This is part of a more general principle that the side with the greater mobility, other things equal, has the better game.

(3) Backward, isolated and doubled pawns are weak.

(4) An exposed king is a weakness (until the end game).

These and similar principles are only generalizations from empirical evidence of numerous games, and only have a kind of statistical validity. Probably any chess principle can be contradicted by particular counter examples. However, from these principles one can construct a crude evaluation function. The following is an example :—

$$f(P) = 200(K-K') + 9(Q-Q') + 5(R-R') + 3(B-B'+N-N') + (P-P')$$
$$-\cdot5(D-D'+S-S'+I-I') + \cdot1(M-M') + \ldots$$

in which :—

K, Q, R, B, N, P are the number of White kings, queens, rooks, bishops, knights and pawns on the board.

D, S, I are doubled, backward and isolated White pawns.

M=White mobility (measured, say, as the number of legal moves available to White).

Primed letters are the similar quantities for Black.

The coefficients $\cdot5$ and $\cdot1$ are merely the writer's rough estimate. Furthermore, there are many other terms that should be included *. The formula is given only for illustrative purposes. Checkmate has been artificially included here by giving the king the large value 200 (anything greater than the maximum of all other terms would do).

It may be noted that this approximate evaluation $f(P)$ has a more or less continuous range of possible values, while with an exact evaluation there are only three possible values. This is as it should be. In practical

---

* See Appendix I.

play a position may be an "easy win" if a player is, for example, a queen ahead, or a very difficult win with only a pawn advantage. In the former case there are many ways to win while in the latter exact play is required, and a single mistake often destroys the advantage. The unlimited intellects assumed in the theory of games, on the other hand, never make a mistake and the smallest winning advantage is as good as mate in one. A game between two such mental giants, Mr. A and Mr. B, would proceed as follows. They sit down at the chessboard, draw for colours, and then survey the pieces for a moment. Then either

(1) Mr. A says, "I resign" or
(2) Mr. B says, "I resign" or
(3) Mr. A says, "I offer a draw," and Mr. B replies, "I accept."

4. Strategy Based on an Evaluation Function.

A very important point about the simple type of evaluation function given above (and general principles of chess) is that they can only be applied in relatively quiescent positions. For example, in an exchange of queens White plays, say, $Q \times Q$ ($\times$ = captures) and Black will reply $P \times Q$. It would be absurd to calculate the function $f(P)$ after $Q \times Q$ while White is, for a moment, a queen ahead, since Black will immediately recover it. More generally it is meaningless to calculate an evaluation of the general type given above during the course of a combination or a series of exchanges.

More terms could be added to $f(P)$ to account for exchanges in progress, but it appears that combinations, and forced variations in general, are better accounted for by examination of specific variations. This is, in fact, the way chess players calculate. A certain number of variations are investigated move by move until a more or less quiescent position is reached and at this point something of the nature of an evaluation is applied to the resulting position. The player chooses the variation leading to the highest evaluation for him when the opponent is assumed to be playing to reduce this evaluation.

The process can be described mathematically. We omit at first the fact that $f(P)$ should only be applied in quiescent positions. A strategy of play based on $f(P)$ and operating one move deep is the following. Let M_1, M_2, M_3, . . ., M_s be the moves that can be made in position P and let M_1P, M_2P, etc. denote symbolically the resulting positions when M_1, M_2, etc. are applied to P. Then one chooses the M_m which maximizes $f(M_m P)$.

A deeper strategy would consider the opponent's replies. Let M_{i1}, M_{i2}, . . ., M_{is} be the possible answers by Black, if White chooses move M_i. Black should play to *minimize* $f(P)$. Furthermore, his choice occurs *after* White's move. Thus, if White plays M_i Black may be assumed to play the M_{ij} such that

$$f(M_{ij}M_iP)$$

is a *minimum*. White should play his first move such that f is a maximum after Black chooses his best reply. Therefore, White should play to maximize on M_i the quantity

$$\min_{M_{ij}} f(M_{ij} M_i P).$$

The mathematical process involved is shown for a simple case in Fig. 2. The point at the left represents the position being considered. It is assumed that there are three possible moves for White, indicated by the three solid lines, and if any of these is made there are three possible moves for Black, indicated by the dashed lines. The possible positions after a White and Black move are then the nine points on the right, and the numbers are the evaluations for these positions. Minimizing on the upper three gives $+\cdot 1$ which is the resulting value if White chooses the

Fig. 2.

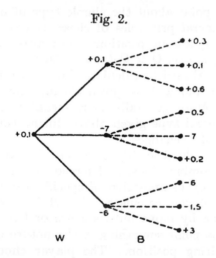

upper variation and Black replies with his best move. Similarly, the second and third moves lead to values of -7 and -6. Maximizing on White's move, we obtain $+\cdot 1$ with the upper move as White's best choice.

In a similar way a two-move strategy (based on considering all variations out to 2 moves) is given by

$$\underset{M_i}{\text{Max}} \; \underset{M_{ij}}{\text{Min}} \; \underset{M_{ijk}}{\text{Max}} \; \underset{M_{ijkl}}{\text{Min}} \; f(M_{ijkl} \; M_{ijk} \; M_{ij} \; M_i \; P) \qquad \dots \dots (1)$$

The order of maximizing and minimizing this function is important. It derives from the fact that the choices of moves occur in a definite order.

A machine operating on this strategy at the two-move level would first calculate all variations out to two moves (for each side) and the resulting positions. The evaluations $f(P)$ are calculated for each of these positions. Fixing all but the last Black move, this last is varied and the move chosen which minimizes f. This is Black's assumed last move in the variation in question. Another move for White's second move is chosen and the process repeated for Black's second move. This is done for each second White move and the one chosen giving the largest final f (after Black's best assumed reply in each case). In this way White's second move in each variation is determined. Continuing in this way the machine works back to the present position and the best first White move. This move is then played. This process generalizes in the obvious way for any number of moves.

A strategy of this sort, in which all variations are considered out to a definite number of moves and the move then determined from a formula such as (1) will be called a type A strategy. The type A strategy has certain basic weaknesses, which we will discuss later, but is conceptually simple, and we will first show how a computer can be programmed for such a strategy.

5. PROGRAMMING A GENERAL PURPOSE COMPUTER FOR A TYPE A STRATEGY.

We assume a large-scale digital computer, indicated schematically in Fig. 3, with the following properties :—

Fig. 3.

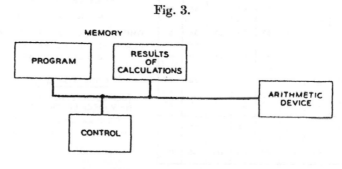

(1) There is a large internal memory for storing numbers. The memory is divided into a number of boxes each capable of holding, say, a ten-digit number. Each box is assigned a " box number ".

(2) There is an arithmetic organ which can perform the elementary operations of addition, multiplication, etc.

(3) The computer operates under the control of a " program ". The program consists of a sequence of elementary " orders ". A typical order is A 372, 451, 133. This means, extract the contents of box 372 and of box 451, add these numbers, and put the sum in box 133. Another type of order involves a decision, for example, C 291, 118, 345. This tells the machine to compare the contents of box 291 and 118. If the first is larger the machine goes on to the next order in the program. If not, it takes its next order from box 345. This type of order enables the machine to choose from alternative procedures, depending on the results of previous calculations. It is assumed that orders are available for transferring numbers, the arithmetic operations, and decisions.

Our problem is to represent chess as numbers and operations on numbers, and to reduce the strategy decided upon to a sequence of computer orders. We will not carry this out in detail but only outline the programs. As a colleague puts it, the final program for a computer must be written in words of one microsyllable.

The rather Procrustean tactics of forcing chess into an arithmetic computer are dictated by economic considerations. Ideally, we would like to design a special computer for chess containing, in place of the arithmetic organ, a "chess organ" specifically designed to perform the simple chess calculations. Although a large improvement in speed of operation would undoubtedly result, the initial cost of computers seems to prohibit such a possibility. It is planned, however, to experiment with a simple strategy on one of the numerical computers now being constructed.

Fig. 4.

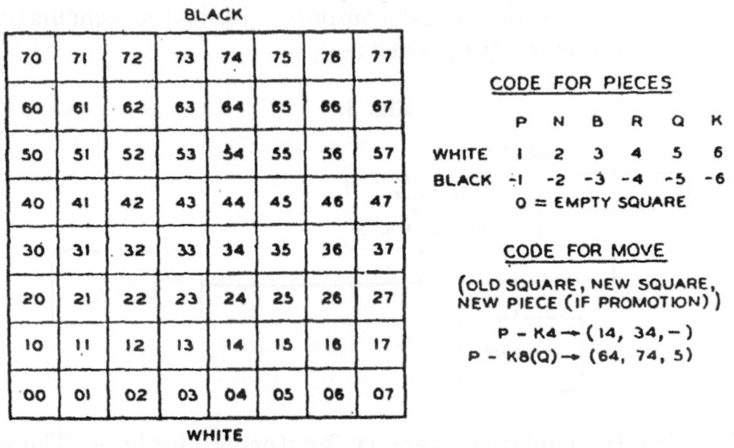

BLACK

70	71	72	73	74	75	76	77
60	61	62	63	64	65	66	67
50	51	52	53	54	55	56	57
40	41	42	43	44	45	46	47
30	31	32	33	34	35	36	37
20	21	22	23	24	25	26	27
10	11	12	13	14	15	16	17
00	01	02	03	04	05	06	07

WHITE

CODE FOR PIECES

	P	N	B	R	Q	K
WHITE	1	2	3	4	5	6
BLACK	-1	-2	-3	-4	-5	-6

0 = EMPTY SQUARE

CODE FOR MOVE

(OLD SQUARE, NEW SQUARE, NEW PIECE (IF PROMOTION))

P – K4 → (14, 34, –)

P – K8(Q) → (64, 74, 5)

A game of chess can be divided into three phases, the opening, the middle game, and the end game. Different principles of play apply in the different phases. In the opening, which generally lasts for about ten moves, development of the pieces to good positions is the main objective. During the middle game tactics and combinations are predominant. This phase lasts until most of the pieces are exchanged, leaving only kings, pawns and perhaps one or two pieces on each side. The end game is mainly concerned with pawn promotion. Exact timing and such possibilities as "Zugzwang", stalemate, etc. become important.

Due to the difference in strategic aims, different programs should be used for the different phases of a game. We will be chiefly concerned with the middle game and will not consider the end game at all. There seems no reason, however, why an end game strategy cannot be designed and programmed equally well.

A square on a chessboard can be occupied in 13 different ways : either it is empty (0) or occupied by one of the six possible kinds of White pieces (P=1, N=2, B=3, R=4, Q=5, K=6) or one of the six possible Black pieces (P=-1, N=-2, . . ., K=-6). Thus, the state of a square is specified by giving an integer from -6 to $+6$. The 64 squares can be numbered according to a co-ordinate system as shown in Fig. 4. The position of all pieces is then given by a sequence of 64 numbers each lying between -6 and $+6$. A total of 256 bits (binary digits) is sufficient memory in this representation. Although not the most efficient encoding, it is a convenient one for calculation. One further number λ will be $+1$ or -1 according as it is White's or Black's move. A few more should be added for data relating to castling privileges (whether the White or Black kings and rooks have moved), and *en passant* captures (*e.g.*, a statement of the last move). We will neglect these, however. In this notation the starting chess position is given by :—

$$4, \quad 2, \quad 3, \quad 5, \quad 6, \quad 3, \quad 2, \quad 4; \quad 1, \quad 1, \quad 1, \quad 1, \quad 1, \quad 1, \quad 1, \quad 1;$$
$$0, \quad 0, \quad 0, \quad 0, \quad 0, \quad 0, \quad 0, \quad 0; \quad 0, \quad 0, \quad 0, \quad 0, \quad 0, \quad 0, \quad 0, \quad 0;$$
$$0, \quad 0, \quad 0, \quad 0, \quad 0, \quad 0, \quad 0, \quad 0; \quad 0, \quad 0, \quad 0, \quad 0, \quad 0, \quad 0, \quad 0 \quad 0;$$
$$-1, -1, -1, -1, -1, -1, -1, -1; \quad -4, -2, -3, -5, -6, -3, -2, -4;$$
$$+1 \ (=\lambda).$$

A move (apart from castling and pawn promotion) can be specified by giving the original and final squares occupied by the moved piece. Each of these squares is a choice from 64, thus 6 binary digits each is sufficient, a total of 12 for the move. Thus the initial move P—K4 would be represented by 1, 4 ; 3, 4. To represent pawn promotion a set of three binary digits can be added specifying the piece that the pawn becomes. Castling is described by giving the king move (this being the only way the king can move two squares). Thus, a move is represented by (a, b, c) where a and b are squares and c specifies a piece in case of promotion.

The complete program for a type A strategy consists of nine subprograms which we designate T_0, T_1, . . ., T_8 and a master program T_9. The basic functions of these programs are as follows :—

T_0—Makes move (a, b, c) in position P to obtain the resulting position.

T_1—Makes a list of the possible moves of a pawn at square (x, y) in position P.

T_2, . . ., T_6—Similarly for other types of pieces : knight, bishop, rook, queen and king.

T_7—Makes list of all possible moves in a given position.

T_8—Calculates the evaluating function $f(P)$ for a given position P.

T_9—Master program ; performs maximizing and minimizing calculation to determine proper move.

With a given position P and a move (a, b, c) in the internal memory of the machine it can make the move and obtain the resulting position by the following program T_0.

(1) The square corresponding to number a in the position is located in the position memory.

(2) The number in this square x is extracted and replaced by 0 (empty).

(3) (a) If $x=1$, and the first co-ordinate of a is 6 (White pawn being promoted) or if $x=-1$, and the first co-ordinate of a is 1 (Black pawn being promoted), the number c is placed in square b (replacing whatever was there).

(b) If $x=6$ and $a-b=2$ (White castles, king side) 0 is placed in squares 04 and 07 and 6 and 4 in squares 06 and 05, respectively. Similarly for the cases $x=6$, $b-a=2$ (White castles, queen side) and $x=-6$, $a-b=\pm 2$ (Black castles, king or queen side).

(c) In all other cases, x is placed in square b.

(4) The sign of λ is changed.

For each type of piece there is a program for determining its possible moves. As a typical example the bishop program, T_3, is briefly as follows. Let (x, y) be the co-ordinates of the square occupied by the bishop.

(1) Construct $(x+1, y+1)$ and read the contents u of this square in the position P.

(2) If $u=0$ (empty) list the move (x, y), $(x+1, y+1)$ and start over with $(x+2, y+2)$ instead of $(x+1, y+1)$.

If λu is positive (own piece in the square) continue to 3.

If λu is negative (opponent's piece in the square) list the move and continue to 3.

If the square does not exist continue to 3.

(3) Construct $(x+1, y-1)$ and perform similar calculation.

(4) Similarly with $(x-1, y+1)$.

(5) Similarly with $(x-1, y-1)$.

By this program a list is constructed of the possible moves of a bishop in a given position P. Similar programs would list the moves of any other piece. There is considerable scope for opportunism in simplifying these programs; e.g., the queen program, T_5, can be a combination of the bishop and rook programs, T_3 and T_4.

Using the piece programs $T_1 \ldots T_6$ and a controlling program T_7 the machine can construct a list of *all* possible moves in any given position P. The controlling program T_7 is briefly as follows (omitting details) :—

(1) Start at square 1,1 and extract contents x.

(2) If λx is positive start corresponding piece program T_x and when complete return to (1) adding 1 to square number. If λx is zero or negative, return to 1 adding 1 to square number.

(3) Test each of the listed moves for legality and discard those which are illegal. This is done by making each of the moves in the position P (by program T_0) and examining whether it leaves the king in check.

With the programs $T_0 \ldots T_7$ it is possible for the machine to play legal chess, merely making a randomly chosen legal move at each turn to move. The level of play with such a strategy is unbelievably bad.* The writer played a few games against this random strategy and was able to checkmate generally in four or five moves (by fool's mate, etc.). The following game will illustrate the utter purposelessness of random play :—

	White (Random)	Black
(1)	P–KN3	P–K4
(2)	P–Q3	B–B4
(3)	B–Q2	Q–B3
(4)	N–QB3	Q × P mate

We now return to the strategy based on an evaluation $f(P)$. The program T_8 performs the function of evaluating a position according to the agreed-upon $f(P)$. This can be done by the obvious means of scanning the squares and adding the terms involved. It is not difficult to include terms such as doubled pawns, etc.

The final master program T_9 is needed to select the move according to the maximizing and minimizing process indicated above. On the basis of one move (for each side) T_9 works as follows :—

(1) List the legal moves (by T_7) possible in the present position.

(2) Take the first in the list and make this move by T_0, giving position $M_1 P$.

(3) List the Black moves in $M_1 P$.

(4) Apply the first one giving $M_{11} M_1 P$, and evaluate by T_8.

(5) Apply the second Black move M_{12} and evaluate.

(6) Compare, and reject the move with the smaller evaluation.

(7) Continue with the third Black move and compare with the retained value, etc.

(8) When the Black moves are exhausted, one will be retained together with its evaluation. The process is now repeated with the second White move.

(9) The final evaluations from these two computations are compared and the maximum retained.

(10) This is continued with all White moves until the best is selected (*i. e.* the one remaining after all are tried). This is the move to be made.

---

* Although there is a finite probability, of the order of 10^{-75}, that random play would win a game from Botvinnik. Bad as random play is, there are even worse strategies which choose moves which actually *aid* the opponent. For example, White's strategy in the following game: 1. P–KB3, P–K4. 2. P–KN4, Q–R5 mate.

These programs are, of course, highly iterative. For that reason they should not require a great deal of program memory if efficiently worked out.

The internal memory for positions and temporary results of calculations when playing three moves deep can be estimated. Three positions should probably be remembered : the initial position, the next to the last, and the last position (now being evaluated). This requires some 800 bits. Furthermore, there are five lists of moves each requiring about $30 \times 12 = 360$ bits, a total of 1800. Finally, about 200 bits would cover the selections and evaluations up to the present calculation. Thus, some 3000 bits should suffice.

6. IMPROVEMENTS IN THE STRATEGY.

Unfortunately a machine operating according to this type A strategy would be both slow and a weak player. It would be slow since even if each position were evaluated in one microsecond (very optimistic) there are about 10^9 evaluations to be made after three moves (for each side). Thus, more than 16 minutes would be required for a move, or 10 hours for its half of a 40-move game.

It would be weak in playing skill because it is only seeing three moves deep and because we have not included any conditions about quiescent positions for evaluation. The machine is operating in an extremely inefficient fashion—it computes *all* variations to *exactly* three moves and then stops (even though it or the opponent be in check). A good human player examines only a few selected variations and carries these out to a reasonable stopping-point. A world champion can construct (at best) combinations say, 15 or 20 moves deep. Some variations given by Alekhine (" My Best Games of Chess 1924–1937 ") are of this length. Of course, only a few variations are explored to any such depth. In amateur play variations are seldom examined more deeply than six or eight moves, and this only when the moves are of a highly forcing nature (with very limited possible replies). More generally, when there are few threats and forceful moves, most calculations are not deeper than one or two moves, with perhaps half-a-dozen forcing variations explored to three, four or five moves.

On this point a quotation from Reuben Fine (Fine 1942), a leading American master, is interesting : " Very often people have the idea that masters foresee everything or nearly everything ; that when they played P–R3 on the thirteenth move they foresaw that this would be needed to provide a loophole for the king after the complications twenty moves later, or even that when they play 1 P–K4 they do it with the idea of preventing Kt–Q4 on Black's twelfth turn, or they feel that everything is mathematically calculated down to the smirk when the Queen's Rook Pawn queens one move ahead of the opponent's King's Knight's Pawn. All this is, of course, pure fantasy. The best course to follow is to note the major consequences for two moves, but try to work out forced variations as they go."

The amount of selection exercised by chess masters in examining possible variations has been studied experimentally by De Groot (1946, *b*). He showed various typical positions to chess masters and asked them to decide on the best move, describing aloud their analyses of the positions as they thought them through. In this manner the number and depth of the variations examined could be determined. Fig. 5 shows the result of one such experiment. In this case the chess master examined sixteen variations, ranging in depth from 1/2 (one Black move) to 4–1/2 (five Black and four White) moves. The total number of positions considered was 44.

Fig. 5.

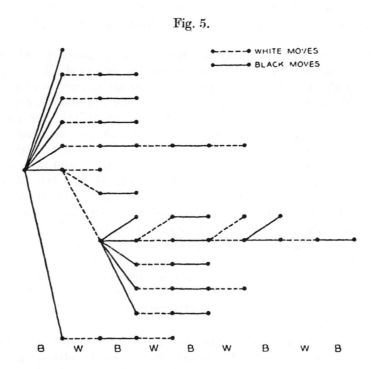

From these remarks it appears that to improve the speed and strength of play the machine must :—

(1) Examine forceful variations out as far as possible and evaluate only at reasonable positions, where some quasi-stability has been established.

(2) Select the variations to be explored by some process so that the machine does not waste its time in totally pointless variations.

A strategy with these two improvements will be called a type B strategy. It is not difficult to construct programs incorporating these features. For the first we define a function $g(P)$ of a position which determines whether approximate stability exists (no pieces *en prise*, etc.). A crude definition might be :

$$g(P) = \begin{cases} 1 \text{ if any piece is attacked by a piece of lower value, or by more} \\ \phantom{1 \text{ }} \text{pieces then defences or if any check exists on a square} \\ \phantom{1 \text{ }} \text{controlled by opponent.} \\ 0 \text{ otherwise.} \end{cases}$$

Using this function, variations could be explored until $g(P) = 0$, always, however, going at least two moves and never more than say, 10.

The second improvement would require a function $h(P, M)$ to decide whether a move M in position P is worth exploring. It is important that this preliminary screening should *not* eliminate moves which merely look bad at first sight, for example, a move which puts a piece *en prise*; frequently such moves are actually very strong since the piece cannot be safely taken.

" Always give check, it may be mate " is tongue-in-cheek advice given to beginners aimed at their predilection for useless checks. " Always investigate a check, it may lead to mate " is sound advice for any player. A check is the most forceful type of move. The opponent's replies are highly limited—he can never answer by counter attack, for example. This means that a variation starting with a check can be more readily calculated than any other. Similarly captures, attacks on major pieces, threats of mate, etc. limit the opponent's replies and should be calculated whether the move looks good at first sight or not. Hence, $h(P, M)$ should be given large values for all forceful moves (checks, captures and attacking moves), for developing moves, medium values for defensive moves, and low values for other moves. In exploring a variation $h(P, M)$ would be calculated as the machine computes and would be used to select the variations considered. As it gets further into the variation the requirements on h are set higher so that fewer and fewer subvariations are examined. Thus, it would start considering every first move for itself, only the more forceful replies, etc. By this process its computing efficiency would be greatly improved.

It is believed that an electronic computer incorporating these two improvements in the program would play a fairly strong game, at speeds comparable to human speeds. It may be noted that a machine has several advantages over humans :—

(1) High-speed operation in individual calculations.

(2) Freedom from errors. The only errors will be due to deficiencies of the program while human players are continually guilty of very simple and obvious blunders.

(3) Freedom from laziness. It is all too easy for a human player to make instinctive moves without proper analysis of the position.

(4) Freedom from " nerves ". Human players are prone to blunder due to over-confidence in " won " positions or defeatism and self-recrimination in " lost " positions.

These must be balanced against the flexibility, imagination and inductive and learning capacities of the human mind.

Incidentally, the person who designs the program can calculate the move that the machine will choose in any position, and thus in a sense can play an equally good game. In actual fact, however, the calculation would be impractical because of the time required. On a fair basis of comparison, giving the machine and the designer equal time to decide on a move, the machine might well play a stronger game.

7. VARIATIONS IN PLAY AND IN STYLE.

As described so far the machine once designed would always make the same move in the same position. If the opponent made the same moves this would always lead to the same game. It is desirable to avoid this, since if the opponent wins one game he could play the same variation and win continuously, due perhaps to some particular position arising in the variation where the machine chooses a very weak move.

One way to prevent this is to have a statistical element in the machine. Whenever there are two or more moves which are of nearly equal value according to the machine's calculations it chooses from them at random. In the same position a second time it may then choose another in the set.

The opening is another place where statistical variation can be introduced. It would seem desirable to have a number of the standard openings stored in a slow-speed memory in the machine. Perhaps a few hundred would be satisfactory. For the first few moves (until either the opponent deviates from the " book " or the end of the stored variation is reached) the machine plays by memory. This is hardly " cheating " since that is the way chess masters play the opening.

It is interesting that the " style " of play of the machine can be changed very easily by altering some of the coefficients and numerical factors involved in the evaluation function and the other programs. By placing high values on positional weaknesses, etc. a positional-type player results. By more intensive examination of forced variations it becomes a combination player. Furthermore, the strength of the play can be easily adjusted by changing the depth of calculation and by omitting or adding terms to the evaluation function.

Finally we may note that a machine of this type will play " brilliantly " up to its limits. It will readily sacrifice a queen or other piece in order to gain more material later or to give checkmate provided the completion of the combination occurs within its computing limits.

The chief weakness is that the machine will not learn by its mistakes. The only way to improve its play is by improving the program. Some thought has been given to designing a program which is self-improving but, although it appears to be possible, the methods thought of so far do not seem to be very practical. One possibility is to have a higher level program which changes the terms and coefficients involved in the evaluation function depending on the results of games the machine has played. Small variations might be introduced in these terms and the values selected to give the greatest percentage of " wins ".

8. ANOTHER TYPE OF STRATEGY.

The strategies described above do not, of course, exhaust the possibilities. In fact, there are undoubtedly others which are far more efficient in the use of available computing time on the machine. Even with the improvements we have discussed the above strategy gives an impression of relying too much on " brute force " calculations rather than on logical analysis of a position. It plays something like a beginner at chess who has been told some of the principles and is possessed of tremendous energy and accuracy for calculation but has no experience with the game. A chess master, on the other hand, has available knowledge of hundreds or perhaps thousands of standard situations, stock combinations, and common manœuvres which occur time and again in the game. There are, for example, the typical sacrifices of a knight at B7 or a bishop at R7, the standard mates such as the " Philidor Legacy ", manœuvres based on pins, forks, discoveries, promotion, etc. In a given position he recognizes some similarity to a familiar situation and this directs his mental calculations along lines with greater probability of success.

There is no reason why a program based on such " type positions " could not be constructed. This would require, however, a rather formidable analysis of the game. Although there are various books analysing combination play and the middle game, they are written for human consumption, not for computing machines. It is possible to give a person one or two specific examples of a general situation and have him understand and apply the general principle involved. With a computer an exact and completely explicit characterization of the situation must be given with all limitations, special cases, etc. taken into account. We are inclined to believe, however, that if this were done a much more efficient program would result.

To program such a strategy we might suppose that any position in the machine is accompanied by a rather elaborate analysis of the tactical structure of the position suitably encoded. This analytical data will state that, for example, the Black knight at B3 is pinned by a bishop, that the White rook at K1 cannot leave the back rank because of a threatened mate on B8, that a White knight at R4 has no move, etc. ; in short, all the facts to which a chess player would ascribe importance in analysing tactical possibilities. These data would be supplied by a program and would be continually changed and kept up-to-date as the game progressed. The analytical data would be used to trigger various other programs depending on the particular nature of the position. A pinned piece should be attacked. If a rook must guard the back rank it cannot guard the pawn in front of it, etc. The machine obtains in this manner suggestions of plausible moves to investigate.

It is not being suggested that we should design the strategy in our own image. Rather it should be matched to the capacities and weaknesses of the computer. The computer is strong in speed and accuracy and weak in analytical ability and recognition. Hence, it should make more use of brutal calculations than humans, but with possible variations increasing by a factor of 10^3 every move, a little selection goes a long way toward improving blind trial and error.

ACKNOWLEDGMENT.

The writer is indebted to E. G. Andrews, L. N. Enoquist and H. E. Singleton for a number of suggestions that have been incorporated in the paper.

October 8, 1948.

APPENDIX.

THE EVALUATION FUNCTION FOR CHESS.

The evaluation function $f(P)$ should take into account the " long term " advantages and disadvantages of a position, *i. e.* effects which may be expected to persist over a number of moves longer than individual variations are calculated. Thus the evaluation is mainly concerned with positional or strategic considerations rather than combinatorial or tactical ones. Of course there is no sharp line of division ; many features of a position are on the borderline. It appears, however, that the following might properly be included in $f(P)$:—

(1) Material advantage (difference in total material).

(2) Pawn formation :
  - (*a*) Backward, isolated and doubled pawns.
  - (*b*) Relative control of centre (pawns at K4, Q4, B4).
  - (*c*) Weakness of pawns near king (*e. g.* advanced KNP).
  - (*d*) Pawns on opposite colour squares from bishop.
  - (*e*) Passed pawns.

(3) Positions of pieces :
  - (*a*) Advanced knight (at K5, Q5, B5, K6, Q6, B6), especially if protected by pawn and free from pawn attack.
  - (*b*) Rook on open file, or semi-open file.
  - (*c*) Rook on seventh rank.
  - (*d*) Doubled rooks.

(4) Commitments, attacks and options :
  - (*a*) Pieces which are required for guarding functions and, therefore, committed and with limited mobility.
  - (*b*) Attacks on pieces which give one player an option of exchanging.
  - (*c*) Attacks on squares adjacent to king.
  - (*d*) Pins. We mean here immobilizing pins where the pinned piece is of value not greater than the pinning piece ; for example, a knight pinned by a bishop.

(5) Mobility.

These factors will apply in the middle game : during the opening and end game different principles must be used. The relative values to be given each of the above quantities is open to considerable debate, and should be determined by some experimental procedure. There are also numerous other factors which may well be worth inclusion. The more violent tactical weapons, such as discovered checks, forks and pins by a piece of lower value are omitted since they are best accounted for by the examination of specific variations.

REFERENCES.

CHERNEV, 1937, *Curious Chess Facts*, The Black Knight Press.

DE GROOT, A. D., 1946a, *Het Denken van den Schaker* 17–18, Amsterdam ; 1946b, *Ibid.*, Amsterdam, 207.

FINE, R., 1942, *Chess the Easy Way*, 79, David McKay.

HARDY and WRIGHT, 1938, *The Theory of Numbers*, 116, Oxford.

VON NEUMANN and MORGENSTERN, 1944, *Theory of Games*, 125, Princeton.

VIGNERON, H., 1914, *Les Automates*, La Natura.

WIENER, N., 1948, *Cybernetics*, John Wiley.

You're not a man, you're a machine.
　　　　　　　　　—George Bernard Shaw (*Arms and the Man*)

Thinking makes it so.　　　　　　　　—Shakespeare (*Hamlet*)

Things are in the saddle and ride mankind.　　—Ralph Waldo Emerson

A Chess-Playing Machine

By CLAUDE E. SHANNON

FOR centuries philosophers and scientists have speculated about whether or not the human brain is essentially a machine. Could a machine be designed that would be capable of "thinking"? During the past decade several large-scale electronic computing machines have been constructed which are capable of something very close to the reasoning process. These new computers were designed primarily to carry out purely numerical calculations. They perform automatically a long sequence of additions, multiplications and other arithmetic operations at a rate of thousands per second. The basic design of these machines is so general and flexible, however, that they can be adapted to work symbolically with elements representing words, propositions or other conceptual entities.

One such possibility, which is already being investigated in several quarters, is that of translating from one language to another by means of a computer. The immediate goal is not a finished literary rendition, but only a word-by-word translation that would convey enough of the meaning to be understandable. Computing machines could also be employed for many other tasks of a semi-rote, semi-thinking character, such as designing electrical filters and relay circuits, helping to regulate airplane traffic at busy airports, and routing long-distance telephone calls most efficiently over a limited number of trunks.

Some of the possibilities in this direction can be illustrated by setting up a computer in such a way that it will play a fair game of chess. This problem, of course, is of no importance in itself, but it was undertaken with a serious purpose in mind. The investigation of the chess-playing problem is intended to develop techniques that can be used for more practical applications.

The chess machine is an ideal one to start with for several reasons. The problem is sharply defined, both in the allowed operations (the moves of chess) and in the ultimate goal (checkmate). It is neither so simple as to be trivial nor too difficult for satisfactory solution. And such a machine could be pitted against a human opponent, giving a clear measure of the machine's ability in this type of reasoning.

There is already a considerable literature on the subject of chess-playing machines. During the late 18th and early 19th centuries a Hungarian inventor named Wolfgang von Kempelen astounded Europe with a device known as the Maelzel Chess Automaton, which toured the Continent to large audiences. A number of papers purporting to explain its operation, including an analytical essay by Edgar Allan Poe, soon appeared. Most of the analysts concluded, quite correctly, that the automaton was operated by a human chess master concealed inside. Some years later the exact manner of operation was exposed (see Figure 1).

FIGURE 1—Chess machine of the 18th century was actually run by man inside.

A more honest attempt to design a chess-playing machine was made in 1914 by a Spanish inventor named L. Torres y Quevedo, who constructed a device that played an end game of king and rook against king. The machine, playing the side with king and rook, would force checkmate in a few moves however its human opponent played. Since an explicit set of rules can be given for making satisfactory moves in such an end game, the problem is relatively simple, but the idea was quite advanced for that period.

An electronic computer can be set up to play a complete game. In order to explain the actual setup of a chess machine, it may be best to start with a general picture of a computer and its operation.

A general-purpose electronic computer is an extremely complicated device containing several thousand vacuum tubes, relays and other elements. The basic principles involved, however, are quite simple. The machine has four main parts: (1) an "arithmetic organ," (2) a control element, (3) a numerical memory and (4) a program memory. (In some designs the two memory functions are carried out in the same physical apparatus.) The manner of operation is exactly analogous to a human computer carrying out a series of numerical calculations with an ordinary desk computing machine. The arithmetic organ corresponds to the desk computing machine, the control element to the human operator, the numerical memory to the work sheet on which intermediate and final results are recorded, and the program memory to the computing routine describing the series of operations to be performed.

In an electronic computing machine, the numerical memory consists of a large number of "boxes," each capable of holding a number. To set up a problem on the computer, it is necessary to assign box numbers to all numerical quantities involved, and then to construct a program telling the machine what arithmetical operations must be performed on the numbers and where the results should go. The program consists of a sequence of "orders," each describing an elementary calculation. For example, a typical order may read A 372, 451, 133. This means: add the number stored in box 372 to that in box 451, and put the sum in box 133. Another type of order requires the machine to make a decision. For example, the order C 291, 118, 345 tells the machine to compare the contents of boxes 291 and 118; if the number in box 291 is larger, the machine goes on to the next order in the program; if not, it takes its next order from box 345. This type of order enables the machine to choose from alternative procedures, depending on the results of previous calculations. The "vocabulary" of an electronic computer may include as many as 30 different types of orders.

After the machine is provided with a program, the initial numbers required for the calculation are placed in the numerical memory and the machine then automatically carries out the computation. Of course such a machine is most useful in problems involving an enormous number of individual calculations, which would be too laborious to carry out by hand.

The problem of setting up a computer for playing chess can be divided into three parts: first, a code must be chosen so that chess positions and the chess pieces can be represented as numbers; second, a strategy must be found for choosing the moves to be made; and third, this strategy must be translated into a sequence of elementary computer orders, or a program.

A suitable code for the chessboard and the chess pieces is shown in Figure 2. Each square on the board has a number consisting of two digits, the first digit corresponding to the "rank" or horizontal row, the second to the "file" or vertical row. Each different chess piece also is designated by a number: a pawn is numbered 1, a knight 2, a bishop 3, a rook 4 and so on. White pieces are represented by positive numbers and black pieces by negative ones. The positions of all the pieces on the board can be shown by a sequence of 64 numbers, with zeros to indicate the empty

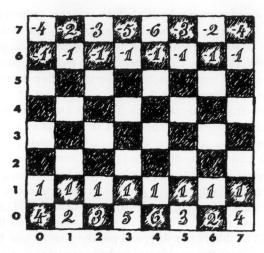

FIGURE 2—Code for a chess-playing machine is plotted on a chessboard. Each square can be
designated by two digits, one representing the horizontal row and the other the vertical. Pieces also are coded in numbers.

squares. Thus any chess position can be recorded as a series of numbers
and stored in the numerical memory of a computing machine.

A chess move is specified by giving the number of the square on which
the piece stands and of the one to which it is moved. Ordinarily two
numbers would be sufficient to describe a move, but to take care of the
special case of the promotion of a pawn to a higher piece a third number
is necessary. This number indicates the piece to which the pawn is converted. In all other moves the third number is zero. Thus a knight move
from square 01 to 22 is encoded into 01, 22, 0. The move of a pawn from
62 to 72, and its promotion to a queen, is represented by 62, 72, 5.

The second main problem is that of deciding on a strategy of play. A
straightforward process must be found for calculating a reasonably good
move for any given chess position. This is the most difficult part of the
problem. The program designer can employ here the principles of correct
play that have been evolved by expert chess players. These empirical
principles are a means of bringing some order to the maze of possible
variations of a chess game. Even the high speeds available in electronic
computers are hopelessly inadequate to play perfect chess by calculating
all possible variations to the end of the game. In a typical chess position
there will be about 32 possible moves with 32 possible replies—already
this creates 1,024 possibilities. Most chess games last 40 moves or more
for each side. So the total number of possible variations in an average
game is about 10^{120}. A machine calculating one variation each millionth
of a second would require over 10^{95} years to decide on its first move!

Other methods of attempting to play perfect chess seem equally impracticable; we resign ourselves, therefore, to having the machine play a reasonably skillful game, admitting occasional moves that may not be the best. This, of course, is precisely what human players do: no one plays a perfect game.

In setting up a strategy on the machine one must establish a method of numerical evaluation for any given chess position. A chess player looking at a position can form an estimate as to which side, White or Black, has the advantage. Furthermore, his evaluation is roughly quantitative. He may say, "White has a rook for a bishop, an advantage of about two pawns"; or "Black has sufficient mobility to compensate for a sacrificed pawn." These judgments are based on long experience and are summarized in the principles of chess expounded in chess literature. For example, it has been found that a queen is worth nine pawns, a rook is worth five, and a bishop or a knight is worth about three. As a first rough approximation, a position can be evaluated by merely adding up the total forces for each side, measured in terms of the pawn unit. There are, however, numerous other features which must be taken into account: the mobility and placement of pieces, the weakness of king protection, the nature of the pawn formation, and so on. These too can be given numerical weights and combined in the evaluation, and it is here that the knowledge and experience of chess masters must be enlisted.

Assuming that a suitable method of position evaluation has been decided upon, how should a move be selected? The simplest process is to consider all the possible moves in the given position and choose the one that gives the best immediate evaluation. Since, however, chess players generally look more than one move ahead, one must take account of the opponent's various possible responses to each projected move. Assuming that the opponent's reply will be the one giving the best evaluation from his point of view, we would choose the move that would leave us as well off as possible after his best reply. Unfortunately, with the computer speeds at present available, the machine could not explore all the possibilities for more than two moves ahead for each side, so a strategy of this type would play a poor game by human standards. Good chess players frequently play combinations four or five moves deep, and occasionally world champions have seen as many as 20 moves ahead. This is possible only because the variations they consider are highly selected. They do not investigate all lines of play, but only the important ones.

The amount of selection exercised by chess masters in examining possible variations has been studied experimentally by the Dutch chess master and psychologist A. D. De Groot. He showed various typical positions to chess masters and asked them to decide on the best move, describing aloud their analyses of the positions as they thought them through. By this procedure the number and depth of the variations examined could be determined. In one typical case a chess master examined 16 variations, ranging in depth from one Black move to five Black and four White moves. The total number of positions considered was 44.

Clearly it would be highly desirable to improve the strategy for the machine by including such a selection process in it. Of course one could go too far in this direction. Investigating one particular line of play for 40 moves would be as bad as investigating all lines for just two moves. A suitable compromise would be to examine only the important possible variations—that is, forcing moves, captures and main threats—and carry out the investigation of the possible moves far enough to make the consequences of each fairly clear. It is possible to set up some rough criteria for selecting important variations, not as efficiently as a chess master, but sufficiently well to reduce the number of variations appreciably and thereby permit a deeper investigation of the moves actually considered.

The final problem is that of reducing the strategy to a sequence of orders, translated into the machine's language. This is a relatively straightforward but tedious process, and we shall only indicate some of the general features. The complete program is made up of nine sub-programs and a master program that calls the sub-programs into operation as needed. Six of the sub-programs deal with the movements of the various kinds of pieces. In effect they tell the machine the allowed moves for these pieces. Another sub-program enables the machine to make a move "mentally" without actually carrying it out: that is, with a given position stored in its memory it can construct the position that would result if the move were made. The seventh sub-program enables the computer to make a list of all possible moves in a given position, and the last sub-program evaluates any given position. The master program correlates and supervises the application of the sub-programs. It starts the seventh sub-program making a list of possible moves, which in turn calls in previous sub-programs to determine where the various pieces could move. The master program then evaluates the resulting positions by means of the eighth sub-program and compares the results according to the process described above. After comparison of all the investigated variations, the one that gives the best evaluation according to the machine's calculations is selected. This move is translated into standard chess notation and typed out by the machine.

It is believed that an electronic computer programmed in this manner would play a fairly strong game at speeds comparable to human speeds. A machine has several obvious advantages over a human player: (1) it can make individual calculations with much greater speed; (2) its play is free of errors other than those due to deficiencies of the program, whereas human players often make very simple and obvious blunders; (3) it is free from laziness, or the temptation to make an instinctive move without proper analysis of the position; (4) it is free from "nerves," so it will make no blunders due to overconfidence or defeatism. Against these advantages, however, must be weighed the flexibility, imagination and learning capacity of the human mind.

Under some circumstances the machine might well defeat the program designer. In one sense, the designer can surely outplay his machine; knowing the strategy used by the machine, he can apply the same tactics at a deeper level. But he would require several weeks to calculate a move, while the machine uses only a few minutes. On an equal time basis, the speed, patience and deadly accuracy of the machine would be telling against human fallibility. Sufficiently nettled, however, the designer could easily weaken the playing skill of the machine by changing the program in such a way as to reduce the depth of investigation (see Figure 3). This idea was expressed by a cartoon in *The Saturday Evening Post* a while ago.

As described so far, the machine would always make the same move in the same position. If the opponent made the same moves, this would always lead to the same game. Once the opponent won a game, he could win every time thereafter by playing the same strategy, taking advantage of some particular position in which the machine chooses a weak move. One way to vary the machine's play would be to introduce a statistical element. Whenever it was confronted with two or more possible moves that were about equally good according to the machine's calculations, it would choose from them at random. Thus if it arrived at the same position a second time it might choose a different move.

Another place where statistical variation could be introduced is in the opening game. It would be desirable to have a number of standard openings, perhaps a few hundred, stored in the memory of the machine. For the first few moves, until the opponent deviated from the standard responses or the machine reached the end of the stored sequence of moves, the machine would play by memory. This could hardly be considered cheating, since that is the way chess masters play the opening.

We may note that within its limits a machine of this type will play a brilliant game. It will readily make spectacular sacrifices of important pieces in order to gain a later advantage or to give checkmate, provided the completion of the combination occurs within its computing limits. For example, in the position illustrated in Figure 4 the machine would quickly discover the sacrificial mate in three moves:

	White	*Black*
1.	R-K8 Ch	R X R
2.	Q-Kt4 Ch	Q X Q
3.	Kt-B6 Mate	

Winning combinations of this type are frequently overlooked in amateur play.

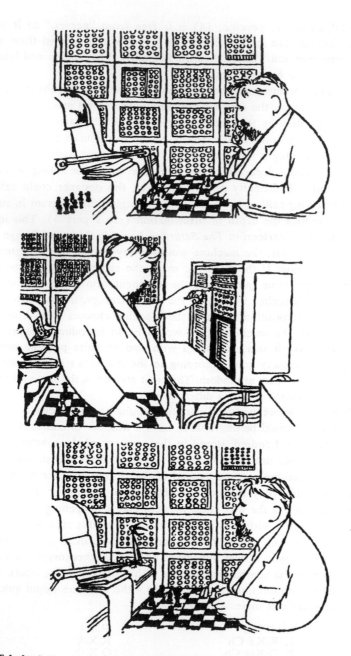

FIGURE 3—Inevitable advantage of man over the machine is illustrated in this drawing. At top human player loses to machine. In center nettled human player revises machine's instructions. At bottom human player wins.

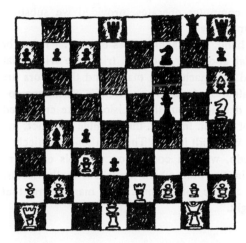

FIGURE 4—Problem that the machine could solve brilliantly might begin with this chess position. The machine would sacrifice a rook and a queen, the most powerful piece on the board, and then win in only one more move.

The chief weakness of the machine is that it will not learn by its mistakes. The only way to improve its play is by improving the program. Some thought has been given to designing a program that would develop its own improvements in strategy with increasing experience in play. Although it appears to be theoretically possible, the methods thought of so far do not seem to be very practical. One possibility is to devise a program that would change the terms and coefficients involved in the evaluation function on the basis of the results of games the machine had already played. Small variations might be introduced in these terms, and the values would be selected to give the greatest percentage of wins.

The Gordian question, more easily raised than answered is: Does a chess-playing machine of this type "think"? The answer depends entirely on how we define thinking. Since there is no general agreement as to the precise connotation of this word, the question has no definite answer. From a behavioristic point of view, the machine acts as though it were thinking. It has always been considered that skillful chess play requires the reasoning faculty. If we regard thinking as a property of external actions rather than internal method the machine is surely thinking.

The thinking process is considered by some psychologists to be essentially characterized by the following steps: various possible solutions of a problem are tried out mentally or symbolically without actually being carried out physically; the best solution is selected by a mental evaluation of the results of these trials; and the solution found in this way is then acted upon. It will be seen that this is almost an exact description of how a chess-playing computer operates, provided we substitute "within the machine" for "mentally."

On the other hand, the machine does only what it has been told to do. It works by trial and error, but the trials are trials that the program designer ordered the machine to make, and the errors are called errors because the evaluation function gives these variations low ratings. The machine makes decisions, but the decisions were envisaged and provided for at the time of design. In short, the machine does not, in any real sense, go beyond what was built into it. The situation was nicely summarized by Torres y Quevedo, who, in connection with his end-game machine, remarked: "The limits within which thought is really necessary need to be better defined . . . the automaton can do many things that are popularly classed as thought."

Memory Requirements in a Telephone Exchange

By CLAUDE E. SHANNON

(Manuscript Received Dec. 7, 1949)

1. INTRODUCTION

A GENERAL telephone exchange with N subscribers is indicated schematically in Fig. 1. The basic function of an exchange is that of setting up a connection between any pair of subscribers. In operation the exchange must "remember," in some form, which subscribers are connected together until the corresponding calls are completed. This requires a certain amount of internal memory, depending on the number of subscribers, the maximum calling rate, etc. A number of relations will be derived based on these considerations which give the minimum possible number of relays, crossbar switches or other elements necessary to perform this memory function. Comparison of any proposed design with the minimum requirements obtained from the relations gives a measure of the efficiency in memory utilization of the design.

Memory in a physical system is represented by the existence of stable internal states of the system. A relay can be supplied with a holding connection so that the armature will stay in either the operated or unoperated positions indefinitely, depending on its initial position. It has, then, two stable states. A set of N relays has 2^N possible sets of positions for the armatures and can be connected in such a way that these are all stable. The total number of states might be used as a measure of the memory in a system, but it is more convenient to work with the logarithm of this number. The chief reason for this is that the amount of memory is then proportional to the number of elements involved. With N relays the amount of memory is then $M = \log 2^N = N \log 2$. If the logarithmic base is two, then $\log_2 2 = 1$ and $M = N$. The resulting units may be called binary digits, or more shortly, bits. A device with M bits of memory can retain M different "yes's" or "no's" or M different 0's or 1's. The logarithmic base 10 is also useful in some cases. The resulting units of memory will then be called decimal digits. A relay has a memory capacity of .301 decimal digits. A 10×10 crossbar switch has 100 points. If each of these points could be operated independently of the others, the total memory capacity would be 100 bits or 30.1 decimal digits. As ordinarily used, however, only one point in a vertical can be closed. With this restriction the capacity is one decimal digit for each vertical, or a total of ten decimal digits. The panels used in a panel type exchange are another form of memory device. If the commutator in a panel has 500 possible levels, it has a memory capacity of log 500; 8.97 bits or 2.7 decimal digits. Finally, in a step-by-step system, 100-point selector switches are used. These have a memory of two decimal digits.

Frequently the actual available memory in a group of relays or other devices is less than the sum of the individual memories because of artificial restrictions on the available states. For technical reasons, certain states are made inaccessible—if relay A is operated relay B must be unoperated, etc. In a crossbar it is not desirable to have more than nine points in the same horizontal operated because of the spring loading on the crossarm. Constraints of this type reduce the memory per element and imply that more than the minimum requirements to be derived will be necessary.

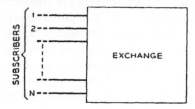

Fig. 1—General telephone exchange.

2. Memory Required for any S Calls out of N Subscribers

The simplest case occurs if we assume an isolated exchange (no trunks to other exchanges) and suppose it should be able to accommodate any possible set of S or fewer calls between pairs of subscribers. If there are a total of N subscribers, the number of ways we can select m pairs is given by

$$\frac{N(N-1)(N-2)\cdots(N-2m+1)}{2^m \, m!} = \frac{N!}{2^m \, m!(N-2m)!} \tag{1}$$

The numerator $N(N-1)\cdots(N-2m+1)$ is the number of ways of choosing the $2m$ subscribers involved out of the N. The $m!$ takes care of the permutations in order of the calls and 2^m the inversions of subscribers in pairs. The total number of possibilities is then the sum of this for $m = 0, 1, \cdots, S$; i.e.

$$\sum_{m=0}^{S} \frac{N!}{2^m \, m!(N-2m)!} \tag{2}$$

The exchange must have a stable internal state corresponding to each of these possibilities and must have, therefore, a memory capacity M where

$$M = \log \sum_{0}^{S} \frac{N!}{2^m \, m!(N-2m)!}. \tag{3}$$

If the exchange were constructed using only relays it must contain at least $\log_2 \sum N!/2^m m!(N - 2m)!$ relays. If 10×10 point crossbars are used in the normal fashion it must contain at least $\frac{1}{10} \log_{10} \sum N!/2^m m!(N - 2m)!$ of these, etc. If fewer are used there are not enough stable configurations of connections available to distinguish all the possible desired interconnections. With $N = 10{,}000$, and a peak load of say 1000 simultaneous conversations $M = 16{,}637$ bits, and at least this many relays or 502 10×10 crossbars would be necessary. Incidentally, for numbers N and S of this magnitude only the term $m = S$ is significant in (3).

The memory computed above is that required only for the basic function of remembering who is talking to whom until the conversation is completed. Supervision and control functions have been ignored. One particular supervisory function is easily taken into account. The call should be charged to

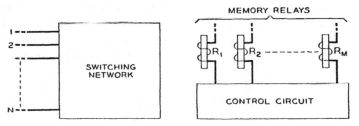

Fig. 2—Minimum memory exchange.

the calling party and under his control (i.e. the connection is broken when the calling party hangs up). Thus the exchange must distinguish between a calling b and b calling a. Rather than count the number of pairs possible we should count the number of ordered pairs. The effect of this is merely to eliminate the 2^m in the above formulas.

The question arises as to whether these limits are the best possible—could we design an exchange using only this minimal number of relays, for example? The answer is that such a design is possible in principle, but for various reasons quite impractical with ordinary types of relays or switching elements. Figure 2 indicates schematically such an exchange. There are M memory relays numbered $1, 2, \ldots, M$. Each possible configuration of calls is given a binary number from 0 to 2^M and associated with the corresponding configuration of the relay positions. We have just enough such positions to accommodate all desired interconnections of subscribers.

The switching network is a network of contacts on the memory relays such that when they are in a particular position the correct lines are connected together according to the correspondence decided upon. The control circuit is essentially merely a function table and requires, therefore, no memory. When a call is completed or a new call originated the desired configuration of the holding relays is compared with the present configuration and voltages applied to or eliminated from all relays that should be changed.

Needless to say, an exchange of this type, although using the minimum memory, has many disadvantages, as often occurs when we minimize a design for one parameter without regard to other important characteristics. In particular in Fig. 2 the following may be noted: (1) Each of the memory relays must carry an enormous number of contacts. (2) At each new call or completion of an old call a large fraction of the memory relays must change position, resulting in short relay life and interfering transients in the conversations. (3) Failure of one of the memory relays would put the exchange completely out of commission.

3. The Separate Memory Condition

The impracticality of an exchange with the absolute minimum memory suggests that we investigate the memory requirements with more realistic assumptions. In particular, let us assume that in operation a separate part of the memory can be assigned to each call in progress. The completion of a current call or the origination of a new call will not disturb the state of the memory elements associated with any call in progress. This assumption is reasonably well satisfied by standard types of exchanges, and is very natural to avoid the difficulties (2) and (3) occurring in an absolute minimal design.

If the exchange is to accommodate S simultaneous conversations there must be at least S separate memories. Furthermore, if there are only this number, each[1] of these must have a capacity $\log \dfrac{N(N-1)}{2}$. To see this, suppose all other calls are completed except the one in a particular memory. The state of the entire exchange is then specified by the state of this particular memory. The call registered here can be between any pair of the N subscribers, giving a total of $N(N-1)/2$ possibilities. Each of these must correspond to a different state of the particular memory under consideration, and hence it has a capacity of least $\log N(N-1)/2$.

The total memory required is then

$$ M = S \log \frac{N(N-1)}{2}. \tag{4} $$

If the exchange must remember which subscriber of a pair originated the call we obtain

$$ M = S \log N(N-1). \tag{5} $$

or, very closely when N is large,

$$ M = 2S \log N. \tag{6} $$

[1] B. D. Holbrook has pointed out that by using more than S memories, each can have for certain ratios of $\dfrac{S}{N}$, a smaller memory, resulting in a net saving. This only occurs, however, with unrealistically high calling rates.

The approximation in replacing (5) by (6), of the order of $\frac{S}{N} \log e$, is equivalent to the memory required to allow connections to be set up from a subscriber to himself. With $N = 10,000$, $S = 1,000$, we obtain $M = 26,600$

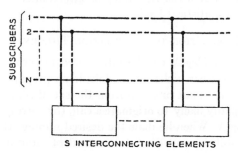

Fig. 3—Minimum separate memory exchange.

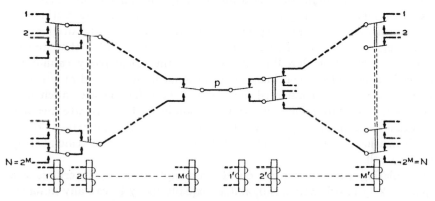

Fig. 4—Interconnecting network for Fig. 3.

from (6). The considerable discrepancy between this minimum required memory and the amount actually used in standard exchanges is due in part to the many control and supervision functions which we have ignored, and in part to statistical margins provided because of the limited access property.

The lower bound given by (6) is essentially realized with the schematic exchange of Fig. 3. Each box contains a memory $2 \log N$ and a contact network capable of interconnecting any pair of inputs, an ordered pair being associated with each possible state of the memory. Figure 4 shows such an interconnection network. By proper excitation of the memory relays 1, 2, $\cdots$, M, the point p can be connected to any of the $N = 2^m$ subscribers on the left. The relays $1'$, $2'$, $\cdots$, M' connect p to the called subscriber on the right. The general scheme of Fig. 3 is not too far from standard methods, although the contact load on the memory elements is still impractical. In actual panel, crossbar and step-by-step systems the equivalents of the memory boxes are given limited access to the lines in order to reduce the contact loads. This reduces the flexibility of interconnection, but only by a small amount on a statistical basis.

4. Relation to Information Theory

The formula $M = 2S \log N$ can be interpreted in terms of information theory.[2] When a subscriber picks up his telephone preparatory to making a call, he in effect singles out one line from the set of N, and if we regard all subscribers as equally likely to originate a call, the corresponding amount of information is $\log N$. When he dials the desired number there is a second choice from N possibilities and the total amount of information associated with the origin and destination of the call is $2 \log N$. With S possible simultaneous calls the exchange must remember $2S \log N$ units of information.

The reason we obtain the "separate memory" formula rather than the absolute minimum memory by this argument is that we have overestimated the information produced in specifying the call. Actually the originating subscribers must be one of those not already engaged, and is therefore in general a choice from less than N. Similarly the called party cannot be engaged; if the called line is busy the call cannot be set up and requires no memory of the type considered here. When these factors are taken into account the absolute minimum formula is obtained. The separate memory condition is essentially equivalent to assuming the exchange makes no use of information it already has in the form of current calls in remembering the next call.

Calculating the information on the assumption that subscribers are equally likely to originate a call, and are equally likely to call any number, corresponds to the maximum possible information or "entropy" in communication theory. If we assume instead, as is actually the case, that certain interconnections have a high *a priori* probability, with others relatively small, it is possible to make a certain statistical saving in memory.

This possibility is already exploited to a limited extent. Suppose we have two nearby communities. If a call originates in either community, the probability that the called subscriber will be in the same community is much greater than that of his being in the other. Thus, each of the exchanges can be designed to service its local traffic and a small number of intercommunity calls. This results in a saving of memory. If each exchange has N subscribers and we consider, as a limiting case, no traffic between exchanges,

[2] C. E. Shannon, "A Mathematical Theory of Communication," *Bell System Technical Journal*, Vol. 27, pp. 379–423, and 623–656, July and October 1948.

the total memory by (6) would be $4S \log N$, while with all $2N$ subscribers in the same exchange $4S \log 2N$ would be required.

The saving just discussed is possible because of a group effect. There are also statistics involving the calling habits of individual subscribers. A typical subscriber may make ninety per cent of his calls to a particular small number of individuals with the remaining ten per cent perhaps distributed randomly among the other subscribers. This effect can also be used to reduce memory requirements, although paper designs incorporating this feature appear too complicated to be practical.

ACKNOWLEDGMENT

The writer is indebted to C. A. Lovell and B. D. Holbrook for some suggestions incorporated in the paper.

A SYMMETRICAL NOTATION FOR NUMBERS

C. E. SHANNON, Bell Telephone Laboratories

The possibility of representing real numbers in various scales of notation is well known. Thus, in the scale r an arbitrary positive number b may be expanded in the form,

$$b = \sum_{-\infty}^{N} a_n r^n, \qquad 0 \leq a_n \leq r - 1,$$

and represented in the "decimal" notation as $a_N a_{N-1} \cdots a_0 \cdot a_{-1} a_{-2} \cdots$. Negative numbers are represented by prefixing a minus sign to the representation of the corresponding positive numbers. Although it seems unlikely that the scale ten will ever be changed for ordinary work, the use of other scales and systems of notation is still of practical as well as mathematical interest. In some types of computing machines, for example, scales other than ten lend themselves more readily to mechanization.

A slight modification of the ordinary expansion gives a representation for numbers with certain computational advantages. Assuming r to be odd, it is seen easily that any positive or negative number b can be represented as

$$b = \sum_{-\infty}^{N} a_n r^n, \qquad -\frac{r-1}{2} \leq a_n \leq \frac{r-1}{2},$$

and we may denote b as usual by the sequence of its digits

$$b = a_N \cdots a_0 \cdot a_{-1} \cdots .$$

Both positive and negative numbers are thus represented by a standard notation without a prefixed sign, the sign being implied by the digits themselves; the number is positive or negative according as the first (nonvanishing) digit is greater or less than zero. Every real number has a unique representation apart from those whose expansion ends in an infinite sequence of the digits $(r-1)/2$ or $-(r-1)/2$, each of which has two representations. If this notation were to be used, a simple notation should be invented for the negative digits which suggested their close relation to the corresponding positive digits. For typographical simplicity we shall here denote the negative digits by placing primes on the corresponding positive digits. The notation for the first nine positive and negative integers with $r = 3, 5, 7, 9$ is as follows:

r	-9	-8	-7	-6	-5	-4	-3	-2	-1
3	1′00	1′01	1′11′	1′10	1′11	1′1′	1′0	1′1	1′
5	2′1	2′2	1′2′	1′1′	1′0	1′1	1′2	2′	1′
7	1′2′	1′1′	1′0	1′1	1′2	1′3	3′	2′	1′
9	1′0	1′1	1′2	1′3	1′4	4′	3′	2′	1′

r	0	1	2	3	4	5	6	7	8	9
3	0	1	11'	10	11	11'1'	11'0	11'1	101'	100
5	0	1	2	12'	11'	10	11	12	22'	21'
7	0	1	2	3	13'	12'	11'	10	11	12
9	0	1	2	3	4	14'	13'	12'	11'	10

In general the negative of any number is found by placing a prime on each unprimed digit and taking it off each primed digit. Arithmetic operations with this system are considerably simplified. In the first place the symmetries introduced by this notation make the addition and multiplication tables much easier to learn. For the scale $r = 9$ these tables are, respectively, as follows:

$+$	4'	3'	2'	1'	0	1	2	3	4
4'	1'1	1'2	1'3	1'4	4'	3'	2'	1'	0
3'	1'2	1'3	1'4	4'	3'	2'	1'	0	1
2'	1'3	1'4	4'	3'	2'	1'	0	1	2
1'	1'4	4'	3'	2'	1'	0	1	2	3
0	4'	3'	2'	1'	0	1	2	3	4
1	3'	2'	1'	0	1	2	3	4	14'
2	2'	1'	0	1	2	3	4	14'	13'
3	1'	0	1	2	3	4	14'	13'	12'
4	0	1	2	3	4	14'	13'	12'	11'

$\cdot$	4'	3'	2'	1'	0	1	2	3	4
4'	22'	13	11'	4	0	4'	1'1	1'3'	2'2
3'	13	10	13'	3	0	3'	1'3	1'0	1'3'
2'	11'	13'	4	2	0	2'	4'	1'3	1'1
1'	4	3	2	1	0	1'	2'	3'	4'
0	0	0	0	0	0	0	0	0	0
1	4'	3'	2'	1'	0	1	2	3	4
2	1'1	1'3	4'	2'	0	2	4	13'	11'
3	1'3'	1'0	1'3	3'	0	3	13'	10	13
4	2'2	1'3'	1'1	4'	0	4	11'	13	22'

The labor in learning the tables would appear to be reduced by a factor of at least two from the corresponding $r = 9$ case in ordinary notation. There is no need to learn a "subtraction table"; to subtract, one primes all digits of the subtrahend and adds. The sign of the difference automatically comes out correct, and the clumsy device of "borrowing" is unnecessary. More generally, to add a set of numbers, some positive and some negative, all are placed in a column without regard to sign and added, e.g. ($r = 9$):

(1')		(1)		carried numbers.
1	3'	1'	2	
2'	3	1	4	
4'	1'	2	3	
3	2'	3'	4	
3	0	0	1'	
1'	2'	1	3'	
1'	4	1	0	

This process may be contrasted with the usual method where the positive and negative numbers must be added separately, the smaller sum subtracted from the larger and the difference given the sign of the larger, that is, three addition or subtraction processes and a sign rule, while with the symmetrical system one standard addition process covers all cases. Furthermore, in such a sum cancellation is very common and reduces considerably the size of numbers to be carried in memory in adding a column; this follows from the fact that any digit cancels its negative and these may be struck out from a column without affecting the sum. If all digits are equally likely and independent, the sum in a column will have a mean value zero, standard deviation $\sqrt{p(r^2-1)/12}$ where p is the number of numbers being added, while in the usual notation the mean value is $p(r/2)$ with the same standard deviation.

Multiplication and division may be carried out also by the usual processes, and here again signs take care of themselves, although in these cases, of course, the advantage of this is not so great.

We may note also that in the usual system of notation, when we wish to "round off" a number by replacing all digits after a certain point by zeros, the digits after this point must be inspected to see whether they are greater or less than 5 in the first place following the point. In the former case the preceding digit is increased by one. With the symmetrical system one always obtains the closest approximation merely by replacing the following digits by zeros. Numbers such as $1.444 \cdots = 2.4'4'4' \cdots$ with two representations are exactly half way between the two nearest rounded off approximations, and in this case we obtain the upper or lower approximation depending on which representation is rounded off. If we were using this notation, department stores would find it much more difficult to camouflage the price of goods with $.98 labels.

We have assumed until now that the scale r is odd. If r is even, say 10, a slightly unbalanced system of digits can be used; for example, 4', 3', 2', 1', 0, 1, 2, 3, 4, 5. The dissymmetry introduced unfortunately loses several of the advantages described above, e.g., the ease of negation and hence of subtraction, and also the round off property.

A more interesting possibility is that of retaining symmetry by choosing for "digits" numbers halfway between the integers. In the case $r = 10$ the possible digits would be

$$a_n = \frac{9'}{2}, \frac{7'}{2}, \frac{5'}{2}, \frac{3'}{2}, \frac{1'}{2}, \frac{1}{2}, \frac{3}{2}, \frac{5}{2}, \frac{7}{2}, \frac{9}{2},$$

and any number b can be expressed as

$$b = \sum_{-\infty}^{N} a_n r^n.$$

In this system the properties of positive-negative symmetry, automatic handling of signs, and simple round off are retained. One curious and disadvantageous feature is that the integers can only be represented as infinite decimals, and this is possible in an infinite number of different ways. For example.

$$0 = \cdot\frac{1}{2}\frac{9'}{2}\frac{9'}{2}\cdots = \frac{1}{2}\cdot\frac{9'}{2}\frac{9'}{2}\frac{9'}{2}\cdots = \frac{1'}{2}\cdot\frac{9}{2}\frac{9}{2}\frac{9}{2}\cdots \text{ etc.}$$

Symmetrical notation offers attractive possibilities for general purpose computing machines of the electronic or relay types. In these machines it is possible to perform the calculations in any desired scale and only translate to the scale ten at input and output. The use of a symmetrical notation simplifies many of the circuits required to take care of signs in addition and subtraction, and to properly round off numbers.

A Method of Power or Signal Transmission to a Moving Vehicle[*]

Claude E. Shannon

Abstract

This note describes a circuit for power or signal transmission or both to an object which may be placed anywhere on a surface in any orientation. The transmission is accomplished without trailing wires or an overhead trolley system. The circuit may have applications in the toy field for remotely controlled automobiles, in factories and warehouses for supplying power to fork lifts and delivery trucks, and in other fields.

The general method has many variants. Perhaps the simplest is shown in Figure 1. The floor is covered with strips of conducting material connected alternately to the plus and minus of the battery. The vehicle has four brushes rubbing on the floor. Three of these are located at the vertices of an equilateral triangle, and the fourth is at the center of the triangle.

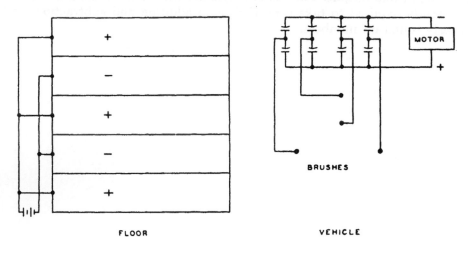

FLOOR   VEHICLE

FIG. 1

The altitude of the triangle is made greater than the width of the strips, and less than 1.5 times this width. In this case it is easily seen that for any orientation of the vehicle, and any position on the floor, at least one brush is contacting a positive strip and at least one brush contacts a negative strip. If the triangle altitude is, say, 1.25 times the strip width there is a margin sufficient to allow for insulating strips between the conducting strips, and to avoid short circuits when a brush passes from one strip to the next.

---

[*]   Bell Laboratories Memorandum, July 19, 1950.

The brushes are connected as shown to eight rectifying elements. These might be, for example, two selenium bridge rectifiers. It will be seen that there is always a forward path from plus battery through the rectifiers, motor, and back to minus battery. All direct paths from plus to minus pass through at least one rectifier in the reverse direction, and therefore do not cause short circuits.

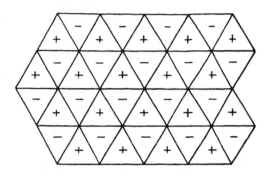

FIG. 2

The general scheme can be varied in many ways. In place of alternate strips, the floor can be made a checkerboard or interlaced triangles, or other patterns (Figure 2). More brushes and other arrangements of the brushes can be used. Those in Figure 3 give a larger margin for error in positioning, or allow narrower conducting strips on the floor at the cost of more rectifiers. The width of the conducting strips can be reduced as much as desired by using a sufficiently large number of brushes. Figure 4 shows a brush arrangement for this. If n brushes are used equally spaced along the arms of a three-pointed star, the ratio of conducting width to insulating width can be reduced to about $4 / n$. In this case the brushes along an arm can be connected together to the same rectifier pair over a length of the arm not greater than the spacing d between conducting segments. Thus as before only eight rectifiers are necessary. In the limit one obtains a group of four continuous linear brushes and very narrow conducting strips.

FIG. 3

Another possibility is that of going to an array of point contacts on the floor, say at the corners of a checkerboard, and to use brushes which cover a sizable area. This would reduce the possibility of accidental short circuits from metal dropped on the floor. The point contacts might even be recessed in the floor and drawn up magnetically when needed.

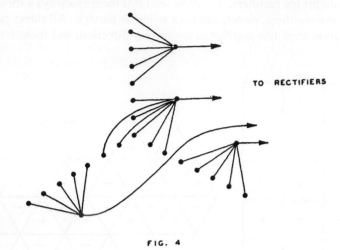

FIG. 4

It may be noted that AC as well as DC may be used from primary power. The rectifiers rectify the AC in their operation, so the motor could be a DC motor. When operated on DC, signalling could be accomplished over the same two-wire circuit by various superimposed AC frequencies, with separating filters on the vehicle.

Presentation of a Maze-Solving Machine*

Claude E. Shannon

This is a maze-solving machine that is capable of solving a maze by trial-and-error means, of remembering the solution, and also of forgetting it in case the situation changes and the solution is no longer applicable. I think this machine may be of interest in view of its connection with the problems of trial-and-error learning, forgetting and feedback systems.

As you can see (Figs. 1 and 2) there is a maze on the top panel of the machine which has a range of 5 × 5 squares. The maze can be changed in any desired manner by rearranging the partitions between the twenty-five squares. In the maze there is a sensing finger, which can feel the partitions of the maze as it comes against them. This finger is moved by two motors, an east-west motor and a north-south motor. The problem facing the machine is to move the finger through the maze to the goal. The goal is mounted on a pin which can be slipped into a jack in any of the twenty-five squares. Thus you can change the problem any way you choose, within the limits of the 5 × 5 maze. I will turn it on so you can see it, in the first place, trying to solve the maze. When the machine was turned off, the relays essentially forgot everything they knew, so that they are now starting afresh, with no knowledge of the maze.

Savage: Does that mean they are in a neutral position, neither to the right nor the left?

Shannon: They are in a kind of nominal position. It isn't really a neutral position but a meaningless one.

You see the finger now exploring the maze, hunting for the goal. When it reaches the center of a square, the machine makes a new decision as to the next direction to try. If the finger hits a partition, the motors reverse, taking the finger back to the center of the square, where a new direction is chosen. The choices are based on previous knowledge and according to a certain strategy, which is a bit complicated.

Pitts: It is a fixed strategy? It is not a randomization?

Shannon: There is no random element present. I first considered using a probability element, but decided it was easier to do it with a fixed strategy. The sensing finger in its exploration has now reached the goal, and this stops the motors, lights a lamp on the finger, and rings a bell. The machine has solved the maze. I will now run the finger, manually, back to the starting point, and you will see that the machine remembers the solution it has found. When I turn it on, it goes directly to the goal without striking the partitions or making side excursions into blind alleys. It is able to go directly to the goal from any part of the maze that it has visited in its exploration. If I now move the finger to a part of the maze that it has not explored, it will fumble around until it reaches a known region. From there it goes directly to the goal.

Now I should like to show you one further feature of the machine. I will change the maze so that the solution the machine found no longer works. By moving the partitions in a suitable way, I can obtain a rather interesting effect. In the previous maze the proper solution starting from Square A led to Square B, then to C, and on to the goal. By changing the partitions I have forced the machine at Square C to go to a new square, Square D, and from there back to the original square, A. When it arrives at A, it remembers that the old solution said to go to B, and so it goes around the circle A, B, C, D, A, B, C, D.... It has established a vicious circle, or a singing condition.

* Transactions 8th Cybernetics Conference, Josiah Macy Jr. Foundation, 1952.

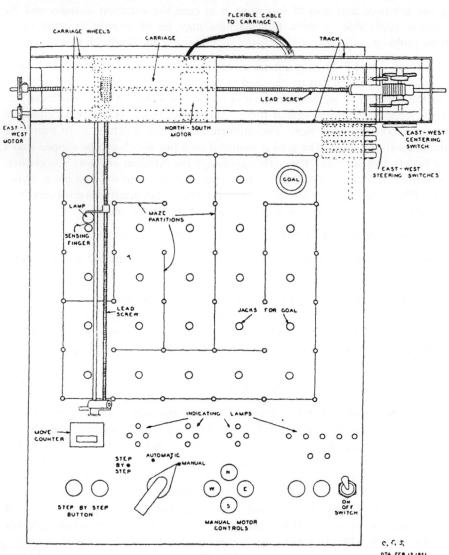

Figure 1

Figure 2

Gerard: A neurosis.

Shannon: Yes.

Savage: It can't do that when its mind is blank, but it can do it after it has been conditioned?

Shannon: Yes, only after it has been conditioned. However, the machine has an antineurotic circuit built in to prevent just this sort of situation.

Mead: After it has done it a number of times?

Shannon: After it has gone around the circle about six times, it will break out. The relay circuit includes a counter which stops this behavior at the twenty-fourth count.

Frank: How many relays are there in it?

Shannon: All told, there are about seventy-five relays.

Savage: It doesn't have any way to recognize that it is "psycho"; it just recognizes that it has been going too long?

Shannon: Yes. As you see, it has now gone back to the exploring strategy.

Teuber: Now, does it have to relearn the entire maze, or can it still utilize some form of it?

Shannon: No. As it stands, it can't utilize any information it had before.

Savage: But it is trying to utilize it, I suppose. It is moving as it would move.

Shannon: As a matter of fact, the old information is doing it harm.

Bigelow: I think it's getting to it.

Shannon: Yes, it is gradually working over toward the goal. I should like to spend the rest of my time explaining some of the things which are involved in the operation of the machine.

The strategy by which the machine operates can be described as follows: There are two modes of operation, which I call the "exploration strategy" and the "goal strategy." They are both quite simple. The exploration strategy is used when it is first trying to find the goal. For each square in the maze, there is associated a memory, consisting of two relays. These are capable of remembering one of four possible directions: north, east, south, or west. The direction that is remembered for a square is the direction by which the sensing finger left the square the last time it visited that square. Those are the only data the machine remembers about the course of the finger through the maze. There are some other memory functions in the computing part of the circuit, but these remembered directions are the data which allow it to reproduce its path at a later time.

Now, let's call the remembered direction for a particular square, D, considered as a vector. In exploration strategy, the machine takes the vector D and rotates it 90° as the first choice when it comes into a square. For example, suppose it left a square in the easterly direction at the last visit. If it comes to that square again, it will try the northern direction as the first choice. If it hits a barrier and comes back, it again rotates 90°, because it has just put this northern direction into the memory, and advancing 90°, it tries the westerly direction, and so on. The choices progress around counterclockwise, starting with the direction by which it left the square last time – with one exception: it also remembers the direction by which it came into the square at the current visit, and on the first rotation of the vector D, it skips that direction of entrance. This is to prevent the path repeating too much. Before that feature was installed, there was a tendency to explore up to a new square, go back through the entire maze, and then go one square further, and so on; and it took a very long time to solve the maze. It required about three times as long as it does now, with this skipping feature added.

When it hits the goal, a relay operates and locks in, and the machine then acts according to the goal strategy, which is also based on this vector D.

In the goal strategy, the machine takes as its first choice direction D, which is the direction by which it left the square on its last visit. This is very simple to do, and it has many convenient features for maze solving, because it cancels out all blind alleys and circular paths. Since a blind alley must be left by way of the same square through which it was entered, the direction D retained for that square will necessarily lead to the goal directly rather than by way of the side excursion into the blind alley. In a similar way, if the machine follows a circular or re-entrant path in exploring its way to the goal, the direction retained for the last fork in this path must be that going to the goal rather than around the side loop. As a consequence, the machine follows a fairly direct path to the goal after it has first found its way there.

The final feature of forgetting is obtained as follows: After reaching the goal, suppose we move the sensing finger to a different point in the maze and start it operating. The machine then starts counting the number of moves it takes, and if it does not reach the goal within a certain specified number of moves, which happens to be twenty-four in this case, the machine decides that the maze has been changed or that it is in a circular loop, or something of that sort, and that the previous solution is no longer relevant. The circuit then reverts to the exploration-type strategy which is mathematically guaranteed to solve any finite solvable maze.

There are a few other points about the machine which may be of some interest. The memory is quite undifferentiated in the sense that I can take the group of wires leading from the rest of the circuit into the memory, shift them over either in the north-south or east-west directions, and the machine will still operate correctly, with no significant change, although the data corresponding to a square are then stored in a different part of the memory.

Another point is that there are, of course, a large number of feedback loops in this system. The most prominent is the feedback loop from the sensing finger through the circuit to the driving motors and back to the sensing finger, by mechanical motion of the motors. Normally, if you have a feedback loop and change the sign of the feedback, it completely ruins the operation of the system. There is ordinarily a great difference between positive and negative feedbacks. This maze-solving machine, however, happens to be such that you can change either or both of the signs in the feedback connections, and the machine still operates equally well. What it amounts to within the circuit is that the significance of right and left is interchanged; in other words, the effect on the strategy if one of the feedback loops is changed is that the advance of 90° counterclockwise becomes an advance of 90° clockwise. If both of them are changed, the strategy is not altered.

Von Foerster: If there are two different ways to reach the target, certainly the machine is only able to find one. Does the possibility point to its making a choice of the better way?

Shannon: No, it does not necessarily choose the best way, although the probabilities are in favor of its choosing the shorter of two paths. Incidentally, the exploration strategy of this machine will solve any maze whether it be simply or multiply connected. Some of the classic solutions of the maze problem are satisfactory only in the case of simply connected mazes. An example is the method of keeping your hand always on the right-hand wall. While this will solve any simply connected maze, it often fails if there are closed loops.

Savage: This cyclical feature that you illustrated occurred because the machine was not then in really searching condition?

Shannon: No, it was in the goal strategy rather than in the exploratory.

Savage: A goal strategy is to go the way you last went, but what are you to do if the attempt to do that is frustrated?

Shannon: Then it returns to the center of the square and advances 90° and tries that direction. But it still remains in goal strategy.

Savage: I see. When it gets into the next square, it tries to go ahead in the accustomed direction?

Shannon: That's right. The purpose of this is that it may have learned most of a maze in its first exploration, but not quite all of it. If we put it into a square it has not visited, it explores around by trial and error until it reaches a familiar square, and from there goes directly to the goal. The previously unknown squares have by this process been added to its previous solution.

Bigelow: You can then put new loops on any known path; it will learn those new loops immediately and not get into trouble. Is that right?

Shannon: That's right.

Bigelow: Because when you come back to the main stream, the search goes in the right direction, if it recognizes that square.

Shannon: I am not sure I understand what you mean.

Bigelow: It forms a single-directional path. Now, then, if you introduce a new path which brings it out of the known path into strange territory, back into the known path again –

Shannon: Such a side path is completely canceled when it has gone into the goal strategy.

Bigelow: But once you start it around that circuit, then the procedure is correct after the starting point.

Shannon: If it is in goal strategy, yes, but not in exploratory.

Bigelow: What would you have to do to minimize running time – in order to make it learn on repeated trials eventually to take the shortest possible path in a more complex maze?

Shannon: I think that would require a considerable amount of memory in the form of relays, because of the need to store up a number of different solutions of the maze as well as additional computing relays to compare and evaluate them. It surely could be done, but it would be more difficult; it would mean a much more complicated machine than this.

Savage: And it would have to decide when to invest the effort to seek a new path. That is really a very important problem in any kind of real human learning. If you can already peel a potato, why should you take the trouble to find a better way to peel it? Perhaps you are already peeling it correctly. How do you know?

Von Foerster: What happens if there is no goal?

Shannon: If there is no goal, the machine establishes a periodic path, searching for the goal; that is, it gradually works out a path which goes through every square and tries every barrier, and if it doesn't find the goal, the path is repeated again and again. The machine just continues looking for the goal throughout every square, making sure that it looks at every square.

Frank: It is all too human.

Brosin: George Orwell, the late author of *1984*, should have seen this.[*]

Von Foerster: And after that? For instance, if you put a goal into the path after the machine has established such a periodic motion, what happens then?

---

[*]   Orwell, G.: *1984*. New York, Harcourt, Brace & Co., 1949 and Signet Books, 1950.

Shannon: When it hits the goal, the machine stops and changes into the goal strategy, and from there on it goes to the goal as placed there. Incidentally, it is interesting to think of this – if I can speak mathematically for a moment – in the following way. For each of the twenty-five squares, the memory of the machine retains a vector field defined over the 5 × 5 maze. As the sensing finger moves through the maze, it continually revises this remembered vector field in such a way that the vectors point along possible paths of the maze leading to the point currently occupied by the finger.

Teuber: If you rotate the field through 180°, would it continue to function?

McCulloch: Suppose you reverse the connections and leave the motor, so that you reverse your direction of rotation; can it still find its way?

Shannon: Only if I reverse some switches within the machine which tell it what square it is currently occupying. If I reverse the motors, I must change these switches to compensate. Otherwise, it would think it was moving one way and put that in the memory and actually be moving in a different direction.

Gerard: That would be like cross-suturing the motor nerves of animals and getting flexion when you want extension.

Bigelow: Have you considered how difficult it would be to have a circuit which, instead of forgetting everything, goes back to the origin and remembers what it did at the first square but tries something else, say, the opposite search sequence? When that produces no new solution, go back where it was, in the second square, but try the opposite, therefore asking for the possibility of replacing each square in its memory as it goes systematically through. In other words, this would require a very small addition of memory because it need only remember the entire past pattern once, but then, having reached the state where goal behavior is no longer a solution (which it knows by exceeding "N" trials), then, instead of erasing its entire thinking, you have a switching technique where it goes back to the origin, and then tests each hypothesis in turn, and finds the particular one to replace.

Shannon: I haven't considered that, but I think it would be rather slow, because there is a great deal of backtracking in that procedure, back to the origin, as it tries out different hypotheses.

Bigelow: If it knows how to get from the origin to the target, does it not always know how to get from the target back to the origin, by a very simple reversal of the switches?

Shannon: No. You see, this vector field, if you like, is unique in going in the direction of the vectors, but going backward, there are branch points, so it does not know where it came from.

Savage: Does this vector field flow into the target from every point?

Shannon: Yes, if you follow the vectors you will get to the goal, but, going in reverse, you may come to branch points from which you may go in any of various directions. You can't say where the sensing finger came from by studying the memory.

Savage: It is not organized around any particular initial point; and that is one of the features of it, that once it has learned the maze, if you start it anywhere where it has been on its way to the maze, it continues; if you start it where it hasn't been, it finds one of those places where it has been, and then continues.

McCulloch: Like a man who knows the town, so he can go from any place to any other place, but doesn't always remember how he went.

A Mind-Reading (?) Machine*

Claude E. Shannon

This machine is a somewhat simplified model of a machine designed by D. W. Hagelbarger. It plays what is essentially the old game of matching pennies or "odds and evens." This game has been discussed from the game theoretic angle by von Neumann and Morgenstern, and from the psychological point of view by Edgar Allen Poe in the "The Purloined Letter." Oddly enough, the machine is aimed more nearly at Poe's method of play than von Neumann's.

To play against the machine, the player should guess out loud either "right" or "left." The center button of the machine is then pressed and the machine will light up either the right or left light. If the machine matches the player, the machine wins, otherwise the player wins. The player should then move the key switch in the direction corresponding to the choice he made. The machine will then register a win for the machine or the player, as the case may be, by shooting a ball into the proper glass tube. The overall score against all players since the machine was started is shown on the two counters visible through the front panel.

The Strategy of Operation

Basically, the machine looks for certain types of patterns in the behavior of its human opponent. If it can find these patterns it remembers them and assumes that the player will follow the patterns the next time the same situation arises. The machine also contains a random element. Until patterns have been found, or if an assumed pattern is not repeated at least twice by the player, the machine chooses its move at random.

The types of patterns remembered involve the outcome of two successive plays (that is, whether or not the player won on those plays) and whether he changed his choice between them and after them. There are eight possible situations and, for each of these, two things the player can do. The eight situations are:

1. The player wins, plays the same, and wins. He may then play the same or differently.

2. The player wins, plays the same, and loses. He may then play the same or differently.

3. The player wins, plays differently, and wins. He may then play the same or differently.

4. The player wins, plays differently, and loses. He may then play the same or differently.

5. The player loses, plays the same, and wins. He may then play the same or differently.

6. The player loses, plays the same, and loses. He may then play the same or differently.

7. The player loses, plays differently, and wins. He may then play the same or differently.

8. The player loses, plays differently, and loses. He may then play the same or differently.

* Bell Laboratories Memorandum, March 18, 1953.

Each of these corresponds to a different cell in the memory of the machine. Within the cell two things are registered: (1) whether, the last time this situation arose, the player played the same or differently; (2) whether or not the behavior indicated in (1) was a repeat of the same behavior in the next preceding similar situation. Thus consider the situation win, same, lose. Suppose that the last time this situation occurred in the game the player played "differently". Then "differently" is recorded in the (1) part of this memory cell. If the preceding time this situation arose the player also played "differently", the (2) part of the memory cell registers this as a repeat. The machine will assume, should this situation arise again, that this is a definite pattern in the player's behavior and will play correspondingly. If the player has not repeated, the machine plays from its random element. The memory cells are always kept up to date. A particular memory cell, for example, will change from one prediction to the opposite in two repetitions of the corresponding situation.

A mathematical analysis of the strategy used in this machine shows that it can be beaten by the best possible play in the ratio 3:1. To do this it is necessary to keep track of the contents of all the memory cells in the machine. The player should repeat a behavior pattern twice, and then when the machine is prepared to follow this pattern the player should alter it. It is extremely difficult to carry out this program mentally because of the amount of memory and calculation necessary.

The ball counter used in this machine for score keeping is an application of the conservation of momentum principle. If a ball is struck against a stationary row of equal balls, the momentum of the first ball is transferred down the line and the last ball in the row moves off with the velocity of the original striking ball. In this counter the momentum is transferred through a row of up to fifty balls!

The random element in the machine is actually a commutator rotating at about 10 revolutions per second. Two brushes separated by 180° bear on this commutator. A copper segment of the commutator contacts the brushes alternately. When the button is pressed and a random choice is to be made, the first brush contacted by the commutator determines whether the choice be "right" or "left". Basically, therefore, the randomness of the device depends on the uncertainty of the interval between moves, the variation of which due to human variability is typically large compared to the tenth of a second period of the commutator.

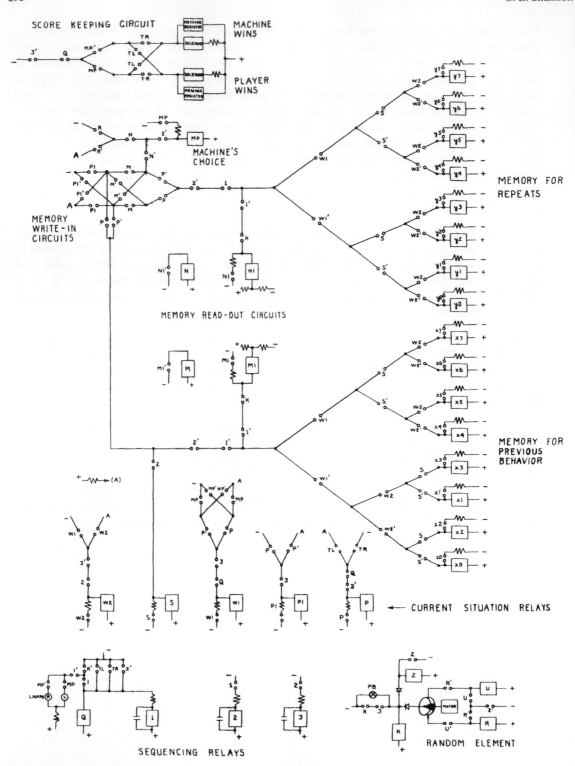

SCORE KEEPING CIRCUIT

MACHINE WINS

PLAYER WINS

MACHINE'S CHOICE

MEMORY WRITE-IN CIRCUITS

MEMORY READ-OUT CIRCUITS

MEMORY FOR REPEATS

MEMORY FOR PREVIOUS BEHAVIOR

CURRENT SITUATION RELAYS

SEQUENCING RELAYS

RANDOM ELEMENT

"MIND READING" MACHINE

The Potentialities of Computers*

Claude E. Shannon

In atomic energy it has been suggested that we have a bear by the tail. In the development of computing machines I think we have something like a very active and rapidly growing cub by the tail. While the advent of computing was by no means as spectacular and dramatic as that of atomic energy, its end effects promise to be quite as important for the average man.

While the front pages of our newspapers have been carrying articles about the latest bomb explosion, inside we find notes about mechanical ''brains,'' the newest high speed calculators, machines playing chess and the like. What are these large-scale computers, and what are their capacities and limitations?

Historically, primitive computing machines such as the Chinese abacus can be traced back almost as far as civilization itself. However, the first real attempt at a modern calculator goes back only about a century to George Babbage, who, far ahead of his time, attempted to develop a machine capable of carrying out a long series of calculations. Financial and technical difficulties prevented the completion of Babbage's dream, and the art lapsed until just before World War II. During the war, with the increased flexibility and speed of electronic devices, it became possible to design modern large scale computers. Since the war the field has been developing at a constantly accelerating rate.

Most of us are familiar with the adding machines used in banks and laboratories for ordinary calculations. How do large-scale computers differ from these? In the first place they are enormously faster — an electronic computer can add two numbers in one ten-thousandth of a second. In a half hour it can perform calculations which would require a mathematician with a desk computer a year to complete. In the second place, they have large internal memories in which they can store data concerning the problem, intermediate results of their calculations and final answers. Finally and perhaps most important, the machines are programmed. This means that it is possible to write out in advance a long series of instructions telling the machine what to do. When this set of instructions, known as the program, is fed into the machine, it faithfully carries them out, one by one, at extremely high speed. The instructions enable the machine to perform all the basic operations of arithmetic, addition, subtraction, multiplication and division and usually various other mathematical operations. The instructions enable the machine to store information in its memory and read it out at a later time. In addition, there are certain very important instructions which enable the machine to make a choice or decision between various lines of behavior. The choice is ordinarily determined by results that the machine will have available only when the time comes to make the choice. In other words, the machine makes a decision which the man who writes the program cannot exactly foresee, since he does not have the data available when writing the instructions on which the decision is to be made. These seemingly innocuous decision instructions can lead, by being compounded, to the machine performing acts which the man who wrote the program foresaw only very vaguely or perhaps not at all, acts akin to thinking, rational decisions, problem solving and learning.

---

* Bell Laboratories Memorandum, April 3, 1953.

While it is literally true that these computers do only what we tell them to do, it is possible to phrase what we tell them to do in such broad terms, involving so many "ifs, ands and buts," that we can hardly say ourselves what we told them to do. It would in fact take a computing machine to find out. Put another way, it is possible to instruct them in certain general principles of behavior, so general that the specific outcome in various situations comes as a complete surprise even to the man who wrote the instructions for the machine. Indeed, the potentialities of programming are so great that we have at present only scratched the surface. Programs have been set up by which machines erase and rewrite parts of their own programs and then follow the instructions which they have written for themselves.

What can we expect in the development of computing machines in the next 20 or 30 years? The computers are largely a result of a cooperation between two groups of scientists- mathematicians and electronic engineers. The engineers construct the machines, and the mathematicians write the programs and use them. We have, then, two main streams of research relating to the hardware on the one hand and the logic on the other. With regard to the engineering aspects, many promising new lines are being explored — one of the most promising is the newly developed transistor which can perform most of the functions of the ordinary vacuum tube used in radios and TV sets and, in enormous quantities, in computing machines. The transistor has many advantages over the vacuum tube such as extremely small size, long life and low power consumption. Another promising recent development is the ferroelectric memory — a device which enables one to store information without power consumption in a very small space. Devices such as these suggest that the computers of the future may be extremely compact and use far less power than they do today. Other research is being carried on toward speeding up the already fantastic speeds of the computers and it is quite possible that in the near future they may operate 10 or even 100 times as rapidly as they do today.

Now let us take a look at the type of research the mathematicians are doing to improve the scope and use of computing machines. This work is aimed at the problems of finding out what computers can do and making it easier to program them.

At the present time, the major use of computers has been in solving mathematical problems involving a great deal of computation. These problems range from such pedestrian activities as tabulating and classifying census figures to solving the nuclear equations arising in atomic work. One of the most significant trends is that because of the high speed of these computers it becomes possible to solve many problems which previously were considered beyond the realm of practical calculation. As an example of this, one of the computers has been set up to solve the equations required for weather forecasting. Previous to the existence of high speed computers it would have taken many months to solve the equations for tomorrow's weather.

While the solving of straightforward mathematical problems is the bread and butter work of the computers, mathematicians are having a field day in exploiting the more general capabilities of these machines. A look at some of the current research will perhaps suggest the general trends we may expect in the future.

A frequently raised question and the cause of much friendly argument is "can computing machines think?". The answer, of course, depends partly on what is meant by "think" and also on whether you mean by "machines" computing machines we have today or machines we expect to have in, say, twenty years. It is certainly possible to program computers in such a way that they act very much as though they were thinking. For example, they can be set up to play various games with a certain amount of skill, games of the complexity of bridge or chess. A computer in England has recently been programmed to play a tolerably good game of checkers, the program consisting of a set of general principles, not specific moves, which the machine applies in whatever situations may arise in the game. Some machines have been built to play games skillfully enough to defeat the people who designed the machines, and here I speak from personal experience.

Another line of research being actively studied today is the problem of language translation by computing machine techniques. While still at a primitive level, it has already been demonstrated that it is possible for suitably programmed computers to give a crude translation from one language to another. The translations at present are faulty, containing many errors of grammar and of meaning, but are still sufficiently good that it is usually possible to understand the intended meaning of the original text. There is no doubt that refinements of the techniques will lead to more and more polished translations, although we hardly expect the machines to give an elegant rendition of, say, Goethe into English in the near future.

Another interesting line of research in the logic of computers is aimed toward making them learn from experience. Here again, the results so far can hardly compare with the abilities of human beings but are nevertheless highly suggestive. To cite some examples, a machine has been developed which solves mazes. A tiny mechanical mouse blunders about in a complicated maze, eventually, by trial and error, finding its way to the "cheese" in the corner. Placed in the same maze a second time, the mouse remembers the proper path and runs directly to the cheese with no mistakes. Its performance is considerably better than that of the average live mouse placed in the same situation.

Still another computer has been programmed to make symbolic shopping tours. Certain parts of its memory represent grocery stores, others hardware stores, and so on. The machine must learn the whereabouts and the products carried by these stores in such a way as to do its shopping efficiently. In this case, the original program of the machine is of a very general and flexible nature. As the machine learns the properties of its environment, it in effect writes for itself a set of much more specific instructions. This seems to me rather close to the manner in which we suppose animals and man adapt to their environment.

An aspect of animal behavior which has sometimes been held to be unique to life forms is the ability to reproduce. Is it possible for machines to duplicate this behavior? One of our leading mathematicians, von Neumann, has studied this problem from the mathematical point of view. Without actually constructing machines which do this, he has set up an abstract mathematical model of certain machines which operate, or should I say "live," in a rather generalized type of environment. One of those machines will collect parts from its environment and assemble them to produce a second machine of the same type, which then starts collecting parts to construct a third machine and so on *ad infinitum*. I hasten to add that this fascinating but somewhat sinister type of machine is not yet in production.

These are just a few of the many directions of research in the potentialities of computers. Dr. Ridenour will undoubtedly tell us in the next talk other more immediate and practical applications of computing machine techniques. Perhaps, however, these few examples will give you some feeling of the immense generality and flexibility of a modern high speed computing machine.

In view of the seemingly limitless potentialities, are there any problems which are difficult or impossible for computing machines to solve? On the abstract mathematical end, the English mathematician, Turing, has given one answer. He has shown that there are certain classes of problems of a very esoteric nature which it is impossible for any computing machine following the present day pattern of organization to solve. A typical problem of Turing's type is to design a machine which can tell, roughly speaking, whether any other machine presented to the first machine will eventually give an answer to the problem proposed it. Turing's results unfortunately give but cold comfort to those of us who wish to find an element of superiority of the human mind over the computing machine, for, as Turing points out, these problems are most likely also unsolvable for a human being.

There is another quite different realm of human activity which it is extremely difficult to duplicate by mechanical means. This is activity relating to artistic creation and aesthetic evaluation. While perhaps not impossible for suitably programmed computers, it will certainly be centuries rather than decades before machines are writing Shakespearean sonnets or Beethoven symphonies. It is here, rather than in the field of reasoning and logical deduction that man can continue to show a clear superiority.

Like many scientific advances, the development of computing machines has implications for man, both good and evil. There can be no turning back. What Wiener has called the Second Industrial Revolution, in which machines take over many of the control functions now performed by men, is already under way. There will be short range problems of technological unemployment and sociological adjustment. These, however difficult they may seem at the time, can in the long run be solved, as they were in the first Industrial Revolution. There will be long range problems of a far more serious nature depending on man's ability to adjust to a world in which his mental powers are somehow devalued. Will he relapse into a Huxleyan Brave New World type of existence or will he be able to redirect his energies to higher cultural and spiritual values?

Throbac I*

Claude E. Shannon

Abstract

Throbac (THrifty ROman-numeral BAckward looking Computer) is a relay desk calculator operating entirely in the Roman numeral system. It performs the four operations of addition, subtraction, multiplication and division. The controls and method of operation are very similar to the Marchant desk calculator.

Operation. The power supply unit is plugged into a 110V AC socket and the cord from the calculator is plugged into any one of the two-prong sockets on the power supply. When the switch on the power supply unit is turned on, the computer is ready for operation.

Addition. To add a series of numbers, first clear the machine by pressing all three clear buttons. Enter the first number on the keyboard and press the + button momentarily. The first number will then appear on the lower or main accumulator dial. Clear the keyboard by means of the Keyboard Clear button, enter the second number on the keyboard and press the + button again. The sum of the first two numbers will then appear on the lower dial. Continue in the same manner for all numbers to be added.

The limit of the lower dial is 79 (LXXIX). Should a sum exceed this limit it will be reduced mod 80. Also, negative numbers will appear in terms of their complements mod 80, thus 95 will appear as 15 (XV), −7 will appear as 73 (LXXIII).

The successive digits (letters?) of a number entered on the keyboard need not be adjacent. For example, XVI can be entered with the X in the left-hand column, the V in the center column and the I in the right-hand column. The machine will accept correctly almost any reasonable notation for a number, not just the standard one. Thus 4 can be entered not only as IV but also IIII (as used on watch dials), IL is interpreted as 49 (XLIX), IIIIIV is interpreted as 0. Its rules of interpretation are as follows:

1. L always counts as +50.

2. X counts as +10 unless followed (not necessarily adjacently) by L, when it counts as −10.

3. V counts as +5 unless followed by L when it counts as −5. (Note that in any reasonably written Roman numeral V will not be followed by X.)

4. I counts as +1 unless followed by V, X or L when it counts as −1.

Subtraction. Enter the minuend in the keyboard and transfer it to the lower dial by pressing the + button. Clear the keyboard and enter the subtrahend there. Press the − button and the difference will appear on the lower dial.

Multiplication. *Before a multiplication be sure to press the clear upper button, even if nothing*

---

* Bell Laboratories Memorandum, April 9, 1953.

is registered in the upper dial. This erases memory of the previous multiplication. Enter the multiplicand in the keyboard. The multiplier is introduced digit by digit, *starting with its right-hand digit,* in the three multiplier buttons on the extreme right of the panel. Thus to multiply 7 by 8, press the Clear upper button, enter VII in the main keyboard and then press in sequence I, I, I, V in the multiplier buttons. Wait for the machine to stop at each stage before entering the next digit. The product will appear on the lower dial.

Division. Enter the dividend in the keyboard and transfer to the lower dial by pressing the + button. Clear the keyboard and enter the divisor there. Press the ÷ button. The quotient will appear in the upper dial and the remainder in the lower dial. *The limit of the quotient dial is 10* (the number of points on the stepping switch that was used). If the correct quotient is greater than 10, only 10 will appear on the upper dial.

General Principles of the Circuit. The central part of the Throbac circuit is a relay counter (see Fig. 1). The lowest section of this counter counts mod 5 and accumulates I's. The next section counts mod 2 and accumulates V's; the final section counts mod 80 and accumulates X's and L's. By entering this counter at appropriate points, I, V, X or L can be added to the number previously registered. When a reversing relay is operated, I, V, X or L can be subtracted from the previous number. Contacts on the relays in this counter control the lights of the lower dial, translating where necessary into standard Roman notation (thus IIII in the accumulator appears as IV on the dial).

A number entered in the keyboard is added into the accumulator by reading off the digits of the number sequentially from right to left and adding them (or subtracting) according to the rules of interpretation listed above. This sequence is controlled by a stepping switch. If in this sequence of additions an L occurs, a relay operates and locks in. The operation of this relay causes any I's, V's or X's thereafter to be subtracted. Other similar relays enforce the other rules of interpretation. When the addition is complete these relays are all automatically reset.

Subtraction is performed similarly but with an inversion of the add and subtract parts of this routine.

Multiplication is performed by successive addition. Pressing the V button, for example, causes the machine to add the contents of the keyboard into the accumulator five times. Here again there is a rule of interpretation, that the I button adds unless X or V has already been pressed. Since the multiplier is fed in from right to left this subtraction occurs only if the I is followed in the Roman numeral by X or V.

Division is accomplished by successive subtraction. When the divide button is pressed, the machine starts subtracting the contents of the keyboard from the number registered in the accumulator. After each subtraction, provided that subtraction did not make the number in the accumulator go negative, one unit is added into the upper dial. When the accumulator does go negative, the subtraction has gone one unit too far. The machine adds back the contents of the keyboard once to make up for this last subtraction and stops.

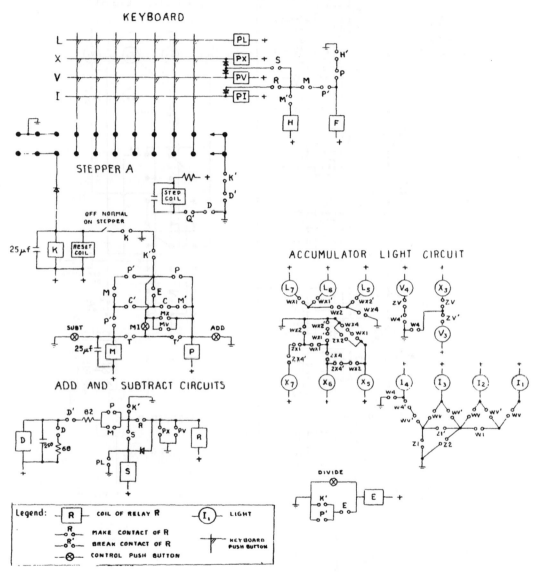

KEYBOARD

STEPPER A

OFF NORMAL ON STEPPER

ADD AND SUBTRACT CIRCUITS

ACCUMULATOR LIGHT CIRCUIT

DIVIDE

Legend:

	COIL OF RELAY R		LIGHT
R	MAKE CONTACT OF R		KEYBOARD PUSH BUTTON
R'	BREAK CONTACT OF R		
	CONTROL PUSH BUTTON		

THROBAC CIRCUIT DIAGRAM

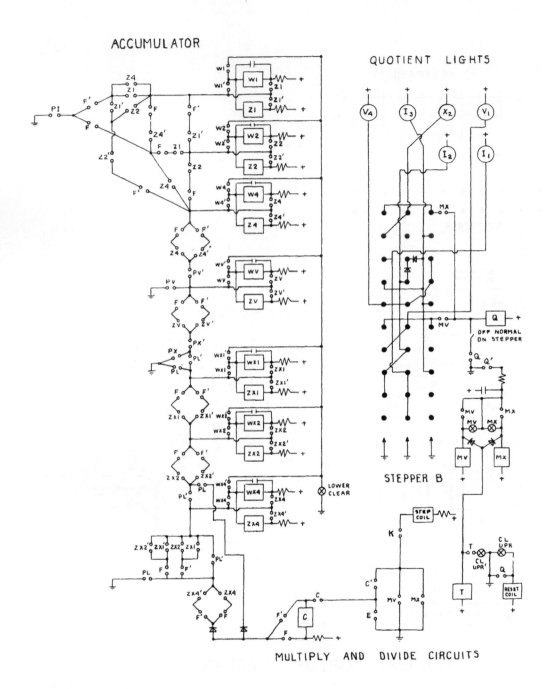

ACCUMULATOR

QUOTIENT LIGHTS

STEPPER B

MULTIPLY AND DIVIDE CIRCUITS

Machine Aid for Switching Circuit Design*

CLAUDE E. SHANNON†, FELLOW, IRE AND EDWARD F. MOORE†, ASSOCIATE, IRE

Summary—The design of circuits composed of logical elements may be facilitated by auxiliary machines. This paper describes one such machine, made of relays, selector switches, gas diodes, and germanium diodes. This machine (called the relay circuit analyzer) has as inputs both a relay contact circuit and the specifications the circuit is expected to satisfy. The analyzer (1) verifies whether the circuit satisfies the specifications, (2) makes systematic attempts to simplify the circuit by removing redundant contacts, and also (3) obtains mathematically rigorous lower bounds for the numbers and types of contacts needed to satisfy the specifications. A special feature of the analyzer is its ability to take advantage of circuit specifications which are incompletely stated. The auxiliary machine method of doing these and similar operations is compared with the method of coding them on a general-purpose digital computer.

INTRODUCTION

SOME OPERATIONS which assist in the design of relay circuits or other types of switching circuits can be described in very simple form, and machines can be constructed which perform them more quickly and more accurately than a human being can. It seems possible that machines of this type will be useful to those whose work involves the design of such circuits.

The present machine, called the relay circuit analyzer, is intended for use in connection with the design of two terminal circuits made up of contacts on at most four relays. The principles upon which this machine is based are not limited to two terminal networks or to four relays, although an enlarged machine would require more time to operate. Each addition of one relay to the circuits considered would approximately double the size of the machine and quadruple the length of time required for its operation. This type of machine is not applicable to sequential circuits, however, so it will be of use only in connection with parts of the relay circuits which contain contacts, but no relay coils.

OPERATION OF THE MACHINE

The machine, as can be seen from Fig. 1, contains sixteen 3-position switches, which are used to specify the requirements of the circuit. One switch corresponds to each of the $2^4 = 16$ states in which the four relays can be put. Switch number two in the upper right hand corner, for instance, is labeled $W + X + Y' + Z$, which corresponds to the state of the circuit in which the relays labeled W, X, and Z are operated, and the relay labeled Y is released.

The three positions of this switch correspond to the requirements which can be imposed on the condition of the circuit when the relays are in the corresponding

state. Since any single relay contact circuit assumes only one of two values (open or closed) the inclusion of a third value (doesn't matter, don't care, or vacuous, as it has been called by various persons) merits some explanation. If the machine, of which the relay circuit being designed is to be a part, only permits these relays to take on a fraction of the 2^n combinations of which n relays are capable, then it will not matter what the circuit does in the excluded states. The user indicates the optional nature of these requirements by placing the corresponding switches in the "don't care" positions. With these options, there is a wider range of circuits satisfying the requirements, and hence more likelihood that a circuit with fewer contacts will suffice. The sixteen 3-position switches thus permit the user not only to require the circuit under consideration to have exactly some particular hindrance function, but also allow the machine more freedom in the cases where the circuit need not be specified completely.

In order to make a machine of this type to deal with n relays (this particular machine was made for the case $n = 4$), 2^n such switches would be required, corresponding to the 2^n states n relays can assume. In each of these states the circuit can be either open or closed, so there are 2^{2^n} functionally distinct circuits. But since each switch has 3 positions, there are 3^{2^n} distinct circuit requirements specifiable on the switches, which in the case $n = 4$ amounts to 43,046,721. Thus, the number of problems which the analyzer must deal with is quite large, even in the case of only four relays.

The left half of the front panel of the machine (see Fig. 1) is a plugboard on which the circuit being analyzed can be represented. There are three transfers from each of the four relays, W, X, Y, and Z brought out to jacks on this panel, and jacks representing the terminals of the network are at the top and bottom. Using patch cords, it is possible to plug up any circuit using at most three transfers on each of the four relays. This number of contacts is sufficient to give a circuit representing any switching function of four variables.

If the specifications for the circuit have been put on the sixteen switches, and if the circuit has been put on the plugboard, the relay circuit analyzer is then ready to operate.

With the main control switch and the evaluate-compare switch both in the "evaluate" position, pressing the start button will cause the analyzer to evaluate the circuit plugged in, i.e. to indicate in which of the states the circuit is closed by lighting up the corresponding indicator lamps.

Turning the evaluate-compare switch to the "compare" position, the analyzer then checks whether the

* Decimal classification: 621.375.2×R257. Original manuscript received by the Institute, May 28, 1953; revised manuscript received June 29, 1953.
† Bell Telephone Laboratories, Inc., Murray Hill, N. J.

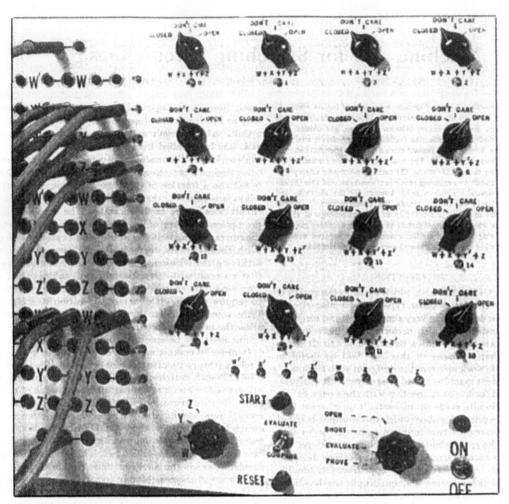

Fig. 1—View of front panel of the relay circuit analyzer.

circuit disagrees with the requirements given on the switches. A disagreement is indicated by lighting the lamp corresponding to the state in question. If a switch is set for closed and the actual circuit is open in that state, or vice versa, a disagreement is indicated, but no disagreement is ever registered when the switch is set in the "don't care" position, regardless of the circuit condition. The compare position, while it gives information equivalent to that given in the evaluate position, gives it in a form more convenient for noticing errors.

After a circuit has been found which agrees entirely with the requirements, the main control switch is then turned to the "short test" position and the start button is pressed again. The machine then determines whether any of the contacts in this circuit could have been shorted out, with the circuit still satisfying the require-

ments. The machine indicates on the lamps beside the contacts which ones have this property.

It may be surprising to the reader that anyone would ever need the assistance of a machine to find a contact which could be shorted out without affecting its circuit. While this is certainly true of simple examples, in more complicated circuits such redundant elements are often far from obvious (particularly if there are some states for which the switches are in the "don't care" position, since the simplified circuit may be functionally different from the original one, as long as it differs only in the "don't care" state). It is often quite difficult to see the simplification in these cases.

The analyzer is also helpful in case the circuit being analyzed is a bridge, because of the complications involved in tracing out all paths in the bridge. The circuit shown in Fig. 2 is an example of a circuit which was not known to be inefficiently designed until put on the analyzer. It determined in less than two minutes (including the time required to plug the circuit into the plugboard) that one of the contacts shown can be shorted out. How likely would a human being be to solve this same problem in the same length of time?

After the short test has been performed, putting the main control switch in the "open test" position permits the analyzer to perform another analogous test, this time opening the contacts one at a time.

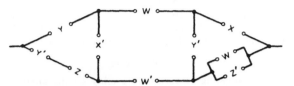

Fig. 2—The relay circuit analyzer was able to simplify this circuit, removing one contact, in less than two minutes total time. Can you do as well?

These two particular types of circuit changes were chosen because they are easy to carry out, and whenever successful, either one reduces the number of contacts required. There are other types of circuit simplification which it might be desirable to have a machine perform, including various rearrangements of the circuit. These would have required more time as well as more equipment to perform, but would probably have caused the machine to be more frequently successful in simplifying the circuit. Using such techniques, it might be possible to build a machine which could design circuits efficiently starting from basic principles, perhaps by starting with a complete Boolean expansion for the desired function and simplifying it step by step. Such a machine would be rather slow (unless it were built to operate at electronic speeds, and perhaps even in this case), and not enough planning has been done to know whether such a machine is practically feasible. However, the fact that such a machine is theoretically possible is certainly of interest, whether anyone builds one or not.

Another question of theoretical interest is whether a logical machine could be built which could design an improved version of itself, or perhaps build some machine whose over-all purpose was more complicated than its own. There seems to be no logical contradiction involved in such a machine, although it will require great advances in the general theory of automata before any such project could be confidently undertaken.

To return to the relay circuit analyzer, a final operation which it performs is done with the main control switch in the *prove* position. Pressing the start button and moving the other 4-position switch successively through the W, X, Y and Z positions, then certain of the eight lamps W, W', X, X', Y, Y', Z, Z' will light up. The analyzer has carried out a proof as to which kinds

of contacts are required to synthesize the function using the method of reduction to functions of one variable, which will be explained in a forthcoming paper. The analyzer here ignores whatever circuit has been plugged in the plugboard, and considers only the function specified by the sixteen 3-position switches. If every circuit which satisfied these specifications requires a back contact on the W relay, the W light will go on, etc.

If, for instance, seven of the eight lights are on, any circuit for the function requires at least seven contacts, and if there is, in fact, a circuit which uses just seven, the machine has in effect, given a complete proof that this circuit is minimal. Circuits for which the machine can give such a complete proof are fairly common, although there are also circuits (which can be shown to be minimal by more subtle methods of proof) which this machine could not prove minimal. An example is the circuit of Fig. 2. This can be simplified by the analyzer to a circuit of nine contacts, but in the *prove* position the analyzer merely indicates that at least eight contacts are necessary. It can be shown by other methods that the 9-contact circuit is minimal. But at any rate, the analyzer always gives a mathematically rigorous lower bound for the number of contacts.

The small size and portability of this machine depends on the fact that a mixture of relay and electronic circuit elements were used. The gas diodes are particularly suited for use where a small memory element having an associated visual display is required, and the relays and selector switches are particularly suited for use where the ability to sequence and interconnect, using only a small weight and space, is required. In all, the relay circuit analyzer uses only 24 relays, 2 selector switches, 48 miniature gas diodes, and 14 germanium diodes as its logical elements.

It may be of interest to those familiar with general purpose digital computers to compare this method of solution of this problem on such a small, special-purpose machine with the more conventional method of coding it for solution on a high-speed general-purpose computer. One basic way in which the two methods differ is in the directness with which the circuits being analyzed are represented. On a general-purpose computer it would be necessary to have a symbolic description of the circuit, probably in the form of a numerical code describing the interconnections of the circuit diagram, and representing the types of contacts that occur in the various parts of the circuit by means of a list of numbers in successive memory locations of the computer. On the other hand, the relay circuit analyzer represents the circuit in a more direct and natural manner, by actually having a copy of it plugged up on the front panel.

This difference in the directness of representation has two effects. First, it would be somewhat harder to use the general-purpose computer, because the steps of translating the circuit diagram into the coded description and of typing it onto the input medium of the computer would be more complicated and lengthy than the step of plugging up a circuit directly. The second effect is in the relative number of logical operations (and hence, indirectly, the time) required by the two kinds of machines. To carry out the fundamental step in this procedure of determining whether the given circuit (or some modification of it obtained by opening or shorting a contact) is open or closed for some particular state of the relays, requires only a single relay operate time for the relay circuit analyzer. However, the carrying out of this fundamental step on a general-purpose digital computer would require going through several kinds of subroutines many times. There would be several ways of coding the problem, but in a typical one of them the computer would first go through a subroutine to determine whether a given contact were open or closed, repeating this one for each contact in the circuit, and then would go through another subroutine once for each node of the network. Altogether this would probably involve the execution of several hundred orders on the computer, although by sufficiently ingenious coding this might be cut down to perhaps 100. Since each order of a computer takes perhaps 100 times the duration of a single logical operation (i.e., a pulse time, if the computer is clock-driven), actually what takes 1 operation time on one machine takes perhaps 10,000 on another.

Since 10,000 is approximately the ratio between the speed of a relay and of a vacuum tube in performing logical operations, this gain of about 10,000 from the directness of the representation permits this relay machine to be as fast at this kind of problem as a general-pupose electronic computer.

This great disparity between the speeds of a general-purpose and of a special-purpose computer is not typical of all kinds of problems, since a typical problem in numerical analysis might only permit of a speed-up by a factor of 10 on a special-purpose machine (since

multiplications and divisions required in the problem use up perhaps a tenth of the time of the problem). However, it seems to be typical of combinatorial problems that a tremendous gain in speed is possible by the use of special rather than general-purpose digital computers. This means that the general-purpose machines are not really general in purpose, but are specialized in such a direction as to favor problems in analysis. It is certainly true that the so-called general purpose machines are logically capable of solving such combinatorial problems, but their efficiency in such use is definitely very low. The problems involved in the design of a general-purpose machine suitable for a wide variety of combinatorial problems seem to be quite difficult, although certainly of great theoretical interest.

Conclusions

An interesting feature of the relay circuit analyzer is its ability to deal directly with logical circuits in terms of 3-valued logic. There would be considerable interest in techniques permitting easy manipulation on paper with such a logic, because of its direct application to the design of economical switching circuits. Even though such techniques have not yet been developed, machines such as this can be of value in connection with 3-valued problems.

Whether or not this particular kind of machine ever proves to be useful in the design of practical relay circuits, the possibility of making machines which can assist in logical design procedure promises to be of value to everyone associated with the design of switching circuits. Just as the slide rule and present-day types of digital computers can help perform part of the routine work associated with the design of linear electrical networks, machines such as this may someday lighten much of the routine work associated with the design of logical circuits.

Computers and Automata*

CLAUDE E. SHANNON†, FELLOW, IRE

C. E. Shannon first became known for a paper in which he applied Boolean Algebra to relay switching circuits; this laid the foundation for the present extensive application of Boolean Algebra to computer design. Dr. Shannon, who is engaged in mathematical research at Bell Telephone Laboratories, is an authority on information theory. More recently he received wide notice for his ingenious maze-solving mechanical mouse, and he is well-known as one of the leading explorers into the exciting, but uncharted world of new ideas in the computer field.

The Editors asked Dr. Shannon to write a paper describing current experiments, and speculations concerning future developments in computer logic. Here is a real challenge for those in search of a field where creative ability, imagination, and curiosity will undoubtedly lead to major advances in human knowledge.—*The Editor*

Summary—This paper reviews briefly some of the recent developments in the field of automata and nonnumerical computation. A number of typical machines are described, including logic machines, game-playing machines and learning machines. Some theoretical questions and developments are discussed, such as a comparison of computers and the brain, Turing's formulation of computing machines and von Neumann's models of self-reproducing machines.

INTRODUCTION

SAMUEL BUTLER, in 1871, completed the manuscript of a most engaging social satire, *Erewhon*. Three chapters of *Erewhon*, originally appearing under the title "Darwin Among the Machines," are a witty parody of *The Origin of Species*. In the topsy-turvy logic of satirical writing, Butler sees machines as gradually evolving into higher forms. He considers the classification of machines into genera, species and varieties, their feeding habits, their rudimentary sense organs, their reproductive and evolutionary mechanisms (inefficient machines force men to design more efficient ones), tendencies toward reversion, vestigial organs, and even the problem of free will in machines.

Rereading *Erewhon* today one finds "The Book of the Machines" disturbingly prophetic. Current and projected computers and control systems are indeed assuming more and more the capacities and functions of animals and man, to a far greater degree, in fact, than was envisaged by Butler.

The bread-and-butter work of large-scale computers has been the solution of involved numerical problems. To many of us, however, the most exciting potentialities of computers lie in their ability to perform non-numerical operations—to work with logic, translate languages, design circuits, play games, co-ordinate sensory and manipulative devices and, generally, assume complicated functions associated with the human brain.

Non-numerical computation is by no means an unproven offspring of the more publicized arithmetic calculation. The shoe is rather on the other foot. A hun-

dred years ago Charles Babbage was inspired in the design of his remarkably prescient analytical engine by a portrait woven in silk on a card controlled Jacquart loom—a device then in existence half a century. The largest and most reliable current information processing machine is still the automatic telephone system. Our factories are filled with ingenious and unsung devices performing almost incredible feats of sensing, processing and transporting materials in all shapes and forms. Railway and power systems have elaborate control and protective networks against accidents and human errors.

These, however, are all special-purpose automata. A significant new concept in non-numerical computation is the idea of a general-purpose programmed computer—a device capable of carrying out a long sequence of elementary orders analogous to those of a numerical computer. The elementary orders, however, will relate not to operations on numbers but to physical motions, operations with words, equations, incoming sensory data, or almost any physical or conceptual entities.

This paper reviews briefly some of the research in non-numerical computation and discusses certain of the problems involved. The field is currently very active and in a short paper only a few sample developments can be mentioned.

THE BRAIN AND COMPUTERS

The brain has often been compared, perhaps over-enthusiastically, with computing machines. It contains roughly 10^{10} active elements called neurons. Because of the all or none law of nervous action, neurons bear some functional resemblance to our binary computer elements, relays, vacuum tubes or transistors. The number of elements is six orders of magnitude greater than our largest computers. McCullough has picturesquely put it that a computer with as many tubes as a man has neurons would require the Empire State building to house it, Niagara Falls to power it and the Niagara river to cool it. The use of transistors in such a comparison would improve the figures considerably, power requirements coming down to the hundreds of kilowatt range (the brain dissipates some 25 watts) and size requirements (with close packing) comparable to an ordi-

* Decimal classification: 621.385.2. Original manuscript received by the Institute, July 17, 1953.
† Bell Telephone Laboratories, Murray Hill, N. J.

nary dwelling. It may also be argued that the increased speed of electronic components by a factor of, say, 10^3 might be partially exchangeable against equipment requirements.

Comparisons of this sort should be taken well salted —our understanding of brain functioning is still, in spite of a great deal of important and illuminating research, very primitive. Whether, for example, the neuron itself is the proper level for a functional analysis is still an open question. The random structure at the neural level in number, placement and interconnections of the neurons, suggests that only the statistics are important at this stage, and, consequently, that one might average over local structure and functioning before constructing a mathematical model.

The similarities between the brain and computers have often been pointed out. The differences are perhaps more illuminating, for they may suggest the important features missing from our best current brain models. Among the most important of these are:

1. Differences in size. Six orders of magnitude in the number of components takes us so far from our ordinary experience as to make extrapolation of function next to meaningless.

2. Differences in structural organization. The apparently random local structure of nerve networks is vastly different from the precise wiring of artificial automata, where a single wrong connection may cause malfunctioning. The brain somehow is designed so that overall functioning does not depend on the exact structure in the small.

3. Differences in reliability organization. The brain can operate reliably for decades without really serious malfunctioning (comparable to the meaningless gibberish produced by a computer in trouble conditions) even though the components are probably individually no more reliable than those used in computers.

4. Differences in logical organization. The differences here seem so great as to defy enumeration. The brain is largely self-organizing. It can adapt to an enormous variety of situations tolerably well. It has remarkable memory classification and access features, the ability to rapidly locate stored data via numerous "coordinate systems." It can set up stable servo systems involving complex relations between its sensory inputs and motor outputs, with great facility. In contrast, our digital computers look like idiot savants. For long chains of arithmetic operations a digital computer runs circles around the best humans. When we try to program computers for other activities their entire organization seems clumsy and inappropriate.

5. Differences in input-output equipment. The brain is equipped with beautifully designed input organs, particularly the ear and the eye, for sensing the state of its environment. Our best artificial counterparts, such as Shepard's Analyzing Reader for recognizing and transcribing type, and the

"Audrey" speech recognition system which can recognize the speech sounds for the ten digits seem pathetic by comparison. On the output end, the brain controls hundreds of muscles and glands. The two arms and hands have some sixty independent degrees of freedom. Compare this with the manipulative ability of the digitally controlled milling machine developed at M.I.T., which can move its work in but three co-ordinates. Most of our computers, indeed, have no significant sensory or manipulative contact with the real world but operate only in an abstract environment of numbers and operations on numbers.

TURING MACHINES

The basic mathematical theory of digital computers was developed by A. M. Turing in 1936 in a classic paper "On Computable Numbers with an Application to the Entscheidungsproblem." He defined a class of computing machines, now called Turing machines, consisting basically of an infinite paper tape and a computing element. The computing element has a finite number of internal states and is capable of reading from and writing on one cell of the tape and of moving it one cell to the right or left. At a given time, the computing element will be in a certain state and reading what is written in a particular cell of the tape. The next operation will be determined by the current state and the symbol being read. This operation will consist of assuming a new state and either writing a new symbol (in place of the one currently read) or moving to the right or to the left. It is possible for machines of this type to compute numbers by setting up a suitable code for interpreting the symbols. For example, in Turing's formulation the machines print final answers in binary notation on alternate cells of the tape, using the other cells for intermediate calculations.

It can be shown that such machines form an extremely broad class of computers. All ordinary digital computers which do not contain a random or probabilistic element are equivalent to some Turing machine. Any number that can be computed on these machines, or in fact by any ordinary computing process, can be computed by a suitable Turing machine. There are, however, as Turing showed, certain problems that cannot be solved and certain numbers that cannot be computed by any Turing machine. For example, it is not possible to construct a Turing machine which, given a suitably coded description of another Turing machine, can always tell whether or not the second Turing machine will continue indefinitely to print symbols in the squares corresponding to the final answer. It may, at a certain point in the calculation, relapse into an infinite intermediate computation. The existence of mechanically unsolvable problems of this sort is of great interest to logicians.

Turing also developed the interesting concept of a universal Turing machine. This is a machine with the property that if a suitably coded description of any Turing machine is printed on its tape, and the machine started at a suitable point and in a suitable state, it will then act like the machine described, that is, compute (normally at a much slower rate) the same number that the described machine would compute. Turing showed that such universal machines can be designed. They of course are capable of computing any computable number. Most digital computers, provided they have access to an unlimited memory of some sort, are equivalent to universal Turing machines and can, in principle, imitate any other computing machine and compute any computable number.

The work of Turing has been generalized and reformulated in various ways. One interesting generalization is the notion of A computability. This relates to a class of Turing type machines which have the further feature that they can, at certain points of the calculation, ask questions of a second "oracular" device, and use the answers in further calculations. The oracular machine may for example have answers to some of the unsolvable problems of ordinary Turing machines, and consequently enable the solution of a larger class of problems.

LOGIC MACHINES

Boolean algebra can be used as a mathematical tool for studying the properties of relay and switching circuits. Conversely, it is possible to solve problems of Boolean algebra and formal logic by means of simple relay circuits. This possibility has been exploited in a number of logic machines. A typical machine of this kind, described by McCallum and Smith, can handle logical relations involving up to seven classes or truth variables. The required relations among these variables, given by the logical problem at hand, are plugged into the machine by means of a number of "connective boxes." These connective boxes are of six types and provide for the logical connectives "not," "and," "or," "or else," "if and only if," and "if-then." When the connections are complete, starting the machine causes it to hunt through the $2^7 = 128$ combinations of the basic variables, stopping at all combinations which satisfy the constraints. The machine also indicates the number of "true" variables in each of these states. McCallum and Smith give the following typical problem that may be solved on the machine:

It is known that salesmen always tell the truth and engineers always tell lies. G and E are salesmen. C states that D is an engineer. A declares that B affirms that C asserts that D says that E insists that F denies that G is a salesman. If A is an engineer, how many engineers are there?

A very suggestive feature in this machine is a selective feedback system for hunting for particular solutions of the logical equations without an exhaustive search through all possible combinations. This is achieved by elements which sense whether or not a particular logical relation is satisfied. If not, the truth variables involved in this relation are caused to oscillate between their two possible values. Thus, variables appearing in unsatisfied relations are continually changing, while those appearing only in satisfied relations do not change. If ever all relations are simultaneously satisfied the machine stops at that particular solution. Changing only the variables in unsatisfied relations tends, in a general way, to lead to a solution more rapidly than methodical exhaustion of all cases, but, as is usually the case when feedback is introduced, leads to the possibility of continual oscillation. McCallum and Smith point out the desirability of making the changes of the variables due to the feedback unbalance as random as possible, to enable the machine to escape from periodic paths through various states of the relays.

GAME PLAYING MACHINES

The problem of designing game-playing machines is fascinating and has received a good deal of attention. The rules of a game provide a sharply limited environment in which a machine may operate, with a clearly defined goal for its activities. The discrete nature of most games matches well the digital computing techniques available without the cumbersome analog-digital conversion necessary in translating our physical environment in the case of manipulating and sensing machines.

Game playing machines may be roughly classified into types in order of increasing sophistication:

1. Dictionary-type machines. Here the proper move of the machine is decided in advance for each possible situation that may arise in the game and listed in a "dictionary" or function table. When a particular position arises, the machine merely looks up the move in the dictionary. Because of the extravagant memory requirements, this rather uninteresting method is only feasible for exceptionally simple games, e.g., tic-tac-toe.

2. Machines using rigorously correct playing formulas. In some games, such as Nim, a complete mathematical theory is known, whereby it is possible to compute by a relatively simple formula, in any position that can be won, a suitable winning move. A mechanization of this formula provides a perfect game player for such games.

3. Machines applying general principles of approximate validity. In most games of interest to humans, no simple exact solution is known, but there are various general principles of play which hold in the majority of positions. This is true of such games as checkers, chess, bridge, poker and the like. Machines may be designed applying such general principles to the position at hand. Since the principles are not infallible, neither are the machines, as indeed, neither are humans.

4. Learning machines. Here the machine is given only the rules of the game and perhaps an elementary strategy of play, together with some method of improving this strategy through experience. Among the many methods that have been suggested for incorporation of learning we have:
   a) trial-and-error with retention of successful

and elimination of unsuccessful possibilities;

    b) imitation of a more successful opponent;

    c) "teaching" by approval or disapproval, or by informing the machine of the nature of its mistakes; and finally

    d) self-analysis by the machine of its mistakes in an attempt to devise general principles.

Many examples of the first two types have been constructed and a few of the third. The fourth type, learning game-players, is reminiscent of Mark Twain's comment on the weather. Here is a real challenge for the programmer and machine designer.

Two examples of the third category, machines applying general principles, may be of interest. The first of these is a machine designed by E. F. Moore and the writer for playing a commercial board game known as Hex. This game is played on a board laid out in a regular hexagon pattern, the two players alternately placing black and white pieces in unoccupied hexagons. The entire board forms a rhombus and Black's goal is to connect the top and bottom of this rhombus with a continuous chain of black pieces. White's goal is to connect the two sides of the rhombus with a chain of white pieces. After a study of this game, it was conjectured that a reasonably good move could be made by the following process. A two-dimensional potential field is set up corresponding to the playing board, with white pieces as positive charges and black pieces as negative charges. The top and bottom of the board are negative and the two sides positive. The move to be made corresponds to a certain specified saddle point in this field.

To test this strategy, an analog device was constructed, consisting of a resistance network and gadgetry to locate the saddle points. The general principle, with some improvements suggested by experience, proved to be reasonably sound. With first move, the machine won about seventy per cent of its games against human opponents. It frequently surprised its designers by choosing odd-looking moves which, on analysis, proved sound. We normally think of computers as expert at long involved calculations and poor in generalized value judgments. Paradoxically, the positional judgment of this machine was good; its chief weakness was in end-game combinatorial play. It is also curious that the Hex-player reversed the usual computing procedure in that it solved a basically digital problem by an anlog machine.

The game of checkers has recently been programmed into a general-purpose computer, using a "general principle" approach. C. S. Strachey used a method similar to one proposed by the writer for programming chess—an investigation of the possible variations for a few moves and a minimax evaluation applied to the resulting positions. The following is a sample game played by the checker program with notes by Strachey. (The white squares are numbered consecutively, 0–31, from left to right and top to bottom. Numbers in parentheses indicate captures.)

While obviously no world champion, the machine is certainly better than many humans. Strachey points out various weaknesses in the program, particularly in certain end-game positions, and suggests possible improvements.

Learning Machines

The concept of learning, like those of thinking, consciousness and other psychological terms, is difficult to define precisely in a way acceptable to the various interested parties. A rough formulation might be framed somewhat as follows. Suppose that an organism or a machine can be placed in, or connected to, a class of environments, and that there is a measure of "success" or "adaptation" to the environment. Suppose further that this measure is comparatively local in time, that is, that one can measure the success over periods of time short compared to the life of the organism. If this local measure of success tends to improve with the passage of time, for the class of environments in question, we may say that the organism or machine is learning to adapt to these environments relative to the measure of success chosen. Learning achieves a quantitative significance in terms of the broadness and complexity of the class of environments to which the machine can adapt. A chess playing machine whose frequency of wins increases during its operating life may be said by this definition to be learning chess, the class of environments being the chess players who oppose it, and the adaptation measure, the winning of games.

A number of attempts have been made to construct simple learning machines. The writer constructed a maze-solving device in which an arbitrary maze can be set up in a five-by-five array of squares, by placing partitions as desired between adjacent squares. A permanently magnetized "mouse," placed in the maze, blunders about by a trial and error procedure, striking various partitions and entering blind alleys until it eventually finds its way to the "food box." Placed in the maze a second time, it will move directly to the food box from any part of the maze that it has visited in its first exploration, without errors or false moves. Placed in other parts of the maze, it will blunder about until it reaches a previously explored part and from there go directly to the goal. Meanwhile it will have added the information about this part of the maze to its memory, and if placed at the same point again will go directly to the goal. Thus by placing it in the various unexplored parts of the maze, it eventually builds up a complete pattern of information and is able to reach the goal directly from any point.

If the maze is now changed, the mouse first tries the old path, but on striking a partition starts trying other directions and revising its memory until it eventually reaches the goal by some other path. Thus it is able to forget an old solution when the problem is changed.

The mouse is actually driven by an electromagnet moving beneath the maze. The motion of the electromagnet is controlled by a relay circuit containing about 110 relays, organized into a memory and a computing circuit, somewhat after that of a digital computer.

MACHINE	STRACHEY
11—15	23—18
7—11	21—17
8—12	20—16 *a*
12—21 (16)	25—16 (21)
9—14 ! *b*	18— 9 (14)
6—20 (16, 9) *c*	27—23
2— 7 *d*	23—18
5— 8	18—14
8—13 *e*	17— 8 (13)
4—13 (8)	14— 9
1— 5 *f*	9— 6
15—19	6— 1 (K)
5— 9	1— 6 ?*g*
0— 5 ! *h*	6—15 (10)
11—25 (22, 15)	30—21 (25)
13—17	21—14 (17)
9—18 (14)	24—21
18—23	26—22
23—27	22—17
5— 8 *i*	17—14
8—13	14— 9
19—23	9— 6
23—26 *j*	31—22 (26)
27—31 (K)	6— 2 (K)
7—10	2— 7
10—15	21—16 ?*k*
3—10 (7)	16— 9 (13)
10—14	9— 6
15—19	6— 2 (K)
31—27 *m*	2— 6
27—31 *m*	6—10
31—26 *n*	10—17 (14)
19—23	29—25
26—31 *p*	

Notes:
a) An experiment on my part—the only deliberate offer I made. I thought, wrongly, that it was quite safe.
b) Not foreseen by me.
c) Better than 5–21 (9, 17).
d) A random move (zero value). Shows the lack of a constructive plan.
e) Another random move of zero value. Actually rather good.
f) Bad. Ultimately allows me to make a King. 10–14 would would have been better.
g) A bad slip on my part.
h) Taking full advantage of my slip.
i) Bad, unblocks the way to a King.
j) Sacrifice in order to get a King (not to stop me Kinging). A good move, but not possible before 19–23 had been made by chance.
k) Another bad slip on my part.
m) Purposeless. The strategy is failing badly in the end game.
n) Too late.
p) Futile. The game was stopped at this point as the outcome was obvious.

The maze-solver may be said to exhibit at a very primitive level the abilities to (1) solve problems by trial and error, (2) repeat the solutions without the errors, (3) add and correlate new information to a partial solution, (4) forget a solution when it is no longer applicable.

Another approach to mechanized learning is that of suitably programming a large-scale computer. A. E. Oettinger has developed two learning programs for the Edsac computer in Cambridge, England. In the first of these, the machine was divided into two parts, one part playing the role of a learning machine and the second its environment. The environment represented abstractly a number of stores in which various items might be purchased, different stores stocking different classes of items. The learning machine faced the problem of learning where various items might be purchased. Starting off with no previous knowledge and a particular item to be obtained, it would search at random among the stores until the item was located. When finally successful, it noted in its memory where the article was found. Sent again for the same article it will go directly to the shop where it previously obtained this article. A further feature of the program was the introduction of a bit of "curiosity" in the learning machine. When it succeeded in finding article number j in a particular shop it also noticed whether or not that shop carried articles $j-1$ and $j+1$ and recorded these facts in its memory.

The second learning program described by Oettinger is modeled more closely on the conditioned reflex behavior of animals. A stimulus of variable intensity can be applied to the machine in the form of an input integer. To this stimulus the machine may respond in a number of different ways indicated by an output integer. After the response, it is possible for the operator to indicate approval or disapproval by introducing a third integer at a suitable point. When the machine starts operating, its responses to stimuli are chosen at random. Indication of approval improves the chances for the response immediately preceding; indication of disapproval reduces this chance. Furthermore, as a particular response is learned by conditioning it with approval, the stimulus required for this response decreases. Finally, there is a regular decay of thresholds when no approval follows a response.

Further embellishments of programs of this sort are limited only by the capacity of the computer and the energy and ingenuity of the program designer. Unfortunely, the elementary orders available in most large-scale computers are poorly adapted to the logical requirements of learning programs, and the machines are therefore used rather inefficiently. It may take a dozen or more orders to represent a logically simple and frequently used operation occurring in a learning routine.

Another type of learning machine has been constructed by D. W. Hagelbarger. This is a machine designed to play the game of matching pennies against a human opponent. On the front panel of the machine are a start button, two lights marked + and −, and a key switch whose extreme positions are also marked + and −. To play against the machine, the player chooses + or −, and then pushes the start button. The machine will then light up one of the two lights. If the machine matches the player, that is, lights the light corresponding to the choice of the player, the machine wins; otherwise the player wins. When the play is complete, the player registers by appropriate movement of the key switch the choice he made.

The machine is so constructed as to analyze certain patterns in the players' sequence of choices, and attempt to capitalize on these patterns when it finds them. For example, some players have a tendency if they have won a round, played the same thing and won again, to then change their choice. The machine keeps count of these situations and, if such tendencies appear, plays in such a way as to win. When such patterns do not appear the machine plays at random.

It has been found the machine wins about 55–60 per cent of the rounds, while by chance or against an opponent that played strictly at random it would win only 50 per cent of the time. It appears to be quite difficult for a human being to produce a random sequence of pluses and minuses (to insure the 50 per cent wins he is entitled to by the theory of games) and even more difficult to actually beat the machine by leading it on to suspect patterns, and then reversing the patterns.

A second penny-matching machine was designed by the writer, following the same general strategy but using a different criterion to decide when to play at random and when to assume that an apparent behavior pattern is significant. After considerable discussion as to which of these two machines could beat the other, and fruitless attempts to solve mathematically the very complicated statistical problem involved when they are connected together, the problem was relegated to experiment. A third small machine was constructed to act as umpire and pass the information back and forth between the machines concerning their readiness to make a move and the choices made. The three machines were then plugged together and allowed to run for a few hours, to the accompaniment of small side-bets and loud cheering. Ironically, it turned out that the smaller, more precipitate of the two machines consistently beat the larger, more deliberate one in a ratio of about 55 to 45.

A still different type of learning machine was devised by W. Ross Ashby who christened it the Homeostat. Homeostasis, a word coined by Walter B. Cannon, relates to an animal's ability to stabilize, by feedback, such biological variables as body temperature, chemical concentrations in the blood stream, etc. Ashby's device is a kind of self-stabilizing servo system. The first model of the Homeostat contained four interconnected servos. The cross-connections of these servos passed through four stepping switches and resistors connected to the points of the steppers. Thus the effect of unbalance in the other three loops on a particular loop depended on the values of the resistors being contacted by the stepper associated with that loop. When any one of the servos was sufficiently out of balance, a corresponding limit relay would operate and cause the corresponding stepping switch to advance one point. Now normally, a servo system with four degrees of freedom and random cross- and self-gain figures will not be stable. If this occurred, one or more of the stepping switches would advance and a new set of resistors would produce a new set of gain figures. If this set again proved unstable, a further advance of the steppers would occur until a stable situation was found. The values of the resistors connected to the stepping switches were chosen by random means (using a table of randon numbers). Facilities were provided for introducing many arbitrary changes or constraints among the servos. For example, their connections could be reversed, two of them could be tied together, one of them held at a fixed value, etc. Under all these conditions, the mechanism was able to find a suitable stable position with all the servos in balance. Considering the machine's goal to be that of stabilizing the servos, and the environment to be represented by the various alterations and constraints introduced by the operator, the Homeostat may be said to adapt to its environment.

Certain features of the Homeostat are quite attractive as a basis for learning machines and brain models. It seems in certain ways to do a bit more than was explicitly designed into it. For example, it has been able to stabilize under situations not anticipated when the machine was constructed. The use of randomly chosen resistors is particularly suggestive and reminiscent of the random connections among neurons in the brain. Ashby, in fact, believes that the general principle embodied in the Homeostat, which he calls ultra-stability, may underlie the operation of the animal nervous system. One of the difficulties of a too direct application of this theory is that, as Ashby points out, the time required for finding a stable solution grows more or less exponentially with the number of degrees of freedom. With only about 20 degrees of freedom, it would require many lifetimes to stabilize one system. Attempts to overcome this difficulty lead to rather involved conceptual constructions, so involved that it is extremely difficult to decide just how effectively they would operate. Our mathematical tools do not seem sufficiently sharp to solve these problems and further experimental work would be highly desirable.

Self-Reproducing Machines

In *Erewhon* the reproduction process in machines was pictured as a kind of symbiotic co-operation between man and machines, the machines using man as an intermediary to produce new machines when the older ones were worn out. Man's part is akin to that of the bee in the fertilization of flowers. Recently von Neumann has studied at an abstract level the problem of true self-reproduction in machines, and has formulated two different mathematical models of such "machines."

The first of these may be pictured somewhat as follows. "Machines" in the model are constructed from a small number (of the order of twenty) types of elementary components. These components have relatively simple functions, for example, girders for structural purposes, elementary logical elements similar to simplified relays or neurons for computing, sensing components for detecting the presence of other elements, joining components (analogous to a soldering iron) for fastening elements together, and so on. From these elements, various types of machines may be "constructed." In particular, it is possible to design a kind of universal construction machine, analogous to Turing's universal computing machine. The universal constructing machine can be fed a sequence of instructions, similar to the program of a digital computer, which describe in a suitable code how to construct any other machine that can be built with the elementary components. The universal constructing machine will then proceed to hunt for the needed components in its environment and build the machine described on its tape. If the instructions to the universal constructing machine are a description of the universal constructing machine itself, it will proceed to build a copy of itself, and would be a self-reproducing machine except for the fact that the copy is not yet supplied with a set of instructions. By adding to the universal machine what amounts to a tape-copying device and a relatively simple controlling device, a true self-reproducing machine is obtained. The instructions now describe the original universal machine with the addition of the tape reproducer and the controlling device. The first operation of the machine is to reproduce this entity. The controlling device then sends the instruction tape through the tape reproducer to obtain a copy, and places this copy in the second machine. Finally, it turns the second machine on, which starts reading its instructions and building a third copy, and so ad infinitum.

More recently, von Neumann has turned from this somewhat mechanical model to a more abstract self-reproducing structure—one based on a two-dimensional array of elementary "cells." Each cell is of relatively simple internal structure, having, in fact, something like thirty possible internal states, and each cell communicates directly only with its four neighbors. The state of a cell at the next (quantized) step in time depends only on the current state of the cell and the states of its four neighbors. By a suitable choice of these state transitions it is possible to set up a system yielding a kind of self-reproducing structure. A group of contiguous cells can act as an organic unit and operate on nearby quiescent cells in such a way as to organize a group of them into an identical unit.

This second model avoids many of the somewhat extraneous problems of locating, recognizing and positioning components that were inherent in the first model, and consequently leads to a simpler mathematical formulation. Furthermore, it has certain analogies with various chemical and biological problems, such as those of crystal and gene reproduction, while the first model is more closely related to the problem of large scale animal reproduction.

An interesting concept arising from both models is the notion of a critical complexity required for self-reproduction. In either case, only sufficiently complicated "machines" will be capable of self-reproduction. Von Neumann estimates the order of tens of thousands of components or cells to obtain this property. Less complicated structures can only construct simpler "machines" than themselves, while more complicated ones may be capable of a kind of evolutionary improvement leading to still more complicated organisms.

CHALLENGE TO THE READER

We hope that the foregoing sampler of non-numerical computers may have stimulated the reader's appetite for research in this field. The problem of how the brain works and how machines may be designed to simulate its activity is surely one of the most important and difficult facing current science. Innumerable questions demand clarification, ranging from experimental and development work on the one hand to purely mathematical research on the other. Can we design significant machines where the connections are locally random? Can we organize machines into a hierarchy of levels, as the brain appears to be organized, with the learning of the machine gradually progressing up through the hierarchy? Can we program a digital computer so that (eventually) 99 per cent of the orders it follows are written by the computer itself, rather than the few per cent in current programs? Can a self-repairing machine be built that will locate and repair faults in its own components (including components in the maintenance part of the machine)? What does a random element add in generality to a Turing machine? Can manipulative and sensory devices functionally comparable to the hand and eye be developed and coordinated with computers? Can either of von Neumann's self-reproducing models be translated into hardware? Can more satisfactory theories of learning be formulated? Can a machine be constructed which will design other machines, given only their broad functional characteristics? What s a really good set of orders in a digital computer for general purpose non-numerical computation? How can a computer memory be organized to learn and remember by association, in a manner similar to the human brain?

We suggest these typical questions, and the entire automata field, as a challenge to the reader. Here is research territory ripe for scientific prospectors. It is not a matter of reworking old operations, but of locating the rich new veins and perhaps in some cases merely picking up the surface nuggets.

BIBLIOGRAPHY

W. R. Ashby, *Design for a Brain* (New York, Wiley, 1951).

E. C. Berkeley, *Giant Brains, or Machines That Think* (New York, Wiley, 1949).

S. Butler, *Erewhon and Erewhon Revisited* (New York, Modern Library Edition, 1927).

J. Diebold, *Automation* (New York, Van Nostrand, 1952).

A. S. Householder and H. D. Landahl, *Mathematical Biophysics of the Central Nervous System* (Bloomington, Principia Press, 1945) pp. 103–110.

S. C. Kleene, *Representation of Events in Nerve Nets and Finite Automata*, Rand Corporation Memorandum RM-704, 1951.

D. M. McCallum and J. B. Smith, "Mechanized Reasoning," *Electronic Engineering* (April, 1951).

Warren S. McCulloch, and Walter Pitts, "A Logical Calculus of the Ideas Immanent in Nervous Activity," *Bull. Math. Biophysics*, (1943) vol. 5, pp. 115–133.

W. S. McCulloch, "The Brain as a Computing Machine," *Electrical Engineering* (June, 1949).

John Meszar, "Switching Systems as Mechanical Brains *Bell Labs. Record*, (1953) vol. 31, pp. 63–69.

A. Oettinger, "Programming a Digital Computer to Learn," *Phil. Mag.*, (December, 1952) vol. 43, pp. 1243–1263.

W. Pease, "An Automatic Machine Tool," *Scientific American*, (September, 1952) vol. 187, pp. 101–115.

C. E. Shannon, *Presentation of a Maze-Solving Machine*, Transactions of the Eighth Cybernetics Conference, Josiah Macy, Jr. Foundation, New York, 1952, pp. 173–180.

C. E. Shannon, "Programming a Computer for Playing Chess," *Phil. Mag.*, (March, 1950) vol. 41, pp. 256–275.

C. S. Strachey, "Logical or Non-Mathematical Programmes," *Proc. of the Assn. for Computing Machinery*, Toronto (1952), pp. 46–49.

A. M. Turing, "Computing Machinery and Intelligence," *Mind*, (1950) vol. 59, pp. 433–460.

A. M. Turing, On Computable Numbers, with an Application to the Entscheidungsproblem, *Proc. Lond. Math. Soc.*, (1936) vol. 24, pp. 230–265.

J. Von Neuman, "The General and Logical Theory of Automata from Cerebral Mechanisms in Behavior," (New York, Wiley, 1951, pp. 1–41.

J. Von Neumann, *Probabilistics Logics*, California Institute of Technology, 1952.

N. Wiener, Cybernetics (New York, Wiley, 1948).

Realization of All 16 Switching Functions
of Two Variables Requires 18 Contacts*

Claude E. Shannon

Abstract

Eighteen contacts are necessary and sufficient to simultaneously realize all 16 switching functions of two variables.

In 1949 the writer gave a switching circuit realizing the 16 Boolean functions of two variables using 20 contacts. Recently a student in the M.I.T. Switching Course found a circuit (Fig. 1) requiring only 18 contacts. We will prove that this is minimal — it is not possible to realize these 16 functions with 17 or fewer contacts.

Suppose there were such a circuit K using 17 or fewer contacts. The circuit K would have 16 terminals on the right corresponding to the 16 functions of two variables and a common terminal A on the left. The open circuit terminal (hindrance 1) need not be connected in any way to terminal A. All the other 15 terminals must have paths (in general through contacts) to A, since each of the remaining switching functions are closed for certain states of the relays x and y. Thus the 15 terminals are nodes of a *connected* network. Each of these terminals is a *different* node since otherwise two of the terminals would correspond to the same switching function. Hence the network K has at least 15 distinct nodes. By assumption it has not more than 17 branches. Now in a connected network the branches B, nullity N, and number of nodes V are related by Euler's formula $N = B - V + 1$. Since $B \leq 17$, $V \geq 15$ we obtain

$$N \leq 3 .$$

We will show by another argument that the nullity $N \geq 4$, thus giving a contradiction and proving that the assumption that the network K contains 17 or fewer elements is impossible.

The nullity of K is the number of independent closed circuits or meshes in K (or more precisely in the linear graph associated with K, obtained by replacing each contact in K by a branch). The nullity of a network may be obtained by determining how many branches must be cut (each cutting operation being made so as to open at least one closed circuit) in order to leave no closed circuits in the network. In Figure 1 the nullity is 4 corresponding to the closed circuits C_1, C_2, C_3, C_4. By cutting, for example, the four branches B_1, B_2, B_3, B_4 all closed circuits are eliminated.

We will show that there exist at least four independent meshes in our assumed network K, and in fact in any network realizing the four particular functions:

---

* Bell Laboratories Memorandum, Nov. 17, 1953.

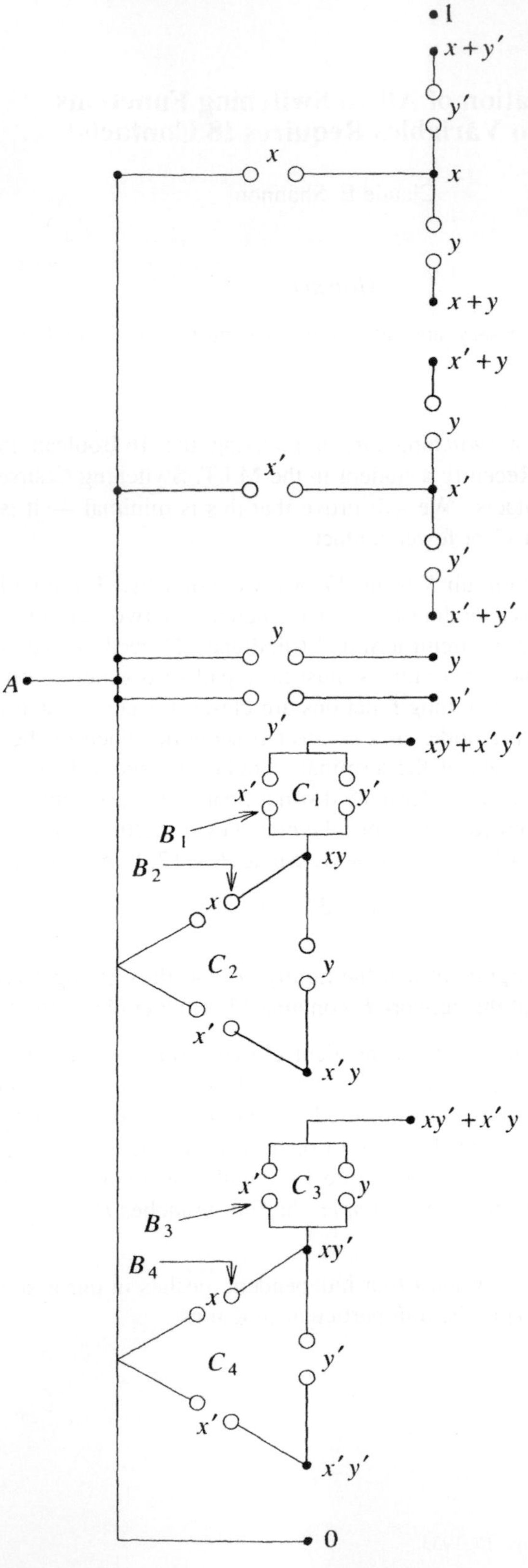

Figure 1

$$f_1 = (x + y)(x' + y') \, ,$$
$$f_2 = (x + y')(x' + y) \, ,$$
$$f_3 = xy \, ,$$
$$f_4 = x'y' \, .$$

Let us suppose that in K these four functions are realized at nodes N_1, N_2, N_3, N_4, respectively.

Consider the node N_1 of K giving the function $(x + y)(x' + y')$. The branches coming into this node may be divided into two classes: branches labeled x or y and branches labeled x' or y'. There is at least one member of the first class since otherwise there would be no connection from this node to the common terminal A when both x and y are closed. Thus it is possible to go from the node in question via a branch of the first class to A along elements of the network. Similarly the second class is not empty (otherwise the node would not be closed to A when both x and y are not operated) and there is a path from the node to A starting through a branch of the second class.

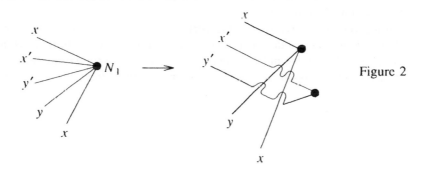

Figure 2

Now separate this node into two nodes, according to the two classes of branches, as typified in Figure 2. This will open a closed circuit of K (because of the two distinct paths from N_1 to A whose existence we have established) and hence reduce the nullity of K by 1. A similar process will be applied to the three other nodes N_2, N_3 and N_4. Each of these separations will reduce the nullity by 1. This will show that the original nullity was at least 4, proving the desired result.

We must first show that the separating process we have applied to node N_1 has not affected the switching functions at the other three nodes. In the first place, functions f_1 and f_2 are disjunctive, so no operating path for f_2 can pass through N_1 (otherwise there would be states of the relays with both f_1 and f_2 closed). Hence this separation does not alter the realization of f_2 at node N_2.

Also the separation does not alter the realization of xy at node N_3. For this would mean that a previous operating path through N_1 to N_3 no longer exists. Such a path must have passed through an x and a y' or through an x' and a y. But, if this were so node N_1 would be closed to A either in the xy' state or else in the $x'y$ state of the relays. This is impossible since then N_1 would not have represented the function $(x + y)(x' + y')$.

Exactly the same argument shows that we have not changed the realization of $x'y'$ at terminal N_4 by the separation process.

Consequently we have, after the separation, a network realizing the functions

$$f_2 = (x + y')(x' + y) \, ,$$

$$f_3 = xy \, ,$$

$$f_4 = x'y' \, ,$$

at nodes N_2, N_3, N_4, respectively and with a nullity one less than that of the original network K.

We now perform a similar operation at N_2, separating the node into two nodes corresponding to branches x or y' and x' or y. By an identical argument this reduces the nullity by one, and does not affect the realization at nodes N_3 and N_4 of xy and $x'y'$.

Now proceed to node N_3 which represents xy. Here again we divide the branches into two classes: x or y' and x' or y. The node is then separated into two nodes. By essentially the same argument this reduces the nullity by one. Also this separation will not affect the realization at N_4 of $x'y'$. For if there were an operating path to N_4 through N_3 which has been broken by this separation it must have passed through either x and y in series or x' and y' in series. In the first case f_4 should not be closed, and in the second case f_3 should not be closed, and hence neither of these assumed paths is possible.

Finally going on to N_4, we divide the branches into the classes x or y and x' or y'. Separating the node into two nodes again reduces the nullity by one. In total we have reduced the nullity by four and since the nullity cannot be negative, the original nullity must have been at least four. This contradicts the original calculation of at most three for the nullity and proves the theorem.

A Relay Laboratory Outfit for Colleges*

Claude E. Shannon and D. W. Hagelbarger

Abstract

An experimental relay kit suitable for use in a college laboratory course in switching is described. Circuit diagrams are given for several circuits that have been set up on the machine. It is suggested that if such a kit were developed and made available to colleges, it would materially aid our long-range policy toward cultivating switching engineers.

An important perennial problem facing the Bell Telephone Laboratories and, in fact, the entire Bell System is that of recruiting a sufficient number of switching engineers. Until recently practically no colleges gave courses dealing with this subject, and even now the number is very small. Many engineering graduates are hardly aware of switching as an important branch of electrical engineering, and one with any training in the techniques is a rare gift indeed. It has been necessary first to sell graduate engineers the idea of switching as a career, and then to train them almost from the ground up.

Bell Laboratories has not been unaware of this problem and has taken several important steps toward its solution. The publication of *The Design of Switching Circuits* by Keister, Ritchie and Washburn has made available an excellent textbook for use in a switching course. The recent survey course for professors in Digital Control Techniques should also stimulate interest in the field and encourage colleges to offer courses in switching. The development of large-scale computing machines has "glamorized" the field of switching and digital devices to a considerable extent. A number of colleges now offer courses in computing machines which at least touch on the subjects of switching and relay circuits.

This memorandum proposes another supplementary attack on the same problem. An important adjunct to any engineering course is a related series of lecture-room and laboratory experiments. Most colleges, even if prepared to give a course in switching, do not have available suitable relay and switch gear for such experiments. It is suggested here that a laboratory switching outfit be developed and made available to colleges. This outfit would consist of about thirty relays and associated switch gear (pushbuttons, indicating lights, stepping switches, dial mechanisms, etc.) mounted on a panel with terminals brought out to a plugboard. By means of patch-cords, these components could be connected up to form a wide variety of switching circuits. The apparatus would be accompanied by a laboratory manual describing many experiments and typical circuits that could be set up, starting with the simplest combinations of relays and switches, and working up to rather involved functional circuits.

Used as laboratory equipment, students would gain valuable experience in actually setting up, observing and trouble shooting physical apparatus. In addition, the output should prove a useful lecture aid; the instructor could set up simple circuits for demonstrations in his lectures.

We feel that a relay plugboard of this sort would also be useful to other groups. It is extremely difficult to design relay circuits completely free of logical errors. If such an outfit

---

* Bell Laboratories Memorandum, Jan. 10, 1954.

were available to relay circuit designers, they could easily make a final check of the logic of their circuits by setting them up on the plugboard. In a way, such an apparatus is analogous, for relay circuits, to the AC and DC network boards widely used in the study of power systems.

It is, of course, not possible at this stage to give an accurate cost estimate of such an outfit. However, existing switch gear usually runs some ten dollars per relay. Using this figure for thirty relays and doubling the figure to account for the other components, the chassis and the patch-cords, we arrived at $600 as a rough estimate, which is probably not off by more than a factor of two. The cost could be reduced by making the outfits in kit form — assembly and wiring to be done by the users. Cost might also be cut by the use of salvage relays from old equipment. This would surely be a more desirable destination for used relays than the Nassau Smelting and Refining Co. In any case, it would seem a good long-range investment for the Laboratories to supply such equipment to colleges at cost or, possibly, free of charge.

The Experimental Model To try out the idea of a plugboard relay outfit, an experimental model has been constructed (see Figures 1 and 2).[1]

This model contains the following components:

24 relays, each with four transfer contacts and each with a permanent series resistance to + battery (for shunt-down purposes as in W-Z pulse dividers).

2 "minor" switches, each having three decks and ten positions. These selector switches have an operate coil which advances the swingers one step for each pulse, and a reset coil which returns the wipers to normal. There is also an off-normal switch.

1 slow pulse source.

1 telephone dial mechanism.

4 message registers.

30 pushbuttons and switches.

30 indicating lamps and sockets.

200 patch-cords of assorted lengths.

All terminals of all components, apart from the lamps, buttons and dial, are connected permanently to jacks of the plugboard. The lamps, buttons and dial have cords attached with plugs on the ends. These components are mounted on the front operating panel in a manner appropriate to the circuit being set up and the plugs from them are plugged into the jacks of the plugboard.

The selection of equipment in the experimental model is, of course, subject to modification as we gain experience. It is possible, with this amount of equipment, to design a wide variety of interesting relay circuits. At a basic level all of the fundamental circuits – series, parallel, shunt-down, pulse dividers, symmetric functions, trees, counters, preference chains, etc. – can be demonstrated. At a more advanced level, functional circuits of some complexity can be designed. Some examples are described briefly in the next section.

---

[1] Editors' note. Figures 1 and 2 are actually photographs of Model 2, rather than the version described in this Memorandum (see Commentary).

Figure 1

Figure 2

In the experimental model, banana plugs are used on the patch-cords. They are so constructed that each plug has a jack at its top end. This allows the plugs to be stacked — any number of connections can be made to the same point.

It is quite easy to set up a circuit on the plugboard. A convenient method is to have two people, one working on the circuit diagram, calling off connections and noting which ones are complete, and the other working at the plugboard. Circuits involving up to five relays can be set up in ten minutes or less. The most involved circuits possible on the machine, using most of the contacts on most of the equipment, can be set up in less than two hours. It would require several days to set up the same circuits with ordinary soldered connections.

This experimental relay board was exhibited to the professors attending the recent course in Digital Control Techniques and received considerable favorable comment. A number of them felt the need for laboratory experiment and indicated a definite interest in obtaining such equipment.

The Laboratory Manual The laboratory manual accompanying the outfit should contain specifications of the components, a description of how circuits are set up on the machine, a series of carefully selected experiments and circuits that can be carried out on the machine, and a number of design problems for the student to solve.

With the equipment available, many interesting circuits can be constructed. The following short list will give some idea of the capacities of the machine.

1. Perpetual calendar. (See appendix.) The telephone dial acts as input, the names of months being written opposite appropriate holes. Any date from 1752 to 2099 may be dialed into the machine, e.g., September 17, 1953. The machine then indicates the corresponding day of the week by lighting one of the group of seven lamps.

2. Dial-pulse register. The board is wired to act as a small dial-pulse register, similar to those used in an automatic office.

3. Nim-playing machine. The machine plays the game of Nim with three piles of up to seven lights in each pile, winning whenever this is possible.

4. Adding circuit. The board can be wired to act as a binary adder similar to those used in computing machines, receiving its input from two sets of pushbuttons and displaying the output on a set of lights. It is also possible to set up a decimal adder with the telephone dial as input.

5. Tic-tac-toe machine. The board can be set up to play Tic-tac-toe against a human opponent, receiving its input from pushbuttons and indicating its move with lights. It will always win if possible, otherwise draw.

6. Automatic elevator. A circuit can be designed for controlling an automatic elevator with four floors and memory of buttons that have been pressed.

7. Miniature telephone exchange. A model exchange with four subscribers can be set up, embodying many of the principles of large offices.

8. Tower of Hanoi. The standard circuits for solving this puzzle can be set up easily on the plugboard.

9. Penny-matching machine. A simplified model of the penny-matching machine circuit can be set up on the machine.

10. Morse encoder. Twenty-six buttons labeled A, B, . . . , Z are available. If one of these is pressed, the machine produces the corresponding Morse code, the output appearing on a light and a buzzer.

11. Morse decoder. (See appendix.) A key is available as input and twenty-six labeled lights as output. If the key is operated (at proper speed) the machine decodes this signal.

It takes a week or more to design and trouble-shoot a circuit of the complexity of those listed above. Writing a good laboratory manual for the outfit would probably require a man year of work.

Relay Plugboards for Hobbyists The idea of a flexible relay outfit has a possible application, on a smaller scale, for children or adult hobbyists interested in experimenting with relay and switching circuits. Because of cost considerations, this problem is entirely distinct from the type of outfit described above. In another memorandum this problem is discussed, and an inexpensive three-relay board is described.

Appendix 1. Perpetual Calendar

This circuit (see Fig. 3) indicates on what day of the week any date (Gregorian calendar) falls. It covers the period from 1752 to 2099. The input is a telephone dial with month labels added according to Table I. The date is dialed in the order:

Nov. 23, 1953 AD.

When the dialing is completed a lamp corresponding to the day of the week lights. The circuit gives the correct day except for the months of January and February 1800 and 1900.[1]

Table I

Possible Values of Letters in Date

Month	Jan	Feb	Mar	Apr	May	June	July	Aug	Sept	Oct	Nov	Dec
M	0	3	3	6	1	4	6	2	5	0	3	5
M(leap year)	6	2										

D_1	$10D_1$ (mod 7)	D_2	C_1C_2	$N(C_1C_2)$	Y_1	Y_2
0	0	0–9	1 7	4	0 – 9	0 – 9
1	3		1 8	2		
2	6		1 9	0		
3	2		2 0	6		

For purposes of discussion we will consider the date to be written:

---

[1] This is because the circuit assumes that 1800 and 1900 were leap years. They were not since 1800 and 1900 are not divisible by 400. A few additional relays could correct this.

$$M\,D_1^{(2)}\,D_2, \quad C_1C_2\,Y_1Y_2 \quad AD$$

where the letters can have the values given in Table I. The day of the week is given by the equation:

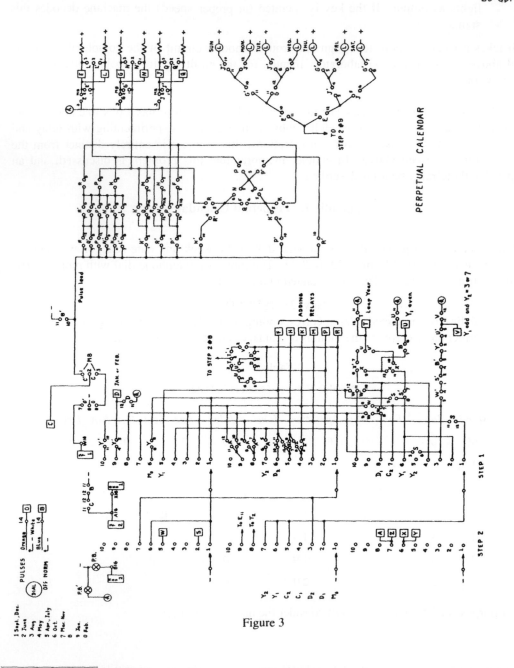

Figure 3

(2) If D_1 is zero it should be dialed, that is, New Year's Day is dialed Jan. 01, 1954.

$$\text{Day of week} = M + 10D_1 + D_2 + N(C_1 C_2) + \left[\frac{50}{4} Y_1 + \frac{5}{4} Y_2 \right] \quad (\text{mod } 7)$$

where

$$\text{Sun} = 0, \quad \text{Mon} = 1, \ldots, \text{Sat} = 6 .$$

The circuit solves this equation as follows. The dial pulses are followed by stepping switch number one (ST1). While the dial is being wound up for the next digit, the previous digit (stored on ST1) is connected through the appropriate translating network to a fast mod 7 adder. ST2 counts the returns to normal of the dial, keeping track of what part of the date is being dialed and controlling the translating networks.

The detailed description will be given by describing the function of each of the relays. The heart of the circuit is the fast mod 7 adder. Relays E, L, G, N, J and Q form 3 WZ pairs. The digits 0 through 6 are binary coded. E and L are the 2^2 digit, G and N the 2^1 digit and J and Q the 2^0 digit. Closing one and only one of the adding relays (R, P, M, K, H or F) and putting a minus pulse on the pulse lead will add 1, 2, 3, 4, 5 or 6 (mod 7) to the number in E, G and J. Removing the minus pulse lets L, N and Q follow E, G and J. The circuit was designed by preparing Table II. The entries indicate for which adder outputs the E, G and J (W relays) relays should be pulsed when it is desired to add the number which is the row label. For example, the entry in column G row 3 indicates that when 3 is to be added the G relay is to be pulsed only when the adder reads 0 or 2. Table III gives circuits which are closed for the values given in Table II. The final circuit was obtained by combining the circuits of Table III with contacts on the adding relays. For instance, if relay K is operated the circuits of row 4 Table III are connected between the pulse lead and the coils of relays E, G and J.

Table II

Values of Adder Output for Which W Relays Should Change

Numbers to be added	J	G	E
		W Relays	
1	012345	1356	36
2	56	012346	2356
3	0123	02	123456
4	3456	35	012456
5	01	123456	0156
6	123456	0246	04

The machine is cleared with the pushbutton P.B. After clearing relays D and C are operated. All other relays are not. Winding up the dial operates relay B; stepping ST2 to its #1 position and resetting ST1. When the dial is released relay 0 follows the dial pulses, stepping ST1 to the dialed position. Relay C is released at the beginning of the first dial pulse. After the last dial pulse one of the adding relays (F, H, K, M, P, R) is closed through the top deck of ST1 (unless Oct. was dialed in which case none is closed since we wish to add zero). When the dial reaches its normal position relay B releases, placing a minus pulse on the pulse lead and adding a number, corresponding to the month dialed, to the mod 7 adder. Releasing relay B causes relay C to operate and hold, then relay 0. If Jan. or Feb. were dialed relay D is locked up and holds until the machine is cleared.

A similar action occurs as each part of the date is dialed. As the dial is wound up ST1 resets and ST2 steps one connecting the proper translating networks between the decks of ST1 and the adding relays. The dial pulses are followed by ST1 and when the dial returns to normal a pulse is put on the pulse lead which causes the mod 7 adder to add the appropriate number.

Relays S, W, X, Y, Z and A are operated by ST2 and make changes in the translating networks. Relays T, U and V are used in calculating the leap year correction and the fractional parts of the largest integer in $\frac{50}{4}Y_1 + \frac{5}{4}Y_2$. If Y_1 is even U locks up. If $Y_1 Y_2$ is a leap year T locks up. If Y_1 is odd and $Y_2 = 3$ or 7 V locks up. The correction is added when the A of AD is dialed. Dialing the D steps ST2 and lights the correct day of the week lamp through a tree on relays E, G and J.

Table III

Circuits on Z Relays which are
Closed for Combinations Given in Table II

Adding Relay	No. to Be Added	W Relays		
		J	G	E
R	1	Q, N', L' (parallel)	Q ∥ (N—L)	(Q ∥ L) — N
P	2	(Q ∥ N) — L	Q, N, L' (parallel)	N ∥ (Q—L)
M	3	—L'—	—Q'——L'—	Q, N, L (parallel)
K	4	L ∥ (Q—N)	(N ∥ L) — Q	Q, N', L (parallel)
H	5	—N'——L'—	Q, N, L (parallel)	—N'—
F	6	Q, N, L (parallel)	—Q'—	—Q'——N—

BO-361720

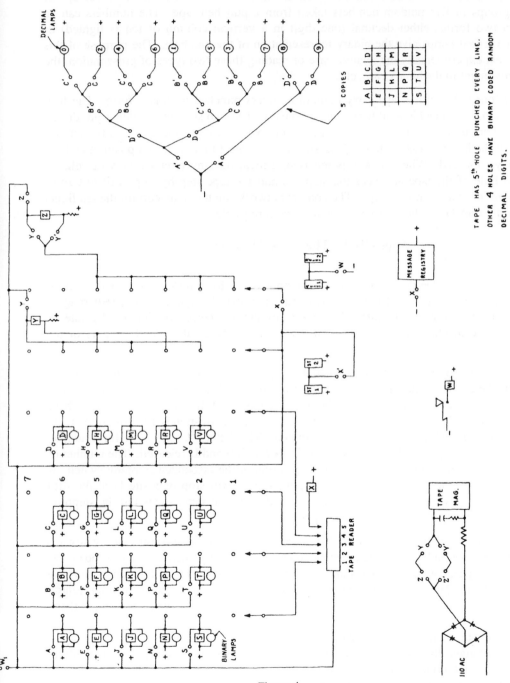

TAPE HAS 5th HOLE PUNCHED EVERY LINE. OTHER 4 HOLES HAVE BINARY CODED RANDOM DECIMAL DIGITS.

A	B	C	D
E	F	G	H
J	K	L	M
N	P	Q	R
S	T	U	V

NUMBER DISPLAY CIRCUIT

Figure 4

Appendix 2. Number Display Circuit

The circuit shown in Figure 4 was designed at the request of J. Karlin. It is set up for displaying groups of five random numbers taken from a punched tape. The numbers can be displayed in two forms, either decimal (one digit in a vertical column of ten is lighted) or binary (four vertical lamps give the binary representation of the number). The purpose of this circuit is to test experimentally the relative ease of reading these two types of presentation, the rate of improvement in the binary case, etc.

The first four holes of the tape carry random numbers punched in binary form. The fifth hole is always punched and is used for control purposes. The two stepping switches are driven in parallel and are used chiefly to steer the random numbers from the tape into twenty memory relays. When the key is pressed the stepping switches are reset to their initial position and the memory relays released. When the key is released, a local buzzing circuit involving relay X and the fifth hole of the tape advances the steppers and the tape step-by-step until five rows have been read into the memory relays. The contact networks on the relay control the ten lights in each column, translating the binary into the decimal representation.

Appendix 3. The Morse Decoder

This circuit decodes the dots and dashes of International Morse into its component letters, which are displayed in a panel of lights. A telegraph key may be operated at speeds ranging from five to forty words per minute. Two switches are set corresponding to the rate of transmission. The machine lights up successively lamps corresponding to the letters of the signal.

The circuit is shown in Figure 5. The machine "copies" one letter behind the transmission; a letter is displayed while the next one is being transmitted. There are two sets of memory relays which are used alternately to register the dots and dashes of the successive letters. These are the relays A, B, C, D and S, T, U, R. A received dot corresponds to a memory relay released, a received dash to the relay being operated. The letter "C" ($-\cdot-\cdot$), for example, would be registered in the ABCD group as A and C operated, B and D released. The number of dots and dashes in a letter corresponds to the final position of the associated stepping switch. If "C" is registered in the ABCD group, the stepping switch will stop opposite D at the fifth level. If "K" ($-\cdot-$) were registered, the relays would be in the same states but the stepping switch would have stopped at the fourth level opposite C.

The circuit has two timing elements. The first measures the length of closure of the key and decides between dots and dashes. The second measures periods when the key is open and decides between spaces within a letter and spaces between letters. These two subcircuits are essentially identical. The dot-dash discriminator, for example, is constructed of three relays. When the key is closed, these start going through a sequence of seven states. The signal that a dash has occurred (rather than a dot) can be made to correspond to any of these states. Early states correspond to short dots and dashes and rapid sending. Later states in the sequence correspond to a longer discriminating time and slow sending. Similar considerations apply to the "key open" measuring device. Receiving a dash corresponds to a ground on the line leading to the stepper wipers going into the memory relays. A space between letters operates relay Q which pulses the WZ pair of relays L and M. This pair of relays determines which of

BO-361721

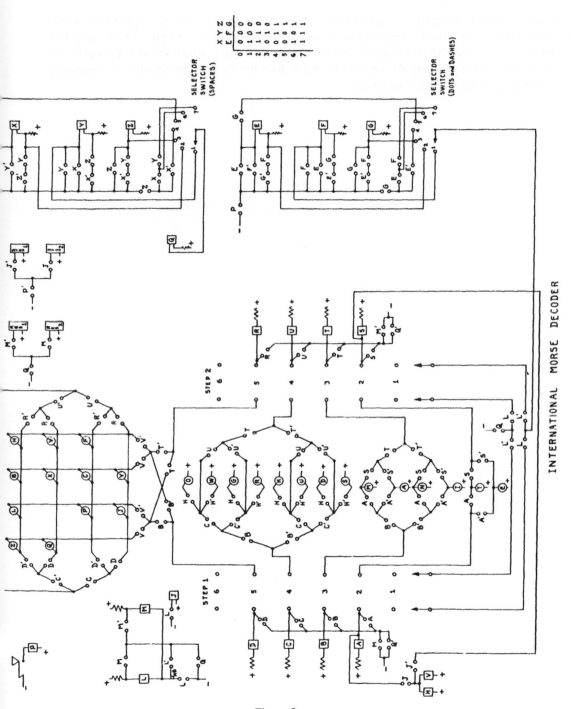

Figure 5

the two sets of memory relays and associated steppers is currently registering the transmitted letter (the other set of memory relays will be connected to the panel of display lights).

When a letter is transmitted, each dot or dash advances the registering stepper one notch. Whether it is a dot or a dash is recorded in the memory relay at each position. When the end of the letter occurs, relay Q will operate, advancing the LM pair, which in turn connects the second stepper for registering the next letter and allows the first set to control the indicating lights and display the letter just received.

AUTOMATA STUDIES

W. R. ASHBY	J. MC CARTHY
J. T. CULBERTSON	M. L. MINSKY
M. D. DAVIS	E. F. MOORE
S. C. KLEENE	C. E. SHANNON
K. DE LEEUW	N. SHAPIRO
D. M. MAC KAY	A. M. UTTLEY

J. VON NEUMANN

Edited by

C. E. Shannon and J. McCarthy

Princeton, New Jersey

Princeton University Press

1956

The preface, table of contents and the two papers by Shannon
are included here.

PREFACE

Among the most challenging scientific questions of our time are
the corresponding analytic and synthetic problems: How does the brain
function? Can we design a machine which will simulate a brain? Speculation
on these problems, which can be traced back many centuries, usually reflects in any period the characteristics of machines then in use. Descartes,
in DeHomine, sees the lower animals and, in many of his functions, man as
automata. Using analogies drawn from water-clocks, fountains and mechanical
devices common to the seventeenth century, he imagined that the nerves transmitted signals by tiny mechanical motions. Early in the present century,
when the automatic telephone system was introduced, the nervous system was
often likened to a vast telephone exchange with automatic switching equipment directing the flow of sensory and motor data. Currently it is fashionable to compare the brain with large scale electronic computing machines.

Recent progress in various related fields leads to an optimistic
view toward the eventual and not too remote solution of the analytic and
synthetic problems. The fields of neuro-anatomy and neuro-physiology,
using powerful tools from electronics in encephalographic studies, have
illuminated many features of the brain's operation.

The development of large scale computers has led to a clearer
understanding of the theory and design of information processing devices.
Programming theory, still in its infancy, is already suggesting the tremendous potential versatility of computers. Electronic computers are also
valuable tools in the study of various proposed models of nervous systems.
Often such models are much too complex for analytic appraisal, and the only
available method of study is by observation of the model in operation.

On the mathematical side, developments in symbolic logic, recursive
function theory and Turing machine theory have led to deeper understanding
of the nature of what is computable by machines. Neighboring fields of
game theory and information theory have developed concepts relating to the
nature and coding of information that may prove useful in automata research.

The problem of giving a precise definition to the concept of
"thinking" and of deciding whether or not a given machine is capable of
thinking has aroused a great deal of heated discussion. One interesting
definition has been proposed by A. M. Turing: a machine is termed capable
of thinking if it can, under certain prescribed conditions, imitate a human
being by answering questions sufficiently well to deceive a human questioner
for a reasonable period of time. A definition of this type has the advantages of being operational or, in the psychologists' term, behavioristic.
No metaphysical notions of consciousness, ego and the like are involved.
While certainly no machines at the present time can even make a start at
satisfying this rather strong criterion, Turing has speculated that within
a few decades it will be possible to program general purpose computers in
such a way as to satisfy this test.

A disadvantage of the Turing definition of thinking is that it is possible, in principle, to design a machine with a complete set of arbitrarily chosen responses to all possible input stimuli (see, in this volume, the Culbertson and the Kleene papers). Such a machine, in a sense, for any given input situation (including past history) merely looks up in a "dictionary" the appropriate response. With a suitable dictionary such a machine would surely satisfy Turing's definition but does not reflect our usual intuitive concept of thinking. This suggests that a more fundamental definition must involve something relating to the manner in which the machine arrives at its responses--something which corresponds to differentiating between a person who solves a problem by thinking it out and one who has previously memorized the answer.

The present volume is a collection of papers which deal with various aspects of automata theory. This theory is of interest to scientists in many different fields and, correspondingly, among the authors are workers who are primarily logicians, mathematicians, physicists, engineers, neurologists and psychologists. The papers include some which are close to pure mathematics; others are essentially directed to the synthesis problem and some relate largely to philosophic questions. There is also a certain amount of overlap, the same problem being handled from somewhat different points of view by different authors.

The papers have been divided into three groups. The first group consists of papers dealing with automata having a finite number of possible internal states. In the usual quantized model of this type, the automaton has a finite number of inputs and outputs and operates in a quantized time scale. Thus, such a device is characterized by two functions of the current state and input, one function giving the next state and the other the next output. Although seemingly trivial at this level of description, many interesting problems arise in the detailed analysis of such machines. Indeed, it should be remembered that essentially all actual physical machines and even the brain itself are, or can be reasonably idealized to be, of this form.

Neurophysiologists have proposed a number of models for the neuron and Kleene, in his paper, investigates the capabilities and limitations of automata constructed from these idealized components. von Neumann, using similar components, allows the possibility of statistically unreliable operation and shows that under certain conditions it is possible, with unreliable components, to construct large and complex automata with as high a reliability as desired. In Culbertson's paper a simple construction is given for an idealized neural network which will react in an arbitrary prescribed manner for an arbitrary lifetime. In all of these papers the notion of universal components plays a significant role. These are components which, roughly speaking, are sufficiently flexible to form devices capable of acting like any machine. Minsky considers the problem of universality of components

and finds conditions which ensure this property. In a paper of a somewhat
different type, Moore studies what can be learned about finite state automata by experiments performed on the inputs and outputs of the machine
(without direct observation of its interior).

The second group of papers deals with the theory of Turing machines
and related questions, that is to say, with automata having an unlimited
number of possible states. The original Turing machine (since then, recast
in many different forms) may be described as follows. Let there be given a
tape of infinite length which is divided into squares and a finite list of
symbols which may be written on these squares. There is an additional mechanism, the head, which may read the symbol on a square, replace it by another
or the same symbol and move to the adjoining square to the left or right.
This is accomplished as follows: At any given time the head is in one of a
finite number of internal states. When it reads a square it prints a new
symbol, goes into a new internal state and moves to the right or left depending on the original internal state and the symbol read. Thus a Turing
machine is described by a finite list of quintuplets such as 3, 4, 3, 6, R
which means: If the machine is in the third internal state and reads the
fourth symbol it prints the third symbol, goes into the sixth internal state
and moves to the right on the tape. There is a fixed initial internal state
and the machine is supposed to start on a blank tape. One of the symbols
represents a blank square and there may be given a state in which the machine
stops.

Turing gave a convincing argument to the effect that any precisely
defined computation procedure could be carried out by a machine of the type
described above. He also showed that the Turing machines can be enumerated
and that a universal machine could be made which, when it read the number of
any Turing machine, would carry out the computation that that machine would
have carried out were it put on a blank tape. His final result was to show
that there did not exist a Turing machine which when confronted with the
number of another machine would decide whether that machine would ever stop.

Any of the present automatic electronic computers is equivalent to
a universal Turing machine if it is given, for example, a means of asking
for more punched cards and for the return of cards it has already punched.
In Shannon's paper it is shown that a universal Turing machine can be constructed with only two internal states, or alternatively, with only two
tape symbols. Davis gives a general definition of a universal Turing machine
and establishes some results to make this definition appear reasonable.
McCarthy discusses the problem of calculating the inverse of the function
generated by a Turing machine, after some argument to the effect that many
intellectual problems can be formulated in this way. Finally, De Leeuw,
Moore, Shannon and Shapiro investigate whether machines with random elements
can compute anything uncomputable by ordinary Turing machines.

The third section of the book contains papers relating more directly to the synthesis of automata which will simulate in some sense the operation of a living organism. Ashby discusses the problem of designing an intelligence amplifier, a device which can solve problems beyond the capacities of its designer. MacKay, dealing with the same general problem, suggests means for an automaton to symbolize new concepts and generate new hypotheses. Uttley studies from a still different point of view the problem of the abstraction of temporal and spatial patterns by a machine, that is, the general problem of concept formation.

It gives us pleasure to express our gratitude to all those who have contributed to the preparation of this volume. The work was supported in part by the Princeton Logistics Project sponsored by the Office of Naval Research. Professor A. W. Tucker, directing this project, has been most helpful. H. S. Bailey, Jr. and the staff of the Princeton University Press, particularly Mrs. Dorothy Stine and Mrs. Jean Muiznieks have been efficient and cooperative. Thanks are also due Dr. Julia Robinson for help with the reviewing and Mrs. E. Powanda for secretarial services.

                                                        John McCarthy
                                                        Claude Shannon

A UNIVERSAL TURING MACHINE WITH TWO INTERNAL STATES

Claude E. Shannon

INTRODUCTION

In a well-known paper[1], A. M. Turing defined a class of computing machines now known as Turing machines. We may think of a Turing machine as composed of three parts — a control element, a reading and writing head, and an infinite tape. The tape is divided into a sequence of squares, each of which can carry any symbol from a finite alphabet. The reading head will at a given time scan one square of the tape. It can read the symbol written there and, under directions from the control element, can write a new symbol and also move one square to the right or left. The control element is a device with a finite number of internal "states." At a given time, the next operation of the machine is determined by the current state of the control element and the symbol that is being read by the reading head. This operation will consist of three parts; first the printing of a new symbol in the present square (which may, of course, be the same as the symbol just read); second, the passage of the control element to a new state (which may also be the same as the previous state); and third, movement of the reading head one square to the right or left.

In operation, some finite portion of the tape is prepared with a starting sequence of symbols, the remainder of the tape being left blank (i.e., registering a particular "blank" symbol). The reading head is placed at a particular starting square and the machine proceeds to compute in accordance with its rules of operation. In Turing's original formulation alternate squares were reserved for the final answer, the others being used for intermediate calculations. This and other details of the original definition have been varied in later formulations of the theory.

Turing showed that it is possible to design a universal machine which will be able to act like any particular Turing machine when supplied with a description of that machine. The description is placed on the tape of the universal machine in accordance with a certain code, as is also the starting sequence of the particular machine. The universal machine then imitates the operation of the particular machine.

Our main result is to show that a universal Turing machine can be constructed using one tape and having only two internal states. It will also be shown that it is impossible to do this with one internal state. Finally a construction is given for a universal Turing machine with only two tape symbols.

---

[1] Turing, A. M., "On Computable Numbers, with an Application to the Entscheidungsproblem," Proc. of the London Math. Soc. 2 - 42 (1936), pp. 230 - 265.

THE TWO-STATE UNIVERSAL TURING MACHINE

The method of construction is roughly as follows. Given an arbitrary Turing machine A with an alphabet of m letters (symbols used on the tape, including the blank) and n internal states, we design a machine B with two internal states and an alphabet of at most $4mn + m$ symbols. Machine B will act essentially like machine A. At all points of the tape, except in the position opposite the reading head and one adjacent position, the tape of B will read the same as the tape of A at corresponding times in the calculation of the two machines. If A is chosen to be a universal Turing machine, then B will be a universal Turing machine.

Machine B models the behavior of machine A, but carries the information of the internal state of A via the symbols printed on the tape under the reading head and in the cell of the tape that the reading head of A will next visit. The main problem is that of keeping this state information up to date and under the reading head. When the reading head moves, the state information must be transferred to the next cell of the tape to be visited using only two internal states in machine B. If the next state in machine A is to be (say) state 17 (according to some arbitrary numbering system) this is transferred in machine B by "bouncing" the reading head back and forth between the old cell and the new one 17 times (actually 18 trips to the new cell and 17 back to the old one). During this process the symbol printed in the new cell works through a kind of counting sequence ending on a symbol corresponding to state 17, but also retaining information as to the symbol that was printed previously in this cell. The bouncing process also returns the old cell back to one of the elementary symbols (which correspond one-to-one with the symbols used by machine A), and in fact returns it to the particular elementary symbol that should be printed in that cell when the operation is complete.

The formal construction of machine B is as follows: Let the symbol alphabet of machine A be $A_1, A_2, \ldots, A_m$, and let the states be $S_1, S_2, \ldots, S_n$. In machine B we have m elementary symbols corresponding to the alphabet of the A machine, $B_1, B_2, \ldots, B_m$. We further define $4mn$ new symbols corresponding to state symbol pairs of machine A together with two new two-valued indices. These symbols we denote by $B_{i,j,x,y}$ where $i = 1, 2, \ldots, m$ (corresponding to the symbols), $j = 1, 2, \ldots, n$ (corresponding to the states), $x = +$ or $-$ (relating to whether the cell of the tape is transmitting or receiving information in the bouncing operation) and $y = R$ or L (relating to whether the cell bounces the control to the right or left).

The two states of machine B will be called α and β. These two states are used for two purposes: First, on the initial step of the bouncing operation they carry information to the next cell being visited as to whether the old cell is to the right (α) or left (β) of the new one. This is necessary for the new cell to bounce the control back in the proper direction. After the initial step this information is retained in the new cell by the symbol printed there (the last index y). Second, the states α and β are used to signal from the old cell to the new one as to when the bouncing operation is complete. Except for the initial step of bouncing, state β will be carried to the new cell until the end of the bouncing operation when an α is carried over. This signifies the end of this operation and the new cell then starts acting as a transmitter and controlling the next step of the calculation.

Machine B is described by telling what it does when it reads an arbitrary symbol and is in an arbitrary state. What it does consists of three parts: printing a new symbol, changing to a new state, and moving the reading head to right or left. This operation table for machine B is as follows.

symbol;	state $\longrightarrow$	symbol;	state;	direction		
B_i;	$\alpha \longrightarrow$	$B_{i,1,-,R}$;	α;	R	$(i = 1, 2, \ldots, m)$	(1)
B_i;	$\beta \longrightarrow$	$B_{i,1,-,L}$;	α;	L	$(i = 1, 2, \ldots, m)$	(2)
$B_{i,j,-,x}$;	$\beta \longrightarrow$	$B_{i,(j+1),-,x}$;	α;	x	$\begin{pmatrix} i = 1, 2, \ldots, m \\ j = 1, 2, \ldots, n-1 \\ x = R, L \end{pmatrix}$	(3)
$B_{i,j,+,x}$;	α or $\beta \longrightarrow$	$B_{i,(j-1),+,x}$;	β;	x	$\begin{pmatrix} i = 1, 2, \ldots, m \\ j = 2, \ldots, n \\ x = R, L \end{pmatrix}$	(4)
$B_{i,1,+,x}$;	α or $\beta \longrightarrow$	B_i;	α;	x	$\begin{pmatrix} i = 1, 2, \ldots, m \\ x = R, L \end{pmatrix}$	(5)

So far, these operations do not depend (except for the number of symbols involved) on the operation table for machine A. The next and last type of operation is formulated in terms of the operation table of the machine being modeled. Suppose that machine A has the operation formula

(6) $A_i; \; S_j \longrightarrow A_k; \; S_\ell; \; \begin{smallmatrix} R \\ L \end{smallmatrix}$.

Then machine B is defined to have

(7) $B_{i,j,-,x}; \; \alpha \longrightarrow B_{k,\ell,+,\begin{smallmatrix} R \\ L \end{smallmatrix}}; \; \begin{smallmatrix} \beta \\ \alpha \end{smallmatrix} \; ; \; \begin{smallmatrix} R \\ L \end{smallmatrix}$

where if the upper letter (R) occurs in (6) the upper letters are used in (7) and conversely.

To see how this system works, let us go through a cycle consisting of one operation of machine A and the corresponding series of operations of machine B.

Suppose that machine A is reading symbol A_3 and is in state S_7, and suppose its operation table requires that it print A_8, go into state S_4 and move to the right. Machine B will be reading (by inductive assumption) symbol $B_{3,7,-,x}$ (whether x is R or L depends on preceding operations and is irrelevant to those which follow). Machine B will be in state α. By relation (7), machine B will print $B_{8,4,+,R}$, go into state β, and move to the right. Suppose the cell on the right contains A_{13} in machine A; in machine B the corresponding cell will contain B_{13}. On entering this cell in state β, by relation (2) it prints $B_{13,1,-,L}$, goes into state α, and moves back to the left. This is the beginning of the transfer of state information by the bouncing process. On entering the left cell, it reads $B_{8,4,+,R}$ and by relation (4) prints $B_{8,3,+,R}$, goes to state β and moves back to the right. There, by relation (3), it prints $B_{13,2,-,L}$, goes into state α and returns to the left. Continuing in this manner, the process is summarized in Table I.

The operations indicated complete the transfer of state information to the right cell and execution of the order started in the left cell. The left cell has symbol B_8 registered (corresponding to A_8 in machine A) and the right cell has symbol $B_{13,4,-,L}$ registered, with the reading head coming into that cell with internal state α. This brings us back to a situation similar to that assumed at the start, and arguing by induction we see that machine B models the behavior of machine A.

To get machine B started in a manner corresponding to machine A, its initial tape is set up corresponding to the initial tape of A (with A_i replaced by B_i) except for the cell initially occupied by the reading head. If the initial state of machine A is S_j and the initial symbol in this cell is A_i, the corresponding cell of the B tape has $B_{i,j,-,R(\text{or } L)}$ registered and its internal state is set at α.

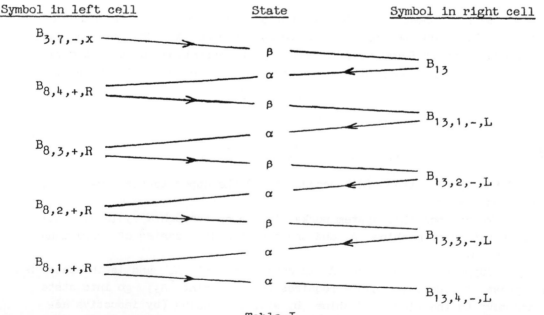

Symbol in left cell   State   Symbol in right cell

$B_{3,7,-,x}$ β

α B_{13}

$B_{8,4,+,R}$ β

α $B_{13,1,-,L}$

$B_{8,3,+,R}$ β

α $B_{13,2,-,L}$

$B_{8,2,+,R}$ β

α $B_{13,3,-,L}$

$B_{8,1,+,R}$ α

α $B_{13,4,-,L}$

Table I

IMPOSSIBILITY OF A ONE-STATE UNIVERSAL TURING MACHINE

It will now be shown that it is impossible to construct a universal Turing machine using one tape and only one internal state.

Suppose we have a machine satisfying these conditions. By registering a suitable "description number" of finite length on part of the tape (leaving the rest of the tape blank), and starting the reading head at a suitable point, the machine should compute any computable number, in particular the computable irrational numbers, e.g., $\sqrt{2}$. We will show that this is impossible.

According to Turing's original conception, $\sqrt{2}$ would be computed in a machine by the machine printing the successive digits of $\sqrt{2}$ (say, in binary notation) on a specified sequence of cells of the tape (say, on alternate cells, leaving the others for intermediate calculations). The following proof assumes $\sqrt{2}$ to be calculated in such a form as this, although it will be evident that modifications would take care of other reasonable interpretations of "calculating $\sqrt{2}$."

Since $\sqrt{2}$ is irrational, its binary digits do not, after any finite point, become periodic. Hence if we can show that with a one-state machine either (1) all but a finite number of the cells eventually have the same symbol registered, or (2) all but a finite number of the cells change indefinitely, we will have proved the desired result.

Assume first a doubly infinite tape — an infinite number of blanks each side of the description number for $\sqrt{2}$. When the reading head enters a blank cell it must either stay there indefinitely or eventually move out either to right or left. Since there is only one state, this behavior does not depend on previous history of the computation. In the first case, the reading head will never get more than one removed from the description number and all the tape except for a finite segment will be constant at the blank symbol. If it moves out of a blank symbol to the left, either the left singly infinite section of blank tape is not entered in the calculation and therefore need not be considered, or if it is entered, the reading head from that time onward continues moving to the left leaving all these previously blank cells registering the same symbol. Thus the tape becomes constant to the left of a finite segment and blank to the right of this segment and could not carry $\sqrt{2}$. A similar situation arises if it emerges to the right from an originally blank cell. Hence the doubly infinite tape is no better than the singly infinite tape and we may assume from symmetry a singly infinite tape to the right of the description number.

Now consider the following operation. Place the reading head on the first cell of this infinite blank strip. The machine will then compute for a time and perhaps the reading head will be transferred back out of this strip toward the description number. If so, replace it on the first cell of the now somewhat processed blank tape. If it returns again off the tape, again replace it on the first cell, etc. The number of times it can be placed

on the first cell in this fashion will be called the reflection number of the
machine and denoted by R. This will be either an integer 1, 2, 3, ...,
or ∞.

      Now consider placing the reading head at its appropriate start for
the description number to compute $\sqrt{2}$. After a certain amount of computation
the reading head will perhaps emerge from the description number part of the
tape. Replace it on the last cell of the description number. Again after a
time it will possibly emerge. Continue this process as long as possible. The
number of times it emerges will either be an integer 0, 1, 2, 3, ..., or ∞.
This number, S, we call the reflection number for the $\sqrt{2}$ description.

      If S is finite and R (possibly ∞) > S, the reading head after
a finite time will be trapped in the part of the tape that originally contained the description number. Only a finite amount of the blank tape will
have been changed and the machine will not have calculated $\sqrt{2}$.

      If both R and S are infinite, the reading head will return in-
definitely to the description number part of the tape. The excursions into
the originally blank parts will either be bounded or not. If they are bounded,
only a finite amount of the blank tape will have been changed as in the preceding case. If the excursions are unbounded, all but a finite segment of
tape will be operated on by the reading head an unlimited number of times.
Since there is only one state and a finite alphabet of tape symbols, the
symbol registered in a cell visited an unlimited number of times must either
come to a constant (the same for all these cells) or else change cyclically
an infinite number of times. In the first case, all the originally blank
tape becomes constant and cannot represent $\sqrt{2}$. In the second case all the
blank tape is continually changing and cannot be the computation of anything.

      If R ≤ S, the reading head eventually moves into the original
blank part of the tape and stays there. In this case it can be shown that
the symbols in the originally blank part become constant. For either it moves
to the right out of the first blank cell into the second blank cell at least
R times, or not. If not the reading head is trapped in what was the first
blank cell after a finite time, and all but a finite amount of tape remains
constant at the blank symbol. If it does move out R times it will not return to the first originally blank cell since R is the reflection number
for blank tape. This first cell will then have registered the result of operating on a blank 2R times (R coming in from the left and R from the
right). The second originally blank cell will eventually register the same
constant symbol, since the same argument applies to it as to the first. In
each case the machine works into the same tape (an infinite series of blanks)
and enters the same number of times (R). This exhausts the cases and completes the proof.

MODELING A TURING MACHINE WITH ONLY TWO TAPE SYMBOLS

It is also possible, as we will now show, to construct a machine, C, which will act like any given Turing machine A and use only two symbols 1 and 0 on its tape, one of which, 0 say, is the symbol for a blank square. Suppose, as before, a given machine A has m tape symbols and n internal states. Let ℓ be the smallest integer such that m is less than or equal to 2^ℓ. Then we may set up an arbitrary association of the m symbols used by machine A with binary sequences of length ℓ, letting however the blank symbol of machine A correspond to the sequence of ℓ zeroes. Basically, the machine C will operate with binary sequences; an elementary operation in machine A will correspond in machine C to stepping the reading head to the right $\ell - 1$ squares (storing the read information in its internal state) then stepping back to the left $\ell - 1$ squares, writing the proper new symbol as it goes, and finally moving either to the right or to the left ℓ squares to correspond to the motion of the reading head of machine A. During this process, the state of machine A is also, of course, carried in machine C. The change from the old state to the new state occurs at the end of the reading operation.

The formal construction of machine C is as follows. Corresponding to states S_1, S_2, ..., S_n of machine A we define states T_1, T_2, ..., T_n in machine C (these will occur when machine C is at the beginning of an operation, reading the first symbol in a binary sequence of length ℓ). For each of these T_i we define two states T_{i0} and T_{i1}. If machine C is in state T_i and reads symbol 0, it moves to the right and goes into state T_{i0}. If it reads a 1, it moves to the right and goes into state T_{i1}. Thus, after reading the first symbol of a binary sequence, these two states remember what that symbol was. For each of these there are again two states T_{i00}, T_{i01} and T_{i10} and T_{i11}. If the machine is in the state T_{i0} for example and reads the symbol 0 it goes to the state T_{i00} and similarly for the other cases. Thus these states remember the initial state and the first two symbols read in the reading process. This process of constructing states is continued for $\ell - 1$ stages, giving a total of $(2^\ell - 1)n$ states. These states may be symbolized by

$$T_{i,x_1,x_2,\ldots,x_s} \qquad i = 1, 2, \ldots, n; \quad x_j = 0, 1; \quad s = 0, 1, \ldots, \ell - 1.$$

If the machine is in one of these states $(s < \ell - 1)$ and reads 0 or 1, the machine moves to the right and the 0 or 1 appears as a further index on the state. When $s = \ell - 1$, however, it is reading the last binary symbol in the group of ℓ. The rules of operation now depend on the specific rules of machine A. Two new sets of states somewhat similar to the T states above are defined, which correspond to writing rather than reading:

$$R_{i,x_1,x_2,\ldots,x_s} \quad \text{and} \quad L_{i,x_1,x_2,\ldots,x_s}.$$

A sequence x_1, x_2, ..., $x_{\ell-1}$, x_ℓ corresponds to a symbol of machine A. Suppose that when machine A is reading this corresponding symbol and is in state i it prints the symbol corresponding to the binary sequence y_1, y_2, ..., $y_{\ell-1}$, y_ℓ, goes to state j and moves (say) right. Then we define machine C such that when in state $T_{i,x_1,x_2,...,x_{\ell-1}}$, and reading symbol x_ℓ, it goes into state $R_{j,y_1,y_2,...,y_{\ell-1}}$, prints y_ℓ and moves to the left. In any of the states $R_{i,y_1,y_2,...,y_s}$ (or $L_{i,y_1,y_2,...,y_s}$), machine C writes y_s, moving to the left and changes to state $R_{i,y_1,y_2,...,y_{s-1}}$ (or $L_{i,y_1,y_2,...,y_{s-1}}$). By this process the binary sequence corresponding to the new symbol is written in place of the old binary sequence. For the case $s=1$, the writing of y_1 completes the writing operation of the binary sequence. The remaining steps are concerned with moving the reading head ℓ steps to the right or left according as the machine is in an R state or an L state. This is carried out by means of a set of U_{is} and V_{is} ($i = 1, 2, ..., n$; $s = 1, 2, ..., \ell - 1$). In state R_{ix_1} the machine writes x_1, moves to the right, and goes into state U_{i1}. In each of the U states it continues to the right, printing nothing and going into the next higher indexed U state until the last one is reached. Thus U_{is} produces motion to the right and state U_{is+1} ($s < \ell - 1$). Finally $U_{i\ell-1}$ leads, after motion to the right, to T_i, completing the cycle. In a similar fashion, L_{ix_1} leads to motion to the left and state V_{i1}; V_{is} gives motion to the left and V_{is+1} ($s < \ell - 1$); finally, $V_{i\ell-1}$ gives motion to the left and T_i.

The initial tape for machine C is, of course, that for machine A with each symbol replaced by its corresponding binary sequence. If machine A is started on a particular symbol, machine C will be started on the left-most binary symbol of the corresponding group; if machine A is started in state S_1, C will be started in state T_1.

Machine C has at most $n(1 + 2 + 4 ... + 2^{\ell-1}) = n(2^\ell - 1)$ T states, similarly at most $n(2^\ell - 2)$ R states and $n(2^\ell - 2)$ L states, and finally $2n(\ell - 1)$ U and V states. Thus altogether not more than $3n2^\ell + n(2\ell - 7)$ states are required. Since $2^\ell < 2m$, this upper bound on the number of states is less than $6mn + n(2\ell - 7)$, which in turn is certainly less than $8mn$.

The results we have obtained, together with other intuitive considerations, suggest that it is possible to exchange symbols for states and vice versa (within certain limits) without much change in the product. In going to two states, the product in the model given was increased by a factor of about 8. In going to two symbols, the product was increased by a factor of about 6, not more than 8. These "loss" factors of 6 and 8 are probably in part due to our method of microscopic modeling — i.e., each elementary

operation of machine A is modeled into machine B. If machine B were
designed merely to have the same calculating ability as A in the large,
its state-symbol product might be much more nearly the same. At any rate
the number of logical elements such as relays required for physical realization will be a small constant (about 2 for relays) times the base two logarithm of the state-symbol product, and the factor of 6 or 8 therefore implies
only a few more relays in such a realization.

      An interesting unsolved problem is to find the minimum possible
state-symbol product for a universal Turing machine.

COMPUTABILITY BY PROBABILISTIC MACHINES

K. de Leeuw, E. F. Moore, C. E. Shannon, and N. Shapiro

INTRODUCTION

The following question will be considered in this paper: Is there anything that can be done by a machine with a random element but not by a deterministic machine?

The question as it stands is, of course, too vague to be amenable to mathematical analysis. In what follows it must be delimited in two respects. A precise definition of the class of machines to be considered must be given and an equally precise definition must be given of the tasks which they are to perform. It is clear that the nature of our results will depend strongly on these two choices and therefore our answer is not to be interpreted as a complete solution of the originally posed informal question. The reader should be especially cautioned at this point that the results we obtain have no application outside the domain implied by these choices. In particular our results refer to the possibility of enumeration of <u>infinite</u> sets and the computation of <u>infinite</u> sequences. They yield no information of the type that would be wanted if <u>finite</u> tasks were being considered; for example, the relative complexity of probabilistic machines which can perform a given finite task and their relative speeds.

This difficulty is implicit in any situation where mathematics is to be applied to an informally stated question. The process of converting this question into a precise mathematical form of necessity will highlight certain aspects. Other aspects, perhaps of equal or greater importance in another situation may be completely ignored.

The main body of the paper consists of definitions, examples, and statements of results. The proofs are deferred to the appendix since they consist in the most part of more or less elaborate constructions which are not absolutely essential for an understanding of the results.

Readers acquainted with recursive function theory will readily see that the results of this paper are actually results in that theory and can easily be translated into its terminology. In the light of this, the proofs of the results take on a dual aspect. They can be considered to be complete proofs, assuming the intuitively given notion of an <u>effective</u> process;[1] or they can be considered to be <u>indications</u> of how the theorems, if they were

---

[1] For discussion of effective processes, see [9] or [2]. The reader who is not familiar with the notion of an effective process is advised to consult one of these before proceeding further. Effective processes are also discussed in [1], [7], and [8].

742

stated formally in the language of recursive function theory, could be proved formally using the tools of that theory. This formalization is not carried out in the paper since it would detract from the conceptual content of the proofs. However, if should be clear to anyone familiar with recursive function theory that the formalization can be carried out.

PROBABILISTIC MACHINES VS. DETERMINISTIC MACHINES

In this section we will first develop a precise definition of a class of computing machines. These machines will have an input and an output. The input will be an infinite sequence of binary digits which may be supplied in two different ways: Either as a fixed sequence (physically we may think of an infinite prepared tape) or as the output of a binary random device (with probability p of producing a 1). In this latter case we have a probabilistic machine. We will next formulate a precise class of tasks that we wish such machines to perform, namely, the enumeration with positive probability of sets of output symbols. The key result of the paper, Theorem 1, is then applied to answer our question. The answer is given in Theorem 2. What it states is that if the random device has a probability p, where p is a <u>computable</u> <u>real</u> <u>number</u> (that is, a real number such that there is an effective process for finding any digit of its binary expansion), any set that can be enumerated by a probabilistic machine of the type considered can be enumerated by a deterministic machine. This does not occur if p is a non-computable real number. Similar results are obtained if the sequential order of the output symbols is taken into consideration. The situation is summarized in Theorem 3.

We shall think of our machines as objects that accept as input a tape printed with 0's and 1's and puts forth as output a tape on which it may print using a finite or countably infinite selection of output symbols $s_1, s_2, s_3 \ldots$ (These symbols may be configurations formed from some finite alphabet.) The machine shall be assumed to have some initial state in which it is placed before any operation is started; (as, for example, a desk calculator must be cleared before a computation). Another requirement that we can reasonably require a machine to satisfy is the following: There is an effective procedure whereby one can determine what the sequence of output symbols $(s_{j_1}, \ldots, s_{j_r})$ on the output tape will be if the machine is presented with the input sequence of 0's and 1's $(a_1, \ldots, a_n)$ in its initial state. This output sequence will be denoted by $f(a_1, \ldots a_n)$. Since we shall be interested only in the relationship between input and output in machines we can abstract away their interior and take this requirement as a definition. (Even though an abstract definition is given at this point, we shall continue to speak of machines in concrete terms.)

DEFINITION: A <u>machine</u> is a function that, for every n, to each n-tuple of 0's and 1's $(a_1, \ldots, a_n)$, associates some finite sequence $f(a_1, \ldots, a_n) = (s_{j_1}, \ldots, s_{j_r})$ consisting of elements from some fixed set S such that the following two conditions are satisfied.

1. $f(a_1, \ldots, a_n)$ is an initial segment of $f(a_1, \ldots, a_n, \ldots, a_{n+m})$ if $(a_1, \ldots, a_n)$ is an initial segment of $(a_1, \ldots, a_n, \ldots, a_{n+m})$.

2. f is a computable function, that is, there is an effective process[2] such that one can determine $f(a_1, \ldots, a_n)$ if $(a_1, \ldots, a_n)$ is given.

This definition is extended to infinite sequences as follows: If $A = (a_1, a_2, a_3, \ldots)$, $f(A)$ is the sequence which has as initial segments the $f(a_1, \ldots, a_n)$.

The operation of the machine can be thought of informally as follows: If it is supplied with input $(a_1, \ldots, a_n)$, it looks at a_1 and prints the sequence of symbols $f(a_1)$ on its output, it looks at a_2 and prints symbols after $f(a_1)$ on the tape to obtain the sequence $f(a_1, a_2)$, ..., it looks at a_n and prints symbols after $f(a_1, \ldots, a_{n-1})$ on the tape to obtain the sequence $f(a_1, \ldots, a_{n-1}, a_n)$ and then stops.

At this point several concrete examples of objects that are machines will be given. These are to serve two purposes, to illustrate the concept of machine introduced and to be referred to later to illustrate new concepts that arise. The examples need not all be read at this point.

MACHINE NO. 1: The output symbols of this machine are to be ordered pairs of integers (a, r). For each input symbol a the machine prints the output symbol (a, r) if a was the rth input symbol on the input tape. In other words, $f(a_1, \ldots, a_n) = ((a_1, 1), (a_2, 2), \ldots, (a_n, n))$.

MACHINE NO. 2: Let g be an integral valued function of positive integers which is computable, that is, there is an effective process for finding $g(n)$ if n is given. Let the machine print the output symbol $(r, g(r))$ after it has scanned the rth input symbol. In this case $f(a_1, \ldots, a_n) = \left((1, g(1)), (2, g(2)), \ldots (n, g(n)) \right)$ and the output is independent of the input. This machine and Machine No. 1 are extreme cases. No. 2 is oblivious of the input and No. 1 essentially copies the input onto the output tape. Note that No. 2 would not be a machine according to our definition if the function g were not computable, for in this case there would be no effective process for determining what the output would be if the input were given.

MACHINE NO. 3: Let the machine print the symbol 0 as soon as it comes to

---

the first zero in the input sequence. Otherwise it is to do nothing. Then $f(a_1, \ldots, a_n) = (0)$ if one of the a_j is a zero. Otherwise the machine prints nothing. This eventuality will be denoted by the "empty sequence," $(.)$, and we have $f(1, \ldots, 1) = (.)$.

MACHINE NO. 4: Let $f(a_1, \ldots, a_n) = (a_1)$. The machine merely copies the first input symbol onto the output tape and then prints nothing.

MACHINE NO. 5: Let the machine print the output symbol r if the maximum length of a string of 1's that the machine has observed is r. For example, $f(1) = (1)$, $f(1, 0) = (1, 1)$, $f(1, 0, 1) = (1, 1, 1)$, $f(1, 0, 1, 1) = (1, 1, 1, 2)$.

MACHINE NO. 6: Let $h(r, s)$ be a computable integral valued function whose domain is the positive integers. The machine prints nothing until it comes to the first 1 in the input; if this 1 is the first input symbol it never prints anything; if this 1 has occurred after r zeroes, it prints the symbol $(1, h(r, 1))$. After the next input the machine prints $(2, h(r, 2))$, after the next $(3, h(r, 3))$ etc. Let the function h_r with r fixed be defined by $h_r(s) = h(r, s)$. Then what this machine actually does is to compute the function h_r if it is presented with an initial string of r zeroes followed by a 1.

MACHINE NO. 7: This machine is given by $f(a_1, \ldots, a_n) = ((1, r_1), (2, r_2), \ldots, (q, r_q))$ where the integer r_s is obtained as follows: Look at the first 100^s digits of $(a_1, \ldots, a_n)$. Let p_s be the proportion of digits that are 1's. Let r_s be the sth digit in the binary expansion of the number p_s. q is the greatest s such that $100^s \leqq n$. A construction similar to this is used in the proof of part of Theorem 1.

      Although the action of a machine is defined only for finite input sequences, it is clear what one of our machines would do if it were fed an infinite input sequence $A = (a_1, a_2, a_3, \ldots)$ and had available an infinite output tape on which it could print. Its action is determined by the fact that we know what its output will be for all finite input sequences. Thus the machine associates to each infinite input sequence an output sequence which may or may not be infinite. For example, if Machine No. 1 is fed an infinite tape on which only 1's are printed, the output sequence will be $((1, 1), (1, 2), (1, 3), \ldots)$. Machine No. 3 gives no output (the empty sequence $(.)$) and Machine No. 4 the output sequence (1) when presented with the same input.

      We wish to consider the set of symbols that occur on the output tape of a machine that is supplied with some infinite input sequence A. (For example, if the output sequence is $(1, 1, 1, \ldots)$ the set of symbols consists of the symbol 1 alone while if the output sequence is $(1, 3, 5, 7, \ldots)$ the set of symbols is the set of all odd integers.) Thus the machine associates to each input sequence A some set of output symbols

which it enumerates. (We do not wish to consider here the order in which
the set is enumerated or whether or not it is enumerated without repetitions.
This will be done later when computation of sequences is considered.)

     For example, Machine No. 1 associates to any infinite input sequence
$A = (a_1, a_2, ...)$ the set of output symbols consisting of all (a_n, n) as
n runs over the positive integers. Machine No. 2 associates any input
sequence to the set of all $(n, g(n))$ as n runs over the positive integers.
Machine No. 3 associates to the input sequence consisting of all 1's the
empty set. To the same input Machine No. 5 associates the set of all positive
integers.

DEFINITION: A machine supplied with the infinite input sequence
$A = (a_1, a_2, a_3, ...)$ will be called an A-machine. It will be said to
A-enumerate the set of output symbols that it prints. A set of symbols is
called A-enumerable if there is an A-machine that A-enumerates the set.
     The sets that are A-enumerable if A is the sequence consisting
of all 1's are usually referred to as recursively enumerable sets. We
shall call them 1-enumerable sets and an A-machine shall be called a
1-machine if A consists entirely of 1's.
     One can associate to each infinite sequence $A = (a_1, a_2, ...)$
the set of all pairs (n, a_n) where a_n is the nth element in the sequence
A and n runs over all positive integers. This set will be called A'.
A sequence A is called computable if there is an effective process by means
of which one can determine the nth term of A for every n. The following
three lemmas will be proved in the appendix, although their proofs are almost immediate.

     LEMMA 1. The sequence A is computable if and only
     if the associated set A' is 1-enumerable.

     LEMMA 2. If A is a computable sequence, any A-enumerable
     set is 1-enumerable (and conversely).

     LEMMA 3. If A is not a computable sequence, there
     exist sets that are A-enumerable but which are not
     1-enumerable.

     Lemma 3 together with the fact that non-computable sequences exist
will be important later.
     We now wish to attach a random device to a machine in order to
construct a probabilistic machine. If one has a device that prints 0's
and 1's on a tape, 1's occurring with probability p and 0's occurring
with probability $1 - p$ $(0 < p < 1)$ and each printing being independent of
the preceeding printings, the output of the device can be used as the input

tape of a machine. The combination of the random device and the machine will
be called a p-machine.

The question asked in the Introduction of whether there are probabilistic machines that are more general than deterministic machines can now
be narrowed down to the more specific question: Can everything done by a
p-machine be done by a 1-machine? (In the next section, it will be shown
that there is little loss of generality in considering the rather narrow
class of p-machines within the larger class of all conceivable probabilistic machines. We shall see that a large class of probabilistic machines
are equivalent (in a sense that will be defined) to 1/2-machines, and many
of their properties can be deduced from the properties of 1/2-machines.)

We must further restrict our question since it is clear that no
precise answer can be given till we have a precise defininition of the task
that the machines are to perform.

The task that the machines in this paper shall be set to perform
is that of enumerating sets. This job is not as specialized as it at first
may seem. For example, a machine can compute a function by enumerating
symbols "f(n) = m"; or can decide the truth or falsity of a statement about
positive integers by enumerating symbols like "P(n) is true" and "P(n)
is false"; or can compute the binary expansion of a real number by enumerating symbols like "the nth digit of r is a".

We already have a definition of what is to be meant by a set of
symbols being 1-enumerable. Namely, a set is 1-enumerable if there is a
machine that has that set as its total output if a tape with all 1's is
fed in as input. It is necessary to have some definition of enumerability
to apply to p-machines so that a comparison can be made between them and
1-machines.

Two definitions will be proposed, p-enumerable sets and strongly
p-enumerable sets. Our original informal question will have been reduced
to the two precise questions: Is every p-enumerable set 1-enumerable?
Is every strongly p-enumerable set 1-enumerable?

It remains to give the two definitions: If one has a given
p-machine, one can assign to each set of possible output symbols its probability of occurrence as total output of that machine. This is the probability that that set will be precisely the set of symbols that occur on the
output tape of the machine if it is started in its initial position, the
random device connected and allowed to run forever. This probability is,
of course, zero for most sets. Several examples will be given, calling upon
the machines that we have used before. We shall assume that they have been
attached to a random device with p = 1/2 and thus have become 1/2-machines.
Machine No. 1 prints any set with zero probability. It should be pointed
out that finite sets cannot occur and that is the reason they have zero probability. However, there are infinite sets that <u>can</u> occur as output but nevertheless do so with zero probability. One should not forget the distinction

between occurrence with probability zero and impossibility of occurrence.
Machine No. 2 prints the set of all $(n, a(n))$ with probability 1 (and
actually with certainty). Machine No. 3 has as output the set consisting
of the symbol 0 alone with probability 1 but not with certainty. Machine No. 5 has as output the set of all positive integers with probability
1, but not certainty; since an infinite sequence of 0's and 1's contains
arbitrarily long runs of 1's with probability 1, but not certainty.
Machine No. 6 puts out the set of all $(n, h(r, n))$ with r fixed and n
running over all positive integers with probability 2^{-r}. In other words,
the machine computes the function h_r (which was defined by $h_r(n) = h(r, n)$)
with probability 2^{-r}.

DEFINITION: For some fixed p, a set S of symbols will be called
strongly p-enumerable if there is a p-machine that produces that set of
output symbols in any order with non-zero probability.

The previous examples showed that the following sets are strongly
1/2-enumerable: The set of all $(n, g(n))$ the set consisting of 0 alone,
the set consisting of all positive integers and the set of all $(n, h(r, n))$
with r fixed.

It is clear how a p-machine could be used to give information
about some strongly p-enumerable set S that it produces with positive
probability. One would operate the p-machine having confidence that the
set it enumerates is S in accordance with the probability of S occurring
as output. So long as S has some positive probability, the p-machine
could be used with some measure of confidence. If the probability of S
occurring as output were zero, one would have no confidence in the machine's
ability to enumerate precisely S. However, it might have a high probability
of being right for any particular output symbol and still enumerate S with
zero probability. So that this situation can be considered, a weaker definition will be given below.

There exists a definite probability that a given p-machine M
will eventually print some given output symbol. Let S_M be the set of all
output symbols that M eventually will print with probability $> 1/2$. For
example, let the machines that have been considered as examples be connected
to a random device with $p = 3/4$, so that they become $3/4$ machines. S_M
for Machine No. 1 is the set of all $(n, g(n))$, for Machine No. 3 is the
set consisting of 0 alone, for Machine No. 4 is the set consisting of 1
alone, for Machine No. 5 is the set of positive integers and for Machine No. 6
is the empty set.

If a p-machine M is started, the probability is $> 1/2$ that
it will eventually print any given element of S_M, while the probability is
$\leq 1/2$ that it will print any given element not in S_M. Thus it is clear how
a machine M could be used to give information about S_M. One would operate

the machine having a certain degree of confidence that any particular element of S_M will eventually occur as an output symbol and that any particular element not in S_M will not occur as output. However, the set S_M itself might occur with probability zero, in which case, one would have no confidence that the machine will enumerate precisely S_M. (It is clear that all this remains true if a number greater than $1/2$ is used in the definition of S_M. All of the following results remain valid in this case.)

DEFINITION: A set of symbols S will be called _p-enumerable_ if there is a machine M such that S is precisely S_M.

The condition that a set be p-enumerable is quite weak and we have thought of no weaker definition that would still ensure that there be a p-machine that give some information about each element of the set. One should note that a p-machine p-enumerates exactly one set while it may strongly p-enumerate many or no sets.

Superficially strong p-enumerability seems a much stronger concept that p-enumerability, and indeed it will be shown that a strongly p-enumerable set is p-enumerable. A bit deeper and perhaps unexpected is the converse result which implies actual equivalence of the two concepts.

To formulate the key result of the paper, which will be used to answer the two basic questions that we have enunciated, one more definition is needed. Let p be a real number, $0 < p < 1$. Then A_p is to be the infinite sequence of 0's and 1's $(a_1, a_2, a_3, \ldots)$ where a_n is the nth digit of the binary expansion of the real number p. That is, $p = .a_1 a_2 a_3 \ldots$. Since A_p is an infinite sequence of 0's and 1's, it can be used as input to machines and we shall speak of A_p-machines, A_p-enumerability, etc.

For any number p between 0 and 1, there are now three concepts, A_p-enumerability, p-enumerability and strong p-enumerability. The first is a strictly deterministic notion while the others are probabilistic.

The key result is:

THEOREM 1: Let S be a set of symbols and p a real number, $0 < p < 1$. The following three statements are equivalent:

1. S is A_p-enumerable
2. S is p-enumerable
3. S is strongly p-enumerable.

A proof of this theorem is given in the appendix but a sketch of the proof will be given after it is shown that this theorem gives immediate answers to our two questions.

First, let p be a non-computable real number between 0 and 1. It is known that such exist and in fact almost all (in Lebesgue measure) numbers are non-computable. The non-computability of p is equivalent to the non-computability of A_p. Then, according to Lemma 3, there exists a set S that is A_p-enumerable but which is not 1-enumerable. This set, because of Theorem 1, is a set which is both p-enumerable and strongly p-enumerable but is not 1-enumerable. Thus, if one admits random devices that will print the symbol 1 with a probability that is not a computable real number, one can construct p-machines that will "enumerate" sets that are not 1-enumerable.

The situation is entirely different if p is a computable real number (in particular if it is 1/2). This is equivalent to A_p being a computable sequence. Theorem 1 shows that any set which is p-enumerable or strongly p-enumerable is A_p-enumerable. Since A_p is computable, Lemma 2 shows that the set must be 1-enumerable. Thus a p-enumerable or strongly p-enumerable set must be 1-enumerable. The conclusion is that if p is restricted to be a computable real number (or in particular is 1/2), a machine with a random device cannot "enumerate" anything that a deterministic machine could not.

Both cases can be summarized in:

THEOREM 2: If p is a computable real number, any p-enumerable or strongly p-enumerable set is already 1-enumerable. If p is not a computable real number, there exist p-enumerable and strongly p-enumerable sets that are not 1-enumerable.

An indication of how Theorem 1 will be proved is given at this point. The proof proceeds by demonstrating statement 3 implies statement 2 implies statement 1 implies statement 3. This chain of implications gives the equivalence.

That 3 implies 2 is proved by showing that if one has a p-machine that has output S occurring with positive probability one can construct a new machine which has output S occurring with probability $> 1/2$. Then every element of S occurs with probability $> 1/2$ and any element not in S occurs with probability $< 1/2$ so that S is p-enumerable. Thus any strongly p-enumerable set is p-enumerable.

That 2 implies 1 is proven as follows: Let a p-machine M be given. We wish to construct an A_p-machine that A_p-enumerates the set S_M. Let us assume that we have an infinite tape on which A_p is printed. By the use of larger and larger initial segments of the infinite sequence A_p, one can compute lower bounds, which are arbitrarily good, for the probability of the truth of statements of the form "By the time n inputs from the random device have occurred M will have printed the symbol s." M

actually does print s with probability > 1/2 if and only if there is an
n such that the above statement is true with probability > 1/2. This in
turn occurs only if some one of the arbitrarily good lower bounds (that we
can compute using initial segments of A_p) for the probability of the above
statement being true is > 1/2. One can compute successively (using larger
and larger initial segments of A_p) all of the lower bounds for the probabilities for every n and every s. As soon as one comes to a lower bound
that is > 1/2, the corresponding symbol s is written down. One sees that
the set of symbols thus enumerated is S_M and the enumeration has been accomplished by a process which is actually an A_p-machine. Thus, any set
which is p-enumerable is also A_p-enumerable.

      1 implies 3 is proved as follows: A p-machine is constructed
which computes with probability > 1/2 the binary expansion of the real
number p. That is, the output of the machine is, with probability > 1/2,
the set of all (n, a_n) where a_n is the nth digit in the binary expansion
of p. The machine that does this is a modification of Machine No. 7. If
the output of this p-machine is used as input of another machine M, the
consequent output will be, with probability > 1/2, exactly what the output
of M would be if it were supplied as input the sequence A_p. If S is
any A_p-enumerable set and M a machine that A_p-enumerates it, the composite machine constructed above is a p-machine that strongly p-enumerates
S. Thus, any A_p-enumerable set is strongly p-enumerable. This proves that
1 implies 3 and the sketch of the proof of Theorem 1 is complete.

      The question that will be considered now is whether the same re-
sults are obtained if one considers the sequential order of the outputs of
the machines instead of only the totality of output symbols. It will be
shown that this situation can be reduced to a particular case of the results
that we have already obtained.

DEFINITION: An infinite sequence of symbols $S = s_1, s_2, s_3 \ldots$ is called
A-computable if it occurs as the output, in the given order, of some A-
machine. It is 1-computable if A consists entirely of 1's. S is
strongly p-computable if there is a p-machine that puts it out, in the
given order, with positive probability. S is p-computable if there is
a p-machine that has as its nth output symbol the nth symbol of S
with probability > 1/2.

      It will be shown that the exact analog of Theorem 2 holds for
these new concepts.

      Let S be a sequence of symbols $(s_1, s_2, s_3, \ldots)$. S' is to
denote the set of all pairs (n, s_n) where n runs over all positive
integers. The following lemmas will be proven in the appendix but are immediate consequences of the definitions.

> LEMMA 4: S is a 1-computable sequence if and only
> if S' is a 1-enumerable set.

> LEMMA 5: If S is strongly p-computable, S' will
> be strongly p-enumerable. If S is p-computable,
> S' will be p-enumerable.

> Applying the preceding two lemmas and Theorem 2 one gets

> LEMMA 6: Let p be a computable real number (in
> particular 1/2). Then any p-computable or strongly
> p-computable sequence is already 1-computable.

PROOF: Let the sequence S be p-computable or strongly p-computable.
Then S' is either p-enumerable or strongly p-enumerable because of
Lemma 5. By Theorem 2, S' is 1-enumerable. By Lemma 4, S must be
1-computable.

This settles the case where p is a computable real number. If
p is not computable, the proof of Theorem 1, given in the appendix, shows
that there is a sequence that is p-computable and strongly p-computable
but not 1-computable. (This sequence is the binary expansion of p.) Combining the two cases, one has the following analog of Theorem 2 for the
computability concepts.

> THEOREM 3: If p is a computable real number, any
> p-computable or strongly p-computable sequence is
> already 1-computable. If p is not computable,
> there exists a p-computable and strongly p-computable
> sequence that is not 1-computable.

As a special case of this one has the result that a 1/2-machine
cannot print out any one particular non-computable sequence with positive
probability.

A MORE GENERAL CLASS OF MACHINES

In this section, a generalization of the result that Theorem 2
gives for p a computable number will be given. A wide class of probabilistic machines, the computable-stochastic-machines or c-s-machines, which
are not covered by our previous definitions, will be defined. A concept of
equivalence for probabilistic machines will be proposed. It will be shown
that any one of the new class of machines defined is equivalent to a 1/2-
machine and as a consequence of Theorem 2, one will have that any set enum-

erated by a machine of this class must already be 1-enumerable. Furthermore, there is an effective process such that if one is supplied with the description of a machine in the class one can find a description of a 1/2-machine equivalent to it and a description of a 1-machine that 1-enumerates the same set that it enumerates.

To simplify the presentation, in this section, only one definition of enumerability, that corresponding to p-enumerability, is considered while the stronger definition corresponding to strong p-enumerability is ignored. It can be shown that the same results hold for the strong definition.

First, the class of stochastic machines will be defined. A stochastic machine is to be an object having a countable set of states X_1, X_2, X_3, ..., a distinguished initial state X_0, and a countable collection of output symbols s_1, s_2, s_3 ... . It is to be supplied with a rule that gives the probability that the machine will be next in state X_p and print output symbol s_q if it has passed successively through states X_0, X_{j_1}, ..., X_{j_n} so far. This probability will be denoted by $P\left(X_{j_1}, ..., X_{j_n}; X_p; s_q\right)$. (The rule need not give an effective procedure for computing the P's.)

To any p-machine M one can associate a stochastic machine in the above sense. The states of the associated stochastic machine are to be finite sequences of 0's and 1's $(a_1, ..., a_n)$ where the initial state is to be the "empty" sequence $(.)$. (What we are actually going to do here is say the "state" a p-machine is in the input sequence that it has received. These may not correspond to the internal states it may have if it is a concrete machine but determine them completely. The probability of going from state $(a_1, ..., a_n)$ to $(a_1, ..., a_n, 1)$ is p and from $(a_1, ... a_n)$ to $(a_1, ..., a_n, 0)$ is $1 - p$. The associated stochastic machine prints on arrival in state $(a_1, ..., a_n, a_{n+1})$ the same thing that the p-machine prints on receiving the $(n + 1)^{st}$ input symbol a_{n+1} after having received $(a_1, ..., a_n)$. Thus the stochastic machine is completely specified. It shall be referred to as the stochastic machine associated with the p-machine M. Thus, p-machines can be identified with special cases of stochastic machines.

When p is a computable number, it is easily seen that the associated machine has the following special property: The function P is computable; that is, there is an effective process such that if one is given a positive integer m, the states X_{j_1}, ..., X_{j_n} and X_p, and the output symbol s_q, one can compute the first m digits of the binary expansion of the number $P\left(X_{j_1}, ..., X_{j_n}: X_p; s_q\right)$. We shall call stochastic machines having this special property computable stochastic machines or c-s-machines. As a direct consequence of the definitions, one has

LEMMA 7: The stochastic machine associated with a
p-machine is a c-s-machine if and only if p is
a computable real number.

The remainder of this section is devoted to showing that the result stated in Theorem 2 for p-machines with p a computable number is
also valid for the much wider class of c-s-machines. That is, any set that
can be enumerated by a c-s-machine is already 1-enumerable.

With stochastic machines and p-machines, one can speak of the
probability of the machine eventually printing the output symbols
s_{j_1}, ..., s_{j_n} (as before we spoke of the probability of a p-machine eventually printing a single symbol s). Since we are having our machines enumerate sets, any two machines that eventually do the same thing with the same
probability can be considered to be identical from the point of view of eventual output. Thus, the following definition will be made:

DEFINITION: Two objects which are either stochastic machines or p-machines
will be said to be _equivalent_ if for any finite set of symbols s_{j_1}, ..., s_{j_n},
they have the same probability of eventually having that set included in
their output. If the machines are M_1 and M_2, this will be denoted by
$M_1 \sim M_2$.

For example, a p-machine and its associated stochastic machine
are equivalent.

One recalls that a p-machine is said to p-enumerate a set of
symbols if every element in that set occurs as an output symbol with probability > 1/2 and any output symbol not in the set occurs with probability
$\leq$ 1/2. The definition can be used directly for stochastic machines and
c-s-machines. If M is a stochastic machine, S_M will be the set of all
output symbols that occur with probability > 1/2, in agreement with the
previous notation for p-machines. S_M is the set of symbols that M enumerates. As an immediate consequence of the definition of equivalence one
has the fact that if $M_1 \sim M_2$, then $S_{M_1} = S_{M_2}$. That is, two equivalent
machines enumerate the same set.

DEFINITION: A set S is c-s-enumerable if there is a c-s-machine M
such that $S = S_M$.

The question that we want answered now is the following: Is every
c-s-enumerable set 1-enumerable? The answer is a consequence of the following which is proved in the appendix.

THEOREM 4: Every c-s-machine is equivalent to a
1/2 machine.

Thus, if M is a c-s-machine, the set S_M that M enumerates
is also enumerated by some 1/2-machine. According to Theorem 2, S_M must
be 1-enumerable. Thus

THEOREM 5: Any c-s-enumerable set is already
1-enumerable.

This is the result that we set out to obtain that any set which
can be enumerated by a c-s-machine can be enumerated by a 1-machine.

The proof of Theorem 4 actually yields more than has been stated.
It might have occured that the proof only demonstrated the existence of a
1/2-machine equivalent to any c-s-machine but gave no effective means of
finding one. This, however, is not true and it does yield an effective
process.

THEOREM 4: (Supplement) There is an effective process
such that if one is supplied with a description of a
c-s-machine, one can produce a description of a 1/2-
machine equivalent to it.

Thus, if one is given a description of a c-s-machine, M_1, there
is an effective process for finding a description of a 1/2-machine M_2
such that $S_{M_1} = S_{M_2}$. This does not yet give an effective extension of
Theorem 5. What is needed in order to obtain that is the following effective
extension of a part of Theorem 1.

THEOREM 1: (Supplement) There is an effective process
such that if one is supplied with a description of a
p-machine M (with p a computable number), one
can produce a description of a 1-machine that
1-enumerates the same S_M that M p-enumerates.

Combining the supplements of Theorem 1 and Theorem 4, one has

THEOREM 5: (Supplement) There is an effective process
such that if one is supplied with a description of a
c-s-machine that c-s-enumerates a set S, one can
produce a description of a 1-machine that 1-enumerates S.

The results at the end of the preceding section about computability
of sequences remains valid for c-s-machines. One defines in the obvious
way c-s-computable sequences. The proofs of Lemmas 4, 5, and 6 are valid
in this case and it follows that any c-s-computable sequence is already
1-computable.

APPENDIX

LEMMA 1:   The sequence A is computable if and only
if the associated set A' is 1-enumerable.

PROOF: Assume that the sequence A = $(a_1, a_2, a_3, \ldots)$ is computable. Define a machine by means of $f(b_1, \ldots, b_n) = ((1, a_1), \ldots, (n, a_n))$. Since
A is computable, this actually defines a machine. The machine 1-enumerates
the set A'. To prove the converse, assume that the set A' is 1-enumerable.
Then there exists a 1-machine whose total output is the set of all symbols
(n, a_n), but perhaps not occurring in the proper order. To determine a_n,
the output tape of the machine is observed until a pair occurs whose first
entry is the number n. This is certain to eventually happen. The second
entry of this pair will be a_n. Thus, there is an effective process for
determining a_n and A as a computable sequence.

LEMMA 2:   If A is a computable sequence, then any
A-enumerable set is 1-enumerable (and conversely).

PROOF: Let the machine M enumerate the set S if the computable sequence
A = $(a_1, a_2, a_3, \ldots)$ is used as input. Because of Lemma 1 there is a
1-machine that has as output the set of all (n, a_n). This output can be
converted in an effective manner into the sequence $(a_1, a_2, a_3, \ldots)$ and
used as input by M. The composite object is a 1-machine that 1-enumer-
ates S. It is clear that the converse is true, that any 1-enumerable set
is A-enumerable. This is true because a 1-machine that 1-enumerates a
set S can be converted into a machine with input, that is oblivious to
that input, and will enumerate S given any input.

LEMMA 3:   If A is not a computable sequence, there
exists sets that are A-enumerable but which are not
1-enumerable.

PROOF: The set A' is such a set.

The concept of "random device" will now be formalized. Let D be
the set of all infinite sequences, A = $(a_1, a_2, a_3, \ldots)$, of 0's and
1's. Let $C(a_1, \ldots, a_n)$ be the subset of D consisting of all sequences
starting with $(a_1, \ldots, a_n)$. D shall be considered to be a measurable
space [5] whose measurable sets are the σ-ring [5] generated by the sets
$C(a_1, \ldots, a_n)$. Let M be a machine (a precise definition has already
been given) and S the set of possible output symbols of M. Let Q_S be
the set of all finite or infinite sequences, $T = (s_{j_1}, s_{j_2}, \ldots)$, whose
elements are in S. Q_S will be considered to be a measurable space whose

measurable sets are the σ-ring generated by the $C(s_{j_1}, \ldots, s_{j_n})$ and the finite sequences. Let R_S be the set of all subsets of S. Let $E(j_1, \ldots, j_n; k_1, \ldots, k_m)$ be the subset of R_S consisting of all subsets of S that contain the s_{j_r} and do not contain the s_{k_r}. R_S shall be considered to be a measurable space whose measurable sets are the σ-ring generated by the sets E.

The machine M associates to each infinite input sequence in D some output sequence in Q_S. This determines a function $f_M: D \rightarrow Q_S$. One also has the mapping $q_S: Q_S \rightarrow R_S$ that takes a sequence into the set of its entries. The composite map $q_S f_M$ will be denoted by h_M. If A is in D, $h_M(A)$ is the set that will be enumerated by M if A is used as input.

The following is an immediate consequence of the definitions.

LEMMA: The maps f_M, q_S, and h_M are measurability preserving.

Let p be a real number, $0 < p < 1$. D can be considered to be the sample space of a random device which prints 1's with probability p and 0's with probability $1 - p$. That is, D is the space of all possible events that can occur if infinitely many independent operations of the random device are observed. There is associated to each p, in a natural manner, a measure m_p on D which assigns to each measurable subset of D the probability that the random device will print an infinite sequence in that subset. [3] Thus m_p induces in the usual way probability measures on the spaces Q_S and R_S. Every measurable subset E of Q_S is assigned probability $m_p(f_M^{-1}(E))$ and every measurable subset F of R_S is assigned probability $m_p(h_M^{-1}(F))$. These induced measures will be referred to as $m_{M,p}$ and sometimes as m_M. It shall always be clear from the context which measure is being used.

The significance of the measures $m_{M,p}$ is clear: If E is a measurable subset of Q_S, $m_{M,p}(E)$ is the probability of the output sequence of M being in E if M is operated as a p-machine; if F is a measurable subset of R_S, $m_{M,p}(F)$ is the probability that the set of output symbols that M will enumerate is an element of F if M is operated as a p-machine.

If U is some subset of S, then $\{U\}$, the set consisting of U alone, is a measurable subset of R_S. Thus, one can in all cases speak of the probability of a p-machine having some set U as output. $E(j_1, \ldots, j_n;)$ is the subset of R_S consisting of all sets that contain

---

[3] For a discussion of this, see [3].

all the s_{j_r}. Since $E(j_1, \ldots, j_n;)$ is measurable, one can in all cases
speak of the probability that a p-machine will eventually print some finite
set of output symbols.

 The proof of Theorem 1 will now be given. First 3 implies 2
will be proven: If a set S is strongly p-enumerable it must be p-enumerable.

 Let M be a machine that strongly p-enumerates the set S, that
is, has S as its total output with positive probability if used with a
random device having probability p of printing 1's. It will be sufficient
to find a new machine M' that has S as output with probability $> \frac{1}{2}$ if
used with a random device having probability p. This machine M' will
also p-enumerate the set S. For every element of S will occur with
probability $> \frac{1}{2}$ and every element not in S will occur with probability
$< \frac{1}{2}$.

 Machines $M(b_1, \ldots, b_n)$ will be constructed which are described
as follows: The output of $M(b_1, \ldots, b_n)$ in response to input $(a_1, \ldots, a_m)$
is the same as the output of M corresponding to input
$(b_1, \ldots, b_n, a_1, \ldots, a_m)$. Thus, $M(b_1, \ldots, b_n)$ acts in its initial
state as if it were M and had already received an input of $(b_1, \ldots, b_n)$.
It is intuitively rather compelling that if the set S occurs as output of
M with non-zero probability, that there will be machines $M(b_1, \ldots, b_n)$
whose output is S with probability arbitrarily close to 1. (Such an
$M(b_1, \ldots, b_n)$ could be taken as M' and the proof of 3 implies 2 would
be complete.) That this actually does occur is seen as follows: Let D_S
be $h_M^{-1}((S))$, that is the subset of D consisting of all sequences that
will give the set S as output when supplied as input to M. Since M produces S with non-zero probability $M_p(D_S) > 0$. Recall that $C(b_1, \ldots, b_n)$
is the subset of D consisting of all sequences that have initial segment
$(b_1, \ldots, b_n)$. The probability that S will occur as output of
$M(b_1, \ldots, b_n)$ is $m_p(D_S C(b_1, \ldots, b_n))/m_p(C(b_1, \ldots, b_n))$. Thus, our task
will be completed if sequences $(b_1, \ldots, b_n)$ can be found such that
$m_p(D_S C(b_1, \ldots, b_n))/m_p(C(b_1, \ldots, b_n))$ is arbitrarily close to 1. Actually, more than this is true.

  LEMMA: Let $B = (b_1, b_2, b_3, \ldots)$ be some sequence
  in D. Then

$$\lim_{n \to \infty} m_p(D_S C(b_1, \ldots, b_n))/m_p(C(b_1, \ldots, b_n))$$

  exists and is equal to 1 for every point of D_S
  and is equal to 0 for every point not in D_S, for
  all B in D except for a set of measure 0.

 This lemma will be proven by setting up a measure preserving
correspondence between the space D, supplied with the measure m_p, and

the unit interval I, supplied with Lebesgue measure; and applying the following result about Lebesgue measure m, which is the precise correlate of
the above lemma.

> METRIC DENSITY THEOREM:[4] Let F be a measurable
> subset of I, x a point of I and $I_n(x)$ a de-
> creasing sequence of intervals whose intersection
> is x. Then
>
> $$\lim_{n \to \infty} m(F \cap I_n(x))/m(I_n(x))$$
>
> exists and is equal to 1 for x in F and 0
> for x not in F, for all points x except for
> a set of measure zero.

The correspondence is set up as follows: Let f: D $\rightarrow$ I be the
map given by

$$f(A) = \sum_{n=1}^{\infty} a_n 2^{-n}$$

if $A = (a_1, a_2, a_3, \ldots)$. Every infinite sequence is taken into that real
number which has the sequence as a binary expansion. The map f is onto
and is 1 - 1 except for a countable set of points. The map f and the
measure m_p induce a measure m_p' on I. If p were $\frac{1}{2}$, m_p' would be
ordinary Lebesgue measure and f would be the correspondence wanted. If
p is not $\frac{1}{2}$, another step must be performed. Let g: I $\rightarrow$ I be given by
$g(x) = m_p'(I_x)$ where I_x is the closed interval from 0 to x. It is
clear that g has the following properties: It is 1 - 1, onto, monotone
and bicontinuous· Let h : D $\rightarrow$ I be the composite map of f and g. h
is the correspondence wanted. It has the following properties:
   No. 1: If E is a measurable subset of D, h(E) as a Lebesgue measurable subset of I and $m(h(E)) = m_p(E)$.
   No. 2: Let $B = (b_1, b_2, b_3, \ldots)$ be a sequence in D. Then
   $h(C(b_1, \ldots, b_n))$ is an interval containing the point h(B) of I.
      It is clear that since the mapping h has these properties, a
statement corresponding to the Metric Density Theorem is true for m_p on D,
and that the lemma stated is included in this statement.
      Thus 3 implies 2 is proven. Actually slightly more has been
proven. What has been shown is that if there is a p-machine that has a
set S as output with non-zero probability, there are p-machines that have
S as output with probability arbitrarily close to 1. It should be noted
that the proof is non-constructive and no effective process is given for
finding such machines.

---

[4] For a proof see Vol. 1, page 190 of [6].

Next 2 implies 1 will be proven: If a set S is p-enumerable, it must be A_p-enumerable.

Let p be any real number, $0 < p < 1$. Let M be any p-machine. To prove that 2 implies 1, it will be sufficient to construct a machine that A_p-enumerates S_M, which is the set that M p-enumerates.

Let n be a positive integer. Let s be a possible output symbol of M. Let $q(n, s)$ be the probability that M has printed the symbol s by the time n input symbols have been scanned. Note that $q(n, s) \leqq q(n + 1, s)$ and

$$\lim_{n \to \infty} q(n, s)$$

is the probability of s being eventually printed. S_M is the set of all s such that

$$\lim_{n \to \infty} q(n, s) > \frac{1}{2}.$$

Thus, S_M is the set of all s such that there exists some n with $q(n, s) > \frac{1}{2}$. Let $B_{n,s}$ be the set of all input sequences $(b_1, \ldots, b_n)$ of length n which will, when supplied as input to M, produce an output containing s. The probability of an element of $B_{n,s}$ occurring as the first n outputs of the random device is precisely $q(n, s)$. Let $q(b_1, \ldots, b_n)$ be the probability of the sequence $(b_1, \ldots, b_n)$ occurring as output of the random device. $q(b_1, \ldots, b_n) = p^r(1 - p)^t$, where r is the number of b's that are 1 and t is the number of b's that are 0. $q(n, s) = \Sigma\, q(b_1, \ldots, b_n)$ where the summation is over all sequences in $B_{n,s}$. Let the binary expansion of the real number p be $.a_1 a_2 a_3 \ldots$. Let $p_m = .a_1 a_2 \ldots a_m$ and $p'_m = .a_1 a_2 \ldots a_m + 2^{-m}$. $p_m \leqq p \leqq p'_m$. A lower bound for $q(b_1, \ldots, b_n)$ is $p_m^r (1 - p'_m)^t$. This will be denoted by $q_m(b_1, \ldots, b_n)$. Let $q_m(n, s) = \Sigma\, q_m(b_1, \ldots, b_n)$ where the summation is over all sequences in $B_{n,s}$; $q_m(n, s)$ is a lower bound for $q(n, s)$. Since $p_m \leqq p_{m+1}$ and $p'_m \geqq p'_{m+1}$, $q_m(b_1, \ldots, b_n) \leqq q_{m+1}(b_1, \ldots, b_n)$ for all sequences and $q_m(n, s) \leqq q_{m+1}(n, s)$. Since $p_m \to p$ and $p'_m \to p$, $q_m(b_1, \ldots, b_n) \to q(b_1, \ldots, b_n)$ for all sequences and $q_m(n, s) \to q(n, s)$. Thus S_M, which is the set of all s such that there exists some n with $q(n, s) > \frac{1}{2}$, is also the set of all s such that exist some m and some n with $q_m(n, s) > \frac{1}{2}$.

Now it is clear from the construction that if one were presented a tape on which the sequence A_p were printed, one could compute successively in an effective manner all of the rational numbers $q_m(n, s)$, for every positive integral n and m and every possible output symbol s. If one writes down the symbol s each time some $q_m(n, s)$ occurs that is $> \frac{1}{2}$, the set that is enumerated is precisely S_M and the process by means of which it is enumerated is an A_p-machine.

Next 1 implies 3 will be proven: If a set S is A_p-enumerable, it must be strongly p-enumerable.

The case of p having a terminating binary expansion must be treated separately. In this case A_p is computable. Then if a set S is A_p-enumerable, it is 1-enumerable because of Lemma 2. Thus, a machine, which is oblivious of input, and which enumerates S, given any input, can be constructed. If the output of a random device having probability p of printing 1 is used as input for the machine, it enumerates S. Thus, S is strongly p-enumerable.

A machine M will now be constructed which has the following property:[5] Let p be a real number, $0 < p < 1$, which does not have a terminating binary expansion. If the output of a random device that prints 1 with probability p is fed into M, the output tape of M will, with probability $> \frac{3}{4}$, be printed with the binary expansion of p. (The $\frac{3}{4}$ is not significant. It can be replaced, uniformly in all that follows, by any X with $\frac{1}{2} < X < 1$).

Let N be a machine that A_p-enumerates the set S. If the output tape of the machine M, supplied with a random device having probability p, is used as input to N, the composite object has as output, with probability $> \frac{3}{4}$, the set S. The composite object will be a p-machine and will strongly p-enumerate the set S. Thus, any A_p-enumerable set will be shown to be strongly p-enumerable if M can be constructed. If this can be done, the two cases, p terminating and p not terminating, will have been covered, so that it is sufficient to construct the machine M.

Let $(c_1, c_2, c_3, \ldots)$ be a computable sequence of rational numbers such that $0 < c_j < 1$ and

$$\prod_{j=1}^{\infty} c_j > \frac{3}{4} .$$

M will be constructed so that it operates as follows: It scans the input from the random device having probability p, and computes the proportion of 1's that one has at the end of each output. It waits till it is certain[6] with probability $> c_1$ what the first binary digit of p must be to have produced the proportion of 1's observed. Then it prints this digit on its output tape. It forgets the proportion it has observed so far and starts computing the proportions of 1's that it next receives from the random device. It waits till it is certain with probability $> c_2$ what the first two binary digits of p must have been to have produced the pro-

---

[5] We are indebted to Hale Trotter at this point for the suggestion that led to the following construction.

[6] Most of the complications of the rest of the proof will be to show that this certainty can be obtained, uniformly in p, even for those arbitrarily close to terminating binary numbers.

portion of 1's observed. It then prints the second digit of the two that
it has on the output tape and starts again. Proceeding in this manner, it
prints on its output tape the correct binary expansion of p with probability

$$> \prod_{j=1}^{\infty} c_j > \frac{3}{4} \ .$$

The precise construction is as follows. Let X_n be the nth
coordinate function on D. That is, if $A = (a_1, a_2, a_3, \ldots)$, $X_n(A) = a_n$.
D is now being considered as the set of all possible output sequences of a
random device.

$$\sum_{j=1}^{n} X_j$$

is the number of 1's that have occurred during the first n operations of
the device and

$$Y_n = \frac{1}{n} \sum_{j=1}^{n} X_n$$

is the proportion of 1's that have occurred. Recall that m_p is the measure on D that is used if the device prints 1's with probability p.
Define the function f as follows:

$$f(m, q, n, r) = m_{\frac{q}{2^m}} \left\{ A: \ | \ Y_n(A) - q/2^m \ | \ > r/2^n \right\}$$

for all positive integers m and n, all $q = 1, \ldots, 2^m - 1$ and all
$r = 1, \ldots, 2^n - 1$. This is the probability of a random device, having
$p = \frac{q}{2^m}$, printing out a sequence of n symbols which has its proportion of
1's deviating from $\frac{q}{2^m}$ by more than $\frac{r}{2^n}$. One easily sees that
f(m, q, n, r) is a rational number and that the function f is a <u>computable</u>
function. Note that $f(m, q, n, 2^n) = 0$ so that if the function g(m, q, n)
is defined to be $\frac{1}{2^n} \left[\text{the least } r \text{ such that } (f(m, q, n, r) < \frac{1 - c_m}{5 \cdot 2^m \cdot n^2}) \right]$
the function is well defined. Since the sequence of c_m has been chosen
to be a computable sequence of rational numbers, the function g is a
<u>computable</u> function which takes on only rational values.

LEMMA: $\lim_{n \to \infty} g(m, q, n) = 0$

PROOF: The theorem on page 144 of [4] shows, if one takes $x = n^{1/3}/(pq)^{1/2}$,
that

$$m_p \left\{ A: \ | \ Y_n(A) - p \ | \ > \frac{1}{n^{1/6}} \right\} \sim \sqrt{\frac{2p(1 - p)}{\pi}} \ \frac{e^{\frac{-n^{2/3}}{2pq}}}{n^{1/3}} = o \ (\frac{1}{n^2})$$

this implies, taking $p = \dfrac{q}{2^m}$, that $g(m, q, n) = o\left(\dfrac{1}{n^{1/6}}\right)$ and in particular
that

$$\underset{n \to \infty}{\text{Lim}} \ g(m, q, n) = 0$$

The operation of the machine can now be described as follows: It
accepts an input sequence $A^1 = (a_1^1, a_2^1, a_3^1, \dots)$ from a random device. It
computes, in order, all of the numbers $Y_1(A^1)$, $Y_2(A^1)$, $Y_3(A^1)$, ...
As soon as it comes to an n such that $|Y_n(A^1) - \frac{1}{2}| > g(1, 1, n)$ (we shall
see that this will occur with probability 1) it prints on its output tape
the first binary digit of the number $Y_n(A)$. We shall see that this digit
will be with probability $> c_1$ the first digit of the number p. It then
accepts a new input sequence $A^2 = (a_1^2, a_2^2, a_3^2, \dots)$ from the random device.
It computes in order the numbers $Y_n(A^2)$ and the numbers $g(2, 1, n)$,
$g(2, 2, n)$ and $g(2, 3, n)$. As soon as it comes to an n such that
$|Y_n(A) - \frac{q}{4}| > g(2, q, n)$ for $q = 1, 2, 3$, it writes the second binary
digit of $Y_n(A^2)$ on the output tape. It will be the second digit of p
with probability $> c_2$. At the mth stage the machine works in a similar
manner. It accepts an input sequence $A^m = (a_1^m, a_2^m, a_3^m, \dots)$, computes
the numbers $Y_n(A^m)$ and when it reaches an n such that
$|Y_n(A^m) - \frac{q}{2^m}| > g(m, q, n)$ for all $q = 1, \dots, 2^m - 1$, it prints the
m^{th} digit of $Y_n(A^m)$ on its output tape. This digit will be the mth
digit of the number p with probability $> c_m$. Thus the machine prints
all the digits of p with probability $> \pi c_m > \frac{3}{4}$.

It remains to verify that the mth digit printed is the mth
digit of p with probability $> c_m$. Define the function U_m on D as
follows: If A is a sequence in D, let $U_m(A) = Y_r(A)$, where r is
the least n such that $|Y_n(A) - \frac{q}{2^m}| > g(m, q, n)$ for all
$q = 1, \dots, 2^m - 1$, if such an integer n exists. Let $U_m(A)$ be undefined
if such an n does not exist. If the sequence A occurs as output of the
random device and is used by the machine, according to the rules of operation that have been given, to determine the mth digit of p, the result
will be correct if and only if $U_m(A)$ is defined and $\frac{q}{2^m} \leq U_m(A) < \frac{q+1}{2^m}$
where q is such that $\frac{q}{2^m} \leq p < \frac{q+1}{2^m}$. (Note that there will be no result if
$U_m(A)$ is undefined.) The probability that $U_m(A)$ is undefined will first
be determined. $U_m(A)$ is undefined if and only if for each n there is some
q such that $|Y_n(A) - \frac{q}{2^m}| \leq g(m, q, n)$. According to the lemma proved,

$$\underset{n \to \infty}{\text{Lim}} \ g(m, q, n) = 0,$$

so that there is some single q_0 such that for all n sufficiently large
$|Y_n(A) - \frac{q_0}{2^m}| \leq g(m, q_0, n)$. But then

$$\underset{n \to \infty}{\text{Lim}} \ Y_n(A) = \frac{q_0}{2^m}.$$

Because of the Strong Law of Large Numbers [4], for every A except a set of m_p-measure zero,

$$\lim_{n \to \infty} Y_n(A) = p.$$

Since p does not have a terminating binary expansion, it is not equal to any of the $\frac{q}{2^m}$ so that $m_p \{A : U_m(A) \text{ undefined}\} = 0$.

Since the probability that U_m is undefined is zero, the probability that $U_m(A)$ has its first m digits correct is 1 minus the probability that it has an incorrect digit among the first m. Thus, it is sufficient to compute the latter. It is

$$\Sigma m_p \left\{ A : U_m(A) \text{ defined } \& \frac{q}{2^m} \le U_m(A) < \frac{q+1}{2^m} \right\}$$ where the sum is over all q such that it is not true that $\frac{q}{2^m} \le p < \frac{q+1}{2^m}$. Each of these terms will be estimated separately and shown to be $\le \frac{1}{2^m}(1 - c_m)$. It will then follow that the sum is $\le 1 - c_m$ and that the probability of the mth digit of $U_m(A)$ being correct is $> c_m$. Thus, all that remains to conclude the proof is the estimation. Take any one of the sets

$$\left\{ A : U_m(A) \text{ defined } \& \frac{q}{2^m} \le U_m(A) < \frac{q+1}{2^m} \right\}$$ such that p is not between $\frac{q}{2^m}$ and $\frac{q+1}{2^m}$. Call this set E. It will be assumed that $p < \frac{q}{2^m}$. A procedure similar to that which follows covers the case $p > \frac{q+1}{2^m}$. Because of the manner in which U_m is defined, the set E is seen to be a disjoint union of sets $C(b_1, \ldots, b_r)$ where the proportion of 1's in the b_j is between $\frac{q}{2^m}$ and $\frac{q+1}{2^m}$.

$\Big($One should recall that $C(b_1, \ldots, b_r)$ is the subset of D consisting of all sequences that have $(b_1, \ldots, b_r)$ as initial segment. For any $(b_1, \ldots, b_r)$, let B be an infinite sequence that has the r-tuple as initial segment. Then E is the disjoint union of the $C(b_1, \ldots, b_r)$ where the $(b_1, \ldots, b_r)$ as such that for each s less than r there is some t, $t = 1, \ldots, 2^m - 1$, such that $|Y_s(b) - \frac{t}{2^m}| \le g(m, t, s)$ while $|Y_r(B) - \frac{t}{2^m}| > g(m, t, r)$ for all t and $\frac{q}{2^m} \le U_n(B) < \frac{q+1}{2^m}.\Big)$ Since $p < \frac{q}{2^m}$,

$$m_p \left(C(b_1, \ldots, b_r) \right) < m_{\frac{q}{2^m}} \left(C(b_1, \ldots, b_r) \right) \text{ if the proportion of } 1\text{'s}$$

in $(b_1, \ldots, b_r)$ is between $\frac{q}{2^m}$ and $\frac{q+1}{2^m}$. Thus, $m_p(E) < m_{\frac{q}{2^m}}(E)$.

But $m_{\frac{q}{2^m}}(E) = m_{\frac{q}{2^m}} \left\{ A : U_m(A) \text{ defined } \& \frac{q}{2^m} \le U_m(A) < \frac{q+1}{2^m} \right\} \le m_{\frac{q}{2^m}}$ $\{A : U_m(A) \text{ defined}\}$. $U_m(A)$ is defined only if there is some n such that $|Y_n(A) - \frac{q}{2^m}| > g(m, q, n)$. Thus, $m_{\frac{q}{2^n}} \{A : U_m(A) \text{ defined}\}$

$$\le \sum_{n=1}^{\infty} m_{\frac{q}{2^n}} \left\{ A : |Y_n(A) - \frac{q}{2^m}| > g(m, q, n) \right\} \le \frac{1-c_m}{5 \cdot 2^m} \sum \frac{1}{n^2} < \frac{1-c_m}{2^m}$$

because of the definition of g(m, q, n). Thus, each term is shown to be
$\leq \frac{1-c_m}{2^m}$ and the proof is complete.

It should be pointed out again that the $\frac{3}{4}$ could be replaced by
any X satisfying $\frac{1}{2} < X < 1$ and that the construction is the same for
all p that do not have a terminating binary expansion. Thus, the following
is true. For any ϵ there is a machine M_ϵ such that if M_ϵ is used as
a p-machine, the output is the binary expansion of p, with probability
greater than $1 - \epsilon$, for any p not a terminating binary.

The proof of Theorem 1 is completed.

LEMMA 4: S is a 1-computable sequence if and only
if S' is a 1-enumerable set.

PROOF: Same as Lemma 1.

LEMMA 5: If S is strongly p-computable, S' will
be strongly p-enumerable. If S is p-computable,
S' will be p-enumerable.

PROOF: Let M be a machine. Modify the M to form the machine M' as
follows: If the output of M in response to some input is $\left(s_{j_1}, \dots, s_{j_n}\right)$,
the response of M' to the same input is to be $\left((1, s_{j_1}), \dots (n, s_{j_n})\right)$.
M' is a machine and if M strongly p-computes the sequence S, M'
strongly p-enumerates the set S'. If M p-computes the sequence S,
M' p-enumerates the set S'.

Let M be a stochastic machine. Let G be the set of all
sequences $X = \left(X_{j_1}, X_{j_2}, X_{j_3}, \dots\right)$ whose elements are names of states of M.
Let $C\left(X_{j_1}, \dots, X_{j_n}\right)$ be the set of all sequences that have $\left(X_{j_1}, \dots, X_{j_n}\right)$
as initial segment. G is to be considered as a measurable space whose mea-
surable subsets are to be the σ-ring generated by the $C\left(X_{j_1}, \dots, X_{j_n}\right)$.
The underlying stochastic process of the machine gives rise in a natural
manner to a measure m on G which associates to each measurable subset
the probability that the machine will pass through a sequence of states in
that subset.[7] Let S be the set of possible output symbols of M. Q_S
and R_S are as before the set of all sequences of elements of S and the
set of all subsets of S, respectively. We have the map $f_M : G \to Q_S$
which associates to each infinite sequence of states the output sequence
that will be printed if the machine passes through that sequence of states.
This combined with the natural map $g_S : Q_S \to R_S$, which takes a sequence

---

[7] For a discussion of this, see [3].

into the set of elements that occur in it, gives rise to the composite map $h_M : G \rightarrow R_S$. If X is in G, $h_M (X)$ is the set of symbols that will be enumerated if the machine passes through the sequence of states X. The map h_M and the measure m on G induce a measure on R_S which will be denoted by m_M. If E is a measurable subset of R_S, $m_M (E) = m (h_M^{-1}(E))$ is the probability that the machine will enumerate a set in E.

Let $E (j_1, ..., j_n; k_1, ..., k_m)$ be the subset of R_S consisting of all subsets of S that contain $s_{j_1}, ..., s_{j_n}$ and do not contain $s_{k_1}, ..., s_{k_m}$. (Either n or m may be zero.) Two stochastic machines M_1 and M_2 have been defined to be equivalent, $M_1 \sim M_2$, if they have the same set S of possible output symbols and $m_{M_1} (E (j_1, ..., j_n;)) = m_{M_2} (E (j_1, ..., j_n;))$.

> LEMMA: If $M_1 \sim M_2$, m_{M_1} and m_{M_2} agree on all sets of the form $E (j_1, ..., j_n; k_1, ..., k_m)$.

PROOF: The proof proceeds by induction on m. It is true for $m = 1$ because $E (j_1, ..., j_n;) = E (j_1, ..., j_n, k_1) + E (j_1, ..., j_n; k_1)$ where the sum is disjoint. m_{M_1} and m_{M_2} agree on the first two sets and thus must agree on the third. The induction from $m - 1$ to m proceeds in a similar manner since $E (j_1, ..., j_n; k_1, ..., k_{m-1}) =$
$E (j_1, ..., j_n, k_m; k_1, ..., k_{m-1}) + E (j_1, ..., j_n; k_1, ..., k_{m-1}, k_m)$, the sum being disjoint. m_{M_1} and m_{M_2} agree on the first two and therefore must agree on the third.

The set of all subsets of R_S of the form $E (j_1, ..., j_n; k_1, ..., k_m)$ is a ring of sets and generates the σ-ring of sets. Thus, if m_{M_1} and m_{M_2} agree on the ring, they agree on all measurable subsets of R_S [5, p. 54]. The converse is trivially true. Thus, we have.

> LEMMA: $M_1 \sim M_2$ if and only if $m_{M_1} = m_{M_2}$.

This shows that $m_{M_1} = m_{M_2}$ could have been taken as definition of equivalence instead of the weaker statement.

In order to prove Theorem 4, that every stochastic machine is equivalent to a $\frac{1}{2}$-machine, a reduction step must be made. The underlying stochastic process of a stochastic machine will be reduced in the usual way to a markoff process.

DEFINITION: A stochastic machine is markoff if:

No. 1: $P \left(X_{j_1}, ..., X_{j_{n-1}}, X_{j_n}; X_p; s_q\right)$ is independent of $X_{j_1}, ..., X_{j_{n-1}}$.

No. 2:   For every X_p there is only one s_q such that
$P\left(X_{j_1}, \ldots, X_{j_n}; X_p; s_q\right)$ is non-zero.

That is, not only is the underlying stochastic process a markoff
process but the symbol printed on arrival in any state depends deterministically
on that state, and depends only on that state.

LEMMA: Every stochastic machine   M   is equivalent
.to a stochastic machine   M'   which is markoff.   If
M   is a   c-s-machine,   M'   can be chosen to be a
c-s-machine.

PROOF: The usual trick of converting a stochastic process into a markoff
process by considering it to be in "state" $\left(X_{j_1}, \ldots, X_{j_n}\right)$ if it has
passed successively through the $X_{j_1}, \ldots, X_{j_n}$ works in this case.   The
states of   M'   are to have names $\left(X_{j_1}, \ldots, X_{j_n}; s_r\right)$.   The probability of
M'   going from state $\left(X_{j_1}, \ldots, X_{j_n}; s_r\right)$ to state $\left(X_{j_1}, \ldots, X_{j_n}, X_p; s_q\right)$
and printing the symbol s_q on arrival is $P\left(X_{j_1}, \ldots, X_{j_n}; X_p; s_q\right)$,   and
all other probabilities are zero.   M'   is a markoff machine and   M ~ M'.
If   M   is a   c-s-machine,   M'   is also a   c-s-machine.   Also, it is clear
that an effective process has been furnished which will supply the description
of   M'   if a description of   M   is given.

Thus, our attention may be restricted to   c-s-machines   that are
markoff.   A simplification in the notation can be made.   The states of a
markoff   c-s-machine can be assumed to be named by the positive integers
and $P(n, m)$ will be used to denote the probability of moving from the
nth   state to the mth   state.   Note that

$$\sum_{m=1}^{\infty} P(n, m) = 1.$$

We shall now use for the first time the fact that the objects
under consideration are   c-s-machines.   This means that there is an effective
process such that if one is given positive integers, r, n and m,   one
can find the first r digits of the binary expansion of $P(n, m)$.   Denote
the rational number $.a_1 a_2 \ldots a_r$ by $P(n, m; r)$ if $(a_1, a_2, \ldots, a_r)$
are the first r digits of the binary expansion of $P(n, m)$. $P(n, m; r)$
is a computable function.   Let $Q(n, m; r)$ be the number $.b_1 b_2 \ldots b_r$
if $(b_1, b_2, \ldots, b_r)$ are the first r binary digits of

$$\sum_{j=1}^{m} P(n, j).$$

Note that $Q(n, m; r) \leqq Q(n, m; r + 1)$ and that

$$\lim_{r \to \infty} Q(n, m; r) = \sum_{j=1}^{m} P(n, j).$$

We now wish to construct a $\frac{1}{2}$ - machine that is equivalent to a given markoff c-s-machine. If this can be done Theorem 4 will be proven since every c-s-machine is equivalent to one that is markoff. The main trick is the use of a random device printing 1's with probability $\frac{1}{2}$ in conjunction with the computable function $Q(n, m; r)$ to obtain events occuring with the probabilities $P(n, m)$. A simplified but relevant example will be given first that will demonstrate the idea involved.

Let us assume that we are given a random device that prints 1's with probability $\frac{1}{2}$ and wish to construct a device that prints 1's with probability p, where p is a computable number. First construct a - 1-machine N_p that generates the binary expansion $.b_1 b_2 b_3 \ldots$ of p. Let the output of our random device be the sequence $a_1, a_2, a_3, \ldots$. Compare the successive approximations

$$.b_1, \ .b_1 b_2, \ .b_1 b_2 b_3, \ \ldots, \ \sum_{r=1}^{n} b_r \, 2^{-r}, \ \ldots$$

that one obtains for the number p by observing the output tape of N_p, with the numbers

$$.a_1, \ .a_1 a_2, \ .a_1 a_2 a_3, \ \ldots, \ \sum_{r=1}^{n} a_r \, 2^{-r}, \ \ldots$$

Eventually, if

$$\sum_{r=1}^{\infty} a_r \, 2^{-r} \neq p$$

(and thus with probability 1), one will come to the first n such that

$$\sum_{r=1}^{n} a_r \, 2^{-r} \neq \sum_{r=1}^{n} b_r \, 2^{-r}.$$

At this point, write down a 1 if

$$\sum_{r=1}^{n} a_r \, 2^{-r} < \sum_{r=1}^{n} b_r \, 2^{-r}$$

and a 0 if the inequality is in the other direction. Thus, since the probability is precisely p that

$$\sum_{r=1}^{\infty} a_r \, 2^{-r} < p$$

and is $1 - p$ that

$$\sum_{r=1}^{\infty} a_r \, 2^{-r} > p,$$

the event "a 1 is written" occurs with probability p and the event "a 0 is written" occurs with probability $1 - p$. (Note that the event "nothing ever happens" occurs with probability 0 but may still occur.) If this process is repeated, the object that is described is a device that prints 1 with probability p.

Furthermore, this construction demonstrates that every p-machine (remember that p is a computable number) is equivalent to a $\frac{1}{2}$ - machine. For any machine M, supplied with the output of the device constructed above, becomes a $\frac{1}{2}$ - machine, and is equivalent to the p-machine that one obtains when one supplies M with the output of a random device that prints 1's with probability p. The construction of a $\frac{1}{2}$ - machine equivalent to a given c-s-machine will be seen to be similar to the above construction.

We shall now assume that we have a markoff c-s-machine M and shall proceed to construct a $\frac{1}{2}$ - machine M' equivalent to it. It can be assumed that the machine M starts in the state 0. Let the output sequence of a random device printing 1 with probability $\frac{1}{2}$ be $(a_1, a_2, a_3, \ldots)$. The probability that the number

$$\sum_{n=1}^{\infty} a_n \, 2^{-n}$$

lies between

$$\sum_{j=0}^{m-1} P(0, j)$$

and

$$\sum_{j=0}^{m} P(0, j)$$

is precisely $P(0, m)$. Let N be a 1-machine that computes in <u>succession</u> the values of the computable function $Q(n, m; r)$ for every n, m and r. The machine M' does the following: At the sth stage, it compares the number

$$\sum_{j=1}^{s} a_j \, 2^{-j}$$

with the first s of the values Q(o, m; r) that N has computed. Using
this process, with probability 1 (but not certainty), these comparisons
will eventually find some number t_1 such that

$$\sum_{r=1}^{t_1-1} P(o, r) < \sum_{n=1}^{\infty} a_n \, 2^{-n} < \sum_{r=1}^{t_1} P(o, r).$$

At this point the machine M' prints what M would print on arrival in
state t_1. Thus M', imitating the first transition of M, has printed
with probability P(o, m) what M would print on arrival in state m.
M' must now imitate the second transition of M. It again accepts an
input $(b_1, b_2, b_3, \ldots)$ from the random device and compares the numbers

$$\sum_{j=1}^{s} b_j \, 2^{-j},$$

this time to the first s values of $Q(t_1, m; r)$ that N produces. With
probability 1, these comparisons will eventually find some integer t_2
such that

$$\sum_{r=1}^{t_2-1} P(t_1, r) < \sum_{n=1}^{\infty} b_n \, 2^{-n} < \sum_{r=1}^{t_2} P(t_1, r).$$

At this point M' imitates the second transition of M and prints what
M would print on arrival in state t_2. Thus, M' has printed with probability $P(t_1, m)$ what M would print on arrival in state m. M' then proceeds in the same manner to imitate the next transitions of M. It is clear
that M' is a $\frac{1}{2}$ - machine that is equivalent to M and also that the
above construction yields an effective process for transforming a description
of M into a description of M'.

The proof of Theorem 4 is complete.

BIBLIOGRAPHY

[1] CHURCH, Alonzo, "An Unsolvable Problem of Elementary Number Theory,"
     American Journal of Mathematics, Vol. 58, pp. 345 - 363 (1936).

[2] DAVIS, Martin, Forthcoming Book on Recursive Functions and Computability,
     to be published by McGraw-Hill.

[3] DOOB, J. L., "Stochastic Processes," John Wiley & Sons, (1953).

[4] FELLER, William, "An Introduction to Probability Theory and its Appli-
     cations," John Wiley & Sons, (1950).

[5] HALMOS, Paul R., "Measure Theory," Van Nostrand, (1950)

[6]   HOBSON, E. W., "The Theory of Functions of a Real Variable and the
      Theory of Fourier's Series," (1926).

[7]   KLEENE, S. C., "Introduction to Metamathematics," Van Nostrand, (1952).

[8]   POST, Emil L., "Finite Combinatory Processes - Formulation I." Jour.
      Symbolic Logic, Vol. 1, pp. 103 - 105, (1936).

[9]   TURING, A. M., "On Computable Numbers, with an Application to the
      Entscheidungsproblem," Proc. London Math. Society, Ser. 2, Vol. 42
      (1936), pp. 230 - 265, and Vol. 43 (1937), pp. 544 - 546.

Some Results on Ideal Rectifier Circuits*

Claude E. Shannon

Abstract

Some results are obtained in the theory of circuits constructed of rectifiers and of rectifiers and relay contacts. Such circuits are shown to be related to partially ordered sets. Upper and lower bounds are found for the number of rectifiers necessary for n-terminal rectifier circuits. A duality theorem is obtained. A partly ordered set analyzer is described.

We consider some properties of circuits made up entirely of ideal rectifiers. By an ideal rectifier we mean a two-terminal element which conducts perfectly in one direction and presents an open circuit for current flow in the other direction.

Consider a circuit, made up of a number of such rectifiers, having n available terminals, T_1, $T_2, \ldots, T_n$. Two of these terminals, say Terminals T_i and T_j, may be related in four different ways.

(1) It is possible for current to pass from i to j and from j to i. This will occur either if they are directly connected internally or if there is a chain of rectifiers all in the same direction from i to j and a second chain all pointed in the reverse direction from j to i. In this case we consider i and j to be the same terminal, and write $T_i = T_j$. In Figure 1, $T_6 = T_7$ and $T_3 = T_4$.

(2) It is possible for current to go from i to j but not in reverse. This will occur if there is a chain of rectifiers running from i to j but no chain in the reverse direction. In this case we will write $T_i > T_j$. In Figure 1, $T_1 > T_3 > T_4$, $T_8 > T_9$, etc.

(3) In the reverse situation, current can go from j to i but not in reverse, and there is a chain of rectifiers from j to i but no reverse chain. Here we write $T_i < T_j$.

(4) It may not be possible for current to go in either direction, there being no oriented chain of rectifiers from i to j and vice versa. This does not necessarily mean that no path exists, but along any path there will be some rectifiers pointed one way and some the other.

The set of terminals $T_1, T_2, \ldots, T_n$ together with the relations $=$, $<$ and $>$ form a partially ordered set, or poset, as defined for example in Birkhoff, *Lattice Theory*. (We interpret his relation $T_i \geq T_j$ to mean either $T_i > T_j$ or $T_i = T_j$.) The transitive and reflexive properties required of a partial order are readily seen to be true for the $>$ relation we have here. For example, $T_i > T_j$ and $T_j > T_k$ imply $T_i > T_k$, since there is a directed path from T_i to T_j whose existence is implied by $T_i > T_j$ together with the directed path from T_j to T_k whose existence is implied by $T_j > T_k$. Also there is no path from T_k to T_i since, if there were, there would also be a path from T_j to T_i, namely from T_j to T_k and thence to T_i. This would imply $T_i = T_j$, contradicting $T_i > T_j$.

---
* Bell Laboratories Memorandum, June 8, 1955.

Figure 1

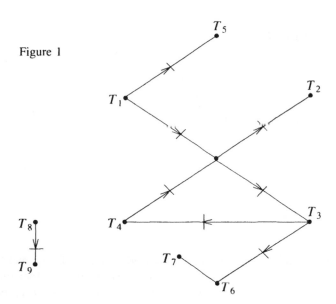

Similar arguments show that the other requirements for a partially ordered set are satisfied, and we have as our first result that any ideal rectifier circuit corresponds in the sense described to a partially ordered set. The partial ordering is, in fact, a complete specification of the external characteristics of the circuit, for it gives complete information as to the current and voltage constraints imposed by the circuit. If for two terminals T_i and T_j we have $T_i = T_j$, then the network imposes the constraint $e_i = e_j$, where e_i and e_j are the potentials of terminals T_i and T_j. If $T_i > T_j$, the network imposes $e_i \leq e_j$, etc. If two different n-terminal circuits impose the same ordering on their terminals T_i, then they are identical in external electrical characteristics.

A finite partially ordered set is conveniently represented by the well-known Hasse diagram (the Hasse diagram for Figure 1 is shown in Figure 2). For a given ordering, the diagram is uniquely determined in its connectivity. Correspondingly, with an ideal rectifier circuit we can find a kind of canonical equivalent circuit which corresponds directly to the Hasse diagram. One way to do this is to determine the partial ordering of the rectifier circuit, construct the corresponding Hasse diagram, and in each line of this diagram place a rectifier oriented downward.

A more direct procedure for obtaining the same result is the following. Construct for the given network N a new network N' according to the following rules. If, in N, $T_i = T_j$, let terminals T_i' and T_j' be directly connected in N'. If, in N, $T_i > T_j$, then connect a rectifier from T_i' to T_j'. If T_i and T_j are incomparable, no connection is made in N'. Now if in N' there are two terminals, say T_i' and T_j', such that there is a rectifier from T_i' to T_j' and also a path from T_i' to T_j' through other terminals, say T_i' to T_a' to T_b' ... to T_j', then delete the rectifier directly connected from T_i' to T_j' (since it is superfluous). Continue this process eliminating all such superfluous rectifiers. When this is done, we obtain a canonical circuit equivalent to the given circuit and having no internal nodes and no redundant rectifiers (that is, rectifiers which may be eliminated without altering the operation of the circuit). This last is true since it is easily seen that if any element is removed, say an element from terminal T_i' to terminals T_j', then it is not possible for current to flow from T_i' to T_j', whereas with the element present it is possible.

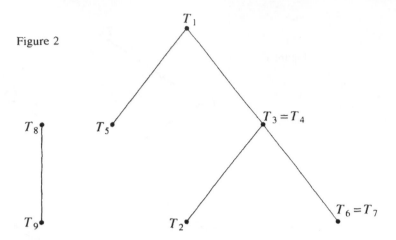

Figure 2

Theorem 1: The normal form of a rectifier network contains fewer rectifiers than any other form of the same network which has no internal nodes (no nodes other than the n terminals). The normal form of an n-terminal network contains at most $[n(n + 1)/4]$ rectifiers.

Here the square brackets mean "the largest integer in."

To prove the first part of the theorem, note first that since the normal form, say N, of a network corresponds to the Hasse diagram of the corresponding partially ordered set, it contains a rectifier for each line of that diagram and consequently for each case of one element "covering" another (being an immediate superior in the ordering). Now consider some other realization N' of the same partial ordering without any internal nodes. Suppose in the ordering T_i' covers T_j'. Then in this second network there must be a rectifier from T_i' to T_j', for if not, in order for current to go from T_i' to T_j', there must be a directed path and since the direct path does not exist it must go through other terminals. This implies that these other terminals lie between T_i' and T_j' in the ordering, contradicting the assumption of T_i' covering T_j'. Thus in N' we may find a rectifier for each line of the Hasse diagram and, in general, others as well. If there are no others, N' is clearly identical with the normal form N; otherwise it contains more rectifiers.

The second statement of the theorem will be proved by induction. The result is obvious for $n = 2$, since the two terminals are then either open, shorted or connected by one rectifier. The worst case is one element and $[2 \cdot 3/4] = 1$. Now, note that the normal form of a network never contains three rectifiers connected in a triangle, that is, three terminals T_i, T_j and T_k with rectifiers between each pair. If there were such a triangle, either the orientation would be around a circle and T_i, T_j and T_k would be considered the same terminal and directly connected, or the orientation would be of the type T_i to T_j, T_j to T_k and T_i to T_k in which case the latter rectifiers would be eliminated as superfluous.

To carry out the inductive step, we consider first the case where n is odd, the result is assumed true for n, and we wish to prove it for $n + 1$. Select the terminal (or one of the terminals), say T_i, with the minimum number of rectifiers connected to it in our $n + 1$ terminal network. This number of rectifiers is less than or equal to $\frac{1}{2}(n + 1)$, for suppose it were greater than $\frac{1}{2}(n + 1)$. Then select one of the terminals, say T_j, connected to T_i through a rectifier. T_j must be connected through rectifiers to at least $\frac{1}{2}(n + 1) + 1$ terminals (including

T_i), none of which can belong to the set connected to T_i, for if one did there would be a triangle of three rectifiers. We thus would have at least $\frac{1}{2}(n + 1) + 1 + \frac{1}{2}(n + 1) + 1$ different terminals, a contradiction. Therefore the terminal T_i adds at most $\frac{1}{2}(n + 1)$ rectifiers. Since, with n odd, $[n(n + 1)/4] + \frac{1}{2}(n + 1) = [(n + 1)(n + 2)/4]$, the inductive step carries through in this case. For the case n even, the same construction is carried out. We can in this case deduce that T_i has at most $\frac{1}{2}n$ rectifiers connected to it, and with n even, $[n(n + 1)/4] + \frac{1}{2}n = [(n + 1)(n + 2)/4]$. This completes the induction and the proof of the theorem.

We can exhibit a partial ordering for any n which in the normal form actually requires $n(n + 1)/4$ rectifiers. For n even, the terminals are divided into two sets of $\frac{1}{2}n$ each. Each member of the first set covers each member of the second set. In the odd case a similar device is used with sets containing $\frac{1}{2}(n + 1)$ and $\frac{1}{2}(n - 1)$ members.

If internal nodes are allowed, it is interesting that an equivalent circuit can often be found with fewer rectifiers than the normal form (which we have shown to be minimal when there are no internal nodes). Indeed, the circuits just described which require $[n(n + 1)/4]$ elements in their normal form can be realized with only n elements by the addition of one extra node, a great reduction when n is large. The extra node I is merely placed between elements of the first and second sets, all terminals of the first set cover I and I covers all terminals in the same set. An interesting unsolved problem is that of finding the least number, G_n, such that any network with n terminals can be realized with not more than G_n elements (allowing internal nodes). Theorem 1 shows that $G_n \leq [n(n + 1)/4]$. We will now show that $G_n \geq (n/2)^{3/2}$ for every n which is the square of a prime, thus for an infinite sequence of values of n. The construction is based on a particular partially ordered set suggested for this purpose by E. F. Moore.

Let the integers from 0 to $p^2 - 1$ be written down in order in a $p \times p$ square array. We construct p^2 subsets of these integers, each subset containing exactly p elements, and such that no two subsets have more than one element in common. Each subset contains one element from each row of the square array. A subset is defined by a pair of integers, a, b for $a, b = 0, 1, 2,..., p - 1$. The subset defined by a, b contains the element in the column numbered $a + rb \pmod{p}$ from the left in the r-th row, where the leftmost column is numbered 0, etc.

There are clearly p^2 subsets each containing p elements. We need to show that no two have more than one element in common. This would require that simultaneously

$$a_1 + b_1 r = a_2 + b_2 r \quad (\bmod\ p)$$
$$a_1 + b_1 s = a_2 + b_2 \quad (\bmod\ p)$$

or, subtracting,

$$b_1(r - s) = b_2(r - s) \quad (\bmod\ p)$$
$$\text{or} \quad (b_1 - b_2)(r - s) = 0 \quad (\bmod\ p)\ .$$

Since p is a prime and r does not equal s, this requires $b_1 = b_2$. In this case we see that $a_1 = a_2$ and the two subsets are identical.

Now consider the partially ordered set containing $2p^2$ elements, the p^2 integers and the p^2 subsets, the ordering being that of inclusion. In the Hasse diagram the p^2 subsets will be on one level and the p^2 points on a lower level. There will be p lines down from each upper point and p lines up from each lower point. The normal form for this as a rectifier circuit would clearly contain p^3 elements. We will show that any circuit realizing this partially ordered set contains at least p^3 elements.

Suppose we have a network realizing this partial ordering. Suppose terminal A (of the upper level) includes in the partial ordering terminal a (of the lower level). Then there is a directed path through rectifiers from A to a. Going along this path from A to a, let us mark the first rectifier such that after passing through this rectifier it is not possible to go in the direction of current flow to any terminal of the lower level except a. This rectifier will, in fact, exist, for if it did not, at terminal a itself it would be possible to go in the direction of current flow to another terminal of the lower level, i.e., one point would include another, which is not true. We assign this rectifier to the pair (A, a). In a similar manner we assign a rectifier to each other pair which are related by inclusion. We now must show that the same rectifier has not been assigned to two different pairs, say (A, a) and (B, b). It is clear from the way the rectifier was assigned that $a = b$, since having gone through it, it is possible to reach only one terminal of the lower level. Since the rectifier was the first at which the destination of the path became unique, just before entering it there must have been a branch path leading to at least one other terminal, say c, of the lower level. It is clear, then, that terminals A and B each include both a and c. This is a contradiction if A and B are different, since two of our subsets do not have more than one point in common. Consequently we have assigned a different rectifier to each of the p^3 inclusion relations and therefore the network contains at least p^3 elements. The number of terminals n is equal to $2p^2$, and hence the number of rectifiers is at least $3n/4$.

Partially Ordered Set Device

A second use of this correspondence between rectifier circuits and partially ordered sets is that rectifier circuits may be constructed to represent and study, analog-computer fashion, various partially ordered sets. The circuit shown in Fig. 3, for example, may be used to represent any partially ordered set within its capacity. Rectifiers with plugs on each end are available to plug into the jacks. By plugging these in, the partially ordered set in question is set up on the machine. If, now, the test lead is applied to any terminal, all gas tubes associated with terminals included in the given terminal (in the ordering) will receive voltage and fire. By reversing the + and − voltage it is possible to isolate all elements including the given element. Simple modification of this circuit allows one to perform more complex operations in the partial ordering, for example, obtaining the set of elements included in both of two given elements or including them. (The greatest and least of these sets are the $\cup$ and $\cap$ of lattice theory.)

Rectifier Contact Networks

So far we have considered networks consisting entirely of rectifiers. One may also consider networks of rectifiers and relay contacts. It is, in fact, often convenient to use rectifiers in relay circuits for the elimination of sneak paths and the like. An n-terminal circuit of rectifiers and contacts on s relays corresponds to a function from a set of s Boolean variables to partially ordered sets with n (labeled) elements. This is evident since for each particular state of the relays we have a pure rectifier circuit corresponding to a partially ordered set. It is easily seen that any such function can be realized by means of a suitable network. One may, for example, construct a tree on the s relays from each of the terminals. Corresponding points of these n trees are connected with a rectifier circuit corresponding to the desired partial ordering for that state of the relays.

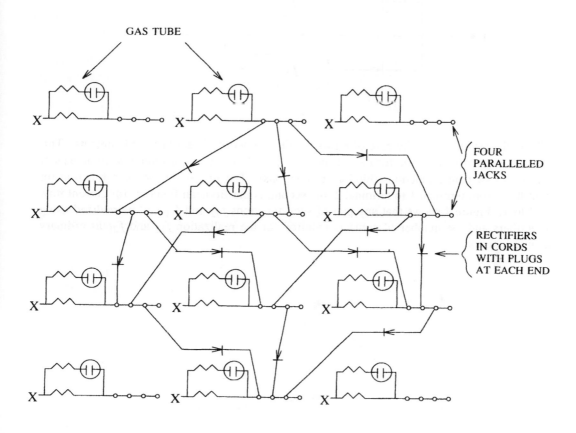

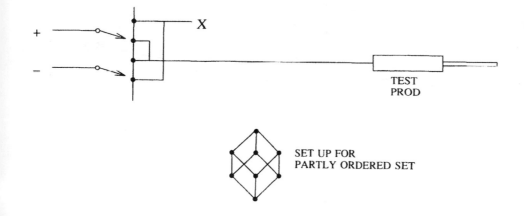

Figure 3

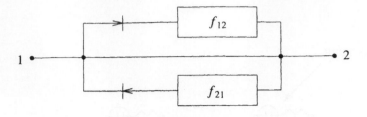

Figure 4

Of particular interest is the case of a two-terminal network of rectifiers and contacts. This may be characterized as above for the special case $n = 2$, or, more conveniently, by means of two Boolean switching functions (hindrance functions). The first is the Boolean function for current flow from terminal 1 to terminal 2; the second is the Boolean function for current flow from 2 to 1. Figure 4 shows that any pair of such functions f_{12} and f_{21} can be realized using two rectifiers and the number of contacts required for the realization f_{12} and f_{21} as ordinary switching functions.

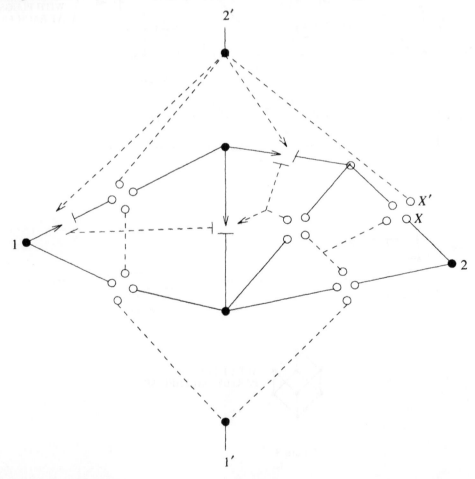

Figure 5

We now give a generalization of the duality theorem for contact networks to the case of networks containing contacts and rectifiers. Let N be a planar network of this type with terminals 1 and 2, and switching functions f_{12} and f_{21}. We construct the dual N' as follows. Let N be drawn upon a plane and the topological dual network drawn superimposed in the usual manner. For each contact in N, place its negative in the corresponding branch of N'. For each rectifier in N, place a rectifier in N' with orientation rotated 90° clockwise from that of N. Let the terminal of N' counterclockwise from terminal 1 of N be labeled $1'$; similarly for 2. An example is shown in Fig. 5, with N solid and N' dotted.

Theorem 2:

$f''_{1'2'} = f'_{12}$, $f'_{2'1'} = f'_{21}$. With proper orientation, dualizing the network negates the two switching functions.

Proof: The proof follows the same line as that for simple contact networks. For current to flow from 1 to 2 in N, there must be a path containing only closed contacts and rectifiers oriented from 1 to 2. This path defines a cut set across N' with every element on the cut set either an open contact or a rectifier pointed in the wrong direction for current flow from $1'$ to $2'$. Thus it is impossible in this state for current to flow from $1'$ to $2'$. In a similar way, when $f''_{1'2'} = 0$ then $f_{12} = 1$, and consequently $f_{1'2'} = f'_{12}$. The similar argument for reverse current flow completes the proof.

The Simultaneous Synthesis of s Switching Functions of n Variables*

Claude E. Shannon

Abstract

Some results are established in the problem of simultaneously synthesizing s functions of n switching variables. Roughly speaking they show that the number of contacts required is about that needed for one typical function of $n + \log s$ variables.

We consider the following problem: Given s switching functions $f_i(x_1, x_2, \ldots, x_n)$, $(i = 1, 2, \ldots, s)$, to find an $s + 1$ terminal contact network (Figure 1) which realizes these s functions between its ground terminal 0 and terminals $1, 2, \ldots, s$ respectively. Let $\lambda_s(n)$ be the least number such that for any choice of the functions f_i the network can be realized with not more than $\lambda_s(n)$ contacts. We wish to investigate some upper and lower bounds for $\lambda_s(n)$, particularly when n and s are large. This is a generalization of the problem treated previously by the author in "The Synthesis of Two-Terminal Switching Circuits" [1], where the function $\lambda_1(n)$ (there called $\lambda(n)$) was studied. The methods we use follow closely those used there and the reader is assumed familiar with that paper.

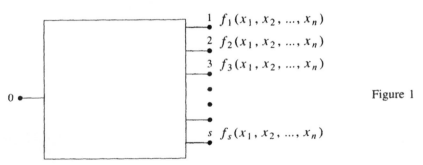

Figure 1

Reference may also be made to the related work of E. N. Gilbert [2] who studies the synthesis of general n-terminal circuits, in which, however, the switching functions between all pairs of terminals are of importance.

As indicated in the synthesis paper [1], a single function of n variables may be realized by cross-connecting suitably between a tree network on $n - m$ of the variables and a network realizing all 2^{2^m} functions of the remaining m variables. If we wish to realize more functions, it is possible to make use of the same network realizing all functions of m variables, provided we supply a different tree for each of the functions we wish to construct, as indicated in Figure 2. Indeed, since the trees are disjunctive, there are no sneak paths back through the trees to cause interference between the functions being realized.

---

* Bell Laboratories Memorandum, June 8, 1955.

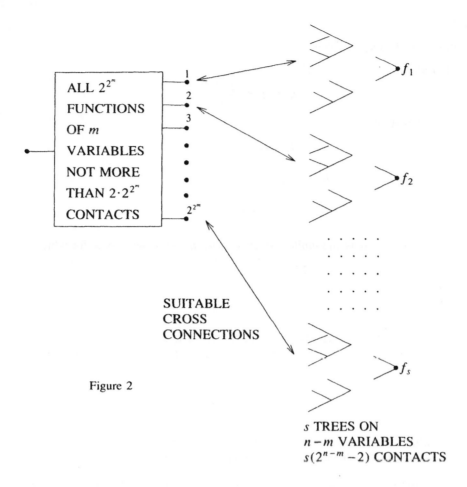

ALL 2^{2^m}

FUNCTIONS

OF m

VARIABLES

NOT MORE

THAN $2 \cdot 2^{2^m}$

CONTACTS

SUITABLE
CROSS
CONNECTIONS

Figure 2

s TREES ON
$n-m$ VARIABLES
$s(2^{n-m}-2)$ CONTACTS

The common network realizing all functions of m variables can be constructed with $2 \times 2^{2^m}$ contacts. The s trees require at most $s(2^{n-m} - 2)$ contacts. Consequently, our total contact requirements are bounded by

$$\lambda_s(n) \leq U = 2 \times 2^{2^m} + s(2^{n-m} - 2) .$$

Our problem is to minimize this upper bound by proper choice of m, which must of course be an integer. If we write $s = 2^d$, then we have

$$U = 2 \times 2^{2^m} + 2^{n+d-m} - 2 \times 2^d$$
$$< 2 \times 2^{2^m} + 2^{n+d-m} .$$

This last is precisely the expression that was minimized in the synthesis paper if we read $n + d$ to be the n there (in proving Theorem 6). The only difference in the problem is that here $n + d$ is not necessarily an integer (since s is not necessarily a power of 2). This does not alter in any way the analysis of this minimizing problem or the upper bounds one may prove concerning the value of U. These may be carried directly from Theorem 6, to give the first parts of the following result.

Theorem:

Let $u = n + \log_2 s$. Then:

(a) For all u,

$$\lambda_s(n) < \frac{2^{u+3}}{u} .$$

(b) For almost all u,

$$\lambda_s(n) < \frac{2^{u+2}}{u} .$$

(c) If $\varepsilon > 0$, for all sufficiently large u,

$$\lambda_s(n) < \frac{2^{u+2}}{u} (1 + \varepsilon) .$$

(d) For $\varepsilon > 0$, there is an infinite sequence of u_i, $u_i \to \infty$ as $i \to \infty$ for which

$$\lambda_{s_i}(n_i) < \frac{2^{u_i+1}}{u_i}(1 - \varepsilon) \qquad i = 1, 2, 3, \ldots$$

provided $n_i + \log s_i = u_i$.

(e) For $\varepsilon > 0$, $\delta > 0$, there exists N_ε such that for $u > N_\varepsilon$ all but a fraction less than δ of the sets of s possible functions of n variables ($n + \log_2 s = u$) require a number of contacts *greater* than

$$\frac{2^u}{u}(1 - \varepsilon) .$$

Part (c), which is not actually given in the Theorem 6 referred to, is, however, implicit in the analysis leading to that Theorem, and might well have been stated there explicitly.

Part (e) of the theorem is a *lower* bound for $\lambda_s(n)$, and remains to be established. The analysis follows that given in the synthesis paper for proving Theorem 7. Gilbert has shown that the number of graphs $G(N, K)$ with N terminals and K branches has the upper bound

$$G(N, K) < 2^{N+K}(N + 2K)^K .$$

Consequently, the number of switching circuits with $s + 1$ terminals and using K total contacts on n relays is less than

$$H = 2^{s+1+K}(s + 1 + 2K)^K (2n)^K . \tag{1}$$

The first terms count the number of graphs and the second term, $(2n)^K$, counts the number of ways we may assign variables to the K branches (any of n variables or their n negatives).

Now the number of possible sets of s switching functions that might be desired for a network is precisely

$$\left[2^{2^n}\right]^s = 2^{s2^n} = 2^{2^u} . \tag{2}$$

Part (e) of the theorem will be proved if we can show that if $K < (1 - \varepsilon)\, 2^u/u$, then the ratio of the expression (1) to the expression (2) is less than δ for u greater than some N.

Making the substitution $K = (1 - \varepsilon) 2^u/u$ in (1) and taking the logarithm,

$$\log_2 H = s + 1 + (1 - \varepsilon)2^u/u + (1 - \varepsilon)2^u/u \left[\log(s + 1 + 2(1 - \varepsilon)2^u/u) + \log 2n\right].$$

For large u, this expression is dominated by one of the form

$$\log H < (1 - \varepsilon_1)2^u/u \log 2^u = (1 - \varepsilon_1)2^u \qquad u > N$$

All the other terms have a lower order of growth as $u \to \infty$, and can be absorbed in the difference between ε and ε_1 when u is sufficiently large. Hence, for large u, $H < 2^{(1-\varepsilon_1)2^u}$ and $H/2^{2^u}$ goes to zero as u goes to infinity, concluding the proof.

To summarize, somewhat roughly, for large n and s, $\lambda_s(n)$ behaves about like $\lambda_1(n + \log_2 s)$, that is to say, like

$$A \, \frac{2^{n + \log_2 s}}{n + \log_2 s} = A \, \frac{s \cdot 2^n}{n + \log_2 s}$$

with A approximately 1.

The reason for this connection between s functions of n variables and one function of $n + \log s$ variables may be seen from Figure 2. If a tree involving $\log s$ variables (if this is not an integer then use the next larger integer) is constructed and the branches are connected to the s terminals of Figure 2, we have, essentially, the canonical circuit of this type for synthesizing one function of $n + \log s$ variables. The contacts used in this additional tree part are in general only a small fraction of the total and hence the similarity in asymptotic behavior.

It should be pointed out that the general design of Figure 2 furnishes a method of attack on practical problems where n and s are small, as well as theoretical results such as the above theorem. When used for actual design purposes, there is a great deal of scope for trial and error and for ingenuity in the specific realization. One may try different variables in the tree part, use different lines of division between the tree and the other network, etc., in an attempt to minimize the circuit.

References

[1]   C. E. Shannon, The Synthesis of Two-Terminal Switching Circuits, *Bell Syst. Tech. J.*, **28** (1949), 59-98.

[2]   E. N. Gilbert, N-Terminal Switching Circuits, *Bell Syst. Tech. J.*, **30** (1951), 668-688.

Concavity of Resistance Functions

C. E. SHANNON AND D. W. HAGELBARGER

Bell Telephone Laboratories, Inc., Murray Hill, New Jersey

(Received August 1, 1955)

It is proved that any network of linearly wound potentiometers and fixed resistors has a curve of resistance *versus* shaft angle which is concave downward.

A S part of a computer, a rheostat having a resistance that was a concave upward function of the shaft angle was needed. After many attempts to approximate it with networks of linearly wound potentiometers and fixed resistors, it became apparent that either it was impossible or that we were singularly inept network designers. Rather than accept the latter alternative, we have proved the following theorem:

Theorem: Let N be a two-terminal network of resistors, $R_1, R_2, \cdots, R_n$ with resistance R between its two terminals. Then $R = R(R_1, R_2, \cdots, R_n)$ is a concave downward function of $R_1, R_2 \cdots, R_n$.

This means that for any two sets of (non-negative) values $R_1, R_2, \cdots, R_n$ and $R_1', R_2', \cdots, R_n'$ we will have:

$$R\left(\frac{R_1+R_1'}{2}, \frac{R_2+R_2'}{2}, \cdots, \frac{R_n+R_n'}{2}\right)$$

$$\geq \tfrac{1}{2}[R(R_1, R_2, \cdots R_n) + R(R_1', R_2', \cdots, R_n')].$$

$$(1)$$

Thinking of these sets of resistances as two points in n-space, this states that the resistance R at the midpoint of the joining line is greater than or equal to the average of the values at the ends.

Before proving the theorem we state two corollaries.

Corollary I: Let $R_{ij} = (\partial^2 R/\partial R_i \partial R_j)$. Then R_{ij} is a negative semidefinite form.

Corollary II: Any network of linearly wound potentiometers[1] on a common shaft and fixed resistors will give a resistance which is a concave function of shaft position.

All three terminals of a potentiometer may be used in the network, since this is equivalent to two rheostats with their wipers connected.

Proof: The right-hand side of Eq. (1) may be interpreted as half the resistance of a series connection of the

---

[1] A linearly wound potentiometer is one whose resistance is a linear function of shaft position.

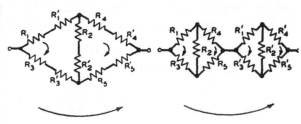

FIG. 2.

network N with $R_1, R_2, \cdots, R_n$ for its elements and the network N with $R_1', R_2', \cdots, R_n'$ for elements. The left-hand term is the resistance of the network N with elements $(R_1+R_1')/2$, $(R_2+R_2')/2$, $\cdots$, $(R_n+R_n')/2$ or (due to linearity) half the resistance with elements R_1+R_1', R_2+R_2', $\cdots$, R_n+R_n'. Thus, to establish Eq. (1), we must show that in Fig. 1 the box at the left has the same or higher resistance than the series connection at the right. A simple special case of these networks is shown in Fig. 2.

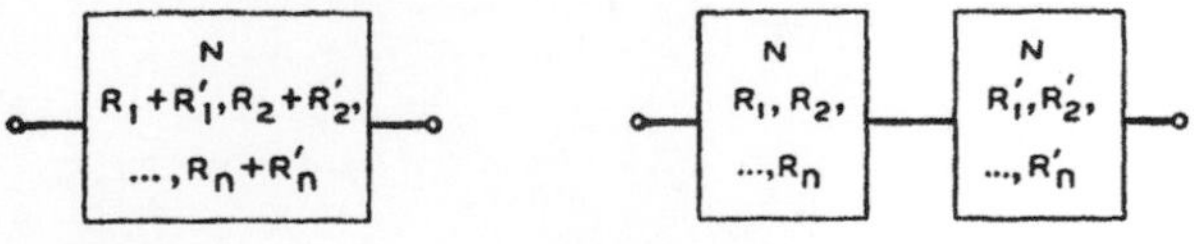

To the network with elements R_1+R_1', R_2+R_2', $\cdots$, R_n+R_n' add the auxiliary circuits shown in Fig. 3 for the particular network of Fig. 2. The additions consist of a set of ideal one-to-one transformers connected across the unprimed elements. A set of independent meshes is chosen for the network N. Suppose elements $a, b, \cdots, k$ form one of these meshes. Then the other winding of transformers connected across elements $R_a, R_b, \cdots, R_k$ are connected in series. This is done for each mesh in the set chosen except the mesh containing the external source. If these series connections are now left open it may be seen that the ideal transformers have no effect whatever and the circuit acts like the left-hand circuit of Fig. 1 or, in the particular case, Fig. 2. On the other hand, if the loops described for these ideal transformers are closed (switches SW_1 and SW_2 in Fig. 3 are closed), the constraints of the circuit are exactly the constraints of the right-hand part of Fig. 1 or, in the particular case, Fig. 2. It may be seen that the ideal transformers imply the mesh constraints for the unprimed elements. The original mesh constraints minus those due to the ideal transformers imply that the primed variables also satisfy these constraints. The mesh through the external source contains the same elements in both cases. Consequently, the current through each element and the voltage across it in Fig. 3 is the same as the corresponding

---

FIG. 1.

Concavity of Resistance Functions

785

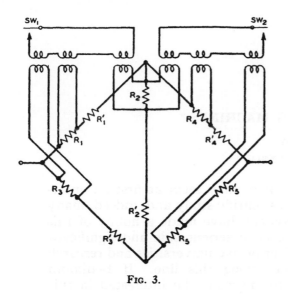

FIG. 3.

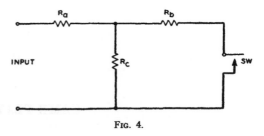

FIG. 4.

current and voltage in Fig. 2 right, and the resistance of Fig. 3 when these switches are closed is the same as Fig. 2 right.

In any linear resistance network, closing a switch reduces (or leaves constant) the resistance. This is more or less evident from physical intuition but follows mathematically by representing the two terminal circuit and switch by its equivalent T structure, Fig. 4. If the original circuit is passive then although the individual resistances R_a, R_b, and R_c may be negative, $R_b + R_c$ is non-negative. The input resistance with the switch open is $R_a + R_c$ and with it closed is $R_a + R_b R_c/(R_b + R_c)$. Now since

$$R_c^2 \geq 0$$
$$R_b R_c + R_c^2 \geq R_b R_c$$
$$R_c \geq R_b R_c/(R_b + R_c)$$
$$R_a + R_c \geq R_a + R_b R_c/(R_b + R_c).$$

Thus closing the switch reduces the resistance. In Fig. 3 this applies to each switch and hence the resistance of the right part of Fig. 2 is less than or equal to that of the left-hand side. This argument, of course, applies to the general networks of Fig. 1 and proves our main theorem.

The ideal transformers in this argument are not really necessary—the argument could be translated into purely mathematical terms. A set of equations is found of the mesh type which can be transformed into those for either of the two circuits in Fig. 1 by making a set of particular resistors (the switches) have zero or infinite resistance. The standard network theorems work for these mesh equations, in particular the result concerning reduction of resistance when a switch is closed. The ideal transformers merely serve as a convenient way of describing how to set up these equations.

Corollary I is a well-known condition equivalent to convexity of a function when these second partials exist.[2] These partials do exist for physical networks, since the resistance R is then a bilinear function of any particular R without poles at finite points.

The second corollary is equivalent to the statement that a convex function in n-space reduces to a convex function of one variable if we move uniformly along a straight line in the n-space.

___

[2] Hardy, Littlewood, and Polya, *Inequalities* (Cambridge University Press, London, 1934), p. 80.

GAME PLAYING MACHINES *

BY

C. E. SHANNON [1]

The design of game playing machines may seem at first an entertaining pastime rather than a serious scientific study and, indeed, many scientists, both amateur and professional, have made a hobby of this fascinating subject. There is, however, a serious side and significant purpose to such work, and at least four or five universities and research laboratories have instituted projects along this line. If Benjamin Franklin were alive today, I am sure he would be interested in this problem for it combines two of his avocations. We are all familiar with his achievements as a scientist and an inventor; it is not so well known that he was also a strong chessplayer. Indeed, he is the author of an engaging essay called "The Morals of Chess"—a blend of diplomacy and chess that might well have been subtitled "How to be Happy Even Though a Chessplayer."

One of the most important technological advances of the last twenty years has been the development of large scale electronic computing machines. These computers are capable of carrying out automatically and at the speed of thousands of operations per second a long sequence of numerical operations. The series of instructions which tells the computer exactly what it should do is called the program. When a computer is to solve a problem, a program must first be devised which translates the solution into a series of simple operations. These basic orders might consist of the elementary operations of arithmetic, addition, multiplication and the like, and also "decision" orders which enable the machine to make a choice between two alternatives, the choice depending upon the results of previous calculations. When the

* Delivered at the 1955 Medal Day Meeting, October 19, 1955, in acceptance of the Stuart Ballantine Medal.

[1] Bell Telephone Laboratories, Murray Hill, N. J.

(Note—The Franklin Institute is not responsible for the statements and opinions advanced by contributors in the JOURNAL.)

Reprinted from JOURNAL OF THE FRANKLIN INSTITUTE,
Vol. 260, No. 6, December, 1955
Printed in U. S. A.

program is introduced into the machine, it carries out the instructions one by one at high speed.

Electronic computers are normally used for the solution of *numerical* problems arising in science or industry. The fundamental design of these computers, however, is so flexible and so universal in conception that they may be programmed to perform many operations which do not involve numbers at all—operations such as the translation of language, the analysis of a logical situation or the playing of games. The same orders which are used in constructing a numerical program may be used to symbolize operations on abstract entities such as the words of a language or the positions in a chess game.

Programming computers to perform such non-numerical tasks is valuable in a number of ways. It widens our understanding of the capabilities of this amazingly flexible tool, the general purpose computer; it seems certain that we have only scratched the surface of the potentialities of such computing devices and each new application leads to new understanding. Also, this wider use of the computers suggests useful changes in their design; new types of orders which will enhance their value in these more unusual programs and even in the ordinary numerical problems. Finally, we hope that research in the design of game playing machines will lead to insights in the manner of operation of the human brain. It would, of course, be naive to expect that the brain operates in a manner similar or even vaguely analogous to that of a machine designed to play a game. It is nevertheless certain that the design of any learning machine will illuminate the path toward the understanding of brain functioning.

Perhaps the earliest game playing machine was the chessplaying Automaton of Maelzel. This was a device constructed in 1769 by the Austrian inventor von Kempelen and exhibited widely in Europe and America by the promoter Maelzel. A large mechanical figure seated at a desk would play chess against human opponents. Before the performance the desk and figure were opened to show that there was no one inside. In its games, the machine usually won. The automaton created quite a sensation at the time and a number of theories were proposed to explain its operation. Among these, for example, was an essay by Edgar Allen Poe who concluded correctly (although in part by fallacious arguments) that the machine was a hoax and in fact was operated by a human chessmaster cleverly concealed inside. This was indeed the case, the effect being produced as in many cases of magical tricks by moving the chessmaster about within the machine as the various compartments and doors were opened for inspection. After many adventures, including some games with the Emperor Napoleon, the automaton ended up in a place called the Chinese museum here in Philadelphia and was finally destroyed by fire in 1854.

A modern counterpart to the Maelzel Automaton came to my

attention a few years ago. A friend in California wrote me that a checker playing machine had been exhibited there both in local department stores and on television. Almost invincible, it had even played the United States checker champion a drawn match and was widely accepted as an authentic electronic computer. Having investigated the problem of programming machines for chess and checkers, I was rather skeptical, particularly in view of the reported strength of play and portability, and suggested an investigation of the device. After considerable detective work, my friend finally tracked down the checker player in an old warehouse. He reported that the only electronic component was an electric fan to keep the concealed human operator cool!

Apart from such hoaxes, game playing machines may be divided into three main types depending on their level of sophistication. The simplest type of machine is that designed for games which have been completely analyzed. By this we mean that a complete strategy of play of relatively simple nature is known, a strategy of play which dictates an appropriate move for each situation in the game. This is the case, for example, in tic-tac-toe, in the match game of Nim and in a number of other mathematical games. In cases such as these, one can translate the known strategy into a program for a general purpose computer or into a special purpose computer so that the machine will make the correct move for each situation in the game. This type of machine will typically play a perfect game. It will win whenever it is possible to win.

One of the first machines of this type was developed about 1914 by a Spanish inventor Torres y Quevedo. It was a machine which played the end game in chess of king and rook against king. This end game is a relatively easy one and the proper moves can be described with only a few simple rules. The Torres machine translated these rules into a switching circuit—while by today's standards the device seems simple, it was certainly a remarkable invention for that period.

Another game susceptible of complete mathematical analysis is the game of Nim and many Nim-playing machines have been constructed. The first, I believe, was one exhibited at the World's Fair in New York in 1939. The game of Nim was analyzed early by mathematicians, who found that the correct strategy of play could be stated quite simply in terms of the binary notation for numbers. Relay circuits are most naturally adapted to the binary notation and consequently it was an easy step to translate the mathematical strategy for Nim into a relay circuit. Most of the Nim machines which have been built play a perfect game in the sense of winning whenever it is possible, but they usually give the human opponent a starting position that he can win if he plays without error. If he makes a single error the machine seizes the initiative and will win the game.[2]

---

[2] Here the speaker demonstrated a small Nim playing machine.

The familiar game of tic-tac-toe is a favorite among amateurs and hobbyists for machine construction. The game can be completely analyzed by enumeration of all possible lines of play. When the symmetry of the board is taken into account the number of such variations is relatively small. One of the earliest tic-tac-toe machines was designed by W. Keister about fifteen years ago and I have here a tic-tac-toe machine using Keister's circuit. In this machine the human player has first move and the machine will always at least draw the game. If the player makes a serious mistake, however, the machine will win. It also has "anti-cheat" features built in. If one attempts to make two moves at once, a "tilt" light goes on.[3]

The second main class of game playing machines relates to games for which a complete analysis is unknown but for which certain general principles of play or maxims of sound strategy are available. This includes most of the games of every day interest such as checkers, chess, bridge, or poker. A machine for playing chess by such general principles would investigate, in a given position, the different moves it could make, the different replies available to its opponent, and so on for two or three moves. At the end of each of these variations it might apply an "evaluation function" to the resulting positions. It would choose as its move that one which leads to the position of highest value, when its opponent is assumed to play in such a way as to minimize this value. This is a kind of *minimax* procedure familiar in the theory of games. Insofar as the evaluation function or the general principles of play are not infallible, a machine designed along these lines would not play a perfect game. It might be expected, however, to make tolerably good moves if the general principles were carefully thought out.

One example of a machine playing by general strategic principles of the type just mentioned is the checker playing routine devised by C. S. Strachey for use on a large scale computing machine. The first game played by Strachey's routine gave the indication of reasonably good play in the opening and middle game but very poor play in the end game. It is evident that a rather different type of program should be used in the later stages of play.

Another checker playing routine has been devised by A. L. Samuel and it is rumored that a match is being arranged between the two machines. There is a possibly apocryphal story with regard to Dr. Samuel's program. When he first introduced it into a computing machine and pressed the start button for the machine to give its first move the computer operated furiously for a few minutes and then printed out "I resign !".

Another quite different general principle type game player was designed by E. F. Moore and myself. It is a special purpose machine

---

[3] Here the lecturer demonstrated the operation of the tic-tac-toe machine.

designed to play a game of Hex. Hex is a game played on a board laid out in a regular hexagon pattern. Two players alternate in playing men on the hexagons. One player uses yellow men and the other uses blue men. The object of the yellow player is to form a connected path of yellow men from the top of the board to the bottom. The object of the blue player is to form a connected path of blue men between the two sides of the board. After some study of this game Moore and I conceived the idea of representing the board by a resistance network and the placement of men by voltages applied to corresponding points of the network; + voltage for the yellow men and − voltage for the blue men. We suspected that certain saddle points in the potential field produced in this resistance network would correspond to good moves in the game. A simple device was built embodying this network and it turned out that the machine played a tolerably good game. It would win when it had first move perhaps 70 per cent of the time against laboratory visitors. With second move its score was perhaps 50 per cent or less. We were often agreeably surprised to find the machine selecting moves which at first looked weak but careful analysis proved sound and strong. Indeed in one early position of the game the machine "discovered" a move which is better than any we had used in that position and which we now normally adopt.

The third and most sophisticated type of game playing machine is one which learns its own principles of play. Only the rules of the game and the desired goal are introduced into the program, together with some general principles of how to improve the play through experience. The machine is then allowed to play many games and by trial and error, by imitation of its opponent, by analysis of its failures or by other means it is supposed to gradually improve its playing skill. Although this problem has been discussed a good deal, no machines quite coming up to these specifications have been actually designed. The problem is one of great difficulty and the cost of carrying out such a research program would be great. However, at a somewhat more elementary level, learning machines have been built. Two examples of these will be described.

D. W. Hagelbarger has developed an interesting device which plays the game of matching pennies against a human opponent. In the ordinary game of matching pennies two players expose coins at the same time. They may arrange to have either the heads or the tails facing up when the coin is exposed. If the two coins are the same, one player wins. If they are different the second player wins. In actual play this results in a kind of psychological outguessing game. The player who can predict his opponent's reactions better will in the long run win. Hagelbarger's machine plays this game substituting lights and switches for the coins. The machine has memory registers in which are stored some of the results of the play against its opponent.

As it plays against the opponent these results are analyzed in the machine in an attempt to find certain patterns or psychological tendencies on the part of the human player. For example, one individual might have a tendency if he had won twice in a row to change from heads to tails. Another individual might have just the opposite tendency. The outguessing machine searches for such tendencies and those that it finds it exploits in future play. Thus, it assumes that in the future the human player will follow the tendencies he has exhibited in the past and the machine plays in such a way as to win if he in fact does so. In actual play the penny matcher has won something like 55 per cent of the time against a wide variety of opponents, definitely better than the 50 per cent it would win by pure chance.

Fascinated by Hagelbarger's machine, I designed a second penny matcher along the same general lines but simplified a great deal with regard to memory capacity and other details. After considerable discussion concerning which of these two machines would win over the other we decided to put the matter to an experimental test. A third small umpire machine was constructed which was able to pass information back and forth between the two machines, keep score, and ensure that the Queensbury rules were followed. The three machines were plugged together and allowed to run for a few hours to the accompanyment of small side bets and large cheering. It turned out that the smaller, presumably less "intelligent" of the two machines beat the larger one in the ratio of about 55 to 45. This was possibly due to its greater speed in altering its conclusions concerning its opponent. Both machines are attempting to find patterns in the other and as soon as one machine finds such a pattern the other machine begins to lose and consequently changes the pattern. Thus the more volatile type has a certain advantage.

The maze solving machine which I have here is another example of a learning machine. While not learning to play a game, it does learn by experience to solve a certain type of problem. A classical psychological learning problem is to place an animal in a maze and observe the time required for it to learn its way to the food box. The maze solving machine is an attempt to dramatize in precisely the same terms how a relay circuit can learn to solve this type of problem. The partitions in the maze can be changed about at will and allow one to set up something like one thousand billion different possible mazes for the machine to solve. On its first trip through, the mouse follows an exploring strategy involving a great deal of trial and error and false moves into blind alleys. Eventually it arrives at a brass disk representing the food box. If we now place the mouse at its original starting point it goes directly to the goal with no false moves. This demonstrates that the relay circuit has learned the correct path. Furthermore if the mouse is placed in any other part of the maze that it has previously explored it will proceed directly to the goal. If it is placed in a part of the maze that it has not previously visited during its exploration phase it will blunder about until it reaches a familiar square and from there it will proceed directly to the goal. If it is now again placed in this region it will go directly to the goal. This shows that it has added the information about this part of the maze to its previous analysis. Finally, if the maze is changed the mouse first tries the old path and when this fails it starts exploring again to find another way to the goal. If the goal is blocked off so that there is no path available the mouse continuously searches through all parts of the maze that it can reach.[4]

While the developments in game-playing machines of the past, particularly in the last two decades, have been interesting and provocative, it seems certain that the next decade or two will make these devices seem primitive. The widespread use of large-scale computers and the rapid advancement of programming theory will surely result in impressive examples of general strategic machines and of game-learning machines.

---

[4] Here the operation of the maze solving machine was demonstrated.

A Note on the Maximum Flow Through a Network*

P. ELIAS†, A. FEINSTEIN‡, AND C. E. SHANNON§

Summary—This note discusses the problem of maximizing the rate of flow from one terminal to another, through a network which consists of a number of branches, each of which has a limited capacity. The main result is a theorem: The maximum possible flow from left to right through a network is equal to the minimum value among all simple cut-sets. This theorem is applied to solve a more general problem, in which a number of input nodes and a number of output nodes are used.

CONSIDER a two-terminal network such as that of Fig. 1. The branches of the network might represent communication channels, or, more generally, any conveying system of limited capacity as, for example, a railroad system, a power feeding system, or a network of pipes, provided in each case it is possible to assign a definite maximum allowed rate of flow over a given branch. The links may be of two types, either one directional (indicated by arrows) or two directional, in which case flow is allowed in either direction at anything up to maximum capacity. At the nodes or junction points of the network, any redistribution of incoming flow into the outgoing flow is allowed, subject only to the restriction of not exceeding in any branch the capacity, and of obeying the Kirchhoff law that the total (algebraic) flow into a node be zero. Note that in the case of information flow, this may require arbitrarily large delays at each node to permit recoding of the output signals from that node. The problem is to evaluate the maximum possible flow through the network as a whole, entering at the left terminal and emerging at the right terminal.

The answer can be given in terms of cut-sets of the network. A *cut-set* of a two-terminal network is a set of branches such that when deleted from the network, the network falls into two or more unconnected parts with the two terminals in different parts. Thus, every path from one terminal to the other in the original network passes through at least one branch in the cut-set. In the network above, some examples of cut-sets are (d, e, f), and (b, c, e, g, h), (d, g, h, i). By a *simple cut-set* we will mean a cut-set such that if any branch is omitted it is no longer a cut-set. Thus (d, e, f) and (b, c, e, g, h) are simple cut-sets while (d, g, h, i) is not. When a simple cut-set is deleted from a connected two-terminal network, the network falls into exactly two parts, a *left part* containing the left terminal and a *right part* containing the right terminal. We assign a *value* to a simple cut-set by taking the sum of capacities of branches in the cut-set, only counting capacities, however, from the left part to the right part for branches that are unidirectional. Note that the direction of an unidirectional branch cannot be deduced

from its appearance in the graph of the network. A branch is directed from left to right in a minimal cut-set if, and only if, the arrow on the branch points from a node in the left part of the network to a node in the right part. Thus, in the example, the cut-set (d, e, f) has the value $5 + 1 = 6$, the cut-set (b, c, e, g, h) has value $3 + 2 + 3 + 2 = 10$.

Theorem: The maximum possible flow from left to right through a network is equal to the minimum value among all simple cut-sets.

This theorem may appear almost obvious on physical grounds and appears to have been accepted without proof for some time by workers in communication theory. However, while the fact that this flow cannot be exceeded is indeed almost trivial, the fact that it can actually be achieved is by no means obvious. We understand that proofs of the theorem have been given by Ford and Fulkerson[1] and Fulkerson and Dantzig.[2] The following proof is relatively simple, and we believe different in principle.

To prove first that the minimum cut-set flow cannot be exceeded, consider any given flow pattern and a minimum-valued cut-set C. Take the algebraic sum S of flows across this cut-set. This is clearly less than or equal to the value V of the cut-set, since the latter would result if all paths from left to right in C were carrying full capacity, and those in the reverse direction were carrying zero. Now add to S the sum of the algebraic flows into all nodes in the right-hand group for the cut-set C. This sum is zero because of the Kirchhoff law constraint at each node. Viewed another way, however, we see that it cancels out each flow contributing to S, and also that each flow on a branch with both ends in the right hand group appears with both plus and minus signs and therefore cancels out. The only term left, therefore, which is not cancelled is the flow out of the right hand terminal, that is to say, the total flow F through the network. We conclude, then that $F \leq V$.

We now prove the more interesting positive assertion of the theorem: That a flow pattern can be found which actually achieves the rate V. From any given network with minimum cut-set value V it is possible to construct what we will call a *reduced* network with the properties listed below.

1) The graph of the reduced network is the same as that of the original network except possibly that some of the branches of the original network are missing (zero capacity) in the reduced network.
2) Every branch in the reduced network has a capacity

* Manuscript received by the PGIT, July 11, 1956.
† Elec. Eng. Dept. and Res. Lab. of Electronics, Mass. Inst. Tech., Cambridge, Mass.
‡ Lincoln Lab., M.I.T., Lexington, Mass.
§ Bell Telephone Labs., Murray Hill, N. J., and M.I.T., Cambridge, Mass.

[1] L. Ford, Jr. and D. R. Fulkerson, *Can. J. Math.*; to be published.
[2] G. B. Dantzig and D. R. Fulkerson, "On the Max-Flow Min-Cut Theorem of Networks," in "Linear Inequalities," *Ann. Math. Studies*, no. 38, Princeton, New Jersey, 1956.

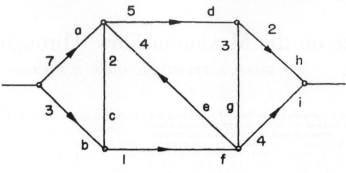

Fig. 1

equal to or less than the corresponding branch of the original network.

3) Every branch of the reduced network is in at least one cut-set of value V, and V is the minimum value cut-set for the reduced network.

A reduced network may be constructed as follows. If there is any branch which is not in some minimum cut-set, reduce its capacity until either it is in a minimum cut-set or the value reaches zero. Next, take any other branch not in a minimum cut-set and perform the same operation. Continue in this way until no branches remain which are not in minimum cut-sets. The network then clearly satisfies the condition. In general, there will be many different reduced networks obtainable from a given network depending on the order in which the branches are chosen. If a satisfactory flow pattern can be found for a reduced network, it is clear that the same flow pattern will be satisfactory in the original network, since both the Kirchhoff condition and the capacity limitation will be satisfied. Hence, if we prove the theorem for reduced networks, it will be true in general.

The proof will proceed by an induction on the number of branches. First note that if every path through a reduced network contains only two or less elements, the network is of the form shown typically in Fig. 2. In general, such a network consists of a paralleling of series subnetworks, these series combinations being at most two long with or without arrows from left to right. It is obvious that for such a reduced network, the theorem is true. It is only necessary to load up each branch to capacity. Now suppose the theorem true for all reduced

networks with less than n nodes. We will then show that it is true for any reduced network with n nodes.

Either the given reduced network with n nodes has a path from left to right of length at least three, or it is of the type just described. In the latter case the theorem is true, as mentioned. In the former case, taking the second branch on a path of length three, we have an element running between internal nodes. There exists (since the network is reduced) a minimum cut-set containing this branch. Replace each branch in the cut-set by two branches in series, each with the same capacity as the original branch. Now identify (or join together) all of these newly-formed middle nodes as one single node. The network then becomes a series connection of two simpler networks. Each of these has the same minimum cut-set value V since they each contain a cut-set corresponding to C, and furthermore neither can contain higher-valued cut-sets since the operation of identifying nodes only eliminates and cannot introduce new cut-sets.

Each of the two networks in series contains a number of branches smaller than n. This is evident because of the path of length at least three from the left terminal to the right terminal. This path implies the existence of a branch in the left group which does not appear in the right group and conversely. Thus by inductive assumption, a satisfactory flow pattern with total flow V can be set up in each of these networks. It is clear, then, that when the common connecting node is separated into its original form, the same flow pattern is satisfactory for the original network. This concludes the proof.

It is interesting that in a reduced network each branch is loaded to its full capacity and the direction of flow i

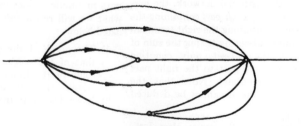

Fig. 2

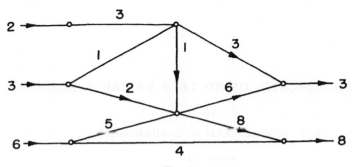

Fig. 3

determined by any minimum cut-set through a branch. In nonreduced networks there is, in general, some freedom in the amount of flow in branches and even, sometimes, in the direction of flow.

A more general problem concerning flow through a network can be readily reduced to the above result. Suppose we have a network with a number of input nodes and a number of output nodes as in Fig. 3. The three nodes on the left are inputs and it is desired to introduce two, three, and six units of flow at these points. The nodes on the right are outputs and it is desired to deliver three and eight units at these points. The problem is to find conditions under which this is possible.

This problem may be reduced to the earlier one by adding a channel for each input to a common left-hand node, the capacity of the channel being equal to the input flow, and also introducing channels from the outputs to a common right-hand node with capacities equal to the output flow. In the particular case this leads to Fig. 4. The network obtained in this way from the original problem will be called the *augmented* network.

It is easy to show that necessary and sufficient conditions for solving this multiple input multiple output problem are the following:

1) The sum of the input flows must equal the sum of the output flows. Let this sum be C.

2) The minimum cut-set in the augmented network must have a value C.

To prove these, note that the necessity of 1 is obvious and that of 2 follows by assuming a flow pattern in the original network satisfying the conditions. This can be translated into a flow pattern in the augmented network, and using the theorem, this implies no cut-set with value less than C. Since there are cut-sets with value C (those through the added branches), the minimum cut-set value is equal to C.

The sufficiency of the conditions follows from noting that 2 implies, using the theorem, that a flow pattern can be set up in the augmented network with C in at the left and out at the right. Now by Kirchhoff's law at the right and left terminals and using condition 1, each added output branch and input branch is carrying a flow equal to that desired. Hence, this flow pattern in the original network solves the problem.

ACKNOWLEDGMENT

This work was supported in part by the U. S. Army Signal Corps, the U. S. Air Force Air Research and Development Command, and the U. S. Navy Office of Naval Research.

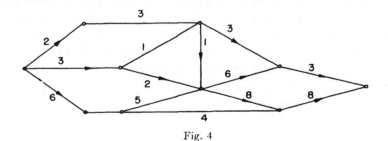

Fig. 4

Reprinted from the IRE TRANSACTIONS OF THE PROFESSIONAL GROUP ON *INFORMATION THEORY* Volume IT-2, Number 4, December, 1956

PRINTED IN THE U.S.A.

RELIABLE CIRCUITS USING LESS RELIABLE RELAYS

BY

E. F. MOORE [1] AND C. E. SHANNON [1]

ABSTRACT

An investigation is made of relays whose reliability can be described in simple terms by means of probabilities. It is shown that by using a sufficiently large number of these relays in the proper manner, circuits can be built which are arbitrarily reliable, regardless of how unreliable the original relays are. Various properties of these circuits are elucidated.

Part I [2]

INTRODUCTION

In an important paper[3] von Neumann considers the problem of constructing reliable computing circuits by the redundant use of unreliable components. He studies several cases, one of which, for example, involves the construction of machines using as a basic component a "Sheffer stroke" organ.[4] Von Neumann shows that under certain conditions it is possible to combine a number of unreliable Sheffer stroke organs to obtain an element which acts like a Sheffer stroke organ of higher reliability. In fact, under certain conditions one can approach perfect operation by means of a sufficiently redundant circuit.

The present paper was inspired by von Neumann's work and carries out a similar analysis for relay circuits. It appears that relays are basically more adaptable to these error-correcting circuits than the neuron-like components studied by von Neumann. At any rate, our results go further than his in several directions.

In the first place, von Neumann needs to assume a certain fairly good reliability in his components in order to get started. With the Sheffer stroke organ, a probability of error less than 1/6 is absolutely necessary, and something like one in a hundred or better is required in the specific error-correcting circuits developed. The methods developed here, on the other hand, will apply to arbitrarily poor relays.

Secondly, the amount of redundancy required in our circuits for a

---

[1] Murray Hill Laboratory, Bell Telephone Laboratories, Inc., Murray Hill, N. J.

[2] Part II will appear in this JOURNAL for October, 1956.

[3] J. VON NEUMANN, "Probabilistic Logics," California Institute of Technology, 1952. (Also Published in "Automata Studies," edited by C. E. Shannon and J. McCarthy, Princeton University Press, 1956.)

[4] The Sheffer stroke is the logical operation on two variables "not A and not B." It has the property that all logical functions can be generated in terms of it. A Sheffer stroke *organ* is a device with two binary inputs and one binary output which performs this logical operation. An unreliable component of this sort would give the proper output only with a certain probability.

given improvement in reliability is considerably different from that required by von Neumann. For example, in one numerical case that he considers, a redundancy of about 60,000 to 1 is required to obtain a certain improvement in operating reliability. The same improvement is obtained in relay circuits with a redundancy of only 100 to 1. We also show that in a certain sense some of our circuits are not far from minimal. Thus, in the numerical case just mentioned, our results show that a redundancy of at least 67 to 1 is necessary in any circuit of the type we consider. Hence, the actual circuits which achieve this improvement with a redundancy of 100 to 1 are not too inefficient in the use of components.

Another difference is that it is not necessary in the case of relays to use what von Neumann calls the "multiplexing system" in order to approach perfect operation on the final output. With his types of elements, the final output (without multiplexing) always has a definite residual unreliability. With the systems described here, this final probability of error can approach zero.

This paper is not intended for practical design purposes, but rather for theoretical and mathematical insight into the problem. There may, however, be some practical applications. The reliability of a commercial relay is typically very high, for example, one failure in 10^7 operations. However, there are cases where even this reliability is insufficient. In the first place, in large-scale computing machines an extremely large number of individual relay operations may be involved in one calculation, an error in any one of which could cause an error in the final result. Because of this, the Bell Telephone Laboratories' computers have made extensive use of self-checking and error-detecting schemes. A second type of situation requiring extreme reliability occurs when human safety is dependent on correct operation of a relay circuit, for example, railway interlocks, safety circuits on automatic elevators and in guided missiles, etc. It is possible that some of the simpler circuits we describe may be of some use in applications such as these. However, the results of this paper will not be directly applicable to actual relays which wear out with age, but only to idealized relays whose probability of failure are constant in time.

IDEALIZED RELAYS

We will prove results only for idealized relays whose failures can be described in one specific manner by means of probabilities. Their description allows only intermittent types of failures, and allows these only under the assumption that the probability of failure remains constant as time passes.

This idealization does not cover such actually possible cases as relays which wear out with age, relays whose windings burn out, or relays which have been wired into the circuit with an imperfect soldered

connection. It is also assumed that the circuit is not improperly designed or improperly wired and that there are no bits of solder to
produce short circuits between different wires.

Since all of the above kinds of errors and failures can actually occur
in practice, using real relays, the results of this paper do not strictly
apply to such real relays. However, the two kinds of failures considered in this paper do actually occur in relays, so the kinds of circuits
suggested are of some possible application.

The first kind of failure allowed is the failure of a relay contact to
close, which in actual relays is often due to a particle of dust preventing
electrical closure.

The second type of failure is the failure of a contact to open, which
in actual relays is usually due to the welding action of the current
passing through the contacts. We shall consider relay circuits in which
the only causes of errors are of these two types—failure of contacts
that should be closed to be actually closed and of contacts that should
be open to be actually open. We will assume, in fact, that there are
two probabilities associated with a contact on a relay. If the relay is

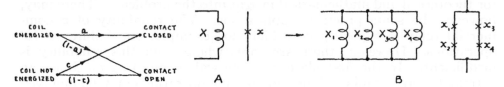

FIG. 1. Schematic representation of the transition probabilities.

FIG. 2. One proposed way of transforming relay circuits
to improve reliability.

energized, the contact is closed with probability a, open with probability $1 - a$. If the relay is not energized, the contact is closed with
probability c and open with probability $1 - c$. If a is greater than c, we
will call the contact a make contact; if a is less than c we call it a break
contact. We assume that different contacts are statistically independent. With actual relays this is probably not too far from the truth
for contacts on *different* relays and, indeed, this is all that is required
for most of the results we wish to establish. In addition, we shall
assume that on the successive times that a relay coil is energized its
closures are statistically independent.

A relay of this type governed by probabilities a and c will be called
a *crummy*[5] relay. Its probability operation may be represented schematically as in Fig. 1. This will be recognized as similar to diagrams
used to represent a simple noisy communication channel, and indeed
such a relay can be thought of as a noisy binary channel. The capacity
of the corresponding channel will be zero if and only if $a = c$. We will

[5] "Crummy = crumby, esp. lousy," Webster's New International Dictionary. We chose
the more modern spelling universally used in comic books.

see later that highly reliable computers can be constructed from a sufficient number of crummy relays if and only if $a \neq c$.

THE GENERAL METHOD OF IMPROVING RELIABILITY

In a general way the analysis we will give depends on constructing networks of contacts which act like a single contact but with greater reliability than the contacts of which they are composed. For example, in Fig. 2A, we have a crummy relay X with a make contact x. This relay might appear as a part of a large computing circuit. In Fig. 2B we replace this by four crummy relays X_1, X_2, X_3, X_4 whose coils in parallel replace the single coil X, and whose contacts are in the series parallel combination shown, this two-terminal circuit replacing the single previous x contact. If each of these four contacts has the probability p of being closed, it is easily seen that the probability of the four-contact circuit being closed is

$$h(p) = 1 - (1 - p^2)^2 = 2p^2 - p^4.$$

This function is plotted in Fig. 3. It will be seen that it lies above the diagonal line $y = p$ for p greater than 0.618 and lies below the line for

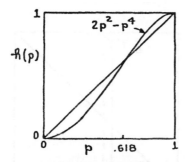

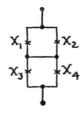

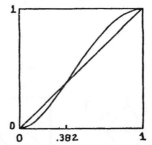

FIG. 3. The function describing the behavior of Fig. 2B.

FIG. 4. Another series-parallel circuit and its associated function.

p less than 0.618. This means that if 0.618 is between the a and c of Fig. 1, Fig. 2B will act like a relay with better values of a and c, that is, values nearer to zero and one. For example, if the individual relays made errors with probabilities $1 - a = c = 0.01$, the circuit of Fig. 2B would make errors when the coils are energized with probability 0.000396, and when the coils are not energized with probability 0.0002. Thus a large improvement in reliability, both when the coil is energized and when it is not energized, is obtained by the use of this circuit.

Figure 4 shows another contact arrangement giving rise to a somewhat different function

$$h(p) = [1 - (1 - p)^2]^2 = 4p^2 - 4p^3 + p^4.$$

Here again, $h(p)$ is the probability of the network being closed, when the individual contacts each have probability p of being closed. The network of Fig. 4 is the dual of that in Fig. 2, and the curve is that obtained by interchanging 0 and 1 in both abscissa and ordinate in Fig. 3.

The bridge network of Fig. 5 gives rise to a symmetrical curve crossing the diagonal at $p = 0.5$. For this network we have:

$$h(p) = 2p^2 + 2p^3 - 5p^4 + 2p^5.$$

All of these networks tend to accentuate the nearness of p to its values 0 or 1 and thus tend to improve reliability. Many other networks have similar properties as we shall see. Furthermore, we will show that it is possible to find a network whose curve, Fig. 6, crosses the diagonal line for a value of p between any two given numbers a and c (no matter how close together) and in fact is less than δ at a and greater than $1 - \delta$ at c, for any positive δ. This means that an arbitrarily good relay can be made from a sufficient number of crummy relays.

It may be seen that this general procedure operates to improve the reliability of either make or break contacts. The only difference is the labeling of the points a and c.

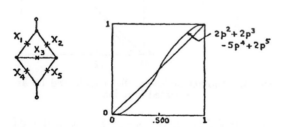

FIG. 5.   A bridge circuit and its associated function.

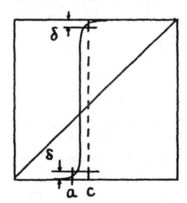

FIG. 6.   The general form of curve of attainable functions.

PROPERTIES OF $h(p)$

Consider any two-terminal network made up of contacts each of which has a probability p of being closed. The network will have a probability, say $h(p)$, of being closed. We wish to investigate some of the properties of $h(p)$.

In the first place, $h(p)$ is a polynomial and may be written as follows:

$$h(p) = \sum_{n=0}^{m} A_n p^n (1 - p)^{m-n} \tag{1}$$

where m is the total number of contacts in the network and A_n is the number of ways we can select a subset of n contacts in the network such that if these n contacts are closed, and the remaining contacts open, then the network will be closed. This is evident since (1) merely sums up the probabilities of the various disjoint ways that the network could be closed.

The first non-vanishing term in (1), say $A_s p^s (1 - p)^{m-s}$, is related to the shortest paths through the network from one terminal to the other —s is the length of these paths and A_s the number of them. This is because in (1) all the elements of a subset which contribute to A_s must actually be on the path (otherwise A_s would not have been the first non-vanishing term). We will call s the *length* of the network. It is evident from (1) that near $p = 0$ the function $h(p)$ behaves as $A_s p^s$.

In a similar way, one can work with the probability of the network being open and write

$$1 - h(p) = \sum_{n=0}^{m} B_n (1 - p)^n p^{m-n} \qquad (2)$$

where B_n is the number of subsets of n contacts such that, if all contacts in a subset are open and the other contacts closed, the network is open. The first non-vanishing term in this series, say $B_t(1 - p)^t p^{m-t}$, relates to the smallest cut sets of the network (sets of contacts which, if opened, open the network). Here t is the number of contacts in these minimal cut sets, and B_t the number of such cut sets. The reason is essentially as before. We will call t the *width* of the network. It is evident that, in the neighborhood of $p = 1$, $h(p)$ behaves as $1 - B_t(1 - p)^t$.

The function $h(p)$ may also be calculated by other means. For example, fix attention on a particular contact in the network, N. Calculate the probability function for the network obtained from N by replacing this contact with a short circuit, say $f(p)$, and for the network obtained from N by replacing this contact with an open circuit, say $g(p)$. Then clearly,

$$h(p) = pf(p) + (1 - p)g(p). \qquad (3)$$

Furthermore we will have, whenever $0 \le p \le 1$,

$$f(p) \ge g(p). \qquad (4)$$

This is intuitively evident since closing a connection certainly cannot decrease the probability of the network being closed. Formally, it follows from the relation (1), noting that the cases where the g network is closed are a subset of those in which f is closed, and consequently the terms in the expression for f dominate those in the expression for g.

If the network in question is planar, it will have a dual. Let $h_D(p)$ be the probability function for this dual network. For each state of the contacts of the original network let us make correspond in the dual network the state in which corresponding contacts have the opposite value.   Then states for which the original network is open correspond to states for which the dual network is closed.   If the probability of closure of a contact in the dual network is $1 - p$, where p is the probability of closure in the original network, then the probabilities of corresponding states are equal.   Consequently we will have

$$1 - h_D(1 - p) = h(p). \tag{6}$$

An example of this relation between the h functions for a network and its dual is given in Figs. 3 and 4.   Either of these graphs can be obtained from the other by inverting, that is, by interchanging 0 and 1 in both abscissa and ordinate.

If the network is self-dual (for example the bridge of Fig. 5),

$$1 - h(1 - p) = h(p). \tag{7}$$

Substituting $p = 1/2$, we find $h(1/2) = 1/2$.

COMBINATION OF TWO NETWORKS

Consider now two networks N_1 and N_2 with functions $h_1(p)$ and $h_2(p)$.   If N_1 and N_2 are connected in series, Fig. 7, the resulting net-

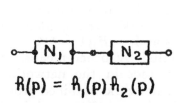

$$h(p) = h_1(p)\, h_2(p)$$

FIG. 7.   Connection of two networks in series.

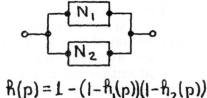

$$h(p) = 1 - (1 - h_1(p))(1 - h_2(p))$$

FIG. 8.   Connection of two networks in parallel.

work will be closed only if both parts are closed.   Hence, the resulting $h(p)$ function will be given by the product $h_1(p)\, h_2(p)$.

If N_1 and N_2 are connected in parallel, Fig. 8, the resulting network will be open only if both parts are open, an event with probability $(1 - h_1)(1 - h_2)$.   Hence, the resulting $h(p)$ function for the parallel network will be $[1 - (1 - h_1)(1 - h_2)]$.

A third method of combining the two networks N_1 and N_2 is by "composition."   By this we mean replacing each element of N_1 by a copy of N_2, as shown for a typical example by Fig. 9.   It is evident that the composite network has an h function given by the composition of the two original h functions:

$$h(p) = h_1(h_2(p)). \tag{8}$$

If N_1 and N_2 are identical and this process is repeated $n - 1$ times, we obtain the nth composition of h with itself, which we denote by

$$h^{(n)}(p) = h(h(h \cdots h(p) \cdots)).$$

The value of $h^{(n)}(p)$ can be found readily from the $h(p)$ curve by the staircase construction shown typically in Fig. 10 for $h^{(3)}(p_1)$. Thus, by composition, a greater improvement in reliability may be obtained with networks whose $h(p)$ curve crosses the diagonal but once. This effect, and the improvement by iteration relating to the staircase construction of Fig. 10, are very similar to situations in von Neumann's approach.

BOUNDS ON $h'(p)$

We will now deduce an interesting inequality concerning the slope of possible functions $h(p)$. As a corollary, we will show that any $h(p)$ function can cross the diagonal at most once.

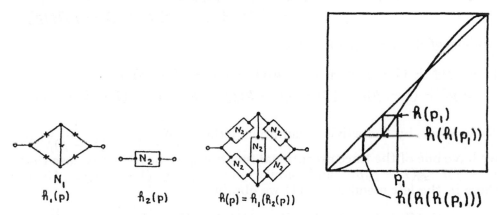

FIG. 9.   Composition of two networks.   FIG. 10.   The effect of iterated composition.

Theorem 1

$$\frac{h'(p)}{(1 - h(p))h(p)} > \frac{1}{(1 - p)p} \quad \text{whenever} \quad 0 < p < 1, \tag{9}$$

provided $h(p)$ is neither identically zero, identically one, nor identically equal to p.

This will be proved by an induction on the number of contacts in the network. We expand $h(p)$ as in (3) except that we expand it about some contact which lies on a path through the network, and then we assume that either the inequality holds for the functions f and g, or that they are among the three exceptional functions, and then we prove the inequality for the function h. But since the contact actually lies on a path, the proof of (4) gives that $f(p) < g(p)$ for all p. Also we cannot have $1 - f(p) + g(p) = 0$ for any p, for if so, we would have $f(p) = 1$ and $g(p) = 0$, which implies there is no path through the network of g, and no cut set through the network of f, and hence $f(p) = 1$ and $g(p) = 0$ for all p, hence $h(p) = p$, contradicting the hypotheses of the theorem.

It can be seen that

$$(1 - p)p(f - g)(1 - f + g) > 0 \text{ whenever } 0 < p < 1, \qquad (10)$$

since each of the terms is positive. Multiplying out,

$$pf - pg - pf^2 + 2pfg - pg^2 - p^2f + p^2g + p^2f^2 - 2p^2fg + p^2g^2 > 0.$$

Rearranging and factoring

$$-pf^2 + (1 - p)pf - (1 - p)g^2 - (1 - p)pg >$$
$$- [p^2f^2 + (1 - p)^2g^2 + (1 - p)2pfg].$$

Adding $pf + (1 - p)g$ to each side,

$$(1 - f)pf + (1 - p)pf + (1 - p)(1 - g)g - (1 - p)pg$$
$$> pf + (1 - p)g - [pf + (1 - p)g]^2 = h - h^2 = (1 - h)h. \qquad (11)$$

Now, since by inductive assumption either $\dfrac{f'}{(1 - f)f} > \dfrac{1}{(1 - p)p}$, or we have one of the three exceptional functions, we have in any case that $(1 - f)f \le (1 - p)pf'$ and similarly $(1 - g)g \le (1 - p)pg'$. Using these in the left member of (11) we obtain

$$(1 - p)p^2f' + (1 - p)pf + (1 - p)^2pg' - (1 - p)pg > (1 - h)h.$$

Dividing by $(1 - p)p$,

$$pf' + f + (1 - p)g' - g > \frac{(1 - h)h}{(1 - p)p},$$

or

$$\frac{d}{dp}(pf + (1 - p)g) > \frac{(1 - h)h}{(1 - p)p},$$

$$\frac{h'}{(1 - h)h} > \frac{1}{(1 - p)p},$$

completing the proof.

If we replace the inequality (9) in the statement of the theorem

by an equality, that is if we set $\dfrac{y'}{(1-y)y} = \dfrac{1}{(1-p)p}$, we have a differential equation, the solutions of which form a one-parameter family
of curves. The inequality (9) states that the permissible h functions
corresponding to contact networks must have slopes greater than these
y curves. If we solve this differential equation for the y curves we
obtain

$$\frac{y(p)}{1-y(p)} = C\,\frac{p}{(1-p)}. \tag{12}$$

This family of curves is plotted in Fig. 11 for $C = 1/4$, $1/3$, $1/2$, 1, 2,
3, 4. Any possible $h(p)$ function must cross curves of this family with

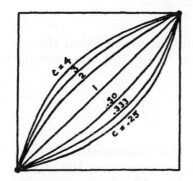

FIG. 11. The family of curves satisfying the equation

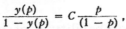

$$\frac{y(p)}{1-y(p)} = C\,\frac{p}{(1-p)},$$

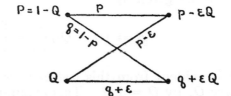

FIG. 12. A binary channel used to obtain an
upper bound on the slope $h'(p)$.

a greater slope. Consequently, any $h(p)$ curve can cross one of these
curves at most once in the open interval $0 < p < 1$. Since the straight
line of slope 1 which goes through the origin is one member of this
family, any $h(p)$ curve can cross this line once at most, say at the point
$p = p_0$. Then applying the staircase construction as shown in Fig. 10,
it can be seen that $h^{(n)}(p)$ approaches 0 as a limit for all $p < p_0$, and
approaches 1 for all $p > p_0$. Thus any network whose $h(p)$ curve
crosses this diagonal straight line can be composed with itself to obtain
a network which improves reliability. In fact if we iterate the composition n times, we will have

$$\operatorname*{Lim}_{n\to\infty} h^{(n)}(p) = \begin{cases} 1 & p > p_0 \\ p_0 & p = p_0 \\ 0 & p < p_0 \end{cases}$$

where p_0 is the (necessarily unique) diagonal crossing point.

It is possible to place an *upper* bound on the slope $h'(p)$ by a curious argument involving information theory.   Consider the binary channel shown in Fig. 12.   The rate of transmission for this channel will be

$$
\begin{aligned}
R &= H(y) - H_x(y) \\
&= -(p - \epsilon Q) \log (p - \epsilon Q) - (q + \epsilon Q) \log (q + \epsilon Q) \\
&\quad + (1 - Q)(p \log p + q \log q) \\
&\quad + Q[(p - \epsilon) \log (p - \epsilon) + (q + \epsilon) \log (q + \epsilon)].
\end{aligned}
$$

For ϵ approaching zero, $(a + \epsilon) \log (a + \epsilon)$ is approximated by its Taylor series

$$
a \log a + (1 + \log a)\epsilon + \frac{\epsilon^2}{a} + \cdots.
$$

Using this in the above for all terms containing ϵ, we find that the constant terms and first order terms in ϵ vanish.   The first non-vanishing terms are given by

$$
R = (Q - Q^2) \frac{\epsilon^2}{pq} = \left[\frac{1}{4} - \left(Q - \frac{1}{2} \right)^2 \right] \frac{\epsilon^2}{pq}.
$$

It is evident from this last expression that R is maximized (when we vary Q) by $Q = 1/2$.   This maximum R is, by definition, the channel capacity C.   Thus as ϵ approaches zero in Fig. 12, the capacity C is asymptotic to $\dfrac{\epsilon^2}{4pq}$.

Now consider a crummy relay which has probability p of being closed when the relay is energized and $p - \epsilon$ of being closed when the coil is not energized.   The relay may be thought of as a communication channel for which the coil is the input and the contact the output.   If ϵ is very small, the capacity will be $\dfrac{\epsilon^2}{4pq}$.   If we have n relays, with the same p and ϵ, the total capacity of this sytem, using the n coils as input and the n contacts as output, is $n\epsilon^2/4pq$, since the capacity of a set of independent channels is the sum of the individual capacities.

We wish to show from these capacity considerations that the probability function $h(p)$ for our contact networks must satisfy

$$
\frac{dh}{dp} \leq \sqrt{\frac{n(1 - h)h}{(1 - p)p}}. \tag{13}
$$

Consider a network N with n contacts and probability function $h(p)$. Let the individual relays and contacts have probabilities p_1 and ϵ as in Fig. 12.   Then the network as a whole acts like a single relay with parameters $h(p_1)$ and $h_2'(p_1)\epsilon$, (when ϵ is small). As such, it has a capacity $(h'\epsilon)^2/4(1-h)h$. This capacity must be less than or equal to that obtained when these n relays are used in the best possible way. Hence,

$$\frac{(h'\epsilon)^2}{4(1-h)h} \leq \frac{n\epsilon^2}{4(1-p_1)p_1}.$$

This being true for any p_1, we have, rearranging terms, the desired result

$$h' \leq \sqrt{\frac{n(1-h)h}{(1-p_1)p_1}}.$$

If this inequality is changed to an equality, we obtain the differential equation

$$\frac{\sqrt{n}\,dp}{\sqrt{(1-p)p}} = \frac{dh}{\sqrt{(1-h)h}}$$

the solution of which is

$$\sqrt{n}\,\sin^{-1}(1-2p) = \sin^{-1}(1-2h) + \theta. \qquad (14)$$

For a given number of contacts n, a possible $h(p)$ curve must cross the corresponding family of curves (14) always with less or equal slope.

Another sort of upper bound on $h(p)$ functions obtained from n contacts can be found by a different argument. A two-terminal network corresponds to a Boolean function of the n contacts involved. However, it is not possible to realize all Boolean functions using only one make contact for each variable. Suppose we ignore these conditions of realizability and consider the class of all Boolean functions of n variables. For any such Boolean function there will be an $h(p)$ function, $h(p)$ being the probability that the function is equal to one if each variable has the (independent) probability p of being equal to one. Which Boolean functions have $h(p)$ functions with the greatest slopes and show the greatest sharpening effect on probabilities?

A Boolean function of n variables will be called a *quorum* function if there is some s, $0 \leq s \leq n$, such that if less than s of the variables are one the function is zero, and if more than s of the variables are one the function is one.

Theorem 2

If the h curve for any quorum function of n variables, say $h_Q(p)$, crosses the h curve of any other Boolean function of n variables, say $h(p)$, then at the point of crossing p_0 we have

$$h'(p_0) < h_Q'(p_0)$$

that is, the quorum function has the greater slope. Furthermore,

$$h(p) > h_Q(p) \qquad 0 < p < p_0$$
$$h(p) < h_Q(p) \qquad p_0 < p < 1.$$

This theorem says that, in a certain sense, the quorum functions are the best of all Boolean functions for our purposes of increasing reliability.

Proof: For any Boolean function of n variables, the $h(p)$ polynomial is made up of a sum of terms of the form $p^i q^{n-i}$, a term of this form for each state of the variables for which the Boolean function has the value one with i of the variables equal to one. A quorum function has the value one for all states with i less than s, say, and zero for all states with i greater than s. Hence the $h_Q(p)$ function is of the form

$$h_Q(p) = \sum_{i=0}^{s-1} \binom{n}{i} p^i q^{n-i} + A p^s q^{n-s}. \quad 0 \leq A \leq \binom{n}{s}$$

Since h is not identical with h_Q but is equal in value to it at p_0, it follows that the h polynomial must miss some terms before (or at) i equals s and have some extra ones after (or at) i equals s. In other words, we can write

$$h(p) = \sum_{i=0}^{n} B_i p^i q^{n-i}$$

with $B_i \leq \binom{n}{i}$ Let $C(p) = \sum_{i=0}^{\tau} B_i p^i q^{n-i} + \alpha p^s q^{n-s}$ where α is B_s or

A, whichever is smaller. Then we will have

$$h_Q(p) = C(p) + \sum_{i=0}^{\tau} D_i p^i q^{n-i}$$

$$\tag{15}$$

$$h(p) = C(p) + \sum_{i=\tau+1}^{n} E_i p^i q^{n-i}$$

where the D_i and E_i are non-negative integers and τ is $s-1$ or s according as B_s or A was smaller.

Now we note that for an expression of the form $u(p) = p^i q^{n-i}$ we have

$$u'(p) = i\, p^{i-1} q^{n-i} - (n-i) p^i q^{n-i-1}$$
$$= \left(\frac{i}{p} - \frac{n-i}{q} \right) u(p) = \frac{i - pn}{pq} u(p).$$

Thus $\dfrac{u'}{u} = \dfrac{i - pn}{pq}$ is a monotone increasing function of i. Now all the terms in the sum in (15) for h_Q correspond to smaller values of i than those in the sum for h. If we let $u_Q(p)$ stand for any term in the sum in h_Q and $u(p)$ stand for any term in the sum in h, we will have

$$\frac{u_Q'}{u_Q} < \frac{u'}{u}$$

and hence there will exist a constant K such that

$$\frac{u_Q'}{u_Q} < K < \frac{u'}{u},$$

and

$$u_Q' < K u_Q, \qquad K u < u'.$$

Summing the first inequality over all the different terms u_Q, and the second over all the u, we obtain

$$\sum u_Q' < K \sum u_Q, \qquad K \sum u < \sum u'.$$

But evaluating at p_0, we have $\sum u_Q = \sum u$, and consequently

$$\sum u_Q' = \sum u',$$
$$h_Q'(p_0) < h'(p_0).$$

The remainder of the theorem follows readily by noting that to contradict it, since the h and h_Q curves are continuous, would require that they cross at a point different from p_0 and in such a way as to contradict the first part of the theorem.

NETWORKS OF A GIVEN LENGTH AND WIDTH

We have seen that the orders of flatness of $h(p)$ in the neighborhoods of $p = 0$ and $p = 1$ are related to the "length" and "width" of the network in question. It is clear that in the case of practical importance, the values of p of interest will be in these neighborhoods, that is, the relays will be initially quite reliable. In this section we will develop some results relating these orders of flatness with the number of elements in the network.

Theorem 3

If a network N has length l and width w it contains at least lw contacts. Equivalently, if $h(p)$ behaves like $A p^l$ near $p = 0$, and if $1 - h(p)$ behaves like $B(1 - p)^w$ near $p = 1$, the corresponding network contains at least lw contacts.

Proof: We associate an integer with each contact in N by the following process. Contacts directly connected to the left terminal of N are labeled "1," contacts connected to those labeled 1 but not already labeled are numbered "2," and so on inductively. In general, a contact will be labeled n if it is possible to find a path to the left terminal through $n - 1$ other contacts but there is no such path through a smaller number.

The set of contacts labeled n for any particular n from 1 to l will be shown to form a cut set of the network. This is true since every path through the network starts at the left terminal with a contact labeled 1 and ends at the right terminal with a contact labeled l or more (if any of the contacts touching the right terminal were labeled with numbers less than l the length of N would be less than l). Along any path, the numbering changes by 0 or ± 1 in going from one contact to the next. Hence every path in going from contacts numbered

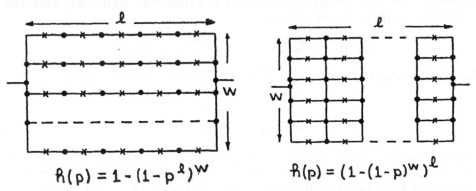

$$\Re(p) = 1 - (1 - p^{l})^{w}$$

$$\Re(p) = (1 - (1 - p)^{w})^{l}$$

Fig. 13.   A series-parallel network of length l and width w.

Fig. 14.   Another series-parallel network of length l and width w.

1 to those with numbers $\geq l$ must pass through every intermediate value. Consequently if all contacts labeled n (for $1 \leq n \leq l$) are deleted from N, all paths are broken and these contacts thus form a cut set.

Since the network is of width w, every cut set contains at least w contacts. Thus there are at least w contacts labeled 1, at least w labeled 2, $\cdots$, and at least w labeled l. The network therefore contains at least wl contacts.

The alternative statement of Theorem 3 follows from remarks made in connection with Eqs. 1 and 2.

It is possible to achieve the "dimensions" l and w with *exactly lw* contacts in a wide variety of ways. For example, we can make a series chain of l contacts and parallel w copies of this (Fig. 13). Dually, w contacts can be paralleled and l copies of this placed in series (Fig. 14).

Theorem 4

A complete characterization of minimal networks with dimensions l and w is the following. Let Y and Z be the terminal nodes, s_0 be the set consisting of Y alone, and s_l be the set consisting of Z alone. In addition to s_0 and s_l there will be $l - 1$ subsets of nodes $s_1, s_2, \cdots, s_{l-1}$. There will be precisely w elements connecting nodes in s_n to nodes in s_{n+1} $(n = 0, 1, \cdots, l - 1)$. Finally, if any node in s_j has m elements connecting it to nodes in s_{j-1}, then it has m elements connected to nodes in s_{j+1} $(j = 1, 2, \cdots, l - 1)$.

This means that any such minimal network with dimensions l and w can be obtained from the network of Fig. 13 by making appropriate connections among nodes in the same vertical line. When all the nodes in each vertical line are connected together, for example, the result is Fig. 14. Another possibility is shown in Fig. 15.

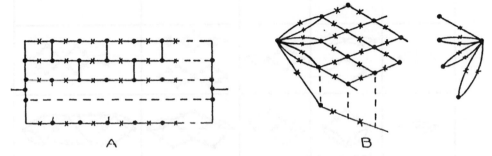

A   B

FIG. 15.   A hammock network of length l and width w.

To show that any minimal lw network is of the form described in Theorem 4, first note that in our preceding proof, each of the numbered cut sets must contain precisely w elements, and these elements must run between elements of lower numbers and higher numbers. The nodes between elements numbered $j - 1$ and j will belong to subset s_j in the above characterization. Now suppose that some node in s_j has m elements going to nodes in s_{j-1} and $m + p$ going to nodes in $s_{j+1}(p > 0)$. The elements numbered $j + 1$ form a cut set of w elements. It is easily seen that if the $m + p$ members of this, going from the node in question, are replaced by the m elements going to nodes in s_{j-1}, then we will still have a cut set but one with less than w elements, a contradiction. Consequently any minimal network of dimensions l and w is of the type described in our characterization.

To show the converse, that any network of the type characterized has dimensions l and w, note first that to go from one terminal to the other the path must pass through nodes belonging to $s_1, s_2, \cdots, s_{l-1}$. Hence any path is of length at least l and the network is of length l. Now consider any cut set c. We will show that c contains at least w

elements. Consider the smallest-numbered contacts of c. Suppose one of these is connected from node A in s_{j-1} to node B in s_j. Then either all elements from B to nodes in s_{j-1} are in the cut set or the one in question is not essential to the cut set and may be eliminated, giving a still smaller cut set. In the former case, this group of elements can be replaced by an equal number, those going from node B to members of s_{j+1}, preserving the cut set property. Proceeding in this way, the cut set is gradually worked over toward the right-hand terminal, either reducing or keeping constant the number of elements in the cut set.

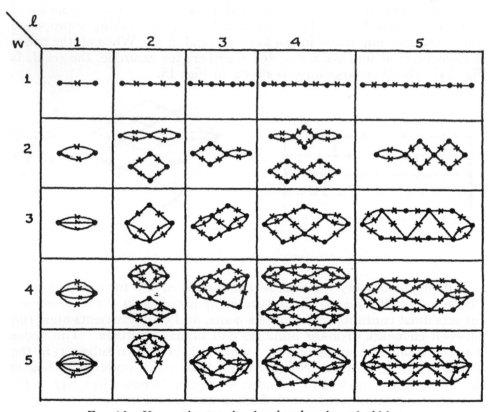

FIG. 16. Hammock networks of various lengths and widths.

When all the elements of the cut set are adjacent to the right-hand terminal there are exactly w members. Consequently there were at least that many in the original cut set, as we wished to prove.

An interesting type of minimal lw network is obtained by putting alternate connections in Fig. 13, leading to the brick-wall appearance of Fig. 15A. When redrawn, pulling together the vertical connections, the network appears as in Fig. 15B, and we will call networks of this type hammock networks. Figure 16 shows some of the simple cases of hammock networks. It will be seen that if both l and w are even, there are two possible hammock networks with these dimensions. If either or both are odd, there is only one. Furthermore, the dual of a hammock network with length l and width w is a hammock network with length w and width l. These hammock networks are, in a sense, midway between the extreme minimal lw networks of Figs. 13 and 14, having half of the connections required to go from Fig. 13 to Fig. 14. In the case where l and w are equal and odd the (unique) hammock network is self-dual.

RELIABLE CIRCUITS USING LESS RELIABLE RELAYS

BY

E. F. MOORE [1] AND C. E. SHANNON [1]

Part II [2]

THE CENTRAL PROBLEM

We now attack our main problem—the design of arbitrarily good circuits from crummy relays arbitrarily poor in reliability.   It will be shown that circuits with the $h(p)$ characteristic of Fig. 6 can be constructed; $h(p)$ rising from a value less than δ at $p = a$ to a value greater than $1 - \delta$ at $p = c$, for any $\delta > 0$, $0 \leq a < c \leq 1$.   We also make estimates of the number of contacts in such circuits in terms of δ, a, and c.

The general design problem will be solved in three stages.   These will be called the *opening, middle game*, and *end game*.   The opening consists of finding a network which, roughly speaking, moves the given a and c over until they straddle the point $p = 1/2$.   That is, a network is designed such that $h(a) < 1/2$ and $h(c) > 1/2$.   This network can then be thought of as a single contact with more suitably placed a and c (at least, more suitable for the method of design being used).

The *middle game* consists of designing a network that can efficiently separate a and c near the value $1/2$ until a is in the general neighborhood of $1/4$ and c near $3/4$.

The *end game* consists of designing a network that will efficiently move points near $1/4$ and $3/4$ toward the ends of the scale, 0 and 1, respectively.

The solution of the general problem is then found by placing a copy of the first (opening) network for each contact of the second (middle game) network.   A copy of this structure is then placed for each contact of the end game network.   The total number of contacts used is clearly the product of the numbers used in each of the three subsidiary problems.

This breakdown into three problems is largely for mathematical convenience.   It is likely that the most efficient possible design frequently would not consist of this composition of three networks.

In many cases, of course, the first part or even the first two parts of the solution are unnecessary since a and c already are separated by $1/2$ and sufficiently far apart.   This indeed will always be true with normal relays.   The general case is chiefly of theoretical interest.   In the cases of practical interest, where a and c are already close to 0 and 1, it will be

---

[1] Murray Hill Laboratory, Bell Telephone Laboratories, Inc., Murray Hill, N.J.
[2] Part I appeared in this JOURNAL for September, 1956.

shown that the circuits proposed for the end game are quite efficient in contacts—they do not contain many more contacts than a provable lower bound for all circuits.

THE OPENING

The first step will be to show that a network can be constructed with an $h(p)$ curve crossing the line $h(p) = 1/2$ in an arbitrary interval and with an average slope in the interval of at least one half. Further, bounds will be obtained for the number of contacts in the network. More precisely, we prove the following result.

Theorem 5

Given a, c with $0 < a < c < 1$, let $b = \dfrac{a + c}{2}$, let $d = $ max $(b,$ $1 - b)$, let $\epsilon = \dfrac{c - a}{4}$, then there exists a network N having fewer than $\left[\dfrac{\log \epsilon}{\log d}\right]$ contacts such that $h_N(a) \leq \tfrac{1}{2} - \epsilon$, $h_N(c) \geq \tfrac{1}{2} + \epsilon$.

Lemma I. There exist two sequences of networks N_0, N_1, N_2, $\cdots$ and M_0, M_1, M_2, $\cdots$ such that for each i:

N_i has i or fewer contacts

M_i has i or fewer contacts

$h_{N_i}(b) < \tfrac{1}{2} \leq h_{M_i}(b)$

$h_{M_i}(b) - h_{N_i}(b) \leq d^i$

and

either M_i can be obtained by shorting between two of the nodes of N_i

or

N_i can be obtained by opening a contact of M_i.

The networks M_i and N_i in this lemma will be derived from a ladder network of the general form of Fig. 17 (with, however, different numbers of horizontal and vertical elements, depending on the value of b,

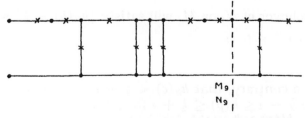

FIG. 17.   A ladder network of the sort used in the proof of Theorem 5.

and possibly starting with a vertical instead of a horizontal group). M_i or N_i is obtained by cutting off the network after i contacts (as shown for M_9 or N_9) and shorting or opening, respectively, the wires that are cut. The infinite network may be thought of as one which crosses $h(p) = 1/2$ at exactly $p = b$. The networks M_i and N_i are finite approximations which cross to the left and right of b.

Proof: Let M_0 be a short circuit and N_0 be an open circuit. These satisfy the conditions for the case $i = 0$, since $h_{M_0}(p) = 1$, $h_{N_0}(p) = 0$.

Then assume the above conditions are satisfied for $i - 1$. If M_{i-1} is obtained by shorting between two nodes of N_{i-1}, let M be the network having a single contact added between these nodes. If N_{i-1} is obtained by opening a contact of M_{i-1}, let M be the network obtained by putting another contact in series with this contact. Then M has i or fewer contacts; shorting the added contact causes M to become M_{i-1}, and opening the added contact causes M to become N_{i-1}. Then by (3)

$$h_M(p) = p \cdot h_{M_{i-1}}(p) + (1 - p) \cdot h_{N_{i-1}}(p),$$

hence $h_{N_{i-1}}(p) < h_M(p) < h_{M_{i-1}}(p)$. If $h_M(b) < \frac{1}{2}$, let $N_i = M$, and $M_i = M_{i-1}$. Then

$$\begin{aligned} h_{M_i}(b) - h_{N_i}(b) &= h_{M_{i-1}}(b) - h_M(b) \\ &= h_{M_{i-1}}(b) - [b\, h_{M_{i-1}}(b) + (1 - b)\, h_{N_{i-1}}(b)] \\ &= (1 - b)\, (h_{M_{i-1}}(b) - h_{N_{i-1}}(b)) \\ &\leq (1 - b)d^{i-1} \leq d^i. \end{aligned}$$

And if $h_M(b) \geq \frac{1}{2}$, let $M_i = M$ and $N_i = N_{i-1}$. Then similarly $h_{M_i}(b) - h_{N_i}(b) \leq bd^{i-1} \leq d^i$. This completes the proof of the lemma.

Lemma II. $h'(p) \geq \frac{3}{4}$ for all p such that $\frac{1}{2} - \epsilon \leq h(p) \leq \frac{1}{2} + \epsilon$.

Since $\epsilon = \dfrac{c - a}{4} \leq \frac{1}{4}$, we have $\frac{1}{4} \leq h(p) \leq \frac{3}{4}$, hence $h'(p) \geq \dfrac{(h - 1)h}{(p - 1)p}$

$\geq \dfrac{\frac{3}{16}}{\frac{1}{4}} = \frac{3}{4}$.

To prove the original theorem, let $i = \left[\dfrac{\log \epsilon}{\log d}\right]$, then $d^i \leq \epsilon$, hence

$$h_{N_i}(b) < \tfrac{1}{2} \leq h_{M_i}(b) \leq h_{N_i}(b) + \epsilon.$$

Let N be whichever of N_i or M_i will satisfy $|h_N(b) - \frac{1}{2}| \leq \dfrac{\epsilon}{2}$, since one of the two must satisfy it.

Then, without loss of generality, it suffices to show only that $h_N(c) \geq \frac{1}{2} + \epsilon$.

Assume the contrary, that $h_N(c) < \frac{1}{2} + \epsilon$. Then since h_N is monotone, we have $\frac{1}{2} - \epsilon \leq h(p) \leq \frac{1}{2} + \epsilon$ for all p between b and c. Hence by Lemma II. $h'(p) \geq \frac{3}{4}$ in this interval.

Hence

$$h(c) = h(b) = \int_b^c h'(p)\,dp \geq \frac{1}{2} - \frac{\epsilon}{2} + \frac{3}{4}\cdot(c-b)$$

$$\geq \frac{1}{2} - \frac{\epsilon}{2} + \frac{3\epsilon}{2} \geq \frac{1}{2} + \epsilon$$

which contradicts the assumption.

THE MIDDLE GAME

The second phase of our approach consists of finding networks which move probabilities just below and just above 1/2 to values beyond 1/4 and 3/4, respectively.   Thus we seek networks for which

$$h(1/2 - \epsilon) \leq 1/4$$
$$h(1/2 + \epsilon) \geq 3/4,$$

and wish to estimate the number of elements used in terms of ϵ.

Networks satisfying our requirements may be obtained by composing a self-dual network with itself a sufficient number of times.   For example, the three-by-three hammock network, Fig. 16, may be used. It is not difficult to show that the $h(p)$ function for this network, as shown in Fig. 18, lies below a straight line of slope 3/2 passing through

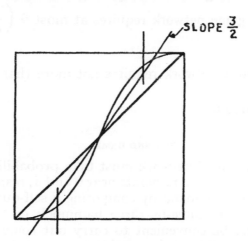

FIG. 18.   The function associated with the three-by-three hammock network.

the point 1/2, 1/2 in the interval $1/4 \leq p < 1/2$, and lies above this straight line in the interval $1/2 < p \leq 3/4$.   This means that composing the hammock network with itself a sufficient number of times to move a point $1/2 - \epsilon$ out to 1/4 will require fewer compositions than if the staircase construction moved along this straight line.   Now, if we move along the straight line starting at $1/2 - \epsilon$, it is evident that after

s compositions (or staircase steps) the point will be moved to $1/2 - \epsilon \times$
$\left(\dfrac{3}{2}\right)^{s}$. If we wish to reach $1/4$, then s compositions will suffice if s
is the smallest integer satisfying

$$\frac{1}{4\epsilon} = \left(\frac{3}{2}\right)^{s},$$

and this same number will surely suffice with the hammock network
since its effect in the staircase construction is stronger. The number of
contacts for an s-fold composition of this hammock network with itself
is

$$N_2 = 9^{s} \le 9 \left(\frac{1}{4\epsilon}\right)^{\frac{\log 9}{\log 3/2}}$$

$$\le 9 \left(\frac{1}{4\epsilon}\right)^{5.41}.$$

The same considerations apply, of course, to moving the point $1/2$
$+ \epsilon$ to $p = 3/4$ and the same network, being self-dual, performs this
function.

Since our ϵ resulting from the opening part of the strategy was
$\dfrac{c - a}{4}$, the middle game network requires at most $9 \left(\dfrac{1}{c - a}\right)^{5.41}$ con-

tacts. The combined network requires not more than $9 \left[\dfrac{\log \dfrac{c - a}{4}}{\log d}\right]$

$\times \left(\dfrac{1}{c - a}\right)^{5.41}$ contacts.

THE END GAME

Our third "end game" network must take probabilities at $1/4$ and
$3/4$ or better and move them to points near 0 and 1, respectively. This
type network will also be found by composing a self-dual network with
itself, in particular the three-by-three hammock or the five-element
bridge. It will first be convenient to carry out some calculations to
determine the rate at which it is possible to approach 0 and 1 in such
cases.

It is sometimes possible to obtain upper or lower bounds on a particular $h(p)$ function in the form of a power of p. For example

$$h(p) \le ap^{r}. \tag{16}$$

If $h(p)$ is composed with itself we obtain, using the fact that $h(p)$ is
monotone:

$$h^{(2)}(p) \le a(ap^r)^r = a^{1+r}p^{r^2}$$
$$h^{(3)}(p) \le a^{1+r}(ap^r)^{r^2} = a^{1+r+r^2}p^{r^3}$$
$$\cdots\cdots\cdots\cdots\cdots\cdots\cdots\cdots\cdots$$
$$h^{(s)}(p) \le a^{1+r+r^2+\cdots+r^{s-1}}p^{r^s}$$

$$= a\,\frac{r^s-1}{r-1}\,p^{r^s}$$

$$= \frac{(a^{\frac{1}{r-1}})^{r^s}p^{r^s}}{a^{\frac{1}{r-1}}}. \tag{17}$$

Now suppose that the original network contains n_1 contacts. When composed with itself s times, the resulting network will require $n = n_1{}^s$ contacts. Eliminating s from (17), we obtain

$$h^{(s)}(p) \le \frac{(a^{\frac{1}{r-1}})^{n^{\frac{\log r}{\log n_1}}}p^{n^{\frac{\log r}{\log n_1}}}}{a^{\frac{1}{r-1}}}.$$

If the direction of the inequality (16) were reversed the result would also be reversed. Furthermore, similar results hold with p replaced by $1-p$.

The three-by-three hammock network, Fig. 16, has the $h(p)$ function:

$$h(p) = 8p^3 - 6p^4 - 6p^5 + 12p^7 - 9p^8 + 2p^9$$
$$= 8p^3 - p^4[6 + 6p - 12p^3 + 9p^4 - 2p^5]$$
$$= 8p^3 - p^4[6(1-p^3) + 6p(1-p^2) + 7p^4 + 2p^4(1-p)].$$

Since the bracketed expression is clearly non-negative,

$$h(p) \le 8p^3 \quad \text{for} \quad 0 \le p \le 1.$$

Hence for the s'th composition, by (17):

$$h^{(s)}(p) \le \frac{1}{\sqrt{8}}\,(\sqrt{8}\,p)^{3^s}.$$

Since each composition multiplies the number of contacts by 9, the total number is $N = 9^s$, $\sqrt{N} = 3^s$.

$$h^{(s)}(p) \le \frac{1}{\sqrt{8}}\,(\sqrt{8}\,p)^{\sqrt{N}}. \tag{18}$$

$$N \le \left(\frac{\log \sqrt{8}\,h^{(s)}(p)}{\log \sqrt{8}\,p}\right)^2. \tag{19}$$

It may be noted that this gives a significant result only when $p \leq \dfrac{1}{\sqrt{8}}$
$\doteq 0.353$.   For larger values of p the upper bound on h exceeds 1.

It should also be pointed out that in this process N must jump by multiples of nine.   If the right member of (19) is given, the number N of contacts required may be up to nine times that defined by the inequality, but this amount will surely suffice.

The dual situation gives an inequality for N:

$$N \leq \left[\frac{\log \sqrt{8}\,(1 - h)^{(a)}(1 - p)}{\log \sqrt{8}\,(1 - p)} \right]^{2}. \tag{20}$$

Returning now to the end-game problem, we wish to improve a probability $p \leq 1/4$ to $h(p) \leq \delta$, say.   This requires by (19) not more than
$9 \left(\dfrac{\log \sqrt{8}\,\delta}{\log \sqrt{2}} \right)^{2}$ contacts.   Since the hammock network is self-dual, similar considerations apply to improving the probability $3/4$ to $1 - \delta$. The same network will effect this improvement.

We may summarize the results obtained by the composition of these three networks in the following manner:

Theorem 6

Given $\delta > 0,\, 0 < a < c < 1$, let $d = \max \dfrac{a + c}{2},\, 1 - \dfrac{a + c}{2}$.

There exists a network such that

$$h(a) < \delta$$
$$h(c) > 1 - \delta$$

using not more than N contacts, where

$$N = 81 \left[\frac{\log \dfrac{c - a}{4}}{\log d} \right] \left(\frac{1}{c - a} \right)^{\frac{\log 9}{\log 3/2}} \left(\frac{\log \sqrt{8}\,\delta}{\log \sqrt{8}} \right)^{2}.$$

This result shows that the equivalent of an arbitrarily reliable relay may be made from a sufficient number of arbitrarily poor ones, and places a bound on the number of them which are necessary.   The bound is undoubtedly quite loose.   In particular the factor 81, which was introduced because things might not "come out even," could probably be reduced a great deal by a more refined analysis.   For particular values of c, a and δ, this factor will be one, and for cases where the factor is large, the substitution of other networks for the three-by-three hammock will often reduce it to a number not far from one, without greatly changing other parts of the bound.

If the relays are initially quite reliable, the first two stages of the above construction can be omitted, the a and c being less than 1/4 and greater than 3/4 at the start.   This of course is the usual practical case. When this is true, and we wish to improve a down to δ_1 and c up to $1 - \delta_2$, not more than the maximum of:

$$9 \left(\frac{\log \sqrt{8} \,\delta_1}{\log \sqrt{8} \,a} \right)^2, \quad 9 \left(\frac{\log \sqrt{8} \,\delta_2}{\log \sqrt{8} \,(1 - c)} \right)^2$$

contacts are required, and if the numbers work out right, the factor 9 may be replaced by a factor as low as one.

In the appendix we develop some similar bounds using general hammock networks.   These bounds are somewhat stronger, both in eliminating the factor 9 and in replacing the coefficient $\sqrt{8}$ by a smaller one.

We will now develop a companion inequality to this giving a *lower* bound for the number of contacts required for a given improvement in reliability.

Theorem 7

Suppose $0 < a < c < 1$ and N is a two-terminal network with $h(p)$ satisfying

$$h(a) \leq \delta_1$$
$$h(c) \geq 1 - \delta_2.$$

Then the number of contacts, n, in the network satisfies

$$n \geq \frac{\log \delta_1}{\log a} \cdot \frac{\log \delta_2}{\log (1 - c)}.$$

For example, if contacts made errors one time in ten, both when they should be open and when they should be closed, we would have $a = 1 - c = 10^{-1}$.   If a network is desired making but one error in 10^6 operations, it will require by this theorem at least

$$\frac{\log 10^{-6}}{\log 10^{-1}} \cdot \frac{\log 10^{-6}}{\log 10^{-1}} = 36 \text{ contacts.}$$

To prove this theorem, let the network N have length l and width w. There is then a path through l contacts from one terminal to the other. The probability that this path will be closed when it should be open is a^l.

If this should occur, the network of course will be closed when it should be open.   Hence

$$\delta_1 \geq al$$

and

$$\log \delta_1 \geq l \log a.$$

Dividing by the necessarily negative $\log a$ reverses the inequality:

$$\frac{\log \delta_1}{\log a} \leq l.$$

The dual argument concerning cut-sets with w elements goes through in a similar fashion to give

$$\frac{\log \delta_2}{\log (1 - c)} \leq w.$$

Since all terms are positive, we may multiply these inequalities and obtain

$$\frac{\log \delta_1}{\log a} \cdot \frac{\log \delta_2}{\log (1 - c)} \leq lw \leq n,$$

using the inequality proved in Theorem 3.

To summarize, the number of contacts n required to improve the probability of error on make from a to δ_1 and on break from $\log (1 - c)$ to δ_2 is something like

$$\frac{\log \delta_1}{\log a} \cdot \frac{\log \delta_2}{\log (1 - c)}.$$

It is never less than this, and for an infinite sequence of increasing values of n only a little greater, as shown for the hammock networks in the Appendix.

COMPARISON WITH VON NEUMANN'S ELEMENTS

As a numerical example, we may consider a case similar to one used by von Neumann, in which he assumes Sheffer stroke organs whose probability of error is $1/200$ and wishes to construct from them a Sheffer stroke organ with a probability of error about 10^{-20}.   He finds that his circuits then require something like 60,000 elements for each desired reliable organ.   It also turns out that the number 60,000 is quite insensitive to the final reliability 10^{-20}, varying only from 32,000 to 69,000 when the final reliability varies from 10^{-17} to 10^{-23}.

As a corresponding problem we may consider relays with initial probabilities of error $a = 1 - c = 1/200$, and ask for circuits which improve this reliability to figures like 10^{-20}.   Since our initial probabilities are relatively good, we need only use the end-game type of analysis.

Let us first consider using the three-by-three hammock networks in composition. If one stage is used, a redundancy of 9 to 1 is involved and the final probability of error is less than $8\left(\frac{1}{200}\right)^3 = 10^{-6}$. If two stages are used the redundancy is 81 to 1, and the final probability of error is less than $8^{-3}\left(\sqrt{8}\cdot\frac{1}{200}\right)^9 = 8\cdot10^{-18}$. Thus with this redundancy of 81 to 1 we are in the general range desired, although still a bit short. Another composition of the three-by-three hammock gives a redundancy of 729 to 1 and the final error probability is less than $4\cdot10^{-51}$!

By using larger hammock networks (see the Appendix for bounds on the error probability), we can hit closer to our mark. Thus, with a ten-by-ten hammock, the error will be less than $2\cdot10^{-19}$ with a redundancy of 100 to 1, while with the eleven-by-eleven the figure is $2.2\cdot10^{-21}$ with redundancy 121 to 1.

In general, in the range where the Sheffer stroke organs require redundancies of 50,000 up to 70,000, crummy relays require redundancies of only 80 to 120, a rather remarkable reduction.

The lower bound for the number of contacts, obtained in Theorem 7, may now be applied to show that the redundancies here could not be improved very much. In fact, in order to obtain a final probability $8\cdot10^{-18}$, at least 55 contacts are necessary (while 81 were used). To obtain $2\cdot10^{-19}$ at least 66 are necessary (100 were used), while for $2.2\cdot10^{-21}$ at least 81 are necessary (121 were used). In all these cases the lower bound is very nearly two-thirds of the actual number.

It is interesting to speculate on why the relays should require so much less redundancy than appears to be necessary for the Sheffer stroke type of synthesis. (It is not certain,[3] of course, that the type of error control used by von Neumann approximates the most efficient use of these elements.) One difference between the two types of component, which may account for this difference, is the following. In both types of machine two processes are involved: first the duplication of variables, that is, obtaining copies of the same variable for use in various parts of the computation, and second, forming logical combinations and functions of several variables. In the case of crummy relays, the errors occur in the duplication of variables. The different contacts on a relay are not in exact correspondence with the coil but are subject to statistical error. However, logical combinations are formed without error; a series combination is an absolutely correct "and" circuit and a parallel combination is always correct as an "or" circuit.

In the case of neuron-type components, the situation is reversed. It is possible to obtain any number of duplications of a given variable

---

[3] In fact, it is not even certain that the methods used in this paper give close to the best possible reduction of errors for relay circuits. Perhaps it is more efficient to redesign the circuit as a whole to get redundancy than to replace each relay by an individual circuit.

by merely branching the line on which it appears. These are all assumed to be identical. However, when a logical combination is made
of two or more variables in a Sheffer stroke or majority organ, statistical
errors occur. Now, in each of the two machines, the statistically unreliable part must be checked by a logical operation involving something
akin to vote-taking. "Sed quis custodiet ipsos custodies?" In the
relay case, the custodians are beyond reproach; in the case of neuron-
like organs, the custodians must indeed be carefully controlled by further custodians. This fundamental difference may be responsible for
the difference in the redundancies and possibly also for the fact that a
certain reliability is necessary in the Sheffer organs in order to control
errors at all, a situation that is not present in the relay case.

It is interesting, in this comparison, that for sufficiently great improvements in reliability the von Neumann circuits will require fewer
elements than the ones we have described. If we take as before $\delta_1 = \delta_2$ and $a = 1 - c = 0.005$, he has approximately $\left(\text{taking the logarithm}\right.$
of his Eq. 27, identifying $p = a$ and ignoring the higher order term
$\left. \log \dfrac{6.4}{\sqrt{n}} \right)$

$$n \approx -3500 \log \delta_1.$$

With our circuits, we have

$$n \approx \tfrac{1}{4} (\log \delta_1)^2.$$

These curves cross at $\delta_1 \approx 10^{-14.000}$! If improvements in reliability
greater than this were desired, the multiplexing circuits would require
fewer elements.

However, the effect of a Sheffer stroke organ could be obtained by
using the circuit of Fig. 19, in which two relays, each having one back

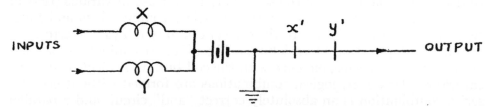

FIG. 19.   Method of making a Sheffer stroke element from two relays.

contact, labelled x' and y', respectively, are connected to act as such an
organ. This circuit as a Sheffer stroke has a reliability only slightly
less than its individual elements and may be used in the type of circuit
proposed by von Neumann. Hence, for the extremely high reliabilities

where the von Neumann circuits have the advantage, it is possible to change over to the first power increase with $\log \delta_1$ using only slightly greater redundancy than the Sheffer stroke elements.

The converse method, attempting to use the relay type correcting circuit for the Sheffer stroke organs, does not appear to be possible. There seems to be no way to make anything which acts quite like a relay from Sheffer stroke organs.

RELAYS WITH UNCERTAIN OPERATE TIMES

The function $h(p)$ associated with a network of contacts can be interpreted in a way somewhat different from that employed above. Suppose that each of the contacts in the network is on a different relay and that these relays are uncertain in their operate times. Let $\varphi(t)$ be the cumulative distribution function for one of the relays; if the relay is energized at $t = 0$, $\varphi(t)$ is the probability that its contact will be closed at time t. The same $\varphi(t)$ is assumed to apply to all the relays and they are assumed statistically independent. Then *the cumulative distribution for the two-terminal network is given by* $h[\varphi(t)]$. The reason for this is that at any time t_1 each of the contacts may be thought of as a contact on a crummy relay whose probability of closure is $p = \varphi(t_1)$. Hence, the probability of the network as a whole being closed at t_1 is $h(p) = h[\varphi(t_1)]$.

The same statements hold even if the relays are both uncertain in time and crummy. In this case, $\varphi(t)$ does not range from zero to one but from the c to a of Fig. 1, when t goes from zero to $+ \infty$.

The results we proved concerning the sharpening of the $h(p)$ curve show in this interpretation that relays of uncertain operate time can be used to synthesize circuits of precise timing. The fact that $h(p)$ crosses the diagonal at most once shows that, in a certain sense, the timing of any two-terminal circuit is less uncertain than its component contacts. In a general way this interpretation indicates that replacing individual contacts by these two-terminal networks should tend to improve timing margins and reduce the probability of errors due to races and the like.

DESIGN OF RELIABLE CIRCUITS IN THE LARGE

Up to now we have been concerned with the problem of designing circuits which would act like a single reliable relay contact. It is not immediately clear that we may replace the relay contacts of a large circuit by the reliable circuits we have developed and necessarily expect the large circuit to behave reliably. The difficulty is that replacing a single contact by a reliable network introduces the possibility of certain race conditions which might conceivably cause errors of a kind not present in the original network. For example, one of our reliable networks might open and close rapidly several times in the transition of its relays from the energized to the non-energized state. If this circuit operated a pulse-counting circuit which could correctly count such a rapid sequence of pulses, it is evident that errors could be introduced. We have not been able to justify the use of these reliable circuits in all cases for just such reasons as these. There are, however, many types of circuit in which such effects cannot occur and there are reasons for believing that even when they can, they will usually not be troublesome. Some possible cases and justifications are as follows.

1. Forward-acting circuit. By this we mean relay circuits in which the relays may be organized in levels. A relay in level n, say, is controlled by a contact network on inputs and relays of levels less than n. This type of organization implies that there are no memory or feedback effects and that race conditions are of no significance for final positions of the relays. It is easy to see that if such a circuit contains N contacts and each of these is replaced by a reliable network with probability less than P of incorrect operation, then the network as a whole will have probability less than NP of failure. This overbound adds the failures of the individual contacts disjunctively and hence pessimistically.

2. "Synchronous" relay circuits. By this we mean circuits operating in a quantized time system and acting somewhat like the neuron models of McCulloch and Pitts[4] or like IBM "selectors." More precisely, contacts can open or close only at integer multiple of the unit T of time, and if at time nT a relay is energized (or not energized), at time $(n + 1)T$ the contacts will have probability a (or c) of being closed. Circuits constructed of such components can be made reliable by techniques we have described, even if memory and feedback are involved. The probability of an error in any calculation performed by such a circuit is, by a slight extension of the previous argument, less than PND, where TD is the duration of the calculation, and P and N are as before.

3. In many ordinary relay circuits the techniques we have described will lead to reliable relay circuits even though feedback and memory are involved. This is because, as we have seen, reliable contact networks tend to sharpen the effective operate time. As the contact network is made more and more reliable it tends to act more and more like a relay with a very definite operate time. If any extra opening and closing occurs, it is with high probability confined to an extremely short time and would not be expected to cause malfunctioning of the circuit. Thus, it is very plausible that even in cases of this sort the techniques we suggest will not, in fact, lead to trouble, particularly if a great deal of improvement in reliability (and hence great sharpening of operate and release times) is involved.

---

[4] W. S. McCulloch and W. Pitts, *Bull. Math. Biophysics*, Vol. 5, p. 115 (1942).

Upper Bounds for the Error Probabilities with l-by-w Hammock Networks

In our standard design method we made use of the three-by-three hammock network, composed with itself many times if necessary, to give increased reliability. This led to easily computed upper bounds for the error probabilities. It is plausible, however, that a more efficient procedure might be to use a larger type of hammock network without the composition.

In this Appendix it will be shown that with a, c, δ_1, δ_2 as before, in a hammock network of length l and width w we have the inequalities

$$\delta_1 \leq \left(\frac{1 - \sqrt{1 - 16a^2}}{4a} \right)^{l-1} wa$$

and

$$\delta_2 \leq \left(\frac{1 - \sqrt{1 - 16(1 - c)^2}}{4(1 - c)} \right)^{w-1} l(1 - c).$$

For a and $1 - c$ small, the right members of these inequalities are approximately $(2a)^{l-1} wa$ and $[2(1 - c)]^{w-1} l(1 - c)$.

To prove these inequalities, first consider the infinite network shown in Fig. 20. All sloping lines here represent contacts with probability

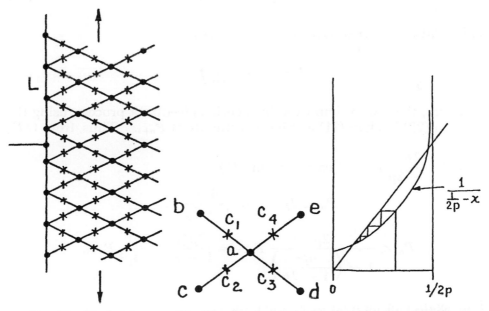

FIG. 20. The infinite hammock network.

FIG. 21. One node of the infinite hammock network.

FIG. 22. The iterative procedure used to improve the bound.

p of being closed. The network is assumed to continue indefinitely at the top, bottom and to the right. The vertical line L at the left is a common connection. Let P_1 be the probability of one of the junction points at distance 1 from L being connected to the line L. Similarly P_2 is the probability for those at distance 2, and P_n for those at distance n. We wish to derive an upper bound for P_n.

In Fig. 21, the node a at distance n will be closed only if node b is closed to L and contact c_1 is closed, or node c is closed to L and contact c_2 is closed, or node d is closed to L and contact c_3 is closed, or node e is closed to L and contact c_4 is closed. An upper bound for the probability for the first of these four events is pP_{n-1}. This also applies to the second event. The last two have upper bounds pP_{n+1}. If we add these (as though they were disjunctive) we have again increased our estimate of the probability P_n (since more than one of these can occur at once). Thus we can say

$$P_n < 2pP_{n-1} + 2pP_{n+1}. \tag{21}$$

Now it is evident that $P_{n+1} \leq P_n$. Using this in the above, we obtain

$$P_n < 2pP_{n-1} + 2pP_n$$

$$P_n < \frac{2p}{1 - 2p} P_{n-1}. \tag{22}$$

This relation, carried back to $P_0 = 1$, gives

$$P_n \leq \left(\frac{2p}{1 - 2p} \right)^n.$$

However, this can be improved by a curious feedback process, using the relation (22) back in (21) as a better estimate of P_{n+1}. Thus, from (22),

$P_{n+1} \leq \dfrac{2p}{1 - 2p} P_n$ and using this in (21)

$$P_n < 2pP_{n-1} + \frac{4p^2}{1 - 2p} P_n.$$

$$P_n < \frac{2p}{1 - \left(\dfrac{4p^2}{1 - 2p} \right)} P_{n-1} = \frac{2p(1 - 2p)}{1 - 2p - 4p^2} P_{n-1}.$$

This again can be used to improve the estimate. To find the result of infinite application of this process, notice that at stage j we have a relation

$$P_{n+1} < \alpha_j P_n.$$

Using this in (21) we have

$$P_n < 2pP_{n-1} + 2p\,\alpha_j P_n$$

and hence

$$P_n < \frac{2p}{1 - 2p\alpha_j}\,P_{n-1}$$

$$\alpha_{j+1} = \frac{2p}{1 - 2p\alpha_j}.$$

This hyperbolic relation between α_{j+1} and α_j is plotted in Fig. 22. If $p < 1/4$, the hyperbola will intersect the straight line $\alpha_{j+1} = \alpha_j$ in two places, namely the roots of

$$2p\alpha^2 - \alpha + 2p = 0$$

$$\alpha = \frac{1 \pm \sqrt{1 - 16p^2}}{4p}.$$

The lower intersection, corresponding to the root $\dfrac{1 - \sqrt{1 - 16p^2}}{4p}$, is a stable point of the iterative process. Starting with any α_0 lying between zero and one, α_n will approach as a limit this root by the staircase process indicated in Fig. 22. It follows readily that

$$P_n \le \left(\frac{1 - \sqrt{1 - 16p^2}}{4p}\right) P_{n-1}$$

and from this that

$$P_n \le \left(\frac{1 - \sqrt{1 - 16p^2}}{4p}\right)^n. \tag{23}$$

Now consider the l-by-w hammock network. This can be thought of as made up of the two parts shown in Fig. 23. The probability of

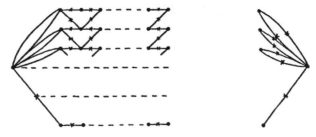

FIG. 23. An l-by-w hammock network is made up of the two parts shown above.

closure for this network is bounded by the inequality

$$h(p) \leq P^{(1)}(2p - p^2) + P^{(2)}(2p - p^2) + \cdots.$$

The last term will be of the form $P^{(w)}(2p - p^2)$ or $P^{(w)}p$, according as w is even or odd. In this expression, $P(j)$ is the probability of the left half of the network being closed to its jth node from the top on the right. The quantities $2p - p^2$ are the probabilities for the parallel connection of two contacts being closed. The terms of the sum therefore correspond to the different ways the network could be closed. Since we have added these, we have an upper bound for the probability.

It is clear that each $P^{(i)} \leq P_{l-1}$ since we may obtain the network of Fig. 20 from the left part of Fig. 23 by adding contacts which will certainly only increase the probability of closure. Consequently, from (23) $P^{(i)} < \left(\dfrac{1 - \sqrt{1 - 16p^2}}{4p} \right)^{l-1}.$ Using this and also strengthening the inequality by deleting the negative p^2 terms, we arrive at the desired result

$$\delta_1 < \left(\frac{1 - \sqrt{1 - 16a^2}}{4a} \right)^{l-1} wa.$$

The dual of a hammock with dimensions l and w is a hammock with dimensions w and l. By duality we obtain

$$\delta_2 < \left(\frac{1 - \sqrt{1 - 16(1 - c)^2}}{4(1 - c)} \right)^{w-1} l(1 - c).$$

It may be noted that for a and $1 - c$ small, these upper bounds become approximately $\dfrac{w}{2} (2a)^l$ and $\dfrac{l}{2} [2(1 - c)]^w$. We conjecture, but have not been able to prove, that for all a and c

$$\delta_1 < \frac{w}{2} (2a)^l$$

$$\delta_2 < \frac{l}{2} [2(1 - c)]^w.$$

Von Neumann's Contributions
To Automata Theory*

Claude E. Shannon

The theory of automata is a relatively recent and by no means sharply defined area of research. It is an interdisciplinary science bordered mathematically by symbolic logic and Turing machine theory, bordered engineering-wise by the theory and the use, particularly for general non-numerical work, of large scale computing machines, and bordered biologically by neurophysiology, the theory of nerve-nets and the like. Problems range from Godel-type questions (relating to Turing machines and decision procedures), to questions of duplication of various biological phenomena in a machine (e.g., adaptation, self-reproduction and self-repair).

Von Neumann spent a considerable part of the last few years of his life working in this area. It represented for him a synthesis of his early interest in logic and proof theory and his later work, during World War II and after, on large scale electronic computers. Involving a mixture of pure and applied mathematics as well as other sciences, automata theory was an ideal field for von Neumann's wide-ranging intellect. He brought to it many new insights and opened up at least two new directions of research. It is unfortunate that he was unable to complete the work he had in progress, some of which is in the form of rough notes or unedited lectures, and for some of which no record exists apart from his colleagues' memories of casual conversations.

We shall not here discuss his tremendously important contributions to computing machines and their use — his ideas on their logical organizations [1], [3], the use of flow diagrams for programming [3], [4], [5], methods of programming various problems such as the inversion of matrices [2], the Monte Carlo method, and so on — but restrict ourselves to the automata area proper.

Reliable machines and unreliable components. One important part of von Neumann's work on automata relates to the problem of designing reliable machines using unreliable components [10]. Given a set of building blocks with some positive probability of malfunctioning, can one by suitable design construct arbitrarily large and complex automata for which the overall probability of incorrect output is kept under control? Is it possible to obtain a probability of error as small as desired, or at least a probability of error not exceeding some fixed value (independent of the particular automaton)?

We have, in human and animal brains, examples of very large and relatively reliable systems constructed from individual components, the neurons, which would appear to be anything but reliable, not only in individual operation but in fine details of interconnection. Furthermore, it is well known that under conditions of lesion, accident, disease and so on, the brain continues to function remarkably well even when large fractions of it are damaged.

These facts are in sharp contrast with the behavior and organization of present day computing machines. The individual components of these must be engineered to extreme reliability, each wire must be properly connected, and each order in a program must be correct. A single error in components, wiring or programming will typically lead to complete gibberish

---

* *Bulletin American Mathematical Society*, volume 64, 1958.

in the output. If we are to view the brain as a machine, it is evidently organized for protection against errors in a way quite different from computing machines.

The problem is analogous to that in communication theory where one wishes to construct codes for transmission of information for which the reliability of the entire code is high even though the reliability for the transmission of individual symbols is poor. In communication theory this can be done by properly introduced redundancy, and some similar device must be used in the case at hand. Merely performing the same calculation many times and then taking a majority vote will not suffice. The majority vote would itself be taken by unreliable components and thus would have to be taken many times and majority votes taken of the majority votes. And so on. We are face to face with a "Who will watch the watchman?" type of situation.

To attack these problems, von Neumann first set up a formal structure for automata. The particular system he chooses is somewhat like the McCullough-Pitts model; networks made up of a number of interconnected components, each component of a relatively simple type. The individual components receive binary inputs over a set of different input lines and produce a binary output on an output line. The output occurs a certain integer number of time units later. If the output were a function of the inputs, we would have a reliable component that might perform, for example, operations of "and," "not," "Sheffer stroke," etc. However, if the output is related only statistically to the input, if, for example, with probability $1 - \varepsilon$ it gives the Sheffer stroke function and with probability ε the negative of this, we have an unreliable component. Given an unlimited number of such unreliable elements, say of the Sheffer stroke type, can one construct a reliable version of any given automaton?

Von Neumann shows that this can be done, and in fact does this by two quite different schemes. The first of these is perhaps the more elegant mathematically, as it stays closely with the prescribed problem and comes face to face with the "watchman" problem. This solution involves the construction from three unreliable sub-networks, together with certain comparing devices, of a large and more reliable sub-network to perform the same function. By carrying this out systematically throughout some network for realizing an automaton with reliable elements, one obtains a network for the same behavior with unreliable elements.

The first solution, as he points out, suffers from two shortcomings. In the first place, the final reliability cannot be made arbitrarily good but only held at a certain level ε (the ε depending on the reliability of the individual components). If the individual components are quite poor the solution, then, can hardly be considered satisfactory. Secondly, and even more serious from the point of view of application, the redundancy requirements for this solution are fantastically high in typical cases. The number of components required increases exponentially with the number n of components in the automaton being copied. Since n is very large in cases of practical interest, this solution can be considered to be of only logical importance.

The second approach involves what von Neumann called the multiplex trick. This means representing a binary output in the machine not by one line but by a bundle of N lines, the binary variable being determined by whether nearly all or very few of the lines carry the binary value 1. An automaton design based on reliable components is, in this scheme, replaced by one where each line becomes a bundle of lines, and each component is replaced by a sub-network which operates in the corresponding fashion between bundles of input and output lines. Von Neumann shows how such sub-networks can be constructed. He also makes some estimates of the redundancy requirements for certain gains in reliability. For example, starting with an unreliable "majority" organ whose probability of error is 1/200, by a redundancy of 60,000 to 1 a sub-network representing a majority organ for bundles can be constructed whose probability of error is 10^{-20}. Using reasonable figures this would lead to an automaton of the complexity and speed of the brain operating for a hundred years with expectation about one error. In other words, something akin to this scheme is at least possible as the basis of the brain's reliability.

Self-reproducing machines. Another branch of automata theory developed by von Neumann is the study of self-reproducing machines – is it possible to formulate a simple and abstract system of "machines" which are capable of constructing other identical machines, or even more strongly, capable of a kind of evolutionary process in which successive generations construct machines of increasing "complexity"? A real difficulty here is that of striking the proper balance between formal simplicity and ease of manipulation, on the one hand, and approximation of the model to real physical machines on the other hand. If reality is copied too closely in the model we have to deal with all of the complexity of nature, much of which is not particularly relevant to the self-reproducing question. However, by simplifying too much, the structure becomes so abstract and simplified that the problem is almost trivial and the solution is unimpressive with regard to solving the philosophical point that is involved. In one place, after a lengthy discussion of the difficulties of formulating the problem satisfactorily, von Neumann remarks: "I do not want to be seriously bothered with the objections that (a) everybody knows that automata can reproduce themselves, (b) everybody knows that they cannot."

Von Neumann spent a good deal of time on the self-reproduction problem, discussing it briefly in the Hixon Symposium paper [8] and later in more detail in uncompleted manuscripts [12].

He actually considered two different formulations of the problem. In the Hixon Symposium paper and in earlier lectures on this subject, a model is discussed in which there are a small number of basic components from which machines are made. These might be, for example, girders, a sensing organ (for sensing the presence of other parts), a joining organ (for fastening other parts together), etc. Machines are made by combinations of these parts and exist in a geometrical environment with other similar parts freely available.

Certain machines, made from these parts, are capable of gathering and working with components from the environment. It is possible also to construct "programmed" machines which follow a long sequence of instructions much as a computer does. Here, however, the instructions relate to manipulating parts rather than carrying out long calculations. The situation is somewhat analogous to that of Turing machines and indeed there is a notion of a *universal constructing machine* which can, by proper programming, imitate any machine for construction purposes. Von Neumann indicates how such a universal machine, together with a program-duplicating part, can be made into a self-reproducing machine.

This model is a very interesting one but, involving as it does complex considerations of motion of parts in a real Euclidean space, would be tremendously difficult to carry out in detail, even if one ignored problems of energy, noise in the environment, and the like. At any rate, von Neumann abandoned this model in his later work in favor of a simpler construction.

The second type of self-reproducing system is described in an unfinished book for the University of Illinois Press. This second model is perhaps a little more suggestive of biological reproduction in the small (say at the cellular or even molecular level) although it is not closely patterned after any real physical system. Consider an infinite array of squares in the Euclidean plane, each square or "cell" capable of being in any of a number of states. The model that von Neumann developed had cells with twenty-nine possible states. Time moves in discrete steps. The state of a cell at a given time is a function of its state at the preceding time and that of its four nearest neighbors at the preceding time. As time progresses, then, the states of all cells evolve and change according to these functional relations. A certain state of the cells is called "quiescent" and corresponds to an inactive part of the plane. By proper construction of the functional equations it is possible to have groups of neighboring "active" cells which act somewhat like a living entity, an entity capable of retaining its identity, moving about and even of reproduction in the sense of causing another group of cells to take on a similar active state.

In addition to the self-reproducing question, he considers to some extent the problem of "evolution" in automata – is it possible to design automata which will construct in successive generations automata in some sense more efficient in adapting to their environment? He points out the existence of a *critical size* of automaton built from a given type of component such that smaller automata can only construct automata smaller than themselves, while some automata of the critical size or larger are capable of self-reproduction or even evolution (given a suitable definition of efficiency).

Comparison of computing machines with the brain. A field of great interest to von Neumann was that of the relation between the central nervous system and modern large-scale computers. His Hixon Symposium paper relates to this theme as well as to the problem of self-reproducing machines. More particularly, the Silliman Memorial Lectures [11] (which he prepared but was unable to deliver) are largely concerned with this comparison.

While realizing the similarities between computers and nerve-nets, von Neumann was also clearly aware of and often emphasized the many important differences. At the surface level there are obvious differences in order of magnitude of the number and size of components and of their speed of operation. The neurons of a brain are much slower than artificial counterparts – transistors or vacuum tubes – but on the other hand they are much smaller, dissipate less power and there are many orders of magnitude more of them than in the largest computers. At a deeper level of comparison von Neumann stresses the differences in logical organization that must exist in the two cases. In part, these differences are implied by the difference in the kind of problem involved, "the logical depth," or the number of elementary operations that must be done in sequence to arrive at a solution. With computers, this logical depth may reach numbers like 10^7 or more because of the somewhat artificial and serial method of solving certain problems. The brain, with more and slower components, presumably operates on a more parallel basis with less logical depth and further, the problems it confronts are much less of the sequential calculation variety.

In the Silliman lectures, von Neumann touches briefly on a curious and provocative idea with some relevance to the foundations of mathematics. Turing, in his well known paper on computability, pointed out how one computing machine could be made to imitate another. Orders for the second machine are translated by a "short code" into sequences of orders for the first machine which cause it to accomplish, in a generally roundabout way, what the first machine would do. With such a translating code the first machine can be made to look, for computing purposes, like the second machine, although it is actually working inside in a different language. This procedure has become a commonplace and very useful tool in the everyday use of computers.

If we think of the brain as some kind of computing machine it is perfectly possible that the external language we use in communicating with each other may be quite different from the internal language used for computation (which includes, of course, all the logical and information-processing phenomena as well as arithmetic computation). In fact von Neumann gives various persuasive arguments that we are still totally unaware of the nature of the primary language for mental calculation. He states "Thus logics and mathematics in the central nervous system, when viewed as languages, must be structurally essentially different from those languages to which our common experience refers.

"It also ought to be noted that the language here involved may well correspond to a short code in the sense described earlier, rather than to a complete code: when we talk mathematics, we may be discussing a *secondary* language, built on the *primary* language truly used by the central nervous system. Thus the outward forms of our mathematics are not absolutely relevant from the point of view of evaluating what the mathematical or logical language *truly* used by the central nervous system is. However, the above remarks about reliability and logical and arithmetic depth prove that whatever the system is, it cannot fail to differ considerably from what we consciously and explicitly consider as mathematics."

In summary, von Neumann's contributions to automata theory have been characterized, like his contributions to other branches of mathematics and science, by the discovery of entirely new fields of study and the penetrating application of modern mathematical techniques. The areas which he opened for exploration will not be mapped in detail for many years. It is unfortunate that several of his projects in the automata area were left unfinished.

Selected Bibliography

1. *Preliminary discussion of the logical design of an electronic computing instrument.* Part I, Vol. I. With A. W. Burks and H. H. Goldstine. Report prepared for U.S. Army Ord. Dept. under Contract W-36-034-ORD-7481 (June 28, 1946, 2d ed. Sept. 2, 1947), 42 pp.

2. *Numerical inverting of matrices of high order.* With H. H. Goldstine. Amer. Math. Soc. Bull. vol. 53 (1947) pp. 1021-1099.

3. *Planning and coding of problems for an electronic computing instrument.* Part II, Vol. I. With H. H. Goldstine. Report prepared for U.S. Army Ord. Dept. under Contract W-36-034-ORD-7481, 1948, 69 pp.

4. *Planning and coding of problems for an electronic computing instrument.* Part II, Vol. II. With H. H. Goldstine. Report prepared for U.S. Army Ord. Dept. under Contract W-36-034-ORD-7481, 1948, 68 pp.

5. *Planning and coding of problems for an electronic computing instrument.* Part II, Vol. III. With H. H. Goldstine. Report prepared for U.S. Army Ord. Dept. under Contract W-36-034-ORD-7481, 1948, 23 pp.

6. *The future of high-speed computing.* Proc., Comp. Sem., Dec. 1949, published and copyrighted by IBM, 1951, p. 13.

7. *Numerical inverting of matrices of high order,* II. With H. H. Goldstein. Proc. Amer. Math. Soc. Vol. 2 (1951) pp. 188-202.

8. *The general and logical theory of automata.* "Cerebral mechanisms in behavior – The Hixon symposium," September 1948, Pasadena, edited by L. A. Jeffress, John Wiley and Sons, Inc., New York, 1951, pp. 1-31.

9. *Entwicklung and Ausnutzung neuerer mathematischer Maschinen.* Arbeitsgemeinschaft für Forschung des Landes Nordrhein-Westfalen, Heft 45. Düsseldorf, September 15, 1954.

10. *Probabilistic logics and the synthesis of reliable organisms from unreliable components,* "Automata studies," edited by C. E. Shannon and J. McCarthy, Princeton University Press, 1956, pp. 43-98.

11. *The computer and the brain.* Yale University Press, New Haven, 1958.

12. Unfinished manuscript for the University of Illinois Press relating to the theory of automata and, particularly, self-reproducing machines.

CLAUDE ELWOOD SHANNON

Computers and Automation—Progress and Promise in the Twentieth Century

The TECHNOLOGICAL PROGRESS of mankind in exploiting its environment may be divided into three main streams of activity. The first and earliest of these relates to exploiting material resources. Man learns to use wood for shelter, develops agriculture for food and the use of metals for tools. In our time this has led to the great industries relating to extraction, manufacturing, and transportation.

The second major stream of activity relates to the exploitation of our energy resources. Early man uses fire for heat, domestic animals supply transportation, and he harnesses both wind and water. The development of the steam engine and the internal combustion engine were important break-throughs in this area, followed by the wonders of electric-power engineering. A most important point in this history was the first industrial revolution, when it became clear that it was possible to replace man's muscle by the power of a steam engine, using a man only to control this energy. Our own century has seen further break-throughs in the exploitation of energy, the use of nuclear power and the promise of solar energy. The rapidity of change on this scientific front can be judged from the fact that while atomic energy is only twenty years old, power engineers tell me that steam-driven generators are now almost obsolete.

The third great stream of technological activity relates to the collection, transmission, and processing of information. Early man learned to communicate with his fellow man by the spoken word and later to use writing and a printed book to record and disseminate knowledge. The great and explosive growth in communication and processing of information, however, occurred in the late nineteenth

CLAUDE ELWOOD SHANNON is Donner Professor of Science at Massachusetts Institute of Technology. This lecture was presented in Hamman Hall at 2:00 P.M., October 12, 1962.

century and in the present century, spurred by the development of electrical technologies. In rapid sequence we had the various powerful communication media—the telegraph, the telephone, radio, and television, together with the information-processing devices of computing machines, control systems, and the like. It is this area of information-processing and communication that I wish to discuss today.

Information, like many other words, has both a popular and a technical meaning. In the popular sense, information is what we find in a book or hear when someone is speaking. Technically, information relates to choosing one possibility from a set or ensemble of various possibilities. The information in a sequence corresponds to the fact that it is this particular sentence chosen from the set of possible sentences. Information is always carried either by means of matter or energy. In the case of a book, it is carried on a material carrier; in a radio wave, on a medium of pure energy. The information, however, is not the underlying carrier but rather corresponds to the particular form or pattern impressed on this carrier as one from the set of possible forms it might assume.

The relations between information, energy, and matter may be illustrated by a little anecdote involving Samuel Johnson. His biographer, James Boswell, tells us that at one time Bishop George Berkeley proposed a philosophy of idealism, suggesting that the real world about us was not, in fact, real, but only ideas in one's mind. When Johnson was asked how he would refute this philosophy the good doctor said, "I would refute it thus," and took a mighty kick at a nearby stone. I don't wish to take a position on idealism versus realism but would like to point out the parts played in this little story by matter, energy, and information. Matter is represented by a stone that Johnson kicked, energy by the muscle power he used to kick it, and information by the thoughts and nerve currents which caused his muscles to so act. The three entities are playing parts here which are entirely typical. Information controls energy which then acts on matter.

In its technical sense, information can be measured much as we measure energy or mass. The unit of information is the bit. It corresponds to the information produced when a choice is made from two equally likely possibilities. If I toss a coin and tell you that it came down heads, I am giving you one bit of information about this event. More complex choices correspond to larger numbers of bits. The unit of information is useful in measuring storage capacity in computers. For example, one might have a computer with a million bits of storage. This means that it can store a million independent yes-or-no decisions.

Again, the measure is useful in communication problems where one is concerned with how much information is produced by an information source and how much capacity may be available in a communication channel. If the capacity of the channel, in bits per second, is less than the rate of production for the source, it is impossible to transmit all the information over the channel. On the other hand, if greater capacity is available than the source rate, it is possible by suitable coding to transmit the information with substantially no errors.

It may be noted that the unit of information says nothing whatever concerning the value or importance of the information. The outcome of a presidential election still corresponds to only one bit if the two candidates are equally likely to win and less if the probabilities are biased. It is analogous to the fact that a gram is the same whether it be a gram of diamonds or a gram of sand.

In the first industrial revolution we have said that man's muscles were replaced by external energy sources. We are now in the midst of what Norbert Weiner has called the second industrial revolution, in which man's control function is replaced by computing devices. This actually started long ago. The Jacquard loom, for example, used a rather sophisticated control system based on punched cards for controlling the harnesses of a power loom. However, automation, like communication, really required the speed and simplicity of electronics for adequate realization.

Automation in this century was initiated on a large scale with the development of the dial system for telephone switching. This was not only efficient and desirable—it was, in fact, absolutely necessary. The present level of telephone traffic, if handled manually, would require the services of almost all the young ladies of suitable age in the country. The telephone-switching system uses electromagnetic relays, a rather slow type of component operating in the millisecond range. The most exciting possibilities in automation and computers stem from the vacuum tube and recently the transistor, those two wonderful devices capable of operating in fractions of a millionth of a second. These can be used for many types of logical operations required in processing and transmitting information.

The development of the transistor was a genuine scientific breakthrough of absolutely first-rate importance. I recall some fifteen years ago when I first saw a transistor and was completely taken with the beauty of its tiny size and small power requirements. It seemed an absolutely ideal component apart from technical difficulties with noise levels and reliability. In the intervening fifteen years our ideas have changed. We now regard the transistor as an easily manageable device but rather large and bulky. Most of it, after all, was empty air, and now we are looking to microminiaturization which reduces size again about as much as the transistor did relative to the vacuum tube.

This highlights an interesting feature of information-processing devices. Information can be carried on almost arbitrarily small bits of matter or of energy. It would seem that the only limits are set by difficulties of manufacture as a practical limit and the presence of thermal noise or quantum uncertainty as a theoretical limit. Nature, however, is still far ahead of us in the miniaturization game. This may be illustrated by a simple calculation. If we regard a neuron in the brain as about the equivalent of a vacuum tube and if we were to build an electronic circuit with as many vacuum tubes as the brain has neurons, this circuit would just about fill the Empire State Building. If it were built with conventional transistor circuitry closely packed, it would still fill an ordinary dwelling. With microminiaturization techniques, it might be reduced to the size of a room. We have at least one linear order of magnitude to go in order to equal nature's amazing circuit. I hasten to add that even if we had these ten billion circuit elements available, we would, by no means, know how to connect them up to simulate a brain. The problem of how the brain operates is still largely unknown.

Perhaps the most exciting developments in the information area relate to the large-scale digital computing machines. While the history of computers can be traced back many centuries, the most important ideas of modern computers were first discovered by the Anglo-Irish mathematician, Charles Babbage, about a century ago. With a remarkable prescience, he discovered the basic principles of a program-controlled computer and spent his life attempting to build one. Unfortunately, like many geniuses ahead of their time, his attempts failed, mainly because of lack of money and because he was attempting to do mechanically something that really required electronics.

Babbage's work was forgotten for some eighty years until about 1940. Then in at least three independent projects the principles of digital computers were rediscovered; at Harvard under Howard H. Aiken, at Bell Telephone Laboratories under George R. Stibitz, and at the University of Pennsylvania under John P. Eckert, Jr., and John W. Mauchly, with a strong assist from John von Neumann. Three programed computers were constructed, soon to be followed by many others at numerous laboratories, each generation of computers producing improvements over the last. The improvements took the form of increased speed, increased capacity, greater flexibility, and greater ease of programing, together with more compact designs and greater reliability. Since that time the dollars involved in computation have just about doubled every two years, and there appears as yet to be no slackening of this exponential increase. In addition to the large-scale computers, there is a vast family of smaller or more specialized devices, and my own feeling is that the surface of this great mother lode has only been scratched.

What are the important features of a large-scale computer? First, it can carry out arithmetical and logical operations at incredibly high speeds. Current models operate in the microsecond range, and in the near future we expect to push toward millimicroseconds. Second, these computers can store and recover large amounts of information, including results of intermediate calculations. Finally, they can carry out a sequence of orders without outside help, this sequence or program representing a very complex calculation. The program can contain decision points, where the further operation depends on the results of previous calculations. Thus, the machine can make a proper choice when the time comes, even though the person who writes the program does not know which choice it will be. Perhaps more than anything else, these decision orders give computers a possibility of simulating in many ways complex logical decisions that we associate with the human mind.

We have had, then, just two decades of development of the computer in the modern era. The first of these, the decade of the forties, witnessed the construction of a large number of computers, each different from all the others, and going by such names as Eniac, Edvac, Univac, Illiac, and even Maniac. Most of these were built at universities and explored the possibilities of various types of logical organization, as well as new types of components such as different kinds of memory. Further, much work was done in learning how to use computers efficiently.

The uses of computers at this time were almost entirely straightforward computation, the solution of complex numerical problems arising in science and commerce.

During the decade of the fifties the development of computers largely passed from the university laboratory to the industrial research laboratory. Large companies began to manufacture computers and sell or rent them as a commercial product. There was still a good deal of research and development of new components, but it was more a matter of perfecting and improving than of innovating.

An important area of research during this period was that of improving communication between man and machine. The very difficult problem of programing was gradually reduced to manageable size. Whereas earlier it was necessary for man to talk in the machines' language, communication is now carried out in a language about halfway between that of the computer and that of man. It is now possible for the average scientist to program his own problem after only a few days of study.

Another trend of growing importance became evident during the decade of the fifties. This was the growing realization that the potential applications of computers were by no means limited to ordinary numerical work—the solution of differential equations, or keeping bank accounts straight. Indeed, computers could be used for all manner of symbolic manipulation, involving abstract entities of almost any sort. Words, musical notes, mathematical expressions, wiring diagrams, or even pictures could be encoded into numbers and stored in a computer. Furthermore, almost any rules of operation or manipulation could be translated into a form understood by a general-purpose computer. Thus the doors were opened for a wild orgy of experimental programing, ranging from such things as playing chess to composing music, from translating languages to medical diagnosis.

So far most of this work must be described as experimental with little practical application. Much of it, in fact, is not intended for application, but rather to gain experience and knowledge relating to the possibilities in this general area. I feel, however, that this line of research is one of the greatest promise—a real indicator of the shape of things to come. It is interesting to take a quick look at some of the experimental programing that has been, or is being, carried out. This is an area in which there is a good deal of scientific wildcatting with many dry holes, a few gushers, but mostly unfinished drilling.

Language translation has attracted much attention, and many research groups are devoted to its study. As yet results are only mediocre. It is possible to translate rather poorly and with frequent errors but, perhaps, sufficiently well for a reader to get the general ideas intended. It appears that for really first-rate machine translation the computers will have to work at a somewhat deeper level than that of straight syntax and grammar. In other words, they must have some primitive notion, at least, of the meaning of what they are translating. If this is correct, the next step forward is a rather formidable one and may take some time and significant innovation.

Many computers have been programed to play various games, such as chess, checkers, bridge, or blackjack. By and large, the machines are now in the middle range of human ability, although in certain games particularly suited to their talents they will outplay any human.

To give just one example, A. L. Samuel has developed a program for playing checkers which plays a first-rate game. While a world champion can beat it, I would certainly bet on the 704 in a strong local tournament such as, say, the Houston Finals. Samuel's program is interesting in several respects. The machine is improving its play by a learning procedure as it plays more games. It remembers parts of previous analyses and uses these later. Thus at times it may be seeing the game twenty or more moves in depth. It also may change its strategy in general form as time goes on.

It is also interesting that Samuel himself was only a beginner at checkers when he designed the program, and the machine beats him soundly. This shows that one can design a machine which does an intellectual task better than one's self, just as we can design steam shovels that lift more or automobiles that go faster than we can.

Another area of programing exploration is that of symbolic mathematics in contrast with solution of numerical problems. One aspect of this relates to the manipulation of expressions that occur in algebra and calculus—problems of factoring expressions, differentiation, and integration. These problems have all been tackled with excellent results. Differentiation is essentially a rote process and mainly, therefore, a matter of translating the rules into a program. Integration and algebraic manipulation often involve trial-and-error procedures and, for the mathematician, experience and insight. Nevertheless, it is possible to set up programs which will carry out these operations with a considerable degree of success. For example, an integration routine developed by Dr. James R. Slagle was sufficiently competent to pass an M.I.T. calculus test on formal integration.

Another aspect of symbolic mathematics is that of discovering and proving theorems, the work of the pure mathematician. It is possible to program a set of axioms and rules of inference into a computer, together with methods of looking for proof, and have it deliver proofs of various theorems. Thus, Hao Wang has programed a part of propositional calculus into a computer in such a way that it can prove many of the theorems in this area.

In particular, it was able to prove all the theorems in a large section of the famous Whitehead and Russell tract, *Principia Mathematica*, and it did this in less than five minutes. The authors of this work must surely have required many months to do the same job.

While on the subject of these rather exotic researches, I would like to mention a number of theoretical studies with biological repercussions. Lead by von Neumann, a number of investigators have studied mathematically and theoretically the matter of self-reproduction in a machine. Without going into details, one might summarize the results by saying that there is no theoretical reason why this should not be possible, although from a practical viewpoint complete self-reproduction by machine is at best a gleam in some mathematician's eye.

Another related question is that of self-repair and self-maintenance together with self-checking of errors in machines. Many computers today have error-checking systems built in, so this is a realized goal. Self-repair is considerably more difficult, but some investigation has been made of this possibility.

Work has also been carried out in the direction of using computers to design various types of electrical circuits. These include such things as relay-switching circuits, diode-logic circuits, linear-filter circuits, and the like. In some cases the circuits designed were actually used in the next generation of computers. Thus we have perhaps the beginnings of self-reproduction in machines.

I should like to mention briefly also a creeping invasion of the arts and professions by the ubiquitous computer. In the arts, some of you may have heard the record *Suite for the Illiac*—music composed by the Illiac computer. While certainly not great music, its very existence brings to mind thoughts of a brave new world.

In the professions, lawyers have been working with the possibility of using computers for the study of legal precedents and other information-retrieval problems. Doctors are studying the possibilities of computers as a diagnostic aid. Teachers are investigating the possibility of teaching machines which may range from a simple question-and-answer device to a full-scale computer acting very much like a private tutor. The second industrial revolution may displace us at all levels, from the factory hand to the skilled professional.

For the most part, computers so far have been used as straight information-processing devices. Instructions are fed in by a human operator and answers typed out for a human operator. The only connection of the computer to the real world is through the operator. A most interesting area of study is that of giving a computer its own sense organs so it has direct knowledge of the outside world, and manipulative means, the equivalent of hands, so that it can act directly on the outside world. Of course, this is done in the automation of factory equipment, but here the outside world is so limited that the machine has very little in the way of freedom of action or of unexpected surroundings. Is it possible to add sense organs and motor organs to a computer so that it is something like the robot of science fiction? One study along this line was carried out by Dr. Heinrich A. Ernst at M.I.T., in which he coupled a mechanical arm of the type used in nuclear research to a computer. The arm was supplied with primitive sense organs of touch and given a program allowing the computer to maneuver the hand with seven degrees of freedom. The hand was able, for example, to feel around on the floor and pick up blocks and then stack them in a tower or to deposit them in a wastebasket. This is only a beginning, and many difficulties are encountered in this line of research. Perhaps the most challenging is that of developing a sense organ comparable to the human eye which can be coupled directly to a computer. Recent studies of the operation of the frog's eye and also work in progress on the abstraction of object content from a picture may eventually alleviate this problem.

The various research projects I have been discussing and many others of similar nature are all aimed at the general problem of simulating the human or animal brain, at least from the behavioristic point of view, in a computing machine. One may divide the approaches to this problem into three main categories, which might be termed the logical approach, the psychological approach, and the neurological approach. The logical approach aims at finding a straightforward method, in logical terms a decision procedure, which will solve all of the problems of a given class. This is typified by Wang's program for theorem-proving in symbolic logic. It is most effective and efficient when it can be done, but not all problems have available a suitable decision procedure. Furthermore, a decision procedure requires a deep and sophisticated understanding of the problem by the programer in all its detail.

The second method, the psychological approach, is often referred to as heuristic programing. It involves a study of how we solve problems, perhaps by subjective or introspective analysis of our own thought processes. We then attempt to translate these heuristic methods of trial and error and the like into a program for a computer. The integrating program of Slagle is an example of this method. I believe that heuristic programing is only in its infancy and that the next ten or twenty years will see remarkable advances in this area. This may also have important fringe benefits in that we may understand far better the processes of creative thinking and perhaps be able to teach them to some extent to others.

The third or neurological approach aims at simulating the operation of the brain at the neural level rather than at the psychological or functional level. Although several interesting research studies have been carried out, the results are still open to much question as to interpretation. While neurophysiologists have uncovered much information regarding the operation of individual neurons and their general patterns of interconnection, the mode of operation of the brain is still a wide-open scientific question. It is not, for example, as yet known where memory takes place or by what means. Thus anyone attempting to construct a neural-net model of the brain must make many hypotheses concerning the exact operation of nerve cells and with regard to their cross-connections. Furthermore, the human brain contains some ten billion neurons, and the simulated nerve nets of computers at best contain a few thousand. Under these conditions one could only hope for the most primitive type of brain activity in the model, and consequently the experimental results are difficult to understand. This line of research is an important one with a long-range future, but I do not expect too much in the way of spectacular results within the next decade or two unless, of course, there is a genuine break-through in our knowledge of neurophysiology.

With the explosive growth of the last two decades in computer technology, one may well ask what lies ahead. The role of the prophet is not an easy one. In the first place, we are inclined to extrapolate into the future along a straight line, whereas science and technology tend to grow at an exponential rate. Thus our prophecies, more often than not, are far too conservative. In the second place, we prophesy from past trends. We cannot foresee the great and sudden mutations in scientific evolution. Thus we find ourselves predicting faster railroad trains and overlooking the possibility of airplanes as being too fanciful.

However, we may certainly expect in the near future to see continued improvements in types of components and surely the development of many new computer components. The next generations of computers will be faster, smaller, with greater flexibility and memory capacity, and more reliable. We may expect the programing to progress so that it becomes easier to communicate with computers using our own language or something close to it. We may expect computers to be applied in many new areas; thus the stock market is planning computer innovations. Many commercial enterprises will find computers efficient and economical.

At the intellectual level and taking a longer-range view, I expect computers eventually to handle a large fraction of low-level decisions, even as now they take care of their own internal bookeeping. We may expect them to be programed for a wide variety of types of symbolic information-processing and general problem-solving, replacing man in many of his semirote activities.

I further expect the development of high-grade sensory and motor organs, the equivalent of the eye and the hand, for computers, leading perhaps eventually to autonomous robotlike devices which might be smart enough to do housekeeping.

Many people are concerned with regard to the impact of automation and computers on our economic and social life. It is clear in the first place that there is no way to stop or slow down this type of scientific research any more than work in any other field of science. Good or bad, these trends will continue. Our computers will become more sophisticated, and our automation will invade more and more areas. As in the first industrial revolution, there will necessarily be technological unemployment, economic hardship during relocation, and the like. But again, as in the first industrial revolution, automation makes possible a larger gross national product for the same total man-hours of work. Thus if we desire a higher average standard of living or more leisure, automation leads in this direction, provided only that we can solve the problem of equitable distribution of this larger work product. This last problem is, of course, most difficult, but, nevertheless, one feels that an intelligent scientific attack on it should lead to a solution.

Another problem often discussed is: What will we do if the machines get smarter than we are and start to take over? I would say in the first place, judging from the I.Q. level of machines now in existence and the difficulty in programing problems of any generality, that this bridge is a long way in the future, if we ever have to cross it at all. I would also suggest that if we can ever make machines much smarter than we are we can also perhaps make them much wiser, and possibly *they* will help *us* find a peaceful coexistence!

CLAUDE SHANNON'S NO-DROP JUGGLING DIORAMA

When Claude Shannon conceived a juggling diorama, he put his hands and head to work on an assortment of chains, rods, bolts and other hardware.

Shannon picked up an interest in juggling as an adjunct to his distinguished career in mathematics and computer science. Professor emeritus at the Massachusetts Institute of Technology, Shannon has received honorary doctoral degrees from Yale, Princeton, Edinburgh and Oxford Universities, among others.

It all started when Betty brought home a little four-inch clown, doing a five ball shower, from the cake decorating store ($1.98). I was both amused and bemused — amused as a long-time amateur juggler who even as a boy wished to run away and join the circus, but bemused by the unlikely shower pattern and the plastic connections between the balls.

A little study of this clown led to the idea of constructing a diorama of numbers juggling, a stationary display of the record number of rings, balls and clubs (and certainly without obvious connections between the props)

By

CLAUDE E. SHANNON
5 CAMBRIDGE STREET
WINCHESTER, MASSACHUSETTS 01890

Official rules in the "numbers game" are hard to find, by no means as well defined as, say, the rules for track and field events. How long must you juggle 'n' rings to claim to be an n-ring juggler? With large numbers, even starting and stopping become major problems as the human hands find difficulty with more than four objects. Jugglers sometimes circumvent these problems with a belt to hold props at the start and an assistant to catch them at the finish.

With rings, Ignatov is quite confident with 11. He includes this often in performance and finishes in elegant fashion, tossing them backward over his head to an assistant with a basket. A fellow Russian, Petrovsky, also does 11 rings, and Albert Lucas has even flashed 12.

With balls the numbers are somewhat less. First, balls collide much more than rings. Also, top professionals tend to concentrate on rings, realizing their greater visual impact. Enrico Rastelli, considered by many the greatest juggler of all time, is credited with juggling 10 balls.

On a recent trip to Europe I met Felix Adanos, a "gentleman juggler" using props such as top hats, canes and champagne bottles. Adanos, in his seventies but still doing juggling dates, was a friend of Rastelli, he said that Rastelli "played with 10 balls but really didn't do them." However, I also talked

Comic strip characters can do anything!

with juggling Historian Hermann Sagemuller, who is writing a biography of Rastelli. He believes Rastelli worked 10 balls well, and also mentioned Jenny Jaeger, the German prodigy, as also juggling ten small leather beanbags.

With clubs, the record seems to be seven by the Rumanian Mitica Virgoaga, using triple spins. His student, Jack Bremlov, later equalled this record, as have a number of others since then.

IJA historian Dennis Soldati gives 11 rings, 10 balls and 7 clubs as the current numbers records, and I used these in constructing my first diorama.

I placed three clowns against a black velvet stage, because it is excellent material for absorbing light. I suspended their props with blackened needles, which were totally invisible from more than a few inches away. The props were half-inch beads for the balls, miniature cake-decorating bowling pins for the clubs, and curtain rings.

Night after night I looked at these frozen jugglers and, Pygmalion-like, wished that they and their props would come to life and actually juggle. This led, finally, to a project requiring several months of work. With the help of assistant Phil Stone and members of my family, it culminated in a display of three animated clowns juggling the record numbers of props.

THE ILLUSION

In this miniature theater, we first hear a German folk song. The curtains open and three tiny clowns are seen, spotlighted against a dead-black background. All of the clowns are juggling in time to the music.

The left-hand clown, "Ignatov," is juggling 11 rings in a cascade pattern with the rings passing from one hand to the other. The rings glow brightly in different colors, and the little juggler's hands seem to be throwing them up while his head moves as though observing their flight.

In center stage, "Rastelli" juggles ten balls, five in each hand in a synchronous pattern. He later changes to an alternating, fountain pattern.

On the right, "Virgoaga" does a cascade of seven clubs using triple spins. The clubs are caught in a flat position, as in human juggling. At the catch, they go through a "glitch" of a small amount of reverse rotation, and then are reversed again in direction and proceed airborne to the other hand.

The amount of motion on this little stage is mind-boggling. In scientific terms, the three clowns and their props appear to move with 96 degrees of freedom.

THE REALITY

How is all this magic wrought? With a bag of cheap scientific tricks and a fiendishly ingenious backstage mechanism. In the first place, the audience sees only what it is supposed to see — the clowns and their props. The stage is completely lined with black velvet, and the scene is illuminated by ultraviolet light, "black light." The combined effect of black light on black velvet can best be

described with a phrase from an old blues tune, 'blacker than the darkest kind of night."

The juggling props are painted with fluorescent paint and glow brightly against the dead-black background. Each juggling clown has a tiny spotlight trained on him.

In **Peter Pan,** Mary Martin flew through the air supported by the great tensile strength of steel wire. Our three performers similarly depend upon steel. In this case, horizontal rods, projecting from slots in the backdrop of the stage, support the jugglers' props.

Behind the backdrop, each of the three jugglers has his own special mechanical system involving a great many sprockets, gears and cams. They all, however, use a chain drive system to move their props. The props are mounted on very thin (.021") steel rods which go through slots in the backdrop and, backstage, through two parallel ladder chains.

For the ball juggler with an even number of balls — five in each hand — there are two sets of chains, each carrying five rods and five balls. For realistic juggling, the balls and hands should describe paths partially in front of the juggler. This cannot be done with the supporting rods for right and left-hand balls parallel — the rods would have to go through the juggler's body. For this reason, the two sets of rods — those for the right hand balls and those for the left hand balls — were brought in from the sides at about 15-degree angles encompassing the clown. Coupling these angled chain systems to the main motor drive required a pair of universal joints.

A friction clutch was introduced between the right and left hand drives. This allows slipping the phase of one hand relative to the other to change from synchronous to alternating variations. The juggler's hands are driven synchronously with the balls and, in fact, the same shafts that carry the lower sprockets extend out to cranks which move the hands in small circular patterns about 1½" in diameter.

The ring juggler with an odd number of rings uses a cascade pattern. This requires the rings to move from hand to hand and therefore the rods, which control the rings, to slide in and out. This is done by having the rods carry small discs which ride against slanting tracks. At the top of the track a choice must be made, to go right or left. The choice is governed by a cam which moves the discs alternately one way or the other. When the disc comes from the right, the cam forces it over to the left, and vice versa. The cam is coupled synchronously to the rest of the mechanism and operates by sliding the shaft that carries the sprockets and chain back and forth.

The club mechanism is still more complex, involving rotation of the clubs as well as three dimensional positioning. The mechanism is similar to that for rings but with the addition of a disc on each of the rods that carry the clubs.

(Continued on next page)

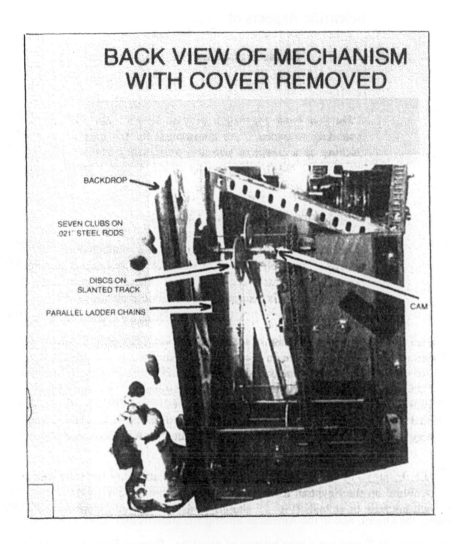

BACK VIEW OF MECHANISM
WITH COVER REMOVED

BACKDROP

SEVEN CLUBS ON
.021" STEEL RODS

DISCS ON
SLANTED TRACK

PARALLEL LADDER CHAINS

CAM

JACK BREMLOV

7

WITH

FIRST IN THE WORLD

This disc rolls against a plane as the chains carry the rods through their cycle. This rotation carries to the club which is frictionally connected to the rod. The clubs normally turn with the rods due to this friction. However, when the strike the clown's hands, slippage occurs and they stop turning, remaining horizontal for a short period, as with real juggling. Without this slippage, the clubs would turn $3\frac{1}{2}$ revolutions from one hand to the other.

The "glitch" holds the clubs back for a half-revolution, giving the triple spins of Virgoaga. The clown's hands are driven by a crankshaft in synchronization with the clubs, and his head is also linked to the system. Three different methods of coordinating clubs and hands were tried before a satisfactory solution was found. The entire effect is quite realistic.

All of the clown and prop motions are driven by one synchronous motor at a rate of 1.3 throws per second for each hand. This is slower than the human rate for numbers juggling of about two throws per second. Experimentation with different speeds indicated that this slower rate gives a better effect. Scaled-down models in general appear too busy unless the time scale is slowed down as well. The music is produced by a Casio "VL-Tone" adjusted to the same timing as the clowns.

The ball and club jugglers are the most interesting of the three. While the ball juggler perhaps gives the most accurate representation of reality, the clubs involve the mot complexity of object movements.

The greatest numbers jugglers of all time cannot sustain their record patterns for more than a few minutes, but my little clowns juggle all night and never drop a prop!

Scientific Aspects of Juggling

Claude E. Shannon

"Do you think juggling's a mere trick?" the little man asked, sounding wounded. "An amusement for the gapers? A means of picking up a crown or two at a provincial carnival? It is all those things, yes, but first it is a way of life, friend, a creed, a species of worship."

"And a kind of poetry," said Carabella.

Sleet nodded. "Yes, that too. And a mathematics. It teaches calmness, control, balance, a sense of the placement of things and the underlying structure of motion. There is a silent music to it. Above all there is discipline. Do I sound pretentious?"

Robert Silverberg, *Lord Valentine's Castle*.

The little man Sleet in Silverberg's fantasy who so eloquently describes the many faces of juggling is a member of a juggling troupe on a very distant planet, many centuries in the future. We shall discuss some of the many dimensions of juggling on our tiny planet Earth from the viewpoints of Darwin (What is the origin of the species *jongleur?*), Newton (What are the equations of motion?), Faraday (How can it be measured?) and Edison (Can American inventiveness make things easier?). But we shall try not to forget the poetry, the comedy and the music of juggling for the Carabellas and Margaritas future and present. Does this sound pretentious?

On planet Earth, juggling started many centuries ago and in many different and distant civilizations. A mural on the Egyptian tomb of Beni-Hassan dating back to 1900 B.C. shows four women each juggling three balls (Fig. 1). Juggling also developed independently at very early times in India, the Orient, and in the Americas among the Indians and Aztec cultures.

The South Sea island of Tonga has a long history of juggling. George Forster, a scientist on one of Captain Cook's voyages, wrote:

"This girl, lively and easy in all her actions, played with five gourds, of the size of small apples, perfectly globular. She threw them up into the air one after another continually, and never failed to catch them all with great dexterity, at least for a quarter of an hour."

The early Greek historian Xenophon, about 400 B.C., describes in *The Banquet* the following incident.

"At that, the other girl began to accompany the dancer on the flute, and a boy at her elbow handed her up the hoops until he had given her twelve. She took these and as she danced kept throwing them whirling into the air, observing the proper height to throw them so as to catch them in regular rhythm. As Socrates looked on he remarked: 'This girl's feat, gentlemen, is only one of many proofs that woman's nature is really not a whit inferior to man's, except in its lack of judgment and physical strength.' "

Fig. 1. Egyptian wall painting, circa 2040 B.C. (Source: unknown.)

This excerpt is interesting at a number of different levels. At the juggler's level, did the girl in fact juggle twelve hoops at once? This is an astounding feat — in the twenty-three centuries since then no one has reached this record, the highest being the great Russian juggler, Sergei Ignatov, who does nine regularly and sometimes eleven in his act (Fig. 2). However, who could ask for better witnesses than the great philosopher Socrates and the famous historian Xenophon? Surely they could both count to twelve and were careful observers.

At a different level, it is amusing to note how Socrates, departing from his famous method of teaching by question, makes a definite statement and immediately suffers from foot-in-mouth disease. Had he but put his period nine words before the end he could have been the prescient prophet of the women's equality movement.

In medieval times court jesters and traveling minstrel troupes often combined the three arts of juggling, magic and comedy. A "Street of the Conjurers," where daily performances could be seen, was a feature of many cities. Early in the present century vaudeville, circuses and burlesque were a spawning ground for jugglers. Many jugglers of this period combined a comedy patter with their juggling and some of the great comedians, Fred Allen (billed as the World's Worst Juggler), Jimmy Savo (I Juggle Everything from a Feather to a Piano!) and W.C. Fields (Distinguished Comedian & Greatest Juggler on Earth, Eccentric Tramp) evolved from this background.

Jugglers are surely among the most vulnerable of all entertainers. Musicians and actors can usually cover their slips but if a juggler makes a mistake "it's a beaut!." This has led through the centuries to a vast number of comedy lines and cover-ups for the missed catch or the dropped club. Books on juggling contain whole sections about how to save face in such situations. La Dent introduced the "Swearing Room," a boldly labeled, screened-off portion of the stage to which he would retreat on missing a trick. Others wear numerous medals which they take off if they make a slip. One writer suggests a large pair of spectacles to put on after an error. There are dozens of comedy lines to be used after an error, e.g., "That's part of the act, folks — the part I didn't rehearse." W.C. Fields was a master of the seemingly wild throws, dropped balls and incredible recoveries. Expert jugglers could not distinguish Fields' intentional moves from actual misses.

This very vulnerability may have led to the dichotomy between the comedy and the technical jugglers. The technicians aim for perfection, striving to keep more and more objects in the air at one time, the "Numbers game" in juggling parlance. Albert Lucas, keeping score

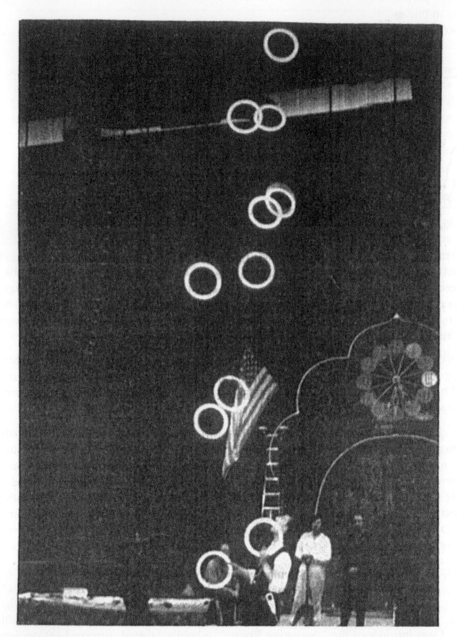

Fig. 2.   Sergei Ignatov took American juggling audiences by storm when he toured this country with the Moscow Circus in 1978. Ignatov demonstrated his mastery of seven balls and five clubs by doing a number of variations with them during his performances. He performed with eleven rings for his show-stopping finale. (Source: Jugglers World Calendar, 1980. Photo courtesy Roger Dollarhide.)

of his own performance, reported "2 misses in 46,000 throws." Outstanding among performers in this area was Enrico Rastelli, who was said to have juggled ten balls. He could do a one-armed handstand while juggling three balls in the other hand and rotating a cylinder on his feet.

There have been many talented women jugglers. We have already mentioned the Grecian lady who was perhaps the numbers champion of all time. Some others are Lottie Brunn (Fig. 3), the only woman to perform solo in Ringling Brothers' center ring, and the child star Trixie from Germany. A photograph in the book *Will Mariner* by Somerville shows a woman on Tonga showering eight balls — an incredible feat (showering being a very difficult way of keeping many balls going).

With the advent of the various electronic media (radio, motion pictures and television), vaudeville and the circuses were doomed and juggling went into decline. This lasted several decades and many of the great jugglers sought greener pastures.

Recently, however, there has been a revival of this ancient skill, particularly among young people of college age. The University of Colorado, Pennsylvania State University, M.I.T., Wesleyan and many other universities have active juggling groups. The market for the professional juggler is still small — some ice shows, Las Vegas floor shows, the Ringling circus. Street performers may be seen in such places as Greenwich Village, Harvard Square and San Francisco. However, the main thrust of juggling today is that it is a challenging recreation for amateurs. It can involve not just one person trying to juggle five balls but two people passing six or more clubs between them, or, indeed, twenty people in a very complex pattern of club passing.

Juggling seems to appeal to mathematically inclined people — many amateur jugglers are computer programmers, majors in mathematics or physics, and the like. One knowledgeable juggler, a mathematics professor himself, told a reporter that forty per cent of jugglers are "algorithmically inclined." In the *New York Times* story, it appeared as "forty per cent are logarithmically inclined." (This curious anagram probably conveyed the meaning better than the original to most readers.) In spite of this appeal to the technical mind, there seems to be very little mathematical or scientific literature relating to juggling.

Juggling also appears to be a skill that very young people can master well. W.C. Fields was a fine juggler at age fourteen. Albert Lucas, one of the world's top performers, was brought up in a circus family and is said to have juggled five balls at age five. He is now nineteen and has performed several years with the Ice Capades (Fig. 4). (Note not only the nine rings but the mouthpiece and ball and the ring on one leg.) Other young performers are Demetrius and Maria Alcarese, who in their teens show excellent potential. In the various 1980 competitions of the International Jugglers' Association, the Juniors (less than three years' experience), Seniors, seven-ball, five-club and team events were all won by young people in their teens or early twenties. Especially impressive were Barrett Felker and Peter Davison who, with Keziah Tannenbaum, won the team event, and battled it out between themselves in five-club juggling. It seems plausible that juggling ability may have its child prodigies in much the same way as music (Mozart, Mendelssohn and Menuhin), mathematics (Pascal, Gauss, Abel) and chess (Morphy, Capablanca, Reshevsky, Fischer). Further, it seems likely that the age of peak ability for juggling may be quite young, as it is for such sports as gymnastics and swimming.

The Tools of Jugglers

It is well known that witches use three basic tools in their craft — the bell, the book and the candle. Jugglers, whom many think are close cousins of witches, also use three basic tools — the ball, the ring and the club.

Fig. 3.   Lottie Brunn was billed by Ringling Brothers as the "Greatest Girl Juggler of All Time." She is also the only female juggler to have performed solo in the center ring. She has appeared at all of the top Las Vegas nightclubs, as well as Radio City Music Hall in New York. (Source: Jugglers World Calendar, 1980. Photo courtesy Lottie Brunn.)

Fig. 4.   Albert Lucas began juggling as a small child, and could juggle five balls by the age
of five. (Source: Jugglers World Calendar, 1980. Photo courtesy Robert Leith.)

Balls are the easiest for learning, and lacrosse balls weighing about five ounces and two and one half inches in diameter are very popular among jugglers. However, all sizes of balls have been used, from jelly beans to basketballs. Recently a record was set in juggling three eleven-pound bowling balls for thirty-seven catches. At the other end of the weight scale, the Mexican juggler Picasso has juggled up to five ping-pong balls by popping them out of his mouth.

Most professional jugglers like rings. If the juggler stands at right angles to the audience, the rings present a large viewing area and are easily seen, as in Fig. 2. Furthermore, when tossed, the area presented to the juggler is less than half that of balls, causing less interference. This probably leads to higher numbers in ring juggling than in ball juggling.

While balls and rings are ancient, it appears that clubs date only to the late 19th century. At that time the art of swinging "Indian clubs" became popular. This is an elegant and demanding art form in itself. It was left to the jugglers, however, to discover the possibilities of tossing clubs, and, even more exciting, exchanging them with partners. The sight of two people with six rapidly spinning clubs being passed back and forth was electrifying. The early clubs were turned from solid wood and were quite heavy. Modern clubs are made of plastic, often with a wooden dowel through the middle, or of fiberglass. They weigh much less than the wooden ones, about nine ounces, and are about nineteen inches long.

We spoke earlier of the witches' basic tools, bell, book and candle. Their secondary instrumentation would have to include cauldron, broomstick and the entrails of a toad. If these seem a bit exotic, consider the objects that jugglers use.

Jugglers will juggle with almost anything — gossamer scarves, kitchen utensils, flying saucers, badminton racquets and flaming torches. One three-ball juggler uses a rubber chicken, a head of lettuce and an M&M candy. Probably the ultimate in choice of weapons is that of the Flying Karamazov Brothers, a totally insane group of performers, mad even by jugglers' standards. They announce that they are going to juggle with a chainsaw and bring out a completely harmless toy chain saw. However, they follow with a real machine operating at full speed and toss this around.

Flying saucers and gossamer scarves involve aerodynamics — the interaction of the object in flight with the air. The most common juggling objects, rings, balls and clubs, are sufficiently massive relative to their surface area, and their speeds sufficiently slow, that such effects can be ignored.

At the instant a juggling object leaves contact with the hand of the juggler it enters the world of analytical dynamics, free of the juggler's control but subject to the laws and theorems of Newton, Euler, Poinsot and Poincare. It seems unlikely that any of these mathematicians ever did a three-ball cascade, but their differential equations describe not only the complex motion of planets and satellites but the "polhodes," "herpholodes" and "invariable lines" of a juggler's club in motion.

What can we learn from mechanical principles about the motion of a club? First, and simplest, its center of gravity will follow a parabolic course. The relation between height and time will be given by $h = \frac{1}{2}gt^2$, where h is measured from the apex of the trajectory and $g = 32\,\text{ft/sec}^2$ is the acceleration of gravity. For example, if a juggler throws a ball two feet in the air and catches it with his hand at the same level, two feet below its highest point, the time of flight would be $2\sqrt{2h/g}$ or .7 seconds. The horizontal distance traveled is of no significance. It will take precisely the same time going straight up and down or to a juggling partner, say six feet away, as long as the vertical travel is the same.

If the object is tossed to a height h_1 and caught after a drop of h_2, the time of flight would be given by $\sqrt{2h_1/g} + \sqrt{2h_2/g}$. In most cases of juggling, h_1 and h_2 are close enough the approximate formula $2\sqrt{2\bar{h}/g}$ can be used, where $\bar{h}$ is the average of the two distances. The following table shows the time of flight F for various values of $\bar{h}$ ranging from six inches (a fast three-ball cascade) to the sixteen feet we estimate for Ignatov's eleven rings in Fig. 2.

$\bar{h}$	6″	1″	2′	4′	8′	16′
F (sec)	.35	.5	.71	1	1.41	2

Much more complex than the motion of the center of gravity is the rotational motion of an object in free flight. This is a subject that was studied extensively by many mathematicians in the 18th and 19th centuries. The motion will depend on the distribution of mass of the body, which can be summarized in its ellipsoid of inertia. It is noteworthy that the three favorite juggling objects are very special with regard to their ellipsoids of inertia. The ball has all three axes of inertia equal, the ring has two equal and the other very small, and the club has two equal and the third very large. These three special situations lead to much more predictable behavior than that of an object with three unequal axes. In the latter case, the object will show stability in rotation about the largest and smallest axes but not about the intermediate one. It is easy and interesting to observe this property. Put a rubber band around a book so it cannot fly open. Now toss it up, with a spin, in each of the three possible ways. The book will spin stably about its shortest dimension and its longest dimension, but when spun about the intermediate dimension will continue turning almost fully around in a most erratic fashion.

Basic Juggling Patterns

"The cross rhythm of 3 against 2 is one of the most seductive known." So wrote Gene Krupa, the great jazz drummer, some forty years ago. Seductive it is, whether it be the Chopin F minor Etude or Krupa's own tom-tom chorus in "Sing-Sing-Sing" with its ever-changing emphasis.

The visual analog of the three against two rhythm is in the juggler's three balls into two hands, the three-ball cascade. This is the first pattern that most people learn and the most fundamental, and it is capable of as many changes as bell ringing.

Fig. 5a shows how the simplest three-ball cascade appears to a viewer. Jugglers can vary the height of the throw, the width of the hands and even reverse the direction of motion. They can make under-leg throws, floor bounces, behind-the-back throws, overhand (claw) catches, "chops," and numerous other variations.

The three against two can be done with clubs, rings, and, in fact, almost anything. The Brothers Karamazov in their act offer the audience a choice of three from a wildly varied assortment of possibilities — such things as hoses, basketballs, clubs, candies, etc. The audience by their applause picks three of these and the "world's greatest juggler" attempts to keep them in the air. Should he fail, he gets a pie in the face.

Many expert jugglers restrict their acts to three-ball variations and entire books have been written on this subject. At the 1980 jugglers' convention there were seventeen entries in the Seniors competition — each entrant was allowed six minutes for an unrestricted act, judged by seven experts and viewed by a sophisticated audience of several hundred of his peers. The acts were all good and ranged from comedy monologues to highly technical exhibitions.

The first prize, however, went to a young man, Michael Kass, who used no props other than

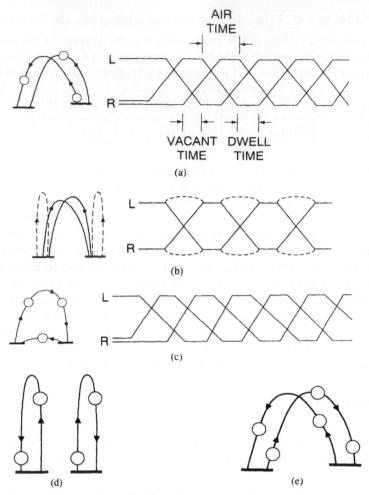

Fig. 5.   (a) Three-ball cascade. (b) Two balls. (c) Three-ball shower. (d) Three-ball fountain. (e) Five-ball cascade.

the three clubs he was juggling as he came on the stage. His routine consisted almost entirely of variations on the three-ball cascade. The clubs were double-spun, thrown behind his back, under his legs, in chops, flats and other variations to the music of Synergy "Synthesizer." His stunning climax came with a series of "foot-drops" where the clubs were dropped to his feet and tossed back into the cascade with a flip of the ankle. The audience was hypnotized and gave him a standing ovation.

While the three-ball variations can be totally fascinating, the juggling repertoire has evolved a vast series of other patterns. A small sampling of these is shown in Fig. 5. The right-hand parts of these diagrams show how the juggled objects progress from hand to hand with time.

The almost trivial example of two balls and two hands (Fig. 5b) is included because of its theoretical importance. It is the simplest case where a choice can be made at each toss — whether to interchange the balls or keep them in the same hands.

The three-ball shower (Fig. 5c) is similar to the three-ball cascade but with different timing — the left to right throw going almost horizontally so that the whole pattern looks more like balls rotating in a circle.

Four balls are usually done in one of two ways: the "fountain" (Fig. 5d) where the two hands are out of synchronism and which, in fact, amounts to two balls in each of two hands which never interchange, or a synchronous movement where the balls can be interchanged or not at each toss.

Fig. 5e shows the pattern for a normal five-ball cascade, a natural generalization of the three-ball. In a multiplex juggle two or more balls may be caught in one hand at the same time. In the 1979 competitions, one of the contestants raised a considerable furor by juggling seven balls with the multiplex system. Multiplex juggling in itself is an interesting and picturesque art but considerably easier than the standard form where only one ball contacts a hand at one time. After some soul-searching, the IJA decided to disallow multiplex juggling in their numbers competitions.

The Uniform Juggle

We shall define a *uniform juggle* as one without multiplexing and with all dwell times the same (D), all flight times the same (F) and all vacant times the same (V). Uniform juggles include many of the most common juggling patterns, the three-, five- and seven-ball cascades, two or three in one hand, the four-ball fountain and many passing routines among two or more jugglers. At a recent juggling convention with perhaps one hundred jugglers on the floor it appeared that 75% or more were working on uniform juggles.

Uniform juggles have good reason for their popularity — all of the hands do about the same thing: they throw balls to the same height, hold them for the same time and are vacant for the same time.

The same uniform juggle, for example the three-ball cascade, may of course appear in a multitude of forms. The juggler may do overhead (clutch) juggling, he may toss the balls under his legs or behind his back or cross his arms in a bewildering fashion. For our purposes we are concerned only with the uniformity of the time parameters D, V and F.

Focusing on the uniform juggle is somewhat akin to the geometer who spends much time with circles and triangles. He is well aware of the existence of other geometric figures, but the simple structure of these leads to elegant mathematical theorems. We shall later give some results relating to generalization to other types of juggles.

Of course a juggle may be uniform only for a period of time. In fact, many juggling routines are made up of segments, which are uniform in our sense, with transitional moves. *The theorems which follow about uniform juggles require only that uniformity last for the period that it would take one ball to visit all the hands* (if it did them all in sequence, that is, $H(D+F)$). These theorems will be first stated and discussed, and later proved in a general argument.

Theorem 1. In a uniform juggle with dwell time D, vacant time V, flight time F, then

$$\frac{F+D}{V+D} = \frac{B}{H} \, ,$$

where B is the number of balls and H the number of hands.

In one sense this theorem seems almost trivial. It states a proportionality between the number of balls and hands, and the total time for each ball circuit ($F+D$) and each hand circuit. It is, however, more subtle than it appears, its proof depending on the uniformity of the juggle for at least H tosses.

Theorem 1 allows one to calculate the range of possible periods (time between hand throws) for a given type of uniform juggle and a given time of flight. A juggler can change this period, while keeping the height of his throws fixed, by increasing dwell time (to increase the period) or reducing dwell time to reduce the period. The total mathematical range available for a given flight time can be obtained by setting $D = 0$ for minimum range and $V = 0$ for maximum range in Theorem 1. The ratio of these two extremes is independent of the flight time and dependent only on the number of balls and hands.

Corollary. In a uniform juggle with a fixed flight time, the range of possible periods is $B/(B-H)$.

For example, in the three-ball cascade a 3-to-1 period (or frequency) ratio is possible; with five balls the maximum ratio is 5-to-3. With larger numbers of balls there is much less range available. At nine, it is 9-to-7. Of course, in actual juggling the possible range will be considerably smaller than these figures — it is not possible to have either zero dwell time or zero vacant time.

Theorem 2. If B and H are relatively prime (have no common divisor) then there is essentially (i.e., apart from labeling) a unique uniform juggle. The balls can be numbered from 0 to $B-1$ and the hands from 0 to $H-1$ in such a way that each ball progresses through the hands in cyclical sequence and each hand catches the balls in cyclical sequence.

Theorem 3. If B and H are not relatively prime, let n be their greatest common divisor with $B = np$ and $H = nq$ (p and q relatively prime). Then there are as many types of juggles as ways of partitioning n into a sum of integers.

For example, if n were 5, a partition into $2+2+1$ would correspond to three disjoint juggles. There would be no possible interchange of balls among these three juggles. Each "2" in this partition would correspond to $2p$ balls circulating among $2q$ hands in a fashion similar to the cases described above, except that at each toss there is a choice of two possibilities. The "1" in this partition would be a cyclical juggle of the type in Theorem 2, with p balls circulating around q hands with no choice.

In the common case of two jugglers, each with three balls (or clubs), we have $B = 6$ and $H = 4$. The greatest common divisor is 2, which can be written as a sum of positive integers in two ways: 2 or $1+1$. The case of 2 corresponds to the jugglers starting simultaneously. Thus at each toss there is a choice of two possibilities: a self-throw or a throw to a partner. In group juggling, incidentally, a downbeat analogous to that of a musical conductor is used to ensure synchronism.

The other partition, $1+1$, corresponds to two jugglers out of synchronism. There is no way to pass clubs from one pair of hands to the other without violating the uniform juggle condition.

The number of partitions of n into a sum increases rapidly with n as the following table shows:

n	1	2	3	4	5	6	7	8	9	10
no. of partitions	1	2	3	5	7	11	15	22	30	42

We now prove these theorems.

Suppose that at time 0 a uniform juggle commences with the toss of a ball. Let us follow this ball for a period of H catches (a time $H(F+D)$). Since there are only H hands and the ball has visited $H + 1$ (counting the one it started with) it must have visited the same hand twice. This is sometimes called the pigeonhole principle in mathematics — if you have $n + 1$ letters in n pigeonholes, there must be some pigeonhole with at least two letters. The pigeonhole principle, or *Schubfachprinzip*, as German writers call it, applies only for finite numbers. The theory of transfinite juggling, like the case of the Giant Rat of Sumatra, is a story for which the world is not yet prepared.

Focusing now on the hand that was visited twice by a ball, suppose the number of catches of the ball was a. Then the time between these catches was $a(D + F)$. Meanwhile, the hand, to satisfy the uniform juggling condition, has made some integer number, say b, catches in the same time, and consequently $b(D + V) = a(D + F)$, or $(D + F)/(D + V) = b/a$, a rational number. In other words, the times related to balls, $F + D$, must line up exactly with the times related to hands, $D + V$, after some integer number of throws.

Let a/b be reduced to its lowest terms, say p/q. Thus p and q would be the smallest number of hand catches and flight times which could return to coincidence.

Now consider the set of all balls, say d_1, thrown at the time t_0. These may be called a synchronous set — with a uniform juggle they will all be caught at the same times and thrown at the same times so long as the juggle remains uniform. Furthermore, no other balls can fall into this time pattern under the uniformity condition. Consider now the subset of balls caught by the hands that caught this synchronous group at a time interval $(D + V)$ after time t_0, that is, the next catches of these hands. These balls also form a synchronous set at a later time. The same may be said for each hand-catching interval $(D + V)$ until we reach $p(D + V)$ from time t_0, the first time it is possible for the original balls to return to the original hands. At this time, all of the original balls *must* have returned to the original hands, since no other balls could have come into synchronism with these and all of these are timed right for these hands.

Consider now the balls thrown by the subset of hands we have been discussing at the time $(D + V)$ after t_0 (one throw after our initial time). This subset must basically parallel the subset we have just described — these balls go to the same next hands and after p throws return as a subset to the same original hands.

Continuing this argument, we obtain pd_1 balls following each other cyclically through p stages, d_1 balls at a time.

If d_1 did not exhaust all of the balls, we carry out the same process with the next balls caught after time t_0. These are, in a sense, totally disjoint from the first subset. They cannot be caught by the hands involved in the first sequence. Consequently we obtain a totally disjoint subset of the balls juggled by a totally disjoint subset of the hands.

Continuing in this fashion, we exhaust all of the balls and all of the hands. The total number of balls, B, is therefore equal to $\sum pd_i$, and the total number of hands, H, $= \sum qd_i$.

The Jugglometer

> "Some son-of-a-bitch will invent a machine to measure Spring with"
>
> e. e. cummings

In order to measure the various dwell times, vacant times and flight times involved in actual juggling, some instrumentation was developed. The first of these devices used three electromagnetic stopclocks, accurate to about .01 seconds (10 milliseconds). These were activated by a relay circuit. The relays were connected to a flexible copper mesh which was fitted over the first and third fingers of the juggler's hand. Lacrosse balls were covered with conducting foil. When one of these was caught it closed the connection between the two fingers, causing a clock to start. Break contacts allowed the measurements of vacant times, and contacts on two hands enabled measurement of flight times. Juggling rings and clubs were also made conductive with foil so that the various times could be measured.

While this system was workable, it required several people to observe and record the observations, and we replaced it with a computerized version using an Apple II computer. This uses essentially the same sensor arrangement, copper sleeves for the fingers connected to the "paddles" of the computer. A computer program displays the time in milliseconds of the various tosses and catches.

Preliminary results from testing a few jugglers indicate that, with ball juggling, vacant time is normally less than dwell time, V ranging in our measurements from fifty to seventy per cent of D. Of course, jugglers have great freedom in changing this ratio, especially when juggling a small number of balls.

With a three-in-one-hand juggle, a dwell of .27 sec. against a .17 sec vacant time was measured. With three clubs, typical figures were .52 sec dwell, .20 sec vacant and .56 sec flight time. Clubs lead to a larger ratio of dwell to vacant time because of the need to stop a club's rotation and start it again. At each catch the spin energy is all dissipated and must be supplied anew at each toss. Curiously, after all of this the club is spinning in the same direction relative to the juggler.

How Much Do Jugglers Weigh?

Watching a competition of jugglers working with eleven-pound bowling balls recently reminded me of an old puzzle which I shall restate as follows.

Claude Crumley comes upon a canyon. He is carrying three copper clappers from his latest caper. Claude weighs 98 kilo and each clapper 1 kilo. The bridge across the canyon can carry 100 kilo. How can Claude cross the canyon?

The intended answer is that Claude walks across doing a three-clapper cascade. I surely hope he doesn't try this, for he would be catapulted into the canyon. All of the gravitational forces on a juggler's objects in the air must be supported basically through his feet, by way of the larger forces downward when he accelerates the objects upward. Put another way, the center of gravity of the entire system, juggler plus objects, would accelerate downward were not an average force of the weight of this system applied upward, and this can only come via his feet. In Fig. 2, Ignatov's feet are pressing down with an average force of his weight plus that of the eleven rings, just as surely as if he had the rings around his neck, and just as surely as Isaac Newton sat under that apple tree.

Why Does Juggling Get So Hard So Fast?

Most people can learn to make 20 or 30 catches of a three-ball cascade within a week or two, and some learn within a few hours. Moving up to four balls (basically two in each hand) again is not extremely difficult. People do this in a few weeks of practice. The five-ball cascade is a different matter indeed. I have asked many five-ball jugglers how long it took them to learn. The answers ranged from six months to two years, and these were talented and dedicated jugglers. Six balls, three in each hand, is again a step forward in difficulty, and seven balls is a point that very few jugglers reach. At the 1980 Fargo convention, a competition was held for juggling seven objects (balls, rings or clubs). Only six entered, and the longest time registered was 5.6 seconds, twenty-six catches. A number of other seven-object jugglers are known who were not entered or present at this convention but the number is very small, probably less than ten. We estimate that fewer than twenty-five people in the United States can juggle seven objects for more than twenty-five catches.

Moving into the stratosphere, we come to the superstars of juggling. Among these is the legendary figure Enrico Rastelli, who was famous for many complex balancing acts and is said to have juggled ten balls. He practiced his craft as musicians do theirs, ten hours a day, and died at only 35. The current world champion in the "numbers game" is undoubtedly the great Soviet star of the Moscow circus, Sergei Ignatov. He juggles nine rings very securely in his act, and can do eleven rings on occasion. Another strong contender is the American, Albert Lucas, who started very young in a circus family and now juggles ten rings. In the picture, he has nine rings but note also the ring rotating on his leg, the ball balanced in his mouth and that he is balanced on one ice skate, truly an incredible juggling feat.

Why does it get so hard so fast?

To begin with, suppose a juggler requires the same dwell time and vacant time whether he is juggling three balls or nine. From Theorem 1, thinking of all terms fixed except the number of balls and flight time, we see that the flight time goes up linearly with the number of balls. Now flight time, as we have seen, increases only as the square root of height of throw, which is proportional to energy. Thus already we are facing energy and height requirements going up roughly as the square of the number of objects juggled.

However, the situation is much worse than this. There is much painful positive feedback at work. First, throwing objects higher will require longer dwell time to accelerate. Second, there is always dispersion in angles of toss. With the same dispersion of angle, the dispersion of where the objects land increases in proportion to the height of throw. The juggler, therefore, will have increasing difficulty in catching, and consume more time. Even more serious is the dispersion in vertical velocity of the toss. This can cause two objects, one thrown a little high and the next a little low, to come down at almost the same time, making it impossible to catch them both.

All of these factors must react on each other — the dispersion of angle and flight time forces greater dwell and vacant time, which in turn requires higher throws. In the higher numbers this vicious loop can only be controlled by the most precise throwing in height, in angle and in tempo.

Bounce Juggling

> "— things never fall *upwards*, you know. It's a plan
> of my own invention. You may try it if you like."
> Lewis Carroll, *Through the Looking Glass*

Bounce juggling is an interesting variety of juggling where the balls are thrown downward and bounced off the floor rather than tossed upward. It is possible to do all of the basic juggling patterns — three- and five-ball cascades and the like — in this upside-down fashion.

There are pluses and minuses to bounce juggling vis-a-vis toss juggling. First, in bounce juggling much of the energy expended on each throw is conserved. Balls of highly compressed rubber ("superballs") will rise to .85 of the original height. This means that the bounce juggler must supply only 15% of the energy that the toss juggler would for a given height of throw. It also probably implies less dispersion in both time and direction, since these tend to be proportional to energy requirements.

On the negative side, in bounce juggling the juggler's own hands interfere with his line of sight to the juggled balls. In addition, the part of the trajectory of the balls which we think most

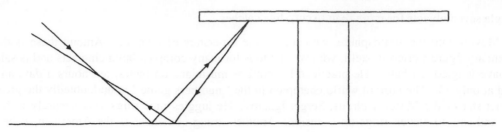

Fig. 6. "Superball" bouncing under tabletop.

optimal for prediction, namely halfway between the toss and the catch point, is now on the floor at a very poor viewing angle. When tossing, the eyes are in a fine position for viewing the tops of the parabolic orbits.

All told, it seems likely that bounce juggling may be easier than toss juggling, but very few people specialize in it. I have seen bounce jugglers work five balls at less than two feet from their bouncing surface — faster than these same jugglers could do a five-ball toss cascade.

There are other intriguing possibilities in bounce juggling. If the juggling ball has a high coefficient of friction with the floor (as do "superballs"), when it is thrown at an angle against the floor a considerable fraction of the horizontal component of energy is turned into rotational energy. If it continues and strikes the floor again, the second bounce appears to be unexpectedly flat. More interesting, however, is to let it hit the underside of a table, Fig. 6. The rotational energy then causes it to very closely return on its original path, bounce again on the floor and return very closely to the hand that threw it. It is possible to bounce juggle several balls this way under a tabletop. Since each one makes three loud clicks on each throw, the audible effect approaches that of a drumroll.

In other words, this situation is a kind of boomerang where one can throw the ball quite arbitrarily and it will come back to the same place except for a slight drop. This is something of a juggler's delight, except that each ball returns to the hand that threw it. To get to the other hand, as in a normal cascade, requires moving the other hand to where the throwing hand was.

A generalization of this automatic return in bounce juggling which, however, gives interchange of hands can be constructed as follows.

If a light ray starts from one focus of an ellipse it will reflect back to the other focus. If that ellipse is rotated about its major axis we have a prolate spheroid, and the light ray from one focus in any direction in three-dimensional space will be reflected back to the other focus.

Although balls do not reflect exactly like light rays, their behavior is fairly close. Imagine a reflecting dish about 20″ long by about 18″ wide shaped as a portion of a prolate spheroid. The two foci would be about 4″ above the surface where the juggler's hands normally are. He can throw a ball anywhere with one hand so long as it hits the dish, and it will automatically come back to the other hand!

The Use of the Lakatos-Hickman Relay in a Subscriber Sender*

Claude E. Shannon

Abstract

A study is made of the possibilities of using the Lakatos-Hickman type relay for the counting, registering, steering, and pulse apportioning operations in a subscriber sender. Circuits are shown for the more important parts of the circuit where it appears that the new type of relay would effect an economy.

---

*   Bell Laboratories Memorandum, August 13, 1940.

A Study of the Deflection Mechanism and Some Results on Rate Finders*

Claude E. Shannon

Summary

1. The deflection mechanism may be divided into three parts. The first is driven by two shafts and has one shaft as output, which feeds the second part. This unit has a single shaft output which serves as input to the third part, whose output is also a single shaft, used as the desired azimuth correction.

2. The first unit is a simple integrator. Its output rate is

$$\dot{y} = \Sigma \, a \frac{R_0}{R_p} \, t_p \ .$$

3. The second part is the same circuit as previous rate finders. Its presence appears to be detrimental to the operation of the system from several standpoints. The output e of this part satisfies

$$e = x + y \ ,$$

$$\frac{R_1}{L_1} x + \dot{x} = y \ .$$

4. The third and most important part of the machine satisfies

$$S \, q + R \, \dot{q} + \frac{L}{\sqrt{1 - \dot{q}^2}} \, \ddot{q} = e$$

in which

$e =$ an input forcing function which, except for transients in the second part and other small effects, is the function whose rate is to be found,

$\dot{q} =$ the rate of e as found by the device (the output of the mechanism is $\sin^{-1} \dot{q}$),

R, L, S are positive constants depending on the gear ratios, etc. in the machine.

5. The mechanism therefore acts like an R, L, C circuit in which the differential inductance is a function of the current

$$\frac{L}{\sqrt{1 - \dot{q}^2}} \ .$$

The system can be critically damped for differential displacements near at most two values of the current.

---

*   Report to National Defense Research Committee, circa April 1941.

6. Omitting the effect of backlash, the system is stable for any initial conditions whatever, with a linear forcing function $e = At + B$. It will approach asymptotically and possibly with oscillation a position where $\dot{q}$ is proportional to $\dot{e}$. An error function can be found which decreases at a rate $-R(\dot{q} - \dot{q}_0)^2$, $\dot{q}_0$ being the asymptotic value of $\dot{q}$.

7. If the system is less than critically damped, ordinary gear-play play type of backlash can and will cause oscillation. This includes play in gears, adders, lead screws, rack and pinions and looseness of balls in the integrator carriages. The oscillation is not unstable in the sense of being erratic, or growing without limit, but is of a perfectly definite frequency and amplitude. This type of backlash acts exactly like a peculiarly shaped periodic forcing function. Approximate formulas for the frequency and amplitude of the oscillation are

$$f_0 = \frac{1}{2\pi} \sqrt{\frac{1}{L_D C} + \frac{R^2}{4L^2}}$$

and

$$I = \frac{\frac{2}{\pi} B_1 + 4 f_0 B_2}{\sqrt{R^2 + (\omega_0 L_D - \frac{1}{\omega_0 C})^2}},$$

B_1 and B_2 being the amounts of backlash in the two driven shafts as measured in a certain manner.

8. Elastic deformations of shafts and plates can be divided into two parts. One is exactly equivalent to the gear type of backlash and may be grouped with B_1 and B_2 above. The other has the effect of altering the parameters R, L, C of the circuit and also adding higher order derivatives with small coefficients. This will slightly alter the time constant and the natural frequency of the system.

9. The manner in which the arcsin function is obtained seems to me distinctly disadvantageous to the operation of the system for a number of reasons, chiefly since to eliminate backlash oscillation it requires high overdamping near $\dot{q} = 0$ and this slows down the response for low target speeds.

10. The general problem of rate finding and smoothing is considered briefly from two angles – as a problem in approximating a certain given transfer admittance and as a problem in finding the form of a differential equation. The first method based on a linear differential equation leads to tentative designs which I think would be an improvement over the present one. The second method indicates the possibility of still more improvement if non-linear equations can be satisfactorily analyzed.

Backlash in Overdamped Systems*

Claude E. Shannon

Abstract

In the report "A study of the deflection mechanism and some results on the rate finder" it is shown that backlash will cause sustained oscillation in a second order mechanical system, providing the equation is less than critically damped. The question of overdamped systems was not completely settled. The present paper is a new attack on this problem.

---

* Report to National Defense Research Committee, June 26, 1941.

Some Experimental Results on the Deflection Mechanism*

Claude E. Shannon

Abstract

In a previous report, "A Study of the Deflection Mechanism and Some Results on Rate Finders," a mathematical study was made of a new type of deflection mechanism. The present paper is a further study of this device and a report on some experimental results obtained on the M.I.T. differential analyzer.

---

* Report to National Defense Research Committee, June 8, 1941

The Transient Behavior of a Large Number of Four-Terminal Unilateral Linear Networks Connected in Tandem*

C. L. Dolph and Claude E. Shannon

Abstract

Asymptotic expressions for the transient response of a long chain of four-terminal unilateral linear networks connected in tandem subject to an initial disturbance are developed and classified according to the characteristics of the common transfer ratio. It is shown that a necessary and sufficient condition for the stability of the chain for all n is that the transfer ratio be of the high pass type.

The mathematical results are applied to chains of self-regulating telephone repeaters.

---

*   Bell Laboratories Memorandum, April 10, 1946.

Review of "Transformations on Lattices and Structures of Logic," by Stephen A. Kiss*

Claude E. Shannon

Published (1948) by Stephen A. Kiss, 11 E. 92 St., New York 28, N.Y. 315 pages + 4-page index + 2-page bibliography + x pages. 6 figures. 7 × 10.

Mathematics develops by successive abstraction and generalization. Modern algebra is particularly subject to this tendency, with many of its concepts, such as those of group and lattice, now permeating the entire range of mathematical thought. In this book Dr. Kiss develops a generalization of Boolean algebra based upon its lattice theoretic properties. Naturally such a work will be of principal interest to the logician and the pure mathematician.

The book falls into three main parts of about the same length. The first consists of an orderly exposition of the pertinent results from modern algebra and lattice theory. In the second part the author defines his generalized Boolean algebras with 4, 8, 16 or generally 2^n elements, and develops their algebraic and lattice theoretic properties. These algebras have a natural and elegant mathematical structure. The third part of the book is an exposition of the calculus of classes and of propositions, and an application of the preceding algebraic theory to an extension of these fields.

Classical Boolean algebra and the calculus of propositions have been applied in such fields as switching theory and the study of nerve networks, and it is possible that the author's extensions of these disciplines may find similar applications. Dr. Kiss conjectures that an adequate description of physical and biological phenomena require 4 and 16 class logics, without, however, developing this thesis. At any rate, considered as a purely algebraic theory, the author has added a significant contribution to mathematical literature.

---

* *Proceedings Institute of Radio Engineers*, volume 37, 1949.

Review of "Cybernetics, or Control and Communication in the Animal and the Machine," by Norbert Wiener*

C. E. Shannon

Published (1948) by John Wiley and Sons, Inc., 440 Fourth Ave., New York 16, N. Y. 194 pages. $6 \times 9\frac{1}{4}$. $3.00.

The last decade has seen a considerable amount of research in a number of closely related fields centering on the general problems of communication and control. The development of large-scale computing machines, of fire-control equipment with its complex predicting and servo systems, and research in communication theory and the mathematics of the nervous system are all parts of this general trend. Professor Wiener has coined the word "cybernetics" from the Greek word for "steersman" to cover this rapidly growing branch of science. Communication engineers have a charter right and responsibility in several of the roots of this broad field and will find Wiener's treatment interesting reading, filled with stimulating and occasionally controversial ideas.

After a lengthy introduction in which he relates his own association with the problems of cybernetics, the author presents some of his central theses: the essential unity of the various disciplines involved, and the need for cross fertilization. Wiener sees the present historical period as one of a second industrial revolution, a revolution in which machines take over the more routine and clerical types of mental work. His outlook for an easy adaptation to this change is justifiably somewhat pessimistic.

His first three chapters are concerned with the relation of statistical theory to the problems of cybernetics. Communication systems, and information processing devices generally, must operate on a statistical ensemble of possible inputs, and the statistical aspects are of paramount significance in the newer theories. One important result of this approach is Wiener's theory of linear least square filters and predictors, of which a summary is given. Wiener also considers some other questions in information theory and makes the interesting conjecture that the paradoxes of the "Maxwell demon" can be resolved by taking into account the information received by the "demon" in entropy calculations. If this could be given experimental verification, it would be of considerable significance in statistical mechanics.

The remainder of the book deals for the most part with problems of the nervous system and analogies between it and computing machines. The author stresses the importance of the feedback concept in understanding teleological behaviour. Many interesting parallels can be drawn between certain nervous diseases, such as ataxia, and unstable oscillations of a servo system. Other pathological conditions are analogous to failures of the internal memory of a computer.

The book, unfortunately, contains numerous misprints, some of which, in the mathematical sections, make for difficult reading. There are also a few errors of the over-simplified statement, for instance the attempt to construct an arbitrary ensemble from a Brownian motion.

---

* *Proceedings Institute of Radio Engineers*, volume 37, 1949.

These criticisms, however, are minor. Professor Wiener, who has contributed much to communication theory, is to be congratulated for writing an excellent introduction to a new and challenging branch of science.

Review of "Description of a Relay Calculator," by the Staff of the [Harvard] Computation Laboratory*

Claude E. Shannon

Published (1949) by the Harvard University Press, Cambridge, Mass. 264 pages + 5½-page index + xvi pages + 37-page appendix. 210 figures. 8 × 10½. $8.00.

The Harvard Computation Laboratory, under the direction of Professor H. H. Aiken, has designed and constructed three large-scale digital calculators. The first of these, Mark I, was described in Volume I of the Annals of the Computation Laboratory. The book under review is Volume 24 in the series and describes the Mark II calculator, which is now in use at the Dahlgren Naval Proving Ground. The recently completed Mark III, largely an electronic rather than relay calculator, will be covered in a later volume.

The Mark II contains some 13,000 relays and is controlled by a routine from punched tape. The speed of elementary operations is as follows: addition, 0.2 sec.; multiplication, 0.7 sec.; division, 4.7 sec.; tape reading, 1.5 sec.; determination of elementary functions, 5-10 sec. Numbers are represented by the "floating-decimal" method, i.e., $\pm p \cdot 10^n$ with p given to ten significant figures and n ranging from -15 to $+15$. The machine is divided into two identical parts which can be used either independently for two problems or together for one.

After describing the general functional organization of the calculator, each of the components is treated in detail down to individual circuit diagrams. The relay circuits involved are often ingenious and exhibit nicely the amazing versatility of these elements. The final chapters deal with operation and problem preparation for the machine. Various general observations scattered through the text will be of interest, for example, the statement that number transfers, additions, and multiplications occur in the approximate ratio 3:2:1.

The book is well illustrated and the style clear and straightforward, if perhaps a trifle dry. Those interested in the design and operation of computers will find it a valuable reference volume, not only in connection with the Mark II calculator, but also with regard to general questions of programming, checking, and methods of implementation that arise with any computer.

Proceedings Institute of Radio Engineers, volume 38, 1950.

The Relay Circuit Analyzer*

Claude E. Shannon and E. F. Moore

Abstract

This memorandum describes a machine (made of relays, selector switches, gas diodes, and germanium diodes) for analyzing several properties of any combinational relay circuit which uses four relays or fewer.

This machine, called the relay circuit analyzer, contains an array of switches on which the specifications that the circuit is expected to satisfy can be indicated, as well as a plugboard on which the relay circuit to be analyzed can be set up.

The analyzer can (1) verify whether the circuit satisfies the specifications, (2) make certain kinds of attempts to reduce the number of contacts used, and also (3) perform rigorous mathematical proofs which give lower bounds for the numbers and types of contacts required to satisfy given specifications.

---

* Bell Laboratories Memorandum, March 31, 1953.

The Relay Circuit Synthesizer*

Claude E. Shannon and E. F. Moore

Abstract

The Relay Circuit Synthesizer is a machine to aid in switching circuit design. It is capable of designing two terminal circuits involving up to four relays in a few minutes. The solutions are usually minimal. The machine, its operation, characteristics and circuits are described.

*   Bell Laboratories Memorandum, Nov. 30, 1953.

Notes to Part B

[1] A Symbolic Analysis of Relay and Switching Circuits

This is Shannon's prize-winning Master's thesis, already mentioned in the biography and interviews at the beginning of this collection and in the Preface to Part B. Shannon returned to this subject in several later papers, notably [50]. In the following years a large number of books appeared, dealing with the problems of constructing an efficient circuit to realize a given switching function — see for example Caldwell [Cald58], Harrison [Harr65], Hennie [Henn68], Keister, Ritchie and Washburn [KeRW51], McCluskey [McCl65] and Phister [Phis58]. More recent books are Davio, Deschamps and Thayse [DaDT78], McCluskey [McCl86], Mead and Conway [CoMe80] and Roth [Roth80]. At the present time, more than fifty-four years after the paper was written, the subject has developed to a point which is hard for the mind to grasp. In 1992 it is possible to manufacture a large-scale integrated circuit containing hundreds of thousands of gates on a single chip, with an automated process that takes as input the logical specification of the desired circuit and produces the chip as output (see for example [LSI91]).

The following hitherto unpublished Bell Laboratories memorandum of Oct. 14, 1940, by John Riordan, provides a correction to the first theorem in Section IV of the paper (see also the footnote to paper [50]).

Series-Parallel Realization of the Sum Modulo Two of n Switching Variables

This memorandum gives a correction to a theorem in Shannon's paper "A Symbolic Analysis of Relay and Switching Circuits," relative to the series-parallel realization of the sum modulo two of n switching variables (defined below).

The theorem is in Section IV and reads as follows:

Theorem: The two functions of n variables which require the most elements in series-parallel realization are the sum modulo two and its negative, each of which requires $3.2^{n-1} - 2$ elements.

It will be shown below that the sum modulo two of n variables and its negative each may be realized by a series-parallel circuit having at most $(10/9) n^2$ elements. It is not difficult to see that there are functions requiring more elements than this in series-parallel realization; in fact, this is required by Shannon's theorem (in his memorandum "The Synthesis of Two Terminal Switching Circuits") that almost all functions of n variables with n large require N elements where N is of the order of $2^n/n$, but it appears difficult to identify the function requiring the most elements in series-parallel realization. The number $3.2^{n-1} - 2$ appearing in the theorem remains as the least upper limit known to the number of elements required in series-parallel realization of an arbitrary function of n variables.

If X_1 and X_2 are switching variables, their sum modulo two and its negative are defined by

$$X_1 \circ X_2 = X_1 X_2' + X_1' X_2 ,$$
$$(X_1 \circ X_2)' = X_1 X_2 + X_1' X_2' .$$

As pointed out by Shannon the sum is associative so that in the case of n variables parentheses may be distributed arbitrarily.

In Shannon's proof, parentheses are placed around the sum of the first $n-1$ variables, hence the validity of the proof as relating to sums modulo two depends upon invariance in the number of elements when parentheses are placed otherwise. This is untrue for $n > 3$; e.g., $n = 4$, denoting the variables X_1 to X_4 by their subscripts only:

$$(1 \circ 2 \circ 3) \circ 4 = [(12' + 1'2)3' + (12 + 1'2')3]4' + [(12' + 1'2)3 + (12 + 1'2')3']4 ,$$

$$(1 \circ 2) \circ (3 \circ 4) = (12' + 1'2)(34 + 3'4') + (12 + 1'2')(34' + 3'4) ,$$

requiring, respectively, 22 and 16 elements.

In general, if s_n is the number of elements for n variables,

$$s_n = 2(s_k + s_{n-k}) , \quad k = 1, 2 \ldots n-1 .$$

It turns out that least values are obtained for $k = [n/2]$ (with brackets indicating "integral part of"). Hence

$$s_{2m} = 2(s_m + s_m) = 2s_m ,$$

$$s_{2m+1} = 2(s_{m+1} + s_m) ,$$

and

$$\Delta s_{2m} = \Delta s_{2m+1} = 2\Delta s_m = 2(s_{m+1} - s_m) ,$$

where Δ is the differencing operator defined by the last expression.

From these and the initial values $s_1 = 1, s_2 = 4, s_3 = 10,$

$$s_n = 4^k + 3r \cdot 2^k , \quad n = 2^k + r , \quad 2^k \le n < 2^{k+1} ,$$

$$= (n-r)^2 + 3r(n-r) = n^2 + rn - 2r^2 .$$

For fixed n, the last expression attains its maximum for $r = n/4$, i.e., $s_n = (9/8)n^2$, but this value of r is impossible for n integral since $n - r = 2^k$. Looking only at the terms involving r, namely $r(n-2r)$, the sum of the factors is $n - r = 2^k$, a constant for given k, and the maximum is attained for $r = n - 2r$ or $3r = n$; the corresponding value of s_n is $(10/9)n^2$. Hence

$$n^2 \le s_n \le \frac{10}{9} n^2 ,$$

the lower limit being attained for $r = 0$, i.e., $n = 2^k$.

J. Riordan

[6] Mathematical Theory of the Differential Analyzer

This paper is based on Shannon's work at M.I.T. on the Bush differential analyzer, a mechanical analog computer for solving differential equations, and establishes the basic theory of such machines. Most analog computers today are electronic, not mechanical — see for example Johnson [John63], or Korn and Korn [KorK72]. So are mechanical computers still of any interest? Well, yes, as is illustrated by an article in today's *New York Times* (Sunday, May 10, 1992, Section 1, page 16) describing a 184-foot Soviet patrol-boat, built in 1985. The main computer on this ship is a mechanical computer using shafts and gears, apparently of the type described in [6] and [13].

[13] The Theory and Design of Linear Differential Equation Machines

A greatly expanded version of the preceding paper. This was originally a restricted war-time report written for the National Defense Research Committee, dated January 1942. It was declassified in Sept. 1946, and is published here for the first time.

[14] (With John Riordan) The Number of Two-Terminal Series-Parallel Networks

The paper by MacMahon in which this problem was first studied (mentioned in Footnote 1) has been reprinted in [MacM78], pp. 617-619. This is Shannon's second published paper, and is also one of earliest papers on combinatorics by his colleague John Riordan. Riordan later wrote two very highly praised books on combinatorics [Rior58], [Rior68]. The enumeration of series-parallel graphs is treated in the first of these books. Incidentally the numbers s_n of series-parallel graphs on n nodes and the associated numbers τ_n are Sequences 466 and 989 in [Sloa73] (see also [Sloa92]). There have been many subsequent papers on the enumeration of series-parallel graphs — see, for example, Carlitz and Riordan [CaRi56], Lomnicki [Lomn72] and Meir and Moon [MeMo90]. Moon [Moon87] gives the asymptotic formula

$$s_n \sim D\, \delta^{-n}\, n^{-3/2}$$

as $n \to \infty$, where $D = 0.2063\ldots$ and $\delta = 0.2808\ldots$.

[42] Network Rings

A hitherto unpublished Bell Laboratories memorandum, dated June 11, 1948. The topological formula for the admittance of an electrical network stated in the first paragraph, and attributed to ''a group of Chinese scientists,'' is in fact much older and is probably due to J. C. Maxwell ([Maxw92], Vol. I, pp. 403-410). There is an excellent treatment of the topological approach to the analysis of electrical circuits in Seshu and Reed [SesR61].

[44] A Theorem on Coloring the Lines of a Network

Shannon first stated this result in an unpublished Bell Laboratories memorandum dated July 8, 1940 (see item [2] of his Bibliography). In current graph-theory terminology, the theorem states that the edge-chromatic number of a multigraph without loops and with maximal degree m is at most $\lceil 3m/2 \rceil$ — see Berge [Berg73], p. 262. For other results on the edge-chromatic numbers of graphs see for example Berge [Berg73], Chap. 12; Bondy and Murty [BonM76], Chap. 6; and Harary [Hara69], Chap. 12.

[50] The Synthesis of Two-Terminal Switching Circuits

A sequel to [1] — see the notes to that paper. The error in [1] mentioned in the footnote on page 22 was discussed in those notes.

[54] Programming a Computer for Playing Chess

The seminal paper on computer chess. An excellent account of the current state of computer chess may be found in the book edited by Marsland and Schaeffer [MarS90]. Chapter 1

[Mars90] gives a brief history, and states that

"Shannon's inspirational work was read and re-read by computer-chess enthusiasts, and provided a basis for most early chess programs. Despite the passage of time, that paper is still worthy of study."

The current computer chess world champion is the machine "Deep Thought" — see [Hsu87], [HsuA90], [HsuA90a].

[55] A Chess-Playing Machine

A popularization of the preceding paper which first appeared in the *Scientific American*, February 1950, and was later reprinted in James R. Newman's *World of Mathematics* (Simon and Schuster, New York, 1956, Vol. 4, pp. 2124-2133). The latter version is reproduced here.

[70] Presentation of a Maze Solving Machine

This paper appeared in the proceedings of a cybernetics conference. The format is explained by the editors (Heinz von Foerster, Margaret Mead and Hans Lukas Teuber) as follows.

"To the reader of this somewhat unusual document, a few words of explanation, and caution. This is not a book in the usual sense, nor the well-rounded transcript of a symposium. These pages should rather be received as the partial account of conversations within a group, a group whose interchange actually extends beyond the confines of the two day meeting reported here. This account attempts to capture a fragment of the group interchange in all its evanescence, because it represents to us one of the few concerted efforts at interdisciplinary communication."

Later in the introduction they refer to

". . . the construction of such likable robots as Shannon's electronic rat described in this volume. The fascination of watching Shannon's innocent rat negotiate its maze does not derive from any obvious similarity between the machine and a real rat; they are, in fact, rather dissimilar. The mechanism, however, is strikingly similar to the *notions* held by certain learning theorists about rats and about organisms in general. Shannon's construction serves to bring these notions into bold relief."

Figure 2, showing Shannon and his mouse (or rat), was not part of the original article but is a Bell Laboratories photograph from May 1952. The caption on the reverse side of the photograph says

"In 1952, Claude E. Shannon of Bell Laboratories devised an experiment to illustrate the capabilities of telephone relays. Here, an electrical mouse finds its way unerringly through a maze, guided by information 'remembered' in the kind of switching relays used in dial telephone systems. Experiments with the mouse helped stimulate Bell Laboratories researchers to think of new ways to use the logical powers of computers for operations other than numerical calculation."

For recent developments in electric mice the reader is referred to the accounts of various "Micro-Mice" competitions that are held from time to time. One such competition is described by Allan [Alan78].

[73] A Mind-Reading (?) Machine

Hagelbarger's machine is described in [Hage54]. For a description of what happened when the two machines played against each other, see "Game playing machines" [99].

[75] The Potentialities of Computers

A hitherto unpublished Bell Laboratories memorandum, dated April 3, 1953. This is a paper to be read at a conference, but we have been unable to identify the name of the conference. (The speaker after Shannon, however, was Louis N. Ridenour.)

[76] Throbac I

We have printed the text of [76] and the circuit diagram from [77], but have omitted the lengthy description of the circuit given in [77].

[85] (With D. W. Hagelbarger) A Relay Laboratory Outfit for Colleges

If all the computers in the world broke down, how many people today could build a machine to play tic-tac-toe, or read Morse code? Even in 1954 Bell Labs was finding it difficult to recruit electrical engineers with an adequate knowledge of switching circuit design. This memorandum describes a relay kit with which students can build machines to

- play nim,
- perform binary or decimal addition,
- calculate the day of the week from the data (a perpetual calendar machine),
- play tic-tac-toe,
- control an elevator,
- act as a telephone exchange with four customers,
- solve the Tower of Hanoi puzzle,
- play the penny matching game (see also paper [11]),
- encode and decode Morse.

A later version of this kit is described in [Hage55]. Figures 1, 2 are actually taken from [Hage55], since the original photographs accompanying [85] were unavailable.

[93] A Universal Turing Machine with Two Internal States

The main theorem of this paper, that a universal Turing machine can be constructed with just two internal states, is (as Shannon proves) the best possible result, since a one-state machine is impossible.

In connection with the final section of this paper, J. H. Conway has pointed out that it is possible to strengthen the result slightly, by proving that a universal Turing machine can be constructed in which only 0's and 1's appear on the tape and no more than four 1's appear on the tape at any given time.

[94] (With Karel de Leeuw, Edward F. Moore and N. Shapiro) Computability by Probabilistic Machines

There has been a great deal of subsequent work on the subject of this paper. See for example Gill [Gill77], and, for a recent survey, Johnson [John90].

[97] The Simultaneous Synthesis of s Switching Functions of n Variables

A sequel to [50].

[99] Game Playing Machines

A survey of a number of game-playing machines, including Shannon's penny-matching and maze solving machines (see [10], [11]), as well as the Moore-Shannon machine for playing Hex, which is not mentioned elsewhere.

[11] (With Peter Elias and Amiel Feinstein) A Note on the Maximum Flow Through a Network

This is a version of the "max-flow min-cut" theorem, one of the most important results in graph theory. It was discovered independently and at around the same time by Ford and Fulkerson [ForF56], [ForF62]. See Berge ([Berg73], Chap. 5), Harary ([Hara69], Chap. 5).

[89] and [90] (With Edward F. Moore) Reliable Circuits Using Less Reliable Relays

Originally entitled "Reliable circuits using crummy relays" [88], rumor has it that the title was changed at the request of the Bell Laboratories Public Relations department. The paper is a sequel to that of Von Neumann [VonN56] (described in the following paper). The main result is the following. Given an unreliable relay, let a (resp. c) be the probability of a contact being closed when its coil is energized (resp. not energized). As long as the contacts are statistically independent and $a \neq c$, it is possible to construct networks out of these relays with reliability arbitrarily close to 1.

Naturally, in view of the importance of this subject for computer design, there have been a large number of sequels and related papers. See in particular Pippenger [Pipp88], Feder [Fede89], and Winograd and Cowan [WinC63]. We cannot resist quoting the first paragraph of the latter:

> "One of the most interesting theoretical questions involved in the design of programs for the construction of reliable automata from less reliable modules has been the possible relevance to the problem of information theory and of coding theory. J. von Neumann's original demonstration of the process whereby reliable automata could be constructed from highly redundant modular assemblies utilized a very primitive error-correcting code and the law of large numbers. The result did not seem to be consistent with the central theory of information theory, C. E. Shannon's noisy-channel coding theorem. This theorem specifies a limit to the redundancy required to obtain any given level of reliable communication through a noisy channel, given sufficiently complex encoding and decoding equipment, and proves

the existence of at least one error-correcting code, with redundancy close to but not less than this limit, that exhibits such reliability. It is the purpose of this monograph to show how this coding theorem may be extended to include the case of computation with noisy modules rather than communication, and how error-correcting codes may be employed in the design of programs for constructing reliable automata from less reliable modules, despite even occasional mistakes in the wiring diagram.''

[114] Von Neumann's Contribution to Automata Theory

References 1 to 10 have been reprinted in Volume V of Von Neumann's Collected Papers [VonN61].

[120] Computers and Automation — Progress and Promise in the Twentieth Century

A talk given at Rice University on October 12, 1962, as part of a symposium on Man, Science, Learning and Education.

[126] Scientific Aspects of Juggling

The following comments are based on information kindly provided by J. P. Buhler (Reed College) and R. L. Graham (AT&T Bell Laboratories).

This article was written in late 1980 and early 1981. It was solicited by, and intended to be published in, *Scientific American,* but for various reasons was never finished. It was widely circulated in typescript form, and influenced a number of people interested in various aspects of juggling. It was written after Shannon returned from the 1980 juggling convention; some of the names of the top performers and estimates of the current state of the art are therefore out of date. As often happened in his career, Shannon was ahead of his time. In the last few years several articles, books, and a respectable Ph.D. thesis on juggling have appeared — see, for example, Austin [Aust76], Beek [Beek88], [Beek89], Buhler and Graham [BuhG84], Donner and Jameson [DonJ], Graham and Buhler [GraB82], Magnusson and Tiemann [MaTi89], Truzzi [Truz79], and Ziethen and Allen [Zie85]. Beek [Beek89] refers to the equation given in Theorem 1 of this article as the ''common equation of juggling.''

The text has been slightly edited. Shannon also intended to include several more illustrations, but these were not available and references to them in the text have been deleted.

[5] The Use of the Lakatos-Hickman Relay in a Subscriber Sender

Unpublished Bell Laboratories memorandum of August 13, 1940. Only the abstract is included.

[7] A Study of the Deflection Mechanism and Some Results on Rate Finders

This and the following two items are unpublished war-time reports dealing with aspects of the mechanical differential analyzer (compare [6], [13]). Only the abstracts are included.

[8] Backlash in Overdamped Systems

See preceding item.

[11] Some Experimental Results on the Deflection Mechanism

See notes to [7].

[30]   (With C. L. Dolph) The Transient Behavior of a Large Number of Four-Terminal Unilateral Linear Networks Connected in Tandem

An unpublished Bell Laboratories memorandum of April 10, 1946. Only the abstract is included.

[74] (With E. F. Moore) The Relay Circuit Analyzer

A Bell Laboratories memorandum, which was subsequently revised and published as [80]. Only the abstract is included.

[84] (With E. F. Moore) The Relay Circuit Synthesizer

Unpublished Bell Laboratories memorandum of Nov. 30, 1953, a sequel to the preceding item. Only the abstract is included.

References

[Alla78]   R. Allen, "Three amazing micromice: hitherto undisclosed details," *IEEE Spectrum*, **15**, (No. 11, Nov. 1978), 62-65.

[Aust76]   H. A. Austin, *A Computational Theory of Physical Skill*, M.I.T. Artificial Intelligence Laboratory, 1976.

[Beek88]   P. J. Beek, "Timing and phase locking cascade juggling," *Ecological Psychology*, **1** (1988), 55-96.

[Beek89]   P. J. Beek, *Juggling Dynamics*, Ph.D. Dissertation, Free University of Amsterdam, 1989.

[Berg73]   C. Berge, *Graphs and Hypergraphs*, North-Holland, Amsterdam, 1973.

[BeCG82] E. R. Berlekamp, J. H. Conway and R. K. Guy, *Winning Ways*, Academic Press, N.Y., 2 vols., 1982.

[BonM76] J. A. Bondy and U. S. R. Murty, *Graph Theory with Applications*, North-Holland, N.Y. 1976.

[Brua74]   R. A. Brualdi, "Networks and the Shannon switching game," *Delta*, **4** (1974) 1-23.

[BuhG84] J. P. Buhler and R. L. Graham, "Fountains, Showers, and Cascades," *The Sciences*, **24** (No. 1, Jan./Feb. 1984), 44-51.

[Cald58]   S. H. Caldwell, *Switching Circuits and Logical Design*, Wiley, N.Y. 1958.

[CaRi56]   L. Carlitz and J. Riordan "The number of labeled two-terminal series-parallel networks," *Duke Math. J.*, **23**, (1956), 435-445.

[DaDT78] M. Davio, J.-P. Deschamps and A. Thayse, *Discrete and Switching Functions*, McGraw-Hill, N.Y. 1978.

[DonJ] M. D. Donner and D. H. Jameson, "Recent progress in juggling robot research," IBM Research Report, Yorktown Heights, NY.

[Edmo65] J. Edwards, "Lehman's switching game and a theorem of Tutte and Nash-Williams," *J. Res. Nat. Bur. Stand.*, **69B** (1965), 73-77.

[Fede89] T. Feder, "Reliable computation by networks in the presence of noise," *IEEE Trans. Inform. Theory*, **35** (1989), 569-571.

[ForF56] L. R. Ford and D. R. Fulkerson, "Maximal flow through a network," *Canad. J. Math.*, **8** (1956), 399-404.

[ForF62] L. R. Ford and D. R. Fulkerson, *Flows in Networks*, Princeton Univ. Press, Princeton, 1962.

[Gill77] J. Gill, Computational complexity of probabilistic Turing machines, *SIAM J. Comput.*, **6** (1977), 675-695.

[GraB82] R. L. Graham and J. P. Buhler, "L'art de jongler," *La Recherche*, **13,** (No. 135, July/August 1982), 856-867.

[Hage55] D. W. Hagelbarger, "A relay laboratory outfit for colleges — mode two," Bell Laboratories Memorandum MM-55-114-14, Feb. 18, 1955.

[Hage54] D. W. Hagelbarger, "SEER, A SEquence Extrapolating Robot," *I.R.E. Trans. Electronic Computers*, **5** (1956), 1-7.

[HamV88] Y. O. Hamidoune and M. Las Vergnas, "A solution to the misère Shannon switching game," *Discrete Math.*, **72** (1988), 163-166.

[Hara69] F. Harary, *Graph Theory*, Addison-Wesley, Reading, Mass. 1969.

[Harr65] M. A. Harrison, *Introduction to Switching and Automata Theory*, McGraw-Hill, N.Y. 1965.

[Henn68] F. C. Hennie, *Finite-State Models for Logical Machines*, Wiley, N.Y. 1968.

[Hsu87] F-h. Hsu, "A two-million moves/s CMOS single-chip chess move generator," *IEEE J. Solid-State Circuits*, **22** (1987), 841-846.

[HsuA90] F-h. Hsu et al., "Deep Thought," pp. 55-78 of [MarS90].

[HsuA90a] F-h. Hsu et al., "A grandmaster chess machine," *Scientific American*, **263** (No. 4, Oct. 1990), 44-50.

[John63] C. L. Johnson, *Analog Computer Techniques*, McGraw-Hill, N.Y., 2nd ed., 1963.

[John90] D. S. Johnson, "A catalog of complexity classes," in *Handbook of Theoretical Computer Science*, ed. J. van Leeuwen, Elsevier, 1990, pp. 69-161.

[KeRW51] W. Keister A. E. Ritchie and S. H. Washburn, *The Design of Switching Circuits*, Van Nostrand, N.Y. 1951.

[KorK72] G. A. Korn and T. M. Korn, *Electronic Analog and Hybrid Computers*, McGraw-Hill, N.Y. 1972.

[Lehm64] A. Lehman, "A solution of the Shannon switching game," *SIAM J.*, **12** (1964), 687-725.

[Lomn72] Z. A. Lomnicki, Two-terminal series-parallel networks, *Advances Appl. Prob.*, **4** (1972), 109-150.

[LSI91] LSI Logic Corporation, *System Building Blocks Catalog 1991*, LSI Logic, Milpitas, Calif., 1991.

[MacM78] P. A. MacMahon, *Collected Papers*, MIT Press, Cambridge, 1978, Vol. I.

[MaTi89] B. Magnusson and B. Tiemann, "The physics of juggling," *Physics Teacher*, **27** (1989), 584-589.

[Mars90] T. A. Marsland, "A short history of computer chess," pp. 3-7 of [MarS90].

[MarS90] T. A. Marsland and J. Schaeffer, *Computers, Chess and Cognition*, Springer-Verlag, N.Y., 1990.

[MaxW92] J. C. Maxwell, *Electricity and Magnetism*, Oxford Univ. Press, 1892.

[McCl65]   E. J. McCluskey, *Introduction to the Theory of Switching Circuits*, McGraw-Hill, N.Y., 1965.

[McCl86]   E. J. McCluskey, *Logic Design Principles*, Prentice-Hall, Englewood Cliffs, N.J., 1986.

[MeCo80]   C. Mead and L. Conway, *Introduction to VLSI Systems*, Addison-Wesley, Reading, Mass. 1980.

[MeMo90]   A. Meir and J. M. Moon, "The asymptotic behavior of coefficients of powers of certain generating functions," *Europ. J. Combin.*, **11** (1990), 581-587.

[Moon87]   J. W. Moon, "Some enumerative results on series-parallel networks," *Annals Discrete Math.* **33** (1987), 199-226.

[Phis58]   M. Phister, Jr., *Logical Design of Digital Computers*, Wiley, N.Y., 1958.

[Pipp88]   N. Pippenger, "Reliable computation by formulas in the presence of noise," *IEEE Trans. Inform. Theory*, **34** (1988), 194-197.

[Rior58]   J. Riordan, *An Introduction to Combinatorial Analysis*, Wiley, N.Y. 1958.

[Rior68]   J. Riordan, *Combinatorial Identities*, Wiley, N.Y. 1968.

[Roth80]   J. P. Roth, *Computer Logic, Testing and Verification*, Computer Science Press, Potomac, Maryland, 1980.

[SesR61]   S. Seshu and M. B. Reed, *Linear Graphs and Electrical Networks*, Addison-Wesley, Reading, Mass., 1961.

[Sloa73]   N. J. A. Sloane, *A Handbook of Integer Sequences*, Academic Press, N.Y. 1973.

[Sloa92]   N. J. A. Sloane, *The New Book of Integer Sequences*, W. H. Freeman, N.Y., in preparation.

[Truz79]   M. Truzzi, "On keeping things up in the air," *National History*, **88** (No. 10, 1979), 45-53.

[VonN56]   J. von Neumann, "Probabilistic logics and the synthesis of reliable organisms from unreliable components," in *Automata Studies*, edited C. E. Shannon and J. McCarthy, Princeton Univ. Press, Princeton, N.J., 1956, pp. 43-98.

[VonN61]   J. von Neumann, *Collected Works*, edited A. H. Taub, Pergamon Press, Oxford, 6 vols., 1961.

[Wels76]   D. J. A. Welsh, *Matroid Theory*, Academic Press, London, 1976.

[WinC63]   S. Winograd and J. D. Cowan, *Reliable Computation in the Presence of Noise*, M.I.T. Press, Cambridge, Mass., 1963.

[ZieA85]   K. K. Ziethen and A. Allen, *Juggling: The Art and Its Artists*, Werner Rausch and Werner Lüft Inc., Berlin, 1985.

Part C
Genetics

Preface to Shannon's Collected Papers (Part C)

This is Shannon's hitherto unpublished Ph.D. dissertation (M.I.T., April 15, 1940).

An Algebra for Theoretical Genetics*

Claude E. Shannon

Abstract

In this thesis, an algebra is constructed for studying the dynamics of Mendelian populations. The symbols of the algebra represent groups of individuals or populations. The indexed symbol λ_{jk}^{hi}, for example, represents a population in which two gene loci are under consideration (the number of loci corresponds to the number of pairs of indices). The number of allelomorphs in each locus is completely arbitrary, as is the recombination value for the loci. The different components of a population symbol, represented by fixing the indices at specific values, are numbers whose values correspond to the fractions of the population with certain genetic formulae. It is convenient in some cases to consider as populations symbols whose components are negative or even complex. Such symbols cannot, of course, represent an actual group of individuals and are called *unrealizable* populations, but their use sometimes facilitates the solution of problems.

Addition of two population symbols, $R\lambda_{jk}^{hi} + S\mu_{jk}^{hi}$, results in a third population symbol which is defined in such a way as to represent the population obtained by merely combining the original populations in fractional proportions corresponding to the scalar coefficients R and S. Cross multiplication of population symbols $\lambda_{jk}^{hi} \times \mu_{jk}^{hi}$ gives a population symbol which is defined in such a way as to represent the expected offspring population when the two original populations are crossmated at random. When two gene loci are considered, this is realized by the mathematical definition

$$\lambda_{jk}^{hi} \times \mu_{jk}^{hi} = \tfrac{1}{2}[p_0\lambda_{\bullet\bullet}^{hi} + p_1\lambda_{\bullet i}^{h\bullet}][p_0\mu_{\bullet\bullet}^{jk} + p_1\mu_{\bullet k}^{j\bullet}]$$

$$+ \tfrac{1}{2}[p_0\lambda_{\bullet\bullet}^{jk} + p_1\lambda_{\bullet k}^{j\bullet}][p_0\mu_{\bullet\bullet}^{hi} + p_1\mu_{\bullet i}^{h\bullet}]$$

in which $p_1 = 1 - p_0$ is the recombination value for the two loci, and replacing an index by a dot indicates summation of the population symbol on that index. Cross multiplication is defined analogously for n loci. It is shown that this algebra is commutative on addition and multiplication, distributive, and associative on addition but not on multiplication. These laws together with two fundamental manipulation theorems: one, that summation of a population on all indices gives unity and two, that inverting the upper and lower rows of indices of a population leaves it unchanged, form the basic algorithms of the algebra.

A number of the well known theorems of theoretical genetics are easily proved by means of this algebra. In addition, a number of new results are found. Completely general formulae for the nth generation offspring under random intermating of an arbitrary initial population are developed both for the cases of two and of three linked factors. For two linked factors, the formula for the nth generation is

$$\mu_{jk}^{hi} = [p_0^{n-1}(p_0\lambda_{\bullet\bullet}^{hi} + p_1\lambda_{\bullet i}^{h\bullet}) + (1 - p_0^{n-1})\lambda_{\bullet\bullet}^{h\bullet}\lambda_{\bullet\bullet}^{\bullet i}]$$

$$[p_0^{n-1}(p_0\lambda_{\bullet\bullet}^{jk} + p_1\lambda_{\bullet k}^{j\bullet}) + (1 - p_0^{n-1})\lambda_{\bullet\bullet}^{j\bullet}\lambda_{\bullet\bullet}^{\bullet k}]$$

---

* Ph.D. Dissertation, Massachusetts Institute of Technology, 1940.

in which λ_{jk}^{hi} is the initial population and p_1 the recombination value. Incidental to this, it is shown that a recombination value $> \frac{1}{2}$ is impossible when there is no interference. Conditions are found for the stability under random intermating of a population when one or more loci are considered. For the case of one locus, three sets of equivalent necessary and sufficient conditions are established.

By means of certain homogeneous γ populations an arbitrary population may be expanded in a finite series displaying its various components. This expansion, together with the multiplication law for the γ populations, displays the elements of this algebra as hypercomplex numbers. It is shown that an arbitrary population may be expanded uniquely as a sum of any n linearly independent populations where n is the number of different possible genetic formulae for the factors considered.

It is possible to write down various types of equations involving known and unknown populations using the operations of addition and cross multiplication. In general, such an equation can be interpreted as a breeding experiment involving one or more unknown populations and resulting in a genetically known population. Methods are developed whereby most such equations can be solved in case a solution exists. Briefly this method of solution may be summarized as follows. By summing on one or more indices of the unknown populations, enough data about them is obtained to uniquely determine any cross products in which they appear. The cross product terms in the original equations then become known and the equations may be solved in exactly the same way as ordinary linear algebraic equations.

In case a selective action exists favoring individuals of a certain genetic constitution, the previous formulae for stability no longer hold. Although this more difficult problem has not been completely solved, a necessary condition for the possible existence of a stable population under an arbitrary given selective action is established, and a formula for this population is developed. This has only been done for the case of a single locus.

A start has been made toward the development of a calculus of populations, i.e., the study of populations which may vary continuously with time. The time derivative of a population is defined. The derivative of a population, although an indexed symbol, is not itself a population. All the ordinary rules of derivation including the Leibnitz rule for the derivative of a cross product of populations are shown to hold true. Also, a population may be expanded in a Taylor series in powers of time, of the same form as the ordinary Taylor series.

1. Introduction

In this paper an attempt will be made to develop an algebra especially suited to problems in the dynamics of Mendelian populations. Many of the results presented here are old in the theory of genetics, but are included because the method of proof is novel, and usually simpler and more general than those used previously.

For the benefit of readers who are not familiar with modern genetics theory, we will first give a brief factual summary of those parts of it which are necessary for our work. Although all parts of the theory have not been incontestably established, still it is possible for our purposes to act as though they were, since the results obtained are known to be the same *as if* the simple representation which we give were true. Hereafter we shall speak therefore as though the genes actually exist and as though our simple representation of hereditary phenomena were really true, since so far as we are concerned, this might just as well be so. We will omit from consideration mutations and phenomena in the sex chromosomes.

Hereditary traits are transmitted by small elements called *genes*. These genes are carried in rodlike bodies known as *chromosomes*, a large number of genes lying side by side along the length of a chromosome. Chromosomes occur in pairs and an individual obtains one chromosome of each pair from his mother and the other from his father.

By the *genetic constitution* of an individual we mean the kind and location of the genes which he possesses. If we represent the different genes by letters, then we may write a *genetic formula* for an individual. Thus considering two chromosome pairs and four gene positions in each chromosome, an individual might have the formula

$$A_1 \ B_1 \ C_3 \ D_5 \qquad E_4 \ F_1 \ G_6 \ H_1$$
$$A_3 \ B_1 \ C_4 \ D_3 \qquad E_4 \ F_2 \ G_6 \ H_2 \tag{1}$$

Here the series $A_1 \ B_1 \ C_3 \ D_5$ represents one chromosome, with $A_3 \ B_1 \ C_4 \ D_3$ the corresponding one of the first pair. $A_1, B_1, C_3, D_5, A_3, B_1, C_4, D_3$ are the genes lying in the positions under consideration. $E_4 \ F_1 \ G_6 \ H_1$ and $E_4 \ F_2 \ G_6 \ H_2$ are the two chromosomes of the second pair. We will sometimes write a genetic formula in one line. Thus (1) would be written:

$$A_1 \ A_3 \ B_1 \ B_1 \ C_3 \ C_4 \ D_5 \ D_3 \ E_4 \ E_4 \ F_1 \ F_2 \ G_6 \ G_6 \ H_1 \ H_2$$

alternate letters being taken from the top and bottom lines of (1).

There is no essential ordering of chromosomes in a pair. That is to say the top and bottom lines of the formula for a chromosome pair may be inverted and still represent the same individual. Thus the formula (1) is identical, for example, with the following:

$$A_3 \ B_1 \ C_4 \ D_3 \qquad E_4 \ F_1 \ G_6 \ H_1$$
$$A_1 \ B_1 \ C_3 \ D_5 \qquad E_4 \ F_2 \ G_6 \ H_2$$

in which we have inverted the first pair.

Certain simple traits are controlled by only one pair of genes lying at analogous points in corresponding chromosomes. Two such corresponding points in a chromosome pair are known as a *gene locus*, and the different genes which may occupy one locus are known as *allelomorphs* or more shortly as *alleles*. In our example (1) the positions occupied by genes C_3 and C_4 constitute a locus. We shall adopt the convention that allelomorphic genes shall have the same base letter with different subscripts. Thus C_1, C_2, C_3, C_4, C_5 represent five alleles. A C gene can only occur in the locus corresponding to C genes.

The *appearance* of an individual depends only on the kinds of genes, not on their positions. Thus an individual with the formula

$$A_1 \ B_1 \ C_4 \ D_3 \quad E_4 \ F_1 \ G_6 \ H_2$$
$$A_3 \ B_1 \ C_3 \ D_5 \quad E_4 \ F_2 \ G_6 \ H_1$$

would *appear* (insofar as the characteristics controlled by these genes are concerned) the same as (1). He would, however, *breed* differently as will appear later. Two such individuals are said to be *phenotypically* the same with respect to these characteristics. They are *genotypically* different; they have different genetic formulae with respect to these loci. Such a situation can occur in a different way. In garden peas there are two alleles which control the size of the plant. These genes we may represent by A_1 and A_2. If a plant has two A_1 genes, it will be tall. If it has two A_2 genes, it will be a dwarf. A plant with one A_1 gene and one A_2 gene is tall, since the gene for tallness (A_1) is, as we say, *dominant* over the *recessive* gene (A_2) for shortness. Thus $A_1 A_1$ plants and $A_1 A_2$ (or $A_2 A_1$) plants are phenotypically the same but genotypically different with respect to tallness.

As we stated above, an individual receives one chromosome of each pair from the corresponding pair possessed by his mother and the other from that of his father. Let us now consider a pair of chromosomes possessed by a parent. In case a phenomenon known as *cross-over* does not occur in the chromosome pair under consideration, an offspring receives an entire chromosome selected at random from these two. We say that the genes in the chromosome are *linked* together, meaning that they tend to be transmitted as a body. Genes located close together in the same chromosome are closely linked; the greater the distance between them, the weaker the linkage. Let us suppose that an individual has the genetic formula represented as follows

$$A_1 \ B_2 \ C_3 \ D_3 \ E_4 \ F_1 \ G_1$$

$$A_2 \ B_2 \ C_2 \ D_1 \ E_6 \ F_1 \ G_2$$

for a pair of corresponding chromosomes. Now, as we have said, in case crossover does not occur, an offspring of this individual will receive either the series

$$A_1 \ B_2 \ C_3 \ D_3 \ E_4 \ F_1 \ G_1 \ \text{ or } A_2 \ B_2 \ C_2 \ D_1 \ E_6 \ F_1 \ G_2$$

and he is equally likely to receive either of these. However, it may happen that a crossover occurs between these chromosomes. If this crossover occurred, for instance, between the C and D loci, he would receive either

$$A_1 \ B_2 \ C_3 \ D_1 \ E_6 \ F_1 \ G_2 \ \text{ or } A_2 \ B_2 \ C_2 \ D_3 \ E_4 \ F_1 \ G_1 \ .$$

There is a definite probability that a crossover will occur between any two gene loci. Determining the relative positions of genes in a chromosome according to such a probability scale is known as *mapping* the chromosome. This has been carried out quite extensively for Drosophila and to a lesser extent for some other plants and animals. The *map distance* between two loci a and b may be defined as follows. Let x measure the actual physical distance along the chromosome and let $p(x)$ be the probability that a crossover occurs between the points x and $x + dx$, providing it is known that no other crossover occurs near to the point x. This last restriction is necessary due to a phenomenon known as *interference* in which a crossover at one point hinders nearby crossovers. The map distance is then given by

$$\int_a^b p(x) \ dx \ .$$

The *recombination value* of two loci is the probability of an odd number of crossovers between these loci. For small distances the probability of more than one crossover is a second order term and the map distance is nearly equal to the recombination value, and both approximate the probability of one crossover between the loci.

If the two genes in a certain locus are identical, the individual is said to be *homozygous* in this factor. Otherwise he is *heterozygous*. The individual (1) is thus homozygous in the B, E, and G factors and heterozygous in all others.

A simple example will perhaps help to clarify these notions. Suppose that two gene loci are under consideration. There are three allelomorphic genes for the first locus, A_1, A_2, A_3; the second locus has four alleles, B_1, B_2, B_3, B_4. The recombination value for these two loci is $1/4$. An individual with the genetic formula

$$\begin{array}{cc} A_1 & B_4 \\ A_3 & B_2 \end{array}$$

is mated with an individual having the formula

$$A_2 \quad B_4$$
$$A_2 \quad B_1$$

What is the probability that an offspring of this mating will have the formula

$$A_3 \quad B_4$$
$$A_2 \quad B_1$$

Stated another way, what fraction of the offspring population should be expected to have this formula?

Evidently an offspring must obtain the A_3 B_4 chromosome from the first parent. The probability that he will get an A_3 gene from this parent is $1/2$ since A_3 and A_1 are equally likely. If he gets this A_3 gene, the probability that he will also get a B_4 gene from this parent is $1/4$, the recombination value, since A_3 and B_4 are in opposite chromosomes. Thus the probability that both events occur is $1/2 \cdot 1/4 = 1/8$. Now our offspring must obtain A_2 and B_1 from the second parent. He will certainly obtain an A_2 since both genes in this locus are of this type. The chance that he obtains a B_1 is $1/2$, since B_1 and B_3 are equally likely. The probability of the combination is therefore also $1/2$. Our final answer is, since the events are independent, $1/8 \cdot 1/2 = 1/16$. If we had asked what fraction would be of the type

$$A_3 \quad B_2$$
$$A_2 \quad B_2$$

then in place of multiplying by the recombination value $1/4$, we would multiply by $1 - 1/4 = 3/4$ since this is the probability that a crossover *does not* occur between the loci.

2. Notation

To non-mathematicians we point out that it is a commonplace of modern algebra for symbols to represent concepts other than numbers, and frequently therefore not to obey all the laws governing numbers. Such is the case in vector algebra, the theory of groups, rings, matrix algebra, in symbolic logic, tensor analysis, etc. In the particular algebra we construct for genetics theory the symbols represent Mendelian populations, and stand for a large group of numbers which describe the genetic constitution of the population. Addition and multiplication are defined to mean simple combination and cross breeding respectively, and it is shown that nearly all the laws of ordinary numerical algebra hold here. One interesting exception is the associative law of multiplication. It is not in general true that

$$(\lambda \times \mu) \times \nu = \lambda \times (\mu \times \nu) .$$

Much of the power and elegance of any mathematical theory depends on use of a suitably compact and suggestive notation, which nevertheless completely describes the concepts involved. We will employ an index notation somewhat similar to that of the tensor calculus, which has proved so useful in differential geometry and in relativity theory. Because the notation employed is so basic to our work we will first explain the meaning of indexed symbols.

Consider, for example, the symbol

$$\lambda^{h\,i}_{j\,k} . \tag{2}$$

Here λ is the *base letter* and $h, i, j,$ and k are indices. Each index has a certain specific range of variation and the different indices may vary independently and even have different ranges of variation. In our work two indices in the same vertical column, such as h and j in (2), will always have the same range, but vary independently over this range. Thus h and j might have the range of values 1, 2, and 3 while i and k have the range 1, 2, 3, 4, ..., 9.

When the indices of (2) take on specific values, e.g., $h = 1$, $j = 3$, $i = 5$, $k = 5$, the symbol

$$\lambda_{3\,5}^{1\,5}$$

represents a number. Symbol (2) thus stands for a whole group of numbers, one for each combination of values of the indices; however, it should not be thought of as a group of separate numbers, but rather as a single entity having components whose values are the different numbers of the array.

When we think of an indexed symbol as representing a whole array of numbers and the indices as variables which assume any of the values in their ranges we say the indices are *live* or *variable*. Occasionally, however, it is desirable to think of $\lambda_{j\,k}^{h\,i}$ (say) as representing a certain specific one of the components. Thus we may set $h = 1$, $i = 3$, $j = 2$, $k = 3$. We say then that we have *fixed* or *killed* the indices at these values; they become *dead* indices. Also we sometimes wish to think of the indices as fixed at some value which is perfectly arbitrary. Without any change of notation we use $\lambda_{j\,k}^{h\,i}$ to represent an arbitrary component rather than the whole set of components. In such a case fixing the indices is purely subjective.

In an equation, although indices represented by different letters may vary independently, a specific letter, e.g., h, must not take on different values in different places. Thus the *sum* of two indexed symbols

$$\lambda_{j\,k}^{h\,i} + \mu_{j\,k}^{h\,i} \tag{3}$$

is an indexed symbol, say $v_{j\,k}^{h\,i}$, whose components are the sums of the corresponding components of $\lambda_{j\,k}^{h\,i}$ and $\mu_{j\,k}^{h\,i}$. For example

$$v_{1\,1}^{1\,1} = \lambda_{1\,1}^{1\,1} + \mu_{1\,1}^{1\,1}$$

$$v_{3\,5}^{1\,2} = \lambda_{3\,5}^{1\,2} + \mu_{3\,5}^{1\,2} \,.$$

On the other hand if

$$v_{j\,k}^{h\,i} = \lambda_{j\,k}^{h\,i} + \mu_{j\,i}^{h\,k}$$

then $v_{3\,5}^{1\,2} = \lambda_{3\,5}^{1\,2} + \mu_{3\,2}^{1\,5}$, etc.

An equation in indexed symbols stands therefore for a large number of ordinary equations, one for each combination of values of the variable indices.

Ordinary multiplication of indexed symbols will be indicated by juxtaposition, e.g., $R_j^i \lambda_k^i$, $R_i^h \lambda_i^h$, $\lambda_i^h \mu_k^i$. Ordinary multiplication means numerical multiplication of the components indicated, and results therefore in another indexed symbol. The multiplications above would result respectively in symbols with indices as follows:

$$\tau_{j\,k}^{i} \,, \quad \rho_{i}^{h} \,, \quad \sigma_{i\,k}^{h\,j}$$

where

$$\tau_{2\,3}^{1} = R_2^1 \lambda_3^1 \,, \quad \tau_{3\,3}^{2} = R_3^2 \lambda_3^2 \,,$$

$$\rho_{2}^{1} = R_2^1 \lambda_2^1 \,, \quad \rho_{3}^{3} = R_3^3 \lambda_3^3 \,,$$

$$\sigma_{4\,3}^{1\,2} = \lambda_4^1 \mu_3^2 \,,$$

etc. There are always as many variable indices in a product as there are *different* variable indices in the factors. Thus $R_j^i \lambda_k^l$ has three independent variable indices i, j, k and hence the product τ_{jk}^i has three indices.

An important operation in indexed symbols is summation on one or more indices. This is so common in our work that we indicate it by replacing the index in question by a large dot. Thus supposing the index h has a range of variation of 1 to 3 and i, a range 1 to 5, then

$$\lambda_{jk}^{\bullet i} = \sum_{h=1}^{3} \lambda_{jk}^{hi} = \lambda_{jk}^{1i} + \lambda_{jk}^{2i} + \lambda_{jk}^{3i},$$

$$\lambda_{jk}^{\bullet\bullet} = \sum_{h=1}^{3} \sum_{i=1}^{5} \lambda_{jk}^{hi} = \lambda_{jk}^{11} + \lambda_{jk}^{12} + \lambda_{jk}^{13} + \lambda_{jk}^{14} + \lambda_{jk}^{15}$$

$$+ \lambda_{jk}^{21} + \lambda_{jk}^{22} + \lambda_{jk}^{23} + \lambda_{jk}^{24} + \lambda_{jk}^{25}$$

$$+ \lambda_{jk}^{31} + \lambda_{jk}^{32} + \lambda_{jk}^{33} + \lambda_{jk}^{34} + \lambda_{jk}^{35}.$$

Most of our indexed symbols will represent populations. Suppose we are considering two different Mendelian factors. Let the first have two alleles, A_1 and A_2, and suppose the second factor has three, B_1, B_2, and B_3. Then any population may be divided into 21 genetically different groups, having the genetic formulae

(1) A_1 A_1 B_1 B_1	(7) A_2 A_2 B_1 B_1	(13) A_1 A_2 B_1 B_1
(2) A_1 A_1 B_1 B_2	(8) A_2 A_2 B_1 B_2	(14) A_1 A_2 B_1 B_2
(3) A_1 A_1 B_1 B_3	(9) A_2 A_2 B_1 B_3	(15) A_1 A_2 B_1 B_3
(4) A_1 A_1 B_2 B_2	(10) A_2 A_2 B_2 B_2	(16) A_1 A_2 B_2 B_2
(5) A_1 A_1 B_2 B_3	(11) A_2 A_2 B_2 B_3	(17) A_1 A_2 B_2 B_3
(6) A_1 A_1 B_3 B_3	(12) A_2 A_2 B_3 B_3	(18) A_1 A_2 B_3 B_3
		(19) A_1 A_2 B_2 B_1
		(20) A_1 A_2 B_3 B_1
		(21) A_1 A_2 B_3 B_2

This population would be represented by the symbol λ_{jk}^{hi}.

The indices h and j correspond to the first locus and since there are two alleles for this factor they each have a range of variation of 1 to 2. The second factor has three alleles and correspondingly i and k range over the values 1, 2, 3. Now, thinking of h, i, j, and k as fixed or dead we define the components of λ_{jk}^{hi} in the following manner. If $h = j$ and $i = k$ then $\lambda_{jk}^{hi} = \lambda_{hi}^{hi} = $ the fraction of the population with the genetic formula A_h A_h B_i B_i. Thus λ_{13}^{13} is the fraction of the population of the type A_1 A_1 B_3 B_3. If $h \neq j$, or $i \neq k$, or both, then λ_{jk}^{hi} represents *one half* the fraction of the population having the formula A_h A_j B_i B_k or, what is the same thing, A_j A_h B_k B_i. Thus λ_{23}^{13} and λ_{12}^{23} are *one half* the fractions having the respective formulas A_1 A_2 B_3 B_3 and A_2 A_1 B_3 B_2.

We shall use Greek letters as base letters for populations, and in general, then, the symbol

$$\lambda_{j_1 \, j_2 \, \dots \, j_s}^{i_1 \, i_2 \, \dots \, i_s} \tag{4}$$

represents a population in which s gene loci are under consideration. The first column of indices, i_1 and j_1, corresponds to the first factor under consideration, the second column to the next factor, etc. Each factor may have an arbitrary number of alleles, and the linkage between any two may be of any value including 50% or random assortment. In case $i_1 = j_1$, $i_2 = j_2, \dots, i_s = j_s$ then $\lambda_{i_1 \, i_2 \, \dots \, i_s}^{i_1 \, i_2 \, \dots \, i_s}$ is the fraction of the population having the formula $(A_{i_1} \; A_{i_1} \; B_{i_2} \; B_{i_2} \; \dots \; S_{i_s} \; S_{i_s})$. If these equalities are not all true then $\lambda_{j_1 \, j_2 \, \dots \, j_s}^{i_1 \, i_2 \, \dots \, i_s}$ is ½ the fraction having the formula $(A_{i_1} \; A_{j_1} \; B_{i_2} \; B_{j_2} \; \dots \; S_{i_s} \; S_{j_s})$. It is helpful in using this notation to note the close connection between the two rows of letters in the indices and the two rows of genes in the chromosomes. The analogue is more than superficial, for we will later show how crossing over, say between the second and third loci, is connected, in this notation, with the symbol $\lambda_{\bullet \, \bullet \, j}^{h \, i \, \bullet}$.

3. Fundamental Theorems

There are two fundamental manipulation laws which we present as theorems because of their importance, although both are almost obvious.

Theorem I.

$$\lambda_{j_1 \, j_2 \, \dots \, j_s}^{i_1 \, i_2 \, \dots \, i_s} = \lambda_{i_1 \, i_2 \, \dots \, i_s}^{j_1 \, j_2 \, \dots \, j_s} . \tag{5}$$

That is, exchanging the upper and lower rows of indices of a population gives an identical population. This is evident from the meaning of the symbols, since a genetic formula $(A_{i_1} \; A_{j_1} \; B_{i_2} \; B_{j_2} \; \dots \; S_{i_s} \; S_{j_s})$ is identical with the formula $(A_{j_1} \; A_{i_1} \; B_{j_2} \; B_{i_2} \; \dots \; S_{j_s} \; S_{i_s})$. This exchange of indices may be carried out independently of the location of the gene loci in question. However, if it is known that certain of the loci are in one chromosome pair, and none of the others are in this pair, further identities will hold. Namely, we may invert the indices corresponding to this chromosome pair and leave the others intact without changing the meaning of the symbol. Thus, if in the population $\lambda_{k \, l \, m}^{h \, i \, j}$, the first two loci are in one chromosome pair, and the third in another, we have:

$$\lambda_{k \, l \, m}^{h \, i \, j} = \lambda_{k \, l \, j}^{h \, i \, m} = \lambda_{h \, i \, j}^{k \, l \, m} = \lambda_{h \, i \, m}^{k \, l \, j} .$$

Theorem II.

$$\lambda_{\bullet \, \bullet \, \dots \, \bullet}^{\bullet \, \bullet \, \dots \, \bullet} = 1 . \tag{6}$$

That is, summation of a population on all indices gives the result one. Obviously the sum of all the fractional parts of the population is unity. Those parts which we have divided by 2 appear in the summation (6) twice, corresponding to an exchange of the upper and lower indices. Thus with the population $\lambda_{j \, k}^{h \, i}$ the term $\lambda_{2 \, 2}^{1 \, 2}$ appears twice in the summation $\lambda_{\bullet \, \bullet}^{\bullet \, \bullet}$, once as $\lambda_{2 \, 2}^{1 \, 2}$ and once as $\lambda_{1 \, 2}^{2 \, 2}$, which are equal by Theorem I.

The significance of summation on a smaller number of indices is also of considerable importance. Consider the population $\lambda_{j \, k}^{h \, i}$. Summation on k gives $\lambda_{j \, \bullet}^{h \, i}$, a symbol with three variable or "live" indices. The reader may verify that if $h \neq j$, $\lambda_{j \, \bullet}^{h \, i}$ represents one half the fraction of $\lambda_{j \, k}^{h \, i}$ which have the formula $A_h \; A_j \; B_i \; \_$, where the $\_$ may be any gene. If $h = j$ then $\lambda_{h \, \bullet}^{h \, i}$ represents half the fraction having the formula $A_h \; A_j \; B_i \; \_$ plus half the fraction of the type $A_h \; A_h \; B_i \; B_i$.

Summing on both k and i we have $\lambda_{j \, \bullet}^{h \, \bullet}$ and this may be shown to have exactly the same meaning as λ_j^h where h and j refer to the same gene locus in each case. That is, summing on a pair of vertical indices is equivalent to eliminating this locus from consideration. Summing on two horizontal indices, j and k, gives $\lambda^{h\,i}_{\bullet\,\bullet}$, a two-index symbol, whose components are the fractions of all *chromosomes* in the population in which genes A_h and B_i both appear. Likewise $\lambda^{h}_{\bullet\,k}$ represents the fraction of all *chromosome pairs* in which A_h is in one and B_k in the other.

Summation on three indices $\lambda^{h}_{\bullet\,\bullet}$ gives a one-index symbol and its components are the gene frequencies of A_1, A_2, ... in the general population. That is, $\lambda^{1}_{\bullet\,\bullet}$ is the sum of the fraction of homozygotes in A_1 and half the heterozygotes having one A_1 gene.

The reader will easily generalize these statements for more complex cases. For easy reference we summarize the above remarks in the following proposition.

Theorem III.

1. If $i_1 = j_1$, $i_2 = j_2$, . . . , $i_{s-1} = j_{s-1}$ then $\lambda^{i_1\ i_2\ \dots\ i_s}_{j_1\ j_2\ \dots\ \bullet}$ is one half the fraction of the population of the type $A_{i_1}\ A_{i_1}\ \dots\ S_{i_s}\ \_$ plus half the fraction of the type $A_{i_1}\ A_{i_1}\ \dots\ S_{i_s} S_{i_s}$. If the conditions above do not hold then it represents one half the population of the type $A_{i_1}\ A_{j_1}\ B_{i_2}\ B_{j_2}\ \dots\ S_{i_s}\ \_$.

2. Summation on two vertical indices is equivalent to eliminating the corresponding locus from consideration.

3. Summing on one index in each column gives the fractions of the chromosome pairs in which alleles with the remaining indices appear.

4. The fraction of $\lambda^{i_1\ \dots\ i_s}_{j_1\ \dots\ j_s}$ having at least one A_h gene is given by

$$2\lambda^{h}_{\bullet\,\bullet\,\dots\,\bullet} - \lambda^{h}_{h\,\bullet\,\bullet\,\dots\,\bullet} .$$

In order to present a rigorous mathematical development it is convenient to consider symbols whose components are not all positive real numbers lying between zero and one. Of course, such a symbol cannot represent an actual group of individuals, but in some cases it is possible to solve problems using these symbols and get an actual population for the final answer. We shall speak of the symbol as a population in either case, but if the symbol *does* correspond to a possible group of individuals we shall say the population is *realizable*. If the components are all real numbers we will say the population is *real*. The use of unrealizable populations also adds elegance and generality to some of our later theorems.

We now introduce an operation between two populations to be known as cross multiplication and written:

$$\lambda^{h\,i}_{j\,k} \times \mu^{h\,i}_{j\,k} .$$

This will be defined in such a way that the cross product of two realizable populations represents the expected offspring if the population in question are cross mated at random. We will first give the definition for the case of two linked factors. Let the probability of *zero* or an *even* number of crossovers between the two factors be $p_0 = 1 - p_1$ and let p_1 be the probability of an odd number of crossovers (i.e., the recombination value). We define the cross product of $\lambda^{h\,i}_{j\,k}$, $\mu^{h\,i}_{j\,k}$ as follows:

$$v_{jk}^{hi} = \lambda_{jk}^{hi} \times \mu_{jk}^{hi}$$

$$= \tfrac{1}{2}[p_0\lambda_{\bullet\bullet}^{hi} + p_1\lambda_{\bullet i}^{h\bullet}][p_0\mu_{\bullet\bullet}^{jk} + p_1\mu_{\bullet k}^{j\bullet}] \qquad (8)$$

$$+ \tfrac{1}{2}[p_0\lambda_{\bullet\bullet}^{jk} + p_1\lambda_{\bullet k}^{j\bullet}][p_0\mu_{\bullet\bullet}^{hi} + p_1\mu_{\bullet i}^{h\bullet}]$$

To prove that this represents the expected offspring population we use the idea of gene-pair frequencies, a generalization of the idea of gene frequencies. We wish to determine the probability that an offspring of mating λ with μ will have the genetic formula $A_h\ A_j\ B_i\ B_k$. One way an offspring may obtain this formula is to get $A_h\ B_i$ from λ and $A_j\ B_k$ from μ. This corresponds to the term

$$[p_0\lambda_{\bullet\bullet}^{hi} + p_1\lambda_{\bullet i}^{h\bullet}][p_0\mu_{\bullet\bullet}^{jk} + p_1\mu_{\bullet k}^{j\bullet}] \qquad (9)$$

in the equation (8). Each of the terms of (9) is a gene-pair frequency. The first is the frequency of the gene pair $A_h\ B_i$ in the population λ. The second is the frequency of the gene-pair $A_j\ B_k$ in μ. The product is then the probability of obtaining an offspring $A_h\ A_j\ B_i\ B_k$ by the method described.

Gene-pair frequency here means the frequency with which this pair of genes occurs together in the same chromosome *after* crossovers have taken place. The term

$$[p_0\lambda_{\bullet\bullet}^{hi} + p_1\lambda_{\bullet i}^{h\bullet}] \qquad (10)$$

actually represents this because, from Theorem III, $\lambda_{\bullet\bullet}^{hi}$ represents the frequency with which A_h and B_i appear together in the same chromosome *before* crossover, and p_0 is the probability that there is no crossover between these factors (or at most an even number of crossovers) so that $p_0\lambda_{\bullet\bullet}^{hi}$ is the probability of getting A_h and B_i together after crossovers if they start together. Likewise $p_1\lambda_{\bullet i}^{h\bullet}$ is the probability of A_h and B_i ending together when they start in opposite chromosomes of a pair. Since these two possibilities are mutually exclusive, and collectively exhaustive, their sum (10) represents the gene-pair frequency of A_h, B_i in λ after crossovers. Similarly the second term of (9) is the gene-pair frequency of $A_j\ B_k$ in μ after crossover and the product of these two is the probability of an offspring getting the pair $A_h\ B_i$ from λ *and* $A_j\ B_k$ from μ. The only other way for an offspring to get the formula $A_h\ A_j\ B_i\ B_k$ is to get $A_j\ B_k$ from λ and $A_h\ B_i$ from μ. This corresponds in exactly the same way to the second term of (8), and we may add the probabilities since the events are mutually exclusive. All that remains to be explained in (8) is the factor $1/2$. In case the equations $h = j, i = k\ do\ not$ both hold then for the components of the offspring population we want half of the fraction of individuals of this type in order to fit our previous definition of a population symbol, and hence this factor. If both these equalities are true then both terms of (8) are identical and we may add, getting

$$v_{hi}^{hi} = [p_0\lambda_{\bullet\bullet}^{hi} + p_1\lambda_{\bullet i}^{h\bullet}][p_0\mu_{\bullet\bullet}^{hi} + p_1\mu_{\bullet i}^{h\bullet}]\ ,$$

which is what we get by the derivation above in this case, since the two "different" possibilities become identical under this restriction and therefore (8) holds for all values of the indices.

For three factors the defining equation of the cross product is

$$v^{hij}_{klm} = \lambda^{hij}_{klm} \times \mu^{hij}_{klm}$$

$$= \tfrac{1}{2}[p_{00}\lambda^{hij}_{\bullet\bullet\bullet} + p_{01}\lambda^{hi\bullet}_{\bullet\bullet j} + p_{10}\lambda^{h\bullet\bullet}_{\bullet ij} + p_{11}\lambda^{h\bullet j}_{\bullet i\bullet}]$$

$$\cdot [p_{00}\mu^{klm}_{\bullet\bullet\bullet} + p_{01}\mu^{kl\bullet}_{\bullet\bullet m} + p_{10}\mu^{k\bullet\bullet}_{\bullet lm} + p_{11}\mu^{k\bullet m}_{\bullet l\bullet}] \qquad (11)$$

$$+ \tfrac{1}{2}[p_{00}\lambda^{klm}_{\bullet\bullet\bullet} + p_{01}\lambda^{kl\bullet}_{\bullet\bullet m} + p_{10}\lambda^{k\bullet\bullet}_{\bullet lm} + p_{11}\lambda^{k\bullet m}_{\bullet l\bullet}]$$

$$\cdot [p_{00}\mu^{hij}_{\bullet\bullet\bullet} + p_{01}\mu^{hi\bullet}_{\bullet\bullet j} + p_{10}\mu^{h\bullet\bullet}_{\bullet ij} + p_{11}\mu^{h\bullet j}_{\bullet i\bullet}] .$$

In this equation p_{00} is the probability of an even number of crossovers between the first two genes *and* an even number between the second and third. If we wish to consider interference effects we cannot merely write $p_{00} = p_0 q_0$ with p_0 the probability of an even number of crosses between the first two loci and q_0 that for the second and third, since the events are not independent. However, defining q_0 as the probability of an even number of crosses between the second and third factors *after it is known* that an even number occurred between the first two would make this valid. Similarly p_{01} is the probability that an even number of crosses occur between the first two factors and an odd number between the second two, etc. The method of formation of the formula is fairly obvious; note first that all permutations of 0, 1 are used on subscripts of the efficient p. Also a 1 corresponds to changing from one row of indices to another, while a 0 corresponds to staying in the same row.

The proof of formula (11), and indeed the general case, is an easy generalization of the method used for two factors. It merely amounts to showing that a term such as

$$[p_{00}\lambda^{hij}_{\bullet\bullet\bullet} + p_{01}\lambda^{hi\bullet}_{\bullet\bullet j} + p_{10}\lambda^{h\bullet\bullet}_{\bullet ij} + p_{11}\lambda^{h\bullet j}_{\bullet i\bullet}]$$

is the gene-triplet frequency for the set A_h B_i C_j after crossovers in population λ^{hij}_{klm}. This the reader will readily verify.

For n linked genes the expression for the cross product of two populations will take the form:

$$v^{i_1 i_2 \ldots i_s}_{j_1 j_2 \ldots j_s} = \lambda^{i_1 i_2 \ldots i_s}_{j_1 j_2 \ldots j_s} \times \mu^{i_1 i_2 \ldots i_s}_{j_1 j_2 \ldots j_s}$$

$$= \tfrac{1}{2}\left\{ [p_{00\ldots 0}\lambda^{i_1 i_2 \ldots i_s}_{0 0 \ldots 0} + p_{10\ldots 0}\lambda^{i_1 \bullet \ldots \bullet}_{\bullet i_2 \ldots i_s} + \ldots + p_{111 \ldots 1}\lambda^{i_1 \bullet i_s \ldots}_{\bullet i_2 \bullet \ldots}] \right.$$

$\cdot$ [same expression with λ replaced by μ and $i_1, i_2, \ldots, i_s$ by $j_1, j_2, \ldots, j_s$] }
   $+ \tfrac{1}{2}$ { same pair of expressions with λ and μ interchanged } .

Although we have spoken throughout as though the factors under consideration were linked and in the same chromosome, this is not necessary. Suppose that in equation (11) the first two genes have a recombination value $p_1 = 1 - p_0$, and that they are located in a different chromosome from the third. Under these conditions it is easy to see that

$$p_{00} = p_{01} = \tfrac{1}{2}p_0 ,$$

$$p_{10} = p_{11} = \tfrac{1}{2}p_1 .$$

Also we have

$$\lambda^{hij}_{klm} = \lambda^{him}_{klj} , \qquad \mu^{hij}_{klm} = \mu^{him}_{klj} .$$

From these equations (11) may be reduced to

$$\tfrac{1}{2}\,[p_0\lambda^{h\,i\,j}_{\bullet\,\bullet\,\bullet\,\bullet} + p_1\lambda^{h\,\bullet\,j}_{\bullet\,i\,\bullet}][p_0\mu^{k\,l\,m}_{\bullet\,\bullet\,\bullet\,\bullet} + p_1\mu^{k\,\bullet\,m}_{\bullet\,i\,\bullet}]$$

$$+\ \tfrac{1}{2}\,[p_0\lambda^{k\,l\,m}_{\bullet\,\bullet\,\bullet\,\bullet} + p_1\lambda^{k\,\bullet\,m}_{\bullet\,i\,\bullet}][p_0\mu^{h\,i\,j}_{\bullet\,\bullet\,\bullet\,\bullet} + p_1\mu^{h\,\bullet\,j}_{\bullet\,i\,\bullet}]\ .$$

So the independence of factors merely simplifies the situation.

In case all three factors are independent,

$$p_{00} = p_{01} = p_{10} = p_{11} = 1/4\ ,$$

and $\lambda^{h\,i\,j}_{k\,l\,m} = \lambda^{h\,i\,m}_{k\,l\,j} = \lambda^{h\,l\,m}_{k\,i\,j}$ etc., so that (11) reduces to

$$\tfrac{1}{2}\,\lambda^{h\,i\,j}_{\bullet\,\bullet\,\bullet}\,\mu^{k\,l\,m}_{\bullet\,\bullet\,\bullet} + \tfrac{1}{2}\,\lambda^{k\,l\,m}_{\bullet\,\bullet\,\bullet}\,\mu^{h\,i\,j}_{\bullet\,\bullet\,\bullet}\ .$$

We have proved the following fundamental result.

Theorem IV. The cross product of two realizable populations represents the expected offspring of these populations when cross mated at random.

Much of our work will now be the investigation of special cases of the general formulae given above. We note at once both from the mathematical definition and obvious genetic considerations the following result.

Theorem V.

$$\lambda^{i_1\,\ldots\,i_2}_{j_1\,\ldots\,j_s} \times \mu^{i_1\,\ldots\,i_s}_{j_1\,\ldots\,j_s} = \mu^{i_1\,\ldots\,i_2}_{j_1\,\ldots\,j_s} \times \lambda^{i_1\,\ldots\,i_s}_{j_1\,\ldots\,j_s}$$

That is to say, cross multiplication is *commutative*.

Let us now consider the case of a single factor, but with, however, any number of alleles. Then the cross product reduces to

$$\nu^i_j = \lambda^i_j \times \mu^i_j = \tfrac{1}{2}\,[\lambda^i_{\bullet}\mu^{\bullet}_j + \lambda^{\bullet}_j\mu^i_{\bullet}] \tag{14}$$

from which we get the following proposition.

Theorem VI. If $\lambda^i_{\bullet} = \mu^i_{\bullet}$ then

$$\lambda^i_j \times \sigma^i_j = \mu^i_j \times \sigma^i_j\ . \tag{15}$$

In other words, if two populations have the same gene frequencies for all alleles of a factor, then they will have the same breeding characteristics when cross mated with another population.

Theorem VII. If $\nu^i_j = \lambda^i_j \times \mu^i_j$ then

$$\nu^i_{\bullet} = \frac{1}{2}(\lambda^i_{\bullet} + \mu^i_{\bullet})\ . \tag{16}$$

This follows immediately from (14) on summing on the index j and noting by Theorem II that $\lambda^{\bullet}_{\bullet} = \mu^{\bullet}_{\bullet} = 1$. This theorem shows that a gene frequency of a cross product is the arithmetic mean of the corresponding gene frequencies of the factors in the product.

We have already indicated in Part II how indexed symbols are added. When our symbols represent populations we shall consider addition only when the sum of the coefficients is unity. The purpose of this restriction is to keep all terms on an actual fractional basis and thus preserve the validity of our theorems. In general this causes little or no inconvenience, as merely dividing by the sum of the coefficients will always normalize in this sense.

We write

$$\lambda_{jk}^{hi} = R_1 \mu_{jk}^{hi} + R_2 v_{jk}^{hi} + \cdots + R_n \sigma_{jk}^{hi} , \tag{17}$$

where $\sum_{i=1}^{n} R_i = 1$, for the "sum" of the populations $\mu, v, \ldots, \sigma$ in the fractional proportions $R_1, R_2, \ldots, R_n$. Note that all terms of a sum must have the same indices (although sometimes an index may be changed in position in the same vertical column). This is part of a useful idea in indexed symbols known as *index balance*.

Index balance serves as a simple partial check on equations. If the indices do not balance in an equation, the equation is certainly wrong (in fact it is meaningless). The results governing index balance for our work may be formulated as follows:

1. Each term in a sum must have the same indices.

2. Each side of an equation must have the same indices.

3. A product (ordinary or cross) has indices corresponding to each *different live* index appearing on any of the factors of the product. (See Part II.)

Index balance applies only to live indices. There is no balance, for example, on the dead indices 0 and 1 on p_{01} in equation (11).

Addition of populations (17) is interpreted very simply as the population obtained by combining random samples of $\mu, v, \ldots, \sigma$ in the fractional proportions $R_1, R_2, \ldots, R_n$.

Theorem VIII. Cross multiplication is distributive on addition, e.g.,

$$\lambda_{jk}^{hi} \times (R_1 \mu_{jk}^{hi} + R_2 v_{jk}^{hi}) = R_1 \lambda_{jk}^{hi} \times \mu_{jk}^{hi} + R_2 \lambda_{jk}^{hi} \times v_{jk}^{hi} . \tag{18}$$

We shall prove the theorem only for this simple case. The method of proof, however, is perfectly general and will apply with any number of indices and any number of terms in the sum. The left side of the equation is, by the definition (8):

$$\tfrac{1}{2} [p_0 \lambda_{\bullet\bullet}^{hi} + p_1 \lambda_{\bullet i}^{h\bullet}] [p_0 (R_1 \mu_{\bullet\bullet}^{jk} + R_2 v_{\bullet\bullet}^{jk}) + p_1 (R_1 \mu_{\bullet k}^{j\bullet} + R_2 v_{\bullet k}^{j\bullet})]$$

$$+ \tfrac{1}{2} [p_0 \lambda_{\bullet\bullet}^{jk} + p_1 \lambda_{\bullet k}^{j\bullet}] [p_0 (R_1 \mu_{\bullet\bullet}^{hi} + R_2 v_{\bullet\bullet}^{hi}) + p_1 (R_1 \mu_{\bullet i}^{h\bullet} + R_2 \mu_{\bullet i}^{h\bullet})]$$

$$= R_1 \{ \tfrac{1}{2} [p_0 \lambda_{\bullet\bullet}^{hi} + p_1 \lambda_{\bullet i}^{h\bullet}] [p_0 \mu_{\bullet\bullet}^{jk} + p_1 \mu_{\bullet k}^{j\bullet}]$$

$$+ \tfrac{1}{2} [p_0 \lambda_{\bullet\bullet}^{jk} + p_1 \lambda_{\bullet k}^{j\bullet}] [p_0 \mu_{\bullet\bullet}^{hi} + p_1 \mu_{\bullet i}^{h\bullet}] \}$$

$$+ R_2 \{ \tfrac{1}{2} [p_0 \lambda_{\bullet\bullet}^{hi} + p_1 \lambda_{\bullet i}^{h\bullet}] [p_0 v_{\bullet\bullet}^{jk} + p_1 v_{\bullet k}^{j\bullet}]$$

$$+ \tfrac{1}{2} [p_0 \lambda_{\bullet\bullet}^{jk} + p_1 \lambda_{\bullet k}^{j\bullet}] [p_0 v_{\bullet\bullet}^{hi} + p_1 v_{\bullet i}^{h\bullet}] \}$$

$$= R_1 \lambda_{jk}^{hi} \times \mu_{jk}^{hi} + R_2 \lambda_{jk}^{hi} \times v_{jk}^{hi} .$$

The theorem on equilibrium of population after random intermating may be easily proved by the methods we have developed. We shall consider a somewhat more general case than is usually used, in that we allow any number of alleles, and also cross breeding between generations (i.e., the generations need not come in distinct steps nor need each individual mate in its own generation).

Theorem IX.

$$R_1 \lambda_i^h \times \lambda_i^h + R_2 \lambda_i^h \times (\lambda_i^h \times \lambda_i^h) + R_3 (\lambda_i^h \times \lambda_i^h) \times (\lambda_i^h \times \lambda_i^h) + \cdots \qquad (19)$$

$$= \lambda_i^h \times \lambda_i^h = \lambda_\bullet^h \lambda_\bullet^i \, .$$

The first term corresponds to a component representing direct offspring of our present population λ_i^h, the second term represents a fraction obtained by mating this offspring with the parent generation, etc. Consider any term of this expression. In order to have a meaning it must have a factor $(\lambda_i^h \times \lambda_i^h) = \lambda_\bullet^h \lambda_i^h$ by (14), but this may be replaced by λ_i^h from Theorem VI since $\lambda_\bullet^h \lambda_\bullet^i = \lambda_\bullet^h$. Hence the number of factors in the product may be reduced by one. Continuing in this manner all terms reduce to the form $R_k \lambda_i^h \times \lambda_i^h$, and by adding we get the desired result.

In particular, if we have "step type" generations this result shows that

$$\lambda_i^h \times \lambda_i^h = (\lambda_i^h \times \lambda_i^h) \times (\lambda_i^h \times \lambda_i^h)$$

$$= [(\lambda_i^h \times \lambda_i^h) \times (\lambda_i^h \times \lambda_i^h)] \times [(\lambda_i^h \times \lambda_i^h) \times (\lambda_i^h \times \lambda_i^h)]$$

$$= \text{etc.,}$$

these expressions being the 2nd, 3rd, 4th, etc. offspring generations, and all of these are equal to $\lambda_\bullet^h \lambda_\bullet^i$. It is obvious that a necessary and sufficient condition for a population λ_i^h to be in this type of equilibrium is that

$$\lambda_i^h = \lambda_\bullet^h \lambda_\bullet^i \, .$$

For two alleles it is well known that this is equivalent to the condition

$$\lambda_1^1 \lambda_2^2 = \lambda_2^1 \lambda_2^1 \, .$$

We now show how this, and the generalized result for any number of alleles, may be obtained.

Theorem X. The three following statements are all equivalent.
(1) $\lambda_i^h = \lambda_\bullet^h \lambda_\bullet^i = \lambda_i^h \times \lambda_i^h$.
(2) $\lambda_h^h \lambda_i^i = \lambda_i^h \lambda_h^h$.
(3) The matrix $\| \lambda_i^h \|$ is of rank one. By $\| \lambda_i^h \|$ is meant the matrix

$$\lambda_1^1 \; \lambda_2^1 \; \ldots \; \lambda_s^1$$
$$\lambda_1^2 \; \lambda_2^2 \; \ldots \; \lambda_s^2$$
$$\cdots \quad \cdot \quad \cdots \quad \cdot$$
$$\cdots \quad \cdot \quad \cdots \quad \cdot$$
$$\lambda_1^s \; \lambda_2^s \; \ldots \; \lambda_s^s$$

In the first place (1) implies (2), for if

$$\lambda_i^h = \lambda_\bullet^h \lambda_\bullet^i \, ,$$

then

$$\lambda_h^h = \lambda_\bullet^h \lambda_\bullet^h$$

and

$$\lambda_h^h \, \lambda_i^i = \lambda_\bullet^h \, \lambda_\bullet^h \, \lambda_\bullet^i \, \lambda_\bullet^i$$

$$= (\lambda_\bullet^h \, \lambda_\bullet^i)(\lambda_\bullet^h \, \lambda_\bullet^i) = \lambda_i^h \, \lambda_i^h \,.$$

Also (2) implies (1). Summing (2) on i gives

$$\lambda_h^h = \lambda_\bullet^h \, \lambda_\bullet^h \,.$$

Hence

$$\lambda_\bullet^h \, \lambda_\bullet^i = \sqrt{\lambda_h^h \, \lambda_i^i}$$

$$= \sqrt{\lambda_i^h \, \lambda_i^h} = \lambda_i^h \,.$$

Thus (1) and (2) are equivalent.

Condition (3) is equivalent to either of these, for if (1) is true then

$$\lambda_i^h = \lambda_\bullet^h \, \lambda_\bullet^i \,,$$

and the elements of the matrix $\|\lambda_i^h\|$ can be written as the product of a number depending only on the row by a number depending only on the column. This is a well known condition that the matrix be of rank not greater than one. The rank is actually one since at least one element is different from zero to satisfy $\lambda_\bullet^\bullet = 1$. Thus (1) implies (3). If (3) is true then each second-order minor of $\|\lambda_i^h\|$ must vanish. In particular we have

$$\begin{vmatrix} \lambda_h^h & \lambda_i^h \\ \lambda_i^h & \lambda_i^i \end{vmatrix} = 0 \,.$$

Hence

$$\lambda_h^h \, \lambda_i^i = \lambda_i^h \, \lambda_i^h \,,$$

so that (3) implies (2). This shows that all the conditions are equivalent and proves the theorem.

If a population is in equilibrium we have

$$\sum_i \sqrt{\lambda_i^i} = \sum_i \sqrt{\lambda_\bullet^i \, \lambda_\bullet^i} = \sum_i \lambda_\bullet^i = \lambda_\bullet^\bullet = 1 \,,$$

but this is not a sufficient condition for equilibrium, as the example

$$\|\lambda_i^h\| = \begin{Vmatrix} \dfrac{1}{9} & \dfrac{1}{6} & 0 \\[2mm] \dfrac{1}{6} & \dfrac{1}{9} & \dfrac{1}{6} \\[2mm] 0 & \dfrac{1}{6} & \dfrac{1}{9} \end{Vmatrix}$$

proves, for here $\sqrt{\dfrac{1}{9}} + \sqrt{\dfrac{1}{9}} + \sqrt{\dfrac{1}{9}} = 1$ while $\begin{vmatrix} \dfrac{1}{6} & 0 \\[2mm] \dfrac{1}{9} & \dfrac{1}{6} \end{vmatrix} = \dfrac{1}{36} \neq 0$ so the population

is not in equilibrium.

In case more than one factor is considered the population will, in general, only reach equilibrium (for gene combinations) asymptotically. Suppose we have two linked factors and assume "step type" generations. The result of random intermating is given by the following result.

Theorem XI. Under random intermating of λ_{jk}^{hi} the nth generation is the population

$$\mu_{jk}^{hi} = [p_0^{n-1}(p_0\lambda_{\bullet\bullet}^{hi} + p_1\lambda_{\bullet i}^{h\bullet}) + (1 - p_0^{n-1})\lambda_{\bullet\bullet}^{h\bullet}\lambda_{\bullet\bullet}^{\bullet i}] \tag{20}$$

$$\cdot [p_0^{n-1}(p_0\lambda_{\bullet\bullet}^{jk} + p_1\lambda_{\bullet k}^{j\bullet}) + (1 - p_0^{n-1})\lambda_{\bullet\bullet}^{j\bullet}\lambda_{\bullet\bullet}^{\bullet k}]$$

and (assuming $p_0 \neq 1$) approaches asymptotically the population

$$v_{jk}^{hi} = \lambda_{\bullet\bullet}^{h\bullet}\, \lambda_{\bullet\bullet}^{\bullet i}\, \lambda_{\bullet\bullet}^{j\bullet}\, \lambda_{\bullet\bullet}^{\bullet k} \quad \text{as } n \to \infty$$

Proof: By definition (8) the first generation is

$$\sigma_{jk}^{hi} = \lambda_{jk}^{hi} \times \lambda_{jk}^{hi} = [p_0\lambda_{\bullet\bullet}^{hi} + p_1\lambda_{\bullet i}^{h\bullet}][p_0\lambda_{\bullet\bullet}^{jk} + p_1\lambda_{\bullet k}^{j\bullet}]$$

$$= [(p_0\lambda_{\bullet\bullet}^{hi} + p_1\lambda_{\bullet i}^{h\bullet}) + (1 - p_0^{1-1})\lambda_{\bullet\bullet}^{h\bullet}\lambda_{\bullet\bullet}^{\bullet i}]$$

$$\cdot [(p_0\lambda_{\bullet\bullet}^{jk} + p_1\lambda_{\bullet k}^{j\bullet}) + (1 - p_0^{1-1})\lambda_{\bullet\bullet}^{j\bullet}\lambda_{\bullet\bullet}^{\bullet k}]$$

so the theorem is true for $n = 1$. We now show that if it is true for the nth generation it will be true for the $(n + 1)$th generation and thus complete the proof by mathematical induction. Assume, then, that the nth generation is

$$\mu_{jk}^{hi} = [p_0^{n-1}(p_0\lambda_{\bullet\bullet}^{hi} + p_1\lambda_{\bullet i}^{h\bullet}) + (1 - p_0^{n-1})\lambda_{\bullet\bullet}^{h\bullet}\lambda_{\bullet\bullet}^{\bullet i}] \tag{21}$$

$$\cdot [p_0^{n-1}(p_0\lambda_{\bullet\bullet}^{jk} + p_1\lambda_{\bullet k}^{j\bullet}) + (1 - p_0^{n-1})\lambda_{\bullet\bullet}^{j\bullet}\lambda_{\bullet\bullet}^{\bullet k}]$$

whence, summing on j and k,

$$\mu_{\bullet\bullet}^{hi} = [p_0^{n-1}(p_0\lambda_{\bullet\bullet}^{hi} + p_1\lambda_{\bullet i}^{h\bullet}) + (1 - p_0^{n-1})\lambda_{\bullet\bullet}^{h\bullet}\lambda_{\bullet\bullet}^{\bullet i}]$$

$$\cdot [p_0^{n-1}(p_0\lambda_{\bullet\bullet}^{\bullet\bullet} + p_1\lambda_{\bullet\bullet}^{\bullet\bullet}) + (1 - p_0^{n-1})\lambda_{\bullet\bullet}^{\bullet\bullet}\lambda_{\bullet\bullet}^{\bullet\bullet}]$$

$$= [p_0^{n-1}(p_0\lambda_{\bullet\bullet}^{hi} + p_1\lambda_{\bullet i}^{h\bullet}) + (1 - p_0^{n-1})\lambda_{\bullet\bullet}^{h\bullet}\lambda_{\bullet\bullet}^{\bullet i}]$$

since $\lambda_{\bullet\bullet}^{\bullet\bullet} = 1$ and $p_0 + p_1 = 1$. Also

$$\mu_{\bullet k}^{h\bullet} = [p_0^{n-1}(p_0\lambda_{\bullet\bullet}^{h\bullet} + p_1\lambda_{\bullet\bullet}^{h\bullet}) + (1 - p_0^{n-1})\lambda_{\bullet\bullet}^{h\bullet}\lambda_{\bullet\bullet}^{\bullet\bullet}]$$

$$\cdot [p_0^{n-1}(p_0\lambda_{\bullet\bullet}^{\bullet k} + p_1\lambda_{\bullet k}^{\bullet\bullet}) + (1 - p_0^{n-1})\lambda_{\bullet\bullet}^{\bullet\bullet}\lambda_{\bullet\bullet}^{\bullet k}]$$

$$= \lambda_{\bullet\bullet}^{h\bullet}\, \lambda_{\bullet\bullet}^{\bullet k}.$$

Now the $(n + 1)$th generation is given by the cross product of the nth generation with itself, i.e.,

$$\mu_{jk}^{hi} \times \mu_{jk}^{hi} = [p_0\mu_{\bullet\bullet}^{hi} + p_1\mu_{\bullet i}^{h\bullet}][p_0\mu_{\bullet\bullet}^{jk} + p_1\mu_{\bullet k}^{j\bullet}]$$

$$= [p_0\{p_0^{n-1}(p_0\lambda_{\bullet\bullet}^{hi} + p_1\lambda_{\bullet i}^{h\bullet}) + (1 - p_0^{n-1})\lambda_{\bullet\bullet}^{h\bullet}\lambda_{\bullet\bullet}^{\bullet i}\} + p_1\lambda_{\bullet\bullet}^{h\bullet}\lambda_{\bullet\bullet}^{\bullet i}]$$

$$\cdot [p_0\{p_0^{n-1}(p_0\lambda_{\bullet\bullet}^{jk} + p_1\lambda_{\bullet k}^{j\bullet}) + (1 - p_0^{n-1})\lambda_{\bullet\bullet}^{j\bullet}\lambda_{\bullet\bullet}^{\bullet k}\} + p_1\lambda_{\bullet\bullet}^{j\bullet}\lambda_{\bullet\bullet}^{\bullet k}]$$

$$= [p_0^n(p_0\lambda_{\bullet\bullet}^{hi} + p_1\lambda_{\bullet i}^{h\bullet}) + (1 - p_0^n)\lambda_{\bullet\bullet}^{h\bullet}\lambda_{\bullet\bullet}^{\bullet i}]$$

$$\cdot [p_0^n(p_0\lambda_{\bullet\bullet}^{jk} + p_1\lambda_{\bullet k}^{j\bullet}) + (1 - p_0^n)\lambda_{\bullet\bullet}^{j\bullet}\lambda_{\bullet\bullet}^{\bullet k}]$$

which is the same expression as (21) with n replaced by $(n + 1)$. This therefore completes the proof. The asymptotic value is obvious since if $p_0 \neq 1$ then as $n \to \infty$, $p_0^{n-1} \to 0$ and $(1 - p_0^{n-1}) \to 1$, so (21) reduces to

$$\lambda_{\bullet\bullet}^{h\bullet} \lambda_{\bullet\bullet}^{\bullet i} \lambda_{\bullet\bullet}^{j\bullet} \lambda_{\bullet\bullet}^{\bullet k} . \tag{22}$$

An obvious corollary is that a necessary and sufficient condition for a population τ_{jk}^{hi} to be stable under random intermating is that it satisfy the conditions

$$\tau_{jk}^{hi} = \tau_{\bullet\bullet}^{h\bullet} \tau_{\bullet\bullet}^{\bullet i} \tau_{\bullet\bullet}^{j\bullet} \tau_{\bullet\bullet}^{\bullet k}$$

or that either $p_0 = 0$ or $p_0 = 1$. If $p_0 = 0$ the expression (21) reduces to its equilibrium value

$$\lambda_{\bullet\bullet}^{h\bullet} \lambda_{\bullet\bullet}^{\bullet i} \lambda_{\bullet\bullet}^{j\bullet} \lambda_{\bullet\bullet}^{\bullet k}$$

at the first generation. If $p_0 = 1$ we have perfect linkage and the expression becomes $\lambda_{\bullet\bullet}^{hi}\lambda_{\bullet\bullet}^{jk}$ as it should, since it then acts like a single factor.

We note that the speed with which equilibrium is approached depends entirely on the value of p_0. If p_0 is small the approach will be very rapid, less so as p_0 becomes larger, or the linkage closer between the factors.

It is interesting to see that with a given population λ_{jk}^{hi}, the equilibrium will be approached more rapidly if there is very weak linkage ($p_0 < \frac{1}{2}$) than if the factors are completely independent, either in different chromosomes or in the same chromosome with $p_0 = \frac{1}{2}$.

Incidentally, if there is no interference between crosses a recombination value $p_0 < \frac{1}{2}$ is mathematically impossible. Suppose the map distance (measured in morgans) between two loci is d. Let this distance be divided into a large number, n, of sections, each of map distance d/n. Then if n is large d/n is small and the probability of a cross in any one section is approximately d/n and approaches this value as $n \to \infty$. The probability of *exactly* s crosses between the two loci is given by

$$\lim_{n \to \infty} \begin{bmatrix} n \\ s \end{bmatrix} (\frac{d}{n})^s (1 - \frac{d}{n})^{n-s} , \tag{23}$$

where $\begin{bmatrix} n \\ s \end{bmatrix} = \dfrac{n(n-1)\ldots(n-s+1)}{s!}$ is the number of ways we can pick out the s sections where the crosses may occur, $(\dfrac{d}{n})^s$ is the probability that these crosses do not occur and $(1 - \dfrac{d}{n})^{n-s}$ is the probability that crosses do not occur in the other $n - s$ sections. This limit may be written as

$$\lim_{n\to\infty} \frac{n(n-1)(n-2)\cdots(n-s+1)}{n\cdot n\cdot n\cdots n}\cdot\frac{d^s}{s!}(1-\frac{d}{n})^n\cdot(1-\frac{d}{n})^{-s}.$$

The first factor approaches the limit 1, the second is a constant $\frac{d^s}{s!}$, the third is (setting $x = n/d$)

$$\lim_{n\to\infty}(1-\frac{d}{n})^n = \lim_{x\to\infty}(1-\frac{1}{x})^{xd} = e^{-d},$$

and the last term approaches 1 since the exponent is a constant. The entire function therefore approaches

$$\frac{d^s}{s!}\,e^{-d}$$

as the probability of exactly s crosses. The probability of an odd number is then

$$p_1 = e^{-d}(\frac{d}{1!} + \frac{d^3}{3!} + \frac{d^5}{5!} + \cdots)$$

$$= e^{-d}(\frac{e^d - e^{-d}}{2}) = \frac{1 - e^{-2d}}{2}$$

which is clearly less than 50% for any real d. In case interference is present we cannot multiply probabilities as we did in (23), since the events are no longer independent and it is at least mathematically possible to have values of $p_1 > \frac{1}{2}$. Thus suppose we have a long chromosome which is very likely to cross over at least once, but one cross strongly inhibits any other crosses for a large distance. It is evident that such conditions would allow recombination values greater than 50%.

In the case when the factors are in different chromosomes, equation (20) can be simplified, due to the fact that

$$\lambda_{jk}^{hi} = \lambda_{ji}^{hk}$$

under these conditions. It follows that

$$\lambda_{\bullet\bullet}^{hi} = \lambda_{\bullet i}^{h\bullet}\ ;\ \ \lambda_{\bullet\bullet}^{jk} = \lambda_{\bullet k}^{j\bullet},$$

so that (20) reduces to

$$\mu_{jk}^{hi} = [p_0^{n-1}\lambda_{\bullet\bullet}^{hi} + (1 - p_0^{n-1})\lambda_{\bullet\bullet}^{h\bullet}\lambda_{\bullet\bullet}^{\bullet i}]$$

$$\cdot[p_0^{n-1}\lambda_{\bullet\bullet}^{jk} + (1 - p_0^{n-1})\lambda_{\bullet\bullet}^{j\bullet}\lambda_{\bullet\bullet}^{\bullet k}].$$

For three linked factors the first-generation offspring of the population λ_{klm}^{hij} is

$$[p_{00}\lambda_{\bullet\bullet\bullet}^{hij} + p_{01}\lambda_{\bullet\bullet j}^{hi\bullet} + p_{10}\lambda_{\bullet ij}^{h\bullet\bullet} + p_{11}\lambda_{\bullet i\bullet}^{h\bullet j}]$$

$$\cdot[p_{00}\lambda_{\bullet\bullet\bullet}^{klm} + p_{01}\lambda_{\bullet\bullet m}^{kl\bullet} + p_{10}\lambda_{\bullet lm}^{k\bullet\bullet} + p_{11}\lambda_{\bullet i\bullet}^{k\bullet m}]. \tag{24}$$

The second random intermating gives

$$[p_{00}(p_{00}\lambda^{hij}_{\cdots} + p_{01}\lambda^{hi\cdot}_{\cdots j} + p_{10}\lambda^{h\cdot\cdot}_{\cdot ij} + p_{11}\lambda^{h\cdot\cdot}_{\cdot i\cdot j})$$

$$+ p_{01}((p_{00} + p_{01})\lambda^{hj\cdot}_{\cdots} + (p_{10} + p_{11})\lambda^{h\cdot\cdot}_{\cdot i\cdots})\lambda^{\cdots}_{\cdots i}$$

$$+ p_{10}((p_{00} + p_{10})\lambda^{\cdot ii}_{\cdots} + (p_{01} + p_{11})\lambda^{\cdot i\cdot}_{\cdots j})\lambda^{h\cdot\cdot}_{\cdots} \tag{25}$$

$$+ p_{11}((p_{00} + p_{11})\lambda^{h\cdot j}_{\cdots} + (p_{10} + p_{01})\lambda^{h\cdot\cdot}_{\cdots j})\lambda^{\cdot i\cdot}_{\cdots}]$$

$$\cdot \ [\text{same expression with } h, i, j \text{ replaced by } k, l, m.].$$

The nth generation has also been determined in this case. It is given by the following proposition.

Theorem XII. Under random intermating of the population λ^{hij}_{klm}, the nth offspring generation is given by

$$\mu^{hij}_{klm} = [p_{00}^{n-1}(p_{00}\lambda^{hij}_{\cdots} + p_{01}\lambda^{hi\cdot}_{\cdots j} + p_{10}\lambda^{h\cdot j}_{\cdot i\cdot} + p_{11}\lambda^{h\cdot\cdot}_{\cdot i\cdot j})$$

$$+ ((p_{00} + p_{01})^{n-1} - p_{00}^{n-1})\left\{(p_{00} + p_{01})\lambda^{hi\cdot}_{\cdots} + (p_{10} + p_{11})\lambda^{h\cdot\cdot}_{\cdot i\cdot}\right\}\lambda^{\cdots}_{\cdots i}$$

$$+ ((p_{00} + p_{10})^{n-1} - p_{00}^{n-1})\left\{(p_{00} + p_{10})\lambda^{\cdot ij}_{\cdots} + (p_{10} + p_{11})\lambda^{hi\cdot}_{\cdots j}\right\}\lambda^{h\cdot\cdot}_{\cdots}$$

$$+ ((p_{00} + p_{11})^{n-1} - p_{00}^{n-1})\left\{(p_{00} + p_{11})\lambda^{h\cdot j}_{\cdots} + (p_{01} + p_{10})\lambda^{h\cdot\cdot}_{\cdots j}\right\}\lambda^{\cdot i\cdot}_{\cdots}$$

$$+ (1 + 2p_{00}^{n-1} - (p_{00} + p_{01})^{n-1} - (p_{10} + p_{00})^{n-1} - (p_{00} + p_{11})^{n-1}) \ \cdot$$

$$\cdot \lambda^{h\cdot\cdot}_{\cdots}\lambda^{\cdot i\cdot}_{\cdots}\lambda^{\cdot\cdot j}_{\cdots}]$$

$$\cdot \ [\text{same expression with } h, i, j \text{ replaced by } k \ l, m].$$

This may be proved by mathematical induction exactly as we proved Theorem XI. The expression approaches $\lambda^{h\cdot\cdot}_{\cdots}\ \lambda^{\cdot i\cdot}_{\cdots}\ \lambda^{\cdot\cdot j}_{\cdots}\ \lambda^{k\cdot\cdot}_{\cdots}\ \lambda^{\cdot l\cdot}_{\cdots}\ \lambda^{\cdot\cdot m}_{\cdots}$ asymptotically as $n \to \infty$. In case the three loci are in different chromosomes it reduces to

$$\frac{1}{16^{n-1}}[\lambda^{hij}_{\cdots} + (2^{n-1} - 1)\left\{\lambda^{hi\cdot}_{\cdots}\lambda^{\cdot\cdot j}_{\cdots} + \lambda^{h\cdot j}_{\cdots}\lambda^{\cdot i\cdot}_{\cdots} + \lambda^{\cdot ij}_{\cdots}\lambda^{h\cdot\cdot}_{\cdots}\right\}$$

$$+ (4^{n-1} - 3 \cdot 2^{n-1} + 2)\lambda^{h\cdot\cdot}_{\cdots}\lambda^{\cdot i\cdot}_{\cdots}\lambda^{\cdot\cdot j}_{\cdots}]$$

$$\cdot \ [\text{same expression with } h, i, j \text{ replaced by } k \ l, m].$$

It is possible to expand a population in a series form which displays the homogeneous components of the population. This series is very similar to the expansion of a Boolean function in Symbolic Logic, and not only throws light on the mathematical nature of the symbols we are using, but is also useful for computational purposes. To develop the expansion we must first define a set of "constants"; homogeneous populations of a certain fixed genetic constitution. These constants will always be represented by the base letter γ, and the indices refer to the particular locus or loci we are considering. All the members of a constant γ population have the same genetic constitution with respect to the factors under consideration.

For a single locus our definitions are as follows:

$$_a^a\gamma_j^i = \begin{cases} 1 & \text{if } i = j = a, \\ 0 & \text{otherwise .} \end{cases} \tag{27}$$

If $a \neq b$ then

$$_b^a\gamma_j^i = \begin{cases} \tfrac{1}{2} & \text{if } i = a \text{ and } j = b \text{, or if } i = b \text{ and } j = a, \\ 0 & \text{otherwise .} \end{cases} \tag{28}$$

Here a and b are dead indices; they represent certain fixed numbers, while the live indices i and j represent any of several values. The dead indices merely serve to distinguish one γ from another and there is, in general, no index balance on them. It will be seen from our definition that $_b^a\gamma_j^i$ represents a population whose members are all of the genetic type $A_a\, A_b$. Thus $_2^1\gamma_j^i$ is a homogeneous population with the formula $A_1\, A_2$.

If we are considering only a single dimorphic factor the series expansion of a population λ_j^i is as follows:

$$\lambda_j^i = \lambda_1^1\, _1^1\gamma_j^i + 2\lambda_2^1\, _2^1\gamma_j^i + \lambda_2^2\, _2^2\gamma_j^i . \tag{29}$$

To prove this it is merely necessary to note that it reduces to an identity for all values of i and j. Thus with $i = 1, j = 1$ all the terms on the right are zero, except the first which reduces to λ_1^1. For $i = 1, j = 2$ only the second term is effective, giving $\lambda_2^1 = 2\,\lambda_2^1\,\tfrac{1}{2} = \lambda_2^1$, etc.

The expansion (29) displays λ_j^i as a population made up of three homogeneous parts $_1^1\gamma_j^i$, $_2^1\gamma_j^i$, $_2^2\gamma_j^i$. The fraction of each type is the coefficient of the corresponding γ in the expansion. For more than two alleles the expansion takes the form

$$\lambda_j^i = \lambda_1^1\, _1^1\gamma_j^i + \lambda_2^2\, _2^2\gamma_j^i + \cdots + \lambda_n^n\, _n^n\gamma_j^i$$

$$+ 2\lambda_2^1\, _2^1\gamma_j^i + 2\lambda_3^1\, _3^1\gamma_j^i + \cdots + 2\lambda_n^1\, _n^1\gamma_j^i \tag{30}$$

$$+ 2\lambda_3^2\, _3^2\gamma_j^i + \cdots + 2\lambda_n^{n-1}\, _n^{n-1}\gamma_j^i .$$

With more than one factor under consideration we define the γ populations according to the following scheme:

$$_{ab}^{ab}\gamma_{jk}^{hi} = \begin{cases} 1 & \text{if } h = j = a, i = k = b, \\ 0 & \text{otherwise .} \end{cases} \tag{31}$$

If $a \neq c$ or $b \neq d$ or both

$$_{cd}^{ab}\gamma_{jk}^{hi} = \begin{cases} \tfrac{1}{2} & \text{if } h = a, i = b, j = c, k = d \text{ or } h = c, i = d, j = a, \ k = b, \\ 0 & \text{otherwise .} \end{cases} \tag{32}$$

Thus $_{32}^{12}\gamma_{jk}^{hi}$ represents a homogeneous population whose members all have the formula $A_1\, A_3\, B_2\, B_2$. Constants for more than two factors are defined in a completely analogous manner. Thus $_{def}^{abc}\gamma_{klm}^{hij}$ is a population whose members are of the type $A_a\, A_d\, B_b\, B_c\, C_c\, C_f$.

The series expansion for more than one locus has the form (taking three factors to be specific):

$$\lambda \begin{smallmatrix} h & i & j \\ k & l & m \end{smallmatrix} = \lambda \begin{smallmatrix} 1 & 1 & 1 \\ 1 & 1 & 1 \end{smallmatrix} \begin{smallmatrix} 1 & 1 & 1 \\ 1 & 1 & 1 \end{smallmatrix} \gamma \begin{smallmatrix} h & i & j \\ k & l & m \end{smallmatrix} + 2\lambda \begin{smallmatrix} 1 & 1 & 2 \\ 1 & 1 & 1 \end{smallmatrix} \begin{smallmatrix} 1 & 1 & 2 \\ 1 & 1 & 1 \end{smallmatrix} \gamma \begin{smallmatrix} h & i & j \\ k & l & m \end{smallmatrix} \tag{33}$$

$$+ \cdots + \lambda \begin{smallmatrix} r_1 & r_2 & r_3 \\ r_1 & r_2 & r_3 \end{smallmatrix} \begin{smallmatrix} r_1 & r_2 & r_3 \\ r_1 & r_2 & r_3 \end{smallmatrix} \gamma \begin{smallmatrix} h & i & j \\ k & l & m \end{smallmatrix} ,$$

where r_1, r_2, r_3 are the number of alleles of the three factors. Each term corresponding to a part of the population homozygous in all factors has the coefficient one; if the corresponding part of the population is heterozygous in one or more factors the coefficient should be two.

The cross product of any two γ population may be written as a linear combination of γ's. Thus

$$\begin{smallmatrix} a \\ b \end{smallmatrix} \gamma_i^h \times \begin{smallmatrix} c \\ d \end{smallmatrix} \gamma_i^h = \frac{1}{4} \begin{smallmatrix} a \\ c \end{smallmatrix} \gamma_i^h + \frac{1}{4} \begin{smallmatrix} a \\ d \end{smallmatrix} \gamma_i^h + \frac{1}{4} \begin{smallmatrix} b \\ c \end{smallmatrix} \gamma_i^h + \frac{1}{4} \begin{smallmatrix} b \\ d \end{smallmatrix} \gamma_i^h . \tag{34}$$

In case some of the numbers a, b, c, d are equal this expression is still true but may be simplified. Thus if $a = b$

$$\begin{smallmatrix} a \\ a \end{smallmatrix} \gamma_i^h \times \begin{smallmatrix} c \\ d \end{smallmatrix} \gamma_i^h = \tfrac{1}{2} \begin{smallmatrix} a \\ c \end{smallmatrix} \gamma_i^h + \tfrac{1}{2} \begin{smallmatrix} a \\ d \end{smallmatrix} \gamma_i^h .$$

For two loci the law of multiplication of the γ's is

$$\begin{smallmatrix} a & b \\ c & d \end{smallmatrix} \gamma_{jk}^{hi} \times \begin{smallmatrix} e & f \\ g & h \end{smallmatrix} \gamma_{jk}^{hi} = \frac{p_0^2}{4} \left[\begin{smallmatrix} a & b \\ e & f \end{smallmatrix} \gamma_{jk}^{hi} + \begin{smallmatrix} a & b \\ g & h \end{smallmatrix} \gamma_{jk}^{hi} + \begin{smallmatrix} c & d \\ e & f \end{smallmatrix} \gamma_{jk}^{hi} + \begin{smallmatrix} c & d \\ g & h \end{smallmatrix} \gamma_{jk}^{hi} \right]$$

$$+ \frac{p_0 p_1}{4} \left[\begin{smallmatrix} a & b \\ e & h \end{smallmatrix} \gamma_{jk}^{hi} + \begin{smallmatrix} a & b \\ g & f \end{smallmatrix} \gamma_{jk}^{hi} + \begin{smallmatrix} c & d \\ e & h \end{smallmatrix} \gamma_{jk}^{hi} + \begin{smallmatrix} e & d \\ g & f \end{smallmatrix} \gamma_{jk}^{hi} + \begin{smallmatrix} a & d \\ e & f \end{smallmatrix} \gamma_{jk}^{hi} + \begin{smallmatrix} a & d \\ g & h \end{smallmatrix} \gamma_{jk}^{hi} \right.$$

$$\left. + \begin{smallmatrix} c & b \\ e & f \end{smallmatrix} \gamma_{jk}^{hi} + \begin{smallmatrix} c & b \\ g & h \end{smallmatrix} \gamma_{jk}^{hi} \right] + \frac{p_1^2}{4} \left[\begin{smallmatrix} a & d \\ e & h \end{smallmatrix} \gamma_{jk}^{hi} + \begin{smallmatrix} a & d \\ g & h \end{smallmatrix} \gamma_{jk}^{hi} + \begin{smallmatrix} a & b \\ e & h \end{smallmatrix} \gamma_{jk}^{hi} + \begin{smallmatrix} a & b \\ g & f \end{smallmatrix} \gamma_{jk}^{hi} \right] .$$

The series expansion and law of multiplication of the γ's display a population as a hypercomplex number, i.e., as a symbol of the form $(a_1 e_1 + a_2 e_2 + \ldots + a_n e_n)$ where the coefficients $a_1, a_2, \ldots, a_n$ are numbers and the symbols $e_1, e_2, \ldots, e_n$ are "unit vectors" with some given law of multiplication such that the product of any two of the e's may be written as a linear combination of e's. It is well known that except for trivial cases and the case of ordinary complex numbers, no law of multiplication preserves all the commutative, associative and distributive laws of ordinary numbers. In our case the associative law of multiplication is sacrificed. Thus the product $(\begin{smallmatrix} 1 \\ 1 \end{smallmatrix} \gamma_i^h \times \begin{smallmatrix} 1 \\ 1 \end{smallmatrix} \gamma_i^h) \times \begin{smallmatrix} 1 \\ 2 \end{smallmatrix} \gamma_i^h$ is, by (34):

$$(\begin{smallmatrix} 1 \\ 1 \end{smallmatrix} \gamma_i^h) \times \begin{smallmatrix} 1 \\ 1 \end{smallmatrix} \gamma_i^h \times \begin{smallmatrix} 1 \\ 2 \end{smallmatrix} \gamma_i^h = \begin{smallmatrix} 1 \\ 1 \end{smallmatrix} \gamma_i^h \times \begin{smallmatrix} 1 \\ 2 \end{smallmatrix} \gamma_i^h = \frac{1}{2} \begin{smallmatrix} 1 \\ 1 \end{smallmatrix} \gamma_i^h + \frac{1}{2} \begin{smallmatrix} 1 \\ 2 \end{smallmatrix} \gamma_i^h ,$$

while on the other hand

$$(\begin{smallmatrix} 1 \\ 1 \end{smallmatrix} \gamma_i^h \times \begin{smallmatrix} 1 \\ 1 \end{smallmatrix} \gamma_i^h \times \begin{smallmatrix} 1 \\ 2 \end{smallmatrix} \gamma_i^h) = \begin{smallmatrix} 1 \\ 1 \end{smallmatrix} \gamma_i^h \times \left| \frac{1}{2} \begin{smallmatrix} 1 \\ 1 \end{smallmatrix} \gamma_i^h + \frac{1}{2} \begin{smallmatrix} 1 \\ 2 \end{smallmatrix} \gamma_i^h \right|$$

$$= \frac{1}{2} \begin{smallmatrix} 1 \\ 1 \end{smallmatrix} \gamma_i{}^h + \frac{1}{2} \left| \frac{1}{2} \begin{smallmatrix} 1 \\ 1 \end{smallmatrix} \gamma_i^h + \frac{1}{2} \begin{smallmatrix} 1 \\ 2 \end{smallmatrix} \gamma_i^h \right|$$

$$= \frac{3}{4} \begin{smallmatrix} 1 \\ 1 \end{smallmatrix} \gamma_i^h + \frac{1}{4} \begin{smallmatrix} 1 \\ 2 \end{smallmatrix} \gamma_i^h .$$

This is a simple example of a multiplication in which the associative law does not hold, and shows that in a cross product of several factors it is essential that parentheses be retained to indicate the order in which multiplication is performed.

The series expansion (33) of a population shows how an arbitrary population may be written as the sum of a set of particular homogeneous populations, the γ's. The choice of this particular set of populations as components was a matter of convenience, not of necessity. We now show that any set of populations satisfying a certain simple condition would do as well.

Consider a set of n populations $\gamma, \mu, \ldots, \sigma$. We omit writing the indices, but there may be any number of loci. We will say that these populations are linearly independent if there is no set of numbers $a_1, a_2, \ldots, a_n$, not all zero, such that

$$a_1 \lambda + a_2 \mu + \cdots + a_n \sigma = 0 \tag{35}$$

for all values of the live indices.

Theorem XIII Any population ϕ may be expressed uniquely as a linear combination of n linearly independent populations, where n is the number of different possible genetic formulae for the factors considered.

To prove this, note that a necessary and sufficient condition that (35) have no solution for the a's (not all zero) is that the determinant

$$\begin{vmatrix} \lambda_{11\ldots1}^{11\ldots1} & \mu_{11\ldots1}^{11\ldots1} & \ldots & \sigma_{11\ldots1}^{11\ldots1} \\ \lambda_{11\ldots2}^{11\ldots1} & \mu_{11\ldots2}^{11\ldots1} & \ldots & \sigma_{11\ldots2}^{11\ldots1} \\ \ldots & \ldots & \ldots & \ldots \\ \ldots & \ldots & \ldots & \ldots \\ \lambda_{r_1 r_2 \ldots r_s}^{r_1 r_2 \ldots r_s} & \mu_{r_1 r_2 \ldots r_s}^{r_1 r_2 \ldots r_s} & \ldots & \sigma_{r_1 r_2 \ldots r_s}^{r_1 r_2 \ldots r_s} \end{vmatrix} \tag{36}$$

be different from zero. In this determinant each population takes on the values of all components in a column; i.e., the values obtained by giving the indices all possible values.

Now the non-vanishing of (36) is also a necessary and sufficient condition for the existence of a unique solution for the b's in the equations

$$\phi = b_1 \lambda + b_2 \mu + \cdots + b_n \sigma ,$$

and this proves the theorem.

In passing we note that if we have linked factors with $r_1, r_2, \ldots, r_s$ alleles respectively then n, the number of different components, is given by

$$n = \frac{r_1 r_2 \ldots r_s (r_1 r_2 \ldots r_s + 1)}{2} . \tag{37}$$

We may think of $2s$ positions in which genes may be placed. There are r_1 possibilities for the first and second positions, r_2 for the third and fourth, etc., and therefore a total of $r_1^2 r_2^2 r_3^2 \ldots r_s^2$. However, as an interchange of the two chromosomes does not affect the genetic constitution we should divide this by two, except for the ones which are homozygous in all factors and were not counted twice. There are $r_1 r_2 \ldots r_s$ types of fully homozygous individuals and we may correct our formula, then, by adding this and then dividing by two:

$$n = \frac{r_1^2 r_2^2 \ldots r_s^2 + r_1 r_2 \ldots r_s}{2} = \frac{1}{2} [r_1 r_2 \ldots r_s (r_1 r_2 \ldots r_s + 1)] .$$

In case the loci are not all in the same chromosome but spread out in a number of different ones, we may evaluate the expression (37) for each chromosome involved and multiply these results.

4. The Solution of Equations Involving Unknown Populations

It is easy to write down equations of various types involving unknown populations. Many of these may be solved for the unknowns in terms of the known populations by means of the theorems we have developed. In general an equation represents some breeding experiment involving a population of unknown genetic constitution resulting in a genetically known population. In the following we shall use the letters ϕ, ψ, χ ... for base letters in unknown populations and λ, μ, ν ... for known populations.

The general method of attack on these problems may be outlined as follows:
1. By summing on various indices we are able to evaluate gene frequencies, gene pair frequencies, etc. for the unknown populations. This ordinarily involves no more than the solution of one or more linear algebraic equations.
2. Knowing these we can evaluate cross products in which the unknowns appear, since a cross product depends only on the values of the population symbol with half the indices dotted.
3. With only linear terms remaining it is usually easy to solve the equations by ordinary methods for algebraic equations.

To illustrate how this is done we shall consider several examples. Suppose first, for simplicity, that only one locus is involved, and that we have the equation

$$R_1 \phi_i^h + R_2 \phi_i^h \times \phi_i^h + R_3 \phi_i^h \times (\phi_i^h \times \phi_i^h) + \cdots = \lambda_i^h , \tag{38}$$

where $\Sigma R_i = 1$, with ϕ_i^h unknown and λ_i^h known.

By Theorem IX this reduces immediately to the form

$$R \phi_i^h + S \phi_i^h \times \phi_i^h = \lambda_i^h ; \quad R + S = 1 . \tag{39}$$

Summing on i we have, by Theorem VII,

$$R \phi_\bullet^h + \tfrac{1}{2} S \phi_\bullet^h + \tfrac{1}{2} S \phi_\bullet^h = \lambda_\bullet^h ,$$

or

$$\phi_\bullet^h = \lambda_\bullet^h .$$

Hence by Theorem VI we may replace ϕ_i^h by λ_i^h in any product. Returning then to equation (39) we have

$$R \phi_i^h + S \lambda_i^h \times \lambda_i^h = \lambda_i^h ,$$

$$\phi_i^h = \frac{1}{R} \lambda_i^h - \frac{S}{R} \lambda_i^h \times \lambda_i^h ,$$

and this must be the unique solution of the equation, if a solution exists. To prove that it is a solution we merely try it in the equation and find that it is satisfied.

A more general equation in one unknown is the following:

$$R \phi_i^h \times (\mu_i^h \times \phi_i^h) + S \phi_i^h \times \phi_i^h + T \phi_i^h = \lambda_i^h . \tag{40}$$

Summing on i:

$$R(\frac{1}{2}\phi_{\bullet}^{h} + \frac{1}{4}\mu_{\bullet}^{h} + \frac{1}{4}\phi_{\bullet}^{h}) + S\phi_{\bullet}^{h} + T\phi_{\bullet}^{h} = \lambda_{\bullet}^{h} ;$$

$$\phi_{\bullet}^{h} = \frac{4}{3R + 4S + 4T}\lambda_{\bullet}^{h} - \frac{R}{3R + 4S + 4T}\mu_{\bullet}^{h}$$

$$= \frac{4}{4 - R}\lambda_{\bullet}^{h} - \frac{R}{4 - R}\mu_{\bullet}^{h} .$$

Replacing ϕ_i^R in each product of (39) by the expression $\frac{4}{4 - R}\lambda_{\bullet}^{h} - \frac{R}{4 - R}\mu_{\bullet}^{h}$ gives

$$\phi_i^h = \frac{1}{T}\lambda_i^h - (\frac{4}{4 - R}\lambda_i^h - \frac{R}{4 - R}\mu_i^h)$$

$$\times [\frac{4}{4 - R}\lambda_i^h \times \mu_i^h - \frac{R^2}{4 - R}\mu_i^h \times \mu_i^h + \frac{4S}{4 - R}\lambda_i^h - \frac{RS}{4 - R}\mu_i^h]$$

as the solution of (39).

It may be easily shown that the above method is applicable to any single equation in one unknown ϕ_i^h providing the coefficient of ϕ_i^h does not equal zero. Such an equation always has a unique solution, although this solution may not always represent a realizable population.

A system of linear simultaneous equations may be solved by the ordinary methods for algebraic equations, since by fixing the indices we actually have such a system of linear algebraic equations. Thus suppose

$$\sum_{i=1}^{n} R_{ij} \,_i\phi_i^k = {}_j\lambda_i^k , \qquad j = 1, 2, \ldots, n \qquad (41)$$

represents a system of equation with $_1\phi_i^k, _2\phi_i^k, \ldots, _n\phi_i^k$ unknowns. The indices i and j here serve to distinguish between the different ϕ and λ populations. The solution of this system is

$$_i\phi_i^k = \sum_{j=1}^{n} \frac{M_{ji}}{|R_{ji}|} \,_j\lambda_i^k , \qquad (42)$$

where $|R_{ij}|$, the determinant of the coefficients, is nonzero, and M_{ji} is the cofactor of R_{ij}.

The reader may verify that simultaneous systems of equations with cross products involving the unknown populations may also be solved by these methods. Turning now to problems involving more than one gene locus the situation becomes a bit more complicated. Suppose again we have the equation in one unknown

$$R\,\phi_{jk}^{hi} \times \phi_{jk}^{hi} + S\,\phi_{jk}^{hi} = \lambda_{jk}^{hi} . \qquad (43)$$

Referring to the definition of a cross product for two factors we see that knowing the two quantities $\phi_{\bullet\bullet}^{hi}$ and $\phi_{\bullet i}^{h\bullet}$ the cross product in (43) is completely determined. Summing, then, on j and k we get

$$R\,\phi_{\bullet\bullet}^{h\bullet}\,\phi_{\bullet\bullet}^{\bullet i} + S\,\phi_{\bullet i}^{h\bullet} = \lambda_{\bullet i}^{h\bullet} , \qquad (44)$$

and we see that to determine $\phi_{\bullet i}^{h\bullet}$ we should find $\phi_{\bullet\bullet}^{h\bullet}$. Summing (44) on i gives us

$$\phi_{\bullet\bullet}^{h\bullet} = \lambda_{\bullet\bullet}^{h\bullet} , \qquad \phi_{\bullet\bullet}^{\bullet i} = \lambda_{\bullet\bullet}^{\bullet i} , \qquad (45)$$

hence

$$R \, \lambda_{\bullet\bullet}^{h\bullet} \, \lambda_{\bullet\bullet}^{\bullet i} + S \, \phi_{\bullet i}^{h\bullet} = \lambda_{\bullet i}^{h\bullet} \,,$$

$$\phi_{\bullet i}^{h\bullet} = \frac{1}{S} \, \lambda_{\bullet i}^{h\bullet} - \frac{R}{S} \, \lambda_{\bullet\bullet}^{h\bullet} \, \lambda_{\bullet\bullet}^{\bullet i} \,. \tag{46}$$

Substituting in (44):

$$\phi_{\bullet\bullet}^{hi} = \frac{1}{S + Rp_0} (\lambda_{\bullet\bullet}^{hi} - \frac{Rp_1}{S} \, \lambda_{\bullet i}^{h\bullet} + R \, \lambda_{\bullet\bullet}^{h\bullet} \, \lambda_{\bullet\bullet}^{\bullet i}) \,. \tag{47}$$

Now from our original equation (43):

$$\phi_{jk}^{hi} = \frac{1}{S} \, \lambda_{jk}^{hi} - \frac{R}{S} \, \phi_{jk}^{hi} \times \phi_{jk}^{hi} \,,$$

and the cross product on the right may be calculated from the equations (46) and (47). This gives the unique solution to the problem.

Generalizing these methods to systems of simultaneous equations in more than one unknown and with any number of gene loci is not difficult. Of course, the equations become larger and more cumbersome, but no new theoretical difficulties appear.

5. Lethal Factors and Selection

The results of a selective action may be calculated by the methods we have developed. Suppose the chances of survival of the types A_h A_i are R_i^h where h and i take values over all alleles. Then starting with a population λ_i^h the population reaching maturity will be

$$\frac{1}{D_1} \, R_i^h \, \lambda_i^h \,,$$

where D_1 is a normalizing factor given by

$$D_1 = \sum_h \sum_i R_i^h \, \lambda_i^h \,. \tag{48}$$

Sums on more than one index are of frequent occurrence in selection work and we adopt the convention that summation on two or more indices simultaneously will be indicated by placing a bar over these indices. Thus (48) would be written

$$D_1 = R_i^{\bar{h}} \, \lambda_i^{\bar{h}} \,.$$

The first-generation offspring of λ_i^h would be

$$\mu_i^h = \frac{1}{D_1^2} \, (R_i^h \, \lambda_i^h) \times (R_i^h \, \lambda_i^h)$$

$$= \frac{1}{D_1^2} (R_{\bar{s}}^h \, \lambda_{\bar{s}}^h \, R_i^{\bar{t}} \, \lambda_i^{\bar{t}}) \,,$$

and if

$$D_2 = D_1^2 \, R_i^{\bar{h}} \, \mu_i^{\bar{h}}$$

then

$$\frac{1}{D_2} \, R_i^h \, R_{\bar{s}}^h \, \lambda_{\bar{s}}^h \, R_i^{\bar{\imath}} \, \lambda_i^{\bar{\imath}}$$

will reach maturity.

The next generation is given by

$$\frac{1}{D_2^2} \, R_j^h \, R_{\bar{s}}^h \, \lambda_{\bar{s}}^h \, R_j^{\bar{t}} \, \lambda_j^{\bar{t}} \, R_i^{\bar{k}} \, R_{\bar{s}}^{\bar{k}} \, \lambda_{\bar{s}}^{\bar{k}} \, R_i^{\bar{\imath}} \, \lambda_i^{\bar{\imath}}$$

etc.

A population will be in equilibrium if and only if the equation

$$\lambda_i^h = \frac{1}{D} \, R_i^h \, \lambda_{\bullet}^h \, \lambda_{\bullet}^i \tag{49}$$

is satisfied. This requires that

$$\lambda_{\bullet}^h = \frac{1}{D} \, R_i^h \, \lambda_{\bullet}^h \, \lambda_{\bullet}^{\bar{\imath}} \tag{50}$$

or

$$\lambda_{\bullet}^h \left(\frac{1}{D} \, R_i^h \, \lambda_{\bullet}^{\bar{\imath}} - 1 \right) = 0 \, . \tag{51}$$

This may be satisfied in two different ways. If none of the $\lambda_{\bullet}^h = 0$, we must have

$$R_i^h \, \lambda_{\bullet}^{\bar{\imath}} = D \, , \tag{52}$$

a system of linear algebraic equations with the unique solution (providing $|R_i^h| \neq 0$)

$$\lambda_{\bullet}^h = k \begin{vmatrix} R_1^1 & R_2^1 & \dots & R_{h-1}^1 & 1 & R_{h+1}^1 & \dots & R_n^1 \\ R_1^2 & R_2^2 & \dots & R_{h-1}^2 & 1 & R_{h+1}^2 & \dots & R_n^2 \\ & & \dots & & & \dots & & \\ & & \dots & & & \dots & & \\ R_1^n & R_2^n & \dots & R_{h-1}^n & 1 & R_{h+1}^n & \dots & R_n^n \end{vmatrix}, \tag{53}$$

where k is a constant determined by the condition $\lambda_{\bullet}^{\bullet} = 1$. Equation (51) may also be satisfied if some of the $\lambda_{\bullet}^h = 0$. We may not divide through by these components, but the remainder gives us a set of, say, $m < n$ equations in the m nonvanishing components which will, in general, have a unique solution.

A population satisfying (49) above would be in equilibrium in the sense that the first-generation *expected* offspring would be of the same genetic constitution. However, this equilibrium may not be stable, for the actual offspring will in general deviate somewhat from the expected offspring, and the population will be stable if and only if this deviation tends to cause the next generation to return to the equilibrium position. The situation may be likened to a ball which may be either balanced on the top of a hill or placed at the lowest point in a valley. In either case the ball is in equilibrium, but only in the valley is it stable, for if given a slight displacement on the hill the ball will tend to run down, while in the valley it tends to return to the lowest point.

Although a set of necessary and sufficient conditions for stability of a population have not been found, we have the following proposition.

Theorem XIV. A necessary condition for stability of a realizable equilibrium population λ_i^h (no gene frequency equals zero) under the selective action R_i^h is that

$$R_h^h < R_s^h , \qquad s \neq h . \tag{54}$$

Proof: Let the R_i^h coefficients be multiplied by such a constant that the equilibrium population satisfies the normalized equation

$$\lambda_{\bullet}^h = R_i^h \, \lambda_{\bullet}^h \, \lambda_{\bullet}^{\bar{i}} , \tag{55}$$

or, since no $\lambda_{\bullet}^h = 0$,

$$R_i^h \, \lambda_{\bullet}^{\bar{i}} = 1 . \tag{56}$$

Let this population take on a small increment $\Delta \lambda_i^h$ with $\Delta \lambda_{\bullet}^{\bullet} = 0$. The result of one generation random intermating of this displaced population $\lambda_i^h + \Delta \lambda_i^h$ is

$$\mu_i^h = \frac{1}{D} \, R_i^h \, (\lambda_{\bullet}^h + \Delta \lambda_{\bullet}^h)(\lambda_{\bullet}^i + \Delta \lambda_{\bullet}^i) ,$$

whence

$$\mu_{\bullet}^h = \frac{1}{D} \, R_i^h \, (\lambda_{\bullet}^h + \Delta \lambda_{\bullet}^h)(\lambda_{\bullet}^i + \Delta \lambda_{\bullet}^i)$$

$$= \frac{1}{D} \, [R_i^h \, \lambda_{\bullet}^h \, \lambda_{\bullet}^{\bar{i}} + R_i^h \, \lambda_{\bullet}^h \, \Delta \lambda_{\bullet}^{\bar{i}}$$

$$+ R_i^h \, \lambda_{\bullet}^{\bar{i}} \, \Delta \lambda_{\bullet}^h + R_i^h \, \Delta \lambda_{\bullet}^h \, \Delta \lambda_{\bullet}^{\bar{i}}] .$$

Now the first term $R_i^h \, \lambda_{\bullet}^h \, \lambda_{\bullet}^{\bar{i}} = \lambda_{\bullet}^h$, and the third $R_i^h \, \lambda_{\bullet}^{\bar{i}} \, \Delta \lambda_{\bullet}^h = \Delta \lambda_{\bullet}^h$ from (56). For small increments the last term is of the second order and may be neglected, so that

$$\mu_{\bullet}^h = \frac{1}{D} \, [\lambda_{\bullet}^h + \Delta \lambda_{\bullet}^h + R_i^h \, \lambda_{\bullet}^h \, \Delta \lambda_{\bullet}^{\bar{i}}] .$$

To evaluate the constant D, we first sum on h:

$$\mu_{\bullet}^{\bullet} = \frac{1}{D} \, [\lambda_{\bullet}^{\bullet} + \Delta \lambda_{\bullet}^{\bullet} + R_h^{\bar{h}} \, \lambda_{\bullet}^{\bar{h}} \, \Delta \lambda_{\bullet}^{\bar{i}}] ,$$

$$1 = \frac{1}{D} \, [1 + 0 + \Delta \lambda_{\bullet}^{\bar{i}}] = \frac{1}{D} ,$$

thus

$$\mu_{\bullet}^h = \lambda_{\bullet}^h + \Delta \lambda_{\bullet}^h + R_i^h \, \lambda_{\bullet}^h \, \Delta \lambda_{\bullet}^{\bar{i}} .$$

We see that the offspring of the displaced population is equal to this population plus an additional increment $R_i^h \, \lambda_{\bullet}^h \, \Delta \lambda_{\bullet}^{\bar{i}}$. Clearly a necessary condition for stability is that this be opposite in sign to the original increment $\Delta \lambda_{\bullet}^h$. Now the original increment was completely arbitrary. Let us fix h and s as two constant indices and suppose the components of the increment were $\Delta \lambda_{\bullet}^h = + \varepsilon$, $\Delta \lambda_{\bullet}^s = - \varepsilon$ and all other components zero. Taking ε positive we have the condition

$$R_i^h \, \lambda_\bullet^h \, \Delta\lambda_\bullet^{\bar{i}} < 0 \,,$$

or

$$(R_1^h \Delta\lambda_\bullet^1 + R_2^h \, \Delta\lambda_\bullet^2 + \cdots + R_n^h \, \Delta\lambda_\bullet^n)\lambda_\bullet^h < 0 \,.$$

For a realizable population $\lambda_\bullet^h$ is positive and all the terms in the parentheses are zero except $\Delta\lambda_\bullet^h$ and $\Delta\lambda_\bullet^s$, giving

$$R_h^h \, \varepsilon - R_s^h \, \varepsilon < 0 \,,$$

or

$$R_h^h < R_s^h \,.$$

This proves the theorem.

For a dimorphic factor this condition is also easily shown to be sufficient for stability; but examples show that it is not always sufficient for more than two alleles. Sufficient conditions (not necessary) for any number of alleles are that

$$R_h^h = K_1 \,, \qquad \text{a constant independent of } h \,,$$

$$R_s^h = K_2 \,, \qquad \text{a constant independent of } h \text{ and } s \,,$$

with $K_1 < K_2$. For then the correction term is

$$\lambda_\bullet^h \, [R_s^h \sum_{\substack{i=1 \\ i \neq h}}^{n} \Delta\lambda_\bullet^i + R_h^h \, \Delta\lambda_\bullet^h]$$

$$= \lambda_\bullet^h [- R_s^h \, \Delta\lambda_\bullet^h + R_h^h \, \Delta\lambda_\bullet^h] = \lambda_\bullet^h \, \Delta\lambda_\bullet^h (K_1 - K_2) \,,$$

which is clearly opposite in sign and less in absolute value than $\Delta\lambda_\bullet^h$.

6. A Calculus of Populations

So far all our population symbols have been constants, i.e., each represented a certain particular population. The manipulation of these discrete sets of numbers constitutes an algebra. Sometimes, however, it is convenient to consider continuous time variations of a population. Such a study leads to a calculus of populations. We have already used, in the preceding section, the idea of an incremental population.

In this section we will define the "derivative" of a population and develop some of the fundamentals of the calculus.

First let us generalize our idea of population to include variable populations, i.e., populations that are functions of time. We indicate this functional dependence by the usual notation, e.g.,

$$\lambda_{jk}^{hi}(t) \tag{58}$$

represents the genetic constitution of the population λ_{jk}^{hi} at the time t. In case no ambiguity is introduced we sometimes omit the argument t, it being understood that

$$\lambda_{jk}^{hi} = \lambda_{jk}^{hi}(t) \,.$$

We define the derivative of a population as the indexed symbol whose components are the time derivatives of the components of the population in question. Thus

$$\frac{d}{dt} \lambda_{jk}^{hi}(t) = \lim_{\Delta t \to 0} \frac{\lambda_{jk}^{hi}(t + \Delta t) - \lambda_{jk}^{hi}(t)}{\Delta t} . \tag{59}$$

We assume the population large enough and the variation of λ smooth enough for the limit to exist in a practical sense.

Note that the derivative of a population is *not* a population. A population has the property $\lambda_{::}^{::} = 1$ while its derivative has the following property.

Theorem XV.

$$\frac{d}{dt} \lambda_{::}^{::} = 0 . \tag{60}$$

This is true if we first sum on all indices and then take the derivative, or vice versa. Both follow immediately on taking the derivative of (6).

As in ordinary calculus we have simple rules for taking derivatives of sums, products, etc. These are all exactly the same as those of ordinary calculus.

Theorem XVI.

1. If $\lambda_{jk}^{hi}(t)$ is a constant,

$$\frac{d}{dt} \lambda_{jk}^{hi} = 0 . \tag{61}$$

2. If

$$\lambda_{jk}^{hi} = R_1 \, \mu_{jk}^{hi} + R_2 \, v_{jk}^{hi} \tag{62}$$

then

$$\frac{d}{dt} \lambda_{jk}^{hi} = R_1 \, \frac{d}{dt} \, \mu_{jk}^{hi} + R_2 \, \frac{d}{dt} \, v_{jk}^{hi} .$$

3. If

$$\lambda_{jk}^{hi} = \mu_{jk}^{hi} \times v_{jk}^{hi} \tag{63}$$

then

$$\frac{d}{dt} \lambda_{jk}^{hi} = \mu_{jk}^{hi} \times \frac{d}{dt} \, v_{jk}^{hi} + v_{jk}^{hi} \times \frac{d}{dt} \, \mu_{jk}^{hi} .$$

The first two of these rules for differentiation are obvious, since by fixing the indices they merely state the ordinary rules for differentiating constants and sums. The third, which is the analogue of the Leibnitz rule for differentiating a product, requires proof. Starting with the definition of a derivative we have:

$$\frac{d}{dt} \lambda_{jk}^{hi} = \lim_{\Delta t \to 0} \frac{1}{\Delta t} [\lambda_{jk}^{hi}(t + \Delta t) - \lambda_{jk}^{hi}(t)]$$

$$= \lim_{\Delta t \to 0} \frac{1}{\Delta t} [\{\mu_{jk}^{hi}(t) + \Delta \mu_{jk}^{hi}(t)\} \times \{v_{jk}^{hi}(t) + \Delta v_{jk}^{hi}(t)\} - \mu_{jk}^{hi}(t) \times v_{jk}^{hi}(t)]$$

where $\Delta \mu_{jk}^{hi}(t) = \mu_{jk}^{hi}(t + \Delta t) - \mu_{jk}^{hi}(t)$ and similarly for $\Delta v_{jk}^{hi}(t)$. Now the first cross product may be multiplied out by our distributive law (Theorem VIII) giving

$$\lim_{\Delta t \to 0} \left[\mu_{jk}^{hi}(t) \times \frac{\Delta v_{jk}^{hi}(t)}{\Delta t} + v_{jk}^{hi}(t) \frac{\Delta \mu_{jk}^{hi}(t)}{\Delta t} + \Delta \mu_{jk}^{hi}(t) \times \frac{\Delta v_{jk}^{hi}(t)}{\Delta t} \right].$$

The third term in general tends to zero with Δt so that our limit is

$$\mu_{jk}^{hi} \frac{d}{dt} v_{jk}^{hi} + v_{jk}^{hi} \frac{d}{dt} \mu_{jk}^{hi},$$

the desired result.

For a population λ_{jk}^{hi} intermating at random this reduces to

$$\frac{d}{dt}(\lambda_{jk}^{hi} \times \lambda_{jk}^{hi}) = 2\lambda_{jk}^{hi} \times \frac{d}{dt} \lambda_{jk}^{hi}.$$

A population whose components are analytic functions of time may be expanded in a Taylor series

$$\lambda_{jk}^{hi}(t) = \lambda_{jk}^{hi}(0) + \frac{d}{dt} \lambda_{jk}^{hi}|_{t=0} \cdot t + \frac{d^2}{dt^2} \lambda_{jk}^{hi}|_{t=0} \frac{t^2}{2} + \cdots,$$

for by fixing the indices we are again merely stating the standard Taylor theorem.

Bibliography

Inasmuch as no work has been done previously along the specific algebraic lines indicated in this thesis, our references must be of a fairly general nature. For a good introductory treatment of genetics, we recommend:

Sinnott, E. W. and Dunn, L. C. Principles of Genetics. McGraw Hill, 1932.

For mathematical treatment of certain phases of hereditary phenomena, the following may be consulted:

Fisher, R. A. The genetical theory of natural selection. Oxford Clarendon Press, 1930, pp. xiv + 272.

Wright, Sewall. *Genetics,* 1921, V.6, Systems of Mating. II. The effects of inbreeding on the genetic composition of a population.

Ibid. pp. 162-166. IV. The effects of selection.

Haldane, J. B. S. The cause of evolution. London, Longmans Green, 1932.

Robbins, R. B. Some applications of mathematics to breeding problems. I. *Genetics,* 1917, 2, 489-504; II. Ibid, 1918, V.3, 73-92; III. Ibid, 1918, V.3, 375-389.

Hogben, L. A matrix notation for Mendelian populations. *Proc. Royal Soc. Edinburgh,* 1933, 53, 7-25.

Notes to Part C

[3] An Algebra for Theoretical Genetics

Since this dissertation is not mentioned in J. Felsenstein's *Bibliography of Theoretical Population Genetics* (Dowden, Hutchinson & Ross, Stroudsberg, Penn., 1981), we wrote to several experts in population genetics, asking if they were aware of this thesis, and if the results were known to them.

Prof. James F. Crow (University of Wisconsin), replied that

"as far as I know, the thesis is entirely unknown to contemporary population geneticists. It seems to have been written in complete isolation from the population genetics community. It is clearly the work of a creative and original mind.

"Curiously, there were two other theses that were written at about the same time and which were also almost entirely ignored at the time. One was by C. W. Cotterman in 1940 (Ohio State University). The other was by G. Malécot in 1939 (University of Paris). Both workers, especially Malécot, have had a great, but belated, influence on modern population genetics. Shannon has likewise discovered principles that were rediscovered later.

"It was already shown by Robbins in 1918 (in papers known to Shannon) that a randomly mating population approaches two-locus chromosomal equilibrium asymptotically. Equation (8) is an extension to mating between populations. If the two populations are identical, so that this is equivalent to random mating within a population, then the unnumbered equation at the foot of the page applies. If this is regarded as a recurrence equation, it is essentially the same as the equation given (I think, later) by Malécot. Equation (11) was new at the time. The three-locus problem was first solved by Hilda Geiringer (Ann. Math. Stat. 16: 390-393, 1945) and more generally and elegantly by J. H. Bennett (Ann. Eugen. 18: 311-317, 1954).

"Shannon's formula on page 18, relating recombination to map distance, with its consequence that in the absence of interference recombination cannot exceed 50%, was not new at the time, having been discovered by Haldane in 1919. This is something that was known to many geneticists, and is further evidence for Shannon's isolation. The treatment of stable and unstable equilibria in Section 5 may have been new at the time. The results are well known now, including Theorem XIV, but I don't know what was known in 1940.

"In 1940 population genetics was dominated by Wright, Fisher, and Haldane, who didn't approach the subject with the precise definitions and clarity that now characterize it. Shannon joins Cotterman, and especially Malécot in treating the subject in the modern manner. For a thesis it seems most remarkable. My regret is that the work of all three did not become widely known in 1940. It would have changed the history of the subject substantially, I think."

Prof. Thomas Nagylaki (University of Chicago), comments that

"this dissertation is in the spirit of Cotterman's, but the latter's is far more penetrating and important, and presents many more applications. Malécot's has all the qualities of Cotterman's and is also mathematically powerful... Everything in the thesis is known now, though some things were new in 1940.

Page 8: The exchange of upper and lower indices for unlinked loci (see the unnumbered display and the discussion above it) is dangerous. The coupling and repulsion phases do have the same gametic output, but the symmetry in this display is not preserved by reproduction. I would use only invariant symmetries, though one might be able to employ this with suitable modifications. But this is not used later in any essential way, so there are no consequent errors.

"Equations (8) and (11) are single-generation transitions. The former generalized Robbins (1918) to multiple alleles and the crossing of two populations; the latter was new. By taking $\lambda = \mu$, we obtain recursions for random mating within a single population; the solutions of (8) and (11) in this case are Theorems XI and XII, respectively. Theorem XI generalized Robbins to multiple alleles; Theorem XII was new. See Dr. Crow's references.

"Pages 27-28. Both Theorem XIV and its proof contain two distinct conceptual errors. From the 'proof' it is obvious that Shannon means that (54) holds for every h and *every* $s \neq h$. In fact, the correct theorem is that (i) the inequality is *not* strict and (ii) the inequality holds for every h for *some* $s \neq h$ (i.e., for every h, there exists at least one s such that $s \neq h$ and the inequality holds). This is not a minor point: there are counterexamples to (54) as stated. The difficulty arises in the analysis of the linearized perturbation equation at the top of page 28. First, Shannon assumes that the deviation of each component of a multidimensional system from a stable equilibrium is reduced monotonically in absolute value. In fact, this is true in one dimension, but holds only asymptotically (when the maximal eigenvalue dominates) in more than one. It is easy to write down a two-dimensional counterexample. Second, there is no justification for using strict inequalities. The case of equality depends on the quadratic terms, and without their analysis nothing can be asserted.

Page 28: The claim in the last paragraph of Section 5 was new and correct, though Shannon's argument does not exclude equality. (Here, this is trivial because with equality there is no selection.)"

We are very grateful to Professors Crow and Nagylaki for their comments.

Permissions

Printed and bound by CPI Group (UK) Ltd, Croydon, CR0 4YY

27/10/2024

14580339-0001